THE
EXTRAORDINARY
BLACK BOOK

Also by JOHN WADE

In REPRINTS OF ECONOMIC CLASSICS

History of the Middle and Working Classes [1833]

[JOHN WADE, EDITOR]

THE

EXTRAORDINARY

BLACK BOOK

AN EXPOSITION OF ABUSES

IN

CHURCH AND STATE

COURTS OF LAW, REPRESENTATION

𝔐𝔲𝔫𝔦𝔠𝔦𝔭𝔞𝔩 𝔞𝔫𝔡 𝔠𝔬𝔯𝔭𝔬𝔯𝔞𝔱𝔢 𝔅𝔬𝔡𝔦𝔢𝔰

WITH A PRECIS OF

THE HOUSE OF COMMONS

PAST, PRESENT AND TO COME

[1832]

AUGUSTUS M. KELLEY · PUBLISHERS

NEW YORK 1970

First Edition 1820

A New Edition 1832

(London: Effingham Wilson, *Royal Exchange*, 1832)

Reprinted 1970 by

AUGUSTUS M. KELLEY · PUBLISHERS

REPRINTS OF ECONOMIC CLASSICS

New York New York 10001

·   ·   ·   ·   ·   ·   ·   ·   ·   ·   ·

S B N   678 00601 6

L C N   79 104006

·   ·   ·   ·   ·   ·   ·   ·   ·   ·   ·

PRINTED IN THE UNITED STATES OF AMERICA

by SENTRY PRESS, NEW YORK, N. Y. 10019

THE

EXTRAORDINARY

BLACK BOOK:

AN EXPOSITION OF ABUSES

IN

CHURCH AND STATE,

COURTS OF LAW, REPRESENTATION,

Municipal and Corporate Bodies;

WITH A PRECIS OF

THE HOUSE OF COMMONS,

PAST, PRESENT, AND TO COME.

A New Edition,

Greatly enlarged and corrected to the present time.

BY THE ORIGINAL EDITOR.

LONDON:

PUBLISHED BY

EFFINGHAM WILSON, ROYAL EXCHANGE.

———

MDCCCXXXII.

FRIENDS OF REFORM. FOES OF REVOLUTION.

BROUGHAM

GREY

LANSDOWNE

THE KING.

ALTHORPE

RUSSELL

BURDETT.

" We must be free or die, who speak the tongue   That SHAKSPEARE spake; the faith and morals hold
Which MILTON held. In everything we are sprung   Of Earth's first blood, have titles manifold.____ "

Engraved for the Extraordinary Black Book from Originals by Percy Roberts.

PUBLISHED BY, EFFINGHAM WILSON, ROYAL EXCHANGE. LONDON, 12 TH MARCH, 1832.

ADVERTISEMENT TO THE NEW EDITION.

THE rapid sale of a large impression of *The Black Book* has speedily afforded an opportunity for again subjecting it to severe revision, and this it has undergone in every department. Besides improving the arrangement, the Lists of Places, Pensions, and Pluralists have been carefully corrected, and the illustrative notes revised. The reductions in salaries and allowances, the settlement of the Civil List, and other economical arrangements of Ministers, either actually effected, or in contemplation, have been noticed.

Besides correction, many parts have been greatly enlarged, as those on the Church, Legal Sinecures, the Bank of England, and East-India Company; in the former a section has been added on the Numbers, Wealth, and Educational Efficiency of the Dissenters; and in the last have been comprised the chief facts and considerations involved in the approaching renewal of the charters of these two powerful associations. In addition, several new chapters have been introduced on subjects of immediate national interest; one on the Origin and Present State of CORPORATIONS IN CITIES AND TOWNS, and on COMPANIES, GUILDS AND FRATERNITIES: these form branches of the ancient institutions of the country, and an account of them was essential to the completeness of our work. A chapter has been added on the Principles of Finance, Abuses in the Government Expenditure, and the Workings of Taxation. Also a Précis of the HOUSE OF COMMONS, Past, Present, and to Come; with details illustrative of the Reform Bill, and the present state of parties and opinions.

In the APPENDIX will be found many new articles and tables of value, as those on the Ecclesiastical Patronage of the Nobility —the House of Lords—Inns of Court—Church Rates—Trinity College—Colonial Statistics —Civil Contingencies — Remarks on the Reports on Irish Tithes—Commissioners of Sewers— Lay and Clerical Magistrates, &c.

Notwithstanding our anxiety to be correct, we cannot be sure that in every case we have succeeded. Our work is an assemblage of facts and principles, and it would be wonderful, if, in so great a number, some errors had not escaped vigilance. Of errors of *intention* we know we are guiltless; of those which have originated in the inaccuracy of the official returns and other sources of information on which we have relied, we cannot be so confident.

All parliamentary and public documents, whatever could throw light on the Ecclesiastical Establishments, the Civil List and Hereditary Revenues, the Courts of Law and Judicial Administration, the Aristocracy, Public Offices, Funding System, Public Revenue, Pensions, Sinecures, and other departments of our work, have been consulted. Our object has been an honest one, and we have sought to attain it by honest means: nothing has been exaggerated, nor has a single fact been wilfully misstated; we needed not the aid of falsehood, our case being strong enough without it, and we refer to the references on our pages to attest the veracity of our sources of intelligence. The statements we have made we shall at all times be ready to defend, but cannot answer for those which have been mistakenly imputed to us. It has unfortunately happened, either from similarity of name or other circumstance, many representations have been placed to our account with which we had nothing in common, and of which any one might be convinced by reference to our publication. In a high quarter we have been most unjustly aspersed : we believe it was unintentional; but, consistently with honour, atonement ought to have been made by open acknowledgement in the same place where the injury was inflicted. Instead of exaggeration we have leaned to an opposite course ; whenever we had doubts, from the absence of authentic information, about the correctness of a statement, we omitted it altogether : if, in the statements of the emoluments of individuals, the errors on the side of *redundancy* were compared with those of *deficiency,* we know—and many names inscribed on our pages know too—which would preponderate. These, however, are the evils of a day, while the good we have done will be lasting. By the improvement of the Game Laws the Aristocracy have torn out one leaf from our pages ; when, in like manner, they have torn out the rest, our labours will cease—and not till then.

The Black Book is the Encyclopedia of English politics for the Georgian era, and will last as long as the abuses it exposes shall endure. It was, originally, brought out in periodical numbers twelve years ago, and laboured under the disadvantages incident to that mode of publication. Defective as the publication was, it excited unusual interest; though ill-arranged, rough in manner, and incorrect in matter, it contained a striking development of Oligarchical abuse, and thus fixed the attention of the public. It was oftentimes reprinted, and upwards of 14,000 copies were sold, almost without the expense of advertisement, or any of those helps from literary notices which are usually deemed essential to give celebrity to the productions of the press. In the edition of last year an endeavour was made to remedy the defects of the first undertaking; in this we flatter ourselves the task has been nearly completed.

The object of the Editor at first was, and. now has been, to show the manifold abuses of an unjust and oppressive system ; to show the dire calamities it has inflicted on the country, and by what ramifications of influence it has been supported.

Government has been a corporation, and had the same interests and the same principles of action as monopolists. It has been supported by other corporations; the Church has been one, the Agriculturists another; the Boroughs a third, the East-India Company a fourth, and the Bank of England a fifth: all these, and interests like these, constituted the citadel and out-works of its strength, and the first object of each has been to shun investigation. We have, however, rent the vail; those who before doubted may, if they please, come and see, and be convinced.

In lieu of the old system we are told a new one is in progress of being substituted; intelligence, not patronage, is to form the pivot of public authority: the idea is a grand one,—it is worthy of the age, and we wait in hope to see it practically realized.

In conclusion we must observe that many opinions have been introduced, from which, we doubt not, our readers will dissent; we regret this, but it is unavoidable. Our object has been Truth, not to compromise with error, nor knowingly pander to any prejudice, aristocratic or democratic. We have an aversion to war, foreign and domestic; nor do we love spoliation either on the part of the People or their Rulers. The land is full of miseries; we share them not, neither do we profit by them; but it is the impulse of our nature to wish to see them alleviated. In place of a bad government we wish a good one substituted; for it is not individuals, but the power of the State, directed by intelligence, which must administer to the maladies of a nation. And even wisdom and good intentions, without co-operation on the part of the community, would be unavailing. Public disorders of long standing and extremely complicated require deliberation as well as remedial applications. But while we crave indulgence for an Administration we believe patriotic, it must be an indulgence accompanied with constant watchfulness, and even suspicion, on the part of the People.

March 16th, 1832.

ADDRESS TO THE NEW EDITION.

IN our Dedication, written about a twelvemonth since, we expressed a want of confidence in the Whig Ministry. In the interval they have gained on our esteem. They mean well, but the difficulties they have to surmount are great. Arrayed against them are all the interests identified with public abuses, and which have so long flourished by the ruin of the country; but they must be compelled to yield. The People are quiescent; it is the quiescence of *hope :* should doubt prevail, they will rise in their might and scatter the band—the factious band that would interpose its selfish ends between the weal of twenty-four millions of persons.

The People have nobly done their duty, and Ministers must do theirs. In the words of their chief, they are individually pledged to the REFORM BILL; it is the tenure of administration. They know their power; and to have held office so long without the *means* and *determination* to accomplish the public wish, would have been basely perfidious,—it would have been treachery to the nation. Their honour is bound up in the Bill—our patriotic Monarch is faithful—the People are unanimous—and it must be carried in all its integrity. Every interest in the empire is abased, shaken, or powerless, except that of Reform, and it must triumph: it is essential to the harmony of the Constitution and the peace of the community.

Hitherto, in their domestic policy, Ministers have claims on the confidence of the public. In Ireland they have endeavoured to substitute national interests and toleration, for the reign of factions and religious feuds. They have not fomented plots, nor sought by new laws to abridge popular liberties. They have entered on the Augean stable of judicial abuses. They have cut down a part of our enormous establishments; they have even touched their own salaries, and meditate further reductions. In the work of economy has consisted their greatest difficulty; it tends to generate opposition and discontent among those who ought to be their servants, and, by impairing future prospects, dilutes the zeal of mercenary supporters; but it has conciliated the esteem of the People.

Abroad they have maintained peace and leaned to the side of constitutional governments. The battle of continental freedom is not yet won. A terrible phalanx is couched in the North and East, which waits only the acquiescence or neutrality of this country to open a new crusade against liberal institutions. While England and France are united, the hordes of Tyrants will not break from their ambush. Englishmen are awake ! Feudal pretexts of national rivalry and hereditary hate will not excite hostile feelings towards a nation with which so many interests in common ought to unite them in amicable bonds. They rightly appreciate the Aberdeen and Wellington school of foreign politics ; they will not again suffer the produce of industry to be squandered and future calamities entailed in support of aristocratic wars,—in support of wars to defend Misrule at home and Despotism abroad !

So long as Ministers pursue national objects, they will be supported. They have opposed to them only that delinquent Muster-roll with whose names are associated every lavish grant —every attack on public liberty—every insolence of authority for the last forty years. That they should be vanquished by a set like this, when supported by the People, is impossible. While, however, we seek for them popular aid, it is, we repeat, an aid accompanied with unceasing vigilance. Government is power, and its agents will luxuriate in the enjoyment without strict responsibility. Its inherent tendency is to abuse, not to improvement. Individuals are slow to reform without imperative motives; governments are still more reluctant: they are always prompt to bequeath the redemption of their follies to their successors; while posterity has cause to lament that justice has not been contemporary with guilt.

March 17th, 1832.

DEDICATION TO THE PEOPLE.

To the People our labours may be fitly inscribed—they are the tribunal of last resort,—also the victims of Misrule,—and to them, therefore, may be properly dedicated a record of the abuses from which they have long suffered, and of the means by which they may be alleviated.

All the blessings the nation ought to enjoy have been intercepted,—the rewards of industry, science, and virtue have been dissipated in iniquitous wars abroad—at home, in useless establishments, in Oligarchical luxury, folly, and profusion.

If we wanted proof of misgovernment—of incapacity and turpitude—Ireland affords a frightful example: it is not Mr. O'Connell who causes her agitation; he is only one of the fruits of Tyranny,—an effect, not the cause, of the disorders, which have originated in the neglect of her vast resources, in an unemployed population, an absentee proprietary, and a plundering church. To the wretchedness of Ireland, England is fast approaching, and

just as little from the efforts of individual disturbers. It is not
the manufacturing, but the agricultural districts which are now
excited; these have always formed the exclusive domain of
the Clergy and Aristocracy;—the rural population is exactly
what tithes, game-laws, the country magistracy, Church-of-
Englandism, and a luxurious and non-resident priesthood have
made them. And what do we behold? The people have risen
against their pastors and landlords, and have resorted to nightly
outrage and revenge—the last resort of the oppressed for wrongs
for which neither remedy nor inquiry has been vouchsafed.

We are not of the number of those who inculcate patient
submission to undeserved oppression. A favourite toast of Dr.
Johnson was, " Success to an insurrection of the BLACKS!"
Shall we say—Success to the rising of the WHITES! We
should at once answer yes, did we not think some measures
would be speedily adopted to mitigate the bitter privations and
avert the further degradation of the labouring classes.

A new era, we are told, is about to commence:—no more
liberticide wars—no more squanderings of the produce of industry in sinecures and pensions—and, above all, reform is to
be conceded. We wait in patience. Our diseases are manifold
and require many remedies, but the last is the initiative of all
the rest, involving at once the destruction of partial interests—
of monopolies, corn-laws, judicial abuse, unequal taxation,—
and giving full weight and expression to the general weal and
intelligence. If Ministers are honest, they deserve and will
require all the support the People can give them to overturn a
system which is the reverse: if they are not, they will be soon
passed under the ban of their predecessors, with the additional

infamy of having deceived by pledges which they never meant to redeem. We have hope, but no confidence.

Public opinion, and not Parliament, is *omnipotent;* it is that which has effected all the good which has been accomplished, and it is that alone which must effect the remainder. Unfortunately, Government can never be better constituted than it is for the profit of those who share in its administration; they have no interest *in change,* and their great maxims of rule are,—first, to concede nothing, so long as it can with *safety* be refused; secondly, to concede as little as possible; and, lastly, only to concede that little when every pretext for delay and postponement has been exhausted. Such are the arcana of those from whom reform is to proceed, and it is unnecessary to suggest the watchfulness, unanimity, and demonstrations by which they must be opposed.

Some of the Ministers are honest—they are all ingenious, and, no doubt, will have an ingenious plan, with many ingenious arguments for its support, concocted for our acceptance, —a plan with many convolutions, cycles, and epicycles—and, perhaps, endeavour to substitute the shadow for the substance! But it will avail them nothing; the balance is deranged, and it must be adjusted by a real increase of democratic power. The remedy, too, must be one of *immediate* action, not of *gradual* incorporation; it must not be patch-work—no disfranchising of non-resident voters—the transfer of the right of voting to great towns—the lessening of election expenses—and stuff of that sort. Such tinkering will not merit discussion, and would leave the grievance precisely in its original state.

We have fully stated our views on the subject in the concluding article of our work : by their accomplishment a real reform would be obtained, and all good would follow in their train. Our last wishes are, that the PEOPLE, to whom we dedicate our labours, will be firm—united—and persevering; and, rely upon it, we are on the eve of as great a social regeneration as the destruction of Feudality, the abasement of Popery, or any other of the memorable epochs which have signalized the progress of nations.

February 1st, 1831.

CONTENTS.

CHAPTER I.

CHURCH OF ENGLAND.

I.—ORIGIN AND TENURE OF CHURCH PROPERTY.

II.—PATRONAGE OF THE CHURCH.

III.—SINECURISM.—NON-RESIDENCE.—PLURALITIES.—
CHURCH DISCIPLINE.

IV.—REVENUES OF THE ESTABLISHED CHURCH.

V.—RAPACITY OF THE CLERGY EXEMPLIFIED.

VI.—ORIGIN AND DEFECTS OF THE CHURCH LITURGY.

CHAPTER II.

CHAPTER III.

CHURCH OF IRELAND.

CHAPTER IV.

REVENUES OF THE CROWN.

CHAPTER V.

CIVIL LIST.

CHAPTER VI.

PRIVY COUNCIL—DIPLOMATIC MISSIONS—AND CONSULAR ESTABLISHMENTS.

CHAPTER VII.

THE ARISTOCRACY.

CHAPTER VIII.

LAW AND COURTS OF LAW.

CHAPTER IX.

PROGRESS OF THE PUBLIC DEBT AND TAXES.

CHAPTER X.

EXPOSITION OF THE FUNDING-SYSTEM.

CHAPTER XI.

TAXATION AND GOVERNMENT EXPENDITURE.

II.—WORKINGS OF TAXATION.

CHAPTER XII.

THE EAST INDIA COMPANY.

CHAPTER XIII.

THE BANK OF ENGLAND.

CHAPTER XIV.

MUNICIPAL CORPORATIONS, COMPANIES, GUILDS, AND FRATERNITIES.

CHAPTER XV.

PLACES, PENSIONS, SINECURES, REVERSIONS, HALF-PAY, AND SUPERANNUATIONS.

CHAPTER XVI.

CHAPTER XVII.

HOUSE OF COMMONS, PAST, PRESENT, AND TO COME.

I.—PROGRESS OF THE CONSTITUTION UP TO THE REFORM BILL.

II.—ADEQUACY OF THE REFORM BILL TO THE WANTS OF THE NATION INVESTIGATED.

APPENDIX.

ADDENDUM.

MINISTERIAL PLANS ON TITHES.

We thought of submitting some observations on the recent reports of the two Houses of Parliament on Irish tithes, and the resolutions founded upon them, but, in looking over what we have written, we find the subject has been nearly exhausted in our copious articles on the united churches of England and Ireland. If the project of Ministers for converting arrears of tithes in Ireland into debts of the crown, and levying them by government process, be enforced, it concedes at once the important principle in dispute as to the *tenure* of church property. If an evasion of tithes may be prosecuted by the attorney-general, like an evasion of the excise or revenue laws, then is the income of the church identified with the income of the State, and the clergy admitted to be the stipendiaries of the public. Nothing, however, we apprehend, will ultimately result from the government measure: these are not the times to harden the tithe laws, and convert what has been hitherto treated as a civil delinquency, when committed by a whole body of Christians, into a criminal charge when committed by an entire kingdom. Ministers in this, as other emergencies, will be compelled to succumb to events. Public opinion obviously points to two inevitable conclusions,—first, the abolition of the Irish protestant establishment as a national church ; and, secondly, the appropriation of the tithes and ecclesiastical revenue to the wants of society, and not suffering the former to be amalgamated with the rents of the landlords.

The increasing numbers and wealth of Dissenters indicate that the fate of tithes in Ireland involves their fate in England. Such are the conflicting claims of religionists that in all measures of general improvement, whether as respects popular education or parliamentary reform, the Government is embarrassed rather than supported by its alliance with any ; and we doubt not the question will soon arise whether it would not be better policy for the State to withdraw its support from the privileged worship, rather than be compelled to adopt the alternative, which will be speedily forced upon its consideration, of granting a common support both to separatists and members of the national church.

In these movements there is nothing to excite alarm ; least of all in the prompt extinction of tithe. It is an impolitic and impoverishing impost condemned by Mr. Pitt and every statesman of eminence, and the only miracle is that it has been so long upheld. The attempt to confound rent with tithe is monstrous. One is as much private property as the wages of the operative, and every one, rich or poor, is alike interested in maintaining its inviolability. The difference between them

is almost as great as that between useful industry and downright robbery ;
or the sinecure of lord Ellenborough and the salary of an efficient
servant of the public.

The most difficult part of the question is the settlement of *existing
interests*. A substantial difference has always appeared to us to
subsist between the claims of the clerical and lay-tithe owner, and
we have expressed as much on a former occasion (*p.* 91). Beyond
a *life interest* we imagine no one would claim a compensation for the
clergy, and even for this it would be fair to accept a *compromise*. It is
a plain case of *bankruptcy*, and in lieu of receiving the *full value* they
must be content with a dividend. If such is their lot, they will not be
alone in misfortune. What a sinking in the condition of most classes at
this moment, and how many fortunes have been cut from under the possessors within the last twenty years ! What fluctuations have been
wrought by changes in the currency, the introduction of machinery, and
improvements in mercantile law ! The clergy cannot expect to be exempt
from the vicissitudes of life. They ought, themselves, to practise the
precepts of resignation it has been their duty to inculcate in others, and
place their affections on treasures more enduring than temporal possessions.

If the occupation of the clergy be gone, it is their own fault, and they
have only themselves to blame. Government has always been prompt
to lend its aid to support the ecclesiastical establishment ; but the days
are past when the " arm of flesh" could be put forth to control the *religious faith* of a nation. The basis of the contract between Church
and State is that the latter shall afford protection, on condition the former
affords spiritual instruction, to the people. If, however, the people
secede from the established communion, or if its ministers, from want of
zeal—correct discipline—or soundness of doctrine—fail to make converts
of the community over which they are the appointed pastors ; why, then,
it may be reasonably inferred that as the duties have ceased, or failed to
be discharged, the stipends annexed to them ought to cease also ; or, at
least, the servants of the fallen or abandoned worship ought only to be
paid temporary allowances—as was the case with the Catholic clergy
at the Reformation—till such time as they can adjust themselves to the
altered circumstances of society

A consideration of a peculiar nature tends to augment the difficulties
of this embarrassing subject, and the apprehensions naturally felt by
many at the sinking state of the Irish protestant establishment. By the
articles of UNION the churches of the two kingdoms are united into
one episcopal church, under the denomination of " the *United* Church of
England and Ireland." It was no doubt esteemed good policy in the
framers of this great legislative measure to support the *weakness* of one
church by the *strength* of the other ; but in the existing circumstances
of the two countries it is likely the English hierarchy will consider it
true wisdom to imitate the example of a certain order of the creation,
remarkable for prescience of coming calamites, and endeavour to scape
from so perilous an alliance !

THE EXTRAORDINARY

Black Book.

CHURCH OF ENGLAND.

RELIGION and the institution of property, the pursuits of science, literature, and commerce have greatly benefited the human race. Christianity is peculiarly the worship of the people: among them it originated, and to the promotion of their welfare its precepts are especially directed. Under the influence of its dogmas the pride of man is rebuked, the prejudices of birth annihilated, and the equal claim to honour and enjoyment of the whole family of mankind impartially admitted.

Men of liberal principles have sometimes shown themselves hostile to the Gospel; forgetting, apparently, that it has been the handmaid of civilization, and that for a long time it mitigated, and, finally, greatly aided in breaking the yoke of feudality. They are shocked at the corruptions of the popular faith, and hastily confound its genuine principles with the intolerance of Bigotry, the oppression of tithes, the ostentation of prelacy, and the delinquencies of its inferior agents, who pervert a humble and consoling dispensation into an engine of pride, gain, and worldliness. In spite, however, of these adulterations, the most careless observer cannot deny the generally beneficial influence of the Christian doctrine, in promoting decorum and equality of civil rights, in spreading a spirit of peace, charity, and universal benevolence.

As education becomes more diffused, the ancillary power of the best of creeds will become less essential to the well-being of society. Religions have mostly had their origin in our depravity and ignorance; they have been the devices of man's primitive legislators, who sought, by the creations of the imagination, to control the violence of his passions, and satisfy an urgent curiosity concerning the phenomena by which he is surrounded. But the progress of science and sound morals renders superfluous the arts of illusion; inventions, which are suited only to the nursery, or an imperfect civilization, are superseded; and men submitting to the guidance of reason instead of fear, the dominion of truth, unmixed with error, is established on the ruins of priestcraft.

Even now may be remarked the advance of society towards a more dignified and rational organization. The infallibility of popes, the divine right of kings, and the privileges of aristocracy, have lost their influence and authority: they once formed a sort of secular religion, and were among the many delusions by which mankind have been plundered and enslaved. Superstition, too, is gradually fading away by shades; and it is not improbable it may entirely vanish, ceasing to be an object of interest, further than as a singular trait in the moral history of the species. Formerly, all sects were bigots, ready to torture and destroy their fellow-creatures in the vain effort to enforce uniformity of belief; now, the fervour of all is so far attenuated, as to admit not only of dissent, but equality of claim to civil immunities. The next dilution in pious zeal is obvious. Universal toleration is the germ of indifference; and this last the forerunner of an entire oblivion of spiritual faith. Such appears the natural death of ecclesiastical power; it need not to be hastened by the rude and premature assaults of Infidelity, which only shock existing prejudices, without producing conviction: while the priesthood continue to aid the civil magistrate, their authority will be respected; but when, from the diffusion of science, new motives for the practice of virtue and the maintenance of social institutions are generally established, the utility of their functions will cease to be recognized.

Sensible men of all ages have treated with respect the established worship of the people. If so unfortunate as to disbelieve in its divine origin, they at least classed it among the useful institutions necessary to restrain the passions of the multitude. This was the predominant wisdom of the Roman government. Speaking of this great empire, in its most triumphant exaltation, GIBBON says, " The policy of the emperors and the senate, as far as it concerned religion, was happily seconded by the reflections of the enlightened, and by the habits of the superstitious part of their subjects. The various modes of worship which prevailed in the known world were all considered by the people as equally true; by the philosopher as equally false; and by the magistrate as equally useful. And thus toleration produced not only mutual indulgence, but even religious concord."* Further on he continues, " Notwithstanding the fashionable irreligion which prevailed in the age of the Antonines, both the interests of priests and the credulity of the people were sufficiently respected. In their writings and conversation, the philosophers asserted the independent dignity of reason; but they resigned their actions to the command of law and custom. Viewing with a smile of pity the various errors of the vulgar, they diligently practised the ceremonies of their fathers, devoutly frequented the temple of the gods, and, sometimes condescending to act a part on the theatre of superstition, they concealed the sentiments of the atheist under the sacerdotal robes. Reasoners of such a temper were scarcely inclined to wrangle about their respective modes of faith or of worship.

* Decline and Fall of the Roman Empire, vol. i. p. 46.

It was indifferent to them what shape the folly of the multitude might choose to assume; and they approached with the same inward contempt and the same external reverence the altars of the Libyan, the Olympian, or the Capitoline Jupiter."

Can it be supposed the statesmen and teachers of the nineteenth century are less adroit and sagacious than those of pagan Rome? Can it be supposed those whose minds have been enlightened by foreign travel, who have witnessed the conflict of opposite creeds, and who have escaped the mental bondage of cloisters and colleges in the freedom of general intercourse, are less penetrating than the magnates of the ancient world? Like them too, they will be equally politic in maintaining an outward respect for the errors of the vulgar. In the prevailing worship they recognize an useful auxiliary to civil government; prosecuting no one for dissent, it can as little offend the philosopher as politician; and the topics of all-absorbing interest it holds forth to every class, divert the vast majority from too intense a contemplation of sublunary misfortunes, or from the painful contrast of their privations with the usurpations and advantages of their superiors.

The policy of governing nations by enlightening the *few* and hoodwinking the *many*, is of very old standing. It is strongly inculcated by Machiavel in his *Prince*, and Dugald Stewart remarks, that public men of the present day mostly hold the *double-doctrine;** that is, they have one set of principles which they openly profess in complacence to the multitude, and another, comprising their real sentiments, which they keep to themselves, or confide to intimate friends. The result of this sinister policy may be constantly remarked in the proceedings of legislative assemblies: in the discussion of questions bearing on the social interests, especially such as involve the principles of government, the theory of morals, or population, there is invariably maintained a conventional latitude, beyond which if any one trespass, it is deemed more creditable to his sincerity than understanding. It is only the vain and superficial who unreservedly assail popular opinions, and prophane with invective and ribaldry the sanctities of religion. Such rash controversialists are ignorant of the *points d'appui* upon which the welfare and harmony of society depend; and though it may happen that honour, philanthropy, or patriotism be sufficient guarantees for the discharge of social duties by some, there are others whose turpitude can only be restrained by the fear of Tyburn or Tartarus. Hence theological inquiries have lost much of their interest, and are, in fact, placed beyond the pale of discussion. The mysteries of religion are well understood by the intelligent of all classes; it is considered for the good of society that some should " believe and tremble," while others enjoy, in private, the consciousness of superior light; and to those who impugn and to those who dogmatise in matters of faith, the same indulgence is extended as to well-meaning disputants, who utter, as new discoveries, commonplace or self-evident truths.

---

* Supplement to the Encyclopedia Britannica.

Having made these general observations on the utility of religion, considered as a civil institution for the government of mankind during a period of ignorance, we shall proceed to our more immediate object— an exposition of the Established Church of this country.

In our elucidations of this important inquiry, it is not our intention to interfere with the doctrines of the national religion. We have heard that there are more than one hundred different sects of Christians : so it would be highly presumptuous in mere laymen to decide which of these multifarious modes of worship is most consonant to the Scripture. A certain Protestant Archbishop said, " Popery was only a religion of *knaves* and *fools ;*" therefore, let us hope the Church of England, to which the Right Reverend Prelate belonged, comprises the honest and enlightened. The main purpose of our inquiries, is not the dogmas, but the temporalities of the Church. To us the great possessions of the clergy have long appeared an immense *waste*, which wanted surveying and enclosing, if not by act of parliament, by the act of the people. Like some of our political institutions, the excellence of our religious establishment has been greatly over-rated ; it has been described as the most perfect in Europe ; yet we are acquainted with none in which abuses are more prevalent, in which there is so little real piety, and in which the support of public worship is so vexatious and oppressive to the community.

Most countries on the Continent have reformed their church establishments : wherever a large property had accumulated in the hands of the clergy, such property has been applied to the service of the nation ; and we are now the only people who have a large mass of ecclesiastical wealth appropriated to the maintenance of an indolent and luxurious priesthood. Even in papal Rome the church property has been sold to pay the national debt ; so that far more property belonging to the clergy is to be found in any part of England of equal extent than in the Roman state. The cardinals of Rome, the bishops, canons, abbotts, and abbesses, have no longer princely revenues. A cardinal who formerly had thousands has now only *four* or *five hundred* pounds a-year. Residence is strictly enforced, and no such thing as *pluralities* is known ; the new proprietors of the Church estates live on them and improve them to the best advantage. In France, there has been a still greater ecclesiastical reformation. Before the Revolution the clergy formed one fifty-second part of the population. The total number of ecclesiastics, in 1789, was estimated at 460,000, and their revenues at £7,400,000. At present the total number of ecclesiastics of all ranks, Protestant and Catholic, is about 40,000, and their total incomes £1,460,000.* Throughout Germany and Italy there have been great reforms in spiritual matters ; the property of the church has been sold or taxed for the use of the state, and the enormous incomes of the *higher* have been more equally shared among the *lower* order of the clergy. In the Netherlands, the charges for religion, which supply the wants of the

* Scotsman Newspaper, May 14, 1831.

whole community, except those of a few Jews, do not, in the whole, exceed £252,000, or 10d. per head per annum, for a population of six millions.* Even in Spain, under the most weak and bigotted government, ecclesiastical reform has made progress. A large portion of the produce of tithe is annually appropriated to the exigences of the State, and the policy adopted of late has dispossessed the clergy of their wealth; and this body, formerly so influential, is now lightly esteemed, and very moderately endowed.

Wherever these reforms have been made, they have been productive of the most beneficial effects; they have been favourable to religion and morality, to the real interests of the people, and even to the interests of the great body of the clergy themselves; they have broken the power of an order of men at all times cruel and tyrannical, at all times opposed to reform, to the progress of knowledge, and the most salutary ameliorations; they have diffused a spirit of toleration among all classes, removed the restrictions imposed by selfish bigotry, and opened an impartial career to virtue and talent in all orders; they have spread plenty in the land by unfettering the efforts of capital and industry, paid the debts of nations, and converted the idle and vicious into useful citizens. Wherever these changes have been introduced, they have been gratefully received by the People, and well they might; for with such changes their happiness is identified, liberty and intelligence diffused.

To England, however, the spirit of ecclesiastical improvement has not yet extended; though usually foremost in reform, we are now behind all nations in our ecclesiastical establishment; though the Church of England is ostentatiously styled the *reformed* Church, it is, in truth, the most *unreformed* of all the churches. Popery, in temporal matters at least, is a more reformed religion than Church of Englandism. There is no state, however debased by superstition, where the clergy enjoy such prodigious wealth. The revenues of our priesthood exceed the public revenues of either Austria or Prussia. We complain of the poor-rates, of superannuation charges, of the army and navy, of overgrown salaries and enormous sinecures; but what are all these abuses, grievous as they are, to the abuses of our church establishment, to the sinecure wealth of the bishops, dignitaries, and aristocratical rectors and incumbents? It is said, and we believe truly, that the clergymen of the Church of England and Ireland receive, in the year, more money than the clergy of all the rest of the Christian world put together. The clergy of the United Church cost at least seven times more than the whole of the clergy of France, Catholic and Protestant, while in France there is a population of 32,000,000; whereas, of the 24,000,000 of people comprising the population of our islands, less than *one-third*, or 8,000,000, are hearers of the Established Religion.

Such a system, it is not possible, can endure. While reform and reduction are in progress in other departments, it is not likely the clergy

* Foreign Quarterly Review, No. X. p. 394.

should remain in undisturbed enjoyment of their possessions. To protect them from inquiry, they have neither prescriptive right nor good works to plead. As a body they have not, latterly, been remarkable for their *learning*, nor some of them for exalted notions of *morality*. It would be unfair to judge any class from individual examples ; but it is impossible to open the newspapers without being struck by the repeated details of clerical delinquency. When there is an instance of magisterial oppression, or flagrant offence, it is almost surprising if some father in God, some very reverend dean, or some other reverend and holy person, be not accused or suspected. In this respect they resemble the clergy of the Church of Rome before the Reformation. It is known that the catholic priesthood in the fourteenth century exceeded all other classes in the licentiousness of their lives, their oppression, and rapacity; it is known, too, that their vices arose from the immense wealth they enjoyed, and that this wealth was the ultimate cause of their downfal.

It is not to the credit of the established clergy, that their names have been associated with the most disastrous measures in the history of the country. To the latest period of the first war against American independence, they were, next to George III. its most obstinate supporters ; out of the twenty-six English Bishops, Shipley was the only prelate who voted against the war-faction.* To the commencement and protracted duration of the French revolutionary war, they were mainly instrumental ; till they sounded the ecclesiastical drum in every parish, there was no disposition to hostilities on the part of the people ; it was only by the unfounded alarms they disseminated, respecting the security of property and social institutions, the contest was made popular. In this, too, the episcopal bench was pre-eminent. Watson was the only bishop who ventured to raise his voice against the French crusade, and he, finding his opposition to the court fixed him in the poorest see in the kingdom, in the latter part of his life appeared to waver in his integrity. In supporting measures for restraining the freedom of discussion, and for interdicting to different sects of religionists a free participation in civil immunities, they have mostly been foremost.

Uniformly in the exercise of legislative functions, our spiritual lawmakers have evinced a spirit hostile to improvement, whether political, judicial, or domestic, and shown a tenacious adherence to whatever is barbarous, oppressive, or demoralizing in our public administration. The African slave-trade was accompanied by so many circumstances of cruelty and injustice, that it might have been thought the Bishops would have been the most forward in their endeavours to effect its abolition. Yet the fact is quite the contrary. They constantly supported that infamous traffic, and so marked was their conduct in this respect, that Lord Eldon was led, on one occasion, to declare that the commerce in human bodies could not be so inconsistent with Christianity as some

---

* Belsham's History of Great Britain, vol. x. page 349.

had supposed, otherwise it would never have been so steadily supported by the right reverend prelates. The efforts of Sir Samuel Romilly and others to mitigate the severity of the Criminal Code never received any countenance or support from the Bishops. But the climax of their legislative turpitude consists in their conduct on the first introduction of the Reform Bill. Setting aside the political advantages likely to result from this great measure, one of its obvious consequences was the destruction of the shameless immoralities and gross perjuries committed in parliamentary elections. Yet the Heads of the Church, in their anti-reform speeches, never once adverted to this improvement; their fears appeared chiefly to centre on the ulterior changes in our institutions which might flow from the Bill, and which might involve a sacrifice of their inordinate emoluments, and under this apprehension they voted against the people and reform.

Public education is a subject that appears to have peculiar claims on the attention of the clergy; unless indeed, as instructors of the people, their functions are extremely unimportant, and certainly, in this world, do not entitle them to much remuneration. Yet this is a duty they have generally neglected. Had not a jealousy of the Dissenters roused them into activity, neither the Bell nor Lancaster plans of instruction would have been encouraged by them. A similar feeling appears to have actuated them in the foundation of King's College, in which their object is not so much the diffusion of knowledge, as the maintenance of their influence, by setting up a rival establishment to the London University. In short, they have generally manifested either indifference or open hostility to the enlightenment of the people, and, in numerous instances of eleemosynary endowments, they have appropriated to their own use the funds bequeathed for popular tuition.

So little connexion is there between the instruction of the people and the Church establishment, that it may be stated as a general rule that the ignorance and degradation of the labouring classes throughout England are uniformly greatest where there are the most clergy, and that the people are most intelligent and independent where there are the fewest clergy. Norfolk and Suffolk, for instance, are pre-eminently parsons' counties; Norfolk has 731 parishes, and Suffolk 510. Yet it has been publicly affirmed, by those well-informed on the subject,* that so far as instruction goes, the peasantry of these two counties are as ignorant as " Indian savages." The same observation will apply to the southern and midland counties, which have been the chief scene of fires and popular tumults, and where the people have been debased by the maladministration of the poor-laws. Compare the state of these districts with that of the north of England, in which it is generally admitted the people are best instructed and most intelligent, and where, from the great extent of parishes, they can have little intercourse with the parsons. Cumberland has 104 parishes, Durham 75, Northumber-

---

* Morning Chronicle, October 21, 1831.

land 88, Westmoreland 32, Lancaster 70, West-Riding of Yorkshire 193, Chester 90. It appears that Norfolk alone has a great many more parsons than all these northern counties, containing about one-third of the population of the kingdom. In Lancashire there are only 70 parsons for a million and a half of people; yet so little detriment have they suffered from the paucity of endowed pastors, that barristers generally consider the intelligence of a Lancashire common jury equal to that of a special jury of most counties.

A feeling of charity is the great beauty of Christianity; it is, indeed, the essence of all virtue, for, if real, it imports a sympathy with the privations of others divested of selfish considerations. The rich and prosperous do not need this commiseration; if they are not happy, it is their own fault, resulting from their artificial desires and ill-regulated passions. But the poor, without the means of comfortable subsistence, have scarcely a chance of happiness, though equally entitled with others to share in the enjoyments of life. It is the especial duty of the clergy to mitigate extreme inequalities in the lot of their fellow-creatures. Yet it is seldom their labours are directed to so truly a Christian object; though wallowing in wealth, a large portion of which is the produce of funds originally intended for the destitute and unfortunate, they manifest little sympathy in human wretchedness. As a proof of their ordinary callousness, it may be instanced that, at the numerous public meetings to relieve the severe distress of the Irish, in 1822, not a single Irish bishop attended, when it was notorious the immense sums abstracted by that class from the general produce of the country had been a prominent cause of the miseries of the people.

The clergy might be usefully employed in explaining to popular conviction the causes of the privations of the people, and in enforcing principles more conducive to their comfort and independence. In the agricultural districts, where their authority is least disputed, and where the sufferings of the inhabitants are greatest, such a course might be pursued under peculiar advantages. Their remissness in this respect is less excusable, since they are relieved from cares which formerly engaged anxious attention. In the time of Hoadley, Barrow, and Tillotson, much of the zeal and talent of the church was consumed in theological controversy: the removal of civil disqualifications has tended to assuage the fervour of ecclesiastical disputation, and the clergy have only tithes, not dogmas, to defend. This tendency to religious tranquillity has been also promoted by the indifference of the people, who discovered that little fruit was to be reaped from polemical disquisitions, which, like the researches of metaphysicians, tended to perplex rather than enlighten. Men now derive their religions as they do parochial settlements, either from their parents or birth-place, and seldom, in after life, question the creed, whether sectarian or orthodox, which has been implanted in infancy. The all-subduing influence of early credulity is proverbial. Once place a dogma in the catechism, and it becomes stereotyped for life, and is never again submitted to the ordeal of examination.

By education most have been misled,
So they believe because they so were bred;
The priest continues what the nurse began,
And thus the child imposes on the man!—*Hind and Panther.*

It is the inefficiency of the clergy as public teachers, the hurtful influence they have exerted on national affairs, and their inertness in the promotion of measures of general utility, that induce men to begrudge the immense revenue expended in their support, and dispose them to a reform in our ecclesiastical establishment. To the Church of England, in the *abstract*, we have no weighty objection to offer; and should be sorry to see her spiritual functions superseded by those of any other sect by which she is surrounded. Our dislike originates in her extreme oppressiveness on the people, and her unjust dealings towards the most deserving members of her own communion. To the enormous amount of her temporalities, and abuses in their administration, we particularly demur. It is unseemly, we think, and inconsistent with the very principles and purposes of Christianity, to contemplate lofty prelates with £20,000 or £40,000 a-year, elevated on thrones, living sumptuously in splendid palaces, attended by swarms of menials, gorgeously attired, and of priests to wait upon their persons, emulating the proudest nobles, and even taking precedence of them in all the follies of heraldry. Beneath them are crowds of sinecure dignitaries and incumbents, richly provided with worldly goods, the wealthiest not even obliged to reside among their flocks; and those who reside not compelled to do any one act of duty beyond providing and paying a miserable deputy just enough to keep him from starving. Contrasted with the preceding, is a vast body of poor laborious ministers, doing all the work, and receiving less than the pay of a common bricklayer or Irish hodman: but the whole assemblage, both rich and poor, paid so as to be a perpetual burthen upon the people, and to wage, of necessity, a ceaseless strife with those whom they ought to comfort, cherish, and instruct.

These are part of the abuses to which we object, and which we are about to expose; and as we intend our exposition to be complete, it may be proper to state the order in which the several subjects will be treated.

1. We shall inquire into the origin and tenure of Church-property, clearly showing that Church-property is public property, originally intended for, and now available to public uses.

2. We shall inquire into the tenure of patronial immunities; exhibit the present state of Church-patronage, and show, by examples, its abuses and perversion to political and family interests.

3. We shall expose the system of Pluralities, Non-residence, and other abuses in Church Discipline.

4. We shall treat on the enormous Revenues of the Established Clergy, from tithes, church-lands, surplice-fees, public charities, Easter-offerings, rents of pews, and other sources.

5. We shall detail some extraordinary examples of Clerical Rapacity,

exemplified in the conduct of the higher clergy, in regard to Queen
Ann's Bounty, and of the Clergy generally, as regards First Fruits,
Moduses, and Tithes in London.

6. We shall advert to the history, origin, and defects of the Church
Liturgy.

7. We shall compare the Numbers, Wealth, Moral and Educational
efficiency of the Protestant Dissenters with the Established Clergy.

8. We shall inquire,—Who would be benefited by a Reform in the
Church Establishment?

Lastly, we shall give a statement of the Incomes of the Bishoprics
and principal Dignities, and an Alphabetical List of Pluralists in
England and Wales, showing the number of livings and other preferments held by each individual, the names of their patrons, their family
connexions, and influence.

I. ORIGIN AND TENURE OF CHURCH PROPERTY.

A late dignitary of the church, the Rev. Dr. Cove, inclines to the
idea that the consecration of a tenth part to the clergy was the consequence of " some unrecorded revelation made to Adam ;" which, he
says, is not only " a most rational, but the most probable solution" of
the origin of tithes. To what parish church Adam paid his tithe, this
zealous partizan of the establishment has left unascertained ; if Adam
paid tithe, he must have paid it to himself, or a very near relation,—
a practice which, if tolerated in his descendants, would render them
less averse from the impost, though it might be far from advantageous to
the church establishment.

The only people who can pretend to place the right to tithe on divine
authority are the Jews ; but such a right, if it ever existed among
them, certainly ceased with their theocracy. The Jews of this day
pay no tithes for the support of their rabbis ; nor, indeed, have any
tithes been paid by this nation since the destruction of the Temple and
consequent dispersion of the tribe of Levi.

It is so inconsistent with reason, that it may be almost affirmed to be
an unquestionable fact, that there never was a religion, either Jew or
Gentile, which could legally claim for its maintenance a tenth part of the
yearly produce of land and labour. For the clergy to be entitled to a
tenth, they ought to form one-tenth of the population ; but there never
was a mode of worship which required one-tenth of the people to be
teachers and ministers. The tribe of Levi had a tenth, because they
formed a tenth of the population, and had no other inheritance ; but
Aaron and his sons had only a tenth of that tenth ; so that the clergy
received no more than the *hundredth part*, the remainder being for
other uses, for the rest of the Levites, for the poor, the stranger, the
widow, the orphan, and the temple.

Christianity contains less authority for tithe than Judaism. Jesus
Christ ordained no such burden ; and in no part of his history is any
compulsory provision for the maintenance of the clergy mentioned.
Both our Saviour and his Apostles unceasingly taught poverty and

humility to their followers, and contempt of worldly goods. Hear their exhortations : " Carry neither scrip nor shoes; into whatever house ye enter, say, Peace." " Take no care of what ye shall eat, nor what ye shall drink, nor for your bodies what ye shall put on." " Beware of covetousness; seek not what ye shall eat, but seek the kingdom of God." " Give alms ; provide yourselves with bags that wax not old, a treasure in Heaven that faileth not." Again, " Distribute unto the poor, and seek treasures in Heaven." And, again, " Take care that your hearts be not charged with surfeiting and drunkenness, and the cares of this life."

In all this there is no authority for tithing, and the fathers of the Church were equally hostile to this species of extortion. The council of Antioch, in the fourth century, allowed the bishops to distribute the goods of the Church, but to have no part to themselves. " Have food and raiment, be therewith content," says the canon. It was only as real Christianity declined, that tithing began. When the simple worship of Christ was corrupted by the adoption of Jewish and Pagan ceremonies ; when the saints and martyrs were put in the room of the heathen deities; when the altars, the bishops, prebends, and other corruptions were introduced; then tithes commenced, to support the innovations on the primitive faith.

It is impossible to ascertain exactly the period when tithes were first introduced into this country. During the first ages of the Church, its ministers were supported by charity, by oblations, and voluntary gifts. According to Blackstone, the first mention of tithes in any written English law is in a constitutional decree made in a synod held A.D. 786, wherein the payment of tithes is generally enjoined. But this was no law, merely a general recommendation, and did not, at first, bind the laity. They are next mentioned in the *Fœdus Edwardi et Guthurni*, or treaty agreed upon between King Guthrun, the Dane, and Alfred and his son Edward the elder, successive kings of England, about the year 900. Guthrun being a Pagan, it was thought necessary to provide for the subsistence of the Christian clergy under his dominion ; accordingly the payment of tithes was enjoined, and a penalty imposed for its non-observance ; which law is countenanced by the laws of Athelstan, and this, according to the Commentator, is all that can be traced out with regard to their legal origin.* In fact, this inquiry, like all others into the early constitutional history of the country, is involved in darkness and contradiction. We are not even satisfactorily informed of the origin of the civil divisions of the kingdom into counties, hundreds, and parishes. These have been commonly ascribed to Alfred ; but the researches of late writers have traced them to a period of much earlier date.

One thing, however, is certain as regards tithes, namely, that in England, in France, and, probably, in all Christian countries, they were divided into four portions : one for the bishop, one for the poor,

---

* Commentaries, b. ii. ch. 3.

one for the repair of the church, and one for the priest. A late writer*
attempts to controvert the fourfold division of parochial tithes; but
the fact rests upon such unquestionable authority, that it may be deemed
a truth placed beyond dispute. Without digressing into any learned
research, it may be observed that the quadrupartite division of tithes is
still retained in many parishes in Ireland; a point which appears to have
been overlooked by the reviewer. In the Diocesan Returns to Parliament
in 1820, the bishop of Clonfert and Kilmacduagh and the bishop of
Kildare remarked that in their dioceses is preserved the old episcopal
establishment of the quarta pars; that is, a portion of the parochial
tithes out of every parish is payable to the bishop.

The right of the poor to share in the tithe is established by the tenor
of ancient statutes made to protect them from the consequences of the
appropriation of parishes by spiritual corporations. After these appropriations had been effected, the religious houses were wont to depute
one of their own body to perform divine service in those parishes of
which the societies had become possessed of the tithes. This officiating
minister was in reality no more than the curate or vicar of the appro-
priators, receiving from them an arbitrary stipend. Under this system
the poor suffered so much, that the legislature was obliged to interpose,
and, accordingly, the 15 Rich. II. c. 6 provides, that in all appropriations
of churches the diocesan shall order a competent sum to be distributed
among the poor parishioners annually; and that the vicar shall be
sufficiently endowed. " It seems," says Blackstone, " the parishes
were frequently sufferers, not only by the want of divine service, but
also by withholding those *alms for which, among other purposes, the
payment of tithes was originally imposed;* and, therefore, in this
act, a pension is directed to be distributed among the poor parochians as
well as a sufficient stipend to the vicar."†

One or two facts well attested are better than a hundred ingenious
deductions and learned conjectures. What we have advanced not only
establishes the original fourfold division of parochial tithes, but also the
right of the poor to a portion of them. It also incidentally establishes
another fact deserving attention, in showing the falsity of those representations made, from time to time, of the *charity and hospitality* of
the abbeys and monasteries. By masses and obits and other sanctimo-
nious pretexts, the monks possessed themselves of a large number of
the benefices in the kingdom; instead of applying the revenues of these
to the purposes of religion and charity, they perverted them to the
enriching of their own fraternities, and a compulsory act of the legislature
was necessary to compel them to restore to the poor a portion of their
rights, and allow a decent maintenance to the parish priest. The little
charity of the religious houses might be inferred from the general
principles of human nature without the aid of facts. It is notorious
that they had become the abodes of luxury, indolence, and crime. Who
would expect from societies so depraved, either charity or hospitality?

---

* Quarterly Review, No. 83.   † Commentaries, b. i. chap. 11.

The rich, the sensual, and vicious, rarely sympathise with indigence. For their own ease, and, as a motive to indifference, they are mostly prompt to calumniate the poor with unjust aspersions, and represent a lively zeal in their welfare, either as undeserved or mistaken benevolence.

The practice of appropriating livings was first introduced by the Normans; and within three hundred years after, the monks had become the proprietors of one-third of all the benefices in the kingdom, and these for the most part the richest. At the dissolution of the religious houses by the 27 and 31 Hen. VIII. these benefices, by the common law, would have been disappropriated, had not a clause been inserted in these statutes to give them to the King in as ample a manner as the abbots, &c. had held the same at the time of their dissolution. Having thus become the proprietor of one-third of the benefices as well as all the plate, revenues and wealth of the abbeys, the manner in which this monarch disposed of the treasure he had acquired accounts for the present state of ecclesiastical property. With a part of it he founded new bishoprics, colleges, and deaneries; large masses of it he gave to courtiers and noblemen; a portion he retained in his own hands, and the remainder applied to the maintenance of the reformed religion. Individuals, corporations, and colleges, who obtained grants from the Crown, obtained, also, all the rights annexed to them; and the present proprietors of the abbey-lands are proprietors of the tithes and benefices formerly attached to these lands. Hence it is so large a portion of the tithes are in the hands of laymen. It is calculated there are 3845 impropriations in England; that is, benefices, in the hands of persons not engaged in the service of religion, but who receive the great tithes, leaving only the vicarial tithes or other minor endowments for the maintenance of the incumbent,

The effect on society of this new disposition of ecclesiastical property has been differently represented by writers. Discontent is inseparable from the reform of every established practice and institution. Those who profit by abuses, and those who are benefited by their removal must view in different lights and hold forth different representations of measures by which they are oppositely affected. With the dissatisfaction of the monastic orders, there can be no surprise; their condition was that of drones forced from the hives in which they had devoured in idleness the fruits of others' industry; but the dissatisfaction of other classes cannot be so readily explained. Mr. Hallam states that the summary abolition of the religious houses led to the great northern rebellion:* it is certain from the popular ballads of the time, this important measure was a subject of regret to the lower orders; and old Harry Jenkins laments that "those days were over in which he used to be invited to the Lord Abbot's chamber, to feast on a quarter of a yard of roast beef and wassail in a black jack." Two reasons may be assigned for the existence of this feeling; either it may be ascribed to

---

* Constitutional History of England, vol. i. p. 77.

the cessation of the almsgiving and hospitality of the conventual bodies, or to the general ignorance of the people. The limited extent of the former has been already shown; if the populace could be conciliated by such miserable charity as we have adverted to, their fatuity may be likened to that of the multitude in more recent times, who are often blinded to their just claims by doles of soup or salt fish, or a bonus of 100 guineas out of an enormous civil list. The extreme ignorance of the people was, doubtless, the principal cause of their hostility to the reformation, and disqualified them from duly estimating the advantages likely to ensue from so great a revolution. While the people continue unenlightened, they must always be subject to their superiors, or those who possess influence enough to delude or direct them. The Forty-Shilling freeholders of Ireland were the alternate slaves of aristocratic landlords and fanatic priests, and in the votes they gave at the instigation of each, as well as in the tameness with which they submitted to be disfranchised, they have manifested a like rational view of their ultimate interests. The monks of the time of Henry VIII. were not less omnipotent over the multitude than the priests of Ireland, or those of Spain and Portugal; under the influence of the former the populace sung out whatever note they were directed; and, unquestionably, such views of the tendency of the reformation would be impressed upon them as best accorded with the interests of their spiritual guides.

To this cause we ascribe the popular feeling as regards the dissolution of monastic establishments. The same spirit opposed the opening of turnpike-roads, and the introduction of the cow-pox and machinery. But it is extremely erroneous to maintain that the Reformation was not a great blessing to the country, and tended, most essentially, to better the condition of the working classes. Had popery (such popery we mean as existed at that day) continued the established religion, the present condition of the people would have been no better than that of the degraded rabble who have restored Don Miguel and Don Ferdinand, and whose miseries, in spite of the almsgiving and hospitality of convents, are sufficiently acute to prevent an increase in their numbers. From the general poverty of the Peninsula, and the state of its agriculture, commerce, and population, fettered and oppressed by aristocratic, ecclesiastic, and corporate immunities, we may form an idea of what England would have been without the Reformation. Knowledge was incompatible with the power of the monks, whose influence was founded on the general belief of miracles, the sanctity of relics, and other pious frauds, to which popular illumination would have been fatal. Without, therefore, the excitement produced by their dispersion, and the freedom of discussion with which it was accompanied, the people would have remained intellectually debased; their ignorance was necessary to the ascendancy of those in whose hands they were, and of course they would have been kept in that state, and withheld from the only means by which their condition in society could be ameliorated. If more substantial benefits have not resulted from the Reformation, it may be easily traced to other causes. That great event certainly put the people in possession, by removing the mental incubus of a degrading superstition, of the most powerful instrument, by which they can be obtained.

It is to be regretted that, at the dissolution of the abbeys, the immense revenue at the disposal of the Crown was not appropriated in a manner more advantageous to the community. One of the great evils in our social economy is the unequal division of property—the vast masses in which it is accumulated by entails and rights of primogeniture in the hands of individuals. This evil was aggravated by transferring the endowments of the monks to the aristocracy, and thus was lost a favourable juncture for obtaining better security for the liberties of the people, by a more equal partition of proprietary influence. Instead of wasting the spoils of the church on rapacious courtiers, it might have been appropriated, as in Scotland, to the establishment of a system of parochial education; or, it might have been applied to sustain the dignity of the Crown, or defray the charges of government without burthening the people, or to other undertakings of general and permanent interest. Of the magnitude of the opportunity thrown away, we may form some idea from the almost incredible wealth of the monastic institutions.

Of the annual value of 388 religious houses, we have no estimate; but, computing the value of these in the same proportion, as of the 653 of which we have the returns, the total revenue of the 1041 houses in England and Wales was £273,106:—a prodigious sum in those days, if we consider the relative value of money, and the smallness of the national income. But incredible as this revenue is, it was only the reserved rents of manors and demesnes, without including the tithes of appropriations, fines, heriots, renewals, deodands, &c. which would probably have amounted to twice as much. Upon good authority it is stated the clergy were proprietors of seven-tenths of the whole kingdom; and, out of the three remaining tenths, thus kindly left to king, lords, and commons, were the four numerous orders of mendicants to be maintained, against whom no gate could be shut, to whom no provision could be denied, and from whom no secret could be concealed.

Mr. Cobbett often amuses his readers by exclamations of astonishment, in contemplating the splendid cathedrals of Lincoln, Ely, Canterbury, and Winchester; considering them incontestable evidence of the great wealth and population of the country at the period of their erection. But it would be quite as correct for future generations to refer to Windsor Castle or Buckingham Palace as evidence of the general contentment and prosperity of the kingdom under the government of the Borough-mongers. The fact is, it was not necessary either the population or general wealth of the community should be very great to enable the Catholic priesthood to erect those magnificent, but comparatively useless, structures. Pious souls! they had possessed themselves of nearly the whole land and labour of the community, and would have grasped the remainder, had it not been for the interference of the legislature. Such have been the religious propensities of the English, at all times, that the fervour of their piety has oftener required checking than encouraging by their rulers. It was with this view the *Mortmain Act* was passed, in the reign of Henry VII. which, by prohibiting the bequest of property to the ecclesiastical bodies, prevented the patrimony of almost every family in the kingdom from being engulphed by the cunning and insatiable monks. Had the vast amount of landed property acquired by spiritual corporations, previously to the passing of this statute, remained tied up in their hands, it must have formed an insuperable obstacle to the developement of the productive powers of the country, and under such a system neither the riches nor numbers of the people could have greatly augmented.

The statements of church property before the Reformation would appear exaggerated, had we not illustrative proof in the present state of Ireland and other countries. The mere remnant of the estates of the church, now held by the Irish Protestant Establishment, is calculated at two elevenths of the entire soil of the kingdom. In Tuscany, before the French Revolution had partially regenerated the dukedom, the priesthood was found, from inquiries instituted by the grand duke, to enjoy seventeen parts in twenty of the land. In Spain and Portugal, and in France, the monopoly of the church was nearly as great.

But we shall now leave the subject. We could not treat on the origin of church property in this country, without adverting to the changes effected by the Reformation. We shall next advert to the tenure on which the property of the church devolved, and continues to be holden by our Protestant Establishment.

It seems almost a work of supererogation to set about proving that the property of the established church is *public property*, the bare terms of the proposition apparently involving the demonstration. What can be understood by an established church, but a church endowed by the state, and, if so endowed, subordinate to the state, and for the benefit thereof? This principle has been recognized in every country in Europe. Wherever church property has been interfered with, (and we know none where it has not been interfered with,) it never appears to have been surmised that the state had not only the power but the right to give a new disposition to ecclesiastical endowments, either by appropriating them to the maintenance of a different religion, or to the necessities of the community. In England this power has been distinctly admitted, as appears from the measures adopted at the Reformation: at that period a commission was appointed to investigate the abuses of the church; a return was made of the value of all monasteries and religious houses, of parochial livings, episcopal and cathedral dignities, and every other species of ecclesiastical revenue, and the whole entered in a book, called *Liber Regalis*, or the King's Book. This important document has been recently reprinted by the Commissioners of Public Records; it is the only authentic survey of the revenues of the church; and the result was, as before described, an entire new disposition of ecclesiastical property. No claim appears to have been set up that the property was sacred, and in every succeeding period it has been treated in a similar manner. It has been always considered public property, and the government, for the time being, whether a monarchy under a Tudor, or a commonwealth under Cromwell, has always exercised the right of applying it to secular uses, or to the maintenance of whatever form of faith might be in vogue, whether Catholic, Protestant, or Presbyterian.

Down to our own time the same principle has been constantly acted upon by parliament. In the numerous acts of parliament, passed within the last thirty years, for regulating the sale and exchange of parsonage-houses and glebe-lands, of mortgages in cases of buildings and repairs, church property is invariably treated as public property, the *ownership* of which is vested in the State. Were it not so, the legislature could have no more right to interfere in the disposal of the property of the church than of the property of private individuals. It could have no right to pass the act for prohibiting the sale of spiritual preferment, by making it penal to present to any benefice for money, gift, or reward. It could have no right to pass the act, by which an incumbent is compelled to pay to his curate the whole, or a proportionate part of the income of his benefice. It could have no right to pass the Church-Building Acts, authorizing the division of parishes, glebes, and tithes; nor the various statutes for regulating the discipline of the clergy, by compelling them to reside on their benefices, or refrain from exercising any trade, or taking any farm of more than eighty acres of land. It is never attempted by such legislative interference, to control the conduct and possessions of laymen. The possessor of an estate can sell it to another in his lifetime, or, after his death, bequeath it to posterity; but the clergy have no such power over their possessions. They have at most only a life-interest; and even of that they may be disinherited at the pleasure of their diocesan. The tenure of their property is similar to that by which any public servant holds the office of Secretary of State, or the Chancellorship of the Exchequer.

The church is now as anxious to disown connexion with the state as it formerly was to claim its alliance and protection. With this view ingenious theories, for they are nothing more, have been put forth to prove that ecclesiastical property has not been derived from any public grant or concession. It has been alleged, for instance, that tithes and other profits of ecclesiastical benefices were not derived from the state, but ,from the bounty of private individuals, by whom such benefices were founded and endowed. This assumption has been refuted by Mr. Eagle in his admirable Legal Argument on Tithes: he has proved by the most incontestable authorities, that parochial tithes formed no part of the original endowment of benefices; that the dowry of churches at the time of their foundation consisted of house and glebe only, and that tithes were subsequently assigned to incumbents by the state. But were it otherwise, and could it be shewn that the gifts of individuals formed part of the endowments of benefices, still the public nature of the purposes to which they were appropriated has made them the property of the public to the exclusion of all other claimants.

Others again attempt to defend the claims of the clergy, upon the principle that they possess *corporate rights*, and hence contend that though the existing race of bishops, deans, prebendaries, rectors, and vicars might compromise their interests with the state, they could have no power to enter into any arrangement for the future, by which their successors might be deprived of the reversion of church property.

To this it has been answered, that bodies politic and corporate are civil institutions created by the law, and what the law has power to create it has power to abrogate. Therefore if the legislature, in the exercise of its undoubted right to dissolve by the law that which was created by the law, should think fit to put an end to the corporate capacity of the clergy, their right to the tithes and other profits of their benefices would necessarily cease. For they could not claim as individuals that which they had held and enjoyed in their corporate capacity only. Their possessions would revert to the state, from which they had been derived, to be disposed of in the manner best calculated to promote the welfare of the nation.

But it is useless to contend with mere legal fictions, shadows, and assumptions. The entire argument on church tithes may be comprised in a very small compass, and rests on recent and indubitable authority. The tenure of ecclesiastical property was prescribed by the Statutes of Dissolution at the time of the Reformation. The legislature of that day made a new disposition of the possessions of the church, and reserved to itself, and has constantly exercised the power of altering that disposition in future. Any title or claim of the clergy antecedent to these acts is superseded on the well-known principle that posterior abrogate prior laws. If the acts of Henry VIII. be invalid, if the parliament of the sixteenth century be deemed to have exceeded its powers, what would be the consequences ? Why precisely those which have been forcibly pointed out by Mr. Eagle. All the grantees, *lay* and ecclesiastical, of the lands and tithes of the dissolved monasteries would not have a shadow of a legal title, and therefore the Duke of Bedford and every other descendant of the grantees would be liable to be called to account for the past rents and profits accruing from their possessions.

To conclude, the established clergy are a great body of public stipendiaries, engaged for the discharge of specific duties ; and their rights and constitution resemble more those of our military establishment than any other department of the national service. Like the army, the clergy have their own laws, and may be tried by their own courts. A regular subordination exists from the lowest to the highest ; from the curates, who are privates in the ecclesiastical corps, to the rectors and vicars, who are regimental officers ; from thence to the bishops and archbishops, who are generals and field-marshals : there are, also, district generals, inspectors, and quarter-masters-general under the names of archdeacons, deans, and prebendaries. The bishops have their regular staff of commissaries, chaplains, secretaries, and apothecaries. No clergyman can be absent without leave, and is liable to be broken or cashiered for neglect of duty. The king is the supreme head of the

Church and the Army; he appoints to all the principal commissions, and in both a plurality of commissions may be holden. Supplies are voted by the parliament for both branches of service; either may be augmented or diminished, or entirely discontinued, as circumstances require. Lastly, the military have the same property in their muskets, barracks, and accoutrements, that the clergy have in their pulpits, tithes, and cathedrals; both may be transferred from the present possessors to others, or sold for the benefit of the community.

Such being the tenure of ecclesiastical immunities, it is mere sophistry to contend that the property of the church is as sacred as any other property. No analogy exists betwixt the rights of individuals, or even of corporations, and the rights of the church, and this view of the subject is confirmed by the history of the church itself, and the example of every European government. If the church ever had an indefeasible claim, it could only have appertained to the catholic church, to which the ecclesiastical revenues were originally granted. But whatever corporate or other rights the catholic church might claim, they were annihilated at the Reformation, and the legislators of that period plainly dealt with the possessions of the clergy, as neither perpetually attached to any particular class of persons, nor to any particular form of worship. They evidently treated church endowments as a sort of *waif* or *estray;* and, in assigning them pro tempore to the protestant establishment, they only assigned them on the terms of a tenancy-at-will, subject to such conditions of occupancy, ejectment, forcible entry, &c. as the parliamentary landlords might think expedient from time to time to promulgate.

ii. PATRONAGE OF THE CHURCH.

If the possessions of the clergy are not inviolate, the rights of patrons appear to have a still less substantial guarantee. It has, however, been affirmed by an eminent ecclesiastical judge, Dr. Lushington,* that, whatever opinion might be held on the general tenure of ecclesiastical property, there could be no doubt advowsons were strictly private property. As this is a point of great importance, it may be proper, before we give an exposition of the present state of church patronage, shortly to elucidate the nature and origin of patronial immunities. Our observations will, of course, apply solely to the rights of private individuals: of the tenure of the patronage vested in the king, the lord chancellor, the bishops, deans and chapters, there cannot be any difference of opinion; all these exercise their patronage *ex officio*, and unquestionably the same legislative power which has authority to regulate the functions of these offices, may make regulations as to the disposition of the ecclesiastical patronage appertaining to them.

A patron, as is well known, is one who has the right to present to ecclesiastical preferment. The exercise of this right is called a *presentation*, and the right itself an *advowson*. When the Christian

---

* House of Commons, April 27th, 1830.

religion was first established in England, the sovereign began to build cathedrals, and afterwards, in imitation of him, lords of manors founded churches on part of their demesnes, endowing them with house and glebe, reserving to themselves and heirs a right to present a fit person to the bishop as officiating clergyman. Hence most advowsons were formerly appendant to manors, and the patrons parochial barons: it was only by the corruptions of later ages the lordship of the manor and the patronage of the church were dissevered, and any one, however mean and disreputable, might, by purchase, aspire to the dignity of patron.

Still such presentative right, however valuable it might be as a provision for relatives and friends, was deemed purely an *honorary* function, from the exercise of which no lucrative benefit ought to accrue to the possessor. For the better security of this principle, severe laws have been enacted to punish patrons who dispose of spiritual preferment from interested motives. If a patron present any person to a benefice for a corrupt consideration, by gift, promise, or reward, the presentation is void, and, for that turn, lapses to the Crown. If a person procure a presentation for money or profit, and is presented, he is disabled from holding the living. Even general bonds given to resign a benefice at the request of a patron, or in favour of some particular person, have been declared a violation of the statutes.* Such transactions have been termed *simony*, from their supposed relation to the offence of Simon Magus, who offered, with money, to buy the Holy Ghost. The design of the Legislature was to prevent the obtrusion of improper persons in the ministry, and guard against the patronage of the Church being perverted to objects of mere lucre in lieu of promoting religion and virtue. For the same salutary end, bishops may refuse to institute the presentee of a patron who is not sufficiently learned, or labours under moral or canonical disqualification.

In practice, however, all these precautions are nugatory, and the laws against simony are as easily evaded as those against usury or the sale of seats in the House of Commons. Preferment in the Church is as regular a subject of sale as commissions in the army; and a patron would as soon think of rewarding an individual for his learning and piety with the gift of a freehold estate as a church living. Hence, the door of the church is open to all, whether they have *a call* or not, provided they possess a *golden key;* and, in the Metropolis, offices are openly kept in which spiritual preferment is sold as regularly as offices in the East Indies, medical practice, or any other secular pursuit. Not unfrequently, a *cure of souls* is brought under the hammer of an auctioneer, and a JEW, who maintains our Saviour was an impostor, may, if he please, purchase the right to select a proper person for the ministry of the Gospel. In short, church patronage is dealt with as a mere commodity , and the produce of tithe and glebe, instead of

---

* 31 Eliz. c. 6; 12 Ann, stat. 2, c. 12 ; also, the cases of Bishop of London *v.* Ffytche, and of Fletcher *v.* Lord Sondes.

being employed as the reward of religious zeal and service, is bought, like a life annuity, as a provision and settlement for families.*

These abuses must always continue while the law tolerates the sale of advowsons; it is in vain to prohibit the corrupt presentation to an ecclesiastical benefice, if a third person may purchase the right to present, and, under the semblance of a gift, convey the benefice to his employer. But such perversion can in no way strengthen the claims of patrons, and entitle them to set up a mere incorporeal immunity as real property. The history of church patronage, as well as the enactments of the law, are repugnant to the idea of treating church patronage as houses and land. In cases of bankruptcy and insolvency, the assignees can neither sell nor present to a vacant ecclesiastical benefice; this is a *personal* function which cannot be delegated or assigned like a mere chattel, but must be discharged by the insolvent himself. Were, therefore, the Church reformed to-morrow, and all its ministers placed on an uniform salary of £250 a-year, the patrons of livings could not claim a compensation for the loss of tithe and church estate. They never, either in law or in equity, had a beneficial interest in the Church; their interests were purely honorary and functional: and were the patronage of livings continued to them under a reformed system, however much the value of advowsons might be depreciated in the market, whatever interest they legally possessed would have been abundantly respected.

Having shortly exhibited the origin and tenure of patronial immunities, we shall next explain the present distribution of church patronage, and the mode and purposes for which it is usually employed.

The patronage of the Church is in the king, bishops, deans and chapters, universities, collegiate establishments, aristocracy, and gentry. The king's patronage is the bishoprics, all the deaneries in England, thirty prebends, twenty-three canonries, the mastership of the Temple,

---

* All the offices of the Church being professedly of a spiritual nature, and executed for spiritual objects, an American bishop, Dr. Hobart, during his sojourn in this country, felt much scandalized by reading the following details of secular traffic in the Morning Chronicle, July 13, 1824:—

"The church livings in Essex, sold on the 1st instant, by Mr. Robins, of Regent-street, were not the absolute advowsons, but the next presentations contingent on the lives of Mr. and Mrs. W. T. P. L. Wellesley, aged thirty-six and twenty-five years respectively, and were as under:—

Place.	Description.	Estimated Annual Value.	Age of Incumbent.	Sold for.
Wanstead	Rectory	.... £653	.... 62	£2,440
Woodford	Ditto	 1,200	.... 58	4,200
Gt. Paindon	Ditto	 500	.... 63	1,600
Fifield	Ditto	 525	.... 59	1,520
Rochford	Ditto	 700	.... 62	2,000
Filstead	Vicarage	 400	.... 50	900
Roydon	Ditto	 200	.... 46	580

The biddings appeared to be governed by the age and health of the incumbents, residence, situation, and other local circumstances, with which the parties interested seemed to be well acquainted."

the wardenship of the collegiate church of Manchester, and 1048 livings. The lord chancellor presents to all the livings under the value of £20 in the king's book, which are about 780; he also presents to six prebendal stalls in Bristol cathedral, and to five in each of the cathedrals of Gloucester, Norwich, and Rochester; the other ministers present to the remaining patronage of the crown. Upwards of 1600 pieces of church-preferment are in the gift of the bishops; more than 600 in the presentation of the two universities; 57 in the colleges of Eton and Winchester: about 1000 in the gifts of cathedrals and collegiate establishments; and the remainder in the gift of the aristocracy and private individuals.

The population-returns of 1821 make the number of parishes and parochial chapelries in England and Wales 10,674; which, divided into rectories and vicarages, exhibit the following classification of parochial patronage :—

In the gift of	Rectories.	Vicarages.
The crown	558	490
The bishops	592	709
Deans and chapters	190	792
University of Oxford	202	112
University of Cambridge	152	131
Collegiate establishments	39	107
Private individuals	3,444	3,175

In addition, there are 649 chapels not parochial, making the total number of benefices in England and Wales, without allowing for the consolidation of the smaller parishes, 11,342. To this number ought to be added 227 new churches and chapels erected under the authority of the Church-Building-Acts, and which must hereafter greatly augment the patronage and revenues of the established church. All these churches and chapels constitute, by the statutes, so many separate benefices, their ministers are incumbents, and bodies corporate, empowered to take endowments in land or tithes.

The benefices now in the gift of the Crown were reservations, when the manors to which they were appendant were granted away, or were acquired by lapse, or conferred on Henry VIII. and his successors, by act of parliament, at the dissolution of the monasteries to which they belonged. The livings belonging to the bishoprics, the deans and chapters, the universities, and colleges, were the gifts of their munificent founders. Those in the hands of private individuals have come into their possession along with their estates, or they have purchased or inherited the advowson dissevered from manorial rights.

Directly or indirectly the entire patronage of the church may be said to be vested in the Crown. No one is eligible to church-preferment, unless first ordained by the bishop; when eligible, no one can enjoy any benefice unless instituted by a bishop: the bishops, therefore, by ordination and institution, have a double power to exclude obnoxious persons: and the bishops themselves being appointed by the king, the latter has, virtually, the whole patronage of the church, having a veto on all ecclesiastical appointments by the aristocracy, the gentry, cathedrals, and other bodies in which church patronage is vested. It is easy to conceive how much the power of the Crown is thereby augmented. The clergy, from superior education, from their wealth and sacred profession, possess greater influence than any other order of men, and all the influence they possess is as much subservient to government as the army or navy, or any other branch of public service. Upon every public occasion the consequence of this influence is apparent. There is no question, however unpopular, which may not obtain countenance by the support of the clergy: being everywhere, and having much to lose, and a great deal to expect, they are always active and zealous in devotion to the interests of those on whom their promotion depends. Hence their anxiety to attract notice at county, corporate, and sessional meetings. Whenever a loyal address is to be obtained, a popular petition opposed, or hard measure carried against the poor, it is almost certain some reverend rector, very reverend dean, or venerable archdeacon, will make himself conspicuous.

It has been before remarked that church patronage is a regular article of sale. Besides being sold for money, spiritual preferment is devoted to political objects, and to the emolument of powerful families, chiefly the nobility. Few individuals attain high honour in the church, unless remarkable for their devotion to government; any show of liberality or independence is fatal to ecclesiastical ambition, as may be instanced in the history of a Watson, a Paley, or a Shipley. On the contrary, hostility to reform, subserviency to ministers, and alacrity in supporting them on all occasions, is sure to be rewarded. We do not think the conduct of the Bishops in voting against the reform bill any objection to this imputation. They, doubtless, calculated, as Lord Brougham remarked, on " tripping up the heels" of the Whig Ministers. That they have mostly thriven by subserviency, will be apparent from adverting to the claims to promotion of the individuals rewarded by mitres under Tory administrations. Two of them are generally known as " the Lady's Bishops," from the nature of the court influence to which it is supposed they were indebted for their exalted stations. Marsh, one of the most orthodox, was a political pamphleteer, who wrote a book in favour of Pitt's war; after which he received a pension, then a bishopric. Blomfield owed his first preferment to a noble lord, whom he had pleased by his dexterity in rendering some Greek verses ; his subsequent elevation is said to have been purchased by a compromise of principle on the catholic question : he did not vote on the first introduction of the reform bill, divided, probably, by a sense of gratitude to his early patron lord Spencer, and uncertainty as to future events. Dr. Monk is also an eminent haberdasher in " points and particles." He was raised to the *throne* of Gloucester, from the deanery of Peterborough and rectory of Fiskerton, and to which elevation it is not unlikely he paved the way by a fulsome dedication of his " *Life of Bentley*" to his friend and patron, the bishop of London. The tergiversations and subserviency of Dr. Philpotts are too notorious to require description. The archbishop of Canterbury is, as far as we know, without any particular trait of distinction, either in his history or character. He was formerly dean of the Royal Chapel, and tutor to the prince of Orange; he seems a man of great singleness of mind; for in one of his charges to the clergy, he deplores the absence of that " humble docility" and " prostration of the understanding" which formerly rendered the people such apt subjects, either of religious or political knavery. The bishop of Durham is of Dutch extraction, and some years since underwent a severe prosecution for non-residence on a benefice in the City, of which he was then incumbent. Burgess is a *protégé* of lord Sidmouth, who is now living in retirement on a pension of £3000 a year, granted for " high and efficient" services to church and state. Coplestone is the writer of a satirical squib, called " Hints to a Young Reviewer," directed against a well-known northern periodical. John Bird Sumner is considered a person of some merit, and has written several articles in the *Edinburgh Encyclopedia.* Carey, too, who was sub-almoner to George III. is also an author and has published a sermon, preached on the occasion of the famous " Jubilee." With the exception of Bathurst and Maltby little is known of the rest; they have mostly been indebted for promotion to marriage, or to their connexions with the aristocracy, either by relationship, or from having filled the office of tutor or secretary in their families. In this roll of services, of accident of birth, of situation, and connexion, there is evidently no claim of public service or utility to entitle the bishops to their princely revenues and vast patronage.

One of the greatest abuses in the disposal of patronage is *monopoly*, in a few individuals, of influence and connexion, sharing among them the most valuable emoluments of the church. In all spiritual offices and dignities, there is a great difference in value, and also in patronage; and the great object of ecclesiastical intrigue is, to secure not only the most valuable, but the greatest number of preferments. Hence arises the present disposition of church property. Scarcely any preferment is held *single;* the sees, dignities, rectories, and vicarages, being mostly held with other good things, and the most valuable monopolized by the relations and connexions of those who have the disposal of them; namely, the Crown, the Bishops, and Aristocracy. The bishops are frequently archdeacons and deans, rectors, vicars, and curates, besides holding professorships, clerkships, prebends, precentorships, and other offices in cathedrals. Their sons, sons-in-law, brothers, and nephews, are also pushed in to the most valuable preferments in the diocese. We shall give an instance of the manner of serving out the loaves and fishes of the church in particular families, from the example of SPARKE, bishop of Ely, who owed his promotion to the circumstance of having been tutor to the duke of Rutland. The exhibition is limited to the two sons and son-in-law of the bishop, without including appointments to distant relatives. In the shiftings, exchanges, resignations, movings about, and heaping up of offices, we have a complete picture of the ecclesiastical evolutions which are constantly being performed in almost every diocese of the kingdom.

1815. The Rev. John Henry Sparke, the eldest son, took his degree of B.A.; he was then about 21; he was immediately appointed by his father to a bishop's fellowship in Jesus College, Cambridge.

1816. He was appointed steward of all his father's manorial courts.

1818. He took his degree of M.A., and was presented to a prebendal stall in Ely Cathedral, on the resignation of the Rev. Archdeacon Brown, who had been holding it one year: he was also presented to the sinecure rectory of Littlebury, and in the following month he was presented to the living of Streatham-cum-Thetford, by an exchange with the Rev. Mr. Law for the living of Downham, which last living had been held for three years by the Rev. Mr. Daubeny, the bishop's nephew, who now resigned it in favour of Mr. Law, and retired to the living of Bexwell.

1819. The Rev. J. H. Sparke had a dispensation granted him from the archbishop of Canterbury, permitting him to hold the living of Cottenham with his other preferments.

1818. The Rev. Henry Fardell, the bishop's son-in-law, was ordained deacon.

1819. He was presented to a prebendal stall in Ely, the degree of M.A. having been conferred on him by the archbishop of Canterbury.

1821. He was presented to the living of Tyd St Giles.

1822. He was presented to the living of Waterbeach, on the resignation of the Rev. Mr. Mitchell.

1823. He resigned Tyd St. Giles, and was presented to Bexwell, on the resignation of the Rev. Mr. Daubeny, the bishop's nephew, who was presented to Feltwell; but in a few weeks, when the value of Feltwell was better understood, Mr. Daubeny was required to resign Feltwell and return to Bexwell. This, it is said, he did with great reluctance; he was, however, presented to Tyd as well as Bexwell, and the Rev. Mr. Fardell was then presented to Feltwell.

1824. The Rev. J. Henry Sparke was appointed Chancellor of the diocese, and this year he resigned the prebendal stall he held, and was presented to the one which became vacant by the death of the Rev. Sir H. Bate Dudley; the house and gardens belonging to the latter stall being considered the best in the College.

1826. The Rev. Edward Sparke, the bishop's youngest son, took his degree of B.A., and was immediately presented by his father to a bishop's fellowship in St. John's College, Cambridge, on the resignation of Charles Jenyns, Esq. a friend of the family, who had been holding it three years. He was also appointed Register of the diocese.

1827. The Rev. J. Henry Sparke resigned the livings of Cottenham and Stretham, and was presented to the rich living of Leverington.

1829. The Rev. J. Henry Sparke was presented to Bexwell.

1829. The Rev. Edward Sparke took his degree of M.A. and was presented to a prebendal stall on the resignation of Rev. Ben. Park (another friend of the family) who had been holding it three years.

He was also this year presented to the living of Hogeworthingham, and to the living of Barley.

1830. He resigned Hogeworthingham, and was presented to Connington. This year he resigned Barley also, and was presented to Littleport.

1831. He resigned Connington, and was presented to Feltwell, at the same time he resigned his prebendal stall, and was presented to the one become vacant by the death of the Rev. George King—the rich living of Sutton being in the gift of the possessor of the latter stall.

1831. The Rev. Henry Fardell resigned Feltwell, and was presented to the rich living of Wisbech.

The Rev. J. Henry Sparke now holds the living of Leverington, the sinecure rectory of Littlebury, the living of Bexwell, a prebendal stall in Ely Cathedral, is steward of all his father's manorial courts, and Chancellor of the diocese. The estimated annual value of the whole, £4,500.

The Rev. Henry Fardell now holds the living of Waterbeach, the vicarage of Wisbech, and a prebendal stall in Ely Cathedral. The estimated annual value of his preferments, £3,700.

The Rev. Edward Sparke holds the consolidated livings of St. Mary and St. Nicholas, Feltwell, the vicarage of Littleport, a prebendal stall in Ely, is Register of the diocese, and Examining Chaplain to his father. The estimated annual value of his appointments not less than £4000.

The bishop's see of Ely and dependencies, £27,742.

Total income of the Sparke family, £39,942.

In the Ordination-Service a bishop is said to be intrusted with office for " the glory of God, and the edification of the Christian flock." He is particularly enjoined not to be " covetous," nor " greedy of filthy lucre," and he promises to be " faithful in ordaining, sending, and laying hands on others." How far bishop Sparke has observed these matters, we shall not presume to say; it is obvious, however, that the faithful discharge of the duties of his office does not allow the " sending" of relations and connexions on the service of the church, unless duly and properly qualified. For any thing we know, his sons and son-in-law may be amply qualified for these numerous endowments ; indeed, they must be men of extraordinary capabilities, to be able to discharge the duties of so many and important offices.

Bishop Sparke is not the only prelate who has shown regard to the temporal welfare of his family. Other prelates seem to agree with lord Plunket and sir R.Inglis, in considering church property of the nature of private property, which cannot be better employed than in providing handsome marriage portions for their sons and daughters. Several prelates are of too recent elevation to have had time to send off numerous branches into the church; but an example or two from their immediate predecessors on the bench will illustrate the ordinary working of the system. The late archbishop SUTTON is an eminent instance of the perversion of ecclesiastical patronage. The Suttons remaining in the church are very numerous; among seven of them are shared sixteen rectories, vicarages, and chapelries, besides preacherships and dignities in cathedrals. Of the *eleven* daughters of the archbishop, several had the prudence to marry men in holy orders, who soon became amply endowed. Hugh Percy, son of the earl of Beverly, married one daughter; and, in the course of about as many years, was portioned off with eight different preferments, estimated to be worth £10,000 per annum; four of these preferments were given in one year, probably that of the nuptials, and intended as an *outfit*. This fortunate son-in-law is now bishop of Carlisle, to which see he was translated from Rochester. According to law he ought to have resigned all the preferments he held at the time of being promoted to a bishopric; but somehow he has contrived to retain the most valuable prebend of St. Paul's, worth £3000 per annum, and also the chancellorship of Sarum. Another daughter of the archbishop married the Rev. James Croft, who is archdeacon of Canterbury, prebendary of Canterbury, curate of Hythe, rector of

Cliffe-at-Hone, and rector of Saltwood—all preferments in the gift of the archbishop. Archbishop Sutton kept a favourable eye towards *collaterals* as well as those in a direct line. A sister married a Rev. Richard Lockwood, who was presented, in one year, with the three vicarages of Kessingland, Lowestoff, and Potter-Heigham: all these livings are valuable, and in the gift of the bishop of Norwich, and were presented by his grace when he held that see. The archbishop left the Rev. T. M. Sutton and the Rev. Evelyn L. Sutton, chaplains to the House of Commons, and a nephew with several livings ; but we cannot state particulars.

The late bishop of Winchester is another instance of a man who provided well for his family out of the revenues of the church. This prelate first held the sea of Lincoln, and changed his name from Pretyman to Tomline, on acceding to a large estate bequeathed by a relation. He had been tutor to the " heaven-born Minister," to whom he was indebted for his earliest preferments. His children, it will be seen, from the subjoined enumeration, are not left destitute in the world.

G. T. PRETYMAN:
Chancellor and Canon Residentiary of Lincoln,
Prebendary of Winchester,
Rector of St. Giles, Chalfont,
Rector of Wheat-Hampstead,
Rector of Harpenden.

RICHARD PRETYMAN:
Precentor and Canon Residentiary of Lincoln,
Rector of Middleton-Stoney,
Rector of Walgrave,
Vicar of Hannington,
Rector of Wroughton.

JOHN PRETYMAN:
Prebendary of Lincoln,
Rector of Sherrington,
Rector of Winwick.

The younger Pretymans had, also, some nice pickings out of the Mere and Spital charities, the wardenship of which the father got hold of by the exchange of a living in his gift; but as the subject has already been before the public, we refrain from dwelling upon it.

The Sumners, Blomfields, and Marshes are growing thick in the church calendar, but, as before remarked, they have been too recently planted to have yet struck their roots wide and deep in the Lord's vineyard. The death of a bishop causes a movement in the church, like a change of ministers in the state. Expectations are excited, numerous removes follow, the adherents and connexions of the deceased are got out of the way as fast as possible, and all vacancies filled with the followers of the new diocesan. No regard is apparently paid to " the faithful ordaining, sending, or laying hands on others ;" the great object is to secure the dignities, the fat living, the fine living, the noble living to the *next of kin.* The excessive greediness of filthy lucre has long been the reproach of the episcopal bench, and it is known that former diocesans of London, Durham, Winchester, and Canterbury, have died loaded with the spoils of the church. The wealth they amassed was due to the poor, to God, and the unfortunate of their own order. In the epistle which is read at their consecration, it is required of them that they should " be given to hospitality:" they, likewise, solemnly promise to assist the " indigent, and all strangers who are destitute of help." But who ever heard of a bishop being generous, of being given to hospitality, or assisting the unfortunate? who ever heard of them employing their immense revenues in any useful work; of their patronage of science, of literature, or the arts? Most of them have been only intent on amassing immense fortunes, and leaving behind them their million or half million, like Jew-jobbers, loan-contractors, and commercial speculators. They live out of the world, consuming, in solitary indulgence, the spoil of the industrious, and without sympathy with the misfortunes and vicissitudes of life. They have no bowels even for the indigent of their own class : in the rich diocese of Durham it is known begging subscriptions are had every year for the poor clergy and their families; and measures introduced into Parliament for the general relief of the inferior clergy have usually failed from the opposition of the higher class of ecclesiastics.

In the disposal of *Parochial Patronage* there is the same abuse and monopoly as prevail in the higher departments of the church. The most valuable benefices, like the most valuable sees and dignities, fall into the hands of those whose chief claims are their families and connexions. By bringing forward the poor livings, it is usual to make out a favourable case for the parochial clergy; but from the small number of individuals among whom parochial preferments are shared, there are few except the curates entitled to much sympathy. We shall illustrate this point by laying before the reader a list of incumbents, selected almost at random, which will at once show the measureless rapacity that directs the disposal of church-preferment.

Robert Affleck, prebendary of York; rector of Silkston, with Bretton-Monk and Stainbury chapelries; rector of East Mediety; rector of West Mediety, Tresswell; perpetual curate of Thockerington; vicar of Westow.

Henry Anson, vicar of Buxton, with rectory of Oxnead and rectory of Skeyton; rector of Lyng with vicarage of Whitwell.

H. Bathurst, archdeacon of Norwich; rector of North Creake; rector of Oby with rectory of Ashby and rectory of Thurne.

J. W. Beadon, precentor and prebendary of Wells; precentor of Brecon; rector of Farley-Chamberl; rector of Christian-Mal.

J. T. Casberd, prebendary of Wells and Llandaff; also, one rectory, four vicarages, and two chapelries.

Charles W. Eyre, prebendary of York; rector of Carlton, in Lindrick; rector of Hooton-Roberts; vicar of Kilnwick-Percy; vicar of Pocklington with the chapelry of Yapham.

John Fisher, archdeacon of Berks; canon-residentiary of Sarum; also, two vicarages and three chapelries.

Dr. Forester, prebendary of Worcester; rector of Broseley; rector of Little Wenlock, with the chapelries of Barrow and Benthall; vicar of St. John's, Worcester.

Dr. Goddard, archdeacon and prebendary of Lincoln; chaplain to the king; vicar of Bexley; vicar of Louth; rector of St. James, Garlichythe, London.

Dr. Goodall, provost of Eton; canon of Windsor; vicar of Bromham; rector of Hitcham : rector of West Ilsley.

Dr. E. Goodenough, dean of Bath and Wells; prebendary of Westminster; ditto of Carlisle; ditto of York: vicar of Wath, All Saints-on-Dearne, with the, chapelries of Adwick and Brampton Bierlow.

W. Goodenough, archdeacon of Carlisle; rector of Mareham-le-Fen; rector of Great Salkeld.

Hon. T. de Grey, archdeacon of Surrey; prebendary of Winchester and chaplain to the king; rector of Calbourne; rector of Fawley with the chapelry of Exburg; rector of Merton.

Earl of Guildford, rector of New and Old Alresford, with chapelry of Medstead; rector and precentor of St. Mary, Southampton; master of St. Cross with St. Faith's.

A. Hamilton, archdeacon of Taunton; prebendary of Wells; chaplain to the King; rector of Loughton; rector of St. Mary-le-Bow, of St. Pancras, and of Allhallows, London.

W. Hett, prebendary and vicar-choral of Lincoln; vicar of Dunholme; rector of Enderby Navis; vicar of St. John's and rector of St. Paul's, Lincoln; minister of Greetwell and Nettleham chapelries; rector of Thorpe-on-the Hill.

Hon. H. L. Hobart, dean of Windsor and of Wolverhampton; rector of Haseley; vicar of Nocton; vicar of Wantage.

Dr. Hodgson, dean of Carlisle; vicar of Burgh-on-Sands; vicar of Hillingdon; rector of St. George's, Hanover-square.

Hon. E. S. Keppel, rector of Quiddenham, with rectory of Snetterton; vicar of St. Mary's and All Saints, Shottisham; rector of Tittleshall with rectories of Godwick and Wellingham.

Dr. Madan, prebendary and chancellor of Peterborough; chaplain to the King; rector of Ibstock, with chapelries of Dunnington and Hugglescote; rector of Thorpe Constantine.

Herbert Marsh, bishop of Peterborough; rector of Castor, with chapalries of Sutton, St. Michael, and Upton; rector of St. Clement and St. John, Terrington.

Dr. Oldershaw, archdeacon of Norfolk, with perpetual curacy of Coston; vicar of Ludham; vicar of Ranworth, with the vicarage of St. Margaret, Upton; rector of Redenhall with chapelry of Harlestone.

Hon. G. Pellew, dean of Norwich; prebendary of York; and rector of St. Dionis Backchurch, London.

F. D. Perkins, chaplain to the King; vicar of Foleshill; ditto of Hatherley-Down; ditto of Sow; ditto of Stoke; rector of Swayfield; ditto of Ham.

Lord Wm. Somerset, prebendary of Bristol; rector of Crickhowel; rector of Llangallock, with chapelries of Llanelly and Llangenneth.

Lord John Thynne, prebendary of Westminster; rector of Kingston-Deverill; rector of Street, with chapelry of Walton.¶

Wm. Trivett, vicar of Arlington; ditto of Willington; ditto of Ashburnham, with rectory of Penshurst; rector of Bradwell.

James Webber, dean of Ripon and prebendary of Westminster; vicar of Kirkham; rector of St. Mary, Westminster.

Fras. Wrangham, archdeacon of York and prebendary of York and Chester; rector of Dodleston; vicar of Hunmanby, with chapelry of Fordon; vicar of Muston.

Abundant other examples of equal or greater enormity will be found in the List of Pluralists subjoined to this Article. But nothing, in a small compass, attests more strikingly the abuses in patronage, and the scan-

dalous manner in which offices are heaped on favoured individuals, than
a comparison of the whole number of ecclesiastical preferments with
the whole number of persons among whom they are divided. This is a
test which may be applied with perfect accuracy. The only description
of ecclesiastics whose number cannot be ascertained with precision are
the curates and the inferior classes connected with cathedral and collegiate churches; the rest may be easily reckoned up from the *Clerical
Guide*, which contains the names of all the episcopal, dignified, and
beneficed clergy. From this work we find that the whole number of
prelates, dignitaries, rectors, vicars, and perpetual curates, in England
and Wales, is only *seven-thousand six-hundred and ninety-four*.
Those who make the established clergy amount to 18,000 must needs
include the parish-clerk, sexton, and grave-digger; but these functionaries of the church not being in holy orders, they certainly ought not
to be included in the ecclesiastical corps, any more than the groom,
valet, or other menials of clergymen. Neither ought curates to be included : they are merely the hired deputies of their principals, without
institution or induction, and always subject to removal at the pleasure
of the bishop or incumbent. Omitting these classes, we affirm that the
whole number of endowed and beneficed clergy is, as we have stated,
7694, and by this diminutive number are the whole preferments of the
church monopolized. These preferments are, as we collect from COVE
and other sources, as under :—

Sees	26
Chancellorships	26
Deaneries of cathedral and collegiate churches	28
Archdeaconries	61
Prebends and canonries	514
Minor canonries, priest-vicars, vicars-choral, and other dignities and offices, without including lay-offices in cathedrals	330
Rectories, vicarages, and chapelries	11,342
Total	12,327

Thus, there are 12,327 places of preferment divided among 7694 individuals, affording nearly two for each. This extraordinary monopoly
of offices accounts for the vast number of pluralists. The whole
number of incumbents in England and Wales is 7191 ; of this number,
2886 hold two or more rectories, vicarages, and chapelries. From data
in the last edition of the Clerical Guide, published in 1829, we have
drawn up the following classification of parochial patronage, exhibiting
the number of individuals and the number of parochial preferments
enjoyed by each.

PAROCHIAL PATRONAGE, *showing the Number of Individuals, and the Number of Rectories, Vicarages, and Chapelries held by each.*

Number of Individuals.	Livings held by each.	Total Number of Livings.
1	11	11
1	8	8
5	7	35
12	6	72
64	5	320
209	4	836
567	3	1701
2027	2	4054
4305	1	4305
7191		11,342

According to strict ecclesiastical discipline, no minister ought to hold more than *one* living;* and, for the better care of the souls of parishioners, he ought to reside on his benefice. Laws have been made, and are still in force,† imposing forfeitures and penalties on clergymen who, having one living, accept another, or who absent themselves from their parishes. These laws, however, in practice, like the representation of the people in the lower house of parliament, are little more than the theory of church government. By dispensations and licenses, a clergyman may hold as many livings as he can get, and he need not reside on any of them. Hence it is that considerably more than one-third of the whole number of incumbents are PLURALISTS. Many have five, four, and three livings. Majendie, late Bishop of Bangor, who died in 1830, held no fewer than ELEVEN parochial preferments. These preferments we presume are held by his successor, and what an extraordinary divine he must be to be able to administer his various episcopal and parish duties! In the above classification are not included cathedral dignities, fellowships in the universities, chaplainships, professorships, masterships of grammar-schools, and other offices held by incumbents, and to which members of the Establishment are exclusively eligible. It merely shows the cutting-up of parochial benefices, and it is hardly necessary to add that those who are in possession of the most valuable and greatest number are connected by birth, marriage, politics, or in some other way, with those who have the disposal of them. Indeed, it is impossible to peruse the list of dignitaries and highly-beneficed clergy, without remarking that many of them are "honourable lumber," who have been turned over to spiritual pursuits from inability to succeed in the

---

* For the sense in which the term *living* has been used in the preceding classification, see the *Explanations* prefixed to the List of Pluralists at the end of this article.

† Statutes 21 Henry VIII. c.13, and 57 Geo. III. c. 99.

more arduous professions of the law, the army, or the navy. In the church, as in the state, those chiefly work for the public who have no other dependence, who are of plebeian extraction, and without support from family interest or aristocratic connexion.

III. SINECURISM—NON-RESIDENCE—PLURALITIES—CHURCH DISCIPLINE.

Sinecurism abounds more in our ecclesiastical than civil establishment. In the church almost every thing is done by deputy,—a consequence naturally resulting from her great wealth ; for where large salaries are annexed, great duties are seldom discharged. Those with large incomes have various reasons for not burthening themselves with official toil. First, they can afford to pay for a deputy ; secondly, they can purchase or influence the connivance of others for neglect of their own duties ; thirdly, they have the means for indulgence and recreation, which, consuming much time, leave little leisure for more serious avocations. Hence has arisen sinecurism in both Church and State ; presenting the singular spectacle of one class receiving the pay, and another, born under less favorable auspices, doing the work for which the pay is received.

Among the different orders of our ecclesiastical polity, there are none, with the exception of the curates and a few beneficed clergy, who reside and do the duties of their parishes ; the remainder being clerical sinecurists, filled with the Holy Ghost, to share in the rich endowments of the church. The bishops are most amply remunerated, and, as is usual in such cases, perform the least service. They employ archdeacons to visit for them ; rural deans and others to preach for them ; and a vicar-general to issue licenses, hold courts, and perform other drudgery ; if otherwise engaged, they employ a brother bishop to ordain for them. They have their own chaplains, commissaries, and secretaries ; in short, their work must be light, and chiefly consists in keeping an eye to the next translation, and the falling in of the rich livings. In the Ordination Service, however, they are enjoined strict and abstemious duties. It is there said a bishop must be " blameless," they are admonished diligently to preach the word, and be conspicuous examples of various Christian virtues." They are now chiefly known among the people by their grotesque attire. They are the only *men* (save exquisites) who continue to dress in imitation of the female sex, or take pains to disguise themselves under uncouth habiliments. The *shovel*, or *coal-scuttle* hat is particularly distinguishable. It is the remains of the old hat worn by Roman Catholic priests in their days of splendour, and still to be seen on the Continent. Under this chapeau is a bush of false hair, plastered and twisted into a most unnatural size and ridiculous shape, resembling any thing but what we may suppose to have been the fashion among the apostles. To these distinctions may be added the long gaiters and " lady's maid apron," from the hips to the knees only, so that the gaiters may not be concealed. These gaiters are of vast importance, importing that the wearers are meek and *lowly*, and constantly *walking about* doing good.* Nevertheless they often ride in dashing style through the streets, attended by grooms in purple liveries, and some of them are very Nimrods in the country.

Many of the church dignitaries are distinguishable by peculiarities of dress, as the shovel hat and kirtle. Their duties are less onerqus than those of the bishops. For instance, what are the duties of the very reverend Dean ? he is chiefly known among sextons and monument-builders. Mr. Gordon, in the debate on the Curates' Salary Bill, said he knew a clergyman who was dignitary in no fewer than six cathedrals. Were there any duties to perform, how could a man discharge the duties of so many different offices, in so many different places, perhaps at the distance of some hundred miles from each other ? Archbishop Cranmer, in a letter to Cromwell, in the reign of Henry VIII., denounces the canons and prebendaries as a " superfluous condition."† He says, a prebendary is neither a " learner nor a teacher, but a good *viander*, who wastes his substance in superfluous *belly cheer*." If they were a " *superfluous condition*" under a Popish regime, they must be much more so under a Protestant establishment. The prebends, however, are very valuable, some of them worth £3000 a year, which will be a good reason with many for retaining them as a part of the venerable establishment. What further adds to their value is, that, being benefices not having cure of souls, they may be held with other preferment without a dispensation for plurality.

The Parochial Clergy are, for the most part, a mass of sinecurists. In one respect, Church of Englandism is an improvement on the original simplicity of the gospel, by rendering the discharge of its duties almost a mechanical operation. No long and expensive course of education is requisite to prepare her ministers : all her service is written ; no extempore preaching or praying ; it requires no mind, merely to be able to read is enough. To perform such a puerile and heartless ceremony, it is not surprising a majority of the clergy conceive it unnecessary to reside on their benefices. Of the violation of the law in this respect, of the penalties incurred by this violation, and of the Bill of Indemnity passed by our immaculate representatives to screen the delinquents, we shall relate an extraordinary example.

It is necessary to premise that, under the 43d Geo. III. c. 84, every spiritual person, possessed of any archdeaconry, deanery, or other dignity or benefice, is required to reside on his preferment ; if he absent himself without license from the bishop, or some special cause of exemption, he is subject to penalties varying from one-third to three-fourths of the annual value of his dignity or benefice, recoverable by action of debt by *any person* suing for the same. This act was passed

---

* The Church and Nothing but the Church, p. 12.
† Bentham's *Church of Englandism*, p. 250, where this curious epistle is inserted at length.

to amend a statute of Henry VIII. as regards the residence of the clergy ; it has been subsequently modified by the 57th Geo. III. c. 99, and was introduced by Sir William Scott, (now Lord Stowell,) and solemnly enacted, in the year 1803, by king, lords, and commons. In the year 1811, Mr. Wright commenced nearly 200 different actions against the incumbents in the dioceses of London, Ely, and Norwich, to recover the penalties under the statute. This gentleman had been secretary to four right reverend bishops—the bishops of London, Norwich, Ely, and some other prelate—and, of course, had enjoyed the most ample opportunities for procuring correct information of the conduct of the clergy. These opportunities appear not to have been neglected. In a series of letters published in the Morning Chronicle, betwixt the 6th November, 1813, and the 11th March, 1814, he favoured the public with many curious disclosures which had come to his knowledge during the discharge of his official duties.

In his letter of November 20th, he says that he has selected from well authenticated documents 10,801 benefices, on which there are only 4,490 incumbents, even said to be resident, so that there are 6,311 confessedly non-resident incumbents ; to supply whose places 1,523 resident curates are employed, which leaves 4,788, which are acknowledged to have neither a resident curate nor incumbent. The whole number of curates, whether resident or not, employed to supply the place of non-resident incumbents, is only 3,730, and only 1,793 of these are licensed ; whereas, according to the canon and statute law, no person has a right to officiate until he is licensed. In one diocese, he says, one-third of the livings have had duty reduced from twice to once on a Sunday ; and in another diocese, one-third of the parsonage-houses were returned in *bad repair*, as an excuse for the non-residence of our gentlemen pastors. Speaking of the *false pretences* made use of by the clergy, in order to avoid residing among their parishioners, and the scandalous lives they lead, he says,—

" Now ill-health of the incumbent himself, or his wife, or daughter, is a common pretext, when no other *legal* cause can be found of avoiding residence. Of *twenty-two* licenses granted in one diocese for this reason, *three* only of the persons are in a state of health to warrant it, and the benefices from which they so absent themselves are very valuable. Whether the ministers whom I thus challenge as using false pretences deserve the imputation, will best appear by the mode of life they adopt. Some live in town during the winter ; and although night air certainly cannot benefit a valetudinarian, they may be constantly seen at card parties, routs, or the theatres. In summer, enjoying the amusements of fashionable watering places ; whilst, too often, their curates, by the parsimonious stipends they afford them, are with a numerous family in a state of the greatest poverty. Others have beneficial schools in the neighbourhood of London. Others are continually to be met with near their residence in more pleasant parts of the country, enjoying the sports of the field, or vigorously endeavouring to detect some poor countryman who may have an unfortunate inclination to taste game ! Others may be seen most days driving their own carriage ! Some are in debt, and some are Curates near the Fens! and all to observers seem *perfectly healthful;* yet a certificate from a medical man is deposited with the bishop that they are not so; probably it is six or eight years before when there might have existed a degree of temporary ill-health, but after the cause ceases, the same plea is continued; and a license once granted, is renewed as a matter of course."—Lett. IV. Jan. 6, 1814.

Thus we see how these reverend gentlemen are employed; not in administering spiritual instruction to the ignorant, comfort to the afflicted, or alms and clothing to the naked. Oh! no; these are ignoble pursuits, the mere theory of the profession. They pretend sickness in order to obtain a license for non-residence, that they may bawl at the card-table, frequent the playhouse, tally-ho, shoot, play at cricket, brandish the coachman's whip, and bully at fashionable watering-places. Remember, these jovial spirits are all filled with the Holy Ghost,—empowered to forgive or not to forgive sins—have the cure of souls; that their poor curates are starving on a wretched stipend, and that, in the maintenance of both, the industrious are deprived of the fruits of their labour, and the necessary comforts of their families wasted in the profligate and dissipated lives of their parochial ministers.

In Letter V. Jan. 18th, 1814, Mr. Wright gives the following statement, collected, he says, with infinite pains, of the state of the ecclesiastical discipline in the small diocese of Ely, in 1813, compared with the year 1728 :—

In 1728.	In 1813.
On 140 livings, 70 Resident Incumbents.	On the same 140 livings, 45 Resident Incumbents.
Thirty-four who reside near and perform the duty.	Seventeen who reside near and perform the duty.
Thirty-one curates who reside in the parish or near it.	Thirty-five curates, some of whom reside eight, ten, or twelve miles off.
The population was 56,944 souls.	The population is 82,176 souls.
The duty was performed 261 times every Sunday.	The service is performed about 185 times every Sunday.
And their income £12,719 per annum.	And their income is now £61,474 per annum.

This is singular—duty neglected in proportion as it became more important and better paid. The population increased one-half, and the number of times service is performed diminished one-third. The revenues increased almost fivefold, and the number of resident incumbents decreased one-third. What sincere and conscientious labourers in the vineyard of the Lord! How strikingly it confirms the observation that "Religion brought forth wealth, and the daughter devoured the mother."

"The number of these (says Mr. Wright, Lett. II.) who have neglected their duty in contempt of the law, and in direct violation of solemn oath and bond, are far more than can be contemplated without a considerable degree of alarm." One vicar obtained a license from a bishop for non-residence on one living, stating that he was going to reside near another in a different part of the kingdom. On inquiring for him at the place where he was supposed to reside, he was gone to a more *fashionable part of the country*. On another, to ' encourage him,' the great tithes were settled, worth near £1200 : when he was instituted, *he took* AN OATH *to reside*, which he afterwards neglected to observe. A rector, holding two valuable rectories worth £1200 per annum, to obtain which he gave bond to the archbishop that he would constantly reside on one, and keep a resident curate on the other, himself preaching on the benefice where he did not reside thirteen sermons every year : this worthy son of the church contrived to evade these conditions, and got a poor devil of a curate to do the work of both livings for £84 a year. Another rector holding two livings, one worth £500, the other £400—he lived 200 miles off, and had neither resident nor licensed curate !

On the subject of *pluralities* and of non-residence together, the Secretary to four bishops says, " In one diocese there are about 216 clergymen, who each hold two livings ; 40 who hold three each ; 13 who hold four each ; 1 who holds five ; 1 who holds six, besides dignities and offices : and although many of these thus accounted *single* benefices are two, three, four, or five parishes *consolidated*, yet a great part of these pluralists do not reside on any of their preferments." In Lett. VII. he says, " I will prove that there are pluralists holding more than *seven benefices* and dignities."

It might be thought these statements of Mr. Wright were exaggerations or the result of personal pique, had they not been fully supported by the Diocesan Returns laid before the Privy Council, and ordered by the House of Commons to be printed. From these returns in the years 1809, 1810, 1811, and 1827, we shall insert an abstract, and then a few explanations : it will shew at once the state of church discipline both at present, and when the Secretary was arrested in his attempt to bring the delinquents to justice.

	CASES OF NON-RESIDENTS IN YEARS			
	1809.	1810.	1811.	1827.
1. Resident on other benefices	1240	1846	2059	2163
2. Absent without licence or exemption	672	650	1033	405
3. Exemptions not notified	817	363	155	9
4. Infirmity of incumbent or family	465	389	396	395
5. Want or unfitness of parsonage-house	944	943	1068	1389
6. Incumbents residing in the neighbourhood, and doing duty	565	348	301	815
7. Unenumerated cases confirmed by the Archb.	54	35	26	13
8. Dilapidated churches	23	34	56	39
9. Sinecures	233	70	68	33
10. Livings held by Bishops	26	35	21	10
11. Recent institutions	—	54	33	71
12. Miscellaneous cases	1271	38	51	41
Total open to connivance	6310	4903	5268	5383
Total of non-residents	7358	5840	6311	6120
Total of residents	3836	4421	4490	4413
Total of residents and non-residents together	11,194	10,261	10,801	10,533

The first of these totals contains the twelve preceding classes, in each class of which there is room for connivance on the part of the bishops to whom the returns are made, and of falsehood and evasion on the part of the incumbents. The second total exhibits the whole number of non-residents; and the fourth, the total number of residents and non-residents together, in England and Wales. Hence it appears, that considerably more than one-half of the whole number of incumbents do not reside on their benefices; receive large salaries for nothing; and the little duty that is performed is performed by their curates.

As the Diocesan Returns for 1827* are the latest printed, it may be proper to exhibit more particularly, as follows, the state of church discipline in that year.

RESIDENTS:

Resident in the parsonage-house ··············	3598	
Resident within two miles of the church or chapel, there being no parsonage-house ··············	815	
Total-residents ····· ·················		4413
NON-RESIDENTS:		
Non-residents exempt ·····················	2619	
Non-residents licensed ····················	2147	
Cases which could not be included among licenses or exemptions························· ··· ·····	1313	
Miscellaneous cases ·························	41	
Total non-residents·····················		6120
Total number of benefices returned··········		10,533

Thus, only 3598 incumbents consider the parsonage-houses good enough to reside in; the rest are absentees. According to Mr. Wright, *want or unfitness of parsonage-house* is a common pretext for obtaining a license for non-residence: in one diocese, he says, one-third of the parsonage-houses were returned in bad repair. In 1827, this aversion of the clergy to their domicile appears to have augmented; in that year 1398, or more than one-eighth of the whole number of parsonage-houses in the kingdom were returned as not fit places for our aristocratic pastors to reside in; or, in other words, as an excuse for a license to desert their parishes, and roam about the country in quest of more lively amusements than churching, christening, and spiritually instructing their parishioners.

Among the clergymen *exempt from residence*, a large portion consists of those who reside on other benefices; that is, holding more livings than one, they cannot, of course, reside on both. The exemptions also include such privileged persons as chaplains to the nobility; preachers and officers in the royal chapels and inns of court; wardens, provosts, fellows, tutors, and ushers in the universities, col-

* Parliamentary Paper, No. 471, Sess. 1830.

leges, and public schools; the principal and professors of the East-India college; and officers of cathedral and collegiate churches. The duties of many of these offices are such as ought to disqualify the possessors altogether from church preferment. For instance, what reason is there in masters of the Charter-house claiming exemptions; in other words, seeking to hold benefices and dignities in addition to their other offices and duties? Surely the management of a great public foundation, with upwards of 800 scholars, and incomes of near £1000 per annum, afford sufficient both employment and remuneration, without incurring the responsibility of a *cure of souls.* The same remark applies to the heads of colleges, and the masters and teachers of endowed charities. With so many friendless curates in the country, starving on miserable stipends, there is no need that any class of persons should be overburthened with duties, or corrupted by the aggregation of extravagant salaries.

Of the other cases of non-residence, mentioned in the above table, we shall offer only some brief remarks. The cases of those who plead *sickness and infirmity* have been sufficiently illustrated by an extract from Mr. Wright, page 34. *Sinecures* hardly need explaining; they are offices yielding masses of pay without any duty whatever. *Livings held by bishops* present a curious anomaly; the right reverend prelates commit the very offence of absenteeism, which it is their duty to prevent being committed by the subaltern clergy of their diocese. Lastly, among the *miscellaneous cases* are included those livings held in *sequestration.* In these instances, the incumbent being insolvent, possession, at the instance of some creditor, had been taken of the benefice, to raise money for the discharge of his debts. In 1811 the number of livings held by sequestration was seventy-eight; in 1827, forty-eight.

Such is a brief exposition of the state of church discipline, as exhibited by official documents, and the averments of Mr. Wright, when that gentleman commenced his actions against the clergy. We have stated that the number of actions amounted to 200; and had Mr. Wright been allowed to recover, the penalties would have amounted to £80,000. To this sum he had an indisputable claim; a claim as sacred as any person can have to an estate devised by will, or on mortgage, or other legal security; his claim had been guaranteed to him by a solemn. act of the legislature. Moreover, this gentleman had been basely treated by the right reverend bishops; and it was partly to indemnify himself for losses sustained in their service, that he endeavoured to recover the penalties to which the clergy had become liable by their connivance and neglect. In Letter I. he says, " At a committee of bishops, after a deliberation of nearly *Two Years*, it was decided that each bishop should give his secretary an annual sum of money. I have received it from not one of them, except my late lamented patron, the Bishop of London."——" Commiseration may have been given, (Letter VII.) but it was all I ever received from any one, and that would have been unnecessary, if the sums had been paid which were acknowledged to be my due."——" Two secretaries have, within the last ten years, fallen victims to depression of mind, arising from a want of sufficient income."

Most merciful bishops! most Christian bishops! What, not pay your poor secretaries their stipends! drive two of them to despair by your barbarous avarice! Surely you might have spared them the odd hundreds, out your 10, 20, and 40,000 pounds per annum. But you are right reverend fathers, you can lisp about charity, turn up your eyes, talk about treasures in heaven, but your treasures are all in this world; there your hearts are fixed upon translations, pluralities, fat livings, and heavy fines on leases and renewals.

These, however, are private anecdotes betwixt Mr. Wright and his right reverend employers. Let us speak to the public part of the question. It is clear, from what has been said, that Mr. Wright was in possession of valuable information; he had resided in the Sanctum Sanctorum of the Temple, and was intimately acquainted with the secret management of the holy church. The clergy were terribly alarmed at his disclosures: they resorted to every artifice to avert the storm, and save their pockets: clubs were formed among the higher order of ecclesiastics: lies and calumnies of every shape and description were vomited forth to blacken the character of Mr. Wright; he was stigmatized as an " informer," who, availing himself of his official situation, was in part the cause of and then the betrayer of their guilt. In short, he became exposed to the whole storm of priestly cunning, malignity, and fury. But facts are stubborn things; and this gentleman had secured too firm a hold of his object to lose his grasp by the wiles and malice of the church. Their guilt was unquestionable; there was no chance of escape from the verdict of a jury; but that protection which it was in vain to expect from an English court of justice, they found in the great sanctuary of delinquency, a boroughmongering House of Commons.

On the 17th November, 1813, Bragge Bathurst brought in a bill to *stay all legal proceedings against the clergy* on account of the penalties they had incurred under the Clergy Residence Act. This bill shortly after passed into a law, almost without opposition. The whigs were silent. Mr. Whitbread and Mr. Brand indeed said something about the absurdity of enacting laws one day, and abrogating them the next; of the injustice of tempting people by rewards, and after they had earned them, interfering to prevent their being granted. But this was all. These gentlemen agreed it was necessary to protect the clergy; and, with the exception of the present Earl of Radnor, we do not find, in Hansard's History of the Debates, a single individual who raised his voice against the principle of this nefarious transaction. Mr. Wright, too, finding it vain to hope for justice from such a source, ceased his communications to the public relative to the clergy: the Parsons' Indemnity Bill passed into a law, and the church received a complete white-washing from the State for all its manifold sins and transgressions.

After the passing of the Bank restriction Act, Gagging Bills, Seditious Meeting Bills, Press Restriction Bills, and of the Habeas Corpus Suspension Bills, it can hardly excite surprise that a bill passed to indemnify the clergy. In the latter case, however, there appears something more unprincipled and contemptible than in the former unconstitutional measures. The law imposing the penalties which Mr. Wright sought to recover had only been enacted in 1803 : the professed object was to remedy the crying evil of *non-residence ;* and to give greater encouragement to prosecutions, the act provided that the whole of the penalties should be given to the informer. Only eight years elapse, an informer comes forward, relying on the faith of parliament ; prosecutions are commenced ; when the legislature interferes —in utter contempt of justice and consistency—belying its former professions, violating its pledge, robbing an individual of his reward, and screens the delinquents which its own laws had made liable to punishment. It is impossible for the people to feel any thing but contempt for such a system of legislation. Laws, it is clear, are not made to principles, but to men, and are only terrible to the weak, not to the wicked.

Since the memorable actions of Mr. Wright, nothing has intervened to improve the state of church discipline. An act of parliament,* passed some years after, was rather in favour of the clergy than otherwise, by abolishing the oaths formerly exacted of vicars to reside, by augmenting the monitory power of the bishops, and increasing the difficulties in the way of prosecution. Accordingly, the great abuses in ecclesiastical discipline remain unabated. Lord Mountcashell states that, since 1814, the number of incumbents has decreased to the amount of 2,500 ;† consequently, there has been a proportionate increase in pluralities. Of the number of resident and non-resident incumbents, the latest returns printed are for the year 1827 ;‡ in that year, we have seen, the returns were from 10,583 benefices in England and Wales, of which benefices 4,413 had resident, and 6,120 non-resident incumbents. Many incumbents who reside on their benefices do no duty ; they are only attracted to their parishes by a fine cover for game, an excellent trout-stream, or, perhaps, they seek a quiet retreat, having worn out the better part of their existence in the dissipation of a town life.

Even those who reside and do duty, and are called the *working clergy,* perform a service requiring so little intellectual exertion, that it hardly merits the remuneration of a tide-waiter. They have scarcely ever occasion to compose and deliver an original sermon. The late Dr. Johnson, before he received his pension, was regularly employed in the manufacture of this description of commodity. The market is now

---

* 57 Geo. III. c. 99, the act which now regulates the residence of the clergy.
† House of Lords, May, 4, 1830.
‡ Parliamentary Paper, No. 471, Sess. 1830. After what has been explained, it is perhaps unnecessary to observe that there are not actually so many individuals as the number of resident and non-resident incumbents in the Returns import. The apparent inconsistency results from *pluralities.* Every benefice with cure has an incumbent ; but, as each incumbent often holds two or more benefices, it reduces the number of individuals to the amount we have stated, (page 30,) namely, 7191.

overstocked; we seldom turn over a newspaper without meeting with advertisements for the sale of MS sermons, which, next to manufactures, seem the most abundant of all things.   Sometimes parcels are advertised in *lithographic* type; this type being an imitation of writing, sermons composed in it pass with the congregation for original compositions, and the minister has the credit of propounding a good discourse, the result of the previous week's hard study and preparation.   A lot of sermons of this description would be invaluable, and might be transmitted from father to son, like a freehold estate.   If they became stale, they might be sold or exchanged with a neighbouring incumbent : this is a common practice with ministers who wish to indulge their parishioners with novelty; they exchange one old batch of sermons for another, from a different part of the country.

But enough of this.   One is at a loss to imagine what the bishops have been doing while the church has been running to seed.   These right reverend prelates are expressly appointed to watch over the morals and conduct of the inferior clergy ; they are amply endowed, and have numerous corps of officers to assist in the discharge of their episcopal functions.   Yet they have been strangely remiss in attention to their subaltern brethren.   Translations have tended greatly to produce this apathy ; they divest the bishops of a permanent interest in their dioceses, and prevent them becoming intimately acquainted with the character and demeanour of incumbents.   Until they attain the summit of prelatical ambition, they consider themselves only birds of passage ; in their sees, what they chiefly take an interest in is, to fill up the vacant commissions, and then keep a steady eye on Durham or Winchester.

Under the primacy of the late Archbishop SUTTON, energetic measures of reform were not likely to be countenanced; the career of this mild but rapacious prelate was not an inapt exemplar of the favourite priestly motto on the Lambeth arms,—" *Unite the meekness of a dove with the subtlety of a serpent.*"   His grace and his grace's family shared too largely in the advantages of the existing system to relish innovation.   His lordship had profound views of the true policy of our spiritual establishment ; was always for yielding a little to keep things quiet, rather than make a noise; knowing that the less was said about the church the more she would shine.   Some of the primate's successors, on the episcopal bench, appear hardly yet so rife in the mysteries of ecclesiastical dominion.   A few years since, Marsh, of Peterborough, was tormenting his clergy with some unintelligible points of doctrine, and Bishop Blomfield lately astounded the inhabitants of London and Westminster with a " Letter on the Profanation of the Lord's Day."   Had the strictures of this right reverend prelate been directed only against the baneful habit of drinking to excess, and other vices which disgrace the Sabbath, they might have passed without animadversion ; but when he assails the Sunday press, and those innocent relaxations, conducive only to health and harmless enjoyment, he betrays a puritanism unsuited to the age.   His lordship seems to opine a poor man is born only to work and pray, while a lord or a bishop may have his concerts, card-parties, and grand dinners every day, not even excepting the seventh. Such idle cant deceives no one; it only excites contempt or disgust. Men's professions now pass unheeded; every thing is put into the scale and taken at its intrinsic worth. People quietly ask why should the clergy take TEN MILLIONS annually out of the produce of land and industry? What services do they render society? Do they instruct the rising generation? No; they teach them little that is useful and a great deal positively injurious. Are they administrators of justice? No; God forbid they should. Are they profound statesmen? Do they often originate or encourage measures for the good of the country? No; they are most miserable politicians, and as to any project for bettering the condition of the great body of the people, they appear not to have a single idea. Well, but they are ministers of religion! Very few of them are so employed, and as to that the Dissenters are not less teachers of their flocks, and they receive no tithes, build their own chapels, and altogether do not cost one-tenth as much as the mere sinecure rectors of the Establishment.

IV. REVENUES OE THE ESTABLISHED CLERGY.

It is impossible to produce a complete and accurate statement of the revenues of the clergy. The bulk of ecclesiastical revenue consists of tithe; but besides tithe, an immense revenue is drawn from other sources. The clergy are almost in entire possession of the revenue of charitable foundations. They hold, exclusively, the professorships, fellowships, tutorships, and masterships of the universities and public schools. Immense landed property is attached to the sees, cathedrals, and collegiate churches. The clergy have also a very considerable income from glebe-lands, surplice-fees, preacherships in the royal chapels, lectureships, town-assessments, Easter-offerings, rents of pews in the new churches, stipends of chapels of ease, chaplainships in the army and navy, chaplainships to embassies, corporate bodies, and commercial companies; besides which they monopolize nearly all profitable offices in public institutions, as trustees, librarians, secretaries, &c.

The bishops, who hold the chief estates of the church, and to whom the parochial clergy, on obtaining licenses for curates and dispensation for plurality, are required by law to state the yearly value of their benefices, could furnish the most valuable information relative to the incomes of the clergy. But even this would be insufficient; nothing would throw complete light on the subject, but every member of the establishment, whether in lay or spiritual capacity, making a return of his income and emoluments. The times, we doubt not, are fast approaching when this defect in public statistics will be supplied, and one of the first objects of a reformed parliament be an inquiry into the amount and distribution of ecclesiastical revenues. Until this period arrive, we are compelled to rely on collateral and inferential evidence. The endowments of the church are nearly as ancient as the first introduction of Christianity into Britain, and we know from the results of recent inqui-

ries into the incomes of grammar-schools and other charitable foundations, which are nearly of cotemporary antiquity, that the increase in
the value of ecclesiastical estates must be immense. The returns in
Liber Regis are usually relied upon, in estimating the revenues of the
church, and, perhaps, with other helps, it is the best authority to which
we can resort. Of the vast increase in the value of land since the *Valor
Ecclesiasticus* was obtained, the history of St. Paul's School affords a
striking and appropriate exemplification. The estates of this foundation
are situated in various parts of the kingdom; in A. D. 1524, they produced an income of £122 : 0 : 11 ; in the year 1820, the yearly income
derived from the same estates was £5252 : 2 : 11½.* Here is an increase
in value of nearly *fifty fold*, under the wasteful and negligent management of a city company. The colleges of Eton and Winchester were
endowed for the education and maintenance of only *seventy poor and
indigent scholars;* their revenues amount respectively to £10,000 and
£14,000 a year. The founder of Hemsworth's hospital in Yorkshire
estimated its revenues not to exceed £70 a year; they are now more
than £2000. Leeds' grammar-school was endowed in the reign of
Philip and Mary, for the maintenance of two masters, and the endowments probably calculated to yield £80 a year; they now produce £1595.
Birmingham grammar-school has a revenue of near £5000 per annum.
The valuation of the rectory of Alresford in the king's book is only £8
a year; the composition now paid for tithes by the parishioners is £300
per annum, being an increase of more than thirty-seven fold. The rectory of Stanhope, Durham county, Mr. Phillpotts admits to yield an
income of £2500; the valuation in *Liber Regis* is £67 : 6 : 8. Ilfracombe, in Devonshire, is returned at £50 : 4 : 4 : the tithes are leased to
a layman, and worth £1000 a year. The tithes of the adjoining parish
of Morthoe are also leased out to a layman for £700 or £800, although
the valuation in the king's book is only £19 : 19 : 3. Besides affording
a curious illustration of the increase in the value of ecclesiastical property, we may observe, in passing, that the two last mentioned parishes
are a curious example of the state of church discipline. Ilfracombe is
attached to a prebendal stall of Salisbury 120 miles distant; Morthoe
belongs to the dean and canons of Exeter; although the tithes are so
considerable, the working minister of each parish receives only a stipend
of £100 a year. In Morthoe the glebe is also leased out,—the vicar,
having no residence, lives five or six miles off, and service is performed
once on Sunday, which is all the return the parishioners receive for
their tithe-assessment of £800 per annum.

Other facts might be cited to illustrate the increase in the value of
church property since the ecclesiastical survey of the sixteenth century ;
but we consider the examples we have selected from various parts of the
kingdom sufficient to afford a criterion of the proportional increase in
the revenues of the church. The increase in population, by increasing

---

* Third Report of the Charity Commissioners, p. 230.

the number of church-fees, has tended, as well as the increased value of land, to swell the revenues of the church, and no doubt many benefices are worth two hundred fold what they were at the time of the Reformation. The vicarage of Hillingdon, held by the present rector of St. George's, Hanover-square, is an instance of the vicissitudes in clerical income. This, it appears, from the original record preserved in the archives of the Dean and Chapter of St. Paul's, was a mere trifle, the great tithes of which, in the year 1281, were bestowed on the Bishop of Worcester towards defraying the expenses of his journeys to the metropolis, and for repair of the church, the small tithes being reserved for the maintenance of a vicar, to be appointed by the Bishop of London. That part of the contract relating to the expense of repairs has always been left to be performed by the parishioners, the Right Reverend Prelates of Worcester contenting themselves with receiving their share of the tithes, and reading a sermon to the inhabitants about once in a twelvemonth. These tithes have been of considerable value, and the management of them not a little extraordinary. The practice has been to let them to the *highest bidder*, by granting a lease of them for three lives, the purchaser paying down, in ready money, about £8000. Even on these terms it is said to have been a profitable bargain ; the last speculator in this spiritual traffic was the late Lord BOSTON, of whom the Bishop demanded the exorbitant sum of £8000, for the insertion of a new life, one of the former having dropt. His lordship neglecting to complete the agreement, the lease was nominally made over to the bishop's daughter, who gave receipts in her own name for the amount of tithes collected.

Affairs continued in this state until the year 1812, when an act of parliament was obtained for enclosing and exonerating from tithes certain lands in the parish of Hillingdon ; which was promptly acted upon, and a distribution of lands took place, by which 765 acres were set apart and appropriated in lieu of rectorial and vicarial tithes for ever. By this arrangement the bishop and vicar have obtained a fine estate in exchange for £16 a year, the valuation of the living in the time of Henry VIII. All parties are more independent of each other—no contention about tithes nor compositions for tithes. The bishop repairs a chapel in lieu of the church ; the vicar is an absentee, leaving a curate for the spiritual welfare of the inhabitants ; and the only parties who have sustained any loss are the poor, in being deprived of the rights of common which their forefathers enjoyed.

Leaving these incidental illustrations of church property, let us endeavour to ascertain, upon some general principle, the amount of the revenues of the clergy. The estimates, by individuals, of ecclesiastical revenues are mostly limited to a valuation of tithe and the landed estates of the church. Of the unfairness of this mode of proceeding we shall hereafter speak ; at present we shall submit to the reader two estimates of the revenues of the church, drawn up on very different principles, and by parties who entertain very different views of the state of our ecclesiastical establishment. The first statement is from the third edition of a work, entitled " Remarks on the Consumption of Public Wealth by the Clergy."

Estimate of the Revenues and Property of the Established Church in England and Wales.

Annual value of the gross produce of the land of England and
Wales £150,000,000
One-third of the land of England and Wales not subject to tithe
for the clergy, being either tithe-free or lay-impropriations 50,000,000

Leaving the amount on which tithes for the clergy are levied 100,000,000
Supposing the clergy to levy one-sixteenth, they get............ 6,250,000

Tithes 6,250,000
Estates of the bishops and ecclesiastical corporations 1,000,000
Assessments in towns, on houses, &c....................... 250,000
Chapels of ease stipends 100,000

Total.................£7,600,000

From the Quarterly Review, No. 58.

Total number of acres in England and Wales 37,094,400
Deduct waste land, about one-seventh...................... 5,299,200

Number of acres in tillage 31,795,200
Abbey-land, or land exempt by modus from tithe, one-tenth 3,179,520

Number of acres actually subject to tithes 28,615,680

This number, divided by 10,693, the number of parishes, gives 2,676 tithable acres to each parish.

In the Patronage of the Crown, the Bishops, Deans and Chapters, the Universities and Collegiate Establishments.

1733 Rectories, containing 4,637,508 acres, at 3s. 6d.............£ 811,563
2341 Vicarages, containing 6,264,516 acres, at 1s. 3d............. 391,532

Annual value of Public Livings................. 1,203,095

In the Gift of private Patrons.

3444 Rectories, containing 9,216,144 acres, at 3s. 6d. 1,612,825
2175 Vicarages, containing 5,820,300 acres, at 1s. 3d............. 363,768
1000 Perpetual curacies, averaging £75 each.................... 75,000
 649 Benefices, not parochial, averaging £50 each 32,450

Annual value of Private Benefices.............. 2,084,043
8000 Glebes, at £20 each 160,000

Total income of parochial clergy 3,447,138
Income of bishoprics......................... 150,000
Ditto of deans and chapters.................... 275,000

Total revenue of the Established Clergy £3,872,138

We shall first solicit attention to the estimate from the Quarterly Review, which is such an unfair and misleading representation of the revenues of the clergy, that we ought almost to apologize to the reader for laying it before him. Arthur Young, who is no bad authority in these matters, says the revenue of the church was five millions in 1790, and how greatly it must since have augmented from the vast increase in population and produce. Notwithstanding the evasions and omissions under the Property-Tax, the returns for 1812* make the tithe of that year amount to £4,700,000, and, allowing for the increase in produce and fall in prices, it is not likely a less sum would be returned at present. During the war, the tithe was usually estimated at one-third of the rent; it is not much less now, but, suppose it only one-fourth, and the rental of England and Wales £31,795,200, or one pound for every acre in tillage; then the whole amount of tithe collected is £7,948,200; from which, if we deduct one-third for lay-tithes and land exempt from tithe, the church-tithes alone amount to £5,297,200.

Upon whatever principle we test the statement in the Quarterly Review, its erroneousness is apparent. The reviewer supposes the rectorial tithes to average only 3s. 6d. per acre, and the vicarial tithes only 1s. 3d. Both these sums are assuredly too low. The vicarage tithes, in consequence of the turnip-husbandry and other improvements in agriculture, are often more valuable than the parsonage. The returns to the circular inquiries by the Board of Agriculture make the tithe throughout the kingdom, in 1790, average, per acre, 4s. 0¼d.; in 1803, 5s. 3½d.; in 1813, 7s. 9½d. Adopting the rate of tithe of 1803, and taking, with the reviewer, the land in tillage at 31,795,200 acres, the whole amount of tithes collected is £10,267,200; from which, if we deduct, as before, one-third for lay-tithes and tithe-free land, the amount of church-tithes is £6,844,800 per annum.

Again: the reviewer greatly misrepresents the proportion between rectories and vicarages. It is well known to every one the impropriate livings barely equal one-third of the whole number. Yet the reviewer makes the number of vicarages 4516; whereas, according to Archdeacon Plymley, there are only 3687 vicarages in England and Wales.† But it suited the sinister purpose of the writer to exaggerate the number of vicarages, in order to calculate the tithes of so many parishes at only 1s. 3d. per acre.

The estimate of the income of the Bishoprics at £150,000 is greatly below the truth. The revenues of the four sees of Winchester, Durham, Canterbury, and London alone exceed that sum. A vast deal of mystery is always maintained about the incomes of the bishops; but the public has incidentally been put in possession of some certain data on this point. In 1829, the late Archbishop Sutton applied for a private act of parlia-

---

* Nos. 248 and 250, for 1814 and 1815.
† Charge to the Clergy of the County of Salop.

ment to raise a loan of £37,000, to assist in altering and improving Lambeth-palace; when it came out that the revenue of the see of this poor member of the " college of fishermen" was ONLY £32,000 per annum. This is the representation of his own officer, Doctor Lushington. Mr. A. Baring stated that the revenue of the see of London would, by the falling in of leases, shortly amount to £100,000 a year.* The Bishop of London, in reply to this, alleged that his income, allowing for casualties, did not amount to one-seventh of that sum. His lordship, of course, meant his *fixed* income, and did not include fines for the renewal of leases, nor the value of his parks, palace, and mansions. We can assure this right reverend prelate that the public never, in truth, thought his income, or that of his Grace of Canterbury, was so extravagantly high as on their own showing they appear to be. The see of Winchester is supposed to be worth £50,000 per annum. In one year the bishop of this diocese received upwards of £15,000 in fines for the renewal of leases.

But let us ascertain the total income of all the sees. In Liber Regis, the King's book, we have an authentic return of the value of the bishoprics in the reign of Henry VIII. As this return was to be the foundation of the future payment of first fruits and tenths, we may be sure it was not too much. However, in these returns, the See of Canterbury is valued at £2682 : 12 : 2 per annum; the See of London at £1000. This was at a time when a labourer's wages were only a penny a day. Now, it appears, from the admissions of Doctor Lushington and the Bishop of London, that the present incomes of these sees are £32,000 and £14,444 a-year. So that one see has increased in value twelve and the other more than fourteen-fold. The other bishoprics have, no doubt, increased in a similar proportion. Hence, as the incomes of the twenty-six sees in Liber Regis amount to £22,855 a-year, their present value cannot be less than thirteen times that sum, or £297,115, instead of £150,000, as stated in the Quarterly Review. This does not include the dignities and rectories annexed to the sees, or held in commendam, nor the parks and palaces, the mansions, villas, warrens, fines for renewals, heriots, and other manorial rights, enjoyed by the bishops, and which would make their incomes equal to, at least, *half-a-million* per annum.

The revenues of the Deans and Chapters may be approximated to on the same principle. Their incomes, like those of the bishops, arise principally from lands and manors, and certain payments in money. In the King's Book, the deans and chapters are valued at £38,000 a-year; consequently, they do not amount, at present, to less than £494,000 per annum, instead of £275,000. But the returns in the Valor Ecclesiasticus are far from complete; several deaneries, prebends, and other offices are omitted; it follows, our estimate is far below the annual worth of the ecclesiastical corporations.

---

* House of Commons, April 27, 1830.

The Reviewer considers each glebe to be worth only £20 a-year; but, when he is desirous of illustrating the penury of the church by comparing its endowments with those of the Church of Scotland, he values the glebes of the latter at £30 per annum. The writer omits to estimate the value of the parsonage-houses : they must be worth something, as they save rent to the incumbents or their curates.

But enough of the estimate in the Quarterly Review. The principles and purposes of this publication are so notorious that every one is on his guard against receiving, implicitly, any representations relative to the church from so suspicious a source. The first statement, from the " Remarks," &c. contains some inaccuracies and omissions which we shall endeavour to supply. Before, however, we submit a complete view of the revenues of the church, it will be proper shortly to advert to some items of ecclesiastical emolument usually omitted in inquiries of this nature.

Besides tithe and the landed estates of the church, there are, as before remarked, various other sources from which the clergy derive very considerable advantages. Of these, the first we shall notice are *Public Charities.* The inquiries by the Royal Commissioners, so far as they have proceeded, tend to confirm the accuracy of Lord Brougham's estimate of the revenues of charitable foundations at nearly *two millions* a-year. From the tenure of charitable endowments, the clergy have almost entire possession of this immense fund. In England and Wales, according to the returns under the Gilbert Act, there are 3898 *school* charities, of which the clergy enjoy the exclusive emolument; and, in the remaining charities, they largely participate as trustees, visitors, or other capacity. The pious credulity of our ancestors induced them to place implicit reliance on the clergy, little foreseeing how their confidence would be abused. Three-fourths of charitable property, at least, were thus placed at the mercy of ecclesiastics. It is certain that, in the inquiries recently instituted into charitable foundations, the worst abuses have been found under their management. The school of Pocklington, in Yorkshire, was a flagrant instance, in which a member of the established church was receiving a snug income of nine hundred pounds a-year for teaching ONE scholar. A right reverend prelate, who had been left IN TRUST, and his family, had appropriated the funds of the Mere and Spital charities. The grammar-schools in almost every town have become mere sinecures, seldom having more than two or three foundation-scholars; and the buildings piously intended for the gratuitous accommodation of *poor scholars*, have been perverted into boarding and pay schools for the emolument of their clerical masters. Bristol and Bath, Birmingham, Wolverhampton, Ripon, and Preston, are striking examples of this sort of abuse and perversion. In the principal foundations in the metropolis and neighbourhood, in the Charter-house, Christ's Hospital, the great schools of Westminster, St. Paul's, Harrow, Rugby, and the Gresham Lectures, they derive great advantages as wardens, visitors, provosts, high masters, senior masters, ushers, lecturers, and assistants. Many of these offices are held by *pluralists*, who are, also, *dignitaries*, and yield salaries of £800 a-year, besides allowances for house-rent, vegetables, and linen, and large pensions of one thousand a-year, or so, on retirement. The present head-master of the Charter-house, and the late and present head-master of St. Paul's School, are examples of this sort of monopoly. In the colleges of Eton and Winchester, again, the established clergy have a nice patrimony. The government of these foundations is vested in a certain number of *reverend* fellows, and a provost, who is a *reverend* also. The value of a fellowship, including allowances for coals, candles, and gown, is about £1000 a-year; and a provostship, in good years, has netted £2500 per annum;* besides which, the fellows generally help themselves to a good fat living or two, which are in the gift of the colleges. Again, the established clergy have exclusive possession of the revenues of the Universities, to the exclusion of dissenters, and all persons of delicate consciences, who are scrupulous about taking oaths, and subscribing to articles of faith they neither believe nor understand.† The value of a university fellowship is generally less than a fellowship at Eton or Winchester; though the incomes of some of the fellows are handsome enough to induce them to prefer celibacy and college residence to a benefice in the country : add to which the professorships and tutorships, which, bringing the possessors in contact with the youth of the aristocracy and gentry, lead to livings and dignities. Numerous livings are also in the gift of the Universities, as well as in the other foundations we have mentioned, believe some of the offices in the Universities are incompatible with church-preferment.

From these details we may conclude the established clergy share largely in the revenues of Public Charities ; supposing the college and school charities average only £175 each, they will produce £682,150 a-year.

CHURCH or SURPLICE FEES, as they are commonly called, form another abundant source of revenue to the clergy. Originally, surplice-fees were paid only by the rich, and were intended for charity : what was formerly a voluntary gift has been converted into a demand, and,

---

* Evidence of Dr. Goodall, Third Report of Education-Committee.

† It is to this hour the practice at one of the Universities, in obedience to the statutes of Laud, to demand of every student on his matriculation, provided he have attained the mature age of *twelve* years, his written assent and consent to all and every of the thirty-nine Articles of religion !—and at the other, where candidates for the degree of Master of Arts are, for the first time, required to subscribe, I can solemnly declare,—from my own positive, personal, knowledge,—that the most reckless levity—the most dangerous trifling with the sacred engagements of truth, are found to prevail on these occasions ! I ask are such the approved methods of laying the foundation of a national morality ? I ask are these mockeries an exemplification of the position so recently pro-claimed by Captain Basil Hall,—that ' it is the aristocratical classes, and they alone, who can give a right tone to manners, by setting the fashion in everything *which is true in principle, or practically wise in morals and in politics ?'—The Church : its Civil Establishment indefensible.*—Hunter, London, 1831.

instead of the poor receiving these donations, they are pocketed by the clergy, and poor as well as rich are now compelled to pay fees on burials, marriages, churchings, and christenings. The total sums netted from this source we have no means of estimating correctly. In London, church-fees are supposed to be equal to one-third of the priest's salary. Besides the regular fee, it is usual, on the burial of opulent people, to get a compliment of a guinea or more for hat-band and gloves : at marriages, five guineas; at christenings, a guinea. In Ireland, the surplice-fees, aided by a few voluntary gifts, form the only maintenance of the catholic priesthood : and, in this country, the total revenue derived from fees and gratuities, is little short of one million a-year. The late Rev. Dr. Cove, whose estimate of church property is seldom more than one-half of its real amount, calculates the annual value of the glebe and surplice-fees of each parish, on an average, at £40 a-year, making, according to him, a tax upon the population of half a million per annum.

EASTER-OFFERINGS, OBLATIONS, &c. form a third source of ecclesiastical emolument. These Offerings, or *Dues*, as they are some-times called, are certain customary payments at Easter and all church-festivals, to which every inhabitant-housekeeper is liable. Their amount varies in different parts of the country. In the North, they commonly pay sixpence in lieu of an offering-hen; a shilling in lieu of an offering-goose or turkey; one penny, called smoke-penny; one penny-halfpenny for every person or communicant above the age of six-teen, and so on. We have no means of judging the annual value of these good things. All that we can say is, that in some parts they are very pertinaciously levied, and considered by the established clergy as part of their " *ancient* rights."* Probably, the value of Easter-offer-ings may be taken at £100,000 a-year.

The LECTURESHIPS, in towns and populous places, are another branch of clerical income. Where there is no endowment for a lecture-ship, the parishioners, if they desire a novelty of this sort, in addition to the ordinary routine of church-service, provide one at their own charge. The value of a lectureship, of course, varies with the number and liberality of the subscribers. No person can officiate as a lecturer unless approved by the incumbent and diocesan. Frequent squabbles arise from this cause; the parishioners choosing a popular preacher, who, from a miserable feeling of jealousy, is not approved by the less gifted incumbent. The lectureships are generally held with other pre-ferments. Their total value may be stated at £60,000 per annum.

The next branch of revenue we shall notice are CHAPLAINSHIPS and those public offices which the Clergy may be said to hold *ex officio*, and to which they have always the preference. The value of chaplain-ships to the nobility, to ambassadors, public bodies, and commercial companies, must be considerable ; but of the value of these, and of the

---

* Trial of Peter Watson, in the Consistory Court of Durham, for the sub-straction of Easter Offerings.

places held by the clergy in public institutions, it is hardly possible to estimate. Suppose £10,000 a-year.

Beside all these sources of ecclesiastical revenue, another and onerous burthen is imposed on the people by the NEW CHURCHES erected under the authority of the Commissioners appointed for that purpose. The sum of £1,367,400 in Exchequer-bills has been already issued in aid of the voluntary contributions towards this undertaking.* The salaries of the secretary, surveyors, office-keepers, and other underlings of this commission cost the country more than £5,000 a-year. One hundred and nine churches and chapels have been completed, and one hundred and five more are in different stages of progress : what is the whole number intended to be erected, or the total expense, nobody can tell, for the Commissioners have been recently *incorporated*, and in all probability their pious labours will be protracted for ages to come. Had the rich clergy contributed their just share to the First Fruits Fund, there would have been no necessity for imposing this additional tax on the public. But the first outlay is far from being the worst part of this extraordinary proceeding. All those new churches and chapels will have to be kept in repair by rates levied on the parishioners—dissenters as well as churchmen, and this, though many have opposed their erection as unnecessary. Then there are the stipends of ministers, clerks, beadles, pew-openers, and though last, not least, the guzzlings and feedings of sextons, churchwardens, and chapelwardens to be provided for ; for though the patronage of the new churches is given to the patron or incumbent of the mother-church, yet the salaries of the minister and other officials, instead of being deducted from the income of the rector or vicar, are to be raised by a charge for the *rents of pews*. Only think of this novel device for augmenting the revenues of the ecclesiastical order ! Notwithstanding the immense sums levied for the maintenance of the established religion, and though the frequenters of the new churches are actually compelled to pay tithes to the incumbents of their parishes, yet they are obliged to contribute an additional sum in pew rents to enjoy the benefit of the national communion, and if they desire a *third* service on Sundays, they must contribute additional for that too.† How much the revenues of the clergy will be ultimately increased from this source, we have not the means of estimating. The incomes settled on some of the new ministers by the Commissioners are very considerable ; that of the minister of St. Peter's, Pimlico, is £900 a year; and those of the rectors of the three new churches in the parish of St. Mary-le-bone are £350 per annum each. Suppose the annual charge of each new church £450 per annum, it will shortly add to the other permanent revenues of the church a yearly sum of £94,050.

---

* Eleventh Annual Report of the Commissioners, Session, 1831.
† Church-Building-Acts the 58 Geo. III. c. 45 ; 59 Geo. III. c. 134 ; 3 Geo. IV. c. 72; 5 Geo. IV. c. 103 ; 7 & 8 Geo. IV. c. 72 ; 9 Geo. IV. c. 42.

We shall now collect the different items and exhibit a general statement of the revenues of the Established Clergy. The sum put down for tithe is church-tithe only, after deducting the tithe of lay-impropriations, and allowing for abbey-land and land exempt by modus from tithe. The church-rates are a heavy burden on the people, but being levied at uncertain intervals, for the repair of churches and chapels, they do not form a part of the personal income of the clergy, and are omitted.

Revenues of the Established Clergy of England and Wales.

Church-tithe	£6,884,800
Incomes of the bishoprics	297,115*
Estates of the deans and chapters	494,000
Glebes and parsonage-houses	250,000
Perpetual curacies £75 each	75,000
Benefices not parochial £250 each	32,450
Church-fees on burials, marriages, christenings, &c.	500,000
Oblations, offerings, and compositions for offerings at the four great festivals	80,000
College and school foundations	682,150
Lectureships in towns and populous places	60,000
Chaplainships and offices in public institutions	10,000
New churches and chapels	94,050

Total Revenues of the Established Clergy··£9,459,565

We are confident several of these sources of emolument are rather under-rated. Perhaps it may be alleged that some items do not properly appertain to ecclesiastical income—that they are the rewards *pro opera et labore* extra-officially discharged by the clergy. But what would be said if, in stating the emoluments of the Duke of Wellington, we limited ourselves to his military pay, without also including his pensions, sinecures, and civil appointments? The sums placed to the account of the clergy are received by them either as ministers of religion, or from holding situations to which they have been promoted in consequence of being members of the Established Church. There are several sums annually raised on the people which we have omitted, but which, in strictness, ought to be placed to the account of the clergy. Large sums are constantly being voted by Parliament for building churches in Scotland, as well as in England; more than £21,000 has been granted for building churches and bishops' palaces in the West Indies; £1,600,000 has been granted for the aid of the *poor clergy*, as they are called, and who have been also favoured by their livings

---

* The see of Sodor and Man is not in charge in the King's Book, and is omitted in this estimate.

being exonerated from the land-tax ; nearly a million has been granted for building houses and purchasing glebes for the clergy in Ireland ; upwards of £16,000 a-year is voted to a society for propagating Church of Englandism in foreign parts ;* and more than £9,000 is granted to some other Society for *Discountenancing Vice*, — a duty which one would think especially merged in the functions of our established pastors. All these sums have been omitted ; they certainly tend to augment the burthen imposed on the public by the Church : but as it is to be hoped they do not all form permanent branches of ecclesiastical charge, they are excluded from our estimate of clerical income.

The next consideration is the *Number of Persons* among whom the revenues of the Church are divided. It has been already shown that the number of prelates, dignitaries, and incumbents, is only 7,694, and by this diminutive phalanx is the entire revenue of £9,459,565 monopolized, affording an average income of £1,228 to each individual. Except the clergy, there is no class or order of men whose incomes average an amount like this. The average pay of officers in the army or navy will bear no comparison with that of the Clergy. Take the legal classes — the most gainful of all professions ; add together the incomes of the lord-chancellor, the judges, the barristers, conveyancers, proctors, special-pleaders, and every other grade of that multitudinous craft — the pettifogger of most limited practice included — and divide the total by the number of individuals, and it will yield no average income like that of dignitaries, rectors, and vicars. Still less will the fees and gains of the medical classes — the physician, surgeon, and apothecary — bear a comparison with the Church. The pensions, salaries, and perquisites of *employés* in the civil department of government are justly deemed extravagant ; but compare the united incomes of these with ecclesiastics, from the first lord of the treasury to the humblest official in the Stamp Office, and the difference is enormous. The Church is a monstrous, overgrown CRŒSUS in the State, and the amount of its revenues incredible, unbearable, and out of proportion with every other service and class in society.

An average estimate of the incomes of the Clergy, however, affords no insight into the mode in which the enormous revenues of the church are squandered among its members. Next to pluralists, the greatest abuse in the establishment results from the unequal amount of income possessed by individuals of the same rank in the ecclesiastical order, and the unequal burthen of duties imposed upon them. The incomes of some bishops, as those of Llandaff, St. Asaph, and Bangor, barely

---

* The efforts to promote Church of Englandism by expensive establishments are attended with as little success in the Colonies as in the mother country. In Upper Canada, out of 235 clergymen, only 33 are clergymen of the church of England. The Moravians are the sect whose mission is most successful in the West Indies. They mix familiarly with the Indians, instruct them in the arts of agriculture and building, and thus hold out to them advantages more readily comprehended than the mysteries of the Trinity, election, and the incarnation.

equal that of a clerk of the Treasury, or of rectors and vicars whose conduct they are appointed to superintend; while the incomes of others exceed those of the highest functionaries in the land. Yet we are told, by Mr. Burke, that the revenues of the higher order of ecclesiastics are to enable them to rear their " mitred fronts in courts and palaces to reprove presumptuous vice." But if one bishop requires a large revenue to support his dignity in high places, so does another. Among the archdeacons is like inequality, their incomes varying from £200 to £2000 a-year. And among the dignitaries and members of cathedral and collegiate establishments is similar disproportion. Many of the deaneries, as those of Westminster, Windsor, St. Paul's, Salisbury, Lincoln, Exeter, and Wells, are very valuable, yielding, probably, to their possessors, incomes of £10,000, £8,000, £5,000, £2,000, £1,900, and 1,500 respectively. The prebendaries and canonries vary in amount from £250 to £2,000 a-year. Some of the precentorships are worth not less than £900 a-year; and many of the chancellorships, treasurerships, succentorships, and we know not how many other official ships, afford snug incomes of £400, £500, and £800 per annum. The minor canons some of them have £250; the vicars-choral £350; the priest-vicars, the chanters, and sub-chanters, and a hundred more popish names and offices, are all amply, though unequally, remunerated for their services.

In the incomes of the parochial clergy there is similar diversity and injustice. Many rectories, as before observed, are more valuable than bishoprics, having incomes from £8,000 to £10,000 a-year. The same may be said of the vicarages, being possessed of large glebes or large endowments, and sometimes both. While, again, it cannot be denied that there are some rectories, and in particular vicarages, whose tithes are in the hands of laymen, and without even a parsonage-house. In some instances, the deficiency of income has been so great, that it has been found necessary to unite the incomes of two or three parishes to produce an adequate maintenance to the officiating minister, who, in the care of so many churches, cannot have time to officiate at any of them properly; and thus, no doubt, are many souls lost which might be saved; some, straying into the fold of sectarianism, become jacobins and dissenters, to the great injury of the mother church, and the eternal reproach of the right reverend bishops, the very reverend deans, the venerable archdeacons, and other reverend dignitaries, who waste, in the pomp, vanities, and luxuries of the world, the sums which ought to be appropriated to the augmentation of these poor livings.

The penury of one part of the church is not less objectionable than the bloated and sinecure opulence of another.* At the establishment of

* The poverty of the Welch clergy is proverbial; many of the curates receive no more than £10 or £15 per annum. They seldom taste animal food, a meagre allowance of bread and potatoes being all their scanty means afford. In North Wales we have heard (*Church Regeneration and University Reform*) there is a clergyman of the establishment who receives no more than the miserable stipend mentioned. He has a wife and six children. In the day-time he con-

Queen Anne's bounty, in the beginning of the last century, there were 5597 livings (above one-half of the whole number) whose incomes did not exceed £50 per annum. The Diocesan Returns in 1809 gave the following classifications of poor livings under £150 per annum : —

	£	Livings.
Not exceeding	10	12
———	20	72
———	30	191
———	40	353
———	50	433
———	60	407
———	70	376
———	80	319
———	90	309
———	100	315
———	110	283
———	120	307
———	130	246
———	140	205
———	150	170

Total........3998

It is by grouping these poor livings with the rich ones, and averaging the whole, that a plausible case is often attempted to be made out in favour of the clergy. One writer, for instance, whose statement has been often quoted, makes the average income of each living in England and Wales only £303 per annum.* The Rev. Dr. Cove, adopting different principles of calculation, makes the average income of the parochial clergy only £255 each.† Both these estimates, it is apparent from what has been advanced, are very wide of the truth. There are 11,342 benefices, and only 7,191 incumbents; and these incumbents engross the entire revenue of the parochial clergy arising from tithe and other sources. Turning to the statement at page 52, and deducting from the total revenues of the established clergy the incomes of the bishoprics and ecclesiastical corporations, it will be found that the parochial 'clergy alone have a total revenue of £8,668,450, which, divided by the number of benefices and the number of incumbents, gives £764 for the average value of each benefice, and £1,205 for the

---

trives to scrape together a few pence by conducting a boat in which passengers cross a river : he is the barber of the village, shaves for a penny every Saturday night; and five evenings in the week he teaches the children of the poor villagers reading and writing, for which he receives a small acknowledgement. O, ye ecclesiastical potentates, ye Blomfields and Sumners, for one moment lay aside your silken attributes, stop your postillions at the foot of Snowdon, and visit a poor afflicted brother !

In Liverpool, Mr. Morgan Jones affirms, within these last five years there have been discovered among the prostitutes of that dissolute sea-port no less than twenty-five young women the *daughters of Welch clergymen.*

* Quarterly Review, vol. xxix. p. 554.
† Essay on the Revenues of the Church, p. 124.

average income of each incumbent. From this enormous income, the paltry stipends of £40 or £60 a-year, paid by some of the beneficed clergy to their curates, are, of course, to be deducted.

The representation which the Quarterly Review, and other misleading publications, is desirous of impressing on the public is, that there are about 10 or 11,000 benefices, held by about as many individuals—rectors, vicars, and perpetual curates—whose average income is the very moderate sum of £255 or £303 each. Such a statement, if true, would render the amount of the revenues of the clergy, and the distribution of these revenues, very little objectionable indeed. But we will soon show this is all mystification and delusion.

The real situation of the Parochial Clergy is this: in England and Wales there are 5098 rectories, 3687 vicarages, and 2970 churches neither rectorial nor vicarial; in all, 11,755 churches.* These churches are contained in 10,674 parishes and parochial chapelries; and, probably, after a due allowance for the consolidation of some of the smaller parishes, form about as many parochial benefices. Now, the whole of these 10,674 benefices are in the hands of 7191 incumbents; there are 2886 individuals with 7037 livings; 517 with 1701 livings; 209 with 836 livings; 64 with 320 livings. Look again, at page 31, and the whole mystery of parochial monopoly is solved. Or let any one look into the *Clerical Guide*, and he will find nearly one-half the whole number of incumbents are pluralists. Some are rectors at one place, vicars at another, and curates at another; some hold three or four rectories, besides vicarages and chapelries; some hold two vicarages, a chapelry, and a rectory; in short, they are held in every possible combination. But what does the secretary to four bishops, Mr. Wright, the "*Informer*," as the late Bragge Bathurst termed him, say on this subject: in one diocese the majority of the clergy held three livings, some five, and some six, besides dignities, and "yet a great part of them did not reside upon any of their preferments."

This is exactly the way in which the property of the church is monopolized. Some persons imagine that there are as many rectors as rectories, vicars as vicarages, prebendaries as prebends, deans as deaneries, &c. No such thing: the 26 bishops, 700 dignitaries, and about 4000 non-resident incumbents, principally belonging to the Aristocracy, enjoy nearly the whole ecclesiastical revenues, amounting to more than NINE MILLIONS, and averaging upwards of £2000 a-year.

And for what service? what duties do they perform? what benefit do the people derive from their labours? The bishops ordain the priests; sometimes visit their dioceses; sometimes preach; and this we believe is the extent of their performances, and which, in our opinion, amount to very little. As to the venerable, very reverend, and worshipful dignitaries, they perform still less. Let any one visit the cathedral or collegiate churches; go into St. Paul's, Westminster Abbey, or York

---

* Archdeacon Plymley's Charge to the Clergy of the County of Salop.

Minster, for instance; and observe what is doing in those places. No service is performed which interests the public. Persons may be found admiring the stone and mortar; but the vicars-choral, the priest-vicars, the chanters, or sub-chanters, or fifth or sixth canons, are very little regarded; and as to the dignitaries themselves, why they are never to be seen; many of them probably reside some hundred miles off, in more pleasant parts of the country, enjoying the amusements of the chase, or whiling away their time at card-tables or watering-places. Then, as to the non-resident incumbents, it must be admitted they are sinecurists, whose duty is performed, and for which they receive the salary, by deputy. Thus, it appears, that these three classes, without performing any duties of importance, absorb almost the entire revenues of the church.

The labouring bees in the established church are the curates, who receive a very small share of its emoluments. In a parliamentary paper, ordered to be printed on the 28th of May, 1830, containing the diocesan returns relative to the number and stipends of curates in England and Wales, we find that, for the year 1827, out of 4254 individuals of that class, there were 1639 with salaries not exceeding £60, and only eighty-four out of the whole number with salaries exceeding £160. There were fifty-nine curates with incomes between £20 and £30, and six with incomes between £10 and £20. There were 1393 curates resident in the glebe houses, and 805 more resident in their parishes. So that, either for want of parsonage-houses, or other cause, a vast number of parishes had neither resident curate nor incumbent. Supposing the stipends of the curates average £75 a-year, which is higher than the bishops, under the 55 Geo. III., have in many cases authority to raise them, their share of the church-revenues amounts only to £319,050. Yet it is this useful and meritorious order which performs nearly the whole service of the national religion.

To the curates we may add the possessors of the *poor livings*, as a portion of the clergy who really discharge some duties for their emoluments. These livings may be considered the mere offal, or waste land of the church, on which those who have neither rotten boroughs nor family influence, are allowed to graze. Their incomes not being sufficient to allow for the maintenance of a curate, many of the incumbents reside on their benefices and perform the duties of their parishes. But even this class is not in the indigent state some persons are apt to imagine. The returns we have cited of the value of poor livings in 1809, were considered, at the time, a gross imposition on the public and parliament. In consequence, however, of these returns, true or false, the incomes of the poor clergy have subsequently been greatly augmented. Besides Queen Anne's bounty, £100,000 has been voted annually by parliament; the benefactions in money, by private individuals, amount to upwards of £300,000; other benefactions, in houses for the residence of ministers, in lands, tithes, and rent-charges, are very considerable: to which we may add the advantages small benefices have derived from being exonerated from the land tax, and from the increase in population, and in the value of tithes from agricultural improvements.

Another point necessary to be borne in mind, in considering the situation of the poor clergy, as they are called, is, that they are, like the non-resident aristocratical incumbents, nearly all pluralists. Few, indeed, only hold one living; and, probably, the whole 3998 livings under £150, are held by 1500 or 2000 individuals. That this is the case, is evident, from the returns made to the Commissioners appointed to exonerate small benefices from the land-tax, and which are now lying before us. In these returns for 1820 we find 2137 livings, or other ecclesiastical benefices of less than £150 in clear yearly value, had been exonerated from the land-tax.* Of 419 benefices exonerated from the land-tax in 1814, there were only ninety-two with incomes of less than £100 each, held *without other preferment*.† Hence we conclude that the poor clergy, whose incomes Dr. Cove made about £80, have, from pluralities, consolidation, and the other advantages mentioned, incomes of at least £150 each, and that, with the exception of curates, there are few poor clergy in England.

We have now afforded the reader, without exaggeration or distortion of facts, a complete and intelligible view of the total amount and disposition of the immense revenues of the Established Clergy. The chief points to be borne in mind are the diminutive number of the beneficed clergy, their sinecurism, and relative efficiency in the discharge of religious duties, and the monstrous inequality in their incomes. These points will best appear from the succinct statement we subjoin.

Statement, showing the Mode in which the Revenues of the Church, amounting to £9,459,565, are divided among the different Orders of Clergy.

Class.		Average income of each individual.	Total incomes.
EPISCOPAL CLERGY,	2 Archbishops ··············	£26,465	£52,930
	24 Bishops ····· ···········	10,174	244,185
DIGNITA-RIES, &c.	28 Deans ·················	1580	44,250‡
	61 Archdeacons ····· ·······	739	45,126
	26 Chancellors ····· ······	494	12,844
	514 Prebendaries and Canons ··	545	280,130
	330 Precentors, Succentors, Vicars-General, Minor Canons, Priest-Vicars, Vicars-Choral,&otherMembers of Cathedral and Collegiate Churches ······	338	111,650

Carried forward £791,085

---

* Parl. papers, vol. xi. No. 303, Session 1820.
† Parl. Papers, vol. xii. No. 474, Session 1815.
‡ The value of the deaneries, prebends, and other dignities, is calculated from the returns in the King's book, allowance being made for the increase in the

Brought forward £791,085

	2886 AristocraticPluralists,mostly non-resident, and holding two, three, four, or more livings, in all 7037 livings, averaging each, tithes, glebes, church-fees, &c. £764	1863 5,379,430
PAROCHIAL CLERGY,	4305 Incumbents, holding one living each, and about one-half resident on their benefices	764 3,289,020
	4254 Curates, licensed and unlicensed, whose average stipends of about £75 per annum, amounting together to £319,050, are included in the incomes of the pluralists and other incumbents.	

Total £9,459,565

Observations.

The above statement affords room for important remarks, in order to distinguish the over from the under paid, and the useful and meritorious from the mere sinecurists, in our ecclesiastical polity.

Every thing in this country is formed upon an aristocratic scale. Because some noblemen have enormous incomes, *ergo* the bishops must have enormous incomes, to be fit and meet associates for them. Thus, one extravagance in society generates another to keep it in countenance; because we have a king who costs a million a year, we must have lords with a quarter of a million, and bishops with fifty thousand a year; and as a consequence of all this, a labourer's wages cannot be more than 10d. a day—he must live on oatmeal and potatoes, and have the penny roll not bigger than his thumb. But why should the income of a bishopric so far exceed that of the highest offices in the civil department of government? Burke's argument is not consistent. A Secretary of State has to show his " front in courts and palaces," as well as a bishop; he is in constant intercourse with dukes and princes,

---

value of ecclesiastical property in the proportion of thirteen to one. The result is, we are aware, an average value greatly below the truth. Some single prebends, as the golden ones of St. Paul's, Winchester, Ely, Lincoln, and Durham, are worth from £800 to £2000 a-year. But, in the absence of more authentic information, we have been reduced to the alternative of either proceeding on the general principle mentioned, or of relying on private reports—and we preferred the former.

yet his salary does not exceed £6000 a year. The bishops have their private fortunes as well as others, and there is no just reason why their official incomes should be so disproportionate to that of a lord of the Treasury, or Chancellor of the Exchequer.

An *Archdeacon* is considered the deputy of the bishop, and assists in the discharge of the spiritual duties of his diocese. As such, we think the deputy ought to be paid out of the income of his principal, and the revenues of the archdeaconries applied to a fund to be raised, in lieu of tithes. Many bishops are not overburthened with duty, and have little need of assistants. One bishop of the United Church, it is well known, spent all his time in Italy, where he dissipated the revenues of an immensely rich see. Some English bishops do not reside in their dioceses. We knew a bishop who resided, within the last eight years, not more than a mile from St. James's Palace ; he lived till he sunk into a state of dotage and imbecility; he was in fact left to the care of a wet-nurse, who treated him like an infant : we never heard the church sustained any injury from the suspended services of this right reverend prelate, and he, or some one for him, continued, till his death, to receive the revenues of his see.

The *Dean and Chapter*, consisting of canons and prebendaries, are considered the *council* of the bishop. This is about as much of a farce as O'CONNELL's great crucifix in Merrion-Square, or the virtues of relics and holy water. It is notorious, the bishop and his chapter are oftener at open loggerheads, than sitting in harmonious conclave to devise measures for the good of the Church. The bishop of St. David's is his own dean, and so endeavours to avoid such unseemly dissensions by being part *council to himself.* One of the most important offices of the dean and chapter, is to *elect* the bishop ; that is choose the appointee of some court favourite, and in the exercise of which franchise, they discharge as virtual functions as the electors of Cockermouth or Ripon, who adopt the nominees of Earl Lonsdale and Miss Lawrence. The deaneries, prebends, canonries, and other cathedral dignities, are in fact honorary offices of great value; they are endowed with vast estates, numerous manors, and other good things, and have valuable livings in their gift; all of which advantages are so much public income idly squandered. We have before adverted to the sinecure nature of these appointments before the Reformation, and, as a further proof that they are offices without duties, we may mention that nominations to them are sometimes suspended. In 1797, when the cathedral of Lichfield was about being repaired, an act of parliament was obtained to defray the expense, by sequestrating the revenues of two vacant prebends. If the duties of these two offices could be suspended for an indefinite term, they might for perpetuity, and the revenues of all similar situations appropriated to the establishment of a fund in lieu of tithes, for the maintenance of the Working Clergy.

Next in order come the *Aristocratic Pluralists.* These are so many clerical sinecurists who receive immense incomes, without rendering any service to the community. They are mere men of the world, whose element is the race-course, the ball-room, and billiard-table. They seldom see their parishes : their residence is in London, at Paris, Naples, or Florence.   If they visit their benefices, it is not in the capacity of pastor, but of surveyor or tax-gatherer, who comes to spy out improvements, to watch the increase of stock and extension of tillage, and see how many hundreds more he can squeeze out of the fruits of the industry and capital of the impoverished farmer.   The poor parishioner, who contributes his ill-spared tithe to the vicious indulgence of these spiritual locusts, is neither directed by their example, instructed by their precepts, nor benefited by their expenditure.

From the preceding table, it is evident that about 2152 incumbents,* and 4254 curates, discharge nearly the entire duties of the established religion ; that their average income is £301, which is more than the average income of the Scotch clergy ; more than the income of the dissenting clergy in England, and the catholic clergy in Ireland; that, therefore, £1,974,503, the total revenue of these classes, constitutes nearly the whole expenditure the national worship requires for its maintenance and the discharge of its spiritual functions.

It is further evident that the Bishops, Dignatories, and Non-resident incumbents, amounting to 6,025 individuals, receive £7,485,062 per annum, or seven-ninths of the revenues of the church ; that these classes hold either merely honorary appointments, discharge no duties, or are greatly overpaid ; that, in consequence, by abolishing non-residence, stalls, and other sinecures, and by reducing the salaries of the higher clergy to a level with those of appointments in the State, or to a level with those of the best paid clergy in Europe, several millions of public income might be saved, to be applied either to the establishment of a fund for the maintenance of the operative clergy, in lieu of tithe and other ecclesiastical imposts ; or, it might be applied, as a great portion of it was originally intended, as a provision for the maintenance of the poor ; or, as a substitute for those public taxes whose pressure on " the springs and sources of industry" tends to produce national poverty and embarrassment.

Further, it is clear, from an impartial inquiry into the origin and tenure of church property, that it has been always considered public property ; that it was dealt with as such in the reign of Henry VIII., and by parliament in the reigns of George III. and IV., and the same policy has been pursued towards ecclesiastical possessions in every European state : that, in consequence, the legislature, after making a provision for the life interests of the present possessors of the church revenues, as was done at the time of the Reformation,† is authorized by

---

* The Diocesan Returns, laid before the privy council, for 1827, state that, of the non-resident incumbents, 1590 *do duty;* but the amount of duty they discharge is not stated. Many incumbents who reside do no duty. Allowing for the non-residents who do duty, and the residents who do none, we believe the number of incumbents, who actually perform the duties of parishes, is not greater than we have mentioned.

† Hallam's Constitutional History of England, p. 78.

precedent and the example of other nations; and may, without injustice or inhumanity, adopt such measures for introducing a new disposition of clerical endowments, as is most conducive to the general interests of the community.

Lastly, it appears, on the authority of the ablest writers on ecclesiastical polity, that a religious establishment of any kind is no part of Christianity—it is only the means of inculcating it; that a church establishment is founded solely on its utility ;* that the public endowment of any church implies, it is intended to be subordinate and auxiliary to the public good; that the endowments of the Church of England were not originally granted for the support of a particular sect of religionists, but the general support and diffusion of the Gospel: that, in consequence, our episcopalian establishment is not an essential part of religion, but a mean of social advantage, and its policy and duration ought to be determined solely by its bearing on the public interest; and, that, on any future interference with the revenues of the church, the two most important considerations are—*first*, that if appropriated to the maintenance of religion at all, they ought to be appropriated to the maintenance of the teachers of Christianity generally, without distinction of creed; and, *secondly,* that the amount and proportion in which they are so appropriated, ought to be determined by one sole object— the only true end of religion, government, law, and every social institution—namely, the general prosperity and happiness of the People.

We cannot, perhaps, more appropriately conclude this section than by a comparative estimate of the cost of Church of Englandism and of Christianity in other countries. England affords the only grand monument of ecclesiastical wealth remaining to shew the intellectual bondage of men in times of superstition, before the more general diffusion of knowledge and education. Except in this country, the people have every where cast off the prejudice impressed upon them during the dark ages, that it was necessary to yield up a large portion of their property and the fruits of their industry, to be consumed by a numerous body of idle and luxurious ecclesiastics. Abroad those clergymen are only respected and supported who zealously labour in their ministry, and are the real spiritual pastors of the people. Formerly clergymen were almost the only persons who knew how to *read and write;* they took an active part in the administration of the laws, and were in universal request as secretaries and clerks. This was some excuse for their number and endowments. But these days are past, and the subjoined comparison will show that the churches of the Roman Catholic faith present as singular a contrast with their ancient endowments as with the present enormity of Church of England opulence.

---

* Paley's Principles of Moral and Political Philosophy, book vi. chap. 10.

Comparative Expense of Church of Englandism and of Christianity in all other Countries of the World.

Name of the Nation.	Number of Hearers.	Expenditure on the Clergy, per Million of Hearers.	Total Amount of the Expenditure in each Nation.
France	32,000,000	£62,000	£2,000,000
United States	9,600,000	60,000	576,000
Spain	11,000,000	100,000	1,100,000
Portugal	3,000,000	100,000	300,000
Hungary, Catholics	4,000,000	80,000	320,000
Calvinists	1,050,000	60,000	63,000
Lutherans	650,000,	40,000	26,000
Italy	19,391,000	40,000	776,000
Austria	18,918,000	50,000	950,000
Switzerland	1,720,000	50,000	87,000
Prussia	10,536,000	50,000	527,000
German Small States	12,763,000	60,000	765,000
Holland	2,000,000	80,000	160,000
Netherlands	6,000,000	42,000	252,000
Denmark	1,700,000	70,000	119,000
Sweden	3,400,000	70,000	238,000
Russia, Greek Church	34,000,000	15,000	510,000
Catholics and Lutherans.	8,000,000	50,000	400,000
Christians in Turkey	6,000,000	30,000	180,000
South America	15,000,000	30,000	450,000
Christians dispersed elsewhere	3,000,000	50,000	150,000

The Clergy of .... 203,728,000 people receive 9,949,000
England and Wales 6,500,000 1,455,316 9,459,565

Hence, it appears, the administration of Church of Englandism to 6,500,000 hearers costs nearly as much as the administration of all other forms of Christianity in all parts of the world to 203,728,000 hearers.

Of the different forms of Christianity the Romish is the most expensive. A Roman Catholic clergyman cannot go through the duties of his ministry well for more than 1000 persons. The masses, auricular confessions, attendance on the sick, and other observances, make his duties more laborious than those of a Protestant clergyman with double the number of hearers: add to which, the cost of wax lights, scenery, and other accompaniments peculiar to Catholic worship. Notwithstanding these extra outgoings, we find that the administration of the Episcopalian Reformed Religion in England to one million of hearers, costs the people fourteen times more than the administration of Popery to the same number of hearers in Spain or Portugal, and more than forty times the administration of Popery in France.

Dissenters, like churchmen, are compelled to contribute to the support of the ministers and churches of the established religion, besides having to maintain, by voluntary payments, their own pastors and places of worship.   In France all religions are maintained by the state, without distinction; all persons have access to the universities and public schools: in England, only one religion is maintained by the state ; and all dissenters from the national worship are excluded from the universities and colleges, and from the masterships of grammar-schools, and other public foundations, endowed by our common ancestors, for the general promotion of piety and learning.

Dr. PALEY, a writer of great eminence, and whose principal work has been adopted as a text-book at Oxford and Cambridge, has shown that it is the policy of every government which endows a particular form of religion, to make choice of that religion which is followed and believed in by a majority of the people.   This principle, however, is not acted upon in this country.   Notwithstanding the immense endowments of the established clergy, their gradation of rank, and protection by the state, it seems that, owing to laxity of discipline, want of zeal, defects in the Liturgy, or other causes, the adherents of the privileged worship constitute a minority of the nation.

England and Ireland are the only countries in the world where a tenth of the produce is claimed by the clergy.   In Popish Italy the ecclesiastical tithe is only a fortieth, and is taken in kind.   A prosecution by a clergyman for tithe is nearly unknown ; whereas, in the United Kingdom, tithe causes, often forming the most costly and intricate source of litigation, are of frequent occurrence.   In France the expense of all religions, Protestant and Catholic, is defrayed out of the taxes, like other branches of the public service.   In the United States of America all the different modes of worship are maintained by their respective followers.

The monstrous excess in the pay of the English clergy appears from comparing their average income, with the incomes of the clergy of equal rank in other countries.   In France an archbishop has only £1041 a-year; a bishop £625; an archdeacon £166; a canon or prebend £100; a rector £48; a curate £31.   In Rome the income of a cardinal, the next in dignity to the pope, is £400 to 500 a-year ; of a rector of a parish £30; of a curate £17 : compare these stipends with the enormous incomes of the English clergy ; and, making allowance for difference in the expence of living in the respective countries, the disparity in ecclesiastical remuneration appears incredible.

V. RAPACITY OF THE CLERGY EXEMPLIFIED.

Though the avocations of the clergy are professedly of a spiritual nature, no class has manifested so greedy an appetite for temporal advantages and enjoyments.   They have been like the daughters of the horse-leech, their cry has constantly been *give! give!*   A brief notice of the application of First Fruits and Tenths, and, subsequently, of parliamentary grants to the augmentation of ecclesiastical revenues, will show as much rapacity on the part of the clergy and as wasteful expenditure of public money on the church as was ever exhibited in the darkest ages of monkish superstition.

First Fruits, as is well known, are the first year's whole profit or value of any spiritual preferment. The *Tenths* are the tenth part of the annual value of each living. Both first-fruits and tenths were formerly paid to the pope. The first-fruits were paid to his Holiness on promotion to any new benefice, and the tenths were an annual income-tax of ten per cent. out of the revenue of the clergy. As the clergy would, when it was contrary to law, persist in the payment of these foreign exactions, Henry VIII. determined, on the dissolution of the monasteries, to keep them to the yoke to which they had voluntarily subjected themselves, and annexed the revenue arising from first-fruits and tenths to the crown ; excepting, however, from the payment of first-fruits, all vicarages under ten pounds, and rectories under ten marks per annum.

According to the valuation in the King's Book, the first-fruits and tenths were paid, as the 1st of Elizabeth has it, to " the great aid, relief, and supportation of the *inestimable* charges of the Crown :" and so continued till the 2d year of queen Anne, 1703, when an act passed giving to a corporation, which was to be erected for the augmentation of small livings, the whole of the first fruits and tenths. This is what is called QUEEN ANNE'S BOUNTY, and amounted to about £14,000 per annum : it has been subsequently increased by an annual grant of £100,000 from parliament and the benefactions of individuals. By another act of the queen, the bishops are required, by oaths of witnesses, to ascertain the clear improved yearly value of every benefice with incomes not exceeding £50 per annum, and certify the same to the exchequer, in order to be discharged from the payment of first-fruits : and all above that value to contribute, by the payment of first-fruits and tenths, to the augmentation of the former.

The object of the queen in establishing this fund was to relieve the *poor* clergy ; the real and only effect has been to relieve the *rich* clergy from a charge to which by law they were liable. In the 26th Henry VIII. a provision was made for revising, from time to time, the valuations under which the first-fruits and tenths were paid. It is probable the clergy of 1703 were apprehensive, as the nation was then engaged in an expensive war, that such a revision might be made ; and in persuading the pious queen to renounce a portion of the hereditary revenue for the sake of " her poor clergy," they artfully contrived to insert a clause (the last in the act) by which the payment of first-fruits and tenths was made *perpetual at the original rate* of valuation !

The cunning of the rich clergy in thus shifting from themselves the burthen of contributing to the relief of their poorer brethren, is only to be matched in degree by the folly shown in the application of the diminished revenue which this trick of theirs still left for the improvement of small livings. At the time when the Bounty-Fund was established, there were, according to the returns, 5597 livings in England and Wales with incomes not exceeding £50, and which the slow operation of the fund, aided by parliament, would not raise to £150 in two centuries. Under such circumstances any rational being would suppose the governors and the legislature, by whom the disposal of the fund was superintended, would have made some inquiry into the condition of these livings. Some of them were of very small extent and scarcely any population; and might, therefore, have been advantageously united with one another or with other parishes. In others, the number of hearers was very great, and the parishes so large, they might have been advantageously subdivided. No attention was paid to these different circumstances. The governors of the bounty proceeded bountifully: they distributed a part of their money, in sums of £200, on any poor living to which any private person would give an equal sum; the rest, and greater part, they distributed *by lot*, letting each poor living take an equal chance for a £200 prize, without any regard to persons or urgency of claim. After this the story of Bridoye deciding suits-at-law by dice, after making up a fair pile of paper on each side, appears no longer an extravaganza. Up to the year 1815 the governors had made in this way 7323 augmentations of £200; but with benefices, as with men, fortune is not proportioned to desert or necessity. Some of the least populous parishes had a wonderful run of luck. In the diocese of Chichester, for instance, the rectory of Hardham, which, in 1811, contained eighty-nine inhabitants, has received six augmentations by lot, or £1200. The vicarage of Loddington, with forty-eight people, has had six augmentations,—£1200. In the diocese of Salisbury, Bremilham drew a prize; it contained fourteen people. Pertwood drew another; it had but twelve people. Calstone had £1000, including a benefaction of £200; its population was nineteen. In the diocese of Winchester, St. Swithin's, with twenty-four people, has received £800; and £200 has been expended on Ewhurst, which has seven people, and the living returned worth £99. In the diocese of York, Butterwick, with sixty-two people, has had five prizes,—£1000; while Armley, with 2941 people, and Allendale, with 3884, have only gained one each. Even in cities, where the scattered condition of the population could afford no pretext against the union of parishes, the same random plan of augmentations has been pursued. In Winchester separate augmentations have been given to seven parishes, the population of which, all united, would have amounted only to 2376, and would, consequently, have formed a very manageable and rather small town parish. In short, the whole of the returns* teem with instances of extravagance, and clearly demonstrate this clerical *little-go* has been managed for a very different purpose than relieving the penury of part of the establishment. Indeed it is supposed that the church looks upon the poverty of some of her members as sturdy beggars look upon their sores, considering them a valuable adjunct for exciting an ill-judged compassion for the whole body, and securing impunity in idleness and over-feeding.

Had it not been for the fraudulent substraction of the higher clergy from the burthen of contributing to the relief of their poor brethren,

---

* Parliamentary Paper, No. 115, Session 1815.

there would have been no need of resorting to eleemosynary aid from parliament.   If the first-fruits and tenths had been paid, subsequently to the gift of Queen Anne, according to the rate which the law provided, that is, according to the *real value of the benefices*, instead of a million and a half, at least thirty millions would have been received from those taxes;* a sum not only quite sufficient to have removed the poverty of all the poor livings in the kingdom, but to have established schools in every parish, and left a surplus beside for building additional churches, or any other useful purpose.

The funds at present in the hands of the governors are very considerable : not long since these faithful trustees for the benefit of the *poor clergy* advanced a loan for the repair of the palace of the rich archdiocese of Canterbury; and it is said they have come to a resolution to discourage as much as possible the purchase of lands, and to make certain annual allowances to clergymen with small livings from the dividend of the stock.   By this latter proceeding the heads of the church have themselves begun to pay the clergy out of the public funds; affording an example, from high authority, of the practicability of this mode of paying the clergy generally.

In the course of the augmentations no security has been taken against *non-residence* or *plurality*.   The governors have gone on increasing the income of two small livings, in order to make each of them capable of supporting a resident clergyman, while, after as well as before the augmentation, one incumbent may hold them together—reside on neither—and allow only a small part of the accumulated income to a curate, who performs the duties of both.

Rapacity and finesse appear inseparable traits in the character of the clergy at all times; and the recent conduct of our spiritual guides in the metropolis is a worthy counterpart to that of the clergy in the time of Queen Anne.   The situation of the clergy of the City of London is different from that of the clergy in other parts of the kingdom.   In the reign of Henry VIII. continual altercations took place between the citizens and their pastors relative to tithes and ecclesiastical dues.   To put an end to these unseemly disputes, the 37th Henry VIII. established a commission, at the head of which was the archbishop, with full power to give to their decrees the force of law, if they were *enrolled in the Court of Chancery* before March, 1545.   By a decree of this commission the tithe of houses and buildings is fixed at the rate of 2s. 9d. for every 20s. yearly rent, and 2d. for each of the family for the four yearly offerings.   Great disputes, however, have arisen between the inhabitants and tithe-holders respecting the validity of this decree ; for it appears, on the authority of Tomline and Raithby, that it never was enrolled agreeably to the obligation of the act.   The clergy, however, have continued to urge their claim to 2s. 9d. in the pound, which they modestly term their " *ancient rights*," and would, doubtless, yield a

very handsome remuneration.   An assessment of 1s. in the pound, as
stated by the City tithe-committee, would, in the smallest and poorest
parishes, yield an income of £500 a-year; and an assessment of 2s. 9d.
would raise the lowest living to £1400 a-year.   To this exorbitant pretension the clergy have long looked with extreme desire, beholding the
increasing wealth and population of the City with feelings similar to
those ascribed by Milton to Satan, when contemplating, with malign eye,
the happiness of our first parents in the garden of Eden.

Though the decree emanating from the 37th Henry VIII. was of
doubtful validity, it has formed the principle on which the assessment has
been raised for the maintenance of the city clergy.   The clergy, indeed,
do not generally exact the 2s. 9d. but content themselves with 2s. 1s. 9d.
or 1s. or, in short, any thing they can obtain,—insisting, however, at
the same time, on their extreme forbearance in thus generously foregoing their "*ancient rights*."   Even the 37th Henry did not intend to
vest in the clergy the 2s. 9d. for their exclusive maintenance, but also
for relieving the poor and repairing the edifice of the church.   This they
have always kept out of sight: the parishioners apparently acquiesced
in their pretended rights; and it was only owing to the ill-timed rapacity
of the Fire-Act Clergy which led to the explosion of their unfounded
claims.   Of the proceedings of the Fire-Act Clergy it may be worth
while to give some account.

After the 37th Henry VIII. the clergy in the city were maintained
by a certain pound-rate levied on the rental of buildings in their respective parishes.   This practice continued till the great fire laid the major
part of the city in ashes, burning down or damaging eighty-five parish-
churches.   After this catastrophe, the legislature enacted that some of
the parishes destroyed should be united ; that only fifty-one churches
should be rebuilt ; and that the ministers of those churches should, in
lieu of their former allowance, receive certain fixed sums, levied by an
equal pound-rate on the houses.   This was the 22d and 23d Charles II.
termed the *Fire-Act*.   The clergy subject to the provisions of this act
were perfectly satisfied, till the effects of the fire began to disappear,
the rents of the houses to rise, and the city to get rich again.   Then
it was our reverend gentlemen became discontented : they saw, with
grudging eyes, the increasing wealth of the capital, of which their fixed
stipends would not allow them to participate ; they talked unceasingly
of their former pound-rate, of their "*ancient rights*," and at length
determined, in good earnest, to apply to parliament.

This was in 1804, and, in consequence, parliament made valuable
additions to their salaries; the lowest incomes were raised to £200 a-
year, and many of the larger parishes, nearly, if not quite, to £600
a-year, exclusive of surplice-fees and other valuable emoluments.   Such
augmentation, to all reasonable men, appeared quite sufficient: not so
to the clergy.   In 1817 they applied for a further augmentation.   This
application was refused.   In 1818 they came forward a third time, with
their famous petition of the 4th February, filled with grievous lamentations about the loss of their "*ancient rights*."   The bubble now burst.

Parliament, disgusted with the rapacity of these " sturdy beggars," determined to refer their petition to a committee.   It was soon discovered their " *ancient rights*" had no foundation ;* that they never were entitled to 2*s*. 9*d*. on the rental, or any part of it; that with the 37th Henry VIII. which they had foisted into their petition, they had nothing to do, except it were to exhibit the craving and rapacious spirit which actuated them.

Various other disclosures were made.   Of the thirty-five *poor* clergymen who had signed the petition, none of them, on an average, was receiving less than £500 a-year.   Twenty-five out of the number were pluralists, and not a few of them the fattest pluralists of the profession. Some of the incumbents received annually £1200, £1500, and even £2000, while they did not pay their curates more than £60, £70, or £80 a-year.†   Instead of residing in the parsonage-house, among the parishioners, the parsonage-houses of many were let to the merchants and manufacturers for counting-houses and warehouses, for which they

---

* Parliamentary Papers, vol. viii. Sess. 1819.

† The incumbents in London are usually careful to select curates whose abilities are not likely to eclipse their own.   Some do not stop here, but actually make personal appearance an object of consideration, always taking care to choose a curate of a less imposing figure than themselves.   Hence many parishes, in order to have a tolerable discourse once on Sunday, and a decent-looking man for a preacher, go to the expense of paying an evening lecturer of their own choice; but here again they are often foiled by the reverend rector, or reverend vicar, refusing to let him preach in his pulpit.   A Reverend Mr. Gunn, a man well remembered by many in London, was once placed in this predicament : he mentioned the circumstance to a former Bishop of London ; on which his Lordship replied, alluding to the rector in question, " Ah, Mr. Gunn, you can shoot too well for him."   The lecturers are paid by voluntary subscription ; the lecturer going round with his subscription-book among the butchers, bakers, and publicans, humbly requesting " Mr. Pumpkin or Mr. Samuel Blewett to put down his name for any trifle he pleases."

Much of the spiritual duty in the metropolis is performed by *job-parsons*. These are unfortunate men, who, being without powerful influence or connexion, are unprovided with a regular curacy or benefice; or, perhaps, some of them have been cast on the world from an unlucky adventure at college, an ungovernable propensity to strong cordials, or an untoward issue of a love-affair in their native parishes.   Whatever is the cause, they are met with in great number in different parts of the town, and may be generally known from their care-worn appearance, soiled linen, and threadbare clothes.   Like coopers, carpenters, and other branches of operatives, they have their *houses of call*, where they inform themselves of the state of ecclesiastical employment and the current rate of remuneration.   It is to these places the well-fed pastors of London resort, when, from *indisposition*—that is the usual pretext—or some unforeseen emergency, they require a deputy, or assistant, to pass through the morning-service.   In this resource they are never disappointed, for, unfortunately, the market is overstocked with labourers in the vineyard, and the unattached sons of the church may be always met with in readiness, like so many ticket-porters, for any half-crown or dollar engagement.

From these traits may be learned the manner in which the churches are served, and the degraded state of discipline in the metropolis, where the revenues are more than ten times sufficient, if properly distributed, to pay for the permanent services of men of first-rate talents, independence, and character.

received exorbitant rents of £200 or £300 a-year. Some of them were archdeacons, royal chaplains, or honourable and very reverend deans; some canons at St. Paul's, some were precentors, prebendaries, and held other dignified situations in cathedral and collegiate churches. Had they not been the most unreasonable and rapacious men breathing, there is little doubt but they would have considered the emoluments arising from their numerous preferments sufficient. But the wealth of India would not satisfy the cravings of spiritual men. Some of them were mean enough to lay in wait for the members going to the House while their petition was pending, and beseech them to support their claims for an increase in their stipends. It reminds us of the monks of St. Swithin's. These gluttons had thirteen dishes a day. Hume relates that they threw themselves prostrate in the mire before Henry II. and, with doleful lamentations, complained that the Bishop of Winchester had cut off three dishes a day. " How many has he left ?" said the King. " Ten," replied the disconsolate monks. " I myself," said Henry, " have only three, and I enjoin the Bishop to reduce you to the same number."

The emoluments of the metropolitan clergy generally exceed those of the provincial clergy. The practice of uniting parishes, which is allowed by 37th Henry VIII. c. 21, when churches are not more than one mile apart, and under the value of £6, has been carried to a great extent in London. The City alone reckons 108 parishes, which have been formed into no more than seventy-eight benefices, having alternate patrons. Some of these livings are very valuable. For instance, the rectory of St. Botolph, Bishopsgate, held by the dean of Hereford, and in the alternate gift of the King and Bishop of London, is worth £2500 a-year. The rectory of St. Andrew's, Holborn, held by the Rev. Mr. Beresford, and in the patronage of the Duke of Buccleugh, is probably worth £3500. In Westminster, the rectory of St. George's, Hanover-square, held by the Dean of Carlisle, and in the gift of the Bishop of London, is worth, at least, £4000 per annum. The living of St. Giles's, held by the Rev. J. E. Tyler, and in the gift of the Lord Chancellor, is another valuable rectory. We could enumerate others, but these must suffice.

In considering the incomes of the metropolitan clergy, it must be remembered that they have many other sources of emolument besides their benefices. St. Paul's Cathedral and Westminster-Abbey have many valuable dignities, equal in value to good livings, and which are principally shared among the London ecclesiastics. Then there are the appointments in the royal chapels, public libraries and museums, and the salaries they receive as ushers, masters, &c. in the numerous and wealthy charitable foundations, and which altogether must make their incomes immense.

From this representation of the situation of the clergy of the metropolis, it is clearly their wisest course to follow the policy of primate SUTTON, and keep quiet. They should constantly bear in mind the fable of the dog with a piece of flesh, and not endanger what they possess by grasping at too much.   But, somehow, the clergy ordinarily evince so little general knowledge, and are so blindly intent on immediate gain, that they usually adopt the most contracted and mistaken views of their permanent interests.   Their conduct in respect of compositions for tithes strikingly exemplifies these traits in the clerical character.   In order to render this part of the subject intelligible, it will be necessary to premise a few explanations.

A real composition for tithes is when an agreement is made between the landlord and parson, with the consent of the ordinary and patron, that certain land shall be discharged from the payment of tithes, by reason of some land, or other recompense, given to the incumbent in lieu thereof.   Such agreements were anciently very frequent, till, by the 13th Elizabeth, it was provided that no composition for tithes should be valid for a longer term than three lives, or twenty-one years.   This tended greatly to restrain compositions, and they are now rarely heard of, unless by authority of parliament.   To establish the validity of these agreements previously entered into, it is necessary to *produce the deed itself*, executed between the commencement of the reign of Richard the First and the restraining act of Elizabeth, or such evidence from whence, independent of mere usage, it may be inferred that the deed once existed.   Now this is often impossible.   Time, as Lord Ellenborough once said, is a greedy devourer of patents and parchments, as of other things, and, probably, in the lapse of 240 years, the deed has been lost or destroyed, or other circumstances utterly preclude the production of the necessary proof.   Clergymen, however, have often been found greedy enough to avail themselves of this strange peculiarity in the law, and suddenly claim the tithes from land that had been exonerated for centuries, and for which there could be no doubt a composition had been once granted.   This was done, not many years since, by some sinecure priests of the cathedral of Exeter.   We well remember the case of Dr. Peplow Ward, the rector of Cottenham.   This was a real composition traced so far back as the middle of the sixteenth century;* the parson claimed his tithes, and kept the land too, given in lieu of them, because the unfortunate owner could not produce the deed of conveyance.

A recent instance of clerical rapacity has been evinced by the dean and chapter of Ely, and was brought before parliament in the session of 1831,† by the owners of Lakenheath-fen, a district of 5000 acres.   The fen-owners claim exemption from tithe by prescription; and the property has been purchased, made the subject of wills, family settlements, and contracts, as tithe-free land.   But the legal maxim is, that the elapse of no time bars the claim of the church, and the petitioners are bound to prove an uninterrupted exemption from the payment of

---

* Hansard's Parliamentary Debates, vol. xxxvii. p. 551.
† Cobbett's Register, October 29, 1831.

tithe for nearly 650 years. The dean and chapter of Ely, who possess the rectory and vicarage of Lakenheath, have availed themselves of this difficulty, to revive their claim of tithe over the fen. For nineteen years have the owners of the fen-land been harassed by their spiritual oppressors; they have already expended £5000 in litigation, and more law is now threatened them; the dean and chapter having granted a concurrent lease of the rectory to Mr. Evans, their solicitor and agent, who has renewed the persecution for the tithe of the fen.

A *modus*, or accustomed rate of payment for tithe, no more than a composition, is never allowed to stand after the clergyman wishes to terminate it, unless it can be proved to have existed prior to A.D. 1189. Day after day rank moduses, as they are called, though they have continued from time out of mind, yet bear evidence of not having existed before the return of King Richard from the Holy Land, are set at naught. Why our legal sages should have adopted this antiquated era for the bounds of legal memory, and to which, for the validity of a custom or prescription, it is necessary to trace an uninterrupted observance, no one can divine, unless it arise from the obvious interest they have in involving every rule regarding the rights of persons and property in the greatest possible obscurity and contradiction. The parsons, however, avail themselves of this dictum, and set aside every customary payment for tithe they do not like, which cannot be proved to have continued, without interruption, from the twelfth century. Hence no modus for hops, turkeys, or other thing introduced into England since that period, is valid. The keenness with which, on various occasions, the clergy have litigated these points is astonishing; and their conduct, both as regards compositions, first fruits, and tithes in London, shows the inherent rapacity of the order, and that there is no stratagem to which they will not resort, in order to avoid payments to which they are justly liable, or to fasten on the public some of their own dormant pretensions. They cannot, therefore, expect any indulgence, nor complain if a similar measure of justice be dealt to them. One mode of retaliation would be to insist on the payment of first fruits and tenths, according to the present value of benefices, whereby the condition of the inferior clergy would be improved out of the redundant incomes of the rich ecclesiastics.

But quite as equitable and a more effective blow might be dealt the priesthood, by the poor insisting on their old common law right to one-third of the tithes of benefices. If the clergy will persist in reviving worn-out claims, why should the people suffer their own just rights to remain in abeyance? That the poor are entitled to one-third of the tithes has been unanswerably proved by Ruggles and Eagle. No time has elapsed to defeat the claims of the poor any more than the claims of the Church. There stands their right, guaranteed to them by the old common law of the land, sanctioned by centuries of uninterrupted usage, and never repealed by any statute of the realm.

VI. ORIGIN AND DEFECTS OF THE CHURCH LITURGY.

New religions are seldom genuine. Like new constitutions of government, they are mostly established by being incorporated with pre-existing opinions and institutions. This observation will appear evident from an advertance to the origin and history of the Church Liturgy, by which will be seen the successive gradations of Paganism, Popery, and Protestantism, through which it has emerged and been transmuted.

Dr. MIDDLETON, an eloquent and learned divine of the Church of England, was the first to lead the way in this inquiry. In his celebrated letter from Rome, he exhibits, in a very perspicuous manner, the great conformity between Paganism and Popery, and proves that the religion of the present Romans is entirely derived from that of their heathen ancestors :—in the use of incense, holy water, tapers and lamps, in their worship; in the practice of pomps and processions, penance, pretended miracles, and pious frauds; in the making of votive gifts and offerings, and erecting rural shrines; in the orders of their priesthood, nuns, monks, and begging friars, and in the use of boys clothed in sacred habits, to attend the officiating priest: all of which he has shown to have been practised by the Pagans, and by the Papists, in imitation of them. But here Dr. Middleton stopped in his comparison, unaware, apparently, that in his zeal to depreciate a rival church, he had furnished weapons of no ordinary temper, with which that to which he belonged might be assailed.

This task has been executed in the well-known work of DE LAUNE, in his Plea for the Nonconformists, where he has exhibited learning and ability not inferior to Dr. Middleton. He shows that in the several particulars of kneeling at the Sacrament, the use of the surplice, the sign of the cross, the rite of confirmation, the use of sponsors in the baptism of infants, of a liturgy or form of prayer, and of altars, the observance of fasts and festivals, the ceremony of marriage, bowing at the name of Jesus, and towards the east, the authority of episcopacy, and the dedication of churches to saints; the church of England symbolizes not with primitive Christianity, but with the idolatrous forms of Popery. Such resemblance ceases to be matter of surprise, when it is known, on the authority of Calderwood, that the English service was put together out of three Romish channels : viz. 1. The breviary, out of which the common prayers are taken; 2. The ritual, or book of rites, out of which the administration of the sacraments, burial, matrimony, and the visitation of the sick, are taken; and, 3. The mass-book, out of which the consecration of the Lord's supper, collects, epistles, and gospels are taken.

The Rubric, or Service-book of Henry VIII.'s time, was no other than the Romish liturgy, partly translated into English. In the reign of Edward VI. the whole was rendered into the vernacular tongue, but otherwise was little altered. This fact was distinctly avowed by the proclamation of the king and council made at the rebellion of some enthusiasts in the West of England, who had been excited thereto by the priests; it is thus: " As for the service in the English tongue, it perchance seems to you a *new service*, and, yet, indeed, *it is no other but the old*, the self-same words in English; for nothing is altered but to speak with knowledge that which was spoken with ignorance, only a few things taken out, so fond, that it had been a shame to have heard them in English."[*] Between that period and the reign of James I. it is true that some alterations were effected, but notwithstanding we find that monarch thus speaking of the same service. " As for our neighbour Kirk of England, their service is an *evil said mass in English;* they want nothing of the mass, but the *liftings*."[†] It is allowed, that after this period there were some other alterations made in the service, but we find that Charles II. in his preface to the Common Prayer, annexed to the Act of Uniformity, thus expresses his opinion: " the main body and essentials of it (as well in the chiefest materials as in the frame and order thereof) have still continued the same unto this day, notwithstanding all vain attempts and impetuous assaults made against it." Now the obvious inference from these testimonies is, that the service of the Church of England, with little alteration, is the same as that of the Church of Rome. But, to show more satisfactorily the resemblance between the two churches, we shall insert the following comparison from an ingenious and elaborate publication, entitled " The Church Establishment founded in Error:"[‡]

" The breviary and calendar of the Church of Rome divides the year into fasts, vigils, feasts, and working days. The same division is adopted by the Church of England, with this exception, that there are less of the former; but of those that are observed they stand in the same order, and are evidently borrowed from the calendar of the Roman Church. Their feasts are divided into moveable and fixed; so are ours; and of thirty-six of them the observance is the same in both churches. The fast-days of both are alike. In the Church of Rome the service itself is divided into matins and even songs; so is ours; theirs is appropriated to the particular feasts, fasts, vigils, &c.; so is ours; the substance of their service consists in collects, confessions, absolutions, psalms, epistles, gospels, prophets, apocrypha, litanies, anthems, &c. so does ours. In the Church of Rome, the people kneel at confession or absolution, repeat after the priest the pater-noster, stand at gloria patri, stand up and repeat the apostle's creed, kneel and repeat after the minister, Lord, have mercy upon us; Christ have mercy upon us; make responses at the saying of the litany, kneel at the altar when they partake of the eucharist, or Lord's supper, kneel and ask mercy and grace after the rehearsal of the decalogue; read the psalms alternately with the priest, verse by verse; sit at reading the lessons, say the psalms to the accompaniment of music, bow to the

---

[*] Acts and Mon. vol. ii. p. 1189; quoted by De Laune.
[†] Calderwood, Hist. Ch. of Scot. p. 256; quoted by De Laune.
[‡] London, E. Wilson, 1831.

east and at the name of Jesus. All this is done in the Church of Rome, and so is it performed in the Church of England. The places of worship which the Church of England at present occupies, and the endowments it possesses, were built, consecrated, and bestowed by the Papists, and as they were dedicated by them to various saints, so they continue dedicated by the Church of England. The Church of Rome has its archbishops, bishops, deans and chapters, prebends, archdeacons, and other graduated dignities; so has the Church of England, which retains also distinguishing habits for each, as formerly practised by the Roman Church. And the ordination services in both churches so closely resemble each other, that, with a few unimportant alterations, they are verbatim the same. A parallel so singular and striking cannot fail to convince every unprejudiced mind, that one system has given rise to the other."—pp. 44-5.

Having gone through the historical part of our inquiry, we shall next come to a notice of the church service as now administered. Apart from the temporalities of the Church, we do not think there is much to give offence in the established worship, notwithstanding its impure and idolatrous origin. Man is said naturally to be prone to religion, and were he deprived of his present idols, it is not improbable he might create others with more onerous pretensions. Those, however, most attached to the national establishment, cannot deny there are defects in its ritual, which, if they could be quietly abscinded, would be a great improvement. The church has partaken, in some degree, of the improvements of the age. It has been argued out of intolerance towards every Christian sect. Some doctrines still retained, as part of the Athanasian creed and Thirty-nine Articles, are viewed, we apprehend, in the same light as special pleading and other legal fictions, rather as curious relics of a past age than as dogmas of practical use and belief. In its rites and ceremonial, the services it exacts are of easy performance to every class. The enforcement of the sabbath is an unmixed good to the industrious orders, while the hebdomadal inculcation of a future state of reward and punishment supports with hope or restrains with fear those who cannot appreciate the claims of a more enlightened morality. Philosophers can hardly begrudge the devotion of one morning out of seven to a parish church; if their feelings are not interested in the iterations of the Liturgy, their souls may be soothed by music and psalmody, and thus be enabled to range, with less disturbance, through the regions of science.

Mere politicians, who usually look on the sanctions of religion as more useful than credible, are little under its influence. The Tories were formerly a godly race of men,—they had religion at the heart, but with the Whigs it never went beyond the lips. Speaking of these once notable factions, the late Mr. Fox observes, " While the Whigs considered all religion with a view to politics, the Tories, on the other hand, referred all politics to religion. Thus the former, in their hatred to Popery, did not so much regard the superstition or even idolatry of that unpopular sect, as its tendency to establish arbitrary power in the state;

while the latter revered arbitrary monarchy as a divine institution, and cherished passive obedience and non-resistance as articles of religious faith."* With few exceptions, both parties are now agreed in treating religion as an engine or ally of the state,—a branch of the police, or civil power, very useful for repressing disorders, or assisting that famous tax machine, a mock representation, in extracting money out of the pockets of the people.

The Church appears inclined to cultivate a spirit of indifference and quietism,—the most favourable course it could take for a lengthened duration. It prosecutes no doctrine, controls, with a gentle hand, the passions of the multitude, gives full scope to the pleasures of the great, and is mostly prompt to throw the weight of its influence into the scale of government. So far is well and judicious. But there are some parts of the Liturgy so staringly preposterous, and so inconsistent with genuine Protestantism, that we think, if they are not shortly got rid of, they must, ere long, attract a dangerous share of popular attention. The reformation of Henry VIII. from the first needed reforming, and, after an elapse of more than two centuries, the task cannot surely be deemed premature.

The portion of the book of Common Prayer, to which we shall first call attention, is the *Church Catechism*. This includes the elements of Church of Englandism, and is of the utmost importance from being first impressed on the minds of the rising generation. To the bad grammar and logic of this manual we do not attach much importance, though, entering as it does into early instruction, it ought to be unobjectionable on these points. But what is more serious, is the impracticable, superfluous and unintelligible matter it contains.

For example:—in the baptismal service, the godfather and godmother renounce, in the name and behoof of the child, " the devil and all his works, the vain pomp and glory of the world, with all covetous desires of the same, and the carnal desires of the flesh;" and this engagement the child solemnly promises to fulfil. But the utter impossibility of performance reduces the whole to an unmeaning ceremony : sponsors offer up their pledges without consideration, and christenings next to marriages are scenes of the greatest levity and indecorum.

That part where the child engages to make " no graven image, nor the likeness of any thing that is in heaven above, or in the earth beneath, or in the water under the earth," is superfluous, inapplicable, and liable to be misunderstood. Though the *golden calf* was never more worshipped than at present, it is the most romote possible from a religious worship. The injunction was delivered to the Jews when they were surrounded by nations of idolators ; but the nearest idolatry is distant from England at least a thousand leagues, and children can find no type of it in this country, except in the productions of the artist, to which they may mistakenly think it applies.

In another place occurs the phrase " all the elect people of God," which savours strongly of that Calvinism against which Lord Chatham directed

---

* History of James II.

his anathema, and which we verily believe, next to the anarchical principles of the French revolutionists, is the most anti-social doctrine ever propagated. Unless religion aids the cause of virtue, it is, comparatively,
valueless ; but the doctrine of election divests the Christian faith of
every moral obligation. Of what importance can an individual's conduct be, if his salvation depends solely on the fiat of a foregone conclusion. In the words of JOHN WESLEY, who has stated the case with
equal force and truth, the sum of all is this : " one in twenty (suppose)
of mankind are elected; nineteen in twenty are reprobated ! The elect
shall be saved, *do what they will*: the reprobate shall be damned, *do
what they can*."* Affirm till doomsday that there can be no election
without faith, and no faith without works, this is the essence of Calvinism ; for which, *diabolism* would be a better name ; and in the worst
and bloodiest idolatry that ever defiled the earth, there is nothing so
horrid, so monstrous, so impious.

Transubstantiation, or the real presence, was the great test of popery
at the time of the Reformation. If a man, like Mr. O'Connell, for
example, were to affirm his belief that the body and blood of Christ are
actually taken and swallowed, at the sacrament of the Lord's Supper,
he was hurried off to the stake, without pity or remorse. Yet, for the
life of us, we cannot attach any other than a real and corporeal interpretation to the following interrogatories in the *Catechism :—*

Question.—What is the inward part or thing signified ?
Answer.—The body and blood of Christ, which are *verily and indeed taken
and received* by the faithful in the Lord's Supper.
Question.—What are the benefits whereof we are partakers thereby ?
Answer.—The strengthening and refreshing of our souls by the body and
blood of Christ, as our bodies are by the bread and wine.

If this is not transubstantiation we do not know how it can be otherwise expressed. But it may be urged, that our apprehensions are
wholly groundless, and no harm is done : that the catechism is intended
only for the instruction of children; that it is mere words learnt by
rote, like the Lord's Prayer, the Apostles' Creed, and the Ten Com-
mandments, at an age when the understanding is so little unfolded that
no ideas are attached to them. Granted : but if the formula is to be so
construed, we think it had better be consigned to the exclusive use
of the dame shools, and the public saved the expense of maintaining so
many well-fed clergymen, chiefly employed in impressing and confirming it on the minds of our juvenile population.

Another *morceau* from the mass-book is retained in the *Visitation
of the Sick ;* in which the Protestant priest actually grants absolution
of sin with as much *sang froid* and authority as Leo. X. The sick person is directed to make a confession of his sins, if he feel his conscience
troubled in any weighty matter ; the priest then tenders a *carte blanche*
in manner and form following : —

" Our Lord Jesus Christ, who hath left power to his church to absolve all sin-

---

* Dr. Southey's Life of Wesley, vol. i. p. 371.

ners who truly repent and believe in him, of his great mercy forgive thee thine offences ; and by his authority, committed to me, *I absolve thee from all thy sins,* in the name of the Father, and of the Son, and of the Holy Ghost.—*Amen.*

In the *Morning Service* is a form of absolution; but the terms in which it is given are less explicit; and the priest only declares a remission of sins to those who truly repent. Considering the era when the Common Prayer was framed, it is not surprising it retains some remnants of the superstition out of which it was fabricated. For aught we know, the power of granting absolution may have scriptural authority ; at all events it must often prove salutary, affording consolation at a moment when human nature most needs support, and compensating for any fears and anxieties which may have been felt during past life, by the certain hope held out of future forgiveness and beatitude.

The mode of filling a Church of England priest with the Holy Ghost, and endowing him with the invaluable elixir to forgive sins, and keep out of hell, or let drop into it whom he pleases, is not less extraordinary than the gift itself. It must be premised that no person can be admitted to any benefice unless he has been first ordained a priest ; and then, in the language of the law, he is termed a clerk in orders. The mode of such ordination is thus described in the Liturgy.

" The bishop, with the priest present, shall lay their hands severally upon every one that receiveth the order of priesthood ; the receivers humbly kneeling upon their knees, and the bishop saying,
" *Receive the Holy Ghost,* for the office and work of a priest in the church of God, now committed unto thee by the imposition of our hands.—*Whose sins thou dost forgive, they are forgiven ; and whose sins thou dost retain, they are retained.*"

Truly this is marvellous in our eyes ! The bare idea of any one who can swallow three bottles of wine, and leap a five-barred gate, being filled with the Holy Ghost, makes the gorge rise. But then the necromancy of this wonderful infusion. The bishop, only imposing his right reverend hands, saying, " Receive the Holy Ghost," and instantly, with the suddenness of the electric fluid, the Holy Ghost passes from the fingers of the bishop into the inside of—perhaps, a Clogher, a Philpotts, a Hay, a Blacow, or a Daniels.

Talk of miracles having ceased,—they are performing daily. Talk of popery, of indulgences, and absolutions. Talk of the poor, naked, godless, unenlightened Indian, who wanders on the banks of the Niger or the Orinoque. Talk of the Chinese, who cuts his deity with scissars, or moulds him in paste. Talk of the wretched Hindoo, who immolates his victim to Juggernaut ; or of the wild Tartar, who worships the invisible Lama. Talk of all or any of these, or go to what age or country we may, for examples of supernatural pretension, can we find any to match this part of the rites of the Church of England ?

We shall now leave to the Reader's further consideration the subject of the church ritual. It is only a work of men's hands, and cannot, of course, claim the same infallibility as the Holy Scriptures. An order in council is any time sufficient authority for introducing alterations in the Liturgy; and, even within our own time, it has been subjected both to curtailment and additions. George IV., it will long be remembered, ordered the name of Queen Caroline to be struck out, as a person unworthy of the prayers of the people. Lord Sidmouth, who now forms a fragment of the *dead weight*, during his secretaryship, directed four prayers to be interpolated, and they form a regular portion of the church service. In the few observations we have ventured to put forward, our purpose has been only to advert to such parts as seemed most startling to vulgar apprehension; and in doing this, we trust, nothing irreverent has escaped us, or in derogation of the general utility of the *Book of Common Prayer*. With all its imperfections we greatly prefer the established ceremonial to the random out-pourings of the conventicle; and think the measured solemnities deliberately framed for the various occasions of life, preferable to those wild exhortations which have no standard but the intellect of the preacher, his thirst of gain or popularity, or the passions and fatuity of his hearers.

VII. NUMBER, WEALTH, MORAL AND EDUCATIONAL EFFICIENCY OF PROTESTANT DISSENTERS.

The Roman slaves were never numbered lest they should discover their power and importance. A similar policy appears to have been observed towards the dissenters. Although we have had three censuses of the people within the last thirty years, in the taking of which various inquiries were made into the numbers employed in different trades and occupations; no inquiry was made into the number of the different religious sects. Were the legislature, in this case, apprehensive that they might be called upon, agreeably to the dogma of Dr. Paley on the policy of patronizing the most popular faith, to commence another religious reformation, by altering the present disposition of ecclesiastical endowments? Whatever may have been the motive, the fact is as stated —that no public inquiry has ever been instituted into the relative number of Separatists and Episcopalians.

In the session of 1829, returns were ordered by the House of Commons of the number of churches and chapels of the establishment, and of the number of places of worship not of the establishment.* With the exception of Lancaster, no returns have yet been published from any other county. The only public document which throws light on the question, is a parliamentary paper, ordered to be printed May 29th, 1812, and re-printed by the Lords in 1818. This document comprises only the results of returns from parishes containing a population of 1000 persons and upwards. In 1881 parishes of this description, containing a population of 4,937,789, there were 2,533 churches and chapels belonging to the established church; the number of persons they would contain 1,856,108: in the same number of parishes there were 3,438 dissenting places of worship. From this it might be in-

---

* Votes of the House of Commons, June 19, 1829.

ferred the number of dissenters considerably exceeds the number of conformists. No doubt many small parishes not included in the return would have a church and not a dissenting chapel. On the other hand, the manufacturing population consists chiefly of dissenters; and it is to be observed, that dissenting chapels are generally more crowded and afford greater seat-room in the same space than the churches of the establishment. A dissenting minister cannot subsist without a large audience, but the income of a Church of England priest is secure, if he have no audience at all, nor even a church to preach in. The structure, too, of churches—the system of proprietary pews—generally empty and locked up to guard against intrusion—the vast space taken up by the mayor's pew, the churchwardens' pew, and other parish officials, leaves little accommodation for the poor, and they have no alternative but to be crammed up—often standing in aisles, or driven to what are called *free-seats*, where they can neither hear nor see—or resort to a dissenting chapel.

In the absence of more complete official returns, the Dissenters them · selves have attempted to solve this important question in public statistics.

The supplement to the *Congregational Magazine* for December, 1829, comprises the results of very elaborate inquiries into the number of the places of worship of different religious persuasions. There are some inaccuracies in this statement which we cannot reconcile; but the data it affords, aided by information from other sources, will enable us to make out a tolerable exposition of the relative numbers, and the religious and educational efficiency of the several classes of religionists.

The great religious denominations of the day are those of the Established Church, the Roman Catholics, and the Protestant Dissenters. The number of churches and chapels of the Establishment is 11,600;* of Roman Catholics, 388:† of Protestant Dissenters, 7,634. Supposing the number of attendants at each place of worship is the same, the following will be the result:—

	Churches, &c.	Attendants.
Established Church	11,600 × 300 =	3,480,000
Roman Catholics	388 × 300 =	116,400
Protestant Dissenters	7,634 × 300 =	2,290,200

---

* Church Establishment founded in Error, p. 86. This estimate, we apprehend, has been founded on erroneous data. In many parishes there is no church at all, though the tithe in these parishes is collected with as much rigour as in the rest. In the fine county of Kent there are *thirteen parishes* which have no churches, and forty-four parishes, each having less than 100 inhabitants, none of whom hardly ever see the face of a parson, and yet who have tithes exacted from them to the last blade of grass. It is obligatory both on bishops and incumbents that parsonage houses should not fall into decay, yet it is a fact that there are 3000 churches and parochial chapels to which neither house nor glebe is attached. With the immense revenues of the established church it must be sickening and disgusting to her best friends, to think how her interests have been neglected by those who have been wallowing in her wealth.

† Catholic Laity's Directory.

It appears from this that, in point of *number*, the advantage is on the side of the national establishment. But from what has been previously observed, it may be presumed that this is a partial mode of stating the question. It is probable the Church of England has the greatest number of ministers and places of religious worship; we doubt, however, its numerical superiority; at all events, the efficiency of an army is not to be estimated by its skeleton regiments, or even by its numerical strength, but by the skill, energy, and devotedness which animate its soldiery. In these points the Dissenters may claim preeminence, as appears from a comparison of missionary and educational exertions.

During the year 1828-9, the Church of England party raised, for missionary purposes, as under:—

	£	s.	d.
Society for Promoting Christian Knowledge—*Foreign Objects*	9,208	9	5
Society for Propagating the Gospel	6,239	10	5
Church Missionary Society	52,080	19	1
	£67,528	18	11

The Protestant Dissenters alone, during the same period, contributed the following sums:—

	£	s.	d.
Wesleyan Missionary Society	41,846	12	10
London Missionary Society	37,207	0	6
Particular Baptist Ditto	9,305	10	2
General Baptist Ditto	1,651	1	6
	£90,010	5	0

Thus it appears, that although the numerical strength of the Church of Englandists exceeds that of the Protestant Dissenters, they do not contribute so much by £22,481 per annum, towards the cause of evangelizing the world, as the non-conformists.

For the mental improvement of their countrymen, the Protestant Dissenters are not less strenuous in their exertions; and on the subject of education, notwithstanding the superior advantages of the Establishment party, they likewise bear the palm.

	Children.
The National School Society educates	704,730
The Sunday School Society educates	720,717*

In exhibiting the exertions of the two great parties of Conformists and Dissenters, we have taken no notice of what is done by the Catholics,

* Church Establishment founded in Error, p. 92.

which cannot be inconsiderable; if, therefore, we add the amount of their efforts to our previous calculation, we shall find that the classes of religionists without public endowments, not only possess the greatest share of Christian zeal, but of moral and educational energy.

With so many things to be proud of, it is not surprising the Dissenters have begun to manifest symptoms of dissatisfaction with the favour shown to the national establishment. Hitherto they have submitted to this inequality in an exemplary manner, and steadily refrained from any thing like political agitation. Some fifty years ago, it is true, their ministers were said to be " men of *close ambition*," and the way in which this imputation was met deserves to be recorded. It was occasioned by the introduction of a bill, in 1772, to relieve dissenters from the hardship of subscribing to the thirty-nine articles. The bill passed the House of Commons, but was lost in the House of Lords by the weight and influence of the episcopal bench, particularly Dr. Drummond, Archbishop of York, who strongly inveighed against dissenters. Pitt, the eloquent Earl of Chatham, in reply to the archbishop, said, " whoever brought a charge against dissenters without proof, defamed." After a pause, he felt the workings of a generous and indignant enthusiasm, and thus proceeded : " The dissenting ministers are represented as men of *close ambition*—they are so, my lords ; and their ambition is to keep close to the college of fishermen, not of Cardinals; and to the doctrine of inspired apostles, not to the decrees of interested bishops. They contend for a spiritual creed and spiritual worship. We have a Calvinistic creed, a Popish liturgy, and an Arminian clergy. The reformation has laid open the Scriptures to all ; let not the bishops shut them again. Laws, in support of ecclesiastical power, are pleaded, which it would shock humanity to execute. It is said, that religious sects have done great mischief, when they are not kept under restraint ; but history affords no proof that sects have ever been mischievous, but when they were oppressed by the ruling church."

The chief oppression of which dissenters have to complain is the injustice of having to pay tithe and church-rates. Building their own chapels and maintaining their own ministers; supporting their own colleges to the number of twenty ; educating upwards of 700,000 children in their Sunday-schools ; and expending nearly £150,000 in diffusing their religious tenets—impose on them duties and sacrifices sufficiently onerous, without being compelled to aid in the support of the Episcopal establishment. It is apparent, therefore, if land-owners, farmers, and politicians were to be silent on ecclesiastical grievances, they would not be much longer tolerated by the vast body of separatists—who in England probably equal, and certainly in the United Kingdom greatly exceed, in number the members of the national communion. The dissenters have already begun to sound the tocsin of discontent, and several papers, extensively circulated, sufficiently indicate the spirit working within them. We subjoin one of these documents.

Twenty Reasons *why Dissenters should not be compelled to pay Church Rates and Tithes, or in any way to support the Church of England.*

1. Because it is a flagrant violation of equity, to compel people to pay for instruction, which they, in conscience, cannot receive.
2. Because it is a denial of our Saviour's interpretation of the law : " All things whatsoever ye would that men should do to you, do ye even so to them; for this is the law and the prophets."—Matt. vii. 12.
3. Because no passage in the Bible sanctions compulsion in supporting religion.
4. Because Christianity is slandered by its professors using compulsion for its support.
5. Because compulsory payments were not known in the purest ages of Christianity.
6. Because the Constitution of the Church of England, with the peculiar *names, titles,* and *offices* of its clergy, has no foundation in the Holy Scriptures.
7. Because no writer in defence of the Church of England, has ever dared to rest its claims upon the declarations of the Holy scriptures.
8. Because the Church of England is a *fearful system of traffic in the souls* of men.—Rev. xviii. 13.*
9. Because the Church of England gives the chief occasion to infidels to slander Christianity as a system of mere Priestcraft,—INFIDELS *of this class are found in every parish.*
10. Relinquishing unscriptural claims would remove a foul blot from the Church of England.
11. Because Dissenters bear all the expenses of their own Colleges, Chapels, Ministers, and Schools.
12. Because Dissenters in the United Kingdom far exceed in number those who attend at church.
13. Because religion flourishes most in the United States of America, without tithes or church rates, but supported by voluntary contributions.
14. Because religion is known to flourish most at those places in the Church of England, in which all their expenses are met by voluntary contributions.
15. Because the system of compulsion leads the clergy grievously to oppress each other.

---

* *St. James's Chronicle,* of Nov. 20 to 23, 1830, contains the following articles of " Property for Sale," advertised and specified in numbers from 1 to 79:—
    20 " Advowsons," income from £300 to £2000 per annum.
    14 " Next Presentations," income from £150 to £700 per annum.
    45 Other " Livings," for sale or exchange, including " a sinecure of two
    — parishes in Ireland," for which " a dispensation has been granted,"
    79 and two Livings, one of £700, the other of £1000 per annum!!
Compare this with the Oath on *Simony.*

16. Because the *curates* of the church are worse paid than any class of educated men; and the majority of them far less than journeymen mechanics.

17. Because the working clergy would be incomparably better supported by free contributions.

18. Because Christianity, left to its own resources, would become universal, as in the first ages.

19. Because no priesthood, in any age or nation, has received tithes to the extent of our clergy.

20. Because the tithes of the Israelites were not for the clergy, but for the whole tribe of Levi, about a tenth of the population, who were not allowed to possess a single acre of freehold land; and these were the judges, magistrates, lawyers, physicians, and instructors of the nation.

A desirable fact to ascertain is, the relative strength of religious sects in the several counties of England. Official returns, as before stated, have been received for the county of Lancaster, (Parl. Paper, No. 664, Sess. 1830,) but for no other county. From these returns it appears the number of parish churches in Lancashire is 65, parochial chapels 157, chapels of ease 59: total number of churches and chapels of the establishment, 281. The total number of dissenting places of worship is 590, and of sectarians 255,411. So that one-fourth of the population of Lancashire are open and professing non-conformists.

We shall conclude with stating the results of the inquiries of the Dissenters on this subject. They have exhibited a statement of the number of church livings and the number of chapels or congregations in each county in England. Their statement, we apprehend, is not far from the truth; it is certainly not exaggerated, as will appear from comparing the results of their inquiries with the official returns for Lancashire. It does not contain the unitarian chapels in England and Wales; this sect has 169 chapels; they are a numerous and increasing body; in Lancashire alone there are 28 congregations of that persuasion, with 5,099 members.

In the next chapter, on the Church of Ireland, we shall endeavour to ascertain the proportion of Conformists and Separatists in the United Kingdom.

CHURCH OF ENGLAND AND DISSENTING PLACES OF WORSHIP.

COUNTIES.	Roman Catholics.	Presbyterians.	Independents.	Particular Baptists.	General Baptists.	Quakers.	Wesleyan Methodists.	CalvinisticMethodists.	Other Methodists.	Missionary Stations.	Total Dissenting Congregations.	Church Livings.
Bedfordshire	1	—	8	21	—	4	35	—	1	1	71	115
Berkshire	6	1	14	11	1	6	34	7	—	1	81	150
Buckinghamshire	1	—	21	28	—	8	25	1	—	37	121	190
Cambridgeshire	1	1	23	19	6	3	29	1	1	1	85	162
Cheshire	7	12	27	5	9	6	48	8	30	1	153	145
Cornwall	2	—	31	12	—	10	219	3	39	4	320	187
Cumberland	4	10	16	8	—	22	32	—	11	2	105	139
Derbyshire	8	7	36	5	11	5	84	3	22	1	182	161
Devonshire	9	15	65	31	—	6	93	—	18	10	247	442
Dorsetshire	7	3	22	5	—	5	21	—	22	3	88	248
Durham	14	7	13	8	—	7	72	—	28	28	177	91
Essex	7	2	64	24	—	20	36	1	—	21	175	413
Gloucestershire	5	4	38	27	—	13	53	11	7	19	177	290
Hampshire	11	4	49	22	1	5	27	6	—	3	128	258
Herefordshire	4	—	11	9	—	4	16	1	—	4	49	201
Hertfordshire	1	1	28	13	1	12	2	4	—	—	62	129
Huntingdonshire	—	1	9	12	1	3	9	1	—	—	36	74
Kent	8	4	44	30	4	9	90	15	—	6	210	395
Lancashire	81	36	88	29	5	25	156	9	75	—	504	287
Leicestershire	7	3	17	13	17	4	68	—	13	2	144	208
Lincolnshire	12	2	18	14	11	9	211	2	24	1	304	598
London and Middlesex	21	15	91	55	2	12	59	22	7	5	289	233
Monmouthshire	4	—	24	28	—	3	10	—	—	3	72	118
Norfolk	8	1	21	32	2	13	74	1	24	5	181	683
Northamptonshire	3	1	35	40	4	7	61	—	—	2	153	303
Northumberland	19	50	8	3	1	4	29	—	22	—	136	97
Nottinghamshire	3	3	12	7	6	3	77	—	41	—	152	178
Oxfordshire	8	3	14	12	—	10	44	—	2	6	99	203
Rutland	—	—	3	1	1	1	7	—	—	—	13	40
Shropshire	7	2	25	15	—	3	32	—	18	—	102	209
Somersetshire	8	7	47	37	—	17	94	3	20	21	254	456
Staffordshire	21	5	32	16	3	6	82	—	41	7	213	178
Suffolk	4	2	33	35	2	10	40	1	—	5	132	486
Surrey	4	1	27	21	—	10	—	11	—	27	101	142
Sussex	6	4	31	13	—	5	20	6	—	2	87	300
Warwickshire	11	5	30	16	7	12	18	2	2	5	108	209
Westmoreland	2	1	12	—	—	11	13	—	1	1	41	68
Wiltshire	3	1	38	31	3	3	37	1	8	4	129	274
Worcestershire	8	8	10	22	—	7	24	3	21	1	104	175
Yorkshire	46	13	154	51	9	64	532	1	147	2	1019	809
North Wales }	6	23	{ 172	52	—	3)	214	300	{ 6	0	{ 1100	299 }
South Wales }			202	107	—	5)			9	0		526 }

VIII.   WHO WOULD BE BENEFITED BY A REFORM OF THE
CHURCH?

A reform of the Church, like most other reforms, would permanently benefit the many, and only temporarily injure the few. The lawn-sleeves, the shovel-hats, silk-aprons, and monopolizing incumbents would be the chief sufferers; while the condition of the most numerous and useful order of the clergy would be improved. Such odious abuses as non-residence and pluralities would be abolished, and the shameful injustice of one man doing the duty and another receiving the reward would be no longer tolerated. Every district, or parish, requiring the services of an officiating clergyman would be provided with one to whom the degrading epithet of " *poor curate*" or " *poor parson*" could never be justly applied. By mitigating the penury of the working clergy, their respectability and influence would be augmented, and every neighbour-hood enjoy the advantages which are known to result from the perma-nent abode of at least one educated, intelligent, and exemplary individ-ual. The clergy alike profess to be engaged solely in the work of religious instruction, and no class can boast superior piety or attainments by which to lay claim to superior reward. Why then should there exist such disparity in income? Why should the rector enjoy his £2000 per annum, the vicar receive but £400, and the curate only £80 or £100?

The equalizing of the value of sees would remove the abuse of *trans-lations*, and thereby effect a great improvement in the bench of bishops. It is only a few lucky individuals who obtain the rich prizes of Canter-bury, Winchester, London, Ely, and Durham, that are benefited by the unequal revenues of the bishoprics. Many prelates have barely income enough to support the dignity of their stations; yet they share, in common with the rest, the public odium attached to their class from the inordinate wealth of their more fortunate brethren. It is this in-equality, and the desire consequently excited *to move* to the wealthier endowments that gives to the bishops their political *animus*, and renders them the most self-seeking men in the country. Without translations they would be as independent in their conduct as the judges are said to be; but with the help of them government has, generally, the power to render them subservient to its purposes.

The exercise of legislative functions by the bishops has become ex-tremely unpopular since their mischievous vote on the Reform Bill. The House of Lords has always been to them the great scene of jobbing, intrigue, and ambition. On no occasion have they done themselves credit there; they appear, indeed, totally void of legislative aptitude, and never, by one act, have they rendered substantial service to the State, or done honour to themselves and the Church. Whether as magistrates or legislators, clergymen are inherently disqualified for the discharge of secular duties. It is not so much in their character of churchmen as of laymen that they have become so universally disliked;

and we verily believe, had they been eligible to seats in the lower house as they are to the upper, the additional opportunity thereby afforded to render themselves odious, would have hastened the downfal of the establishment. Besides the deprival of their legislative functions, a substantial improvement in the prelacy would consist in the *abolition of their patronage.* As it is, a rigid discharge of their duties is often incompatible with their interests, or at least their feelings. Their proper functions are the superintendence of the subaltern clergy of their dioceses; but many of these clergy have been promoted by themselves to their benefices; they are their very good friends, and not a few their own flesh and blood. How, in such cases, can it be expected they will be strict in the enforcement of pastoral duties; that they will not be indulgent in the granting of licenses for non-residence, and dispensations for pluralities; or that they will insist on the payment of suitable stipends to the curates. A bishop, like a pope, ought to have *no relations,* and thus escape, as Benedict II. remarked of the successors of St. Peter, the opprobrium of perverting the patronage of the church to the aggrandizement of his family. Under the existing system the chopping, exchanging, bargaining, and moving about, that ensue in a diocese on a translation or consecration, are a disgrace to the church, and render the discharge of episcopal duties more like a game on the chessboard, in which the *rooks, knights,* and other prime pieces, represent the " kit and kin" of the new diocesan.

The unequal extent of benefices has been urged in favour of ecclesiastical reform. In most cases, the extent of the livings is made to answer antiquated boundaries of parishes, by which, sometimes five or six churches are to be seen within a mile of each other, in a thinly populated country, while, again, parishes of from eight or ten miles in length afford but the accommodation of one church to a large population. Thus the distribution of the churches and livings bears no proportion either to the inhabitants or the acres, as will appear from the following list:—

	Inhabitants.	Sq. Miles.	Livings.	Av. Inh.	Av. Miles.
England and Wales	12,912,106 and	58,554 ..	10,872 ..	1.187 and	5.38
Bedfordshire	70,213 and	463 ..	115 ..	610 and	4.00
Durham	207,673 and	1,040 ..	91 ..	2.282 and	11.42
Lincolnshire	283,058 and	2,748 ..	598 ..	473 and	4.59
Northumberland	195,965 and	1,850 ..	97 ..	2.020 and	19.07
London and Middlesex	2,370,225 and	282 ..	250 ..	9.490 and	1.12
Lancashire	1,052,859 and	1,831 ..	287 ..	3.665 and	6.38
Huntingdon	48,771 and	370 ..	74 ..	659 and	5.00
Rutland	18,487 and	149 ..	40 ..	462 and	3.72
Norfolk	344,368 and	1,710 ..	683 ..	504 and	2.50

Anomalous and disproportionate as are these numbers, the above remark is still more strikingly displayed by reference to individual cases; thus the livings of—

Easton Neston	Northamptonshire contains	137	inhabitants.
Eaton-sacon	Bedfordshire ——	2,039	ditto.
Eccles	Lancashire ——	23,331	ditto.
Ecclesfield	Yorkshire ——	7,163	ditto.

Edburton	Sussex	contains	92	inhabitants
Edgcot	Northamptonshire. ——		67	ditto.
Egmore	Norfolk	——	47	ditto.

" Thus we see," as observed by the author from whom the preceding statement is copied, " that the State provides the same extent of accommodation for 47 as for 23,331 persons, so that as far as secular authority is concerned for the religious instruction of the people, a large proportion of them are wholly unprovided for; while, on another portion, its goodness is showered to redundancy. And should the former class think it necessary to have a second church in the same parish, they can have no clergyman to perform the services therein without an increase of their ecclesiastical burdens, notwithstanding they may already raise £3,000 per annum, for the purpose of an adequate supply of religious instruction. That income is the freehold of the rector, and any other instruction than what he can afford in a church not large enough to contain one-tenth part of the inhabitants, at a distance of five or six miles from many of their homes, must be paid for by a separate imposition."— *Church Establishment founded in Error, p. 70.*

Having adverted to the benefits the church would derive from ecclesiastical reform, let us next advert to those it would confer on the community.

In the first place the abolition of non-residence, of pluralities, of sinecure offices in cathedrals, and the reduction of extravagant incomes, and the substitution, in lieu of these abuses, an uniform and graduated rate of payment to the different order of ecclesiastics, proportioned to rank and duty, would not only effect a vast improvement in church discipline, but a saving of at least *seven millions* per annum of public income. Away then would go the TITHE,—the most unjust and impolitic impost the ingenuity of rulers ever devised for tormenting God's creatures, and crippling national resources. Of course we do not mean the tithe would be *simply repealed ;* that would be merely throwing so much additional rent into the pockets of the land-owners without benefiting the farmer or general consumer of his produce. The tithe is a tax, and forms part of the public income levied for public purposes. Its simple removal, without purchase or commutation, would only yield so much increase of revenue to be lavished on opera dancers and Paganinis ; or dissipated in gaming-houses, in concerts, coteries, and grand dinners; or wasted at Paris, Florence, and Naples, and which had better continue to be spent, as much of it now is, by sinecure silk-aprons and non-resident pluralists, at Bath, Cheltenham, and Tonbridge. The measure contemplated by the people is the *sale of the tithe* outright to the landowners, or its commutation by a land-tax. This would be a real reform ; the other is only delusion.

With such a resource as church property would yield, all the rabble of taxes might be repealed which now weigh down to annihilation the springs and sources of industry, and oppress a man's " house, even his heritage." The farmers and working agriculturists would share in the general benefit, not only by an increase of profits and wages and the mitigation of public burthens, but also by the extinction of an inquisitorial impost, whose pressure augments with every increase in industry, skill, and capital. For the tithe is not, as it has been alleged, a rent-charge imposed on the land, it is a virtual income-tax levied on stock and industry. A rent-charge is paid by reason of the land, but tithes are not, but by reason of the stock and labour of the occupier. If there be no annual increase, no profit made, or crop planted, no tithe can be demanded; but for non-payment of a rent-charge, he on whom it is settled, may enter upon and possess the land; whereas, he that claims tithe can only avail himself of the produce.

Nothing can more pointedly illustrate the stagnating influence of our aristocratic institutions on the mind and energies of the community than the continuance of the tithe-tax so long after its impolicy and injustice have been demonstrated. Even Mr. Pitt, who, throughout his political life was the slave of a paltry ambition for place, and the tool of a despicable faction, meditated its removal. It has been denounced by Bishop Watson, by Dr. Paley, by Burke, by Malthus, and every writer and statesman with the least pretensions to intelligence and patriotism It is supported by the example of no country in Europe. Though England swarms with separatists, and can hardly be said to have a national religion, yet, for the maintenance of one handful of spirituals, the whole nation is insulted and the operations of rural industry fettered and impeded.

Our neighbours, the Scotch, have long since wiped out this abominable stain. Among them tithe is a valued and commuted rate of payment, forming a trifling and invariable impost, to the extent of which, alone, the landlord can ever be made liable to the church. This reform they commenced about the time they got rid of prelacy and cathedrals, in the days of JOHN KNOX. With this superiority Scotland would be the land to live in, were it not for her rag-money, her myriads of *legalists* and placemen, her host of servile writers, the barrenness of her moors and mountains, and the griping keenness of her population. " Strange as it may seem," says lord BROUGHAM, in one of his eloquent harangues, " and to many who hear me incredible, from one end of the kingdom to the other, a traveller will see no such thing as a bishop— not such a thing is to be found from the Tweed to John o'Groats : not a mitre, no nor so much as a minor canon, or even a rural dean—and in all the land not a single curate—so entirely rude and barbarous are they in Scotland—in such utter darkness do they sit that they support no cathedrals, maintain no pluralists, suffer no non-residence; nay, the poor benighted creatures are ignorant even of tithes ! Not a sheaf, or a lamb, or a pig, or the value of a plough-penny, do the hopeless mortals render from year's end to year's end ! Piteous as their lot is, what makes it infinitely more touching is to witness the return of good for evil, in the demeanour of this wretched race. Under all this cruel neglect of their spiritual concerns, they are actually the most loyal, contented, moral, and religious people any where, perhaps, to be found in the world."*

Bishop Watson, said " a reformer, of Luther's temper and talents, would, in five years, persuade the people to compel parliament to abolish tithes, to extinguish pluralities, to enforce residence, to confine episcopacy to the overseeing of dioceses, to expunge the Athanasian creed from our Liturgy, to free dissenters from Test-Acts, and the ministers of the establishment from subscription to human articles of faith."— *Letter to the Duke of Grafton.*

Mr. Burke said, he " wished ministers to preach the gospel with ease, but their possessions to be such that the pastor would not have the inauspicious appearance of a tax-gatherer."—*His Works,* vol. x. p. 146.

The progress of public reform is at a snail's pace, and so numerous and strong are the holds of abuse, that many pitched battles have to be fought before a single inch can be gained from the waste of corruption. But the interests identified with a reform of the church are so many, important, and self-evident, that we feel certain it is a measure that cannot be much longer averted. The Archbishop of Canterbury, we are sure, may save himself the trouble of putting forward his cunningly-devised scheme for a *composition* for tithes, for a limited period, at a fixed rate of payment. The country will never sanction any plan tending to give permanency to an odious impost which, to our great opprobrium, has long been suffered to survive the natural term of its existence. The worthy primate seems to feel that the foundations of Mother Church are giving way, and he, doubtless, deems it good foresight in himself and brethren to lay hold of something certain for at least the next twenty years, the probable term of their earthly pilgrimage. But he may rely upon it the owners and occupiers of land, in England, will not be so easily overcome by ecclesiastical artifice as some of them have been in Ireland : a man must be totally regardless of the aspect of the times, he can know nothing of the state of opinion, as indicated by private conversations, by proceedings at public meetings, by newspapers, by parliamentary debates, by the petitions from Rochester, Devonshire, and other parts of the kingdom, who is not convinced that tithes, two years hence, will neither impoverish the soil nor reproach the wisdom of domestic policy : the attention of the people is rivetted on the vast possessions of the church, and to them they look as the best resource in their privations and difficulties. In the language of Scripture, and of the followers of Sir Walter Raleigh, they may truly exclaim, " Come hither, all ye that are heavy laden,—Here is the real *El Dorado* for reducing the boroughmongers' debt, and lightening the burden of taxation. Here is the fund for colonizing, for miti-

---

* Trial of John Ambrose Williams, for a libel on the Clergy of Durham, Aug. 16th, 1822, p. 43. The defendant had given umbrage to the haughty clergy of the Palatinate by commenting, in a newspaper, on their servile conduct in prohibiting the bells to be tolled on the occasion of the death of the Queen of George IV.

gating poor-rates, repealing corn-laws, and creating employment; and none but fools look for any other!"

Considering, then, a great bettering in the condition of the operative clergy,—the improvement of church discipline,—the abolition of tithes, —and the saving of many millions of public income, as the certain and prominent advantages of ecclesiastical reformation, we will next advert to one or two interests in society which, at first sight, appear to present some obstruction to this salutary revolution.

First, of the rights of *lay-impropriators*. It is necessary to bear in mind the distinction which has been before adverted to between the tithes of the church and the tithes of laymen. These last are considerable, amounting, perhaps, to one-fourth or one-fifth of the whole tithes of the kingdom. They have been estimated—though, we think, on incorrect principles—to be worth £1,752,842 per annum.* Now, these tithes are unquestionably of the nature of *private property*, and bear no analogy to clerical tithes. How they originated has been explained, (page 12,) but that has no bearing on their present tenure. We must take things as we find them, and adopt such rights of property as the laws and usages of society recognize, without ascending to their remote origin. Upon this principle we quickly discern the different tenure of church and impropriate tithes. The former have always been dealt with as a portion of the public income, payable to certain persons while engaged in the service of such form of worship as the State choose to patronize; the latter has been considered a rent-charge due to individuals, and with which the legislature had no concern. Hence the parliament has no more thought of interfering with impropriate tithes than with the estates in land obtained at the Reformation. The tithe-owner has dealt with them as part of his patrimony, which he could rightfully sell or devise to whom he pleased, and which immunities of ownership have been shown not to appertain to ecclesiastical possessions. To sequestrate lay-tithes would be gross spoliation, but, in the secularization of church-property, the legislature would only exercise an authority it has always possessed; and, were the life-interests of present possessors fairly commuted, neither loss nor injustice would be sustained by any person. It follows, impropriate tithes do not at all enter into the question of church reform; they must continue a charge on land, or lands liable thereto may be exonerated on such terms as can be agreed upon by the landlords and lay-impropriators.

Next, as to the interests of *private patrons* in advowsons. A right of presentation, in its origin and in acts of the legislature, has been shown to have been always considered merely an *honorary* function, which ought not to be exercised for gain or family interests, but the promotion of religion and virtue. Private patrons, therefore, could not expect to be indemnified for the loss they would sustain by ecclesiastical reform, according to the present value of benefices. All they could expect would be the continuance to them (as was the case in Scot-

---

* Quarterly Review, vol. xxix. p. 556.

land) of the right of nominating the ministers of the Reformed Church, subject, as at present, to the approval of the bishop. For the public to purchase their interests, according to the present value of tithes and church-fees, would be nothing less than at act of NATIONAL SIMONY ; it would be converting a spiritual function into a temporal possession, and the state committing the very crime in wholesale which had been condemned and punished when perpetrated in a less degree by individuals.

Nothing has yet been said of the provision for the Established Clergy, to be substituted in lieu of tithes and church estates,—whether they ought to be paid stipends by Government, or out of the poor-rates, the county-rate, or some other rate levied expressly for the purpose, or whether they ought to be supported by the voluntary contributions of their hearers. The discussion of these matters will be time enough, when the people, or their representatives, have determined upon the secularization of church property. The proceedings of the Church-building Commissioners offer an example which some may think it wise to follow. They have shown not only how episcopalian churches may be built by subscription, but how the minister's stipend may be paid out of pew-rents, and other voluntary contributions, without the aid of the compulsory and odious provision of tithes. It may be thought a similar plan might be extended to all the churches of the establishment; but, for our parts we are in favour of a national religion—a Liturgy – and an endowed clergy ; provided the endowment is moderate —fairly apportioned among the working clergy—and does not exceed about a million and a half per annum. A public worship protected by the state has formed, with few exceptions, a part of every well-ordered community. The French *tried* to do without it; the experiment was productive of enormous crimes, and after floundering for a time in the waves of anarchy, they were compelled again to resort to the aid of spiritual faith. Religion contains now little to give offence to the most liberal mind ; it is not, as formerly, like the demon of some German story—recluse, bloody, and unrelenting; its worst features—bigotry and intolerance—have been removed by the progress of science and philosophy, and what remains may be considered a good with scarcely any admixture of evil.

Whether, however, we have an endowed clergy or not, no fear need be entertained about the interests of religion suffering. The fear at present is all the other way, lest a people evidently verging into the gloom of *puritanism*, may not afterwards recoil into the opposite extreme of licentiousness and unbelief. This has been termed an age of *cant*, and every thing tends to show its ascendancy. Nothing but cant can live in literature, the drama, trade, or politics. Let any one deny the popular faith, and the doors of the legislature are closed upon him ; he is a " doomed man," whose future life is " bound in storms and shallows," and he is shunned as if he had caught the plague from some infectious lazaretto. This is the state of opinion among the lower and middle orders ; among the higher, there is less scrupulosity; and a lord or a gentleman of £10,000 a year may admire Voltaire, Diderot, or Spinoza, without being ejected out of the pale of social communion.

While men's fortunes depend on their faith, we may be sure there will be enough of it, or at least, the profession. Like the French satirist, every one thinks it necessary *he should live*, and of course will adopt the means essential to the end in view. It is possible, however, the artificial encouragement of devotion may produce it in excess, beyond the wants of the state, and thus generate the extreme to which we have adverted at the Restoration of Charles II. There is always some danger in meddling with spiritual opinions as with temporal interests; and many may think the wisest course to be adopted towards religion would be to follow the policy recently become popular in respect of trade—*leaving it free ;* neither attempting to depress one sect by the drawback of civil disabilities, nor to encourage another by the bounty of protection. It is certainly a fact that religion will generally abound in proportion to the wants and demands of society; where there is much ignorance and mental debility, there will, as there ought, be much faith; on the other hand, where there is a strong and enlightened reason, the motives for good conduct will be sufficiently apparent, without being aided by the hopes and fears of superstition.

However, as before hinted, we are not the partizans of a *free-trade in religion*, and think a worship patronized by the state is best, provided *it be cheap*. Our reason for this preference may be somewhat peculiar, and not shared in by our readers. We prefer an established worship, not less as a means of maintaining a rational piety, than as a counterpoise to fanaticism. Without religion at all, men are seldom better than beasts; but if their rulers have no control over the popular faith, the people will be at the mercy of every pretender, whose warm imagination or an over-weening conceit may have filled with the delusion of a divine commission. With an endowed corps of ecclesiastics the state possesses a medium through which religion may be kept in countenance among the higher classes, (adopting the slang of aristocracy,) and its temperature among the lower be regulated. Of course we mean a race of clergymen differently qualified from the present. These, good easy souls! have little influence or authority; they have ministered away their flocks, and remain themselves objects of derision or cupidity, not veneration.

With the near and long-standing example of the Presbyterian establishment, North of the Tweed, it is surprising the task of ecclesiastical reform has made no progress either in England or Ireland. In the Kirk of Scotland, it has been already remarked, there are no bishops, nor dignitaries, nor tithes. The incomes of the national clergy are paid by the Court of Session out of a fund formed from the ancient tithes of the country. Some of the benefices being considered of too small value, they were, in 1810, augmented by an annual grant, from Parliament, of £10,000, which made the poorest livings worth £150 a-year, and the income of some of the ministers are considerably more, amounting to £300 or £350. Exclusive of house and glebe, the average income of the clergy is £245, which to 948 pastors, makes the whole annual expenditure on the Kirk only £234,900. This cannot be considered extravagant to a ministry with upwards of a *million and a half of hearers;* and upon the whole there are many things to admire in the Scotch Establishment. The Scots do not pay a quarter of a million for *lawn-sleeves;* nor half a million for cathedral and collegiate sinecurists. There are no curates; the parochial clergy reside upon their benefices; exhorting, catechising, instructing, and performing all those duties to their parishioners, for which they receive their incomes. The Scotch Church, though it cannot now be termed *poor,* yet its wealth is not so exorbitant as to corrupt its ministry. The wealth of the English Church is the source of all its vices—sinecurism, pride, luxury, and inefficiency.

The Dissenters afford an example of the efficient support of religion without any compulsory provision. In England and Wales there are upwards of 9,000 ministers supported by Dissenters. This is certainly not done at a less expense than £120 each, or rather more than a million per annum. Again, America is another proof of what can be done by voluntary contributions. There are not less than 11,000 ministers of all denominations in the United States, the great majority of whom derive their subsistence from the free-will offerings of the people, independent of legislative provision. The option left to the people has not operated to the decay of virtue or religion; on the contrary, religion flourishes among them to an extraordinary extent—it pervades all ranks and conditions of men—it is associated with all their pursuits—not, indeed, as a second head of the social body, dividing the intellect and strength of its frame, but as a pursuit distinct from political combinations, altogether a personal concern, and, therefore, purposely discarded by the constitution. Notwithstanding this absence of state-worship the United States have become a mighty empire, which, in spite of the solemn pedantries of Capt. Basil Hall, may be advantageously compared with any other in the world, whether measured by the standard of morals, personal prowess, commercial enterprize, or national wealth and power.

We have now done, and having finished our exposition of the Church of England, can truly say we have " nothing extenuated, nor set down aught in malice." Our statements we know cannot be impugned ; but it is possible our opinions may be misunderstood. It may be thought we are Jacobins, Liberals, or worse. Of this we take no note, knowing we are as good subjects as true Christians. We have no dislike to the Church, but we object to it as we do to the borough system, because it does not reward merit, and oppresses the honest and industrious. Our humble endeavour has been to expose the corruptions of the establishment. If the duties of the Church be of importance to Government, or to the interests of religion and morality, it is a strong reason for reforming, not protecting its abuses. It must be clear to the most common observers it cannot long continue in its present state. Without adverting to the number of dissenters—to defects in discipline,—the

Liturgy—ill-proportioned revenue—or the conduct of the clergy themselves, the mere fact of a body of men, not exceeding *eight thousand* in number, and of no great social importance—claiming in the most vexatious manner a tenth of the natural and artificial produce of a soil, raised for the support of FOURTEEN MILLIONS, is so staringly outrageous, as to throw all argument out of court, and leave the Church a barefaced and unparalleled oppression, without precedent or palliative. Further reasoning on such a subject is out of place, and the only question is—Who will rise to abate the colossal nuisance ? Will Government timely interfere and afford the Church a chance of prolonged duration, under a less obnoxious form, or will it supinely wait and behold it swept off in a whirlwind, leaving " not a wreck behind," by a simultaneous rush of the TIERS ETAT ?

If the Church is to be saved it must be saved by a wisdom very different from that which directs the councils of the heads of the Establishment. They are obviously as insensible to the position in which they stand as the child unborn. Only think of the nature of the bills introduced by them last year for the reform of the Church. The character of one — that for a composition for tithe—has been already noticed. Of the remaining two, one is for *augmenting* the incomes of vicarages ; the other for shortening the time of prescription in cases of moduses and exemptions from tithes. In the last is a proviso which prevents it from interfering with any suit which may be commenced *within three years.* Ah, my Lords Bishops, the crisis will be past long before. Do not, we beseech you, lay the flattering unction to your souls that there will be litigation about moduses, prescription terms, and *nullum tempus* maxims three years hence. Your days are assuredly numbered ; your lease is expired. The fatal vote given on the Reform-Bill has sealed your doom, and no depth of repentance can again establish you in the estimation of the people. Solemn pledges will be demanded from a reformed parliament that tithe shall be abolished, and that haughty prelates shall cease to haunt the chambers of legislation. A terrible storm is impending over the Church, and nothing can avert its destructive ravages save a timely abandonment of all that has long excited popular indignation—its enormous wealth—its avarice, pride, and self-seeking—its insolent and oppressive power.

LIST

OF

BISHOPS, DIGNITARIES, AND PLURALISTS

OF THE

CHURCH OF ENGLAND.

EXPLANATIONS.

THE name of the Pluralist comes first. After the name comes the first living of the Pluralist in *italic*, and an initial letter denoting its title—namely, r. for rectory, v. for vicarage, c. for chapelry, p. c. for perpetual curacy, d. for donative, d. r. for district rectory, and d. c. for district chapelry. The name of the Patron is put after the living or livings, supposing more than one living, of which the same person is patron. *Abp.* is put for archbishop, *bp.* for bishop, *archd.* for archdeacon, *dn.* for dean, *ch.* for chapter. When a living is in the gift of the University of Oxford, *Oxon* is put; when of the University of Cambridge, *Camb.* When a *nobleman*, as the duke of Newcastle, or the marquis of Exeter, is patron, the *of* in the title is omitted both for brevity and propriety. The " of " expresses territorial jurisdiction, but as peers do not possess such authority at the present day, the term by which it is implied may be properly dropped.

In the language of churchmen a living or benefice, which are synonymous, is a *rectory* or *vicarage* only ; but many chapelries are equally entitled to fall under this denomination, and have been so considered. There are free chapels perpetually maintained, and provided with a minister, without charge to the rector or parish. In some places chapels of ease are endowed with lands and tithes ; they have by custom a right to a distinct minister, to baptize, to administer sacraments and burial : such parochial chapelries differ only in name from parish churches. *Parish* is a vague term. In the north, parishes comprise thirty or forty square miles, which is seven or eight times the area of parishes in the south. Under 13th Charles II. certain townships and villages are allowed to maintain their own poor ; hence these townships became so many distinct parishes. There are 200 *extra-parochial* places, many of which are as large as parishes ; these are exempt from poor-rate, because there is no overseer on whom the magistrate can serve an order ;—from militia, because no constable to make a return ; from repairing highways, because no surveyor. The 37 Hen. VIII. c. 31, (also 4 and 5 Will. & Mary,) allows the union of churches, when not more than one *mile* apart, and under value of £6. Under these acts churches have been united : the city of London reckons 108 parishes, forming no more than 78 benefices ; in Norwich, 70 parishes have been compressed into 37 benefices. Contrary to the rule of ecclesiastics, we have considered all parishes held *cum*, or with another, distinct benefices ; the only reason for an opposite course is, that they form only one presentation, though such presentation is often held by *two* patrons, who present alternately ; and many of such consolidated parishes (Upham *cum* Durley, for instance,) have two churches, and two sets of overseers and churchwardens.

The *district rectories* and *district chapelries,* established in such parishes as have been divided into ecclesiastical districts by the Royal Commissioners for

Building New Churches, under the authority of powers granted to them by Parliament, form so many distinct livings or benefices, each having a separate maintenance for a minister, independent of the mother church.

Apart, then, from the corruptions and mystification of the Church, we have deemed every parochial preferment, chapelry, vicarage, or rectory, a *living;* and we consider every clergyman a *pluralist* who holds two such preferments, whether separate or united. A *curacy,* without any great impropriety, might be styled a living, as a stipend is, or ought to be, annexed to the office, adequate to the maintenance of at least one individual : but as curates are removable at the pleasure of incumbents, they are excluded from our *List,* which includes only beneficed clergymen.

The abuse of holding *two* livings or more is so prevalent, that to have enumerated all the transgressors (about 2880 in number,) would have extended our List to an inconvenient length, without corresponding utility; our object has been to exhibit the more flagrant breaches of ecclesiastical discipline ; and with this view, we have restricted ourselves to such shameful monopolists among the parochial clergy as hold *three or more* preferments. We have also included the bishops and principal dignitaries of the church.

The 21 Hen. VIII. c. 13, prohibits a person holding a second benefice when the first is worth *eight pounds* in the King's Book. But a man, by dispensation, may hold as many benefices, without cure, as he can get ; and, likewise, so many with cure as he can get, all of them, or all but the last, being under the value of eight pounds ; provided the person to be dispensed withal be not otherwise incapable thereof. By the 41st Canon, however, of 1603, the two benefices must not be farther distant than *thirty miles ;* and persons obtaining dispensation, must at least be M.A. But the provisions of this canon are not regarded or enforced in the courts of law ; and the privileges, *ex officio,* entitling to grants of dispensation, are so numerous, and the facilities for obtaining them, through favour or evasion, so easy, that there can hardly be said to exist a practical check to the most aggravated cases of plurality.

In the disposal of every living, three parties are principally concerned : *first,* the patron ; *second,* the incumbent ; *third,* the bishop. The patron is the person in whom the right of presenting to a living is vested. The person nominated by the patron is the incumbent. The office of the bishop is to grant institution to the living to which the incumbent is presented. By refusing institution, the bishops have a veto on appointments by patrons ; this veto, however, is rarely exercised, and it is seldom that the patron and the diocesan are at issue. The most important personage in the affair is the patron. It will be seen from the *List* that the patronage is sometimes in individuals—sometimes in public bodies. Sometimes the incumbent is his *own* patron, and presents himself ; sometimes the incumbent's wife is patron, and presents her husband ; sometimes the husband and wife are co-patrons. In some instances the patronage is divided, the nomination being in one party and the appointment in another. Many *ladies* are patrons, and though otherwise ineligible to the exercise of civil rights, no doubt they are well qualified to select spiritual persons for the cure of souls.

Nearly all the livings in the metropolis, and the most valuable livings in the large towns in the country, are in the gift of the crown, which adds enormously to its influence. The patronage not in the crown is chiefly in the aristocracy and gentry, the universities, and the bishops. The patronage of the aristocracy and gentry is chiefly bestowed on the members of their own families ; the patronage of the universities on the members of those places ; the patronage of the bishops on their connexions and relations to the hundredth degree. A great mass of patronage, however, remains, which cannot be disposed of in any of these ways ; for though the families of the aristocracy have been recently proved to be, on the average, more prolific than those of the democracy, they are not sufficiently so to fill all offices in the army, navy, law, church, and public departments ; and, consequently, there is a surplus patronage to be brought into the market, which is disposed of, like other commodities, to the highest bidder.

It would have been more satisfactory, had we been able to state the *present value* of livings; but there is no authentic data for the purpose : parliamentary returns, it is true, have been made of the *poor* livings, but none of the *rich* ones ; and there have been returns of the *number* of all livings above and below the value of £300, having non-resident incumbents: returns were also ordered in the session of 1830 of the value of livings in the gift of the crown. These last returns have not yet been made, or at least printed : they would add something to our knowledge of the present value of church-property ; but what the public wants is the separate value of every see, dignity, benefice, and ecclesiastical preferment, and the *proportion* in which, and number of individuals among whom, they are shared. By such data would be shown what the Church of England really is, and indisputably prove the existence of those enormous abuses, which, in our preliminary article, we have fully proved to pervade the ecclesiastical establishment.

We have only one more remark to make, and that refers to our accuracy. The movements that are daily and almost hourly occurring in the Church, from deaths, translations, resignations, and exchanges, render it probable that alterations have intervened since our List was sent to the press. But this does not defeat our object. If one pluralist has been removed another has succeeded. So that our List will continue to exhibit a correct picture of ecclesiastical patronage as long as the present system of church discipline is tolerated.

Adams, J. C. *Saxleby*, r. lord Aylesford. *Shilfon*, c. *Anstye*, c. the King.

Affleck, R. preb. of York ; *Silkston*, r. *with Bretton, Monk, and Stainborough chapelries*, abp. of York. *Treswell, East Mediety*, r. *West Mediety*, r. dn. and ch. of York and Mr. Stevenson. *Thockerington*, p. c. Prebendary. *Westow*, v. abp. of York.

Alban, T. *Llandrillo*, v. bp. of St. Asaph. *Eaton*, v. H. and W. Lloyd. *Snead*, c. P. Morris.

Aldrich, W. *Boyton*, r. lord Rous. *Stowe-Market*, v. *with Stowe-Upland*, c. Mr. Aldrich.

Allen, R. *Driffield*, r. precentor of York. *Whaream Pier*, v. Misses Isted and Englefield. *Little*, p. c. unknown.

Allen, S. *Haslingfield*, v. C. Mitchell. *Lynn, St. Margaret and St. Nicholas*, c. dn. and ch. of Norwich.

Allen, D. B. preb. of St. David's and Brecon. *Burton*, r. sir W. Owen. *Manordiffy*, r. *Llandewn Welfrey*, r. the King.

Allen, S. *Dunton*, v. T. W. Coke. *Wolterton*, r. *with Wickmere*, r. earl of Oxford.

Allfree, E. M. minor canon of Rochester ; *Canterbury, St. Andrew*, r. *and St. Mary, Bredon*, r. abp. of Cant. and dn. and ch. of Cant. *Strood*, r. dn. and ch. of Rochester.

Alison, A. preb. of Sarum ; *Ercall*, v. H. Pulteney. *Roddington*, r. the King.

The pluralist is senior minister of the episcopal chapel, Canongate, Edinburgh, and a native of Scotland ; being related to the late bishop Douglas, that prelate gave him a stall in his cathedral, and procured for him the vicarage of High Ercall, in Shropshire, to which was afterwards added the rectory of Roddington, in the same county. Mr. Alison is the author of a work on *Taste*.

Allington, W. *Bardford Lit.* r. *Twywell*, r. J. Williamson. *Swinhop*, d. Mrs. Allington.

Anson, H. *Buxton*, v. *with Oxnead*, r. *and Skeyton*, r. lord Anson. *Lyng*, r. *with Whitwell*, v. T. Anson.
   Uncle of earl of Lichfield, master of the buckhounds. Another uncle is rector of Longford, and rector of Sudbury, of which benefices Mr. Coke of Norfolk, and lord Vernon, both connected with the family by marriage, are respectively the patrons.

Ashfield, C. R. *Great Blakenham*, r. Eton Coll. *Dodington*, r. duke Buckingham. *Stewkley*, v. bp. of Oxon. *London, St. Benet Finck*, c. dn. and canons of Windsor.

Apthorpe, F. preb. of Lincoln ; *Bicker*, v. dn. and ch. of Lincoln. *Farndon*, v. *with Balderton and Fiskerton*, chapelries, preb. of Lincoln. *Gumley*, r. dn. and ch. of Lincoln.
   The grandfather of this gentleman was a merchant at Boston, in America. His father was rector of St. Mary-le-Bow, and had the valuable prebend of Finsbury, in St. Paul's. His brother-in-law, Dr. Cory, is master of Emanuel College, Cambridge. Another brother-in-law is master of Shrewsbury grammar-school.

Atlay, H. *Great Casterton*, r. *Pickworth*, r. marq. Exeter. *Great Ponton*, preb. of Sarum.

Astley, H. N. *Foulsham*, r. sir H. Astley. *Little Snoring*, r. *with Bashan*, v. bp. of Norwich.

Atkinson, R. *Musgrove*, r. bp. of Carlisle. *Upelby*, c. J. B. Elliot. *Claxby with Normanby*, r. Rd. Atkinson.

Bagot, Richard, bishop of Oxford and dean of Canterbury.
   Brother of lord Bagot and of sir C. Bagot, ambassador to the Netherlands, who married a daughter of lord Maryborough.

Bankes, E. king's chaplain and preb. of Gloucester and Norwich ; *Corfe Castle*, r. Henry Bankes, M.P.
   Son-in-law of lord Eldon. The inhabitants of Corfe Castle must feel greatly indebted to the late member for Dorsetshire : he appoints one of his sons to watch over their spiritual welfare, and sends another into the house of commons to take care of their temporal affairs.

Baker, T. canon res. of Chichester; *Bexhill*, v. *Rodmell*, r. bp. of Chichester. *Falmer*, v. earl Chichester.

Barker, F. H. *St. Alban's, St. Stephen*, v. A. Fisher. *North Church*, r. the King. *Steppingley*, r. duke of Bedford.

Barker, T. *Acaster Malb.* v. T. B. Thompson. *Kilburn*, p. c. *Thirkleby*, v. abp. of York.

Barrington, viscount, preb. of Durham; *Sedgefield*, r. *with Embleton*, c. bp. of Durham.

Bathurst, Henry, bishop of Norwich : *Sapperton*, r. earl Bathurst.

Bathurst, H. archdn. of Norwich ; *North Creake*, r. earl Spencer. *Oby*, r. *with Ashby*, r. *and Thurne*, r. bp. of Norwich.

Barrow, R. vic. chor. Southwell ; *Barnoldby le Beck*, r. *Halloughton*, p. c. *South Muskham*, v. *Rampton*, v. *South Wheatley*, r. Southwell, Collegiate chapter.
   The small collegiate church of Southwell has attached to, in the gift of the chapter and prebendaries, twenty-seven livings, amongst them several of the large and populous parishes : of these there are four resident incumbents,

very few of them have any resident officiating minister, and almost all, if not all, of the parsonage houses have been suffered to fall into decay. The following particulars will exemplify the state of ecclesiastical discipline.

In the gift of the Chapter :—

    7 Rectories .... None resident.
    4 Vicarages .... One resident.
    3 Perpetual Curacies .... One resident.
    1 Chapelry........................ Not resident.

In the gift of Prebendaries :—

    11 Vicarages .... Three resident.
    4 Ditto .... Believe none resident.

Many of these are held by clergymen living in Southwell, who are pluralists, and several of the curates also live in Southwell, so that the people of the parishes never see their ministers except on a Sunday in the pulpit. That they find Southwell more agreeable than living in a retired village is possible; but ought they not to remember that their duty is to visit the sick and afflicted, and to go about doing good. They are thus suffered to neglect their duty, and to let fall down their houses, because they are in the gift of the church, and yet they expect to be esteemed and their delinquencies overlooked.

Bartlett, T. *Canterbury All Saints*, r. *All Saints St. Mary's church*, r. *All Saints St. Mildred*, r. lord Chan. *Kingston*, r. sir E. Brydges.

Bartlett, W. P. *Great Cranford*, v. G. T. Brice. *Cranford*, r. earl Berkeley. *Worth Maltravers*, v. rev. T. C. Bartlett.

Bastard, J. *Stratfieldsay*, v. *Stratfieldsay Turgis*, r. lord Wellington. *Belchalwell*, r. *Fifehead Neville*, r. lord Rivers.

Basnett, T. G. vic. chor of Southwell; *Bonsall*, r. dn. Lincoln. *Edingley*, v. *Halam*, p. c. Southwell College.

Beadon, F. *North Stoneham*, r. J. Fleming. *Sulham*, r. J. Wilder. *Titley*, p. c. Winton College.

Chancellor and canon res. of Wells. Several other Beadons are in the church, who are indebted for their preferments to the late bishop of Bath and Wells, who had been tutor to the duke of Gloucester.

Beauclerk, lord F. *Kempton*, v. *Redburn*, *St. Alban's*, *St. Michael*, v. lord Verulam.

Beauchamp, Brian, *Cove*, c. chapel in Tiverton. *Hawkridge*, v. *with Withypoole*, c. Miss Wood. *Thoverton*, c. vic. Thoverton.

Beauchamp, T. W. H. *Chedgrave*, r. *Langley*, c. *Buckenham Ferry*, r. *with Hassingham*, r. sir T. B. Proctor.

Becher, J. T. preb. of Southwell; *Hoveringham*, p. c. sir R. Sutton. *Thurgorton*, p. c. Trinity Coll. Camb. *Farnsfield*, v. Southwell Coll.

Beckett, G. preb. of Lincoln; *Barnsley*, p. c. abp. of York. *Epworth*, r. the King. *Gainsborough*, v. preb. of Corringham.

Beeke, H. dean of Bristol.

Beevor, Miles, *Bircham Newton*, r. earl Orford. *Toft Bircham*, r. sir T. Beevor. *Hethell*, r. *Ketteringham*, v. E. Atkins.

Bellaman, J. *Ewerby*, v. lord Chan. *Kirkby Green*, v. the King. *Kyme South*, c. sir A Hume.

Belfield, F. *St. Martin*, r. viscountess Sandwich. *Stoke Gabriel*, v. *Exbourne*, r. F. Belfield.

Beynon, T. archdn. of Cardigan, preb. of St. David's and Brecon;

Llanfchangel Aberbythych, r. bp. of St. Asaph. *Llandevey,*
p. c. *Llanvihan Kilwayn,* r. *Penboyr,* r. *with Ydrindod,* c. earl
Cawdor.

Berkeley, H. R. fell. of Winton Coll. ; *Cotheridge,* c. Himself.
Shelsea Beauchamp, r. lord Foley. *Onibury,* r. bp. of Hereford.

Bertie, hon. F. *Aldbury,* r. *Wooton,* p. c. *Wigtham,* r. earl Abingdon.

Bethell, Christopher, D.D. bishop of Bagnor ; *Kirkly Wiske,* r. duke
of Northumberland.

Biddulph, T. T. *Bristol, St. James's,* c. corp. of Bristol. *Durston,* d.
rev. R. Gray. *Lyneham,* c. Mr. Long.

Binney, H. *Hackthorne,* v. *Hanworth Cold,* r. Rt. Cracroft. *West
Moulsey,* p. c. rev. Dr. Binney.

Birch, Samuel, D.D. president of Sion Coll. preb. of St. Paul's, and
professor of geometry at Gresham College ; *St. Mary Woolnoth,
and St. Mary Woolchurch,* r. *London,* the King and Mr.
Thornton alternately; the former this turn.

As this gentleman is one of the Gresham professors, a short notice of the present state of the college may not be out of place. Sir Thomas Gresham, the
munificent founder of the Royal Exchange, for the convenience of commerce,
was also the founder of a college for the advancement of learning; the rents
of the former were bequeathed for the maintenance of the college; seven
learned men were perpetually to reside there, for the cultivation of science ;
and during term time—every day—they were to deliver, in English and Latin,
gratuitous lectures to the public, on astronomy, civil law, music, rhetoric,
geometry, divinity, and medicine. All the remains of this endowment are the
professors, their salaries of £100 per annum each, and an obscure nook in the
south-east angle of the Exchange, adjoining the premises of our publisher;
no lectures are delivered, or none that the public think worth hearing. An
attempt was lately made to revive the college by removing the lectures to
the London Institution. It failed, we believe, from the reluctance of the professors to concur in the new arrangement. The fact is, the Gresham lectures
have degenerated into a city job ; the professors had received their appointments
as sinecures, through personal favour or relationship, and had not sufficiently
devoted themselves to scientific pursuits to be prepared to convert their professorships, as the founder intended, into chairs of efficient popular instruction. It
is not pleasant to be always reverting to abuses; but there is such a principle
of vitality in them that it is only by repeated exposures they can be rooted out.

Birch, Thomas, D.C.L. dean of Battle, archdeacon of Lewes; *West-
field,* v. bp. of Chichester.

Blandford, Joseph, *Carlton in Moreland,* v. w. *Stapleford,* c. lord
Middleton. *Kirton,* r. *Mapplebeck,* c. duke Newcastle. *Wellow,*
c. hon. and rev. J. L. Saville.

Blomberg, F. W. canon res. of St. Paul's, deputy clerk of the king's
closet, chap. in ord. to H. M.; *Bradford,* v. w. *Atworth, Holt,
Stoke, Wraxhall, Winsley, and South,* chapelries, dn. and ch. of
Bristol. *Shepton Mallett,* r. the King.

Blomfield, Charles James, D.D. bishop of London, provincial dean of
Canterbury, and dean of the chapels royal.

Bower, H. *Orchard Portman,* r. *Taunton, St. Mar.* r. *Staple Fitz-
poine,* r. E. B. Portman.

Bowes, T. F. F. chaplain to the king; *Cowlam,* r. *Cake,* r. B. F.
Bowes. *Barton le Clay,* r. the King.

Bradley, W. *Baddesley Ensor,* p. c. Inhabs. of Polesworth. *Mere-vale,* c. D. S. Dugdale. *Whitacre Over,* c. earl Howe.

Brice, J. *Aisholt,* r. Incumbent. *Grenton,* r. S. Kekewich. *Catcott,* p. c. lord Henniker.

Bromley, W. D. *Bagginton,* r. *Oxhill,* r. rev. W. D. Bromley. *Copesthorne,* c. D. Davenporte.

Brown, H. *Ayleston,* r. *with Little Glen,* c. *Lubbesthorpe,* c. duke Rutland. *Hoby,* r. Incumbent.

Father-in-law of the rev. Gilbert Beresford, rector of St. Andrew's, Holborn, by whom Ayleston was resigned on account cf the distance.

Brown, L. R. *Carlton,* r. *with Kelsale,* r. rev. B. Bence. *Prestbury,* v. Mrs. Leigh. *Saxmundham,* r. D. L. North. *Thorington,* r.

Browne, J. H. archdeacon of Ely; *Cotgrave,* 1st *Mediety,* r. 2d *Mediety,* r. *Eakring,* r. earl Manvers.

Browne, W. *Charsfield,* p. c. W. Jennens. *Great Glemham,* c. *with Little Glemham,* r. D. L. North. *Marlesford,* r. A. Arcedeckne.

Buckle, W. *Banstead,* v. rev. W. Buckle. *Pirton,* v. Christ Church, Oxon. *Shireborn,* v. lord Macclesfield.

Bulwer, A. *Haydon,* r. W. W. Bulmer. *Cawston,* r. Pemb. Hall. *Corpusty,* v. sequestrated.

Burgess, Thomas, D. D. bp. of Salisbury, and provincial precentor of Canterbury.

Burgess, Geo. *Atherington,* r. Fra. Bassett. *Halvergate,* v. bp. of Ely. *Moulton,* v. *Tunstall,* c. rev. H. Anguish.

A relation of the bishop of Salisbury and of the duke of St. Alban's. The bishop is the son of a grocer at Odiham, Hants, where he was born, about 1755. His first patron was the bishop of Durham, who gave him a prebend, first in the cathedral of Salisbury, and afterwards at Durham. At Durham he continued till the administration of Mr. Addington (now Sidmouth), who had been his companion at Winchester College, conferred on him, in 1802, the See of St. David's. In 1796, the bishop married a Miss Bright of Durham, half-sister of the marchioness of Winchester.

Burrard, Geo. *Middleton-Tyas,* r. the King. *Yarmouth,* r. *Shalfleet,* v. sir H. B. Neale.

This pluralist is also a magistrate and a king's chaplain. He is brother to sir H. Burrard Neale and to lady Rook, who has a pension, and son-in-law to admiral Bingham.

Butler, Samuel, D.D. archdn. of Derby, preb. of Lichfield; *Kenilworth,* v. lord Chan.

Several more Butlers are in the church. Dr. Butler is head master of Shrewsbury grammar-school. He married a daughter of Dr. Apthorpe, a pluralist. His son, W. Butler, is author of a pamphlet on the French Revolution.

Bull, archdn. D.D. preb. York, canon res. of Exeter, archdn. of Barnstaple; *Lezant,* r. bp. of Exeter.

Butler, W. J. *Nottingham, St. Nicholas,* r. *Thwing,* 1st *Midiety,* r. 2d *Mediety,* r. lord Chan.

Calvert, W. *Childerly,* r. *Hunsdon,* r. *Pelham Stocking,* r. Nicholas Calvert.

Candler, P. *Burnham Market,* v. lord Chan. *Little Hautboys,* r. *Lammas,* c. rev. P. Candler. *Letheringsett,* r. Mrs. Burrell.

Carr, G. *Great Eversden,* v. lord Chan. *Little Eversden,* r. Queen's Coll. *Ipswich, St. Margaret,* c. rev. W. Fonnereau. *Ipswich, St. Mary,* c. Parishioners.

Cage, Ed. *Bearsted,* v. dn. and ch. of Rochester. *Badlesmere,* r. *Eastling,* r. *Newnham,* v. *cum Leveland,* r. lord Sondes.

Campbell, C. *Wesenham, All Saints,* v. *St. Peter,* v. *Shingham,* r. *Beechamwell, All Saints,* r. the King.

Canon, R. *Broxholme,* r. *North Carlton,* p. c. lord Monson. *Westbury-on-trim,* p. c. *with Minehampton,* c. G. Edwards and J. Baker, alternately.

Cantley, T. *Cambridge, St. Clement,* Camb. *Griston,* v. bp. of Ely. *Gawston,* v. R. Huddleston.

Carey, Wm. bishop and archdeacon of St. Asaph.

Carr, Robert James, bishop of Worcester, canon res. of St. Paul's, and clerk of the closet to the king.

The prelate is brother of sir H. W. Carr, the gentleman who married Perceval's widow alluded to in the *Pension List.*

Capper, G. *Blackenham, Lit.* r. *Gosbeck, St. Mary,* r. T. Vernon. *Wherstead,* v. the King.

Capper, J. preb. of Chichester; *Ashurst,* r. duke Dorset. *Wilmington,* v. hon. G. A. H. Cavendish. *Lollington,* v. bp. of Chichester.

Casberd, J. T. preb. of Wells and Llandaff; *Eglwystowis,* r. R. Jones. *Llanover,* v. ch. of Llandaff. *Llantude,* v. *Penmark,* v. dn. and ch. of Gloucester. *Lysevanoth,* v. lord Plymouth. *Mamlad,* c. *Trevethan,* c. vic. of Llanover.

Champness, T. minor canon, Westminster and Windsor; *Cottesford,* r. Eton Coll. *Upton,* v. the King. *Fulmer,* c. *Wyrardsbury,* v. *with Langley,* c. dn. and canons of Windsor.

Chaplin, W. *West Halton,* r. abp. of Canterbury. *Raithby,* r. *with Hallington,* r. *and Maltby,* c. lord Chan. *Hougham,* v. sequestrated.

Several more Chaplins in the church; they are cousins of the late archbishop Sutton.

Chandler, G. dean of Chichester; *Southam,* r. *Marylebone, All Souls, Langham Place,* r. the King.

Chester, W. *Denton,* r. abp. of Cant. *Woodrising,* r. J. Weyland. *Walpole, St. Peter,* r. the King.

Clarke, J. S. canon of Windsor, dep. clerk of the closet to the King, chap. in ord. to H. M. *East Preston,* w. *Hove,* v. *Tillington,* r. lord Egremont.

Son of the late rev. Edward Clarke, rector of Buxted, Sussex; he was formerly a chaplain in the navy, and owed his appointment in the royal household to his intimacy with admiral Payne. He is author of a Life of Nelson, and established the periodical miscellany the Naval Chronicle.

Clapham, Samuel, *Christchurch,* v. *with Bransgore,* c. *and Holdenhurst,* c. dn. and ch. of Winton. *Gussage, St. Mic.* r. I. and R. Randall. *Great Ouseborn,* v. the King.

This gentleman is a native of Leeds, Yorkshire, where he was educated. He was first patronized by lord Loughborough, then lord chancellor, who presented nim to the living of Great Ouseborn. As a remuneration for his Abridgement of the Bishop of Winchester's (Pretyman) Elements of Christian Theology, that prelate obtained for him the vicarage of Christchurch and the rectory of Gussage. He is an acting magistrate for the county, and compiled an Index to Burn's and Williams's Justice, Blackstone's, Hawkins', &c. law-books.

Clarkson, T. *Hinxton-Combes*, v. *Swovesey*, v. Camb. *Acton Scott*, r. R. J. Stackhouse.

Cleaver, J. F. preb. of Southwell. • *Holme Pierrepont*, r. earl Manvers. *Appleton-in-the-Street*, v. *Amotherby*, c. Camb.

Cleaver, J. *Edwinstow*, v. *Ollerton*, c. *Carburton*, c. *Polethorpe*, c. dn. and ch. Lincoln.

Cleaver, J. F. canon and reg. of St. Asaph. *Corwen*, r. *Rug*, c. bp. St. Asaph. *Great Coxwell*, v. bp. of Sarum.

The pluralists owe their preferments to their father, the bishop of St. Asaph, who died in 1815. The bishop was tutor to the marquis of Buckingham, with whom he went to Ireland during his viceroyship. His brother was first made bishop of Ferns, then archbishop of Dublin. He himself first obtained a prebend of Westminster, was next elevated to the see of Chester, and, after one or two more moves, to the see of St. Asaph. He married a Miss Asheton, sister of Wm. A. of Lancashire, from whom the present are descended.

Cobbold, T. *Ipswich*, *St. Mary Tower*, c. Parishioners. *Welby*, r. rev. N. White. *Woolpet*, r. rev T. Cobbold.

There are three more Cobbolds in the church, one vicar of Selbourne, and a witness at the Winchester trials under the special commission; a riotous assemblage of farmers and labourers had endeavoured to compel the reverend gentleman to consent to reduce his tithes from £600 to 400 a-year, the last—four pounds a week—being deemed sufficient remuneration to a parish priest in the opinions of the rural logicians. In the existing state of popular feeling, how is it possible for the tithe system to be upheld? it does not answer a single good purpose; and its compulsory exaction is wholly impracticable. The ends of religion can never be furthered by an impost which generates social animosity, and tends to exhibit ministers and parishioners more in the relation of wolves and sheep than pastors and their flocks.

Cockburn, Wm. dean of York.

Coldham, J. *Anmer*, r. J. Coldham. *Snettisham*, r. H. Styleman, *Stockton*, r. P. Randall.

Combe, E. *Barrington*, p. c. rev. Dr. W. Palmer. *Donyatt*, r. *Earnshill*, r. *Drayton*, p. c. R. T. Combe.

Colson, T. M. *Pilesdon*, r. *with Stratton*, c. hon. C. Damer. *Chaminster*, c. Mr. Trenchard. *Linkenholt*, r. Mrs. Worgan.

Collet, A. *Aldringham*, c. *with Thorpe*, c. *Great and Little Linstead*, c. lord Huntingfield. *Heveningham*, r. the King.

Collett, W. *Swanton Morley*, r. sir J. Lambe. *Surlingham*, r. rev. W. Collett. *Egmere*, r. T. W. Coke.

Last year the parishioners of Surlingham gave to the rector the alternative of either accepting a compensation for tithes, or gathering *them in kind;* the reverend pluralist dexterously endeavoured to ward off this blow, by sowing division in the enemy's camp; and in a hand-bill, signified his intention to distribute, as a gift, among the " poor and deserving families" of his parish, all the eggs, milk, pigs, poultry, and fruit, which would in future belong to him, as small tithes, on the occupations of certain of the *rebels* whose names were mentioned." A very adroit stratagem this! but it is a pity the worthy rector did not think of the " poor and deserving families" before the FIRES, and the union of the labourers and farmers. Other parsons have endeavoured to conciliate their parishioners, by circulating hand-bills, in which they try to prove that tithes are good things for the labourers—that they do not oppress the farmer, being only *part of his rent*, which if not paid to the incumbent, would be exacted by the landlord—and that the *average* incomes of the beneficed clergy are so small that it is impossible they should be objects of cupidity with any reasonable person. All these sophistries we have exposed; it is not the *average* income of the clergy, but the total amount of the revenues of the church and the *unequal* distribution of them that are objected to; neither is it meant that tithe should be simply abolished—that would certainly only add to the rents of the landlords—but that it should be *commuted* for an equivalent and less objectionable assessment, levied on the landed interest, and this commutation be available to the relief of the productive classes.—On these matters, see p. 53,55, and p. 88.

Corbett, S. LL.D. *Kirkhamwith,* r. chan. du. Lancaster. *Scrayingham,* r. *with Leppington,* c. the King. *Wortley,* c. rec. of Tankersley.

Cooke, G. *Rissington Wick,* r. the King. *Cubbington,* v. *Honingham,* p. c. I. H. Leigh.

Professor of natural philosophy, and keeper of the archives in the University of Oxford.

Copleston, Edw. bishop of Llandaff and dean of St. Paul's.

Crabbe, Geo. *Trowbridge,* r. *Staverton,* c. *Croxton Kerrial,* v. duke of Rutland.

A popular poet, who was chaplain to the late duke of Rutland, from whom he obtained his preferments, and whose funeral sermon he preached at Belvoir.

Crawley, C. *Broadwater,* v. Miss Mills. *Flaxley,* d. sir J. Crawley. *Stow, Nine Churches,* r. rev. J. L. Crawley.

Croft, James, archd. and preb. of Canterbury. *Cliffe-at-Hone,* r. *Saltwood,* r. w. *Hythe,* c. abp. of Cant.

Married a daughter of the late archbishop Sutton.

Crook, Ch. *Bath, St. Peter and St. Paul,* v. *St. Mary Mag. Ch. St. Michael,* r. *Widcombe,* c. Mayor and Corporation.

Cust, Henry, *Cockayne-Hatley,* r. *Sywell,* r. *Raisen Mid. Tupholm,* v. earl Brownlow. *Willoughby, St. Helen,* r. lord Gwydyr.

Dallen, J. vic. chor. York. *Rudston,* v. *Trinity in Goodramgate,* r. *St. John Delpike,* r. *and St. Maurice without Monk,* v. abp. of York.

Dampier, J. *Codford, St. Peter,* r. H. Kellow. *Langton Matravers,* r. Incumbent. *Pitcombe,* c. *Brewham,* c. sir R. C. Hoare.

Davies, G. J. *Grovenhurst Superior,* r. Trustees. *Marfleet,* c. H. Grylls. *Sutton,* c. H. Broadley.

Davy, Geo. M.A. dean of Chester; vacated by Dr. Phillpotts.

Davy, C. *Barking,* r. *Combes,* r. *Badley,* c. earl Ashburnham.

Dawson, F. *Chiselhurst,* r. *Hayes,* r, *Orpington,* (sinecure,) r. *with Down,* c. abp. of Cant.

Day, G. minor canon of Norwich. *Barton Bendish,* r. sir H. Berney. *Hemblington,* c. *Norwich Eaton,* v. dn. and ch. of Norwich.

Day, J. *Seething,* c. *St. Peter, Mundham,* c. Corp. of Norwich. *Yelverton,* r. lord Chan.

Digby, C. canon of Windsor. *Chiselboro',* r. *with West Chinnock,* c. *Middle Chinnock,* r. *Penselwood,* r. lord Ilchester.

Dillon, H. L. *Carhampton*, v. Mrs. Langham. *Carhampton*, p. c. H. P. Wyndham. *Litchet*, r. W. Trenchard.

Dixon, W. H. preb. of York and Ripon. *Bishopsthorpe*, v. abp. of York. *Cawood*, c. preb. of Wistow. *Mappleton*, v. archdn. E. Riding. *Topcliffe*, v. dn. and ch. of York.

Doveton, J. F. *Betchworth*, v. dn. and ch. of Windsor. *Burnet*, r. Corp. of Bristol. *Mells*, r. *with Leigh on Mendip*, c. T. G. Horner.

D'Oyley, Geo. *Lambeth*, r. *with Stockwell*, c. *Sundridge*, r. abp. of Cant.

Chaplain to the archbishop of Canterbury, and christian advocate in the University of Cambridge.

Dudley, J. *Humberstone*, v. Incumbent. *Sileby*, v, W. Pochin. *Himby*, r. earl Dudley.

Dowland, J. J. G. *Broad Windsor*, v. the King. *Turnworth*, v. bp. of Sarum. *Winterbourne Whitchurch*, v. E. M. Pleydell.

Edge, W. *Hollesley*, r, *Noughton*, r. *Nedging*, r. rev. W. Edge.

Ellis, J. *Llangamdimell*, v. *Llankerrig*, r. bp. St. David's. *Llanbadrig*, v. the King. *Wooten Waven, with Uttenhall*, c. King's Coll. Cambridge.

England, W. archdn. of Dorset. *Ower Moine*, r. *Winterbourne Carne*, r. *and St. Germain*, r. lady Damer. *West Stafford*, r. Mrs. Floyers.

Fardell, H. preb. of Ely. *Wisbech*, v. *Waterbeach*, v. bp. of Ely.

See a chronological statement of the progress of this gentleman in the church, p. 25.

Fellowes, J. *Bramerton*, r. *Easton*, r. *Mottisham Mantby*, r. R. Fellowes. *Bratton Clovelly*, r. bp. of Exeter.

Field, R. *Mendlesham*, v. Pearson and Wyatt. *Sutton, All Saints*, v. Oxon. *Ramsholt*, c. J. Pennington.

Finch, H. *Oakham*, v. *with Barleythorpe*, c. *and Brooke*, c. *Langham*, c. *Eggleton*, c. lord Winchelsea.

Finch, H. *Great Melford*, v. *Little Melford*, r. W. F. Finch. *Longstanton, All Saints*, bp. of Ely.

Nine Finches in the church, with eighteen livings, besides dignities. Most of them are *honourables*, and branches of the family of lord Winchelsea.

Fisher, John, archdn. of Berks, can. res. of Sarum. *Gillingham*, v. w. *East and West Stover*, c. *Motcombe*, c. *Osmington*, v. bp. of Salisbury.

Fisher, Jona. P. D.D. can. res. of Exeter. *Farringdon*, r. *Rockbear*, v. bp. of Exeter.

Fisher, P. *Elton*, r. Messrs. Shafto and Hogg. *Whapload*, v. the King. *Stoke Canon*, d. dn. and ch. of Exon.

Thirteen more *Fishers* with benefices and offices. They are all, we suspect, relations of the late bishop of Salisbury, and are an instance of that monopoly which is the disgrace of the establishment. The bishop was preceptor to the princess Charlotte of Wales and the Duke of Kent. Having obtained a prebend of Windsor and the archdeaconry of Exeter, he was, in 1803, promoted to that see; and, in 1808, translated to Salisbury. The patronage of the diocese is forty livings and thirty-five prebends, from which fund he made a comfortable provision for his family. *P. Fisher*, beside his three livings, has a prebend at

Norwich, and another at Salisbury, and is head master of the Charter-house. This man is really insatiable. His salary at the Charter-house is £800 a year, with a house, candles, vegetables, and an allowance for linen. He had a nephew lately on the foundation, and two sons exhibitioners at the Universities, with allowances of £80 a year from the charity.

Fletcher, W. chan. of d. of Carlisle, and preb. of York. *Bromfield*, v. *Dalston*, v. *Lazonby*, v. bp. of Carlisle.

Fly, H. D.D. sub-dean of St. Paul's, London. *Trinity, Minories*, c. the King. *Willesdon*, v. *Kingsbury*, p. c. *with Twyford*, c. dn. and ch. of St. Paul's.

Forester, T. preb. of Worcester. *Broseley*, r. *Little Wenlock, with Barrow*, c. *and Benthall*, c. lord Forester. *Worcester, St. John Bedwardine*, v.

Foxton, G. *Queensbury*, v. *with Ragdale*, c. E. Loveden. *New Town*, r. bp. of St. Asaph. *Twining*, v. Christ-church, Oxon.

Frome, R. *Folke*, r. rev. W. Chafin. *Goathill*, r. earl Digby. *Mintern*, r. Mrs. Sturt.

Gabell, H. D. *Ashow*, r. C. Leigh. *Binfield*, r. *Winchester, St. Laurence*, r. lord Chan.

Gaisford, T. dean of Oxford.

Garnier, Thomas, *Bishop's Stoke*, r. *Brightwell*, r. *Foxhall*, c. bp. of Winton.

The patronage of the church is an excellent resource for comfortable marriage-settlements. A son of the pluralist married a daughter of Brownlow North, late bishop of Winchester, and was portioned off with the rectory of Droxford, a prebend of Winchester, and the mastership of St. Cross's Hospital, which has great patronage. A daughter married Thomas, second son of the late lord Walsingham, who is archdeacon of Surrey, prebendary of Winchester, rector of Colbourne, and king's chaplain. A son of this last is prebendary of Winchester, and rector of Alverstoke and of Havant. The Norths, who are numerous in the church, are relations of the former bishop of Winchester, and had more than *thirty livings* shared among them.

Geldert, J. *Aldfield*, c. Mrs. Laurence. *Barnwell*, c. *Cambridge Less*, c. *Kirk Deighton*, r. rev. Dr. Geldart.

Goddard, C. archdn. and preb. of Lincoln, chaplain to the king; *Bexley*, v. viscount Sidney. *Louth*, v. preb. of Louth. *London, St. James's, Garlichythe*, r. bp. of London.

Goddard, E. *Eartham*, v. preb. of Eartham. *Easthampstead*, r. Chr. Ch. Oxon. *Pagham*, v. *with Bognor*, c. abp. of Cant. *Sidlesham*, v. preb. of Sidlesham.

Goodacre, W. *Mansfield Woodhouse*, p. c. *Skegly*, p. c. duke Portland. *Sutton Ashfield*, p. c. duke Devonshire.

Goodall, J. provost of Eton Coll. canon of Windsor; *Bromham*, v. *Hitcham*, r. Eton Coll. *West Ilsley*, r. dn. and cns. of Windsor.

The rev. pluralist being the head of a great public school, we shall give a brief account of one of these foundations, the boasted nursery of our *legislators and statesmen*. They are receptacles of abuse, and present a singular contrast to similar institutions in a neighbouring country; while the latter produce philosophers, heroes, and patriots, the former send forth a plentiful crop of exquisites, air-gun shooters, and at best pedants and Payleyean politicians. From the seed sown such fruit may be expected; the scholar's time is misspent in grammatical and metrical trifling, and little is read or studied but Horace,

Virgil, and Homer. Leaving these matters, let us come to the foundation of Eton and its management.

Eton college is situated near Windsor, and was founded by Henry VI. for the education of *seventy poor and indigent scholars*, who were enjoined by the founder to swear they had not *£*3 : 6*s*. a year to spend. The exact amount of the revenues it is not easy to ascertain, as it is a fact carefully concealed by the heads of the college; but, according to the evidence of Mr. Hinde, they amount to considerably more than £10,000 a year, and arise from various manors, estates, rectories, and tenements belonging to the foundation. The government of the college, and the management of this large income, is vested in the provost and *seven fellows*; the salaries of the latter, according to the statutes, are £10 a year, and of the former double that sum. The bishop of Lincoln is visitor. Besides the foundation scholars there are more than 400 *oppidens*, or town scholars, who pay for their education; though, like the rest of the boys, they are entitled to *gratuitous* instruction. The scholars are instructed by masters and assistants, who in fact do all the business of the college, and, as is usual in such cases, get the worst paid; the head master receives only £63 a year; the under master fares still worse and is paid in a trifling "*allowance of bread and beer.*"[*]

The more interesting subject for inquiry is, what becomes of the revenue when all the work is done at such a cheap rate? Nearly the whole of this, at the present, appears to be divided betwixt the provost and the fellows; the share of the former in *good* years has amounted to £2500; but the incomes of the latter are made up of such variety of items, they are not easily estimated. It is certain, however, their incomes are enormous. Besides the total income of the college, thirty-seven livings, some of which, worth £800 per annum, are in the gift of the fellows; they have the power of presenting themselves to one of these livings, which of course would not be the worst. They receive about £550 in money annually from the fines; a yearly stipend of £50; and a liberal allowance for gowns, coals, candles, &c. Moreover, they generally confer some office on themselves in the college, as bursar, precentor, sacrist, or librarian; for which they receive a salary. These are the principal items; but it is impossible to discover exactly what the fellows receive in all: their gross incomes cannot be much less than £1000 a year each.

After *Dr. Goodall* has taken the lion's share, and the fellows nearly as much as they please, the remainder is applied to support the establishment. According to the statutes, the scholars ought to be fed, clothed, educated, and lodged, free from expense; they have reduced their meals to two, namely, dinner and supper; clothing they have none; for their education they pay a gratuity of six guineas to the master, and their other yearly expenses amount to about *sixty pounds*; while, at the same time, they swear, or ought to swear, they have not *three pounds six shillings a year to spend!*

These exactions are, however, so shameless, unjustifiable, and so directly in the teeth of the statutes, that when any person ventures to object to their payment, to prevent enquiry, the charges are remitted. The indulgence is extended to a very small number; and to prevent such a dangerous example spreading through the school, the fact is carefully concealed from the rest of the boys. That this illegal demand for teaching may excite as little notice as possible, it is always thrust into the bill of the person with whom the boys board.[†]

Such is a brief account of the royal college of Eton. It only now remains to point out the more flagrant abuses which prevail in its management, and the manner the *poor* have been robbed of their rights and interests in this celebrated foundation.

First, instead of the revenues being expended in feeding, educating, and clothing, "*seventy poor and indigent scholars*," they are divided among eight clerical sinecurists; and children of opulent persons, who can afford to pay £70

---

[*] Third Report of the Education Committee, Sess. 1818, p. 72.
[†] Third Report of Education Committee, p. 71, evidence of the Rev. Dr. Goodall.

a-year for their education, are alone admitted to the benefits of the foundation. The statutes provide, that one-third part of the yearly saving shall be placed in the treasury, for the use of the college ; although there has been annually a surplus revenue to a very considerable amount, instead of being applied to the enlargement of the college, or any other laudable object, it has been divided and pocketed by the reverend fellows and the provost ; one hundred marks, too, piously left to clothe the " *poor and indigent scholars,*" have, in like manner, been shared as lawful plunder by the same reverend persons. In consequence of the spoliation of Edward the IVth. the number of fellows was reduced from ten to seven ; but although the revenues have increased so enormously, that they would very well support the old statutable number, yet they have for centuries been kept at the present amount, contrary to the intentions of the founder. Finally, the reverend fellows have all sworn not to obtain a dispensation for the holding of livings ; or, if obtained, not to use it ; yet, notwithstanding their oaths, notwithstanding the dreadful maledictions of the founder, such has been their greediness for the emoluments of the church, that they have obtained a dispensation to hold church preferment ; and the right reverend visitor has sanctioned this infringement of the ordinances of Henry VI.

Goodenough, E. dn. of Bath and Wells, and preb. of Westminster, Carlisle, and York ; *Wath, All Saints on Dearne,* v. *Adwick,* c. *Brampton Bierlow,* c. Christ Ch. Oxon.

Goodenough, S. J. preb. of Carlisle; *Broughton Poges,* r. rev. J. Goodenough. *Hampton,* v. the King.

Goodenough, William, archdn. of Carlisle, *with Mareham le Fen,* r. *and great Salkeld,* r. bp. of Carlisle.

Three more Goodenoughs ; they are of the family of the late Bishop of Carlisle. The prelate obtained the deanery of Rochester in 1802, and in 1808 was promoted to the See of Carlisle, through the interest of lord Sidmouth, his brother having married the sister of the *letter-of-thanks-man.*

Gordon, G. dn. of Lincoln; *Harbling,* v. *with Briggend,* c. bp. of Lincoln. *Whittington,* r. dn. of Lincoln. *Ledgbrook,* 1*st and 2d Mediety* r. *with East Allington,* c. lord Chan.

Gordon, G. *Bentley Fenney,* r. Dr. Gordon. *Muston,* r. lord Chan. *Whittington,* c. dn. of Lincoln.

Gower, G. L. *St. Mabyn,* r. *St. Michael Penkevil,* r. lord Falmouth. *Tatsfield,* r. *Titsey,* r. W. L. Gower.

Grant, J. T. *Merston,* r. *Wrabness,* r. The King. *Butterleigh,* r. lord Chan.

Grant, R. fellow of Winton Coll. ; *Bradford Abbass,* v. marquis Anglesea. *Clifton Maybank,* r. Winton Coll. *Portsea, St. Paul's,* p. c. vicar of Portsea.

Gray, Robert, bishop of Bristol, and prebendary of Durham.

Green, J. C. *Rillington,* v. the King. *Thornton-le-Moor,* r. bp. of Ely. *Birdsall,* p. c. marquis Hertford. *Whaream-in-the-Street,* v. lord Middleton. *Rustington,* v. bp. of Chichester.

Grey, hon. Thomas de, archd. of Surrey; *Calbourne,* r. *Fawley,* r. *with Exbury,* c. bp. of Winton. *Merton,* r. lord Walsingham.

The honourable, venerable, and reverend pluralist is, also, a king's chaplain, and prebendary of Winchester. He is uncle of lord Walsingham, and related to the Norths and Garniers, whom see. Three more Greys are in the church ; one of them is brother of the earl of Stamford, and is rector of Wickham and prebendary of Durham. Another relation of the earl has a living worth £1500 a-year.

Grey, hon. E. dean of Hereford, and prebendary of Hereford ; *St. Botolph, Bishopsgate,* r. bp. of London and the King alternately.
Youngest brother of earl Grey, who married, firstly, Miss Croft, by whom he had a family of ten children, nine of whom survive ; secondly, Miss Adair, the daughter of Sir R. Adair, the minister to Belgium, by whom he had also a family ; and, thirdly, the very reverend dean married Miss Innes, the daughter of an opulent merchant, formerly M.P. for Grampound.—A bishop, lord chancellor, or first lord of the treasury, with vast patronage and a host of expectants about him, always appears to our mind like the man at the head of the table with a fine turkey before him, which he is prepared to carve for the benefit of his family and guests. " Which part do you prefer—here is a leg—the wing or the apron." Just so in the distribution of public offices and preferments ; there is a benefice for one, a dignity for another, and an embassy, secretaryship, or commissionership for a third. We do not in this place complain ; earl Grey has certainly lost no time in moving his brother nearer to Durham or Winchester ; but it is not the advancement of the meritorious—though they be *relatives*—but the worthless that excites indignation. With the exception of the dispute about the payment of the stipend of the minister of the new church, the dean, like his predecessor in the parish of St. Botolph, bears an exemplary character, and the public is gratified rather than otherwise by his promotion.

Griffith, C. preb. of Brecon ; *Disserth,* r. bp. of St. David's. *Glondegla,* p. c. bp. of St. Asaph. *Llanvayes,* v. archdn. of Brecon.

Guildford, earl of, *Alresford, New and Old,* r. *with Medsted,* c. *Southampton, St. Mary, prec. and r. St. Cross, with St. Faith's Master,* bp. of Winchester.
The family, of which his lordship is the head, was some years since widely ramified in the church, engrossing upwards of thirty livings and dignities. These numerous preferments were derived through *Brownlow North,* uncle of the present lord Guildford and former bishop of Winchester. The bishop was a younger brother of lord North, the minister under whose administration the inglorious war was waged against the independence of North America. The bishop owed his promotion to his brother, and his advancement to the bench was much resisted by the minister's colleagues, on account of his youth. Lord North, however, observed—" that when he should become of more matured age, he would not have a brother prime minister." Under such powerful auspices the bishop rose rapidly in the church. He was first preferred to a canonry of Christ Church, Oxford. A few months afterwards he was pushed into the deanery of Canterbury, and the following year advanced to the diocese of Lichfield and Coventry. Soon after he was translated to Worcester, and in 1781 to the rich See of Winchester, which he held more than forty years, and must have netted from the revenue of his diocese upwards of one million and a half principal money.

Haden, A. B. *Ware,* c. O. Crewe. *Saddington,* r. *Wednesbury,* v. the King.

Haggitt, D'Arcy, *Branxton,* v. dn. and c. of Durham. *Cornhill,* c. W. N. Darnell. *Pershore St. Andrew,* v. *and Holy Cross,* c. *with Besford,* c. *Bricklehampton,* c. *Defford,* c. *and Penvin,* c. dn. and cns. of Westminster.

Harbin, J. *North Barrow,* r. E. B. Portman. *Kingston,* r. Mr. Harbin. *Wheathill,* r. Mrs. Phillips.

Harvey, B. *Alsager,* c. lord of the Manor. *Blackmore,* v. the King. *Doddinghurst,* r. J. Henrick.

Hasted, H. *Bury St. Mary,* c. Corporation. *Chedburg,* r. *with Ickworth,* r. chap. of Worcester. *Braisworth,* r. marquis Cornwallis. *Horningsheath,* r. lord Bristol.

Hett, W. *Enderby Navis*, r. Incumbent. *Greetwell*, c. ch. of Lincoln. *Lincoln, St. John in New*, v. *and St. Paul*, r. archd. of Lincoln. *Dunholme*, v. the King. *Nettleham*, c. chanc. of Lincoln. *Thorpe-on-the-Hill*, r. chap. of Lincoln.

Three rectories, a vicarage, and two chapelries, are not enough for this reverend pluralist. He is prebendary and vicar choral of Lincoln, and chaplain to the marquis of Stafford. His recommendation to *all* these good things are— The Genuine Tree of Liberty, or the Royal Oak of Great Britain; a political squib of 1793; a Fast-day Sermon; Letter upon Restrictions on Dissenting Teachers, &c.

Holdsworth, Robt. preb. of Exeter; *Brixham*, v. *with Kingsweare*, c. the King. *Dartmouth, St. Sav.* c. Corporation. *Townstall*, v. *Churston Ferrers*, c. corp. of Clifton.

Hales, R. *Hemesby*, v. J. T. Hales. *Herringswell*, r. H. Sperling. *Hillington*, r. sir W. J. B. Folkes.

Hamond, R. *Beechamwell St. John and St. Mary*, r. J. Molleaux. *Pensthorpe*, r. *East Walton*, v. *Gayton Thorpe*, r. A. Hamond.

Hanbury, T. *Burrough*, r. *Somerby*, v. *Langton Church*, r. *with Langton Tur*, c. *and Thorpe Langton*, c. W. Hanbury.

Hankinson, r. *Pentney*, c. sequestrated. *Walpole St. Andrew*, v. T. Hankinson, *West Bilney*, p. c. J. Dalton.

Harries, G. preb. of St. David's. *Letterston*, r. *Llanwair*, c. *Nolton*, r. *Rock*, c. *Rupa Castle yn Graig*, v. lord Chan.

Harries, J. *Langattock*, r. earl Abergavenny. *Llandett*, r. T. H. Gwynne. *Newcastle in Emlyn*, c. *with Bettws*, c. *and Llalestone*, c. T. Lewis.

Hawkesley, J. W. *Knotting*, r. *with Souldrop*, r. rev. J. W. Hawkesley, *Melchburn*, v. lord St. John. *Turvey*, r. D. C. Higgins.

Heathcote, G. archdn. of Winchester, fellow of Winton Coll., treasurer of Wells Cathedral. *Andover*, v. *with Foscot*, c. Winton Coll. *Hursley*, v. *Otterburn*, c. sir G. Heathcote.

Hewgill, F. *Littleborough*, p. c. J. Hewett. *Soundby*, r. *North Wheatley*, v. lord Middleton. *Sturton in the Clay*, v. dn. and ch. of York.

Hill, R. *Berrington*, r. *with Little Ness*, c. *Sutton St. John*, r. *Thornton Mayow*, r. lord Berwick. *Great Bolas*, r. sir R. Hill.

Several other Hills in the church. The pluralist is uncle of lord Hill, commander of the forces, and of Rowland Hill, the well known dissenting preacher.

Hobart, hon. H. L. *Haseley*, r. the King. *Nocton*, v. dn. and ch. of Cant. *Wantage*, v. dn. and cns. of Windsor.

This hon. and very reverend pluralist has two deaneries, that of Windsor, the other of Wolverhampton. A brother is canon of Hereford, and rector of Beer Ferrers; of which rectory, his nephew, the duke of Buckingham, is patron. Another *Hobart*, a son, we suspect, of the plural dean, has a valuable rectory, and prebend of Wolverhampton.

Hodgson, R. dn. of Carlisle. *Burgh on Sands*, v. lord chan. *Westminster, St. George's, Hanover-square*, r. *Hillington*, v. bp. of London.

Nephew of Porteus, late bishop of London. Many other Hodgsons, with livings, offices, and dignities.

Hodson, G. *Birmingham, Christ Church, c. Colwick,* v. *with Frodswell, c.* bp. of Lich. and Cov. *London, St. Katharine Cree,* v. Mag. Coll.

Holland, W. Wm. vic. of Chichester cath. *Bapchild,* v. *Burpham,* v. dn. and ch. of Chichester. *Chichester St. Andrew and St. Martin,* r. dn. of Chichester.

Holland, S., M.D. precent. and preb. of Chichester. *Beaudesert,* r. *Poynings,* r. *Warehorn,* r. the King.

This is a remarkable instance of the secular uses to which church property is applied by those who have the disposal of it. The reverend pluralist was originally a physician; but, happening to marry a daughter of lord Erskine, while his lordship held the great seal, he took holy orders, with a view to qualify himself for a share of the good things in the gift of his father-in-law. Erskine gave him the three rectories, worth about £2000 a-year, during the short period of his chancellorship. *Doctor* Holland has written a book to vindicate the clergy from the charge of neglecting their duties. Who may the preceding pluralist of this name be?

Holt, J. *Elston,* r. W. B. Darwin. *Gringley,* v. Camb. *Kelstern,* v. sir J. C. Hawkins. *Wrawby,* v. *with Brigg, c.* Clare Hall, Camb.

Hoste, J. *Barwick in Brakes,* v. Mrs. Hoste. *Longham, c. Wendling,* r. T. W. Coke.

Housen, H. vicar choral of Southwell. *Bleasby,* v. *Howerby,* r. *with Beesby in the Marsh, c.* Southwell, v. prec. and preb. of Normanton. *Aslacton,* p. c. Southwell Coll.

Howard, J. *Fundenhall,* d. T. T. Burney. *Morley, St. Botolph and St. Peter.* r. B. N. Cooper. *Tacolneston,* r. Mrs. Warren.

Howard, R. D.D. *Denbigh,* r. bp. St. Asaph. *Llandegfan,* r. *with Beaumaris, c.* Llanvewgan, c. R. W. Bulkeley.

Howes, F. min. can. of Norwich. *Attlebridge,* v. *with Alderford,* r. *Bawburgh,* v. *Norwich, St. George, col. r.* dn. and ch. of Norwich.

Howes, T. *Fritton,* r. T. L. Hodges. *Tharston,* v. bp. of Ely. *Thorndon,* r. rev. T. Howes.

Howley, Wm. primate of all England; consecrated bishop of London, 1813, and elevated to the primacy in 1828, on the decease of archbishop Sutton.

We have nothing to add to our notice, page 24, of this prelate. It may be inferred, from the strictness with which the preserves are watched at Addington, and the severe persecution of poachers, that his grace is very fond of *game.*

Hudleston, A. *Bownes,* r. *Morresby,* r. *Whitehaven St. Nicholas, c.* lord Lonsdale.

Hume, T. H. treas. and can. res. of Sarum. *Figheldean,* r. Treas. of Sarum, *Kewstoke,* v. lord Chan. *Stratford-under-Castle, c.* dn. and ch. of Sarum.

Huntingford, G. H. bishop of Hereford; consecrated bishop of Gloucester, 1802; translated 1815.

Hurt, T. *Lindby,* r. *Papplewick, c.* hon. F. Montague. *Scrooby,* v. *with Sutton-on-Lound,* v. duke of Portland.

Jacob, S. S. *Waldershore,* v. *Whitfield,* p. c. abp. of Cant. *Woollavington,* v. dn. and cans. of Windsor.

Ibbotson, J. *Ayton*, p. c. rev. W. Marwood. *Newton*, p. c. rev. S. Shepherd. *Nunthorpe*, p. c. T. Simpson and W. Richardson.

Ibbotson, T. *Garton*, v. the King. *Lowthorpe*, p. c. sir A. Quentin. *Skerne*, p. c. R. Arkwright.

Jenkinson, J. Banks, bishop of St. David's, dean of Brecon, and dean of Durham.

Jepson, G. preb. and vic. chor. of Lincoln. *Ashby Pueror*, v. *Glenthan*, v. *Normanby*, v. dn. and ch. of Lincoln. *Lincoln St. Botolph*, p. c. preb. of St. Botolph.

Inman, G. *Kilnsea*, v. L. Thompson. *Skefling*, v. rev. N. Holme. *Easington*, v. abp. of York.

Johnson, P. *Beeston*, r. *Sustead*, p. c. the King. *Ingworth*, r. W. Wyndham.

Jones, H. *Lewisham*, v. lord Dartmouth. *Talgarth*, v. dn. and cans. of Windsor. *Mablethorpe*, r. *with Stane*, r. col. Jones.

Iremonger, L. preb. of Winchester. *Wherwell*, preb. sin. *Goodworth Clatford*, v. J. Iremonger. *Kevil*, v. *Wanborough*, v. dn. and ch. of Winton.
Brother-in-law of lord Gambier, who has a nephew with three livings.

Karslake, W. *Culmstock*, v. dn. and ch. of Exeter. *Dalton*, r. J. Cleveland. *Loxbeare*, r. sir T. D. Acland.

Kaye, John, bishop of Lincoln, ditto prebendary, and provincial chancellor of Canterbury.

Keith, P. *Marr*, p. c. earl Kinnoul. *Ruckinge*, r. *Stalisfield*, v. abp. Cant.

Kelly, A. P. *Barnham*, p. c. *Little Hampton*, v. bp. Chichester. *Hoxton*, c. archdn. of London.

Kempthorne, J. preb. of Lichfield. *Gloucester St. Michael*, r. *and St. Marg. de Grace*, c. lord Chan. *Northleach*, v. *Preston*, v. bp. of Gloucester. *Wedmore*, v. dn. of Wells.

Kent, G. D. preb. of Lincoln. *Newton*, r. T. Smith. *Lincoln St. Martin*, v. bp. of Lincoln. *Scothern*, v. lord Scarboro'. *Conisholme*, r. hon. Mr. and Mrs. Robinson. *East Winch*, v. E. Kent.

Kett, W. *Darsham*. v. Sir J. Rous. *Shottisham*, r. Mr. Kett. *Waldringfield*, r. N. Randall.

Keppel, hon. E. G. *Quiddenham*, r. *with Snetterton*, r. *Shottisham All Saints*, v. *and St. Mary*, v. earl of Albermarle. *Tittleshall*, r. *with Godwick*, r. *and Wellingham*, r. T. W. Coke.
Third son of lord Albemarle, master of the horse, and brother-in-law of Mr. Coke, of Norfolk.

Kidd, T. *Croxton*, r. sir G. W. Leeds. *Eltisley*, v. lord Chan. *Norwich*, St. *Swithin*, r. bp. of Norwich, *sequest.*

Kipling, C. *Coston*, r. *Newport Pagnall*, v. lord Chan. *Wolverton*, v. *with Stratford Tony*, c. W. Drake.

Kipling, J. *Chearsley*, c. sir C. Dormer. *Chilton*, p. c. *Oakley*, v. sir J. Aubrey. *Upper Winchendon*, p. c. sir C. Cave.

Knatchbull, W., D.D. *Aldington*, r. *with Smeath*, c. abp. Cant. *Bircholt*, r. lady Bankes. *Wesbere*, r. lord Chan.

Kynaston, sir E. chap. in ord. to H.M. *Farnham, St. Genev.* r. *with Risby,* r. *Kinnersley,* v. the King. *Hordley,* r. J. K. Powell.

Lade, W. *Graveney,* v. *with Goodnestone,* r. *Wickhamtreux,* r. J. Lade, *Knowlton,* r. sir N. D'Aeth.

Langdon, G. *Houghton,* r. E. M. Pleydell. *Milton Abb.* v. lord Dorchester. *Weston-Patrick,* p. c. W. T. L. Wellesley.

Landon, W. dn. of Exeter and preb. of Sarum. *Bishopstone,* r. preb. of Bishopstone. *Branscombe,* v. dn. and ch. of Exeter. *Croft,* r. *with Yarpole,* c. Mrs. Johnes.

Lates, J. J. *Charlton Abbot,* c. F. Pyson. *Sudely,* r. lord Rivers. *Winchcombe,* v. *with Gretton,* c. lord Tracey.

Law, G. H. bishop of Bath and Wells; consecrated bishop of Chester, 1812.

Law, Henry, archdeacon of Wells and canon residentiary.

Lax, W. *Ippolitts,* v. *with Great Wymondley,* v. *Marshworts,* v. Camb. *Orwell,* v. rev. J. H. Renouard.

Lee, H. fellow of Winton Coll. and preb. of Hereford. *Ash,* r. *Frimley,* p. c. *Hound,* v. *with Bursledon,* c. *and Hamble,* p. c. Winton Coll.
    See Bishop Sumner for an account of Winton College.

Lewis, D. C. min. can. of Windsor. *Colnbrook,* c. Pem. Coll. Oxon. *Newington,* v. Eton Coll. *Ruislip,* v. dn. and ch. of Windsor.

Lewis, J. *Buttsbury,* c. rev. D. Lloyd. *Ingatestone,* r. N. W. Lewis. *Ravenhall,* r. C. W. Western.

Leyson, T. *Bassalleg,* v. bp. Llandaff. *Panteague,* r. *Treddunnock,* r. C. H. Leigh.

Linton, H. *Dinton,* v. *with Great Teffont,* c. Mag. Coll. Oxon. *Fritwell,* v. *North Aston,* v. T. F. Willes.

Long, R. C. *Dunston,* c. Misses S. and G. Long. *Illington,* r. Mrs. Kellett. *Newton Flotman,* r. Miss Long. *Swarsthorpe,* r. rev. R. C. Long.

Lord, J. *Berfreyston,* r. Oxon. *Northiam,* r. Miss Lord. *Drayton Parslow,* r. rev. J. Lord.

Lowe, J. *Tankersley,* r. *Swinton,* c. *Wentworth,* p. c. earl Fitzwiiliam. *Brotherton,* v. dn. and ch. of York.

Lowndes, R. *Astwood,* v. the King. *North Crawley,* r. Miss Duncombe. *Farley,* r. Oxon.

Lucas, G. *Caifield,* r. *Stokesby with Heringby,* r. W. Downs. *Billockby,* r. *Filby,* r. C. Lucas.

Luxmore, C. S. dean, with Heullan, v. annexed, chanc. of see of St. Asaph, and preb. of Hereford. *Bromyard, 2d Port,* r. and v. *West Cradley,* r. bp. of Hereford. *Daroven,* r. *Gurlsfield,* v. bp. of St. Asaph.

Luxmore, John, joint regist. of Hereford, preb. of St. Asaph. *Berriew,* v. bp. of St. Asaph.

Three more Luxmores in the church. They are sons and nephews of the late bishop of St. Asaph. The prelate owed his promotion to his connexion with the family of the duke of Buccleugh. He first obtained the living of St. George the Martyr, Queen's-square, which he vacated upon being presented to the neighbouring rectory of St. Andrew's, Holborn, which he held, *in commendam*, with the see of Hereford. To the last see he was translated from the diocese of Bristol, before which he held the deanery of Gloucester. He was translated to St. Asaph in 1815. The progress of the bishop, like most of his brethren, may be generally traced from the number of relations and dependents which they leave behind them in possession of the most valuable preferments in their gift.

Madan, Spencer, preb. and chan. of diocese of Peterborough, chap. in ord. to the King. *Ibstock*, r. *with Hugglescote*, c. *Dunnington*, c. bp. of Rochester. *Thorpe Constantine*, r. W. P. Inge.

Son of the late bishop of Peterborough, nephew of the late bishop of Lichfield, and cousin of the marquis Cornwallis. Except a *fast-day sermon* or two, we do not know any other claim of this reverend pluralist to his appointments. His uncle, the bishop, to whom he is chiefly indebted for his preferments, was, at first, intended for the bar, and, with that view, entered himself a student of the Temple; but the elevation of his uncle to the archbishopric, on the death of Dr. Secker, opened a more lucrative prospect, and he devoted himself, without any particular call that way, to the church. His first preferment was the rich rectory of Wrotham, in Kent, soon after which he obtained a prebend of Westminster, and shortly after succeeded Dr. Moore in the deanery of Canterbury. On the translation of bishop Hurd, he was raised to the *throne* of Lichfield and Coventry; and, on the death of bishop Douglas, he succeeded him as dean of Windsor, which he vacated for the richer deanery of Durham.

Maddy, J. *Somerton*, r. Incumbent. *Stansfield*, r. *Hartest*, r. *Boxted*, r. the King.

Markham, Robert, archd. of York, and canon. res.

Maltby, Edward, bishop of Chichester, and preacher to Society of Lincoln's Inn : consecrated in 1831.

Manning, H. C. *Burgh Castle*, r. the King. *Thetford St. Cuth.* c. *and St. Peter*, r. duke Norfolk. *Santon*, r. Corp. of Thetford.

Mapleton, J. H. *Southwark, Christchurch*, r. Trustees of Marshall's charities. *Whaddon*, v. New Coll. Oxon. *Mitcham*, v. Mrs. Simpson.

Marsh, Herbert, bishop of Peterborough, professor of divinity, Cambridge.

Marsham, hon. and rev. J. *Allington*, r. earl Romney. *Wateringbury*, v. dn. and ch. of Rochester. *Kirby Overblow*, r. earl Egremont.

Canon of Windsor, prebend of Bath and Wells, ditto of Rochester. Brother of lord Romney.

Marsham, C. *Cavenfield*, v. dn. and ch. Rochester. *Edgcott*, r. *Stoke Lyne*, v. J. Coker. *Islington*, v. dn. and cans. Windsor.

Marsham, E. *Sculthorpe*, r. sir G. Chadd. *Wramplingham*, r. *Stratton Strawless*, r. R. Marsham.

Massingberd, F. C. *Calceby*, v. *Dribg*, r. *Kettlesby*, r. *South Ormesby*, c. C. B. Massingberd.

Mavor, W. *Bladon*, r. *Hurley*, v. *Woodstock*, c. duke of Marlborough. This is the well-known compiler of useful books, and a native of Aberdeen. He was, at first, a schoolmaster, and being employed by the duke of Marlborough to instruct the junior branches of the family in writing, he obtained such favour as to get a title for holy orders. Soon after he was rewarded with the livings of Hurley and Woodstock.

Methold, T. preb. of Norwich. *Apsal-stoneham*, r. W. Middleton. *Kilverton*, r. lord Chan. *Wetheringsett*, r. Mrs. Close.

Millard, C. F. *Henley*, v. *Norwich St. Giles*, r. *and at Palace*, d. dn. and ch. Norwich. *Hickling*, v. Mr. Micklethwaite.

Miller, E. *Chesterton*, c. lord Willoughby de Broke. *Radway*, v. *Ratley*, v. lord Chan.

Millers, G. min. can. of Ely. *Hardwich*, r. *Runham*, v. *Stanford*, v. bp. of Ely.

Mills, T. chap. to the King. *Bumpstead Helion*,, v. Camb. *Little Henney*, r. *Stutton*,, r. N. Barnardiston.

Mitford, J. *Benhall*, v. W. Mitford. *Weston, St. Peter's*, r. the King. *Stratford St. Andrew*, r. chan. of du. of Lancaster.

Monk, John H. bishop of Gloucester, and prebendary of Westminster : consecrated in 1830.

Monins, J. *Charlton, near Dover*, r. *Ringwould*, r. rev. J. Monins. *Fawkenhurst*, r. *Hurst*, r. Miss Carter.

Moore, G. *Croxby*, r. lord Chan. *Lincoln St. Margaret, with St. Peter, p. c.* precent. and preb. Lincoln Cath. *Ownby*, r. chan. du. of Lancaster.

Moore, R. preb. of Canterbury. *Eynesford*, r. *Hollingbourn*, r. *Hunton*, r. *Latchingdon*, r. abp. of Cant.

Morgan, H. H. can. res. of Hereford. *Fownhope*, v. *Wolhope*, v. dn. and ch. of Hereford. *Moccas*, r. sir G. Cornwall.

Mounsey, G. *Forest*, c. lord Derby. *Fairfield*, p. c. Trustees. *Rushton Spencer*, c. lord Macclesfield.

Mount, C. *Bath, Christchurch*, c. rev. C. A. Moysey. *Hannington*, v. R. Montgomery. *Helmdon*, r. *Suttesbury*, r. Oxon.

Moysey, C. A. archdn. of Bath, preb. of Wells. *Bath, Wolcot*, r. dame Gay. *Boarhunt*, d. T. Kethwayte. *Southwick*, d. Mr. Thistlethwayte.

Mucklestone, J. F. preb. and vic. of Lichfield, and preb. of Wolverhampton. *Tong*, p. c. G. Durant. *Weeford*, c. chan. of Lichfield. *Wybunbury*, v. bp. of Lich. and Cov.

Mules, J. H. *Abbot's Isle*, v. dn. and ch. of Bristol. *Broadwater*, c. *Broadway*, c. rev. W. Palmer. *Ilminster*, v. H. Hanning.

Murray, Geo. bishop of Rochester, dean of Worcester, rector of Bishopsbourne, and chaplain to abp. of Cant.

Nelson, J. vic. chor. of Lincoln. *Ruskington*, v. the King. *Searby*, r. *Wellingore*, r. dn. and ch. of Lincoln. *Snarford*, r. sub-dn. of Lincoln. *Lincoln St. Mark*, p. c. precent. of Lincoln.

Nevile, viscount, *Byrling*, v. *Holveston*, r. *with Burgh Apton*, r. *Otley*, r. lord Abergavenny.

Third son of the noble patron. Another son is vicar of Trant, in Sussex, and rector of Birling, in Kent.

Newsam, Clement, *Harbury*, v. Miss Newsam. *Portbury*, r. *with Tickenham*, v. bp. of Bristol.

Nicholas, John, D.D. *Bremilham*, r. lady Northwich. *Fisherton Ange*, r. W. H. F. Talbot. *Westport*, v. *with Brockenborough*, c. lord Chan.

Nicolay, G. F. L. one of the brethren of St. Katharine; *Little Marlow*, v. rev. G. F. L. Nicolay. *London, St. Michael Royal and St. Martin Vintry*, r. abp. Cant. and bp. Worcester, *ult.*—See Nicolay, in the *Place List*.

North, Henry. *Heacham*, v. H. Spelman. *Great Ringstead, St. Andrew and St. Peter*, r. H. Styleman.

Northcote, Hugh, *Dowlan*, p. c. *Monkoakhampton*, r. *Okhampton St. James*, r. *Upton Pyne*, r. sir H. Northcote.

Nott, G. F., D.D. preb. of Winton, Chichester, and Sarum. *Harrietsham*, r. All Souls' Coll. *Woodchurch*, r. abp. of Cant.

This gentleman has been for a long time missing; should this meet his eye, we beg to inform him, that the parishioners of Woodchurch are very desirous of seeing him, and they wish to know where he may be found; they have been served with notices for the payment of tithes by the solicitor of the reverend pluralist, who has only been *once* in the parish during the whole of last reign, aad that for a day only.

Oakes, James. *Gipping*, d. C. Tyrrel. *Thurston*, v. *Rattlesden*, r. James Oakes, esq. *Tostock*, r. Mr. Moseley.

Oldershaw, John, D.D. archdn. of Norfolk, *with Coston*, p. c. *Ludham*, v. bp. of Norwich. *Ranworth*, v. *with Upton, St. Margaret*, v. bp. of Ely. *Redenhall*, r. *with Hailestone*, c. duke of Norfolk, on nom. of bp. of Norwich.

Onslow, G. W. *Send*, v. *with Ripley*, c. earl Onslow. *Wisley*, r. *with Perford*, v. *Shalford*, v. *with Bramley*, c. lord Chan.

Onslow, R. F. archdn. of Worcester, preb. of Sarum. *Kidderminster*, v. w. *Lower Mitton*, c. lord Foley. *Newent*, v. hon. E. Foley.

The venerable archdeacon is son of the late dean of Worcester, whose father was a lieutenant-general, and brother of the famous Arthur Onslow, who was forty years speaker of the Collective Wisdom. A. C. Onslow, rector of St. Mary, Newington-butts, of which benefice the bishop of Worcester is patron, is a brother of the archdeacon.

Oxenden, Mont, *Bonington*, r. T. Papillon. *Luddingham*, r. lord Chan. *Wingham*, p. c. sir H. Oxenden.

Palmer, G. *Leominster*, v. Eton Coll. *Parham*, r. baroness Zouch. *Sullington*, r. N. Tredcroft.

Parkinson, J. D.D. *Brocklesby*, r. lord Yarborough. *Healing*, r. rev. R. Parkinson. *Immingham*, v. W. Amcotts.

Parkinson, T. D.D. preb. St. Paul's, chan. of dioc. of Chester, archdn. of Leicester; *Kegworth*, r. *with Isley Walton*, c. Christ Coll. Camb.

257 livings are in the gift of the University of Oxford, and 292 in the gift of Cambridge. The livings are situate in different parts of the country ; many of them in the metropolis. Some of the livings are annexed to the provostships and professorships of the different colleges, but for the most part they are in the gift of the fellows. By the statutes of the universities the holding of a fellowship is incompatible with the holding of a college living. When, however, a living is *more* valuable than a fellowship, a fellowship is vacated for the sake of being eligible to the living.

Parsons, H. preb. of Wells; *Durleigh*, v. Mr. Dunning. *Goathurst*, r. lady Tynte. *Wembdon*, v. C. K. Tynte.

Payne, Henry Thomas, can. res. of St. David's, preb. of Brecon; *Devunnuck*, v. *with Blaen Glyn Tavy*, c. bp. of Gloucester. *Ystradvellty*, p. c. *Llanbedr*, r. *Patricio*, p. c. duke Beaufort.

Pearce, Thomas, *Folkstone*, v. *Hawkinge*, r. abp. of Cant. *Hartlip*,
v. dean and c. of Roch. *Merston*, r. lord Chan.

Pearson, H. dean of Salisbury.

Pellew, hon. G. D.D. dn. of Norwich, preb. of York; *London, St.
Dionis Backchurch*, r. dn. and can. of Cant.

This honourable and very reverend dignitary is son of lord Exmouth, who
has a pension of £2000 a-year, and son-in-law of lord Sidmouth, who has a
pension of £3000 a-year. He was originally intended for the legal profession,
but his abilities not-lying that way, he was, after eating a few terms, turned
over to the church. His progress in this line has been very successful: in 1819
he was presented to the vicarage of Naseing, worth £1200 a-year; next year he
was presented to the rectory of Sutton, said to be worth £4000 a-year; and,
within a few months after he had a prebend's stall in St. Paul's: these appear
to have been subsequently resigned or negotiated for his present preferments.

Penrice, Charles, *Smallburgh*, r. bp. of Norwich. *Witton*, r. *with
Brundall*, r. *and Little Plumstead*, r. J. Musket.

Pepys, H. preb. of Wells; *Aspeden*, r. lord Hardwicke. *Westmill*, r.
Moreton, r. St. John's Coll.

Percy, hon. Hugh, D.D. bp. of Carlisle, chan. of Sarum, preb. of
St. Paul's.—See page 26.

Perkins, F. D. chap. in ord. to H. M.; *Down-Hatherley*, v. *Sow*, v.
with Stoke, v. *Swayfield*, r. lord Chan.

Perkins, John David, D.D. *Dawlish*, v. bp. Exon. *Exeter, St. Laurence*, r. *Manhead*, r. lord Chan.

Pett, Phineas, D.D. archdn. of Oxford, can. of Christ Church, preb. of
Sarum. *Chilbolton*, r. bp of Winton. *Newington*, r. abp. of Cant.

Phillpotts, Henry, bishop and treasurer of Exeter, and prebendary of
Durham.

The honest retraction of an error does credit to the heart and understanding;
but if a man from mercenary motives suppresses or disguises—for he cannot
abandon them—his convictions, he is a traitor to truth, and merits the most igno-
minious brand that public opinion can inflict. The most charitable cannot put
a favourable construction on the conduct of Dr. Phillpotts, and he is given up,
by all parties, as one guilty of unpardonable crimes. The first exploit we remember of this spiritual adventurer was a pamphlet imputed to him in defence of the
Manchester massacre, in which 800 poor creatures, men. women, and children,
were killed, cut-down, and maimed, under the sabres of a ferocious yeomanry.
He next signalized himself by his writings against catholic emancipation, and
finally astonished people by voting for a minister, at Oxford, who was favourable to the catholic relief bill. Thus he was all things to all men, and at last
receives his reward—universal contempt and a mitre! As the political bishop
had succeeded in fastening on the See of Exeter, we would have suffered him
to have held Stanhope rectory too, with the fine house to live in he had built
at an expense of £12,000: there appeared a paltriness in the Whigs attempting
to blink the transaction by suffering the prelate to exchange the rectory with
Mr. Darnell for a stall at Durham.

Pierce, W. M. *Burwell*, v. *with Walmsgate*, c. *Goulsby*, v. M. B.
Lister. *Fulletby*, r. bp. of Lincoln.

Plater, Charles Eaton, *River*, v. *Whitstable*, c. abp. of Cant. *Sea-
salter*, v. d. and c. of Cant.

Plimley, Henry, chan. of diocese of Chichester, preb. of Chichester;
Cuckfield, v. *Shoreditch*, v. bp. of Chichester.

Polson, J. H. P. preb. of Exeter; *Exeter Major*, r. d. and c. of
Exeter. *Upton Helion*, r. Jos. Polson, esq.

Poore, J. *Bicknor*, r. lord Chan. *Murston*, r. St. John's Coll. *Rainham*, v. abp. of Cant.

Potchett, William, preb. of Sarum; *North and South Grantham*, v. *with Great and Little Gunnerby*, v. *Londonthorpe*, v. and *Braceby*, v. cath. of Sarum.

Pott, Jos. Holden, archdn. of London, preb. of St. Paul's, chan. of Exeter Cath.; *Kensington*, v. bp. of London.

Poulter, Edm. preb. of Winton; *Alton*, v. *with Holybourn*, c. dn. and can. of Winton. *Meonstoke*, r. *with Soberton*, c. bp. of Winton.

Pratt, J. S. preb. of Peterboro'; *Maxey*, v. *Paston*, r. *with Werrington*, c. dn. and cns. of Peterboro'. *Peterboro'*, &c. v. bp. of Peterboro'.

Preston, W. preb. of York; *Bulmer*, r. earl Fitzwilliam. *Butterwich*, c. Parson Foord. *Ergham*, r. T. Grimstone. *Sculcoates*, v. the King. *Whenby*, v. W. Garforth. *Wold Newton*, v. hon. M. Langton.

Pretyman, G. T. chan. and can. res. of Lincoln, preb. of Winton; *Chalfont St. Giles*, r. *Wheathampstead*, r. *with Harpenden*, r. bp. of Lincoln.

Pretyman, John, preb. of Lincoln; *Sherrington*, r. *Winwick*, r. bp. of Lincoln.

Pretyman, Richard, prec. and can. res. of Lincoln; *Middleton Stoney*, r. *Walgrave*, r. *with Hannington*, v. bp. of Lincoln. *Wroughton*, r. bp. of Winton.

Having, at page 27, noticed the numerous ecclesiastical emoluments of the Pretymans, we shall only give some account of the rise of the bishop, to whom the family is indebted for its preferments. Tomline, formerly Pretyman, the late bishop of Winchester, was the son of a tradesman at Bury St. Edmund's, at the grammar-school of which town he and his brother, Dr. John Pretyman, the archdeacon of Lincoln, received the elements of their education; after which they removed to Cambridge. The bishop was distinguished at the university as a good classical scholar and expert arithmetician. Having the good fortune to become tutor to " the Heaven-born minister," he soon experienced the patronage of his pupil, who appointed him his private secretary, and gave him a prebendal stall in the church of St. Peter, Westminster. In 1787 he was made bishop of Lincoln, to which preferment was added the deanery of St. Paul's; and on the death of Dr. Randolph, he was offered the See of London, but that dignity he declined, from an expectation of something more substantial, in which calculation he was not disappointed; for, on the death of Brownlow North, he obtained the rich See of Winchester, the *summum bonum* of episcopal ambition.

Price, Morgan, *Knebworth*, r. *Letchworth*, r. R. W. Lytton. *Llangedwyn*, c. sir W. W. Wynne. *Tallachdu*, r. Parson Griffiths.

Proby, Charles, can. of Windsor; *Tachbrook Bishops*, v. Lichfield Cath. *Twickenham*, v. d. and can. of Windsor. *Waddesden*, 3rd Port, r. duke Marlborough.

Probyn, John, archdn. of Llandaff; *Abbenhall*, r. E. Probyn. *Mathern*, v. *with Caerwent*, v. archdn. of Llandaff.

Proctor, Joseph, D.D. preb. of Norwich; *Conington*, r. *Gidding Steeping*, r. J. Heathcote.

Prosser, Richard, D.D. preb. of Durham, *with Easington*, r.
Radcliffe, John, *Doddington*, v. *Teynham*, v. archdn. of Cant. *Limehouse*, r. Brazenose Coll.
Ramsden, W. B. *Croxton All Saints*, v. Christ Coll. *Great Stambridge*, r. govs. of Charter House. *Little Wakering*, v. St. Bart. Hospital. *Witcham*, v. d. and c. of Ely.
Randolph, J. H. preb. of St. Paul's; *Burtan Coggles*, r. lord Chan. *Fobbing*, r. the King. *Nothall*, v. bp. of London.
Randolph, T. preb. of St. Paul's, and chap. to the King; *Great Hadham*, r. and *Little Hadham*, c. bp. of London.
Raymond, Oliver, *Belchamp Walters*, v. *with Bulmer*, v. *Middleton*, r. Trustees of S. R. Raymond.
Rennell, Thomas, D.D. dn. of Winchester, preb. of St. Paul's. *Barton Stacey*, v. dn. and ch. of Winton.

The prebend was resigned to Dr. Rennell, by his father, on his obtaining a fellowship in the university. Having obtained the patronage of the Grenvilles, he was presented to a living in the city, and, in 1798, was made master of the Temple. On the death of Dr. Holmes he was presented to the deanery of Winchester. The dean married a daughter of judge Blackstone, by whom he has a son, who is also in the church. He was suspected of being concerned in a foolish book, called the *Pursuits of Literature*, but this charge he publicly disavowed. He is the author of several political sermons, one delivered in Winchester cathedral, in 1793, on the *Violence and Blood Guiltiness of the French Revolution;* another thanksgiving sermon for the success of his majesty's arms, preached before the Collective Wisdom, 1798. We mention these forgotten squibs, thinking they may afford a hint to spiritual aspirants, who may seek to avail themselves of passing events, by serving up *au rechauffé* the labours of the venerable dean.

Rice, hon. E. dn. of Gloucester, and precentor of York. *Great Rissington*, r. lord Dynevor. *Oddington*, r. precentor of York.
Brother of lord Dynevor, and brother-in-law of the Markhams.
Richards, Charles, preb. of Winton. *Chale*, r. Incumbent. *Winchester, St. Bartholomew*, v. the King.
Richardson, J. vic. chor. of York. *Crambe*, v. *Hutton's Ambo*, p. c. abp. of York. *Fryston Ferry*, v. vic. chor. of York. *Heslington*, v. *Huntington*, v. York Cath.
Rodney, hon. Spencer, *New Romney*, v. All souls Coll. *Swarraton*, r. A. Baring, M.P. *Wonstow*, v. T. Swineston.
Brother of lord Rodney, a pensioner; another brother vicar of Eye, of which the lord Chancellor is patron.
Roles, William, *Raunds*, v. *Upton Lovel*, r. *Sharncot*, r. lord Chan.
Rolfe, Robert, *Caldecot*, r. Mrs. Tynte. *Cockley Cley*, r. R. Dashwood. *Hempnall*, v. John T. Mott. *Yaxley*, r. *Thurgarton*, r. bp. of Norwich.
Rooke, George, *Wolford*, v. *with Burmington*, c. *Woolvercot*, c. Merton Coll. *Yardley Hastings*, r. marquis Northampton.
Rowley, Joshua, *East Bergholt*, r. *with Brentham*, r. Incumbent. *Stoke by Nayland*, r. sir W. Rowley.
Royle, James, *Islington*, v. the King. *Stanfield*, r. rev. W. Newcome. *Wereham*, p. c. *with Wretton*, c. Edw. W. Pratt.

Rycroft, Henry, preb. of Lincoln. *Greetham,* r. *Mumby,* v. bp. of Lincoln.

Ryder, hon. Henry, D.D. bp. of Lichfield and Coventry, *with Pitchley,* r. *annexed,* and prebendary of Westminster.

Brother of lord Harrowby, and uncle of lord Sandon, M.P. late secretary to the India Board. The prelate was raised to the see of Gloucester on the translation of Huntingford to the neighbouring bishopric of Hereford, from which Luxmore had been removed to St. Asaph. It is necessary to attend to these translations, as they afford an important key in the disposal of patronage; the successive removes of bishops and dignitaries generally being indicated by trails of relations left behind in possession of the most valuable preferments.

Sandiford, P., D.D. *Ashbury,* r. bp. of Bath. *Fulmodeston,* r. *with Croxton,* v. Corpus Christi Coll. *Newton in the Isle,* r. bp. of Ely.

Sargent, J. *Graffham,* r. *Woolavington,* r. *with Punton,* v. J. Sargent, esq.

Savory, Samuel H. *Barmer,* c. earl Oxford. *Houghton-in-the-Hole,* v. marquis Cholmondely. *Twyford,* r. G. Thomas.

Seale, J. B., D.D. *Anstye,* r. Camb. *Stisted,* r. abp. Cant. *Willingale Spain,* r. bp. of London.

Simms, W. Eratt, *Nayland,* c. sir W. Rowley. *Santon Downham,* p. c. lord Cadogan. *West Bergholt,* r. W. Fisher. *West Toft,* r. J. Mosely.

Simpson ,T. *Boynton,* v. *Carnaby,* v. *Fraisthorpe,* c. sir G. Strickland. *Auborn,* p. c. dn. of York.

Singleton, Thomas, archdn. of Northumberland *with Elsdon,* r. annexed, preb. of Worcester.

Skurray, Francis, *Horningham,* p. and p. c. dn. of Sarum. *Lullington,* r. marq. Bath. *Winterbourne Abbas,* r. *and Steepleton,* r. Lincoln Coll. Oxon.

Slaney, Richard, *Kemberton,* r. *with Sutton Maddock,* v. P. Broughton. *Penkridge,* p. c. *with Coppenhall Hay,* c. *Dunston,* c. *and Woodbaston,* c. sir E. Lyttleton.

Sleath, John, D.D. head master of St. Paul's School, preb. of St. Paul's, and chaplain to the King.

As Dr. Sleath is high master of St. Paul's school, we cannot help adverting to the abuses in the management by the Mercer's company of that munificent foundation of dean Colet. The landed revenues of the school amount to upwards of £6000 per annum; and by the aid of sundry outgoings in dinners, committees, pensions, repairs, gratuities, and medals, it is contrived that the expenditure shall nearly equal the income. It is now admitted, the charity was intended for all who could avail themselves of it, whether *rich or poor;* why then should the benefits of so wealthy a foundation, situated in the centre of the metropolis, be limited to the precise number of 153 scholars? The company are invested with full authority to modify the statutes of the school, as the changes of the times may require. When the number 153 was fixed, the income of the foundation was not one-fiftieth part of its present amount, and that number was fixed solely from a superstitious notion of the founder.*

But if the company are scrupulous about violating the ordinances of dean Colet, it is strange they have already violated so many. The dean ordained

---

* Account of Public Charities, abridged from the Commissioners' Reports, with Notes and Comments, by the Editor of the " *Cabinet Lawyer,*" p.15.

that, every morning, the children should be at the school by seven o'clock; that, thrice every day, prostrate, they should say their prayers; that, at Childermas-day, they should "come to Paule Church and hear the *Childe Bishop's* sermon, and after be at the *high-mass*." Are these things observed?

The statutes of St. Paul's school are venerated in the same way, we suspect, as those of the colleges of Eton and Winchester; just as much of them is observed as suits the interest of those having the management, the rest is given to the winds. On this principle the high-master's salary of a *mark a week* is interpreted to mean £613 per annum, besides gratuities; and the surmaster's salary of 6*s.* 8*d.* a week £300 per annum. From what part of the ordinances the annual gold medal to the accountant-surveyor, or the fee of one guinea for attendance on committees is derived, we have not been able to discover.

From the evidence of the high-master, Dr. Sleath, it appears, the children mostly belong to the clergy, the professional gentlemen, and medical men in the neighbourhood, and to gentlemen in Doctors' Commons. It has been suggested the instruction of the school should embrace reading, writing, and mathematics, but we have not heard this plan has been adopted. There certainly appears no just reason why the education of the school should be limited to the acquirement of Latin and Greek. Dean Colet contemplated no such restriction when he said, "*desiring nothynge more thanne* EDUCATION *and bringing uppe children in good manners and literature.*" Without deviating from the literal expression, education might be interpreted to include many other branches of knowledge beside an acquaintance with the learned languages.

The profusion in the expenditure of the school is wholly indefensible. There can be no doubt but the same number of boys might be taught Latin and Greek at a much less sum than was paid in pension to the late high-master; but it is mostly thus in foundations under the management of corporate bodies; no efforts to economize or to multiply the objects of the charity. If there be a surplus revenue it is sure to be exhausted in the expenses of committees, law-agency, and surveyors' charges; in extra repairs and improvements; in ostentatious buildings; in luxurious feasting for the parties and their friends; and in pensions and gratuities. There is never too much—generally too little, and the charity in debt.

Smith, S., D.D. dn. of Christchurch, preb. of York. *Daventry*, p. c.
    Dry Drayton, r. Oxon.

Smith, Sidney, preb. of Bristol, and canon res. of St. Paul's. *Foston*, r.
    lord chan. *Londesboro'*, v. duke of Devonshire.

Somerset, lord Wm. preb. of Bristol. *Crick Lowel*, r. *Llangattock*, r.
    with Lonelly and Llangennett, c. duke Beaufort.

Sparke, Bowyer Edward, D.D. bishop of Ely; consecrated bishop of
    Chester, 1809.

Sparke, J. H. preb. and chan. of the diocese of Ely. *Leverington*, r.
    with Parson Drove, c. *Littlebury*, sinecure, r. bp. of Ely.

Son of the preceding; the father had the good fortune to become tutor to the duke of Rutland, and his advancement followed of course. From the deanery of Bristol he was raised to the see of Chester; and, on the death of Dr. Dampier, removed to the valuable see of Ely. Besides an immense revenue and numerous cathedral appointments, he has one hundred and eight livings in his gift. For an account of the preferments the rev. prelate has heaped on his family see p. 25.

Spooner, William, archdn. of Coventry, preb. of Lichfield. *Acle*, r.
    lord Calthorpe. *Elmdon*, r. L. Spooner.

Spry, J. Hume, D.D. preb. of Canterbury. *Hanbury*, v. bp. Lich.
    and Cov. *St. Marylebone*, r. the King.

The commissioners of woods and forests purchased of the duke of Portland the advowson of the opulent and populous parish of Mary-le-bone, out of the produce of the crown lands, for £40,000; this was considered less than the value, but his grace was content to make a sacrifice, rather than the patronage of so important a district should fall into the hands of dissenters.

Stabback, William, *East Anstye,* r. corp. of Exeter. *St. Stephen,* r. bp. of Exeter. *Sancread,* v. dn. and ch. of Exon.

Stanhope, hon. F. H. R. *St. Buryan,* d. and r. *with St. Levan,* c. the King. *Cattan,* r. *Wressle,* v. lord Egremont.

Stawell, Wm. M. *Creacombe,* r. rev. W. Karslake. *Filleigh,* r. *with East Buckland,* r. earl Fortescue. *High-Bickington,* r. rev. W. Stawell.

Stevens, Robert, D.D. dn. of Rochester, preb. of Lincoln. *West Farleigh,* v. dn. and ch. of Rochester.

Stopford, hon. R. B. preb. of Hereford, can. of Windsor, chap. in ord. to H. M. *Barton Seagrave,* r. duke Buccleugh.

Strong, Philip, *Aston Abbots,* v. lord Chesterfield. *Colchester, St. Michael, Mile End,* r. *Myland,* r. countess de Grey.

Stubbin, N. J. *Higham,* v. *Offton,* r. *with Little Bricet,* c. *Somersham,* r. Trustees.

St. John, J. F. preb. of Worcester; *Chaddesden,* c. H. Gilbert. *Powick,* v. *Severnstoke,* r. lord Coventry. *Spondon,* v. *with Locker,* c. *and Standley,* c. D. W. Lowe.

Sumner, C. H. V. *Farmborough,* r. G. H. Sumner. *Newdigate,* r. lord chan. *Newington Butts, Trinity,* c. rec. of Newington.

Sumner, Charles Rich. D.D. bishop of Winchester, sub-dean of Canterbury, prelate of the order of the garter, and visitor of Winchester College.

The right rev. prelate being visitor of Winchester College it may not be improper to call the attention of his lordship to the abuses which have crept into the foundation, and which in the exercise of his power of inspection and superintendence he may have authority to reform. The college was founded by William of Wykham, in the fourteenth century, and, like that of Eton, intended for the education of seventy " poor and indigent scholars." So careful was the founder to confine the benefits of his institution entirely to the *poor,* that the boys, when they attain the age of fifteen, solemnly swear they have not *three pounds six shillings* a year to spend; and it is expressly ordered, if ever any scholar come into the possession of property to the amount of five pounds a year, he shall be expelled. The management of the college is vested in the warden, the bishop of Hereford, and ten reverend divines, termed " fellows," subject to the visitation of the bishop of Winchester. The warden, fellows, and scholars, all swear to observe the statutes, " according to their plain, literal, grammatical sense and understanding." Peculiar privileges are secured to the founder's kin, ten or twelve of whom were lately upon the foundation. The revenue of the college amounts to about £14,000, and the expenditure to £11,000. The value of a fellowship, according to the evidence of Mr. Williams, is four or five hundred pounds a year, with meat and drink gratis in the college; also the use of knives, forks, plates, and as many church livings as they can obtain. The emoluments of a warden are double those of a fellow, with travelling expenses, &c. The scholars are chosen yearly, by six electors; their ordinary fare is bread and butter to breakfast: beef, bread, and cheese to dinner; mutton, bread, and cheese to supper, with beer at every meal. They have no spoons, knives, nor forks, nor vegetables of any sort, *allowed by the statutes,* but they have salt and wooden trenchers found, and one gown is given annually to each scholar for clothing. The allowance for the sustentation of the boys may be varied agreeably to the statutes, according to the price of corn and provisions.

Such we collect from the Third Report of the Education Committee, to be the history and nature of this foundation, which has been very strangely perverted and abused. First, instead of the scholars being "poor and indigent," they are all children of *opulent persons;* some, we suspect, of noble families, who, at the time they solemnly swear they have not *three pounds six shillings* a year to spend, are paying ten guineas a year to the masters, and the average of their other expenses exceeds fifty. By a liberal translation of the warden, who has sworn to observe the statutes according to their *literal and grammatical sense, one hundred shillings* are considered equal to £66 : 13 : 4. It is strictly enjoined that no boy shall be admitted above twelve years of age. This is wholly disregarded. The incomes of the fellowships are augmented to four or five hundred pounds a year, by a liberal interpretation of the term describing their money payments : while the strictest construction is adopted towards the scholars and founder's kin ; the latter continuing only to receive their old statutable allowance of *forty shillings a year*. Thus, too, while the scholars are refused the convenience of knives, forks, spoons, plates, &c. on the ground that such articles of furniture were unknown in the time of William of Wykham, the fellows are allowed those accommodations, although the fellowships were endowed at the same early period. That a surplus revenue of three or four thousand pounds may be divided betwixt the warden and fellows, the parents of the scholars pay between sixty and seventy pounds a year for their education ; although it was intended by the founder they should be instructed and maintained gratuitously.

During the inquiries of the Education Committee, a singular sort of delicacy was manifested by the heads of this college to screen the abuses of the institution from investigation. They affected to be extremely willing to give every possible information relative to the college ; but unfortunately they had sworn, conformably to the statutes, not to disclose the *private affairs* of the college ; and until their scruples relative to this *moral and religious obligation* were removed, they could not, forsooth, submit their concerns to the investigation of the commtttee. Now, this would have been all well enough, had it not been notorious that the warden and fellows, on every occasion, when it suited their interest, had shown the greatest contempt both for the oaths and ordinances of the founder ; nay, with so little respect had these precious relics been treated by the reverend hypocrites, who affected to be suddenly seized with a profound veneration for them, that they had been left exposed to the boys of the school, who scrawled upon them whatever nonsense they pleased. But the truth is, they wished to avoid inquiry,—as well they might ; and they attempted to play off the same artifice on the committee, in the construction of the statutes, which enabled them to deprive the scholars of knives, forks, vegetables, and the kinsmen of the founder of their yearly incomes.

Sumner, John Bird, D.D. bishop of Chester, *with Waverton,* r. annexed, preb. of Durham.

Surtees, J. preb. of Bristol; *Banham,* r. The King.　*Bristol, St. Augustine,* v. *and St. Mark,* c. lord Chanc.　*Taverham,* 1*st and* 2*d Mediety,* r. bp. Norwich and Mrs. Branthwayte alt.

　Brother-in-law of lord Eldon.　For another brother-in-law of the ex-chancellor see M. V. Surtees, *List of Places.*

Sutton, Charles, D.D. *Aldeburgh,* r. duke Norfolk.　*Holme* (near the Sea) v. *with Bishops Thornham,* v. bp. of Norwich.　*Norwich, St. Geo. Tombla,* r. bp. of Ely.

Sutton, E. L. one of the six preach. of Canterbury, and chaplain to the House of Commons; *High Halden,* r. *St. Peter's,* v. abp. of Cant.

Sutton, Robert, preb. of Ripon; *Falford,* c. York, *St. Michael in Spurrier Gate,* alias *St. Michael at Ousebridge,* r. lord Chan.

Sutton, T. M. preb. of Westminster, and chaplain to the House of Commons; *Great Chart,* r. *Tunstall,* r. abp. of Cant.

　Other Suttons are in the church, with one or two livings. Most of them, but we cannot discover how many, are related to the late primate Sutton, whose mode of disposing of church patronage has been described, page 26. The archbishop, like many other *noble persons*, was indebted for his education to the Charter House, which opulent foundation was intended only for the "*maintenance and education of* POORE CHILDREN," and "the relief of poore, fatherless, decrepit, aged, sick, infirm, and impotent persons." On entering holy orders, his grace obtained some ecclesiastical preferment, and soon after, by his affinity to the Rutland family, was raised to the see of Norwich, with which dignity he was permitted to hold the deanery of Windsor. On the death of archbishop Moore, in 1804, his lordship, by the special favour of George III., was elevated to the primacy. It is observable that a short time before the following panegyric on his grace appeared in the *Pursuits of Literature*, a work ascribed to Mr. Mathias, privy clerk to queen Charlotte:—"He is a prelate whose amiable demeanour, useful learning, and conciliating habits of life, particularly recommend his episcopal character. No man appears to me so peculiarly marked out for the highest dignity of the church, *sede vacante*, as Dr. SUTTON." This puff direct, and the writer, availing himself of those opportunites which his situation afforded, is supposed to have materially contributed to the sudden exaltation of the archbishop. The patronage of the archbishopric is 131 livings, an archdeaconry, and three prebends. Out of this fund his grace was enabled to provide comfortably for his numerous offspring.

Swainson, C. preb. of Hereford; *Clunn*, v. *with Bettws*, c. *Edgton*, c. *Llanvair Waterdine*, c. *and Shipton*, c. earl Powis.

Swan, Francis, *Kirton*, v. *with Brothertoft*, c. Mercers' Comp. Lond. *Lincoln, St. Pet. Arc.* r. *and at Goats*, p. c. Prebendary. *Winteringham*, r. rev. J. L. Saville.

Tanqueray, Edward, *Ridgmont*, v. Sequest. *Tampsford*, r. the King. *Tingrith*, r. Mr. Treven.

Taylor, C. D.D. preb. of Hereford and chanc. of the dio. Hereford; *Madley*, v. *with Tibberton*, c. *Stanton, St. Michael*, v. dn. and ch. Hereford.

Templer, G. H. preb. of Wells; *Shapwick*, v. Incumbent. *Thornford*, r. Mrs. Sampson.

Tennyson, G. D.D. *Benningworth*, r. R. Ainstie. *Great Grimsby, St. James*, v. *and St. Mary*, v. G. R. Heneage. *Somersby*, r. R. Burton.

Thackeray, J. R. *Downham Market*, r. Miss Franks. *Hadley*, d. J. Penny. *Wiggenhall, St. Mary Magdalen*, v. Mrs. Gorforth.

Thompson, John B. *Luddesdown*, r. rev. Dr. R. Thompson. *Shropham*, v. Corp. of Norwich. *Thompson*, c. S. Hethersett.

Thornhill, John, *Cockfield*, r. *Staindrop*, r. marquis Cleveland. *Middleton in Teesdale*, r. the King.

Thorpe, C. archdeacon of Durham; vice Prosser, resigned.

Thurlow, Edward S. preb. of Norwich; *Eastwn*, r. *Stamfordham*, v. lord Chanc. *Houghton-le-Spring*, r. bp. of Durham.

Three more Thurlows in the church, one a pluralist. Houghton-le-Spring, next to Brentford, is the highest valuation in the king's book, and rated at £124. The *pedigree* of these preferments will be seen by referring to Thurlow in our *Place List*.

Thynne, lord John, preb. of Westminster; *Backwell*, r. *Kingston Deverill*, r. *Street*, r. *with Walton*, c. marquis of Bath. Third son of the patron and son-in-law of the rev. C. C. Beresford.

Tickell, John A. *Castle Acre*, v. T. W. Coke. *Hempstead*, near *Holt*, v. *Wighton*, v. dn. and ch. of Norwich.

Timbrill, J. D.D. archdn. of Gloucester, *with Dursley*, r. annexed, *Beckford*, v. *with Alston Underhill*, c. *Bradforton*, v. *with Aldington*, c. rev. Dr. Timbrell.

Tredcroft, Robert, preb. of Chichester; *Fittleworth*, v. bp. of Chichester. *Tangmere*, r. duke Richmond. *West Ichenor*, r. lord Chanc.

Trevelyan, Walter, preb. of Wells; *.Henbury*, v. *with Aust*, c. and *Northwick*, c. lord Middleton. *Nettlecombe*, r. sir J. Trevelyan.

Treweeke, George, *Illogan*, r. lord de Dunstanville. *Manselgamage*, v. *St. Menver*, v. sir J. G. Cotterell.

Trivett, W. *Arlington*, v. *Willingdon*, r. Chichester Cath. *Ashburnham, with Penshurst*, r. dn. and ch. of Cant. *Bradwell*, r. the King.

Turner, Richard, preb. of Lincoln; *Great Yarmouth*, p. c. dn. and ch. of Norwich. *Ormesby*, *St. Margaret*, v. *and St. Michael*, v. *with Scroteby*, c. *Swelling*, r. Incumbent.

Turner, Samuel, *Attenborough*, v. *with Bramcote*, r. F. Foljambe. *Nettleton*, r. rev. W. Jackson. *Rothwell*, r. lord Middleton. *Tealby*, v. G. Tennyson.

Turton, Thomas, dn. of Peterborough, preb. of Lincoln, reg. prof. of div. Cambridge. *Somersham*, r. *with Coln St. Helen*, c. *and Pidley*, c. annexed; *Gimmingham*, r. *with Trunch*, r. Cath. Hall, Camb.

Underwood, T. can. res. of Hereford. *Lugwardine*, v. *with Bartestry*, c. *Dewchurch*, c. *Hentland*, c. *Langarrow*, c. *and St. Veep Wennard*, c. dn. and ch. of Hereford. *Ross*, r. and v. bp. of Hereford.

Van Mildert, W., D.D. bishop of Durham and custos rotulorum.

Vansittart, W., DD. preb. of Carlisle, master of Wigston's Hosp. Leicester. *Waltham Abbas, with Shottesbrook*, r. A. Vansittart.

Vernon-Harcourt, hon. Edward Venables, primate of England, and lord almoner to the King.

Vernon, hon. J. S. V. preb. of Southwell. *Barton in Fabis*, r. abp. of York.

Vernon, L. V. chan. of the church of York, archdn. of Cleveland. *Kirby in Cleveland*, sinecure, r. *Stainton, St. Winifrid*, v. *Stokesley*, r. abp. of York.

Vernon, W. Venables, can. res. of York. *Etton*, r. *Wheldrake*, r. abp. of York.

Six more Vernons, with valuable preferments. They belong to the family of the archbishop of York. The Venables are also relations of the archbishop. The right rev. prelate is the younger son of the late lord Vernon by his third wife, the sister of the first lord Harcourt. He married a sister of the marquis of Stafford, by whom he has several children, all well provided in church and state. The first preferment of the bishop was a canonry in Christchurch; he was next advanced to the bishopric of Carlisle, on the removal of Douglas to Salisbury; and, in 1807, he succeeded Markham in the see of York. The patronage of his grace is 80 livings, 50 prebends, besides precentorships and sub-deaconries. We subjoin the following estimate of the gleanings of the archbishop and *five* sons during his primacy :—

Revenues of the archdiocese, 23 years	£26,000 —	598,000
L. Vernon, chancellorship, prebend, and two rectories, 10 years	3,000	30,000
W. Vernon, prebend and three rectories, 10 years	2,500	25,000
C. Vernon, one rectory, 10 years..............	2,000	20,000
G. Vernon, chancellor of diocese	1,800	1800
E. Vernon, registrar of diocese................	2,000	2000
	£37,300	676,800

Vevers, Richard, *Saxby*, r. lord Harborough. *Stoke Albany*, r. *Wilbarston*, v. lord Sondes.

Vevers, R. W. *Coates*, v. sequestrated. *Marton*, v. bp. of Lincoln. *Somershall*, r. lord Chesterfield.

Vincent, Wm. preb. of Chichester, *London, Allhallows, Great and Less*, r. abp. of Cant.

Son of the late Dr. Vincent, head-master of Westminster school, dean of Westminster, King's chaplain, and rector of Allhallows. The son has apparently succeeded to most of his father's preferments. The doctor was patronized by lord Sidmouth, from whom he received a prebend in the collegiate church of Westminster. He preached and published several *loyal sermons*, which were carefully distributed by the Association for the " Protection of Property," at the Crown and Anchor Tavern.

Vivian, J. W., D.D. min. can. of St. Paul's. *London, St. Austin and St. Faith*, r. *Mucking*, v. dn. and ch. of St. Paul's.

Wakeham, H. *Culford*, r. *with Ingham*, r. *and Timworth*, r. bp. of Lich. and Cov.

Walker, A. J. *Bishops Stone*, r. *Llangua*, r. *Yazer*, v. U. Price.

Walpole, Robert, *Itteringham*, r. *with Mannington*, r. lord Orford. *St. Mary-le-bone, Christchurch*, d. r. the King.

Ward, Wm. D.D. bishop of Sodor and Man, preb. of Sarum. *Great Horkesley*, r. countess de Grey.

Warneford, S. W., D.D. *Burton on the Hill*, r. *with Moreton in Marsh*, c. *and Lower Slaughter*, c. *Liddiard Millicent*, r. rev. Dr. Warneford.

Warren, J. dean of Bangor.

Watson, J. J., D. D. archdn. of St. Alban's, preb. of St. Paul's. *Digswell*, r. Incumbent. *Hackney*, r. S. Tyssen.

Watson, Richard, preb. of Wells and Llandaff. *Dingestow*, v. *with Tregan*, c. arch. and ch. Llandaff. *Penrice*, v. *Undy*, v. bp. Llandaff.

Watson, Robert, *Barlavington*, r. *South Bradon*, sinecure, r. lord Egremont. *Egdean*, r. *Hardham*, r. sir G. F. Goring.

These Watsons are relicts of the late Dr. Watson, bishop of Landaff, archdeacon of Ely, rector of Knoptoft, professor of divinity in Cambridge, with the rectory of Somersham, in Huntingdonshire, annexed. The bishop had been tutor to the late duke of Rutland, who gave him the rectory of Knoptoft, and next exerted his influence for his advancement to the bishopric of Landaff. Here the prelate became stationary : his politics did not exactly accord with the Toryism of George III., and the doctrines advanced by him in the American war and during the French Revolution, prevented his translation to a richer see. Neither his ambition nor cupidity, however, appear to have been less than those of his brethren. In the *Posthumous Memoirs* published by his son, he complains bitterly that his " public services" had not been sufficiently rewarded, though possessed of the numerous preferments mentioned. He also declaims lustily against the statesmen of his time, declaring that they " sacrificed their public principles to private ends, and their honour to their ambition," and that their " patriotism was merely a selfish struggle for power." In the latter opinions all men had reason to concur, unless those blinded by prejudice or personal attachment.

Webb, Richard, min. can. of St. Paul's, Westminster, and Windsor. *Kensworth*, v. dn. and can. of St. Paul's.

One might exhibit a curious and authentic account of the private history of this minor canon of three churches ; but we wish to avoid *personal* details relative to the clergy. First, because to enter into the private history of the clergy would far exceed our limits. Secondly, because we had not materials for so doing, unless we chose to rely on reports and statements which we had no means of verifying. Lastly, and this is our principal reason, the best authenticated private details serve only to expose individuals, not the system ; whereas our object has constantly been to expose the system, not the individuals composing it. As a body, no doubt the clergy have improved in external demeanor as well as other classes of the community. Modern manners do not sanction the gross vices which were common forty or fifty years ago ; and for sake of social intercourse the priesthood have found it necessary to conform to the altered fashion of the times. The clergy, therefore, do not frequently come intoxicated to church, nor reel into the streets in open day-light : still some of them, according to Mr. Beverly, continue addicted to hard drinking. " I have been acquainted," says he, " with drunken clergymen at Cambridge, and the intoxication of one, in particular, was so remarkable, that I have often wondered how he was able to clear his head for the Sunday morning's duty, after the Saturday night's debauch. I state it also as a notorious fact, that at the present moment there are priests in that University remarkable for their intemperate habits. There was in existence, within these five years, a clerical club, consisting of not more than six members, who used to meet at a tavern every Sunday evening, after their days' labours, and indulge in compotations worthy of the hard-drinking parsons of Queen Anne's reign."

Webber, Charles, archdn. and can. res. of Chichester. *Amport*, v. *with Appleshaw*, c. dn. and ch. of Chichester.
Webber, E. *Bathealton*, r. bp. of Bath. *Runnington*, r. the King. *Thorne, St. Margaret*, c. archdn. of Taunton.
Webber, James, preb. of Westminster, dn. of Ripon. *Kirkham*, v. Christ Church, Oxon, *Westminster, St. Marg.* r. dn. and ch. of Westminster.
Welby, John Earle. *Haceby*, r. W. G. Welby. *Harston*, r. the King. *Stroxton*, r. sir J. E. Welby. *West Allington*, r. dn. and ch. of Exon.
Welfitt, William, D.D. preb. of Canterbury. *Elmstead*, v. *Hastingleigh*, r. abp. of Cant. *Ticehurst*, v. dn. and ch. of Cant.
Wellesley, hon. G. V., D.D. preb. of Durham, chap. in ord. to H. M. *Bishop's Wearmouth*, r. bp. of Durham. *Chelsea*, r. lord Cadogan. *Therfield*, r. dn. and ch. of St. Paul's.
Brother of lady Ann Culling Smith, and the Duke of Wellington, whom see in our *Place List.*
Wells, George, preb. of Chichester. *Billinghurst*, v. sir H. Goring. *Wilson*, r. C. Goring.

Westcombe, Thomas, min. can. of Winton. *Preston, Candover,* v. *with Nutley,* c. dn. and ch. of Winton. *Winchester, St. Peter Stoke,* r. *with St. John,* r. lord Chan.

Weston, C. F. *Melton Ross,* p. c. Prebendary. *Ruckland,* r. *with Farforth,* r. *and Marden Well,* c. lord Yarborough. *Somerby,* r. *with Bagenderby,* r. the King.

Wetherell, Henry, archdn. of Hereford and preb. of Gloucester. *Kentchurch,* r. the King. *Kingstone,* v. dn. of Hereford.

Whichcote, Francis, *Aswardby,* r. *Deeping, St. James,* v. *Swarby,* v. sir T. Whichcote.

Whinfield, H. *Battlesdon,* r. *with Potsgrove,* r. sir G. P. Turner. *Tyringham,* r. *with Filgrave,* r. Wm. Praed.

Whalley, R. T. preb. of Wells. *Ilchester,* r. *Yeovilton,* r. bp. of Bath.

Whistler, W. W. *Hastings, All Saints,* r. *and St. Clements,* r. sir G. Webster. *Newtimber,* r. N. Newnham.

Whitcombe, Francis, *Ferring,* v. Prebendary. *Lodsworth,* c. S. W. Poyntz. *Stanlake,* r. Magdalen Coll.

White, Henry, vic. of Lichfield Cath. *Chebsea,* v. *Dilhorn,* v. *Ridware Pipe,* c. dn. and ch. of Lichfield.

Whittingham, Paul, min. can. of Norwich. *Martham,* v. *Norwich, St. Saviour,* r. *Sedgford,* v. dn. and ch. of Norwich.

Wickham, Thomas, preb. of Sarum. *North Newington,* v. *with Little Knoyle,* c. preb. of Sarum Cath. *Yatton,* v. *with Kenn,* c. preb. of Yatton.

Wilkins, G., D.D. preb. of Southwell. *Lowdham,* v. *Nottingham, St. Mary,* v. *and St. Paul,* c. *Snenton,* p. c. Earl Manvers. *Wing,* r. lord Chan.

Wilkinson, W. F. *East Harling,* r. W. F. Wilkinson. *North Walsham,* v. *with Antingham, St. Margaret,* r. Queen's Coll. Cam. *Norwich, St. Benedict,* c. *and St. Laurence.* r. Parishioners.

Wilkinson, M. W. *Harescombe,* r. *with Pitchcombe,* r. Mrs. Parnell. *Redgrave,* r. G. St. Wilson. *Uley,* r. lord Chan.

Willoughby, H. P. *Birthorpe,* r. *Burythorpe,* c. lord Chan.

Wingfield, Thomas, *Stapleford,* v. *Teigh,* r. lord Harborough. *Tickencote,* r. J. Wingfield.

Wintle, Robert, preb. of St. Paul's. *Compton Beauchamp,* r. Mr. Wright. *Culham,* v. bp. of Oxford.

Wodehouse, hon. A. *Bixton,* r. *East and West Lexham,* r. *with Litchans,* r. *Kimberley,* v. *with Barnham Broom,* r. lord Wodehouse.

Wodehouse, C. N. preb. of Norwich. *Geldestone,* r. lord Chan. *Murningthorpe,* r. the King.

Wodehouse, Thomas, can. res. of Wells. *Norton,* r. *Stourmouth,* r bp. of Rochester.

Wodehouse, hon. W. *Carlton Forehoe,* r. lord Wodehouse. *Hingham* r. *Falmouth,* r. hon. and rev. W. Wodehouse.

The hon. and rev. A. Wodehouse, who has four rectories and a vicarage, is the son of lord Wodehouse, the patron, and son-in-law of sir T. Beauchamp.

Proctor. W. Wodehouse is another son of the noble lord. Several more of the family are well provided in church or state, but a notice of them does not belong to our present subject.

Wollen, W., D. D. *Bridgewater*, v. *with Chilton Trinity*, v. *Kilton*, v. the King.

Wood, George, *Cann. St. Rumbold*, r. *Dorchester, Trinity*, v. *Shaftesbury, St. Rumbold*, r. lord Shaftesbury.

Wood, J., D.D. dean of Ely. *Freshwater*, r. St. John's Coll. Camb.

Wood, Peter, preb. of Chichester. *Broadwater*, r. *Rusper*, r. Mr. Wood.

Worsley, Ralph, sub-dean of Ripon. *Finchley*, r. bp. of London. *Little Ponton*, r. rev. Dr. Dowdeswell.

Woodcock, H. preb. of Sarum, can. of Christ Church. *Longparish, or Middleton Prebend*, lady Churchill. *Michaelmarsh*, r. bp. of Winton.

Woodhouse, J. C. dn. of Lichfield and Coventry.

Woodward, W. P. preb. of Chichester. *Plumpton*, r. Mrs. Woodward. *West Grinstead*, r. Mr. Woodward.

Woolcombe, Henry, *Ashbury*, r. the King. *High Hampton*, r. J. M. Woolcombe. *Pillaton*, r. W. Helgar.

Worsley, H., D.D. *Gatcomb*, r. Mr. Campbell. *St. Lawrence*, r. hon. C. A. Pelham. *Woolverton*, r. Messrs. R. and J. Clarke.

Wrangham, Francis, archdn. of East Riding of York and preb. of York and Chester. *Dodleston*, r. dn. and ch. of Chester. *Hunmanby*, v. *with Fordon*, c. *Muston*, v. H. S. Osbaldeston.

Wrench, J. G., D.C.L. *Blakeney*, c. Haberdashers' Comp. London. *Salehurst*, v. S. Micklethwait. *Stowting*, r. rev. Dr. Wrench.

Wrey, B. W. *Combintenhead*, r. *Tawstock*, r. *Temple Imp.* c. sir B. Wrey.

Wright, Thomas, *East Claydon*, v. *Middle*, r. *and Steeple*, v. Mr. Vacknell.

Wyndham, T. T., D.D. *Hinton Admiral*, p. c. G. J. Topps. *Melcombe*, r. *with Radipole*, c. W. Wyndham. *Pimperne*, r. lord Rivers.

Yonge, Denys, *East Anthony*, v. R. Carewe. *West Putford*, r. lord Clinton. *Willoughton*, v. King's Coll. and lord Scarborough, alt.

Yonge, James, *Cockington*, c. *Tormoham*, c. rev. R. Mallock. *Stockley Pomeroy*, r. bp. of Exeter.

Yonge, William, Chan. of d. of Norwich. *Hillburgh*, r. earl Nelson. *Swaffham*, v. *with Threxton*, r. bp. of Norwich.

Several more *Yonges* in the church. They are, by marriage, relations of earl Nelson, prebendary of Canterbury, and a pensioner to the amount of £5000 per annum.

VALUATION OF SEES AND DIGNITIES IN THE KING'S BOOK.

THE only authentic return of the amount of church revenues is the *Valor Eccle-siasticus*, of the time of Henry VIII. This document is incomplete even for the period it was obtained, many deaneries and ecclesiastical dignities having been omitted ; and it is still less applicable to the present, owing to the vast alteration in the value of land and tithe. Still it is the only authentic basis for estimating the value of sees and dignities ; and, aided by information from other sources, we may form an estimate of the incomes of the bishops, deans, archdeacons, precentors, chancellors, and other cathedral and diocesan officials.

In the parliamentary session of 1830, Dr. Lushington admitted the income of the See of Canterbury amounted to £32,000, and the bishop of London admitted his income amounted to about £15,000. Thus it appears from the subjoined table of the valuations in *Liber Regis* that these sees have increased in value twelve and fourteen fold. The revenues of other sees and dignities being derived from sources similar to those of Canterbury and London, the incomes of any of the bishoprics, dignities, and offices in the subjoined statement may be calculated to have augmented in a similar ratio. In some instances we have only been able to insert the *year* when the dignity was received by the present possessor ; the value not being returned in the King's Book.

If churchmen demur to our mode of calculating their incomes, our reply is— let us have an authentic and authorised return of the amount of ecclesiastical revenues. Till then we must depend on collateral and inferential evidence.

King's Book.

Canterbury :

Archbishop	£2682	12	2
Dean	1827		
Archdeacon	163	1	10

Prebendaries.

Wm. Welfitt	1786
Geo. Moore	1795
Chas. Norris	1799
Earl Nelson	1803
Robt. Moore	1804
Walt. Brown	1804
J. E. Boscawen	1822
Archdn. Croft	1822
W. F. Baylay	1826
John Russell	1827
J. Hume Spry	1828
John Peel	1828

York :

Archbishop	1610	0	0
Dean	308	10	7
Chancellor of the Church	85	6	8
Precentor	96	4	2

King's Book.

Sub-dean	£50	14	2
Succentor	8	0	0

Archdeacons.

Robt. Markham	90	3	1
Fras. Wrangham	62	14	7
L. Ver. Harcourt	36	0	10
Wm. Barrow	61	0	10

Canons Residentiary.

Archdeacon Markham	82	11	3
W. Ver.-Harcourt	40	0	1
Charles Hawkins	14	8	4
W. H. Dixon	32	10	5

Prebendaries.

Hon. J. Lumley Savile	14	9	9
H. Kitchingman	17	17	1
Samuel Smith	9	17	1
Lamplugh Hird	17	17	1
Hon. A. Cathcart	43	19	1
Robert Affleck	2	17	1
W. R. Hay	19	10	10
Edward Otter	34	11	8
William Preston	14	8	9
R. Carey	42	17	1

	£	s	d
Hon. H. E. J. Howard ..	11	3	9
Archd. Wrangham	35	0	0
Dean of Wells	6	0	0
Walter Fletcher	34	7	3
John Bull..............	37	15	5
Theophilus Barnes	38	16	0
Dean of Norwich........	65	16	0
Charles W. Eyre........	74	7	1
G. P. Marriott..........	32	13	4
Henry John Todd	38	17	11
Henry Markham........	10	2	6
Hammond Roberson	8	0	0
John Lowe	33	11	8
T. Hutton Croft	47	16	3
G. H. Vernon, *Chanc.* 1818			

Lonton:

	£	s	d
Bishop	1000	0	0
Dean	210	12	0
Chancellor	33	0	0
Precentor	46	7	6
Treasurer..............	37	0	0

Archdeacons.

	£	s	d
G. O. Cambridge........	60	0	0
Jos. Holden Pott	23	13	4
I. J. Watson 1816			
Hugh C. Jones..........	52	0	0
W. Rowe Lyall..........	50	0	9

Canons Residentiary.

	£	s	d
Very Rev. the Dean	10	5	0
Thos. Hughes	6	0	0
F. W. Blomberg	7	17	1
Sydney Smith	7	13	4

Prebendaries of St. Paul's.

	£	s	d
William Gibson	8	6	8
Robert Watts	5	15	10
Dean of Winchester	10	2	6
Thomas Wintle	12	0	0
George Secker..........	13	13	4
William Wood..........	6	0	0
Richard Lendon	7	1	3
Thomas Randolph	34	8	9
W. S. Goddard ········	8	6	8
Bishop of Carlisle	39	13	4
A. R. Chauvel..........	28	15	10
Samuel Birch	5	6	8
John H. Randolph	5	6	8
Archdeacon Pott........	19	17	6
John Sleath	5	6	8
Dean of Christ Church ..	11	6	8
Archdeacon Watson	14	6	8
Sir Herb. Oakeley, Bt. ..	21	6	8
Jon. Tyers Barrett	12	0	0
H. Handley Norris......	8	5	5
C. E. J. Dering	46	0	0
Charles Wodsworth	5	6	8
William Hale Hale......	11	10	10
John Smith	17	19	2
T. Hartwell Horne	13	6	8
John Lonsdale..........	28	0	0

Minor Canons of St. Paul's.

	£	s	d
H. Fly, *Sub-dn. & 1st Can.*	24	17	11
H. J. Knapp.... 2d do ..	20	6	3
W. Holmes...... 3d do ..	20	6	3
R. H. Barham .. 4th do..	13	16	5
W. J. Hall...... 5th do..	15	9	9
J. W. Vivian.... 6th do..	16	15	11
J. Lupton ...... 7th do..	15	9	9
J. T. Bennett ... 8th do..	17	11	8
R. C. Packman.. 9th do..	14	9	9
E.G.A.Beckwith 10th do..	16	16	8
E. J. Beckwith..11th do..	13	10	10
C. Packe ......12th do..	13	8	6
S. Lushington, *Chancellor* 1828			

Durham:

	£	s	d
Bishop 1821	1	2	
Dean, Bishop of St. David's 1827			

Prebendaries.

David Durell................	1801
Bishop of Bristol	1804
R. Prosser	1804
Bishop of Chester.............	1820
J. Savile Ogle	1820
Th. Gisborne	1823
G. Townsend.................	1825
Wm. S. Gilly	1826
G. V. Wellesley.............	1827
Charles Thorp	1829
Bishop of Exeter	1831
Samuel Smith	1831

Archdeacons.

	£	s	d
C. Thorpe..............	100	0	0
Thos. Singleton	36	13	4

Winchester:

	£	s	d
Bishop 2873	18	1	
Dean, Thomas Rennell.........1805			

Prebendaries.

Edm. Poulter	1791
Robt. Barnard	1793
Lord Walsingham..............	1807
Geo. F. Nott	1810
W. Harrison	1820
Rd. Cockburn	1825
G. Pretyman	1825
Ch. Richards.................	1827
Edw. James	1828
Wm. Dealtry	1830
William Vaux	1831
Thos. Garnier................	1831

Archdeacons.

	£	s	d
Lord Walsingham	91	3	6
Ven. Chas. J. Hoare	67	15	2

Bangor:

	£	s	d
Bishop 1830			
Dean	22	17	3
Chancellor	0	3	4
Precentor..............	0	4	2

	£	s	d
Treasurer	0	18	9
Archdeacon	13	3	4
Prebendaries.			
Henry Warren	29	16	8
H. W. Majendie	8	5	7
Canons.			
T. Roberts ....1st Can...	0	3	4
R. Williams ..2d do....	0	3	4
R. Newcome ..3d do....	0	3	4
Senior Vicar Choral.... }	17	0	5
Junior Vicar Choral.... }			

𝕭at𝔥 and 𝖂ells:

	£	s	d
Bishop	533	1	3
Dean and Canon Res....	121	7	6
Sub-dean of Wells	21	15	7
Chancellor of the Church	40	5	0
Precentor	24	6	3
Treasurer	62	2	3
Archdeacons.			
Henry Law	144	2	11
C. A. Moysey	25	15	0
A. Hamilton	83	7	6
Canons Res. of Wells.			
Henry Gould	4	0	0
Frederick Beadon	24	0	0
Thos. Wodehouse	4	0	0
Ch. Henry Pulsford	5	6	8
H. W. Barnard	42	0	4
Archdeacon Law	1828		
Prebendaries of Wells.			
W. F. Browne	7	16	3
Thomas Heberden	6	6	10
Hon. J. Marsham	7	0	0
Henry Parsons	6	13	4
J. Thos. Casberd	5	6	8
John Williams	7	14	4
Edward Willes	5	6	8
Brook H. Bridges	14	0	0
J. Watson Beadon	15	16	0
Edward Edgell	5	6	8
John Lukin	5	6	8
George H. Templer	5	6	8
Thomas Williams	5	6	8
Joseph Drury	22	8	9
J. W. Hoskins	5	6	8
W. Hen. Turner	5	6	8
Richard Watson	22	15	5
William Lucas	4	0	0
Francis Goforth	9	0	0
Charles Johnson	8	13	4
William Gimingham	5	6	8
R. P. Whish	7	9	9
Thomas S. Escott	4	0	0
Robert Forster	4	0	0
W. P. Thomas	1	0	0
Wad. Knatchbull	5	6	8
Francis Warre	5	6	8
Geo. M. Coleridge	20	10	0

	£	s	d
Master of Balliol	22	0	0
George Vanbrugh	4	13	4
Rob. Vanbrugh Law	11	13	4
Archdeacon Moysey	5	6	8
Henry Pepys	3	7	6
Miles Bland	5	6	8
Samuel Blackall	5	6	8
Chas. Edm. Keene	38	0	7
Archd. of Taunton	1	5	7
W. A. Fitzhugh	11	6	8
Henry Hoskins	6	12	1
William Bowe	22	0	0
W. B. Whitehead	11	4	2
Charles M. Mount	5	6	8

𝕭ristol:

	£	s	d
Bishop	£327	5	7
Dean, H. Beeke	1814		
Prebendaries.			
H. J. Ridley	1816		
William Bond	1818		
John Surtees	1821		
Lord W. Somerset	1822		
Samuel Lee	1831		
Henry Harvey	1831		
Archdeacon of Dorset....	82	12	8

𝕮arlisle:

	£	s	d
Bishop	£420	13	3
Dean, R. Hodgson	1820		
Prebendaries.			
Adn. Markham	1801		
S. J. Goodenough	1810		
W. Vansittart	1824		
Dean of Wells	1826		
Archdeacon, S. J. Goodenough	..1831		
Chancellor, W. Fletcher	1814		

𝕮hester:

	£	s	d
Bishop	£420	0	0
Dean, G. Davys	1831		
Prebendaries.			
Archd. Clarke	1801		
James Slade	1816		
Archdn. Wrangham	1825		
Wm. Ainger	1827		
G. B. Blomfield	1827		
Robt. V. Law	1829		
Archdeacons.			
Unwin Clarke	1801		
John Headlam	1826		

𝕮hichester:

	£	s	d
Bishop	677	5	3
Dean	58	9	4
Precentor	35	0	10
Chancellor of the Church	27	7	1
Treasurer	62	6	8

Archdeacons.

Charles Webber	38	3	4
Thomas Birch	39	15	0
Chancellor of the Diocese 1822			

Canons Residentiary.

Archdeacon Webber	16	13	6
Thomas Baker..........	12	0	0
Charles E. Hutchinson ..	10	0	0
Charles Webber, jun. 1829			

Canons Non-residents.

Thomas Heberden	11	17	4
Treasurer of Church	20	0	0
Chanc. of Church	8	0	0
R. Constable............	6	0	0
George Fred. Nott	18	13	4
James Capper	2	13	4
Barre Phipps..	4	15	0
Precent. of Church......	20	13	4
John G. Challen	11	0	0
William Woodward	13	0	0
Thomas Valintine	9	10	0
Charles Gray	13	6	8
Edmund Cartwright	16	10	5
Hugh James Rose	2	3	4
George H. Webber......	4	10	0
Peter Wood	18	6	8
George Shiffner	2	6	8
Edward Fulham	9	16	8
W. St. A. Vincent	10	0	0
J. Lettice	0	16	8
S. J. Tufnell............	0	10	0
Chancellor of Diocese....	4	6	8
R. Tredcroft............	2	13	4
Richard Bingham	10	2	8
David Williams	13	6	8
George Wells	10	5	0
Henry Atkins	9	16	8

𝕰𝖑𝖞:

Bishop................£2134	18	0	
Dean, James Wood 1820			

Prebendaries.

Archdeacon Cambridge 1795	
George L. Jenyns..............1802	
John H. Sparke................1818	
Henry Fardell 1819	
W. W. Childers................1824	
E. B. Sparke 1829	
Benj. Parke 1831	
Wm. French 1831	
Archdeacon 97 5 2	

𝕰𝖝𝖾𝖙𝖊𝖗:

Bishop, H. Phillpotts 1830			
Dean, W. Landon 158	0	0	

Canons Residentiary.

Precentor, Thomas Bartlam	99	13	4
Chanc. of the Ch., Adn. Potts	59	0	0

Treasurer, The Lord Bishop	32	7	3
Sub-dean, J. Parker Fisher	22	10	0

Archdeacons.

John Moore	60	15	10
R. H. Froude	37	19	7
John Sheepshanks	50	6	5
George Barnes..........	49	0	0
15 Prebendaries, £4 each.			

𝕲𝖑𝖔𝖚𝖈𝖊𝖘𝖙𝖊𝖗:

Bishop £315	7	3	
Dean, E. Rice 1825			

Prebendaries.

Hon. D. Finch 1792	
G. W. Hall....................1810	
T. Selwyn 1814	
E. Bankes 1821	
Adn. Wetherell..........,......1825	
J. H. Seymour 1829	
Archeacon 64 10 0	

𝕳𝖊𝖗𝖊𝖋𝖔𝖗𝖉:

Bishop £768	11	0	
Dean....................	38	6	3
Chancellor	14	3	4
Precentor..............	21	9	7
Treasurer	9	10	10

Archdeacons.

J. J. Corbett	32	10	10
Henry Wetherell........	41	17	11

Canons Residentiary.

T. Underwood	14	0	0
John Clutton	7	13	4
Hen. C. Hobart	1	17	8
H. H. Morgan..........	4	10	0
Arthur Matthews	3	0	5

Canons or Prebendaries.

John Wall	1	19	2
J. Walker Baugh	11	13	1
R. Wetherell	15	0	0
Love Robertson	28	12	6
Samuel Picart..........	7	1	0
Christ. Swainson........	12	10	0
Edward Barnard........	10	7	6
Hon. R. B. Stopford	17	18	1
James Garbett..........	7	10	0
Dean of St. Asaph	15	0	2
Henry Hoskins	11	6	8
H. Huntingford	15	5	0
Charles Taylor..........	20	0	0
Harry Lee	10	13	6
Archdeacon Clarke......	17	18	9
James Wetherell........	6	10	0
Hon. J. Somers Cocks ..	2	10	2
James Johnson	2	12	11
Fred. Twisleton	3	9	7
Hon. Hen. Rodney......	11	4	4
K. E. Money	15	5	0

	£	s.	d.
Dean of Hereford	2	7	8
John Clutton, jun.	2	3	4

𝕷𝖎𝖈𝖍𝖋𝖎𝖊𝖑𝖉 & 𝕮𝖔𝖛𝖊𝖓𝖙𝖗𝖞:

	£	s.	d.
Bishop	559	17	3
Dean of Lichfield	40	0	0
Precentor	40	0	0
Chancellor	40	13	1
Treasurer	56	13	4
J. Newling	34	0	0
Spencer Madan	23	0	0
Geo. Hodson	30	0	0
Archdeacons.			
Samuel Butler	26	13	4
William Spooner	45	9	2
Edward Bather	19	0	0
George Hodson	30	16	10½
Prebendaries of Lichfield.			
J. F. Muckleston	0	10	0
Dean of Bangor	8	0	0
Thomas Wythe	10	0	0
William Walker	10	11	5
Archdeacon Butler	2	3	4
W. G. Rowland	6	13	4
Sir Her. Oakeley, Bt.	2	0	0
Chancellor Law	1	0	0
Thomas Cotton Fell	13	6	8
Watson W. Dickins	10	0	0
T. R. Bromfield	0	3	4
Simeon Clayton	5	0	0
The Lord Bishop	20	0	0
John Kempthorne	2	13	4
Francis Blick	1	6	8
Archdeacon Spooner	2	0	0
Archdeacon Bather	2	13	4
J. F. Muckleston, *Succen*	14	0	10

𝕷𝖎𝖓𝖈𝖔𝖑𝖓:

	£	s.	d.
Bishop	824	4	9
Dean and Canon Res.	203	9	7
Archdeacons.			
Charles Goddard	179	19	2
H. Kaye Bonney	60	12	3
Henry V. Bayley	25	17	8
Justly Hill	87	14	7
J. B. Hollingworth	64	14	2
T. Kaye Bonney	87	19	2
Precentor	40	13	8
Chancellor of the Church	42	7	4
Sud-dean	2	8	4
Prebendaries.			
George Jepson	1	0	0
Maurice Johnson	3	0	0
William Hett	2	16	8
George Moore	32	0	0
John Humphrey	7	15	2
Richard Turner	25	6	4
L. C. Humphrey	33	18	6
Frederick Apthorpe	30	11	3

	£	s.	d.
George D. Kent	0	3	4
Robert Pointer	9	10	0
R. Williams	15	14	2
Archdeacon H. Bonney	45	3	3
James Cullum	14	10	0
W. W. Drake	7	7	6
John Pretyman	36	0	0
C. A. Wheelwright	12	18	9
C. Webb Le Bas	12	5	0
J. H. B. Mountain	16	10	2
Sir C. Anderson, Bt.			1812
Henry Craven, Ord.	21	13	1
Dean of Rochester	29	10	2
Archdeacon Goddard	36	3	4
J. Henry Batten	5	5	5
Charles Turnor	19	0	0
William Palmer	5	12	1
Edward Fane	19	14	2
John Bouverie	4	9	4
George Beckett	38	16	8
Henry Rycroft	22	13	4
Theodore Bouwens	26	7	3
Edward Edwards	13	13	11
Archdeacon of Stow	20	0	10
Archdeacon T. Bonney	5	5	3
Nathaniel Dodson	11	0	0
Francis Swan, jun.	9	3	5
Fred. Borradaile	7	3	4
Edward Warneford	24	0	0
The Lord Bishop	17	7	6
J. Hobart Seymour	27	6	3
Thomas Turton	20	0	0
Fras. V. Lockwood	12	10	0
John Maul	33	2	3
John Graham	4	0	0
Edward Smedley	11	19	7
Peter Fraser	10	19	2
(Vacant.) *Leighton*	68	16	0

𝕷𝖑𝖆𝖓𝖉𝖆𝖋𝖋:

	£	s.	d.
Bishop	154	14	2
Precentor	6	0	0
Chancellor	2	13	9
Treasurer	12	2	11
Archdeacon	38	12	8
Prebendaries.			
William Williams	1	6	8
John Fleming	4	0	0
W. B. M. Lisle	3	10	7
Richard Watson	3	5	5
John F. Parker	3	17	1
H. Handley Norris	1	3	4
J. Thomas Casberd	4	0	0
Thomas Gaisford	5	6	8
Edward James	0	18	1

𝕹𝖔𝖗𝖜𝖎𝖈𝖍:

	£	s.	d.
Bishop	834	11	7
Dean, George Pellew			1828

Prebendaries.
E. S. Thurlow 1788
J. Procter 1798
T. Methold..................1804
Philip Fisher................1814
C. N. Wodehouse............1817
Ed. Bankes 1820

Archdeacons.

J. Oldershaw	143	8	4
Henry Bathurst	71	1	3
H. D. Berners	89	2	1
George Glover	76	9	4

Oxford:
Bishop 381 11 0
Canons of Christ Church.
F. Barnes 1810
E. C. Dowdeswell.............1808
Hen. Woodcock...............1824
W. Buckland.................1825
E. B. Pusey 1828
Edw. Burton 1829
R. W. Jelf 1830
John Bull 1830
Archdeacon 71 6 0

Peterborough:
Bishop 414 17 8
Dean, T. Turton 1830
Prebendaries.
Spenc. Madan 1800
S. Pratt 1808
Wm. Tournay 1817
T. S. Hughes................1827
John James 1829
W. Macdouall 1831
Archdeacon 122 7 1
Chancellor.
Spenc. Madan 1794

Rochester:
Bishop 358 14 0
Dean, Stevens 1620
Prebendaries.
Hon. J. Marsham 1797
Hon. F. Hotham 1807
Matthew Irving.............1824
W. F. Baylay................1827
John Griffith 1827
Prov. of Oriel 1828
Archdeacon 34 14 9

Salisbury:

Bishop	1385	5	0
Dean and Canon Res.	204	10	0
Precentor	69	6	8
Chancellor of the Church.	56	6	10
Treasurer	101	3	1

Archdeacons.

John Fisher	54	18	6
Liscombe Clarke	70	11	8
W. Macdonald	64	18	9

Canons Residentiary.

T. H. Hume	101	3	1
Archd. Fisher	30	3	4
Archd. Macdonald	29	0	0
Matthew Marsh	35	16	3
Hon. F. P. Bouverie	43	12	6
W. L. Bowles	6	10	0
Subdean	1	13	4
Succentor	13	0	0

Prebendaries.

Archibald Alison	14	13	4
W J. Kerrich	19	10	0
Henry Hetley	7	0	0
John White	18	0	0
Francis Saunders	3	4	2
Jarvis Kenrick	63	13	4
Martin Whish	32	0	0
Prof. Civil Law, Oxford .	39	6	3
A. E. Howman	30	0	0
Bishop of Sodor and Man	25	16	0
Robert Morres	16	0	0
George Fred. Nott	20	0	0
John Salter	17	10	0
Henry Woodcock	18	16	8
Dean of Exeter	19	9	2
J. T. Hurlock	52	11	5
Archd. Onslow	62	0	0
William Fisher	50	0	0
Frederick Browning	36	0	0
John Still	35	15	5
Edward Fane	10	0	0
Thomas H. Mirehouse	24	5	10
H. W. Majendie	20	0	0
The Lord Bishop			
William Potchett	32	9	2
Edward Bouverie	17	0	0
John Bright	29	3	1
Archdeacon Clarke	28	19	2
G. A. Montgomery	8	0	0
Thomas Tyrwhitt	4	13	4
Charles Grove	2	0	0
Edw. C. Ogle	52	0	0
W. S. Goddard	22	5	7
Edward Berens	20	0	0
Herbert Hawes	32	1	10
George Stanley Faber	20	0	0
Francis Lear	5	0	1

St. Asaph:

Bishop	187	11	0
Archdeacon	74	15	7
Dn. and Chan. of Diocese.	45	11	5
Precentor	40	0	0
Chanc. of the Church....	37	13	4
Treasurer	18	6	8

Prebendaries.			
C. Robson	9	5	5
H. Horsley	9	5	5
J. H. M. Luxmoore	3	6	8

Cursal Canons.

Roger Clough	2	6	8
H. H. Edwards	2	6	8
Rowland Williams	2	6	8
J. Francis Cleaver	2	6	8
Rowland Wingfield	2	6	8
W. Williams	2	10	7
T. G. Roberts	2	6	8

St. David's:

Bishop	426	2	1
Precentor	20	6	10
Chanc. of the Church	17	17	1
Treasurer	24	18	6

Canons.

Preb. of, 5th Cursal	1800
Archdn. of Brecon	1805
Archdn. of Carmarthen	1810

Archdeacons.

St David's	56	8	8
Brecon	40	0	0
Cardigan	18	0	0
Carmarthen	16	0	0

Worcester:

Bishop	929	13
Dean of Rochester	1828	
James Meakin	1804	
F. St. John	1804	
Wm. Digby	1813	
Down. Forester	1815	
Henry A. Pye	1818	
John Davison	1825	
Christ. Benson	1825	
G. Faussett	1827	
Adn. Singleton	1829	
Hon. J. S. Cocks	1830	

Southwell Collegiate Chapter.

Prebendaries.

William Dealtry	5	2	0
Henry Smith	5	0	0
Archdn. Barrow	2	11	3
J. T. Becher	13	4	7
James Jarvis Cleaver	22	19	7
E. G. Marsh	9	17	11
Robert Chaplin	27	19	7
George Wilkins	22	6	0
Charles Nixon	1	2	6
Frederick Anson	24	10	0
John Rudd	8	17	6
C. Boothby	32	5	3
T. Percival	23	11	4
Fitzgerald Wintour	15	7	11
Thos. H. Shepherd	16	15	10
C. Vernon-Harcourt	48	1	3

Brecon Collegiate Chapter.

Prebendaries.

Bishop of St. David's	47	0	0
Precentor	18	0	0
Chancellor	34	0	0
H. Davies Morgan	7	0	7
W. Morgan	3	6	8
D. Williams	7	13	4
Richard Venables	1	6	8
Archdeacon Beynon	7	6	8
Archdeacon Payne	2	0	0
W. J. Rees	9	15	4
D. R. Allen	13	0	0
W. A. Barker	3	17	3
C. Griffith	5	0	0
J. Jones	12	9	4
J. Drake	6	13	4
J. Holcombe	10	0	0
Charles Thorp	5	8	9
Edward Owen	13	6	8
Jeremiah Jackson	1	7	1
J. Davies	12	0	0
John Hughes	7	6	8
L. Llewellin	15	0	0

CHURCH OF IRELAND.

HAVING, in the preceding chapter, given a detailed account of the general principles and management of the Church of England, it will not be requisite to be equally copious in our exposition of the Irish Protestant establishment.

In the past and present state of Ireland we have a striking illustration of the tendency of the government that is said to " *work well*," and the wretchedness of her population, her tithe-system, her vast tracts of land, either ill-cultivated or totally unproductive, her judicial and magisterial administration, her insurrections, factions, burnings, desolations, and bloody domestic outrages,—all symptomatic of a community entering on the first stages of civilization,—afford irrefragable proof of the excellencies of the good working government. In England, it is true, there are grievous abuses in the absorption of public money by the Aristocracy, in the denial of justice by the cost and uncertainty of legal decisions ;—in the tolerance of commercial monopolies, in corn-laws, partial taxation, and other oppressions ;—but these sink into insignificance when contrasted with the sufferings of Ireland. There the natural order of society has been inverted, and the government for many years existed, not for the benefit of the people, but the people existed solely for the benefit of the government.

Among the various forms under which oppression has been carried on, the most conspicuous is the Church Establishment ; one is at a loss to conceive for whose benefit this institution exists in Ireland. Is it for the benefit of the clergy, the people, or the state ? If by the former is meant those who minister religious instruction, it can hardly be said to be of advantage to them. The teachers of religion in Ireland are nearly all Catholics, a vast majority of the people are of the same persuasion, and what religion there is the expense is chiefly defrayed by voluntary contributions. Neither the really operative clergy, therefore, nor the people, benefit by the church establishment. With respect to the state, the advantage appears not less equivocal. The alliance betwixt *church* and *state* is founded on reciprocal benefits—that, on the one hand, the state shall give its civil protection to the church, and, on the other, the church shall aid in sustaining the state, by its influence over the people : —this is the basis of the compact ; and it follows, when the church loses its influence, when it loses the adherence of a majority of the population, when it is no longer able to sustain the state, the compact is dissolved ; it has no claim for protection, and its alliance becomes a source of weakness instead of power.

Such is the actual condition of the Irish church, such the advantages it confers on the government; it adds little to its authority, affords no aid to the civil magistrate, neither the law nor its ministers are rendered more sacred by its influence—quite the reverse. Authority is degraded and abhorred in Ireland, solely on account of the ecclesiastical establishment: it is the colossal grievance of the country, the source of all its factions, murmuring, and discontent. Why then, it may be asked, is the establishment maintained? On what principle or pretext is it justified? The godly cannot defend it from piety, the politician from reasons of state, nor the patriot for the blessings it confers on the community. Whose interest, then, is identified with the odious system? The only rational answer that can be given to this question is the fact, that there is, in Ireland, as in this country, an *oligarchical interest*, which has entwined itself round her institutions, and whose support is incompatible with public liberty and happiness. For many years Ireland was the prey of a favoured caste, a selfish and bigoted faction, who divided her as a spoil; and such was the wretched policy of the general government, that it was weak and unprincipled enough to avail itself of the folly and cupidity of such agents to preserve a precarious sovereignty—when, too, its frown would have made the same creatures, who were ready, at any time, to sacrifice their country for a pension or a place, instrumental to her greatness and welfare. Under the Wellington and Grey administrations attempts have been made to introduce a more impartial and enlightened system; with what success time must develope; but it is apparent, so long as her ecclesiastical establishment is continued—it is vain to expect contentment and tranquillity.[*]

The Irish branch of the United Church is more pregnant with abuses even than its sister establishment in England; presenting a more revolting spectacle of inordinate incomes, of lax discipline, of laborious duties without adequate remuneration, and of an immense ecclesiastical revenue levied under circumstances of greater insult, partiality, and oppression. The points most deserving attention in the exposition of these subjects are, *first*, the revenue of the Irish Protestant establishment; *secondly*, the number of individuals among whom this revenue is divided; *thirdly*, the hardships and impoverishment resulting not less from the amount than the mode in which the clerical income is

---

* While the Catholic religion maintains its influence over the popular mind, we esteem it quite impossible for any government permanently to maintain its authority without conciliating the priesthood. Lord Grey ought to make a provision for the Catholic clergy out of the tithes; or send over to Dublin his grace of Norfolk, or other popish viceroy, who believes with O'Connell in the *real presence*. The Irish proprietary, too, have evinced a singular want of political philosophy. The late lord Liverpool stated that nineteen-twentieths of the property of Ireland belonged to protestants; but how can they expect to enjoy their possessions in peace if they continue to differ from their peasantry in *points of faith*. A gentleman ought to be superior to the prejudices of sects whether Catholic or Protestant; in such matters it is best to follow the multitude, or those who cultivate his domains. Voltaire built a church for his neighbours at Ferney, and occasionally preached there.

levied; *fourthly*, the patronage of the Irish church; *lastly*, the diminutive portion of the population who derive even a semblance of benefit from the intolerable burthen imposed on the land and industry of the community. We shall touch on these several heads of inquiry as briefly as possible, confining ourselves strictly to such facts as illustrate the state of the church.

To begin with our first topic—*the Irish Church Revenue.* Within the last ten years a mass of important details has been laid before parliament relative to the estates and revenues of the Protestant establishment; but, either from inability or reluctance in the parties interested to communicate the requisite information, our knowledge is still far from complete and accurate on this interesting branch of public statistics. Upon the authority of documents so communicated we shall, however, in great part, found our exposition; and thus, by relying on the statements of the clergy themselves, their registrars, and other dependent officials, we shall at least avoid the imputation of having arrived, through a prejudiced medium, at an exaggerated result.

We shall commence with the revenues of the Episcopal Clergy. The incomes of the bishops are derived principally from land, but partly from tithe. In some dioceses, in the West of Ireland, *a fourth part of the tithes* of almost every parish is paid to the bishop; affording decisive testimony of the ancient fourfold division of parochial tithes, and of the veracity of the allegation of those who affirm that the poor were formerly entitled to share equally with the bishop and priest in the produce of this impost. The practice, however, is not universal; and the revenues of the bishoprics chiefly arise from their immense landed estates. In the session of 1824, returns were made to parliament of the number of acres attached to the several Irish sees.* These returns are very incomplete, and were mostly compiled by the registrars from the fallacious representations of the tenantry. Three dioceses, Dromore, Down, and Raphoe, made no return at all; alleging that, on examining the leases of the church lands, it was found they did not mention " the number of acres demised." In the return from Armagh, it is remarked that the number of acres has been calculated from the representations of the tenants, but " the lands have *never been surveyed.*" Of the magnitude of the errors in these reports, we may judge from the fact subsequently ascertained, that, in one of them there was a trifling omission of *thirteen thousand acres.* Enough, however, may be collected from them to show the vast extent of ecclesiastical property : in fact, it is clear that the bishops' lands are held, leased, and managed much upon the same liberal scale and principle that lands are in Australia, Canada, and Nova Scotia; and the conjectural estimates by Wakefield, and other statists, of what their immense incomes, either actually are, or might be made, under an improved system of tenure and cultivation, are not remote from the truth. We shall insert the

---

number of acres returned by fourteen sees; the acres are Irish, which makes the amount about one-third less than it would be in English acres.

Number of Acres of Land belonging to fourteen Irish Sees.

Name.	See.	Quantity of See-Lands.
Lord J. G: Beresford, D.D.	Armagh	63,270
Power Le Poer Trench, D.D.	Tuam	49,281
Richard Ponsonby, D.D.	Derry	94,836
John Leslie, D.D.	Elphin	31,832
James Verschoyle, D.D.	Killala	34,672
Lord Robert Tottenham, D.D.	Clogher	27,070
Nathaniel Alexander, D.D.	Meath	18,374
George De la Poer Beresford, D.D.	Kilmore	47,361
Richard Whately, D.D.	Dublin	21,781
Samuel Kyle, D.D.	Cork and Ross	22,755
John Brinkley, D.D.	Cloyne	15,871
Richard Laurence, D.C.L.	Cashel	13,392
Robert Fowler, D.D.	Ossory	13,391
Hon. R. Bourke, D.D.	Waterford	9,996

Total, in Irish acres · · · · · · 463,962*

Mr. Leslie Foster, one of the barons of the Irish exchequer, estimates the lands belonging to *all* the sees to amount to 617,598 Irish acres, which are equal to about 990,000 English acres.† This does not include the demesne lands attached to the episcopal residences, and which, by the same authority, are said to vary from 100 to 500 acres each; making the entire patrimony of the bishops about 623,598 acres, or, according to Beaufort's map of Ireland, one nineteenth of the entire soil of the kingdom. This, it must be allowed, is enough for the maintenance of twenty-two bishops, especially when it is considered a population of *eight millions* is to be supported out of the remainder.

However, the area grasped by the right reverend fathers affords an inaccurate idea of their incomes. Mr. Baron Foster supposes the average value of the see-lands to be 20s. per acre. Even at this low rate, the bishops' lands, if out of lease, would yield a total revenue of £623,598, averaging £28,340 to each prelate. Some of the wealthier sees, as those of Derry, Armagh, Tuam, and Elphin, would have incomes, respectively, of £94,836, £63,270, £49,281, and £31,832, exclusive of what might be derived from tithes, patronage, and other sources. But the nature of ecclesiastical tenures precludes the bishops from realizing incomes to this amount. It scarcely ever happens the occupying tenantry are the bishops' tenants; the immediate lessees hold

---

* Parliamentary Papers, vol. xxi. No. 402, Session 1824.
† Parliamentary Papers, vol. ix. page 75, Session 1825.

from the bishops for the term of 21 years; the bishops renew the leases from year to year, always leaving 21 years unexpired; the rent reserved to the bishops is mostly the old rent payable in the time of Charles II., which has become almost nominal, and the real incomes of the bishops proceed from the *annual fines* for renewing the leases. Now these fines usually amount to about one-fifth of what an ordinary landlord would receive for rent. So that, if the actual worth of the see lands be £623,598, the sum ordinarily received does not exceed £124,719.

We have thought it expedient to explain this, because it is a subject on which there has been a great deal of misapprehension. The fact is, the spiritual tenures are one great obstacle to agricultural improvement in Ireland. The Church is a principal proprietor of the soil, but the vast tracts she holds can never be cultivated to advantage under the uncertainties of the existing system. Much of the land is rough pasture, bog, and mountain, which requires, in the first instance, a great expenditure to render productive; but who would risk capital in the undertaking with a lease which, by law, cannot *exceed twenty-one years;* or with a certainty of having a fine levied on its renewal, augmented in exact proportion to the money and labour expended in improvement? Again, an ecclesiastical tenant is never sure of his landlord, being constantly liable to be changed, not only by death but translation. New lords, as the proverb says, often bring new laws. Although the usual course is to renew every year at one-fifth of the real worth, yet some prelates act differently; they will have surveys made—demand exorbitant fines—or wait the fall of the leases, which are relet at a nominal rent, perhaps, to their own relations. From these causes arises the non-improvement uniformly remarked in the condition of the church lands. It is a great obstacle to the public prosperity of Ireland, and the practice is as little favourable to the interests of the bishops as to those of the lessees, by rendering the incomes of the former not only less than they otherwise would be, but uncertain, varying, as they do, with the amount of the fines, or perhaps they lose the fines altogether, the tenants electing to run out their leases, and thus the advantage stands over to the succeeding diocesan.

In spite of these drawbacks, the bishops, from estates, tithes, brokerage in livings and other means, contrive to make a very profitable crusade. In the *Edinburgh Review* (vol xliii. p. 483) their incomes are stated to average £10,000 a year each, or £220,000 in the whole. The patronage of an Irish bishop, of which we shall hereafter speak, is nearly as valuable as the income of his see. The vast revenues appendant to the bishoprics may be inferred from the immense wealth the prelates leave behind them. A former Bishop of Clogher, (the predecessor of the *soldier-bishop,*) who had been Cambridge tutor to lord Westmoreland, went over to Ireland without a shilling, and continued in his bishopric for eight years, and, at the end of that time, died worth between £300,000 and 400,000. It was stated, by Sir John Newport,* that

---

* Parliamentary Debates, vol. viii. p. 837.

three bishops, in the last fifteen years, had left the enormous sum of £700,000 to their families.

The career of Warburton, the predecessor of Dr. Brinkley in the see of Cloyne, is an example of the sudden acquisition of wealth by the Irish bishops. Warburton, whose real name was Mungan, died in 1826. He was the son of a poor road-way piper, in a little village in the north of Ireland. He was a Roman Catholic, and intended for that Church. On the continent, where he was sent to study at one of the Catholic colleges, before the building of Maynooth, he was thrown, by accident, into the society of the earl of Moira, and having won his favour, was induced to change his destination from the Roman to the Protestant Church. He was, after taking orders, appointed chaplain to a regiment in America, and there he married his first wife, a lady said to have been particularly recommended by lord Moira. That lady soon after dying, he married his second wife, now his widow. With her he changed his name to Warburton. He became dean of Ardah, then bishop of Limerick, and from thence was translated to Cloyne. He was a man of courteous manners, and much esteemed in the higher circles. His ruling passion was the acquisition of riches, which the retired situation of Cloyne afforded him opportunities for indulging. From the hour of his arrival there he continued to amass wealth, and the result was he left £120,000 among his children, three sons and one daughter, one of whom is a colonel in the army, another a major, another in the church, and the daughter married archdeacon Mansell. The bishop was unexceptionable as a private individual, and strict in the observance of religious forms, but he was neither respected nor esteemed in his neighbourhood. He drained the diocese of an immense annual sum, but he returned no part of it in works of charity. He abstracted himself from all society, and held his station more as a petty despot, exacting a subsidy from the toil of the people, than as a Christian pastor, in daily communicating with his flock, to whose care a great revenue was entrusted, as the steward for the children of want and misfortune. His palace was more like a rack-rent farmer's house than a gentleman's mansion. The coldness and apathy of the people at his funeral formed the best comment on his life and character.

Such is the general run of Irish prelates; without the claim of public services or superior mental endowments, they succeed to honours and vast revenues, obtained through intrigue, family connexion, or political interest, and die loaded with spoil, either on a foreign soil, or amidst the scorn and hatred of the people whom they have impoverished and oppressed. Only a month ago we passed over, in Kent, the remains of Dr. Bennett, Warburton's predecessor. He was buried in an obscure grave in Plumstead church-yard, with a common stone slab over him. He died in 1820, after holding the see of Cloyne twenty-six years, and draining at least a quarter of a million from the Irish soil. Yet he must have been an *absentee*, otherwise he would have been buried in his cathedral, or among the clergy of his diocese.

Let us resume our inquiries into the ecclesiatical revenues of Ireland.

Of the extent of the estates of the *Deans and Chapters*, we have no means of forming an estimate, there having been no return laid before parliament of the real property of the ecclesiastical corporations.   Many of the dignities as well as the sees are known to be extremely valuable. The Deanery of Down, for example, in 1790, was worth £2000 per annum; in 1810, it let for £3700.*   The archdeaconry of Armagh is returned at £1662 per annum;† the chancellorship £2385, and the precentorship £2350.   By comparing the cathedral and collegiate establishments of Ireland with those of England, it may, perhaps, be possible to form a conjecture of their relative value.   In England the income of the Deans and Chapters is £494,000 : but, as the number of members of these corporations is double what it is in Ireland, it is probable their endowments exceed in the same proportion.   We may, therefore, conclude that the Deans and Chapters have estates and endowments a little exceeding those of the Irish Bishoprics, and producing a total revenue of £250,000 per annum.

Next in order let us advert to the incomes of the *Parochial Clergy*, from tithes and glebe.   Ireland contains 18,000,000 of English acres of land, of which 900,000 pay nothing to the church; 4,000,000 pay from endowments about one-third of their tithes, and the remaining 13,000,000 and upwards are liable to pay full tithes.   The share which the clergy actually derive from the soil will be best ascertained from the valuations of the Tithe Commissioners, acting under the authority of Mr. Goulburn's statute.   Compositions under this act continue in force twenty-one years when *the original right to tithes revives*, and vary in amount every third year, if the average price of wheat or oats fluctuate one-tenth.‡   Had this act been exclusively framed by a conclave of tithe-eaters, it could not have more adroitly guaranteed their interests; and this is strikingly exemplified by the provision which provides that the tenant may deduct his share of the composition from the landlord's rent, and, if in arrear, it must be paid in preference to *debt, rent, or taxes*—that is, the parson's claim must have priority of that of a creditor, the landlord, or even the KING.   It is a very cunningly devised measure for perpetuating, without lightening, a most grievous burden.   A design is entertained by the Heads of the Church to introduce a similar project into England, but we trust the intention will be frustrated.   Its direct tendency is to fasten on the community the tithe-tax like the land-tax; with this difference, that the latter is paid by the landlord, but the former would have to be paid by the tenants, and augment with every increase in capital and industry.   Its tendency is also to make the pastors completely independent of their congregations, converting the former into annuitants who derive their incomes as independently of their parishoners as if paid out of the public treasury.   The motives for residence will be still further lessened;

* Wakefield's Statistical Account of Ireland, p. 469.
† Parliamentary Paper, No. 328, Sess. 1831.
‡ The Composition-Act, 4 Geo. IV. c. 99, s. 43.

many parsons before, from having few or no hearers, had little inducement, from the claims of duty, to reside on their livings, but now they
will not even have the tithes to look after,—no need of watching the
growth of potatoes, the increase of farm stock, nor extension of tillage;
their composition-money, like the rent of the absentee-landlord, may
be remitted whole and entire to them at London, Paris, Bath, or whatever place they may select as best calculated for unobserved luxurious
indulgence.

However, let us attend to the *workings* of this precious scheme of
Lord Wellesley's Irish administration, and the light it throws on the
value of parochial tithes. But first we must give the reader an idea of
the rapacious manner in which church-preferment has been cut up in
Ireland; how the parishes have been compressed into unions; how the
unions have been dovetailed into enormous pluralities; how the pluralities and unions together have been tacked to dignities and offices;
and how all these good things, like so many bunches of grapes on a
string, have been heaped on the Beresfords, Trenches, Saurins, and
Plunkets, as the means whereby the resources of the country may be
absorbed.

Be it known, then, that there are in Ireland 2450 parishes. Now,
as no parish (though some districts or portions of land are) is wholly
exempt from the payment of tithes, each parish ought to have at least
one resident minister, one church, one parsonage-house, and one glebe.
This is the ecclesiastical state which ought to subsist. Instead of which
there are only, according to clerical authority, *one thousand and
seventy-five* rectors, vicars, and perpetual curates in all Ireland, and
of these not more than two-thirds are said to reside on their benefices.[*]
In the whole 2450 parishes there are only 1100 churches, and of these
churches 474 have been built within the last century by means of grants
of *public money*. There are only 771 glebe-houses, and though there
are some benefices with two or three glebes, containing 4000 acres,
there are many parishes without any glebe at all, the land, through
negligence or abuse, having been lost or alienated, it not being unusual
to find a patch of ground, designated as glebe, situate in the middle of
a gentleman's lawn or part of his demesne, to which he lays claim in
virtue of some patent right, granting him the lands and tenements of a
church for ever. It follows from this that there are more than three
parishes to every resident incumbent; there is less than one church to
every two parishes; and, if every parish had its pastor, as it ought,
there would be nearly four parsons to live in every glebe-house.

To accommodate these dilapidations and inconsistencies the policy of
consolidating the parishes into UNIONS has been resorted to. As in
many parishes there were neither hearers nor a church, there could be
no need of the services of an officiating minister. In these parishes it
would have been *rational* either to have abolished the tithe or applied
the produce of it to some other purpose than the support of a sinecure

---

[*] Ecclesiastical Register of Ireland for 1830, p. 33.

rector or vicar. But this did not accord with the temporal interests of the church. Hence the expedient of *unions of parishes ;* that is, clusters of parishes, in various numbers, from two to a dozen and more, have been compressed into a *single* benefice, forming one presentation, held by a single incumbent, and this incumbent, perhaps, a pluralist, holding two or more of these ecclesiastical conglomerations. In England a similar abuse prevails ; it frequently happening that two or more rectories, vicarages, or parochial chapelries are held *cum,* or with, others, forming a single benefice ; but the instances are neither so numerous nor outrageous as in Ireland. In the latter country unions may be found thirty-six Irish miles in length, containing as many square miles of territory as some of the petty kingdoms under the Heptarchy. One union, that of Burnchurch, in the diocese of Ossory, formed by an act of the privy council, and in the gift of the king and the bishop alternately, consists of no fewer that *thirteen parishes.* Here is a benefice ! If a man is fortunate enough to obtain, as is not impossible, two or three such benefices, he is more like a bishop at the head of a diocese than a parish priest.

Of the whole 2450 parishes there are only 749 held *single,* the remaining 1701 parishes having been consolidated into 517 unions, forming, in the whole, 1266 parochial benefices. The territorial contents of the benefices vary in different districts. According to Mr. Erck, in the northern, southern, and eastern provinces, they average 6544 Irish acres, or upwards of ten square miles, with the exception of those in the dioceses of Clogher and Killaloe, and in the three western dioceses of Elphin, Clonfert, and Killala, where they average from 10 to 12,000 acres ; in the dioceses of Derry, Kilmore, Raphoe, Ardfert, and Achonry, they average from 12 to 15,000 acres ; and in the western diocese of Tuam they average the enormous area of 25,800 acres. The union benefices have been constituted under different authorities, by parliament, by charter, by act of council, by license of the bishops ; and some are of such ancient date that the period and mode of their origin cannot be traced. All the unions are permanent except those under episcopal authority, which enure only during the life of the incumbent, when the parishes may revert to their original state. But if an union has been once formed it is generally continued to successive incumbents, and it is not likely the bishops will dissolve them, especially if they happen to be, as is mostly the case, the patrons. In fact, it is by the heads of the church, whose duty consisted in the maintenance of more strict ecclesiastical discipline, that the abuse of unions has been chiefly encouraged. Of the 517 unions 230 are of episcopal creation, and 126 more have been established under an authority almost identical with that of the bishops,—namely, the privy council of Ireland. We subjoin a classification of the unions now subsisting, as we collect them from the *Ecclesiastical Register,* for 1830, pp. 14, 15.* So long

---

* This work is by John C. Erck, A. M., LL.B. and published in Dublin. It s an elaborate and well-compiled performance, abounding in much curious and

established and intimately cemented have some of these unions become, that the boundaries of the parishes of which they consist it is extremely difficult, if not impossible, to trace ; and there are among the apologists of ecclesiastical abuses those who would avail themselves of this circumstance, and boldly affirm that the parishes in some unions are not distinct parishes, only *town lands,* and this though the denomination and names of the parishes are fully set forth in the titles of every incumbent !

A Statement exhibiting the Number of Unions, the Number of Parishes in each, and their Denominations.

Number of Parishes in each Union.	2	3	4	5	6	7	8	9	10	11	13	Total of Benefices.	Total of Parishes.
Parliamentary Unions	2	4	1		3							10	38
Charter Unions	5	8	4	3	3	1	1					25	98
Privy Council Unions	46	34	19	12	7	2	4	1			1	126	440
Episcopal Unions	119	51	29	16	5	3	3		2	2		230	704
Immemorial Unions	49	34	18	13	5	5		1	1			126	421
Total..	221	131	71	44	23	11	8	2	3	2	1	517	1701

Having explained the nature of unions and their territorial magnitude, the reader will be better enabled to judge of the value of Irish benefices, and he must be convinced what a fortunate aspirant he must be who happens to be presented with two or more such benefices, besides dignities and offices, especially if he have not—as is possible—a church in any of them to preach in, nor a single Protestant to whom he need read prayers. In Ireland, as in England, there is great disparity in the value of livings ; some are extremely small and insignificant, while others, according to the admission of his grace of Armagh, are worth £2300 per annum. We are as averse to the penury of one part of the church as to the corruptive opulence of another ; for we dislike all extremes of condition, and are quite of Agur's opinion in thinking that neither excess of riches nor poverty is for the good of individuals. The list of parishes we subjoin has been taken almost at random from the Parliamentary Returns of the amount of compositions for tithe : it will show the actual sums now paid by parishes in lieu of tithes, and, as the UNIONS are enclosed in crotchets, it will be seen what monstrosities some of them are. The composition-rent put down is for *clerical* tithes only ; the amount paid for impropriate tithes is omitted, as not

useful information, of great interest to those enjoying and aspiring to ecclesiastical emoluments ; but, having been edited under the sanction of the Board of First Fruits, the Editor has been careful not to afford the slightest glimpse of the discipline and immense amount and mal-administration of the revenues of the Irish church.

forming part of the income of the incumbent. In some unions all the parishes have not yet compounded; in others the compositions have been annulled by the bishops, (who have a veto on these agreements,) as not being adequate to their reputed value. The names of the patrons and present incumbents have been collected from the *Ecclesiastical Register* of Ireland.

STATEMENT *of the Sums agreed to be paid, under the Composition-Act, by several Parishes in lieu of Tithes, and the Names of the present Incumbents and Patrons.*

[Those Parishes marked ‡ are not compounded for.]

Incumbent.	Patron.	Parish.	Amount of Composition.
Edward Hincks	*Trin. Col. Dublin*	Artrea	£738
Francis Hall	*Trin. Col. Dublin*	Arboe	507
Charles Atkinson	*Archb. Armagh*	Creggan	1050
Hon. C. Knox	*Archb. Armagh*	{ Carnteel	406
		Aughaloo	609
E. Stopford	*Archb. Armagh*	Derrynoose	646
G. Blacker	*Archb. Armagh*	Drumcree	650
J. Campbell	*Archb. Armagh*	Forkhill	650
W. Pinching	*Bp. Clogher*	Carrickmacross	646
J. G. Porter	*Bp. Clogher*	Donaghmoine	953*
W. Athill	*Bp. Clogher*	Findonagh	600
		{ Kells	553
T. De Lacy	*Bp. Meath*	{ Duleene	200
		{ Rathboyne	270
		{ Burry ‡	
W. Kellett	*The King*	Moynalty	550
W. Pratt	*Bp. Meath*	Enniskeen	900
R. Symes	*Bp. Connor*	Ballymoney	1015
A. Leslie	*The King*	Ahoghill	1015
G. Macartney	*Marq. Donegal*	{ Skerry	419
		Racavan	295
W. Knox	*Bp. Derry*	Ballynascreen	623
A. Ross	{ *Skinner's Com. London*	} Banagher	650
A. W. Pomeroy	*Bp. Derry*	Bovevagh	580
J. W. Ormsby	*Trin. Col. Dublin*	Cappagh	1000
W. Knox	*Bp. Derry*	Clonleigh	840
R. Babington	*Bp. Derry*	Cumber Lower	560

* The lay tithes of this parish have been compounded for £476, making the total amount of composition £1429 a year.

Incumbent.	Patron.	Parish.	Amount of Composition.
F. Gouldsbury	Bp. Derry	Cumber Upper	£740
A. T. Hamilton	Marq. Abercorn	Donagheady	1350
Sir J. Leighton	The Lightons	Donaghmore	1440
S. Brownlow	Bp. Derry	Leekpatrick	646
J. S. Knox	Bp. Derry	Magheara	1015
O. M. Causland	Bp. Derry	Tamlaghfinlagan	1000
J. Jones	Bp. Derry	Urney	700
R. Allott	The King	Raphoe	900*
J. Usher	Trin. Col. Dublin	Raymochy	650
E. Bowen	Marq. Abercorn	Taughboyne, All Saints	1569
H. E. Boyd	Bp. Dromore	Drumaragh	937
G. Crawford	Bp. Ardagh	Clongesh	461
		Killoe	535
W. Bourne	Duke of Leinster	Rathangan	553
H. Joly	Duke of Leinster	Clonsast	628
		Ballinakill	65
J. D. Wingfield	Lord Digby	Geashill	1292
R. Vicars	The King	Coolbanagher	276
		Ardea	259
Hon. J. Bourke	The King	Aghavoe	789
		Comer	969
G. Stevenson	Marq. Ormonde	Callan	550
		Coolagh	383
		Tullomain	105
		Tullaroan ‡	
		Killaloe ‡	
		Ballycallan ‡	
J. B. Ridge	The King	Eirke	692
M. Monck	Bp. Ossory	Rathdowny	750
		Glashare ‡	
		Kildelgy ‡	
H. P. Elrington	Bp. Ferns	Templeshambo	1200
P. Browne	The King	Kilmackclogue	234
		Magloss	55
		Kilkevan	369
		Kilnehue	465
W. Hore	Bp. Ferns	Kilrush	694
M. Charters	Bp. Ferns	Clone	332
		Kilbride	203
		Ferns	270†

* This is an union containing *six* more parishes, but as they have not compounded, their names are omitted.

† Ferns has compounded for its impropriate tithe for £553, making the annual sum payable by this parish for lay and ecclesiastical tithes £823.

Incumbent.	Patron.	Parish.	Amount of Composition.
H. Moore	Bp. Ferns	Carnew	£830
A. Lord	Archbp. Cashell	Templetonhy	500
		Loughmore	249
		Another parish ‡	
J. Pennefather	Archbp. Cashell	Killoscully	323
		Kilvolane	461
		Kilnerath	303
		Kilcomenty	323
T. P. Le Fann	Bp. Emly	Abington	650
		Tough	250
C. P. Coote	Bp. Emly	Doon	830
W. Galway	Bp. Emly	Kilmastulla	318
		Templeichally	406
Lord Brandon	Lordship of Castle Island	Castle Island	638
		Ballyncushlane .	460
		Dysert	173
		Killentierna	823
B. Denny	Sir E. Denny	Ballynahaglish .	230
		Anna	332
		Cloherbrien	332
		Caher	226
		Killencan	160
		Glanbeagh	130
Vicars Choral	Vicars Choral	Lismore ‡	
		Mocollop	1569
J. Scott	The King	Tubrid	955
		Ballybacon	461
T. G. Laurence	Bp. Cork	Moviddy	507
		Kilbonane	208
		Aglish	379
W. Harvey	Bp. Cork	Kilnaglory	325
		Athnowen	425
J. Jervois	Bp. Cork	Kilmichael	692
		Macloneigh	250
A. Trail	The King & Bp.	Skull	850
T. Kenny	Bp. Cloyne	Donoughmore	1100
Hon. G. de la P. Beresford	Bp. Cloyne	Inniscarra	636
		Malthy	513
J. Hingstone	Bp. Cloyne	Whitechurch	784
J. Hingstone	Bp. Cloyne	Aghabullogue	750
A. Champagne	Bp. Cloyne	Castlelyons	571*
M. Purcell	Fitzgerald	Dungourney	664

* The lay-tithes of this parish have been compounded for £1142, making the yearly composition for impropriate and clerical tithes £1713.

Incumbent.	Patron.	Parish.	Amount of Composition.
T. Newneham	Bp. Cloyne	Kilworth	£170
		Macroney	230
		Leitrim	230
		Kilcrumper	220
J. Lombard	Bp. Cloyne	Kilshannick	738
E. Palmer	Bp. Killaloe	Modreeny	533
		Arderony	307
G. Holmes	Bp. Killaloe	Kilmore	323
		Kilnaneave	315
		Lisbonny	323
E. Price	Bp. Killaloe	Aglishcloghane	161
		Lorrha	438
		Dorrha	415

From the above statement it appears that the amount of composition-money paid in lieu of tithes, in some unions, amounts to £1410, £1407, £1554, £1569, and £1758; and that *single* parishes have come down to the tune of £1050, £1200, £1350, and £1440, in order to rid themselves of the worldly visitations of the spiritual locust. These sums, it must be remembered, are not the conjectural estimates of individuals imperfectly informed of the worth of parochial tithes; they are public and authentic returns, founded on an average and impartial valuation. It must, also, be borne in mind that the composition is a net payment, obtained without the trouble of collecting the tithes, or the expense of proctors or middlemen, and the receipt of which is better secured than the landlord's rent or public taxes.

Many of the incumbents enjoying these really fat livings, are *pluralists*, holding other parochial benefices, beside dignities and offices. The names of the *honourable* Charles Knox, the *honourable* George de la Poer Beresford, the *honourable* Joseph Bourke, and other well-known signatures, are quite sufficient to indicate their connexions with the episcopacy and aristocracy of Ireland. It would require pages fully to set forth the families, connexions, and influence; the sinecures, places, offices, and pensions by which some of these *honourables* have sent forth their absorbents into the substance of Church and State. There is one man, however, JAMES HINGSTONE by name, who, as far as we know, is not of *noble blood*, unless it be by some left-handed tilt; yet he seems to have reaped a plentiful harvest. He has compounded for the tithes of two parishes, that of Whitechurch for £784, and that of Aghabullogue for £750, making a snug income of £1534 per annum. But this is far from being the extent of his good fortune. He is, also, rector of Subulter, and prebendary and vicar-general of Cloyne. His son, James Hingstone, is vicar of Clonmult, and vicar-choral of the cathedral church of St. Colman's. It were easy to give similar illustrations of others, but this must suffice.

Mr. Goulbourn's *bait* has taken so well that nearly two-thirds of all the parishes in Ireland have compounded for their tithes: the progress of the measure, up to the present, will appear from the subjoined statement, exhibiting the number of parishes, in each diocese, that have compounded in the four provinces, the proportion between lay and ecclesiastical tithe, and the total amount of the compositions for both descriptions of tithe.

PROVINCE OF ARMAGH. Diocese.	Parishes.	Lay Tithes. £	Clerical Tithes. £	Composition. £
Armagh	48 ..	— ..	19,292 ..	19,292
Clogher	28 ..	1,291 ..	12,257 ..	13,548
Meath	137 ..	11,212 ..	21,406 ..	32,618
Down and Connor	40 ..	1,139 ..	13,622 ..	15,061
Derry	42 ..	— ..	22,990 ..	22,990
Raphoe	14 ..	352 ..	7,424 ..	7,777
Kilmore	19 ..	874 ..	4,813 ..	5,688
Dromore	9 ..	2,128 ..	2,647 ..	4,775
Ardagh	21 ..	2,303 ..	4,793 ..	7,097
PROVINCE OF DUBLIN.				
Dublin	91 ..	4,031 ..	15,035 ..	19,066
Kildare	36 ..	2,089 ..	7,363 ..	9,452
Ossory	61 ..	1,550 ..	15,557 ..	17,107
Ferns and Leighlin	103 ..	7,181 ..	27,989 ..	35,170
PROVINCE OF CASHEL.				
Cashel and Emly	93 ..	5,083 ..	19,555 ..	24,638
Limerick, Ardfert, and Aghadoe	128 ..	7,016 ..	24,349 ..	31,366
Waterford and Lismore	52 ..	2,386 ..	12,500 ..	14,886
Cork and Ross	65 ..	4,022 ..	23,282 ..	27,305
Cloyne	57 ..	4,345 ..	18,629 ..	22,975
Killaloe and Kilfenora	121 ..	3,676 ..	23,355 ..	27,032
PROVINCE OF TUAM.				
Tuam	60 ..	2,945 ..	11,450 ..	14,396
Elphin	54 ..	2,377 ..	6,817 ..	9,194
Clonfert and Kilmacduagh	59 ..	86 ..	8,636 ..	8,723
Killala and Achonry	15 ..	1,098 ..	2,593 ..	3,691
TOTAL	1,353	67,494	326,363	393,857

From the results of the compositions already entered into it is easy to calculate the value of tithes in all Ireland. Of the 1353 parishes, the average rate of composition for each parish, for impropriate tithe, is £50, for church tithe £241, and for ecclesiastical and lay tithes together £291. Supposing the whole 2450 parishes to compound for tithes at the same average rate, the annual value of impropriate tithes is £122,500, of church tithes £590,450, making the total burden imposed by tithes, lay and ecclesiastical, on the entire kingdom, amount to £712,950 per annum. The average tithe for the whole kingdom would probably exceed the sum here stated; since it is known the most fertile districts have been the most backward in compounding for their tithes.

The ecclesiastical tithe of £590,450 per annum constitutes only one item in the yearly emoluments of the parochial clergy. They have, also, glebe-houses, extensive glebes, minister's money, and church-fees. In Ireland, " all things seem oddly made and every thing amiss."

Many benefices have neither glebe-house nor glebe-land ; while others have two glebe-houses each, and two or more glebes, comprising a superficial area of 2000 acres.   One-third of the benefices are destitute of any glebe whatever, and, consequently, of any residence ; while the remaining two-thirds of the benefices are estimated to possess glebe-land to the enormous extent of 91,137 acres.   Supposing, with Mr. Baron Foster, the glebe to be worth, on an average, only £1 per acre, it forms a very considerable addition to the yearly revenue of the beneficed clergy.

Another source of clerical emolument is that termed *minister's money*, intended as a substitute for tithe, and which, as we have no assessment levied in the same way in England, it will be proper to explain.   In cities and towns corporate, where there are small or no tithes, a power is vested in the Lord Lieutenant, authorising, by a commission, valuations to be made, from time to time, of every house; upon a return of such valuations, in which no house may be *rated above* £60, the Lord Lieutenant and six more of the privy-council are empowered to assess each house, in a yearly sum, for the maintenance of the incumbent.   Under this authority valuations have been made of the parishes in the cities of Dublin, Cork, Waterford, and Limerick, and the towns corporate of Drogheda and Clonmel ; and it is from the proceeds of these assessments that the incumbents of forty-eight city parishes are paid their stipends.   We have not any public return of the incomes allotted to the ministers of these towns and parishes ; if they average £500 each, it makes an addition of £25,000 a-year to the revenues of the parochial clergy.   The clause which provides that no house shall be rated *above sixty pounds* originated, no doubt, in the same selfish policy that dictated the abolition of the tithe of pasture, and shows, in every measure, how scrupulously have been considered the interests of the wealthy Protestants, when the burden even of main-taining the established church of the ascendant party was thrown, with unequal weight, on their poor and politically-disfranchised catholic brethren.

The yearly sums derived from *church-fees* we can only conjecture. They do not, of course, from a vast majority of the population being separatists from the endowed worship, form so productive a source of emolument as in England.   But, supposing the *million* of Protestants of different sects, in Ireland, pay for marriages, christenings, and burials only 5s. a-head, surplice-fees yield an income of £250,000. Without including, then, the emoluments derived by the parochial clergy from the dignities and offices they hold, from being masters of diocesan-schools, vicar-general or surrogate of a diocese, or official chap-lain at the Castle ; their total revenue, from the four sources of tithes, glebe-land, minister's money, and church-fees, cannot be less than £956,587.   If to this sum we add the incomes of the episcopal clergy and the deans and chapters already ascertained, we shall have the total amount of the burden imposed on Ireland by its Protestant establishment as follows :—

Revenues of the Established Church of Ireland.

Archbishops and bishops, average income of each £10,000 · ·		£220,000
Estates and tithes of the deans and chapters · · · · · · · · · · · ·		250,000
Ecclesiastical rectors, vicars, and perpetual curates :—		
Tithes ·	£590,450	
Glebe-lands ·	91,137	
Ministers' money ·	25,000	
Church-fees ·	250,000	
		956,587
Total ·		£1,426,587

Here is, certainly, a noble revenue for the maintenance of a little insignificant church, with barely more than half a million of hearers. The established church of Scotland, with a *million and a half* of followers, is now considered amply endowed, although its revenues do not exceed £234,900, or one sixth of those of Ireland. The sums expended on the established priesthood of Ireland are nearly equal to one-half the amount of the revenue paid into the Exchequer, on account of public taxes for the maintenance of an army of 30,000 men, for defraying the expense of police and justice, for the support of the local administration, for defraying the interest of the public debt of Ireland, and its proportional contribution to the exigencies of the general government. It ought never to be forgotten that the immense income lavished on a luxurious priesthood, whose duties prescribe to them charity, humility, and self-denial, is wrung from a poor distressed population, of whom hundreds perish annually from sheer want of the necessaries of life, and the vast majority of whom—so little have they been benefited by the instructions of their well-paid spiritual guides—are in such a state of ignorance and destitution that they are little better fed, clothed, and lodged than the beasts of the field !

Our next inquiry is the *Number of the Clergy*, among whom the revenues of the Irish Church are squandered. The policy of the church, like that of the City companies and all corporations, has been to keep their numbers as *few*, and render their revenues as productive as possible. Formerly there were thirty-two dioceses in Ireland ; these, either by parliamentary authority or by annexing sees to others by way of commendam, have been compressed into eighteen suffragan bishoprics. Thus the work of uniting sees has been nearly as rife as that of uniting parishes. The deans and capitulary bodies are kept up as in England, though their functions are little more than nominal, and the sinecure offices and dignities appendant to them serving only to augment the otherwise redundant incomes of the priesthood. The deans and chapters are endowed in some instances with tithes, in others with lands, and in most cases with both ; but their possessions are, for the most part, divided, the dean having one part alone in right of his deanery, and each member of the chapter a certain part in right of his office. Of the thirty chapters, eighteen consist of the four offices of precentor, chancellor, and archdeacon, and of prebendaries, varying, intermediately, from one, as in the case of Dromore, to twenty, as in the case of St. Patrick's, Dublin. The chapters of Waterford and Kilfenora are without any prebends, and in the chapter of Kildare the eight prebendaries, although they have a voice in the election of a dean, yet form no constituent part of the chapter, which is composed of other officials and four canons.

The precentor, or chantor, is generally the first member of the chapter; his duties, in the old religious houses in papal times, were important and various, consisting in the care of the choir-service, in presiding over the singing men, organist, and choristers, paying their salaries, and keeping the seal of the chapter and chapter-book. In these cathedrals, where a choir-service is still maintained, of which there are only a few in Ireland, the precentor has the superintendence of the choir, but in all others it is a mere title of honour, without any duty whatever attached to the office. The same may be observed of the chancellors of cathedral churches, the treasurers, provosts, and prebendaries, many of whom are without cure or ecclesiastical jurisdiction, and have nothing whatever to do for their emoluments and patronage, unless it be in taking their turn of preaching in the cathedral, and that is mostly performed by deputy.

A dignity without cure is not incompatible with a parochial benefice, and both may be holden together without any dispensation for plurality; for though the dignitaries gain possession of office by institution, they are not instituted to the *cure of souls.* The cure attaches not to any office of the chapter as such; yet it is to be observed that there are no fewer than *two hundred and nineteen dignities and offices,** to which either, by charter or other means, *one or more* parishes with cure have been annexed, and of which parishes the tithes and emoluments are received by the collegiate sinecurists, and the duties, where any exist, are mostly discharged by a stipendiary curate. The fortunate possessors of these plural offices and parishes being eligible to other benefices, one individual may concentrate in his own person scores of dignities, offices, and livings, and enjoy an aggregation of ecclesiastical income and patronage almost incredible.

Next let us advert to the number of the parochial clergy, consisting of all ecclesiastical rectors having cure, vicars, and perpetual curates, and of whom there are, according to Mr. Erck, exclusive of ninety-eight dignitaries having cure, *one thousand and seventy-five.* The assistant curates, amounting to five hundred and fifty, do not, of course, form a part of the beneficed clergy; they are only deputies, removable at pleasure, and discharging the duties, at very miserable stipends, which ought to be discharged by their principals, who receive ample remuneration. Of lay-rectors, or laymen, possessing tithes as a lay-fee, there are seven hundred and eighteen. These, not being in orders, form no part of the ecclesiastical corps; they are usually denominated *impropriators,* as being, according to Spelman, improperly possessed

* Ecclesiastical Register of Ireland, p. 24.

of the tithes of the church; inasmuch as it severs *labour from reward,—* a principle which ecclesiastics profess to repudiate, though it is notorious, the most amply endowed incumbents of the United Church of England and Ireland are as justly obnoxious to the opprobrium of being *impropriators* as the secular parsons—having, by the intervention of curates and other devices, unknown before the Reformation, contrived to rid themselves entirely of every particle of spiritual duty.

The whole number of beneficed parochial clergy, without including collegiate officials, is then only 1075, according to the admission of the editor of the Board of First Fruits. This diminutive phalanx one would think quite small enough, in all conscience, to monopolize the cure of the 2450 parishes of Ireland. But the fact is, the number of individuals is not so numerous by a great many. We have seen that 1701 parishes have been compressed into 517 benefices. Some parishes are both rectorial and vicarial; that is, the same parish has a rector and vicar, united in the same person, and which, we suspect, reckon *two* in Mr. Erck's enumeration of 1075. Then how many are PLURALISTS? The *Ecclesiastical Register* informs us, page 32, *one hundred and thirty-five* benefices are held with other benefices by faculty, dispensation, or permission of their diocesans. This reduces the number of individuals to 940. There appear to be 587 parishes where the vicarial are united with the rectorial tithes, or where both descriptions of tithe are united in the incumbent. It is probable, we think, the entire number of rectories, vicarages, and perpetual curacies are possessed by not more than 700 individuals, who also enjoy the chief offices in cathedrals, the diocesan schools, and public institutions of a religious and literary character.

From the *Ecclesiastical Register*, and other sources, we collect that the number of preferments in Ireland—episcopal, collegiate, and parochial—possessed by the established clergy, is—

Sees	22
Deaneries	33
Precentorships	26
Chancellorships	22
Treasurerships	22
Archdeaconries	34
Provostships	2
Prebends and canonries	188
Rural deans	107
Vicars choral	52
Choristers	20
Choir readers and stipendiaries	12
Diocesan schools	30
Offices in consistorial courts	175
Benefices consisting of a single parish	749
Parishes compressed into 517 benefices	1701

Total of offices enjoyed by the established clergy ··3195

Thus it appears there are 3195 offices shared among about *eight hundred and fifty* individuals, whose aggregate ecclesiastical revenue amounts to £1,426,587, averaging £1678 to each person. Such proportions between numbers, offices, and revenue are certainly without parallel. There is no example any where of 850 persons possessing, in see-lands and glebes, one-eighteenth part of the soil, and claiming one-tenth of the produce of the remainder, which supports eight millions of people. No country, however debased by superstition, ever abandoned so large a portion of its real property, in addition to a tenth part of the national income, for the maintenance of a priesthood, forming less than a nine-thousandth part of the population.

It is not, however, the average income of either the Irish or English ecclesiastic that constitutes the principal abuse in their respective establishments. Although both churches might very well spare *two-thirds* of their aggregate revenues, and enough remain for the adequate remuneration of spiritual service, still it is not the redundancy of their united incomes that is so objectionable as the unequal and inhuman manner in which they are possessed by candidates of the same grade and pretension. We have before enlarged on this point in our exposition of the Church of England; we have there shown how masses of pay and pluralities of office are heaped on clerical sinecurists enjoying high connexions and influence; while the most useful and meritorious labourers in the ministry, divested of patronage, are kept in the most miserable poverty and dependence. Precisely the same injustice predominates in the Irish church. In the latter the grievance is more intolerable, for, in Ireland, church-patronage is chiefly in the hands of ecclesiastics, and it is invariably observed that the clergy have less regard for their brethren, and are more blindly intent on promoting their own personal and family interests than laymen.

We shall insert a tabular representation of the patronage of the Irish church; the number of parishes in Ireland is greater than appears from the subjoined statement, as is evident from the *Ecclesiastical Register*. But it is a point on which there is much difference of opinion, originating in the uncertain boundaries of parishes, and the extraordinary manner they have been consolidated, to serve the purposes of clerical rapacity.

Irish Church Patronage.

DIOCESES.	Patronage of Bishops.	Patronage of Crown.	Others.		Impropriate without Churches or Incumbents.
			Lay	Uni-versit	
Armagh	60	13	22	5	
Cashell and Emly					
Clogher	34	1	2	4	
Clonfert and Kilmacduagh	43	3	14		
Cloyne...........................	107	10	9		11
Cork and Ross	94	8			
Derry	33	3	9	3	
Down and Connor..................	53	12	36		10
Dromore	23		2		
Dublin...........................	144	15	16		
Elphin...........................	72	2	1		
Kildare	30	27	24		
Killala and Achonry..............	48	4			
Killaloe and Kilfenora...........	131	10	36		17
Kilmore	33	3	2	1	
Leighlin and Ferns	171	18	19	1	13
Limerick, Ardfert, and Aghadoe	34	27	65		
Meath	69	81	37		35
Ossory...........................	76	26	30		
Raphoe	15	6	3	7	
Tuam and Ardagh..................	72		10		
Waterford and Lismore	43	24	30		9
	1392	293	367	21	95

Patronage of Bishops............ 1392
Ditto Crown.................... 293
Ditto Lay 367
Ditto University 21

2168

The Irish bishops have a far greater proportion of patronage than the English bishops: the former have the gift of 1392 livings out of 2168; the latter have only the gift of 1290 out of 11,598. The livings, too, in the gift of the Irish bishops are far more valuable. Those in the gift of the Archbishop of Cashel are worth £35,000 per annum; those in the gift of the Bishop of Cloyne, £50,000; of Cork, £30,000; and of Ferns, £30,000. In the see of Cloyne ONE living is worth £3000, one worth £2000, and three worth £1500 each. A living of £500, as we have seen, is but a middling one in Ireland, and any thing beneath it is considered very low.

The king's ministers nominating the bishops, and these having the disposal of all the livings, with the exception of a few belonging to the Universities, lay lords, and those that are tithe free, nearly the whole of the tithes and church revenues of Ireland are in the gift of the crown. Hence we may see how discouraging was the prospect of ecclesiastical *reform* under Tory ministers. The Irish sees were almost in the exclusive possession of their thick-and-thin supporters, in the families of the Beresfords, the Clancartys, Balcarrases, Mayos, Northlands, Rodens, Hoaths, Kilkennys, Caledons, &c. among whom one looks in vain for a single scholar or celebrated divine. Indeed the Irish Protestant Establishment formed a convenient and almost inexhaustible [fund for parliamentary corruption; and appointments to it, like those in the Colonies, being out of sight of the English public, were often made without any regard to decency. Thus a lieutenant in the navy has been made an archbishop; a member of the House of Commons, a dean; a proprietor, and it is said editor, of a newspaper, a chancellor; and an aide-de-camp at the Castle, a rich rector. Such men as Sir Harcourt Lees, the heroes of Skibbereen and Newtonbarry, and Warburton and Percy Jocelyn, having attained preferments in the church, are still more illustrative. All the Irish representative prelates voted against the Reform Bill on its first introduction. Lord MOUNTCASHEL stated, in the House of Lords, that he knew an archdeacon in Ireland who kept one of the best *packs of fox-hounds* in the country. Another clergyman, not seven miles distant from the former, had, also, a pack of fox-hounds, with which he regularly hunted; and he knew of a clergyman who, after his duties in the church had been performed, used to meet his bro-ther-huntsmen at the *communion-table, on the Sunday*, and arrange with them where the hounds were to start for next day. Can these things be, when it is alleged by Sir Robert Peel, that the church has no support to depend upon but her " own purity?"

However, the love of sporting is not confined to the clergy of the sister kingdom. The English spirituals have also a taste for rural sports, and a good pack of fox-hounds is deemed a suitable appendage to a cure of souls, as will be seen from the following notice: " To be sold, the next presentation to a vicarage, in one of the midland coun-ties, and in the immediate neighbourhood of one or two of the *first packs of fox-hounds* in the kingdom. The present annual income about £580, subject to curate's salary. The incumbent in his 60th year."— *Morning Herald, April 15, 1830.*

But it is not these matters which engage our attention; we should care little about the sporting propensities of the parsons if they would leave to the industrious the produce of their labour. So far as manners and morals are concerned, the different sects of religionists may be left to watch each other; and that they will do with the most lynx-eyed attention. Only read what Mr. Beverley has written on this subject in his " Letter to the Archbishop of York."

" It surely is not very edifying to behold a clergyman following the hounds, and though the fox-pursuing parsons are of a different opinion, and defend the practice with orthodox arguments, yet they cannot per-suade the people to agree with them; in vain do they sing a song con-cerning ' manly sport—no harm,' &c.; for their parishioners will not listen to such trash, but indignant at the indecencies of their rectors, turn away in disgust to find better examples amongst the methodists and independents.

"But indecent and unpopular as is the spectacle of a fox-hunting parson, perhaps one's bile is not a little agitated in these exhibitions, by that sort of *vestiary hypocrisy* with which they choose to decorate the scandal: for it seems to be a received dogma of ecclesiastical decorum, that a parson is not to hunt in a *red* coat; provided only the *scarlet* does not appear, the reverend successor of the Apostles may leap over hedge and ditch without the slightest impropriety: give these successors of the Apostles a black or dark grey jacket, a pair of white corderoy breeches, and handsome top-boots, and then you save the character of the church; but if a young priest were to give the view-holloa in a *red* coat, all men would be shocked, and I suspect that ere long a grand and verbose epistle would come to him from Bishopthorpe.

"The same farce in clothing is kept up throughout; at balls the successors of the Apostles must appear clad in black, or any of the shades of black. Thanks, however, to the ingenuity of tailors and haberdashers, such exquisite tints have of late years been discovered in silk stockings and silk waistcoats, such delicious varieties of light black, raven black, French black, and French whites—the black has been softened into winning lavender-tints, and the white has been so dexterously made to blush a morning blush, that it requires very great ingenuity to discover a layman from a priest in a brilliant ball-room. These, however, who are more apostolical, take the bull by the horns, and venture to place *black-tinted buttons on the breasts of their shirts*, a mark of the priestly office not easily to be mistaken! Of such a toilet there is great hope, and it would be a shame indeed if the black-button-bearing priests did not become rich pluralists at last."

Mr. Beverley of Beverley is such a nice connoisseur in *drapery*, that we suspect him of being a bit of an exquisite himself: he is evidently an intense evangelical, and, for aught we know, may be a believer in Mr. Irving's new revelation of a "gift of tongues."

Non-residence of the Irish Clergy.

It is a curious fact that, during the sway of the Catholic Church, no man was permitted to hold a benefice who did not perform the duties of it upon the spot, and it was left for the Reformation, which is said to have established religion in greater perfection, to entitle a man to a large income for the cure of souls in a district which he never visited. A great proportion of the Irish Bishops, Dignitaries, and Incumbents, are *absentees;* many of them whiling away their time on the Continent, and others dissipating their large revenues in the fashionable circles of Brighton and London. With the single exception of the Bishop of Kildare all the archbishops and bishops have each, within their respective dioceses, an episcopal residence, or see-house, with parks, chases, and demesne-lands attached. Yet they spend little or none of their time in Ireland in superintending the clergy. The families of some prelates reside constantly in England, and the only duty performed by the bishop is to cross the water in the summer months, take a peep at the "*palace*," and then return to give grand dinners, and mingle in the gaieties of the metropolis, for the remainder of the year. The late Earl of Bristol, Bishop of Derry, resided twenty years abroad, and during that time received the revenues of his rich diocese, amounting to £240,000. This Right Rev. Prelate was the intimate associate of Lady Hamilton, the kept-mistress of Lord Nelson. The bishop lived in Italy, spending his princely income, wrung from the soil and labour of Ireland, among the fiddlers and prostitutes of that debauched country. The great primate Rokeby resided at Bath, and never visited Ireland. The parochial clergy are not more exemplary. Upwards of *one-third* of the whole number of incumbents do not reside on their benefices. Some of them, with incomes of £5,000 or £10,000 a-year, are living in France, with their wives and families. Others live at Bath, on *account of the gout*. Most of them never see their parishes, deriving their incomes through the medium of agents, or of tithe-farmers, and engaging a curate at some £30 or £50 a-year to attend *once* on each Sunday to read prayers ; often, perhaps, only to the parish clerk.

According to the *Diocesan Returns,* in 1819, the following was the state of the provinces, as regards parochial residence and duty : —

The province of Ulster, containing 443 parishes or unions, had 351 incumbents resident, or *near enough to do duty*.

The province of Leinster, 281 parishes or unions, with 189 incumbents resident, or near enough to do duty.

The province of Munster, 419 parishes or unions, with 281 incumbents resident, or near enough to do duty.

The province of Connaught, 95 parishes or unions, with 65 incumbents resident, or near enough to do duty.

Thus, in 354 parishes or unions, there was neither an incumbent resident, nor near enough to do the duty of his benefice. These returns make the number of incumbents, resident and non-resident, amount to 1240. It is unnecessary to explain, after what has been already stated, that there are not actually so many individuals. The deception results from pluralities. Every benefice with cure has an incumbent; but, as each incumbent often holds two or more benefices, or is rector and vicar of the same parish, it reduces the number of individuals to the amount previously stated, namely *seven hundred*.

One great excuse for the neglect of duty by the protestant clergy is that they have scarcely any duty to perform. Notwithstanding all the inducements offered by the established religion, notwithstanding its monopoly of tithes, honours, power, and emoluments, it has scarcely any followers. A protestant is as rare to be met with in Ireland, as a JEW in England. Out of a population of eight millions, there are little more than half a million communicants of the state religion. The consequence is, that the church establishment is little better than an enormous sinecure, *a prodigious job*, carried on for the benefit of a few hundred individuals, to the impoverishment, disunion, and degradation of all the rest of the nation. The Irish Church has been aptly compared to some Irish regiment, in which there was the whole train of officers, from the colonel downwards, but only ONE *private*. Just so with the ecclesiastical establishment; there is the whole apparatus of bishops, deans, archdeacons, prebendaries, canons, rectors, and vicars; there are all these still, and, what is better, there are all the tithes, houses, gardens, glebe lands, cathedrals, and palaces : all these remain ; but the PEOPLE— those for whose benefit they were originally intended, they have adhered unflinchingly to their old communion. Why then should not the revenues and church lands follow them—the OWNERS, for whose benefit they were first granted ? Why keep up twenty-two bishops where there are scarcely any parsons ? or why maintain these parsons, with large endowments, when they have lost their flocks ? There are scores, aye, hundreds of well paid rectors and vicars, without a single protestant hearer ; there are *thirteen hundred and fifty parishes*, without even a church to preach in ; yet in all these parishes the tithes are levied or compounded for to the utmost farthing.

The anomalous state of the Irish Church has not escaped the notice of foreigners ; and in the pleasant and instructive ' Tour of a German Prince,' there are some curious details. " I took," says the writer, " advantage of the acquaintance I made to day to gain more information of the actual proportion between Catholics and Protestants. I found all I had heard fully confirmed, and have gained some further details ; among others, the official list of a part of the present parishes and livings in the diocese of Cashell, which is too remarkable not to send it to you, though the matter is somewhat dry, and seems almost too pedantic for our correspondence.

	Catholics.	Protestants.
Thurles ······ has ····	12,000 ············	250
Cashel ··············	11,000 ··········	700
Clonhoughty ··········	5,142 ············	82
Coppowhyte ··········	2,800 ············	76
Killenoule··············	7,040 ············	514
Boherlahan ·········	5,000 ············	25
Feathard ············	7,600 ············	400
Kilcummin ··········	2,400 ·········	
Meckarty ············	7,000 ············	80
Golden ··············	4,000 ············	120
Anacarty ············	4,000 ············	12
Donniskeath ··········	5,700 ············	90
New Erin············	4,500 ············	30

In thirteen districts 78,182 Catholics and 2879 Protestants.

" Each of these districts has only one Catholic priest, but often *four* or *five* Protestant clergymen ; so that on an average, there are scarcely twenty persons to each Protestant congregation. Kilcummin is the place I mentioned to you, where there is not a *single parishioner*, and the service, which according to law must be performed once a-year, is enacted in the ruins with the help of a Catholic clerk.   In another, called Tollamane, the same farce takes place.   But not a whit the less must the non-attending parishioners pay the *utmost farthing of their tithes and other dues ;* and no claims are so bitterly enforced as those of this Christian church : —there is no pity, at least none for Catholics.   A man who cannot pay the rent of the church land he farms, or his tithes to the parson, inevitably sees his cow and his pig sold, (furniture, bed, &c. &c. he has long lost,) and himself, his wife, and probably a dozen children thrust out into the road, where he is left to the mercy of that Providence who feeds the fowls of the air and clothes the lilies of the field."—*Tour in England, Ireland, France,* v. ii. pp. 50–51.

Well may this lively tourist exclaim, " What an excellent contrivance is a state religion !"

Oppressiveness of the Tithe System.

Hardship and impoverishment result not less from the amount than the *mode* in which the ecclesiastical revenues are levied in Ireland. By the *Tithe Composition Act,* an attempt was made, without at all lessening the amount of the burthen, to avert the occurrence of those disgraceful scenes, which so frequently accompanied the collection of the tithe-tax.   Under the authority of this statute, it has been seen, many parishes have compounded with the incumbent for tithe ; but as these compositions can only be entered into for a *limited term,* and as the rate of them varies with the fluctuations in the value and quantity of produce, the whole kingdom may be still considered to labour under the curse of an impost, whose pressure increases with every increase of capital and industry.   The expedient of compounding was early and readily adopted in the disturbed districts of Clare and Galway ; and throughout the extensive districts of the dioceses of Clonfert, Kilmacduagh, and Killaloe, composition rent has continued to be promptly and willingly paid.   But the measure has not been equally successful in other parts.   In the county of Carlow, King's County, Queen's County, Kilkenny, and part of Tipperary ; in fact, through the finest lands of the kingdom, composition has slowly and reluctantly advanced.

One circumstance especially deserving notice in the history of the tenth exaction, is, the abolition of *tithes of agistment,* which leaves tillage lands alone liable to the burthen.   This selfish and partial enactment of the Irish parliament shows clearly enough how necessary it is that the different classes of society should be represented in the legislature ; otherwise they are sure to be sacrificed, without regard to justice or humanity, to the exclusive advantage of the ruling power.   The abolition of tithe of pasture causes the revenues of the clergy to be principally drawn from tithe of corn, and of the cattle, pigs, poultry, and potatoes of the cotter tenantry.   While tithes of agistment were paid, the burden, in part, fell upon the opulent grazier,—the landed aristocracy of Ireland; but now the burden presses with disproportionate weight on the poorer cultivators of the soil. Owing to the increase in the numbers, skill, and industry of this class, the quantity of agricultural produce has been augmented a hundred fold, and in the same proportion has augmented the revenue of the church. While the Irish cultivator has been adding to his income by industry, and by the abridgment of the comforts and enjoyments of his family, he has been constrained, also, to add proportionately to the income of the Protestant priest, whose religion he does not profess, and whose intolerant dogmas long withheld from him his civil immunities.

The amount abstracted from the just rewards of industry is not the entire evil of the tithe oppression. Another class of evils results from the variety of ecclesiastical rights, and consequent variety of laws, and the interminable litigation which these laws incessantly occasion. The perplexities arising from this source are infinite, and it frequently happens the same ground is impoverished by the successive levies of the archbishop, bishop, dean and chapter, the rector and vicar. This is the case in most parts of the diocese of Clonfert, and to show the fleecing and harassing nature of the system we cannot do better than insert an extract from the letter of a clergyman and magistrate of Ireland, addressed to Mr. Secretary Stanley, and read by Lord Melbourne on the motion for the appointment of the Tithe Committee.

" The broken and irregular character of tithes, in the rust of its great antiquity, renders the variety and number of claims on the land both harassing and vexatious; the frequency of calls, and the uncertainty of receivers, are so varied and perplexing as to occasion much annoyance to the poor. There are a vast number of instances in my own parish, where one poor man, whose whole tithes annually do not amount to more than 1s. 8d. per acre and yet subject him to have his cow, sheep, pig, or horse, taken and driven to pound six times in the year for tithes, and liable, on each and every driving, to a charge of 2s. 6d. driver's fees, besides expense of impounding, and waste of time from his labour in seeking the person duly authorised to give him a receipt. He is liable to be summoned, moreover, and decreed for vestry cess, once in the year, making annually seven calls, on account of the Church, to his little plot of ground; besides, his little holding is liable to two calls in the year for Grand Jury public money, and frequently two calls more for Crown and quit rent. Thus eleven calls are made upon his small holding in the year, besides his landlord's rent, and for sums trifling in themselves, but perplexing and ruinous in the costs which attend them. Surely such are hardships that ought to be removed.

" Throughout the diocese of Clonfert and Kilmacduagh, in which this parish is situated, the Bishop takes one-fourth of every titheable acre of land. The county is very much broken up amongst cotter tenantry, holding small plots of an acre each, with a cabin or cottage upon it. The whole diocese is compounded for at an average rate of about one shilling per acre."—*House of Lords, Dec.* 15, 1831.

In England, where, in many parts, a man cannot cut a cabbage, pull a carrot, or gather a bunch of grapes, without giving notice to the parson, the system is sufficiently intolerable;* but in Ireland, from the mode of collecting tithes, those evils are aggravated tenfold. The Irish clergy generally employ an agent, called a *proctor*, who, immediately before harvest, estimates the barrels of corn, tons of hay, or hundred weight of potatoes, he supposes are on the ground, and, charging the market price, ascertains the amount to be paid by the owner. This notable agent generally holds his session on Sunday, at a pot-house, where he meets the farmers. As the terms are seldom agreed upon at the first meeting, others follow, and the *reckonings*, on these occasions, are always paid by the farmers, which add not a little to their charges. The parson sometimes leases the tithes out to the proctor, at a fixed rent, like a farm; while the latter, who, in that case, is called the middle proctor, not unfrequently relets them to another. In the south, the tithe is set out and sold by *public auction on the premises*. And, in Connaught, it is customary to call a sale before the harvest, at which the tithe is sold to any person who chooses to collect it.

Under such a system, it is easy to conceive what the Irish must endure. Nothing escapes the vigilance of the spiritual locust, or his agent. No bog, however deep – no mountain, however high—nor heath, nor rock, whatever industry may have reclaimed, or capital fertilized— all is liable to the full penalty of having been made available to the uses of man. From the proctors and middle proctors, neither lenity nor indulgence can be expected. These men, to whom the odious office of reaping the fruits of the industry of others has been delegated, are, probably, strangers in the parish, without motive for cultivating the friendship of the people, and having farmed the tithe for a stipulated sum, it is to be expected they will collect it with the utmost rigour, in order to realize the greatest profit from their bargain. The most distressing scenes are sometimes witnessed from their relentless proceedings, and the tithes not unfrequently collected with the aid of a constabulary or military force. The half-famished cotter, surrounded by a wretched family, clamorous for food, frequently beholds the tenth part of the produce of his potatoe garden, carried off to fill the insatiable maw of clerical rapacity. " I have seen," says Mr. Wakefield, " the cow, the favourite cow, driven away, accompanied by the sighs, the tears, and the imprecations of a whole family, who were paddling after, through wet and dirt, to take their last affectionate farewell of this their only benefactor at the pound gate. I have heard, with emotions which I can scarcely describe, deep curses repeated from village to village, as

---

* Lord Mountcashel, in his speech on Church Reform, May 4, 1830, relates a curious anecdote, illustrative of the luscious keenness of the English clergy after tithes. His lordship had been recently in company with a clergyman, while looking after his *tenths:* and when the man in orders met a goose with its goslings, he stopped to count the progeny, and would cry, " *Ah! there's one for me.*" Or, if he overtook a sow with her litter, he summed them up, with the observation, " *Ah! there are two for me.*" The *noble lords* were highly diverted with this example of ecclesiastical cupidity : they laughed heartily, and our readers may laugh too—if they like.

the cavalcade proceeded. I have witnessed the group pass the domain walls of the opulent grazier, whose numerous herds were cropping the most luxuriant pastures, whilst he was secure from any demand for the tithe of their food, looking on with the utmost indifference."—*Statistical Account of Ireland,* vol. ii. p. 466.

To spare the rich and plunder the poor is certainly not Christianity ; it is more like Church of Englandism, which, by the union of church and state, has perverted the pure and charitable faith of Christ into a tremendous engine of political guilt and spiritual extortion.   There is, we are assured, plenty of law in Ireland, as well as in this country, to punish injustice : there is no *wrong,* we are told, *without a remedy ;* the courts of justice are open, as the hypocrites say in England, for the punishment of either magisterial or clerical delinquents.   All this sounds wells on paper, or in the bloated harangues of an attorney-general ; but it is mere mockery and insult when offered to the victims of oppression.   Law, in both countries, is for those who can pay for it —the rich, not the poor.   The poor cotter, oppressed or defrauded by the exaction of the tithe-proctor, to the value of £10, cannot buy a chance of redress in the lottery of the law for less than £60.   By victory or defeat he is equally and irremediably ruined.   What resource, then, have men whose possessions probably do not amount to half that sum ?   None.   The way to courts of justice, through the impassable barrier of attorneys' and lawyers' fees, is *over a bridge of gold ;* and to point out these tribunals for redress, either to English or Irish poor, or even to those moderately endowed with wealth, is, in other words, to point out to a man the shortest way by which he may bring himself to the jail and his family to the workhouse.

Proportion of Catholics and Protestants in Ireland.

It has latterly become as essential a part of the system to conceal the number of followers of the Irish Protestant church, as the amount of its revenues.   When the last census was taken, it had been easy to ascertain the respective proportions of Catholics, Episcopalians, Presbyterians, and other Dissenters ; but government, for obvious reasons, declined making such classification.   The witnesses examined by parliamentary committees in 1825, evinced much diversity of opinion.   Mr. O'Connell thought the Protestants of all sects did not exceed a million.*   Mr. Leslie Foster supposed them to amount to 1,270,000.   Mr. Mason, who had spent much time in enquiries of this nature, calculated the proportion of Catholics to Protestants as $3\frac{1}{6}$ to 1, which estimate he founded on returns from 300 parishes, or about one-eighth of the whole number.†   Another account, which professes to be founded on the best information, gives the following estimate :—The census made the population amount to 6,800,000 ; if divided into fourteenths,

---

* Parliamentary Papers, vol. ix. p.83, Session, 1825.
† Ibid, p. 308.

it was estimated one-fourteenth belonged to the established church, or 490,000 souls; Presbyterians, and other Dissenters, formed another fourteenth; so that there remained 5,820,000 Catholics. The population has since increased to at least eight millions; and, supposing the proportion continues the same, there are now 571,428 Episcopalians, an equal number of Dissenting Protestants, and 6,857,143 Catholics.

If to the Catholics and Dissenting Protestants of Ireland we add the vast body of Separatists in England, we shall find that together they form an overwhelming majority of the population of the two kingdoms; and that, therefore, the existing Protestant establishment, having only a minority of the people attached to its communion, is not, according to the maxim of PALEY, entitled to the support and protection of government. One writer makes the excess of non-conformists over the conformists, in both countries, to amount to *four millions;* but as there is no certain data whereby this question can be accurately decided, we decline offering an opinion on the precise numerical superiority.

How, in Ireland, the followers of the established church have come to bear so small a proportion, and of the church of Rome so large a one, can only be accounted for by the observation of a celebrated writer, that you may persecute a doctrine up to any number of adherents; and the converse—pamper it down to any number. The selfish and intolerant spirit which so long swayed the destinies of the sister kingdom, by drawing a broad line of distinction betwixt the dominant and proscribed faith, rendered defection from the latter next to impossible. A sense of common injustice cemented more strongly the bonds of union among the Catholics, and gave to their civil disabilities the semblance of a martyrdom, which no one, by apostacy, could escape, without suspicion of being influenced by sordid considerations. Hence, a close and indignant sentiment was fostered, sufficient not only to withstand the claims of the reformed worship, but the influence of property, and the coercive power of authority. Fidelity to the religion of their fathers was identified with fidelity to their countrymen; and no one could secede, without being exposed to the double opprobrium of national treachery and selfish hypocrisy. It follows, that the sectarian missionaries, spread through Ireland, have had little success among the Catholics, and the proselytes they have made have been chiefly picked up in the less guarded folds of the established pastors.

The Catholic religion, however, has not only kept its relative position, but has actually gained ground; for, during the last half century, the proportion of Protestants has declined. In 1766, the Protestants formed nearly *one-half* the population; in 1822, they formed only *one-seventh;* while the Catholics had more than quadrupled from 1766 to 1822, the Protestants had scarcely doubled. This striking fact will be more evident from the following statement, drawn up partly from parliamentary returns, and partly from the estimate of Dr. Beaufort, and other well-informed individuals.

	Year 1766.	Year 1792.	Year 1822.
Protestants····	544,865	522,023	980,000
Catholics ····	1,326,960	3,261,303	5,820,000
Total····	1,871,725	3,783,326	6,800,000

The increase of Protestants from 1792 to 1822 is chiefly ascribed to the exertions of the *Methodists.* It affords a striking illustration of the efficacy of tithes, and large ecclesiastical endowments, in promoting religion; for it is clear, from the above, that the state worship has declined, in spite of its enormous emoluments. Those who are zealous for the promotion of religion, ought not to defend either the Irish or English establishment; for, under both branches of the united church, the number of their members has relatively decreased. Pure Christianity, indeed, can never flourish under the auspices of wealth and power; its precepts and origin are in perfect contrast to the titles, pomps, and vanities of the world. It has no connexion with bishops, nor courts, nor palaces; it was cradled in indigence; it flourished from persecution, it denounced the cant of hypocrites, and never allied itself with the Scribes and Pharisees of authority. They may, indeed, baptize state religions under the name of Christianity, but it has little to do with them; they are only heathen institutions, and their followers more the disciples of Mahomet than of Jesus Christ.

Little more than one-fourteenth of the population of Ireland belongs to the state religion, yet the teachers of this fraction of the community claim *one-tenth* of the produce that feeds the whole EIGHT MILLIONS! Surely if church property was intended for the maintenance of religion, it was intended for the religion of the PEOPLE, not for an insignificant minority of them.

But the misappropriation of ecclesiastical wealth is far from being the extent of the injustice sustained by the Irish and their *real* pastors. The important statute of the Session of 1829 was, no doubt, a great boon to the aristocracy and gentry, by qualifying them for seats in parliament and civil offices; still, as various penal statutes in force against the priesthood were left unrepealed by the *Catholic Relief Act,* they continue to sustain great hardship and opprobrium. Some of the penal acts remaining in force are very unjust and even cruel in their provisions: for instance, if a Catholic priest from inadvertency or misinformation marry two Protestants, or, a Protestant and Catholic, he is liable to a penalty of £500, or, according to a decision of an Orange Chief Justice, he is liable to suffer DEATH. The clergy are not allowed to officiate in any place with steeple or bells; they are prohibited from appearing abroad in the costume of their order; they cannot be guardians, nor receive the personal endowment of any Catholic chapel, school-house, or other pious or charitable foundation. If they do not disclose the secrets of auricular confession, which their religious tenets prohibit them from disclosing, they are liable to imprisonment; if a Jesuit enter the kingdom he may be banished for life, and any person entering such religious order is guilty of a misdemeanor. * No Catholic in Ireland is allowed for his defence to have arms in his house, unless he have a freehold of £10 a-year or £300 personal property. In Cork, Drogheda, and other cities and towns they continue to be ineligible to be members of the municipal corporations of those places. And, though a Catholic is liable to parish cess, he is disabled from voting at vestries on questions relating to repairs of churches. Lastly, no Catholic of the United Kingdom is eligible to the offices of Lord Chancellor, Keeper or Commissioner of the Great Seal, Lord-lieutenant, Deputy or Governor of Ireland, or High Commissioner in Scotland ; nor to any office in the ecclesiastical courts; in the universities; the colleges of Eton, Westminster, and Winchester.

The Catholic clergy are in number between 2000 and 3000, constantly residing among their flocks and ministering to their spiritual comforts. From the absence of any permanent provision for maintenance, and the general poverty of their followers, they live in indigence and hardship. Their chief dependence is on fees for burials, marriages, and christenings, gifts on confessions, and bequests for the celebration of masses for the *repose of the dead*. Hence they have seldom the means of comfortable subsistence, are often without a decent place for religious worship, are overpowered by calls for religious exertion, live in misery, and die at last without ever tasting those emoluments which formerly belonged to their church, and are now showered on the Jocelyns, Warburtons, Plunkets, Beresfords, Magees, Trenches and Knoxes, of the Establishment.

Although Dissenters are equally with Catholics separatists from the establishment, they have been much more favourably treated by government and the legislature. The ministers of the Presbyterians, the Seceders, and Protestant Dissenters, are in fact so many pastors paid by the State receiving annually large sums for their maintenance from the Irish civil list and from grants by parliament. The *Regium Donum* was granted by William III. in the year 1690, to the Presbyterians ; it first amounted to £1200, and was augmented by George III. in 1784, to £2200 per annum. In 1792, by authority of the King's letter, £5000 was charged on the civil list to be annually paid to Protestant Dissenting ministers, and £500 more to that class of Dissenters denominated Seceders. The annual grant from parliament to the Dissenters commenced in the session of 1804. It first amounted to £4,160, and ever since has been gradually augmenting : in 1816, it amounted to £12,228, in 1825, to £13,894, and in 1831, the sum of £14,860 was voted.† The total amount of the annual sums which have been paid to the ministers of the three denominations of Dissenters in Ireland, by payments out of the civil list, and by grants out of public taxes, is £751,452 : 10 : 1¼.

So it is plain the Irish Dissenters have been receiving tribute from

---

* Catholic Relief Act, 10 Geo. IV. c. 7, ss. 29—36.
† Parliamentary Report, No. 337, session 1831.

the State, if not in tithes, in something else. How they reconcile this provision with their doctrinal profession of the independence of their pastors of all secular interference and support we cannot affirm. There has been some discussion among them, we know, on this very point, and we shall be curious to learn whether profit or principle will triumph.

Management of the First Fruits Fund.

With so large a portion of the national wealth placed at the disposal of the clergy, the very least we might have expected the Legislature to do was to enforce the payment of all the taxes to which by law the Church was liable. We have already seen by what artifice the English ecclesiastics avoided contributing their full share to the *First Fruits Fund ;* we shall now show that a similar but more flagrant evasion of their pecuniary obligations has been long tolerated on the part of the Irish clergy.   Having already explained the nature of the annats (page 65) it will be only necessary here to remark that a similar usage formerly prevailed in both England and Ireland ; with this difference, that the Irish clergy paid in lieu of the tenth, only a twentieth of the annual value of each benefice to the Pope. In the reign of Henry VIII. when the papal rights were extinguished, an act passed for annexing to the crown the revenue arising from first fruits and tenths, and the same provision was made, as in England, for ascertaining, from time to time, their real annual value. This arrangement continued till the year 1710 : when Queen Anne, acting under the advice of her Tory ministers, remitted the twentieths to the clergy, rich and poor, without distinction, and gave the first fruits, alone, to form a fund for *building churches, purchasing glebes and glebe-houses,* augmenting poor livings, and other ecclesiastical improvements. The management of the fund was vested in trustees, consisting of the higher dignitaries of the church, and principal law-officers of the crown, who were empowered to " *search out the just and true value*" of the benefices of which they were to levy the first year's income from each incumbent who came into possession.   The valuation under which the first fruits were levied when they were given to the trustees, was the same as in the time of Henry VIII. and was not only very low, but did not include more than *two-thirds* of the benefices of Ireland. It was of course the duty of the Board of First Fruits to promote the objects of the fund, to have remedied the inaccuracies, and supplied the omissions in the original valuation; but this has never been done, and up to this day the first fruits are levied according to the defective valuation at the time of the Reformation. Owing to this mode of procedure, instead of the produce of the first fruits being the real worth of every vacant benefice and dignity, it is a mere nominal sum paid by the clergy. The bishop of Derry, with a revenue of £12,000, pays only £250 first fruits ; the see of Clogher, worth £7000, pays only £350 ; and the see of Cloyne, worth £6000, pays only £10 : 10. It is calculated that, at a fair valuation of Irish benefices, omitting those under £150 a-year, the first fruits would produce £40,000 a-year: whereas, in the ten years ending January, 1830, they produced only £5,142 : 15. ; from which £740 was to be deducted for salaries.* During this period of ten years, fifteen bishoprics and four archbishoprics had become vacant, and the successors thereto liable to the payment of first fruits.

Can it be believed that the Imperial Parliament would sanction such an evasion of their duty by the rich clergy of Ireland? Such, however, has been the fact. Sir JOHN NEWPORT, every session for the last twelve years, has been making motions to establish the integrity of the First Fruits Fund; but his laudable endeavours have seldom met with the support of more than *thirty* or *forty* honourable members. But this is not the worst trait in the proceedings of the Collective Wisdom of the Nation: they have actually voted large sums out of the pockets of the people for the very objects for which this fund was appropriated. In the twenty years ending in 1822, the grants of parliament to the trustees of First Fruits in Ireland, towards building new churches, glebe-houses, and purchasing glebes, amounted to £686,000. Thus has £34,300 a-year been levied on this tax-paying aristocratic gulled nation, merely to save the richest church in the world from contributing to its own necessities. How much more has been levied by parochial taxation on the unfortunate population of Ireland, for the repair of churches and cathedrals, we have not the means of estimating. It is well known the sums raised for this purpose constitute one of the many grievances of the sister kingdom, the hardship of which is aggravated by the Catholics being excluded from voting in parish vestries when the church-cess is imposed. Had the Commissioners of First Fruits done what the law not only authorized, but required them to do, there would have been no need of church-rates, nor grants from parliament. Why the Commissioners have not done their duty and made a fair valuation of benefices is manifest enough; they are the patrons, holders, or expectants of large preferments, and a just valuation would be a tax upon THEMSELVES! Ought, however, " the Guardians of the Public Purse" to have sanctioned this selfish breach of trust? Ought they, whose business is to watch over the interests of the people, yearly to have voted away the public money, for objects for which there was already a legal and adequate provision? No innovation, nothing untried was to be attempted; the only measure requisite was that they should enforce the *law of the land*, for which, on other occasions, they profess such profound veneration. It is to the deficiencies of First Fruits, and the consequent non-residence of the clergy, for want of parsonage-houses and glebes, that the decay of Protestantism has been ascribed by their servile defenders: hence a regard to the interests of our " holy religion" one would have thought a sufficient motive for our virtuous representatives to interfere.

---

* Votes and Proceedings of the House of Commons, May 18, 1830.

The most curious incident regarding the annats is the result of the endeavours of Mr. Shaw Mason, the Remembrancer of First Fruits in Ireland, to obtain a more authentic valuation.   When the subject began to excite attention, this gentleman, the words of whose patent empowered him " to collect, levy, receive, and examine the just and true value of first fruits," preferred a memorial to the Board, setting forth his authority and expressing his willingness to exercise it as his duty required.   The announcement caused not a little alarm, the four archbishops at the time not having paid in their arrears.   A report was made to the local government, who, after referring the matter to the attorney and solicitor generals for their opinions, intimated to Mr Mason if he persevered in his design of enforcing the payment of First Fruits at their real value, they would *deprive him of his patent office*, which he held at the pleasure of the Crown.*   The subject has been subsequently revived by the marquis of Anglesey, but with no better success; Messrs. Blackburn and Crampton, the attorney and solicitor generals of Ireland, having delivered an opinion in accordance with that previously given by lord Plunket—namely, " that the crown is not now entitled to *re-value* any benefice of which a valuation has heretofore been made and certified."†

So the matter rests ; the rich clergy enjoy, undiminished, their princely revenues, and the public remains liable to the burthen of contributing towards the purchase of glebes and houses for Irish parsons, many of whom have already half a dozen houses, residing in none of them, and 4000 acres of glebe.

Promotions in the Irish Church.

An important document was laid before the House of Commons in the session of 1831, (Parl. Paper No. 328.)   It is a return made on the subject of the First Fruits in Ireland, containing a statement of the wealth and other information connected with that establishment. From the information spread over its 134 pages, is given the following abridgement of facts.

Since the month of August, 1812, to which date the returns go back, we find that there were 26 promotions, or translations, to the bishoprics, thus:—Lord John George Beresford, archbishop of Armagh, in 1822, having been raised to the see of Clogher only in 1819, and to the archbishopric of Dublin in 1820 ; Percy Jocelyn to the see of Clogher in 1819, and Lord Robert Tottenham to the same see in 1822 ; William Magee to the see of Raphoe in 1819, and William Bissett to the same see in 1822 ; Nathaniel Alexander to the see of Meath in 1823; Richard Mant to the see of Down and Connor in 1823; no episcopal promotion in Derry; ditto in Kilmore; John Leslie to the see of Dro-

---

* Mr. Spring Rice, House of Commons, May 18, Session 1830.
† Parl. Paper, No. 185, Session 1831.

more in 1812, and James Saurin to the same see in 1819; Lord John George Beresford to the archiepiscopal see of Dublin in 1820, and William Magee to the same in 1822; in Kildare no episcopal promotion; Robert Fowler to the see of Ossory in 1813; Lord Robert Tottenham to the sees of Leighlin and Ferns in 1820, and Thomas Elrington to the same sees in 1822; Richard Lawrence to the sees of Cashel and Emly in 1822; Thomas Elrington, in 1820, to the see of Limerick, and John Jebb to the same in 1822; hon. R. Bourke to the see of Waterford in 1813; in Cork no episcopal promotion; Charles M. Warburton from Limerick to Cloyne in 1820, and John Brinkley to the same see in 1826; Richard Mant to the see of Killaloe in 1820; Alexander Arbuthnot to the same see in 1823; and the hon. R. Ponsonby in 1828; Power-le-Poer Trench to the archbishoprick of Tuam and see of Ardagh in 1819; John Leslie, in 1819, to the see of Elphin; in Clonfert no episcopal promotion; in Killala no episcopal promotion.

It will be seen at once that these names are principally those of *aristocratical* houses, or of families possessed of *parliamentary interest;* perhaps the only one of the whole in which such interest did not influence the selection is that of Dr. Brinkley, who was elevated to the see on account of his great talent.

The yearly incomes of the archbishops are stated to be—Armagh, £15,080 : 15 : 6; Tuam, £5,548 : 19 : 11; Cashel, £3,500 and upwards, while of Dublin no return is made; of the others, Clogher is returned £9,000 late currency; Derry, £10,000 and upwards, late currency; Meath, £5,815 : 14 : 5; Raphoe, £5,379 : 14 : 1; Leighlin and Ferns, £5000 to a fraction; Ossory, £3000 to a fraction; Dromore, £4,863 : 3 : 5; Waterford, £5000 exact money; Cork, £3000 ditto; Limerick (renewal fines, nearly as much more, not included) £2,915 : 19 : 8½; Cloyne, £2000 " and upwards at the least;" Killala, £4,600; from the dioceses in Tuam there is no return made, " as there is no record of the value of the several bishopricks and dignitaries of the province in the registrar's office."

A curious fact observable throughout the return is, the number of individuals of the same *name* as the bishop who had the good luck to get into livings soon after his attainment of the episcopal dignity; for example:—

Knox in possession of Derry at the commencement of these returns; then follow—J. Spencer Knox, June, 1813, rectory of Fahan, £360 a-year; August same year, hon. Charles Knox, rectory of Urney, £700 a-year; June, 1814, W. Knox, rectory of Upper Brandony, £396 : 18 : 6 a-year; same date, hon. Edm. Knox, rectory of Tamlught O'Crilly, no amount specified, but 564 acres of church land in the city and county of Londonderry; James Spencer Knox (again) two more rectories, Magheras and Kilnonaghan, £1,365 : 7 : 7½ per annum, and 926 acres of church land; April, same year, Wm. Knox, rectory of Fahan, £360 a-year; October, same year, William (the same perhaps) Knox, rectory of Tamlaghtard, £425 per annum; August, 1821, W. Knox (again!) rectory of Clonleigh, £840 a-year, and 427 acres of church land;

October, 1822, W. Knox (the fifth time), rectory of Ballinascreen, £623 : 1 : 6½ and 543 acres; and, finally, in June, 1830, the last presentation returned Edmund J. Knox, rector of Killown, £160 a-year. Altogether, the Knoxes have got since 1812 (mention is not made in these returns of what they had before) £5,230 : 7 : 8 per annum, and 3,555 acres of land, besides the annual income of one of which no return is made. There are two Knoxes in Dromore with 1,082 acres.

W. Magee, see of Raphoe, 1819, May, 1820, John Magee, rectory and vicarage of Mevagh, £375 a-year; July, 1825, John Magee again, prebend of Killyman, £276 : 18 : 5½, and 450 acres. Let us here follow his lordship to the see of Dublin, whither he was translated in 1822. W. Magee, vicarage of Finglas, March, 1823, no annual value stated; April, 1826, T. P. Magee, rectory and vicarage of Inch, and vicar of Kilgorman, £365 : 9 : 4½ a-year; T. P. Magee, December, 1826, prebend of Tipperkiven, £127 : 10, and 78 acres; T. P. Magee (third time), same month and year, curacy of St. Michael, Dublin, no amount stated; May, 1829, T. P. Magee (fourth), prebend of St. John's, no value stated; January, 1830, W. Magee, rectory of Dunganstown, no value returned; April, 1830, T. P. Magee (fifth time), prebend of Wicklow, so much talked of, value not stated. T. P. Magee seems either a very fortunate gentleman, or the brightest ornament of the church, judging from the number and rapidity of his promotions, for in addition to those conferred upon him by his father, we find him appointed, in April, 1830, archdeacon of Kilmacduagh.

Waterford and Lismore.—Hon. Richard Bourke to the see in 1813; we have, in Feb. 1817, Hon. George Bourke, a prebend and rectory; in Sept. 1819, the same individual to two rectories and two vicarages, value £471 : 14; a third time, in Aug. 1819, to the prebend and rectory of Leskan, no value stated; again in December, same year (for although the "Hon." is here dropped, it is evidently the same favoured gentleman), to the prebendary and rectory of Kilgobenet, no value stated, and yet a fifth time, in August, 1827, to a precentorship and a rectory, value £1,569 : 4 : 7 per annum. There is also the Hon. Joseph Bourke in October, 1829, to a chantorship, value not stated.

In *Cork* the Hon. R. Laurence was in possession in 1812, since which the promotions of the St. Laurences have been between three individuals : the treasurership in 1815; a vicarage, June, 1818, £461 : 10s. : 8d.; a rectory and three vicarages in the same month and year (not the same person, however), value £1,365 : 17s. : 7d. per annum; a vicarage, in June, 1823, £461 : 10 : 2; at this time Edward made way for Robert, and got instead, three months after, a prebend and four rectories, value £1,162 : 10 : 8 a year, making "a difference" of £700 per annum in his favour; May, 1825, a vicar choralship; and July, 1826, a rectory and vicarage, value not given; in the diocese of Ross, attached to that of Cork, there are ten promotions of the St. Laurences, the value of four of which, the only ones stated, is £1435 per annum.

Kildare.—Dr. Lindsay, in possession of the see in 1812. June,

1815, Charles Lindsay, prebend, rectory, and vicarage of Harristown, and second canonry of St. Bridget's, £220: April, 1828, Charles Lindsay (again), archdeaconry, value not stated, and March, 1823, Charles Lindsay (fourth time,) canonry of St. Bridget's, value not stated.

Ossory.—R. Fowler to the see in 1812; in April, 1824, Luke Fowler gets a union, consisting of a prebend, four rectories, and four vicarages, value annually £874 : 4 : 3; and in March, 1828, Luke Fowler gets two more vicarages, no value stated.

Ferns and Leighlin.—Thomas Elrington to the see in 1821. Dates of the promotions of H. P. Elrington: July, 1823, a prebend and vicarage, no value stated: October, 1824, a precentorship, rectory, and vicarage, £1,200 a year; February, 1824, three vicarages and a rectory, £609 : 4. : 7. per annum.

In 1819 we find Power le Poer Trench in the sees of Tuam and Ardagh; then follow, November, 1820, Hon. C. P. Trench, a rectory and vicarage, £461 : 10 : 9; November, 1821, ditto, an archdeaconry; May, 1825, ditto, a prebendary: same date, W. le Poer Trench two rectories, value £315 : 4 : 7; and October, 1830, ditto, a rectory and vicarage, no value stated, but 523 acres of church land.

In *Killala and Achonry* the Verschoyles are numerous enough to justify a suspicion that they are related to the diocesan; there is one with six vicarages at one promotion; he has also an archdeaconry, a provostship, a prebend, and a vicarage; another of the same name, with a "sen." attached to it, has four vicarages and a prebend, value £949 : 16 : 5 per annum, and 727 acres of church lands.

Meath.—N. Alexander to the see, 1823; James Alexander to the rectory and vicarage of Killucan, 1828.

R. Mant, Down and Connor, 1823; R. M. Mant, archdeacon, 1828; R. M. Mant (the same), vicarage of Billay, 1823.

In *Dromore*, James Saurin, to the see in 1819; November, 1821, Lewis Saurin, rectory of Morin; and July, 1827, James Saurin, vicarage of Seagor, £500 a year.

Cloyne.—Bishop Warburton was translated from Limerick, in 1812, and in March, 1822, his second gift of a living went to Charles Warburton, to the value of £323 : 1. ; 6½. annually.

In 1820, Richard Mant was appointed to the see of Killaloe and Kilfenora; a promotion of R. M. Mant is found, three rectories and two vicarages, value £498 : 8 : 2 in July, 1821.

Even a cursory glance at these returns shows the reader how numerous in the church are the *Beresfords :* of that name there are an archbishop and a bishop; and in the dioceses, six in number, where they chiefly abound, they possess not less than fourteen livings, of which only four have their value annexed, amounting to £1,857 : 11 : 2; and 64,803 acres of land ! !

The other names which occur most frequently beside those we have stated are Tottenham, Stopford, Ottiwell Moore, Porter, St. George, Pakenham, Langrishe, Brabazon, Alexander, Hamilton, Pomeroy,

Stewart, Torrens, Ponsonby, Wingfield, Dawson, Montgomery, Bernard, and Brooke.

We subjoin the summary of the returns : from which it appears—

1st. That between the month of August, 1812, and the date of this return, 1,383 spiritual promotions, comprehending the same number of benefices, have taken place within the several dioceses in Ireland.

2d. That the 1,383 benefices, to which promotions have been so made, contain 353 dignities, including the archbishoprics and bishopricks, and 2,061 parishes, &c.

3d. That 297 of the aforesaid dignities, and 405 parishes have been taxed, and are paying first fruits to the amount of £9,947 : 11 : 3½ ; and that the remainder of said dignities and parishes are either exempted from payment, under the statute of Elizabeth, or have never been taxed and put in charge.

4th. That valuations have been made, under the Tithe Composition Act, in 1,194 of the above-mentioned parishes, to the annual amount of £303,620 : 0 : 6½.

5th. That 1,034 of the said parishes have glebes annexed to them, amounting to 82,645 acres ; and that the see lands on promotions occurring amount to 410,430 acres.

6th. That the total number of acres contained in both glebe and see lands, as referred to in this return, amount to 493,075 acres ; and

7th. That the total number of acres belonging to the several sees in Ireland, with the exception of the dioceses of Down and Connor, Raphoe and Dromore, amount to 489,141 acres ; the pecuniary values of which have not yet been officially ascertained.

Intolerance towards Dissenters and Roman Catholics.

Before concluding our account of the United Church of England and Ireland, we cannot help shortly adverting to the slow steps by which religious toleration has been established in this country. Looking back to the history of the Dissenters, we see with what difficulty freedom of thought has been wrung from the prosecuting grasp of what is considered a reformed Establishment. It was not till the Revolution of 1688 that the public worship of the Dissenters was tolerated ; and the Act of Toleration at that period required them to take certain oaths and subscribe to the doctrinal articles of the Church of England. The same act, so much extolled, requires the places of worship to be registered, and the doors kept unlocked during the time of service. Even liberty of worship, under these suspicious and odious restrictions, it was subsequently attempted to abridge. In the latter part of Queen Anne's reign, an act passed, called the *Occasional Conformity Bill*, making it a crime in any person, in any office under government, entering a meeting-house. Another bill, denominated the *Schism Bill*, passed in 1714, suffered no Dissenter to educate his own children, but required them to be put into the hands of a Church of Englandist, and forbad all tutors and schoolmasters being present at any dissenting place of worship.

The last attempt upon this body was the memorable bill of Lord Sidmouth in 1810. The meditated encroachment upon their liberties was worthy of the sinister statesman from whom it emanated. The Dissenters, to their immortal honour, rushed forward at once to repel this aggression on their rights. Had they suffered their ministers to be placed at the mercy of the *Quarter Sessions*, the magistrates, no doubt, would not only have judged of their fitness for the ministry of the Gospel, but also of their fitness for the ministry of the Boroughmongers.

This disgraceful spirit of legislation is now only matter for history. The repeal of the Corporation and Test Acts and the Catholic Relief Act have scarcely left any trace of the formidable penal code which, for a long time, interdicted to a large portion of the community not only the enjoyment of their civil immunities, but the free disposal of their persons and property. Both Dissenters and Roman Catholics may still complain of not being eligible to fill the office of lord chancellor, or be a member of the privy council; they may complain of being excluded from the national universities, and may think it a hardship in case they fill any judicial, civil, or corporate office, that they cannot appear in their *official costume*, nor with the *insignia of their office* at their own places of worship; but these are trifling grievances, scarcely worth mentioning. They are subject to no test on account of *religious belief*; and it may be now truly said that, with the exception of JEWS and openly professing INFIDELS, the honours and advantages of the social state—so far, at least, as spiritual dogmas are concerned—are fairly opened to every candidate.

For this salutary triumph we have been indebted solely to *secular* wisdom, not to any generous concession or enlightenment proceeding from our established instructors. The Church has always shown itself more tenacious of its monopoly than even the Aristocracy. Of the lofty tone of intolerance maintained by some of our high dignitaries, to a recent period, we have a rather amusing instance in the conduct of DR. KIPLING, the late Dean of Peterborough, and which we shall shortly relate. The Rev. Mr. Lingard, the distinguished Roman Catholic historian, had, it seems, in his Strictures on Professor Marsh's " Comparative View," &c. used the words " *new* Church of England" once, and oftener " the modern Church of England." To consider the Church of England " new" or " modern" appeared a mortal offence in the eyes of *Dean Kipling*. He wrote a furious letter to Mr. Lingard; quoted a passage from Hawkins; and threatened to prosecute him if he did not, within a limited time, prove what the Dean intimated it was impossible for him to prove. Whether the Dean afterwards relented, or whether Mr. Lingard proved that the Church of England, as being the offspring or daughter of the Church of Rome, which, in many respects, she so much resembles, was " new," we are ignorant. Did our limits permit, we would insert the Very Rev. Dean's loving epistle. It would show what a meek, gentle, Christian spirit may still rankle in the hearts of some of our church dignitaries. It would show to what expedients these worthies would resort to uphold their faith, or, more correctly, their temporalities, were they not restrained by the march of philosophy and the public mind. It is impossible to read *Dean Kipling's* letter without feeling persuaded that, had Mr. Lingard had no better barrier for his personal safety than the tolerant spirit of the writer, he might still be liable to be hung up by the middle, with an iron chain, and roasted before a slow fire, according to the orthodox piety of olden time.

Men ought always to set their faces against prosecution for *opinions*, whether instituted under pretence of heresy, sectarianism, Judaism, or even infidelity. Under any of these forms it is the same mischievous and dogmatical principle. What difference, for instance, is there in the principles of a prosecution instituted at this day for Judaism or infidelity, and a Popish prosecution instituted in the reign of Queen Mary on account of the *real presence*. In both cases difference of opinion is combated by corporeal infliction; the Papist punished by fire, the modern intolerant by fine, imprisonment, or civil disability. The difference in the punishment makes no difference in the motive; in both cases it is combating *mind* by physical force, and he who employs such a weapon is as deeply immersed in the night of Popery, as Bishop Bonner, who laboured to convert the miserable victims of his cruelty by a vigorous application of birch to the posteriors.

The ingenuous mind revolts from the idea of maintaining opinions by *force*: to say that any class of opinions shall not be impugned, that their truth shall not be called in question, is at once to declare that these opinions are infallible, and that their authors cannot err. What can be more egregiously absurd and presumptuous? It is fixing bounds to human knowledge, and saying that men cannot learn by experience; that they can never be wiser in future than they are to day. The vanity and folly of this is sufficiently evinced by the history of religion and philosophy. Great changes have taken place in both; and what our ancestors considered indisputable truths their posterity discovered to be gross errors. To continue the work of improvement, no dogmas, however plausible, ought to be protected from investigation; and the only security of the present generation against the errors of their progenitors, is modestly to admit that, in some things, they may possibly yet be mistaken.

The Papists are not the only class of religionists obnoxious to the reproach of uncharitable tenets. H U ME justly remarks that *toleration* is not the virtue of priests of any denomination; and this is amply confirmed by the history of the Scottish, Romish, and English churches. They have all *shed blood*, tortured, and punished, when circumstances gave them an ascendancy. The reason is obvious. Religion is more the result of *feeling* than of *understanding;* and, it may be expected that its most intense professors should be more prompt to use the vulgar weapons suggested by passion and violence, then listen to the dictates of reason and humanity.

Crisis of the Irish Church at the close of 1831.

In Ireland ecclesiastical oppression appears to have reached its term of duration. When a people become unanimous, their fiat is omnipotent and without appeal. It is this which will abase the usurpations of the Boroughmongers, and the same power has decided the fate of the Irish Protestant clergy. At the time we are writing there is all but a national insurrection against the tithe system. In Queen's County, in Kilkenny, Clare, and Tipperary, the resistance to clerical oppression is nearly unanimous—and the spirit is rapidly spreading to other counties. The incomes of many of the clergy have become merely nominal; instead of seizing and selling the produce of others, they are compelled, as a means of temporary subsistence, to bring their own domestic chattels under the hammer of the auctioneer. Yet the law is in their favour; the courts have power to decree and the sheriffs to seize the goods of the refractory. But who will buy—*who dare bid at a tithe auction?* There is the rub. Laws and acts of parliament are empty sounds—they are mere " ink and parchment unless guaranteed by public opinion." The police, the magistracy, and an army of 30,000 men are powerless against six millions united.

Ministers, finding the battle is lost, have brought the subject before parliament. But it may be doubted whether their views are yet commensurate with the vastness of the undertaking. The Protestant church may be considered virtually dissolved ; in fact and opinion it is gone. It has fallen, not so much from its secular oppression as its monstrous incongruities, and from its failing to answer one object— moral, social, or political—for which a church was ever established and supported. A composition for tithe, for the benefit of the priesthood, is out of the question; nothing remains but a general commutation with the landed interest for the benefit of the public—we say the *public*, because the fee simple of church property is not in the clergy, but in the community at large. The example of Scotland must be followed and improved upon. An equal provision or NONE for the pastors *of all sects*, a provision for the poor and for popular education, are the fragments to be seized out of the wreck of the establishment. At all events, in the approaching transition, the tithes must not be suffered to *slip into the rents* of an absentee proprietary. No! Ireland must have the benefit of the TWO MILLIONS* now spent in other climes. It

---

* Mr. Leader estimated the sum annually drawn out of Ireland in tithes and the rents of glebe and bishops' lands at £1,785,000. (House of Commons, December 11th, 1831.) Our previous statements from official returns will have satisfied our readers that this is not an exaggerated estimate.

would clothe her nakedness, reclaim her wastes, appease her hunger, and civilize her generous but yet barbarous population.

A system like that described in preceding pages could not, by possibility, be lasting. It contained within itself the seeds of destruction. Yet it has been long and obstinately persevered in through midnight outrage, assassination, and massacre. To enforce this abominable oppression 26,000 persons have been butchered in twentys and tens within the last thirty years.* Surely this hecatomb of victims is large enough to appease the Moloch of ecclesiastical cupidity. Horrible as the system has been, the mere proposition for reform has been delayed to the twelfth hour. So long as the people only suffered, their cries were unheeded. But the clergy themselves are now the victims; they have lost their incomes; they did very well without churches and congregations, but they cannot do without tithes; so the legislature flies to their relief. The millions pleaded in vain, but their handful of oppressors is listened to. Is this justice? No! it is only fear and selfishness. Nevertheless, like good Christians, we must pardon injuries—forget the past—and provide for a better futurity.

While we fervently hope to see the condition of Ireland improved by the cultivation of her vast resources, by the improvement of her laws and magistracy, by the annihilation of factious interests, and by a provision for her destitute poor, still we cannot help entering our protest against the repeal of the UNION. Had not the decree against the Boroughmongers gone forth, we might have embraced such an alternative; but as the days of the Oligarchy are numbered, we can see no good reason for separating the destinies of Ireland from those of England. It is useless to disguise—the ultimate object sought by the Repealers is the erection of Ireland into an independent state under the presidentship, kingship, or something else of the " Liberator:" but men, we trust, are too enlightened to be ridden over rough-shod, either by the wiles of priests, of mendicant patriots, or military adventurers. We do not inquire what individuals—but what the people would gain by this revolution? From Britain it would sever the right arm of her power; and what advantages would Ireland reap by a separate existence? She does not possess, within herself, the elements to constitute an united, prosperous, and enlightened community. Supposing, for a moment, she escaped a century of civil war, and forthwith passed under the yoke of the " ex-king of Kerry," with a deplorably ignorant population for his lieges—a fanatical, but richly endowed priesthood, as they would be with the lands and tithes of the Protestant establishment—for the servile instruments of his sovereignty—what a spectacle would she present! Under such a regime, it is easy to discern insuperable obstacles to every social improvement. For ages she would be no better under her *new* autocrat, than Portugal under Don Miguel, or Naples under the sway of a Bourbon. Every sincere well-wisher to the greatness and happi-

---

* Statement made at the Aggregate Meeting, Dublin, August 2nd, 1831.

ness of England and Ireland must deplore the idea of dismemberment:
united, they may be a source of mutual light and power; dissevered,
they would be the luminary of day and lamp of night struck from their
orbits. Such an event holds out no remedy for any specific evil;
whatever measures for the good of Ireland could be effected by the
senate of College-green, may be effected by the reformed parliament of
the united kingdom; and this without the delay, clash, and conflict
inseparable from rival legislatures. A dissolution, therefore, of the
empire cannot be sought as the mean of public good, but as a mere
stalking-horse to selfish aggrandisement.

Under an enlightened general government, England and Ireland may
pull together for the mutual advantage of both, and, we trust, by speedy
and effective reforms, so unfortunate a catastrophe as a legislative separation will be averted. It cannot be forgotten how Ireland was governed
by her own parliament — the most corrupt, selfish, and ignorant set of
legislators that ever assembled between four walls. For what then
should it be revived? The true policy for tranquillizing the country
and disarming faction is obvious; remove grievances and confer benefits.
Instead of burthening the yet struggling manufactures and agriculture
of the Irish with *additional taxes,* as was sought to be done by the
Wellington ministry, a resource ought to be sought in the crown-lands
of Ireland, and in the wasted estates of the Church, in the million of
neglected acres possessed by absentee bishops, and in the million and
more worth of land and tithe possessed by the collegiate bodies and non-
resident incumbents. Here is the panacea for cementing the UNION,
producing contentment, and supplying the wants of an impoverished
Exchequer.

The besotted tyranny which has impeded the prosperity of Ireland
will hardly be credited by posterity. Her population is only *half-
civilized;* in religion, manners, and domestic habits, no better than
the rabble of the Peninsula; while her lands in whole districts are as
little cultivated as the wilds of Tartary. We do not allude to the bog
and mountain wastes; and these, in great part, continue such from an
obstinate legislation which tolerates, year after year, the remains of
baronial tenures;—but would it be believed that there is, or was, so
recently as 1821, a tract of country in the south of Ireland, occupying
800 square miles of territory, in which there is not a single resident
gentleman, nor clergyman, nor a single road fit for a wheel-carriage to
pass? This is the testimony of Mr. Baron FOSTER; and hear it,
Boroughmongers! you, who have expended millions to fortify Canada,
as you did the Netherlands, for a *rival* power, and to provide colonial
sinecures and offices in sugar islands, converted into *hells* for the infliction of torture on your fellow-creatures,—hear, and *look at home,* how
you have governed and elicited the resources of our great dependency,
placed at the threshhold, in the very bosom of the empire!

Who can revert to the history of the Oligarchy without indignation?
Rotten boroughs and tithes, as much as sinecures, pensions, and exor-
bitant salaries, have been the great obstacles to sound national policy.
The holders and expectants of these have been ever bandied together, no

less by a sense of common iniquity than common interest, to oppose every salutary amelioration. On every public occasion, on every general election, the priest and the placeman united to oppose the enemy of imposture and peculation: from these no hope of good could be indulged; but the people have at length risen in their might, and the days of misrule will speedily end.

Conclusion.

We have now fairly brought forward whatever can elucidate the present state of the United Church of England and Ireland, and its claims to the support and veneration of the community. Those whose vocation is to mislead and delude may attempt to impugn our statements and calumniate our motives; but their labour will be vain, unless they can disprove our FACTS. We have trusted to nothing apocryphal, and rarely depend on the testimony of individual observers. Our statements have been chiefly drawn from the admissions of the parties who wallow in the corruptions of which we complain,—from official returns to parliament,—and other accredited sources of information. On the results derived from these we have occasionally submitted reflections, the justice of which we leave to the reader's consideration.

If such ecclesiastical establishments as we have exposed be much longer tolerated in their existing state, the people will evince a patience and fatuity far exceeding any previous estimate. No doubt there are mysteries in the art of governing, as well as truths in science, that have not yet been discovered. It is impossible to foresee what unheard-of wiles, delusions, and influence, priestly cunning may bring into play to stifle the claims of truth and justice. A nation, which, from groundless fear of change, was deluded into the support of a *thirty year's* war against human rights and happiness, and had entailed upon it a debt of eight hundred millions, may, by some new fascination, be brought to tolerate a church that absorbs annually ELEVEN MILLIONS of public income, ostensibly for religion, though it is religion's most dangerous foe, and not one hundredth part of which rewards the labours of those really engaged in clerical duty. A pretended anxiety for our spiritual welfare, will, however, no longer serve for a cloak to temporal rapacity. The repetition of such detected knavery would be a national insult and impertinence: some new-fangled scarecrows, therefore, must be devised, other than the dangers of irreligion and democratic encroachment, to consecrate hereafter the oppression of tithes and the absurdities of rotten boroughs.

Secular abuses sink almost into insignificance when compared with those of the church establishment. *One hundred and thirteen* privy councillors receiving £650,164 a-year out of the public taxes, was an astounding fact; but we are sure, and those who have honoured us with attention in the preceding exposition, we are convinced, will believe us when we affirm it would be easy to select a smaller number of sinecure ecclesiastics who receive more and do less than this devouring clan of Oligarchs.

DIGEST of the IRISH BENEFICES, from the DIOCESAN RETURNS.

DIOCESES.	Benefices with Cure constituting Benefices of Souls.	Number of Parishes constituting Benefices.	Churches.	Benefices without Churches.	Unions.	Glebe Houses.	Benefices without Glebe Houses.	Benefices without Glebe Lands.	Incumbents resident.	Incumbents absent.
Armagh	78	103	81	1	11	74	4	4	67	11
Cashell and Emly	57	131	40	17	31	34	23	15	34	23
Clogher	44	46	51	4	2	31	13	3	25	19
Clonfert and Kilmacduagh	14	61	15	1	14	8	6	0	9	5
Cloyne	78	123	59	20	27	22	55	33	33	45
Cork and Ross	77	107	65	14	18	30	47	28	31	46
Derry	54	57	54	2	2	44	10	3	38	16
Down and Connor	79	123	81	5	26	45	34	28	54	25
Dromore	23	26	25	0	1	16	7	4	15	8
Dublin	87	151	83	11	28	41	46	38	49	38
Elphin	37	91	30	7	17	16	6	15	19	18
Kildare	43	72	28	19	19	12	31	20	18	25
Killala and Achonry	20	52	20	0	12	15	4	1	14	6
Killaloe and Kilfenora	51	129	50	5	36	39	12	9	36	15
Kilmore	33	41	36	0	6	23	10	0	20	13
Leighlin and Ferns	92	182	95	6	45	39	53	38	69	23
Limerick, Ardfert, and Aghadoe	105	165	69	5	39	37	68	51	50	55
Meath	101	211	94	11	42	83	18	6	76	25
Ossory	59	135	47	13	22	35	24	13	33	26
Raphoe	26	31	32	0	1	23	8	2	20	6
Tuam and Ardagh	49	124	47	3	27	33	15	6	31	18
Waterford and Lismore	63	98	38	18	27	17	35	26	22	41
	1270	2259	1140	192	453	717	529	343	763	507

REVENUES OF THE CROWN.

ROYALTY, after all, is an expensive government! What is a king without an aristocracy and a priesthood? and what are any of these, unless supported in splendour and magnificence? It is a system in which men are sought to be governed by the senses rather than the understanding, and is more adapted to a barbarous than civilized state. Pageantry and ceremony, the parade of crowns and coronets, of gold keys, sticks, white wands, and black rods; of ermine and lawn, and maces and wigs;—these are the chief attributes of monarchy. They are more appropriate to the state of the king of the Birmans or of the Ashantees than the sovereign of an European community. They cease to inspire respect when men become enlightened, when they have learnt that the real object of government is to confer the greatest happiness on the people at the least expense: but it is a beggarly greatness, an absurd system, that would perpetuate these fooleries amidst an impoverished population,—amidst debts, and taxes, and pauperism.

In treating of the revenues of the crown it will be important to observe the distinction between the ancient patrimony of the sovereign, denominated the hereditary revenues, and the modern parliamentary grant, substituted in lieu of them, called the *Civil List*. Of the nature of the latter—the various charges upon it in the maintenance of the king's household and other disbursements—of its extravagant amount during the profligate reign of George IV. and of the total burthen entailed by the royal expenditure on the people, we shall treat in the next chapter. In the present we shall confine ourselves to an exposition of the amount, the application, and management of the hereditary revenues; consisting of the landed possessions of the Crown, of Admiralty droits, Gibraltar duties, Leeward-Island duties, the property of persons dying intestate without heirs, forfeiture in courts of justice, the incomes of bishoprics during vacancies, surplus of the Scotch civil list, profit on waifs, shipwrecks, treasure-trove, and other minor sources. The other branches of the hereditary revenue, arising from the excise, wine licenses, and post-office, it does not fall within our purpose to investigate; they have been carried to the general account of taxes, and disbursed, we believe, as honestly as other portions of the public income.

Parliament having granted a specific annuity, out of the taxes, for the support of the dignity of the Crown, the public was led to believe, during the two last reigns, that the produce of the hereditary revenues had been appropriated to the wants of the state. This, it will be shown in the sequel, was a complete and egregious delusion. It will be seen that the ancient revenues of the Crown were left at the uncontrolled disposal of ministers. That they were chiefly expended in objects personal to themselves, the king, or royal family; in pensions and grants to their parliamentary supporters, their relatives, and adherents; in the purchase of tithe and church-patronage; in occasional charitable donations, ostentatiously granted, under pretext of mitigating the sufferings of distressed artizans and manufacturers; in payments into the privy purse, for the more lavish support of court prodigality; in the building and pulling down of palaces; in payments for defraying the expense of the royal household, and other outgoings, which ought to have been defrayed out of the civil list: in short, it will be seen that, for seventy years, the public was not only burthened with an enormous provision for a civil list, but, by an extraordinary kind of Tory management, failed to derive any advantage from those funds, in lieu of which a civil list had been specially granted.

For obvious reasons, the leading men in the House of Commons always manifested great reluctance to touch on these subjects. Although it is well known that, allowance being made for difference in the value of money, and the charges transferred to other funds, the income of George IV. exceeded that of his predecessor by more than HALF A MILLION, not one of the people's advocates—not even the more ostentatious patriots—Brougham, Hume, Russell, or Graham—ever brought the shameless extravagance fairly before the country. It is possible, as we have hinted, there may have existed reasons for this complacence towards royal profusion. In spite of the encroachments of the Oligarchy, a king of England possesses great power, and has abundant means of rewarding expectants and supporters: he is not only the fountain of honour, but enjoys, nearly, all the patronage in church and state; and the more virtuous aspirants in public life may have felt reluctant to shipwreck all hope of once basking in the sunshine of the court. However, we feel no restraint from these considerations. Moreover we consider the sovereign, like other state functionaries, only the servant of the public: and the public sustaining a great burthen on his account, under the pretext that the duties of his office are essential to the welfare of the people, they have clearly a right to be informed of the amount and mode of his outgoings. In what follows it will be seen what a lavish expenditure has been tolerated during a period when successive ministers have been loud and vehement in professing a desire to reduce every establishment to the lowest possible scale, and when it has been often openly and boastingly alleged that economy and retrenchment had been carried to the utmost limit compatible with national service. Our exposition will also throw light on the workings of the borough-government in its highest departments, and uncover many streamlets of corruption which meandered through the upper stratum of our boasted Constitution.

The new disposition made of the hereditary revenues by the Civil List Act of 1831, and which continues in force during the life of the king, we shall notice in its proper place; at present we shall give a brief exposition of those ancient endowments of the monarchy which long formed a principal source of ministerial influence and parliamentary corruption. First of the

CROWN LANDS.

These constitute the remains of the ancient patrimony of the sovereign, originally intended to maintain the dignity and defray the expense of the executive government. Formerly, the kings of England, as of other European states, were supported from the soil, and not by the system of revenue which has been organized in latter times. Manufactures and commerce were almost unknown; of money there was little, and scarcely any imposts. Gradually kings found out the means of supplying their wants by loading their subjects with taxes, which rendered the revenue derived from their private domains of less importance ; and hence, contemporaneously with the progress of fiscal oppression, we may date the neglect and alienation of the hereditary revenues. The chief remains of these possessions are the crown lands, consisting of parks, forests, chases, manors, fisheries, and royalties ; extensive estates, numerous church livings, fee-farm-rents, light-house dues, mines of coal, tin, and copper. The property is situate in almost every part of the kingdom, but principally in the metropolis and vicinity ; much of it is in Wales ; and there are extensive estates in Ireland. The history and management of these royal endowments, their subserviency to political purposes, and their present state and value, we shall shortly describe. It is a subject of much novelty, and one with which even public men have not taken great pains to be informed. Our information is mainly derived from the Reports of the Commissioners of Woods and Forests, from a publication entitled, " Observations on the landed Revenue of the Crown," written by a nephew of the celebrated Viscount Bolingbroke, and from the able speech in the session of 1830, of Mr. D. W. Harvey, the member for Colchester.

William, of Normandy, possessed a landed revenue of £400,000 a-year. From that period the territorial income of the sovereign declined, till the reign of Henry VIII., when, by the sequestration of the wealth of the religious houses, it was again augmented. The public revenue of Queen Elizabeth amounted only to £500,000, of which £132,000 was the produce of the crown estates. During the Commonwealth a commission was appointed by Cromwell to ascertain the extent of the crown lands throughout the kingdom ; and, though the disturbed state of the country, and the jealousy with which the new government was regarded, did not afford him an opportunity of making that property produce as much as it would have done in more tranquil times, yet he disposed of crown property to the amount of two millions sterling. In Cornwall there were 52 honours, manors, and estates belonging to the Crown, of which Cromwell disposed of five or six ; but only three or four of the whole number are now remaining in the hands of government. These alienations by the Protector were, after the restoration, made subservient to a system of royal favour and proscription. Those who were artful enough to seize the proper moment for apostatizing from republicanism to royalty were never disturbed in their purchases ; while others, who were either too tenacious of their principles, or had committed themselves too deeply by the part they took in the civil war, were compelled to surrender the crown property. Neither Chares II. nor James II. could resist the solicitations of rapacious courtiers, and the hereditary estates were leased, for long terms, to the great families at almost nominal rents.

But the greatest inroads on the crown estates were committed about the era of the Revolution of 1688. Such was the rapacity of the patriots of those days, and their ingenuity in devising new taxes to defray the royal expenditure, that William III. was induced to grant nearly the whole of the crown estates to his supporters in parliament. One family, that of Portland, obtained a grant of five-sixths of the whole county of Denbigh. In the next reign a compact was, for the first time, entered into between the sovereign and the people, by which a civil list amounting to nearly £700,000 was given to Queen Anne, as a commutation for the land and other revenues enjoyed by her predecessors ; and the preamble of the Act is worthy of notice, for its object was stated to be " to defray part of the expense of government, and *lessen the burthen on the subject* by means of the preservation and improvement of the crown lands." How public burthens have been lessened by this and subsequent engagements with the sovereign for a civil list will be strikingly illustrated in the sequel. For the present let us continue our narrative.

In the agreement with Queen Anne, it was settled that no crown estate should be leased at a rent less than one-third of its clear annual value ; the remaining two-thirds being left to the disposal of ministers, who thereby were enabled to benefit their friends. Indeed, they often neglected the injunction of the statute, by granting long leases at a rent of a mark, 6s. 8d., 13s. 4d. or other nominal consideration. These abuses afforded a pretext to Shippen, Lockhart, and other members, disappointed in not being permitted a share in the spoil, for introducing a bill, the object of which was the resumption of the crown property obtained by the *heroes* of the glorious Revolution. The bill passed the Commons, but found its grave among the delinquents it was meant to reach, and where many similar acts of utility have been entombed.

From this period nothing more was heard of the crown lands till the accession of George III. ; when it was settled that no lease of them should be granted for less than one-eighth of their annual value ; the other seven-eighths to be taken in fines. Such, however, was the profligacy of ministers, that they first let the land almost for nothing, and, after taking an estimate of it at that rate, *sold it for nothing.* Thus an estate that was worth £5,000, was leased at a rent of £10, and afterwards sold for £200. An estate, comprising the whole of Piccadilly from Park-lane to Swallow-street, together with all the back lanes, was absolutely sold to the Pulteney family, six years after a lease had been granted at the rent of £12 : 16 : 10. for £500. This lease is now nearly expired. The fine park of Bowood, in Wiltshire, after being leased at £30 a-year, was sold for £468 : 10. The manor of Spalding, of the annual value of £4,000, which, after being held by the trustees of the Earl of Dalkeith for no consideration at all, was leased to the Duke of Buccleuch at £5 per annum, and afterwards entirely severed from the crown without any inquiry whatever. In Yorkshire, the estate of Seaton, and another place, together with the alum-works, were sold to Lord Mulgrave for £27,000, the annual value of which was £2,296, including the alum-works, estimated at £20,000. It does not appear what became of the proceeds of the sale, except that they were paid into the Treasury; they may remain there still, but it is certain they have never been applied to any *known* public purpose. An estate, forfeited by the Earl of Derwentwater, worth £9,000 per annum, was sold to two of the Commissioners of Woods and Forests for £1,000. This was too gross to escape, and two members of the " Collective Wisdom," having dabbled in the transaction, were expelled, and two others reprimanded. It is difficult to say whether the Whigs or Tories *sported* most in these land jobs, but the Whigs had certainly the best of it in the reigns of William III. and the two first princes of the Hanover family.

In 1770 the manor of Newark was granted to the Duke of Newcastle, first Lord of the Treasury, and a nobleman, according to the testimony of the first Earl of Chatham, much addicted to mendacity.* The rent reserved on this grant to the Pelhams was £482, and according to law the fine should have been £3374, instead of which only £200 was paid. The lease was renewed by Lord Granville, in 1806, for a term of thirty years, at a rent of £2000 ; the property now consists of 960 acres, covered with dwellings, tolls of bridges, fisheries, and markets, and yields to the proprietor £4000 a-year ; and were it let, without reference to electioneering purposes, would yield £7000 a-year. But the great object of the crown-lessee is to maintain his political influence in the borough ; for which purpose this property is under-let in small portions to yearly tenants, who are thus constrained to vote for any person the Duke of Newcastle thinks fit to nominate. A striking illustration of the Duke's influence was afforded in the year 1829. Sir W. H. Clinton, differing in opinion with the noble boroughmonger, on the Catholic question, he was compelled to resign his seat for Newark ; when his lordship, forthwith, posted down Mr. Sadler as the retiring member's accredited successor. Some of the inhabitants, not liking the idea of a total stranger being crammed down their throats so unceremoniously, rebelled against their lord, voting for Mr. Sergeant Wilde, the opponent of the duke's nominee. This was not to be borne : immediately after the election notices of ejectment were served on the

---

* Lord Melbourne's Diary, p. 376.

rebels ; the duke justifying his vindictive proceeding on the tyrant's plea—that he had a right to do " what he pleased *with his own ;*" affording a practical commentary of the vast utility of the constitutional maxim, which declares it to be a " high infringement upon the liberties of the people for any PEER *to concern himself in the election of members* of the House of Commons."

Leaving the noble trader in boroughs, we shall proceed with others. In Lincoln, there was a crown estate valued at £937, let to Sir W. G. Guise, at £37 a year, as a means of political corruption. The estate of Rosedale, in the mountain recesses of Yorkshire, was held by forty tenants, whose leases expired in 1816, and have since held, from year to year, to the great deterioration of the land. Instead of dividing this property to suit the tenants, many of whom would have been purchasers, it was put up in *one lot*, on the last day of December, when the ground was covered with snow. The reserved bid was £70,000 ; only £37,000 was offered. These reserved bids are injurious, for they prevent competitors from coming forward. Property at Esham was let to Sir John Shaw for £3920 : the crown lessee put it up to sale in lots, and obtained biddings to the amount of £25,000 and upwards : this, it must be observed, was during the excitement produced by paper-money and war prices. In 1815 a lease was granted to Sir John Throgmorton, at a rent of £115, of property of which the estimated value, upon oath, was £1104. Another property of great importance, called Sunk Island, had been lately rescued from the sea. In the report of the commissioners it is described as a parcel of sandy land, at the mouth of the river Humber. From 1771, it was leased for thirty-one years. In 1802, another lease was granted for thirty-one years, at a rent of £700 for the first year, £2000 for the second, and for the remainder of the term £3100. In the second year of his lease the tenant went to an expense of £10,000, in making banks and in other improvements, and the estate is now let by him for £10,000 a-year. The Reverend John Lonsdale is the crown-lessee, and, apparently, a good judge in land speculations. This estate consists of 6000 acres of the finest soil in the kingdom, tithe free, and worth fifty shillings an acre. In 1812, freehold estates to the amount of £1084 of yearly value were sold at twenty years' purchase ; the manor of Eltham, with royalties, lands, &c. for £569 ; King's Cliffe £148 ; the manor of the Chapter of Beverley, with all rights, courts, demesnes, and tenements belonging, for £224 ; and part of the race-course of Newmarket for £154. All these were sold at twenty years' purchase, the land-tax having been previously bought by the Crown at *thirty-nine* years' purchase *from itself*, and sold again at *twenty years'* purchase. It is needless to remark that manors are highly desirable investments ; with courts and royalties annexed, they give a local distinction and importance to the purchasers.

We shall next enter the domain of Woods and Forests, abounding with similar examples of waste and mismanagement as those already cited. Here, again, we meet with the Duke of Newcastle. A broad riding-way was cut for his Grace through Sherwood-forest : the timber cut down was given to his lordship, and the pailing raised at each side of the way was charged to the *public* at £1787. Another nobleman had a right of pasturage for one horse, in Wolmar-forest, and, for the pasturage of this *single horse*, not less than 450 acres of forest-land were appropriated. Rockingham-forest and an estate adjoining were let to Lord Westmoreland at less than *one farthing an acre!* The interests of the crown in this property were valued, so long ago as 1704, at £50,000; they were bought, by Lord Westmoreland, for £10,038, in 1796, though the money was not all paid till 1809. With so much indulgence and profuse generosity is it surprising the crown lands have contributed so little to relieve public burthens? Sherwood-forest contains 95,000 acres, and, from 1761 to 1786, the disbursements for management exceeded the receipts by £9037. Some trees, which were blown down in the forest, were valued at £2457; but the produce was only £850, the rest being expended in *fees and allowances* to officers. In the forest of Littlewood there were 5424 acres, and not less than *seventy officers.* During the last-mentioned period the receipts for the crown property, in Wales, amounted to £123,717; the expense of management to £124,466; so that the exchequer was minus, by the principality, £749!

Very inadequate considerations appear to have been received for the *leases of houses* in the metropolis. In 1815, there were no less than thirty-one houses, in Piccadilly and the neighbourhood, let for £125 a-year, a property which, in 1786, was valued at £600, and must now be worth many thousands. Nineteen houses were let in Holborn, near the Turnstile, for £564 and £100 premium, which were worth at least from £100 to £130 each. In the Spring-garden-terrace were three messuages, well worth £200 each, all let for £200 and a fine of £500. Other houses, in Piccadilly and Pall Mall, have been disposed of on terms equally low; the rents must be merely nominal, nothing like what the houses are really worth. A house, No. 17, Charles-street, has been let, upon a thirty years' lease, at £110 a-year. Within a month after the completion of the lease, the tenant let it for £230 a-year; thus clearing more than cent. per cent. by his speculation. The ground-rents of the Crown, in London, produced, last year, £105,000. Reckoning, with the late Mr. Huskisson, the buildings at only *five times* the value of the ground-rents, the rental of the Crown, when the leases fall in, will be £525,000. What a means of *influence* in the capital! what accommodation it enables ministers to afford their friends and supporters!

Indeed, it is important to remark who are the tenants of the crown property. Mr. Harvey justly observed that it presented a source of corruption sufficient to contaminate any parliament, and pervert its members to any purpose. Most of the parties involved in the preceding transactions were *peers of the realm* or members of parliament. Out of four hundred and eight tenants to the rental of £200,000 a year, in 1786, upwards of *two hundred* were men of TITLE. Among them were the Duke of St. Alban's, Earl Bathurst, Viscount Bacon, the Duke of Gloucester, the Duke of Newcastle, the Earl of Lichfield, and many other noble lords; for, to speak truth, they were as "thick as the peerage could make them." It cannot be supposed these great personages would condescend to the humble office of land-jobbers, unless something very substantial was to be gained by it. It is not unusual for peers of parliament and honourable members to take leases of the crown-estates at a low consideration, and then re-let them to sub-tenants at exorbitant rents; but it is not likely they would submit to the trouble and degradation of acting as middle-men, unless the profit was really magnificent.

We must now turn over another leaf. It has been seen on what very low terms Messieurs the Commissioners let and sold the crown lands; we shall, per contra, show how very lavish they have been when they had any thing *to buy*,—a residence, for instance, for a brother placeman, or a piece of church-patronage, or a parcel of land to round off the parks, or to improve the view from the palaces, or the unfinished house of an insolvent prince, or a needy peer. Whether they had authority so to apply the proceeds of the land-revenues may be doubted, but that they have done so is certain, and here follows a brief chronicle of a few of their performances.

Within a short distance of Virginia Water was a public-house, the *Wheat Sheaf;* to remove this vulgarity from the favourite resort of the late king it was bought for £5000, and let to Ramsbottom, the brewer, and a M. P. for £50. At Egham, premises were bought for £1100, for which no person, when they were offered for sale, would give £500. The sum of £21,000 was paid for Mote-park. The house of Lord de Clifford, in Spring-gardens, was bought for £4000 for an *auditor's office*, while the government was letting houses of their own in the same place, and equally fit for the purpose, at £100 a year. In Pimlico, £26,000 was paid for premises to enlarge the mews. In Windsor, a house was purchased from the Honourable John Coventry for £7000, and sold afterwards to the Honourable Mr. Westenra for £6000. A sum of £56,566 was lent to the Duke of York to build a house. Government bought it for £81,000, and sold it again to the Marquis of Stafford for £72,000. In 1805, the *Black Bear*, in Piccadilly, was let under the Crown at a rent of £108; but it became desirable to resume the premises, and the interest of the lessee was valued at £3000. In 1809, the Duke of Richmond disposed of a house to the commissioners for £5000; but they took the precaution of saying to his Grace, you must give us back £700 of this for damage done in 1791, and so the sum paid was reduced, in this way, to £4300. The *perpetual advowson* of the rectory of St. Mary-le-bone was bought of the Duke of Portland for the sum of £40,000. According to the explanation of Lord Bentinck, his father accepted this diminutive consideration rather than the living should fall into "*bad hands*,"—the Dissenters, who had offered a larger sum.* The bargain has not been very advantageous to the public. The expenses incurred in one year subsequent to the pur-

---

* House of Commons, March 30, 1830.

chase were £10,000. The receipt from pews was only £800, and the rector was paid £2000 a year. But an important object was gained by this contract. Ministers secured the ecclesiastical patronage of one of the largest and richest parishes in the metropolis.

Having given specific examples of the management of crown property, and the purposes to which it has been applied, we shall next advert to the general income and expenditure arising from this source.

The property in Ireland has scarcely yet been noticed. It is of the same description as that in England, consisting of estates, composition-rents, quit-rents, and rents of plus acres. The gross proceeds from these sources, in 1796, were £61,340. Since then part has been sold, leaving the Irish rental in 1829, £56,354.

The average receipts from the crown lands in both kingdoms, from 1793 to 1829, has been £560,000 per annum. Of this income a very small portion indeed has been available to the public service. In the last three years £1,500,000 was received, and not a *single farthing* was paid into the Exchequer. During the whole term of twenty-six years only £234,000 has reached the Treasury, the remaining balance of upwards of fourteen millions having been expended in the notable bargains of the commissioners already mentioned, in metropolitan improvements, on the royal parks and palaces, in pensions and compensations, and in the salaries of officers and charges of management.

The average expenditure in the three years 1827, 1828, 1829, in the collection of rents, law expenses, and other charges, was £169,020, being, within a trifle, 20 per cent. on the entire produce of the crown lands. The office of Woods and Forests, including salaries of commissioners, clerks, &c. costs upwards of £18,000; in addition to which £6000 and more is annually paid for law charges, and to auditors and assistants. But the greatest and most objectionable objects of disbursement have been the parks and palaces. The total of the ordinary expenditure on St. James's and Hyde Parks, Richmond, Hampton-court, Bushy, Greenwich, and Windsor Parks, was, in 1826, £48,810. In 1827, the expenditure, ordinary and extraordinary, amounted to £92,200. In 1828 it was £116,143. The sums lavished on the palaces have been really prodigious. For the repairs and alterations of Windsor Castle £771,000 has been granted, and still *unfinished*. £270,670 has been expended in furniture for the castle, and £10,000 more is required. Of the sum expended £1768 was for *kitchen furniture*. The total expenditure on the castle in furniture and building is estimated to amount to £1,084,170.* The estimated expense of repairing and improving that ill-situated pile, Buckingham-Palace, was £432,926; but this did not include the expense of the SCULPTURE of a *marble archway*, alone, to cost £35,000, and the commission of architects and clerks, amounting to £63,243 more. Lord Duncannon, this session,

---

* Parliamentary paper, 271, Sess. 1831.

required £78,750 additional, to complete this monstrous undertaking, which does not include the charge for furnishing the palace.*

The formation of Regent-street was estimated to cost £368,000. From first to last it has cost £1,833,000. The rents of the houses do not exceed £36,000, being under 2 per cent. per annum on the outlay. Had not this undertaking been left to the management of Mr. Nash, it might, by this time, have produced three or four times the present rental. The Charing-cross improvements were estimated to cost £850,000, they have already cost £1,147,000. The Strand improvements are estimated to cost £748,000, but Mr. Arbuthnot *now* admits there will be an exceeding on this estimate of £95,000.

With the purpose of the street-improvements no fault can be justly found. Some of them already are, and others no doubt will be, both useful and ornamental to the Metropolis; and if the land-revenue had not be drawn upon, recourse must have been had to the consolidated fund. The chief objections that can be urged against them are the disproportion between the original estimate and the expenditure; the questionable taste displayed in some of the plans, and to the individuals employed to superintend their execution. For example, Mr. Nash, according to the report of a parliamentary committee, " became a lessee of the Crown while acting as its agent and surveyor, and in his capacity of the crown-surveyor actually reported on the buildings *erected by himself*, upon the ground of which he was the lessee."† Other and more serious charges have been alleged against this gentleman, but as they have not been so clearly established we pass them over.

Throughout we have used the term *crown lands;* they are in fact not the lands of the Crown, but of the public. Ever since the reign of Queen Anne a *life-annuity* has been granted to the sovereign in lieu of the produce of the hereditary revenues. Hence results the mal-appropriation in lavishing these funds in aid of the royal expenditure. Surely the civil list of the late King was ample enough, not only to defray his personal outgoings, but to maintain his own establishments. The

---

* The *palace jobs* have yielded splendid pickings to the upholsterers. Messrs. Morel and Seddon's estimates for furnishing Windsor Castle amounted to £143,000, which were paid to them; but the bills they delivered were for £203,963, leaving a balance of £60,963. A parliamentary committee demurred to the payment of so large a balance over the estimates. Certain persons, deemed competent judges, were appointed to examine the charges for selected articles of furniture which the committee thought would be a criterion whereby to judge whether the general charges of the bills were extravagant. But the gentlemen nominated by the Treasury to appraise, after a preliminary inspection, declined the task, the furniture being of that peculiar sort, they were incapable of forming an estimate of its value. Messrs. Morel and Seddon next delivered a statement of the sums actually expended by them in materials, labour, and trade charges, and the profit accruing, which statement was verified by an inspection of their books by Mr. Abbott, an accountant. Witnesses were then examined as to the FAIR PROFIT which *ought to be charged* by upholsterers, and the result was the bill of Morel and Seddon, originally £203,963 : 6 : 5, was reduced to £179,300 : 13 : 9.

† Parl. Paper, No. 343, vol. iii. Session 1829.

acts of parliament, establishing the administration of the Woods and Forests, require that the revenues arising therefrom shall be expended in objects of *public utility.*   Was the purchase of Claremont, as a residence for Prince Coburg, or the giving of a slice off Hyde-park to the Duke of Wellington, to round the area of Apsley-house, objects of this nature? Or can the parks and palaces be considered such? These last are often very haughtily and insultingly described as solely for the use, recreation, and enjoyment of the King. Let the King then defray, we say, the expense of them.   During the late extravagant reign the people were very contemptuously treated as regards these matters. They were often capriciously excluded from the parks; prohibited from being seen in *certain walks*—restricted from entering here or walking there—and all these fantastic regulations to interdict the enjoyment of their own property, and the expense of maintaining which was defrayed out of their own pockets.   Waterloo-place, Regent's Park, and Windsor-park, afford examples of royal or official whims which will be easily recollected.   Under William IV. there appears a disposition to conciliate popular feeling, but the treatment of the public by his predecessor was intolerable.

We shall now lay before the reader a return of the present income and expenditure on account of the crown lands.   It is for the year ending 5th January, 1829, and it is abstracted from the last triennial Report of the Commissioners of Woods and Forests.   After that we shall subjoin an estimate of the present value of the crown estates, submitted, by Mr. Harvey, to the House of Commons, March 30th, 1830.

INCOME AND EXPENDITURE OF THE LAND-REVENUES.

ORDINARY INCOME.

Total balances, 5th January, 1828		£79,057	3	0¼

England and Wales.

Fee-farm rents ....£	6,401	13	8
Leasehold rents......................	138,164	17	11½
Profits of mines, manors, &c...........	12,315	18	0½
Light-house-dues, &c.................	14,705	0	1
Fines	13,027	15	4
Sales of old materials, &c.............	3,471	2	0
	188,086	7	1

Ireland.

Quit, crown, and composition rents, and rents of plus acres............	56,354	16	7

Island of Alderney.

Rents, tithes, royalties, and harbour-dues.............................	127	0	0

Isle of Man.

Tithes, quit rents, and alienation-fines..	1,428	7	1
	57,910	3	8
The royal forests, parks and woodlands	39,972	15	8

Total ordinary receipts, including balances.......... £362,926 9 5½

EXTRAORDINARY RECEIPTS.

Sales of estates and unimprovable rents in England and Wales	139,704	11	1¼
The like in Ireland	22,949	2	1
Deposits upon sales to be paid	169	17	7
Total income for the year ending January 5, 1829....	£525,750	0	3

ORDINARY EXPENDITURE.

Ancient stipends, including payments to schools, chapels, churches, &c	£7,486	7	10
Collection of rents, including allowances to receivers	4,241	9	8¼
Local disbursements by receivers, and allowances to tenants	4,094	1	4¼
Expenses of the establishment of Woods and Forests, including salaries of commissioners, clerks, surveyors, officers, &c	18,574	6	7
Salaries to auditors and assistants	837	1	8
Law-charges	6,292	5	8
Payments to architects, surveyors, &c. expenses of journeys, and other bills	2,849	0	2
Fees on acts of parliament, enrolling of leases, &c.	3,637	0	2
Rates, taxes, superannuation-allowances, &c	10,807	19	6¼
Expenses on the royal forests, parks, and woodlands	83,797	3	7¼
Total ordinary expenditure	£142,616	16	4¼

EXTRAORDINARY EXPENDITURE.

St. James's, Greenwich, Hyde, Windsor, and other royal parks	68,388	7	3
In purchase of estates and payments to Board of Works for Buckingham-palace	137,623	13	4
Transferred to the Regent-street fund	116,306	9	3
	464,935	6	2¼
Balance, 5th January, 1829	60,814	14	5½
	£525,750	0	7¾

ESTIMATE *of the Value of the Crown Lands, independently of the Woods and Forests, and of that Portion which may be considered to belong exclusively to the Royal Person.*

One hundred and thirty manors and royalties, at £1000	£130,000
Annual rental of estates, £600,000, at 25 years' purchase	15,000,000
Middlesex, ground-rents £50,000 per annum, at 40 years' purchase	2,000,000*
Rents from houses, say £20,000 per annum, at 18 years' purchase	360,000
Carried forward	£17,490.000

* Mr. Harvey committed an oversight in estimating the Middlesex ground-rents at £50,000 per annum. Last year they produced £105,000, and when the leases fall in will be worth, according to the estimate of Mr. Huskisson, £500,000. Instead of *two*, their present worth is, at least, *four millions.*

Brought forward....£17,490,000

Waste lands in forests not fit for oak timber, 86,000 acres, at £5 per acre	430,000
Church livings	100,000
Fee-farm-rents, and other unimproveable payments, in England and Wales, at least £6000, at 25 years' purchase	150,000
Allotments under 485 inclosure acts, at £500	242,500
Irish estates	2,000,000

Total......£20,412,500

N. B. *The above estimate is exclusive of mines of coal, tin, and copper, and also of the Duchy of Lancaster, £30,000. Davenant, in his* Treatise on the Lands of England, *estimates the common rights of the Crown at 300,000 acres.*

The estimate of the value of the land-revenues does not include the royal forests. In some of these are intermingling rights, and the Crown has no property in the soil. Such are New Forest and the forests of Epping, Sherwood, and Dean Forest; all the rights possessed by the Crown consist of the right of herbage for the deer, although in the great forest of Sherwood, comprising a sheet of land of 95,000 acres, not a single deer is kept. In the New Forest, out of 90,000 acres, the Crown has the right to enclose periodically 6,000 acres, which may be dissevered from the pasturage for the growth of timber. The most valuable property undoubtedly consists of the estates and leaseholds alone worth upwards of *twenty millions* sterling. These might be sold without encroaching on any possession in the least conducive to the dignity and enjoyment of the sovereign. What *dignity*, indeed, can there be in the king or his servants being jobbers in land, or hucksters in the sale of houses, leases, and ground-rents?

It is not, however, the dignity nor the comfort of the king, but the patronage of his ministers, that is at stake. The preceding narrative has shown what an endless source of jobbing the crown-lands have been for centuries; of jobbing the most foul, rapacious, and iniquitous. Not only have the commons, but the distinguished names of the peerage — the great historical cognomens—been implicated in these peculating transactions. This description is not ᴜmited to the times of the Edwards and Henries, when there was ᴴho law to contravene the sovereign's pleasure, or the sordid practices of his servants, but applies to the period subsequent to the Revolution, when the constitution is supposed to have been purified and perfected. Acts of parliament, indeed, were passed prescribing the minimum of rent (relatively to the full value) at which the crown-farms should be let,—namely one-third before the reign of George III. and one-eighth after the accession of the said king, stating, too, that, under the former regulation, two-thirds of the valued rack-rent, and, under the latter, seven-eighths should be paid in the shape of fine. But what of these statutory restraints? They were all set at nought; the " creatures were at their dirty work" again; and, in most cases, the rents reserved and the fines exacted were merely nominal. May it not be said, after this, that *ministerial responsibility* is a farce, and that it is sheer fatuity to expect justice will be enforced against public defaulters, when the accused and his judges are alike participant in the delinquency ?

The sale of the crown-lands would not only cut off a dangerous source of ministerial influence, but render them more conducive to national wealth, and effect a saving in the public expenditure. That costly establishment, the Board of Woods and Forests, is in future, it appears, (House of Commons, Dec. 9, 1831,) to be consolidated with the Board of Works, whereby the expense of two boards will be saved. Mr. Huskisson long depastured in this retreat, and retained to the last a singular partiality for the existing mode of administering the crown property. In the debate on Mr. Harvey's motion, he observed that the House had no right to dispose of the hereditary revenues of the Crown *without its consent.* No one could gainsay this constitutional truism. No doubt an act of parliament would be requisite, and every one knows an act of parliament is not law till it receives the royal assent. In this, then, there is nothing peculiar. But the importance ascribed by this wily and selfish politician to the fact, that the royal forests formed a valuable *nursery for the growth of timber,* seemed a little inconsistent with his favourite principles of free trade. England depends much more on the produce of her looms and steam-engines than of her woods and forests; though we should be sorry, for the sake of merely increasing national capital, to see, throughout the country, the latter entirely superseded by the former. Agreeably with the dogmas of the school of which Mr. Huskisson was long a professed disciple, our supply of timber would be most advantageously obtained from the wastes of Canada and Norway, where it can be cheapest produced; while our own acres are best appropriated to the growth of *cheap bread* for the artisan and manufacturer.

DROITS OF THE CROWN AND ADMIRALTY.

The next and most important branch of the hereditary revenues of the Crown is the droits of admiralty. These *droits,* or rights, are received by the king in his capacity of lord high admiral; the duties of which office are discharged by five lords commissioners. The principal sources whence the droits are derived are the following :—all sums arising from wreck and goods of pirates; all ships detained previously to a declaration of war; all coming into port, either from distress of weather, or ignorant of the commencement of hostilities; all taken before the issuing of proclamation; and those taken by non-commissioned captors are sold, and the proceeds form droits of the crown and admiralty.

From this description of the sources whence the droit revenue is constituted, it evidently appears little better than buccaneer or piratical plunder, obtained under circumstances little creditable to any government to sanction. Ships detained previously to a declaration of war, coming into port ignorant of hostilities, or taken before the issuing of a proclamation, are all considered lawful prizes: the sufferers, in these cases, violate a law of which they are ignorant, and of which it is impossible they should have any knowledge. They are caught in a spider's web impervious to the sight. An *ex-post-facto* law, or the laws of the Roman tyrant, who placed them so high that they were illegible to the beholder, were not more unjust and tyrannical. In the course of the late war—in the attack on the Danes, and the seizure of the Spanish ships—we had two memorable instances to what base purposes this principle may be applied. In the attack upon Copenhagen, government might be actuated by its fears as well as its cupidity; it might dread the Danish ships of war falling into the hands of Bonaparte; though, in either case, it was equally disgraceful to a great nation to be excited to an act of flagrant injustice and violation of international law. But what can be urged in defence of the attack on the Spanish ships in 1805? The object, in this case, unquestionably, was plunder for the droit-fund. There could be no fear of the Spanish ships joining the enemy, because they were merchantmen, and not ships of war. We were at peace; the Spanish envoy, in London, and the English ambassador, at Madrid, were carrying on a negotiation, and yet, under these circumstances, a squadron of ships of war was fitted out; the homeward-bound Spanish fleet, from South America, loaded with treasure, attacked, the crews massacred, the ships burnt, and the proceeds of this unhallowed enterprise condemned as *rights of the Crown!*

Posterity, in looking to the foreign and domestic policy of England for the last forty years, under the influence of Tory principles, will be at a loss which most to condemn—the encroachments on the liberties of the people, or the atrocious attacks on the right of other states. The balance of iniquity seems nearly equal. At home, the liberty and property of the people have been assailed by the Bank-Restriction-Act, Seditious Meetings Bills, new Treason Acts, and acts for the curtailment of the freedom of the press. Abroad, we may reckon among the catalogue of offences, the attacks upon Copenhagen and the Spanish fleet, and the affair of Terceira: to which may be added, our slow and reluctant recognition of the independence of the new States of South America—our suspicious neutrality, when the liberties of Italy and Spain were subverted by the interference of foreign armies—our non-interference in behalf of the heroic Poles, in their glorious struggle for national independence—and the promptitude with which we have mostly availed ourselves of every pretext for either openly supporting or covertly aiding the old European despotisms in their machinations against popular rights.

To return, however, to the droits of Admiralty. The monies accruing from the droits, as well as the crown-lands, and other branches of the hereditary revenue, were ostensibly conceded to the public, in lieu of the grant of a fixed sum for the civil list. But instead of being made available to the national service, they have, prior to the commencement of the present reign, always been kept in the back ground, and indirectly expended, without either the people or their representatives having any control over them, further than an occasional return of the objects on which they had been lavished. The management of the fund was not more extraordinary than its application. It was not paid into the Exchequer, like the taxes, but remained in the hands of the registrar of the high court of Admiralty, the receiver-general of droits, the commissioners of prizes, and the Bank of England. There was no responsibility attached to the persons receiving or issuing this money. No account was kept of the receipts and outgoings at the Treasury. It was drawn out of the Bank of England, not on the authority of the privy-seal, but of a warrant under the sign manual only. In short, it was a fund wholly out of the control of parliament, and entirely at the disposal of the ministers of the Crown : it might be expended on the hirelings of the press, in rewarding spies and informers, in purchasing votes of members of parliament, in bribery at elections, in minions or mistresses, or any other purpose of royal or ministerial corruption.

The specific objects for which the Admiralty droits were granted to the Crown were for " *guarding and maintaining the rights and privileges of the seas ;** so that the whole of the fund, agreeably to its original destination, ought to have been expended on the ships, officers, and men of the English navy. How differently it has been applied we shall proceed to illustrate ; instead of being devoted to maritime objects, it has been dissipated in rewarding the questionable services of individuals—in discharging the arrears of the civil list—in payments to Sir William Knighton, for the use of the *privy-purse*—in advances to different branches of the royal family—paying tradesmen's and physicians' bills—defraying the expense of visits from foreign princes, and of royal visits to Ireland, Scotland, and Hanover—and, in general, in discharging any casual debt or expense which the caprice or extravagance of royalty and its servants might incur.

In looking over the returns to parliament of the disbursements to individuals, the first that struck us as singular were two payments to the editor of a *ministerial* newspaper, namely, to Dr. *Stoddart*, now Sir John Stoddart, and a judge in the island of Malta. Next we came to a grant to Sir *Home Popham*, to indemnify him for losses he had sustained in his famous smuggling voyage. This gallant officer, it seems, had entered various investments outwards, in a ship called *Etrusco*, commanded by Sir Home, and bound from one of the ports of Italy to the East Indies. Captain Robinson, appointed on that station for the prevention of smuggling, seized the vessel; and her cargo, value £25,000, being contraband or smuggled goods, was condemned as good and lawful prize. Dr. Lushington having moved for various papers relative to this transaction, it appeared, by a warrant of the Treasury, signed Charles Long and others, as lords of the Treasury, that the loss of £25,000 sustained by Captain Popham, *in smuggling*, was made up to him by a grant of the same sum out of the *Droits of Admiralty*. When all the documents relative to the affair were upon the table in the house, and Mr. C. Long and Sir Home Popham, being both members, were present, Dr. Lushington moved " That Sir Home Popham, in being detected in

---

* Lord Brougham, Parliamentary Debates, vol. xxi. 245.

knowingly carrying on an *illegal* traffic, had acted in contempt of the laws of his country, contrary to the duty of a British subject, and to the disgrace of the character of a British officer ; and, further, that the grant of £25,000 by Mr. Long to him out of the Droits of Admiralty, had been a gross misapplication of the public money." After solemn debate on this question, not a single fact being denied or disputed, ' the Guardians of the Public Purse' fully acquitted Sir Home Popham and Mr. Long of all blame, by a majority of 126 to 57 ! When one member of parliament could thus give to another such a sum of money as £25,000 out of the Droits of Admiralty, it accounts for that *loyal* clamour which was so often heard in Parliament, of this fund being the *private* property of the king.

The way in which the *Reverend W. B. Daniels*, the author of a work on " Rural Sports," became entitled to £5077 out of the fund for the maintenance of maritime rights, is worth describing.

A Mr. Jacob, the owner of the privateer *Daphne*, captured, in 1799 or 1800, the French vessel *Circe*, worth £30,000, which was condemned as lawful prize, and all claim to the contrary disregarded. The year and day for appeal having transpired, the condemnation became final, and £15,000 was shared among the captors. Ten thousand pounds more lay ready to be distributed. At this point of time, information was laid against Mr. Jacob, for having disregarded the 33d of Geo. III. by which the muster of the crew of a privateer before sailing is enacted. On the *letter* of this law they were convicted ; the £10,000 stopped ; and the £15,000 recovered ; all of which became Droits of Admiralty. The mere ignorance of the law was admitted as no excuse for Mr. Jacob, and the result to him was, besides the loss of his prize, costs to the amount of £1700, and utter ruin. From having been in a respectable trade, he was thrown into gaol, and reduced to beggary. But on whose authority does the reader imagine Mr. Jacob and his family were reduced to beggary ? Here it will be necessary to introduce the *Rev. Mr. Daniels.* This gentleman, after publishing his work on " Rural Sports," had been confined for debt, and reduced, as Lord Brougham stated, to the condition of a ' primitive Christian.' After all other attempts to patch up his broken fortune had failed, he, at last, turned a broker in evidence, and procured two men, of the names of Thatcher and Guzman, one of whom had been convicted of perjury, and the other had been flogged at the cart's tail, to swear as much as was necessary to convict Mr. Jacob. For this signal service, the Reverend Mr. Daniels received £5077 out of the Admiralty Droits, and the first of his witnesses £87 : 13 : 7, as a *gratuity for evidence given !*

Besides the payment to Sir Home Popham, and Messrs. Stoddart and Daniels, there are others quite as extraordinary and unaccountable. There is a sum of £2250 granted to Sir George Young, on the 20th of September, 1803, being one-third of the Dutch ship Frederick, taken at the Cape. The item is remarkable, because at the time Sir George is represented capturing ships at the Cape, he was serving in parliament as member for Honiton, filled a lucrative situation, and, on failing in a subsequent election, was appointed governor of that Colony. The Earl of Dunmore is also down for the sum of £2792, under similar circumstances. Lord Stowell is inserted for £932, " for services in deciding upon cases relative to American captures." There are two grants to Lord Keith of £20,521 and £1800, to make up losses he had sustained from an action brought against him for *wrongfully* detaining an American ship at the Cape of Good Hope. There is a grant of £700 to one Captain Temple, to defray the expenses of a prosecution for the alledged murder of a seaman, of which crime he had been acquitted; and another grant of £219 to a Turk, for some losses he had sustained at Constantinople.

The objects for which all these grants have been made appear very questionable and mysterious. Let us now come to the larger sums. To that pious nobleman, Lord Gambier, the great patron of Bible Societies, and to Lord Cathcart, is the enormous sum of £348,621, as their share of the *prize-money* at the memorable expedition to Copenhagen. There is another enormous payment to one John Alcock, " to be by him paid over to the merchants, &c. trading to Spain, whose property had been sequestered in 1796 and 1797." Another singular item of £54,921 is entered as an " indemnification to sundry commanders of his Majesty's ships for condemnations, by a Court of Vice-Admiralty, at Cape Nicola Mole, *afterwards found not to have jurisdiction.*" A sum of £887 to Captain Spencer, in the year 1807, pursuant to his Majesty's warrant; £10,000 and £1900 to William Bourne and others, as commissioners of Spanish and Portuguese property.

The complexion of all these grants is bad enough. We shall now speak of the immense sums taken out of this fund by the different branches of the Royal Family; and the reader must bear in mind that these grants are independent of the enormous incomes they derive from parliamentary grants. The droits have formed an inexhaustible mine for relieving the necessities of the king, the regent, the princes and princesses, in all their embarrassments. The facility with which money was granted by different ministers from this fund, rendered economy on their part wholly unnecessary. Prior to 1812, there had been taken from the droits the enormous sum of £760,000, simply for the payment of the tradesmen's bills of the king's household. The sums granted in aid of the civil list, from 1793 to 1818, amounted to £1,324,000. The sums paid during the same period, to different branches of the royal family, amounted to £266,331 : 17 : 3. Besides these sums, £58,000 was granted to defray the expenses of additional buildings and furniture at Brighton. The sum of £14,579, for additional expenses in the household, occasioned by the visits of foreign princes. The expenses of the *royal visits* to Ireland, Scotland, and Hanover, amounting to £70,000, were paid out of the Admiralty droits. From the same inexhaustible fund is the royal dole of £5000 to the *poor of Spitalfields.* Doubtless this act of charity would have been more gracious had the donation proceeded from the privy purse instead of from a fund which, if it does not belong to the nation, unquestionably belongs to the ships, officers, and seamen of the navy. The last payment out of the droits we shall notice is one in 1829, to John Calvert, Esq., £9,166, to defray the expenses incurred in fitting up and finishing the house of his Royal Highness the Duke of Clarence.

With the exception of the very inadequate payments to captors, we have mentioned the principal purposes to which the droits have been appropriated since the commencement of the late war. The following statement, abstracted from a return to parliament, will show the total produce of this great naval or rather ministerial fund, from 1793 to 1818:—

A SUMMARY ACCOUNT *of all Monies received as Droits of the Crown and of the Admiralty, from the 1st of February,* 1793, *to the 29th of May,* 1818.—*Ordered to be printed, June,* 1818.

	£	s.	d.
Registrar of the High Court of Admiralty ········	5,077,216	9	0
Receiver-General of droits ····················	489,885	10	9
Commissioners for the care of Dutch droits ······	1,286,042	6	10
Commissioners for the care of Spanish droits ······	1,293,313	19	7
Commissioners for the care of Danish and other droits	348,261	6	5
Total········£	8,494,719	12	7

A period of peace is not favourable to an accumulation of Admiralty droits. Accordingly we find, from the date of the above return up to the last annual return to Parliament, the proceeds from naval droits have not averaged more than £120,000 per annum.

FOUR-AND-A-HALF PER CENT. DUTIES.

Notwithstanding the efforts of political writers to expose the manifold abuses of an antiquated system, an immense number remain, of which the public have no knowledge, and of which they have scarcely any means of obtaining information. Where, for instance, previously to the expositions afforded by this publication, could satisfactory information be obtained relative to the crown lands, the civil list, droits of Admiralty, and the other branches of the hereditary revenues of which we are about to treat? Correct information on these subjects can only be acquired from parliamentary reports and papers, to which few persons have access, and still fewer leisure and desire to peruse and digest their voluminous contents. Unquestionably this was a defect in the political knowledge of the people, which we have attempted to remedy, and we have little doubt that the mystery which has heretofore involved the crown revenues, and concealed their amount and application from the community, will be hereafter dissolved.

After the Admiralty droits, the next considerable branch of revenue, at the disposal of ministers, was the Four-and-a-Half per Cent. Leeward-Island Duties. This fund produces from forty to fifty thousand pounds a-year, and consists of a tax of $4\frac{1}{2}$ per cent. imposed on produce in the island of Barbadoes and Leeward Isles. It was created by a colonial law of Barbadoes, nearly two hundred years ago, and, by the terms of the act, was to be applied to the erection of *public buildings, the repair of courts, and other colonial purposes.* In the reign of Charles II. it was seized by the courtiers, and continued to be abused till the reign of Queen Anne ; when, on a representation of the abuses of the fund, it was formally renounced by the queen and parliament in favour of the island of Barbadoes, and the original purposes of the act creating it. It again fell into abuse ; the natural children of the king and royal dukes, the members of both houses of parliament, their relatives and connexions, having got almost entire possession of the fund. The parties in the smuggling transaction related above are inscribed here. The gallant Sir Home is dead, but his pension of £500 survives, being a reversion payable to his widow. The Countess of Mansfield, the mother of the anti-reforming peer who made so stout a stand against the second reading of the Reform Bill on its first introduction, is quartered on the Barbadoes planters for £1000 per annum.

The late General Crauford was a pensioner, till his death, on this fund, to the amount of £1200 a-year. The way in which this officer entitled himself to £1200 a-year for life is deserving of attention. Many people yet remember the fatal expedition to Walcheren, when forty thousand men were suffered to perish in that pestilential climate, owing to the incapacity of Lord Castlereagh and the duplicity of Mr. Canning. When this business became matter of discussion in the House of Commons; when it was made apparent to every man in England that it was to the squabbles and ignorance of these men that this great national calamity was to be attributed ; it was, nevertheless, resolved, by a majority of two hundred and seventy-five, to negative the censure which was moved by Lord Porchester against ministers on that occasion. But the triumph of ministers did not stop here. A vote of *approbation* of the ministers was absolutely moved and adopted by a majority of two hundred and fifty-five. The member who had the effrontery to move this vote of approbation was General Crauford. But this officer had a further claim on ministerial gratitude : he had recently become connected by marriage with the Duke of Newcastle; he represented and commanded the parliamentary interest of that nobleman ; he had *eight votes* to give to ministers on any occasion.

Many other names, not without celebrity, are inscribed on the $4\frac{1}{2}$ per cent. duties. The famous pension to *Edmund Burke* continues to be paid out of this fund. It is entered to " *the executors of Mrs. Burke* £2500," and the date of the grant being the 24th of October, 1795, the public, up to this time, has paid, in principal money, £87,500. How much the world has benefited by the labours of Mr. Burke may be collected from the sublime events daily transpiring in Europe. The sole object of this celebrated renegade in his later writings

and speeches was to stop the progress of knowledge and liberty—to perpetuate the old feudal despotisms—and he might as well have attempted
to stop the progress of the great deep. All he effected was to delay
their *fall*, and so far as he contributed to that he was instrumental in
the useless sacrifice of millions of lives. Events have proved this to be
the issue of all the efforts of this infatuated oracle—for oracle he is
thought by some—and the services of both him and his followers will
appear to posterity as ill-timed as the vain endeavours of those who, in
the later ages of idolatry, sought to oppose the subversion of a barbarous worship. The defect of Burke and his admirers is their blindness
to the fact that the world is undergoing as great a revolution as when
the popular mind was converted from Paganism to Christianity.

Lady *Augusta de Ameland* received a pension of £1292 from
the 4½ per cent. fund to the period of her death in 1830. All we know of
her ladyship is that she was united to the Duke of Sussex, in Italy, by
a sort of Gretna-Green marriage, and afterwards repudiated in consequence of that offspring of German pride and feudality—the royal mar-
riage-act. Next follow the five Misses *Fitz-Clarence*, £2500
—the natural daughters of the king, by Mrs. Jordan. The Duchess of
Gloucester, £1000; the Princess of Hesse-Homberg, £1000; Lord
Hood, £1500; Sir William Sydney Smith, £1250; the Earl of Chatham, 3000; and, in trust for Lady G. Tekell, £300; and for the *seven*
children of Lady Lucy R. Taylor, £139 : 10 each. Lady Hester Lucy
Stanhope brings up the rear with a pension of £900 ; she is the niece of
the " Heaven-born minister," and the same lady, we believe, who
astonishes travellers by acting the Amazon, dressing in man's attire,
and living somewhere about Mount Sinai or Tadmor, in the deserts of
Arabia.

These, we apprehend, are sufficient for specimens. We have passed
over several names totally unknown to us, and, we believe, the public.
So eager have the *higher orders* been to be established on this fund, that
pensions have been granted upon it in reversion, and others charged
upon it have not yet become payable. Of this latter class is the memorable provision for Lady Grenville, of £1500 per annum for life, in the
event of her surviving Lord Grenville. Since Lady Grenville obtained
this grant, she has succeeded to the great possessions of her brother,
Lord Camelford. Lord Grenville holds a sinecure of £4000 out of the
taxes as Auditor of the Exchequer. His eldest brother, the late
Marquis of Buckingham, besides his great estates, held the enormous
sinecure of the Tellership of the Exchequer, worth £30,000 per
annum. Lord Braybrooke and Lord Carysfort, who married sisters
of Lord Grenville, hold, each of them, through the interest of the
family, sinecures that are worth some thousands a-year ; and yet, after
all, the devoted planters of Barbadoes are to be mortgaged for £1500
more for life. As there has lately been a great strain upon the borough
establishment, we really wonder the Grenvilles have not been summoned to its aid : there is no family on whose services the Oligarchy
has so just a claim ; for they are completely bound up with the system

of the last forty years; and now that it is perilled all the veterans, the Sidmouths, Eldons, and the rest, who have retired loaded with spoil, ought to be again brought into active service—without pay!

The whole amount of pensions payable out of the Leeward-Island duties is £27,466, and £15,338 more in salaries. The entire produce of these duties from 1760 to the present is about £2,546,484, more than two-thirds of which sum have been lavished on court favourites and the members and supporters of the Oligarchy. Ministers having been frequently rated concerning the application of this jobbing fund, an act was passed, in 1825, prohibiting the grant of pensions from it in future, and providing that the surplus should be appropriated to the support of the *ecclesiastical establishment* in the West Indies. By this transmutation, nothing was gained to the public; and the ministers lost no portion of their influence, only their patronage became *spiritual*, instead of secular. A scion of Mother Church was planted in a distant land, which, no doubt, will emulate its parent in all her manifold virtues. As we have omitted, in our exposition of the *Church of England*, to give an account of the staff, corps, and endowments of this distant branch of the church establishment, we shall insert it in this place:—

Bishop of Jamaica	£4,000	
Archdeacon of Jamaica	2,000	
Seven clergymen, at £300 each	2,100	
		£8,100
Bishop of Barbadoes	4,000	
Archdeacon of Barbadoes	2,000	
Archdeacon of Antigua	2,000	
Thirteen clergymen, at £300 each	3,900	
Three catechists, at £100 each	300	
		12,200
		£20,300

These worthy gentlemen, after ten years' service, are to have *retiring allowances:* their salaries have hitherto been paid out of the taxes; the 4½ per cent. fund being so deeply mortgaged in pensions, there is no surplus from it applicable to the purpose.* And the proceeds arising from the *smuggling transactions* in sugar and ginger, in which the Wellington ministers were detected, do not appear to have been applied either to the support of the West-India church-establishment or any other public object. But this is another of those secret modes of *raising the wind* with which the public is totally unacquainted, and which it will be necessary to explain.

It had been usual to remit the 4½ per cent. duty in the produce of the Leeward Islands, in sugar and ginger; which, like other commo-

---

* Parliamentary Paper, No. 561, Session 1830.

dities from the British plantations, were sold for home-consumption at the *long price*—the duty included ; and the duty paid over, as by private merchants, to the customs.   This continued until the year 1828 ; previously to which, it has been seen, the surplus of the 4½ per cent. duty had been appropriated to the support of the West-India church establishment.   Ministers appear not to have relished the loss of their old fund ; they had, it is true, exchanged *lay* for *ecclesiastical* patronage, but they seem to have been anxious to secure both.   For this purpose, they hit upon a most extraordinary expedient.   They first submitted *a case* to the Attorney and Solicitor Generals, requesting their opinion whether sugars, granted to the king in kind, and not specially subject to any duty, are liable to the payment of any custom-duty ?*   The lawyers, no doubt foreseeing what sort of answer would be most agreeable to their clients, replied in the negative.   Upon this, directions were forthwith given to admit the sugars sent in payment of the Leeward-Islands duty without charging the duty of customs, which had been heretofore paid as on all other imported sugars.   By this contrivance, Ministers obtained the command of a fund unknown to their predecessors, amounting to betwixt *thirty* and *forty thousand pounds* per annum—the amount of duty remitted, and precisely to the same amount the general revenue of the country suffered by the defalcation in the produce of the customs appropriated by parliament to the public service,   To what extent this evasion of the payment of parliamentary duties, and the raising of money by the power of prerogative, might have been pushed it is impossible to foresee.   Ministers might not only have imported sugars in payment of the 4½ per cent. duty, custom free, but they might, also, by stretching their principle a little further, have imported sugars generally, *for sale*, duty free, and, by retailing them at the usual price, and appropriating the duty, raised a fund for pensions and grants to any amount.

The more we reflect on this affair, the more we are astonished. The idea of the ministers of a great country turning *smugglers ;* of resorting to the age of the Tudors and Plantagenets for precedents ; of seeking to evade, under shelter of the quibbling opinions of lawyers, the payment of duties imposed by themselves, and devoted to the national service, staggers belief.   It establishes, with infinitely greater force than any argument of ours, the vast importance attached, by the servants of the Crown, to those secret and uncontrolled sources of influence we have been exposing, and how essential they deem the exclusive management of them to the *working* of the machinery of government.   To shew that our exposition of the transaction is not exaggerated, we shall insert the opinion entertained of it by Sir James Graham, and expressed in the following resolution submitted by him to the House of Commons, on the 2d of July, 1830 :—

" That to exempt from duty any article of merchandize imported for the Crown, but not intended for the use of the Sovereign, is an

* Treasury Minute, dated 15th April, 1828.

extension of the King's prerogative of dangerous example; and that to levy the parliamentary duties payable upon such articles when sold for home-consumption, and *appropriate the amount thereof without the knowledge and consent* of parliament, is an unconstitutional violation of the privileges of this House."

It is impossible to ascertain all the funds considered at the irresponsible disposal of ministers during the long reign of the Tories. The appropriation of the surplus of the French claims is another instance of the power of a *Treasury Minute* to raise supplies in case of emergency. In this case, a finance-committee ascertained that a sum of £250,000 had been, by a mere order of the treasury, paid over, without the consent of parliament, to the commissioners of woods and forests, by the commission for liquidating the claims of British subjects on the French government, and subsequently expended in the alterations at Buckingham House.*

We have little further to add respecting the 4½ per cent. duties. Mr. Creevy, the late member for Appleby, calculated that these duties, from the accession of George III. to the year 1812, had produced £1,600,000. A statement, by the same respected gentleman, of the purposes to which this enormous sum had been applied, is not more extraordinary, we believe, than correct; and with it we shall conclude our account of one of the most famous jobbing-funds of the Crown:—

Pensions to persons in this country············	£740,000
Special and secret service-money··············	326,000
Salaries to the Governors of Leeward Islands····	400,000
For civil list expenditure ·····················	170,000
To different Secretaries of the Treasury, supposed for electioneering purposes ··············	48,000

SCOTCH CIVIL LIST—GIBRALTAR DUTIES—ESCHEATS—DUCHIES OF CORNWALL AND LANCASTER—FINES AND PENALTIES.

The Scotch Hereditary Revenue forms a *fourth* fund at the disposal of ministers, over which, previously to the accession to office of lord Grey's ministry, there was no legislative control further than when grants had been irrevocably made from it, they were, pro forma, submitted to parliament. It yields, annually, above £100,000, and accrues chiefly from crown-rents, customs, hereditary excise, fines, and forfeitures. About• *two-thirds* of the produce are paid in pensions, the remainder in donations to the episcopal clergy, to the Caledonian hunt, for providing coach-houses and stables for the barons of the Exchequer, and other objects of apparently no public utility. Scotland has lately got rid of the Tory incubus by which she was long deluded and oppressed. Prior to this relief she seldom petitioned for political reform, and the spring of her scribbling and clamouring loyalty may be easily divined, since in no other part of the United Kingdom was loyalty so well paid,

---

* Mr. Angelo Taylor, House of Commons, June 23, 1828.

for in no other part were there such ample funds to reward devotion to ministers. The annual value of places and pensions shared among Scotch freeholders and burghmongers was estimated at £1,750,000, equal to half the rental of the kingdom. In the *Third Report of the Committee on Public Expenditure*, in 1808, it is remarked that Scotch pensions, which, at the commencement of the reign of George III. amounted only to 19, in the year 1797 had swelled to 185, and, in 1808, to 351, two-thirds of these pensions being granted to females!

A fifth source of royal income is the surplus of the *Gibraltar Duties.* It is provided, by the original charter, granted to this place, by Queen Anne, in 1704, that, for the augmentation of trade, no duty or imposition shall be imposed upon any vessel trading or touching at the port; and that the goods and chattels of the inhabitants shall enjoy an immunity from taxation. In violation of these chartered privileges various taxes have been imposed, and the chief portion of the proceeds therefrom, during the late reign, were paid over to Sir William Knighton for the use of the king's privy purse. These taxes were levied without the authority of parliament, merely on the authority of the governor; and some recent impositions appear a tax on *liberty of conscience,*—one being a capitation-tax, of ten dollars each, imposed on Roman Catholics and Jews. Taxes have also been imposed on licenses to sell spirits, fishing-boats, lighters, and billiard-tables. The surplus of the Gibraltar Duties produced, over and above salaries and charges from 1760 to 1830, nearly two hundred thousand pounds; in the year ending 5th of January, 1830, they produced £11,498, of which £5000 was paid into the privy-purse. The collector of these imposts resides, we believe, in Lincoln's Inn, and executes his duty by deputy.

The estates of lunatics, bastards, and others dying intestate and without heirs, form a sixth branch of the casual revenues of the Crown, under the denomination of *Escheats.* The proceeds from this source are considerable, amounting, in the reign of George III. to £323,424.* The King's share of the estate of Mr. Newport, a lunatic, amounted to £113,000. Poor TROUTBACK's money shared a similar fate—but here " hangs a tale," which we must explain, and for which purpose we shall first call in Mr. Waggoner.

" Mr. Frederick Matthew Waggoner called in and examined.

" Do you know any thing of the proceedings that have been had with respect to Mr. *Troutback's* will?—I do; he bequeathed £2000 for erecting an *Orphan Hospital,* and the whole of his money, amounting, with accumulations, to upwards of £100,000, to trustees, for erecting an additional wing, or separate building, to the charity school of St. John of Wapping, and for maintaining and educating poor children of that parish.

" Are there as many poor children as would require the funds to educate ?— Yes ; *more within the parish.*

" Do you think £5000 a-year would not educate the poor of the parish ?—The will is for the *education, clothing, and maintenance.*

---

* Parliamentary Paper, No. 1, Session 1820.

" What has been done with respect to it?—We understand that it has been set aside by the Court of Chancery; and that the testator having no next of kin, the money *has gone to the Crown."*—Report of the Education Committee, 1816, page 289.

Sure enough the *" money has gone to the Crown."* The will was set aside by Lord ELDON, and the property applied to liquidate the royal debts. It was a windfall to the Sovereign, of which, as Mr. Tierney remarked, the public would never have obtained any knowledge, had not the civil list been in arrear, and it became necessary to apply to parliament for an additional allowance.* How the civil list became in arrear it may be worth while explaining. In 1816 the late King, then Regent, had incurred an enormous debt in consequence of living, as he mostly did, in a profuse and riotous manner. The Lord Chamberlain applied to the Lords of the Treasury to know how this debt was to be discharged. The Lords of the Treasury, after much consultation, determined that the debt, amounting to £277,000, should be defrayed partly out of the money bequeathed by Mr. Troutback, for *charitable uses,* partly out of the Droits of Admiralty.† Thus, the money piously left to *clothe, educate, and maintain poor children,* was applied to pay the furniture-bills, tailor-bills, haberdasher-bills, and bills perhaps of a still less creditable description, of the Prince Regent. It vexes one to see to what base purposes the best of things may be perverted. How many poor children of Wapping the money of Troutback would have preserved from the gallows and transportation it is impossible to say; but it is certain, had George IV. been more frugal, or a Prince who thought the welfare of his subjects of more importance than vicious indulgence, the money of Troutback, notwithstanding any informality in his will, would have been suffered to go to the noble objects for which it had been so generously bequeathed.

A *seventh* source of royal income is from the duchies of Cornwall and Lancaster. When there is no Prince of Wales, or during his minority, and there is no Duke of Cornwall of a proper age to receive the revenues amounting to £15,000 a-year, they are claimed by the crown. The duchy of Lancaster yields an income to the King of £10,000 per annum. Both sums are paid into the *privy-purse*—the nature of which will be explained in the next chapter.

The remaining branches of the Crown-revenues are too unimportant to claim particular exposition. They accrue principally from fines and forfeitures in courts of justice, from green-wax money, from the sale of spices in the Molucca Islands, and from quit-rents and confiscated estates in the West Indies. We shall subjoin a statement of the produce of these and other branches of the Crown-revenues during the entire reign of Geo. III. from Parliamentary Paper, No. 1, Session 1820.

---

* Hansard's Parl. Debates, vol. 34, p. 272.
† Treasury Minute, Parl. Paper, vol. 1, Session 1820.

AN ACCOUNT *of the Total Produce of all Funds at the Disposal of the Crown, and deemed not to be under the immediate Control of Parliament, from the Accession of George III. to the Year* 1820.

	£	s.	d.
Droits of the Admiralty and Droits of the Crown from 1760 to 1820	9,562,614	4	6¼
4½-per-Cent. West-India Duties, from 1760 to 1820	2,116,484	0	0
Amount of the surplus of Gibraltar Revenues, remitted to England, from 1760 to 1820, after discharging garrison-expenses ....,...............	124,256	10	7
Scotch Civil-List Surplus, from 1760 to 1820, now appropriated as it may arise, under the Act 50 Geo. III. c. 111, in aid of the Civil-List in England	207,700	0	0
Escheats to his Majesty, in cases of illegitimacy or otherwise, from 1760 to 1820	214,647	15	0
Escheats to his Majesty, being the property of alien enemies, from 1760 to 1820	108,777	17	8
French West-India Islands, funds arising by sale of lands in the islands; ceded at the peace of 1763..................	106,300	0	0
Minorca, Martinique, St. Croix, and St. Thomas, and from the settlement of Surinam, while the same were in the possession of his Majesty—Revenues arising from these Islands	159,816	0	7
Quit-Rents, &c. in the British Colonies, and from all other sources not before enumerated, from 1760 to 1820—casual revenues arising from.................................	104,865	3	2½

Total......£12,705,461 11 7

In the reign of George IV. the same sources of casual income yielded about a million and a half, forming, with the income from the Crown-lands, during the period from 1760 to 1830, a total sum of at least THIRTY-FIVE millions. All this mass of unappropriated revenue was left at the disposal of the minister of the day, and the parliament exercised no control over it, further than that, for the last ten years, it was permitted, as matter of courtesy, annually or triennally, to look at the accounts after the money had been expended or granted away. The manner in which these great funds were managed and dissipated has been, we trust, sufficiently illustrated in the course of this chapter. With the exception of the sums expended in metropolitan improvements, they have been expended in additional grants to the royal family and in pensions to the aristocracy, to ministers, their friends and supporters. They have formed a *practical* branch of the English government, of which Mr. Justice Blackstone failed to give any account to his readers, and we have little hesitation in affirming that they had no inconsiderable influence in the ruinous policy of the late reigns. The royal expenditure always formed a gulph which no man could fathom, and the hereditary revenues were a never-failing source for supplying the prodigality of the king and his servants. Of the studied mystery maintained on these matters we shall cite an instance. In 1777, during the American war, the king's debts amounted to £618,000; papers were produced containing a disguised statement how this incumbrance had been incurred: vast sums were expended in *secret service* money, and half a million was stated under the head of the *board of works*: but then, as Mr. Belsham observes, no one could tell on what palace, garden, or park, the money had been laid out.   In short, there is too much reason to suppose that the debts of George III. were mainly contracted in support of the system of war and injustice in which ministers were engaged, in obtaining the baneful influence which silences all opposition, which swept away all traces of public liberty, and laid the foundation of present distress and embarrassments.

The parliament of 1820 was guilty of a culpable dereliction of duty in not seizing the opportunity, presented by the commencement of a new reign, to bring under its immediate cognizance and control the hereditary revenues.   Instead of availing itself of the occasion, they were left, as before, to the irresponsible disposal of ministers.   After what has been said, it will not be difficult to divine the reasons for this omission; but the people had another and opposite interest.   To the misapplication of the Crown-revenues may partly be ascribed the long postponement of the great measure of Parliamentary Reform; and, therefore, the public cannot help feeling grateful to William IV. in having patriotically surrendered, during his life, to public uses, nearly the whole of these abused funds, in lieu of leaving them to be lavished on court favourites and hireling legislators.

CIVIL LIST.

HAVING fully explained the nature, amount, and application of the ancient hereditary revenues, we next come to the modern parliamentary grant, substituted in lieu of them, denominated the *Civil List*, which is a sum yearly set apart from the general income for the personal maintenance of the sovereign, and to support the honour and dignity of the Crown.

Since the Revolution of 1688, it has been usual, at the commencement of a new reign, to enter into a specific arrangement with the king, by which the hereditary revenues of the Crown are surrendered in exchange for an equivalent life-annuity. A similar course has been pursued in respect of William IV.; but before explaining the alterations and arrangements introduced into the new civil list, it will be convenient to premise some explanations of the chief departments of the royal expenditure,—the king's household establishment; the privy purse; pensions on the civil list, and other branches of disbursement; and conclude with some observations on the character and policy of the last two monarchs, and the total expense their profusion entailed on the country.

The first and most important charge on the civil list is the *royal household.* This forms a ponderous establishment, and affords, by a reduction of useless offices and extravagant salaries, scope for retrenchment. It is the great nursery of indolence, parasites, and courtiers. It is formed upon manners and customs that have long since expired,— upon old baronial customs and arrangements. It not only retains traces of its feudal origin, but it is formed also on the principle of a body corporate; and has its own law-courts, magistrates, and by-laws.

In ancient times, these establishments were supported on a system of *purveyance* and *receipt in kind!* The household was then vast, and the supply scanty and precarious. The king's purveyor used to sally forth from under the gothic, portcullis, to purchase provisions, not with money, but power and prerogative. Whole districts were laid under contribution by the jackals of the royal table, who returned from their plundering excursions loaded with the spoils, perhaps, of a hundred markets, which were deposited in so many caverns, each guarded by its respective keeper. Every commodity being received in its rawest state, it had a variety of processes to pass through before it was prepared for the king and his guests. This inconvenient mode of receipt multiplied offices exceedingly; and hence has arisen the butchery, buttery, pantry, and all that "rabble of places," which, though profitable to the holder, and expensive to the state, are almost too mean to mention.

Let us hear what BURKE said on this subject, in his *reforming days* :—" But when (says he) the reason of old establishments is gone, it is absurd to preserve nothing but the burthen of them. This is superstitiously to embalm the carcass, not worth an ounce of the gums that are used to preserve it. It is to burn precious oils in the tomb: it is to offer meat and drink to the dead,—not so much an honour to the deceased as a disgrace to the survivors. Our palaces are vast *inhospitable halls :* there the bleak winds, ' there Boreas, and Eurus, and Caurus, and Argestes, loud,' howling through the vacant lobbies, and clattering the doors of deserted guard-rooms, appal the imagination, and conjure up the grim spectres of departed tyrants,—the Saxon, the Norman, and the Dane ; the stern Edwards and fierce Henries,—who stalk from desolation to desolation through the dreary vacuity and melancholy succession of *chill and comfortless chambers.* When this tumult subsides, a dead and still more frightful silence would reign in the desert, if, every now and then, the tacking of hammers did not announce that those constant attendants on all courts, in all ages, JOBS, were still alive; for whose sake alone it is that any trace of ancient grandeur is suffered to remain. These palaces are a true emblem of some governments ; the inhabitants are decayed, but the governors and magistrates still flourish. They put me in mind of Old Sarum, where the representatives, more in number than the constituents, only serve to inform us that this was once a place of trade, and sounding with the ' busy hum of men,' though now you can only trace the streets by the colour of the corn; and its sole manufacture is in members of parliament."* The royal abodes at present, we apprehend, are neither so ghostly, chill, nor comfortless, as here described, otherwise the public has been saddled with the enormous bills of Messrs. Wyattville, Nash, and Seddon, to very little purpose.

The great branches of the household are under the direction of the lord chamberlain, the lord steward, and the master of the horse. The office of the *lord chamberlain* is to take care of all the officers and servants belonging to the king's chambers, except those belonging to the king's bed-chamber, who are under the groom of the stole. He has the oversight of the officers of the wardrobe, of tents, *revels,* music, comedians, handicrafts, and artizans ; and, though a *layman,* he has the oversight of all the king's chaplains, heralds, physicians, and apothecaries. It is his office to inspect the charges of coronations, marriages, public entries, cavalcades, and funerals ; and of all furniture in the parliament-house, and rooms of address to the king.

---

* Works of Burke, vol. iii. pp. 277-8.—Speech on Economical Reform.

The *lord steward* has the estate of the household entirely committed to his care, and all his commands in court are to be obeyed; his authority reaches over all officers and servants of the king's house, except those of the king's chamber and chapel. The counting-house, (where the accounts of the household are kept,) the treasurer of the household, comptroller, cofferer, and master of the household, clerks of green cloth, &c. are under his control.

The *master of the horse* has the charge and government of all the king's stables and horses. He has also the power over equerries, pages, footmen, grooms, farriers, smiths, saddlers, and all other trades any way connected with the stables. He has the privilege of applying to his own use one coachman, four footmen, and six grooms, in the king's pay, and wearing the king's livery. In any solemn cavalcade, he rides next behind the king.

Beside these officers, is the lord privy seal, whose office is to put the seal to all charters, grants, and pardons, signed by the king   Before the privy seal is affixed to any instrument, it receives the royal sign manual; it then passes under the signet, which is a warrant to the privy seal; after the privy seal, it receives the great seal from the lord chancellor, which is the *finale*. The performance of these different formalities costs the public, perhaps, £20,000 a-year, while the whole of the duties might be discharged as well by any honest man and his clerk for about £400 a-year. The remaining functionaries are the lord president of the council, whose office is to manage the debates in council, to propose matters from the king, and to report to him the resolutions thereupon ; the commissioners of the treasury are also considered part of the household : but these, as well as some of the preceding officers, more properly appertain to the civil departments of government, and have been so considered in the new arrangement of the civil list.

The little necessity for this immense household establishment was evident during the limitations on the Regency. At that time the regent discharged all the duties of the executive with only his establishment as Prince of Wales. It did not appear then, no more than now, there was any want of attendance to give dignity and efficiency to the first magistrate. Burke mentions, in his time, that at least one-half the household was kept up solely for *influence.* He also mentions that one plan of reform, set on foot by lord Talbot, was suddenly stopped, because, forsooth, it would endanger the situation of an *honourable member who was turnspit in the kitchen !* Whether the duties of this important office continue to be discharged by a member of the *honourable house* we are not sure; but, in looking over a list of the household, we observe that two *noble lords* occupy situations little inferior in dignity and utility : the duke of St. Alban's is *master of the hawks,* salary £1372, and the earl of Lichfield is *master of the dogs,* salary £2000. These offices sound rather degrading to vulgar ears ; but "love," as the poet says, " esteems no office mean ;" and no doubt it is the love of the sovereign rather than £3000 of the *public money* which actuates these noble personages. In 1811 there were no fewer than *twenty-six* peers and *four* commoners who held situations in various departments of the household.

The parade of useless offices is not less great, and still more ridiculous, in the counties palatine of Durham and Chester, and the duchies of Lancaster and Cornwall, and the principality of Wales. These have all separate establishments, sufficient for the government of a kingdom, while their jurisdiction is confined to a few private estates. There are courts of chancery, ecclesiastical courts, chancellors, attorney-generals, solicitor-generals, privy councillors, registrars, cursitors, prothonotaries, auditors, and all the other mimicry of royal government. They bring nothing into the public treasury, but greatly add to the patronage of the Crown, whose dignity they degrade. In one part of his kingdom the sovereign is no more than Prince of Wales; go to the north, and he dwindles down to the duke of Lancaster; turn to the west, and he appears in the humble character of earl of Chester; travel a few miles farther, the earl disappears, and he pops up again as count palatine of Lancaster. Thus does the king, like Matthews in the play, perform all the different characters in his own drama.

Before the reign of George III. no such thing as a *privy purse* was known. The king's income was always considered public property attached to the office, but not to the person of the monarch. The first time any mention is made of the privy purse, is in Mr. Burke's bill, in 1782, and then again in the 39th of Geo. III.; but it was not till the time of the regency, when it was vested in the hands of commissioners, that it was recognised as a fixed annual sum, the private property of the king. But though this anomaly has been only recently acknowledged by any public act, it has been deemed a fixed charge on the civil list for the last seventy years. When the sum of £800,000 was set apart for the royal expenditure, the king was at liberty, with the advice of his ministers, to apply what portion of it he thought proper for his *private use.* The sum at first set aside for this purpose was £48,000; and the king's family increasing, it was extended to £60,000. No part of this fund is applied to defray the expense of the household, nor of any other function of the regal office; it is limited entirely to personal expenses, and may be more properly denominated the king's *pocket money* than his privy purse. Why it should be separated from the general income of the civil list, unless to gratify a puerile avarice in the monarch, it is not easy to conjecture. From this source, and the revenues of the duchies of Cornwall and Lancaster, the private property of the king is supposed to accumulate.

The next considerable charge on the civil list consists of *pensions* payable chiefly to servants of the household, and to the personal favorites of the sovereign and his ministers Up to the time of the 22 Geo. III. commonly called Mr. Burke's act, court pensions were granted without limit and controul. In that act it was provided the amount granted on the English civil list should be reduced to £95,000; the same principal of limitation was subsequently applied to the Scotch and Irish civil lists; the pensions to be granted on the former being limited to £25,000, and on the latter to £50,000, making the total amount of pensions chargeable on the civil lists of the United Kingdom £170,000. At this amount the civil list pensions stood on the accession of the king. After the death of George IV. the Court Pension list was published, and excited in the public mind a considerable sensation. Most of the " splendid paupers" inscribed upon it had never been heard of beyond the purlieus of the court; two thirds of them were *females;* many were the late king's *personal* friends, or the apothecaries, relatives, and *attachés* of successive viceroys of Ireland, and of the great burghmonger of Scotland; some were the mothers, sisters, and nieces of peers, ministers of state, and great borough proprietors in England : but in the whole number there was hardly one (Robert Southey perhaps excepted) eminent for science, literature, or the arts, or distinguished by any kind of public worth or claim. Worthless, however, as the elect of court favour were, their annuities have been continued to them during their lives, under an impression that to rescind them might be productive of individual distress, and a departure from established usage on the accession of a new sovereign. But in the sequel it will be seen that the Court Pension list, in future, is not to exceed £75,000 per annum.

The remaining charges on the civil list consist of certain ancient payments for charity; a sum for special service at the disposal of the lords of the Treasury; and the secret service money of the Treasury.

Other charges heretofore paid out of the civil list have been transferred to the consolidated fund; such were the payments to the judges, to the lords of the Treasury, to foreign ministers, to the speaker of the House of Commons, to the universities, and various miscellaneous items to the city of London, and corporations in the country. The amount of these, and also the expenditure under the several heads of the civil list we have described, will appear from the official documents which will be subjoined to this article. At present let us give a brief summary of the progress and augmentation of the civil list, and an account of its present settlement.

From the year 1804 to 1811, the average annual expenditure of the civil list amounted to £1,102,683. On the commencement of the Regency, this branch of expenditure increased enormously. From 1812 to 1816, the average annual expenditure of the civil list was £1,371,000, being an increase of £268,317 over the expenditure of George III. This augmentation arose chiefly from the profusion in the royal household; from the expense of furniture and tradesmen's bills; of upholsters, jewellers, glass and china manufacturers, builders, perfumers, embroiderers, tailors, and so on. The charge for upholstery, only for three quarters of a year, was £46,291; of linen-drapery, £64,000; silversmiths, £40,000; wardrobe, £72,000. To provide for these additional outgoings, Lord Castlereagh introduced the Civil-List-Regulation-Bill of 1816. By this Bill, no check is imposed on the profusion of the court; it only provides that various fluctuating and other charges, heretofore paid out of the civil list, should be transferred to the consolidated fund, or provided for by new grants from parliament : in other words, that the civil list should be *augmented to the amount of its increased expenditure.* By this arrangement, an additional burden was imposed on the public, amounting to £255,768, being the total of the charges of which the civil list was relieved.

Among the charges transferred from the civil list was £35,000, payable to the junior branches of the royal family, and which was to be paid out of the consolidated fund; also salaries, to the amount of £3,268, to certain officers and persons. All the charges, for the outfit of ministers to foreign courts, or presents to foreign ministers, incidental expenses in the Treasury, deficiencies of fees to secretaries of state, and in the law department, amounting to £197,000, were to be provided for by new grants from parliament. Various charges for furniture and other articles, heretofore provided by the lord chamberlain for public offices ; the expense of collars, badges, and mantles for the orders of the Garter, Bath, and Thistle ; and all expenses for repairs of public offices and buildings at the Tower, Whitehall, and Westminster ; for works in St. James's Park and private roads, estimated at £25,000, were to be provided for by new grants ; the total deduction of charges being, as before stated, £255,768.

Now it is obvious that to the amount of these charges the income of the Crown was augmented, and that the scale of extravagant expenditure, in the first four years of the Regency, from 1812 to 1816, formed the basis on which the civil list of George IV. was provided. On the accession of the late king, in 1820, no alteration was proposed in the Civil-List-Regulation-Bill of 1816 ; it passed, as is observed by the writer of a ministerial pamphlet of the day, with " the entire approbation of *all parties;* that is, " *all parties,*" without inquiry or examination, concurred in making a permanent addition to the king's income of a *quarter of a million* over that enjoyed by his predecessor.

But to judge of the immense disproportion in the incomes of the two sovereigns, it is necessary to advert to the *alteration in the value of money.* The average expenditure of George III. from 1804 to 1811, was £1,102,683. The average price of wheat, from 1804 to 1811, inclusive, was 87s. 6d. per quarter. The average price of wheat, during the ten years of the last reign, from 1820 to 1830, was 58s. 4d. per quarter ; indicating a rise in the value of money, as measured by corn, of above 33 per cent. The price of labour, profits, tithes, rents, and interest, all fell in nearly the same proportion ; so that it would not be too much to reckon an income of £67 equivalent to an income of £100 in the period selected for comparison ; and, conseqently, that the expenditure of George III. of £1,102,683, in a depreciated currency, was not more than an expenditure of £638,797 at the value of money during the last reign. Had, therefore, the civil list of George IV. been fixed at the same nominal amount as the civil list of George III. it would have been virtually 33 per cent. greater ; but, besides being fixed at nearly the same nominal amount as that of his predecessor, *one-fourth less was to pay out of it ;* so that the real addition to the income of

George IV. was not less than fifty-eight per cent.— an arrangement, we are told, with the " entire approbation of all parties."

The extravagant nature of the settlement of the civil list of George IV. must be plain: we have compared it with the latest expenditure of George III. and, allowing for the alteration in the currency and the charges transferred to other funds, the difference was more than half a million. George III. was by no means a *cheap sovereign ;* but in considering his expenditure, it ought to be borne in mind that he was liable to many outgoings from which his successor was exempted. Of this nature, were a large family—sums expended in the improvement of Windsor-castle—the charge of furnishing and decorating the apartments in the palaces for the princesses—their removal to and from Windsor, estimated at £20,000—the journeys to Weymouth about general Garth's affair—and furnishing apartments in Kensington-palace for the Princess of Wales ; all which tended to swell the royal expenditure in the seven years selected for comparison.

But it is proper to observe respecting this pattern-king, as many considered George III., that his income never equalled his expenditure. Allowing for the sums granted by parliament to liquidate the debts of the civil list during his reign, amounting to upwards of THREE MILLIONS AND A HALF, it renders the disparity between his actual expenditure and that of his successor less than we have mentioned. George IV. incurred *no debts* after the settlement of his civil list, and the course adopted to avoid future incumbrances was *first,* by relieving the civil list of all public charges of an expensive and fluctuating amount; and *secondly,* by granting to the king an allowance framed on the most extravagant scale of expenditure ever known in this country, and such as experience had shewn to be adequate to his most lavish demands. By these precautions, and with the hereditary revenues always ready to meet any unexpected outgoing, it would have been wonderful had not the scheme realised the expectations of the projectors. Another feature in lord Castlereagh's bill was the appointment of a new officer under the name of *auditor* of the civil list. The latter regulation can excite no surprise, for it cannot be forgotten that in all attempts to economize by Tory ministers they generally contrived to keep up the same amount of patronage by new creations. An instance of this occurred on the abolition of certain sinecures in 1817, when a bill, the 57 Geo. III. was immediately introduced to provide *pensions* in lieu of them. Another instance was afforded in the consolidation of the revenue departments of England and Ireland, when a vice-treasurer and his deputy were appointed, with a salary of £3000 a-year, apparently for no other object than to keep up the patronage of the Treasury. Again, when the further granting of pensions from the Leeward-Islands-fund was prohibited, ministers set up the West-India church-establishments. The ostensible functions of the auditor of the civil list were to superintend the accounts of the lord chamberlain, lord steward, and master of the horse ; but certainly these were the duties which ought to have been performed by the heads of these departments, and for which they receive their salaries. Was it probable the public would be better secured against profusion in the royal expenditure when confided to the watchful vigilance of a commoner than when confided to three peers of the realm? The precaution was futile, but answered the purpose of a pretext for dipping into the pockets of the people. Mr. Herries was the first auditor appointed; his previous office, commissary-in-chief, had been abolished, and, we presume, ministers were at a loss how otherwise to dispose of him.

The Whig ministry have annexed the auditorship to the Treasury, by which a saving of more than £1500 a-year has been effected.

CIVIL LIST OF WILLIAM IV.

Having adverted to the civil lists of the two last reigns, let us next advert to the civil list arrangement concluded with the present King. WILLIAM IV. is so deservedly popular for his firm and enlightened adherence to the great renovating measure of parliamentary reform, that we are sure the people will not begrudge his Majesty any income conducive to his personal comfort and real dignity. But it is not our province to act the part of parasites, who mislead monarchs and ruin empires, but to submit to our readers the truth, and nothing but the truth. We shall then briefly state the arrangement of the civil list established by 1 Will. IV., c. 25., and which received the royal assent April 22, 1831.

The leading principle of the framers of the act was to relieve the civil list of every charge not strictly connected with the royal expenditure. Hitherto many expenses had been included in the civil list which had no immediate connexion with the king's household or the regal office; expenses which, in fact, were the expenses of the civil government of the country, and as such ought always to have been under the cognizance, and subject to the control of parliament. All charges of this description have been dissevered and transferred to the consolidated fund, to be provided for out of the general produce of the taxes. In lieu of the civil list consisting of nine classes of payment, they have been reduced to the five following; *first*, the privy purse of the King, £60,000, and the establishment of the Queen, £50,000, making the total sum allotted to this class £110,000 per annum. *Second*, the salaries of the royal household, including the departments of the lord chamberlain, £64,450, lord steward, £36,500, master of the horse, £28,500, and master of the robes £850, making the total sum allotted to this class £130,300. The *third* class consists of the expenditure in the several departments in the second class, amounting to £171,500. The *fourth* class consists of royal bounty, alms, payments to the poor of London, special service, and home secret service money, amounting to £23,200. The *fifth* and last class is pensions, which is limited to £75,000. The mode in which the reduction has been effected under this head, was by consolidating the three pension lists of England, Ireland, and Scotland in one alphabetical list, and by providing that pensions to the amount of £75,000 on the first part of the alphabetical list should be charged on the civil list, and the remainder, to the amount of £95,000, be charged on the consolidated fund.   By this arrangement the public will receive the benefit of the pensions which fall in from that part of them which are charged on the consolidated fund, while the King has the advantage of the vacancies which occur in those payable from the civil list.

RECAPITULATION.

		£	s.	d.
First Class.	For their Majesty's Privy Purse ····	110,000	0	0
Second Class.	Salaries of His Majesty's Household ··	130,300	0	0
Third Class.	Expences of His Majesty's Household··	171,500	0	0
Fourth Class.	Special and Secret Service ··········	23,200	0	0
Fifth Class.	Pensions ·······················	75,000	0	0
		£510,000	0	0

An important question now arises—What is the amount of saving effected by the new arrangement? There has been a *shifting of weights* we have seen, there has been a transfer of charges from one fund to another, but the vital question to the public is, how much less will the support of the new king cost than the old.   Let us enquire.

The civil list granted to William IV. is £510,000; the civil list granted to his predecessor (the Irish civil list included) was £1,057,000; the difference is £547,000.   But the saving is by no means to the amount of this difference.   The civil list of the King has been relieved of four entire classes of disbursement, the expenditure in which amounted to upwards of £400,000, and which are now provided for by annual grants from parliament.   Notwithstanding this, we find, on comparing the corresponding classes of the two lists, that there has been an absolute and positive reduction.   In the second class the reductions have been to the amount of £10,300; in the third class to the amount of £37,500; in the fourth class to the amount of £3000; and in the fifth class to the amount of £95,000.   In the first class there has been an augmentation to the amount of £50,000 on account of the establishment of the Queen.   The net reduction in the royal expenditure, below the amount in the preceding reigns, is £95,000.

We have now submitted, as clearly and correctly as we are able, from the official returns to parliament, the new arrangement of the civil list. In our opinion, it is a material improvement on those which have preceded it, and does credit to Earl Grey's administration.   It is simpler in form and more economical.   The cutting down of the infamous pension list is not only a saving, but a *constitutional* improvement in the executive government, by destroying the miasm of the court atmosphere. Other advantages have accrued: the masses of revenue, the nature of which was explained in the last chapter, have been withdrawn from the irresponsible disposal of ministers.   By the transfer of charges to the consolidated fund, a sum of no less than £696,000 has, for the first time, been brought within the cognizance and control of parliament, and which cannot fail, ultimately, to lead to a very considerable reduction of expenditure.

Against these advantages we have only two drawbacks to mention. First, it does not appear from the civil list act, the revenues of the duchies of Cornwall and Lancaster have been included in the surrender of the hereditary and casual revenues of the crown. The income from these royal appanages, we believe, is about £25,000 per annum. The king enjoys the revenue of the former in the absence of a Prince of Wales, and of the latter in his own right as Duke of Lancaster. They are considered by some as the private property of the sovereign, and, as such, not within parliamentary cognizance any more than the income of his grace of Norfolk, or any other nobleman. But we cannot see the reasons for this construction. The king is only known in his public capacity of chief magistrate, and we apprehend the revenues of Lancaster and Cornwall might have been as legally surrendered as the casual and hereditary revenues. The duchies are notoriously great nurseries of abuse and sinecurism, and have long wanted bringing before the public.

The second objection we have to urge is, our apprehension lest the hereditary revenues have not been sufficiently secured from ministerial grasp. In the twelfth section of the Civil List Act various powers are reserved to the Crown, among others, to grant rewards out of the admiralty droits for meritorious conduct. May not this leave a door open for the future encroachments of the servants of the king on these funds? However, this is a contingency, which can only occur from the supineness of the legislature.

We repeat, therefore, in spite of these drawbacks, that the Whig civil list is a substantial improvement on its predecessors. Many, however, will still think, and we think so too, that the allowance of more than half a million per annum for the maintenance of one man is a very great sum. But it is necessary to bear in mind the state and institutions of the society in which we live. No one can reasonably expect that a king of England should have a less annual income than the greatest of his subjects. Before reducing lower the royal income, we must reduce the incomes of the grandees of the church and aristocracy, by the amputation of tithes and corn laws. Till then we do not imagine his Majesty could well discharge the duties of his high station with a smaller revenue; especially while he has the gorgeous civil list of the *citizen* king of the French to keep him in countenance. While, therefore, the monarchical and aristocratic institutions of the country subsist, the people will be compelled to make a great pecuniary sacrifice to mere state and graduated rank, and be under the necessity of declining the tender of the worthy Scotchman, who offered to discharge all the duties of the regal office for £300 a year, and find good security for the performance!

ROYAL DEBTS AND EXPENDITURE DURING THE LATE REIGNS.

The state of the civil list has varied so much during the reigns of George III. and IV., that it may be useful to give a brief sketch of the total amount of public money applied to the support of this department of expenditure, and in extricating the Crown and the members of the royal family from pecuniary embarrassments.

At the commencement of the reign of George III. the king accepted the fixed sum of £800,000 per annum in lieu of the hereditary, temporary, and other revenues. This sum was successively augmented by parliament as follows:

1 Geo. III. c. 1.	£800,000
17 Geo. III. c. 21.	100,000
44 Geo. III. c. 80.	60,000
52 Geo. III. c. 6.	70,000
Surplus of exchequer fees, applied by 23 Geo. III. c. 82.	50,000
Surplus of Scotch revenues, applied by 50 Geo. III. c. 87.	10,000

In 1804, when £60,000 was added, the civil list was relieved of annual charges to the amount of £82,000. The debts of the king, paid by parliament, were as follows:

In 1769	£513,511
1777	618,340
1784	60,000
1786	210,000
1802	990,000
1804	591,842
1805	10,458
1814	118,857
	£3,113,061

Parliament granted, towards the extraordinary expenses of 1814, £100,000, making £3,213,061; and in January, 1815, there was a further debt on the civil list to the amount of £421,355. To these grants to the king must be added the monies granted to the royal family, and to defray those charges of which the civil list had been relieved, amounting to £9,561,396.[*] Besides which there was applied, either in aid of the civil list, or to liquidate arrears thereon, £1,653,717 out of the hereditary revenues.[†] So far brings the royal expenditure to January, 1815. In the following year the civil list expenditure amounted to £1,480,000; making the total expenditure, from the accession of George III. to January, 1816, £64,740,032.

This brings us down to the period when there was a general parliamentary investigation of the civil list; and when it was settled on the basis on which it continued, without material alteration, till the recent demise of the Crown. As we have before explained the profuse character of lord Castlereagh's settlement, and the vast augmentation the

---

[*] Parl. Report on the Civil List, Session 1815.—Ordered to be reprinted July 6, 1830.
[†] Ibid. p. 5.

civil list received, we shall not repeat our statement, further than by recapitulating the chief provisions.

In 1816 the civil list was relieved of public charges to the amount of £255,768, and the future provision for it was fixed at the sum of £1,083,729. £100,000 more was granted for the support of the establishment of George III. at Windsor-Castle, and £10,000 per annum to Queen Charlotte, afterwards continued to the Duke of York, for superintendence. In the same year £60,000 was voted for the establishment of the Princess Charlotte and Prince Coburg. With the exception of the saving of £10,000, by the premature death of the Princess of Wales, in 1817, all these arrangements continued until the accession of George IV. in 1820, when the civil list was fixed at £1,057,000, and so continued to the end of that monarch's reign.

Having obtained the ordinary charges of the civil list, we next inquire, what extraordinary aids flowed into this insatiable gulph. Like his predecessor, George IV. was constantly receiving, in addition to his regular income, *refreshers* out of the Admiralty droits, Gibraltar duties, and other branches of the hereditary revenues, either in aid of the privy purse, to defray travelling expenses among his lieges, or to meet extra outgoings in the household. Besides these, many items ordinarily inserted in that annual budget of miscellanies, the *civil list contingencies*, ought in justice to be placed to the account of the sovereign. Then, again, what masses of money have been swamped in the royal palaces. Upwards of £600,000 has been already granted for the repair and improvement of the Pimlico residence. On Windsor-castle the sum already expended amounts to £894,500;* and £190,670 more is requisite to finish this gothic barbarism. It is said that the pavilion at Brighton cost a million of money; and on the *cottage* in the Great Park half a million was expended. For the two last facts we have no official authority, but they are traits of extravagance not improbable in a king who, in one year, spent £5000 and more in the single article of *robes ;* whose stud of horses, though he seldom journeyed beyond the limits of his own pleasure-grounds, was upwards of 200 ; and whose *old clothes,* white kid inexpressibles with white satin linings included, after his death, actually sold in the *heap* for £15,000! Such are the blessings conferred by a monarch of taste, who, through the agency of servile ministers and a patient people, obtained ample means to gratify his most fantastic desires.

Nothing has been yet said of the burthen imposed by the younger branches of the royal family. The pensions of these are paid out of the consolidated fund, and form a distinct charge from the civil list. The annuities payable at the time of the late demise, exclusive of military pay and official emoluments, amounted to £248,500 per annum.

Every change in the personal relations of the royal family entails additional expense on the community, whether it be a marriage, a christening, or a burial. In the first case, there is a grant for an

---

* Parl. Report, No. 27, Sess. 1831.

outfit ; in the second, a grant for *support and education ;* and in the last, a provision for the servants of the deceased. The public is now paying upwards £30,000 per annum for the servants of George III., Queen Charlotte, and Queen Caroline.* In 1825 an annuity of £6000 a-year was granted to the Duke of Cumberland, to *support and educate* his son, Prince George-Frederick-Alexander-Charles-Ernest-Augustus of Cumberland, (gracious heaven, what a long name this child has got); in the same year a like annuity to the Duchess of Kent, for Alexandrina-Victoria, which, in 1831, was augmented to her royal highness by an additional grant of £10,000. One might suppose these high personages had never been married, and the fact of having offspring was among the accidents of life for which they were totally unprovided.

People naturally wonder what becomes of the heaps of money abstracted from them in taxes; they are, in fact, only imperfectly acquainted with the costliness of the institutions under which they live, and the profusion with which the produce of their industry and skill is lavished: we shall, however, endeavour to open their eyes on these subjects. Let us see, then, what has been the total cost of the two last reigns ; after the preceding explanations the reader will be better able to comprehend and verify the subjoined recapitulation.

SUMMARY *of the Royal Expenditure, from the Accession of George III. to the Death of George IV.*

From the accession of George III. to January 5, 1815, the income of the civil list, and parliamentary grants to liquidate debts thereon.. ....£51,623,564		
Parliamentary grants to the royal family, and for judges and other services, of the charge for which the civil list was relieved	9,561,390	
Monies applied out of the hereditary revenues...........	1,653,717	
Debts on the civil list, January 1815................	421,355	
Civil list expenditure for the year ending January 5, 1816	1,480,000	
TOTAL royal expenditure from the accession of George III. to the year 1816		64,740,026
From 1816 to 1820, the income of civil list by 56 Geo. III. c. 46	4,334,916	
Windsor-castle establishment during the same period, including allowance for *custos*	440,000	
Parliamentary grants for pensions, salaries, and services, of which the civil list was relieved..........	1,358,072	
Pensions and official salaries of the royal dukes and princesses, including Prince Coburg and Queen Caroline	1,335,344	
Monies applied in aid of the king and royal family from the hereditary revenues	350,000	
Revenues of the Duchies of Cornwall and Lancaster ..	100,000	
Allowance to Queen Charlotte to her death in 1818 ..	116,400	
TOTAL royal expenditure, from 1816 to 1820		8,034,332
Carried forward....£72,774,358		

---

* Annual Finance Accounts, Session 1830, p. 134.

	Brought forward £72,774,358
From 1820 to 1830, the income of the civil list, by 1 Geo. IV. c. 1	10,570,000
Parliamentary grants for pensions, salaries, and services, of which the civil list was relieved..........	3,397,680
Pensions, salaries, and allowances of the royal dukes and princesses, including Prince Coburg	3,575,000
Monies appropriated to the use of the king and royal dukes, out of Admiralty droits and Gibraltar duties	150,000
Revenues of the duchies of Cornwall and Lancaster paid into the privy purse	250,000
Allowances to the late servants of George III., Queen Charlotte, and Queen Caroline	350,000
Expense of repairing and improving Buckingham-palace, to 1830.....................................	496,269
Grants for the alteration and improvement of Windsor-castle, to January 5, 1830.......................	527,500
TOTAL royal expenditure, from 1820 to 1830....	———— 19,316,449

GRAND TOTAL of the Royal Expenditure, from the
accession of George III. to the death of
George IV.. £92,000,807

The pensions and official emoluments of the royal dukes, from first entering into public life to the year 1815, are not included; and there are various fees and perquisites of which they were in the receipt, and annuities to the princesses on the Irish civil list, of which we have not been able to obtain authentic returns. The total amount of the incomes of the king and royal family, for the last seventy years, cannot have been less than £100,000,000 sterling, making the average expenditure of a single family £1,428,571 per annum.

The people of England have been so long familiarized to the lavish expenditure of their rulers, that we fear they are unable to appreciate the importance of ONE HUNDRED MILLIONS of money. The best way to bring the mind rightly to estimate the magnitude of this sum, is, to reflect for a moment on the amount of evil it might have averted, or the good it might have accomplished, had it been judiciously appropriated to the attainment of objects of national utility. An annual revenue of £1,428,571 is equal to one-third of all the sums levied in poor-rates during the two reigns, and would maintain two millions of poor people. By the saving of such a sum how many trumpery taxes might have been repealed, which harass and impede the industrious citizen! What a fund it would form to mitigate the sufferings constantly recurring from changes in the seasons and the vicissitudes of commerce! It is calculated that the annual application of a quarter of a million would enable to emigrate the whole of the redundant industry yearly accumulating from the progress of population. How much more, then might be effected by the application of £1,428,571 per annum. What an impulse it would give to our mercantile navy, by creating employment for shipping in the conveyance of settlers:— what stores—what implements of agriculture, and other necessaries, it would furnish to families! Internal industry would be stimulated; new communities founded; the waste and desolate parts of the earth reclaimed and peopled; and by opening new channels of employment and demand, some of the evils, which most embitter our social state, alleviated.

A republican, perhaps, would contend that nearly the whole of the hundred millions might have been saved to the community, and point to the people of the United States of America for an example of frugal government. Their king only costs five thousand a-year, instead of a million; and their other functionaries are equally cheap and reasonable. As for lords of the bed-chamber, grooms of the stole, master of the hawks, master of the robes, and other masters and lords, they have none of these things. And where is the loss they have sustained? Their government never appeared deficient in dignity or efficiency at home or abroad; and the duties of the executive magistracy have been discharged quite as well as in this country.

There is much truth in this; but the British people seem to have a taste for monarchy, and it is a point now hardly disputed, that every community has a right to choose its own form of government. It is true our chief magistrate is not the most efficient of public servants; neither fighting the battles of the country, conducting its negotiations, nor personally exercising judicial administration. Still, we do not consider him quite so useless in his station as "the gilded globe on the dome of St. Paul's," to which the capital "of the Corinthian column" has been rather absurdly compared. Every society must have a head— a king, president, or dictator; and, in fixing the amount of his revenue, it is necessary to have regard to the state and income of his subjects. A richly endowed church and aristocracy demand a richly endowed king *to match* : simultaneously with the curtailment of the income of the monarch ought the revenues of the priesthood and nobility to be curtailed, by the abolition of tithes, the repeal of corn-laws, and a more equal partition of national burthens.

The superior income of the sovereign, however, does not comprise all the advantages he enjoys over his lieges. The king pays no house-rent or taxes; and if he travels he pays no turnpikes. If he marries there is an outfit; if he has a child there is a portion; if he dies he is buried at the public charge, his widow receives £100,000 a year out of the taxes, and has two splendid mansions wherein to mourn her loss. Thus all the relations and vicissitudes of life are so amply provided for that one is at a loss to conceive what the king can have to pay, or on what objects his immense income can be expended. Here is certainly a mystery. The conclusion seems to be, that the functions of the regal office have degenerated into etiquette; and the exalted individuals who discharge them have become, as one of the number observed, little more than a *ceremony*, whose duties are nominal, and whose outgoings—great though they be—consist only of trappings, attendance, and pageantry.

In what, for example, consist the duties of a king of the old European fashion?—At first sight they appear great and manifold: he holds courts and levees.—opens and prorogues parliament—chooses ministers of state—examines and signs all public grants and documents. These functions appear quite sufficient to occupy the attention of one individual; but if we examine them more closely, we shall find they are vain, shadowy, and unimportant.

What, for instance, is a *court?*—A pageant, a farce, in which a train of useless officers, gaudily attired, assemble, and those who have obtained an appointment, a pension, or place, express their gratitude by kissing the royal hands!

What is a *levee?*—A larger muster, a presentation of titled mendicants and others, who move in procession before the king: they bow, and he bows, and sometimes smiles; they pass on, another and another, as " great a fool as t' other ;"—and this is a levee.

How does the king authenticate public documents? He writes W. R., or W. REX, at the top or bottom of a piece of parchment, vellum, or paper: this was done by a *machine* in the last reign, and many were in hopes that it would have been retained, and a similar contrivance extended to other regal functions, by which the monarch would have been able to retire on half-pay, or with a superannuation allowance.

What is the opening of parliament?—The king going in great state to the house of peers; reading about a dozen lines prepared for him by his ministers, containing nothing either rich or rare, and then returning in the same state.

What is a prorogation?—Much the same as the last; with this difference, that the rogues are sent to kill partridges, instead of being called together to talk, and talk, and nothing but talk.

How does the king choose his ministers? He does not choose them at all; they are chosen by a majority of the parliament, which is chosen by one hundred and fifty-four individuals called boroughmongers, who have been chosen by God knows whom, but who appear to have been a visitation inflicted on the people as a punishment for apathy and gullibility.

Are not kings the fathers of their people?—They are so called, but they are very unlike fathers, since, instead of feeding and protecting their children, their children feed and protect them.

Kings are called the sovereigns of their respective states?—They are so styled, certainly, but this is another fiction of feudality and priestcraft. The sovereignty is in the people; and, as every day affords experimental proof of the truth of this position, there are now few to call it in question.

Such is a catechism of the duties and attributes of what may be denominated feudal kings: as to *citizen kings*, our experience of them is yet too limited to decide whether or no they are an improvement. But of the elder sort it may be truly affirmed they have little claim on the gratitude of mankind: formerly they were great destroyers of their species, and latterly they have been great consumers of victual. " When we see," says Rabelais, " the print of Garagantua, that has a mouth as large as an oven, and swallows at one meal twelve hundred pounds of bread, twenty oxen, a hundred sheep, six hundred fowls, fifteen hundred horses, two thousand quails, a thousand barrels of wine, six hundred peaches, five hundred pine-apples, &c. &c. who does not say— That is the mouth of a KING ?"

POLICY AND CHARACTER OF THE TWO LATE REIGNS.

Having dwelt so long on the pecuniary affairs of the late reigns, our readers will, perhaps, have patience with us while we submit a few strictures on their political and social bearing.

The personal character of George III., and the predominant maxims of his reign, are too well known to require elucidation in this place ; but one part of his policy has either not obtained the attention it deserves, or is not so generally understood. It is thought this prince, like his predecessor, was held in thraldom by the boroughmongers : this is an error. Although the intellectual endowments of the king were not of a high order, he is entitled to the praise of being the first of his race who, if he did not emancipate himself from, at least lightened, the yoke imposed on the executive by the aristocracy.

The great families who had mainly contributed to the Revolution of 1688 claimed, for their services, an exclusive right to the government of the kingdom; having averted the despotism of the Stuarts, they sought to establish a despotism in themselves, and transmit the *divine right* of power, wrested from the monarch, to their own posterity. Parliamentary reform had not been agitated ; and the people being of little political importance, the sovereign was the only obstacle to this oligarchical pretension. Hence their intrigues and encroachments were exclusively directed against the Crown. They sought to render the regal office a mere name; the king a puppet, to be moved by wires, of which they held the strings, to be brought out, like the unfortunate Montezuma, on *show days*, decked out in the habiliments of royalty, to inspire the multitude with respect for authority. William III. groaned under this system ; Queen Anne patronized its opponents ; the first and second George, having little knowledge of our institutions, and by nature not much qualified for the exercise of authority, submitted to it quietly ; but to the credit of George III., he openly rebelled against aristocratic usurpation. The king perceived, and his mother, the princess-dowager, in concert with lord Bute, demonstrated to him the galling bondage in which his predecessors had been held by the arrogance of the Devonshire, the Pelham, the Portland, and other towering families. " George," said the princess, " be KING ;" and the prince obeyed her constant exhortation, and became so not only in name but reality. The design was laudable, and even constitutional ; the king his prerogatives, and the people their representatives, being the whole creed of reformers. But it was only the first, not the second, the king regarded ; while grasping at the prerogatives of the Stuarts, he was equally averse to the rights of the Commons.

Lord Bute was appointed the first minister on the new system. Being a man of little capacity, ignorant of public affairs, and the management of parties, he was compelled to retire. But the king did not abandon his object. Partly by the untractableness of his own character, partly by the adroitness with which he played the factions against each other, but most of all from the immense increase in the power of the Crown, from taxation, the augmentation of the peerage, the establishment of the banking interest—aided with the money-jobbers, contractors, and speculators, he succeeded in breaking the aristocratic fetters. His independence may be dated from the American war. That contest was purely his own. It is even said he first suggested the stamp-duty. So much, however, was it considered the king's *personal* quarrel, that those who did not concur in it were branded as *disloyal.*

The last attempt of the aristocracy to reduce the king to a state of pupilage was made in 1783, by the famous India Bill of Mr. Fox. This great measure, framed by Mr. Burke, was intended to establish a counterpoise to the influence of the Crown, by vesting the patronage of India in fifteen individuals chosen by parliament ; in other words, by the coalition administration. Nothing could have been devised more effectual for the purpose ; for it would have placed the sovereign of England at the mercy of the sovereigns of Bengal, and erected a mound from which the palace of St. James's might always be maintained in dutiful and respectful obedience. But the king penetrated the snare that was laid for him ; and, by a vigorous exertion of court influence and the artful excitement of popular clamour, the bill was thrown out, and the Whigs, driven from power in disgrace, sunk into complete insignificance. Their union with lord North exposed to the country the profligacy and rottenness of their public principles. It was the death-blow to party. " From the moment," says the bishop of Llandaff, " the coalition was formed betwixt lord North and the men who for many years had reprobated in the strongest terms his political principles, I lost all confidence in *public men.* I clearly saw that they sacrificed their public principles to private pique, and their honour to their ambition." The observations of Sir N. Wraxall are to the same purport. Mr. Nicholls, in his " Recollections," says, " from the death of lord Rockingham they became a *faction,* and their efforts were no longer employed for the attainment of any great public object." These writers speak from contemporary impression, and consequently represent the general feeling excited by their conduct.

The subsequent history of this party is too fresh in public recollection to require illustration. There are some Whigs yet, as there are some Jacobites, Bourbonites, and Johannites; for sects and parties hardly ever become extinct, however absurd their dogmas. But upon the whole, both Whiggism and Toryism may be considered defunct superstitions ; and the impostures having been unmasked, men are now only shocked at the grossness of the idolatary by which they had been so long enslaved.

Upon the conduct of the Whigs, in their endeavours to controul the executive, one or two observations may be made. That the influence of the Crown, after its enormous augmentation during the American war, required abridgement, there can be no question ; but the means employed for this purpose were highly objectionable. The Whigs attempted to throw the weight into the wrong scale ; they saw the preponderance of the Crown, but were insensible or indifferent to the humiliation of the People : they looked only to themselves, and instead of raising the popular branch of the constitution, sought only their own aggrandizement, and, by providing sinecures and places for their adherents, balancing the patronage of the monarch. Hence the real friends of the people viewed their policy not only with contempt but abhorrence ; for it contained no invitation to popular support—no guarantee for public liberty, and was merely the selfishness of party struggling for the influence and emoluments of regality.

Yet the Whigs have complained of *ingratitude*, of the people having been *deluded* from their " NATURAL LEADERS !" But is not this a faithful history of their conduct ? Is it not notorious, from the Revolution to the end of the last reign, the people had no alternative, save despotism in the sovereign, or despotism in an oligarchy ? Is it surprising that they revolted from both these propositions ; that they repulsed with equal scorn the open partizans of absolute power, and those who, under hollow and hypocritical professions, sought to inveigle them out of their liberties, or render them the passive instruments of personal ambition ? From such " natural leaders" it was time the people separated, and established a party for themselves. That the secession was at length accomplished, may be ascribed to the persevering and patriotic efforts of sir Francis Burdett and the electors of Westminster, who were the first successfully to erect the standard of revolt from aristocratical domination.

These strictures on the aristocratical factions, it is needless to remark, apply only to their public conduct during the period under review. Both Tories and Whigs have recently undergone a change for the better ; the administration of lord Wellington was better than any preceding administration formed from the same class of politicians : many Tories avow sentiments which their predecessors would have repudiated with horror ; and the existing Whig ministry we feel confident, from all we can observe up to the moment we are writing, (December 22d, 1831,) is sincerely bent on reforming the popular branches of our institutions, on reducing the government expenditure, and on improving— if that be possible—the condition of the great body of the people of the United Kingdom. The fact is, there has been a progression (sir C. Wetherell would say, a retrocession) of parties ; the more liberal Tories have adopted the sentiments of the Whigs, and the Whigs have adopted the sentiments of the more intelligent Radicals. But to what is the change to be ascribed ? Why solely to EVENTS—events too obvious to be here enumerated. Had the people remained quiescent, the Whigs would have continued Whigs still, and the Tories would have been unchanged. But the people have become enlightened from ex-

perience of the evils inflicted by bad government; they have tasted of
the forbidden fruit of knowledge—of that fruit which many would gladly
have kept out of their reach; they have, in short, read the *Black Book*,
and the consequence is, they no longer continue the duped spectators
of the *tracasseries* of faction; they will no longer suffer the legislature
of a great empire, instituted solely for their service and benefit, to be
merely an arena for aristocratic contention, intrigue, and selfish ambition; they care nothing about *men* — who is in or who is out, but
insist on the adoption of measures advantageous to themselves—and
these measures are an efficient reform of an insulting mock representation—of an oppressive church—of an absurd and plundering legal system
—of monopolies and taxes partial and unjust. More of these subjects
hereafter; at present let us return to our task, from which we have
deviated in order to escape for a moment the tedium of statistical detail.

The great theme of the panegyrists of George III. is his private
virtues. For a king to discharge his duty to the people, it is not sufficient that he is neither passionately addicted to wine, nor women, nor
gaming, and that he does not amuse himself occasionally, after the fashion
of the East, by cutting off the heads of his lieges. Betwixt private
men and those who fill important public stations there is a wide difference. The former may live and die as it has pleased Heaven to
make them, and society has no right to complain, provided they observe
the laws, and neither burthen the parish nor their friends. But the
condition of a king is widely different: he has no privilege to be inept;
he is the *retained* servant of the community, who has grave duties to
discharge, and, his fees being enormous, it is not sufficient he is harmless and inoffensive, he ought to be actively beneficial. To judge of the
blessings accruing from the reign of George III. it would be sufficient
to contrast the state of the country when he ascended the throne with
the condition to which it was reduced when his intellectual twilight
subsided into total darkness. It is hardly possible to imagine how any
career could have been more reckless, profligate, and regardless of ultimate consequences than that which entailed the paper currency, the
monstrous debt, the poor-rates, and a vastly increased population dependent for subsistence on the uncertain demands of commerce and manufactures. Private virtues are a poor set-off against national calamities,
especially if produced by inveterate obstinacy and error, as was unquestionably the case with the two great ruinous wars—those against
America and France—in which George III. was engaged. Although
the mental endowments of the king were very moderate, and he possessed
no strength or originality of mind to carry him beyond the notions of
religion and politics impressed during his education, yet, like others of
the same intellectual grade, he had a quick sense of whatever tended to
interfere with his own interests. He fully comprehended the effect
likely to be operated on the *status* of his order by the French revolution. When that mighty movement began to manifest itself, he put
(says Mr. Nicholls) Burke's incendiary publication into the hands of
every one he met. He said to every courtier who approached him, " If

a stop is not put to French principles there will not be a king left in Europe in a few years." In fact, he was the greatest alarmist in his dominions. Mr. Burke and the duke of Portland were only second and third to him. Mr. Pitt was averse to the war, but acquiesced from that truckling love of place, which was the prominent feature of his own character and that of most of his adherents. In like manner the Grenville Whig administration consented to abandon Catholic Emancipation, on the condition of royal service. But the renunciation was not sufficiently explicit to satisfy the jealous scruples of the king.

To conclude, George III. was not a *tool* of the boroughmongers, but a leading and active partner in the Oligarchy. He left the Crown to his successor in more complete sovereignty—more independent of aristocratic influence—disputed title—favouritism, or any other control, than it had been held since the conquest. His reign (as Bishop Watson observes) " was the triumph of Toryism. The Whigs had power for a moment—they quarrelled amongst themselves, and thereby lost the king's confidence, lost the people's confidence, and lost their power for ever; or, to speak more philosophically, there was neither Whigism nor Toryism left; excess of riches and excess of taxes, combined with excess of luxury, had introduced universal *selfism*."*

As we consider the next reign nothing more than an elongation of that of George III.—the government being conducted on precisely the same principles and maxims—we shall be very brief in our notice of it.

George the Fourth always appeared to us nothing more than a *man of pleasure*, whom the accident of birth had made a king. His means of indulgence were ample, and he did not spare them. At first he affected Whigism; but this might arise from his favourite companions in horseracing, drinking, and intriguing being of that persuasion. Still he appears to have been one of the orthodox sort; for, like the party gene-

---

* Anecdotes of the Life of Bishop Watson, p. 194. This work, with the *Memoirs of Sir N. Wraxall,* and the admirable *Recollections of the Reign of George III.* by Mr. Nicholls, comprise valuable materials for forming a true estimate of the public men and measures that distinguished the last century. They have, we believe, been either unnoticed or greatly misrepresented by the reviewers; but this is a point of no great consequence, since Truth is in her nature buoyant and insinuating, and must ultimately triumph over every disadvantage. The monopoly of the press, like every other monopoly opposed to the general welfare, is fast tending to a consummation. The *Memoirs of Lord Waldegrave* is another useful publication for illustrating the factious nature of the government from the Revolution, and the entire want of public principle in the men who directed it. It is impossible to help commisserating the situation of George the Second, surrounded by venal statesmen, not one of whom would render him the least service without first bargaining for a batch of places and pensions for his relatives and dependents. Even Chatham, with whose name it had been usual to associate better things, appears, from the noble author, to have been no better than his compeers, and ready at any time to sacrifice his public duty to his selfishness and ambition. These repeated disclosures must, at length, convince the most incredulous; and all classes allow that the government, for the last century and a half, has been the prey of mercenary adventurers, whose sole objects were to plunder the people and tyrannize over the monarch.

rally, he only adhered to his Whig principles while out of place, and became a Tory on his accession to power.   But the politics of princes and poets are seldom worth investigating ; whatever a King of England may profess while heir-apparent, or whatever popular principles may be held by a Whig lord while out of office, the only principles compatible with the borough system, and on which they can act on the assumption of power, are those of TORYISM—that is corruption and intimidation; and this is no new discovery, since Mr. Pitt declared, almost fifty years ago, that no *honest man* could carry on the government without a reformed parliament.

In the choice of his ministers, as in other things, the king considered his personal ease.   At the commencement of the Regency, a slight effort was made to bring into the administration his early friends ; but, finding them fastidious, pragmatical, and disposed to meddle in his household establishment, the design was abandoned, and never again seriously resumed.   Castlereagh, Canning, Huskisson, and Sidmouth were the most appropriate servants for a voluptuous monarch.   These men held no principles that could interfere with his most lavish desires; their objects were limited to the enjoyment of power and its emoluments : how little they cared about the general weal may be instanced in the fact that, though they managed the affairs of the empire during a long period of profound peace, they never set about reforming the most glaring and admitted abuses in its public administration, not even endeavouring to reform the currency, economize the expenditure, reduce the debt, improve the laws, nor the commercial system, for even that originated in another quarter.   Their object was only to carry on the government and enjoy the spoil, and this they were ready to do by the aid of any shallow and temporary expedient, totally regardless of the ultimate loss and misery it might entail upon the country.   There is one event connected with Canning deserving of notice, since it evinced both discernment and firmness of mind in the sovereign.   When the poor drivelling statesmen, Eldon, Bathurst, and Melville—the Polignacs and Peyronnets of the cabinet—refused to act with Mr. Canning as First Lord of the Treasury, as much, we believe, from personal jealousy as aversion to his more liberal ideas, the king stood manfully and magnanimously by his minister; and it is due to some of the Whigs to say, that they did not refuse their aid in the moment of peril.   Mr. Canning was the best of his set, but not to be greatly admired for his patriotism : he was clever and accomplished, but a political adventurer merely, whose polar star was his own aggrandizement; had he lived, he would not, we apprehend, have been long premier, and, before his death, he evinced symptoms that showed he would prove neither a very useful nor very profound statesman.

It is not our intention to enter into any personal history or delineation of George IV. ; for, in truth, we have nothing to communicate on these points but what is known to all the world.   He always appeared to us to afford a striking confirmation of LAVATER's theory—his physiognomy and conduct being in such admirable keeping.   Some have imagined a resemblance between him and the Emperor Tiberius. Both disappointed the expectations formed of them previous to their accession to power. One lived secluded from the sight of his subjects at the island of Capri ; the other at Windsor. Women, wine, and mere sensual indulgence formed their chief employment and amusement. Neither of them knew *how to forgive,* and both were implacable in personal resentments. The persecution, by the King, of the unfortunate Caroline, and all who supported her, was mean, ungenerous, and unrelenting. His love of dress and etiquette was coxcomical, and detracted from the regal dignity. His love of seclusion is not difficult to explain : George IV. was a *spoiled child,* who, through life, had been accustomed only to do what ministered to his own gratification. In his latter days, neither his vanity nor desires were likely to be flattered by a frequent appearance in public ; age had deteriorated his charms and enfeebled his powers, and to mingle among the " high-born dames" of the aristocracy, to select an object to whom to cast the royal handkerchief, was not among his urgent necessities.

To conclude : " GOD is just in all his ways !" George IV., Lord Castlereagh, Mr. Canning, and Mr. Huskisson are all gathered to their fathers, and will soon be forgotten. They lived for *themselves,* and the public will not cherish any lasting or grateful remembrance of their memories. The monarch expired on a *chaise percée*—what a death-bed for an " *exquisite !*" Lord Castlereagh perished by his own hands. Mr. Canning, after indulging in some unseasonable jokes on the infirmities of poor Ogden—of which no doubt he repented—died of internal inflammation. Mr. Huskisson's death was deplorable. But what ought we to learn from these catastrophes ? — Neither to envy the great, nor refuse sympathy to the unfortunate !

CIVIL LIST ACCOUNTS.

No. 1.

Expenditure in the Department of the Lord Steward of his late Majesty's Household.—*Parl. Paper, No.* 17, *Sess.* 1830.

	1820. £	1823. £	1826. £	1829. £
Bread	1,422 ..	1,377 ..	1,946 ..	2,565
Butter, Bacon, Cheese, and Eggs	2,405 ..	2,507 ..	4,264 ..	4,269
Vegetables	307 ..	382 ..	546 ..	679
Butcher's Meat	5,785 ..	4,741 ..	7,132 ..	7,283
Poultry	3,467 ..	2,624 ..	3,315 ..	2,922
Fish	1,768 ..	1,574 ..	1,619 ..	1,325
Ale and Beer	2,491 ..	2,438 ..	2,746 ..	2,466
Wax Candles	3,011 ..	3,021 ..	3,692 ..	3,813
Tallow Candles	989 ..	663 ..	655 ..	720
Grocery	2,414 ..	2,714 ..	2,666 ..	3,222
	24,059	22,041	28,601	29,264

	£		£		£		£
Brought over......	24,059		22,041		28,601		29,264
Oilery	1,518	..	1,606	..	1,134	..	1,446
Fruit and Confectionary	622	..	521	..	445	..	1,056
Milk and Cream....................	718	..	725	..	1,046	..	1,246
Wines, Liqueurs, Spirits, Mineral Waters, Corks, Bottles, &c.	8,732	..	4,480	..	5,539	..	7,161
Lamps	7,030	..	6,580	..	5,184	..	6,758
Washing Table Linen	1,702	..	1,805	..	2,290	..	2,582
Fuel	7,194	..	7,478	..	6,314	..	7,665
Stationary	628	..	445	..	572	..	697
Turnery	206	..	251	..	272	..	340
Braziery, Ironmongery, and Cutlery ..	367	..	730	..	693	..	769
China, Earthenware, and Glass	1,641	..	494	..	1,040	..	860
Linen............................	3,317	..	2	..	34	..	337
The Royal Gardens	19,831	..	13,782	..	15,187	..	13,309
Maunday Expenses	283	..	274	..	274	..	272
Royal Yachts	1,107	..	387	..	—	..	—
H. R. H. the Duke of Cumberland	—	..	319	..	—	..	—
Board Wages to Servants	3,111	..	3,286	..	3,283	..	3,313
Travelling Expenses of ditto	480	..	361	..	318	..	357
Allowance for Table Beer............	608	..	427	..	439	..	301
Salaries to Extra Servants, pay of hired Assistants, &c...................	1,354	..	2,004	..	1,900	..	2,622
Board Wages to Yeomen of the Guard	2,230	..	2,315	..	2,230	..	2,230
Compensation in lieu of Articles formerly issued in kind	5,542	..	3,549	..	3,183	..	2,783
Sundries and Disbursements..........	12,495	..	7,492	..	8,213	..	8,212
Amount paid in each year...........	104,789		81,372		88,210		93,597

Board of Green Cloth, 15th Sept., 1830.   THOMAS MARRABLE.

No. II.

Expenditure incurred in the Department of his late Majesty's Robes.

1820...............................	£3,513 0 2½
1821...............................	5,249 16 11
1822...............................	4,625 12 5
1823...............................	4,632 18 10½
1824...............................	6,152 6 3½
1825...............................	4,773 15 2
1826...............................	5,687 15 8
1827...............................	6,819 19 6
1828...............................	5,955 18 3
1829, ending 5th January, 1830........	6,673 17 5

Office of Robes, 13th Sept. 1830.   TIM. BRENT.

No. III.

Expenditure of the Master of the Horse's Department.

	1820. £	1823. £	1826. £	1829. £
Liveries	7,729 ..	7,530 ..	9,057 ..	7,560
Forage	6,556 ..	5,010 ..	6,368 ..	6,308
Farriery	1,566 ..	906 ..	1,103 ..	1,217
Horses	6,682 ..	5,392 ..	5,687 ..	3,246
Carriages	8,354 ..	944 ..	3,782 ..	4,029
Harness	798 ..	472 ..	785 ..	702
Saddlery	2,053 ..	1,820 ..	817 ..	1,906
Bitts and Spurs	181 ..	48 ..	117 ..	143
Whips	129 ..	135 ..	133 ..	165
Lamps, Gaslights, &c.	505 ..	580 ..	1,012 ..	1,108
Coals and Wood	838 ..	1,076 ..	1,299 ..	1,251
Stationary	99 ..	53 ..	48 ..	57
Turnery Articles	152 ..	208 ..	190 ..	196
Candles and Soap	165 ..	158 ..	172 ..	167
Washing	120 ..	121 ..	132 ..	140
Ironmongery	48 ..	105 ..	65 ..	79
Allowances for Lodging	— ..	439 ..	367 ..	477
Sundry other small expenses*	637 ..	576 ..	607 ..	649
Travelling expenses and disbursements†	1,600 ..	1,487 ..	1,984 ..	1,701
Post horses	649 ..	652 ..	1,488 ..	1,130
King's Plates	2,126 ..	2,126 ..	2,336 ..	2,338
Stud Bills	6,705 ..	621 ..	1,666 ..	1,196
Hunt Ditto	3,654 ..	3,673 ..	4,313 ..	4,588
Treasury and Exchequer Fees	586 ..	400 ..	494 ..	641
	51,932	34,532	44,024	40,994
Deduct Proceeds of useless Horses sold	915	2,179	2,856	1,226
Net Expense	51,017	32,353	41,168	39,768

Master of the Horse's Office, 1st Sept. 1830.   R. W. SPEARMAN.

No. IV.

An Account of the Application of the Monies paid from Admiralty Droits, Gibraltar Duties, and other Funds than Civil List, at the disposal of the Crown, between 1820 and 1830.

	£
The expenses of his late Majesty's journey to Ireland	58,261
Ditto .... ditto .... to Scotland	21,439
Ditto .... ditto .... to Hanover	13,206
	92,906

* These expenses are such as water-rent, pew-rent, sand, wheeler's work, sweeping chimneys, blacking, spirits of wine, and in short all articles not included in the foregoing heads.

† The disbursements included in the charge for travelling expenses are those of the clerks of the stables, for women employed to clean the stable-servants' rooms, make the beds, &c. and the allowances to servants in lieu of hair-powder, wigs, and silk stockings.

£

Brought over.............. 92,906

The expense of ntting up the state rooms at St. James's 54,947
The expense of certain repairs to the Royal Lodge in Windsor Great Park 14,966
The expense of repairing the stables at Brighton 7,113
The expense of furnishing the Royal Mews at Pimlico 10,083
The amount issued to his late Majesty's privy purse.................. 86,573
The amount issued by his late Majesty's command as contributions to
   charities 17,648
The expense of furñiture purchased for Windsor Castle 10,000
The expense incurred on account of the visit of the Queen of Wirtemberg 16,206
The expense of fitting up the apartments of his present Majesty as Duke
   of Clarence 9,166
The amount advanced to the executors of H. R. H. the Duke of York .. 6,440

326,055

Of the foregoing Amount, there was applied,—

To Privy Purse ....£ 86,573
To Charities 17,648
Services conducted by the Lord Chamberlain...................... 110,024
  -    -   -   Lord Steward...................... 46,956
  -    -   -   Master of the Horse 14,459
  -    -   -   Office of Works 22,080
For the Journey to Hanover 13,206
Expenses of Yachts, Pursuivants, &c. connected with the Journeys to
   Ireland and Hanover... 1,011
For expenses connected with the Journey to Ireland, incurred by the
   Irish Government 7,653
To the Executors of H. R. H. the Duke of York 6,440

£326,055

Whitehall, Treasury Chambers, ⎰
   26th October, 1830.   ⎱   GEO. R. DAWSON.

No. V.

ROYAL FAMILY.

Return of all Sums of Money paid from the consolidated Fund to the
several Branches of the Royal Family, exclusive of the Civil List.—
Parl. Paper, No. 186, *Sess.* 1831.

	Pension.	Granted.
Duchess of Kent	6,000..	58 Geo. III.
Princess Victoria for education...................	6,000..	6 Geo. IV. *

* By an act of the Session of 1831 an additional annuity of £10,000 is granted
to the Duchess of Kent; £4000 thereof to be paid during the life of her royal
highness, and £6000 during the life of the Princess Victoria.

The provision for the queen, by 1 and 2 Will. IV., c. 11, in case she survives
the king, is an annuity of £100,000 ; also Marlborough House and the rangership of Bushy Park.

Duke of Cumberland	6,000..	{ 46 Geo. III. / 47 Geo. III.
Ditto	15,000..	{ 18 Geo. III. / 1 Geo. IV.
Prince George for education	6,000..	6 Geo. IV.
Duke of Sussex	6,000..	{ 46 Geo. III. / 47 Geo. III.
Ditto	15,000..	{ 18 Geo. III. / 1 Geo. IV.
Duke of Cambridge	6,000..	{ 46 Geo. III. / 47 Geo. III.
Ditto	15,000..	{ 18 Geo. III. / 1 Geo. IV.
Ditto	6,000..	1 Geo. IV.
Duke of Gloucester	14,000..	{ 46 Geo. III. / 47 Geo. III.
Duchess of Gloucester	9,000..	52 Geo. III.
Ditto	4,000..	{ 50 Geo. III. / 1 Geo. IV. *
Princess Elizabeth of Hesse Hombourg	9,000..	52 Geo. III.
Ditto	4,000..	{ 56 Geo. III. / 1 Geo. IV.
Princess Augusta	9,000..	52 Geo. III.
Ditto	4.000..	{ 56 Geo. III. / 1 Geo. IV.
Princess Sophia	9,000..	52 Geo. III.
Ditto	4,000..	{ 56 Geo. III. / 1 Geo. IV.
Prince Leopold	50,000..	56 Geo. III. †
Princess Sophia of Gloucester	7,000..	{ 46 Geo. III. / 47 Geo. III.

TOTAL........£210,000

No. VI.

WINDSOR CASTLE AND BUCKINGHAM PALACE.
Windsor Castle.

Expenditure for the building, which has already received the sanction of parliament	£594,000	0　0
Additional sum which has been sanctioned for additional works by the report of the select committee in 1830, is	177,000	0　0
For the building ————	771,000	0　0

* In case of the demise of any of the four princesses, or upon the marriage of any one of them, on the payment of a marriage portion of £40,000, the interest of such princess so dying or being married shall cease, and the annuity of £36,000 shall accrue and remain in the three other princesses ; but none of the above princesses can receive more than £12,000 each, under the provisions of the Act 52 Geo III. c. 57, s. 2.

The Duchess of Gloucester and the Princess of Hesse Hombourg receive, in addition to their annuities out of the consolidated fund, a pension of £1000 each out of the 4½ per cent. Leeward Island duties.— *Parl. Paper, No.* 284, *Sess.* 1831.

† Prince Leopold resigned his pension in July, on accepting the crown of Belgium ; stipulating for annuities for his servants, and the keeping up of Claremont House.

Amount already granted for furniture, is £267,000 0 0
Further amount required 13,670 9 2
            For furniture .. ——————— 280,670 9 2
The amount which has been already granted
  for the purchase of land and houses, is.................... 33,500 0 0

TOTAL sum required...................................... 1,084,170 9 2
The amount already granted being.......................... 894,500 0 0

There is still required 190,670 9 2
On account of which it is proposed to grant
  in 1831, for the building as recommended by
  the select committee of 1830 .... 50,000 0 0
To pay the charge already incurred for furniture beyond the grant.................... 3,670 9 2
For furniture required for new rooms 10,000 0 0
                     —————— 63,670 9 2

Leaving to be granted in future years, according
  to the report of the select committee of 1830 .... 127,000 0 0

Buckingham Palace.

The amount required towards defraying the
  charge incurred of debt for work done and
  contracts made prior to the appointment of
  the select committee in 1831, is 100,000 0 0
Windsor Castle, as above 63,670 9 2

To be granted in 1831 .... 163,670 9 2

     Whitehall Treasury Chambers,   *Parliamentary Paper, No. 271.*
       27th September, 1831.

No. VII.

ANCIENT PAYMENTS heretofore charged on the Civil List of England,
  Ireland, and Scotland, but now payable out of the Consolidated
  Fund: with Notes on the Origin of some of these Annuities.

The Clerk of the Hanaper (expenses) ....·................ 2,000 0 0
The Chief Justice in Eyre, North of Trent.................... 2,110 10 6
The Chief Justice in Eyre, South of Trent.................... 2,155 16 10
       The Chief Justices in Eyre are to be abolished on the ex-
       piration of existing interests.
Master of the Hawks 1,372 10 0
       King James II. by Letters Patent, dated 5th July, in the
       third year of his reign, granted to Charles Duke of St.
       Alban's, and the heirs male of his body, the offices of master
       and keeper of the Hawks of his said Majesty, his heirs
       and successors, after the decease of Thomas Felter and
       William Chiffinch, who then held those offices, and with
       the same allowances as were enjoyed by them, viz. £30 per
       month of twenty-eight days, and 10s. a day; and, also, £800
       per annum, that is, £50 per annum each for four Falconers,
       and £600 for the provision and maintenance of Hawks;
       in all, £1,372 : 10s.

	£	s.	d.
Keeper of the Lions in the Tower, including *extra allowance for the maintenance of the animals*	435	16	3

The King having presented the Tower Menagerie to the Zoological Society, the public, in future. will be saved the salary of the keeper; also the charge for *extra allowance to the animals.*

	£	s.	d.
Knight Harbinger (to cease on expiration of the existing interest)	140	13	5
Keeper of the Tennis Courts (to cease on expiration of existing interest)	89	1	3
Keeper of Records, Tower, including Clerks	1,236	5	4
Keeper of Records, Court of Exchequer	851	7	0
Mayor, Aldermen, and Sheriffs of London, for Imposts on Wine	95	16	6

University of Oxford; viz.

	£	s.	d.
For a Preacher..........perpetuity	8	10	0
Professor of Divinity ....ditto	11	13	8
— Law...........ditto	37	5	0
— Physic.........ditto	37	1	0
— History ....ditto	379	10	0
— Botany.........ditto	189	4	0

University of Cambridge ; viz.

	£	s.	d.
On a perpetuity	8	10	0
For a Preacher	8	10	0
Professor of Divinity	11	13	8
— Law	37	1	0
— Physic	37	1	0
— History	379	10	0
— Botany	189	4	0
Emanuel College, Cambridge, perpetuity	14	16	10

These university endowments are royal grants, the earliest instituted by Margaret, countess of Richmond, mother of Henry VII. The professorships of history were established by George I. and the professorships of botany by George III.

	£	s.	d.
Dean and Chapter of Lichfield, perpetuity	6	5	0
Vicar of Lichfield	9	17	3
Master of the Temple	26	3	7
Reader at Hampton Court Chapel	38	1	0
Fellows of Eaton, perpetuity	39	3	8
Dean and Chapter of Westminster, for French Ministers, Savoy	42	9	0
Ministers, Isle of Man	93	19	0

Charles II. by Letters Patent, in the 27th year of his reign, granted an annuity of £100, to be paid for ever, to the poor Ministers of the Isle of Man, out of the Hereditary Excise.

	£	s.	d.
Bishop of Chester, for four Preachers	187	14	0

Queen Elizabeth established four Preachers in the county of Lancaster, to be nominated by the Bishop of Chester for the time being. Letters of Privy Seal have been issued at the commencement of each reign ever since for the payment of £200 per annum to the Bishop of Chester, for the use of these Preachers.

	£	s.	d.
Vicar of the Tower..............perpetuity	4	1	4
Minister of St. Botolph, Aldgate......ditto	5	9	0
Churchwardens of St. John the Baptist, for the Poor, perpetuity	6	4	3
Ditto........St. Michael, Cornhill......ditto......ditto..	10	10	3
Ditto........St. Magnus ....ditto......ditto..	19	1	6
Schoolmaster of Southwell, perpetuity	8	6	6
Corporation of Dartmouth....ditto	37	1	0

The first grant to this Corporation was dated A.D. 1481;

it was for the building of a strong Tower, and for the furnishing and keeping in repair a chain to secure the
harbour.

Mayor of Macclesfield......................................   35   1   6
>   Macclesfield is a Chapelry in the large Parish of Prest-
> bury. The Chapel was built by Edward I. and endowed
> by Edward VI. with £56 : 6 : 8 per annum for ever. James
> I. in consideration of the smallness of the stipend, added
> £50 per annum during pleasure. The grant has been
> renewed at the commencement of each reign, by letter
> patent, directing £50 yearly to be paid to the Mayor for
> a " preacher to instruct the people of the town of Maccles-
> field and the neighbouring villages in the true knowledge
> of God according to the doctrine of the Church of En-
> gland."

Corporation of Lyme Regis..................................   95 19   0
Ditto...................for repairing the Pier 95 19   0
Corporation of Berwick, for repairing a bridge over the Tweed..   93 19   0
Christ's Hospital   360   4   3
College of St. David's.....................................   400   0   0
Representative of Sir John Hynde Cotton, perpetuity..........   3 19 11
Heirs of Colonel Fairfax ....ditto   71   9   0
>   A grant of Charles II. dated in 1660, and originally
> charged on the Custom Duties of Hull.

Heirs of Nicholas Yates, perpetuity 79 11   6
>   A grant of James II. to Nicholas Yates and his heirs,
> in consideration of Francis Yates and Margaret his wife,
> having been particularly instrumental in the preservation
> of King Charles II. from the hands of the Rebels after
> the battle of Worcester, and not having received any marks
> of favour, by reason that the said Francis died soon after
> the Restoration, leaving his son Nicholas an infant.

IRISH CIVIL LIST.

	£	s.	d.
Clerk of the Crown and Hanaper............................	886	12	4
Deputy......ditto	96	4	0
Constable of the Fort of Hillsborough (hereditary)*	216	3	4
Master of the Riding House	200	0	0
Physician to the State....................................	325	2	4
Surgeon to the State......................................	325	2	4
Master and Composer of Music.............................	88	1	0
Deputy.......ditto	88	1	0
Attendant on Balls	91	16	4
Kettle Drummer	61	16	4
Serjeant Trumpeter	61	16	4
5 Trumpeters..................at £17 : 7 each	86	15	0
7 Violins......................at 17 : 7 each	121	9	0
2 Tenors ....at 17 : 7 each	34	14	0
2 Hautboys....................at 17 : 7 each	34	14	0
2 French Horns................at 17 : 7 each	34	14	0
4 Bass Viols ....at 17 : 7 each	69	8	0
Dulcimer	8	9	8

---

* All charges on the Irish Civil List which follow this, expire on the cessation
of existing interests.

Usher to Council Chamber	266	10	4
House and Wardrobe Keeper, Dublin Castle	535	10	0
Assistant........ditto	132	16	4
Housekeeper of the Phœnix Lodge	39	8	8
Inspector and Director of the Gardens, ditto	39	8	8
The Chief Chamberlain	47	6	0
Chief Serjeant at Arms	92	6	4
Second ditto	354	17	8
Clerk of the Council	1,249	18	4
Compiler of Dublin Gazette	276	18	8
Joint Solicitor in Great Britain	361	7	0
Keeper of Records, Birmingham Tower	461	11	0
Keeper of State Papers	461	11	0
Constable of the Castle of Dublin, including Lodgings	401	11	0
Constable of the Castle of Limerick	336	18	8
Constable of the Castle of Castlemain	184	12	4
Chairman of Committees, late House of Lords	1,332	5	8
3 Messengers, late House of Lords, at £65 : 4 : 8 each	195	14	0
3 Doorkeepers.........ditto........ 65 : 13 each	196	19	0
Housemaid	6	7	4
2 late Masters in Chancery, at £96 : 4 each	192	8	0
Seneschal of his Majesty's Manors	276	18	8
Customer of Wexford	9	4	8
Customer of Waterford	13	17	0
Searcher of ditto	6	3	4
Customer of Youghall and Dungarvan	381	11	0
Comptroller of Cork	461	11	0
Comptroller of Kinsale	92	6	4
Customer of Killybegs	92	6	4
Comptroller of ditto	92	6	4
Customer of Galway	12	6	4
Customer of Drogheda, Dundalk, and Carlingford	376	3	4
Searcher of Dundalk and Carlingford	4	12	4
Searcher of Carrickfergus	6	3	4
Searcher of Strangford and Donaghadee	929	4	8
Commissioner of the Board of Works	553	17	0
One other........ ....ditto	369	4	8
One other............ditto	369	4	8

SCOTCH CIVIL LIST.

His Majesty's Commissioner to the General Assembly of the Church of Scotland	1,950	0	0
The Hereditary Usher of the White Rod	242	15	0
Ten Chaplains...........at £50 each	500	0	0
Six Trumpeters ....at 16 : 16 : 4 each	100	18	0
Limner	276	10	0
Hereditary Keeper of the Palace of Holyrood House	45	10	0
Under Keeper of ditto	50	0	0
The Porter of the said Palace	37	15	6
Under Falconer	50	0	0
First Physician	97	0	0
Second Physician	50	0	0
Apothecary	40	0	0
Clock-maker	16	13	4
Master of the Wardrobe	53	0	0
First Underkeeper of ditto	37	10	0

Second Underkeeper of Wardrobe	20	0	0
Deputy Keeper of Regalia	300	0	0
Clerk of the Stores	30	0	0
Historiographer	184	0	0
Secretary to the Order of the Thistle	276	10	0
Dean of the Order of the Thistle	50	0	0
Usher to the Order of the Thistle	27	0	0
The Principal Masters and Professors of the University of St. Andrew's	1,010	0	0
The Principal and Professors of the Marischall College in Aberdeen	1,397	0	0
The University of Glasgow, for their Professors	1,360	0	0
The University of Edinburgh, for the Professors and for the Botanic Garden and Museum	1,819	3	0
The Procurator for the Church, for defraying the charges of Church affairs in Scotland, with the salaries of the Officers	1,100	0	0
Charities and bounties to such indigent and necessitous persons as shall be approved of by the Barons of Exchequer in Scotland, and to be distributed amongst them quarterly; including £120 as salary to the Almoner and Deputies	2,250	0	0
The General Assembly of the Church of Scotland	1,950	0	0
John James Edmonstone, Esq. retired allowance as late Sheriff Depute of the Shire of Bute	138	5	0
King's Plate, to be run for at Edinburgh	100	0	0
Ditto Royal Company of Archers, or Body Guard	20	0	0
Ditto Caledonian Hunt	100	0	0
For the Clerks of the Auditor, until the office shall be regulated on the cessation of the existing interest	230	0	0

Whitehall, Treasury Chambers,
30th March, 1831.

PRIVY COUNCIL, DIPLOMATIC MISSIONS,

AND

CONSULAR ESTABLISHMENTS.

A BRIEF notice of these subjects will appropriately follow our preceding exposition of the hereditary revenues and civil-list. The number of members of the Privy Council is indefinite, and at the pleasure of the king; the privy counsellors of William IV. amount to 192, comprising the royal dukes, the archbishops, the ministers, the chief officers in the royal household, the heads of the law-courts, and all the principal nobles and commoners who hold, or have held, the more important situations in the civil, military, and diplomatic service of the government. They sit during life, or the life of the king who nominates them, subject to removal at his majesty's discretion. They are bound by oath to advise the king, without partiality, affection, and dread; to keep his council secret, to avoid corruption, and to assist in the execution of what is there resolved. To assault, wound, or attempt to kill a privy counsellor, in the execution of his office, is felony.

Although the ostensible duties of the council are, to advise the king in affairs of state, yet this duty is seldom discharged; and a privy counsellor, as such, is as little the adviser of the sovereign as a peer of the realm, who is denominated the hereditary adviser of the Crown. The really efficient and responsible advisers of the king are the ministers, especially that portion of them constituting the cabinet. No privy counsellor attends in council, unless expressly summoned for the occasion; and summonses are never sent except to those counsellors who, as members of the administration, are in the immediate confidence of his majesty. The privy council, then, is an institution of state, without salaries and without duties; and, as such, would require no notice in this publication. Authors who amuse themselves and their readers in describing that " shadow of a shade," the English constitution, make a great parade of the grave functions and high privileges of " his majesty's most honourable privy council;" but practice is as widely different from theory, in respect of this, as in respect of the representative branch of the government.

Although the privy council *ex officio* is little more than a nonentity, yet, from extrinsic circumstances, it is a body of great interest, and some account of it is strictly relevant to our purpose.   Nearly the whole of the privy counsellors do now, or have held important offices in the state ; and, in consequence of these offices, have contrived to concentrate, in their own persons, a miscellany of pensions, salaries, sinecures, and grants, which is almost incredible.   The mass of taxes consumed by George III. and IV. having been set forth, we may, as an appropriate sequel, set forth the mass of taxes annually consumed by those " grave and reverend seignors," who were fortunate enough to enjoy the greatest share of the favour and confidence of those monarchs.

Our task will be much abbreviated by the exposition, in the session of 1830, of the present first lord of the admiralty.   In a committee of supply on the 14th of May, SIR JAMES GRAHAM moved " for a return of all salaries, profits, pay, fees, and emoluments, whether civil or military, from the 5th of January, 1829, to the 5th of January, 1830, held and enjoyed by each of his Majesty's most honourable Privy Council, specifying, with each name, the total amount received by each individual, and distinguishing the various sources from which the same is derived."   After urging a variety of cogent arguments in support of the propriety and utility of his motion, Sir James made the following extraordinary statement, founded on documents in his possession, and which statement was not contradicted.

" He had divided the Privy Counsellors into classes, excepting from each the Royal Family, because they, having a certain income under the assignment of Acts of Parliament, there was nothing mysterious about them ; and, in many cases, these assignments had been made under the sanction of bills, which had themselves undergone discussion in the House. He, therefore, excluded them altogether from his calculations upon this occasion. The total number of Privy Counsellors was 169, of whom 113 received public money. The whole sum distributed annually amongst these 113 was £650,164, and the average proportion of that sum paid to each yearly was £5,753. Of this total of £650,164, £86,103 were for *sinecures,* £442,411 for active services, and £121,650 for *pensions,* making together the total which he had stated. Of the 113 Privy Counsellors who were thus receivers of the public money, thirty were *pluralists, or persons holding more offices than one,* whether as sinecurists or civil and military officers. The amount received by the pluralists was £221,133 annually amongst them all, or £7,331, upon an average, to each annually. The number of Privy Counsellors who enjoyed full or half-pay, or were pensioned as diplomatists, was twenty-nine, and the gross amount of their income from the public purse was £126,175, or, upon an average, a yearly income to each individual of £4,347 a year. The whole number of Privy Counsellors who were members of both Houses of Parliament was sixty-nine, and of those forty-seven were PEERS, whose gross *income from the public purse was* £378,846, or, upon an average to each, £8,060 a year. The remaining twenty-two were of the House of Commons, and the gross amount of their receipts was £90,849, or, upon an average to each individual, £4,128 a year. It appeared then that there were 113 Privy

Counsellors receiving the public money, of whom, sixty-nine were members of either house of Parliament. He had already stated that sixty-nine were in the receipt of public money by way of salary ; the total number of Privy Counsellors in the House of Commons was thirty-one, and of these twenty-two were charged upon the public purse. In this analysis there might be some inaccuracy ; but if its accuracy were denied, his answer, short and conclusive, was—grant this motion, and prove the error to the public satisfaction."

The motion was not granted ; in lieu of it the then chancellor of the Exchequer substituted and carried a motion, *of his own*, for a return of salaries and emoluments above £250, held by all persons in the civil departments of the United Kingdom. The honourable member had moved for the return of the public emoluments of 169 individuals, and Mr. Goulburn overwhelmed him with a return of 2000. It was serving him, as Sir James remarked, when he called for a glass of wine, with a glass of wine diluted with a bottle of water.

In fact, it was a complete avoidance of the object sought by the member for Cumberland. Mr. Goulburn said it would be *invidious* to produce a return of the emoluments of the Privy Council alone. What ! more invidious than to move for and obtain, as was the case in 1806, of a return of the pensions and emoluments of the royal Dukes ! Or more invidious than to seek and obtain, as was the case in 1822, a return of the pensions and emoluments of the honourable members themselves ! George IV. had often submitted to such invidious proceedings—his income and expenditure too—the amount of his tailors' bills—his upholstery bills—the outgoings in his household—even down to the consumption of pickles and potatoes—had all been sifted and overhauled, oftener than once, and no one thought it invidious. Receiving annually a great mass of public money, which imposed a heavy burthen on the people, they had a right to look into his majesty's affairs, just in the same way as they had a right to look into the affairs of these privy counsellors. But the chancellor of the Exchequer wished to screen the most honourables, by mixing them up with the clerks, and tidewaiters, and other subalterns, who serve not so much for present pay, as the hope of obtaining higher and more lucrative appointments. It was a dextrous diversion of the enemy's attack, worthy of the sublime genius who framed the Irish Tithe Composition Act. Precisely the same manœuvre is resorted to by the apologists of the ecclesiastical establishment to conceal the enormous revenues of the clergy. They have a great repugnance to giving separate statements of the incomes of the bishops, the dignitaries, and aristocratic pluralists ; they like to see them all *lumped together*, those with high connexion and influence, and those with none,—and then, after exaggerating their numbers two-fold, they call upon you to look and sympathize at the miserable pittance allotted to the sons of Mother Church ! But this will not do. It is not the *average* but the *disproportion* that shocks public feeling. A friendless incumbent or poor clerk cannot make his miserable stipend go a jot farther in the purchase of the necessaries of life, because there is some court bishop or court judge with ten or twenty thousand a year. What the community revolts at is the total burthen imposed by the whole number of spiritual and lay placemen, chiefly by the exorbitant emoluments of a few favoured individuals.

The first lord of the admiralty never published a list of the cormorants of the Privy Council, many of whom still continue members of that august body, in the full enjoyment of their ' blushing honours;' but, as they have ceased to exercise the same influence on national affairs since the accession of the Whig ministry, it is unnecessary to notice them here individually, and we shall content ourselves with recording their names in our *Place and Pension List.*

AMBASSADORS AND DIPLOMATIC MISSIONS.

There is, we will venture to affirm, no branch of our multifarious civil services which required to be more keenly investigated, and more unsparingly cut down than our foreign embassies. The Whigs have paired off a little of the exuberance of these dazzling employments; but their reductions ought to have been carried still lower. The embassy to the court of France is still continued at £11,400 a year, independently of a splendid house to live in, bought with the public money; that to Russia as much, with £1000 a year additional for house rent; to Austria, £11,050; to Turkey, £7,350; to Spain, £7,350; and the ministers to the new states of America have £4,000 a year and upwards: and these exclusive of allowances for outfits, for presents, for the charge of journeys to and fro, for postage, for mourning-dresses, for birth-day fêtes, for illuminations, or any other casual outgoing. No other country makes such extravagant allowances to her ministers. Few native noblemen of any of the courts here enumerated are able to vie, in household expense, with men possessing such princely incomes; and it cannot be politic in England to place her representatives in a point of view so invidious towards the communities among which they sojourn. In fact, it is said that hints have, at various times, been transmitted to the government of this country upon the annoyance which is often felt abroad at the unequalled revenues allowed by Great Britain to her diplomatists at foreign courts, for the support of what she calls her *dignity.* Now, the best kind of national dignity is that which renders justice, and demands it—that which is upheld by the urbanity and knowledge of the public officers who represent their nation amongst foreigners; and, after the common decencies of respectable life have been furnished, little if any thing is gained, by mere extravagance and ostentation, to the interests or dignity of a great people. America allows her envoys and plenipotentiaries about £2000, and secretaries of legation £321 per annum; and her dignity and interests are adequately sustained and represented.

Nothing, indeed, can be plainer than if men of a high order of talents, but of private station in society, were to be selected for foreign missions, two good effects would follow. The national business would be incomparably better done, and the extravagance of the diplomatic service might be corrected without a murmur. It is far otherwise when men of *noble birth* but mean capacity, make *love* to the appointment, and are chosen : that is the secret of our vast expenditure in diplomacy. The borough system has been at the bottom of this abuse, as of every other ; and if the puppets of that system did not always succeed in shutting the doors of Parliament against popular representatives, it is certain that they kept the representation of the sovereign elsewhere very snugly and comfortably to themselves.

In the whole range of the public service, nothing accords so well with the taste and acquirements of the aristocracy as this vice-regal mimicry and ostentation. The chief qualifications of an ambassador are that he should be able to bow gracefully, be six feet high, of portly presence, and keep a good table for the entertainment of absentee lords and ladies ; as to real business, it is done by the secretaries : and if any thing extra occurs, there is a special mission for the purpose. Some of the most famous jobs in the history of corruption have been got up under the pretext of an embassy. Witness the mission of the late Mr. Canning to Lisbon. It is well known that the son of this gentleman was in a declining state of health, and required a milder atmosphere ; when the father was sent ambassador to Lisbon, where there was *actually no court*, at an expense to the country of eighteen thousand pounds. Again, in 1821, when a negotiation was on foot to bring the Grenvilles into the administration, one of the stipulations was, that a member of the family, Mr. Henry Wynn, should be sent on a mission to Switzerland, with a salary of £4,000, and this large allowance was justified on the pretext that it was necessary to enable the minister to maintain a liberal hospitality towards his countrymen abroad. And sure enough the hospitable disposition of this young gentleman was soon called into exercise, for he had scarcely arrived at his destination before his brother, Sir Watkin Williams Wynn, Lady Harriet Williams Wynn, and eight more Wynns repaired to Berne, to share the hospitalities of the generous youth, provided out of the taxes of the people of England !

But even these jobs are nothing to those perpetrated in the latter days of Toryism, under the pretext of missions to South America, and to the particulars of which we shall introduce the reader from a parliamentary paper, No. 318, of the session of 1830.

As a sample of the enormous charge of these diplomatic missions, we shall first cite the Mexican embassy. In the year 1825, Mr. Morier received, for five months' service as Mexican commissioner, £3,655 salary, and £1,670 expenses. In the next year, the same gentleman received, for three months' service, £3,594 ; making a total of £8,917 for eight months in two years. This, one would think, quite enough for the cost of one mission, but it was not so : Mr. Ward, the second commissioner, received a much larger remuneration for the same services, in the same year, in the same place. In 1825, this gentleman received £10,920 ; in 1826, £5,598 ; in 1827, £2,523, exclusive of £825 passage-money, making, with other items, a charge of not less than £19,808 for twenty-five months' services of Mr. Ward alone. But even this did not include the entire cost—there was a secretary attached to the mission. This gentleman was a Mr. Thompson, who charged £100 per month salary for his services, and actually, in addition, asked for compensation—for what? Why, for his salary *as clerk in the Audit Office* while he was absent on other duties. The same modest officer also charged £1,607 for the cost of a trip to Guatemala, which he fancied to take. This made an entire charge of £31,857 in two years for one mission to Mexico.

One object of Mr. Ward's mission, according to the explanation of Mr. Goulburn, was to ascertain *what the expense of these South American embassies might be;* and it must be allowed that Mr. Ward went the right way to work to make them very comfortable appointments for his successors, by not fixing the standard at too meagre a scale; and if the gentlemen who succeed him can only get up a book beside, as their predecessor has done, they will be very productive excursions indeed.

The next mission deserving attention is that to Columbia. Our envoy there was a Mr. Cockburn, who, in 1825, received an outfit of £3,000. In 1826, he went to South America, landed at the Caraccas, and never advanced to Bogota: he remained three weeks at the house of the consul, and then returned. For this excursion, he received a year's salary, £6,000; allowance for house rent, £600; expence of conveying him out, £450. Next year he started again for Bogota, never reached his destination, returned to London after an absence of seven months, to announce his own movements instead of transmitting despatches in the usual way, charging £3,376 for this trip. He thus crossed the Atlantic twice, at the public expense, without ever penetrating to the capital to which he was officially appointed; he was the first year three weeks in America, and the second nine weeks; and for his services altogether he received £13,000. It might be thought after this we had done with this gentleman, but something remains—he applied for *farther remuneration,* and actually received £1,664 to " complete his allowance;" and then this highly efficient envoy extraordinary rested from his labours on a pension of £1,700 a year.

Next we come to Mr. Chad, who was recalled from Dresden, to proceed forthwith to Bogota. He got £1,666 for an outfit in the year 1828, together with £1,374; and in 1829, £2,062, although he never left London. Mr. Turner got, in 1829, £2,500 for this same mission, besides a large sum for house-rent, he never having been in Columbia at all; and £528 for his voyage out. In this manner Mr. Cockburn received £15,000 for going out, but never entering the capital; Mr. Chad got £5,002 for *preparing* to go out, but never going at all; and Mr. Turner, £4,955 for undertaking the voyage: whether this last gentleman has arrived at his destination, or absconded, or deviated into a more pleasant tour through Switzerland or Italy, does not appear. So much for the Columbian mission.

Next let us advert to the mission to Buenos Ayres. The first on the roll is Lord Ponsonby, who received an outfit of £2,500, salary £5,000, and an allowance for house-rent £500. These allowances are a little extravagant, but his lordship, unlike the Chads and the Cockburns, did arrive at his post. We cannot say the same of his successor, Mr. Henry Fox, the near relation of a well-known duchy sinecurist Mr. Fox received an outfit of £1,500 for Buenos Ayres, in 1828, at the time he was in Italy, in the receipt of a salary; and, in 1829, an advance of £1,000, though it did not appear, when the return was made, he had yet taken a step towards his American journey. There is similar profusion in the missions to Brazil and Panama, but the instances we have cited are sufficient specimens of the lavish proceedings in this branch of the foreign department. It is to be hoped our Whig ministers, who showed up these doings with great gusto *while out of place*, will not follow the profuse example of their predecessors in office.

CONSULAR ESTABLISHMENTS.

These form minor diplomatic appointments, ostensibly established to watch over the interests of commerce, assist and facilitate the transactions of merchants in foreign parts. The duties being light, and the remuneration considerable, they form a favourite branch of ministerial patronage, and situations therein are mostly obtained by individuals connected with the aristocracy or possessing parliamentary influence. At present the chief objections to the consular establishments are their superfluous number—the expenses they entail on the country in extravagant salaries, pensions, and superannuations—and the unfitness of many persons forced into the situation from the operation of the influence to which we have adverted. In the United States of America, for example, we have eight consuls, besides consuls-general, enjoying salaries of £800 a-year. Both in America and Europe the office of consul-general is unnecessary; at all events such a functionary might be dispensed with, where we had a regular ambassador and his staff at an enormous charge. Where, for instance, can be the utility or necessity of having a consul-general in Paris? We have an ambassador there, with a salary of £10,000 a-year, a secretary of the embassy, and many other individuals attached to the legation in that city; and amongst them, no doubt, a fit individual might easily be found to do the duty at a salary of £500 per annum, for discharging which the present consul-general receives £1200. At Naples we have a consul-general, with £1200 a-year, when the whole trade of the kingdom, with all the ports in the world, does not exceed £1,000,000 per annum. But then the climate of Naples is *salubrious*, and it is sometimes convenient to have a sinecure retreat there for an indolent official or satiated epicure of the "higher orders." The consul-general at Washington has a salary of £1600 a-year. This appears wholly indefensible. In dear countries there is some necessity for high salaries to meet the increased expenditure; but in cheap countries like America there can be no pretext for an exorbitant allowance. £1600 a-year is equal to the salary of the chief justice of the United States, and this amount is paid to a consul-general—an officer who, in fact, has nothing to do.

A change of questionable utility was introduced in 1825, in the mode of remunerating consuls; in lieu of payment by fees, fixed salaries were substituted: but, under some pretext or other, fees still continue to be exacted, and the charges altogether imposed by these functionaries on commerce are very considerable. The money paid to the consuls of Columbia alone amounts to a charge of four per cent. on the traffic carried on between the two countries. The whole amount of our exports and imports to South America is about eleven millions; and our consular and diplomatic establishments in these states cost £60,521, the former £27,241 and the latter £33,100. In the trade with some states these expenses are particularly exorbitant. For instance, the consular and diplomatic per-centage on our trade with Mexico is £1 : 0 : 7, on that with Guatemala £10 : 17 : 2; our exports and imports to the former amounting to £731,000, the diplomatic cost to £4,400, and the consular expense to £3000; while our trade to Guatemala amounts only to £13,813, and the consular expense is £1500. There is no necessity for these charges, which result solely from negligence and abuse in the foreign department, from extravagant salaries, from the appointment of consuls to places where none are required, and from the plural appointments of consuls, vice-consuls, and consuls-general, when a single individual would be amply sufficient for the discharge of official duty.

The little duty these gentlemen discharge may be inferred from the fact that many hold other situations, apparently requiring their entire personal attention, while others hold the appointment of consul in America or distant parts of Europe, and reside constantly in the metropolis. In 1792 the total charge of our diplomatic and consular establishments, including pensions, amounted to £113,927; in 1829, the same establishments cost £366,000; and the charge of the consular department alone was £121,820, being nearly £8,000 more than the charge of both establishments just before the French revolutionary war. We shall conclude the chapter with subjoining a few documents abstracted from parliamentary papers, which will illustrate and authenticate our previous exposition, and show the present state of this branch of the national expenditure.

SALARIES *and Pensions to Ambassadors and Consuls.*—Parl. Paper, No. 305, Session 1830.

Year.	Salaries to Ambassadors.	Salaries to Consuls.	Pensions to Retired Foreign Ministers.	Pensions to Consuls.	Charge for Diplomatists and Consuls.
1822	£144,135	£30,076	£52,206	£1,190	£305,772
1823	139,366	29,740	52,503	1,036	332,453
1824	136,511	33,091	53,547	890	361,728
1825	132,301	52,625	55,938	1,368	418,637
1826	142,584	49,975	53,450	3,370	459,538
1827	132,553	51,100	62,318	3,370	412,159
1828	133,163	50, 26	56,772	4,270	407,117
1829	132,149	49,342	54,719	4,870	366,004

SALARIES *and* Allowances *for* House-rent *of Diplomatic Servants abroad.*—Parliamentary Report, No. 337, Sess. 1831.

Residence.	Character.	Salary.	Allowance for House-rent
France.	Ambassador	£10,000	
	Secretary of Embassy	1,000	
	First Attaché	400	
Russia.	Ambassador	10,000	£1,000
	Secretary of Embassy	1,000	
	First Attaché	400	
Austria.	Ambassador	9,000	900
	Secretary of Embassy	900	
	First Attaché	250	
Turkey.	Ambassador	6,500	
	Secretary of Embassy	800	
	First Attaché	250	
Spain.	Envoy and Min. Plenipo.	6,000	500
	Secretary of Legation	550	
	First Attaché	250	
Prussia.	Envoy and Min. Plenipo.	5,000	500
	Secretary of Legation	550	500
	First Attaché	250	
Washington.	Envoy and Min. Plenipo.	4,500	500
	Secretary of Legation	550	
	First Attaché	200	
Naples.	Envoy and Min. Plenipo.	4,000	400
	Secretary of Legation	500	
	First Attaché	—	
Portugal.	Envoy and Min. Plenipo.	4,000	400
	Secretary of Legation	500	
	First Attaché	—	
Brazil.	Envoy and Min. Plenipo.	4,000	500
	Secretary of Legation	550	
	First Attaché	250	
Holland.	Envoy and Min. Plenipo.	3,600	400
	Secretary of Legation	500	
	First Attaché	—	
Belgium.	Envoy and Min. Plenipo.	3,600	400
	Secretary of Legation	500	
	First Attaché	—	
Sweden.	Envoy	3,000	400
	Secretary of Legation	500	
Denmark.	Envoy	3,000	400
	Secretary of Legation	500	
Bavaria.	Envoy	3,600	500
	Secretary of Legation	500	
Sardinia.	Envoy	3,600	500
	Secretary of Legation	500	
German Diet.	Min. Plenipo.	2,600	300
	Secretary of Legation	400	
	Attaché and German Translator	200	
Wurtemburg.	Min. Plenipo.	2,000	300
	Secretary of Legation	400	
Saxony.	Min. Plenipo.	2,000	300
	Secretary of Legation	200	
	Carried forward....	£103,550	7,800

Residence.	Character.	Salary.	Allowance for House rent
	Brought forward.............£103,550		.. 7,800
Tuscany.	Min. Plenipo.	2,000....	300
	Secretary of Legation	400....	300
Switzerland.	Min. Plenipo...........................	2,000....	250
	Secretary of Legation	400	
Greece.	Minister Resident	2,000....	200
	Secretary of Legation	400	
Mexico.	Min. Plenipo...........................	3,600....	400
	Secretary of Legation	600	
	First Attaché..........................	200	
Columbia.	Minister Plenipotentiary	3,600....	400
	Secretary of Legation	600	
	First Attaché	300	
Buenos Ayres.	Minister Plenipotentiary	3,000....	300
	Secretary of Legation	500	
Albania.	Agent	1,000	
	Salaries.............£124,150		9,950

These salaries and allowances for rent are exclusive of charges for outfit, journeys out, postage, and other incidental expenses, which swell to a considerable amount the civil contingencies of the year. After three, four, or seven years service, it has been usual to grant retiring pensions to foreign ministers of £2000 or £1500 a-year; but from a letter of Lord Palmerston's, dated August 31, 1831, it appears ministers have determined to act on the following resolutions of Sir H. Parnell's finance committee of 1828:—" 1. That no person whatever shall be entitled to receive a diplomatic pension until the expiration of fifteen years from the date of his first commission, nor unless he shall have actually served ten years. 2. That no person shall be entitled to a pension of the first class (£2,000 a-year), unless he shall have actually served three years as ambassador at some foreign court. 3. That pensions to envoys and ministers plenipotentiary at the greater courts shall not exceed 1500 a-year, and shall not be granted until after five years' residence in that capacity at a foreign court. 4. That pensions to envoys and ministers plenipotentiary at other courts, and to ministers, shall not exceed £1000 a-year after a similar period of residence. 5. And last, that pensions in the remaining class shall not exceed £800 a-year under the same conditions as to time of residence."—*Parliamentary Paper, No.* 337, *Sess.* 1831.

ARISTOCRACY.

ALMOST imperceptibly to ourselves, we are drawn through the different departments of our undertaking in heraldic order: first, we explored the Church in all its ramifications; next the revenues of the Monarch; afterwards the monarch's chief council, and his representatives in the persons of his ambassadors, envoys extraordinary, and ministers plenipotentiary; and now we come to the Aristocracy, which, according to the established rules of precedency, ought to follow the Clergy and the Crown.

Before entering on the more serious details of our present subject, we cannot help pausing a moment, on the threshold, to felicitate ourselves and readers on the triumphs already achieved by the progress of knowledge. Three centuries are only a step in the history of nations, yet, within that period, how many fictions of feudality and priestcraft have been dissipated, and which are now only reverted to as sources of amusement, like the delusions of witchcraft and demonology. Only think of the supremacy of the Clergy, in the fifteenth century, when they enjoyed almost impunity for every crime, by exemption from secular jurisdiction. It strikingly demonstrates the influence of *mind* over ignorance; for ecclesiastics, at that era, as much excelled the laity in mental attainments as in the magnitude of their possessions. Such pre-eminence is either lost or fast disappearing: in science and information they are manifestly behind other classes of the community; their moral influence is insignificant; the chief advantages they retain are their revenues, and the permanent enjoyment of these not being founded on any claim of right or social utility, public conviction has decreed against them, and the general verdict waits only to be carried into execution,

Among the fictions of Regality the most preposterous was the claim of *divine right*, which has become too common place a drollery even for mirth. Still it cannot be forgotten, that, so recently as the last of the Stuarts, this dogma had many disciples, and some remains of this singular faith are now to be found. An attempt has been made to erect a new idol in the pretensions of *Legitimacy*: but, in an age of discussion, imposture cannot long maintain its ground, and this was soon trampled under foot. Previously to the introduction of this idolatry, the English had shown their contempt for hereditary right by the transfer of the crown to the Prince of Orange; the French subsequently by the expulsion of Charles X. and the adoption of Philip I.; and the non-interference of the European powers in the mighty movement of 1830 has put an everlasting seal on this species of secular superstition.

Let us next advert to the fictions of the Third Estate : by some accident the English Aristocracy have contrived to retain a greater proportion of their ancient influence and endowments than any other privileged order of the community. The circumstances to which this may be ascribed appear principally the following. First, the English nobility had the good sense to give up in time a portion of their more revolting usurpations, by which they have been enabled to preserve entire, in a more palmy state of enjoyment and for a longer term, the remainder, than any similar class in Europe. Secondly, at an early period of our annals they obtained a hold on popular support, by aiding the people in resisting the encroachments of the clergy and the prerogatives of the Crown. Lastly, and latterly, the more enlightened portion of them have conciliated the favour of the influential classes by the adoption of liberal principles, and by impressing them with the belief that a conservative principle identifies the immunities of their 'order' with the general peace and welfare. Some of these sources of respect and power are manifestly losing ground in popular estimation. For what services the Aristocracy have rendered to civil liberty they have been amply remunerated by the long exercise of the political franchises of the People, by the receipt of enormous rents, and by the absorption of public taxes. The assumption of a community of interest with the People is partly belied by their own legislative acts, in which they obviously consider they have an interest different from that of other classes of society. In short, the time has arrived, when the power and institutions of the privileged orders may be fitly passed in review; they have already conceded many immunities, and it is not improbable the period has arrived when they will be called upon to make further concessions to the spirit of the age.

There was a time, as every body knows, when LORDS were petty despots on their domains. They had their dungeon-castles, in which they could, at their own arbitrary will, torture, imprison, and even execute, their fellow-creatures. They could, when it suited their sovereign pleasure, sally forth on the public highways, and, with impunity, rob and maltreat whatever luckless traveller they happened to meet. They had even immunities still more revolting to human feeling. One, it is true, can hardly bring the mind to believe that such monstrous usages as those which gave rise to *borough-English* and *child-wit* ever existed; yet that they did is unquestionable, and the memorials of these customs, subsisting in the borough of Stafford, in the county of Essex, and other parts of the kingdom, place the facts beyond dispute. By the former usage the lord claimed the trifling perquisite, on the occasion of a marriage on his estate, of sleeping the first night with the bride ; and the latter designates a penalty which a woman had to pay who had suffered herself to be begotten with child *without the lord's permission.*

Thank heaven our seigneurs have abated something of their ancient privileges ; still the bare knowledge that such usages once existed—that they are associated with the *name*—is sufficient to make the mere titles of lord, baron, and duke, an offence—an insult to human reason—an abomination—which modern and civilized Europe ought no longer to tolerate.

Having adverted to a few of the ancient impostures and usurpations, chiefly to show to what a depth of degradation human nature may be reduced, we shall proceed to illustrate the immunities and advantages enjoyed by the Aristocracy, and which they have been enabled to arrogate and maintain by a monopoly of political power. It is a subject of vast importance, and one, we believe, when fairly placed before our countrymen, about which there will hardly exist diversity of opinion.

In contemplating the English government, one peculiar feature may be remarked in every branch of our civil and ecclesiastical polity : in each branch there is an entire departure from the original object of its institution. In the ecclesiastical state, no such abuse as clerical sinecurists was formerly known ; every order had some duties to discharge, for which they received their incomes : but now we find that the episcopal, dignified, and one-third of the parochial clergy receive FOUR OR FIVE MILLIONS annually, for which it is hard to say any service whatever is rendered to society. The House of Commons, originally intended to represent the property, intelligence, and population of the state, has become the mere organ of the Aristocracy ; who, according to the constitution, ought not to have the least influence over its deliberations. The executive, by the delegation of its powers to ministers and judges, exhibits a similar dereliction from civil and military duties : and, lastly, in the House of Peers we find a corresponding abandonment of civil functions; the dukes, earls, and barons had all, formerly, as their names import, important duties to discharge in the commonwealth.

The object of reform is not to destroy the established church, pull down the two houses of parliament, nor invade the rights of the Crown ; but to restore, as far as the altered state of society will allow, those different orders to the exercise of their legitimate authority.

Of the different innovations on the ancient system, there is none more flagrant than those of the Aristocracy : it has swallowed up not only the rights of the people, and the prerogatives of the Crown, but also the immunities of the church. At no former period of history was the power of the Aristocracy so absolute, nor did they enjoy a tithe of their present advantages. During the Norman Kings, and the first kings of the house of Plantagenet, down to the passing of *Magna Charta*, though the power of the Crown, in many instances, proved but a feeble barrier to the encroachments of the barons, yet, when united with the influence of the clergy, it was at all times able to set some bounds to their authority. After the passing of the Great Charter, the growth of manufactures, and the diffusion of knowledge among the people, gave rise to the Commons. This order, unknown to the preceding period, gradually rose into great importance, and ultimately became able not only to prescribe bounds to the Aristocracy, but also to the Monarch.   Under the tyranny of the Stuarts, the Commons brought one monarch to the block, and abolished the House of Peers.   But its ascendancy was of short duration.   The return of Charles II.—the restoration of the rotten boroughs, which had been struck out of the representation during the protectorship of Cromwell, to the right of returning members of parliament,—the introduction of parliamentary corruption in the reign of Charles II.—more systematically and openly practised under William III. and perfected under the administration of Walpole, in the reign of George II.—completely annihilated the powers of the Commons, and gave to the Aristocracy its uncontrolled and irresponsible ascendancy.

Having obtained the power, the Aristocracy have exercised it as uncontrolled power usually is exercised, namely, solely for their own advantage : they have rid themselves of what duties were anciently annexed to their order, and monopolized nearly all the honours and emoluments of society.

The ancient nobility had not only to provide a sufficient military force for the defence of the kingdom, but they had also the administration of justice, the coining of money, and, in short, the whole internal government of the country committed to their care.*   On such conditions, their estates were originally granted : these they retain ; but as to the duties annexed, they have placed them on the shoulders of the other classes of the community.   It is the Commons now, who either discharge, or pay for being discharged, all the duties of the state.   If we only examine the list of taxes, as we shortly intend to do, we shall find that the aristocracy have, comparatively, exempted themselves from impost, while the burthen falls exclusively on the people.   The duties imposed by the *corn-laws* are a tax paid directly for the support of this order ; while, with the exception of the land-tax, a trifling impost, all other duties, the assessed taxes, excise, customs, stamps, post-office duties, fall with disproportionate weight on the middling and working classes, and scarcely touch the massive incomes of the nobility.

This is one of the great evils resulting from the political supremacy of the peerage.   Instead of bearing the burthen of taxation, which, in fact, is the original tenure on which they acquired their territorial possessions, they have laid it on the people.   Nothing can be more unjust and oppressive.   The comforts of one class ought never to be encroached upon, while another class remains in the enjoyment of redundant luxuries.   It is the legitimate object of good government to prevent the extremes of wealth and indigence, and diffuse equally, through all classes, the bounties of nature.   But the aristocratic system is the reverse of this principle.   It weighs chiefly on want and penury ; it

---

* Blackstone's Comment. b. iv. ch. iv. and v. and Smith's Wealth of Nations, b. iii. ch. iv. where the nature of the ancient tenures is investigated.

tramples on those already depressed ; and crushes, almost to annihilation, the most useful classes by its unceasing exactions.

It is not our purpose to investigate the utility and origin of an hereditary privileged class. It is, no doubt, a questionable hypothesis—not supported at least by the cotemporary illustration of many noble families—that wisdom and fitness for the administration of national affairs are inheritable endowments. Besides which, men seldom take pains to cultivate superfluous acquirements: consequently, it is a strong objection to hereditary honours, that those born to them have no necessity for cultivating the virtues by which, perhaps, they were originally acquired. A principal motive for the institution of hereditary right has ceased to be of weight. Originally it was intended to guard against disputed succession, and prevent the division of powers essential to the security of communities and property. But the introduction of the representative principle in governments, the more general diffusion of intelligence, of habits of order, of respect for individual claims, has rendered these precautions no longer essential to the maintenance of social institutions. Leaving, however, the general discussion of the question, we shall proceed to notice, categorically, the real and practical grievances entailed on the commons of England by the advantages and immunities of the Aristocracy.

I. RIGHT OF PRIMOGENITURE AND ENTAILS.

For the last ten years a great deal has been written and said, and justly too, on the evils of monopolies ; but hardly any one has touched upon the monopoly of land. Many, even of the Aristocracy, have been zealous and persevering in their endeavours to establish unrestricted freedom in commerce ; they perceived the advantages of liberty in the exchange of commodities, but they have been indifferent or silent on the advantages of liberty in the exchange of the soil. Yet, what is the right of primogeniture and the law of entail, but a monopoly as grievous and pernicious as that of the Bank of England and East India Company ? What right had an assembly of half-civilized men, some five hundred years ago, to tie up the great estates of the country in perpetuity; to enact that, whatever changes of society might intervene, they should never be subdivided, nor severed from their lineal heirs as long as they endured ? Was not this creating a monopoly? Did it not interpose insuperable obstacles to the sale and division of property—keep up the price of land to an artificial height—impede fair competition—limit the market of buyers—and impose restrictions on the freedom of those who might be disposed to sell?

Moreover, the statute *De donis*, or of "Great Men," as it is frequently called, perpetuated a LANDED INTEREST ; that is, an order of men with interests distinct from those of the community, and who, armed with the power of the state, have been able to treat with special favor their peculiar class, by imposing upon it lighter burthens, by protecting it from competition, and other expedients which tended directly to their own greatness and emolument by the sacrifice of the general welfare.

The motives which originated this feudal institution, as before observed, have, in great part, ceased to exist. In the disorderly era of Edward I. the right of the first-born to the undivided possession of his ancestor was a *law of peace ;* and, by consolidating indisputably the power which the entire property gave in the hands of a single person, it was a *law of security.* To divide the inheritance was to ruin it, and to expose the dwellers upon it, who depended on the proprietor for protection, to be oppressed and swallowed up in the desolating incursions of neighbouring and ferocious rivals. In the existing state of society no such pretexts can be urged. The poor as well as the rich enjoy personal security, and the owner of a single acre of land is as secure in the enjoyment as the owner of 100,000. The right of primogeniture, however, still subsists; and as, of all institutions, it is the most adapted to flatter the pride of great families, it will be tenaciously upheld by the Aristocracy. In other respects it is an unmixed evil; it is even injurious to the real interests of the landowners; for nothing can be more contrary to the welfare of a numerous family than a right which, in order " to enrich one, beggars all the rest of the children;" and reduces them to the alternative of obtaining subsistence either as mendicants or depredators on the bounty and involuntary contributions of the community.

The same reasoning applies to ENTAILS, which are the natural consequence of primogeniture. They were introduced to preserve the lineal succession of which primogeniture first gave the idea, and to hinder any part of the original patrimony from being conveyed out of the proposed line, either by gift, devise, or alienation, either by the folly or by the misfortune of any of its successive possessors. When great landed estates were a sort of principality, such curtailed inheritances might not be indefensible. Like what are called the fundamental laws of some communities, they might frequently hinder the security of thousands from being endangered by the incapacity or extravagance of one man. But, in the existing state of Europe, when property is so well secured, when small as well as great estates derive their security from inviolable laws, nothing can be more absurd than such defensive restrictions. They are founded upon the most absurd of all suppositions, the supposition that every successive generation of men have not an equal right to the earth and to all that it contains ; but that the property of the present generation should be fettered and regulated by barbarians who died centuries ago. Entails, however, are still respected in England; and it is only in particular cases, by means of legal fictions, prompted by the spirit of commerce, and new views of social expediency, that estates tied up by them can be alienated.* They are deemed essential to the maintenance of the monopoly of the aristocracy in the enjoyment of political power,

---

* Humphreys on the Laws of Real Property, 2d edit. p. 31.

honour, dignities, and offices; having usurped many advantages over their fellow citizens, lest their poverty should render them ridiculous, it is thought reasonable that they should have others. It is, however, an oppressive and indefensible grievance. In the present state of society there is no utility in guaranteeing to particular families the perpetual enjoyment of vast masses of property—that this property shall not be liable to the ordinary vicissitudes of life—that it shall not, like personal estates, either be deviseable or saleable—and that all, except members of the privileged order, shall be irrevocably interdicted from ever becoming proprietors of the soil—of that soil which is the common inheritance of the whole community.

Other evils result from this feudal institution. Primogeniture enriches one, and leaves all the other members of a family destitute. Hence they are thrown, like mendicants, on the public for support; but they are unlike mendicants in this—that the public has no option, whether they will support them or not. The Aristocracy, usurping the power of the state, have the means under various pretexts, of extorting, for the junior branches of their families, a forced subsistence. They patronize a ponderous and sinecure church-establishment; they wage long and unnecessary wars, to create employments in the army and navy; they conquer and retain useless colonies; they set on foot expensive missions of diplomacy, and keep an ambassdor or consul, and often both, at almost every petty state and every petty port in the world; they create offices without duties, grant unmerited pensions, keep up unnecessary places in the royal household, in the admiralty, the treasury, the customs, excise, courts of law, and every department of the public administration: by these and other expedients, the junior as well as elder branches of the great families are amply provided for out of the taxes. They live in profusion and luxury; and those by whom they are maintained alone subsist in indigence and privation.

It is only in the less civilized states of Europe, in Hungary, Bohemia, Poland and Russia, that primogeniture is retained. Countries enjoying the benefits of political regeneration have abolished this remnant of feudality, and introduced the law of equal partibility. The happy effects of this reform are visible in the condition of France and the Netherlands; in the greater harmony subsisting among the different classes of society—in the absence of the miserable jealousy and exclusiveness that embitter domestic intercourse in England—in the public spirit, unanimity, and personal independence of the inhabitants, produced, no doubt, by a conviction of common interests, reciprocal obligations, and equal participation in all the advantages and enjoyments of the social state.

II. PRIVILEGES OF PEERS.

There are other laws originating in the same aristocratic spirit, and directed to the maintenance of similar exclusive privileges, as those described in the last section. Such are the Insolvent Laws. Lest the dignity of a peer should be violated, his person is privileged from arrest for debt. Why should this be tolerated? He is not ostensibly entrusted with representative functions, like the members of the lower house. He represents only himself, with the exception of the sixteen peers of Scotland and the twenty-eight peers of Ireland. Why, then, should his person be protected from imprisonment, if he is so inexcusably improvident, with all the advantages he enjoys, as to incur debts he cannot pay? A *Scotch peer*, though not one of those sitting in parliament, is privileged from arrest, as appears from the case of Lord Mordington. This lord, who was a Scotch peer, but not one of those who sat in parliament, being arrested, moved the Court of Common Pleas to be discharged, as being entitled, by the Act of Union, to all the privileges of a peer of Great Britain; and prayed an attachment against the bailiff; when a rule was granted to show cause. Upon this, the bailiff made an affidavit, that when he arrested the said lord he was so mean in his apparel, as having a worn-out suit of clothes, and a dirty shirt on, and but sixteen-pence in his pocket, he could not suppose him to be a peer of Great Britain, and, therefore, through inadvertency, arrested him. The Court discharged the lord, and made the bailiff ask pardon.

A peer, sitting in judgment, is not required to give his verdict upon oath, like a commoner, but upon his *honour*. What a stigma on the other classes of the community! Just as if a peer alone had *honour*, and all others were base perfidious slaves, from whom truth could only be extorted when they had been forced into the presence of their Creator.

A member of the lower house is the deputy or representative of others, and cannot delegate his powers; but a peer represents only himself, and may vote by proxy on any question, even though he has never been present to discuss its merits.

If a thief breaks into a church, and steals the surplice or cushion, it is not like stealing a ledger or cash-box from a shop or counting-house —it is *sacrilege*. If a man scandalizes a peer by speaking evil of him, it is not common scandal, it is *scandalum magnatum*, that is, great scandal, subjecting the offender to indefinite punishment.

If a peer job in the funds, as many of them do; or if he get up bubble companies, as some of them have done, to dupe credulous people; and if he involve himself in debt by these fraudulent practices, you cannot imprison him to enforce payment; neither can you make him a bankrupt, and sequestrate his estates. The property of a peer, like his person, has a *dignity* about it, and must not be violated. You may knock down Nathan Rothschild, though he is a very rich man, or a worshipful alderman, or even a right honourable lord mayor, and the justices will only charge you a few shillings for the liberty you have taken; but if you knock down a peer, though he is ever so insolent, it is almost as bad as murder.

Peers being great landowners, therefore land, as well as their persons, enjoys immunities which do not attach to chattel property. A noble lord may run into as much debt as he pleases, and then, with impunity, defraud all his creditors. He may live in the utmost profusion; he may borrow money to support his extravagance, or for providing portions for younger children, making the most solemn promises, or even giving his *written* engagement to repay it; or he may raise loans, and with these loans buy houses and land, and when he dies leave the houses and land purchased with this borrowed money to whom he pleases: and in all these cases the lenders who have trusted to the honour of a peer have no power to touch a shilling worth of his real estates.

These are a few of the privileges of peers; we shall proceed to illustrate other results of aristocratic legislation.

III. INJUSTICE OF ARISTOCRATIC TAXATION.

Nothing can demonstrate more incontestibly the necessity of the different interests in society being represented in the general government than the course of fiscal legislation. The political power of the state, we need not repeat nor explain, is in this country consolidated in the aristocracy. If we only glance at public burthens we shall see with what admirable adroitness they have been distributed, so as to press as lightly as possible on those who imposed them, and with disproportionate weight on those who had no share in their imposition. Does not this show better than all the general reasoning in the world the utility of universal representation; otherwise, whatever interest is unprotected will assuredly be sacrificed, and this injustice will be perpetrated by the dominant party, however exalted this dominant party may be by birth, by station, by education, by wealth, or other adventitious circumstance.

Let us appeal to facts in illustration of this principle. The landed interest is the primary interest of the Aristocracy; whatever tends to enhance the value of land or its produce tends directly to augment their incomes. Hence, their leading policy has been to protect agriculture, to encourage husbandry, by abstaining from burthening it with imposts, to impose no additional tax on land, and above all things to secure the *home market* against competition from abroad. For this latter purpose they have passed laws the most unjust and outrageous; the importation of some articles they have absolutely prohibited; others they have loaded with heavy duties; so that they have been able to sell their own produce at a monopoly price.

The following list of articles of foreign production, and the import duties to which they are subject, will show to what extent the landowners have availed themselves of political power to promote their own interests, by excluding foreign competition.

	£	s.	d.
Bacon, per cwt.	1	8	0
Beer, per thirty-two gallons	2	13	0
Butter, per cwt.	1	0	0
Bristles, not sorted, per lb.	0	0	3
Bristles, sorted	0	0	4
Cider, per ton	21	10	4
Cheese, per cwt.	0	10	6
Cucumbers, *ad valorem*	20	0	0
Eggs, for every 120	0	0	10
Hay, per load	1	4	0
Hair, cows and oxen, per cwt.	0	2	6
Hair-powder, per cwt.	9	15	0
Hops, per cwt.	8	11	0
Hemp-seed, per quarter	2	0	0
Hemp, undressed, per cwt.	0	4	6
Lard, per cwt.	0	8	6
Madder, per cwt.	0	6	0
Mules and asses, each	0	10	6
Horses, each	1	0	0
Oil, rape and linseed, per ton	39	18	0
Peas, per bushel	0	7	6
Perry, per ton	22	13	8
Potatoes, per cwt.	0	2	0
Seeds, clover, hay, &c.	1	0	0
Spirits, foreign, per gallon (I. M.)	1	2	6
Rum, per gallon	0	8	6
Tallow, per cwt.	0	3	2
Tares, per quarter	0	10	0
Timber, per load	2	15	0

Wheat 16s. 5d. a quarter to 1s. according as the price rises from 61s. to 70s. a quarter.

Barley 13s. 10d. a quarter to 1s. according as the price rises, from 32s. to 40s. a quarter.

Oats 10s. 9d. a quarter to 1s. according as the price rises from 24s. to 31s. a quarter.

Beef, lamb, mutton, pork, sheep, and swine are prohibited to be imported, by 6 Geo. IV. c. 117.

While the landowners have been strenuously exerting themselves to close, hermetically, if possible, the home market against foreign agricultural produce, they have, with admirable consistency of policy, been at the same time endeavouring to throw it wide open for the admission of foreign manufactures. This places their conduct in a most conspicuous light. Surely, if a free trade in manufactures was for the benefit of the community, so was a free trade in the produce of the soil. But, then, our feudal Solons do not deal in cotton, nor silk, nor hardwares ; they are only dealers in corn, and that makes all the differeace. The working and effects of this abominable system has been justly and spiritedly versified in the following lines :—

> Ye coop us up and tax our bread,
>   And wonder why we pine ;
> But ye're fat, and round, and red,
>   And fill'd with tax-bought wine.
>
> Thus twelve rats starve, while three rats thrive,
>   (Like you on mine and me) ;
> When fifteen rats are caged alive
>   With food for nine and three.
>
> Haste ! havoc's torch begins to glow,
>   The ending is begun ;
> Make haste ! destruction thinks ye slow ;
>   Make haste to be undone !
>
> Why are ye call'd ' my Lord' and ' Squire,'
>   While fed by mine and me :
> And wringing food, and clothes, and fire
>   From bread-tax'd misery ?
>
> Make haste, slow rogues, *prohibit* trade,
>   Prohibit honest gain ;
> Turn all the good that God hath made
>   To fear, and hate, and pain.
>
> Till beggars all—assassins all,
>   All cannibals we be ;
> And death shall have no funeral
>   From shipless sea to sea.—*Corn-Law Rhymes.*

It is not a difficult problem to ascertain the annual burthen imposed on the community by the corn-tax. It appears, from the resolutions submitted to the House of Commons by Lord Milton, that the average price of wheat in this country, in the year ending February 1830, had been 64s. 2d. per quarter. The average price on the Continent and in America, during the same period, had been 46s. 3d. per quarter. Now, if there were no restrictions on the importation of corn, the price in England would be nearly the same as in Poland or in the United States ; but, in consequence of the boroughmongers tax, the price is about 20s. per quarter higher : so that, if the annual consumption of corn by the community be 48 millions of quarters, they pay exactly so many pounds additional, in order to swell the rents of the land-owners.*

A tax upon bread is the most oppressive and unjust that could be imposed on the industrious classes. A man with £50 a-year consumes,

---

* We suppose all our readers have read Colonel Thompson's *Catechism of the Corn Laws,* price six-pence. His *True Theory of Rent,* price three-pence, is another admirable publication. The public is indebted to this gentleman for having placed the science of Political Economy on its legs again : it now stands much where it did when Adam Smith left it, after a perilous escape through the thick cloud of darkness in which it had been enveloped by the misleading subtleties of Mr. Ricardo and his followers.

individually, as much bread as a man with £50,000, and consequently sustains as great an annual loss by the artificial enhancement of its price. All taxes on articles of ordinary consumption fall in the same disproportionate manner. They are like a fixed per-centage on income, levied indiscriminately on every person, without regard to large or small revenues. Sugar, tea, and malt are articles of general use; and the labourer and artisan contribute exactly in the same proportion as a lord on their individual consumption of those commodities. In fact, it is to duties of this description the Aristocracy have always shown a marked partiality; the excise, it is known, being the most productive branch of the revenue. Mr. Pitt used to say that the high price of labour in England arose chiefly from the excise; three-fifths of the wages of a poor man passing into the exchequer. But no such proportion of the incomes of the Aristocracy flows into the public treasury.

Yet it is the incomes of the landed interest, as we shall briefly illustrate, which form the most legitimate and unexceptionable fund for taxation. A person who employs himself in making a pair of shoes or inexpressibles adds nothing to the value of the leather or cloth beyond the price of his labour. Land, however, is a more profitable material to work upon; yielding not only a produce adequate to defray the expenses of its culture, but also a surplus; and this surplus constitutes the landlord's rent. But the soil of every country belongs to the people; consequently, the rent or surplus revenue it yields is not so much the property of a particular class of individuals as of the whole community. It follows that the landowners are only so many *pensioners* or *sinecurists*, paid out of a revenue which originally constituted the sole fund out of which all the exigencies of state were provided. Instead of the " Lords of the Soil" taxing every article we eat and drink, and impeding, with vexatious imposts, every operation of industry, they ought to have laid a direct tax on rent, which would have been easily and economically collected. They have acted quite the reverse. The Land-Tax continues to be levied at this day according to the defective valuation in the reign of William III.; and, in 1798, it was made perpetual at 4s. in the pound on the inadequate estimate of the rental at the Revolution. In France the *foncier*, or land-tax, amounts to one-fourth of the whole annual revenue;* in England it does not amount to a sixtieth part. The proportion of our excise, customs, and assessed taxes to similar taxes in France, is as forty-five to twenty; while the proportion of the public revenue of the former to that of the latter is as three to two.

Need we say any thing further to illustrate the tendency of aristocratic taxation, or the selfish purposes to which the political power of the Oligarchy has been perverted? Yes, we shall briefly add a few more facts.

---

* Lowe's Present State of England, p. 318.

When the income-tax was imposed, or rather when it was screwed up by the Whigs, in 1806, lands and tenements were assessed at 2s. in the pound. Precisely the same assessment was laid on incomes arising from professions, trade, or other vocation. Thus was as heavy a tax levied on revenue not worth five years' purchase as on revenue worth thirty years' purchase; in other words, the tax was *six times heavier* on the industrious than on the unproductive classes of the community. A merchant, attorney, tradesman, or shopkeeper, whose income depended entirely on his personal exertions—which ceased at his death—and by savings from which he could alone make a provision for his children after his decease, was taxed six times to the amount of the landowner, by whom the burthen was imposed—whose property was entailed, and protected from all liability for debts however extravagantly incurred.

If the Boroughmongers ever charge themselves with any burthens, they are always prompt to get rid of them the first opportunity, though they touch them ever so lightly, and have been rendered necessary by their own infatuated measures. Thus, immediately after the peace, before any reduction in the public establishments, or in the amount of the monstrous debt they had contracted, the income-tax was abolished. Again, the duty on horses employed in *husbandry* has been long since repealed, but the *malt-tax* is still continued, and the beer-duty—the most unfair and oppressive of all duties—was only repealed within these two years.

From some duties the peerage is exempted altogether. A lord of parliament sends and receives all letters *free of postage;* he usually franks the letters of all his relatives and friends; he enjoys, also, the privilege of sending a letter from London by the post on *Sunday*—a sort of sabbath-breaking which would be considered impiety or perhaps blasphemy in another person.

It would be tedious to go through the whole roll of taxes, to show how indulgent our legislators have been to themselves and how unjust towards the rest of the community. If a lord by inheritance succeed to an estate worth £100,000, he has not a shilling to pay to government. If a rich merchant dies, and bequeaths as much to his children, they are taxed to the amount of £1500, or, if there is *no will*, to the amount of £2250. If a poor man buy a cottage for £10, he has 10s. or one-twentieth part of the purchase-money, to pay for a conveyance. If a nobleman buy an estate worth £50,000, the stamp-duty is only one-hundred-and-eleventh part of the purchase-money, or £450. A similarly unequal tax is incurred in borrowing *small* sums on bond or mortgage, while special favour is shown to those who borrow *large* sums. If a man has eight windows in his house he is assessed 16s. 6d.; if he has *one* more he is charged 4s. 6d. for it. If a lord has 180 windows he is charged £46 : 11 : 3; and if he has *one* more he is charged only 1s. 6d.; and he may have as many more additional windows as he pleases at the same low rate of assessment. If a poor man's horse, or his ass, pass through a toll-bar there is something to pay, of course;

but if a lord's horse pass through, provided it is employed on the lord's land, there is nothing to pay. If a cart pass through a toll-bar, loaded with furniture or merchandize, there is something to pay for the cart, and something extra to pay according as the wheels are broad or narrow; but if the cart is loaded with manure for his lordship's estate, the *cart is free*, and the wheels may be any breadth the owner pleases without liability to extra charges. If a stage-coach, or hackney-carriage, which a tradesman sometimes indulges in, pass through a turnpike, it must pay toll every time it passes; but the carriage of a lord or gentleman may pass through 100 times a day, if he please, for once paying. The tax on a nobleman's carriage is, per year, six pounds; the tax on a glass-coach, which a poor man keeps to get a living by, and which is hired by those who cannot afford to keep a carriage, is, per year, about £160; the tax on a stage-coach, which is paid by those who cannot afford to hire even a glass-coach, is, per year, about £260. A Paddington stage, running every hour, pays, daily, for *mile-duty*, 12s.; while some stages run more than 100 miles daily; if 100 miles, then the daily mile duty is 25s., which must all be paid by the passengers who cannot ride in their own carriages, which travel without duty. Riding or walking, eating or drinking, there is inequality. If a poor person refreshes himself with a glass of spirits (though beer would be better for his health and pocket) he is taxed seventy per cent; but if he takes a glass of wine, which is a lord's drink, he is only taxed seventeen per cent. Lords do not smoke, though they sometimes chew, therefore a pipe of tobacco, which is a poor man's luxury, is taxed 900 per cent. If a poor servant-girl advertises for a place *of all work*, she is taxed 3s. 6d.; if a lord advertises the sale of an estate he pays no more. The house-tax falls heavily on the industrious tradesman, but lightly on the lord and esquire; the former must reside in town, and occupy spacious premises, which make his rent large, and the tax being proportionate, it deducts materially from income, while the latter may reside in the country, occupy a fine mansion, and not be rented more than £50 per annum. Lastly, lords, sinecurists, pensioners, and gentlemen may retire to Paris, Florence, or Brussels, for any thing they have to do, or any good they are capable of doing, by which they avoid house-tax, window-tax, and almost every other tax; but the tradesman and shopkeeper are *adscriptæ glebæ*,— they must stick to their counting-houses and warehouses, and expiate, by toil and frugality, the follies and extravagance of their rulers.

These are a few specimens of our fiscal regulations, and must, we imagine, demonstrate, practically, to merchants, copyholders, shop-keepers, tradesmen, and the middling and working orders generally, the advantages of having a *friend at court*—that is, of having political rights—that is, of having real representatives—that is, of not being taxed without their consent—that is, of having a reform in the Commons House of Parliament, instead of leaving public affairs to the exclusive management of noble lords and their nominees.

IV. ARISTOCRATIC GAME-LAWS.

A salmon from the pool, a wand from the wood, and a deer from the hills, are thefts which no man was ever ashamed to own.—*Fielding's Proverbs.*

We learn from this old Gaelic apophthegm,—the sentiment is very ancient,—that an exclusive right to game and other *feræ naturæ* does not rest on the same basis as property. Mankind will not be easily convinced that stealing a hare or partridge is as criminal as stealing a man's purse. While this continues the popular feeling, it is vain to multiply acts for the preservation of game. Laws, to be efficacious, should be in accordance with public opinion; if not, they only disturb the peace of society, excite ill-blood and contention, and multiply instead of diminishing offences.

Since the preceding edition of this work was printed in 1831, the legislature, by the Game Act of last session, has torn out one of the leaves of *The Black Book:* we then declared that, for this single object— that of getting rid of the demoralizing, detestable, ferocious, and pre- posterous game code ; we said " for this one object alone, without adverting to the church, the rotten boroughs, the dead weight, or other national grievance; only to sweep away this one national stigma would be well worth the *three days' fight* of the Parisians, or even the four days' battle of the Belgians." Our declarations may have hastened the abatement of one of the most insolent oppressions ever exercised over a civilized people, and accelerated the introduction of the new measure by which qualifications to kill game are abolished, and game is allowed to be sold like other commodities, by taking out a license. These con- cessions have removed the chief objects of our former animadversion, and, therefore, what we have to say will be rather for the benefit of the next than of the present generation; our purpose will be to place on record a specimen of the revolting tyranny exercised over the people of England by an usurping Oligarchy even to the last days of its existence.

Be it known then that the Boroughmongers, down to the twelfth hour of their reign, persisted in claiming for *game* greater protection than had ever been awarded to property; they persisted in having it considered as something more inviolate and sacred than household goods; they arbitrarily fixed on certain fowls of the air and beasts of the field, and these, in their sovereign pleasure, they decreed should be endowed with peculiar privileges distinct from all others; in a word, that they should be *aristocrats* like themselves, and it should be highly criminal in any base-born man to *kill them, or eat them, or buy them, or sell them, or carry them,* or even to have them in his possession, or to have in his possession any engine or instrument by which the dear and favoured creatures might be slain, maimed, or injured. In pursuance of these lordly whims they framed a code of laws to which we will venture to say, in subtlety and refinement of insult, nothing equal could be found in the records of the vilest despotism ever established to experiment on the

limits of human endurance; we will venture to say that, in no other
country in the world, with the least pretence to freedom and civilization,
was there to be found a body of laws so partial, so repugnant to the
common sense and subversive of the common rights of mankind, as the
game laws of the English aristocracy!

To enforce their haughty immunities the Boroughmongers fixed on
certain fantastic conceits, which they called *qualifications* to kill game.
These qualifications were not founded on any rational consideration of
wealth, intelligence, or social usefulness. A rich merchant or manufacturer had no right to kill game; his warehouses might be filled with
valuable merchandize; he might give employment to thousands of
people, as some of them do in the North, yet he had no privilege to
meddle with the aristocrats of the air nor of the field! His wealth was
base—it was not feudal, it had not been acquired by war, plunder, and
confiscation, and did not qualify to spring woodcocks, no, nor even to
pop at a snipe, nor a teal, nor a quail, nor a land-rail. A *parson*,
however, who had a living worth £150 per annum, though his estate was
only for life, might kill as much game as he pleased.

But the sages of the King's Bench (blessed be their names!) were
more indulgent than the boroughmongering parliament: they determined
that even plebeians should have a little *sport*, and accordingly ruled that
a qualified person might take out a tradesman, stock-broker, clothier,
attorney, surgeon, or other inferior person *to beat the bushes, and see a
hare killed*, and he should not be liable to penalty. But beware of the
man-traps and spring-guns of the law; if any of the aforesaid ignoble
beings ventured to meddle, without first being *invited* by a lord or gentleman so to do, he was fined, or else imprisoned in the House of Correction.* Ah, these boroughmongers, how they have stabbed us! how
they have kicked us! how they have laughed at us!

Although an unqualified man was not allowed to kill game, it might
be thought, by a rational mind, he would be permitted *to buy* it of those
who were. No, he was not. What, the lords of the soil become
dealers and chapmen! degrade grouse and black-cock into mere commodities of traffic, like broad cloth and calico! Impossible! Therefore
they passed laws that game should neither be *bought nor sold;* that
higglers, victuallers, poulterers, pastry-cooks, and other mean persons
should not carry it, nor have it in possession, nor should any unqualified
person have in his possession any deadly or dangerous weapon for its
injury or destruction. If an unqualified person were *suspected*—barely
suspected, mind—of having game, or any dog, gun, or snare for killing
or wounding it, his house might be SEARCHED, and if any net or snare,
pheasant, partridge, fish, fowl, or other game were found, the offender
might be forthwith carried before a justice and fined, or sent to the
House of Correction, and there whipped and kept to hard labour. If a
man only happened to spoil or *tread* on the egg of a partridge, pheasant,
mallard, teal, bittern, or heron, he was fined or imprisoned. But if he

---

* 5 Ann, c. 14, and decisions thereon; Loft, 178; 15 East Reports, 462.

went forth in the night for the third time, with the full intent of catching an aristocrat bird, a coney, or other game, he was *transported beyond the seas for seven years*, or imprisoned, and kept to hard labour, in the House of Correction for two years; and if he ran away in order to avoid this merciful infliction, or resisted the land-owner or his servants, either with club, stick, or stone, rather than be apprehended, he was guilty of a misdemeanour, subjecting him either to transportation or imprisonment.

Now, mark the commentary afforded by the NIMRODS themselves on these arrogant and savage enactments. Within very few years three parliamentary committees were appointed to inquire into the state and administration of the game-laws; the results of their inquiries were—that poaching could not be prevented—that buying and selling game could not be prevented—that the game-laws were the fruitful sources of crime and immorality, and filled the gaols with delinquents,* and that the only means of remedying the evils were by allowing game to be openly sold like other commodities, and by altering the qualifications, so that every owner of land might not only have the liberty to kill game on his own estate, but be empowered to grant a similar indulgence to any other individual. Instead of acting on the knowledge so communicated, or the suggestions recommended; instead of repealing the laws which were the sole cause of game being so highly prized, and of the deadly nocturnal encounters between keepers and poachers; instead of doing any of these, the only measures that were carried—and which, by the by, still remain in force—were the 7 & 8 Geo. IV. c. 29, and the 9 Geo. IV. c. 69, which greatly augmented the sanguinary character of a code already too ferocious, and the everlasting opprobrium of the misnamed free and enlightened community by which it was tolerated.

But observe what was disclosed respecting the *sale of game*, about which the descendants of the Normans appeared so extremely fastidious. From the inquiries of the committee of the House of Lords, in 1828, it was discovered that game was a regular article for sale in all the principal markets of the metropolis: the penalties, indeed, which were imposed on the traffic were easily evaded; since, by one sapient and moral act of our legislators, the 58 Geo. III. if a person, who had incurred them to any amount, would only *inform* of some other person who had bought or sold game within the preceding six months, his penalties were remitted and he received the informer's reward, for this *neighbourly*, and, as it was often practised, friendly treachery. One salesman sold, on the average, 500 head of game in a week; in one year he sold 9628 head of game. The sale was mostly on commission, at two-pence or three-pence a head. It naturally excited surprise how all these waggon loads of game could be conveyed to London, and by whom

---

* In England and Wales in 1830, the number of convictions for criminal offences was 12,805. The number of convictions under the *Game Laws* was 1987, being nearly one-sixth of the total number of offenders of every description.

supplied. The poor labourer, mason, or weaver, who perilled his life, his limbs, and his health, in the covert attempt to catch a hare or partridge, could not possibly be adequate to support a commerce like this. No, it was not done by poaching exactly; the *wholesale* dealers were the law-makers themselves—those who had interdicted the traffic— NOBLE LORDS and MEN OF TITLE, who had condescended to supply the London poulterers and salesmen with game, on commission, as a means of augmenting their territorial revenues.

This perhaps is enough by way of *record* of the proceedings of the boroughmongers and their game laws, which Mr. Justice Blackstone denominated a " bastard slip of the forest laws." But the fact is, they were a refinement in insult on the savage code of William Rufus. The territorial jurisdiction of the forest-laws, though extensive enough in all conscience, had its local boundaries; at least, it did not extinguish the old common-law right every proprietor exercised to kill and have all animals, *feræ naturæ*, found on his own land. These inroads on the most obvious rights of property and the common sense of mankind, were left for a much more recent period,—a period subsequent to the glorious Revolution of 1688: for, though the Qualification Act was passed in the reign of Charles II. the statutes which first made it penal to *sell* game, or for an unqualified person to have game in his possession, were not passed till the reigns of William III. and George II.

V. INCOMES OF THE ARISTOCRACY.

We are not partizans of Agrarian laws, and we believe the number of political reformers of any sect is extremely diminutive who wish to see or who ever expect to see a Spencean division of property. Industry, perseverance, sobriety, and prudence will mostly acquire wealth, and deserve to acquire it, and to enjoy it, and to transmit the enjoyment, after death, to those they most esteem. These are elements of society which few, indeed, would ever wish to see violated. They are primary laws of social organization, of which every one almost instinctively feels the justice and utility.

Neither are there many, we apprehend, who wish to abolish civil distinctions. A legislator sufficiently wise and experienced to discharge his high functions; a judge or magistrate qualified by probity and learning to adjudicate civil and criminal wrongs; a great public officer meriting and filling a high civil appointment; or a great commander, able and brave, to direct the military power of the state: these are all distinctions which every one must respect and venerate ; and if it be necessary to distinguish the holders by other symbols than the official titles—by a velvet cap, a coronet, or ermined robe, with two, three, or four guards, or a golden epaulette—they will respect and venerate these too. Nay, there are not many, we believe, who care because there is " my lord" this, or " his grace" of that, or the " most noble" t' other thing; these are not matters of pith and moment—they are too childish, we would hope, either to mislead the beholder, or corrupt the possessor.

It is not civil distinctions, but the nuisance of civil usurpations the just and enlightened wish to see abated. An aristocracy of office, of acquirement, and desert, is a natural aristocracy; but an aristocracy of birth is a feudal barbarism which honours the shadow in place of the substance, and dissevers merit from its just reward. Hereditary right to property we can comprehend, but hereditary right to be legislators, bishops, post-captains, military commanders, and secretaries of state, shocks common sense. One is a private immunity, transmissible from father to son; the other are public functions, which can never be alienated to any order of men; they belong to the living, and cannot be bequeathed and regulated by the dead; they are adjuncts to the present not to a past generation.

The claims of property are so self-evident, and have formed, in all ages and in all places, (Sparta alone perhaps excepted,) so inseparable an adjunct to the social state, that one would have thought their utility would never have been called in question. Yet it is a fact—and it has not escaped the observant attention of the Editor of the *Morning Chronicle*—that there are many in both France and England who dispute the advantages of so old fashioned an institution. The followers of St. Simon and Mr. Owen are deeply impressed with the evils resulting from the individual or competitive system, and to escape them would fly to remedies by which they would be augmented a hundred fold. Crime, penury, and ignorance exist to a frightful extent; they have always existed—but evils which are now partial would, under the proposed " New State of Society," become universal. Without the stimulus of property there could be no industry—no eminence moral or intellectual. Who would sedulously devote themselves to the useful arts, to agriculture, manufacture, medicine, or navigation, if superior application, superior enterprize, or superior endowments were not rewarded?

For competition Mr. Owen would substitute *co-operation*. But do not the several classes of society already co-operate to the common advantage of all? One class is occupied in rural industry, another in manufactures and commerce, another in science and letters. Each is rewarded—not always perhaps, but mostly—in proportion to desert: but the claims of merit would not be recognized under Mr. Owen's system; the indolent would reap the rewards of the industrious, the vicious of the more deserving. This is not co-operation, it is *corporation*, the principle of the old monastic institutions and commercial monopolies—associations of whose stagnating, debasing, and injurious tendency the world has already had sufficient experience.

We always respect the motives of men whom we see constantly devoting their means and energies to the good of mankind, and should, therefore, regret to utter any thing harshly of Robert Owen. There is at all events no *imposture* about him: his propositions are brought openly forward, and he challenges inquiry and discussion : submitted to such a test, good may result from them, but they cannot possibly be productive of lasting evil. There is one suggestion we cannot help offering to this gentleman,—namely, that if he were to aim at *less*, he would accomplish *more*. The idea of abrogating the empire of the laws, of abolishing the right of property, and of resolving old communities into little bartering co-operative societies, are projects too wild and puerile to be thought of a moment. But, if in lieu of these, Mr. Owen would endeavour to improve the system of education throughout the country by impressing on parents and teachers, more strongly than it now is, the vast influence of external circumstances in the formation of the juvenile character, some good might result from his zealous exertions.

We have thought it advisable to preface this section, by glancing at some of the novel opinions abroad on a delicate subject, lest our present purpose might be misconstrued.

Our intention is to say something of the *possessions* of the Aristocracy, and we were apprehensive lest it might be imagined we meditated spoliation, or beheld, with jealous eye, the magnitude of their acres and rental. All such constructions we disclaim. It is nothing to us, nor is it much to the public, that the marquis of Stafford has £360,000 per annum ; the duke of Northumberland, £300,000 ; the duke of Buccleugh, £250,000 ; and that there are other dukes and marquesses with nearly as much. Such magnificent revenues are not enjoyed by noblemen alone. There are lords of the loom in Lancashire and Yorkshire who have accumulated incomes nearly as great, and, perhaps, not more humanely nor honourably. But, if such masses of wealth be evils, they are evils which would remedy themselves, were they not fostered and upheld by vicious legislation. Abolish the laws which consecrate these vast accumulations and minister to family pride and personal caprice, and the mere diversities in the characters of succeeding possessors would soon disintegrate the great properties.

It is neither the mansions nor parks of the peerage that excite popular cupidity; it is the hereditary monopoly—not by constitutional right, but usurpation—of the political franchises of the people which begets hostile feelings ; because it enables the privileged legislators to tax others and not themselves—to engross all public honours, offices, and emoluments—in a word, to make all the great social interests of a vast community, of which, in number, intellect, and even wealth, they constitute a most insignificant portion, subservient solely to the purposes of their own vanity, folly, indulgence, and aggrandizement. Here is the national grievance ; and let us inquire whether, from the adventitious circumstance of property, they have any claim to inflict this great wrong on society.

The most authentic data for ascertaining the distribution of the property and revenue of the different classes of society are the returns under the property-tax. But it is to be observed that these returns only include the annual value of property liable to the tax, and, consequently, do not exhibit the annual value of the smaller incomes, nor the amount of that great mass of revenue accruing from the wages of labour. Bearing this in mind, we shall submit a statement of the annual income arising from property, professions, public annuities, profits in trade, pensions, and offices : and the amount of the gross assessments on the several descriptions of revenue arising from the different sources of income. The return is for the year ending April 5th, 1815—the last of the income-tax—and is abstracted from the Parliamentary Paper, No. 59, Session 1823. We have omitted shillings and pence, which make some trifling inaccuracies in the totals, and, to render the statement more intelligible, have added the titles of the schedules and rate of assessment from the 48 Geo. III. c. 65. The rise in the value of the currency has probably depressed the nominal amount of incomes below the contemporary increase in produce and industry; but, as this change affected all classes alike, with the exception of annuitants and those enjoying fixed money payments, it has not materially altered the relative *proportions of revenue*, as exhibited by the returns of 1815, possessed by the different divisions of the community. Here follows the statement:—

	Schedules.	Annual Value.	Gross Assessments.
(A.)	—Lands, tenements, and hereditaments, for every 20*s.* of the annual value 2*s.*	60,138,330	5,923,486
(B.)	—Occupiers of lands, dwelling-houses, and tenements, 1*s.* 6*d.* ; Scotland, 1*s.*	38,396,143	2,734,450
(C.)	—Annuities and dividends arising out of any public revenues, 2*s.*	28,855,050	2,885,505
(D.)	—Increase and profits from professions, trade, or vocations, 2*s.*	38,310,935	3,831,088
(E.)	—Public offices, pensions, and stipends, 1*s.* 6*d.*	11,744,557	1,174,445
	Total	£177,451,015	£16,548,984

The most important item for our purpose is the property charged in schedule A. consisting of lands and tenements which were assessed on the rack rents, and profits from mines and quarries. Under this head the assessment charged on land, houses, mines, &c. appears, from the parliamentary return, to which reference has been made, to have been as follows:—

	£
Lands chargeable under the general rule	39,405,705
Houses so chargeable	16,250,399
Particular properties chargeable on the annual profits, viz. tithes, manors, fines, quarries, mines, iron works, and non-enumerated profits	4,473,224
	£60,138,330

From this it appears that the entire rental returned in the last year of the property-tax was £39,405,705, and which has been reduced since the peace, in the opinion of Mr. Lowe, to twenty-five millions. Now the question is, what portion of this rental is received by the four hundred and eighteen members of the *House of Peers*. The Scotch and Irish peers, to the number of one hundred and eighty, who only sit in the Upper House, by their representatives, we exclude from consideration; the object being to get at the incomes of those who exercise the political power of the empire. For this purpose it will be necessary to analyze the component parts of the landed interests, and separate the peers from those who share with them the territorial revenues of the kingdom.

The number of baronets is 658, and many of them enjoy landed incomes as great or greater than lords. Then there is the *squirearchy*, more numerous than Pharoah's host, who draw freely from the surplus produce of the soil. To these must be added the great loan-contractors, merchants, manufacturers, and others, appertaining to the monied, mercantile, and trading classes, many of whom possess extensive estates, and who rival, and, in part, have superseded the ancient nobility. Dr. Colquhoun supposed the gentry, and the classes we have enumerated, as enjoying large incomes, to amount to 46,861, and their incomes, from land and other sources, to amount to £53,022,110. Besides which, allowance must be made for the estates of the younger children of noble families, and for lands appertaining to lay and ecclesiastical corporations, and to charitable foundations. From all these considerations we should conclude that the rental of peers, sitting in parliament, does not exceed *three millions per annum.* Some of the members of the Upper House, we are aware, enjoy vast revenues, but the average income of each, from the soil, does not exceed £7,177.

Mr. Hallam says the richest of the English aristocracy derive their possessions from the spoils of the Reformation. He ought, also, to have added the spoils of the crown-lands, for they have helped themselves freely to the possessions of both church and king, as well as the people. The Bentinck, the Pelham, and other families inherit vast properties from leases and alienations of the royal domains. The houses of Cavendish and Russell, it is well known, made their acquisitions at the Reformation. The foundation of the Fitzwilliam estates was advantageous purchases at the same era. The Lonsdales have dug out their wealth from coal mines. The Buccleugh property has been an accumulation from heiresses, including here in England the possessions of the duke of Montague. The Gower estates have, also, mainly come by marriages; but the grand augmentation was by the canal-property of the late duke of Bridgewater, to which are now to be added the Sutherland estates of the present marchioness—a principality in themselves. The Grosvenor riches came mainly from an heiress, who brought, in marriage, the London building land about two generations back. The Northumberland estates are, principally, the old feudal inheritance of the Percys. In the whole peerage there are only eighteen commercial families, and these form the only houses which can be said to have acquired their wealth by habits of peaceful and honest industry.

Granting, then, that by means of marriages, and other favourable circumstances, some few of the nobility have accumulated vast revenues, still there are others whose poverty is notorious, and, altogether, they do not enjoy a landed revenue exceeding three millions per annum. What right, then, it may be inquired, have an Oligarchy of 418 persons, possessing so small a share in the general wealth of the community, to monopolize political power. Three millions per annum is not one-hundredth part of the annual revenue of the kingdom.* Yet, to a body of men, having so diminutive a stake in the general weal, are confided the destinies of the empire.

The revenues derived by the peerage from the taxes and church revenues have been estimated to amount to £2,825,846 per annum, being nearly equal to their territorial revenue. This vast addition to their legitimate income they have been able to acquire from having usurped the franchises of the people. Whether the sum they draw from the church estates and the public is more or less, it is not our present purpose to investigate. Our object has been to demonstrate that the wealth of the peerage, of which they can justly claim the possession, is insignificant, when compared with the entire wealth of the country; and that the aristocracy, by direct or indirect means, exercising the political power of the state, the government, as at present constituted, neither represents the number, intellect, nor property of the community. The two former propositions have been often demonstrated, but the latter was a desideratum in general information.

There is another mode of viewing the distribution of the revenues of society, which it will, perhaps, not be unpleasing to our readers, if we submit to their consideration. The whole social fabric rests upon the industrious orders, and, we believe, they are only imperfectly acquainted with the magnitude of their power and resources. The late Dr. Colquhoun, who was a bold, but, as experience has proved, a very shrewd calculator, formed an estimate of the number and income of the different classes into which the community is divided. From the data exhibited by this gentleman, in his "Treatise on the Resources of the British Empire," we have drawn up a statement which will afford a curious insight into the subject about which we are occupied. It is hardly necessary to remark that the Doctor's conjecture of the incomes of the clergy is greatly below the truth. Indeed, it is to be observed that all statistical tables, drawn up prior to the restoration of a metallic currency, are chiefly useful in showing *proportions*, and do not express the present numerical value of either income or property.

---

* Lowe's Present State of England, App. p. 65.

Different Classes of Society, and their respective Incomes.

DESCRIPTION OF PERSONS,	Number of Persons, including their Families and Domestics.	Total Income of each class.
Royalty	300	£ 501,000
Nobility	13,620	5,400,000
Gentry, including baronets, knights, country gentlemen, and others having *large* incomes	402,535	53,022,590
Clergy :—Eminent clergymen	9000	1,080,000
Lesser ditto	87,000	3,500,000
Dissenting clergy, including itinerant preachers	20,000	500,000
State and Revenue, including all persons employed under government	114,500	6,830,000
Pensioners, including those of Greenwich, Chelsea, and Kilmainham Hospitals	92,000	1,050,000
Law :—Judges, barristers, attorneys, clerks, &c.......................	95,000	7,600,000
Physic :—Physicians, surgeons, apothecaries, &c....................	90,000	5,400,000
Agriculture :—Freeholders of the better sort	385,000	19,250,000
Lesser Freholders	1,050,000	21,000,000
Farmers	1,540,000	33,600,000
Trade:—Eminent merchants	35,000	9,100,000
Shopkeepers, and tradesmen retailing goods	700,000	28,000,000
Innkeepers and publicans, licensed to sell ale, beer, and spirituous liquors	437,000	8,750,000
Working Classes :—Agricultural labourers, mechanics, artizans, handicrafts, and all labourers employed in manufactures, mines, and minerals	7,497,531	82,451,547
Paupers, vagrants, gipsies, rogues, vagabonds, and others supported by criminal delinquency	1,548,500	9,871,000

The preceding statement affords room for curious and important inferences. The industrious orders may be compared to the soil, out of which every thing is evolved and produced ; the other classes to the trees, tares, weeds, flowers, and vegetables, drawing their nutriment, supported and maintained on its surface. Leaving out of consideration the professions of medicine, law and religion, and the unproductive or ornamental parts of society, let us attend to the number and incomes of the following orders:—

	Numbers.	Incomes.
Freeholders of the better sort	385,000	£19,250,000
Lesser freeholders	1,050,000	21,000,000
Farmers........................	1,540,000	33,600,000
Eminent merchants	35,000	9,100,000
Shopkeepers.....................	700,000	28,000,000
Innkeepers and publicans........	437,000	8,750,000
WORKING CLASSES	7,497,531	82,451,547

These may be considered the active machinery—the solid substratum —upon which the social pyramid is based. When mankind attain a state of perfectibility; when vice, crime, and ignorance are more circumscribed; when we shall seldom require physic to cure diseases, laws to punish offences, or the terrors of superstition to deter from evil; these will be the chief classes in existence. They are the chief classes which ought to exist in a perfect state. The other classes have mostly originated in our vices and ignorance. As mankind become more perfect, or, which is the same thing, as knowledge is more extensively diffused, then will the honorary, legal, medicinal, and ecclesiastical classes disappear: having no employment, their name and office will cease in the social state.

It is from the useful classes the public revenue, for the maintenance of the army, navy, and general government is chiefly extracted. We have before shown the iniquitous principle on which our fiscal regulations have been framed, owing to the political ascendancy of the Aristocracy. Nearly all our taxes are taxes on the ordinary transactions of business, or on the ordinary articles of consumption; and press on the industrious like an inquisitorial and remorseless income-tax, levied without distinction of small or large revenues. It has been the gradual working of this oppressive system that has mainly produced the revolting extremes now observable in the condition of different classes of the community, that has enabled one class to riot in profusion and the wanton enjoyment of redundant incomes, while others have been steeped in indigence, subjected to unceasing and unrequited toil, and barely able to procure the commonest necessaries. That this is not assertion merely, we will demonstrate by an appeal to facts; we will show that the imposts, which constitute almost the entire revenue, are chiefly levied on the property, avocations, and consumption of the working and mercantile orders of the community. The produce of the customs and post-office is usually referred to as an exponent of commercial activity; that of the excise as the index of internal comfort and enjoyment—and for this reason; that the last, which constitutes considerably more than one-third of the public income, is chiefly contributed by the great body of the people.

Statement of the Gross Produce of Taxes for the Year ending 5th January, 1831, *chiefly paid by the Industrious Classes.*—Annual Finance Accounts, Session 1831.

Windows	£1,185,478	8	4½
Inhabited houses	1,361,825	0	5¼
Probates of wills and letters of Administration	903,938	10	0
Legacies	1,223,260	11	6
Bills of exchange	458,511	8	6
Bankers' notes, including compositions for duties thereon	110,647	3	8
Receipts	220,960	16	10
Marine insurances	220,007	15	6
Fire insurances	768,855	6	9
Stage coaches	418,604	9	6½
Post-office	2,053,720	11	2¼
Tea	3,387,097	13	9½
* Coffee	579,844	19	7
Sugar (exclusive of drawbacks)	4,776,568	0	0
Malt	3,505,453	14	7
Hops	121,451	8	1½
Beer (duty ceased October 10th, 1830)	2,390,310	18	4¼
Spirits (British)	3,708,713	0	6¼
Spirits (Foreign)	4,081,281	11	3
Licenses	737,497	11	0½
Soap	1,513,149	19	9¼
Butter	102,881	18	10
Cheese	55,093	12	9
Corn, grain, meal, and flour	798,082	6	7
Eggs, bacon, and hams	20,700	14	0
Tallow	180,947	0	0
Tobacco and snuff	2,938,050	10	10
Wines of all sorts	1,575,438	6	9
Coals and culm, carried coastwise, (duty ceased March 1, 1831)	979,197	5	6

Total......£40,337,574 19 7½

Thus on the gross receipt of revenue for Great Britain of £54,995,262, the sum of £40,337,574, is levied either wholly or very disproportionately on the necessaries of the industrious orders, and does not touch the luxuries of the great, unless the articles of wines, snuff, and tobacco can be considered such. The duties on wills and legacies, on bills, notes and receipts, on fire and marine insurances, on postage and stage coaches, fall heavily on the mercantile and manufacturing classes. The taxes on articles of daily use and consumption operate, as before observed, like an undiscriminating income-tax, augmenting in the exact ratio of every individual's unavoidable expenditure. This monstrous state of our fiscal system is solely owing to non-representation, and consequent monopoly

---

* The custom duties are for the United Kingdom ; the duties of excise, taxes, and stamps are for Great Britain only.

of political power by the Aristocracy, which has enabled them to throw the public burthens on the productive classes. Those who are the chief source of the wealth of the community, and who defray the charges of the general government, have had no efficient control over its administration ; nay, have often not been treated with ordinary courtesy, and by an usurping Oligarchy the inferior orders have been considered little better than an ignorant rabble !

> " How various and innumerable
> Are those who live upon the rabble !
> 'Tis they maintain the Church and State,
> Employ the priest and magistrate ;
> Bear all the charge of government,
> And pay the public fines and rent,
> Defray all taxes and excises,
> And impositions of all prices ;
> Bear all the expense of peace and war,
> And pay the pulpit and the bar ;
> Maintain all churches and religions,
> And give their pastors exhibitions !"

The aristocratic privilege of an exclusive right to impose taxes, and comparative exemption from their pressure, is strikingly evinced in the present partial mode of rating to the *inhabited house duty*, the splendid seats of the nobility and gentry. In Chester, which contains many residences of a very high class, there is but one mansion, (Eaton, we believe,) assessed so high as £300 a-year. That magnificent palace would be under-assessed probably at £10,000. In Westmoreland, which contains Lowther Castle, as fine a place or nearly so as Eaton, there is not one house assessed so high as £200. In Durham, which contains Raby Castle, and Lambton Castle, and Wynyard, and Ravensworth, and Brancepeth Castles—to say nothing of other mansions—the two first we believe, nearly equal to either of those before mentioned—there is not a *single house* assessed so high as £100, and but two above £70 per annum, which last is about the rate of assessment of our friend Loudon in his little cottage at Bayswater. In the rich and fine county of Hereford, containing Eastnor Castle, there is not a single house assessed so high as £90 per annum, and but three at or above £70. In Leicestershire, which contains Belvoir Castle, there is not an assessment so high as £200 per annum. In Northamptonshire, containing Althorp and various other fine seats, there is but one house rated so high as £110 per annum. In Northumberland, which contains Alnwick Castle, there are but two assessments of £200 and upwards. In Oxfordshire, which contains the stately and far-famed Blenheim, there is but one assessment so high as £300. Lastly in Yorkshire, which contains Wentworth Castle, and Harewood House, and Castle Howard, to say nothing of other numerous and splendid seats, there is not a single house assessed so high as £400 per annum, and but four so high as £300.

Compare these assessments of the Aristocracy with the sums levied on the Shopocracy, as the middle orders have been termed, in the metropolis and manufacturing towns, and we shall find additional reasons for the political representation of all interests in the great council of the nation.

VI. INCREASE OF THE PEERAGE.

The members of the Upper House, succeeding to legislative functions by hereditary right, are exempt from the salutary influence which controls the deliberations of a representative assembly. Their interests are purely oligarchical, and severed from the general interests of the community. It cannot, therefore, excite surprise that any augmentation in a body of exclusives like this—separated from the mass of society by education, by family pride, by privilege, and usurped power — should be viewed with dislike and apprehension.

Other reasons render an increase in the aristocratic branch of parliament inimical to general feeling. It has been ascertained that the nobility afford a striking illustration of Mr. MALTHUS's theory of population.* Possessing, in abundance, the comforts and conveniences of life, they are placed in those circumstances most favourable to a full development of the procreative principle, and it is a singular confirmation of the doctrine of the enlightened writer that noble families are actually as prolific as those of the United States of America. Peers are mostly marrying men. After visiting the European capitals, and committing a few follies and eccentricities, they usually settle down at about twenty-five or twenty-eight years of age, and the results, on the average, are a progeny of five children, or about twenty-five per cent. more than other people. The eldest inheriting the estate, the rest would be destitute, were not the parents, by means of their vote and borough-interest, able to quarter them on the public. Hence it is the people contemplate, with feelings corresponding to those entertained by an Irish absentee who sees the increase of his cotter tenantry, any unavoidable addition to the peerage ; knowing that, in consequence of primogeniture and entail-laws, another family will be thrown upon them for support, and that their own chance of honourable promotion in the army, navy, civil departments, or other branch of national service, is impeded by new rivals, with whom exists no prospect of equitable competition.

Having explained one or two of the popular objections to an increase of the peerage, we shall briefly notice the extraordinary augmentation it has undergone during the reigns of George III. and George IV.

A creation of peers generally takes place on the accession of a new family, the commencement of a new reign, or when some political measure is to be carried. On the death of Elizabeth, the peers only amounted to fifty-six. James, being the first of a new dynasty, raised the number to one hundred and five ; and Charles I. to one hundred and thirty-five; Charles II. created fifteen dukes, (six of whom were his natural children,) one marquess, thirty-seven earls, three countesses, two viscounts, and twenty-nine barons. At the Revolution of 1688, William III. to ingratiate himself with the great families, raised eight

---

* Edinburgh Review, No. 162, p. 316.

powerful earls to dukedoms ; created eighteen earls, three viscounts, and nine barons. Anne increased the peerage to one hundred and seventy. The accession of the Hanover family rendered new creations necessary : George I. either created or elevated no fewer than forty-nine peers. George II. left one hundred and eighty-four. It is evident that the great increase of the peerage was in the reign of George III. being more than doubled. In 1777 a batch of peers was drafted from the Commons to the Lords, to effect a ministerial majority. This expedient was frequently resorted to by Mr. Pitt. In 1797 ten peers were made. He nearly created the order of marquesses : he made ten marquesses in England where there was but one, and nine in Ireland where there was none—all men eminent, of course, for their *services*. Knighthood was still more profusely lavished. In short, he was as prodigal in wasting the honours of the Crown as the money of the people, and for a similar purpose.

The peers created during the reign of George III. have been classified as follows :—

Landed commoners	46
Irish peers	56
Scotch peers	24
Law	25
State	25
Army	13
Navy	10
Younger sons and younger branches of peers	17
Renewals	7
Confirmations	7
Peeresses	5
	235
Extinctions	74
Addition	161*

George IV. added 64 members to the Upper House.† In this number are included individuals who have been raised to the peerage, or in whose favour an abeyance has been terminated, as well as peers of Scotland and Ireland who have obtained English baronies. No notice, however, is taken of Scotch peerages which have been recently restored, nor of the creations of peers of Ireland ; of claims to English peerages which have been admitted, nor of elevations of English peerages to higher honours. The average rate at which peers have been created during the last two reigns has been about four per annum ; and was the same rate of increase to continue for the next century, it would double the existing number of parliamentary lords.

Toryism being the ascendant school of politics during the last reigns, the character of the peers created was of course determined by that of the minister from whom the honours were obtained. The effect of this

* Quarterly Review, No. 84, p. 314.
† Letter to the Duke of Wellington on creating Peers for Life.

was strikingly evinced on the first introduction of the Reform Bill into the House of Lords. Of the *old* peers of the United Kingdom, there was a majority of two *for* the second reading of the bill. Of the *new* peers of the United Kingdom created subsequent to 1792, the majority was *against* the second reading of the bill, and their number was only balanced by the creations under the Whig ministry. The subject will be made clear from the following statement copied from a recent publication.*

	Voted against the Bill.	Voted for the Bill.
Peers of the United Kingdom created previously to the end of 1792..........................	79	81
Peers of the United Kingdom created subsequently to 1792 (including the creations during the administration of Earl Grey)............	66	66
Archbishops and Bishops....................	21	2
Representative Peers for Scotland	12	4
Representative Peers for Ireland	19	4
Royal Dukes	2	1
	199	158

It thus appears that of 54 votes against the bill there were 43 which were the votes of—

21 Bishops against 2 ; being above 10 to 1.
12 Scotch peers against 4 ; being 3 to 1.
19 Irish against 4; being nearly 5 to 1.

The inference from which representation is that the bill was defeated in 1831 by the bishops, and the Irish and Scotch peers, who had obtained their promotions or been elected under Tory influence.

The necessity of an augmentation of the peerage to balance the anti-reform interest created subsequent to 1792, became manifest ; it was not only essential to strengthen the ministry and carry the bill, but also to effect those ulterior improvements in public administration of which this great national measure is justly considered the parent.

The abolition of an hereditary peerage in France cannot fail to have the greatest influence on the future status of the ' order,' and will probably lead to the abolition of an institution in other countries so little consonant to the existing state of society. Because one man is a great lawyer, statesman, or commander, it is no pledge that his lineal descendant will be gifted with the same endowments as those which entitled his progenitor to the exercise of legislative functions. A senate, or upper chamber for life, consisting of individuals eminent for wisdom, experience, or national services, is a defensible institution; but to make them hereditary, and erect legislators into a *caste*, is quite as preposterous as to make the functions of the astronomer royal heredi-

---

* Letter to Earl Grey on the Adjustment of the House of Peers.

tary, or the colleges of surgeons and apothecaries. Such manifest irrationalities must speedily disappear from European communities.

VII. SOURCES OF ARISTOCRATIC MONOPOLY.

The magnitude of the territorial revenues of the Aristocracy is not such as to be in extreme disproportion with the incomes of many others in a community of great commercial opulence, and forms not any portion of the vice of their institution. Whether some noble lords have augmented their rental out of the spoils of the Church and the Crown is a question merely of historical curiosity, and can never be of any practical utility: it is occasionally adverted to as a set-off to oligarchical pride and pretension; beyond which it has no available application. By the law of England, the quiet possession of an estate for *sixty years* gives a clear and valid title; and we believe there are few noblemen who cannot adduce legal proof of the undisturbed enjoyment of their parks and mansions for a much longer period. So far, then, as the *acres* are concerned they are perfectly safe; whatever political changes may intervene—and great ones are impending—the legitimate incomes of the peerage can never be endangered, unless they blindly and pertinaciously oppose a regeneration which the wants of the age render indispensable; unless they emulate, in fatuity and crime, CHARLES CAPET and his guilty accomplices.

Aristocratic monopoly and abuse do not result from enormous landed revenues, but from hereditary rights of legislation, from primogeniture and entail-laws, and from nomination boroughs. None of these, however, are essential constituents of an upper chamber; only two-thirds of the nobility are entitled, by birth, to seats in parliament; primogeniture and entails are feudal barbarisms void of utility in modern society; and the usurpation of the franchises of the people is such a manifest subversion of constitutional immunities, so inimical to the general freedom and prosperity, that it cannot be defended on any pretext of justice or expediency. Abolish these corruptions, and all things will work together for good, without spoliation, without civil convulsion; and the Devonshires, the Lansdownes, and Northumberlands enjoy, undisturbed, their wide-spread domains, and retain, without murmur or complaint, their social distinction and supremacy.

The great fount of evil has been the decayed boroughs; these have been the Pandora's box, from which have flowed national calamities, desolating wars, lavish expenditure, and the monstrous debt and dead weight. They have been the obstacles to every social melioration— civil, commercial, legal, and ecclesiastical. By means of them, the nobility have been enabled to double their private revenues, appropriating to themselves the dignities and livings of the church; pensions and grants out of the public purse; and filling, with their connexions and dependants, every lucrative office in the army, navy, and public administration. There are only two descriptions of offices, namely, those requiring talent and industry, the duties of which cannot be discharged by deputy, that the boroughmongers have denied themselves.

Unfit for the higher stations in courts of law, they have condescended to fill the profitable situations of clerk, registrar, messenger, usher, or receiver, and carry bags and wands in the trains of those whose ability alone made them their superiors, and to whom they were compelled to pay this homage as a penalty for their own indolence and cupidity.

In consequence of the boroughs, all our institutions are partial, oppressive, and aristocratic. We have an aristocratic church, aristocratic bar, aristocratic taxation, aristocratic corn-laws, aristocratic laws of property, and, till recently, aristocratic game-laws; in short, the aristocratic spirit pervades every thing—all is privilege, prescription, monopoly, association, and corporation. But why, it may be asked, has it so long continued,—why did not a wealthy, spirited, and enlightened community exert itself long before to abate the general oppression? The chief reason was this—we had also an ARISTOCRATIC PRESS! By this little key-stone was the entire Gothic arch of antiquated abuse and imposture upheld.

How has it happened the Aristocracy have been so extremely sulky in regard to the memorable events of July 1830; that they have kept their purse-strings so tight; that they kept aloof from all participation in the general exultation? Did they consider, as Napoleon did, that " a revolution in France is a revolution in Europe?" This second national uprising, however, was attended with no popular massacre, no confiscation, no obtrusion of infidelity; all was brave, wise, and moderate —merely a great community rising, with one accord, to defeat an insane attempt to subject it to the yoke of despotism and superstition. Yet they sent forth no *carmen triumphale* on the sublime occasion. Is it possible that they contemplated, at a distance, the mighty swell which was to submerge their own proud pretensions? If it were so, does it not show that their interests are personal; that they are not in common with the people; that they are merely a corporation in the state, and that they feel their corporate immunities imperilled? But what is it which renders them insulated monopolists—strangers in the land? It is not the magnitude of their estates, for they are not objects of popular concern. No; it is not what they rightfully possess, but what they have surreptitiously obtained—the franchises of the people, and the money of the people, which make them fastidious and apprehensive. Be just and fear not, is our advice, and they are still safe !

LAW

AND

COURTS OF LAW.

THE independence of the judges has so long formed a current theme of praise, that it appears almost presumptuous to call it in question. Yet the difference between them and other functionaries is not so apparent as is generally assumed. It is true, the judges hold their situations for life, unless guilty of some flagrant impropriety; but the same may be said of other appointments under the Crown, the possessors of which are seldom disturbed, so long as they correctly discharge their duties; or if they are, they invariably receive a superannuation allowance, or compensation, equivalent to the loss they have sustained. As respects, then, the tenure of office, the sages of the law cannot arrogate a great pre-eminence over other placemen: as respects those causes which ordinarily influence individual conduct—the lure of ambition— the temptation of lucre—and the seduction of indolence—they have still less to pride themselves. A judge, like a bishop, may be *translated* from a lower to a higher dignity—from a judgeship to a chief-justiceship, from that to a peerage or a seat in the cabinet; he may be removed from an office of £5,500 per annum to one of £10,000, and boundless patronage: he may be taken from a court where he is overwhelmed with the claims of duty, to one where the most important duty he has to discharge is to receive his salary. How then can it be alleged the judges are independent and exempt from ministerial influence, when the ministers have similar alluring temptations to hold out to the bench as other functionaries, and similar means of rewarding subserviency?

Other causes operate unfavourably on judicial appointments. Instead of the individuals elevated to the bench being a selection from the entire Bar, of men the most distinguished for ability, probity, and experience, the choice of the ministry is limited to men of their own party. A Tory minister never chooses a Whig judge; nor the contrary. This tends to lower the character of the judges in public estimation, by clearly evincing that politics, as well as legal fitness, have a share in ministerial promotions. It also instils into the minds of both expectant judges, and of men already on the bench, a party feeling fatal to strict justice on political questions. So well established is this fact, lord Brougham has remarked that it is notorious, whenever a question comes before the tribunals, whether it be upon a prosecution for libel, or upon any other matter connected with government, the council, at their meetings, take for granted that they can tell pretty accurately the leaning of the court, and predict exactly which way the consultations of the judges will terminate. It is very unfortunate the judges should be always on the ministerial side of politics; but there is no help for this, while they continue to be selected on the exclusive principle. They have their opinions on public questions as well as other men; they know they fill a certain situation, and they cannot forget by whom they were placed there, or for what reason.

With these remarks we shall leave the venerable occupiers of the Bench, on whom we had no intention of offering any observation; but in some way their situation obtruded itself on our notice, on first entering on the consideration of the important subject of this chapter. We shall now proceed briefly to notice the more prominent abuses in the laws and their administration.

The whole body of English Law is divided into two kinds—the Common and the Statute Law. The Common Law is founded entirely on custom or precedent, and the decisions in the courts of justice. It is not founded on Acts of Parliament, nor on legislative enactments; it is recorded in no public document; the only memorials of its existence are to be found in traditional maxims, records of pleas, books of reports, or the treatises of men eminent in the profession. It is evident that laws originating and preserved in this manner, must be vague, obscure, often absurd, and even contradictory. The Common Law is, in fact, a monument of the opinions, errors, knowledge, and ignorance of every period of society; it has flowed down the stream of time, accumulating like a mighty river, and carrying along vestiges of the learning and ignorance, folly and wisdom, of every age through which it has passed.

How unworthy such an incongruous mass must be of the present age; how inapplicable to the usages of society; and how difficult it is for any individual to obtain a knowledge of such an *onus camelorum*, it is unnecessary to describe. Unsuitable as such a system of law is, to fulfil the ends for which all laws were originally intended, it forms a very considerable part of the laws of this country. It is in virtue of the common law that the eldest son inherits from his father; that property may be purchased and transferred by writing; that a deed is void if not sealed and delivered; that money lent upon bond is recoverable by action of debt; and that a breach of the peace is punishable with fine and imprisonment. These are doctrines not established by any written statute or any legislative enactment, but depend solely upon immemorial usage.

So much for the Common or Unwritten Law; next for the Statute-Law, which exhibits a still more frightful chaos. Statute-Law consists of all those acts, edicts, and statutes, made by the king, with the consent of the lords and commons in parliament assembled. The oldest of these now extant, and printed in the statute-books, is *Magna Charta*, as confirmed in parliament by 9 Hen. III. There were doubtless many acts before that time, the records of which are now lost; and which most probably were the foundation of some of the maxims in the old Common Law.

No man‘in England professes to be acquainted with the Statute-Law —not even the Lord Chancellor nor the Lord Chief Justice. It is such a prodigious compilation, that a knowledge of it is wholly unattainable. No one knows exactly what is law in England; though every individual is presumed to be acquainted with it, and ignorance is admitted as no excuse for its violation. Any one may become a legislator for the whole country; he has nothing to do but to turn to the statute-book; he will there find laws in abundance, of which no man has any knowledge; he may adduce them as the law of the land; he cannot be contradicted, unless some subsequent statute can be found by which it is repealed, and which it would probably require a year's labour to discover. In some respects the statute-book may be compared to the scriptures. It contains many good maxims and excellent precepts; but, as a whole, it is contradictory, obscure, and inapplicable to the age. What one part affirms, another part denies. Laws may be adduced from it, like texts from the Bible, proving any thing and every thing, adapted to all times, principles, and occasions: one affords profitable employment for one hundred thousand wrangling lawyers; the other profitable employment for as many polemical divines: one is termed the perfection of human wisdom; the other a bright emanation from the Deity!

How ignorant the most eminent in the profession are on the subject we may gather from a speech of the late Lord Stanhope, on the revision of the Statute-Book. Some of the most striking facts mentioned by his lordship we will here insert. Conformably with a motion of his lordship, the judges were directed to prepare a bill, reducing into one act all the acts imposing the punishment of pillory. At the end of the bill the judges inserted some observations, stating that pillory was the punishment for some offences not merely by statute but at common law; and also they could not say whether there might *not be statutes on the subject which had escaped their attention.* Their surmise was just; for Lord Stanhope afterwards discovered two more statutes, passed in the reign of Geo. II. which had wholly escaped their researches. Here then was an instance of the twelve judges not being able to discover all the acts inflicting a single punishment.

The same noble lord, wishing to ascertain how far the judges were agreed as to what was the law on several particulars, put to them various questions. For instance, he asked whether a person digging the brick earth from his own field, there manufactured into bricks, and sold, thereby made himself a trader liable to the bankrupt-laws? The judges of the Common Pleas were clearly of opinion one way, the judges of the King's Bench were as clearly of opinion another. Lord Thurlow was reputed a most admirable common lawyer; but he was worsted on one occasion, in a dispute which he had with Lord Stanhope, on the subject of a statute; Lord Stanhope proving to be right, and old Thrumbo wrong. This, says Lord Stanhope, was a great feather in my cap. One day as these noble lords were sitting together on the wool-sack, Lord Thurlow said, " I should be ashamed of myself if I was not accurately acquainted with the common law; but as to your d—d statute-book it is impossible to be acquainted with it." His. lordship also related another anecdote of the celebrated Mr. Dunning, afterwards Lord Ashburton. Lord Stanhope consulted Mr. Dunning on a certain statute regulation relative to the excise, and his answer was, " Now I'll tell you all about it; but I never do answer these general questions when applied to by others. I always tell them, shew me the statute to which you refer, and I will *expound* it for you, but that is all I can do." Now this was doing about as much as we could do ourselves, or as much as any person could do who has a tolerably clear head, and not much disturbed by worldly affairs.

The fact is, the lawyers and judges, in many cases, are as ignorant of the law as their clients and suitors. When a statute is produced, they can *expound* it, as Mr. Dunning terms it; so perhaps may any person who can read and understand the English language; but as to knowing whether it is the law of the land, whether it has been repealed or modified by any subsequent enactment, they are frequently as ignorant as the gaping spectator who looks upon them as infallible and inspired guides. We do not, however, accuse them of wilful ignorance; we do not say that, like the Fellows of Eton College, they are *willingly* ignorant of the statutes; they are generally men of laborious pursuits, who spare no pains to obtain a knowledge of the law; but we accuse them of a culpable indifference to the defective state of the statute-book, of either by their silence or open, hostility opposing every attempt to reduce it into an intelligible form, originating either in a rooted prejudice against the reform of any thing and every thing, or solely from a wish to maintain the pecuniary interests of a multitudinous and rapacious profession.

When a legal question is brought before the courts, deviating in any degree from the ordinary routine, it is seldom decided instanter. The counsel open the case,—they, in fact, instruct the judges,—they refer to precedents and statutes, as they have been instructed by their attorneys, who have, perhaps, been instructed by their clients; the judges then say they will *take time to consider;* and after going home and moleing their way through a labyrinth of reports and acts of parliament, they obtain a twinkling of light, return into court, and adjudicate the subject in dispute to the best of their ability.

Such is the immense number of law-books and their ponderous size, that it would require the age of the patriarchs to acquire a knowledge of them. They are literally Ossa piled on Pelion, a huge unformed mass, which no man can fathom. There is a little *Aldine compilation,* Viner's Abridgement, comprised in twenty volumes folio, which it is considered necessary for every lawyer almost to know by heart. Gracious heaven! only think of that! Mind, too, this is a mere abridgement—

bare memoranda of the great originals; and had it been continued to the present time, it would have amounted to more than one hundred folio volumes, necessary to be carried either in the head or the pocket of every English lawyer. The most condensed edition of the Statutes at Large yet given to the public, occupies thirty-nine volumes in quarto; seven volumes and a half of which comprise the acts from Magna Charta to the end of the reign of George II., the remaining thirty-one and a half being filled with those of the two last reigns. Since the Union with Ireland, a huge closely printed volume has been published every one, two, or three years, and the average number of public acts passed in each of the last twenty-eight years amounts to one hundred and forty. It is calculated that at the end of the present century, the statutes will occupy one hundred ponderous quarto volumes, and the number of public acts will amount to fourteen thousand. The present generation complain of being overwhelmed with law, but what will be the situation of posterity?

We have said nothing yet of *Reports of Cases*. These form an indispensable part of a lawyer's knowledge. It is well known that decisions in courts of justice become a part of the law; and when a point has once been decided, it must be determined in the same way again, unless the precedent can be proved clearly erroneous. Reports of these decisions are published annually; they already amount to upwards of two hundred and eighty volumes, exclusive of those which relate to election, admiralty, and ecclesiastical law. But this is not all: they are going on increasing amazingly; every year adds eight more to the original stock; so that in twenty years there will be one hundred and sixty, and within the century seven hundred and twenty additional volumes, making one thousand volumes of reports, which, with one hundred quarto volumes of statutes, will form a lawyer's library, that it is not only necessary he should read, but digest, and, if possible, understand.

This is English law, the perfection of human wisdom! Let us, however, pause a moment, to reflect on this mass of legal lumber, this grossly absurd system of legislation. It is considered a settled maxim in jurisprudence, that every state within the limits of its own territory ought to exact, and its subjects to yield, obedience to all its laws. The foundation of the obligation on the part of the people is that the legislative authority on its part is presumed to have made the laws so CLEAR, that every member of the community either knows them or must be *culpably inattentive if he do not*. This principle is undeniable. It would never do to allow *ignorance* to be an excuse for the violation of laws. But how can any person be acquainted with English law? How can the legislature have gone on for centuries legislating on such an absurd presumption, and presuming that every individual in the empire was acquainted with their enactments? How can men of business read, digest, and understand one thousand volumes of reports, and one hundred quarto volumes of statutes? How can the people understand the law, when even the judges, whose whole lives are devoted to the subject, are in the most pitiable state of perplexity, uncertainty, and contradiction? Can any thing in the whole world be imagined more completely absurd and ridiculous? Had the whole system been blindly scraped together from every age, nation, and tribe in the universe, from the farthest extremity of Siberia to the remotest deserts of Garamantes, it could hardly have presented a more confused and hideous jumble than the Statute and Common Law of England.

One cause of this profuse, headlong, and inconsistent course of legislation has been the reckless facility with which parliament has multiplied laws oh a given subject, when a general enactment might have been framed adequate to the several occasions. Since the beginning of last century 4000 bills for enclosures of wastes in as many parishes have been passed, proving to demonstration the want of a general law on the subject; while, in the whole of that time, not a step has been taken towards enacting such a law, and so saving the community the prodigious waste of private funds and public time consumed in the passing of so many different statutes. The same observation applies to the innumerable acts passed for lighting towns with gas, and for the purposes of police and local improvements. Upwards of fifty acts have passed relative to game; forty-eight relative to parliamentary elections; and seventy-six indemnifying Dissenters for not qualifying themselves for offices and employments. There are many acts of a temporary and local nature. No fewer than sixty acts have passed for the recovery of small debts in different parts of the country, and fifty of them during the last two reigns. There are some acts relative to the baking of bread, and prohibiting the bakers from selling it unless it has been baked twenty-four hours. About the packing of butter there are somewhere about a dozen different acts; as though it were necessary to instruct people to pack butter by act of parliament. One act on this subject relates to the packing of butter at Malton, in Yorkshire; another to the packing of butter in the city of York, a few miles distant; and another on the same subject for Ireland. Innumerable laws have been enacted relative to the woollen, linen, and cotton manufactures; the whale, cod, herring, and pilchard fisheries; cheese, lace, sugar, glass, and almost every article of wear or consumption has been the object of parliamentary regulation. The whole of the statutes on wool amount to 987; on the subject of gold and silver 290; on tobacco 460; on the fisheries 970; and on a variety of other subjects in proportion. Relative to the poor there are 350 public acts; besides 135 local acts. By some of these acts the poor are farmed out, by others flogged. Of these local acts five passed in the reign of George II.; the remaining 130 in the reigns of George III. and George IV. Besides the number of acts, other causes of the confusion and perplexity of the Statute-Book arise from the immense number repealed and re-enacted, and then partly repealed again, with a "so far as," and "so forth;" also from the mass of altering, amending, and explaining acts; of acts, for instance, for "removing doubts," for "rectifying mistakes," for "relieving from the provisions," for "de-ferring the commencement," for " facilitating the execution,"—to say nothing of acts of total repeal. No fewer than 1874 acts were repealed in the reigns of George II. and III. ; 419 in the former; and 1455 in the reign of the latter ; which made Lord Stanhope remark, "they had been passing bills by waggon loads, and repealing them by cart loads."

Some efforts were made during the reign of George IV., under the auspices of Sir Robert Peel and the Marquis of Lansdowne, to reduce the Statute-Law within more reasonable limits. The parliament, dissolved in 1826, repealed, modified, or consolidated upwards of 1000 statutes. One act, the 3 Geo. IV. c. 41, repeals upwards of 200 statutes, or parts of statutes, relative to the export and import of merchandize ; the commerce of aliens and denizens, the guaging of wine, and other mercantile regulations. The Custom Act consolidated 450 acts of parliament into one ; the Jury Act 30 ; the Bankrupt Act 20 ; and the acts on larceny, malicious mischief, and forgery, have effected a considerable compression. From a table of repealed acts prefixed to Evan's *Collection of Statutes*, it appears that during the short interval from the 4th to the 10th of George IV., 1,126 acts of parliament were wholly, and 443 partly, repealed, making a total of 1569 : of these 1344 related to the empire at large, and 225 solely to Ireland. Still the evil is of such magnitude that there is scarcely perceptible diminution in its amount; nor do we anticipate—for reasons we shall hereafter explain—any decided improvements in jurisprudence, either from the consolidatory acts, or from the other projects of legal reform now in progress.

Nothing has tended so much to swell the Statute-Book as the enormous increase in taxation, and the consequent increase in the number of Revenue-Laws. During each of the last twenty-eight years, the number of acts passed, which relate strictly to the revenue, has amounted to forty ; and those which are connected with them indirectly, and but for them would never have existed, to nearly twenty more ; which comprises about half the whole number of laws annually enacted. The acts lately in force with regard to spirits alone amounted to 140 ; an attempt has been made to consolidate them, but as new acts are yearly being added, both as regards spirits and custom duties, the merchant and trader will soon be involved in as great a labyrinth as ever. The stamp-acts amount to more than 150, and they still remain unconsolidated. So do the innumerable acts relative to the coin. Soap, candles, and the distilleries are under excise lock and key ; and, in many instances of exciseable manufacture, it is impossible to carry on the different steps of the process with advantage, from the delay and interruption from the visits of the excise. What a bungling piece of legislation have been the attempts to regulate the malt-duties, hackney-coaches, and the vend of coals !

On the middling classes these laws are peculiarly oppressive ;—and yet they have been unceasingly told, that a *reform in parliament would do no good!* Would it not, we ask, relieve them from the vexatious inquisition and endless interruption and restraint on the operations of trade under which they now labour ? Would it not, in short, cause an entire revision of that cumbersome and absurd system of jurisprudence which we have attempted to describe;—reduce the Statute-Book to one-hundredth part of its present bulk ; consolidate the almost innumerable local acts into more general laws ; and abolish all those unjust and impolitic enactments which interfere with industry and commerce. Such numerous laws are no doubt useful to the profession ; they afford a fruitful and endless source of litigation ; they are *glorious* things, as Lord Stanhope remarked, for attorneys, conveyancers, special pleaders, barristers, and so forth, but most inglorious and calamitous for the people.

We shall only make one or two more remarks on Statute-Law, and these refer to the language and manner in which acts of parliament are drawn up. It is evident that all laws ought to be intelligible to those on whom they are intended to operate ; otherwise, it is wilfully creating an ignorance which will not be admitted as any excuse for their violation. It is difficult to see why laws could not be so clearly and simply worded as to be intelligible to ordinary capacities, without the assistance of either attorney or lawyer. They involve no abstract theorem of science ; they are a mere statement of facts, requiring something to be done or not to be done ; which, really one would think, might be made intelligible without the continual assistance of interpreters, at an enormous expense. The obscurity and perplexity of statutes arise principally from a perverse deviation from the ordinary language of civil life, an overwhelming verbosity and endless repetition of " he, she, they," " him, her, it, and them," the " aforesaid," and " so far as," the " so forths," &c. which render the whole so involved and perplexed, that one would suppose the legislature, instead of endeavouring to render the laws as lucid as possible, had purposely involved them in the greatest possible darkness. From the habitual indulgence of fiction and tautology the minds of lawyers—for they are lawyers who draw up acts of parliament—become so inveterately alien to truth and simplicity that they cannot be otherwise if they would ; and, accordingly, we find in those cases, when their intention has really been to be intelligible, that their language involves so much complexity—there are so many crochets and puzzles—that they entirely fail in their purpose, and defy comprehension by ordinary minds. We shall give an instance of this from one of Sir Robert Peel's consolidatory acts, the 7 & 8 Geo. IV. c. 28 ; which is the more remarkable, because the express object of it is to obviate obscurity and misapprehension, by giving a simple and general rule for the interpretation of criminal statutes. The clause to which we allude is the 14th, and expressed as follows :—" Whenever this or any other statute relating to any offence, whether punishable upon indictment or summary conviction, in describing or referring to the offence, or the subject matter on or with respect to which it shall be committed, or the offender or the party affected or intended to be affected by the offence, hath used, or shall use words importing the singular number or the masculine gender only, yet the statute shall be understood to include several matters as well as one matter, and several persons as well as one person, and females as well as males, and bodies corporate as well as individuals, unless it be otherwise specially provided, or there be something in the subject or context repugnant to such construction; and wherever any forfeiture or penalty is payable to a party aggrieved, it shall be payable to a body corporate in every case where such body shall be the party aggrieved."

An *unlearned* person might possibly guess at the intended meaning of this explanatory rule, and a lawyer no doubt—and this would be deemed by him its chief excellence—would be able to draw from it a dozen different interpretations, according as they best suited the purposes of his client.

Things the most heterogeneous are frequently jumbled together in the same act of parliament, and the title is often as remote as possible from the subject matter of the statute. These are called "Hodgepodge Acts," and are very numerous. Who, for instance, would expect to find the regulations under which petitions may be forwarded to members of parliament, in an act for laying an *additional duty upon tea and sugar?* The commencing clause of the statute, under which Vauxhall and other theatres and places of entertainment are licensed, is as follows:—" Whereas, the advertising a reward with no questions asked, for the return of things lost or stolen, is one great cause and encouragement of robberies, be it enacted," &c. Many may recollect that Sir R. Peel, on introducing to parliament his bill for amending the larceny-laws (March 9th, 1826), cited the title of one single act, which embraces no fewer than the following bizarre miscellany:—the continuing several laws therein mentioned; the carrying of sugars in British-built vessels; the encouraging the importation of naval stores; preventing frauds in the admeasurement of coals in the city of Westminster; and preventing the stealing or *destroying of madder roots.* Another act he referred to forms a still more whimsical olio, and is intituled "An Act for better securing the duties of customs on certain goods removed to London; for regulating the fees of officers in His Majesty's customs in the province of Segambia, in Africa; for allowing the Receiver-General of Fees in Scotland proper compensation; for the better preservation of hollies, thorns, and quick-sets in private grounds, and trees and underwood; and authorising the exportation of a limited quantity of barley from the Port of Kirkgrow." Such acts run very much like cross-readings in a newspaper, and those who wish for further amusement of the sort will find it in Mr. Wickens's publication on the *Division of Labour in Civil Life,* where the subject is pursued to a greater extent than our limits will admit.

Notwithstanding the laborious and tiresome precision of statutes, they frequently comprise the most egregious blunders. There is a singular instance of one in the 53d George III.: by the 18th section, one half the penalty is to go to the king and the other half to the informer; but the penalty happened in this case not to be a fine, but fourteen years' transportation; so that fourteen years' transportation were to be equally divided between Messrs. Byers and Co. and his Majesty!

Perhaps our readers may deem this too old a blunder to illustrate the deliberative wisdom of the law-makers of the reign of William IV. If so, we shall give them an example of legislative aptitude from one of the most important acts' of the session of 1830—that for Consolidating and Amending the Laws on Forgery. This statute was drawn, we believe, by Messrs. Hobhouse and Gregson, and was some years in preparation, under the auspices of Sir R. Peel; it received the tinkering of Sir James Scarlett, between whom and the gentlemen by whom it was framed, some difference of opinion respecting its provisions arose, which could only be terminated by an appeal to Lord Tenterden, who felt himself bound to decide, notwithstanding his well-known partiality, against Sir James. Well, this act so patronised, elaborated, revised, quarrelled about, and arbitrated, is at length brought forth, passed, and is now the law of the land; and we will venture to say a more defective and bungling piece of legislation is not to be found in the great book of conundrums and absurdities itself. What the public expected was an act that would comprise the entire statute-law of forgery; unless this was attained, little benefit could result from adding one more statute to the 400 previously existing. Instead of consolidating the law, it merely embodies the whole or part of the provisions of *twenty-seven* statutes out of the mass; all the acts relative to the forging of stamps, seamen's warrants, plate-marks, and on the post-office, remain scattered, as heretofore, through the boundless waste of the Statutes at Large, to be applied or not, as it may happen, by judges and lawyers. Incompleteness is not the worst defect in this statute; some of its provisions are obviously incompatible, and the commencing part of the act seems to have been entirely lost sight of when the concluding part was agreed upon. For proof of this compare the following sections, nearly the first and last, in the statute.

" § II. And be it enacted, That if any person shall forge or counterfeit, or shall utter, knowing the same to be forged or counterfeited, the great seal of the United Kingdom, his Majesty's privy seal, any privy signet of his Majesty, his Majesty's royal sign manual, any of his Majesty's seals appointed by the twenty-fourth article of the Union to be *kept, used, and continued in Scotland,* the great seal of Ireland, or the privy seal of Ireland, every such offender shall be guilty of high treason, and shall suffer death accordingly."

" § XXIX. And be it enacted, That this act *shall not extend to any offence committed in Scotland* or Ireland."

Here we see in the second section a specific punishment assigned for the commission of an offence in Scotland; and in a subsequent section it is expressly declared the act shall not extend to any offence committed in Scotland or Ireland. What the judges will make of this inconsistency, when it comes before them, it is impossible to foresee: we suppose we shall have another act or two to " *explain*" or " *amend,*" &c.; and so our legislature proceeds, heaping one act upon another, making delightful work for lawyers, and " raining," as Mr. Bentham expresses it, " snares among the people."

Sir James Scarlett, to be sure, is not a paragon of legislators any more than of attorney-generals. The act for *Improving the Administration of Justice* will not be soon forgotten by the profession : this act, among other changes, altered the period of commencement of the terms. But no sooner was the act in force than it was discovered to be pregnant with the most ludicrous errors ; the framer of the statute was clearly ignorant of the *changes of the moon*—of that common astronomical knowledge which is contained in every almanack ; the consequence was that the courts would have been involved in the greatest confusion, had not another statute been precipitately brought in to remedy the blunders of the first.

One cause of such blundering legislation is to be found in the vicious mode of transacting business in the House of Commons. It is well known law-making is a sort of *after-dinner amusement*, which commences when gentlemen have taken their wine—when the theatres have closed — and the night-houses are thrown open for the reception of customers. It cannot be matter of surprise if, under such unfavourable circumstances, the nocturnal occupations of the Collective Wisdom exhibit strange examples of forgetfulness, haste, and confusion. We, indeed, are often astonished things are not worse, when we reflect on the course of parliamentary proceedings—no division of labour, or exclusive devotion to legislative duty—all chance medley, helter skelter, volunteer and amateur exertion—the chief manager straining every nerve to get through public business before the setting in of the Dog-days — stratagems to steal a march to avoid some economical proposition for a reduction of the estimates—packing a house for a job or private bill—jaded ministers dropping in late from their offices or a protracted cabinet-council—country gentlemen from a tedious morning-waiting at the Treasury for places and appointments—lawyers from the courts—and the sons of riot reel in at midnight, from the saloons and club-houses, in quest of divertisement—and thus business goes on, and a house is formed of men distracted with their individual avocations, or suffering from lassitude and over-excitement. They talk and talk, it is true, without end, as people mostly do when not fully master of their subject ; but their ideas are crude—there has been no preparation or concentration of thought—and all their doings bear evident marks of the intellectual chaos from which they spring. We had a ludicrous illustration of what we are stating in the session of 1830: the House was in a committee, and had been hotly debating, as usual, to no purpose, for the space of six hours, when the chairman got up, and with great gravity said, " he should be extremely obliged by any honourable member informing him what they had all been talking about !"

Such mode of legislation has striking results: it impoverishes the people by litigation, and multiplies and augments the emoluments of a mercenary profession. In the number and magnitude of inns of court, law institutions, and other public buildings the legal classes rival the ancient religious houses; and their unavoidable and constant intervention in all the affairs and transactions of civil life gives them an influence equal to that of the priesthood in the ages of superstition. In the metropolis are nine superior courts, four ecclesiastical courts, twenty courts for recovery of small debts, besides courts of oyer and terminer, courts of general and quarter sessions, coroner-courts, and courts of petty sessions for the purposes of police. Attached to these courts are eight hundred officers, exclusive of judicial functionaries. To these may be added 500 barristers-at-law, 3000 certificated attorneys, 130 conveyancers and equity draftsmen, 67 special pleaders, 84 proctors, 40 public notaries, 6000 clerks and assistants, besides doctors-at-law, serjeants-at-law, and king's counsel, making a legal phalanx, in the metropolis, of nearly 10,000. In the country they are not so concentrated, but more numerous. From " Clarke's Law List" it appears there are, in the country, including England and Wales, 4500 attorneys and conveyancers who have taken out certificates. The number of clerks and assistants cannot be estimated at less than 9000 ; so that the number of persons in the country, in the legal department, is 13,500 ; and if we add 10,000 for persons of a similar description in the metropolis, we have a total of 23,500 persons, whose sole employment is to render the laws intelligible, and justice attainable to the people of England and Wales.

This estimate, we are persuaded, is a great deal below the truth : many attorneys in town employ more than twenty clerks, and the majority of them employ three or four. Perhaps it would not be too much to estimate the total number of counsel, attorneys, clerks, assistants, &c. in England and Wales, at thirty thousand. In this enumeration are not included the justices of peace, amounting to 4,500, nor the judges in the different courts, the sheriffs, nor any portion of the magistracy, whose office it is to administer justice, and who employ an innumerable number of clerks and assistants. The classes we have mentioned form only that branch of the profession who owe their origin, in a great measure, to defects and obscurities in our judicial administration. It is the duty of the legislature to render the laws so clear, and the form of proceeding so simple, that persons of ordinary comprehension would generally be able to understand the one and pursue the other, without the aid, in every case, of a legal adviser.

The adage says—*Many hands make light work ;* but the maxim is reversed in law ; and the swarm of practitioners is a principal cause of the multiplication of suits, their protracted duration, and consequent pressure of business in the courts.

Dr. Colquhoun estimated the total income of the legal classes, when the amount of property and professional practice was greatly less than at present, at £7,600,000 per annum; and two-thirds, probably, of this sum are absorbed by *legalists* resident in London.

However, this can be only considered a vague approximation. In our list of places we shall give an account of the emoluments and incomes of the chief justices, the lord chancellor, the judges, and several other well-known individuals; but the incomes of the profession generally, of counsellors, special pleaders, conveyancers, and attorneys, are so various, that it is impossible to fix on any average amount. Sir

Samuel Romilly, it is credibly reported, netted £15,000 annually from his professional avocations. There are other counsel who, probably, make ten or twelve thousand a-year; others, a half, a third, a fourth, or twentieth part of that sum; and others, again, who make nothing. Sir James Scarlett has received as much as £400 with a brief on the northern circuit; and Sir E. Sugden, we believe, received £3000 with his brief, in the case of *Small* v. *Atwood*. In the incomes of attorneys are great diversities. Some few, in London, make ten or eleven thousand pounds a-year; a great many more about three or four thousand pounds; and some obscure practitioners do not clear more than £100 a-year. Their clerks experience similar variety of fortune. Some are starving on a paltry £50; others living comfortably on £200; and others sumptuously on a £500 salary.

The emoluments and salaries of the masters, registrars, and clerks in Chancery; of the judges in the Admiralty, and ecclesiastical courts, and of the law-officers of the Crown, have been more than doubled since the commencement of the revolutionary war. In 1792 the salary of the chief justice of the King's Bench was £4,000; of the Common Pleas £3,500; of the chief baron of the Exchequer, £3,500; all these have been respectively augmented to £10,000, £8,000, and £7,000 per annum; and the salaries of the puisne judges and barons of the three superior courts have been raised from £2,400 to £5,500 per annum each.* All the judges have patronage—that of the chief justice very valuable; they have, also, some fees remaining, though the principal portion has been commuted. It has been related of these exalted personages, that, at the time sixteen journeymen boot-closers were committed to Newgate for a conspiracy to raise their wages, they were sitting in their chambers in Serjeant's Inn conspiring to raise their own salaries, in consequence of the rise of the *necessaries of life*. This anecdote reminds us of the fable of the Wolf and the Shepherd. A wolf, says Plutarch, happening to put his head into a hut, where some shepherds were regaling on a leg of mutton, exclaimed—*Ah! what a clamour you would have raised had you caught me at such a banquet!* The demeanour of the sages of the law would be something similar; they would declaim eloquently on the evils of *conspiring* when committed by workmen, though it might be done by themselves with impunity.

An important fact connected with legalists is, the enormous increase in their number within the last ten years. In 1820 we were engaged in an inquiry similar to the present; and we find, in the interval, the number of attorneys in the metropolis has augmented *fifty per cent*. There has, no doubt, been a corresponding increase in the country, and in other branches of the profession; and far exceeds the contemporary increment in property and population. It arises, we presume, from the increasing number and perplexities of the laws, which have rendered additional guides, commentators, expounders, and interpreters indispensable; or, it may have arisen from the large fortunes suddenly amassed

---

* Parliamentary Paper, No. 532, Session 1830.

by dealers in legal subtleties, which have tempted more than a fair proportion of the community to embark in so lucrative a calling. Whatever may be the cause, it is not creditable to our judicial administration; nor is it a flattering symptom of social happiness and improvement.

The increase of litigation, and, consequently, of profit to the profession, is demonstrated by the increase of business in the superior courts, as is shown by the following statement of the number of causes entered for trial:—

Years.	King's Bench.	Common Pleas.	Exchequer.
1823	1474	445	162
1824	1695	472	222
1825	2164	500	157
1826	3112	1021	245

The vast number of bankruptcies and insolvencies of late years must have tended enormously to the emolument of the legal profession, and have rendered them the richest class in the community. The number of persons who took the benefit of the Insolvent Act, amounted in 1820, to 2482; in 1825, to 3665; and in 1830, to 4379.* The number of bankrupts, in 1814, was 1612; in 1820, 1381; in 1826, 2582; in 1829, 1654.† All these breakings up yield an abundant harvest of spoil to the gentlemen of the long robe. In most bankruptcies the solicitors, the bar, the commissioners, the accountants, and auctioneers divide the assets. Very few estates pay any thing worth a man's while going after. Under the late administration of the bankrupt-laws, a man had nothing to do but to get into credit to as large an amount as possible—buy goods in every place—turn merchant—ship off such goods to every quarter of the world—fly *kites* in every possible way—keep no books, or those so confusedly that no man, called in by the name of an accountant, could make head or tail of them—carry this system of buying, and exporting, and kite-flying to its utmost extent—purchase goods on credit at any price, and for the greatest length of time—declare his insolvency—go into the Gazette; the solicitors, the bar, the commissioners, the accountants, and the auctioneers would set to work; the larger the amount of the man's debts so much the better for the legal, accounting, and auctioneering agents. In such case, the professional men called it *a good fat bankruptcy*: and, if they could get it into chancery, so much the better; and, in general, it was contrived that *a good fat bankruptcy* should get into chancery. The result, in general was—ten or twelve years' meetings of commissioners, actions, bills in chancery; and at length, when the legalists had absorbed the estate, they tired, and the creditors were told, " Here, gentlemen, are the accounts!"

Mr. Montague justly characterised a commission of bankruptcy " a tribunal in which the minimum of justice was administered at the maximum of expense." All the commissioners were either very old or

---

* Parliamentary Paper, No. 141, Session 1831.
† Parliamentary Paper, No. 280, Session 1830.

very young men, whose only pretensions were the friendship of the chancellor, or the friendship of some friend of the chancellor, or others connected with the government.   They were all either counsel or solicitors, whose sole object was to gain as much money in as little time as possible.   Some of them understood the art of accomplishing this so well as to have been known to boast of pocketing thirty guineas a day. These, however, were only ignoble quarry, compared with the *great fee-gatherer* himself.   It appears, from a parliamentary return, that the several sums sacked by the *purse-bearer* to the lord chancellor, in the year ending 30th April, 1830, amounted to £4081.*   In the same year, the sealing of 4861 writs, at 3s. 3d. each, produced £789, which was shared between his lordship, chaff-wax, sealer, and porter.   From returns in the same year, the masters in chancery appear to net £4000 per annum, their chief clerk upwards of £1000, and the copying clerk £500 and more.   Mr. Wellesley, in a book lately published by him, on the court of chancery, states that the litigation into which he had been forced had cost him £20,000 in four years, and a sum of equal amount had been paid out of the estates of his children.   Mr. Davies, the late tea-dealer, of Philpot-lane, was put to an expense of £32,000 by a chancery commission, appointed to ascertain whether he was in a *sound state of mind.*   Sir E. Sugden stated, not long since, that the equity proceedings, under the will of Mr. Thelluson, had been as productive to lawyers as many principalities to their sovereigns.   The cause of *Small v. Attwood,* it is calculated, will swamp £100,000 in law expenses.   But we must return to the subject from which we have digressed.

The fraud, impoverishment, and desolation resulting from the administration of the Debtor-Laws are almost incredible.   In the processes issued against the person, lawyers and attorneys are the parties who chiefly profit.   From returns of affidavits of debts, it appears, in two years and a half, 70,000 persons were arrested in and about London, the law-expenses of which could not be less than *half a million.*†   In the year 1827, in the metropolis and two adjoining counties, 23,515 warrants to arrest were granted, and 11,317 bailable processes executed.‡ Thus were eleven thousand persons deprived of their liberty on the mere declarations of others, before any trial or proof that they owed a farthing !   So gainful is the trade to attorneys, that they frequently buy up small bills for the purpose of suing the endorsers, and bring nine or ten actions on each.   One house alone has brought five hundred actions in this way, and most of them for sums under £20.

The sum on which arrest is allowed has been gradually augmented to £20 ; but this is too small, and the consequence is, the prisons are crowded with debtors for the most paltry amounts.   The number of persons committed to the five principal prisons of the metropolis, exclusive of crown debtors, and those imprisoned for contempt, averages 5000

---

* Parliamentary Paper, No. 626, Session 1830.
† Mr. Hume, House of Commons, February 19, 1827.
‡ Parliamentary Paper, No. 149, Session 1827.

per annum.   Of these more than *one-third are for sums under* £20. In the years 1826-27, the Court of Requests for the city of London imprisoned 753 persons for various terms, from twenty to one hundred days, for sums under £5.   In the same year, the Court of Requests for Southwark ordered 9758 executions, and 1893 persons were actually imprisoned for debts amounting only to £16,442.*   From 1823 to 1831 the Southwark Request Court committed to the Borough compter and county gaol 8096 persons; of these 3139 were for debts not exceeding *twenty shillings.*†

The minor tribunals for facilitating the recovery of small debts we do not think entitled to the praise usually awarded them.   They foment domestic animosities, promote law-suits, and encourage a trumpery system of credit, which is ultimately ruinous both to the retail trades-man and his customers.‡   Neither are they so economical a resource as is generally imagined; the costs of proceedings in them usually amounting to a tax of *twenty-five per cent.* payable either by creditor or debtor.   A debt can seldom be recovered in the Marshalsea or Palace Court for less than £8, even if no resistance is offered.   In the several courts of request for the city of London, Middlesex, West-minster, and the Borough, the expenses of recovering a debt of 40s. or under, is at least 11s.; above that sum, twice as much.   Such a system can be no advantage to *trade ;* it only tends to fill the coffers of attorneys and clerks of courts, by the ruin of the industrious classes. Only think of the fees received in the request court of Southwark amounting, in one year, to £4255, of which £2475 arose from debts of 40s. or under.   In four years, the fees received, in the request court of the City, amounted to £7322.§   Our legal institutions are chiefly beneficial to those under whose auspices their rules and modes of procedure have been framed and regulated.   Hence the circuity and expense of law-suits.   No prudent man ever thinks it for his interest to sue for a debt below £15; the costs in prosecuting for a small debt being equal to a large one, owing to the proceedings being the same, and the pleadings as voluminous for the recovery of a few shillings as £100.   In the King's Bench, the expenses of recovering a debt under £5, even if no defence is made, and judgment goes by default, are not less than £15; if defendant appear, and, as is not uncommonly the case, puts in a dilatory plea, they are increased to £20; and, by taking out a writ of error, they are still further augmented.   The following receipt has been often given to debtors, who wish to be troublesome, and to weary out their creditors by an expensive process :—

When arrested and held to bail, and after being served with a decla-

---

* Parliamentary Paper, No. 487, Session 1828.

† Parliamentary Paper, No. 240, Session 1831.

‡ Treatise on the Police and Crimes of the Metropolis, by the Editor of the Cabinet Lawyer, where the tendency of the debtor-laws is more fully inves-tigated.

§ Report on Small Debts, Parliamentary Paper, vol. iv. Session 1823.

ration, you may plead the general issue, which puts you on for trial sooner than any other plea; but, if you wish to vex your plaintiff, and put him about, put in a special plea; if you are in custody, order your attorney to plead in person, this will cost you £1 : 1, and run your plaintiff to £30 expense. If you do not intend to try the cause, you have no occasion to do any thing more till the plaintiff gets judgment against you, which he must do the term after you have put in a special plea. The plaintiff is obliged to send you a paper book, which you must return to his attorney with 7s 6d. otherwise you will not put him to more than half the expense. When he proceeds and gets judgment against you, then order your attorney to search the Final Judgment Office, in the Temple; when searched, and found they have got final judgment signed against you, then give plaintiff's attorney notice for him and your attorney to be present with the master at the time the plaintiff taxes the costs; at which time your attorney must have a writ of error with him to give to the plaintiff's attorney before the master, at the time the master taxes the costs; it will put the plaintiff to great expense, which he will have to pay, or go the ground over again. The writ of error will cost you £4 : 4 by a London attorney; but, if you wish to be more troublesome, make the writ returnable in parliament, which will cost you £1 : 1 more, and your plaintiff £100. If he has the courage to follow you further, you may then file a bill in Chancery or Exchequer; if he does not then give his answer, your bill will get an injunction against him: you may then get an attachment from the court where your bill was filed, and take his body for contempt of court. The costs incurred by plaintiff and defendant, respectively, will then be as follow:—

Plaintiff's Costs.	£	s.	d.	Defendant's Costs.	£	s.	d.
Answer to Special Plea ..	30	0	0	Special Plea	1	1	0
Ditto Writ of Error	100	0	0	Paper Book..............	0	7	6
Ditto Bill in Chancery....	100	0	0	Writ of Error............	4	4	0
Ditto Bill in Exchequer ..	84	0	0	Returnable in Parliament..	1	1	0
				To Bill in Chancery	12	0	0
	£314	0	9	To Bill in Exchequer	6	6	0
					£54	19	6

This is a fine exemplification of law, and shows how much greater are the advantages offered to finesse and knavery than to integrity and plain dealing. Some restraints are laid on frivolous writs of error by 6 Geo. IV. c. 96, but in other respects the above outline is a substantially correct exposition of the legal resources available to the unprincipled debtor for harassing his creditor.

SUMMARY OF LEGAL ABUSES AND DEFECTS.

In the preceding exposition our principal objects have been to give a general idea of the laws of England; secondly, of the number and gains of the individuals engaged in their administration; thirdly, of the abuses and defects in those laws especially intended for the benefit of trade; and, lastly, we have brought together a multitude of facts, to exemplify the emoluments and salaries of judges and the fees of lawyers and attorneys, in order to show the mass of interest-begotten prejudices that must interfere with, if not be absolutely arrayed against efficient reform in the judicial system. After proceeding thus far, we still despair of bringing the remainder of our subject within reasonable limits. Lord Brougham, after an extraordinary speech of six hours' duration, was compelled to leave various departments of legal delinquency unexplored, though equally claiming the attention of his powerful mind. All that our circumscribed space will permit is an indication or digest of the more prominent defects, and this we shall endeavour to comprise in the present section. Abuses often exist only because they are concealed, and the first step to their reform is general publicity.

JUSTICES OF THE PEACE.—These are virtually appointed by lords lieutenant of counties; for, though the lord chancellor issues the commission, it is the lord lieutenant who designates the persons comprehended in it. Hence an important source of aristocratic influence; which is exerted in raising to the magisterial bench gentlemen who have distinguished themselves by their political opinions or activity in local contests. The tenure of office is fully as secure as that of the judges; whatever be the conduct of a justice, he is seldom removed; and lord Eldon laid it down as an inflexible rule never to strike a magistrate off the list, either for private misconduct or party feeling, until he had been convicted of some offence by the verdict of a court of record, and such conviction, it is notorious, is almost unattainable. Hence these petty judges may be considered as so many irremoveable and irresponsible functionaries, and the great power confided to them in the administration of the game laws, the punishment of theft and assaults, and the granting of licenses is very liable to be abused. Numerous instances of abuse were cited by lord Brougham, in his great speech of the 7th of February, 1828. Still we do not agree with this eminent personage in thinking, as he seems to incline, that a *stipendiary* magistracy, consisting of lawyers, would, in lieu of the unpaid magistracy, afford the best security for a pure and independent administration of justice. *Costly* justice, no doubt, is better than *cheap* injustice. But lawyers have their prejudices as well as sporting parsons and sporting squires; and we think justice would be quite as corrupt when paid for as when administered gratuitously, unless there were responsibility. This would be best obtained by the entire publicity of justiciary proceedings;—here is the best guarantee against abuse in all functionaries of whatever rank or degree. Clergymen might be disqualified for the magisterial office as for other lay functions, and greater facilities afforded for removing from the commission of the peace justices guilty of misconduct. With these reforms the magistracy would be made a much less objectionable branch of domestic judicature, especially as a material source of their misdoings has been curtailed by the opening of the beer trade and the improvement of the game laws.

DIFFERENT LAWS IN DIFFERENT PLACES.—Nothing can be more inconsistent than the different modes of inheritance and tenure in the different districts of the country. In the county of Middlesex the eldest son succeeds to the estate; cross over the Thames, into Kent, and all the sons succeed to the ancestor's inheritance in equal shares; proceed a little to the westward, and another law prevails, the youngest son inheriting the land to the exclusion of the other children. What can be the motive for perpetuating these divers usages—the relics of a barbarous age—in a country subject to the same general government? But even the customs of gavelkind and borough-English are not so inconvenient as those which regulate the customary tenures in a thousand different manors. In one manor copyhold property is not devisable by will; in another it may be so conveyed. In one manor a devise is not valid, if made longer than two years before the testator's decease; so that it is necessary for wills to be *renewed every two years;* in another one year; in a third three years are the period; while in many there are no such restrictions. In some manors the eldest daughter succeeds to the exclusion of her sisters, as the eldest daughter (in default of male heirs) succeeds to the crown of England; in other manors all the daughters succeed jointly, as co-parceners, after the manner of the common law. In some manors a wife has for dower one-third of the tenement, as in case of freehold. In others she has, for her free bench, one half; and again, in some, she takes the whole for life, to the exclusion of the heir. The fines on death or alienation vary; the power and manner of entailing or cutting off entails vary; the taking of heriots and lords' services varies.* There are as many or more of these local laws than in France, in the *Pays de Coutûme,* of which four hundred have been enumerated, so as to make it the chief opprobrium of the old French law, that it differed in every village. Is it right that such varieties of custom should be allowed to have force in particular districts, contrary to the general law of the land? Is it right that, in London, Bristol, and some other places, the debts due to a man should be subject to execution for what he owes himself, while in all the rest of England there is no such resource; although in Scotland, as in France, this most rational and equitable law is universal?

All these varieties of tenure and diversities of liability are only so many traps to the ignorant and unwary, and so many impediments to the transmission and circulation of property. They embarrass commerce, by making it difficult—in some cases impossible—for a man to get the full value of his property, or dispose of it at all. For copyhold property is not liable even for specialty debts, nor can it be extended by elegit; and thus, absurd and unjust as is the law which prevents

---

* Lord Brougham, House of Commons, Feb. 7, 1828, printed speech, p. 45.

freehold property from being charged with simple contract debts, it goes further in this instance, and exempts the copyhold from liability, even to those of the highest nature, a judgment itself not giving the creditor any right of execution against it. The obvious remedy to be adopted in this case is to give all parts of the country the same rules touching property ; and, therefore, lord Brougham, in his memorable speech, proposed an assimilation of the laws, affecting real estates, all over the kingdom, to take place after the elapse of a fixed period.

DIFFERENT LAWS FOR DIFFERENT PERSONS.—Sir Wm. Blackstone was very fond of asserting that the Crown and people were, in law, on an equal footing, and that the King, in a court of justice, was no more considered than a subject. This is not correct. It is true a person injured, in his property, by the Crown, may proceed by a *petition of right*, having first obtained the consent of the attorney-general ; but the attorney-general may refuse his fiat, and then the subject is without remedy, except the hopeless resource of an impeachment of the officer of the Crown. Again, in cases where the Crown is interested, the Crown has a right, at the mere suggestion of the attorney-general, to call for a *trial at bar ;* and thus the subject be obliged to bring all the witnesses up, from Cornwall, perhaps, or some other remote county. After all this expense is incurred, by reason of the Crown demanding a trial in London, where the other party is not known, and not in Cornwall, where both parties are known, the Crown may withdraw the case from the consideration of the jury, after the examination of all the witnesses, even at the moment that the jury are, with their backs turned, deliberating about their verdict.

But it is said the Crown *pays expenses ;* the subject, however, has his own expenses to pay. As the Crown is above receiving costs, so it is exempt from paying them. The reason of this practice it is not easy to discover. One cannot see how the dignity of the Crown is exalted by not receiving costs, when they reflect that, by the Crown, is meant the revenue raised from the people for the public service, and that, consequently, the non-payment of costs to the Crown is an increase of the people's burthens. But, even if we admit the propriety of the Crown's receiving none, it would by no means follow that it should pay none to the subject, who is in a widely different predicament. All this, however, arises out of notions derived from the *feudal times*, when the Crown was in a situation the very reverse of that in which it stands at present, its income then arising almost entirely from a land-revenue. There is now no reason why it should be exempt from paying, or disabled from receiving, in all cases where costs would be due between common persons. Indeed, there has been of late years an exception made in the crown-law on this head, but so as to augment the inequality complained of. In all stamp prosecutions, the costs of the Crown are paid by the *unsuccessful defendants ;* so far does it stoop from its former dignity ; but not so low as to pay the defendant a farthing of his costs, should he be acquitted.

We shall only mention one more case to illustrate the legal disparity between the King and the people. Whenever a special jury is summoned in a Crown case, and all the twelve jurors do not attend, a tales cannot be prayed to let the cause proceed, without a *warrant from the attorney-general;* so that it is in the power of your adversary to refuse this at the time it may be most for his advantage so to do; while you have no option whatever, in case it should be for his interest to proceed, and for yours to delay. A singular instance of oppression, under this usage, was related by Lord Brougham, in the celebrated speech to which we have referred. A person named Lowe, with four smugglers, was prosecuted in the Court of Exchequer. The accused were acquitted on the second trial, and Meade, one of the witnesses against them, and others connected with him, were prosecuted for perjury; eighteen indictments were found at the sessions, and the Crown at once removed the whole, by *certiorari,* into the Court of King's Bench. There they were all to be tried. Meade was the first tried, and clearly convicted. The other seventeen were then to be tried, and Mr. Sergeant Jones called them on; but the Crown had made the whole eighteen special jury causes; a sufficient number of jurymen did not attend; Mr. Sergeant Jones wanted to pray a tales, and *the Crown refused a warrant.* "Thus," says lord Brougham, " an expense of £10,000 was incurred, and a hundred witnesses were brought to London, all for nothing, except, after the vexation, trouble, and delay already endured, to work the ruin of the prosecutor, who had been first harassed upon the testimony of the perjured witnesses. The poor Yorkshire farmer, whom the villain had so vexed, had no more money to spend in law; all the other prosecutions dropped; Meade obtained a rule for a new trial, but funds were wanting to meet him again, and he escaped. So that public justice was utterly frustrated, as well as the most grievous wrong inflicted upon an individual. Nor did it end here; the poor farmer was fated to lose his life by the transaction. Meade, the false witness, and Lowe, the farmer, whom he had informed against, and who was become the witness against him upon the approaching trial, lived in the same village; and one evening, in consequence, as was alleged, of some song, or madrigal, sung by him in the street, this man (Meade) seized a gun, and shot Lowe, from his house, dead upon the spot. He was acquitted of the murder, on the ground of something like provocation, but he was found guilty of manslaughter, and such was the impression of his guilt upon the mind of the court, that he was sentenced to two years' imprisonment. A case of more complicated injustice—one fraught with more cruel injustice to the parties, I never knew in this country, nor do I conceive that worse can be found in any other. We may talk of our excellent institutions, and excellent some of them certainly are, though I could wish we were not given to so much Pharisaical praising of them; but if, while others, who do more and talk less, go on improving their laws, we stand still, and suffer all our worst abuses to continue, we shall soon cease to be respected by our neighbours, or to receive any praises, save those we are so ready to lavish upon ourselves."—pp. 50-1. So much for the even-handed justice, lauded by Mr. Justice Blackstone, between the Crown and the people!

FINES AND RECOVERIES.—It is well known if a person has an estate *in fee*, that is, the absolute and unconditional possession of it, he can sell or devise it as he thinks proper; but, if he has an estate in tail, he cannot deal with it in this manner. He must first go through certain forms, in order to make himself absolute master of his estate : he must levy a fine, as it is called, which destroys the expectant rights of the issue in tail; or he must, by means of a recovery, get rid of those rights and of all remainders over. But this must be done through the Court of Common Pleas, at certain seasons of the year ;—and why, it may be asked, should there exist a necessity for going there ? Why force tenants-in-tail into court for mere form's sake ? In case of bankruptcy the necessity for these forms is not felt. A trader, who is tenant-in-tail, commits an act of bankruptcy, and, by the assignment under the commission, not only the interest vested in him is conveyed, but all the remainders expectant upon it are destroyed for the benefit of his creditors, and the estate passes to the assignees, free of all restriction. Why, then, may not the possessor of an estate do that for himself which the law permits to be done for an insolvent tradesman and his creditors ? So, too, a man and his wife cannot convey an estate of the wife without a fine or a recovery ; neither can the wife be barred of her dower without a similar proceeding. There is certainly nothing very real in a fine, and, as to recoveries, they proceed upon a mere fiction. They go upon the ground of compensation in value being made to the remainder claimants, whose right they cut off, and who, but for this fictitious suit, would have a right to take the estate after the decease of the tenant-in-tail. They are said to recover compensation in value ; and from whom do they recover it ? Why the common vouchee, who is the *crier of the court* of Common Pleas, and who, like the man at the Custom-House, obliged to take all the oaths other people do not like, lies groaning under the weight of all the liabilities he has incurred to all the claimants in tail since he became crier, and answerable for the millions of property, the rights to which, in remainder, have been barred, he not being worth a shilling !

The abolition of these ridiculous forms was recommended upwards of one hundred and fifty years since, and still remained to be enforced by the eloquence of lord Brougham. They have no earthly use but to raise money by way of fees ; and which, besides creating expense and delay, and oftentimes preventing tenants-in-tail from passing their property by will, which they cannot do if they die before suffering the recovery, they give rise to questions in law, often puzzling, always dilatory and expensive. The mere forms of fines and recoveries cost £70,000 per annum over and above what deeds, operating in the same manner, would cost; and a round sum must be allowed for the litigation which doubts on these assurances are yearly occasioning. Mr. Campbell introduced a bill for abolishing fines and recoveries, which has been hanging on the tenter-hooks during the two last sessions of parliament, owing to the rejection of the Reform Bill by the Lords.

AGREEMENTS FOR LEASES AND CONVEYANCES.—A pregnant source of legal suits is the law with respect to sales, leases, and other conveyances. Thus, if you agree with a person to give him a lease, though he, under the agreement, becomes your tenant, he is your equitable tenant only, but not your legal tenant. He may be possessed of a written agreement, signed and sealed, for a lease of ten years, and may occupy under it, but he has no lease which a court of law can take notice of; and, if an ejectment is brought, he must go out. He may go into a court of equity on his agreement, if that is any comfort to him; he may apply for a decree against you to perform your agreement; but till then his claims are not recognized in a court of common law. If an injunction be brought, the expenses are further multiplied. Why, it may be asked, should not the agreement, such as here described, be as good as a lease; when, in substance, it is the very same thing, and only wants a word added or left out to make it the same in legal effect? A case, illustrative of this subject, happened to lord Brougham, on the York circuit. An agreement had been entered into, and possession given; but, because it did not contain words of present demise, it was no lease, and therefore the tenant could not stand a moment against the ejectment that was brought, but was driven into the Court of Chancery, where the other party could just as little stand against him. How much inconvenience, expense, and delay, then, might be saved, if such an agreement were pronounced equivalent to a lease!

Again, on the same principle of avoiding multiplicity of suits, why, in ejectments, should two processes be requisite to give the plaintiff his remedy? As things now stand, after a man has succeeded in one action, and established his title to the possession, he must have recourse to another, to recover that which he ought to have obtained by one and the same verdict that established his title—the mesne profits. Why could not the same jury settle the matter at once? Why is an individual driven to maintain two actions for the purpose of obtaining one and the same remedy? Or why should not the jury that tries the right also assess the damage? Mr. Tennyson's bill, which was intended to remedy some part of this evil, is only permissive; it ought to have been compulsory. It is partial, and it is only recommendatory, and its recommendations are not always attended to, because the lawyers, having the choice, do not think fit to pursue that which is the least profitable; they choose the two actions, when one would suffice for the interests of justice—for the interests of the plaintiff and defendant—for all interests, except those of the practitioners.

ARREST FOR DEBT.—Unless in cases of grossly improvident conduct, or fraudulent concealment of property from the just claims of creditors, imprisonment of the person for debt, either on mesne process or in execution, seems not defensible. In practice, the power of arrest is often perverted to purposes foreign to its ostensible object. It has been resorted to as a means not of recovering a just claim, but to prevent a just claim being preferred; and the same artifice of a false allegation of debt has been frequently employed to remove a person out of the way who happened to be troublesome, or that some criminal intention might be effected during his incarceration. But, however wicked or spiteful the motives of any one in so employing the process of the law, there being a probable cause of detention, and the process not being abused, no action lies against the wrong doer. If he have no accomplices, so as to fall within the charge of *conspiracy*, he is safe. To the wealthy all these inconveniences are trivial; but how does such a proceeding operate on a poor man, or a tradesman in moderate circumstances? He has no facilities for obtaining bail; if he has, he pays one way or another afterwards for the favour; and, if he cannot procure it, he must go to prison. And on what ground of common sense does the law in this matter rest? Why should it be supposed that a man, owing twenty pounds, will leave his house, his wife, his children, his country, his pursuits, and incur, voluntarily, the punishment awarded for great crimes, by banishing himself for life? Yet the law always proceeds on the supposition that a man will *run away* the moment he has notice given him of an action for debt. Some men might possibly act thus, but their conduct forms the exception, not the rule; and it is neither wisdom nor humanity to denounce a penalty against all men in order to meet a case not likely to occur once in a thousand times. Non-payment of debt, if a crime at all, is a crime against *property only*: and, perhaps, it would be enough to allow property to answer for it: and there is this peculiarity between it and other crimes against property, that it is committed with the mutual consent of the parties. Goods sold on credit are mostly charged extra; this extra charge is the premium exacted by the creditor on account of the risk of repayment; and, having thus fixed the equivalent for his chance of loss, it seems super-erogatory in the law to grant him, in addition, the power of *ex post facto* punishment, of the amount of which he is the sole judge, merely because he has failed in a voluntary adventure, into which he had been tempted to embark, from the prospect of reaping a greater profit than is charged by the ready-money tradesman. Creditors rarely derive any advantage from imprisonment beyond the indulgence of vindictive feeling, which it is inconsistent with the true ends of public law to encourage. Those who do benefit by it are usually the most unfair and ungenerous, who, by a sudden arrest, often embarrass and prejudice all the other parties interested. To the debtor, the consequences are peculiarly hurtful—personal degradation—augmented incapacity and diminished inclination to satisfy his prosecutor—and the contraction of habits inconsistent with future intregrity and industry.

INCONSISTENT LIABILITIES OF PROPERTY FOR DEBTS.—In pro-portion as, before the debt has been proved, the person and property of the party charged should be free from all process not necessary to prevent evasion; so, after judgment, ought the utmost latitude be given to obtain satisfaction from all the defendant's property whatever—

land, goods, money, and debts—for to himself they no longer belong. To allow any distinction between one kind of property and another seems the height of injustice. Yet this is of hourly occurrence in the frustration of a creditor after he has obtained judgment, and taken out execution. His debtor has a landed estate; if it be copyhold, the creditor cannot touch it in any way whatever; if it be freehold, he may take half by elegit, and receive the rents and profits, but no more, in the lifetime of his debtor. The debt for which he has received judgment may be such that the rent of the land will not even keep down the interest; still he can take nothing more; he cannot turn the land into money: so that, when a man sues for a thing detained unlawfully, (a horse, for instance,) you give him money which he does not ask; and when he asks for money by suing for a debt, you give him land which he does not want. But if his debtor die before judgment can be obtained, unless the debt is on bond, he has no remedy at all against any kind of real property of any tenure; nay, though his money, borrowed on note or bill, has been laid out in buying land, the debtor's heir takes that land wholly discharged of the debt!

But not only is land thus sacred from all effectual process of creditors, unless the debtor be *a trader*, the great bulk of most men's personal property is equally beyond reach of the law. Stock in the public funds—debts due in any manner of way—nay, bank-notes, and even money—are alike protected. A man may owe a hundred thousand pounds in any way, and judgment may have passed against him over and over again; if he have *privilege of parliament*, live in a furnished house or hotel, and use hired carriages and horses, he may have an income from stock or money lent, of twenty thousand a-year, and defy the utmost efforts of the law; or if he have not privilege, he may live abroad, or within the Rules, and laugh at all the courts and all the creditors in the country. So absurd are the laws in this respect, that if a person borrow a thousand pounds, and the creditor has obtained judgment, the sheriff's officer appointed to levy upon his personalty may come into his room, and take a table or a desk; but if he sees the *identical thousand pounds lying there*, he must leave it—he touches it at his peril:—" For this quaint reason," says Lord Mansfield, " because money cannot be sold, and you are required, by the writ, to take your debt out of the produce of goods sold."

Lord Brougham, in concluding his observations on these barbarous, absurd, and aristocratic laws, eloquently apostrophises—" who is the innovator—he who would adhere to such rules in violation of the manifest intent and spirit of our old law, or he who would re-adjust them so as to give it effect? In ancient times there were none of those masses of property in existence which are exempt from legal process. When the law, therefore, said, " Let all a man's goods and chattels be answerable for his debts," it meant to include his whole personalty at the least. Things have now changed in the progress of society; trade has grown up; credit has followed in its train; money, formerly only used as counters, has become abundant; bankers' accounts have been invented; paper currency and the funds have been created. Three-fourths of the debtor's personalty, perhaps nine-tenths, now consist of stock, money, and credit; and the rule of law, which leaves those out of all execution, no longer can mean as before—" Let *all* his personalty be liable"—but, " Let a tenth-part of it only be taken." Can there be a greater change made upon, or greater violence done to, the old law itself, than you thus do by affecting to preserve its letter? The great stream of time is perpetually flowing on; all things around us are in ceaseless motion; and we vainly imagine to preserve our relative position among them, by getting out of the current and standing stock still on the margin. The stately vessel we belong to glides down; our bark is attached to it; we might " pursue the triumph, and partake the gale;" but, worse than the fool who stares, expecting the current to flow down and run out, we exclaim—Stop the boat!—and would tear it away to strand it, for the sake of preserving its connexion with the vessel. All the changes that are hourly and gently going on in spite of us, and all those which we ought to make, that violent severances of settled relations may not be effected, far from exciting murmurs of discontent, ought to be gladly hailed as dispensations of a bountiful Providence, instead of filling us with a thoughtless and preposterous alarm."—*Speech on the present State of the Law*, p. 109.

But the imperfect recourse against the debtor's estate, although the grand opprobrium of the debtor-laws, is by no means its only vice: the unequal distribution, in case of insolvency, is scarcely a less notable defect. Only traders, or those who voluntarily take the benefit of the act, are compelled, when insolvent, to make an impartial division of their property. All others may easily, and with impunity, pay one creditor twenty shillings in the pound, and the others sixpence, or nothing. So, when a man dies insolvent, his representatives may, by acknowledging judgments, secure one creditor his full payment at the expense of all the rest. Thus, lax and impotent as the law is against property, wide as are its loop-holes for fraud and extravagance to escape by, utterly powerless as is its grasp to seize the great bulk of the debtor's possessions, against his *useless* PERSON *it is powerful and unrelenting.* The argument used is, that the concealed property may thus be wrung from him: the principle, however, of the law, and on which all its provisions are built, is, that the seizure of the body works a satisfaction of the claim; and this satisfaction is given alike in all cases—alike where there is innocent misfortune, culpable extravagance, and guilty.embezzlement. " Surely," says the great Advocate, whose words we are copying, " for all these evils the remedy is easy. Let the whole of every man's property, real and personal—his real, of what kind soever, copyhold, leasehold, freehold; his personal, of whatever nature, debts, money, stock, chattels—be taken for the payment of all his debts equally, and, in case of insolvency, let all be distributed rateably; let all he possesses be sifted, bolted from him unsparingly, until all his creditors are satisfied by payment or composition; but let *his* PERSON *only be taken when he conceals his goods, or has* *merited punishment by extravagance or fraud.* This line of distinction is already recognised by the practice of the Insolvent Courts; but the privilege of the Rules is inconsistent with every principle, and ought at once to be abrogated as soon as arrest on mesne process is abolished."*

INSECURITY OF PROPERTY.—Our aristocratic legislators have always manifested the greatest repugnance to admit the slightest change in existing institutions, under an alleged apprehension it might endanger the security of individual possessions. Nothing, however, can be imagined less secure than the condition of *real property*, as explained by the Law Commissioners, in their report to Parliament. It staggers one to comprehend how the law of any country could get into such a state, or how it has worked or been so long tolerated. The deeds, it seems, are endless, countless, and exceedingly complex, and, after all, do not give a legal title to the subject. A lord chancellor has been heard declare that there was scarcely a *legal title to an estate in England.*† This defect appears to be remedied by a system of trusts, under which every thing, if not actually in the stomach, is at least within the jaws of the great Leviathan of Chancery. Then there seems to be no way in which the exact tenure of any piece of property can be ascertained, except by getting and studying all the deeds which may have ever been executed respecting it. And, after all, a flaw may be overlooked, and a flaw once is a flaw for ever: for time cures little or nothing in a legal title.

LAWS OF MARRIAGE.—The contract of marriage can only be lawfully entered into by strictly complying with certain religious ceremonies. Unless a special license has been obtained, banns must be previously published, and the nuptials must be solemnized in a church or chapel of the establishment, and by a minister of the establishment. These obligations sometimes entail great hardship on parties by whom they have been unintentionally violated. Parents may rear families, and honour them as legitimate, and afterwards discover they have been living in concubinage, and nourishing a spurious offspring, merely from having been mistaken in supposing a priest to have been ordained, or a chapel to have been licensed. No allowance is made even for Dissenters, though their faith is tolerated; they must join in the ritual of the privileged worship, however repugnant to their conscience, on pain of their marriages being invalid. But mark the inconsistency of the law: parties have only to cross the border to Scotland, where marriages may, with impunity, be contracted in contempt of English ceremonies —without publication of banns—or the payment of surplice-fees, and such marriages are recognized as lawful in an English court of justice.‡

---

* This arrest, the end of which, it is to be hoped, fast approaches, was not generally given by the common law. The *capias ad respondendum* is given in Debt and Detinue, by West, 2 (13 Ed. I.) cap. 11, in case only so late as 19 Hen. VII. c. 9.

† Edinburgh Review, No. 101, p. 129.

‡ Lord Stowell's judgment, in *Dalrymple v. Dalrymple.*

Another hardship may be mentioned, though it cannot be ascribed to the ecclesiastical monopoly of marriages by the established clergy, but to the decisions of the courts on the law of settlement. The hardship to which we allude is the fact that an English woman, marrying a native of Scotland or Ireland, loses all claim to parochial relief in England, and may be passed, like an Irish or Scotch vagrant, to the birth-place of the husband.—7 *Barnw. & Cress.* 615.

Now, too, that religious disabilities are abrogated, measures ought to be adopted to mitigate the severity of the law in regard to marriages celebrated by Roman Catholic priests ; and, in certain cases, to render valid marriages solemnized by ministers of that persuasion. In Ireland, by the law as it now stands, a Catholic priest, in celebrating marriage between a Protestant and Catholic, commits a capital felony, *punishable with death*. By another statute, for the same offence, he is subject to a penalty of £500 : so that, agreeably to the observation of a distinguished Irishman, a Catholic priest may be first hanged, and called upon after to pay a fine of £500. The poor Irish, who flock over to this country, from early habit mostly prefer being married by a Catholic priest. Such marriage is invalid, even between two Catholics. The consequence is, the husband may desert his wife when he pleases, and leave his children utterly destitute ; for they have no claim on parochial aid in England, not even if they have an English mother.

Costs of Law-suits.—It is related by Swift, of Captain Lemuel Gulliver, that his father was ruined by *gaining a law-suit*. Notwithstanding the imputed selfishness of mankind, their addiction to litigation is a strong proof of disinterestedness, or at least shows they care less for money than the indulgence of vindictive feeling, or the acknowledgement of an unprofitable right. The doors of courts of justice are armed with terrors, threatening destruction to all who enter therein, yet they are beset with applicants for admission. Law, proverbially uncertain, is morally certain of inflicting loss on all parties ; for, victor or vanquished, we are sure to be out of pocket. This singular issue results from the rule which allows no more than *taxed costs* to a successful litigant, leaving him to pay the difference between them and the law-charges of his legal adviser. It often happens that a person who sues for a debt of £10 or £15—and the majority of suits are for such diminutive sums —and gains the day, *with costs*—is minus three or fourfold as much for his own share of the expenses. But on this point we shall extract a passage, the first sentence of which we are sure—coming as it does from such high authority—is well worth the ordinary fee of 6s. 8d. to every one with the least disposition to unnecessary litigation. Speaking of the excess of costs which a suitor is obliged to pay his attorney, over and above what he can recover from his antagonist, Lord Brougham says,—

" This is so certain, and so considerable, that a man shall in vain expect me to recommend him either to bring forward a rightful claim, or to resist an unjust demand for any such sum as twenty, or even thirty pounds—at least, upon a calculation of his interest, I should presently declare to him he had much better say nothing in one case, and pay the money a second time in the other, even if he had a *stamped receipt in his pocket*, provided his adversary were a rich and oppressive man, resolved to take all the advantages the law gives him. I have here before me some samples of taxed bills of costs, taken quite at random, and far from being peculiar cases in any one respect. There is one of £428, made out by a very respectable attorney, and from which the master deducted £202; of this sum £147 were taken off, which had been paid for bringing witnesses. In this other, amounting to £217, £76 were taxed off; and, in a third, of £63, there were nearly £15 disallowed; it was an undefended cause, to recover £50: had the defendant been obstinate and oppressively inclined, he would have made the extra costs a good deal more than the whole debt, although the suit was in the Exchequer, where the taxation is known to be more liberal. We had lately, in the King's Bench, a bill of above £100, to recover £19, and probably, of that £100 not above £60 would be allowed. As things now stand, a part of this master evil is inevitable; for if practitioners were sure of receiving all their bills, they would run up a heavy charge wherever they knew the case to be a clear one. But, as the fundamental principle for which I contend is to alter no part of the law by itself, or without considering all the other parts, there can be no difficulty, consistently with this doctrine, to enlarge the allowance of costs as soon as other amendments have prevented the abuse of litigation by professional men. Some erroneous rules of taxation may, even in a partial or insulated reform, be altered. Whatever is fairly allowed, as between attorney and client, should be allowed between party and party, except only such needless charges as have been ordered expressly by the client himself. There can surely be no reason for disallowing, as a general rule, all consultations, often absolutely necessary for the conduct of a cause, generally more beneficial than much that is allowed; nor can it be right that so little of the expense of bringing evidence should be given, and that the cost of preparing the case, by inquiries, journeys, &c. should be refused altogether. The necessary consequence of not suffering an attorney to charge what he ought to receive for certain things, is that he is *driven to do a number of needless things*, which he knows are always allowed as a matter of course, and the expense is thus increased to the client far beyond the mere gain which the attorney derives from it."

Thus it appears attorneys are placed in a similar predicament to what medical men were, prior to Lord Tenterden's decision in their favour, when they were compelled to seek a remuneration for attendance on their patients, through the medium of unnecessary draughts, or exorbitant charges for drugs. It is due, indeed, to the respectable part of the legal profession to say that they are not entirely to blame for the monstrous bills they deliver to their clients. A shameful system of extortion prevails in the courts, and many of the fees exacted by the officers, during the see-saw of a cause, can be considered nothing but legalized robbery of the suitor. In the Common Pleas, the prothonotaries charge 8*d*. per folio of seventy-two words, on all pleadings entered; and if the declaration and issue, or declaration and judgment, be of different terms, the 8*d*. is doubled. In the King's Bench 4*d*. per folio is charged. The entry, by them so called, is, in fact, nothing more than *imprinting a stamp* by a clerk in the office; the attorney performing the drudgery of engrossing or entering the proceedings on the roll. The charges for passing records and setting down causes are a grievous burthen. They are passed by an officer, whose clerk charges from 30*s*. and upwards. If the cause is not tried on the day on which it is set down, the marshal must be paid for his deputy *marking the cause* as a remanet; for the first of which he charges 6*s*. and for all after the first 4s. After the holidays, a fee of 10s. 6d., 6s. 8d., or 3s. 4d., according to usage, is extorted, at each office, for opening them. All these court-fees tend to swell an attorney's bill, though he has advanced the money for them, as well as the lawyer's fee, out of his own pocket.

LAW OF DEBTOR AND CREDITOR.—If there was any country in which a man, in order to recover a debt of £6 or £7, must begin by expending £60 or £70—where, at the outset, he had to run the risk of throwing so much good money after bad—it would at once be said that, whatever other benefits or advantages that country enjoyed, at least it was not fortunate in its system of law. But if it were added that, in addition to spending £60 or £70, a man must endure great difficulties, anxiety and uncertainty, infinite bandying to and fro, and moving about from province to province, and from court to court, before he could obtain judgment, then our envy of the country where such administration of the law existed, would be further diminished. And if, in addition to all this, after expending £60 or £70 in looking after the recovery of £6 or £7, a man's adversary should have the power of keeping his property out of the way, and beyond reach, so that, after all, the plaintiff should not receive some part of his debt, the case would be still worse. And further, in addition to this, if, in the same country, in cases where a man was so circumstanced as to be able to recover and receive his debt, and where the debtor was solvent, and prepared to pay, the individual should receive, it was true, his £6 or £7, but should not receive the whole £60 or £70, which he had spent in costs, although there was judgment in his favour, but should receive the amount wanting £20, so that he should have spent £13 or £14 out of his pocket, over and above the amount of the debt which he recovered, after being exposed to a variety of plagues, and the annoyances of these proceedings; if he were told of such a case, would not the natural inquiry be, "Whether it was possible that such a country existed?"— We should immediately pronounce that, if so, it must be in a most barbarous state; that it must be a poor country, for no commercial country, having interests extensive and important, would endure such a state of things. Nevertheless, the country where this state of things exists is that in which we now live!—England!*

This pointed and forcible delineation of the working of the debtor-laws—indisputably the worst in Europe—will be readily comprehended from our previous illustrations. It is the substance—the bare bone and muscle—of a splendid passage in Lord Brougham's second great philippic on legal abuses. The abilities of this extraordinary man have raised him to the head of the judicial administration, and few have profited more than he has done by existing defects; yet it is to him, next to Bentham and Romilly—posterior in time, but hardly in power—the country is mainly indebted for the reforms in progress, and the improve-

---

* Lord Brougham, House of Commons, April 29, 1830.

ments which must, ere long, be introduced through the entire legal system of the empire.

ABSURDITIES AND DELAYS IN ADMINISTRATIVE JUSTICE.

Magna Charta says that justice shall neither be denied, sold, nor delayed. With the single exception of guarding the country from foreign aggression, the only object for which governments have been instituted is the administration of justice. It is to attain this end that all taxes and contributions from the people were originally intended. They were not meant to support useless placemen and pensioners, nor to maintain standing armies, nor to defray the interest of debts contracted in unnecessary wars : but to protect every individual in the community from oppression. Justice ought not only to be speedy, but, above all things, cheap. To render the expense of legal process exorbitant, is not delaying—it is absolutely denying justice to all but the rich : it is affording the protection of the law to those least in need of its aid, and refusing it to those most exposed to oppression.

In England, justice is not only delayed, but, from its dearness, often unattainable. These evils result from causes much too numerous and complex to be here specified; but the most palpable appear to be the unequal distribution of business in the several courts of law—the consumption of the time of the judges in matters either irrelevant or derogatory to their more important functions—the monopoly of practice vested in different classes of practitioners—the retention of useless, absurd, and antiquated forms of procedure—the confusion, obscurity, and inconsistencies in the laws themselves—and, in short, from the entire fabric of judicial administration being inadequate and unsuitable to the wants of the age, and only adapted to a state of society wholly different from that which now exists.

To point out the manifold absurdities of the legal system we shall make no pretension; still we cannot help noticing the more striking anomalies.

If, for example, twelve judges were necessary to administer justice, centuries ago, why not nearly double the number at the present? Consider the augmentation in wealth, commerce, and population ; consider the increase of lawyers, attorneys, criminals, and suitors; why not a corresponding increase in judges? But then there were only twelve apostles to preach the gospel, therefore there must be only twelve judges to preach the law. What a reason for JOHN BULL—yet he swallows it.*

If circuits have been gradually altered from septennial to annual, and from annual to twice in a year, and three times in the home circuit, why not go on? Why not have gaol deliveries as frequently in the

---

* *Better late than never*—In the Session of 1830, an additional judge was added to each of the three superior courts of King's Bench, Common Pleas, and Exchequer, but the augmentation, we apprehend, is not commensurate to the wants of the community.

country as in London ? Why should a man be confined six months before trial in Yorkshire, and only six weeks in London ? Why, again, should a person, charged with an offence in one part of the metropolis, be imprisoned only four or five weeks, while, under precisely similar circumstances in another part, he is imprisoned two or three months ? Are we never to have uniformity in justice—are the claims of common sense to be for ever stifled by the logic of lawyers, the allegations of custom, antiquity, and local usage ?

If the lord-chief-justice require three or four assistants, why not a lord chancellor similar aid ? Does it require more grave deliberation to adjudicate trumpery suits of £10 or £15 than suits which can never be commenced for less than £100 ? Does it require a greater mass of collective wisdom to administer a written, fixed, and known law than one only inscribed on sand—remarkable for complexity—often to fabricate on the spur of the occasion—and having no immutable standard beyond the varying conscience and intelligence of the judge ? Shame on the legislature, which tolerates, year after year, a system so repugnant to reason !

If it be necessary to have circuits to administer common law, why not equity ? This is the practice in some of the states of North America ; and why should not the precedent be followed, although the people of those countries be so deplorably unfortunate as neither to have a national debt, an established Church, nor hereditary Peerage.

If the evidence of a Gentoo, a Jew, or a Turk may be received in judicial administration, why should the judges suffer the ends of justice to be defeated by rejecting the testimony of an Englishman who happens not to believe in the divine authority of the Holy Scriptures, but who is assuredly as good a Christian as the infidels we have mentioned ?

Why should justices of peace, in quarter sessions, have such great power over the *person* and none over *property* ? Is it a less serious thing to transport a poor man from his country, his wife, and his children, for fourteen years, than to decide a few pounds' debt, a trespass, tort, or other civil injury ? If the country magistracy are not learned enough to administer the laws of property, why not simplify them ? or, why not let them have the aid of an assistant barrister, and thereby expedite justice, save enormous expense to suitors, and lighten the pressure of business at the assizes ? Would not this be a more practicable and economical improvement in domestic judicature than the introduction of an entirely new machinery of local tribunals, as a great, but, as we humbly think, in this point, a mistaken man has recently proposed ?

Again : the meaning of wills, bonds, and other legal instruments being of such vast importance, why are they not punctuated and drawn up according to the ordinary rules of composition, to prevent misapprehension ? Is the contrary course followed as more conducive to obscurity and litigation ?

Lastly, we may inquire, why do attorneys and solicitors delay their suits and impoverish their clients by cramming their briefs into the bags of what are called king's counsel, or leading counsel, who are so over-whelmed with business that they have seldom time to read them—to master the law respecting them—or be present in court when the cause comes on, while there are hundreds of worthy men at the bar, with leisure, talent, and industry, but failing opportunity, name, or con-nexion, who are condemned to penury and obscurity ? Are lawyers all ARISTOCRATS; are they like the rich clergy, without bowels for the more unfortunate brethren of their own order ?

These are a few of the incongruities in the administration of justice which present themselves to the contemplation of an impartial observer. But the Court of Chancery has unquestionably been the least defensible part of our judicial system, and the most pregnant in abuse and delay. Before this tribunal a cause might be pending for years, and, even after it had gone through, and was so far matured as to be what the lawyers call *ripe for decision*, it might wait three years for judgment. Mr. Williams relates a singular instance of dilatoriness in this court: the suit involved considerable property, of which part was a windmill.* A bill was filed in 1703 ; in 1796, the cause had progressed as far as the master's office, where it was stationary till 1815, when it was found, on inquiry, the windmill had disappeared, and there was no longer any trace of its existence. Time, it seems, had been at work, while equity wes sleeping. The immense mass of property locked up in chancery almost exceeds belief. In the year 1756, the amount of suitors' effects fell short of three millions ; in 1829, they had accumulated to £38,886,135.† Of this enormous sum there is more than one-third which, from the procrastinated delay of suits, should either have belonged to persons deceased without representatives, or persons living, but ignorant, from the books not being open to them, of their claims altogether, or, if acquainted with their claims, ignorant in what manner or names their property is vested.

Now, to people living out of the atmosphere of corruption and in-trigue, there appeared little difficulty in suggesting remedies for this monstrous oppression. 1. By separating the political from the judicial character of the lord chancellor, and clothing him with that independence in the exercise of his legal functions, which is considered so great an excellence in the *status* of the common-law judges. 2. By separating the appellate jurisdiction in the House of Lords, and abolishing the absurdity of appeals from the lord chancellor on the bench to the lord chancellor on the woolsack. 3. By the relieving of his lordship of his duties in bankruptcies, which was the more reasonable, since the exer-cise of jurisdiction therein was comparatively of recent occur-rence.‡ Lastly, by a thorough reform in the offices of the masters and registrars.

---

* House of Commons, Delays in Chancery, Feb. 24, 1824.
† Parliamentary Paper, No. 282, Session 1830.
‡ The power of the lord chancellor to adjudicate in bankruptcy was granted by a statute of Henry VIII. but it was never exercised till the time of Lord Chancellor Nottingham.

These reforms were recommended over and over again by Mr. M. A. Taylor, Mr. John Williams, and others during the ascendancy of the Tories; and the only reasons we could ever discover why they were not adopted may be comprised in a very small compass. Our readers are aware what a tempting acquisition the see of Canterbury is to all aspiring churchmen; and what an itching the Philpotts and Blomfields have to clutch the magnificent revenues and patronage of the arch-diocese. Well, what Lambeth is in the Church, the Chancellorship is at the Bar. It is the glittering prize of ambitious, intriguing, and time-serving lawyers; it is the goal of desire to all gentlemen of the long-robe, for every one has more or less confidence in his good fortune and abilities, and few but hope to reach it at last. Hence there was little prospect of effective reform in equity, while Tory law-craft was so predominant in the legislature. But the dynasty of the anti-reformers has expired in principle, if not in its personal representatives; and the accession to power of Earl Grey's ministry has been signalized by some vigorous innovations on judicial abuses. Lord Chancellor Brougham was pledged by his previously expressed opinions to the Herculean task, and he has entered upon it by clearing off the vast arrear of business accumulated by his predecessors, and by projecting efficient reforms in the constitution of his court. The establishment of a Court of Bankruptcy has removed one of the popular objections we have enumerated to the practice in chancery; but this is only one of a series of renovating measures intended to apply to the offices of the masters and registrars, and other branches of the equity department. We shall conclude the section with a few remarks on the economy, and next on the judicial improvement effected by the first of Lord Brougham's legal reforms.

The bankrupt business of the metropolis has hitherto been transacted by seventy commissioners, appointed for that purpose by the Lord Chancellor, who held their offices during pleasure. They were paid by fees out of the bankrupt estate. The average income from these fees to every commissioner, by a return made to the House of Lords, was £389 : 5 : or, according to the secretary of bankrupts' return, in round numbers, £380. The total expense, therefore, of the seventy commissioners, at an average of £380., was £26,000. The other expenses under the old system, together with the sum paid to the commissioners, were estimated by Mr. Vizard at £70,000.

The salaries of the judges, commissioners, and registrars under Lord Brougham's act are:—

Chief Judge	£3,000
Three Puisnes, at £2,000.	6,000
Six Commissioners, at £1,500.	9,000
Two Registrars, at £800, (exclusive of fees)	1,600
Eight Deputy Registrars, at £600.	4,800
Secretary of Bankrupts (exclusive of fees)	1,200
First Clerk	500
Second Clerk	300
Total	£24,000

The office fees of suing out a commission under former practice were as follows :—search for docket, 1s. ; bond, 7s. ; petition for commission, 11s. ; fiat answering petition, or filing affidavit, £1 : 2 ; commission and hanaper fee, £5 : 2 : 8 ; tin-box, 2s. ; if a private suit, £2 : 2 : 6 ; messenger, when the Chancellor was in the country, £1 : 5 ; office copy of petitioning creditor's affidavit, 3s. 2d. Under the new act a *fiat* is substituted for a commission, for which the fee is £10, and various other sums payable to secretary of bankrupts. A sum of £20 is payable to the secretary of bankrupts' account by the assignees. It is impossible, however, to exhibit an accurate comparison of the expense of proceedings under the old and the new system ; some of the charges are contingent, others terminable, and others depend on the number and length of copies, affidavits, folios, &c. Compensations are to be provided for fees and offices abolished, and the remuneration to the official assignees is discretionary in the commissioners.

The opinion of some persons is that the expenses of a proceeding in the smaller bankruptcies, where the assests do not exceed £4000, will be nearly equal to what they were under the former system ; but it is impossible to arrive at an accurate conclusion on this point, till the new machinery has been brought fairly into operation. It is certain, however, that there will be no future harvest of spoil, like that of Howard and Gibbs, when £20,000, was netted ; nor even like that of Chambers, when £10,000 was swamped by the legal, accounting, and assignee agencies.

One striking advantage of the Bankruptcy Court is, that it substitutes a tribunal effective for its purpose for one notoriously ineffective. There will be also greater responsibility in the judges, as well as increased despatch in their proceedings. A saving of time is a saving of expense to suitors, as well as of that which is more painful than expense— doubt and anxiety. So far the improvement is positive. But ought not a tribunal, which costs £24,000 a-year in fixed salaries, to have been final in its adjudications? Why such a gradation of appeals from a commissioner to a Sub-division Court, from thence to the Court of Review, and upwards—though the cases of such higher appeals are limited by the act—to the Lord Chancellor and the House of Lords ?

The branch, however, of the new arrangement about which we have any serious misgivings, is not the *judicial*, but the ministerial or *accounting* department. Will the official assignees be less costly and more expeditious than the creditor assignees have been ? May they not be as dilatory in settling accounts as masters in Chancery ? or may they not in certain emergencies employ the proceeds of the bankrupt estate in a stock-jobbing or mercantile adventure in preference to the payment of them promptly into the Bank of England?—*Nous verrons*, as the French say.*

---

* The number of bankruptcies has declined of late years. It may be partly ascribed to the less commercial speculation and adventure, and partly to the enormous expense attending bankrupt proceedings. If the decline in bankrupt-

OPPRESSIONS UNDER THE EXCISE-LAWS.

We have already made some remarks on the multiplicity and inquisitorial nature of the Revenue-Laws. Excise informations, of which we are going to give some account, are the practical consequences of these laws.

These informations are filed in the Court of Exchequer for real or supposed frauds on the revenue. The prosecutions are almost invariably instituted either on the testimony of hired spies or the Excise-officers. They form a principal source of emolument to the law-officers of the Crown. Every prosecution costs the country about fifty guineas. Of this sum ten guineas are for a brief to the Attorney-General; to the Solicitor-General, ten guineas; to two counsel, eight guineas each; to two other counsel, four guineas each. And to these sums must be added another item of £7 : 13 : 6 for the court-crier. Let the case be ever so simple, this is the usual array of counsel which appears for the Crown; and against which the accused has to contend. In one year there have been no less than 761 informations under the Excise-Laws, and the law-expenses on each case were not less than £120, making an annual sum of more than £120,000. The solicitor for the excise has almost unlimited power in these matters, and exercises the functions of both judge and jury. The petitions that are sent to the Board are referred to him; and which for the sake of his own emolument it is generally his interest to reject. The nature of such proceedings will be best illustrated by examples, selected from many others, which have been brought before the Parliament.

The first case we shall mention is that of Jeremiah Abell, a small farmer, in Norfolk. This man was prosecuted by the Excise for penalties to the amount of £1000, on account of an alleged smuggling transaction. He was able to prove, most distinctly, by seventeen witnesses, against the single testimony of the informer, that he was thirty miles from the place where the offence was sworn to have been committed. When the case was tried, his counsel most unaccountably consented to compromise the matter with the Board for £300, contrary to the express injunction of the defendant. Afterwards, the matter slept for a year, when Mr. Abell was taken into custody; and, at the time his case was mentioned in the House, he had been confined sixteen months in Norwich goal. Of his innocence there could not be the slightest doubt. He had the most satisfactory evidence to prove that the informer was at Norwich at the very time he had sworn to have been thirty miles from that place, watching the defendant and six others engaged in smuggling.

---

cies continue, the Court of Bankruptcy will become little better than a sinecure establishment. But, perhaps, the greater cheapness and dispatch of the new tribunal may augment the number of bankruptcies, by abstracting from the business of the Insolvent Court, and lessening compromises between creditors and debtors, which have been frequently resorted to, to avoid an expensive procedure.

Mr. Henty, another sufferer, and a most respectable gentleman of Sussex, had a very narrow escape from a gang of wretches patronised and employed by the Excise. He was found guilty of an attempt to defraud the revenue, and sentenced to pay fines and costs to the amount of £2400. The evidence on which he was convicted was of the most infamous description, and such as none but the agents of an odious system would ever think of employing. One of them was accused of an atrocious murder at Greenwich; others were afterwards convicted of perjury; some transported for robbery; and others (there being seven witnesses in all) we believe, were hanged. The conduct of the Excise in this case was the more unjustifiable, because they had been apprised of the characters of these miscreants: nevertheless, the solicitor commenced his prosecution against Mr. Henty, and on their evidence he was found guilty. When an indictment for perjury was preferred, the Excise came forward, and offered bail for them ; and no doubt they would have absconded, and Mr. Henty been deprived of all means of proving his innocence, had they not been committed to prison on a charge of felony.

Frequently, Excise prosecutions originate in the conspiracies of base wretches, who, for the sake of the reward, or to gratify their malice, unite to ruin particular individuals. As an instance of this sort, we select the following :—A man took a range of obscure and dilapidated buildings in London, for the pretended purpose of becoming a brewer of ale, and immediately set to work to draw honest tradesmen into his snares. By an act of parliament, a penalty is imposed on those who sell treacle or molasses to brewers. This miscreant, to accomplish his purpose, used to frequent those shops which were left under the super-intendence of apprentices and children; he procured a small quantity of these articles to be sent to him, and then gave information that the parties had sold them to a licensed brewer. Another case of the same stamp:—A respectable and industrious tradesman of Colchester, Mr. Underwood, had on some account or other incurred the hatred of a notorious smuggler, who made a vow that by some means he would accomplish his destruction. This, he thought, could not be more effectually done than by putting him in the hands of the Excise. He accused Mr. Underwood of being engaged in a contraband trade. Two informations were filed in the Exchequer ; one for the condemnation of Mr. Underwood's vessel, the other to recover the penalty of the bond which all masters enter into not to be concerned in any smuggling transaction. When the case came to be heard, the smuggler admitted that the information was false and malicious, and, of course, Mr. Underwood was acquitted ; but he had incurred expenses to the amount of £327 in triumphing over the malice of his enemy. He had no redress for his loss ; and his only resource was to commence an unprofit-able prosecution against the smuggler for perjury. At the same place, a brewer, having lent a friend his copper, was prosecuted for that friend's brewing a quarter of malt. The penalty for his *friendship* was £100 ; and the first intimation of it being incurred was an appalling bill of forty or fifty folios in length. He applied to the Board, who consented to remit the penalty, provided he paid £30, and what *small* costs might have been incurred in the prosecution. Three months after, he received a bill from a solicitor, in which these small costs were charged £46.

Persons are frequently dragged into the Court of Exchequer without knowing for what offence, when it had been committed, or who is the informer. In the case of Mr. Waithman, a handkerchief was brought into his house not worth thirty shillings, by a person in his employ, at the solicitation of a friend in the country. An information was laid against him, and a penalty of £200 demanded, which was afterwards softened down to £100, as a particular favour to the worthy alderman.

We shall only mention one more case of Exchequer process; that of a Captain Bryan. This gentleman was called on for a penalty of £200, two years after he thought the transaction had been entirely settled. On a petition to the Board, the penalty indeed was remitted; but a bill of costs was brought forward by the solicitor to a nearly equal amount. The misfortune of this gentleman originated in mistake in the report of the ship's cargo. The error was explained to the commissioners of Excise, who appeared perfectly satisfied, and the Captain concluded the matter was at an end. Two years were suffered to elapse, when the unsuspecting Captain was surprised with an Exchequer process, showing that an action had commenced against him to recover the penalty for the infraction of the Excise-Laws. The Captain, as we have said, petitioned; the penalty was remitted: but the solicitor brought in his bill of costs to the amount of £160 : 5, and his own solicitor's costs amounted to £89 : 5 : 9 more.

A serious evil resulting from the Excise system is the power vested in the Commissioners of Excise or Lords of the Treasury to mitigate penalties or stay proceedings against offenders at their discretion. This enables them to make the most odious distinction between persons supposed to be friendly or hostile to the government. We had a singular instance of this in the case of Mr. ABBOTT, brewer and magistrate, of Canterbury. This man had for a long time been selling, according to Lord Brougham's statement, *rank poison* in the beverage of the people. It appears he had been selling a liquor resembling beer, manufactured from beer-grounds, distillers' spent wash, quassia, opium, guinea pepper, vitriol, and other deleterious and poisonous ingredients. The officers of Excise having examined this worthy magistrate's premises, found 12 lbs. of prepared powder, and 14 lbs. of vitriol or copperas, in boxes, which, if full, would have contained 56 lbs. Proceedings were instituted against him by the Board. The penalties he had incurred amounted to £9000; and the case being notorious and atrocious, the Commissioners appeared determined to levy them with rigour. Mr. Abbott, however, was a *loyal man* and an *active magistrate;* and he prevailed upon some other loyal men to write on his behalf to the Lords of the Treasury. Among other persons who stepped forward in behalf of this *virtuous* magistrate, were the very reverend the Dean of Canterbury, Dr. Gerard

Andrewes, Mr. Baker, M.P., and the late Sir William Curtis. All these were loyal men and true ; and, in their letters to the Lords of the Treasury, spoke in the highest terms of the public and private virtues of the *good* Mr. Abbott. Mr. Baker styles him " my much esteemed and valued friend, Mr. Abbott." Sir William Curtis was still more eloquent and touching ; stating that he was a very long acquaintance of fifty years, and a " most honourable and virtuous old man." The reverend Dean went on in the same strain ; stating that he was a " *good neighbour* of his, and an useful magistrate ;" and that he should regret were his " usefulness and respectability diminished by a matter that concerned ONLY ALE-DRINKERS !"

Only think of this ! Here is a man, a very reverend dean, who regrets that a *good neighbour of his* should be dragged before the public merely for poisoning *ale-drinkers*. Had Mr. Abbott been poisoning *wine-drinkers*, we imagine his crime would have appeared very different in the eyes of the reverend dean. It is related of a right reverend bishop, in the House of Lords, that he once remarked that he did not know what the people had to do with the laws but to obey them. One is at a loss to conceive where these notions have been taken up; they certainly belong to another age, or at least to another country than England. For our part, we can only ascribe this unseemly insolence of the clergy to the undeserved respect which they have been accustomed to receive from the people, and which has begotten in them a feeling of superiority to which, above all men, they have the least claim, either on account of their knowledge or virtues, or any other qualification useful or ornamental. The views of some of them in respect of the people are very little more elevated than those of the nobles of Russia towards their boors. We remember an anecdote of a Russian officer travelling through Germany, who, on account of a trifling delay or provocation, shot his postillion. The circumstance exciting some noise, the officer was given to understand that, though such things might do very well in Russia, they could not pass in Germany with impunity. The officer, considering the interruption impertinent, demanded the *price* of a German postillion, and said he would *pay for him*. This was not much worse than Dr. Andrewes's notion of the social importance of ale-drinkers.

To return, however, to the *good* Mr. Abbott : so many testimonies, from such quarters, to his various excellences were not to be neglected. The Treasury, without seeking any more evidence, but merely at the instigation of their political friends, ordered the proceedings to be stayed, and penalties to the amount of £9000 were softened down to £500.

The recent case of Leaf and Coles,* the extensive dealers in contraband silks, is an instance of the power of the Treasury to mitigate penalties. The transactions of these persons had been to an enormous extent, to the great detriment of the home manufacture of silk, and the

---

* House of Commons, Dec. 9, 1831.

ruin of the fair trader. The penalties Leaf and Company had incurred by their illicit practices amounted to £25,000; the Treasury, or, more correctly, the attorney-general, compromised with the delinquents for £20,000, and returned them their smuggled silks valued at £5,000 more. It was no case for mercy; justice and the interests of commerce required that the utmost forfeiture should have been exacted.

The examples we have given will, we apprehend, be sufficient to exemplify the nature of Excise informations. The proceedings of the Court of Star Chamber, of the Inquisition in Spain, or *Lettres de Cachet* in France, were not more diabolical and oppressive than those which often occur in this country to uphold an oppressive system of taxation. Much of the evil results from the endeavours of the Aristocracy to throw a disproportionate share of public burthens on the industrious classes, by taxing heavily all articles of general consumption. Tea, spirits, and tobacco are the chief articles in which frauds on the revenue are attempted; and these are respectively taxed 100, 520, and 900 per cent. on the cost price. It is the high amount of duties which renders smuggling and adulteration so profitable that all attempts to suppress them prove unavailing. Three-fourths of the whole quantity of tobacco consumed in Ireland is smuggled;* and one-third of the tea sold in England is the produce of adulteration. What blessed effects are these of our fiscal regulations; especially coupled with the fact that the expense for the prevention of smuggling alone amounts to £700,000 per annum.

PROSPECTS OF LEGAL REFORM.

England is not less a law-ridden than a priest-ridden country; and we regret that Lord Brougham cannot devise plans of reform having a less tendency to increase the number and emolument of a profession already too predominant. It has been remarked, by the venerable father of jurisprudence in Europe, and we may add America—Mr. Bentham, that lawyers oppose improvement from the same motives workmen oppose the introduction of machinery,—they *are apprehensive it would lessen their employment.* Undoubtedly it would have this effect; for the great object sought to be attained is to simplify and expedite judicial proceedings, by which, unnecessary delay and expense may be avoided. The late Mr. Roscoe, in his Life of Leo X. (vol. iv. p. 179,) relates an anecdote of that pontiff which is applicable both to the law and priestcraft of this country. Cardinal Bembo having on one occasion quoted a passage from the Evangelists, he was interrupted by his Holiness, who said " It is well known to all ages how profitable this *fable of Christ* has been to us."—Our lawyers may say the same: the cart-load of legendary rubbish they profess to expound is, doubtless, very profitable to them, but a serious loss and inconvenience to the community.

---

* Sir Henry Parnell on Financial Reform, p. 49.

It by no means follows, because there are laws, there should be a host of legalists to interpret them. The causes which render English laws difficult and unintelligible are obvious, and have been explained. It arises from the unfathomable chaos in which they exist, their multiplicity, their contradictions, and the uncouth and nonsensical jargon in which they are expressed. All these are defects which would be speedily obviated by a government that represented the mind, the wants, and interests of society. The Statute-Book, and the mass of decisions engrafted upon it, we verily believe, might be compressed into an octavo volume, and rendered so plain and readable as to form an appropriate class-book in every seminary of education in the kingdom. Sad calamity this for the gentlemen of the bar! Their occupation would be curtailed; their wigs and gowns cease to be venerable; and all their learned lore be as much out of date as the cocked hats and ruffles of the last generation, Can we wonder, therefore, at their hostility to improvement? They have a great stake—not in the country, but the law; and we may generally reckon upon them for our opponents: though it is rather too much that they should accuse (as some of them do) the reformers of being irrational and visionary, while their own mountebank profession is the reverse of both reason and common sense.

Between jurisconsults in this country and on the Continent there is a marked difference: by the latter, law has long been treated as a rational science; by the former, it is considered nothing more than a mass of precedents, conundrums, forms, and technicalities—an art or mystery, by dabbling in which men may soon become rich. A few illustrious exceptions there are, no doubt, to this description; but this is the general character of the fraternity; their object is to gather fees, not study the principles of jurisprudence. Hence it is not from the profession we anticipate a systematic and effective reform in our judicial administration;—though, if any *unlearned* person venture to suggest improvements, the whole craft is in arms, and ready to devour him. So far as the practice of the profession is concerned, lawyers are the fittest persons to expound it; but so far as regards any thing new,—a *code*, for instance, or a different mode of administering justice,—they are the last persons in the world who ought to be consulted. For our parts, we should as soon think of advising with the disciples of IGNATIUS LOYOLA about the institutions of the order of Jesuits as with lawyers on the subject of legal reform.

Yet it is to lawyers the great work of legal amendment is confided, and from them alone are the people to expect reform in our judicial system. Nothing but disappointment, we fear, will flow from this source. All the law-lords, with the splendid exception of Lord Chancellor Brougham and, perhaps, Plunket, are opposed to reform. Sir James Scarlett suggested some minor improvements, during his attorney-generalship—the best of which was the limiting the power of arrest for debt to £100 and upwards; but it is evident he views, with no favourable eye, innovations on the great field of his triumphs. Only think of this gentleman's defence of *special pleading*, the absurdities of which are enough to make a horse laugh; a drizzling maze of empyrical inventions, circuitous procedure, and unintelligible fiction, calculated for no purpose but to fortify monopoly and wrap justice in deceit and mystery. With such obstacles and prejudices what can be anticipated but delay and evasion without end, and ultimate failure at last?

The Common-Law Commissioners are not expected to conclude their inquiries in less than three years, and the Commissioners of Inquiry on the Laws of Real Property in less than twelve years.* At the expiration of these periods what may be anticipated? The accumulation of innumerable volumes of reports, and the useful suggestions they contain, buried in as impenetrable a mass as the laws whose abuses they are meant to set forth; and, after all this expenditure of time, labour, and money, it is probable no measures of reform will be founded upon them. They will share the fate of the Chancery Report, made six years ago, of the volumes without number of Reports on Public Charities, on the state of Ireland, the state of the finances, the poor, and other national subjects, in which there is much research and many useful suggestions, but they are never reduced to practice.

Next let us advert to the reformatory labours of the late Secretary of State. The consolidation acts of Sir Robert Peel are, no doubt, improvements; but the progress of the Right Hon. Gentleman was much too dilatory, and his plan of proceeding deficient in comprehensiveness. The entire body of criminal law ought to have been taken up at once by a select body of individuals competent to the undertaking, and digested into a simple and uniform code, accessible and intelligible to the whole community. Granting, some thirty years hence, Sir Robert might have finished his task, still it appears to us the criminal law would be nearly in as great a state of obscurity, contradiction, and perplexity as at present. We shall cite an example, from the Forgery Act, to illustrate the working of this tinkering legislation.

In the twenty-third section of the act it is provided that the punishments of the 5 Eliz. c. 14, so far as they have been adopted by *other acts*, shall be repealed, and other punishments substituted in lieu of them. Now, as these *other acts* remain on the statute-book, without reference to the 1 Will. IV. c. 66, by which they have been altered, how is it possible this fact should be known to any person who happens to refer to them? This appears to us a convincing proof of the perplexities which will pervade the criminal statutes after the process of consolidation has been completed. They will be a sealed book, as heretofore, to all but lawyers and judges: in short, the legislature appears to proceed on the principle that laws are framed for the benefit of the profession only, not for the people; but surely the penal code,

---

* Law Magazine for January, 1830.

which affects every member of society, ought to be constituted for a very different purpose. Again, how little is the advantage of consolidating the statutes, if the decisions engrafted upon them, and which are as valid a portion of the law as the statutes themselves, are not incorporated ? It will be all labour in vain, and " confusion worse confounded !"

In our humble opinion a different course might be pursued with advantage in the great work of legal reform. In the first place, it appears inquiries are not so much needed as *remedies ;* abuses in our judicial system are not far to seek—they are obvious, and so are the means of reforming them. Why, then, not dispense with those voluminous reports and endless researches ? A commission might have been appointed to consolidate and simplify the criminal law—another the civil law—another the law of property—and another the laws which regulate civil and criminal procedure, and each commission ought not only to have incorporated the statutes relative to the several departments of jurisprudence, but also the decisions of the judges founded upon them, and which have become part of the law of the land. When each commission had finished its task, their labours might have received the fiat of the legislature. It is only, we imagine, by some such effective measures the laws of England can be made, within a reasonable time, worthy of the opulent and enlightened community for whose benefit they are intended.

But it is high time we concluded this long article. When the first Common-Law Report was presented to the Duke of Wellington, his only remark is said to have been—" Too much of it,—too much of it,—a d——d deal too much of it." We fear a remark of the same tenor may escape some of our readers, owing to the prolixity of our lucubrations. But the importance of the subject must form our apology. The dearness and delay of justice are national grievances of long standing. It appears, from *Whitlocke's Memorials,* Oliver Cromwell presented a petition to the Collective Wisdom of his day, praying that " a speedy consideration might be had of the great oppressions, by reason of the multiplicity of unnecessary laws, with their intricacies and delays, which tend to the profit of some particular men, but much to the expence and damage of the whole." The Lord Protector, later in life, triumphed over every difficulty ; but the lawyers gave him most trouble, and he was constrained at last to acknowledge they were too many for him.

** The subjoined statements are principally abstracted from Returns to Parliament in the session of 1830 and 1831, and will confirm and illustrate the preceding exposition of our judicial administration. In some of the documents we have left out the shillings and pence to save room, which makes trifling inaccuracies in the summing up.

JUDGES' SALARIES.

SALARY and ALLOWANCES received, in the Year 1792, by each of the JUDGES of the Exchequer, King's Bench, and Court of Common Pleas; and the Salary and Allowances paid in 1829.

	1792. £	1829. £
KING'S BENCH:		
Chief Justice	4,000	10,000
Puisne Judges, each	2,400	5,500 *
COMMON PLEAS:		
Chief Justice	3,500	8,000
Puisne Judges, each	2,400	5,500
EXCHEQUER:		
Chief Baron	3,500	7,000
Barons, each	2,400	5,500 †

In addition to the Salaries and Allowances paid in 1792, the Judges of the several Courts were remunerated by Fees, the amount of which, received by each, is not known. The Judges derive no emolument from such source at present.

COURT OF CHANCERY.

RETURN of the Total Amount of the Effects of the Suitors of the Court of Chancery, in the Years 1756 to 1829 inclusive.

	£	s.	d.
In the year 1756 the total amount of suitors's effects was	2,864,975	16	1
—— 1766	4,019,004	19	4
—— 1776	6,602,229	8	6
—— 1786	8,848,535	7	11
—— 1796	14,550,397	2	0
—— 1806	21,922,754	12	8
—— 1816	31,953,890	9	5
—— 1818	33,534,520	6	10
—— 1819	32,848,815	13	4
—— 1820	33,258,897	17	11
—— 1821	34,693,735	10	10
—— 1822	35,683,034	5	6
—— 1823	36,988,481	19	9
—— 1824	37,635,924	13	0
—— 1825	38,224,834	18	4
—— 1826	38,223,602	0	1
—— 1827	38,060,055	4	1
—— 1828	38,266,438	9	10
—— 1829	38,386,135	19	5

---

* In addition to these salaries, the second judge of the King's Bench receives an ancient fee of £10 per term, or £40 per annum, in respect of his labour in giving charge to the grand jury, and pronouncing judgment against malefactors; payable out of the fines, forfeitures, penalties, and compositions in the Court of King's Bench.

† The Chief Baron and Barons of the Court of Exchequer receive, in addition to the above salaries, an annual allowance of £17 : 10 : 8 for stationery, payable, by the Usher of the Exchequer, out of annual grants by parliament.

AN ACCOUNT *of the several Sums of Money received by the* PURSE-BEARER *to the Lord Chancellor, during Three Years, commencing May* 1st, 1827 ; *distinguishing the Amount received from Public Seals and from Private Seals.*

Years.	Total.	Public Seals.	Private Seals.
	£	£	£
1828	3604	481	3123
1829	3766	320	3445
1830	4081	396	3685

In the third column are included the receipt and docquet fees, which are paid whether the instrument is sealed at public or private seal.

There were sealed, at private seal, from 1st May, 1827, to 30th April, 1828, 3704 writs, at 3s. 3d., amounting to £601 : 18 ; from 1st May, 1828, to 30th April, 1829, 4937 writs, at 3s. 3d., amounting to £802 : 5 : 3 ; and from 1st May, 1829, to 30th April, 1830, 4861 writs, at 3s. 3d., amounting to £789 : 18 : 3. This sum of 3s. 3d. is thus appropriated :—the Lord Chancellor, 2s. ; sixpenny-writ duty, 6d. ; chaff-wax, 3d. ; sealer, 3d. ; porter, 3d.

MASTERS IN CHANCERY.

AN ACCOUNT *of the Sums of Money received by Master* STRATFORD *and his Clerks, from his Office, in one Year, ending in* 1830.— Parl. Paper, No. 361, Session 1830.

	£	£
The Master:		
For copies of papers and other proceedings, including particulars	2071	
Warrants	676	
Swearing affidavits, answers, and examinations	48	
Reports and certificates upon orders made upon petitions or motions	200	
Reports and certificates made upon hearing causes	184	
Sales and other matters	84	
		3265
The Chief Clerk:		
On copies of reports, &c.	118	
On swearing affidavits, &c.	6	
On reports and certificates made upon petitions or motions	60	
Ditto on hearing causes	46	
Sales and other matters.	258	
Gratuities	583	
		1074
The Copying Clerk:		
For copies	431	
For transcripts and ingrossments	17	
		448
Total		£4789

The master's salary, received quarterly from the Exchequer, is £87 : 6 per annum; and for robe-money, from the Hanaper-office, £6 : 8 : 10 per annum.

The master's salary, received from the suitors' fund, in the Accountant-General's Office, half-yearly, is £600 per annum.

The clerks have no salaries ; they are remunerated solely by fees, partly belonging officially to the chief clerk, and partly by a participation of the master's fees, regulated by usage or particular agreement between him and his clerks ; and varying in different offices.

*** Returns were made, to the House of Commons, of the emoluments of the other Masters in Chancery ; but, as the sources whence they arise and their amount are similar to Master Stratford's, we omit them, to save room.

An Account of the Sums paid in the Year 1829, and the Total Sums paid from 1826, for Compensations for Loss of Fees, under Authority of 6 Geo. IV. c. 96, intituled, " An Act for preventing frivolous Writs of Error."

	1829.			Total, from 1826.		
	£	s.	d.	£	s.	d.
The Hon. Thomas Kenyon, filacer, exigenter, and clerk of the outlawries in the Court of King's Bench	5,463	7	0	16,590	8	8
Henry Edgell, Esq. clerk of the errors in the Exchequer Chamber	2,521	16	11½	 8,339	19	5
*Cursitors for London and Middlesex :						
Robert Talbot, Esq.	1,176	11	5¾	 3,629	18	5¾
Hon. William Henry John Scott	1,176	11	5¼	 3,629	18	5¾
William Villiers Surtees, Esq..............	1,176	11	5¼	 3,629	18	5¾
Richard Wilson, Esq.	1,176	11	5½	 3,629	18	5¾
Ushers of the Court of Exchequer :						
Richard Grey						
John Morris...............................	} 15	1	6	 50	16	6
William Broadhurst						
Lewis Williams						
William Stewart Rose, Esq. clerk of the pleas of the Court of Exchequer..............	65	4	0	 100	4	0
	£12,771	15	3½	..£39,601	2	6

Filacer, exigenter, and clerk of the outlawries in the Court of King's Bench, appointed by the Lord Chief Justice.

Clerk of the errors in the Exchequer Chambers, appointed by the Lord Chief Justice of the Common Pleas.

Cursitors for London and Middlesex, appointed by the Lord Chancellor.

Ushers of the Court of Exchequer, appointed by the Chief Usher, who holds his office in fee, under grant from the Crown, temp. Henry II.

Clerk of the Pleas of the Court of Exchequer, appointed by the Chancellor of the Exchequer.

IMPRISONMENT FOR DEBT.

Number of Persons committed for Debt to the several Prisons of the Metropolis in the Year 1827, and the Sums for which they were committed.—Parl. Paper, No. 76, Session 1828.

	For sums above £100.	For sums between £50&£100.	For sums between £50&£20.	For sums under £20.	Total.	In custody Jan. 1, 1828.
King's Bench Prison	474	354	550	213	1591	.. 674
Fleet Prison	206	141	223	113	683	.. 253
Whitecross-street Prison	206	273	816	600	1893	.. 378
Marshalsea Prison..........	20	30	166	414	630	.. 102
Horsemonger-lane Prison ..	57	58	134	923	1172	.. 105
Total........	963	856	1889	2263	5969	..1512

₊ From Parl. paper, No. 632, Sess. 1830, it appears 1563 persons were

* We should like to be informed what course the cursitors intend to pursue, in consequence of the alterations made by the act of 1830, for the more effectual

committed to Whitecross-street prison for various terms from one to ten days; the total amount of their *debts* was £2,071 : 10 : 2; the amount of their *costs* £746 : 6 : 6.

Number of Persons DISCHARGED FROM PRISON *under the Acts for the Relief of Insolvent Debtors since the constitution of the present Court in 1820; and the Number who have been ordered to be* DETAINED IN CUSTODY *for contravening the provisions of the Acts for the Relief of Insolvent Debtors.*

In the Year	Ordered to be Discharged Forthwith.				Ordered to be Discharged at some future Period.				TOTAL.
	In London.	On Circuit.	Before Justices.	TOTAL.	In London.	On Circuit.	Before Justices.	TOTAL.	
1820	830	—	1,495	2,325	61	—	96	245	2,482
1821	2,347	—	2,516	4,863	219	—	208	427	5,290
1822	2,074	—	2,499	4,573	161	—	221	382	4,155
1823	1,811	—	2,047	3,858	181	—	202	383	4,241
1824	1,745	318	1,255	3,318	142	18	115	275	3,593
1825	1,955	1,342	73	3,370	126	161	8	295	3,665
1826	2,429	1,865	89	4,383	110	183	5	298	4,681
1827	1,929	1,988	89	4,006	90	128	10	228	4,234
1828	1,913	1,459	112	3,475	127	131	6	264	3,739
1829	2,067	1,580	100	3,747	158	152	10	320	4,067
1830	2,056	1,823	111	3,990	189	191	9	389	4,379
1831 to June 30th	781	749	90	1,620	107	28	2	137	1,757
				43,528				3,652	47,083

The commissioners in the remarks appended to this return, observe that " they have not the means of ascertaining the number of Insolvent Debtors who *have paid dividends*," but they " communicate the subjoined statements which may perhaps assist, in some measure, towards the subject under inquiry:

" Total number of cases in which assignees have accepted and taken their appointments 10,271
" Total of Assignees to whom money has been paid out of Court.... 1,783
" N.B. Of 10,271 assignees, 8,492 *have filed no accounts.* Of the accounts filed there are 932, in which a balance in hand *appears* arising from monies not received out of Court."—*Parl. Pap. No.* 141, *Sess.* 1831.

Administration of Justice in England and Wales. By that act, the cursitorial department of Wales is annexed to the four cursitors for London and Middlesex. But surely these gentlemen, who, for several years, have been receiving an annual compensation for the losses sustained by the *Writ of Error Act*, will make some return to the public from the additional gains accruing to them from the new arrangement.

We believe the plain English of the above is that 47,083 persons have passed through the Insolvent and Circuit Courts; that the average expense of the discharge of each is £256 ; that their debts together amount to at least *four millions*, and that the dividend received by the creditors on this immense sum was about ONE FARTHING IN THE POUND. What an admirable system of Debtor Laws for this commercial, manufacturing, and trading community ! ! !

We are aware this statement is not strictly accurate, but it is an approximation to the truth. There are no means of ascertaining precisely the average dividend realized from the estates of insolvents, since there are no official returns of the sums received by assignees out of court, nor of the amount derived from the property of insolvents acquired subsequently to their discharge. But it is well known the Insolvent Debtors' Act has degenerated into little more than a series of unprofitable forms and ceremonies ;* the *getting-up* of the schedule is such that very little accrues to the creditor from the assets ; and the short imprisonment of the debtor operates neither as disgrace nor improvement. The act certainly *empties the gaols;* but if this be an advantage it would be much better policy never to fill them, rather than resort to a preventive which does not correct the defaulter, and only renders him a worse member of society. Offers of compromise are not so frequent in consequence of the act ; and Sir Peter Laurie stated to a parliamentary committee, that tradesmen charge ten per cent. more for their commodities on account of the facilities it afforded to the escape of debtors. This is a pretty heavy tax on the paying part of the community—for those who do pay must make up for the loss sustained by those who do not—tending greatly to lessen consumption, and consequently the returns and profits of vendors.

Tradesmen are mostly inclined to severer laws towards debtors; they appear not to be aware that all laws would become unnecessary by a simultaneous decline in the custom of credit. That credit can be avoided entirely, even in retail trade, we do not believe : this is the opinion of the best informed merchants and tradesmen of the metropolis ; persons of the greatest respectability often take the longest credit, to the great profit of their domestics : but what we reprobate is its universal practice ; its not being the exception but the rule of trade—and then having recourse to oppressive and inefficient laws to supply the place of individual prudence.

---

* Treatise on the Police and Crimes of the Metropolis, p. 129. By the Editor of the *Cabinet Lawyer*.

PROGRESS

OF THE

PUBLIC DEBT AND TAXES.

THE annual income of a nation consists of the united produce of its
agriculture, manufactures, and commerce.   Taxes are a certain proportion of the annual income levied for the public service.   In other words,
they are a certain proportion of the income of the labourer, the farmer,
the merchant, and manufacturer, abstracted for the use of the government.   The portion of income the different classes can appropriate to
this purpose, without creating national poverty and misery, is limited.
If taxation be carried beyond this limit, the necessaries of life of the
labouring classes will be abridged, the profits of trade and agriculture
will be so far reduced, that capital will diminish, or cease to be employed, or transferred to countries where it will be more productive.
England, in the privations of the people—the protracted stagnation of
industry, only interrupted by transitory gleams of prosperity—the
embarrassments of the agricultural, commercial, and manufacturing
classes—the emigration of capital—and the inability of the farmer,
unaided by the artificial high prices produced by corn-laws, to cultivate
the soil—exhibits all the evils of a country suffering from the pressure
of overwhelming taxation.
     Some, indeed, contend that taxation has no share in producing these
calamities.   The fallacy of this will easily appear.   Taxation being a
certain portion of the income of every individual, the evils it produces
will be obvious, by considering the different effects produced by this
portion of the annual income remaining in the hands of individuals, and
being paid to government.   In the former case, the income of every
individual would be increased, the labourer and artizan would have a
greater command over the necessaries of life; the profits of the farmer,
merchant, and manufacturer augmented; their capital increased, consequently commerce and the means of creating employment extended.
But this is not all; supposing public burthens reduced, there would be

fewer placemen, pensioners, collectors of taxes, soldiers and sailors to be supported. These classes might be returned to the plough or the loom, and occupied in the pursuits of commerce and the cultivation of the earth. There would be no want of capital for these undertakings. The abolition of taxes would create capital. In short, the general effect of a reduction of taxes is this : the power of production and consumption, or, in other words, the quantity of employment and the means of subsistence are augmented.

It is a favorite dogma with some, especially those who live on the public, that taxes return to those from whom they are collected ; which is about as good as the defence of a housebreaker, who, convicted of carrying off a merchant's property, should plead he did him no injury, for the money would be returned to him in purchasing the commodities he dealt in. But it may be asked of those who maintain this position, in what manner are the taxes returned ? Certainly, taxes are paid in money; this money is again paid to the servants of government; these again pay it to the cultivator of the soil and manufacturer ; and in this manner, it may be said, that taxes return to those from whom they were collected. But on this latter part of the operation it must be observed, that before either the cultivator or manufacturer can re-possess himself of his portion of the taxes, he must part with a certain quantity of his commodities in exchange ; so that tax-paying revolves itself at last into the industrious giving a certain portion of their produce for the maintenance of government.

Here is the true source of the privations and embarrassments of the country. The portion of every man's produce levied for the support of government, of pensions, placemen, sinecurists, and standing armies, has invaded the funds necessary for the comfortable subsistence of the labourer, and for carrying on the trade, commerce, and agriculture of the kingdom.

Having alluded to the general effect of taxation, let us consider those measures by which the present enormous load of debt and taxes has been incurred. The principles on which government has been conducted have not varied since the Revolution of 1688 to the present time. The wars waged have generally commenced for trivial and unattainable objects,—and these objects have generally not been attained; under pretence of guarding against distant and improbable dangers, the country has been involved in present and imminent ones; passion and pride, rather than any views of national advantage, have been the actuating principles of government ; and as they engaged in war rashly, they persevered in it obstinately, and rejected more favourable terms of pacification than they were afterwards under the necessity of accepting. In short, our wars have been wars of ambition and oligarchical selfishness, of pride, folly, and despotism, originating in, and carried on by, the corrupt state of the representation. Let us endeavour to give some idea of the cost of these parliamentary wars from the Revolution, as evinced by the increase of taxation and the National Debt.

WILLIAM THE THIRD'S REIGN, FROM 1688 TO 1702.*

The public income at the Revolution amounted to £2,001,855. At the death of William it had increased to £3,895,205, being nearly doubled. This augmentation arose from various new duties; especially the excise on salt, the distillery, and the malt-tax. The other sources of revenue were the customs, land-tax, poll-taxes, a tax on births, marriages, and burials, hearth-money, the post-office, and other smaller duties. The total sums raised by taxes and by loans, during this reign, were as follow;

Customs	£13,296,833	14	6
Excise	13,649,328	0	5½
Land-taxes	19,174,059	8	3½
Polls	2,557,649	7	7¼
Burials, births, marriages, and bachelors, &c.	275,517	18	1
Various articles, including permanent loans and temporary loans unpaid............	23,093,980	16	7½
	£72,047,369	5	6¾

Of the fourteen years of this reign, nearly ten were years of war. The military and naval expenses amounted to £44,847,382, being more than one-half the whole expenditure of government. After all the blood and treasure expended by William, his ambition and revenge remained unsatisfied ; and the ostensible object of the war, the curbing the ambition of Louis XIV. unattained. Speaking of the conclusion of this contest at the treaty of Ryswick, Smollett observes,—" Such was the issue of a long and bloody war, which had drained England of her wealth and people, almost entirely ruined her commerce, debauched her morals by encouraging venality and corruption, and entailed upon her the curse of foreign connexions, as well as a national debt, which was gradually increased to an intolerable burthen."— *Continuation of Hume,* vol. i. p. 330.

The funding system, and the mode of raising money by lotteries and exchequer-bills, commenced in this reign.

QUEEN ANNE'S REIGN, FROM 1701 TO 1714.

The revenue, at the commencement of this reign, amounted to £3,195,205. At the period of the union with Scotland, in 1709, the revenue of England amounted to £5,691,803. The sums received into the Exchequer, during twelve years and three-quarters, were—

---

* The amount of revenue, and the estimate of the naval and military expenses, from the Revolution to the end of the reign of George II. are taken from Dr. Colquhoun's Treatise on the Resources of the British Empire.

Customs ···· ····························· £15,113,811
Excise ··································· 20,850,909
Land-tax ····· ························ 12,285,909
Miscellaneous, including Post-Office, Stamps, and
    smaller loans of the Revenue ···············   5,261,346
Amount of Loans··························· 59,853,154

                                  Total······£122,373,531

Of the thirteen years of this reign, twelve were years of war. The military and naval expenses amounted to £58,560,581. The object of Queen Anne's wars, like those of her predecessor, purely continental. They were terminated by the disgraceful treaty of Utrecht, in 1712, when our allies were ignominiously abandoned. The peace establishment of this period is estimated at £1,965,605.

George the First's Reign, from 1714 to 1727.

On the death of Queen Anne, the National Debt amounted to £52,145,363 ; but though her successor enjoyed a period of uninterrupted tranquillity, no effort appears to have been made to reduce it. On the 31st of December, 1727, the principal amounted to £52,092,235 ; the interest to £2,219,551. The aggregate sum which passed into the Exchequer of George I., during a reign of twelve years, three months, and ten days, amounted to £79,832,160. The revenue at the time of his death amounted to £4,162,643.

George the Second's Reign, from 1727 to 1760.

The prosperous state of the country, for the first twelve years of profound peace at the commencement of this reign, might have admitted of a considerable reduction of the debt, had not Sir Robert Walpole, a profligate statesman, been minister. Instead of expending the surplus revenue in the liquidation of the debt, it was employed in parliamentary corruption. During ten years, from 1707 to 1717, *secret service money* amounted only to £337,960. From 1731 to 1741 it cost the nation £1,453,400. This augmentation is ascribed to the increased pay Sir Robert gave to the *honourable* members for their votes and speeches in support of his administration. The whole of the debt paid off in this long peace, amounted only to £5,137,612, the interest of which was £253,516.

The wars of George II. commenced in 1739, and were concluded at the peace of Aix-la-Chapelle, 1748. The total expense of these contests is estimated, by Dr. Colquhoun, at £46,418,680. The nation gained nothing by all this expenditure of treasure. The war originally arose with Spain : that nation claiming the right of searching all

English vessels navigating the American seas. This subject, which formed the ground of the war, was never mentioned at the peace of Aix-la-Chapelle no more than the *right of search*, which originated the war with the United States of America, was mentioned at the treaty of Ghent. The only advantage the English gained was the *glory* of placing Maria Theresa, grand duchess of Tuscany, on the throne of Germany, in opposition to the King of Prussia.

In the interval of peace, to the commencement of war in 1755, there was a trifling reduction of the debt to the amount of £3,721,472, and the interest of the capital was reduced from 4 to 3 per cent.

The expense of the second war, called the seven years' war, amounted to £111,271,996. This contest first commenced about the respective boundaries of the French and English in the deserts of Canada. It has been called the war of *catskins*—the possession of a few furs being really the object which involved the two countries in hostilities. On this frivolous pretext commenced a war then unexampled in magnitude and expense ; its ravages extended to Europe, and even to the other side of the globe in the East Indies. It is worthy of remark, too, that on the continent, George II. took the part diametrically opposite to the part he had taken in the former contest. The war of 1740 was for the humiliation of the King of Prussia ; the war of 1755 for his aggrandizement !

It will be proper to notice particularly the state of the debt, finances, and peace establishment at the conclusion of this reign. They are thus stated by Dr. Colquhoun :—

Public Revenue.		Peace Establishment.	
Customs	£1,985,376	Civil List	£836,000
Excise	3,877,349	Navy	900,000
Stamps	263,207	Army	900,000
Land-tax, (deducting de-		Ordnance	80,000
ficiencies)	1,737,608	Miscellaneous	50,000
Miscellaneous	650,000		
Total	£8,523,540		£2,766,000

	Principal.	Interest.
Debt at the conclusion of the peace of 1762	£146,682,843	£4,840,821

GEORGE THE THIRD'S REIGN, FROM 1760 to 1820.

Mr. COKE, of Norfolk, when he characterized this monarch's reign as the most sanguinary and disastrous of the English annals, was not far from the truth. In the course of it were three principal wars: the American war, the revolutionary war, and the war of 1815. All these wars were waged against human liberty and happiness ; and the two last commenced on a principle which we would fain hope is now disclaimed by every government in Europe—namely, the right of one nation to interfere with another in its domestic affairs. We will state the cost of each, as shown in the sums raised by taxes and loans.

AMERICAN WAR.

Years.	Revenue.	Loan.
1775	£10,138,061	
1776	10,265,405	£2,000,000
1777	10,604,013	5,500,000
1778	10,732,405	6,000,000
1779	11,192,141	7,000,000
1780	12,255,214	12,000,000
1781	12,454,936	12,000,000
1782	12,593,297	13,500,000
1783	11,962,718	12,000,000
1784	12,905,519	12,879,341
1785	14,871,520	10,990,651
	£142,975,229	£93,869,992

The American war terminated in 1783; but as the loans of the two following years were raised to wind up the expenses of that struggle, it is proper they should be included. The total expense of the American war will stand thus:—

Taxes... £142,975,229
Loans.. 93,869,992
Advances by the Bank of England 110,000
Advances by the East-India Company 3,200,000
Increase in the unfunded Debt 5,170,273

£242,265,494

Deduct expense of a peace-establishment for eleven
years, as it stood in 1794 .... £113,142,403

Net cost of the American war.................£129,123,091

This, then, is the sum expended by the Boroughmongers in an attempt to enslave the colonies. George III. boasted that he was the last man in his dominions to subscribe to the peace with America: he left his people burthened with a debt of *one hundred and thirty millions*, as the price of the obstinacy of one man, and an abortive attempt to impose on a brave people the tyrannical principle of *taxation without representation.*

The second war was still more atrocious than the first; it was a war not merely against liberty, but the principles of liberty; it was a barbarous and gigantic effort of the privileged orders to prevent the amelioration of society, and to render mankind the eternal victims of ecclesiastic and aristocratic oppression. As the war of 1793 was more diabolical in its objects than the contest with America, so we should say, had its calamities only extended to its authors, has it been more justly ruinous in its consequences. Let us endeavour to estimate the cost of this liberticide and Vandal contest. We shall state the sums raised by taxes, and the debt contracted each year from its commencement, and then deduct the probable expenditure of the country, had no such war existed.

The account of sums raised by taxes is taken from Dr. Hamilton's *Inquiry into the National Debt*, p. 203, third edition. The amount of debt contracted, including navy and exchequer bills funded, is also taken from the same writer, p. 320. The short peace of Amiens, and the interval betwixt the exile and return of Bonaparte from Elba, may be considered rather a suspension of hostilities than a period of peace; therefore we have considered it as one uninterrupted war from 1793 to 1815, having the same objects—the maintenance of the usurpations of the Clergy and Aristocracy.

Years.	Taxes. £	Loans. £
1793	17,656,418	25,926,526
1794	17,170,400	——
1795	17,308,411	51,705,698
1796	17,858,454	56,945,566
1797	18,737,760	25,350,000
1798	20,654,650	35,624,250
1799	30,202,915	21,875,000
1800	35,229,968	29,045,000
1801	33,896,464	44,816,250
1802	35,415,296	41,489,438
1803	37,240,213	16,000,000
1804	37,677,063	18,200,000
1805	45,359,442	39,543,124
1806	49,659,281	29,880,000
1807	53,304,254	18,373,200
1808	58,390,255	13,693,254
1809	61,538,207	21,278,122
1810	63,405,294	19,811,108
1811	66,681,366	29,244,711
1812	64,763,870	40,743,031
1813	63,169,845	54,780,324
1814	66,925,835	63,645,930
1815	69,684,192	70,888,402
	£952,929,653	£764,859,036

After making some deductions on account of the operations of the *loyalty loan*, and the transfer of annuities, the total debt contracted from 1793 to 1815, amounts to £762,537,443. If to this sum be added the increase in the unfunded debt during that period, and the additional sums raised by taxes in consequence of hostilities, we shall have the total expenditure, owing to the French war, as follows:—

Debt contracted from 1793 to 1815 ••••••	£762,537,445
Increase in the unfunded debt, ditto ••••••	50,194,060*
War-taxes ••••• ••••••••••••ditto ••••••	614,488,459†

Total expense of the French war ••£1,427,219,964

Two objections may be made to the fairness of this statement. First, the amount of debt redeemed during the war, by the operation of the *Sinking Fund*, ought to be deducted from the amount of debt contracted. The second objection arises from the mode of negotiating loans. In each loan, the capital funded exceeds the sum actually advanced to government. In some loans, government acknowledges itself debtor £100, when only from £54 to £60 is actually received. Hence it follows that, from the debt contracted since 1793, ought to be deducted the difference betwixt that debt and the sums which passed into the Exchequer.

After admitting deductions from the charges of the war on this account, and the operation of the sinking fund, we must be allowed to make a trifling addition. The loans raised for Ireland, guaranteed by Britain, amounted to £103,032,750 : the sums actually received on account of these loans to £64,750,000. The revenue of Ireland, in 1791, amounted to £1,190,684. Owing to the increase of the Irish revenue during the war, the war-taxes of Ireland cannot be estimated at less than £80,000,000. After these deductions and additions the account will stand thus:—

Sums raised on account of loans ••••••• ••••	£506,081,267
Sums raised on account of Irish loans ••••••	64,750,000
War-taxes in England •••••• •••••••••••	614,488,459
Ditto in Ireland ••••••••••••••••••••••	80,000,000
Increase in the unfunded debt •••••• ••••••	50,194,060
	1,255,513,786
Deduct sums paid to the Commissioners for the reduction of the debt •••• •••••••••••	173,309,383
Total••••••	£1,082,204,403

---

* The unfunded debt in 1793.......... £14,902,635
    Ditto   1815.......... 65,096,695 increase as above.—*Dr. Hamilton's Inquiry*, p. 338.

† This sum is obtained by deducting, from the total amount of taxes during the war, the taxes which would have been raised had the expenditure of 1793 continued.

The statement is now divested of every extraneous item, and, reducing it to its lowest amount, *one thousand and eighty-two millions two hundred and four thousand four hundred and three pounds* remains as the sum actually received and expended on account of the war with France, from 1793 to 1815. On an average of the twenty-two years, from 1793 to 1815, it is a war expenditure of nearly fifty millions; and this is the sum which the tax-ridden, law-ridden, priest-ridden, deluded people of England yearly contributed out of the produce of their industry, agriculture, and commerce, to prevent an independent state altering the form and meliorating the abuses of its government.

Can we wonder, after the tremendous sacrifice in pursuit of this unrighteous object, at the terrible calamities with which the country is afflicted ? Can we wonder at our exhausted, impoverished, and embarrassed condition ? More than *one hundred millions* expended in an abortive attempt to enslave the American colonies; more than *one thousand millions* expended to re-establish feudal and ecclesiastical tyranny in France. This forms the financial history of the public debt and taxes—of the ELEVEN HUNDRED MILLIONS *expended in the wars of despotism.* And what has been the result of this lavish waste of national resources ? The answer is—the three immortal days of Paris—the triumph of Belgium—the regeneration of Europe—and the complete—the full—the glorious establishment of those very principles the English Aristocracy vainly sought to exterminate.

When we look back to the history of the last century—the wars of madness, ambition, and tyranny which have been waged ; when we reflect on the millions expended in these wars—the fruits of unexampled industry, skill, and enterprise ; when we think of our present situation—the piercing privations of the bulk of the community—the discontent and disunion among all classes—the abuses pervading every department of our social and general administration—Ireland on the point of rebellion or separation ;—when we think, we repeat, on these things, and contrast them with the situation of glory and happiness England might have attained under a wise and honest government, administering her exhaustless resources in the promotion of the arts of peace, instead of slaughter, bondage, and devastation ; we feel not less indignant at the wickedness of our rulers than the apathy which has so long tolerated their folly and their crimes.

EXPOSITION

FUNDING SYSTEM.

ALTHOUGH the feudal system was a barbarous social institution, it possessed the advantage of entailing on the fomenters of war its unavoidable cost and calamities. The old barons used to arm themselves and vassals at their own expense, and support them during the contest. There was then no standing army nor permanent revenue,— those who tilled the land fought the battles of the country. Under such a system, wars could neither be very long in their duration, nor very remote in their objects. Foreign expeditions suited as little to the national resources as the avocations of the people. The only time that could be spared to settle public quarrels was between seed-time and harvest, and the only treasure they could be provided with before-hand was the surplus produce of the preceding year. Hence, wars were generally either carried on languidly, or were of short duration. Their operations were frequently interrupted by truces, and sometimes discontinued through mere feebleness. A warlike leader was often stopped short in his victorious career, either from the want of resources, or the necessity of allowing his followers to return home to provide subsistence for the following season.

The state of the sovereign was as little favourable to protracted contests as the condition of his lieges. His revenue was derived partly from lands reserved as a royal demesne, and partly from feudal casualties, and afforded a slender provision for maintaining the royal dignity, and defraying the ordinary expenses of government, but was altogether inadequate to the support of numerous and permanent armies. Supplies from the people were obtained to a certain extent; but the people neither possessed the means, nor, happily, had acquired the habit of granting liberal supplies. Princes, under any emergency, real or supposed, or actuated by any scheme of ambition, had recourse either to borrowing or *pawning*. The loans which they raised were partly compulsory, and, as the repayment was ill secured, the rate of interest was high. Sometimes the jewels of the crown were pledged, and sometimes the crown-lands were mortgaged. In this manner, the revenues of most of the powers of Europe were anticipated and encumbered.

A new state of society introduced a new mode of supporting war. Instead of borrowing on their *own credit*, sovereigns learnt to borrow on the credit of *posterity*. The issue of war no longer depended on a single battle or successful irruption, but on the length of the public purse. It was not money, however, that formed the sinews of war, but *credit*. Credit superseded money, and modern policy found out the expedient of supporting wars for temporary objects, and entailing the burthen of them on future generations. This system possessed too many facilities to be abandoned, or not to be carried to the utmost extent of which it was capable. And, accordingly, we find wherever the system of borrowing and funding has been introduced, it has gone on with an accelerated velocity till the payment of the principal became quite chimerical, and governments were obliged to compound with their creditors for the interest.

The debt of this country, which was inconsiderable at the Revolution, has increased, in less than a century and a half, to its present magnitude. The increase during every reign, except the pacific reigns of George I. and George IV. has been greater than the preceding. The increase, during every war, has been greater than during the preceding. The increase, during the latter period of every war, has been greater than during the earlier period. The increase, by every hostile interference or warlike demonstration, has been greater than administration held forth when the measure was undertaken. The part of the Debt paid off, during peace, has borne a small proportion to that contracted by the preceding war.

These are the general characteristics which have marked the progress of the funding system: it has been the national spendthrift vice that has operated on the public welfare like the addiction to some baneful passion in an individual; indulgence augmented appetite, till, at length, the malady has reached a state of virulence which precludes all hope of cure or alleviation. As to the liquidation of the debt, that is an idea we believe not a single person to entertain; all that the most reasonable look forward to is postponement, until such a crisis in public affairs occurs, as will demonstrate to all parties the expediency of coming to terms—*of a compromise*, for mutual safety and advantage. We are now in the *seventeenth year of peace*, and, comparatively, no portion of the debt has been redeemed by actual payment; the reduction in the annual charge has been chiefly effected by the conversion of stocks of a high into those of a lower denomination,—a mode of procedure accompanied with serious suffering to particular classes of annuitants, and accomplished by ministerial combinations in the money-market, for artificially forcing up the prices of stocks, hardly justifiable. Before, however, adverting particularly to the redemption of the debt, let us give a few explanations of the funds and government paper.

By the term *Fund* is usually meant a real sum of money or store of treasure, reserved for a specific purpose, but so far as the term is applicable to the debt of England, it is purely an abstraction. In lieu of calling the Debt the Funds, it is more correct to call it the Public Annuities or the National Annuities. The obligation to pay a perpetual annuity of an enormous amount is, in fact, all that remains of that vast mass of capital swallowed up and lost under the donomination of the Debt, and which has been dissipated in the ruinous foreign wars and domestic profusion detailed in the last and preceding chapters.

The *Sinking Fund*—of which we shall, by and by, give a curious history—means a sum of money set apart for the purpose of discharging the public debt. Generally speaking, we mean, by the Funds, those large sums which have been lent to government, the record of which is preserved in the books of the Bank of England, and for which the lenders, or their assigns, receive interest from the public revenue. The term *Stock* is used nearly in the same sense; but is more strictly applicable to the different branches of the Debt, bearing different or the same rate of interest; as the 3 per Cents Reduced, or the $3\frac{1}{2}$ per Cents, and which together constitute the aggregate public debt. It is, also, applied to the sums which form the capital of the Bank, the East-India Company, the South-Sea Company, and other public companies, the proprietors of which are entitled to a share of their respective profits.

Although the public creditor cannot demand payment of the capital debt, the mode of transferring it, even in small sums, is so conveniently arranged, and the dividends so regularly paid, that it is considered an eligible property. The value of the Funds is liable to considerable fluctuation. It depends chiefly on the proportion between the interest they bear and the profit which may be obtained by applying capital to other purposes. It is influenced by the plenty or scarcity of money; and it is impaired by any event which threatens the safety or weakens the credit of government. It is always much higher in time of peace than in time of war; and is affected by every event, and even by every report, in time of war, favourable or unfavourable. False reports are frequently raised by knavish people for that purpose.

In the early part of the Funding System, a separate account was kept of éach loan, and of the tax imposed for payment of the interest. This method was afterwards found inconvenient, as the produce of some of the taxes fell short of the expected sum, while that of others exceeded it, and the multiplicity of funds produced confusion. To obviate this inconvenience, the different funds were united, and to each various branches of revenue were appropriated, charged with the payment of the annuities.

Besides the funded debt, is a large sum due by government under the name of the *Unfunded Debt*. It arises from any national expense, for which no provision has been made, or the provision has proved insufficient, or not forthcoming at the time wanted. During the latter periods of the late war, and for a few years following the return of peace, its amount considerably exceeded fifty millions; in 1815 it was at the highest, and had reached a sum greatly beyond the entire amount of the debt at the accession of George II., being more than $67\frac{1}{2}$ millions. Of late years the amount of the unfunded or floating debt has not exceeded half that sum. The form in which it mostly exists is that of *Exchequer bills*. These were first issued in 1696, and being intended as a temporary substitute for money during the recoinage at that period, some of them were so low as £10 and £5. There are none issued now under £100, and many of them are for £500, £1000, and still larger sums. They bear interest, at a certain rate per day, for £100; and, being distributed among those who are willing to advance their value, they pass from hand to hand like bank-notes. After a certain time, they are received in payment of taxes, or other moneys due to government; and the interest due on them, at the time, is allowed in the payment. The Bank often engages to receive them to a certain extent, and thereby promotes their circulation; and the daily transactions between the Bank and the Exchequer are chiefly carried on by bills of £1000 deposited in the Exchequer by the Bank, to the amount of the sums received by them on account of government. New Exchequer-bills are frequently issued in discharge of former ones; and they are often converted into funded debt, by granting capital, in some of the stocks, on certain terms, to such holders as are willing to accept it.

Besides Exchequer-bills there are *Navy-bills* issued from the Navy-Office, to answer any purpose in that branch of public expenditure; and they bear interest after a certain date, if not discharged. *Ordnance-bills* or *Debentures* are issued from the Ordnance-Office, for supplying deficiencies in that branch of expenditure. *Victualling* and *Transport Bills* are issued from the respective offices in the same manner. In addition to the principal branches of the unfunded debt, there is always a number of demands on the public for bills accepted by the Treasury, army charges, and miscellaneous services of various kinds. These are daily fluctuating, and their amount at any particular time cannot be easily ascertained.

Our next object will be to exhibit a brief statement of the progress of the Debt, and its successive augmentations and diminutions during different reigns and periods of war and peace, and the total amount at the present time.

SUMMARY *of the Progress of the Debt from the Commencement of the Funding System, at the Revolution, to the 5th January*, 1831.

	Principal.	Interest.
National Debt at the Revolution of 1688··	£ 664,263	£ 39,855
Increase during the reign of William III.	15,730,439	1,271,087
Debt at the accession of Queen Anne····	16,394,702	1,310,942
Increase during the reign of Queen Anne	37,750,661	2,040,416
Debt at the accession of George I.······	54,145,363	3,351,338
Decrease during the reign of George I.··	2,053,128	1,133,807
Debt at the accession of George II.······	52,092,235	2,217,551
Decrease during the peace···········	5,137,612	253,526

Debt at the commencement of the war of 1739 ··················	46,954,623	1,964,025
Increase during the war··············	31,338,689	1,096,979
Debt at the end of the war, 1748 ······	£78,293,312	£3,061,004
Decrease during the peace ············	3,721,472	664,287
Debt at the commencement of the war, 1755	74,571,840	2,296,717
Increase during the war ··············	72,111,004	2,444,104
Debt at the conclusion of the war, 1782··	146,682,844	4,840,821
Decrease during the peace ············	10,739,793	364,000
Debt at the commencement of the American war, 1776···················	135,943,051	4,476,821
Increase during the war ··············	102,541,819	3,843,084
Debt at the conclusion of the American war, 1783 ··············· ·······	238,484,870	8,319,905
Decrease during the peace ············	4,751,261	143,569
Debt at the establishment of the Sinking Fund, 1786 ···················	249,175,323	10,774,398
Increase from 1786 to 1793 ··········	5,131,112	94,577
Debt at commencement of the war of 1793	254,306,435	10,868,975
Increase to the peace of 1801··········	293,591,441	12,438,767
Debt at the peace of Amiens, 1801 ····	547,897,876	23,307,742
Increase during the peace ············	81,569,653	3,735,883
Debt at the renewal of the war, in 1803..	629,467,529	27,043,625
Increase during the war ··············	491,940,407	16,940,954
Debt at the peace of 1815············	1,121,407,936	43,984,579
Increase during the peace, to 1819 ····	108,987,631	5,202,771
Debt, January 5, 1819··············	1,230,395,567	49,187,350
Deduct Debt redeemed by Sinking Fund	389,637,049	15,815,001
Net unredeemed Funded Debt of the United Kingdom, January 5, 1819 ··	840,758,518	33,372,349*
Net unredeemed Funded Debt of the United Kingdom, January 5, 1831 ··	757,486,996	27,399,575†

* Parliamentary Paper, No 35, Session 1819.
† Annual Finance Accounts, p. 145, Session 1831.

The unfunded debt, consisting of Exchequer-bills, amounted, January 5th, 1831, to £27,271,650, the interest of which, added to the interest of the funded debt, and the charges of management make the aggregate annual charge on account of the funded and unfunded debt, £28,349,754.

The diminution in the annual charge of the Debt, during the seventeen years of peace, may be ascribed, in a considerable proportion, to the reduction of the rate of interest on the 5 and 4 per cent. stocks, and on Exchequer-bills, and to the falling in of terminable annuities. A further diminution was effected in the session of 1830, by the conversion of the New Fours into a three-and-a-half per cent. stock. Altogether, the savings effected by these conversions amount to three millions and a half per annum; and the total reduction in the annuity, payable to the public creditor, amounts to four millions and a half.* It appears, then, the diminution in the annual charge of the Debt has not been the result of ministerial economy and retrenchment, but of the internal state of the country—*the redundancy of unemployed capital,* which by lowering the rate of interest, and thereby enhancing the price of the funds, enabled government to offer to the holders of stock, of a high denomination, the option of being either paid off at par, or the acceptance of a lower rate of interest.

A desirable fact to ascertain is, the permanent charge entailed on the community by the war of 1793. From the extensive inquiries of the Finance Committee of 1828, this subject may be correctly illustrated. The annual augmentation of the permanent charge of the debt, between 1792 and 1816, was £22,744,360.† To this must be added, the charge for the half-pay and pensions of the army and navy and civil retired allowances, called the dead weight, amounting to £5,363,640 per annum. We must, also, allow for the increase in salaries, in civil and colonial establishments, which were a consequence of hostilities. The results will be best expressed in a tabular form.

Permanent Burthen entailed on the Country by the Revolutionary War, from 1793 to 1815.

Interest of the debt contracted during the war	£22,744,360
The annual charge for half-pay, pensions, and superannuation allowances, amounting, in 1830, to £5,363,640; but consisting almost all of life annuities, may be computed equal to a permanent burthen of	2,250,000
Exclusive of this last item, the expenditure of the army and navy is greatly augmented since 1792, partly from the extension of our foreign possessions, and partly from the augmented military force kept up in Ireland and Great Britain.—On account of the war, say	2,500,000
Increase of Civil List, salaries and pensions	2,000,000
Other charges not enumerated	1,000,000
Total	£30,494,360

* Viscount Goderich, House of Lords, May 5, 1830.
† Fourth Report of Select Committee on Public Income and Expenditure, p. 20.

Such is the amount of the annual burthen entailed on the country by the last war of the Aristocracy. Yet the Oligarchy have the meanness to refuse £250,000 a year for the purposes of emigration. They have even the baseness to complain of the amount of *poor-rates ;* they grumble to pay a few millions per annum for the relief of the aged, the infirm, and destitute, while they have wantonly burthened the community with a perpetual incumbrance of upwards of THIRTY MILLIONS per annum in war and devastation. Although they have thus mortgaged for ever national resources, happiness, and enjoyments, they aggravate the calamities they have created, by clinging with the grasp of death to enormous salaries, sinecures, and unmerited pensions. Can any one who has a head to think, or heart to feel, suppress indignation in contemplating this unexampled record of infatuation, injustice, and oppression ?

PLANS FOR THE REDEMPTION OF THE DEBT.

Having given a general illustration of the nature of the Funds, and of the progress and present amount of the Debt, our next object will be shortly to notice the empyrical projects set on foot and countenanced by the Aristocracy for its redemption.

Although the Sinking Fund, established under the auspices of Mr. Pitt, was founded on an egregious misapprehension, yet, if we examine the subject attentively, we shall find that ministers had similar reasons for adhering to it that they had for adhering to any other branch of expenditure. First, the keeping up of a Sinking Fund was a pretext for keeping up taxation. Secondly, the management of the fund was a pretext for keeping up a certain amount of patronage, fees, and emoluments. Lastly, the Sinking Fund left a surplus sum at the disposal of ministers, ready to be applied to any casual object they might think expedient. They might employ it to subsidize foreign despots, to enter on new wars, or to supply deficiencies in the civil list, or any other department of expenditure. That the money was voted for other purposes formed no security that it would not be so applied ; experience having shewn that ministers never hesitated to encroach on the Sinking Fund when it suited their necessities.

These, we apprehend, formed some of the reasons for maintaining the Sinking Fund, long after its fallacy had been demonstrated. Some reluctance, too, was no doubt felt to abandon a scheme of finance which had been panegyrized by many distinguished individuals ; and, in fact, the history of the Sinking Fund is the most striking proof of the gullibility of our " great men," that can any where be found ; and it is chiefly for the purpose of illustrating the superlative abilities of hereditary legislators, that we are induced to devote any space to the exposition of such a barefaced subject.

Mr. Pitt's plan of a Sinking Fund was, to set apart a portion of the surplus revenue, to accumulate by *compound interest,* and, after the expiration of a certain period, to apply the aggregate amount of interest and principal to the liquidation of the debt. To show the fallacy of this scheme, it will be necessary to premise a few explanations on the nature of interest.

Interest is of two kinds, either simple or compound ; simple interest is that which is allowed for the use of the principal only ; compound interest, called also interest on interest, is that which is allowed for the use of both principal and interest taken together. If money be lent at simple interest, suppose five per cent. per annum, it will double itself in twenty years ; that is, if the interest be forborn that time, it will equal the principal. If money be laid out at compound interest, on the same terms, it will double itself in little more than fourteen years ; so that the different rate at which money increases by simple and compound interest is very considerable. To illustrate this by an example, we will suppose £100 lent at five per cent. compound interest, for one hundred years. At the expiration of the first fourteen years (omitting the fraction of a year) it would amount to £200 ; at the expiration of the second fourteen years to £400 ; at the expiration of the third fourteen years to £800 ; and so on, doubling itself at the expiration of every fourteen years, till, at the expiration of the one hundred years, it would have increased to the sum of £14,112 ; while, had the same money been put out at simple interest, it would have amounted only to £600 ; £500 being the interest of £100 for one hundred years, at five per cent. per annum.

Now, it is on this power of money to accumulate, at compound interest, that the Sinking Fund was established. Dr. Price, an expert arithmetician, calculated that a penny, or a farthing, we forget which, laid out at compound interest at the birth of Christ, would, at the time he wrote, have accumulated to several *globes of gold, each globe as large as the earth.* This was really prodigious ; and the Doctor was so pleased with the result, that he thence conceived the idea of redeeming the national debt. He thought that if a sum of money, no matter how small, could only be once laid out at compound interest, it would, in a century or so, amount to a sum equal to the debt itself, and by means of which the debt might be discharged. All the Doctor wanted was TIME ; money he did not want, except a farthing or a penny to begin with. Nothing could be more alluring ; to pay off the debt by so small a sum as one penny, seemed, next to a sponge, the cheapest way imaginable.

Doctor Price communicated his scheme to Mr. Pitt, who appears to have been as much captivated as the Doctor with the discovery. This was in 1786 ; a time favourable for the experiment, the country being at peace with all the world, commerce and agriculture just recovering from the depression of the American contest, and, what was more, there was a surplus revenue of nearly a million to begin with. This sum, it was resolved, should be set apart to " fructify" by the miraculous powers of compound interest, agreeably to Dr. Price's calculations. Commissioners were appointed to take charge of the sacred deposit, which, on no pretext, was to be violated: and thus did the Sinking Fund, which, like little David, was to bring down the Goliah of the debt, commence.

All at once, however, the people were seized with a strange panic; from entertaining the most gloomy apprehensions that the debt would never be paid, they began to fear it would be paid *too soon;* the globes of gold had so bewildered the public mind, that it was apprehended, from the sudden payment of the debt, the country would be overwhelmed with money and unemployed capital. To avert so dire a calamity, Mr. Pitt announced his intention to pay off £4,000,000, annually, and no more. Here the subject rested for some years, and we must beg leave to rest also. Having stated fairly the principle of the Sinking Fund, we must now expose its fallacy as applicable to the reduction of the debt. It is due, however, to Dr. Price to observe that there was nothing wrong in his principles, that the effect of compound interest was correctly as he had calculated, and that he was only wrong, like many other well-meaning theorists, in his application of them.

The first objection to the scheme of Dr. Price was the length of time that must elapse before it attained its object. Any plan for the reduction of the debt, founded on an adherence to a particular system of finance, the continuance of a certain amount of taxation, or the duration of peace, was hardly likely to be realized in practice. These were all liable to change; yet a permanency in them was necessary to complete the original plan of the Sinking Fund. The sum set apart was on no pretext to be violated; war might arise demanding additional sacrifices, the ability of the country to support taxation might decrease, or there might arise new chancellors of the exchequer with new schemes of finance, yet none of these were to interfere with the fund. That a plan depending on such contingencies should be realized appears highly improbable.

Waving, however, the objection as to *time*, we will suppose the plan in actual operation; we will suppose a million set apart to accumulate by compound interest, till it equal in amount the debt it is intended to liquidate. Now, it is obvious, if the debt be very large, the Sinking Fund must be very large also; but, supposing the debt amounts to 800 millions, one cannot conceive how any Sinking Fund, long before it equals in amount the debt it is intended to discharge, can be employed, or in whose hands it can be invested. Suppose the fund amounts only to 200 millions, how can any government employ such a sum? To whom are they to lend it? If they lend it to individuals they will want security, not only for the interest but the principal. But the only adequate security would be land; commercial security would hardly be satisfactory; and, it is obvious, if landed security alone be accepted, the advance of 200 millions would make government the mortgagees of nearly all the land in the kingdom. Such a state of things is chimerical, and, consequently, any Sinking Fund founded upon it must be chimerical also.

Instead of reducing the debt in this way, it is easy to conceive another far more economical and equally efficacious. Suppose the money forming the fund had not been raised in taxes, but left in the hands of the people to be employed in trade and manufactures; then suppose, at the expiration of a certain time, a sum is levied in taxes equal in amount to what the Fund would have attained; it is obvious, on this supposition, the debt would be equally reduced; but, in this case, there would be no Sinking Fund,—no commissioners,—no drawing money in shape of taxes, and returning it again in shape of loan;— in a word, there would be no delusion.

Though the principle here illustrated is that on which the Sinking Fund was founded, it is not that according to which it has been conducted. The money forming the fund has never, in fact, been lent to individuals, but employed in the purchase of stock at the market-price. The interest of stock so purchased has been added to the fund, and the total employed in the purchase of more stock; so that, by continually adding the interest of the debt redeemed to the principal of the fund, the effect has been the same as money accumulating at compound interest. If we compare this mode of employing a Sinking Fund with the former, we shall find that, if the first was chimerical, the second was useless, serving no object further than entailing an unnecessary expense on the public for management.

Suppose at the end of the year there is a surplus revenue of one million in the Exchequer; then, agreeably to the system pursued by our statesmen for many years, this million is paid to commissioners, who employ it in the purchase of stock, the stock so purchased and interest forming together the Sinking Fund. But, instead of the million being vested in Commissioners, suppose it is employed by the Chancellor of the Exchequer in the purchase of stock, where, it may be asked, would be the difference? In both cases the same amount of debt is redeemed, and the interest of the redeemed debt, being laid out in the purchase of more stock, accumulates in a compound ratio.

It is in the latter way the Americans have managed the reduction of their debt; and by which they have almost effected its extinction. When there is a surplus in the treasury, after defraying the charges of government, it is applied directly to pay off such portions of the debt as have been advertised to be paid off, and on which the interest afterwards ceases to be paid. Indeed, the principle is so plain that it is astonishing how it can ever have been misapprehended. It is obvious to the meanest capacity that, if a sum of money be owing, on which interest is payable, the gain is equal, whether we pay a part of our debt, or lend, to a third person, a sum of equal amount. Government, however, acted as if there were some substantive difference in the two cases, and they were supported for years in the egregious blunder by the " Collective Wisdom of the nation."

We have not yet conducted the reader to the chief absurdity in the Sinking Fund. We have been all along supposing an *actual surplus revenue*, and considering the most advantageous mode of employing this surplus; but the fact is, there never was any such surplus, except during the first few years after the establishment of the fund. Every year government incurred debt, and this debt it attempted to pay by *borrowed money ;* that is, it borrowed money of A to pay B, and in this consisted the GRAND BUBBLE of the Sinking Fund.

The late Professor Hamilton was the first writer who exposed the delusion of the Sinking Fund, and showed incontrovertibly that it was by the application of a surplus income only that the debt could be reduced. By persisting in the financial error we have endeavoured to explain, an enormous expense was incurred in the charges of management, and this was not the extent of the evil. The Sinking Fund was a principal cause of the augmentation of the debt. So enormous was the blunder, that no one felt any concern about the increase of this national incumbrance; whatever might be the amount, it was conceived the Fund would be adequate to its redemption. Hence public credit became as unlimited as public credulity. Men, in other respects enlightened, were deceived, and it would be easy to cite, from the speeches of distinguished living statesmen, the most extravagant encomiums of this great fiscal deception. But the subject has ceased to be of intense interest, and is chiefly valuable as an additional testimony of those epidemic aberrations to which human nature, in all ages, has been exposed. Even Lord Grenville has lived to discover and acknowledge he was deceived by the Sinking Fund; and this appears not the only error of the Pitt system, of which his lordship appears likely to survive the refutation.

We have still left the more lamentable part of the business unnoticed; the public has not only incurred a great loss from the charge of managing the Sinking Fund, but also from the *additional sums borrowed* for its maintenance.

In every loan the contractors have a profit at the expense of the public, and the greater the loan the greater their gain, and consequently the public loss. From 1793 the Sinking Fund was supported by *borrowed money ;* besides the loan for the public service, an additional sum was raised for the Fund. Had there been no such Fund, the annual loans would have been less by the amount of the sum paid to the commissioners for the redemption of the Debt. The question then is, supposing the sum borrowed for the Fund, since 1793, be 250 millions, how much has the public lost by the operation ?

Professor Hamilton answered this question. He ascertained the total loss to the public, by annually borrowing additional loans to support the delusion of the Fund, at THIRTY MILLIONS. The interest of thirty millions, at five per cent. per annum, is a million and a half. A million and a half then is the gain of the loan-contractors, and the annual loss entailed on the country by the farce of a Sinking Fund.

A question may be here asked,—If we had had no Sinking Fund, in what way were we to look forward to the redemption of the Debt? Our opinion is that, in case of a surplus revenue, it ought to have been applied to the purchase of stock at the market price, and a portion of the Debt cancelled equal to the amount of stock purchased. But we are not much in favour of government having a surplus revenue to dispose of, but think it better that taxes should be remitted to the amount of the surplus ; or, in case the times are favorable to an effort for the reduction of the Debt, that it should be made by a direct assessment on the community expressly for the purpose.   The advocates of a surplus revenue think it tends to support public credit ; but the surest mode of supporting public credit is to contribute, in all possible ways, to promote public prosperity.   Public credit obviously depends on the abundance of public wealth ; in other words, on the ability of the community to support the burthens necessary to pay the interest, or ultimately the principal of the debt ; and this ability is augmented, not by taking money from the people, but by leaving it in their pockets : it is not by tying up capital in a sort of mortmain, in the hands of government commissioners, that national wealth is amassed, but by leaving it to be employed in the extension of commerce, manufactures, and agriculture. Every shilling levied in taxes takes from productive capital, thereby impoverishing the country, and lessening the security of the public creditor.

In short, we trust the people have learnt wisdom by experience, and they see the policy of keeping every administration in a kind of *strait waistcoat*, neither suffering them to have a surplus revenue, nor surplus military force, nor surplus power of any kind, beyond the current exigencies of the state, at their disposal.   Without this precaution, the country is sure to be drawn into some wanton and profligate crusade. All governments are prone to war, because it augments patronage and emolument, and gratifies pride, insolence, and ambition.   If we have not been involved in hostilities ere this, it has been more owing to the protecting Ægis of our pecuniary embarrassments than the absence of inclination in our rulers.   Can it be supposed we should not have been embroiled about Portugal, Turkey, France, Italy, or Belgium, had not the Exchequer been empty ?   A surplus revenue, however, under the pretext of a Sinking Fund, at all times supplies the needful, and it is easy to foresee, from past experience, were such a fund tolerated, it would be dissipated in domestic profusion or foreign aggression.   As to really applying the fund to the redemption of the debt, it is mere delusion : the Oligarchy, notwithstanding the solemn ejaculations of many of them about preserving, *inviolate*, *public faith*, have got a more efficient receipt for reducing the Debt than paying it off, as soon as the necessities of their unprincipled system demand the application.

DEAD-WEIGHT ANNUITY PROJECT.

We are induced shortly to notice this project, because it is the most recent, and, we believe, the last attempt which will ever be made to play tricks of legerdemain in matters of finance.

In the year 1822 a plan was adopted for relieving the country, in some degree, from the immediate pressure of the Dead Weight, by extending the payment of it over a longer series of years than the natural duration of the lives of the individuals holding half-pay, pensions, and allowances, under this denomination, would extend to. For this purpose an annuity of £2,800,000 was appropriated, out of the existing revenue, for 45 years, and vested in trustees for the discharge of the then payments, which, for that year, were estimated at £4,900,000, subject to yearly diminution by the death of annuitants. It was computed, that, according to the ordinary duration of human life, these annuities for the lives of the then holders would be equal to the annuity of £2,800,000 for forty-five years. The trustees, were, therefore, empowered to sell, from time to time, such portions of this annuity as would provide the funds required for the payment of the dead weight, according to a computation made of the amount which would, probably, be due in each year. The act by which this arrangement was sanctioned took effect from the 10th of October, 1822.

The trustees failed in their first negotiation, which was entered into with some public companies, and ultimately made an engagement with the Bank of England, for supplying the funds required for six years, by the transfer to that corporation of an annuity of £585,740, part of the above £2,800,000. The terms of the sale were settled by actuaries on either side, according to the current value of the public stocks. The sum which the Bank undertook to provide in the period specified was £13,089,419, the last payment upon which was made in July, 1828.

Now, to the measure of raising money by the sale of a temporary annuity there is no objection, when practised by the state, no more than by an individual : it may be resorted to, in order to meet an extraordinary charge; and to diffuse the charge at a diminished rate, for each year, over a longer space of time. But the framers of the dead weight expedient sought by the means of it to create *an addition to the income of the state*, whereby a Sinking Fund of five millions might be provided, notwithstanding a considerable reduction of the taxes then existing. It was in this the delusion consisted. The money for the reduction of debt was certainly forthcoming, by the sale of the annuity, and, therefore, positively applicable to the purchase of stock in the market; but the sale of the annuity was itself a *creation of debt*, and it was, therefore, not correct to call that a Sinking Fund which only served to extinguish, in one shape, a debt which it established in another.

Such an intricate contrivance was evidently a revival, in a new shape, of the fundamental error of the Sinking Fund, namely, an attempt to extinguish debt by *borrowed money*, and, like that famous juggle, it entailed an unprofitable charge on the country for management. As the objectionable part of the project has been abandoned, under the recommendation of Sir Henry Parnell's Finance Committee, it is not necessary further to expose its fallacy. We may, also, congratulate our readers on the virtual relinquishment of the Sinking Fund ; since, by the 10th Geo. IV. c. 27, which came into operation July the 5th, 1829, it is provided that the sum, in future, applicable to the reduction of the debt, shall be merely what happens to be the actual annual surplus revenue above the expenditure of the United Kingdom. The actual surplus revenue, for reasons assigned in the last section, will, we trust, be kept at a minimum, at which point, or below, it seems to have arrived; being at present (Jan. 1832) something worse than nothing, or, as algebraists term it, a " negative quantity."

A mere detail of the fiscal blunders and oversights of the Oligarchy would form a most ludicrous display of human folly and presumption. It can never be forgotten that the Omnipotent Parliament of 1810 actually passed a resolution that a pound note and a shilling were equal in value to a guinea, though the latter was openly and publicly sold for *twenty-eight shillings!* Then think of the conduct of the " Guardians of the Public Purse" in granting *annuities on lives.* The Tory statesmen of Oxford and Cambridge appear to have been wholly ignorant that the average duration of human life, especially in females, had greatly extended of late years; and, in consequence, up to the year 1829, and until they were apprised of the circumstance by a private individual, continued to grant life annuities on the most disadvantageous terms, and by which, for many years, an annual loss of £100,000 was sustained by this tax-paying community.

It would be easy to cite similar examples of the waste of public treasure through mere incapacity in our rulers; but it is necessary to conclude. Our exposition of the origin and downfal of the great Sinking Fund bubble, which deluded the country for nearly half a century, cannot fail to be amusing and instructive. If we revert to the history of the Boroughmongers, we shall find that their system has been carried on for many years by a series of moral, political, and financial bubbles. The French war was all a bubble. It commenced under the pretext of protecting property and averting infidelity and immorality. These, however, were mere bubbles; the real objects being to prevent reform in the representation, the administration of justice, and the tithe oppression. Abuses in all these were endangered by the principles of the revolution; but then, government could hardly go to war on the barefaced pretext of supporting them, so they went to war on the pretext of supporting *religion* and *social order.* New circumstances require new delusions. The country is now at peace; but we shall be marvellously surprised, if some new bubble is not blown to justify interference with the regenerated states of the Continent and the New World.

NEW SUGGESTIONS FOR LIQUIDATING THE DEBT.

All idea of liquidating the Debt, by the operation of the Sinking Fund, being abandoned, it may be concluded this great national incumbrance is destined to be a perpetual burthen entailed on succeeding generations. This, it must be confessed, holds out a discouraging prospect for the future. Let us, however, inquire if it be not possible to imagine a course of public affairs which would tend to the just and natural extinguishment of the Debt; or, secondly, let us inquire if such changes in the monetary system of Europe may not supervene, as would constitute an equitable claim for a reduction in the amount of the annuity payable to the public creditor. Although there are few questions in public economy that have excited more intense inquiry than the progress and final issue of our funding system, still we think there are one or two views of the subject which have been overlooked by political writers, and which we shall beg leave briefly to submit to our readers' consideration.

Lord Goderich has justly remarked, (House of Lords, May 7, 1830,) that it is not the magnitude of the capital of the debt, but the amount of the dividends which form a question of interest. A public creditor is not, like a private creditor, entitled to demand payment of both principal and interest: all to which he has compulsory claim is the regular payment of his dividend. A greater amount of capital is only important to the public inasmuch as it imposes a heavier burthen in the charges of management payable to the Bank of England. The vital consideration is the amount of the perpetual annuity entailed on the country: whatever tends to lessen this charge relieves the public; and let us see what system of policy would most effectually promote so desirable a consummation.

The interest of money has been gradually falling for centuries; and, from the augmentation of capital, it is not possible to assign the minimum;—it may be depressed to one, or even a half per cent.; or money may become so redundant, that, instead of the payment of interest for the use, a *premium* may be given merely for its safe custody. How far this reduction may be still carried depends entirely on the management of public affairs. Let us suppose our rulers have resolved, all at once, to carry on the government on principles of justice and wisdom, without regard to the partial interests of the Church, the Aristocracy, or any other section of society; let us suppose they are resolved to give full scope for the augmentation of national wealth, by the abolition of commercial and charted monopolies—by the repeal of the Corn Laws, and of all such taxes and restrictions as impede the development of industry: let us suppose that government is resolved to make all reasonable concessions for the attainment of internal quiet and contentment, by the extension of the elective franchise—the improvement of the judicial administration—the abolition of partial and oppressive laws—the reduction of exorbitant salaries, the extinction of sinecures, the rescinding of unmerited pensions, and the relinquishing of unprofitable and useless colonies: let us further suppose that government is resolved to pursue a system of impartial justice towards Ireland, remove all pretext for popular agitation, and cultivate, to the utmost advantage, her vast resources: lastly, let us suppose that government is so wholly intent on promoting the general welfare, that they are resolved to remove all restrictions on the freedom of discussion, and allow the utmost latitude, without regard to considerations personal to themselves, for the free investigation of every question in the least relevant to the public happiness; especially of such questions as elucidate the causes of the poverty and privations of the great body of the community.

Now, supposing such a liberal and enlightened policy to be pursued by the government, the consequences would be most extraordinary.

Contentment and confidence would pervade all, and every obstacle to the full development of industry removed, commerce, manufactures, and agriculture attain an unexampled state of prosperity. The country would be inundated with wealth, and the mass of unemployed capital would be so great, that interest would be merely nominal. But would not ministers take advantage of such a favourable crisis in national affairs to reduce the Debt? Assuredly they would. All the stocks would rise above par, and they might either pay the public creditor his principal, or compel him to accept a lower rate of interest. It is in this way, merely by the operation of good government, by adopting measures to promote internal concord and prosperity, that the Three per Cents might be reduced to two, one, or even a half per cent.; and this is what we call the *just and natural extinguishment of the Debt!*

The unsettled state of Europe may postpone for a time the decline in the interest of money; but such is the intelligence and desire of accumulation pervading all classes, that we consider it an event of certain occurrence. Under this impression, we do not concur in the wisdom of the plan adopted by the Chancellor of the Exchequer in 1830, for the conversion of the Four per Cents. Agreeably to Mr. Goulbourn's scheme, an option was given to the holders of the New Fours to accept a Five per Cent. stock, *irredeemable* for a long term of years. The chief saving to the public from this arrangement was a diminution in the amount of the capital of the debt; but this, as before remarked, is an unimportant consideration, and only affects the amount of per centage payable to the Bank for management. The great object for a financer to aim at is a reduction in the public annuities; but this reduction is foreclosed, by creating an irredeemable fund; and the country is precluded from deriving advantage from the augmentation of national wealth and consequent declension of the interest in money.

Let us next advert to the other contingency to which we alluded, as likely to operate, an equitable reduction in the monetary charge of the debt—*namely, a rise throughout Europe in the value of the precious metals.* That such a rise is in progress is highly probable, for the following reasons:—1. The unsettled state of South America during the last twenty years, and consequent interruption to the working of the gold and silver mines. 2. The increased consumption of the precious metals, from the diffusion of greater wealth and luxury. 3. The increased demand for them, owing to the increase of population, commerce, and commodities. 4. The general substitution of a metallic for a paper currency in England, America, and the continental states. All these causes obviously tend to enhance the value of the representative medium; and, should they continue to operate, they must eventually work a dissolution of money engagements; for it cannot be supposed that if a pound weight of silver attain as great an exchangeable value as in the reign of the EDWARDS, that either nations or individuals shall be bound by contracts made under circumstances so widely different. Such a revolution in the instrument of exchange, or even an approximation to it, could never have been foreseen, either by creditor or debtor; and the fulfilment of his obligations by the latter being rendered impracticable, by vicissitudes which he could neither foresee nor control, both equity and reason would relieve against them.

The practical application of this reasoning, to the reduction of the Debt, is too obvious to need explaining.   It is a crisis wholly distinct from such as occur from the issue or withdrawal of Bank paper, or the rise or fall of mercantile credit.   These are the local and ordinary fluctuations of the commercial world with which all mankind are familiar ; but a rise or fall in the universal standard of value, from the general causes mentioned, is an event of a different nature.   It is unnecessary, however, to pursue the subject further till the fact of a general rise in the value of the instrument of exchange has been ascertained, and the returns which the Marquis of Lansdowne moved for in the session of 1830, relative to the produce of the American mines, will tend far to its elucidation.

We have thus shortly explained the two sources whence, by possibility, relief may come to this tax-paying community ; but we candidly confess we have not much faith either of them will be realized.   That the Oligarchy will ever pursue such a course of policy as is most likely to diffuse general intelligence, contentment, and wealth, is inconsistent with all experience of their former conduct.   Unfortunately, the government, in its unreformed state, only embodies the partial interests of the Aristocracy, and those interests are incompatible with the general interests of the community.   Hence we conclude, the Manichæan principle of the constitution will triumph to the end of the chapter, and that the funding system will ultimately terminate by a *violent death*. The nature of its final dissolution, the hypocrisy and injustice by which it will be preceded, and the calamities it will entail on the country, we shall set forth in the next and concluding section.

CATASTROPHE OF THE FUNDING SYSTEM.

The natural and inevitable tendency of debt, either in nations or individuals, is bankruptcy.   Efforts will be made, by the Oligarchy, to avert, as long as possible, this lasting reproach of their unprincipled policy ; they will try to economize in this, and retrench in that ; they will be like beasts of prey environed by the hunters, they will seek escape on all sides, but, finding every outlet closed against them, they will then resort, as the only refuge from the difficulties in which they have wantanly involved themselves, to their last expedient—an *attack on the funds*.   Perhaps it will not be this session of parliament, nor the next ; but, that the period is approaching, we feel as confident as that we are now writing.   It is the most feasible of all projects : it would attack a mass of property, and of individuals that are incapable of resistance, who are not represented, and who would sink as silently as a stone dropped into the great deep.   Moreover, it would be the salvation of the system ; it would not touch the Church, nor the Aristocracy, nor the Rotten Boroughs, nor the Sinecures, nor the Barracks ; all the abuses of administration would be saved and perpetuated, for the affliction of the world and posterity. We do, however, trust there is sufficient justice and humanity in the nation to avert the perpetration of this national crime, which would afford complete impunity to those whose mal-administration has, alone, rendered it necessary. The man who first suggests a confiscation of the funds, under the pretext of *equitable adjustment*, unaccompanied with a radical change in our institutions, ought to be ejected from political communion as the worst enemy of Reform and the People. Let us, however, shortly consider the degree of injustice, the extent of suffering, and the misgovernment that would be perpetuated by the adoption of such a mean of surmounting the public difficulties.

Three points present themselves for consideration : 1st. The obligation imposed on the community to keep faith with the public creditor. 2d. The extent of distress and suffering which would be occasioned by a breach of this obligation. 3d. And lastly, The facilities it would afford for the perpetuation of an usurped and pernicious power.

With respect to the *first*, it is certain that funded property stands on a higher and more legitimate basis than any other description of property in the kingdom. It is created by *recent* acts of parliament, of the *meaning* and import of which there can be no difference of opinion : the present possessors of this property hold it by fair and lawful assignment, and the whole nation are *living* witnesses of the contract and execution. The estates of the Church, of the Aristocracy, and even of individuals, are not secured and attested by such strong and solemn authority. The Church has, at least, only a *life-interest* in its possessions, and this under the express stipulation of discharging the religious duties of the community. The estates of the nobility are of extremely dubious origin, mostly obtained by plunder and confiscation, and then held under the tenure of defending the country in war, of coining money, administering justice, and preserving the peace ; all which duties they have long ceased to discharge. Next, as to the estates of individuals : they have, in many instances, been obtained without valuable consideration, or are held by a fraudulent and imperfect title ; none of which can be alleged against funded property. It follows from this that there is no description, even of *real* property, which might not be seized with a greater semblance of justice than that of the fundholder, and that any the least encroachment on the funds would be a more flagrant outrage on all those ties by which property is made sacred and secure, than could in any other way be perpetrated.

We come next to the second consideration,— *The extent of distress and suffering consequent on a breach of faith with the national creditor.*

It is a most mistaken idea to suppose that the great mass of funded property belongs principally to monied men and capitalists. These have rarely much property in the funds ; if they have, it is only a portion of their unemployed capital, which they occasionally lodge there for a few days or weeks, to accomplish some stock-jobbing speculation, or till they find for it a more profitable investment.   Neither has the Aristocracy or Church considerable deposits in the funds : most of the former, from waste and extravagance, are steeped in debt and mortgage, and, notwithstanding their enormous incomes, from rents, tithes, and taxes, they have hardly a shilling to spare for necessary expenses ; and the rich Clergy, from similar want of prudence and economy, are in a not less embarrassed predicament.   The great bulk, therefore, of property permanently invested in the public securities is trust-property ; property left for charitable uses ; property belonging to suitors in Chancery ; small sums belonging to officers retired from service in the army and navy ; the funds of friendly societies and savings' banks ; and a vast number of small annuitants, consisting of minors, orphans, widows, old maids, bachelors, and families retired from business and the world, whose sole dependence is on the receipt of their half-yearly or quarterly dividends, and who having vested the whole proceeds of a weary life on the faith of the nation, any attack on the funds would, to them, be as sudden and overwhelming as a stroke of lightning.

On this part of the subject we have authentic data to proceed ; we know, from accounts laid before parliament, the number of public annuitants, and the amount of property vested in the funds on account of benefit societies, savings' banks, and suitors in Chancery.   From a parliamentary paper, (No. 41, Session 1830,) it appears the total number of persons receiving half-yearly dividends, on the different stocks, constituting the Public Debt, amounts to 274,823 ; of which number there are who received,—

Not exceeding	£5	83,609 persons.
Not exceeding	10	42,227 ditto.
Not exceeding	50	97,307 ditto.
Not exceeding	100	26,316 ditto.
Not exceeding	200	15,209 ditto.
Not exceeding	300	4,912 ditto.
Not exceeding	500	3,077 ditto.
Not exceeding	1000	1,555 ditto.
Not exceeding	2000	450 ditto.
Exceeding	2000	161 ditto.

Several annuitants have property in two or more separate stocks, as in the three per cents. and three-and-a-half per cents. so as to receive dividends quarterly : suppose nearly one-third are of this description, and, instead of 274,823, there are only 200,000 national creditors, who share among them the whole interest of twenty-eight millions, payable on the public debt ; in which case each receives, on an average, only £140 a-year.

Think of the consequence of extinguishing, or even abridging these petty incomes !   What impoverishment and destitution it would create among widows, orphans, the aged, and infirm.   How many funds, destined for charitable uses, or for mutual assurance against misfortune, and amassed with difficulty out of the earnings of the industrious, would be violated! From official returns, in 1829, it appears there are, in the United Kingdom, half a million of contributors to Savings' Banks, whose deposits amount to upwards of 17 millions. In 1830 the number of depositors in Savings' Banks in England only, was 367,812; their total investments £13,080,255, averaging £34 to each depositor. The number of members of Friendly Societies, in 1815, amounted to 925,429;* and the property belonging to them, vested in the funds, amounted to 40 millions. These funds have been raised and guaranteed by special acts of parliament, so that to encroach on them would be a shameless and flagrant violation of the public engagements.

It is not, however, the public annuitants only that would suffer by the measure we are considering; the calamity in its direct and indirect consequences would fall almost exclusively on the *middling and industrious orders.* Nearly the whole interest payable on the Debt is expended in support of the domestic trade, manufactures, and agriculture of the kingdom. A large portion of the revenue of the higher classes is consumed abroad, in the support of menial servants, or in articles of luxury, which create hardly any traffic or employment; whereas the incomes of the public annuitants are chiefly spent among ourselves, in the employment of the artisan and labourer, and in dealings with the grocer, baker, butcher, linen-draper, victualler, builder, carpenter, &c. It follows that any diminution in a revenue so expended would inflict incalculable mischief on the whole internal trade and economy; it would be the most hurtful of all remedies that could be applied to our embarrassments; for there is no other description of property, the violation of which would cause such wide-spread misery, distress, and mercantile stagnation. A man, therefore, who brings forward such a scheme must not only be an enemy to the general welfare, but he must be thoroughly depraved, and an alien to all those principles of justice and feelings of humanity which fit an individual for social communion and intercourse.

We come to the third and last consideration, namely,—*The facilities a breach of national faith would afford for the perpetuation of usurped and pernicious power.*

If established authority be adverse to the general interests, whatever tends to its continuance and support is pernicious;—whatever adds to the power of the weak and unprincipled is criminal. If the government of this country be so administered as to be unjust and oppressive, what-

---

* Parliamentary Report, No. 522, Session 1825. From Mr. Pratt's Tables for 1831 it appears there are 4,117 Friendly Societies in England, and probably the number of members, since 1815, has augmented to 1,500,000, with a corresponding increase of funds. It is gratifying to observe the progress of Friendly Societies and Savings' Banks in both Great Britain and Ireland. Their success must be satisfactory to those who consider the working people deficient in prudence and foresight. The truth is, they only require to be made acquainted with their real interests, and then, like the more educated, they would doubtless pursue them.

ever tends to avert its reform or prolong its existence must be reprobated by every patriotic mind. Now it is certain that to tolerate any
the least attack on the funds would place an uncontrolled and almost
unlimited power at the mercy of the administration. Should ministers
be once allowed openly to reduce or to tax the public annuities, or to
encroach upon them under any form, they would possess an inexhaustible resource for domestic profusion and future war. The whole
interest of the Debt would be at their mercy, and, in gradually reducing
it, they would have the means, for a century longer, to pursue the same
career of folly and injustice which they had pursued in the century that
is past. Thus the Debt, instead of an incumbrance, would be a *real
treasure*, to which they could resort on every emergency. No matter
how small the tax at first imposed ; if the principle be once admitted,
they might gradually augment their exactions on the public creditor ;
the machinery would be made, and would only require *working ;* in a
word, it would be merely retaining the money in their own hands,
instead of paying it half-yearly to the fundholder.

The first step in this proceeding would be the most delicate, and
require great caution and considerable hypocrisy in the execution.
First, probably, only a tax of one per cent. or even a quarter per cent.
would be proposed, accompanied with deep expressions of regret on the
imperious necessity that had rendered necessary such a painful alternative. Having got the handle to the axe, they would proceed with a
slow but sure step, screwing up the fund-tax, like the income-tax, till
at length it equalled, in amount, the dividends, or, in a word, expunged
the Debt !

Such a villainous procedure would, doubtless, raise a great outcry ;
many would exclaim against the violation of *public faith*, and of the
injustice of sacrificing *a part for the whole ;* but ministers would easily
find excuses. They would first eat up all their former declarations on
the great advantages of *national integrity*, and would expatiate on
the great advantages of *national bankruptcy*. They would plead the
alteration in the currency as one pretext for their injustice ; they would
urge the great law of *self-preservation*, which forbids either individuals
or nations to bind themselves to their own destruction ; they would
enlarge on the impolicy and unreasonableness of adhering to engagements that would destroy the sources of productive industry, and,
ultimately, entail ruin on all classes, even the annuitants themselves.
Lastly, they would plead the example of other states, of their " magna-
nimous and august allies,"—the members of the Holy Alliance and
Protocol conferences,—all of whom had been once or twice bankrupt,
and necessitated to compound with their creditors. The knavery and
sophistry of such reasoning would be apparent to all ; but the *majority*
being benefited by the injustice, it is probable they would be inclined to
wink at the transaction, and the poor fundholder become the scape-goat
of the community.

It may appear improbable, at first sight, that a government, founded
on the basis of a regard to " property, morality, religion," and an

abhorrence of " blasphemy," should resort to such a disgraceful expedient, to such unprincipled sophistry; especially, too, as a breach of national faith would be a violation of the principle to which they have been accustomed, on all occasions, to ascribe the prosperity, glory, and independence, of the empire. This, certainly, at first view, appears improbable; but, if we examine the subject more closely, we shall find that it is not without precedent, and that it would be less inconsistent with former *practices* than former *professions* of our rulers.

First, there is the Bank Restriction Act of 1797. This measure, in its nature, was full as unprincipled an attack on the rights of private property and the sacredness of previous engagements as a breach of national faith could possibly be. Secondly, there are various suspensions of the Habeas Corpus Act—the passing of bills of indemnity for all sorts of crimes—the forging of French assignats—the attack of Copenhagen—the blowing up of the Spanish ships, and the affair of Terceira: all these measures are so atrocious, so repugnant to every principle of law, humanity, and justice, that it would be chimerical, in the highest degree, to suppose that the men who could advise and participate in them, would be scrupulous in the observance of their engagements with the public creditor.

Yet the shame, the disgrace, the infamy of a breach of faith would be so great; it would lay bare so completely the unprincipled policy of the last forty years; it would so entirely unmask the principles of the Oligarchy, exposing them to such execration and derision, that we may expect it to be staved off to the last day; and when, at length, it is attempted, it will be disguised, under a thousand pretexts, to hide its deformity from the world. Come, however, it must; for there is no other alternative likely to be adopted; the contest is betwixt rent and tithe, and high official emoluments on one hand, and the payment of the dividends on the other: to pay the latter the former must be sacrificed. But can any one doubt the issue of the conflict? Can it be doubted which party will go to *the wall*, should the Borough proprietors continue to monopolise the franchises of the people? The lords of the soil possess all *political power;* they have the boroughs, the barracks, and the powder-mills at their command; they will take care of THEMSELVES; and, judging from the facts we have enumerated, there is no reason to suppose their love of justice is so extreme as to induce them to abandon their ALL to preserve inviolate public faith.

Before, however, the fundholders are sacrificed, all other classes will be *degraded:* so loth will be the Boroughmongers to touch their great stalking-horse of public credit, that they will endeavour to support it on the ruins of the other orders of society. First, probably, as being most exposed to their attacks, the poor-rate will be attempted; next in order come the other *unrepresented* interests of the community, the profits of all the productive classes—the farmers, merchants, and tradesmen. If the degradation of these classes, if the appropriation of the whole of their revenue, except that portion necessary to a bare subsistence, be insufficient, then the fundholder will be assailed, rather than rent and tithe should be materially reduced. This is what we call the CATASTROPHE OF THE FUNDING SYSTEM. Without a parliamentary reform all classes will be sacrificed to the preservation of the Aristocracy. When the full payment of the dividends encroaches on the sources of their own incomes, they will be forcibly reduced, and the only favour shown to the fundholder will be that of being *last devoured!*

We have thus briefly traced what appears likely to be the catastrophe of the funding system, the consequence of an attack on the funds, its flagrant injustice, the distress and suffering it would occasion, and the lasting impunity it would afford to corruption and misgovernment. We were anxious to do this at the present moment, because if by any unforeseen event the hopes of the nation should be a second time shipwrecked in regard to the " *Bill*," and the Tories regain their ascendancy, it is not improbable the desperate expedient of robbing the fundholder would be tried, in order to silence the cry of a starving population for economy and reform. We trust, however, the public will be on its guard against this horrible project; like all frauds, it will be clandestinely and insidiously introduced; therefore it behoves them to be constantly on the alert. So long as the Debt is *safe*, it is the best ally of the People, but the moment it is violated, it is the best ally of Corruption.

If a general sacrifice be required to save the country, a change in the representation is an indispensable preliminary. The House of Commons, in lieu of representing the people, represents only the government which it ought to control, in the various branches of the executive, the aristocracy, the church, the army, navy, and public offices. Embodying such partial interests, the general weal must be invariably compromised, and no equitable settlement can be made. Admit the intelligence and property of the nation to have their due weight in the public councils, and the best and most salutary measures must necessarily be adopted, and equity and safety found for all.

This is all the people require; they do not want *pity* nor *charity ;* and those who, during their periodical sufferings, are constantly preaching PATIENCE to a famishing population, would do well to change the word for JUSTICE from their rulers. Justice from oppression is a virtue; patience under undeserved suffering a crime!

TAXATION

AND

GOVERNMENT EXPENDITURE.

———————◆———————

GENERAL PRINCIPLES OF TAXATION AND FINANCE.

WE cannot do better than preface the subjects of this chapter by stating a few general principles of taxation and finance; they are principally taken from Adam Smith and Dr. Hamilton, and for the most part are so self-evident that it is superfluous to adduce any argument in their support or elucidation; and the others may be inferred by a very obvious train of reasoning. Yet measures inconsistent with them have not only been advanced by men of reputed abilities, but have been acted on by successive administrations, annually supported in parliament, and extolled in political publications. This may create a necessity for a few explanatory observations, and which we shall subjoin in a separate paragraph immediately after each consecutive proposition.

I. The annual income of a nation consists of the united produce of its agriculture, manufactures, commerce, and industry. This income is the source from which the inhabitants derive the necessaries, comforts, and luxuries of life; distributed, according to their stations, in various proportions, and from which the public revenue, necessary for civil government and external administration, is derived.

In every nation a part of the annual income must be withdrawn from the inhabitants for the support of the army and navy, the administration of justice, and other public purposes. The sum thus withdrawn, however reasonable and necessary, is abstracted from the *funds* which supply the *wants* of the people, and, consequently, lessens their means of enjoyment. Taxation, therefore, though necessary, is a positive evil, and it is a poor set-off to allege against this evil that it may, when gradually augmented, operate as a motive to greater industry and economy in the people. The natural desire of advancement in life and to participate in its pleasures, are sufficient inducements to frugality and industry without the artificial goad of the tax-gatherer. But taxes have not only encroached on luxuries, but on the comforts and necessaries of the productive classes, and it is mere sophistry to allege that they are either *harmless* or *beneficial;* that they either return by *other channels,* or are a *spur to industry.* That which is taken and *consumed* can never be returned by any channel ; and that can never form a *spur to industry,* which lessens the rewards by which industry is excited and put in motion.

II. The portion of national income, which can be appropriated to public purposes, and the possible amount of taxation, *are limited;* and we are apparently advanced to that limit.

That the amount of taxation is limited, and that we have reached that limit, is pretty evident from the generally low rate of profits and wages. The burthens which peculiarly press on productive industry have been enumerated (p. 279). " When," says Mr. M'Culloch, " the taxes which affect the industrious classes are increased, such increase must either immediately fall wholly on profits or wages, or partly on the one and partly on the other. If it fall on profits, it makes, of course, an equivalent deduction from them ; and if it fall on wages, it proportionally depresses the condition of the great body of the people."*
We have arrived at the anomalous state in finance when two and two do not make four. Were additional taxes imposed, instead of increasing, they would probably diminish the total amount by impairing the sources from which they would be derived. The effect of *augmented* taxes beyond national ability was finely exemplified in the case of Ireland. The revenue of Ireland, in 1807, amounted to £4,378,000. Between that year and the conclusion of the war taxes were imposed, which, according to the calculations of chancellors of the exchequer, were to produce £3,400,000, or to augment the revenue to the extent of £7,700,000. What was the result? Why, that in the year 1821, when that amount ought to have been paid into the Treasury, the whole revenue of Ireland amounted only to £3,844,000, being £553,000 less than in 1807, previously to one farthing of these additional taxes having been imposed. Take another example of the effect of a seasonable reduction of taxes in the United Kingdom. Between the years 1823 and 1827 taxes were repealed to the amount of £9,182,571, but the nett loss sustained by the revenue was only to the amount of £3,308,316 : the enormous difference of £5,874,255 being made up by increased consumption. The Whig ministry repealed duties to the amount of £4,477,000 in 1831, but the depression in all the great branches of national industry has prevented the loss sustained by the revenue from being supplied by increased consumption in the proportion experienced by their predecessors.

III. The subjects of every state ought to contribute towards the support of the government as nearly as possible in proportion to their respective abilities; that is, in proportion to the revenue which they respectively enjoy under the protection of the state. The expense of

---

* Principles of Political Economy, 2nd Edit. p. 493.

government to individuals is like the expense of management to the joint tenants of an estate, who are all obliged to contribute in proportion to their respective interests in the estate. In the observance or neglect of this maxim consists what is called the *equality* or *inequality* of taxation.

IV. The tax which every individual is bound to pay ought to be certain and not arbitrary. The time of payment, the manner of payment, the quantity to be paid ought all to be clear and plain to the contributor and to every other person. When it is otherwise, the tax-payer is put more or less in the power of the tax-gatherer, who can either aggravate the tax on any obnoxious contributor, or extort, by the terror of such aggravation, some perquisite or advantage to himself.

The Assessed Taxes, especially the inhabited house duty, and most duties of Excise, contravene this principle.

V. Every tax ought to be so contrived as both to take out and keep out of the pockets of the people as little as possible, over and above what it brings into the public treasury of the state. A tax may either take out or keep out of the pockets of the people a great deal more than it brings into the public treasury in the four following ways :—*First*, the levying of it may require a greater number of officers, whose salaries may eat up the greater part of the produce of the tax, and whose perquisites may impose another additional tax upon the people. *Secondly*, it may obstruct the industry of the people, and discourage them from applying to certain branches of business which might give maintenance and employment to great multitudes. While it obliges the people to pay, it may thus diminish, or perhaps destroy, some of the funds which might enable them more easily to do so. *Thirdly*, by the forfeitures and penalties which those individuals incur who attempt unsuccessfully to evade the tax, it may frequently ruin them, and thereby put an end to the benefit which the community might have received from the employment of their capitals. *Fourthly*, by subjecting the people to the frequent visits and odious examination of the tax-gatherers, it may expose them to much unnecessary trouble, vexation, and oppression; and though vexation is not, strictly speaking, expense, it is certainly equivalent to the expense at which every man would be willing to redeem himself from it.

Our Excise and Custom Duties, which form the great sources of public income, are mostly a violation of this principle of Dr. Smith. The two principal objects of our aristocratic legislators have been, *first*, to tax necessaries, not luxuries ; *secondly*, to tax industry, not property. Thus they have been cutting away, not at revenue, but the sources of revenue; they have been reaping the seed, not the ripened fruit, and have finally exemplified the Fable of the Goose which laid golden eggs. Those who recommend a direct tax on property are right ; nothing less will enable the country to meet its pecuniary difficulties, and get rid of the waste and folly of our fiscal administration.

VI. In time of war taxes may be raised to a *greater height* than can be easily borne in *peaceable times ;* and the amount of the additional taxes, together with the surplus of the peace establishment, applied for defraying the expense of the war.

It is not intended to affirm that the power of a nation to bear taxes is increased in consequence of its being engaged in war. The contrary is always the case. Labour, agriculture, commerce, and manufactures, are the sources from which all revenue is derived. Some of them may be ameliorated, but they are depressed on the whole, and do not attain the *solid prosperity* they would have attained, had not war intervened. But the necessity of the war, real or imaginary, has a powerful influence on the public mind, and reconciles the community to submit to privations, which, in peaceable times, would be accounted insupportable. The latter is the sense in which the proposition is intended to be understood.

VII. The expense of modern wars has been generally so great, that the revenue raised within the year has been insufficient to pay it; hence the necessity of having recourse to the system of funding, or anticipation.

Various causes may be assigned for the increased expense of modern wars : the nature of our military weapons ; the entire separation of the character of the soldier from that of the citizen ; the system of colonies and foreign settlements, in consequence of which a contest, that a few centuries ago would have been decided by a battle on the frontiers of the contending nations, now extends the ravages of war to every part of the globe : and, since the imaginary system of the *balance of power* has prevailed, large sums have been granted by states, like England, more *opulent* than *wise*, as subsidies to others, supposed to be interested in the common cause. While these causes have led to great expense, the increase of national wealth has supplied the means, and the Rulers of this nation, in particular, by artfully supporting the illusion of a Sinking Fund, and a well regulated system of transfer of stock, have been able to draw forth a larger proportion of the wealth of the people than any other government in the world.

VIII. In every year of war, where the funding system is adopted, the amount of the public debt is increased ; and the total increase of debt, during the war, depends on its duration, and the annual excess of the expenditure above the revenue.

IX. In every year of peace, the excess of the revenue above the expenditure ought to be applied to the discharge of the national debt ; and the amount discharged during any period of peace depends upon the length of its continuance, and the amount of the annual surplus.

X. If the periods of war, compared with those of peace, and the annual excess of the war expenditure, compared with the annual savings during the peace establishment, be so related, that more debt is contracted in every war than is discharged in the succeeding peace, the consequence is a *perpetual increase* of debt ; and the ultimate consequence must be, its amount to a magnitude which the nation is unable to bear.

XI. The only effectual remedies to this danger are the extension of the relative lengths of the periods of peace ; frugality in peace establishments ; lessening the war expenses ; the increase of taxes, whether permanent or levied during war.

XII. If the three former of these remedies be impracticable, the last forms the only resource. By increasing the war taxes, the sum required to be raised by loan is lessened. By increasing the taxes in time of peace, the sum applicable to the discharge of debt is increased. These measures may be followed to such an extent, that the savings, in time of peace, may be brought to an equality with the surplus expenditure in time of war, even on the supposition that the periods of their relative duration shall be the same, for centuries to come, that they have been for a century past.

The difficulty, and even impossibility, of a further increase of taxes has been considered. Every new imposition, as the limit to taxation approaches, becomes more oppressive and more unproductive; and if Government adhere to an expenditure beyond the ability of the country to support, it is impossible to escape *national*, or more properly *government bankruptcy*. So long as the practice was followed of defraying almost all the war expenses by loans, and imposing taxes only for the *payment of interest*, the burdens of war were so lightly felt, that the promptness of the Aristocracy to engage in war was scarcely under any restraint. Had the supplies been raised within the year, and most of them by *direct taxation*, the pressure would have been so great, that it would have probably stimulated the people to restrain their rulers from engaging in hostilities for remote and delusive objects. Justice to posterity required this. Every generation has its own struggles and contests. Of these and these only it ought to bear the burden ; and the great evil of the Funding System is, that it enables nations to transfer the cost of present follies to succeeding generations.

XIII. When taxation is carried to such an extent that the supplies adequate to meet a war expenditure are raised within the year, the affairs of the nation will go on under the pressure of existing burdens, but without a continual accumulation of debt, which would terminate in bankruptcy. So long as taxation is below this standard, accumulation of debt advances; and it becomes more difficult to raise taxation to the proper height. If it should ever be carried beyond this standard, a gradual discharge of the existing burdens will be obtained ; and these circumstances will take place in the exact degree in which taxation falls short of or exceeds the standard of average expenditure.

XIV. The *excess of revenue* above expenditure is the only *real Sinking Fund* by which public debt can be discharged. The increase of the revenue and the diminution of expense are the only means by which this Sinking Fund can be enlarged, and its operation rendered more effectual ; and *all schemes* for discharging the National Debt, by Sinking Funds operating by compound interest, or in any other manner, unless so far as they are founded on this principle, are illusory.

Both these propositions have been sufficiently established in our exposition of the Funding System.

ABUSES IN THE EXPENDITURE OF GOVERNMENT.

The labours of Mr. Hume and Sir Henry Parnell are an instance of what the ability and perseverance of a few individuals may accomplish. It is not, however, so much the good effected as the evil prevented that entitles them to the gratitude of the country. Under the long leaden and unprofitable administration of Lord Liverpool, all the great branches of public expenditure had been annually augmenting; and how far this progression would have extended, had not Mr. Hume, supported by a small phalanx of honest persons, commenced his exposures, it is impossible to say. His mode of attack could not be parried: though an unofficial man himself, he showed as intimate acquaintance with the details of the public accounts as John Wilson Croker, Peregrine Courtenay, or any other veteran placeman. Even Sir T. Gooch and Lord Wharncliffe were constrained to admit the value of his services, and the reductions effected in the public departments, prior to the formation of Earl Grey's ministry, are chiefly attributable to him and the gentleman we have mentioned.

In the course of this section we purpose to bring together some of the more palpable abuses in the government expenditure, and for a knowledge of many of which the public is indebted to a valuable work of Sir Henry Parnell, *On Financial Reform*. We intend to avail ourselves of this gentleman's publication, though we cannot say the member for Queen's County is an object of our exclusive admiration: he is too much of a *doctrinaire* for us, and appears to repose too implicit confidence in the dogmas of the Ricardo school,—the disciples of which know as much about the internal state of the country, and the causes and remedies of its embarrassments, as the natives of Kamschatka. But this infirmity of the honourable Baronet does not impair the utility of the facts he has published, nor depreciate the important information collected by the Finance Committee of 1828, over which he so ably presided.

The following is Sir Henry Parnell's list of the several departments entrusted with the business of expending the public money, pursuant to the general appropriation of it by parliament:—

1. The Treasury, including the Commissariat Department in 1827, £80,542
2. The Exchequer 48,000
3. The Audit-Office in 1828.................................. 32,977
4. The Bank of England, do.................................. 267,597
5. The Commissioners of the Sinking Fund, do................ 10,350
6. The Civil Department of the Army, do. 108,837
7. Do. of the Navy, do. 179,647
8. Do. of the Ordnance (the Tower and Pall Mall,) do........... 57,961

£779,911

The expense of the Treasury department was, in 1797, only £44,066; so that it has nearly doubled; although the revenue, the superintending of which constitutes the chief business of the treasury, was as great as in 1827. Does not this show the profusion with which salaries have been increased, and offices multiplied? There are no fewer than fifteen clerks in the treasury, who receive salaries amounting to £1000; five of these fifteen receive £1,500 a-year each and upwards. Their duties are little more than nominal; they seldom attend their offices but to look over the newspapers; many of them hold two or more offices and sinecures; yet with all their official appointments, so little are they engaged in the public service, that they may be mostly seen driving about town in their stanhopes, and whiling their time in the club-houses.

The Exchequer.—This is one of the most absurd and lucrative establishments under government. As the chief duty of the exchequer is that of superintendence, in taking care that there are no issues of public money by the Treasury contrary to parliamentary direction, it ought to be discharged by a very few officers, or altogether abolished. However, neither economy nor common sense are objects sought to be attained. The forms by which business is carried on are extremely anti-- quated and ridiculous, and as remote from modern practice as the conveyance of merchandize by packhorse and bells is from the cheapness and despatch of a rail-road. Our limits will only admit of a brief description of the constitution of this office, and the mummery and nonsense daily perpetrated there.

The Exchequer is divided into seven different departments; the tellers, the pells, the king's remembrancers, the lord treasurer's, the auditor's office, the tally-court, and the pipe-office. The pipe-office alone has seven subsidiary absurdities; among these are the clerk of the nichills, the clerk of the estreats, and the cursitor baron; besides which, are eight sworn attorneys, two board-end clerks, and eight clerks attached to the sworn attornies. From the inquiries of a parliamentary commission, it seems these are nearly all sinecurists. Two of the witnesses examined had been in the office, one eight and the other twenty-five years, and they stated, during that time, five out of the eight attornies never came near the office, living in the country at a considerable distance from London. The duties of their clerks were not more onerous. Three of them were at school long after being appointed to their situations. One of them admitted that, subsequently to his nomination, he was five years at school at Chelsea, two years in a conveyancer's office, and that he now practised as a barrister, and might look into the office once in a month. The board-end clerks laboured under similar lack of duties; and as to the clerk of the *nichills*, the name is sufficient to indicate his heavy and responsible functions.

One of the duties of the Exchequer is, yearly to send down five great rolls of parchment to the sheriffs, containing accounts of supposed debtors to the crown during the last 300 years. The sheriff is bound to summon a jury, in order to ascertain what money is due to the crown on the roll. The sending of the roll down and up again, occasions considerable expense, and is as useless a task as the labours of Sisyphus. The farcical ceremony of passing the sheriffs' accounts is of a piece with the rest, and resembles a game on the draught-board. Under the pretence of testing the account, the practice is to throw, in the presence of the cursitor baron, small copper coins behind a hat, from one little square of the cloth on the table to another; when the sheriffs' accounts are correct, a person cries out " *tot;*" when inaccurate, another person cries " *nel;*" and according as these words are uttered, the copper coins are shifted from one part of the chequers to another. All these antics were, probably, of use prior to the invention of arithmetic and book-keeping, but are now as irrelevant as the idle pageant of a coronation or lord mayor's show.

The manner in which the public money is paid in to the tellers is a similar burlesque on real life. There are four tellers, and each has a little pew or cabin, in which he or his deputy sits, with a suitable complement of clerks, for the purpose of receiving the produce of the taxes nominally paid to him, but in reality to the clerks of the Bank of England, three of whom attend in an adjoining room to receive the money paid out of the Bank to be paid into the Bank again. The tellers, under the mockery of receiving the stamp, excise, and other duties, sign a parchment, written in a mixture of Latin or Saxon, or other jargon, which is as unintelligible to any one but a teller as the unknown tongues of Mr. Irving. They next pass a roll through a pipe into a room below, and there it is cut into a particular shape, and carried to the auditors of the Exchequer. A wooden tally was formerly used, which, within the last two years, has been exchanged for one of parchment. But the inconvenience and absurdity of the formality is so great, that Exchequer payments have been lately abolished, and they are now managed by clerks of the Treasury.

From Madox's *History of the Court of Exchequer*, it appears, scarcely any alteration has been made in this department since the reign of Henry II. The reason is obvious enough. There are vested rights, claims of seniority, and reversionary interests in the way; and no reform can be introduced till all these expectancies are satisfied, and it has been the policy hitherto to take special care such expectancies never shall be satisfied, by promptly filling up every vacant appointment the moment it occurs. The most valuable sinecures in the Exchequer are held by peers and their relatives, and the emolument, fees, and patronage are so great, that it can hardly excite surprise the carnival doings we have described have been so carefully preserved.

For the gratification of tax payers we subjoin a statement of the sums annually swamped in the " great Exchequer job."

	£	s.	d.
Auditor's Office			
Salaries	13,004	9	2½
Contingencies unknown from the want of documents, *in an office professing to check all the other departments of the state.*			
Pells' Office. Salaries £7,606 9 10			
Contingencies 70 15 3			
	7,677	5	1

Carried forward....£20,681 14 3½

			Brought forward....£20,681	14	3½

Tellers' Offices.

	£	s.	d.
Marquis Camden's Salaries	5,700	0	0
Contingencies	312	2	11
	6,012	2	11
Earl Bathurst's Salaries	5,800	0	0
Rt. Hon. Charles Yorke's Salaries	5,768	5	4
Spencer Percival, Esq.'s Salaries	5,396	14	0
Four Money Porters	1,020	4	0
Contingencies of the four departments, exclusive of stationery, the expense of which is unknown	113	4	3
	£44,792	4	9½

Of this sum about one-fourth is paid for *sinecures,* so complete, that in the words of the return, " the Teller is empowered by his patent to appoint a deputy, who transacts all the business of the office. The Teller himself does not, nor has it been usual for him, to execute any part of it whatsoever."

The Auditor is virtually a sinecure; the *money porters,* who perform the heavy drudgery of carrying slips of paper and parchment, are paid indifferently well; and there are five heads of offices who have deputies to act for them " in the general superintendence of the office during any occasional absence."

The following gives an account of the salaries received for " responsibility," and of those paid for work.

		£	s.	d.
Total expense in salaries		44,296	2	4½
Four Tellers at £2,700 per annum	£10,800			
One Auditor	4,000			
Five Heads of Departments	5,400			
Four Money Porters........£1,020 4 0				
Deduct as wages ....· 320 4 0				
	700			
Salaries { for Sinecures or " Responsibility"		20,900	0	0
Salaries { for Work		23,396	2	4½

The Commissioners of 1831 recommend that the whole of the present machinery should be entirely swept away, and suggest the erection of a new office upon a new system—but then, agreeably with the established routine in such cases, the public will have to provide double—salaries for the new, and pensions and compensations for the old officials !

The Audit Office.—This is as snug and delightful a retreat as any in the public departments. Were a proper system adopted in keeping the public accounts, this office might be dispensed with. In 1806, an attempt was made to improve the audit department, and the way this was set about is a very apt specimen of the mode of reforming government abuses in those days. A chairman of the Board was created, salary £1,500; four new members, each £1,200; a secretary, a foreigner, £1,000; six inspectors, each £600; and eight additional examiners; with numerous other appointments, which increased the expense from about £14,000 to £38,000; and after all the establishment was made less efficient than under the old and less expensive system.

Civil Department of the Army.—The office of paymaster of the forces is a sinecure. The business is performed by a deputy and three cashiers. As each of these persons has a power of drawing money out of the Bank of England on his own order, the effect of the office being a sinecure is to diminish considerably the security of the public.* It is also attended with this further inconvenience, that it multiplies the number of imprest accountants, and thus augments the difficulty of establishing a proper system of keeping the public accounts.

The account called *Army Extraordinaries* is liable to great abuse and mystification. Under this head, payments are made which have nothing to do with the army; the sums voted by parliament seldom exceed £900, while the sum expended commonly amounts to three millions. This scheme serves to conceal from the public a great deal of wasteful and illegal expenditure; for instance, the sum paid at home to colonial agents, and the sum drawn from abroad for colonial expenses, although they are wholly for civil colonial purposes, are paid as army extraordinaries, and without any previous vote of parliament; which is thus, according to the testimony of Sir H. Parnell, mislead by the annual production of an account with " a perfectly false title."

The employing of *Commissioners of Accounts* abroad was suggested in consequence of the great accumulation of accounts during the war; but, since the conclusion of it, the motives which originated the plan have gradually ceased to have any force, and therefore the public ought to be saved the expense of such useless functionaries. Where too is the necessity for incurring the expense of having *army agents ?* The accounts of the paymasters of regiments are examined at the War-office, and not by the agents; and all the agents do for the public is to receive money from the paymasters of the forces, and to pay with it the drafts of the regimental paymasters: the other duties are private, and for the benefit of officers of the army.

Royal Military Academy, Woolwich.—This establishment might be appropriated to much better purposes than the nursing of some dozen or so artillery and engineer officers. Long after the peace the Academy was maintained at an annual expense of £20,000 and upwards; the average cost to the public of the cadets admitted to commissions in the army, in 1820, was £920 each. The charge for civil officers, professors and masters, for the year ending in 1831, was £3402. Even this is too much; especially as the knowledge taught at the Academy is quite elementary, and might just as well be learnt at any private mili-

---

* Sir H. Parnell on Financial Reform, p. 141.

tary school.   If instruction were made to begin at the Academy just where it stops at present, that is, when the cadets are seventeen or eighteen years old, then there might be some reason in keeping it up; because the instruction afforded to officers might be of such a description in the higher branches of military art, as could not be attained elsewhere.

Department of the Navy and Dock Yards.—The first lord commissioner of the admiralty has a salary of £4,500, with an official residence, and four other commissioners £1,000 a-year with an official residence each; the first secretary £3,000, the second do 1,500; the comptroller of the navy has £2,000, with a residence, the deputy-comptroller of ditto, £1,200; besides which, are an immense number of commissioners of the navy, and commissioners of the dock-yards with salaries of £1,000 each.   A most objectionable office kept up by the Tories was the treasurership of the navy—a mere sinecure; it has been consolidated by the Whigs with the vice-presidentship of the Board of Trade.

The expenditure in the Royal Dock-yards and arsenals is most lavish in storekeepers, clerks, chaplains, surgeons, measurers, master-attendant, master-shipwright and others, many of whom are apparently kept up for mutual superintendence, and forming a gradation of office and multiplication of expense wholly unnecessary.   Not a single trade is carried on without a master; there is a master-smith, bricklayer, sailmaker, rigger, rope-maker, painter, and others; they have each £250 a-year, and many of them have not above four or five men under their superintendence.   How differently private and public business is conducted, was strikingly shown in the evidence of Mr. Barrow.   There is a private builder who employs 250 shipwrights: he has one foreman, one measurer, two clerks, and ten labourers.   In Woolwich yard, which comes the nearest to it, there are 248 shipwrights, eighteen clerks, six masters' of trades, eight foremen, eight measurers, eleven cabin-keepers; besides surgeons, boatswain, wardens, and other people.   The whole establishment of the officers, clerks, and other salaried persons at the dockyard, amounts to £155,000, and the amount of wages paid for work done by artificers and labourers, &c. is £502,000.   It thus appears that for every three pounds and a quarter paid to the men, there is a pound paid for superintendence.

The *Paymaster of the Marines* has a salary of £1,000, for the discharge of duties which might be very well annexed to the Navy-office. " As to the reasons," says Sir H. Parnell, " that are given to the contrary, they are so plainly nothing more than ingenious pretexts for maintaining a lucrative office, that it would be a waste of time to notice them."

The naval accounts, as indeed all the accounts of the public offices, are kept on a confused and most inconvenient principle, from the want of a well-arranged plan of book-keeping.   Each description of expenditure has its distinct set of books, making thirty-three in all, and tending greatly to the increase of expense by the multiplication of clerks.   At present the payment of officers and seamen's wages is made in the presence of four clerks, in order to have three clerks checking the accuracy of every sum paid by the fourth. As these clerks are selected from different branches, and as each keeps a book, so many books are kept in triplicate, that they amount, in the whole, to 1580 supernumerary volumes.

Increase in Peace Establishments.—The following comparison of the peace establishments of 1792 and of 1831 is very instructive.

	Year 1792.		Year 1831.
Army	£2,330,349	......	£ 6,991,163
Navy	1,985,482	......	5,309,605
Ordnance	444,863	......	1,613,908
Total charge....	£4,760,694	......	£13,914,676*

It thus appears the peace establishment of 1831 exceeds that of 1792 nearly threefold, and that, since 1815, upwards of 250 millions have been expended on soldiers, sailors, ships, and artillery; although we have been all the time in a state of general tranquillity. The only ground on which it is attempted to justify the expenditure, so enormously great in comparison with that of any former peace establishment, is the expediency of being at *all times prepared for war.* So that after expending upwards of eleven hundred millions in the purchase of a secure and lasting peace; after sacrificing millions in fortifying Belgium against French aggression; after erecting splendid and costly monuments to commemorate the glorious triumphs of Waterloo: after all these efforts, glories, and sacrifices, we cannot yet sit down in safety, without bristling on all sides with cannons and bayonets. Is this, we ask, any proof of progression in human affairs? Is this the boasted " *settlement of Europe?*" Are these the blessings of legitimate and constitutional monarchies? Are nations, in their relations to each other, always to exemplify the condition of man in a state of nature, with couched lance, watchful eye, and trembling heart, fearing to be the victim of beasts of prey or of the tomahawk and scalping-knife of his not less savage fellow-creature? If these are all the guarantees of social happiness which aristocratic governments can give, we say,— Away with them! let us try new men, new principles, and new institutions!

A principal cause of the vast increase in the military expenditure of the country is the number and establishments of the army. From the inquiries of the Finance Committee, it appears that, in 1792, the number of all ranks in the army was 57,251; and that, according to the statement of Sir H. Parnell, they were distributed as follows :—

---

* Annual Finance Accounts, p. 21. Sess. 1831.

Officers and Men

Great Britain	17,007
Ireland	11,901
East Indies	10,700
Canada, Nova Scotia, and Bermuda	6,061
Gibraltar	4,221
West-India Islands	6,886
New South Wales	475
	57,251

In 1828, the number of all ranks was 116,738; the distribution was as follows :—

Great Britain	29,616
Ireland	23,969
Colonies	37,037
East Indies	26,116
	116,738

The chief part of the increase is accounted for as under :—

Increase in the New Colonies	17,112
Increase in the Old Colonies	849
Increase in Great Britain	9,094
Increase in Ireland..........................	10,363
Increase in the East Indies	14,287
	51,705

Allowing that the extent of our foreign possessions has rendered necessary an increase in the army, this does not apply to the *household troops*, as they are never sent abroad in time of peace. Yet it is in this branch of the service, and in dragoons, that there has been the greatest augmentation. The following statement shows the increase of life and foot guards and cavalry at the two periods :—

	RANK and FILE.		Officers and Non-Commissioned Officers in 1830.	Total of Men and Officers in 1830.	Increase in Rank and File in 1830.
	1792.	1830.			
Life Guards	411	688	187	875	277
Horse Guards ..	261	344	86	430	83
Dragoon Guards .	696	2,268 ⎱	1,506	9,326	⎰ 1,972
Dragoons	2,080	5,152 ⎰			⎱ 3,072
Foot Guards	3,126	5,760	848	6,608	2,634
Total Number ..	6,574	14,212	2,627	17,239	8,038

These are the most expensive classes in the army, and chiefly kept for *domestic use.* The sums saved by the reduction of the cavalry force would be very considerable, since the expenses of every horseman are nearly as great as those of the junior clerks in the public offices, some of whom have been so unsparingly reduced that their superiors might enjoy, undiminished, their overgrown emoluments. The expense of a dragoon and horse, exclusive of forage, &c. is £57 a year, and of a life and horse guardsman £75 a year; whilst the charge for infantry of the line is only £31 per man.

The guards are chiefly intended for the maintenance of the peace in the metropolis, for the protection of the Bank, the Tower, and royal palaces. But there can be less need of this expensive corps now we have a military police, for the security of property and persons, and ready to aid the established authorities in case of civil commotion. Surely 4000 constables, trained, organised, and barracked, and under the entire control of Ministers, might enable them to dispense with at least one regiment of the household force.

Many millions have been unnecessarily expended, since the Peace, on our maritime establishments. In 1830, 30,000 seamen were voted, and £1,657,601 to defray the charges of their wages and victuals. With the exception of Russia and the United States, the naval force of every other power is less than at the breaking out of the war in 1793. Neither Spain nor Holland has any navy of consequence; and France, which at the commencement of the Revolution had eighty efficient ships of the line, has now not more than forty. What occasion, then, can there be for Great Britain to expend annually £1,300,000 on her dock-yards, and incur a naval expenditure, altogether, of more than five millions?

Expenditure of the Colonies.—These are a tremendous burthen on the resources of the mother country, chiefly to provide governorships, secretaryships, registrarships, agencies, and sinecures for the Aristocracy and their connexions. No parliamentary document shews what the whole expense is that is paid by English taxes on account of the colonies. It is generally estimated that from two to three millions are paid for the army, navy, and various civil charges; but in addition to this the public pay full two millions more for sugar and timber than they ought to pay, in consequence of the increased prices occasioned by the protection given to the colonists by the higher duties imposed on these articles when imported from foreign countries.*

There are only three ways that the Colonies can be of any advantage. 1. In furnishing a military force; 2. In supplying the parent state with a revenue; 3. In affording commercial advantages.

Instead of furnishing a military force, the colonies are always a great drain upon our military resources, particularly in war, when they occupy a large portion of the army and fleet in their defence. With respect to revenue, it has been declared, by the act of the 18 Geo. III. that no taxes or duties shall be levied on the colonies, except

---

* Sir Henry Parnell on Financial Reform, p. 234.

for their use. As to commercial advantages, if the colonial trade were quite free, our commercial relations with the colonies would resemble the intercourse between ourselves and independent countries; and, with our unrivalled superiority in capital, manufactures, machinery, and skill, what have we to fear from unrestricted competition? What have we lost by the independence of the United States? Nothing: the nobility have lost provincial governorships; but the population of both countries has been enriched and benefited by the vast augmentation in their mercantile intercourse.

The rage for colonies has been one of the great big blunders of our national policy, originating in the vain glory of conquest and aristocratic cupidity. England has neither conferred nor derived social happiness from territorial acquisitions. We may have imparted strength to others, but have received in return only the disease of monopolies and vast individual accumulations. How, indeed, could the results have been more favorable? A great nation, possessing within herself the resources of wealth and civilization, what advantage can she derive from exhausting her energies in rearing to maturity and fostering ingratitude in the unfledged offspring of future empires? Between old and infant communities there is not reciprocity of interest; the latter participate in the benefits of the experience, laws, institutions, warlike power, and riches of the former without yielding countervailing advantages: it is strength allying itself to weakness—the full-grown oak bending to the palsying embrace of the creeping ivy.

So convinced are we of the fatuity of our conduct in this respect, that we are sometimes inclined to think that we should have been a happier community had our sway never extended over the border. Scotland has benefited by the Union: her soil has been fertilised by our capital, and her greedy sons have enriched themselves by sinecures and pensions, the produce of English taxes; but what has England gained from the connexion? The generous and intellectual character of her Saxon race has not been improved by amalgamation with Scotch metaphysics, thrift, and servility. Again, what benefits have we derived from the conquest of Ireland? Her uncultivated wastes, too, will be made fruitful by English money, unless the connexion be prematurely severed: but what boon in return can she confer on England? Her miserable children have poured out their blood in our wars of despotism; our rich Aristocracy have been made richer by the rental of her soil; and the aggregate power of the empire has been augmented: but we seek in vain for the benefits communicated to the mass of the English population. Certainly we do not recognise them in the degraded situation of the "men of Kent," depressed by competition with the Hibernian peasantry; neither have the moral habits of our rural and manufacturing population been bettered by commingling with the wretched and half-civilized emigrants from Munster and Connaught.

But these, at best, are only unprofitable lamentations; it is vain to repine at remediless evils; the union of England, Scotland, and Ireland, is, we presume, indissoluble : we are married, as the saying-is, for better and worse, and we must make the best of an unprofitable alliance.

The chief advantage to be derived from colonies is in rendering them a desirable refuge to a redundant population. But the Aristocracy decline making them subservient to the purposes of an extensive plan of emigration, because *of the expense ;* it would be a sacrifice not for the benefit of themselves, but of the industrious orders, and this they begrudge; they prefer subduing the clamours of a starving people by special commissions and improved *man-traps* rather than by providing the means by which the unemployed labourer and artisan may transport his superfluous industry to the banks of the St. Lawrence and the shores of Australia.

Although the Oligarchs are so parsimonious when the welfare of the people is concerned, they are reckless enough about expense when it ministers only indirectly to their own gratification and ambition. It appears, from the inquiries of the Finance-Committee, that the collective expenditure of five of our colonies has exceeded, on an account of ten and more years, the colonial revenues applicable to the discharge of it, so as to have constituted a deficiency of £2,524,000, and that this deficiency was paid by the Treasury, although the surplus expenditure had been incurred without previous communication with ministers ; nor does it appear ministers had any previous knowledge either of the amount of the colonial revenues or the charges upon them. Can any thing more strikingly show the careless and lavish system on which the affairs of the nation have been conducted ? We subjoin an abstract of the returns to parliament of the colonies to which we have alluded. It will be seen that the surplus revenue of the crown colonies above the civil expenditure amounted to £1,453,842, and this was all which remained applicable to a military expenditure of £3,733,939, leaving £2,280,097 to be paid out of the assessed taxes, the excise, and custom-duties of the people of England.

Statement of the Revenue and Expenditure of Five Crown Colonies referred to in Mr. Herries's Letter to Mr. Wilmot Horton, of the 24th March, 1827.—Parl. Paper, No. 352, Sess. 1830.

Colonies.	Years.	Revenue.	Civil Expenditure.	Military Expenditure.
Ceylon · · · · · · · · · · · ·	13	4,384,407	3,097,571	2,570,107
Mauritius · · · · · · · · · ·	12	1,723,114	1,829,508	795,575
Cape of Good Hope · ·	11	1,333,441	1,062,670	277,015
Malta · · · · · · · · · · · ·	10	2,378,114	2,384,197	88,994
Trinidad · · · · · · · · · ·	12	405,513	396,711	2,248
		£ 10,224,589	8,770,747	3,733,939

Of these colonies, three of them—Ceylon, Mauritius, and the Cape of Good Hope—are chiefly of use to the East-India Company, who ought to defray the charges of their military protection.   Many other of our colonies are equally valueless as objects of national utility.   Of what use is the retention of the Ionian Islands, with Malta and Gibraltar in our hands ?   The settlements at Sierra Leone and on the west coast of Africa ought to be abandoned, having entirely failed in the attainment of the object intended.   No reason can be shown why Canada, Nova-Scotia, and other possessions on the continent of America, would not be as available to British enterprise, if they were made independent states.   Neither our manufactures, commerce, nor shipping would be injured by such a measure.   On the other hand, what has the nation lost by Canada?   According to Sir H. Parnell, fifty or sixty millions have been already expended ; the annual sum payable out of English taxes is full £600,000 a-year; and there has been a plan in progress for two or three years to fortify Canada, at an estimated cost of three millions.   Either the Boroughmongers or the people must have been absolutely mad to tolerate for so many years such useless waste of public resources.

The Slave-Trade.—On this subject Sir H. Parnell says,—" The great sum of £5,700,000 has already been expended in carrying into effect the measures of government for co-operating with other countries in putting down the slave-trade, and the annual current expenses amount to nearly £400,000.   But the attempt appears to have altogether failed.   The governments of France, Spain, and Portugal, according to the Parliamentary Papers, make no efforts whatever to enforce the laws for putting down the traffic ; and the persons in authority in Cuba and Brazil not only neglect to execute the laws, but in some cases have been engaged in it themselves.   So that our treaties and laws, where such parties are concerned, are so much waste paper, and spending money to try to give effect to them is perfect folly.   The African Institution say, in their twentieth report, ' The slave-trade has increased during the last year ; and, notwithstanding the number of prizes taken, it continues to rage with unabated fury.'   Surely here are sufficient reasons for saving £400,000 a-year, now expended to so little purpose."—*Financial Reform,* pp. 231, 232.   Human suffering is equally painful to bear, whether inflicted on this or the other side of the globe, on black or white men, and we should be sorry, even for the sake of economy, that any measures should be adopted tending to revive the hellish traffic in Negroes.   But, after all, we ought to look *at home.* The horrors of the ' middle passage ' did not transcend those of the infernal FACTORY SYSTEM : in the former adults were the chief victims sacrificed to the Moloch of wealth ; in the latter it is helpless infancy. If one remonstrate with any of the CRŒSUSES of the North on the cruelty of exacting such long and severe hours of labour from children and apprentices, their only defence is,—" If we did not do it, others would—we should be *undersold in the market.*"   So with them it is a mere question of political economy—of profit and accumulation of capi-

tal—not of humanity. But we shall take leave to tell these lords of the
loom that they have another alternative ; they might be content with
amassing something less, as a passport into the aristocratic circle, than
a million or a million and a half of money by mutilating, misshaping,
and abridging the lives of God's creatures : but this they will not do ;
they will persist in realizing their cent. per cent., and rather than forego
it will have their ' pound of flesh,'—they will see orphans' eye-balls start
from their sockets, and their tendons crack, through unwholesome long-
protracted toil—and this too in a country where society is hourly threatened with dissolution—where internal peace and the security of property
are endangered by the multitude of unemployed artizans !

Expense of Civil Government.—The expense of conducting the civil
government of the country, including the king, the three secretaries of
state, lord-lieutenant of Ireland, the Mint, and judicial establishments,
is about £2,000,000. The progressive increase of expense, in some
departments, is as follows :—

	Year 1706.	Year 1829.
Home Department	£14,423	£31,916
Foreign Department......	34,495	65,681
Colonial Department	9,111	39,824
	£58,019	£137,221

Thus, it appears, the charge of these three departments has more
than doubled since 1796—a period of hostilities.

Lord-Lieutenant of Ireland.—The vice-regal government of Ireland
costs the country £100,000 per annum. This is extravagant, as it is
well known that Irish affairs are chiefly managed at Whitehall. The
keeping up this mimic sovereign tends to keep up those symbols of separation and hostility which a more rational policy would endeavour to
obliterate. For any other purpose, in the present state of intercourse,
we might as well have, once more, a lord-president at York—a king in
Edinburgh—or a separate court for the marches of Wales, at Ludlow,
or Monmouth. What then can be urged to justify the lord-lieutenancy ?
It has been alleged indeed by Irish secretaries, who receive £4000 a-year,
that it is beneficial to the tradesmen of Dublin, among whom the money
granted for the vice-regal establishment is expended. So then the community must be robbed of £100,000, that the Dublin shopkeepers may
profit the odd farthings. This is the favourite round of arguing by corruptionists ; they always deem it a sufficient justification for pillaging
the people, if a portion of the spoil be returned to them in the way of
alms or Christmas doles. By acting on this principle, the pride and
interests of aristocratical government are both favoured ; and the people,
injured by its rapacity, are insulted by its compassion. But in this way
the influence of the lord-lieutenant's salary is, as regards the prosperity
of a great city, contemptible : his whole salary, if spent in Dublin, is not
equal to half the receipts of one of the ten thousand gin-shops in London.

If, however, the effect was greater, the process is dishonest. If the lord-lieutenancy is necessary as an instrument of government—which has never been satisfactorily proved—it ought to be retained; if not, there is no earthly reason why the shopkeepers of Dublin should be supported by taxing the shopkeepers of the other towns of the empire. The viceroyship is a precious jewel in the eyes of the Aristocracy, and that it will not willingly be abandoned, we believe; but where pretexts are seen through easily, it is, perhaps, prudent to abstain from them. The man who merely robs you, does not offend you so much as the man who both robs you and insults your understanding by an awkward attempt at deceiving you.

Expenses of a Coronation.—The ministers of George IV. asked Parliament for a grant of only £100,000, to defray the expenses of his coronation; but the ceremony turned out something like palace-building, the actual cost greatly exceeding the estimate, amounting to £238,000.* The jewels of the crown were valued at £65,000, and 10 per cent. interest was paid to Rundell and Bridge for the loan of them. Either for the gratification of the monarch or his courtiers, the crown was kept four years, at an annual charge to the public of £6500; and it was only in consequence of a seasonable motion of Mr. Hume the royal bauble was at last divested of its borrowed plumage.

Upon the coronation of William IV. the Whigs certainly curtailed materially both the folly and expense of the feudal pageant, to the no small mortification of the antiquated admirers of chivalry, Punch, and Bartholomew fair. But it is time the *oiling* and *kissing* and other tom-foolery, perpetrated in the Abbey by the right reverend bishops, were omitted, and the whole reduced to a simple and economical process of inauguration. The king, the magistrates, and public officers take the needful oaths on the accession, and a coronation confirms nothing; it affords no stronger guarantee either on the part of the king or the people; it is an unmeaning ceremony, fit only to be exhibited among slaves, or a priest-ridden rabble, by an Eastern despot. It is something still more objectionable. Formerly it might be of use, when it was really what it professed to be—a solemn compact between the king and his lieges; but it has since degenerated into a mere mockery of sacred things, of religious rites, vows, and pledges.

Kingly governments are sinking fast in general estimation, and it is bad policy to depreciate monarchy lower by obtruding it in its most absurd and revolting forms. Instead of expending a large sum on a senseless spectacle, we would beg in lieu to suggest that the commencement of every new reign be commemorated by the building of a bridge, the construction of a rail-road, the completion of a Thames-tunnel, the foundation of an university, or any other undertaking of national utility.

---

* Hansard's Parliamentary Debates, New Series, vol. ix. p. 1107.

WORKINGS OF TAXATION.

An important circumstance has been remarked by sir H. Parnell connected with the pressure of taxation, namely, the effect of monopolies and protections in raising the prices of commodities which are the subjects of them. These monopolies and protections impose, by increased prices, burdens on the public which neither fill the exchequer, nor forward any purpose of national utility, but support favoured trades. If the effect of the corn laws is, at least, to raise the price of corn five shillings a quarter, this advance on the annual quantity consumed, taken at 50,000,000 quarters, creates a charge on the public of £12,500,000 a year. If the protecting duties on East India and foreign sugars advance the price of sugar only one penny a pound, this advance on the quantity annually consumed, namely 380,000,000 pounds, is, on the public, £1,500,000 a year. If the East India Company's monopoly makes the price of tea (exclusive of duty) double what it is at New York and Hamburgh, as is the case, it imposes a tax of at least £2,000,000 a year in the form of increased price; and the monopoly of the timber trade, enjoyed by the shipowners and Canada merchants, costs the public at least £1,000,000 a year: so that by these monopolies and protections 17 millions a year are taken from the pockets of the people, just as if corn, sugar, tea, and timber were taxed to that amount, and the produce paid into the Treasury.

Relief to the country is not so much to be expected from a reduction in the amount of taxation as the adjustment of its pressure. The taxes which have been repealed are considerable, and further reductions, with the present scale of expenditure, might render loans necessary to supply the deficiency. The people, however, may be greatly benefited by a *commutation of taxes*, and by imposing those essential to the expenditure of government on the classes and interests best able to support them. We shall in this section shortly notice a few of the taxes which require either to be repealed or modified.

To begin with SOAP, which, as the *cholera spasmodica* has reached our shores, is rendered more than ever essential to health and cleanliness. On hard soap (the revenue on soft soap is next to nothing) the duty is three pence per pound, or 110 to 130 per cent., in some cases more. The duty is too high, and the regulations for collecting it lead to frauds of the grossest description. There is no duty in Ireland, and it is notorious that a large quantity of soap is smuggled back again from that country into England. There is no fixed rule for the collection of the tax: there are no less than seven different modes of levying it: in London there is one way, in Liverpool another, in Hull a third, and so on. This is meant to avoid fraud, and the result is to invite it, and, of course, to harass the fair trader. Mr. Thomson mentioned two Liverpool houses (House of Commons, March 26, 1830) which contrived to carry on an extensive business with government capital, by a dexterous management of the drawback allowed on the exportation of soap to Ireland.

The duty of £4 : 10 per ton on HEMP is injudicious; for it is a tax on a raw material not produced at home, and of the first necessity for shipping and domestic uses. But while we tax the article in its raw state, we admit it in a manufactured form for the use of the marine, if purchased and manufactured *abroad*: thus giving a premium to the foreign manufacturer and discouraging our own. The timber duties are liable to similar objections, but the subject has been so frequently before the public we shall pass on to the SILK DUTIES, which, as justly remarked, are a fine specimen of fiscal absurdity.

First, there is a duty on manufactured silk, to protect the weaver; then, there is a duty on thrown silk, to keep him down, and to protect the silk-throwster; then, there is a duty on raw silk, to contract the operations of both weaver and throwster. Common sense would say, abolish the raw silk-duties at all events; but Common Sense has never been finance minister, and indeed very seldom in the Cabinet in any capacity.

The MALT LAWS will of course be revised. It is an act of justice due to the malster, to the public, and to the agriculturist. The duty on TEA must stand over till the East India Company's charter is settled, when we may expect something better than an infusion from *sloe-leaves* to breakfast; prior to the settlement of the Charter any reduction in the duty would only tend to augment the dividends of the proprietors. The duty on GLASS does not admit of delay; the gross produce is about one million, but nearly half of this sum is either returned or lost in the charges of collection. Lord Althorp proposed to repeal the glass duty, but having been bothered out of the tax on *stock-jobbing* by Messrs. Goulburn and John Smith, he was compelled to retain it, as also the duty on tobacco.

The duties on different kinds of PAPER vary from 50 to 150 per cent. They form a portion of the mass of taxes imposed on knowledge and the diffusion of information. The payment of the duties is the least part of the evil; the paper-maker is harassed like the malster by an infinity of forms—in giving notice to the exciseman—in reweighing the paper before the supervisor—in lettering the rooms of his manufactory—in numbering his vats, chests, presses and engines—in taking out licenses— and in procuring and pasting labels on every ream—and for neglect of any of which he is liable to ruinous penalties. Why is the paltry PAMPHLET DUTY retained? It produces only about £1,000 per annum, which is much less than might be obtained by compelling noble lords and honourable members to pay the postage of their private correspondence. Yet for this insignificant sum the booksellers throughout the kingdom are hampered with forms of entry at the Stamp Office, which, if they do not observe, they must pay forfeit, or what is worse, memorialise the Honourable Board, *alias* the Honourable Solicitor of Stamps. The duty on ADVERTISEMENTS ought to be regulated, but in what way we are unable to suggest. It is certainly unfair that a short advertisement should pay as much as a long one, or that an advertisement for a place, office, or employment should pay as much as one for a loan of money, or the sale of an estate.

The produce of the duty on SEA POLICIES has diminished, although the amount of ship's tonnage entered inwards and outwards has increased. The high rate of duties has driven insurers to make their policies in America, Holland, and Germany, where they could insure at a cheaper rate. In these times of low profits a difference in price of one-quarter or one-half per cent. is sufficient to influence the determination of commercial business.* The case of FIRE INSURANCES is still more flagrant. The premium in London on common risks is 1s. 6d. and upon that 3s. duty must be paid to government. A tax of 200 per cent. obviously prevents many from insuring; those who are willing to pay 1s. 6d. per cent. to the offices do not like to pay twice as much more for pensions and palace buildings. The consequence is that it is only the great properties which are insured, the smaller are left to Providence. A man with a large house and valuable furniture insures, but a man with a cottage does not: thus prudence is taxed where it ought to be specially encouraged.

The unequal mode of assessing the *inhabited house duty* has been before alluded to ; also the *mileage duty* on stage-coaches (pp. 267–280) and the unfair advantage possessed by *real* over *chattel* property. The estates of the aristocracy pass to their descendants without payment of either *probate* or *legacy* duty ; but the property of the merchant, trader, or mechanic, being mostly personal, is subject to both, and cannot be left to children and friends without payment of a tax, varying from one to ten per cent. The whole of the STAMP DUTIES require regulation, and the public has long indulged a hope that the task ere this would have been accomplished. The duty on deeds and other legal instruments should be more regular in its ascent, and not fall so heavily on property of small value. The representatives of a deceased person must swear to the amount of his property without *deducting debts ;* and although the duty is afterwards returned (but with considerable trouble and expense), it frequently inconveniences the poorer classes, who may not have the immediate means of paying the probate duty, without which they cannot act. The *license duties* fall very unequally ; many classes, and these best able perhaps to bear a deduction from their incomes, are wholly exempt. Then why should an attorney be subject to an annual duty, while the barrister, physician, and medical practitioner escape altogether? Or why should the large fundholder, or the army and naval half-pay, and civil superannuation people, receive their dividends and pensions without giving a stamp, especially as government will not receive its own taxes without charging the payer with the receipt-duty.

Ireland has been so impoverished by tithes and absenteeism that her contributions to the wants of the state have been *personal* rather than *pecuniary*. She was exempt from the property tax, and still is from the assessed taxes. Why, however, the gentry should escape direct taxation as well as agistment tithe, cannot be so easily explained, unless from the circumstance of Ireland having been till lately a close borough.

---

* C. P. Thomson, House of Commons, March 26, 1830.

There may be valid grounds for exempting a poor country from duties on articles of consumption; but income arising from property is really more valuable (will go farther) in a poor country than in a rich one.

TAXES ON NEWSPAPERS.—The heavy duty on newspapers, whether considered as a source of revenue, or, in its injurious tendency, to restrict the diffusion of intelligence, is the most objectionable part of our fiscal system. A fourpenny stamp, on an article which sells for sixpence, is a tax of 200 per cent. Some of the weekly papers endeavour to evade this onerous impost, by selling a larger paper at a higher price, which reduces the per centage, the duty not being an ad valorem one; but they are subject to the disadvantage of a more limited sale, owing to the higher price of their publications.

A reduction in the duty would be more than compensated by an increase in the circulation of papers; but then the object of the government has been not so much to realize revenue as to *control public opinion*. Our limits do not admit of our treating this subject so fully as it deserves; nor is it necessary, after the able and conclusive exposition it has undergone in other publications; we shall, however, submit a few brief observations:—1. On the influence of the high stamp-duties on the state of the newspaper press. 2. On the consequences of restricting the sale of cheap political pamphlets, subjecting them to the same duty as the regular journals. Our arguments will be addressed to those who feel an interest in social improvement, not to those who seek only to thrive by abuse and oppression.

The first and most obvious effect of the high duty is, by enhancing the price, to curtail the benefit of newspapers, whether as the source of innocent amusement or useful instruction, to the more opulent classes. But the newspapers depending for support upon what may be termed the *proprietary* of the country, they will, of course, be conducted on such principles and in such spirit as is likely to be most agreeable to the interests, the prejudices, and passions of their subscribers. Hence the predominant character of the press has been ARISTOCRATIC: and it seldom compromised the favour of its chief patrons by the fearless exposition of any political abuse, superstitious error, commercial or chartered privilege, private vice, or public oppression, in which they were especiaily interested.

But the Press being under the influence of the opulent, it leaves the indigent, as we shall term them for brevity, without protection. They may be calumniated with impunity, as they often are; their motives, views, and conduct may be distorted, and they have no effective means— no organ—by which they can set themselves right with the community. Hence it is that the great mass of society—the industrious and trading classes—those numerous and useful orders, which constitute the bone and muscle of the social state—are no more represented—their interests are no more maintained, by the daily journals, than they are by the Commons' House of Parliament.

Of late years a great deal has been said of the advantages of commercial freedom and unrestricted competition; but is a monopoly of knowledge less pregnant with mischief than a monopoly of corn or other article of general consumption ? The exclusive privileges of Oxford and Cambridge have been objected to as well as of the Bank and East-India Company ; but how does it happen there is so little outcry against the Press? The reason is obvious enough ; the Press is the *common crier ;* but, though loud and prompt in proclaiming the abuses of others, it has been marvellously silent concerning its own. How much the monopoly of the great brewers was reprobated, even by most of the journals; but the public injury, from this source, was limited and unimportant, contrasted with that originating in the monopoly of the Press. No doubt the beverage of the people was diluted and adulterated, but this evil, at the worst, was local in its effects ; it was not like the Press, whose despotic authority is not limited to the metropolis, nor the provinces, nor even the empire, but extends to every corner of the globe.

The provincial press takes its tone and character from the London prints ; some of the country papers follow in the wake of the *Times,* some the *Morning Chronicle,* some the *Sun,* some the *Courier,* and some other journals; but all have their guide and prototype in the metropolis, from whom they cut or copy their opinions. From this sort of paternity and connexion arises a most portentous danger to the liberties and prosperity of the empire. The Press has been designated a *fourth estate,* next in influence and importance to King, Lords, and Commons. But, Great GOD ! only think of what this *fourth estate* consists—twelve daily papers established and carried on solely for gain—whose proprietors are unknown—whose editors are unknown—whose reporters are unknown—in short, belonging and attached to which there is not the slighest thread of responsibility, whatever may be the character and magnitude of their delinquency. Upon this vacillating and intangible pivot one-fourth—aye, a great deal more—of the government of this great empire depends. What nonsense it is to complain of the Treasury boroughs, of Gatton, or Midhurst, or of rotten boroughs with only a dozen electors, while an overwhelming influence like this is tolerated ! What dolts ministers would have been, had they exclusively concerned themselves about the influence to be derived from these sources, and not availed themselves of the more potent agency which might be derived from the Press. And do we suppose that Government alone may avail itself of this power; that great commercial companies, loan-mongers, speculators in the funds, and getters up of bubble companies may not resort to similar aid ? Assuredly not; for we know the contrary; we know that the Press has been the great agent not only in the oppressions of the Oligarchy, but in the fraudulent devices by which one portion of the community has plundered another.

Only place at our disposal, out of the secret service money, £20,000 per annum; a few judgeships and offices in the Colonies; a few leases of houses and crown lands in the metropolis ; a few livings and dignities in the Church; a few places in the Customs, Excise, and judicial administration ; and a few appointments to the magistracy and shrievalties in the country : let us, we repeat, have these things in our gift, and we will engage to make the boasted FOURTH ESTATE of this realm as subservient as the most corrupt and despotic minister could desire. We do not mean to affirm we would render the Press undisguisedly prostituted to the Government; we would further its ends in a much more adroit and effective manner; nor would we go openly with bribe in hand, for, in that case, the sly rogues would bruit our offer, knowing they would gain more by proclaiming it, and boasting of their incorruptible integrity, than accepting our tender: we would not adopt any such vulgar mode of procedure; nevertheless, we would accomplish our employer's purpose. If the premier wished to interfere with France, or Belgium, or to get up a war of any sort, we would render the undertaking popular to his heart's content; if he wished to set his face against the reform of domestic abuses, we would convince ninety-nine out of every hundred that our institutions had stood the test of ages, and are the best the wit of man ever devised; if he wished to hunt down a troublesome individual, we would render the caitiff an exile from all decent and respectable society; if he wished to destroy all public spirit in the people, we would throw such discredit on every meeting and association for a patriotic object, that the parties thereto should appear nothing better than gaping idiots or poverty-stricken knaves, whose sole purpose was the plunder of the RICH !

All this we would do, and more, and the great beauty of our doings would be that they should be so dexterously managed that they would neither bring scandal on ourselves, our employer, nor the agents of our *Diabolism*. The only machinery necessary to put in motion would be simply a well-directed MENSONGE, with which gentlemen connected with the " respectable part of the Press" are well acquainted. It would consist of an artful and incessant grinding of paragraphs—an amplifying and improving, or, if an opponent, a garbling, curtailing, and suppressing of speeches—the omission, misrepresentation, or blazoning, as the case might be, of all public meetings and proceedings— in short, in picturing every thing and person on the *broad sheet* in such a way that they should be viewed through a multiplying glass, or the right or wrong end of the telescope, as might best suit the purpose of our employer.

All this we should be able to effect without fear of detection or exposure: we would manage the Press with less noise than the famous William Holmes in the *olden time* managed the orgies of St. Stephen's; the close monopoly affords every facility for bribery and concealment ; and though these diverging rays of intelligence, the country papers, would partake, equally with the rest, of the impulse given at the primal source, they would be as unconscious of the presence, as unparticipant in the favours of the great operator at the focal point.

Perhaps our almost allegorical description of the relation in which the journals stand to the community may not be fully comprehended by all our readers; but it would be a more invidious task than we should like, to illustrate our subject by practical examples. What we have said applies to the Press in its corporate and irresponsible capacity; of the individuals connected with it, they are, we believe, as estimable as any other class ; and some there are, we know, animated by an almost enthusiastic devotion to popular rights and social happiness.　It is not their faults exactly that they are placed in a *false position*, in respect of society; that from the operation of the stamp duty excluding competition, they have been raised into great and hazardous undertakings, which renders it almost madness, and something like breach of trust to the proprietors, to indulge their private sentiments at the risk of compromising the partial interests on which the prosperity of the journals confided to their management notoriously depends.

This is the most that can be said in extenuation of their timid, see-saw, and compromising conduct; and after all, it does not lessen the magnitude of the evil under which the public suffers.　That this evil exists, and to an enormous extent, we shall establish, from the present state and management of *The Times*.　This journal exercises an irresponsible power, dangerous to the interests of society; and were this power exercised in opposition to the government—which, by the by, is not likely, as this journal has evinced a fixed determination to stick to the dynasty de facto, whether Tory or Whig—it would be dangerous even to the government.　Had we the option, whether, as an instrument of the general happiness, we would prefer the return of 100 honest members to parliament from the unrepresented towns, or we would have the Times at our beck, we should unhesitatingly say, give us the beldame of Printing-house-square, with her good name, her Medusean front, her quiver of poisoned arrows, her subtlety, literary tact, experience of town, and general acquaintance with all the springs of life and action.　The influence she is enabled to exercise over public opinion is incredible, and can only be appreciated by those habituated to observe social movements, and the agency by which they are produced.

It is because a newspaper has such power, which may be directed to a beneficial or malignant purpose, that we consider the state of the Press objectionable.　Irresponsible authority is as objectionable in the gentlemen of the Press as in the Boroughmongers, and for the remedy of this literary usurpation we know nothing so well adapted as the *opening of the trade*, by means of minor publications.　The suppression of the cheap political pamphlets by lord Castlereagh always appeared to us both unjust and impolitic.　Sedition and licentiousness might have been effectually restrained without destroying an instrument which, ultimately, might have been made subservient to the attainment of the most salutary ameliorations.　It is the imposition of the *stamp duty*, not the demand of security of which we complain ; the former completely interdicting, to a vast majority of the community, a source of amusement and intellectual improvement.

Some of the most dangerous popular errors, we are convinced, were eradicated solely by the agency of the cheap tracts.　Among these we reckon the prevailing opinions on *Catholic Emancipation*.　Before the establishment of the weekly pamphlets the mass of the population was decidedly anti-catholic, and hardly less obstinate in their prejudices than

Lord Eldon or Sir C. Wetherell.   A prodigious change was effected in
the character of the people in another respect.   During a scarcity, or
high prices, the rage of the labouring classes was mostly vented on the
butcher, baker, and farmer; such senseless outrages are now never heard
of.   The introduction of *machinery*, for obvious reasons, was opposed
by the mass of the people.   It was impossible they should at first be
reconciled to inventions which, though tending to the general advantage,
by the multiplication of commodities at a cheaper rate, yet, if they did
not deprive some classes of the means of subsistence, degraded them
into lower stations.   It was natural, therefore, they should resist this
innovation; and, in so doing, we believe, they did no more than the
legal, ecclesiastical, or any other class would have done, had their interests been sacrificed, though that sacrifice were made for the general
good.   It was necessary, however, the principle should triumph.   The
people resisted; severer laws were made against frame-breakers, and a
terrible sacrifice was made at York: but all this would have been ineffec-
tual, had not another cause interfered.   This cause, we verily believe,
was the introduction, by Mr. Cobbett, of the *two-penny trash;* which
demonstrated that, however injurious the employment of machinery
might be to particular branches of industry, yet, inasmuch as it augmented the supply of food and clothing, consequently rendered them
cheaper to all classes, it must be ultimately beneficial.   We are convinced if pamphlet writing had continued unchecked during the last
twelve years, the effects of the knowledge it would have spread, and the
discussion it would have excited, would have saved the country from
the ' *Swing fires,*' and those outrages against the machinery and property of individuals who suffer as much as their unfortunate work-people
from the manifold difficulties in which we have been involved by a long
course of misgovernment.

Much has been said about the pernicious, dangerous, and absurd
doctrines which were propagated.   It might be the case; with important truths, error also might be inculcated; ideas beneficial to society
might be accompanied with others of a contrary tendency.   This, however, was matter of opinion; and a more proper subject for discussion
than coercion.   Admitting that cheap publications were injurious as
well as beneficial, it afforded no argument whatever for their suppression.   The same objection might be made to plays, novels, romances,
and almost every other publication; the same objection might be urged
against the amusements of the theatre: all these, no doubt, are productive of evil as well as good to the community; but who ever, on that
account, thought that they ought to be suppressed?   Who ever expects
to see any improvement unaccompanied with some countervailing disadvantage?   The only principle in this, as in every other case, is to balance the good against the bad; and it was on this principle the fate of
the cheap publications ought to have been determined.

It is unnecessary, we think, to say any thing more in defence of
political pamphlets.   We were desirous of submitting a few observations,
because it is generally understood Ministers have some measure in contemplation by which the future state of the Press is to be regulated.

There appear only two courses open to them to pursue; either we must have a *restricted* or *free trade* in politics. Public opinion has declared against the former,—it would require a literary preventive service to enforce it, and after all the people would obtain the contraband commodity, though, perhaps, both dear and deleterious ; whereas, by open competition, the cheapest and best, in the long run, would possess the market.

We have not dwelt much on the fiscal part of the subject; it has been better done by others than we could do it, and, moreover, is exhausted ; beside we have not so bad an opinion of Ministers as to think that the loss or gain of the revenue will form a material item of consideration when the question is whether a great community shall be informed, or remain in ignorance of its real and permanent interests.

There is one point we have omitted to notice ; namely, the opinion entertained that the reduction of the stamp-duties would inflict serious pecuniary loss on the newspaper press. We cannot foresee such result ; our impression is, that both the public income and the newspaper proprietary would gain by the alteration. Under the existing system the circulation of the journals is chiefly confined to the opulent ; were the price reduced one-half many would take in two or more papers who only take in one : hundreds of thousands who are restricted to an hour's inconvenient and hasty perusal, or obliged to resort to a coffee-house, news-room, or alehouse, would become subscribers to a paper for their exclusive use, or for the morning, after-dinner, or evening amusement of their families. The consequence would be a prodigious increase of sale, and, of course, revenue. The *Times*, which now circulates 7000 or 8000, would circulate 20,000 or 30,000, and the *Morning Chronicle* and other journals would have a corresponding augmentation of demand. That there would be increased competition we believe, but it would be a competition of *opinion* rather than of *profit*. The old journals would retain their supremacy,— the result of great capital—admirable business arrangements--literary connexion—valuable correspondence in every part of the globe—and long established channels of circulation. Against such advantages new rivals might contend, but they would contend with the odds greatly against them, and if they succeeded, their success would be the result rather of the special favour of the gods than of any other favouring circumstance.

To conclude, we think, by a reduction of the newspaper duties, a vast social benefit would be conferred, without inflicting loss on any class of individuals, or even the Chancellor of the Exchequer. It would be like the discovery of some new and useful invention, which brings within the reach of the whole community an article of luxury or comfort that had previously been confined to the richer classes. Were newspapers sold for threepence, every respectable family could afford its daily journal, and every working man his weekly one ; their circulation would be as great in England, in proportion to the reading population, as in France or the United States. The advantages that would result—moral, social, and political—are too obvious to be enforced.

EAST-INDIA COMPANY.

———

AMONG the monopolies and privileged communities which impede individual enterprise and national prosperity, the East-India Company and
the Bank of England stand pre-eminent : these have formed the out-
works, the strongholds, of the Borough System ; and, by their
connexions and interests, added greatly to that mass of influence by
which the latter has been supported. Both these powerful associations
have become more like petty states, acknowledging a feudatory dependence to the supreme power, than companies of traders, originally
incorporated for commercial purposes. Both have risen from very
humble beginnings, and perhaps it would not be easy to strike the
balance of turpitude by which their power has been respectively acquired. Both have been nurtured under the fostering care of the
Oligarchy, to which, under particular emergencies, they have been
indebted for assistance ; and, probably, it is from a knowledge of this
paternal obligation, that these chartered bodies feel such a lively interest in the permanency of the existing system, and that whenever any
popular movement indicates proceedings hostile to the government, they
are instantly alarmed, and the Bank and the India-House immediately
placed in a defensive attitude.

Both the Bank and the East-India Company claim particular attention,
from the period having arrived about which their charters expire ; and
the legislature, either in the session of 1831 or the following year, will
have to determine their future immunities, and the relative position in
which they are to stand to the government and the community.

Before entering on the exposition of the present state of the East-
India Company, it will be proper to give a brief outline of the history
of this powerful association, and briefly indicate those extraordinary
events by which a few traders in mace, nutmegs, and ginger, have
been able to extend their sway over 120 millions of inhabitants, whose
happiness depends on their wisdom and justice. In giving this notice,
we shall enter into no detail of Asiatic triumphs, of battles and sieges.
We have little taste for these things at best, but still less when the
combatants are unequally matched,—when we should have to present a
counterpart to the conquest of Peru and Mexico by the Spaniards,—
exhibit the conflicts of wolves and sheep, and show how a handful of
crafty, hardy, and unprincipled Europeans wrested a mighty empire
from the feeble grasp of the artless and effeminate Hindoos. Leaving

out, therefore, with one or two exceptions, military details, which in justice ought never to have formed part of the history of the East-India Company, we shall confine ourselves principally to the civil transactions of this association.

The first attention to the India trade appears to have been attracted by the success of the Dutch merchants. These rapacious traders, having supplanted the Portuguese in that part of the world, had an entire monopoly of the trade, and availing themselves of the exclusive possession of the market, exacted exorbitant prices for the productions of the East. To frustrate their avarice, and obtain some share in this lucrative traffic, the merchants of London despatched a mission to the Great Mogul, to obtain from him a grant of commercial privileges to the English. The success of this mission was not known till the year 1600 ; but, in the mean time, the lord mayor, aldermen, and other principal merchants of the city, to the number of 101, assembled in Founders' Hall, and established an association for trading to India, for which they subscribed a capital of £33,133. To this society, and in the year mentioned, Queen Elizabeth granted the first charter of incorporation, with the exclusive privilege to trade to all parts of Asia, Africa, and America, for fifteen years, and the company to be managed by a chairman and twenty-four directors chosen annually. The capital of the corporation amounted to £70,000. They fitted out four ships of the burthen of 240, 260, 300, and 600 tons. The value of the ships' stores and provisions, of the merchandize forming the cargoes, and of the bullion, was estimated at £68,373.

This expedition was tolerably successful, brought home valuable cargoes of merchandize, and succeeded in establishing factories at Bantany, and on the Molucca Islands. But, notwithstanding the success of this undertaking, no great effort was made to follow it up, and for several years after, the trade and capital of the Company gradually declined. In 1606, only three ships were fitted out. In 1608, the Company having subscribed a capital of £33,000, for a fourth voyage, the whole of their ships were either wrecked in India, or on their voyage home. Next year they were more fortunate, and their ships bringing home a valuable cargo of mace and nutmegs, they divided a profit of 211 per cent. Encouraged by this success, the Company solicited the renewal of their charter, and seemed resolved to push the trade with spirit. They built the largest ship that had ever been constructed in England for commercial purposes, being no less than 1000 tons burthen. King James and his court attended the launch, and named her *The Trade's Increase.*

Unfortunately this vessel was lost, and Sir Henry Middleton, her commander, soon after died of grief. The trade subsequently declined, for which various causes may be assigned. The rivals of the Company, the Dutch and Portuguese, made use of every expedient avarice and treachery could suggest, to impede their success ; besides which, we may add, the erroneous principles on which the different voyages were undertaken. Instead of the trade being conducted upon a joint-stock on account of the whole Company, every individual was privileged by the charter to subscribe as much or as little as he pleased, or nothing at all, for every voyage. The disadvantages of this system in an incipient and difficult undertaking became apparent; and, in 1612, it was determined to have no more separate voyages, but to open a subscription for a joint capital to continue for four years. Upon this principle the affairs of the Company assumed a new aspect ; and in a very short time they had established more than twenty factories, in different parts of the Mogul's dominions, and the islands in the Indian seas.

In 1616, when they proposed to raise a new capital, all ranks crowded into the subscription, which, at the time of closing it, amounted to £1,629,040, being the largest capital that had ever been subscribed in any part of Europe for a joint-stock trade. Among the subscribers were 15 dukes and earls, 13 countesses, 82 knights, including judges and privy counsellors, 18 widows and maiden ladies, besides clergymen, physicians, merchants, tradesmen, and others without any denomination ; in the whole 954 subscribers. The stock of the Company sold for 203 per cent. The total value of their property, at this time, was estimated at £400,000. And it was stated by the deputy-governor, that they gave employment to 10,000 tons of shipping, 2500 seamen, 500 ship carpenters, and 120 factors in India.

In 1652 the Company obtained considerable privileges in Bengal through the skill of their surgeons, in curing a certain disease in the Mogul court, and which disease was little known in Europe, though afterwards of frequent occurrence in sea-ports and large capitals. In 1655, the trade was thrown open for three years, but closed again in two years on it being alleged that evils had resulted from the free-trade. In 1669 the Company received two canisters containing 143½ pounds of tea, which is supposed to have been the first importation of this article from any part of the Indies. It was partly given away in presents, and partly consumed in the India-House for the refreshment of the committees.

In 1676, the trade of the Company having been very successful for many years, they were enabled, out of their accumulated profits, to double their capital to £739,782, upon which the market price of their stock, which had been under par, immediately rose to £245 per cent. The ships in their employ amounted to from 30 to 35, of from 300 to 600 tons, and carrying from 40 to 70 guns. In the year 1680, the company sent a ship to trade with China. The whole of that trade had heretofore been monopolized by the Dutch and Portuguese. About this time they acquired the privilege to coin money, not resembling British money, at Bombay and other places in India. The Company consisted of 600 members, who were entitled to votes in proportion to their shares ; hence it happened that some had to the amount of sixty votes : —every member, moreover, had liberty to carry on trade on his own private account, to the extent of one-fifth of his stock in the Company's capital.

In 1698, the English factory obtained permission to purchase three small villages, extending in all about three miles along the east bank of the Ganges, and about one mile back from it, for which they agreed to pay annually to the Nabob 1195 rupees. This diminutive acquisition was the handle to the axe and commencement of the territorial aggrandizement of the Company, by which they were afterwards enabled to hew down the entire Mogul empire. The ground on which these villages stood forms the site of the great city of Calcutta, containing 600,000 inhabitants.

Some jealousy, about this time, began to be entertained at the increasing power of the Company; and the Government intimated to the association that a large sum would be expected for the public service, in consideration of a parliamentary confirmation of their privileges. They offered to advance £700,000 at an interest of 4 per cent. provided their charter was fully confirmed by parliament. Meanwhile several opulent individuals offered to advance £2,000,000, provided they were invested with all the privileges of the India trade, as heretofore enjoyed by the Company. Parliament accepted the larger sum, though at double interest, and a bill was ordered to be prepared for incorporating the subscribers. The Company, not to be outdone by their opponents, then proposed a loan of £2,000,000, but this availed them nothing. The government was favourable to the opposing interest, and it prevailed. So great were the advantages anticipated by the nation from the new association, that the subscription of two millions was filled up within a few days after the books were opened. The greatest part of this sum was subscribed by foreigners. The king himself was an adventurer to the extent of £10,000.

The charter of the original Company had not yet expired, and a most ruinous contest ensued betwixt the rival associations. More than sixty ships are said to have been employed by the contending interests in the India trade. The glut of India goods, joined to other causes, produced by this rivalship, reduced the value of the stock of the old Company, which had been as high as 500 per cent., to 39 per cent. Both parties at length seem to have discovered the ruinous tendency of this contest, and an union was effected in 1702, by a tripartite indenture, wherein Queen Anne, the old Company and the new Company were partners. According to this instrument, the two Companies bind themselves to have at least one-tenth of their exports in English manufactures, and after the expiration of seven years they are to be called " *The United Company of Merchants of England trading to the East Indies,*" which is their present designation.

In 1766, the Company, in consequence of their territorial acquisitions, raised their dividend from 6 to 10 per cent. and shortly after to 12½ per cent. In India this year, their power was exposed to hazard by the abolition of the *double batta,* or allowance to officers in the field : it originated a serious mutiny in the army, but was subdued by the firmness of Lord Clive, and many officers cashiered. The celebrated Hyder Ali, who from a subordinate rank had raised himself to the throne of Mysore, began about this period to menace the sway of the Company.

In 1779, the time for the renewal of the charter approaching, the Company prudently prepared for that event, by a present to the public of three seventy-four gun ships, besides a large sum of money in bounties to 6000 seamen. Notwithstanding this bonus, in 1781 notice was given to the Company by Government, that on the expiration of the charter their exclusive privileges should cease, unless they would agree to pay £1,000,000 into the exchequer, restrict their future dividend to 8 per cent. and pay three-fourths of the surplus profits, over and above that dividend, into the Treasury. After much discussion, the demand for the renewal of the charter was reduced to £400,000, the other conditions remaining unaltered; and the Company were required to submit all political despatches to ministers, who were to decide on all questions relative to peace and war.

In 1789 the decennial settlement of lands commenced in Bengal and Bahar, and was completed in 1793, when the settlement was made perpetual. By this settlement, which produced such an important change in the landed tenure of a vast territory in India, the zemindars, who were in fact the revenue agents of the Mogul government, usually hereditary and possessed of great power and influence, but not *owners* of the soil, which they could neither sell nor alienate, were declared the actual land-owners, and from them the principal revenue of India was to be derived in the shape of land-tax. The poor ryots or peasantry, who were, next to the sovereign, the real owners of the land, as much as the feudal nobility of England or Hungary, and who could not be dispossessed of it so long as they paid their public assessments, were at once transmuted into the *tenants* of the zemindars or tax-gatherers. The objects of this sweeping innovation were *financial* and of disastrous issue. The zemindars, obliged to go through the legal formalities to collect their levies from the ryots, were unable to pay their taxes to the government, whose proceedings were summary. Their lands were gradually sold for the arrears of taxes, and passed into the hands of absentee landlords; in a few years almost all the zemindars disappeared. No improvement took place in the condition of the ryots, who were more oppressed by the middlemen above them than they had been by the tax-gatherers of the Mogul.

About this period, the affairs of the East-India Company, and the transactions in Hindustan, began deeply to interest the public, and every session of parliament produced new investigations on this important subject. From merchants, the Company had risen into sovereign princes, and, instead of being occupied with the ginger and pepper trade, they were wholly absorbed in schemes of territorial aggrandizement. Occupied unceasingly in war—buying and exchanging territory—making treaties of partition—hiring troops to the native princes—establishing monopolies—and fomenting hostilities among the nabobs and subahdars, that these short-sighted princes, after weakening each other by their animosities, might fall an easy prey to the superior policy of the common invader. These avocations ill comported with the commercial character, and it was a little inconceivable how men, whose knowledge,

it may be supposed, was principally confined to making out invoices,
bills of lading, or book-keeping by double entry, could discharge these
royal functions.

In 1783, Mr. Fox introduced his famous India Bills, the general
objects of which were to divest the company of their administrative
functions—to prohibit them from making war, unless in self-defence—
from making treaties of partition—hiring troops to the native princes—
and every illegal present was to be recoverable by any person for his
own benefit. These provisions sufficiently indicate the prevalent abuses.
They were opposed by Mr. Pitt, then out of place, an oppositionist and
reformer. The question agitated the whole nation ; and such was the
outcry raised by the Company against the pretended violation of their
charter—representing such a precedent as endangering the security of
all the corporations in the kingdom,—that they finally prevailed,
and the bills, though passed in the Commons, were rejected by the
Lords.

Next [year a dissolution of parliament and change of ministers having
taken place, Mr. Pitt introduced a new bill for the better government of
India. Many of the provisions of this bill were similar to those of the
bill of Mr. Fox. The most important difference related to the appointment of the Board of Control. The commercial affairs and territorial
possessions of the Company were to continue in their hands, subject
to the superintendence of a board of commissioners appointed by the
Crown.

The next subject of any interest is the trial of Warren Hastings.
This gentleman had presided over India thirteen years, and arrived in
England on the 16th of June, 1785. On the 26th of the same month,
Mr. Burke, who had brought heavy accusations against him in the preceding session, gave notice of his intention to impeach him for high
crimes and misdemeanours, alleged to have been committed in India.
After long debates in this and succeeding sessions, the prosecution was
sanctioned by the Commons, and, in 1787, articles of impeachment were
sent to the Lords. The trial was protracted from year to year, till the
23d of April, 1795, when the accused was acquitted, on the payment
of his fees, of all the charges preferred against him. The Company, in
consideration of the services of this officer, discharged the expenses he
had incurred by the prosecution, amounting to upwards of £70,000, and
settled upon him an annuity of £5000.

In 1793 the charter of the Company was renewed, and their exclusive privileges continued to them until the first day of March, 1814.
In this act a clause was inserted to restrain the belligerent propensities
of the Company's servants, but it appears not to have been much
regarded. In 1792 Tippoo Saib was despoiled of half his dominions, and
compelled to deliver two of his sons into the hands of the Marquis
Cornwallis, as hostages for the performance of a treaty by which he
engaged to pay £1,600,000 in money to the Company. In 1799 this
prince was again attacked by Lord Mornington, now Marquis Wellesley,
under pretext of having entered into negotiations with the French, and

some of the native princes, for the entire expulsion of the English from India. This war completed the destruction of the sultan. His capital of Seringapatam was taken by assault, himself slain in its defence, and his dominions dismembered. His descendants are now supported by pensions payable by the *ci-devant* dealers in mace and cloves.

The Company having obtained possession of the different members of the Mogul empire, in 1803, completed their conquests by attacking the Mogul himself in his capital of Delhi. This monarch and his family were also placed upon the pension-list of the Company.

We shall only mention a few more facts connected with the Company's history till the opening of the trade in 1814. By the act of 1784 the fortunes acquired in India were to be ascertained on the return of each servant of the Company to England; this clause was repealed two years after by 26 Geo. III. c. 57. By the 29 Geo. III. c. 65, they were authorised to add one million to their capital stock. The new stock being subscribed at 174 per cent. produced £1,740,000, which raised their joint-stock to five millions. In 1793 they were authorized to add another million to their capital by subscription, making it £6,000,000, its present amount. This additional stock produced £2,000,000, being subscribed at 200 per cent.

In 1797 valuable concessions were made to the Americans with regard to the India trade. They were permitted to carry on trade with the Company's territories in India, in articles not prohibited by law, on paying only the duties paid by British vessels. These advantages were not neglected by the Americans. In a few years the trade of the United States in India equalled nearly one half the trade of the Company. It was singular policy to admit a foreign state to the participation of the India trade while our own merchants were excluded.

In 1803, during the alarm of an invasion, the Company, at a general court, came to a resolution to present to government 10,000 tons of shipping to guard the coast, and to be maintained at their own expense. In the years 1808 and 1809 the Company lost four outward-bound and six homeward-bound ships. The value of the ships and cargoes was estimated at two millions.

We have now mentioned the more important facts in the history of the East-India Company to the year 1813, when the exclusive privileges of this association were in part abolished. Prior to that time private traders were not wholly excluded from the India trade. By the 17th clause of the act of 1793, the Company were obliged to appropriate 3000 tons of shipping for carrying out goods belonging to private merchants and manufacturers. The act of 1813 continues to the Company the revenue and territorial acquisitions in India, and the exclusive monopoly of the China trade; but the trade to India, subject to certain restrictions and regulations, is thrown open to the enterprise of individuals. These immunities were conceded to the Company until the 10th of April, 1831, absolutely, and afterwards, until three years' notice be given by parliament, and the debt due from the public to the Company be paid.

INDIAN WARS AND TERRITORIAL ACQUISITIONS.

No external dominion in the East can endanger the security of the Anglo-Indian empire. All the native princes have either been absolutely conquered, reduced to a state of dependence, or have been so completely humiliated and divested of offensive power, as to render entirely hopeless every chance of successful opposition to the British government. In 1815 the Ghorkas, who possess the kingdom of Nepaul, on the northern frontier of Hindustan, made a show of contesting the sovereignty of the Company, but they were completely defeated by Lord Hastings, and compelled to purchase peace by the cession of a large tract of territory. The Burmese were the last nation who gave us any uneasiness. They have been represented as a warlike people, and at one time meditated nothing less than an eruption into the province of Bengal. Rangoon, their capital, was occupied by a British force; and in 1826, after a teasing warfare, they submitted to the terms imposed by the invading army, by which the Company has become possessed of the provinces of Arracan and Tenasserim, including nearly the whole line of coast which previously belonged to the Burman empire.

Of the Mahratta chiefs, Scindia alone retains the full military as well as civil government of his territory. The courts of Holkar and of Guicowar, the rajah of Berar and of the smaller principalities, exercise the civil functions of royalty, but are not tolerated in the possession of an armed force. They have each, by the cession or conquest of a part of their territories, purchased military protection from the Company. The Rajpoot chiefs, who occupy the north-west frontier of Hindustan, are tributary either to the Company or to the states of Scindia and Holkar. Of the Mahometan governments, the king of Oude, the Nizam, the rajahs of Mysore and Travancore, and the nabob of Bhopaul, are the principal states whose civil independence is recognized, and these are in such a defenceless condition as to be entirely dependent on the forbearance of the Company for the continuance of their sovereignty.

From foreign rivalry and interference the English have no cause of apprehension. The only colonies which now belong to other European nations are Pondicherry and Chandernagore, to the French; Goa, to Portugal: Tranquebar and Serampore, to the Danish government; and Chinsurah, to the Dutch. The population of the territories directly subject to Great Britain has been estimated at 80,000,000 of souls; while the population of those states which enjoy civil independence, but have been deprived of a military force, has been computed to amount to 40,000,000. The territory extends over an area of 585,000 square miles; and the total territory dependent, directly or indirectly, upon the Company, amounts to about 1,180,000 square miles. Such is the mighty empire, for the government and interests of which parliament will be shortly called upon to legislate.

We have not yet adverted to the means by which this vast dominion has been acquired. In our narrative of the commercial progress of the Company we forbore to enter into the black page of Indian wars and politics. Unparalleled crimes, violated treaties, blood, treachery, and devastation, form the chief materials of Indian history: — crimes, abhorrent even to a nation of barbarians, disgraceful to a civilized state, and horrible when perpetrated by the agents of a Christian country. There was not a single state, we are assured by Burke, prince, or potentate, with whom the Company had come in contact, that they had not sold; not a single treaty they had ever made, that they had not broken ; not a single prince or state, who ever put any trust in the Company, who was not utterly ruined ; and that none were, in any degree, secure or flourishing, but in the exact proportion to their settled distrust and irreconcilable enmity to this nation.

Indian delinquency is of no grovelling kind ; it soars far above all precedent of ancient or European turpitude. Faith, justice, and humanity, were mere pretexts for rapine and violence. When these would not serve for the spoliation of the native powers, imaginary crimes were laid to their charge. Plots and rebellion, which, in England, have often been the pretexts for destroying the liberties of the people, in India were the pretexts for plunder and devastation. These, when no other offered, were the standing resources of the Company. When money had been thought to be heaped up any where, its owners were invariably accused of treason, and the only security for their allegiance was sought in reducing them to indigence. In England poverty is considered symptomatic of a traitorous disposition, in India it was riches; and the native prince had no chance of living free from the endless accusations, exactions, and even *torture*,* of his oppressors, till he had stripped himself of the sordid wealth which excited their cupidity.

The most profitable merchandize of the Company was the nabobs and subahdars or viceroys. These princes, the rightful sovereigns of Hindustan, were sold and re-sold like *cattle in a fair;* even the Great Mogul himself, the descendant of Tamerlane, was included in the general traffic. This potentate, venerable for his years, and accomplished in all the oriental literature, was sold to his own minister. He was knocked down for the revenue of two provinces. Some princes were sold to their own children; the Company, exciting the children to a parricidal war against their parents, put them in possession of their dominions, on condition of hereafter being tributary and dependent on the Company. We could mention several instances of this mode of carrying on the royal slave-trade, but we will pass them by, in order to relate a more sweeping sale of Governor Hastings.

---

* After taking possession of the palace of the Begums—the mother and grandmother of our *ally*, the nabob of Oude—in 1782, two old domestics of the Begums were tortured to elicit an account of the Begums' treasure. Above £500,000 was paid, but the ill treatment continued, with the hope of extracting more money, when, it being found unavailing, they were set at liberty.

This man, who on one occasion received a present of £100,000 from the nabob of Oude, was the great salesman of Indian territory. We have seen that all the expenses of his prosecution were paid, and he was rewarded with an annuity of £5000 per annum for his *faithful services* in India. The province of Bengal, over which he presided, and the territory annexed to it, is larger and more populous than France, and formerly contained a landed interest, composed of a numerous nobility and gentry, of freeholders, lower tenants, religious communities, and public foundations. Under the English administration, these provinces had fallen into great decay, and a strong representation was made of its causes. Mr. Hastings, instead of administering any remedy to the disorders, determined, at one blow, to dispossess all the ancient proprietors. The incredible fact is, he set up the whole landed interest of a kingdom larger than France to public auction. He set up, says Burke, the whole nobility, gentry, and freeholders to the highest bidder.* No preference was given to the zemindars, the ancient proprietors. They were compelled to bid for their own property against every usurer, jobber, speculator, or European servant; or they were obliged to content themselves, in lieu of their extensive domains, with their house and such a pension as the state auctioneer thought fit to assign. Several of them, in lieu of their hereditary lands, contented themselves with a pension, of which, under a new stretch of rapacity, they were subsequently deprived.

For the calamities inflicted on this devoted region by avarice and ambition, few compensatory advantages have been rendered. Scarcely a single trace is to be found of the superiority of our civil administration, nor a record of usefulness and generosity. Almost every village in England attests the former sovereignty of the Romans by the ruins of some work of power or utility; but the future Hindoo will in vain seek for mementos of our sway, in the bridges we have built, the navigations we have opened, or the highways we have constructed. All former conquerors of Hindustan—the Arab, the Tartar, and the Persian, left behind them some monument of either state or beneficence; but were we to be driven out of India this day, nothing would remain to tell that it had been possessed, during the inglorious period of our dominion, by any thing " better than the ourang-outang or the tiger." Our only principle of government has been a system of IMPOSTURE, and our countrymen have visited India not to benefit the natives, but *themselves*. Their object is to amass fortunes, and they resort thither in endless flights, like birds of prey and passage. All discussion, all enquiry, all familiar intercourse with the people they prey upon is discouraged, lest it should betray the secret of our strength, and the delusion upon which the Indian empire is established.

Our military triumphs have been as void of true glory as our civil administration. The feeble and indolent Hindoos were an unequal

---

* Works of Edmund Burke, vol. iv. p. 85.

match for the energy, artillery, and tactic combinations of Europeans: the greatest obstacles they could oppose to their invaders were the fatigue of long marches and a destructive climate. To meet them in the field was synonymous with defeat, dispersion, or capture. Hence our most signal victories, in the East, have been little more than so many *battus*—the " slaughter of some hundred deer."

In the " Life and Correspondence of Sir Thomas Munro," recently published, we have striking illustrations of Indian warfare. The Mahrattas were always reckoned among our most formidable opponents, and the battle of Assaye, the most brilliant of the eastern triumphs of the Duke of Wellington. Yet it appears these warriors, in this famous conflict, kept so far aloof from close collision with our troops, as to inflict no wound either with bayonet or bullet. Speaking of this battle, in a letter to Colonel Read, Sir T. Munro says, " At the battle of Assaye, the severest that took place in the course of the war, I do not recollect, among all our killed and wounded officers, one that suffered from a *musket-ball or a bayonet*, a convincing proof that the Mahratta infantry made very little serious opposition. Its discipline, its arms, and uniform clothing I regard merely as the means of *dressing it out for the sacrifice*."

In the " Correspondence" are several letters from the Duke of Wellington, then Colonel Wellesley, which throw an instructive light on the reckless, plundering, and destroying system which marked our Asiatic triumphs. In one letter Colonel Wellesley recommends, in dashing style, the " *cutting up*" and " *hunting out*" the natives. To be sure these were thieves, and it might be quite in keeping with Indian justice to do execution upon them without trial, judge, or jury.

In another letter Colonel Wellesley signalizes the exploits of a brother officer, by the following graphic description :—

" Colonel Montresor has been very successful in Bulum; *has beat, burnt, plundered, and destroyed in all parts of the country*. But I am still of opinion that nothing has been done which can tend effectually to put an end to the rebellion in Bulum, and that the near approach of the rains renders it impossible to do THAT, which alone, in my opinion, will ever get the better of Kistnapah Naig."[*]

We may recognize, in these military sketches, the same fierce and determined spirit which so promptly turned Huskisson to the right about, and dismissed from the Irish viceroyship that gallant soldier the Marquis of Anglesey. Bonaparte was certainly as regardless of human life as any pestilent conqueror that ever desolated the face of the earth; but there is one letter of Colonel Wellesley, which, it must be allowed, evinces as much barbarous indifference to the common feelings of humanity as ever Napoleon did in the worst of his Egyptian slaughterings. We shall give the letter entire. The colonel was at the time pursuing his operations against Dhoondee.

---

[*] Supplement to the Life of Major-General Sir T. Munro, vol. iii. p. 120.

" Camp at Soodnetty, Aug. 1st, 1800.

" DEAR MUNRO,—I have received your letters of the 22d and 23d ; I have sent orders to the commanding officers at Hullihall and at Nuggar to furnish ammunition in moderate quantities, on the requisition of your amildars ; in any quantities you please, on your own. Don't press Hullihall too much, as I know they are not very well supplied there. Take what you please from Nuggar. *I have taken and destroyed Doondiah's baggage and six guns, and driven into the Malpurba (where they were drowned) about* FIVE THOUSAND PEOPLE: *I stormed Dummull on the 26th July.* Doondiah's followers are quitting him apace, as they do not think the amusement very gratifying at the present moment. The war, therefore, is nearly at an end ; and another blow, which I am meditating upon him and his bunjarries, in the Kentoor country, will most probably bring it to a close. I must halt here to-morrow, to refresh a little, having marched every day since the 22d July ; and on the 30th, the day on which I took his baggage, I marched twenty-six miles ; which, let me tell you, is no small affair in this country.

" My troops are in high health and spirits, and their *pockets full of money, the produce of plunder.* I still think, however, that a store of rice at Hullihall will do us no harm, and, if I should not want it, the expense incurred will not signify."

The man who could write this deserves that his name should be inscribed on the same roll with Attila and Zinghis Khan. It is only, however, a proof of the brutalizing tendency of war ; for we never heard that Colonel Wellesley had either less or more humanity than the usual run of conquering heroes. But how horrible to boast of having driven five thousand people into a river, where they were drowned! Then with what gusto the future Prince of Waterloo talks of *plunder*, and of *burning*, and *destroying*. These excerpts are enough to illustrate Asiatic triumphs.

GOVERNMENT AND PATRONAGE OF INDIA.

The present frame of India government was established under the act of 1784, and modified, by subsequent acts for the renewal of the charter, in 1793 and 1813. Under the authority of these acts, by the institution of the Board of Control, such superintendence of the affairs of India is vested in the ministers of the Crown as precludes misgovernment without their concurrence. The Board is appointed by the King, and consists of twelve commissioners, of whom the two Secretaries of State and the Chancellor of the Exchequer are *ex officio* members ; the president of the Board is the responsible officer, but the assistance of two other members is necessary to render its proceedings valid. The Board is invested with a control in all matters relating to the government of India, whether civil, military, or financial. It has access to all records, and may require abstracts and statements respecting all affairs not strictly commercial. No despatches relating to government or revenue can be forwarded to India without its approval. It may even originate instructions, and the Court of Directors, though they may remonstrate,

cannot alter them. All despatches received from India must be immediately submitted to the Board; nor can any public disclosure of their
contents take place, except under its authority. No war can be undertaken in India without its sanction. It may grant licenses to individuals
to reside in India, and to ships to trade, when such licenses have been
refused by the Directors. So extensive, indeed, have been the powers
committed to it, that, whatever may have been the ·complexion of the
Company's measures in India, their responsibility is shared by the Board
of Control, and, through it, by the king's ministers at home.

Subordinate to the Board of Control are the administrative bodies
emanating from the Company. The first in responsibility and power is
the Court of Directors, consisting of twenty-four members. They are
elected by the General Court of Proprietors, who meet four times
a-year, and to whom it belongs to declare the dividend, to appoint a
committee to frame by-laws, to control all grants above a certain
amount, and to receive reports from the Directors respecting the
general state of the Company's concerns. No proprietor is entitled to a
vote unless he be possessed of £1000 East-India stock; and the qualification of a Director is £2000 stock. Six Directors go out annually
in rotation, so that four years is the period of service for each Director;
no Director can be re-elected until he has been out of the direction for
at least one year; thirteen Directors form a Court, and the presence of
that number is necessary to give effect to all orders and instructions
which do not emanate from the secret committee. The business of the
Company is chiefly conducted by committees and sub-committees, to
which are permanently allotted certain defined duties, and which are
composed of Directors appointed in the order of their seniority.

In India, the administration of each of the three presidencies of
Calcutta, Madras, and Bombay is vested in a Governor and Council,
consisting of three members. The Commander-in-Chief may be a
member of Council, without regard to the term of his residence; but
no civil servant of the Company can become member of Council until
he has served ten years in India. The Government of Calcutta is
supreme over the other governments in matters relating to peace, war,
and revenue. All the proceedings of the governments in India must
be recorded by minutes, with a statement of the reasons upon which
they have been founded, for the purpose of checking maladministration.
The governments are entrusted with the entire control over the army,
and with the imposition of taxes, in all the dominions of the Company,
except the towns of Calcutta, Madras, and Bombay; and their regulations have the authority of law, until reversed by instructions from
home. The Governor-General is empowered to apprehend all suspected
persons, and either to send them home to be tried in England, or,
having forwarded copies of all depositions in their case, to retain them
for judgment in India. Except in case of invasion, or of the most
urgent necessity, the Governor-General is restrained from declaring
war until the sanction of the Directors and of the Board of Control
has been received. The commercial and financial concerns of the

Company in India are superintended by a Board of Trade and a Board of Revenue. The collection of the revenue is conducted by British collectors, aided by British assistants ; but all the inferior business of this department is transacted by natives.

There are three different classes of courts of justice in India. In the first are the King's Courts, or Supreme Courts of Judicature, whose jurisdiction extends to all British-born subjects residing in the provinces, but, in suits between natives, is limited to the immediate vicinity of the presidencies. The courts which administer justice in those cases in which the natives are concerned are of two kinds, civil and criminal. Each kind consists of a supreme court, with courts of circuit and subordinate tribunals, down to institutions analogous to our Courts of Request and petty sessions. In all the courts Europeans preside, except those of the lowest description, in which there are native judges. Justice is administered according to the Mahummudan law, modified by a regard to Hindoo usages and by the regulations of the British Government. The natives have lately been rendered capable of sitting on juries, and it may be hoped that the introduction of this institution will tend to exalt the character of the people, to curb that disposition to pervert justice which is the great political vice of the East, and to supply the deficiencies under which an European judge must always labour, in weighing the evidence of a people with whose habits and ideas he can be only partially acquainted.

Such is a brief outline of the system under which the Indian empire is administered. Like most constitutions, it sounds well on paper, and does not appear liable to serious objections ; but the general government at home is a striking instance how widely the principles of a constitution may differ from its practical administration. It is only an intelligent Hindoo, or some one actually cognizant of our India policy, who could give adequate testimony to the good or evil it confers on the native population. Unfortunately the authorities at Calcutta do not tolerate the publication of an *Extraordinary Black Book* there, nor hardly a Times newspaper, otherwise one might become acquainted with the working of the Leadenhall administration.

One of the best criterions of good government is the excellence of the judicial system. That of India has always been represented corrupt and oppressive. The administration of justice is the most lucrative profession in the east as well as in England. According to a statement of Mr. Hume, in the House of Commons, suitors in India are obliged to pay to government on the sum sued for from 50 to 7 and 6 per cent. and a fine is levied on all debts sued for, decreasing as the amount increases ! Every document requisite to the progress of a suit, the citations, examinations, and depositions of witnesses, are all to be written on stamped paper ; thereby increasing the expenses to an enormous total. These expenses amount to a virtual denial of justice, and, in the course of a long life, a man could scarcely expect to see any termination of suits ; in a word, it is the English chancery system—that admirable contrivance for spunging clients—operating in

India. The police is established on the Sidmouth or Villele system. A corps of spies is attached to every preventive establishment, and there is no *Habeas Corpus Act* to expedite judicial sentences. Persons are frequently taken up, and months elapse before any information is exhibited against them. In the interval they are confined in crowded and unhealthy prisons, where death not unfrequently overtakes them; or, after enduring the aggravated misery of imprisonment, nothing whatever appears against them, and they are liberated. For these blessings the Hindoos pay annually about £1,785,000, which is a greater expense than all the law-officers in Europe.

Leaving for the present any further strictures on the general government of India, let us advert to the important subject of *India influence and patronage.*

The whole patronage of India, civil and military, is vested in the Court of Directors, with the exception of the appointments of bishops, and of the judges of the Supreme Courts of Judicature. The Governors in India and the Commander-in-Chief are named by the Company, but their appointment must be sanctioned by the king. The king also possesses the power of removing any civil servant from his office in India. With these exceptions, the entire civil, naval, and military patronage of India vests in the Company, and exceeds in amount the patronage of the Crown before the French revolutionary war. Of the extent of this patronage we may form some idea from the number of persons in the Company's service. We have no means of stating exactly the number of persons employed by the Company, but the following is an estimate when the revenues and possessions of the east were much less than at present.

Civil Service.	Persons either in the service of the Company or connected with and employed in their affairs in England	2,146
	Persons in India employed in the judicial, clerical, diplomatic, commercial, and revenue departments	1,056
	Seamen employed and reared in the Company's service in 115 ships, about	25,000
Military and Naval Service.	British military officers in the Company's service commanding European troops	1,000
	British officers and cadets in the Company's service commanding native troops	3,000
	British non-commissioned officers and soldiers in the service of the Company	16,000
	British officers in the Company's naval department in India	113
Natives in the service of the Company.	Natives employed in various departments in the civil service of the Company	12,362
	Natives employed in the Indian armies	140,000
	Natives employed in the naval service estimated at about	800
	Total	201,477

All the salaries in India are on a much more extravagant scale than in England. Of the above 201,477 persons in the service of the Company, at least 6000 in the civil and military departments at home and abroad, enjoy emoluments from £200 to £10,000 a year, exclusive of the Governor-General. The salary of the Governor-General of Bengal is £25,000 a year, and three counsellors with a salary of £10,000 a year each. The salary of the Chief Justice of the Supreme Court of Judicature at Calcutta is £8000 a year, with three other judges at £6000 a year each. By the act of 1813, the salary of a bishop in India is £5000 a year, and of three archdeacons £2000 a year each. The expense of outfit, &c. of different officers was fixed by the same act, as follows:—

Governor-General of Fort William, in Bengal	£5000
Each of the members of council there	1200
Commander-in-Chief of all the Forces in India	2500
Chief Justice of the Supreme Court at Fort William	1500
Each of the Puisne Judges there	1000
Governor of Fort St. George	3000
Each of the Members of Council there	1000
Commander-in-Chief there	2000
Chief Justice of the Supreme Court there	1200
Each of the Puisne Judges there	1000
Governor of Bombay	2500
Each of the members of council there	1000
Commander-in-Chief there	1500
Recorder there	1500
Governor of Prince of Wales's Island	1200
Recorder there	1000
Bishop	1200
Each of the Archdeacons	500

The allowance for the outfit, &c. of those officers is about one-fourth the amount of their salaries, exclusive of other emoluments. According to a statement in the *East-India Register*, the allowances per month to general and regimental officers when in the field, were on the Bengal establishment, as follows:—

General officer on the staff	£662	10	0
Colonel not on the staff	156	5	0
Lieutenant-Colonel	123	15	0
Major	93	15	0
Captain	51	7	6
Captain-Lieutenant	43	17	6
Lieutenant	31	15	0
Ensign	25	0	0
Adjutant	28	7	6
Quarter-Master	14	12	6
Surgeon	51	7	6
Assistant ditto	31	15	0

The allowance to officers on the Fort St. George and Bombay Establishments, was nearly the same as the above. The sums granted by way of superannuation allowance to officers and servants of the Company are very considerable. They are fixed according to the following scale, by the 53d George III. c. 155.

Proportion of salary.

If an officer or servant shall have served with diligence and fidelity in the Company's service for ten years, and being under 60 years of age, shall be incapable, from infirmity of mind or body, to discharge the duties of office............	One-third.
If above 10 years and less than 20......................	One-half.
If above 20 years	Two-thirds.
If such officer or servant shall be above 60 years of age, and he shall have served 15 years or upwards, without infirmity of mind or body	Two-thirds.
If 65 years of age, or upwards, and he shall have served 40 years or upwards	Three-fourths.
If 65 years of age, and he shall have served 50 years or upwards	The whole.

From the preceding details, some idea may be formed of the immense value of India patronage, and the wide field it opens for providing for children, relatives, and dependents. The trade of the Company has never been an object of so much importance as the military appointments to an army of 150,000 men, the filling up of vacancies in the judicial and police departments, and the numerous situations in the collection and expenditure of a revenue of 24 millions per annum. It is the annual value of these different situations which constitute the *real profit* of the Company.

It is evident that the excellence of our administration in India will depend upon the employment of individuals recommended by integrity and talent. In theory this principle appears to have been admitted by the Directors in 1793, when, by one of their by-laws, it was enacted that each Director, ten days after his election, should take oath to receive no emolument, perquisite, or pecuniary gratification, for any appointment in India. Little regard was paid to this obligation, and so early as 1798 it was notorious that a very extensive and systematic traffic was carried on for places in India. Several attempts were made, real or pretended, by Committees of the House of Commons, also by committees appointed by the Court of Directors, to discover the individuals implicated in these practices. On one occasion it was proposed that each Director should take oath he had not received any reward for any appointment he had made; but this was rejected by a large majority, and the sale in offices continued by public advertisement and otherwise, till at last an office was openly established for the sale and purchase of India patronage.

The practice was shameless and notorious; but it does not appear to have been completely laid bare, till the memorable disclosures in 1809, relative to Mrs. Clarke and the Duke of York. In that year it was discovered that the improper disposal of India patronage had not been confined to the honourable Directors, but extended even to the right honourable President of the Board of Control. The then president was Lord Castlereagh. This minister, by the agency of a common place-broker, attempted to purchase, for a writership in India, a seat in parliament for his friend Lord Clancarty. Here was corruption three deep. It was a dereliction of his duty as a minister of the Crown; a shameless abuse of his trust as President of the Board of Control ; and a daring attack on the *purity* (bah !) of the Commons' House of Parliament. Such was the description of this transaction given by the late Lord A. Hamilton. Lord Castlereagh, however, was defended on the ground of the *notoriety* of the practice. Some of the members said that selling seats in the House of Commons was as *notorious as the sun at noon-day* : this could not be denied, for it was well known that the Secretary of the Treasury was in the constant practice of buying seats for the adherents of ministers. This being the case, there appeared injustice in making an example of the President of the Board of Control ; and the motion was got rid of by moving the order of the day.

The fact of Lord Castlereagh having a writership at his disposal to purchase a seat in the House of Commons, shows how ministers may avail themselves of even subordinate appointments in India. The Directors have the patronage of the East at their disposal ; but, indirectly, ministers participate in its advantages. The latter we have seen have a negative on the appointments of the principal servants of the Company, besides which the general superintendence they exercise over India affairs, through the medium of the Board of Control, renders it highly improbable the Directors should neglect to provide for any individual backed by a ministerial recommendation ; more especially as the favour might be so easily returned.

We may conclude this part of our subject with remarking that the whole patronage and influence of India is so much added to that of the general government of the empire. The India-House is little more than a branch of the general administration, where a part of the business of the Government is transacted, and with which it is almost as much connected as with the Home-office or Treasury department. The case of the notorious Paul Benfield strikingly illustrates the reciprocal workings of the two systems. This man, whose " offal," Burke said, " ought to have fed the region kites," had at one time no fewer than eight members in parliament, and he attempted to bring in one of his agents for the City of London. These members were returned at Benfield's expense to support the Pitt Ministry ; and in return for this support Mr. Pitt allowed Benfield to set up some imaginary and exaggerated pecuniary claims against the Nabob of Arcot.*

The great mass of influence arises from appointments in India, but the political influence of the Company is very considerable from the vast number of individuals employed in their different warehouses and establishments in London. All the influence they possess is employed in

---

* The commissioners appointed to investigate the debts of this Nabob finished their labours in the course of 1830, having consumed in the inquiry exactly a quarter of a century. One of the principal commissioners died almost immediately after concluding this notable job. The claims set up against the Nabob amounted to £30,404,919 ; the commissioners allowed £2,686,146.—*Parl. Rep. No.* 114, *Sess.* 1830.

support of their parliamentary interest. Whenever a labourer comes into the service of the Company he is required to state for what place he has a vote for a member of parliament: his name is then registered with this specification; and on an election he is told that he will be spared from his situation to give his suffrage, if he will vote according to orders; disobedience being supposed to be punished by dismissal from his office. The number of individuals thus kept in political subjection to the Company is about four thousand.

This practice needs no comment. It sufficiently identifies the East-India Company with Government, and we may consider the revenue of Hindustan, as well as the revenue of England, as forming a part of that immense expenditure by which the Borough System has been supported.

TERRITORIAL REVENUES OF INDIA.

The fiscal system of India is distinguished by a peculiarity which is without parallel in Europe. The rental of the soil, in lieu of being monopolized by an oppressive aristocracy, is applied to defray the charges of government, the support of a military force, and the expense of the judicial administration. The Hindoos are, happily, unacquainted with the custom-duties, the excise-duties, and assessed taxes, which weigh down industry and abridge enjoyments in England. In the East, the state takes about one-fifth of the gross produce of the land, and that satisfies nearly all its wants. Other taxes are inconsiderable; as the transit-duties, stamps, licenses, and judicial fees. The monopoly of salt and opium is also a source of income. But the principal source of revenues is the land-tax, which constituted the only rent payable by the cultivators of the soil, under the Hindoo and Mohummudan sovereigns.

The gross revenues of India, in the year 1827, amounted to £23,383,497; the expenditure, inclusive of the interest of the debt, to £23,323,179. The chief items of expenditure are the military, civil, and revenue establishments; salaries, pensions, superannuation-allowances, and stipends payable to deposed princes.

The total amount of territorial debts in India, in the same year, was £42,870,876; the interest of the debt £1,749,068. By some writers the debt of India is considered to operate in the same way as the debt in England; by rendering a large class of persons interested in the permanency of the British power. This is a one-sided view of the question, which it is hardly worth while stopping to answer. Creditors may feel an interest in their debtors, of the same kind as that which subsists between a lord and his vassal; but this sort of relation does not tend to increase mutual attachment. A government, by incurring debt, may create a partial interest in its stability, but this advantage must be far more than counterbalanced by alienating the vast majority, in consequence of the additional burthens which the debt renders necessary; and, in the foreign transactions of such a government, its power and influence are weakened by a knowledge of its financial encumbrances.

Leaving, however, this matter, as irrelevant to our immediate purpose, let us continue the inquiry into the finances of India. The Company have never been able to realize a surplus revenue from their territorial possessions. All the income they have derived from Indian taxation has been expended in defraying the salaries of their servants, in the maintenance of a numerous army, and other establishments necessary to the preservation of their power. The only source of surplus income for the payment of the interest of their capital stock, and other outgoings, has been the *commercial profits* arising from their exclusive privileges. The nature of these profits it will be proper to explain, as well as the mode in which the China trade is conducted, in order to prepare the way for a few observations on the renewal of the Company's charter.

COMMERCIAL INTERCOURSE WITH THE CHINESE.

The foreign trade with China is restricted to the port of Canton by the Chinese government. It is a source of considerable revenue to the government of China, and of the most valuable patronage, which is sold by the government to the highest bidder. Hence it follows that the local authorities are greatly interested in maintaining the trade, which, from the same cause, is subjected to heavy taxes and extortions. The inhabitants, also, of Canton and its neighbourhood, as well as the numerous classes employed in the culture and manufacture of tea, have a deep interest in the trade; every interruption of which causes great individual distress.

Foreigners are interdicted by Chinese regulations from going within the walls of Canton. The place of their abode is a small suburb, and their residence there is authorized only for the period of the shipping season; but these limitations are not rigorously enforced, the Company's servants going when they please to Canton, and some private merchants residing there throughout the whole year.* Security must be given for the payment of the custom-duties before a ship is permitted to trade, and this security also includes responsibility for the good conduct and submission to the laws of the ship's company. The only persons whom the Chinese government accepts as security is a sort of mercantile corporation or fraternity, called the "Hong merchants," formerly ten in number, but reduced by bankruptcies to seven. These become security for the Company's ships in rotation; the whole of the Company's trade being apportioned among the seven Hong in shares.

Besides the members of the Hong, other persons, designated as "Outside merchants" and "Shopmen," are allowed to trade with foreigners; their traffic is chiefly with the officers of the Company's ships, private traders, and the Americans. They are not allowed to trade in certain

---

* Report of the Select Committee of the House of Commons on India Affairs, Sess. 1830, Nos. 275 to 277.

articles, as tea, raw silk, cloths and woollens, all of which are, by Chinese edicts, reserved exclusively to the Hong.

The Hong merchants are by law mutually responsible to each other for a limited amount, but this regulation is not invariably enforced. They are stated to be fair and liberal in their conduct. A similar opinion, though with less confidence, has been expressed respecting the outside merchants. No one is responsible for the debts of the latter, and foreigners are warned of this by official notifications.

The Company's trade at Canton is managed by an establishment of supercargoes and writers, twenty in all, with two inspectors, whose duty it is to examine into and report upon the qualities of all teas offered for sale to the Company. Three or four of the senior super-cargoes are annually formed into a Select Committee, who, under the orders of the Court of Directors, conduct the whole of the Company's affairs in China.

Most of the witnesses examined by Parliamentary committees concur in stating that business at Canton may be conducted with greater facility and expedition than in almost any other part of the world; much of which is said to be owing to the transactions connected with each ship being all managed by the same person, the security merchant. It was further stated that the Hong had occasionally aided the operations of commerce by advancing money on loan to foreigners.

COMMERCIAL PROFITS OF THE COMPANY.

The commercial profits of the Company are chiefly derived from their monopoly of the trade *in tea*. The following statement shows the difference between the prime cost of tea at Canton and its price at the East-India sales in London, from which an estimate may be formed of the profit on this article:

Tea purchased at Canton.

Years.	lbs.	Prime cost. £	Average price per lb.	
1824–25	28,697,088	1,900,866	1s. 4d.	nearly.
1825–26	27,821,121	1,729,949	1s. 3¾d.	,,
1826–27	40,182,241	2,368,461	1s. 2d.	,,
1827–28	33,269,333	2,086,971	1s. 3d.	,,

Sales in England.

Years.	lbs.	Sale price. £	Average price per lb.	
1825–26	27,803,668	3,872,685	2s. 10d.	nearly.
1826–27	27,700,978	3,485,092	2s. 6d.	,,
1827–28	28,120,354	2,358,955	2s. 5d.	,,
1828–29	28,230,383	3,286,272	2s. 4½d.	,,

It thus appears the Company charge considerably more than 100 per cent. additional to the prime cost on all the teas consumed in the kingdom. It is almost the only article of traffic in which they realize a profit. Their exports to China consist principally of woollens, by which branch of trade they sustain an annual *loss*, though, as we shall show presently, this loss, by an evasion of the Commutation Act, is thrown upon the British public.

The Company has lately sent little merchandize to India, except military stores, which, being charged to the territorial account, do not enter into a statement of commercial profits. It imports, however, to a considerable amount, from that country, raw silk, indigo, and other articles. Whether there is profit or loss in the trade it is difficult to determine from the accounts submitted to parliament.*

In addition to the profits on its trade, the Company is entitled to a certain duty upon goods imported by the private and privileged trade, warehoused and sold through its medium. From the gross profits arising from this trade, a large deduction is to be made for the expense of freight and demurrage, amounting, in 1829, to £662,964. After paying all the other expenses of the commercial establishment, interest on the bond-debt, &c. the dividend remains to be provided. The capital stock of the Company is £6,000,000 ; so that at 10½ per cent. it requires a net profit of £620,000 per annum to pay the dividend.

Now these preliminaries bring us to the consideration of a very important issue between the public and the East-India Company. The Company, we have seen, has not realized a surplus revenue from their territorial acquisitions ; that has been all expended in the charges of war and government. *Commercial profits*, then, are the only source from which the Company has a surplus-revenue to pay the dividends and support their home-establishments. But, it appears, the profits of the Company on the several branches of trade, are either none at all, or very unimportant, except in the single article of TEA. So that, in fact, it is the people of England who pay the dividends of the proprietors, and other outgoings, in the monopoly price of their teas. Let us inquire whether this is conformable to the agreement between the Company and the public.

The Commutation Act, the 24th Geo. III. c. 38, provides that there shall be at least four sales in every year, at which there shall be put up such quantities of tea as shall be judged *equal to the demand;* that the tea so put up shall be sold, without reserve, to the highest bidder, provided an advance of one penny per pound shall be bid upon the *prices at which the same shall be put up;* and that it shall not be lawful for the Company " to put up their tea for sale at any prices which shall, upon the whole of the teas so put up, at any one sale, exceed the *prime cost* thereof, with the *freight* and *charges* of importation, together with lawful *interest* from the time of the arrival of such tea in Great Britain

---

* Considerations relative to the Renewal of the Company's Charter. By W. S. O'Brien, M.P.

and the common premium of insurance, as a compensation for the sea-risk incurred therein."

Here are the terms of the contract between the community and the merchants of Leadenhall: the latter are to supply the former with a quantity of tea adequate to their demand, and, to prevent extortion in the price, all the items of charge which the Company, in addition to the prime cost, are allowed to include in the put-up price, are distinctly specified; but there is no item for the *Company's dividends*, and it was certainly never intended they should be paid out of the profits of the tea-trade. All the legislature contemplated was to reimburse the Company the prime cost of their teas and reasonable charges, but never that they should be enabled to realize an exorbitant profit applicable to their general expenditure. That this profit has been realized is proved from a statement submitted to the Committee of the House of Commons, which shows that the profits on the China trade for the last fifteen years amounted to £16,971,316. Had the trade with China been open, the Company must have been satisfied with the ordinary mercantile profit; they could not have taxed the public to the amount of upwards of one million per annum, to provide a fund not only for the payment of the dividend upon India Stock and the interest of their bond debt, but also materially to aid their wasteful Indian expenditure.

There is another transaction, though not so important as the preceding, on which the principle of the Commutation Act has been contravened. The Company have long taken credit for having persisted in the export trade to China at a considerable *loss*; and this their advocates would have the community to believe has been done for the sake of promoting the sale of British manufactures. From the statements of Mr. Marjoribanks (Report on the China Trade, page 32) it appears the losses on the Company's exports, from 1820 to 1829, averaged about £17,000 per annum, and that for the twenty-six preceding years they amounted to £64,000 per annum. But at whose expense does the reader imagine these losses have been incurred? Why, at the expense of the people of the United Kingdom. The way this has been effected is by adding the losses on exports to the price of the tea in China; thus if the Company export goods to the value of £1000, which, when sold in China, produce only £800, the quantity of tea purchased with this sum is valued by them at £1000, and this amount is charged in the upset price; although, as we have ssen above, that they are restricted by Act of Parliament from putting up their tea at more than "prime cost." There cannot be a more direct violation of the statute, which seems to have been framed with the express view of guarding against such practices. The servants of the Company endeavour to justify these proceedings on the ground of the exports being made for the express purpose of providing funds in China for the purchase of tea; but this is no apology for the infringement of a positive contract. Besides, there can be little doubt that the loss on the export trade results from the wasteful and injudicious manner in which it is conducted;

otherwise how does it happen that the Americans carry on the same trade in the same commodities with a profit?

In 1813 the trade to India was thrown open to private merchants, but was still, in some measure, impeded by enactments which required that all ships passing to the eastward of the Cape of Good Hope should exceed 350 tons of burthen, and which rendered it necessary to procure a license to trade from the Court of Directors, or, upon their refusal, from the Board of Control. They also provided that certain articles of Indian produce should be brought to the port of London alone. British ships were still prevented from trading between ports without the kingdom, and places within the limits of the East-India Company's charter. These restrictions were much relaxed in 1823. The export of military stores to India is reserved to the Company, but ships, without limitation to burthen, may clear out, unlicensed, for any place eastward of the Cape of Good Hope, except for minor ports between the Indus and Malacca. A license is still necessary to proceed to any other except the four principal settlements—Calcutta, Madras, Bombay, and Prince of Wales's Island, within these limits. Vessels returning from India may now be admitted to entry in any of the warehousing ports of Great Britain, and trade is permitted between foreign ports and places within the limits of the Company's charter.

The Company reserve to themselves all the trade between the United Kingdom and China, excepting only a small portion allowed by way of privilege to the commanders and officers of their ships. Licenses are granted by the Company to all .Indian ships, denominated " Country Ships," to trade between India and China, and to export from China a limited quantity of tea, with permission to dispose of it to any intermediate port between China and the port in India to which the ship may be destined. These licenses do not include the Cape of Good Hope, the Company themselves supplying that settlement with tea at *high prices*, notwithstanding the agreement they made some years since to put up their teas for sale at the Cape at an advance not exceeding six per cent. on the costs and charges of importation.*

Let us now advert to the different results arising from the different principles on which the trade to India and China has been conducted.

The effect of opening the trade to India has been greatly to increase its amount. The highest value of goods exported to India in any year between 1792 and 1811 did not exceed £2,475,987 (the exports of 1808). It will be seen, hereafter, that this amount is less than one half of the value of the present exports. The increase has chiefly taken place in the export of cotton-manufactured goods. Previous to 1813 the amount of cotton goods exported to India was very trifling. They now fall very little short of £2,000,000 in value annually. This augmentation may partly be attributed to the extraordinary improvement which has taken place in our manufactures, attended by a great reduc-

---

* Report of Commons' Committee, Sess. 1830, Nos. 405, 627, 2078.

tion of prices, and to the extension and consolidation of the British power in India.

The following statements show at once the comparative exports and imports of the Company and the free and privileged trade in their transactions with India and China.

Exports by the Private Trade.

Years.	Total to India and China. £	By the Private Trade. £
1825	3,918,071	2,574,660
1826	4,468,883	2,625,888
1827	5,201,599	3,903,006
1828	5,212,353	4,085,426

Exports by the East-India Company.

Years.	Merchandize for Sale. £	Stores. £	Total. £
1825–26	754,832	501,518	1,256,350
1826–27	826,055	907,833	1,733,888
1827–28	494,922	807,354	1,302,276
1828–29	636,441	462,369	1,098,810

Imports from India and China.

Years.	By the Company. £	By the Private Trade. £	Total. £
1825	5,375,492	5,178,925	10,554,417
1826	5,076,360	5,162,509	10,688,869
1827	6,148,077	4,514,661	10,662,738
1828	5,576,905	5,643,671	11,220,576

These statements show clearly the benefits which have resulted to the community from the opening of the trade to India, and the outlet it has afforded to British industry and manufactures. From the first, it appears, the exports by the private trade to the East nearly *doubled* in four years; while from the second it appears the exports of the Company, during the same period, and under similar favourable circumstances, have *declined* rather than augmented. What more can be required to establish the advantages of free trade, and the greater results which may be anticipated from the frugality, activity, and enterprise of individuals than from the expensive, negligent, and drowsy proceedings of chartered monopolies?

It is worthy of observation that the most enlightened servants of the Company doubted whether the natives of India would ever be brought to consume largely European manufactures. Experience has falsified their representations. Similar results may be confidently expected from the opening of the trade to China.

RENEWAL OF THE CHARTER OF THE EAST-INDIA COMPANY.

Such improvements in the national representation, as would insure an honest and enlightened government, would render unnecessary any great changes in the scheme of our Indian administration. Ministers, having the control of the affairs of India, are responsible for their management; and, provided the people of England had an adequate control over them, there would be little risk of misgovernment, either in Great Britain or her great dependency. But if a system is tolerated, which admits of the accession to power of corrupt and incapable men, the calamity is felt in every part of the empire. Hence, the happiness of the vast population of Hindustan, no less than that of the United Kingdom, is identified in the great question of parliamentary reform.

The government of India, it appears to us, must always be so constituted as to be subordinate to the general government. Equality would generate rivalry; rivalry, hostility; and this last be the source of mutual weakness and annoyance. All these evils are obviated by the supremacy of the Board of Control. The sovereigns of Leadenhall-street can never compete with the sovereigns of Downing-street; yet, though the dependence of the former is secured, it is not so far merged in the latter as to preclude them from the exercise of a distinct and separate administration.

Another advantage results from the existing system in the division of *India patronage.* Supposing the Company deprived of their territorial authority, by whom could the immense patronage of India be exercised? It was the principle of the India bills of Mr. Fox to vest the patronage of India in a Board, emanating from parliament and independent of the Crown; but, in the present constitution of the House of Commons, this was only adding to the power and emolument of the Aristocracy. Again, to vest India patronage in ministers would be not less objectionable; it would form an enormous addition to the overwhelming influence of the Crown. The Court of Directors, however, though they have some interests in common with the Oligarchy and executive government, are not directly identified with either; they are a different power, based on different interests; their constituency are neither pot-walloppers, burgage-holders, nor freeholders—they are proprietors of India Stock; and this is a qualification from which neither the peerage nor the House of Commons derive their ascendancy. Under this arrangement a diversion of influence is obtained, and the danger to public liberty, which might result from consolidating the patronage of India with that of the United Kingdom, is in some measure averted.

In our opinion, then, the Company ought to retain their political sovereignty, and for this plain reason—that we do not see by what other constituted authority their functions could be discharged with less danger to the community. But though we think the general plan of the Indian government cannot be greatly improved, we are not insensible to the defects in its practical administration. The different departments of the Company's administration, we have little doubt, are more pregnant with abuse, if that be possible, than the borough system itself. But this is a question wholly distinct from that we have been investigating, and into the merits of which we are not prepared to enter. There are, however, a few points bearing on this branch of the subject so notorious, that we cannot forbear noticing them, trusting that they will receive modification in the approaching renewal of the Company's charter.

For instance, it appears a monstrous abuse that the Directors, who are only chosen for four years, should virtually exercise their functions for life. Of the twenty-four directors, six are obliged to retire every year in rotation; but, instead of withdrawing entirely, they secede for one year only, being sure, as a matter of course, of being re-elected for another four years when the period of probation expires, and so on to the end of their lives, through the influence of their co-directors : for which purpose their names are enrolled on what is termed the "House List," in Leadenhall-street.

The number of proprietors of India-Stock is about 2,200. In the choice of directors, £1,000 stock gives one vote; £3,000 stock two votes; £6,000 stock three votes; and £10,000 stock four votes. This is the principle of the select-vestry system, without the same justification. There is nothing analogous to it in the election of members of parliament, and it is as unsuitable in the choice of the governors of an empire, as if the members of the House of Commons were each to have votes proportioned to the magnitude of their rent-roll.

Among the prerogatives which the Company exercise, one is justly objectionable, namely, the power of denying to British subjects permission to reside in India. By the 53d Geo. III. c. 155, heavy penalties are imposed upon any British subject who shall proceed to India without license from the Directors or Board of Control. The local governments are also empowered, if they see fit, to send home any European residing there, even though in possession of a license. It is also enacted that no British subject shall reside in the interior, at a greater distance than ten miles from the presidencies, without a certificate of leave from the local authorities. Till a very late period, no European was allowed to hold lands either as proprietor or upon lease. By a recent regulation, however, of the present governor-general, the indigo planters have been permitted to take leases of lands from the natives for the cultivation of the plant.

Such restrictions are an arbitrary abridgment of the rights of locomotion and enterprise, for which we have never seen any adequate justification. No danger can possibly result from the free settlement of Englishmen in India. The whole European community scattered through this vast region, exclusive of those in the service of the company, does not exceed 3,000, and any increase in their number, so as to excite apprehension, is wholly improbable. Were it not so, the Company can have no right to exercise an authority injurious both to their fellow subjects and the native population, merely for the sake of perpetuating their own power.

Neither is there policy nor justice—if such principles can ever be disjunctive—in keeping in a state of civil and political disfranchisement that numerous and respectable class denominated "East-Indians." These are Christian men, born of English parents, or the descendants of English parents; yet not being considered "British subjects" in the decisions of the Supreme Court, are withheld from the benefits of the laws of England.* Their thraldom is most irksome and anomalous. In conformity with the tenor of parliamentary enactments relative to Hindustan, professors of the Hindoo religion are governed in their civil relations by Hindoo law; professors of the Mohummudan religion by Mohummudan law; and both Hindoos and Mohummudans are subject in criminal matters to Mohummudan law—both civil and criminal being modified by the regulations of the East-India Company. But the unfortunate East-Indians do not fall within the circle of any of these codes of jurisprudence. Not being Hindoos they cannot regulate social duties by Hindoo law; not being Mohummudans they cannot regulate them by Mohummudan law; and not being British-born subjects they cannot enjoy the benefits of English law. They are, in fact, placed without the social pale, and governed in the relations of life by whatever rule any judge may frame on the spur of the occasion. But this does not include the whole of their grievances : they are proscribed from all superior and covenanted offices in the Civil, Military, and Marine services ; they are not considered eligible even to those subordinate employments in the Judicial, Revenue, and Police Departments, which are open without reserve to the Hindoo and Mohummudan. We cannot believe the charter of the Company will be renewed without these unjust distinctions being modified, and the East-Indian race considered, as they ought to be, by the double ties of civil rights and consanguineous claim, the connecting link between the parent state and native population.

Lastly, the operations of the Press in India require a more constitutional guarantee than the fiat of the governors and governor general. During the viceroyship of Lord William Bentinck, the literary and political press of Calcutta has made rapid progress, and has not been disturbed by the arbitrary interference of government. But this is too important an engine to be dependent on the uncertainties of individual character. Those who have embarked their property in the India press ought to have a more valid protection than a system of licenses and censorships, which may be granted or refused—enforced or suspended, as suits the varying purposes of the president and council.

Having shortly noticed the political part of the India question, let us come to the commercial branch of the subject. This is the main point of interest to the people of Great Britain. Comparatively to them, the future territorial government of Hindustan is unimportant,, but every inhabitant of the United Kingdom is deeply interested in a free trade to China; and we sincerely trust this interest will not be compromised—that there will be no renewal of the Company's charter, without an entire abolition of their commercial monopoly.

A defence of some kind may be always devised by artful persons for every abuse and every oppression; but we cannot collect from the inquiries of the Parliamentary Committees that the least plausible case has been made out to justify the commercial privileges of the Company.

---

* Second Petition of the East-Indians, Alexander's East-India Magazine, January, 1832.

There is nothing in the constitution of the Chinese government, in its peculiar policy, in the local usages of the natives, nor in their anti-commercial spirit to interdict the opening of the trade. Both the public officers of China and the people are a thrifty race, and the same motives of interest which actuate the British merchant, concur to induce them to desire a more extended mercantile intercourse with this country.

Why then should this spirit—the mutual interests of two empires—be cramped by the costly and cumbersome incubus of Leadenhall-street? The Court of Directors have sufficient to engage their attention in the discharge of their political functions, without being fettered by mercantile pursuits ; and the sooner they divest themselves of the remnant of their commercial character, the better for both England and Hindustan. The Company has become a great political government, and is no more adapted to the pursuits of commerce than the imperial parliament.

The trade with China neither requires the capital nor united action of a privileged association. The French, the Dutch, the Swedes, the Danes, the Austrians, and Americans, all resort to Canton, and none of them carry on the intercourse through the intervention of an exclusive company. The Dutch trade, which is the most important, used to be conducted by a privileged company, but it is now thrown open. The free trade of the Americans with China has greatly augmented since 1814 ;—and, what is most extraordinary, they actually export to Canton British manufactures—manufactures which the English merchant is interdicted exporting, and which the Company cannot export with *a profit*, owing to their circuitous and costly mode of transacting business —to the unfitness of their institutions for commercial purposes.

But any over-weening conceit in which the Company may have indulged as to the superior advantages resulting from their exclusive management of the China trade, must be destroyed by their existing differences with the Chinese authorities. It is not the Americans, nor the Dutch, but their own establishment at Canton which is embroiled with the native government. So far as information has yet been communicated, the fault appears all on their side ; the Chinese, by the reduction of one-third of the duties on British ships, in 1830, and by taking off an additional duty imposed on cotton, have manifested a strong desire to cultivate the friendship of England. These concessions, however, have been met by a series of insults and encroachments on the part of the Company's servants, which are the more provoking, because they appear to have been wanton, puerile, and unnecessary. For instance, they have persisted in the use of *sedan chairs*, and the introduction of " foreign women" into Canton, contrary to the express usages of the country, and the rules laid down by public proclamations.*
The dignity and firmness with which the gentlemen of the " Select Committee" endeavoured to support these innovations have been quite in keeping with the innovations themselves. They first issued a " protocol"—yes, by the powers, a protocol in China!—intimating their deter-

---

* Lord Ellenborough, House of Lords, December 13th, 1831.

mination to suspend all commercial intercourse with the Chinese, August 4th, 1831 : but this announcement failing to make the expected impression on " the Celestial empire," they issued another, intimating their intention *not* to suspend commercial intercourse at the period mentioned. We believe the desire of the " Select" now is to have a couple or two of British frigates at their disposal, to bombard Canton ; or—if that be possible—to throw a few Congreve rockets into Pekin, or against the Great Wall. But the Emperor may be perfectly easy on this head ; if his Celestial Majesty knew as well as we do how essential an ingredient his tea-plant is in the dividends of the East-India proprietors, he would laugh—if such a movement be consistent with Chinese gravity—at the fulminations of Messrs. Lindsay and his brethren, who appear to have performed, at the British factory, the parts of Captain Bobadil and Ben Jonson's " Angry Boy" with marvellous precision.

After such experience of the mercantile abilities of the Company, and of their address and wisdom in managing their Chinese intercourse, we imagine it cannot be any longer a question whether their commercial privileges ought to be renewed. We think decidedly not. The interests of the public are directly opposed to the monopoly. For years we have been paying double the prices for our teas we ought to pay; double the prices that are paid on the Continent and America ; where there are no privileged associations. And for what purpose are the people of the United Kingdom subjected to this extortion ? Why, in addition to our other burthens, should we be made to pay two millions per annum for the benefit of the Company ? We are becoming a sober people—a tea-drinking nation, and why should this improvement in national character be obstructed by overgrown monopolists ? The reason is this : The finances of the Company are embarrassed. They cannot pay their DIVIDENDS out of fair mercantile profits, and they seek to pay them out of the produce of a poll-tax levied on the people of England !

Here is the gist of the matter at issue between the Company and the public. The question is not the policy of a *free-trade* with China ; on this point no well-informed person can entertain a doubt : the interests of commerce, the interests of the people at large, and the public revenue of the country would all be promoted by free trade ; but then how are the Company's dividend, the interest of their bond debt, and other out-goings to be paid ? They have no surplus territorial revenue ; the profits of the TEA-TRADE are the sole dependence of the proprietary. This is the rub ! But what, it may be asked, have the community to do with the pecuniary difficulties of a junta of ambitious and improvident speculators ? What is India to England ? Some thousands of adventurers have amassed princely fortunes there by rapine and extortion, and have returned to spend them in this country, to add to the aristocracy of wealth already too predominant. Beyond this we have derived no advantage from our eastern acquisitions—neither true glory nor national happiness. Why should we then be called upon to make a sacrifice ? If the Company cannot maintain their association without public support ; if they cannot carry on trade to advantage, without privileges hurtful to the community ; if they cannot enter into fair competition with individuals, let them retire from the contest—let them DISSOLVE, and leave commerce to be pursued by others on more prudent and economical principles.

Only think of the situation of that most patient of all animals, the British public, in this business. The boroughmongers levy a *hundred per cent. tax on tea* for the support of extravagance and the payment of *their* dividends, and the Company a monopoly tax to the same amount, and for similar purposes. How finely is JOHN BULL crucified between the *exclusives* of Leadenhall and the oppressors of Downing-street! If to these agreeables, we add the extra sugar-tax he is compelled to pay for the benefit of the West-India flaggellants, with what gusto he must needs swallow his morning and evening beverage ; what fervent ejaculations he must utter over his *cups* for their prosperity and the permanence of oligarchical government !

There is, however, one resource to the Company, in lieu of the profits of the exclusive trade to China—they may RETRENCH. Like their prototype, the Borough-System, they are embarrassed from a long course of war and prodigality, and they must economize. The people of England will never submit to be taxed for the maintenance of their territorial sovereignty and patronage. They must reduce still further than they have yet done their military, civil, judicial, and revenue establishments; they must curtail enormous salaries, and their " *dead weight ;*" be less lavish in granting pensions, superannuations, and allowances to relatives and dependents. And if all this is not enough, they must reduce their dividend, and instead of bartering offices and appointments in India for the benefit of themselves, sell them openly and fairly to meet their expenditure. At all events, they may rely upon it, that they will not be allowed to tax the community, neither one, two, nor three millions per annum after the 10th of April, 1834.

––––––

In support of the allegations at the close of this article, we ought to have mentioned a few facts confirmatory of our opinions, which we were well enabled to do from the inquiries of parliamentary committees.

We have said that we are becoming a " tea-drinking nation;" here is the proof from the statement submitted to the Commons' Committee, by Mr. Crawford, of the comparative consumption per head, of tea and coffee in Great Britain, France, and the United States.

	Tea.			Coffee.		
	lbs.	oz.	dwts.	lbs.	oz.	dwts.
Great Britain	1	7	8	0	10	14
France	-	-	-	0	9	13
United States	0	9	4	2	1	11

Several statements were submitted to the Committee, with a view of showing the amount of the tax entailed on the community by the Company's exclusive privilege ; by one witness it was estimated at

£1,500,000 per annum; by another at £1,727,934, and by a third at £2,588,499.

For a comparative statement of the prices at which teas are sold by the Company, and on the continent, and in America, we must refer to the statement of Dr. Kelly, No. 4709, of the Lords' Committee. The prices at the Company's sales in London, exclusive of government duty, are about double those in the countries mentioned.

From a statement of Mr. Melvill, auditor-general to the Company, it appears, the gross revenue of Bengal, Madras, and Bombay in the year 1828, was £22,551,617; of this revenue, £15,384,528 was the produce of the land-tax : the charge of *collecting* the revenue, pensions, &c. £5,524,728, and this enormous charge although three fifth parts of the revenue arise from the direct tax on land ! The charge for collecting the revenue of the United Kingdom—which is justly considered extravagant enough—amounted, Jan. 5th, 1831, on the gross income of £59,308,872, to £3,713,944.

The following returns, by the auditor-general of the Company, exhibit a statement of the military charges, the general civil charges, and the judicial charges of the three Presidencies for the year 1828 :—

	Military Charges.	General Civil Charges.	Judicial Charges.
Bengal	£4,747,224	£1,791,508	£1,247,436
Madras	3,926,267	360,484	377,158
Bombay	2,111,222	542,202	312,222
Total	£10,784,713	£2,694,204	£1,836,816

Can any one believe the Company will not be able to find resources from such lavish outgoings, without a monopoly profit on the consumption of tea ?

As every information which relates to the Company will speedily be of intense interest, we subjoin a few more statements; they were prepared by the Company for the Parliamentary Committee on East India affairs, and laid before that committee. It will be seen from the estimates of the auditor that the charges of the Company at the expiration of their charter will exceed their revenues by £827,300 ; so that there will be no *surplus* to pay the dividends without the monopoly profit on tea. But, we again beseech the sovereign Directors not to " lay that flattering unction to their souls," but to look to their wasteful expenditure, especially the civil branches of it.

It appears from the returns of the revenue of the United Kingdom for Jan. 1832, that the expenditure exceeds the income by £21,000 ; and from the depression in all the great branches of national industry, there is little prospect of the country being able to support additional burthens. How then can it be expected, the people will suffer themselves to be heavily taxed to support the Indian empire—a foreign dependency, chiefly valuable for the patronage it vests in 24 merchants. Rather than such a sacrifice should be made, it would be better to abandon Hindustan to its native sovereigns—the Mogul, the Nabobs and Subahdars.

ESTIMATE *of the Revenues and Charges of India, under the several heads, whether payable in India or in England, as they will probably stand at the expiration of the Company's Charter.*

REVENUES.

	Bengal.	Madras.	Bombay.	Penang, Malacca, and Singapore.	Total.
	£	£	£	£	£
Mints, Post-office, stamps, judicial	431,250	80,895	53,939	..	566,075
Land revenue	6,785,000	3,127,931	1,501,047	39,638	11,453,617
Customs	697,910	458,403	334,365	..	1,490,678
Ceded territory,(including the Burmese cessions)	479,167	..	..	..	479,167
Salt	1,820,832	314,590	16,705		2,152,127
Opium	1,427,917	..	..	..	1,427,917
Marine	29,709	5,877	15,280	..	50,866
Subsidies	..	308,579	..	..	308,579
Bank profits	..	7,191	..	..	7,191
	11,671,785	4,303,466	1,921,327	39,639	
Total estimated revenues in India					17,936,217

The rate of exchange observed in this account is 1s. 11d. the Sicca rupee.

CHARGES.

	Bengal.	Madras.	Bombay.	Penang, Malacca, and Singapore.	Total.
	£	£	£	£	£
Civil charges (including provinc. battalions), &c.	687,846	246,441	406,440	93,798	1,434,526
Mints,Post-office & stamps	145,592	45,876	32,268	..	223,736
Judicial	855,906	281,135	213,226	..	1,350,267
Land revenue and customs	1,331,145	839,428	486,620	..	2,657,193
Ceded territory (including Burmese cessions)	103,500	..	..	..	103,500
Salt	730,360	64,901	..	..	795,261
Opium	560,587	..	..	..	560,587
Marine	72,525	14,120	145,885	..	232,530
Buildings, &c.	327,922	62,170	99,701	..	489,793
Military	3,258,536	2,249,012	1,274,719	14,583	6,796,150
Amount which it is estimated will be annually set apart to meet the claims upon the Tanjore revenues	..	57,500	..	..	57,500
	8,073,919	3,860,584	2,658,859	108,381	14,701,743
Interest on debts	1,967,966	177,086	18,054	..	2,162,206
	10,040,985	4,037,570	2,676,913	108,381	

	£
Total estimated charges in India	16,863,949
Expense of St. Helena	90,054

Political charges incurred in England, including invoice amount of
stores consigned to India   1,720,405

Cost of remitting funds from India to meet the territorial advances
in England, being the difference between 1*s.* 11*d.* per Sicca rupee,
the rate which it is here supposed the remittances would realize,
and the average rate at which the advances in England are made   89,109
(N. B.—These advances are estimated at £1,000,000 per annum,
and are exclusive of the political charges defrayed in England.)

Grand total of charges   18,763,517

Deduct revenues   17,936,217

Estimated excess of charge   827,300

*The following are the proportions of the above Charges, which may
be payable in England: viz.—*

Interest on debts, part of the £2,162,206 stated under	£	£
that head.......................................	875,000	
Expenses of St. Helena	90,054	
Political charges incurred in England	1,720,405	
		2,685,459

(Errors excepted.)

East-India House,   JAMES C. MELVILL,
29th July, 1831.   Auditor India Accounts.

TERRITORIAL DEBT OF INDIA.

*Prospective Estimate of the Territorial Debt of India at the close
of the Company's present Term, calculating the Sicca rupee at
1s. 11d. instead of the rates of exchange fixed by the Board of
Commissioners for the Affairs of India.*

	Bengal.	Madras.	Bombay.	Total.
	£	£	£	£
Debts at 4 per cent.	208,275	28,359	292,22	328,854
Ditto 5 ditto	28,453,287	2,446,420	..	30,899,707
Ditto 6 ditto	8,621,874	273,090	182.951	9,077,915
Ditto 8 ditto	44,237	377,508	170,881	592,626
Ditto 10 ditto	1,773	..	..	1,773
Treasury notes	125,851	..	..	125,851
Total debts bearing interest....	37,455,304	3,125,377	446,052	41,026,733
Debts not bearing interest	5,321,933	831,236	429,102	6,582,271
Total territorial debt..........	42,777,237	3,956,613	875,154	47,609,004

(Errors excepted.)

East-India House,   JAMES C. MELVILL,
29th August, 1831.   Auditor India Accounts.

BANK OF ENGLAND.

THERE is a class of politicians in this country with just one idea; and that idea is, there is nothing good in public economy unless it be conducive to the accumulation of capital. The distribution of wealth is a consideration of no importance; their only object being to heap it up in masses, no matter how disproportioned, provided the total amount is augmented. For this purpose, they have been always recommending the indefinite enlargement of farms, the substitution of machinery for manual labour, and the establishment of banks of credit and paper-money. That their principles are true in the abstract, and that the application of them, within certain limits and under certain circumstances, would be beneficial, we have little doubt; but their unqualified and precipitate adoption would, in our opinion, be productive of disastrous consequences. In every case, we believe, they tend to augment the aggregate wealth of the community, but not the aggregate amount of social happiness. National happiness, however, is more important than national wealth; and a system which would compromise the former for the attainment of the latter, sacrifices the end to the means. The direct tendency of the principles of the Economists is to destroy the intermediate links of society; or, more correctly, to consolidate them in one end of the chain;—to replace the feudal aristocracy, from which Europe has suffered so much, with a monied aristocracy more base in its origin, more revolting in its associations, and more inimical to general freedom and enjoyment.

The history of banking affords an apt illustration of the practical tendency of the unqualified dogmas of the Ricardo school. Banking has always been the favourite invention of these theorists, as tending most effectually to the extension of credit, the development of industry, and accumulation of capital. These are its natural results; but such advantages may be more than counterbalanced by an alloy of accompanying evils. In England, we consider the system of credit founded on bank paper to have been the chief auxiliary and main stay of the reckless and unprincipled government of the last forty years. It was this which enabled ministers to build up the baseless superstructure of the Funds, which must ultimately fall, not on its guilty authors, but on those who have unwarily confided in their delusive representations. It was this which enabled them to destroy the currency of 1797, to substitute, for 26 years, in place of the universal medium of exchange, a forced inconvertible representative, which raised prices to an unnatural height, altered the standard of value, by which all existing contracts and engagements were violated; and then, when the profligate errors so committed were to be repaired, the country was again dragged through a series of changes and calamities not less unjust and ruinous than those it had previously suffered. These are not the only evils of the banking system; it has demoralized the country and exercised a baneful influence on internal economy, by giving an undue ascendancy to particular branches of industry—the commercial and manufacturing, for instance; it has given an artificial impulse to population,—multiplying the number of the people beyond the means of permanent employment and subsistence; it has created a vast monied interest, whose sole element is war, gambling, and speculation; it has been a principal cause of over-trading, of mercantile revulsions and vicissitudes, and the endless source of frauds, litigation, arrests, insolvencies, and bankruptcies.

These evils, it will be alleged, are not inherent in banking, but have been the consequences of banking not being conducted on *sound* principles. What the sound principles of banking are the professors of the " science of exchanges" have not yet distinctly laid down. One of the sound principles of the Bullionists in 1810 was that bank paper should always be *convertible* into coin at the will of the holder. But experience proved that this was no effectual guarantee against over-issues. The paper of the Bank of England and of the provincial banks was so convertible in 1825; but it did not avert the commercial crisis which arose out of the redundant issue of their notes and bills of exchange. The fact is, the political economists are wise *after the event*, like many other people with much less pretensions to depth and comprehensiveness. While the banking system was in its full career of fallacious prosperity, they never forewarned the community of its disastrous consequences; they were as little gifted with foreknowledge as others, and, like others, only learnt from experience. Similar results have flowed from other branches of their science. They discovered that a *saving* might be effected by farming on a great scale, and by manufacturing on a great scale; but they could discern nothing further: they could not discern the political, the social, and moral calamities which would flow from the aggregation of great capitals in agricultural and manufacturing industry.

It is this want of foresight of practical evils which ought to make us cautious in adopting the maxims of the Economists. France has recently passed through the same ordeal as England. During the summer of 1830, she suffered from precisely the same causes as those which produced such wide-spread distress in this country in 1811, 1815, and 1825; and the sudden collapse of an extensive system of banking, credit, and mercantile paper, by occasioning great pecuniary embarrassments, threatened, at one period, to impede the full triumph of her glorious revolution.

We shall, however, leave these general topics to come to our more immediate object,—the origin and present state of the powerful corporation in Threadneedle-street—the great foster-parent of banking, credit, and paper-money in this country. In treating of the Bank of England, there appear to be three objects particularly deserving of attention. *First*, a brief outline of the history and connexion of the Bank with government. *Secondly*, the enormous profits it has derived, and the immense wealth it has accumulated from that connexion. *Thirdly*, its present state and influence. We shall treat on these subjects as briefly as possible, so as to put the reader in possession of the most important facts necessary to a knowledge of them.

The Bank had its origin in war and taxation; and was originally projected by one Paterson, a Scotch speculator, who was afterwards engaged in the disastrous project of colonization at Darien. William III. who introduced standing armies, the excise-laws, the funding system, and other calamities, wanted money to carry on a *vigorous* war against the French. An act passed, inviting people to make voluntary advances to the amount of £1,500,000; and, for securing the payment of the interest, taxes were laid upon beer, ale, and other liquors. Upon condition of £1,200,000 of this sum being advanced within a certain time, the subscribers were to be incorporated; and, this being done, the incorporation took place, and the subscribers were formed into a trading company, called, " The Governor and Company of the Bank of England." The charter of corporation was executed July 27, 1694; and directs, among other things, that a governor or deputy-governor, and twenty-four directors, shall be chosen for conducting the establishment; that thirteen or more of them (the governor or deputy-governor being always one) shall constitute a court for the management of the affairs of the Company; that the qualification of the governor shall be at least £5000 stock; deputy-governor £3000; directors £2000 each; and every elector £500; that four general courts shall be held every year, when the majority of electors present may make bye-laws for the government of the corporation; and that " no dividend shall at any time be made by the said governor and Company save only out of the interest, profit, or produce arising by or out of the said capital, stock, or fund, or by such dealing as is allowed by the act of parliament." For the £1,200,000 lent to government, they were to receive yearly £100,000; £96,000, the interest at eight per cent. and £4000 for the charges of management. Their loan to government might be redeemed on a year's notice; and, in that case, the charter and company to expire.

Such is the origin and constitution of the Bank; on which, one or two remarks may be made. It is clear, from the act of incorporation, (the 5 & 6 William and Mary,) that nothing more than the establishment of a company of traders, or pawnbrokers, was intended; and that it never was surmised that they would ever form a part of, or have any dominant influence in, the government. The act specifies, very particularly, the sort of trade they were to carry on : they were not to trade in goods or merchandise, but to employ their capital in advancing money on goods and *pledges*,* in discounting bills of exchange, and the buying and selling of gold and silver bullion; with a permission, however, to sell such goods as were mortgaged to them, and not redeemed within three months after the expiration of the time of redemption.

But, still further to confine these traders and pawnbrokers to their province, and prevent any further connexion with the executive, of which the parliament of that day appears to have been somewhat apprehensive, the same law of William and Mary imposes a penalty upon the Directors if they purchase, on account of the corporation, any crown lands, or if they advance to his Majesty any sum of money, by way of loan or anticipation of any branch of the public revenue, other than on such funds only on which a credit is or shall be granted by parliament. Contrary to this clause, and notwithstanding the penalty, the Directors continued to make advances from time to time, on treasury bills, to the year 1793. In that year, Mr. Bosanquet was governor; he had some doubt of the legality of these advances, and applied for a bill of indemnity: the Bank having then become an essential part of the government, this was easily obtained; and an act was passed to protect the governor and company from any penalties they had incurred, or might incur in future, on account of any advances to government.

There are few facts in the early history of the Bank meriting particular notice. During the great re-coinage of 1696, the company was involved in considerable difficulty, and was even compelled to suspend payment of its notes, which were at a heavy discount. Owing, however, to the skilful management of the directors and the assistance of government, the Bank got over this crisis. But it was at the same time judged expedient, in order to enable the copartners to withstand any subsequent pressure, to augment their capital to £2,201,171.

In 1745 the alarm occasioned by the advance of the Highlanders under the Pretender, led to a run on the Bank; and, in order to gain time, the Directors resorted to the expedient of paying in *shillings and sixpences!* During Lord George Gordon's riots in 1780, the Bank incurred considerable danger. Had the mob attacked the establishment at the commencement of the riots, before it was put into a state of defence, the consequences might have been fatal. Subsequently a military force has been nightly placed in the Bank as a protection in case of emergency.

The next circumstance deserving notice is the increase in the denomination of the notes issued by the Company. For above sixty years, no notes were issued for a less sum than *twenty-pounds*; and these were made payable to the bearer on *demand*; and for the amount of which

---

* It was only during the commercial crisis of 1826 that Lord Liverpool discovered the Bank was empowered to make advances on goods and merchandise; the Directors, it appears, were as little aware of this dormant privilege as his Lordship, having been too much occupied with their more ostentatious and profitable dealings with the Treasury, to attend to the humble avocation set forth by the *three balls*.

notes, in the legal coin of the realm, the Company was liable to be sued and arrested. As the Bank enlarged its advances to government, it became necessary to lower the denomination of its notes. A different reason has been assigned; but this, no doubt, is the true one. It is clear, indeed, that the real capital of the Bank being a limited sum, it could only have money to lend to government by increasing its fictitious capital; in other words, by extending its issue of paper; which again could only be done by lowering the denomination of its notes. While £20 notes alone were issued, their circulation, from their amount, being limited to the commercial and trading classes, no great quantity of paper could possibly be emitted; but when notes of the value of 15, 10, 5, and 1 pound were issued, their circulation extending through all classes of the community, the issue of Bank paper would proportionately increase. Government, therefore, in order to obtain advances from the Bank, readily permitted the issuing of notes of smaller value. In the war of 1755, the Bank began to put out notes of the value of £15; and before the conclusion of that war, notes of the value of £10. At the commencement of the Anti-Jacobin war, in 1793, they were still further indulged, and allowed to issue £5 notes; and, lastly, in the year 1797, came the £1 and £2 notes. Rents, wages, salaries, taxes, and every thing else, could now be paid in Bank paper; and the Restriction-Act having protected the Bank from the necessity of taking up their own notes, they were issued in prodigious quantities; and in exactly the same proportion the Bank enlarged its advances to Government. The following statement, extracted from the report of the Committee of the House of Lords, in 1819, of the amount of Bank paper in circulation in different years; and of the amount of the sums advanced to government on exchequer-bills, and other government securities, will show the connexion which has subsisted between the issue of paper and advances to government:—

	Bank Notes.	Advances.
1794	£10,963,380	£ 8,786,514
1795	13,539,160	11,114,230
1796	11,030,110	11,718,730
1814	25,511,012	33,607,300
1815	27,155,824	27,156,000
1816	26,681,398	26,042,600
1817	27,339,758	25,399,510
1818	27,954,558	27,002,000

Having shown the causes which led to the issue of small notes, and the connexion betwixt the issue of Bank paper and advances to government, we shall now mention some other points connected with the history of this Company.

Without the assistance of the Bank the immense fabric of debt and taxation could not have been reared. Of this government appears to have been soon sensible, from the numerous laws enacted for its protection and encouragement. To prevent competition from the Mine Adventure Company, which had commenced banking, and began to issue notes, it was provided by the 6th of Anne that no other banking company of more than *six persons*, should issue notes payable in less than six months. Innumerable acts have passed, imposing the penalty of death for forging Bank notes ; others, the punishment of transportation, on persons uttering, or having them in their possession. The English code has been made the bloodiest in the world, in order to uphold the Oligarchy and the paper system, and its laws more savage than those of Draco. But of these, and also the Restriction Act, we shall speak shortly ; let us now only attend to those laws for upholding the credit of its paper.

After the Restriction-Act, the Bank ceased to be an independent company; it might be considered a government office, of which the governor and directors had the management; and which issued a *forced* government paper. Paper issued under such circumstances would necessarily depreciate ; and this was an evil which it was of importance to government, as far as possible, to prevent. Having by *force* kept bank-notes in circulation, it seemed a slight extension of the same desperate principle to attempt also by *force* to maintain their credit. Various laws were passed for this purpose. After the Restriction-Act, a law passed to protect debtors from arrest, who tendered payment in notes, though they still continued liable to a common action for debt, to compel payment in guineas. This was the first attempt of the borough-mongers to render Bank-paper a *legal tender*, and equivalent to gold. In 1810, when paper had depreciated 30 per cent., and guineas sold for from 25s. to 28s. in bank-notes, a law passed to punish persons pursuing this traffic, and imposing penalties on those who sold them for their *real* value in paper. Tenants, who offered notes for rent, were protected from distress, though liable to a common action of debt or ejectment. At length, in 1811, Lord King having given notice to his tenants to pay their rents in guineas, the legal coin of the realm, an act passed to protect persons, tendering payment in notes, from all further proceedings. This was nearly the climax. Bank paper was now a *legal tender* to all intents and purposes; and by the fiat of the Oligarchy, old rags were metamorphosed into gold. Even this was not enough to satisfy the omnipotent parliament ; they actually passed a resolution, declaring a one-pound bank-note and a shilling equal in value to a guinea, though the latter was openly selling for twenty-seven shillings !

Let us now revert to the capital part of Bank legislation—the *Restriction-Act*. By turning to the preceding page, and observing the amount of the Bank advances to government in the year 1796, and reflecting on the various laws enacted in favour of the Company, it will appear that an intimate connexion and mutual dependence had been created betwixt the Bank and Government, before the Restriction-Act, in 1797 ; that law, however, fairly incorporated the Bank with church and state. The causes which produced the stoppage were

briefly these:—From the commencement of the year 1797, great
apprehensions were entertained of a French invasion : the people were
alarmed for the stability of the government: consequently for the
stability of the Bank, which depended upon the government : a run upon
the Bank ensued; the credit of the establishment was endangered ; and
suspicion, which PAINE justly denominates credit asleep, was now
awakened.   The run on the Bank continued hourly to increase, till
Saturday the 25th of February, 1797.   This was the last day the Bank
was compelled to pay their notes on demand, agreeably to the tenor of
their notes, and the conditions on which they had been issued.   The
alarm not being likely to subside, and the run continuing to increase till
the latest hour the Bank was open, on the next day, *Sunday,* an order
was issued from the Privy Council, requiring the Bank to *forbear issuing any more cash,* till the sense of parliament could be taken on
the subject.   This order, as might be expected, was instantly obeyed, a
few days more would have drawn out of the Bank coffers the last farthing of cash and bullion.   The Company wished anxiously to conceal
the amount of specie in their possession at the time of the stoppage :
but, by an ingenious calculation of Mr. Allardyce, this point was subsequently ascertained almost to a certainty.   It appears, that, on the
25th of February, the last day of payment, the notes in circulation
amounted to £8,640,250, and the total amount of cash and bullion in
the Bank, to only *one million two hundred and seventy two thousand
pounds.*

   The Bank, like true traders, has always manifested great anxiety
about the *credit of the house,* and endeavoured to make it appear that
the stoppage did not originate in the necessities of the Bank, but the
necessities of the government. In the resolutions of a court of directors,
on the 25th March, 1797, affixed to the second report of the Bank
committee of 1819, it is said, "That the restriction on cash payments
was altogether a measure of *state necessity.*"   Whether it originated
in the necessities of the Bank, or of the boroughmongers, or both—
the latter appears most probable—it is not very material to inquire :
but it appears that on the last day of payment the Bank had little
more than a *million* of cash and bullion to pay more than *eight
millions* of their notes ; and how, under such circumstances, the Bank
could have met their creditors, or what could have protected them from
arrest for debt, but the interference of government, it is not easy to
conceive.

   But the fact is, the stoppage was concerted betwixt Mr. Pitt and the
directors.   Sometime before the order in council was issued, Mr. Bosanquet and other directors had had repeated interviews with that
minister to consult how the run could be stayed, and the Company
saved from impending bankruptcy.   The last interview was on the 22d
of February ; the Directors were then in a terrible fright ; they told the
minister they were " alarmed for the safety of the house ;" and asked
him, when " he would think it necessary to interfere."   Pitt interfered
on the following Sunday ; a singular day for the consummation of this

extraordinary transaction. Immediately after, the Bank had recourse to a great deal of dissimulation to disguise their insolvency from the public. On the 2d of March, six days after the stoppage, a court of proprietors was called. Mr. Bosanquet, who waited on the Minister to express his fears for the " safety of the house," and to know when Government would interfere, was present. After expatiating on the THEN *prosperous state* of Bank affairs, this gentleman told the proprietors that he earnestly hoped they would soon be *permitted* to pay their notes, as usual, in cash. Thanks were then voted to the directors for *complying* with the order in council, which empowered them to violate their engagements to the public with impunity, and refuse payment for their notes. All this was excellent. Mr. Bosanquet " earnestly hoped" that they would be *permitted* to do that which he had earnestly petitioned Mr. Pitt they might be protected from doing ; and the proprietors gravely thanked the directors for *complying* with their own earnest request!

The Order in Council, requiring the Bank to issue no more cash, was issued on the 26th of February. The Restriction-Act received the royal assent on the 3d of May, and was to continue in force till the 24th of June, that is, only for *fifty-two days*. On the 22d of June, two days before the expiration of the original act, it was renewed till one month after the next session of Parliament. This was the *first* renewal ; the *second* renewal was in 1798, to continue till *one month* after the signing of a definitive treaty of peace. Peace came in 1801 ; but, before the expiration of the month, the *third* renewal was passed, to continue till the 1st of March, 1803 ; before that time, notwithstanding peace continued, a *fourth* renewal passed to continue till six weeks after the next session of Parliament. In the interim war broke out ; the *fifth* renewal followed as a matter of course, and to continue till the singing of a definite treaty of peace. In 1814, plaguy peace came again to put these delusions to the test ; but before the expiration of the six months, the *sixth* renewal passed, to continue only one year. In 1816, the country being at peace, every one expected the law would expire : when lo ! it was renewed the *seventh* time, for two years ! In 1818, it was again renewed, for the *eighth* time, for one year ; and in 1819, it was renewed for the *ninth* time, and the Bank protected from payment of its notes in statutable coin for four years.

This was the last renewal, the Bank in 1823 resuming payments in specie, after a suspension of twenty-six years. It was thought by many, and confidently predicted by some, such an event could not possibly happen. These views were fallacious, originating in misconception ; all that was requisite to enable the Bank to fulfil its engagements were a general peace, public confidence, and such a favourable state of the exchanges as would enable it to obtain a supply of the precious metals adequate to meet the probable demand for gold in lieu of paper. These circumstances concurring at the period fixed for the resumption of cash-payments, the Bank resumed its ancient course of business, and an event to which such undue importance had been previously attached, was actually consummated without exciting the least interest or attention.

One of the greatest calamities resulting from the suspension of cash-payments by the Bank, and consequent inundation of the country with small notes, was the vast increase in the number of prosecutions for forgery. It appears, from returns to parliament, that, in the interval from 1797 to 1818, the Bank instituted 998 prosecutions either for forging, uttering, or having forged notes in possession. The results of these prosecutions were a dreadful sacrifice of human life; and it has been calculated that four hundred victims were offered up in the space of twenty-one years to the MOLOCH of paper money. As a set off against this terrible calendar, it is proper to mention that there was an abatement in the number of Mint prosecutions.

Another evil may be justly charged to the vast amount of paper issued by the Bank of England; the great extent of their circulation gave them a complete control over the national currency, which enabled them, at their own arbitrary discretion, merely by contracting or enlarging their issues, *to determine the prices* of all articles of consumption and merchandize. Thus was a company of traders, without responsibility or peculiar fitness for so grave a function, and whose conduct experience proved not to be always influenced either by absolute wisdom or disinterestedness, empowered to entail on the body of the people a plenty or scarcity of the necessaries of life, and on the commercial public the most sudden and disastrous vicissitudes.

Our next object will be to give an account of the BANK PROFITS, and the enormous wealth it has acquired since the suspension of cash-payments.

The profits of the Bank arise from various sources. First, from the interest of their notes in circulation, which, in some years, as in 1817, amounted to more than twenty-nine millions. Secondly, from balances of public money. These balances arise from the public dividends, payable by the Bank, but unclaimed, and from the produce of different taxes paid into the Bank, and which have not been drawn out for the service of government. On an average of ten years, from 1806 to 1816, the balances amounted to £11,000,000, on which the Bank gained an interest of five per cent. per annum. The amount of public balances has since fallen considerably; in 1825 they amounted at an average to £5,247,314; and in 1829 to £3,862,656.

The third source of profit is the interest on their capital and savings. The Bank's permanent capital amounts to £14,686,800, lent to government at an interest of 3 per cent. The fourth source of profit is from the management of the public debt. From a late act for the management of the debt, the Bank is paid £340 per million per annum, when its amount shall be 400 millions, and not exceed 600 millions: and £300 per million on such part of the debt as exceeds 600 millons.

Besides these sources of profit, the Bank derives a profit from its trade in bullion, the destruction of its notes, and the private deposits of individuals. It also has a profit, at the rate of £805 : 15 : 10 per million, for receiving subscriptions on loans contracted for by government.* All these form the gross profits of the Bank; from which, in order to form an estimate of their annual gain, it is only necessary to deduct the amount of their expenses, the stamp-duty on their notes, and the interest of their cash and bullion, which constitute their unproductive capital.

First, as to the expenses of the Bank. The Committee of Public Expenditure stated, in their Report in 1807, " that the number of " clerks employed in the Bank, exclusively or principally in the public " business was,

<blockquote>

" In 1786 · · · · · · · · · · · · · · · · · · 243
" 1796 · · · · · · · · · · · · · · · · · · 313
" 1807 · · · · · · · · · · · · · · · · · ·, 450
</blockquote>

" whose salaries, it is presumed, may be calculated at an average " between £120 and £170, for each clerk, taking them at £135, " which exceeds the average of those employed in the South-Sea " House, the sum is · £60,750 " at £150, the sum is · 67,500 " at £170, the sum is · 76,500 " either of which two last sums would be sufficient to provide a super-" annuation fund."

The total expense for managing the public business, the salaries of the governor, directors, &c. as stated by the same report, are as follows :—

<blockquote>

Salaries to governor, deputy-governor, and directors £8,000
Incidental expenses, about · 15,000
Additional buildings and repairs · · · · · · · · · · · · · · · · 10,000
Law expenses, and loss by frauds and forgeries, about 10,000
Largest estimate for clerks · · · · · · · · · · · · · · · · · · 76,500

Total · · · · · · £119,500
</blockquote>

Owing to the increase of Debt and other causes, Mr. Ricardo supposed that the number of clerks employed in the public business had increased from four hundred and fifty to between five and six hundred. The expenses estimated by the committee, in 1807, at £119,500, he calculated to have increased, in 1816, to £150,000. He states, the total number of clerks employed by the Bank in the whole of their establishment, at one thousand. Half of this number is employed in the public business, and the other half in the private business of the Bank. The expenses of the Company may be supposed to bear some proportion to the whole number of clerks employed. And, according to this rule, Mr. Ricardo says that, " as £150,000 has been calculated to be the expense attending the employment of five hundred clerks in the public business, we may estimate a like expense to be

---

* During the continuance of the income-tax, the Bank had an allowance of £1250 per million, or one-eighth per cent. for receiving the produce of that impost. It had also another source of profit from lotteries; for issuing the tickets and paying the prizes it received £1000 for each lottery.

incurred by the employment of the other five hundred, and therefore the whole expenses of the Bank, at the present time, about £300,000, including all charges whatsoever."—*Secure and Economical Currency*, p. 71, 2.

This estimate includes every charge : the expense of managing the public business, the salaries of the governor, directors, and clerks : stationery, incidental expenses, additional buildings, and repairs ; together with law-expenses, loss by frauds, forgeries, and every other expense incurred in conducting the business of the establishment.

The next subject forming a part of the outgoings of the Bank is the stamp-duty. The Bank, till lately, has always been particularly favoured in the composition which they paid for stamp-duties. In 1791 they paid a composition of £12,000 per annum, in lieu of all stamps either on bills or notes. In 1799, on an increase of the stamp-duty, this composition was advanced to £20,000, and an addition of £4000 for notes issued under £5, raised the whole to £24,000. In 1804, an addition of not less than 50 per cent. was made to the stamp-duty ; but, although the Bank circulation of notes under £5 had increased from one and a half to four and a half millions, the whole composition was only raised from £24,000 to £32,000. In 1808, there was a further increase of 33 per cent. to the stamp-duty, at which time the composition was raised from £32,000 to £42,000. In both these instances the increase was not in proportion even to the increase of duty ; and no allowance whatever was made for the increase in the amount of the Bank circulation.

It was not till the Session of 1815, on a further increase of the stamp-duty, that the new principle was established, and the Bank compelled to pay a composition in some proportion to the amount of its circulation. The composition is now fixed as follows :—Upon the average circulation of the preceding year, the Bank is to pay at the rate of £3,500 per million, on their aggregate circulation, without reference to the different classes and value of their notes. The establishment of this principle it is calculated caused a saving to the public, in the years 1815 and 1816, of £70,000. By the neglect of this principle, which ought to have been adopted in 1799, Mr. Ricardo estimated the public to have been *losers*, and the Bank consequently *gainers*, of no less a sum than *half a million*.

The last subject for which an allowance is to be deducted from the gross profits of the Bank, is for their unproductive capital, namely, their cash and bullion. At the stoppage in 1797, the Bank stated in their accounts, laid before parliament, that their cash and bullion, and their bills and notes discounted, together amounted to £4,196,080. They also gave a scale of discounts from 1782 to 1797, and a corresponding scale of the cash and bullion in the Bank for the same period. By comparing these numbers with each other, and some parts of the evidence, Mr. Allardyce discovered the whole secret the Bank wished to conceal—namely, the amount of cash and bullion in their coffers. According to this gentleman's calculation, as before mentioned, the cash and bullion of the Bank, on the 26th February, 1797, was reduced as low as one million two hundred and seventy-two thousand pounds. Subsequently the Bank increased its stock of cash and bullion; and on the average of the eighteen years, from 1797 to 1815, Mr. Ricardo conjectured it amounted to about three millions.

We have now mentioned all the circumstances necessary to form an estimate of the net profits of the Bank. We have mentioned all the sources whence the gross profits are derived, and also the different items of their disbursements. Proceeding on these principles, Mr. Ricardo calculated the clear gains of the Bank from the time of the suspension of cash payments, in 1797, to the year 1816. The results of his calculations were communicated to the Bank Committee of the House of Lords in 1819. We shall insert his statement, exhibiting at one view the amount of bonuses and increase of dividends to the proprietors, the new stock created, and the increased value of the original capital. It is Mr. Ricardo who is interrogated.

" Do you believe the following account to be an accurate account of the profits of the Bank since the Restriction, namely,

In bonuses and increase of dividends................£7,451,136

New Bank-stock (£2,910,600) divided among the proprietors 7,276,500

Increased value of capital of £11,642,000, (which on an average of 1767, was worth £125, and which is now worth £250,) that is............................... 14,553,000

Making in all, on a capital of £11,642,000, a gain in 19 years of £29,280,636

" I have no reason to doubt it; I believe it is accurate as far as I recollect." —*Minutes of Evidence*, p. 191.

This statement, we conceive, needs no explanation. In bonuses and an increase of dividends, the Bank gained £7,451,136. The new Bank-stock created, at £250 per cent. is worth £7,276,500. The original capital of £11,642,000, has increased in value £14,553,000. The total gain of the Bank on a capital of eleven millions, is more than *twenty-nine millions*. This is the Bank prize-money, the SPOIL OF WAR, the clear gains from the loans, lotteries, and taxation of the " Pitt and Plunder system." The brief history of the Bank, for nineteen years after the stoppage in 1797, is this : they have hanged and transported about EIGHT HUNDRED PERSONS, and in addition to their old dividend have made a profit of near THREE HUNDRED PER CENT !

COLQUHOUN had some reason when he said the Bank was the richest establishment in the world. We here see the amount of its vast profits during twenty years of blood, rapine, and injustice. The ability of the Bank to expend nearly a *quarter of a million* in hanging and transporting their fellow-creatures can no longer excite surprise. At the conclusion of the war in 1815, the Bank could have divided more than one hundred per cent. without encroaching on their permanent capital: in other words, they could have granted £100 to every holder of Bank-stock to the amount of £100, and yet not encroached on the original capital of the Company. If they made a division of one hundred per cent. bonus, they would still have had an unappropriated income of £542,000, which would have enabled them to increase their permanent dividend from ten to fourteen and a half per cent. If they had divided only a bonus of seventy-five per cent. they would retain a surplus capital exceeding that of 1797, and an unappropriated income of £673,000, which would enable them to raise their dividend from ten to fifteen and a half per cent. If the profits of the Bank had continued, and no addition been made to the present dividend of ten per cent. the accumulation of the surplus profit in forty years would have given to the Bank a disposable fund of more than *one hundred and twenty millions.**

According to the charter, all profits and advantages arising out of the management of the Bank ought to be divided, from time to time, among the proprietors, in proportion to each person's share and interest in the stock of the Company. This law has never been observed by the Directors: the concern has been carried on, and no statement of its affairs, nor the surplus savings, has ever been submitted to the proprietors. Mr. Allardyce, in 1801, and subsequently Mr. Young and other proprietors, have attempted at different times to compel the Governor and Directors to make a declaration of the affairs of the Bank; but these gentlemen appear to have considered it more prudent policy to conceal, as far as possible, their gains from the public. The rotten-boroughs have not been more intimately identified with the past system of misgovernment than the Bank of England. It is to the war, commenced by the Oligarchy in 1793, the Bank is indebted for its enormous wealth and inordinate gains. It is to this war the Bank was indebted for the Restriction-Act, which enabled it to raise the circulation of its notes from 12 millions to 27 millions. It was the war which raised the unredeemed public debt from 220 to 850 millions; of this debt the Bank has had the management, and for which it has received from the public about £300,000 per annum, whereas the receipt on account of the debt in 1792 was only £99,800. It is to the war, too, the Bank was indebted for the increase in the amount of public deposits. In 1792 the deposits were probably less than four millions. In and since 1806, to the peace, they exceeded eleven millions. From this source alone, Mr. Ricardo calculated that, in the ten years from 1806 to 1816, the Bank gained £5,500,000. It is to the war the Bank has been indebted for an annual dividend and bonus on its capital to the amount of 10, 12, and in some years as high as 17

---

* Ricardo on a Secure and Economical Currency, p. 84.

per cent. Lastly, the Bank is indebted to the war for clear savings, from the year 1797 to the year 1816, to the enormous amount of £29,280,636.

We are not greatly in favour of *ex post facto* laws, nor bills of pains and penalties, but should there ever be any thing like an *equitable adjustment*, a refunding or surrendering of surreptitious gains, the Bank will certainly have to yield up the most freely next to the Church and the Aristocracy.

At the end of this article are inserted several accounts laid before Parliament by the Bank in 1830, exhibiting their own statements of their past proceedings, the profits they have realized, and their existing transactions with the Government. Between the estimate of the Bank of the amount of their profits and the estimate of Mr. Ricardo, we do not find any material discrepancy. The Bank make their aggregate gains, exclusive of their ordinary dividend of 7 per cent. £16,619,526. If to this sum we add the difference between the value of their capital of £11,642,400 in 1797, and the value of their present capital of £14,553,000, we shall find that the prosperous career of the Bank has not been exaggerated.

The charter of the Bank, when first granted, was to continue for eleven years certain, or till a year's notice after August 1st, 1705. The charter was further renewed in 1697. In 1708 the Bank having advanced £400,000 for the public service, without interest, the exclusive privileges of the Corporation were prolonged till 1733. After further renewals, in consequence of advances in 1800, the charter, having then twelve years to run, was prolonged till the expiration of twelve months' notice to be given after August 1st, 1833, and till the payment by the government of the debt owing to the establishment. The last renewal is by 40 Geo. III. c. 29, and in consideration of an advance to the public of three millions for six years without interest.

It is reasonable to expect the Bank charter will not be again renewed without an entirely new arrangement far more favourable to the public interests than that now subsisting. The Bank annually receives about £257,000 for its trouble in paying the dividends. It holds balances of public money, free of interest, averaging three or four millions. These balances are employed in discounting bills at the rate of four per cent. yielding a revenue of £160,000, which, being added to the £257,000, makes an annual sum of £417,000 derived from its dealings with the Treasury. This has been always deemed a most extravagant remuneration, and has never been defended even in the House of Commons, except on the groundless plea, that it was binding on the public so long as the present charter had to run.

These do not constitute the whole of the advantages of this long favoured establishment : it enjoys various exclusive privileges in carrying on the trade of banking. By the act of Anne, before cited, no corporate body or partnership, consisting of more than *six persons* other than the Bank of England, is allowed to carry on the business of banking. After the panic of 1826, this privilege was so far relaxed as to allow the establishment of banking firms of more than six partners, at places exceeding the *distance of sixty miles* from London ; provided such firms had no establishment *as bankers* in the metropolis.

Why should these restrictions be tolerated in favour of an overgrown corporation, which has already profited so much by its exclusive immunities ? They form, moreover, the chief obstacle to the improvement of the system of banking in both the country and metropolis, by discouraging the establishment of joint-stock associations. Could banking firms be opened in the metropolis with an indefinite number of partners, on the plan of the Scotch banks, their credit would rest on such a sure and extended basis, that they might fairly compete with the establishment in Threadneedle-street for a share of the public business ; Government would be relieved from its dependence on a single fraternity ; and, in lieu of paying the Bank £257,000 per annum for the payment of the dividends, it is not improbable the whole sum might be saved, and the business transacted for the sake of the profit which might be realized from holding the balances of the public money and unclaimed lottery prizes and dividends.*

The Bank has never conducted its affairs either on such liberal or enlightened principles as to become entitled to peculiar favour from the community. Notwithstanding the enormous profits of this great corporation, it has constantly manifested an eagerness for gain, and impatience for the profitable employment of its capital, which could hardly have been exceeded by a private establishment. In 1822, with a view of extending their discount, they lowered the rate of interest from five to four per cent., and extended the term of discount from sixty to ninety days. In 1823, they contracted for a portion of the dead-weight annuity, by imposing upon themselves the obligation of advancing an annual loan for several years ; which engagement was clearly at variance with the legitimate principles of banking. At the close of the same year, they announced their intention to lend money on mortgage, which was a deviation from one of their oldest established rules. Lastly, in 1825, they came forward with a proposition to lend money on government securities, and upon their own stock.

By these expedients they were enabled greatly to extend the circulation of their notes ; but their resources, contrary to all sound maxims, were tied up in inconvertible securities, so that they were less able to discharge their proper functions as bankers. What was worse, the greedy example was followed by the country bankers ; and thus the race commenced between them, which could push out the most paper, till they brought upon the country the disastrous mercantile revulsion of 1825-6.

---

* Memorial of Country Bankers, addressed to the Lords of the Treasury, May 9, 1828.—*Parliamentary Paper*, No. 328, Sess. 1828.

THOUGHTS ON A NEW BANK OF ENGLAND.

Notwithstanding the errors of business and of political meddling with which the Bank Directors may be justly charged, it may be doubted whether the country would be benefited by any attempt to set up a rival establishment. A banking firm of undoubted stability is essential to the functions of government for the receipt and disbursement of the public revenue, and for the management of the national currency. But would it be possible to form an association, better adapted for these purposes than the Bank of England? In the first place with respect to the circulating medium. The Bank enjoying the exclusive privilege of issuing notes in the metropolis, it possesses a complete control over the circulation directly in London and indirectly in the provinces; and it can only arise from a mistaken cupidity or culpable remissness of duty in the Directors if the general circulation is either redundant or deficient —if it is not maintained precisely in that state which the wants of commerce and the course of the exchanges require. But such corrective power over the currency can only be advantageously exercised by a single association. Supposing two chartered bodies had concurrent authority in the issue of notes, they would either pursue their business in opposition or concert: if the former, then would there be a contest between them, which could get out the greatest amount of paper; if the latter, then the case would not be altered from what now exists—it would still be virtually one body, only acting under two denominations, the New Bank of England and the Old Bank of England.

Next as to experience in banking business. In this the Bank could not possibly be excelled by a new establishment. The Direction, it cannot be denied, consists of the *élite* of the commercial world; moreover they inherit, in virtue of their offices, all the wise saws, maxims, and precepts accumulated by their predecessors for the last hundred and forty years, and which, we presume, are carefully treasured up for reference in the Bank parlour, inscribed on tablets or other tangible record.

The last and most important consideration, with respect to any new association, which should undertake to be the national banker, would be the *security* it could afford. A sum of four or five millions, which is the average amount of the government balances, ought not to be entrusted to any mushroom establishment. On this head the Bank appears wholly unexceptionable. Just let us see by fair appraisement how much the " Old Lady" would yield, providing all her effects were brought under the hammer of alderman Farebrother. Lot the first, is that solid capital of £14,686,800, lent to Government at three per cent. and which at the present market price of £195 per hundred pound stock is worth exactly £29,619,260. The second lot is the surplus of profits, &c. after paying all outstanding demands; owing to the extreme reserve of the Old Girl the value of this assortment cannot be stated—common report says betwixt two and three millions: according to her Ladyship's inventory in 1819 (No. II. at the end of this article,) she had a nice balance in her favour of £5,202,320. Supposing we take the Old Dame at her word—here are two articles alone worth £34,821,580. Besides which, is the immense pile in Threadneedle-street, consisting of innumerable vaults, rotunda, cashier, court, committee and tellers' rooms, and a floor of apartments more spacious and intricate than the Cretan labyrinth, together with the site of eight acres, fittings up and Corinthian columns included—all which could not be appraised at a less sum than two millions, and with the preceding constitutes a substantial security to the amount of nearly thirty-seven millions, and must be amply sufficient to satisfy the most scrupulous tax-payer in the kingdom.

Though the Bank of England possesses the recommendations we have mentioned to the office of national banker, yet the Government is not dependent upon or at the mercy of the Corporation. When the charter has expired, the Bank proprietary become nothing more than a common partnership trading upon a joint-stock. Government, by granting a charter of incorporation to a new association, and transferring to it the exclusive privileges of issuing notes, of retaining the public balances, and of paying the public dividends, might, at one blow, destroy two-thirds at least of the business and revenue of the Threadneedle-street establishment. This we advert to lest it might be thought on the renewal of the Bank charter, the Directors had power to prescribe their own terms to Government: the power is all on the other side—in the hands of ministers, and if they do not exercise it for the public benefit, they will not have faithfully discharged their duty to the community. The relation in which the Bank stands to the public is nothing more than that of a number of private individuals entitled to no special favour; whatever privilege they enjoy, they ought to pay for; for whatever work they perform, they ought not to receive more than a reasonable compensation. Upon this principle let us inquire what ought to be the main conditions of the future contract between the Bank and Government.

First, the Bank ought to account to the public for the profits arising from the exclusive privilege of issuing notes, after deducting a reasonable sum for trouble and incidental expenses.

Secondly, the Bank ought to pay a per-centage for the average amount of public balances it holds and employs in banking.

Thirdly, if the composition paid by the Bank in lieu of stamp duties be inadequate, it ought to be augmented.

Fourthly, the Bank ought not to charge a greater sum per million for the payment of the dividends than is an equitable consideration for trouble and loss of time.

Fifthly, the Bank being invested with important public trusts, and having the control of the national currency, and as any error of judgment committed by the Directors, might be productive of disastrous consequences, it is highly expedient their affairs and proceedings should be at all times known, so as to be constantly open to public and parliamentary observance and discussion.

Sixthly, if the suggestion which has been made and appears judicious, be adopted, of making a Bank of England note a *legal tender* when offered by the country banks, the concession of so great and advantageous a privilege would justly claim a bonus from the Bank to the public ; especially as it would tend to augment the circulation of their notes, and accelerate the spread and establishment of their branch institutions.*

Lastly, the Bank charter ought only to be renewed for a short term of years. For this three reasons may be assigned. First, it would tend to keep the Bank dependent upon and under the control of the legislature. Secondly, the peculiar and changing state of the country at the present moment is a strong objection both against granting and accepting long leases by public bodies. Thirdly, there is no public reason for renewing the charter for a long term. In this respect the Bank and East India Company materially differ; the affairs of the former are all *at home*, and may be wound up any time in six months; the affairs of the latter extend to the other side of the globe, and require years.

Upon the conditions we have thus shortly sketched, the Bank charter might be renewed, with advantage to the Corporation, the Government, and the community.

Dividends on Bank Stock, from the Establishment of the Company to the present time.

	Years.	Dividend.		Years.	Dividends.
	1694	8 per cent.	Lady-day	1747	5 per cent.
	1697	9 —	Ditto	1753	4¼ —
	1708 } Varied from 9		Michaelmas	1753	5 —
	1729 } to 5½ per cent.		Lady-day	1754	4½ —
Lady-day	1730	6 —	Michaelmas	1764	5 —
Michaelmas	1730	5½ —	Ditto	1767	5½ —
Lady-day	1731	6 —	Ditto	1781	6 —
Michaelmas	1731	5½ —	Lady-day	1788	7 —
Lady-day	1732	6 —	Ditto	1807	10 —
Michaelmas	1732	5½ —	Ditto	1823	8 —

---

* The private bankers in London and in the country have reason to be jealous of the increasing business and importance of the Bank of England. The branch banks must ultimately prove dangerous rivals in the large provincial towns. In the metropolis the number of private accounts that have been opened with the Company since the great commercial crisis of 1825 is immense. Many who continue to keep accounts with the private firms only do so to the extent of what may be termed their circulating cash ; the mass of their unemployed capital being deposited in the more secure and unfathomable vaults of Threadneedle - street. By this division of confidence the private banks get only the most trouble-some and least profitable part of the banking business.

No. 1.

A RETURN *of the Number of Persons convicted of Forgery, or passing Forged Notes and Post Bills of the Bank of England, in each Year, from* 1791 *to* 1829, *inclusive.*

Years.	Capital Convictions.	Convictions for having Forged Bank Notes in possession.	Total Number of Convictions each Year.
1791—1796	nil.	nil.	nil.
1797	1	- - -	1
1798	11	- - -	11
1799	12	- - -	12
1800	29	- - -	29
1801	32	1	33
1802	32	12	44
1803	7	1	8
1804	13	8	21
1805	10	14	24
1806	nil.	9	9
1807	16	24	40
1808	9	23	32
1809	23	29	52
1810	10	16	26
1811	5	19	24
1812	26	26	52
1813	9	49	58
1814	5	39	44
1815	8	51	59
1816	20	84	104
1817	33	95	128
1818	62	165	227
1819	33	160	193
1820	77	275	352
1821	41	93	134
1822	16	- - -	16
1823	6	- - -	6
1824	5	- - -	5
1825	2	- - -	2
1826	18	4	22
1827	24	- - -	24
1828	10	- - -	10
1829	13	1	14

The Bank of England does not possess the means of stating or distinguishing the punishments inflicted for the said crimes.

No. II.

AN ACCOUNT *of the total Amount of Outstanding Demands on the Bank of England, and likewise the Funds for discharging the same;* 30*th Jan.* 1819.

Dr. - - The Bank, - - 30th January, 1819. - - Cr.

	£.		£.
To Bank Notes out ...	26,094,430	By Advances on Government Securities; viz.	
To other Debts; viz. Drawing Accounts Audit Roll .... Exchequer Bills deposited .... And various other Debts	7,800,150	On Exchequer Bills, on Malt, &c. 1818. Bank Loan, 1818 .. Supply, 1816, at £4 per cent......... Growing Produce of the Consd.Fund to 5th April, 1819, and Interest due, and Loans to Government on Unclaimed Dividends	8,438,660
	33,894,580		
Balance of Surplus in favour of the Bank of England, exclusive of the Debt from Government, at £3 per cent. £11,686,800 .. And the Advance to Government, per 56 Geo. III. cap. 96. at £3 per cent. £3,000,000	5,202,320	By all other Credits, viz. Cash and Bullion .. Exchequer Bills purchased, and Interest .... Bills and Notes discounted .... Treasury Bills for the Service of Ireland Money lent, and various other Articles	30,658,240
	£ 39,096,900		39,096,900
		By the permanent Debt due from Government, for the Capital of the Bank, at £3 per cent. per annum .	11,686,800
		By the Advance to Government, per Act 56 Geo. III. cap.96, at £3 per cent. per annum............	*3,000,000

Bank of England,
22d February, 1819.

WILLIAM DAWES,
Accountant General.

* The Bank capital, on which the shareholders divide, has been increased from £1,200,000 in 1694 to £14,553,000 in 1832. This increase has been effected either by additional subscriptions of stock, or by adding to their capital accumulated profits. In 1781 the Bank added to their capital, from profits, 8 per cent. or, £862,400 ; in 1816, which was the last addition, 25 per cent. was added, or, £2,910,600, raising their capital to the present amount of £14,553,000.

No. III.

AN ACCOUNT *of Money paid or payable at the Bank of England, for the Management of the Public Debt, in the year* 1829, *together with an Account of all the allowances made by the Public to the Bank, or charged by the Bank against the Public, for transacting any Public Service in the year* 1829, *describing the nature of the service, and the Amount charged thereon in the said year, and including any Sum under the denomination of House-money, or House Expenses; and also, any Sum under the denomination of Charges of Management on South-Sea Stock, and stating the aggregate amount of the whole.*

	£.	s.	d.
Charge for Management of the Unredeemed Public Debt for one year, ending the 5th April, 1830, being the annual period at which the accounts are made up, as directed by the Act of 48 Geo. 3, c 4.	248,417	17	2¾
Ditto, ditto, for one year ending ditto, on sundry Annuities transferred to the Commissioners for the Reduction of the National Debt, for the purchase of Life Annuities per Act of the 48 Geo. 3, and subsequent Acts	2,922	11	9
Charges of Management, being part of an entire yearly fund of £100,000 enjoyed by the Governor and Company of the Bank of England, originally by the Act of the 5th and 6th of William and Mary, c. 20, confirmed to the said Governor and Company by several subsequent Acts, and lastly, by the Act of the 39th and 40th Geo. 3, c. 28, as per return made to the Honourable House of Commons, on the 21st of June, 1816	4,000	0	0
Ditto, ditto, on £4,000,000 South Sea Stock, purchased by the Governor and Company of the Bank of England of the South Sea Company, and transferred by them to the said Governor and Company, in pursuance of the Act of the 8th Geo. 1, c. 21, and which charges of management were assigned by the said South Sea Company, to the said Governor and Company, out of a Sum of £8,397 : 9 : 6 per annum, then paid by the Public to the said South Sea Company, for charges of management on their funds, as per Return made to the Honourable House of Commons, on the 21st June, 1816	1,898	3	5
	£257,238	12	4¾

Bank of England,	T. RIPPON,
11th of March, 1830.	Chief Cashier.

No. IV.

An Account of all distributions made by the Bank of England amongst the proprietors of Bank Stock, whether by money payments, transfer of 5 per cent. annuities, or otherwise, under the heads of bonus, increase of dividend, and increase of capital, betwixt 25th February, 1797, and 31st March, 1830, in addition to the ordinary annual dividend of 7 per cent. on the capital stock of that Corporation, existing in 1797, including therein the whole dividend paid since June, 1816, on their increased capital; stating the period when such distributions were made, and the aggregate amount of the whole.

In June, 1799 :
£10 per cent. Bonus in 5 per cents. 1797, on £11,642,400, is £1,164,240
May, 1801 :
£5 per cent. ditto, in Navy 5 per cents, ditto................ 582,120
November, 1802 .
£2½ per cent. ditto, ditto, ditto............................ 291,060
October, 1804 :
£5 per cent. ditto, Cash, ditto............................. 582,120
October, 1805 :
£5 per cent. ditto, ditto, ditto 582,120
October, 1806 :
£5 per cent. ditto, ditto, ditto 582,120

From April, 1807, to Oct., 1822, both inclusive. { Increase of Dividend at the rate of £3 per cent. per annum on £11,642,400, is, 16 years.......... 5,588,352

From April, 1823, to Oct., 1829, both inclusive. { Increase of Dividend at the rate of £1 per cent. per annum on £11,642,400, is, 7 years 814,968

In June, 1816..............Increase of Capital at 25 per cent. is 2,910,600

From Oct., 1816, to Oct., 1822, both inclusive. { Dividend at the rate of £10 per cent. per annum on £2,910,600, increased Captal, is, 6½ years 1,891,890

From April, 1823, to Oct., 1829, both inclusive. { Dividend at the rate of £8 per cent. per annum on £2,910,600, increased Capital, is, 7 years 1,629,936

Aggregate amount of the whole £16,619,526

Annual Dividend payable on Bank Stock in 1797, on a Capital of £11,642,400, at the rate of £7. per cent. per annum. 814,968

Annual Dividend payable since June, 1816, on a Capital of £14,553,000, to October, 1822, inclusive, at the rate of £10 per cent. per annum 1,455,300

Annual Dividend payable from April, 1823, to 31st March, 1830, both inclusive, on a Capital of £14,553,000. at the rate of £8 per cent. per annum 1,164,240

WILLIAM SMEE, Depy. Acct.
Bank of England, 26th April, 1830.

No. V.

An Account *of the Amount of Bank Notes in Circulation on the undermentioned Days; distinguishing the Bank Post Bills, and the Amount of Notes under Five Pounds, with the Aggregate of the whole.*

	Notes of £5. and upwards.	Bank Post Bills.	Bank Notes under £5.	TOTAL.
	£.	£.	£.	£.
1792 February 25	10,394,106	755,703	....	11,149,809
August 25	10,281,071	725,898	....	11,006,969
1793 February 26	10,780,643	647,738	....	11,428,381
August 26	10,163,839	674,375	....	10,838,214
1794 February 26	10,079,165	618,759	....	10,697,924
August 26	10,060,248	567,972	....	10,628,220
1795 February 26	12,968,707	570,456	....	13,539,163
August 26	10,939,880	518,502	....	11,458,382
1796 February 26	10,266,561	643,133	....	10,909,694
August 26	8,981,645	549,690	....	9,531,335
1797 February 25	8,167,949	474,615	....	8,601,964
August 26	9,109,614	524,587	9,34,015	10,568,216
1798 February 26	10,856,188	551,549	1,442,384	12,850,085
August 25	9,997,958	553,236	1,639,831	12,191,025
1799 February 26	10,576,510	607,907	1,451,728	12,636,145
August 26	11,260,675	653,766	1,345,432	13,259,873
1800 February 25	13,106,368	723,600	1,406,708	15,236,676
August 26	12,221,451	823,366	1,690,561	14,735,378
1801 February 26	12,975,206	954,982	2,647,526	16,577,514
August 26	11,715,665	759,270	2,495,386	14,970,321
1802 February 26	12,038,970	803,499	2,616,407	15,458,876
August 26	12,801,746	772,577	3,312,790	16,887,113
1803 February 26	11,796,424	820,039	2,960,469	15,576,932
August 26	12,413,924	776,030	3,846,005	17,035,959
1804 February 25	12,054,943	848,894	4,673,515	17,577,352
August 25	11,766,628	743,841	4,813,525	17,323,994
1805 February 26	11,403,290	1,029,580	4,801,596	17,234,466
August 26	11,182,188	718,510	4,395,480	16,296,178
1806 February 25	11,994,350	725,736	4,428,360	17,148,446
August 26	14,141,510	702,425	4,228,958	19,072,893
1807 February 26	12,274,629	724,485	4,206,230	27,205,344
August 26	15,077,013	725,262	4,231,837	20,034,112
1808 February 26	13,746,598	742,671	4,103,785	18,593,054
August 26	12,440,930	795,102	4,129,234	17,365,266
1809 February 25	12,730,999	944,727	4,338,951	18,014,677
August 26	13,255,599	880,104	5,221,538	19,357,241
1810 February 26	13,650,592	907,620	5,871,069	20,429,281
August 25	16,078,390	1,145,832	7,221,953	24,446,175
1811 February 26	15,110,688	1,133,419	7,140,726	23,384,833
August 26	15,203,611	1,016,303	7,573,201	23,723,115
1812 February 26	14,523,049	1,059,854	7,415,294	22,998,197
August 26	14,873,705	987,880	7,621,525	23,482,910
1813 February 26	14,567,267	1,034,882	7,705,322	23,307,471
August 26	14,975,479	1,015,616	8,033,774	24,024,869
1814 February 26	15,632,250	1,091,242	8,371,923	25,095,415
August 26	18,066,180	1,246,479	9,667,217	28,979,876
1815 February 25	16,394,359	1,184,459	9,094,552	26,673,370
August 26	16,332,275	1,115,079	9,576,695	27,024,049

NO. V. CONTINUED.

	Notes of £5 and upwards.	Bank Post Bills.	Bank Notes under £5.	TOTAL.
1816 February 26	15,307,228	1,336,467	9,036,374	25,680,069
August 26	16,686,087	1,286,429	9,103,338	27,075,854
1817 February 26	17,538,656	1,376,416	8,143,506	27,058,578
August 26	20,388,502	1,712,807	7,998,599	30,099,908
1818 February 26	19,077,951	1,838,600	7,362,492	28,279,043
August 26	17,465,628	1,627,427	7,509,782	26,602,837
1819 February 26	16,307,000	1,622,330	7,317,360	25,246,690
August 26	16,972,140	1,468,920	7,216,530	25,657,590
1820 February 26	15,402,830	1,421,160	6,745,160	23,569,150
August 26	16,047,390	1,633,730	6,772,260	24,453,380
1821 February 26	14,372,840	1,615,600	6,483,010	22,471,450
August 26	16,095,020	1,634,260	2,598,460	20,327,740
1822 February 26	15,178,490	1,609,620	1,384,360	18,172,470
August 26	15,295,090	1,610,600	862,650	17,768,340
1823 February 26	15,751,120	1,742,190	683,160	18,176,470
August 26	17,392,260	1,763,650	550,010	19,705,920
1824 February 26	17,244,940	2,198,260	486,660	19,929,800
August 26	18,409,230	2,122,760	443,970	20,975,960
1825 February 26	18,308,990	2,334,260	416,880	21,060,130
August 26	17,091,120	2,061,010	396,670	19,548,800
1826 February 26	21,100,400	2,487,080	1,367,560	24,955,040
August 26	18,172,160	2,040,400	1,175,450	21,388,010
1827 February 26	18,787,330	2,052,310	668,910	21,508,550
August 26	19,253,890	2,270,110	483,060	22,007,060
1828 February 26	19,428,010	2,329,880	416,890	22,174,780
August 26	19,016,980	2,417,440	382,860	21,817,280
1829 February 26	17,402,470	2,444,660	357,170	20,204,300
August 26	17,164,940	2,030,280	334,190	19,529,410
1830 February 26	17,862,990	2,284,520	320,550	20,468,060

Bank of England,
   11th March, 1830.

WM. SMEE,
Dep. Acct.

POSTSCRIPT.

Our strictures on the Bank of England have been thought a little too severe. It is hardly necessary to remark that we have spoken of the Directors in their corporate, not in their individual capacities. The Bank has frequently been controlled by circumstances which it had little share in producing, and the ultimate consequences of which, actual experience could alone demonstrate. The Directors are often placed in an awkward dilemma, in which their duty to the proprietors, whose servants they are, prescribes one thing, and the interest of the public another; it is not surprising, then, if it sometimes happen that the common weal suffers in order that the dividends may be augmented. What we are now stating applies with equal propriety to the East-India Company. We should just as soon think of charging the present Directors of either association with the delinquencies of their predecessors, as of laying on William IV. the crimes of Richard III. or Henry VIII. The able men mostly chosen for the management of both companies, and the successful manner in which their affairs have been conducted for the benefit of their respective constituencies, often appears to us a strong argument in favour of that principle of representation for which the nation is now contending.

MUNICIPAL CORPORATIONS,

COMPANIES, GUILDS, AND FRATERNITIES.

———

The boroughs, the church, and corporations, have long formed the feet of clay, on which the Tory Oligarchy has been borne up. It has had other supports in judicial abuses and commercial monopolies, but these have been the main pillars of its strength. Now, however, that Gatton and Old Sarum are on the eve of being divested of their mysterious influence, it is not improbable that the kindred nuisance of municipal bodies, of town-councils, guilds, fraternities, and brotherhoods will be abated, either by intire abolition, or thorough reform in their institutions. They have had their day and their use: at present they are only shadows of former power—historical landmarks which, like the remains of a Roman encampment or baronial residence, serve to indicate an age, that with its customs, manners, and establishments is fast descending into " the tomb of the Capulets."

The public mind, however, is not likely to be a precipitate innovator either on corporate or other institutions consecrated by " hoar antiquity." In addition to the strength they derive from early associations, they are fortified by the difficulty of concentrating general attention on a specific object. More than half a century was consumed in discussion and exposition to prepare the people for the removal of the disabilities of the Catholics, and upwards of two centuries in rousing such an united expression of feeling as is essential to the attainment of Parliamentary Reform. The stream of popular opinion is of immense volume, requiring energetic and long-continued efforts, to direct it into new and more fertilizing channels.

Decayed boroughs and corporations, where they are not identical, may be justly deemed of twin origin, and resemble each other in their chief characteristics. Formerly the commonalty of bodies corporate, in the same manner as the parliamentary electors of a borough, included the whole of the free inhabitants, who represented the property, intelligence, and population within their jurisdictions. But this municipal concentration of wealth and power has ceased to subsist; corporations no longer embody the opulence, numbers, or respectability of the cities and towns in which they are placed ; they have degenerated into mere juntos, having no more community with the people than the voters of Malmsbury or Calne with the general mass of the inhabitants. Such is the state of the corporations of London, Dublin, Edinburgh, Bristol, Bath, Liverpool, and Leeds; they consist of little knots of persons, not uniformly of the first class either for wealth or intelligence, who have succeeded to their corporate immunities by right of paternity, conviviality, congeniality of politics or religion, or some other claim very different from that of popular suffrage. So constituted, they form petty oligarchies in the midst of their respective communities, with which they wage a constant war of oppression and annoyance, and to whose welfare they are often as much opposed as the great parent oligarchy of the Boroughmongers has long been to that of the nation.

The late elections offer a striking example of the hostile interests which separate corporations from their fellow citizens. In all the places mentioned above, the municipal bodies made the most strenuous efforts to return anti-reform candidates. It was the same at Oxford and Cambridge, the clerical corporations of the Universities not yielding to their lay-brethren in the expression of aversion to " the BILL."

Now, whence does this arise ? How does it happen that the privileges of the chartered bodies are always felt to be at variance with the general weal, and that corporators and boroughmongers are always found in close alliance ? A common danger ordinarily unites men in a common defence, and this, we apprehend, is the cause of the coalition. Both parties are sensible of their social insignificance ; both are conscious of having long monopolized the rights of others ; and both feel that reform would be destructive of their exclusive interests and pretensions. Hence their confederacies on all occasions. Abuse must ever depend upon abuse for support. The compact is a diabolical one,—it is the same which sometimes bands together the outcasts of society,—a general consciousness of turpitude, with a consciousness of the necessity of fraternizing for common safety.

It is not merely as the uniform opponents of civil and religious liberty, nor as the petty local oppressors and prosecutors within their precincts, nor as the vexatious enemies of the freedom of industry, that corporations are to be charged as arch-delinquents to society. They are justly obnoxious to imputations of a darker complexion. It is well known that corporate bodies are the principal trustees of charity estates all over the kingdom; they are, also, the trustees of town and church-lands, of loan-monies and of immense funds bequeathed for the purposes of education, and for the clothing and maintenance of the orphan, the aged, and infirm. It is in these capacities their chief malversations consist, in the jobbing, peculation, and wasteful administration of the vast funds entrusted to them for pious and charitable uses. But before adverting to this part of the subject and to the general abuses of corporate establishments, it will be convenient to premise a few observations on the origin of municipal institutions, and also of those subordinate associations denominated guilds and fraternities.

ORIGIN OF CORPORATIONS, GUILDS, AND FRATERNITIES.

According to Dr. Smith, the origin of municipal corporations was very little posterior to that of cities and towns. After the fall of the Roman empire the proprietors of land generally lived in fortified castles on their own estates, while the towns were chiefly inhabited by tradesmen and mechanics, who appear to have been of servile or nearly of servile condition. This is apparent from the tenor of many ancient charters that concede to townspeople the *right to give away their daughters in marriage*, and bequeath their property to their children without consent of their lord, and which could hardly have been deemed immunities to any class of people had they been previously raised above the condition of bondsmen or villains. Their occupations were not more elevated than their social state, and consisted in travelling with their goods from place to place, and fair to fair, like hawkers and pedlers of the present times. In these peregrinations, they were subject to various exactions by the lords of the manors, through which they passed under the denomination of passage, pontage, lastage, and stallage. Sometimes the king, sometimes a great lord who had, it seems, upon certain occasions authority to do this, would grant to particular traders, especially those living on their own demesnes, a general exemption from taxes. Such traders, though in other respects of base condition, were upon this account denominated free-traders. They in return usually paid to their protector a sort of annual poll-tax; for, in those times of barbarous violence, protection was never afforded without compensation.

Under the favouring auspices of the monarch, the townspeople, by successive encroachments, emancipated themselves from the yoke of personal servitude to the barons. They also commuted the various imposts to which they were liable for a fixed tribute or rent, for the due payment of which the burghers were jointly and severally responsible. Nor was this all. They were generally, at the same time, erected into a commonalty or corporation, with the privilege of having magistrates or town-council, of making by-laws for their own government, of building walls for their own defence, and of reducing all their inhabitants under a sort of conservative discipline, by obliging them to watch and ward. These immunities had become essential to their new condition of freedom; for having cast off the yoke of former masters, they were left to provide for their own internal order and security.

It would be neither compatible with our limits, nor is it essential to our purpose, to continue at greater length the history of corporations. Those who are desirous of more detailed information, may consult Madox's " *Firma Burgi*," and Brady's " Treatise of Cities and Boroughs." There can we apprehend be little doubt of the republican character of their first institution ; every free burgess being a member of the corporation, and participating either directly or by representation in municipal government. They also shared in the general government of the country, by the privilege conceded to them in the thirteenth century of sending citizens and burgesses to parliament. The successive steps by which their immunities were principally curtailed were, 1. The Mortmain Acts, which interdicted the bequest of property, both to lay and ecclesiastical corporations, for charitable uses ; 2. The restriction of monopolies in the sale of manufactures and commodities—which had become extremely oppressive to the rural population, and enabled the burgesses to indemnify themselves for the exactions they had suffered in a preceding age under the sway of the feudal proprietary; 3. and lastly, was the introduction of the statute of *Quo Warranto* in the reign of Edward the First, which compelled corporations to produce the charter or title under which they exercised their jurisdiction. The popular constitution of corporate bodies was ultimately destroyed through the agency of this law. Its professed object was to restrain the undue assumptions and remedy the disorders and irregularities in the exercise of municipal privileges ; but it was perverted into a fruitful source of revenue by succeeding monarchs, especially by Charles II., who by compelling the surrender of all the charters in the kingdom and granting for money new powers to *select bodies* in corporations, introduced or confirmed all these usurpations which are still maintained against the common rights of the people.

This was not the only result ; for, by a manœuvre of the Collective Wisdom of the day, the chief part of the inhabitants of cities and towns were deprived of their *political*, as well as municipal franchises. A book was written, by Dr. Brady, to prove that the word commonalty in a charter meant corporation, or the " *governing part* " of the people ; and, in pursuance of this new doctrine, the committees of the House of Commons, in the course of about twenty years, deprived the body of the people of a great number of boroughs of their elective rights, and confined the franchise to a small corporation, consisting generally of less than twenty-four persons. One part of the injustice is likely to be remedied by the Reform Bill, which will deprive close and self-elected juntos of the power they have long exercised with great profit to themselves, of making members of parliament, and restore to the inhabitants generally their ancient privilege of choosing representatives.

Let us next advert to the origin of the *Guilds, Companies,* or *Fraternities,* which still exist in the principal cities and towns, especially in London, Bristol, Preston, and Newcastle; and which form a curious and interesting branch of our domestic history. These societies, or mysteries, are of very ancient institution, and may be traced with certainty to a period anterior to the Conquest. In the British Museum are preserved several Saxon deeds which Dr. Hickes has transcribed into his *Thesaurus,* exhibiting the ordinances of two Saxon guilds. From these ancient documents, it would appear, that guilds were originally established by the mutual agreement of friends and fellow-workmen, and had no further object than the relief of the brethren in times of distress, and perhaps, the protection of the associated members against the lawless attacks of powerful neighbours. Certain pious offices, however, were the never-failing concomitants of these institutions, and they were mostly dedicated to some patron saint. After the Conquest, they were established for the express promotion of religion, charity, or trade, and were supported either by specific contributions from the members in money or goods, or by lands assigned to them by the founder.* In order to erect a corporation, no other authority in ancient times was requisite in many parts of Europe, but that of the town corporate in which it was to be established. In England, indeed, a charter from the king was likewise necessary. But this prerogative of the crown seems to have been reserved, rather for extorting money from the subject than for the protection of the common liberty against such exclusive companies. Upon paying a fine to the king the charter seems generally to have been readily granted; and when any particular class of artificers or traders thought proper to act as a corporation without a charter, such *adulterine* guilds as they were called, were not always disfranchised on that account, but obliged to fine annually to the king for permission to exercise their usurped privileges.† The immediate inspection of all corporations, and of the by-laws which they might think proper to enact for their own government, belonged to the town-corporate in which they were established; and whatever discipline was exercised over them proceeded commonly not from the king, but from the parent corporation of which these subordinate ones were only parts or members.

The rules of several of the ancient fraternities are preserved, and they obviously include the same objects of mutual assurance against the misfortunes of life which now form the basis of the institutions of Friendly Societies. Sir F. Eden, indeed, appears strongly inclined to trace the origin of benefit clubs to the guild foundations. The following ordinances of St. Catharine's guild at Coventry, which was founded in the reign of Edward III affords strong confirmation of this conjecture, and are well deserving the attention of the antiquarian. They are cited at length by Dugdale, who speaks of them as very memorable, and " manifesting the decent government, ceremony, devotion, charity, and amity of those times."

" If a member suffer from fire, water, robbery, or other calamity, the guild is to lend him a sum of money without interest.

" If sick or infirm through old age, he is to be supported by his guild, according to his condition.

" No one notorious for felony, homicide, lechery, gaming, sorcery, or heresy is to be admitted.

" If a member fall into bad courses, he is first to be admonished, and if found to be incorrigible, he is to be expelled.

" Those who die poor and cannot afford themselves burial, are to be buried at the charge of the guild."

The chaplain is not to frequent common taverns. Mass was said, every day, and there were four solemnities or feast days every year.

---

* Blomefield's History of Norfolk, vol. iii. p. 494.
† Madox *Firma Burgi,* p. 26.

The guilds were encouraged by persons of rank. From the North-umberland Household Book, we learn that the Earl and Countess of Northumberland and their eldest son were members of St. Christopher's Guild, at York ; and paid annually each 6s. 8d. They each received yearly from the guild two yards of cloth ; whether this was an article usually allowed to the members of such societies, or whether it was merely a compliment to a person of distinction cannot be ascertained.

The ancient associations, whether distinguished by the name of Guild, Fraternity, Mystery, Company, or Brotherhood, seem to have been no less addicted to feasting and conviviality than their descendants of Merchant Tailors' or Drapers' Hall. They generally assembled once a year, for the purpose of acting some interlude or pageant. There is a curious description in the *Liber Niger* of the anniversary feast of the guild of the Holy Cross at Abingdon ; from which Blomefield probably took the following account which he has given of that festival. He says " the fraternity held their feast yearly on the third of May, the invention of the Holy Cross ; and then they used to have twelve priests to sing a *dirige*, for which they had given them four pence a-piece ; they had also twelve minstrels, who had 2s. 3d. besides their dyet and horse-meat.   At one of these feasts, (A.D. 1445,) they had 6 calves valued at 2s. 2d. a-piece ; 16 lambs, 12d. a-piece ; 80 capons, 3d. a-piece ; 80 geese, 2d. a-piece ; 800 eggs, which cost 5d. the hundred ; and many marrow bones, creame and floure ; besides, what theyre servants and others brought in : and pageants, plays, and May-games, to captivate the senses of the zealous beholders." Nor were the Guild-halls, of which vestiges may be found in many of our most insignificant villages, exclusively appropriated to the festivities celebrated at the expense and under the patronage of the companies. As most of these common-halls were well provided with household utensils, especially those requisite for culinary purposes, it was not uncommon for the inha-bitants of a village, upon weddings and christenings, to hold their feast at the Guildhall.* Sometimes, however, the smaller parochial guilds were so poor, that they could not afford to have a mustering place, but met at the members' houses. In general they were in a better condition and possessed or hired a hall near the church, which, Sir John Cullum remarks, was " convenient for them, as their business was to pray as well as eat."

However, we have not yet adverted to the main objects for which the fraternities were instituted, and which were neither convivial, pious, nor charitable ; they were meant for the advancement of trade, and the per-fection of the mechanical arts. It was for these purposes the numerous companies in the city of London were first incorporated ; exclusive privileges being granted to them, that they might perfect themselves in their respective mysteries or occupations, so that the public might be guarded against fraud and adulteration, and not suffer either from the knavery or unskilfulness of traders and workmen. In the early stages

---

* Sir Frederick Eden's History of the Poor, p. 598.

of industry and commerce such a policy might be defensible. It tends, by a recognized division of labour, to improve useful vocations ; and, moreover, as the members of these associations were also united on the principles of a Friendly Society, that circumstance gave them a claim to the protection of authority. But the immunities conceded to them ought to have been limited to a term of years, and not made perpetual ; they ought to have been terminal, and granted on the same principle as the rights of a patentee, or of an author of a literary production. Without this precaution the incorporated companies were sure to degenerate into so many combinations against the public ; whose interests and policy would be to preserve to themselves an exclusive market, to guard against competition from superior and cheaper workmen, and to retail their own industry and commodities at monopoly prices. These results were, in fact, speedily experienced, and we find the trade societies at a very early period notorious for the fraud and extortion they practised on the body of the community. For instance, we read that in the year 1285 Edward I. took away the charter of the city of London, and dismissed the mayor from office for taking bribes of the bakers to permit them to make their bread *short of weight ;* but, it is added, the city soon after recovered it, by making concessions and presenting the king with a *purse of money.* It is not an easy task to maintain individuals at all times in a course of honesty, but it is far more difficult when they are confederated. The example just cited was anciently a frequent mode of replenishing the royal treasury ; the charters were seized under the pretext of some delinquency, and then returned after a pecuniary mulct ; the offenders being allowed to resume their iniquitous career.

Although the civil immunities of the guilds are nearly worn out, we sometimes meet with attempts to annoy the public by re-asserting them, both in the country and the metropolis. An effort of this kind was made some years since by the Merchant Tailors of Bristol, which terminated in the ruin of their society. The history of the Company is singular, and, as it will illustrate our subject and exemplify the present state of many similar fraternities in the kingdom, we shall shortly advert to it.

The company of Merchant Tailors derived its origin from a charter of Richard II., dated 16th October, 1399. It was granted to two burgesses of Bristol, in consideration of their having founded a chapel to celebrate divine service for the good of the king and the brotherhood. The fraternity was incorporated, with power to choose a master from their number, and to purchase lands and tenements for the maintenance of the society's chapel. In the hall of the company are preserved the various deeds by which its possessions have been conveyed down from the original trust to the present feoffees. The last conveyance of the buildings, estates, and other property was in 1802, and was executed, among others, to Mr. Isaac Amos, who is the only surviving member. This gentleman, who is a resident housekeeper in Bristol, gives the following reasons for the condition into which the society has fallen.

About forty-five years ago the association, which was then composed of a great number of members, insisted that every person carrying on the trade of a tailor in Bristol was under a legal obligation to become a freeman of the company, for which the fee of 40s. was payable by such as were qualified by apprenticeship or birth, and £30 by others who purchased their freedom. This claim was resisted, and a suit instituted by the company to try the question, which was determined against them. From that time it has ceased to be an object to become a member of the company, which has accordingly received no accession to its number, and Mr. Amos has outlived all the old members.

The company having lost all claim to fees, its sole dependence has been the rents and premiums accruing from estates. These are considerable, and situate in several parishes of Bristol; they have been demised on leases of 99 years, with heavy premiums, and the reserved rents amount only to £55 per annum, An almshouse has been established for the reception of the decayed members, and is supported out of the funds of the society. The hall, formerly the scene of the festive celebrations of the worshipful fraternity, has been converted into a source of profit, by being let out for the use of any ephemeral pageant—lectures on astronomy—the French players—or a sparring exhibition; and the spacious kitchens are hired to dress dinners for the ancient lodge of Freemasons, the society of Odd Fellows, or some other of the whimsical associations which are found among the Bristolians. The last public act of the society was to let a piece of ground in Horsefair, for which a rent of 10s. was reserved, and a premium of £200 received; what became of the premium cannot be ascertained, as the practice has been to *destroy the accounts* immediately after being audited. Indeed, it is a curious incident in the latter days of the company, that Messrs. Palmer and Amos were for some time the only surviving members, and that until the death of Mr. Palmer, they were alternately master and treasurer, and each, in his capacity of master, audited the treasurer's accounts!

We have thus shortly adverted to the history and present state of one of the ancient guilds, and some curious legal questions here present themselves, namely, in what capacity does the society now exist, and to whom do its possessions belong? Whether the Merchant Tailors' Company has existed at all as a corporation since the dissolution of such religious fraternities under 39th Henry VIII. may, perhaps, be a subject of doubt, as there appears neither a re-grant nor recognition on the part of the Crown to set up the civil part of the establishment in its corporate capacity. If the company is to be considered as a corporation, it is apprehended that, as a corporation *aggregate*, it must have become dissolved by the death of all its members but ONE; and, in such case, as the use was limited so as to become vested in the corporation, an escheat of its property may be considered to have taken place. If it is not to be considered as a corporation, but a mere self-constituted community of individuals, it seems doubtful whether the legal estate was carried out of the feoffees, and whether the trust has not entirely failed and become extinguished by the non-existence of the object for which it was created, namely, the Company of Tailors; and hence arises the difficulty in whom the title to the property, hitherto regarded as belonging to the company, has legally vested. These points can only be resolved by a competent tribunal, and we doubt not their decision would involve the existence of many similar associations in the kingdom.

MANAGEMENT AND REVENUES OF THE CITY COMPANIES.

In the city of London are upwards of seventy companies of an origin and institution analogous to the Merchant Tailors of Bristol. The several professions and trades in the city are incorporated into distinct fraternities, consisting mostly of a livery and freemen, governed by a master, wardens, and court of assistants, which last appears an encroachment on the rights of the freemen: indeed, courts appear to have been unknown prior to the accession of the Scottish dynasty, when they were obtained probably through corruption or intrigue. Persons exercising any trade in the city, not free of one of the companies, are liable to penalties. The livery are chosen from the freemen, and enjoy important privileges in the election of members of parliament and the principal city officers. Refusing to serve on the livery subjects to a penalty, and a fine is payable by each person taking up his livery, varying from £3 to £200.

The power of the incorporated trades to inflict penalties for not being of their fraternity is, occasionally, productive of hardships, for which it is impossible to discover any pretext of utility. Not long since a poor old Irishman was getting a scanty living in the city by shaving and hair-cutting, but not being a freeman, for the profits of his trade were inadequate to the purchase of that qualification, he was proceeded against by the ancient Corporation of Barbers. The fine was inflicted; and the worshipful Company actually took their unfortunate brother of the soap-suds in execution, and kept him in prison about four months. How much longer he would have been an inmate of the " stone jug," as the gaol is called, cannot be conjectured, had not Mr. Barrett made several applications to the clerk of the company, and procured his liberation. Another instance is worth mentioning, but in doing so we do not mean to cast any imputation upon the company exercising the power of exclusion, which they undoubtedly possess. A poulterer was sued in the Mayor's Court for having a stand in Leadenhall-market—not because he was not a freeman of London, but because he was not a freeman of the Poulterers' company—and the customary penalties were ordered to be paid. Whitecross-street prison became the refuge of the unsanctioned poulterer, who still remains locked up for the infraction of the company's by-laws.

Such arbitrary interferences with the freedom of industry are wholly indefensible at this period; and we are glad to learn that Sir James Scarlett intends to bring before the Legislature the subject of corporation abuses. Undoubtedly the companies were originally instituted for the double purpose of protecting the community against fraud, and their respective mysteries from deterioration; with the exception, however, of the Apothecaries and Goldsmiths these duties have ceased to be exercised. Indeed, as the companies are now constituted, it is impossible such functions could be discharged; in many of them not a single member is of that trade the name of the company imports, which, we believe, is the case of the Merchant Tailors' and Mercers', most of whom are merchants of the first class, bankers, and insurance-brokers. Like ancient bodies generally the duties have been suffered to expire, while the appropriation of the revenues, salaries, and fees has been carefully preserved, or enormously augmented.

The revenues of the city companies are very great, and principally arise from the management of charitable trusts. The aggregate incomes of the twelve principal companies is supposed to amount to £500,000 per annum. Out of these revenues the splendid halls of the fraternities have been erected, sumptuous entertainments given, and the enormous emoluments of their clerks, amounting in some instances to £3,000 or £4,000 a-year, paid. As trustees they have the letting of a large portion of the houses, offices, wharfs, and warehouses in the metropolis; in the country they have numerous manors and estates, messuages, tenements, church livings, and impropriate tithes, and vast sums vested in the public funds. The masters, wardens, and assistants are the virtual disposers of this property; they have the letting of the lands and tenements; they contract for repairs, alterations, and improvements; they present to the livings and receive the tithes and dividends. They also select the objects of their charities; and interpret the will, deed, or letter patent by which they were created. The commonalty of the Companies have no share in these functions; the power is engrossed by the parties mentioned, who elect themselves, forming a secret and perpetual conclave, into which no one is admitted, unless connected by ties of friendship or consanguinity.

It is the arbitrary exercise of these unauthorized powers that has tended to generate the hostile spirit which now subsists between the governing juntos and the liveries of several of the companies. Some intelligent and spirited gentlemen of one of the principal companies, the Merchant Tailors', have, in fact, hoisted the standard of rebellion against their oppressors, and are fully intent, either by legal or more effective means, of obtaining a restitution of usurped rights. From what we know of the chartered privileges of some of the companies we are well convinced of the validity of the claims of the non-contents, and we heartily wish them success in their laudable exertions. It would, indeed, be a lasting reproach to the general body of the livery of London, and not at all in accordance with the reputation they bear for intelligence and independence, if, while the great Oligarchy of the state is about being reformed, they suffered the little miniature types among themselves to continue, without undergoing a similar process of regeneration. But it is not merely the recovery of just rights, they have objects of substantial utility to attain. The trust-revenues of the companies are enormous ; for want of due responsibility in the administrative committees they are, for the most part, lavishly and improvidentially squandered ; in lieu of being judiciously appropriated to the objects for which they were charitably bequeathed, they are expended in personal indulgence, in political intrigue, in conciliating the favour of strangers, and in providing lucrative appointments for relatives and dependents. The courts too ought to be opened, and self-elected cabals no longer have the power of passing oppressive by-laws, of declaring new forms of eligibility, of arbitrarily accepting or rejecting candidates for their livery, or imposing upon them new and exorbitant fines.

Constituted as these bodies are, no opportunity is afforded to detect or punish their delinquencies. They form, in short, a great blot in our social economy, which, by some oversight, has escaped those gradual reforms that have been partially, at least, introduced into other departments of public administration. Of the power and constitution of the several branches of the general government, and of the way in which the functions of each is administered, ample information, for the most part, is laid before the public ; but of the proceedings of corporations no one knows any thing. There is no publicity—no control—nor responsibility any where. All that is known of them is that they have a perpetual generation among themslves—that they have many good things in their gift, which they either appropriate to their own use, or bestow on those with whom they are intimately connected—that they have much feasting and banquetting at other people's cost, and that they maintain a reserved and pompous demeanour towards those from whom they originally derived their power, and for whose benefit they were created.

The members of the Merchant Tailors' Company, to whom allusion has been made, have endeavoured, through the medium of the press, and by instituting proceedings in a court of law, to reform the abuses of their Company, and to stimulate the members of the other incorporated trades to corresponding exertions. From a statement published by these gentlemen in *The Free Inquirer* it appears that the annual revenues of the twelve principal companies of the city of London exceeds *five hundred thousand pounds ;* one hundred thousand of which is expended in luxurious entertainments, by a select class, called councillors or assistants; and near forty thousand pounds is divided yearly by the Twelve Legal Pillars, who condescend to *stand* for and act as clerks, to the no small annoyance of those who make inquiry into their own corporate property.

In addition to the twelve worshipful brotherhoods, as they are designated, there are sixty minor companies—the Stationers, Apothecaries, Dyers, Armourers, Sadlers, Cordwainers, &c. whose united incomes yield another half million; the disbursement of which no one hears of, no printed account has ever been known to be circulated, and no answer is ever made to any but the privileged class; as this revenue cannot be allowed much longer to remain in such profound secrecy, and in such

corrupt hands, Mr. Franks has suggested that it be formed into a general fund for the education of the youth of both sexes, and the support of
the poor of the city.

The chief facts to be borne in mind relative to the city companies
are the following :—

1.—That the whole of the companies, with the exception of the Goldsmiths, Stationers, and Apothecaries, have ceased to exercise any
control over the trades they bear the title of, or to which they
may be considered allied.

2.—That nearly the entire site of the city of London belongs to these
powerful and disgracefully-conducted monopolies.

3.—That most of the property has been jobbed or under-let to the private friends of the respective courts.

4.—That the courts of the companies are mostly controlled by stock-
jobbers, parsons, and lawyers.

5.—That the whole of the bequests, in lands, houses, and money, left in
the fourteenth, fifteenth, and sixteenth centuries, has increased
from fifty fold to a hundred fold.

6.—That the population of all the parishes within the jurisdiction of the
city of London amounts only to 123,198.

7.—That the annual revenues of the City Companies exceed £1,000,000.

Of these Companies, there is scarcely one in the immunities of
which the liveries at large are allowed fairly to participate, and in which
the election of the master, warden, and courts are made conformably
with the constitutional laws and charters. They are mostly managed by
cabals, consisting of two or three families and their favourites, who have
succeeded to the possessions and privileges of their societies, with a regular, and, apparently, as indefeasible a claim as any legitimate despot
succeeds to his sovereignty. To these authorities the liveries have
hitherto bowed, with the patience of serfs, and submitted not only to be
deprived of the more substantial enjoyments of their respective corporations, but also to be disseized of their elective franchises, in the
appointment of masters, wardens, assistants, and committees.

The chief reason which can be alleged for this supineness, is the
ignorance in which the liverymen have been kept of the rights and
powers they legally possess. With one or two exceptions, the charters
of the companies have *never been published*, but, for reasons too obvious to mention, have remained under an impenetrable veil, either
among the records in the Tower of London, or the strong boxes of the
several courts of assistants, whose uncourteous demeanor, together with
that of their clerks and underlings, to members seeking information, is
only equalled by the patient endurance of the latter, in submitting for so
long a period to their usurped authority. The advantages that would
result to the liverymen and freemen by the restitution of their ancient
rights, those rights of superintending their fiscal administration, and of
choosing their officers and courts, (if the last be a legal part of their
institution) are both numerous and important.

In the first place, the governors would be made responsible to the governed, and a few individuals no longer be allowed to pervert the revenues and influence of the societies to their own private purposes of favouritism, intrigue, and aggrandizement.

Secondly, and agreeably to their original institution, every member would be equally and alike a brother of the fraternity, eligible to elect and be elected to all places of trust, patronage, and emolument.

Thirdly, exclusive and disqualifying by-laws, intended to deprive the general body of the liverymen of their rights, could not be enacted; neither could arbitrary and oppressive fees on apprenticeships, freedoms, and liveries, be enforced: these unjustifiable extortions have been often screwed up and levied, merely to minister to a lavish expenditure in objects wholly foreign to the interests of the fraternities.

Finally, an efficient and watchful control would be established over the management of the numerous charitable trusts, and ample revenues of the companies.

The last would be one of the most important advantages resulting from the re-establishment of the general rights of the fraternities. The practice of *self-auditing* and *self-election* has long precluded the members of the companies from a knowledge of their own affairs; and it is only by the recent inquiries of the Charity Commissioners, that authentic information has been obtained of the magnitude of their revenues, patronage, and possessions. From these inquiries it appears that nearly the whole of the land and houses in London has been left in trust of the City Companies, for charitable uses; that they also possess, in the same capacity of trustees, in the country, numerous manors, estates, messuages, church livings, and tithes of parishes; that the revenues arising from this property amount, in several instances, to £20,000 or £30,000 per annum, and that not one-twentieth part of this income is expended on the poor, or other objects for which it was benevolently bequeathed. It is seldom the courts increase the amount of their eleemosynary disbursements; notwithstanding the vast augmentation of value in the trust-property, they neither multiply the objects of their charities, nor increase the allowances originally fixed by the donors, in total ignorance of the future produce of their bequests. The objects on which the surplus revenues are principally expended, consist of the expenses of committees, law-agency, and surveyors' charges; in pretended repairs and improvements; in ostentatious buildings; in luxurious feasting for the parties and their friends; and in extravagant pensions and gratuities to favourite servants and dependents. For these purposes the revenues are never too much—generally too little,—and they are compelled to resort to the monstrous expedient of taxing their disfranchised brethren, to supply the deficiency.

CORPORATIONS OF CITIES AND TOWNS.

A reform of municipal institutions is an undertaking only second in importance to that of the general government. The power of the barons against which corporations were directed, has yielded to that of the state, and the remnants of these confederacies, by the assertion of ancient immunities, tend to disturb the peace and order of the realm. They are too insulated amidst the general wealth and population to strengthen the executive power. They represent no great social interest; the real aristocracy of cities and towns keeps aloof from them, either from disgust at their petty cabals, or contempt for their paltry duties. Instead of being the enlightened governors within their respective limits, they are only oppressors; instead of being faithful trustees, they are notorious plunderers of the widow and orphan; instead of being the centres of local government, of police and judicial administration, they are the sources of disorder, tumult, and prosecution. Wherever we find a corporation, we may generally rely on finding a town ill-governed—the inhabitants divided into rancorous parties—the prisons dilapidated and without discipline—the quarter and petty sessions of the peace ill-conducted—and every office of dignity or authority, from the worshipful recorder to the turnkey, filled up, not from the fitness of the individuals selected, but from personal connexion or influence. All these evils have mostly their origin in one source—the absence of popular control: with hardly an exception the members of all corporations are self-elected; hence their interests are partial, not public; hence every office is made a job of, every magisterial function, whether the granting of a license or the adjudication of an assault, is made a favour or an offence.

That these prefatory criminations have some foundation, we shall endeavour to show by briefly glancing at the constitution and management of some of the principal corporations. Our notice will necessarily be very brief, and not at all proportioned to the magnitude of the subject; but perhaps we shall be able, aided by our previous representations, to give a general idea of the existing state of municipal institutions, which may lead to more perfect and comprehensive inquiries. We shall commence with the corporation of the city of London, not only because it is under our more immediate observance, but because it is the first in rank, antiquity, and importance.

The corporation of London, we believe, is more popular in its constitution than any other in the empire. It is formed, as is well known, on the model of that of the state, consisting of three orders; but it is superior to the state, in the absence of those gross incongruities in its constituent bodies which impair the excellence of parliamentary representation. We may also observe respecting the city corporation, that it is more *pure* and *perfect* in its practical administration than any other municipal body of the kingdom. We are well aware what we are now stating; we make the assertion with a full knowledge of city jobbing—of the London Bridge committee—of the Gresham Lectures—of Mansion House dinners—and of the well known fact that from £4,000 to £5,000 per annum is expended by the committees of the Common Council alone; still we affirm that in no other corporation, nor in the general government, nor in the Colonies, is so much *work* performed at so small a cost. The duties of the corporation are very great, not only in matters relative to the magistracy, police, and local improvements of the city, but also in those which relate to the commerce, navigation, and shipping of the port of London ; and in the due discharge of many of which the kingdom at large, as well as the metropolis, is deeply interested.   That these functions should be all executed without expense, without remuneration direct or indirect, is what no reasonable person can expect.

Notwithstanding these excellences, the metropolitan corporation is full of anomalies, or, if the reader pleases, defects.   We cannot stop to enumerate all these, nor to comment upon them, but we will mention the two principal.

First, as regards the local boundary or civil jurisdiction of the corporation.   This comprehends only the nucleus or inner circle of this vast metropolis; all the *living* portion, the great mass of the opulence, respectability, and population of the capital, is placed without the curtilage of corporate authority, which includes within its legislative cognizance little more than an assemblage of shops, counting-houses, offices, wharfs and warehouses.   The evils that result from this cause, whether as respects the conflicting powers of the county and city magistrate, the police, or the composition of the elective bodies of the city, are too well known to require description.

The *second* great anomaly we shall notice, is that which respects the qualification of the city constituency.   As this is now regulated by the statute of the 11th George I. neither *residence* nor householdership confers the right of suffrage either for a member of the corporation or of the House of Commons.   Freemen and liverymen constitute the only two classes of electors, the former of the aldermen and common council ; the latter of members of parliament, lord-mayor, and chief city officers. Now it certainly appears indefensible that a householder should not share equally in the local government with the freemen and liverymen. The rights of both freemen and liverymen may be obtained without any direct or permanent interest in the weal of the city.   Freedoms are acquired by purchase or gift, as well as by birth or apprenticeship.   The rights of the livery or *badgemen* depend on still less valid qualifications ; they are conferred or not at the pleasure of the courts of assistants ; or the franchises of the livery may be acquired by purchasing a certain dress, in some companies at an exorbitant price, and in others no money will purchase it, unless the party be known to have imbibed a certain political or religious faith. *

If there be injustice in withholding elective rights from householders, the civic disfranchisement of resident freemen is still less defensible. Several of the livery companies were only made such within the last century.   None of the companies form a part of the corporation ;† nor is it necessary the liverymen should be resident in the city ; yet in them is exclusively vested the power of choosing the city officers and the members of parliament.   Such an anomaly exists in no other city

---

* Evidence in support of the Franchise of Resident Freemen, p. 26.
† Newell's Evidence, &c. p. 10.

in England. Of the twenty-four cities represented in parliament, there is not one, with the exception of London, where the freemen are disqualified by statute from choosing their representatives.

The utility of the existence of many civic immunities at all is very questionable; they are often an obstacle to the general prosperity and the free exercise of industry. According to the present law of the corporation respecting resident housekeepers carrying on trade in the city of London, they are called on to pay £34 : 11; they cannot continue without being also free of a company, which increases the amount of money paid to £50. The Reform Bill, by conferring the parliamentary franchise on householders, will correct some portion of the injustice we have represented.

Corporation of Bristol.—This corporation ranks the second in the kingdom, and its defective constitution has been practically exemplified during the late tragical proceedings. The civil government of the city is vested in the corporation, consisting of a high steward, the mayor, recorder, aldermen, sheriffs, common council, town-clerk, chamberlain, and subordinate functionaries. The mayor and sheriffs are chosen annually on the 15th of September. The sheriffs are elected from the members of the common council, which body is limited, by the charter of Queen Anne, to forty-two. There are twelve aldermen chosen by the twelve wards into which the city is divided. They are constituted preservers of the public tranquillity, with the power of justices of the peace, and enjoy all the privileges and authority of the aldermen of London.

In point of opulence, the Corporation of Bristol is supposed to rank among the most wealthy bodies corporate of the kingdom. In 1778, Mr. Barrett estimated the annual income of the Corporation at £14,000, arising from the several estates they possess, from those for which they act in trust, with the rents of the several markets, the profits arising from town duties, and other sources of income. It has subsequently increased, Mr. Evans conjectures, in his History of Bristol, to £18,000. There is little doubt it is a great deal more from the augmented value of property, and the Corporation having abandoned, *without the city*, the former practice of letting their estates on lives, with merely fines for renewals. A considerable portion of the city estate is derived from the charter of John, and claimed by them under the title of " lords of the waste," and including what is now Queen-square, Princes-street, King-street, and part of St. Augustine's Back, the Key, Grove, and the Back. Out of the Corporation income £1,500 is annually given to the mayor for the better support of the dignity of his office, and £500 to each of the sheriffs. Between £3,000 and £4,000 is expended in salaries and other expenses incidental to the municipal government of the city. The finances of the Corporation are managed by the chamberlain of the city, which office is one of considerable trust and importance. He gives a bond of £3,000 for the execution of his duties with care and fidelity, and is obliged, by the statute, to render an account of the revenues of the Corporation, together with their application, in one month after the feast of St. Luke.

Bristol is a county corporate ; that is, besides the city properly so called, certain lands and districts adjacent are comprised within its jurisdiction. The freedom of the city is obtained by hereditary right, by serving an apprenticeship of seven years if the indenture be registered at the council-house, by marrying a freeman's daughter, and by purchase. The last charter granted to the city of Bristol is dated the 24th of July, 1710, by which the former grants and privileges are confirmed, and the mayor and other officers of the Corporation allowed to execute their respective offices without the approval of the Lord Chancellor, which by the charter of Charles II. was ordered to be first obtained. Had the constitution of the Corporation been popular enough to conciliate the confidence of the citizens, it is impossible the civic authorities should have been so void of resources as they appear to have been during the late riots. Beside, the Corporation is accused of not administering their numerous charitable trusts either wisely or faithfully. The *Free* Grammar School in Unity-street is a monstrous abuse.* It was endowed by Robert Thorne, for the " better education and bringing up" of the youth of the city. Under the auspices of the Corporation it has been perverted into a splendid boarding-school establishment, to the great emolument of the Rev. Dr. Goodenough, and accommodation of the children of the magnates of Bristol.

Corporation of Liverpool.—Liverpool is an ancient borough by prescription, but incorporated by a series of charters granted from the reign of King John in 1208, to the reign of George II.† By the latest charter it is provided that the body corporate shall consist of forty-one persons, composing the common council, out of whom shall be annually chosen a mayor, recorder, and two bailiffs. All who have passed the chair are styled aldermen. The mayor, recorder, and aldermen are magistrates for Liverpool, and the four senior aldermen are coroners.

Previously to the reign of Charles II. the freemen at large exercised the right of choosing their own corporate officers ; but since that period, here, as in many other places, the corporate body assumed the power of filling up all vacancies within themselves. The free burgesses have, however, reclaimed part of their rights.‡ Members of parliament are chosen by the free burgesses not receiving alms. All persons who are born free, who have served an apprenticeship under freemen, or who have obtained their freedom by grant or purchase from the corporation,

---

* Abridgement of the Reports of the Royal Commissioners on Public Charities, by the Editor of the *Cabinet Lawyer*. This work has been called " national," and may be had of the publisher of the *Black Book*. From the valuable notes and comments of the editor we have been indebted for much of our information relative to the present state of corporations.

† Account of Liverpool, by Smithers, p. 47.

‡ Aikin's History of Manchester, p. 345.

have the right of voting.   A freeman of Liverpool is also a freeman of Bristol, and of Waterford and Wexford in Ireland.

The principal points that have, from time to time, been in dispute between the burgesses and corporation are these:—1. The right of making by-laws by the common council, without the assent or participation of the burgesses. 2. The plan adopted by the common council of electing their own members, or filling up vacancies in their own body. 3. The balancing of the corporation accounts without public audit by the burgesses at large.* These points have been the subject of expensive litigation; the right of making by-laws was decided in favour of the burgesses by the verdicts of two juries at Lancaster; on which occasion Mr. Erskine was their counsel.   A third trial was moved for by the corporation, which the Court of King's Bench, on what grounds does not appear, thought proper to grant.   But the expenses incurred in these proceedings, which were sustained by individual burgesses, added to the consideration that the law has prescribed no limit to the authority of a court in remanding a cause for trial whenever it is not satisfied with the verdict, deterred the burgesses from further prosecution of their claim; and the common council, notwithstanding the opinion of the two juries, still continue to exercise the exclusive power of the corporation in the same manner as before these proceedings were instituted.†

Annual accounts, however, of the corporation receipts and expenditure are now regularly published.   The income of the corporation amounts to £60,000, chiefly from fines for renewal of leases, rents, town dues, anchorage, weighing machine, &c.   The mayor, the recorder, and the aldermen are magistrates for Liverpool, and the four senior aldermen are coroners for the time being.

Corporation of Bath.—The civil constitution of this city as now administered was established by the charter of Queen Elizabeth, dated the 4th of September, 1590, by which the municipal government is vested in a mayor and four aldermen at the least, and not exceeding ten at the most, assisted with twenty of the chief citizens, to be called a common council, and a majority of these (whereof the mayor for the time being is to be always one) may make laws, let the city lands, impose fines, and create, from among the inhabitants, free citizens and burgesses, whom they may bind with an oath to obey all lawful commands.   On Monday before the feast of St. Michael, the mayor, aldermen, and common council, are to choose from among themselves the mayor for the ensuing year, and also elect a recorder, common clerk, chamberlain, constables, and other inferior officers, with two sergeants of the mace.   Persons refusing to take these offices (except those of recorder and town-clerk) may be fined.   The mayor is constituted coroner of the city and clerk of the market.

---

* Smither's Account of Liverpool, p. 59.
† Aikin's History of Manchester, p. 607.

Previous to this charter all preceding grants to Bath were vested in the *whole of the citizens*, who enjoyed the privilege of attending all meetings for making regulations for the internal government of the city, of being consulted in the formation of local institutions, of assenting to the appointment of parliamentary representatives, and of investing strangers with the rights and privileges of citizenship. These powers, for greater convenience, were usually delegated to a chosen body of themselves, the mayor always presiding at their head. But, in the course of time, the body so chosen to represent the citizens assumed a *prescriptive* right to the exercise of their delegated powers, independent of the suffrages of their fellow-townsmen, and, in order effectually to fortify their usurpation, they obtained the charter of Elizabeth, by which the popular constitution of Bath was subverted, and instead of it was substituted a perpetual oligarchy of self-elected individuals.

From this time the freemen of Bath were divided into two classes ; the smaller one, which included only those who were of the *community*, (after Elizabeth's charter denominated the *Corporation*,) and the more numerous class, distinguished from the stranger or inhabitant of other places by the grant of some trifling local privileges ; of these the chief seems to have been a certain interest or privilege of pasture in the grange of Barton or Bath-common.

The freedom of the city is obtained either by *servitude* or *purchase*, or both. The term of *servitude* must be seven years, under a freeman, residing in the city, who is to cause the indenture to be registered within one month after the sealing of the same, in default whereof the apprentice does not gain his citizenship at the conclusion of the term. The freedom by *purchase* can be granted by the corporation, on the payment of a sum not less than £5 (£70 is, we believe, generally paid) into the coffers of that body ; of this, however, the resident freemen do not participate.

The income of the corporation arises from several sources ; such as the private baths in Stall-street; the rent of the pump amounting to £840, (*Warner's History*, p. 337 ;) assessments for supplying the inhabitants with water from the adjoining hills : fines on the renewal of leases ; and the profits of the weighing machine in the Saw-close.

The ecclesiastical patronage is confined to the rectorship of Bath, with Widcombe annexed, and the mastership of St. John's Hospital, both valuable benefices.

The mayor is allowed the sum of 400 guineas to defray the expenses of his mayoralty, chiefly incurred in support of *ancient hospitality*.

The inhabitants of Bath are not represented in parliament, but the corporation, whose members are usually kept *below* the number to which they are restricted by their charter, returns two representatives.

About the middle of last century, the different trades exercised in Bath were in the hands of distinct fraternities, the members of which wore gowns, had their processions and feast-days, and claimed exclusive privileges in the pursuit of their respective vocations. These societies had all sprung up about the year 1600, without charter or act of parliament. In 1765, they were all extinguished by the firmness of one Glazeby, a tailor, who persisted in following his calling within the prohibited jurisdiction. A trial ensued in a court of law, when it was determined these mushroom companies had no legal existence.

There have been some royal grants to Bath subsequent to the charter of Elizabeth, but their provisions do not materially affect the constitution of the city as then established. In 1794, the number of city justices was augmented from two to nine, and power was granted to two aldermen, during the sickness, absence, or inability of the mayor, to appoint another alderman to act in that capacity.*

Corporation of Preston.—Preston is a market town, borough, and parish. It was incorporated by Henry II. in 1160, and the privileges and free customs granted by this and subsequent royal grants were confirmed by charter of 36th of Charles II.

The body corporate consists of a mayor, recorder, seven aldermen, and seventeen capital burgesses, who, together, form the common council of the borough. The mayor, and two town-bailiffs, and two sergeants are elected annually, upon the Friday preceding the festival of St. Wilfrid, who was formerly lord of this town, and they are invested, on the 12th of October following, by a jury of twenty-four guild burgesses. The members of the council, with the exception of the mayor, retain their seats for life, or during the pleasure of a majority, and vacancies are supplied by the *remaining members*. The town sends two representatives to parliament, and affords the nearest practical example of universal suffrage in the kingdom; every male inhabitant, whether housekeeper or lodger, who has resided six months in the town, and who has not, during the last twelvemonth, been chargeable to any township as a pauper, having a right to vote for two candidates at elections. This principle was established by a decision of the House of Commons, on an appeal, in the year 1766, and has ever since been acted upon.

The burgesses are entitled by the charter of Henry II. to have a GUILD MERCHANT, with the usual franchises annexed, of safe transit through the kingdom, exemption from toll, pontage, and stallage; liberty to buy and sell peaceably; and power to hold a guild for the renewal of freedom to the burgesses, the confirming of by-laws, and other purposes. This privilege is still made the occasion of great festivity. For a long time after their first institution, the guilds were held at irregular periods, but they have now for more than a century been celebrated every twentieth year; the last was held in 1822. The several trades of Preston are incorporated. Twenty-five chartered companies go in procession on the guild festival.

Corporation of Lichfield.—The city of Lichfield was anciently governed by a guild and guild-master, which had their first establishment in the reign of Richard II. in the year 1387. Soon after the dis-

---

* Abridgement of the Charity Reports: Notes of the Editor, p. 237.

solution of the guild, by act of parliament, 2 Edward VI. a charter of incorporation was granted to this city by the same king; which was to consist of two bailiffs and twenty-four burgesses; twelve of whom had been masters of the guild. Several other charters were granted by succeeding sovereigns, the provisions of which were confirmed by that of Charles II. and the constitution of the city as now existing determined.

This charter, dated November 5, 1664, directs that two bailiffs shall be annually elected by the brethren on St. James's day; that the senior bailiff shall be nominated by the bishop, keep a part of the seal and be escheator; that the bailiffs, at the expiration of their offices, shall be justices the succeeding year, and shall, together with the then bailiffs, hold courts of record, &c. have the use of fines and dues; that there shall be twenty-one brethren elected from among the citizens, and so called to aid and assist the bailiffs, as the common-council of the city; that the bailiff, or any of the brethren, shall be liable to be removed by a majority of the body; and upon the death or removal of any, others shall be elected by the like authority. It empowers the bailiffs and brethren to hold courts of gaol delivery; to award judgment of death or other punishment; and also to elect a recorder, steward, and common clerk: but none of these officers are to act without having first obtained the approbation of the Crown. They may also annually elect a sheriff, and any one refusing to serve may be fined or imprisoned, and excluded from all the privileges of the city.

Under the authority of the charters granted to this city, the several fraternities and Companies were formed of saddlers, glovers, whittawers, tanners, smiths, bakers, coopers, cutlers, &c. A list of these and their by-laws may be found in Harwood's History of the " City and Antiquities of Lichfield."

Corporation of Stafford.—The earliest incorporation of this borough was by charter of King John, in 1208. This charter was confirmed, and new privileges granted, by that of Edward VI. under which the government is constituted of a mayor, recorder, ten aldermen, ten common-councilmen, a town-clerk, and two sergeants-at-mace. The borough sends two members to Parliament, and has done so since the 23d of Edward I. The right of election is in the mayor, aldermen, and resident burgesses, not receiving parochial relief. The sons of burgesses, and those who have served apprentice seven years in the borough, have a right (upon the demand thereof) to be made burgesses. Though the electors claim to be independent of the personal influence of a patron, it appears, from the declarations of a lately elected member, they are accessible to an influence of a not less undignified description. The ancient custom of Borough English, by which the youngest son succeeds to property, in preference to the elder children, prevails in Stafford.

Corporation of Northampton.—Northampton is both a town incorporate and a borough. It was first incorporated by Henry II. and since confirmed by several successive charters under different reigns, and the privileges of the town much enlarged. By a charter granted in the first of King John, the burgesses were freed from all toll, lastage, and murage throughout England, with the privilege of enjoying these and other liberties in as ample a manner as the citizens of London, paying into the king's exchequer £120 at Michaelmas, in every year. These liberties were continued and enlarged by further grants of Henry III. and Edward I. By charter of Henry VII. the mayor and his brethren, late mayors, are to name and choose forty-eight persons of the inhabitants, which forty-eight persons, together with the mayor and his brethren, and such as have been mayors and bailiffs, should hereafter yearly elect all the succeeding mayors and bailiffs. Before this period, it is stated, in *Whalley's History of Northamptonshire*, vol. i. p. 433, that the mayor and bailiffs were elected by all the freemen in St. Giles's church-yard, the election being often attended with tumults and quarrels. By charter, bearing date 3d August, 15th Charles II. the government of Northampton is committed to the mayor and two bailiffs, and such as have been mayors and bailiffs, and a common council of forty-eight burgesses, usually called the company of forty-eight; and of these, together with the recorder, chamberlain, and town-clerk, the corporation now consists. Those who have served the office of mayor are called aldermen. The recorder and town clerk are usually continued for life, but are re-chosen every year, and at their first appointment must be approved by the king. The mayor for the time being, with the last mayor, and one other member of the corporation, elected by the mayor, aldermen, and bailiffs, are justices of the peace within the town for that year. Freemen not resident may be elected to offices in the corporation, and must pay a fine if they refuse to serve.

Northampton sends two representatives to parliament. The electors, by prescription, are every freeman of the town, whether resident or not, and every inhabitant householder not receiving alms. By a resolution of the House of Commons, persons receiving an annual donation at Christmas are disqualified from voting. This, Oldfield remarks, in his History of Boroughs, vol. ii. p. 329, is not only repugnant to what may be called the common law of committees, but expressly contrary to the decisions on the Bedford petitions in 1755 and 1792 ; when it was determined that persons receiving *charity* were not thereby disqualified from voting, but that receiving *alms* was a disqualification.

Corporation of Gloucester.—The town of Gloucester was erected into a city and bishopric, in 1542, by charter of Henry the Eighth. The inhabitants obtained several other charters before and subsequently to this period ; but that by which the city is now governed was granted by Charles the Second, in 1672, and cost the citizens upwards of £600. By this charter, the corporation must consist of thirty members at the least, but not to exceed forty, of which the mayor and aldermen are twelve, and the rest form the common council. Vacancies are to be filled up by the *remaining corporators ;* and this principle of self-election seems to have been generally introduced into the charters of municipal bodies granted in this and the three preceding reigns, and was intended, as *the charters allege, to avoid the tumults* which had heretofore accompanied elections on more popular principles. The mayor, bailiffs, and chamberlain, are chosen by twenty electors, consisting of the mayor, aldermen, senior sheriff, and senior members of the common council. The other principal officers of the city, either by charter or prescription, are the high steward, the recorder, the two members of parliament, the town-clerk, and the twelve aldermen, out of whom the mayor is chosen. That alderman who was last elected is generally coroner, and president of the hospitals.

Every soon of a burgess is free-born, and, as such, is entitled to his freedom. Each burgess has free common all the year in the Townham and in Portham, after the hay is carried away, which franchise was purchased of the abbey of St. Peter, A.D. 1237: also in Oxclose, Meanham, and Little Meadow, after the first vesture is taken off. The freemen had also, anciently, certain exclusive privileges of fishing in the Severn.

Corporation of Leeds.—Leeds was first incorporated by Charles I. in 1626. A second charter was given to it by Charles II. in 1661, and a third by James II. in 1684. But, in 1689, the second charter was restored by William III. under which the town is at present governed. The corporation consists of a mayor, twelve aldermen, and twenty-four common-councilmen, who fill up the vacancies in their body, and annually elect the mayor from the aldermen by a majority of votes; but the election is merely pro formâ, as the senior alderman is always chosen. There are also a recorder and town-clerk. The mayor and aldermen are justices of peace within the borough, which is co-extensive with the parish, and divided into ten chapelries or townships, including the town properly so called.

The character of the Corporation of Leeds does not form an exception to that of municipal bodies throughout the kingdom; it is exclusive and intolerant: latterly it has received a slight infusion of Whiggism; still we believe the great and influential body of Dissenters have failed to derive any advantage from the abrogation of the sacramental test, and continue excluded from all part and parcel in its councils and proceedings. The relation indeed in which the Corporation stands to the inhabitants at large, precisely corresponds to that of the general government to the people of the empire. It is placed in the midst of a numerous, intelligent, and opulent population, of whose interests and sentiments it has long ceased to be the organ or representative; the same want of reciprocity between the governors and the governed is the pervading characteristic of the sway of the Oligarchy. We need not add that both require to be adjusted.

It is unnecessary, we apprehend, to extend our enquiries to other corporate bodies; those of which we have given an account will be sufficient to afford an insight into the general state of municipal franchises and institutions. Our preceding exposition may not be strictly correct in every particular, but we have had access to and availed ourselves of the best information open to the public. There is one circumstance indeed peculiar to all these privileged confederacies—and it is a very suspicious one, to say the least of it—they are all apprehensive of investigation into their chartered immunities. We had an instance of this in the treatment the Rev. Mr. Seyer received from the Bristol Corporation. This gentleman was desirous of publishing a correct version of the charters of that city, apparently for no other purpose than as a literary or antiquarian curiosity. He applied to the corporation for permission to inspect the originals in their possession; the question was debated in common-council, and the *application refused.* Who could tell what might be the result? The citizens might claim some obsolete franchises, or the worshipful body lose part of their revenues. The example of Newcastle-upon-Tyne was relied upon. After Mr. Brande had published the history of that place, the corporation lost a large portion of the town-duties. It is true the Corporation of Newcastle had *wrongfully levied these duties*—but what of that? They had always been received, and paid without grumbling, till they incautiously permitted the historian to look into their archives, and expose their injustice.

We shall conclude with submitting two propositions for the reform—for we would not have them abolished—of Corporate Bodies.

First, we would apply to corporations the same talisman of PUBLICITY, both as respects their proceedings and finances, which has contributed so much to improve the administration of national affairs. An act of parliament for this purpose, we are convinced, would be attended with the most beneficial consequences. We are aware of no good reason why corporate bodies should be exempt from the obligation imposed on the king's ministers. The corporation of a city or town stands in the same relation to the inhabitants as the imperial government to the people of England. The Chancellor of the Exchequer brings forward his annual statements of debts and credits, of income and expenditure, and lays them before the nation, and the same duty ought to be discharged by every chamberlain, or other equivalent officer, to the whole city, borough, guild, or fraternity, by which he is appointed. Such a reform would check negligence and abuse, and maintain a spirit of inquiry into the administration of all corporation funds.

Secondly, we would abolish the system of SELF-ELECTION, and render corporations responsible to the intelligence and proprietary of the communities of which they have assumed the control and government. The practice of *breeding-in* is as unfavourable to the growth and improvement of public bodies as of animals and vegetables. A mutuality of feeling, a reciprocration of favour and obligation, are necessary between the different classes of every society, from that of a city or town to the entire kingdom. As it is, corporations form so many petty oligarchies, scattered through the country—the mere cess-pools of all that is corrupt, servile, and intolerant—and the exercise of whose sway, within their respective local jurisdictions, is more insulting and oppressive than that of the feudal lords, whose domination they have supplanted.

These changes may be considered by the apostles of an expiring faction as a violation of chartered rights, or "corporation robbery," but happily we have reached a crisis when eloquent declamation on these topics can no longer command a numerous audience.

THE CITY'S ESTATE.

The Chamber of London annually makes a return to parliament of the income and expenditure of the corporation. We subjoin an abstract of the receipts and expenditure of the city, as published by the auditors, Messrs. Williams and Barrett, for the year ending December 31st, 1828.

ABSTRACT OF THE RECEIPTS.

	£.	s.	d.
Balance in hand on the 31st December, 1827	549	10	8¾
Rents and Quit Rents	46,853	19	10
Markets, Tolls, Offices, and Bequests, heretofore called Rent Farms	62,301	7	4¼
Brokers' Rents and Admissions	2,557	0	0
Freedoms Sold	8,900	0	0
Freedoms, Enrolments, &c.	1,391	1	10
Casual Receipts	1,851	13	5½
Rents and Navigation of the River Thames	1,272	11	6
Sales and Alienations of Offices	50	0	0
Fines for Leases	1,791	16	8
Insurances of Officers' Lives	304	16	9
Interest on Government Securities	1,055	19	11
Sale of Premises	82	10	0
Money borrowed	46,000	0	0
	£174,962	8	0½

ABSTRACT OF THE PAYMENTS.

	£	s.	d.
Orphans' Fund	11,500	0	0
Rents and Quit Rents, Taxes, &c.	2,359	15	1¼
Mansion-House Expenses	2,964	5	0
Expenses of Magistracy and Police	9,938	7	5
Expenses of the several Prisons	20,296	4	1
Conservancy of the River Thames	4,281	18	9
Artificers' and Tradesmen's Bills	6,350	11	4
Market Charges	3,794	7	10
Law and Parliamentary Expenses	5,907	11	2
Return of Duty on Corn imported	559	3	3
Charitable Donations, Pensions, &c.	1,757	2	5
Salaries and Allowances	22,744	14	1
Disbursements—Court of Aldermen	395	19	10
Disbursements—Court of Common Council	9,704	19	10½
Purchase of the Right of Alienation of the Officers of the Lord Mayor's Household	7,719	9	10
Bequests	786	5	6
Interest and Annuities	13,696	19	2
Purchase of Securities	1,879	2	10
Debts discharged	16,250	0	0
Removal of Fleet Market	31,000	0	0
Balance in hand, 31st December, 1828	173,976	17	6
	985	10	6½
	£174,962	8	0½

R. CLARK, *Chamberlain.*

DR. BRADY'S INTERPRETATION OF COMMUNITATIS.

At page 455 we alluded to the interpretation given by Dr. Brady of the word " commonalty," and the use made of that interpretation to deprive burgesses at large of their elective rights.   So far as this matter is connected with the existing state of corporate bodies we do not attach much importance to it ; for we think the merit of public institutions ought to be tried by their aptitude to present circumstances, without reference to antiquity or their derivative authority; and whether corporations claim the power they exercise from right or usurpation, is of comparative indifference.   The real question is, can they be reformed and made more conducive to social utility ?   Other persons view these subjects in a different light, and it is for them we refer to Dr. Brady's commentary.   It was made the foundation of a sweeping measure of disfranchisement, and still continues the only legal defence of municipal oligarchies.   The subject will be readily understood by the following quotations.

Warwick.

" 1628. *May* 31, Mr. Hackwill reported from the Committee of Privileges the case for this borough :
" *Question,*
" *Whether the election to be made by the* Mayor *and* Common Council, *or by the Commons in general ?*
" *Upon the Question it was resolved,*
" *That the right of election for the Town of Warwick belongs to the* Commonalty."

Commons' Journals, 4 Chas. I.

The following are Dr. Brady's remarks on this decision of the Committee of the House of Commons :

" *The ground of this popular error was, That this Committee (notwithstanding the two great antiquaries,* Sir Robert Cotton, *and* Mr. Selden, *and the oracle of law* [*so called*] Sir Edward Coke, *were members of it) did not truly* understand the meaning *of the words* communitatis civitatum et burgorum, *the commonalty of cities and burghs; which* always signified *the* mayor, aldermen, *and* common council, *where they were to be found, or the steward or bayliff, and* capital burgesses, *or in short the* governing part *of cities and towns, by what persons soever they were governed, or names and titles they were called and known, which hath been sufficiently evinced by what has been said before in this Treatise, on that subject.   So that, if the* communities *of cities and burghs had been* truly understood, *the Committee ought to have determined, and the House resolved, That the right of election in very many, if not in most, or all cities and burghs, ought to have rested in the governing part of them, which is always a select number.*"—Treatise of Cities and Boroughs, By Robert Brady, Doctor in Physick, 1704.

Dr. Brady possessed considerable shrewdness, and his situation of Keeper of the Records in the Tower afforded him opportunity for learned research, but it did not become him to speak contemptuously of such men as Cotton, Coke, and Selden; nor had he good grounds for the inference he made, as appears from the following extract from another part of his " Treatise :"-

" *In the 29th of Edward the First,* John Blund *was chosen Mayor* per Commune Consilium Elye Russell tunc Majoris, *and the Aldermen there named, and the Sheriffs,* per assensum Duodecim proborum hominum singularum Wardarum, *by assent of Twelve good Men of every Ward. In the 31st of the same King, also in the 32d and 33d,* John Lincoln *and* John Blund *were the third and fourth time chosen, by Twelve* bonos & legales homines de qualibet Warda summonitos ; *twelve good and lawful men summoned out of every Ward."—*Ibid. p. 22.

By a reference to page 12 of Newell's " Evidence of the Elective Franchise in London," it will be seen that Brady has not given the 27th and 28th of Edward the First, because both those records prove that those elections were made by the *whole commonalty ;* he also puts the 31st of Edward I. in the sleight of hand way,—*In the* 31*st of the same King*—and there leaves it, for the reader to suppose that the election in that year was made in the same way as in the 29th, while he must have known that the record of that year shews, that the election was made by the mayor, aldermen, sheriffs, and the *whole commonalty.* He also states that John Lincoln and John Blund were a third and fourth time chosen, whereas John Lincoln never was a mayor at all. This is quite enough for the accuracy and authority of this learned " Doctor in Physick."

PLACES, PENSIONS, SINECURES,

COMPENSATIONS, REVERSIONS,

HALF-PAY, AND SUPERANNUATIONS.

So far we have penetrated into the recesses of the Oligarchy! Our first entrance was into Holy Church, passing, with fear and trembling, through the venerable cathedrals, the collegiate establishments, the stalls, chapters, cloisters, and parsonages—glancing, as we proceeded, at the lawn sleeves, silk aprons, shovel-hats, surplices, hat-bands, and gloves. Next we ventured into the precincts of royalty, surveying the pomp and gorgeous pageants of courts and palaces; loitering, as we went along, in the pleasant retreats, in the woods and forests, the manors, chases, and crown-lands; afterwards we entered the domains of feudality, looking over the inheritances and possessions of the Percys, the Wentworths, Cavendishes, Pelhams, and other lords of the soil. Next, we plunged into the rookery among the wigs and gowns, the owls and owlets of Westminster; passing over thence into the treasury, the exchequer, and admiralty; from which we proceeded eastward into the purlieus of the India House and Threadneedle-street; and finally concluded our exploratory researches among the muniments, charters, trusts and revenues of Companies, Guilds, and Corporations.

After all this long and devious tour, without mentioning sundry off-sets and ramblings by the way, our readers, we fear, are only yet imperfectly acquainted with the System; they comprehend only its geography—its general departments and divisions—and know nothing of the various *living creatures*—the birds and beasts, and creeping things it contains. Our next object, therefore, will be, to introduce them into the *menagerie* of placemen, pensioners, sinecurists, reversionists, compensationists, superannuationists, and what not; first, describing their classes, genera, and species; and, afterwards, concluding with a catalogue of their names and qualities. This department of our work will be found a museum of rarities, embracing every link in the human creation, every description of men, women, and children. Like the ark of Noah, there has been nothing too great or mean in nature to find admission. It exhibits all the vice, the caprice, and injustice, of aristocratic government: the highest services to the state almost without notice, and the greatest gifts of the Crown lavished on profligacy, servility, and intrigue. It exhibits indolence and luxury devouring the bread for which poverty and industry have toiled, and for which they are now starving. It exhibits the strength, arcana, and machinery of the English government. It is a real picture of our boasted constitution—if not by law, as by practice established ; and is a source whence a foreigner may draw far more correct notions of the checks, balances, and supports of the government, than from the visionary and panegyrical descriptions of Blackstone and De Lolme.

Before giving a list of the public cormorants, let us briefly describe their orders and degrees, beginning with the host of placemen filling the public offices.

From returns to parliament, it appears there are 22,912 persons employed in the public departments, whose salaries amount to £2,788,907.* This does not include the immense number of persons employed in courts of law, the royal household, nor the colonies, and which, if included, would almost double the number of functionaries and their emoluments. The following exhibits a statement of the principal branches of revenue, in which this vast army of tax-gatherers and collectors is distributed, and a comparison of their relative numbers and emoluments in 1797 and 1827.

	YEAR 1797.		YEAR 1827.	
Offices.	No. of Persons.	Salaries.	No. of Persons.	Salaries.
Customs....United Kingdom ...	6,004† ..	£338,648	.... 11,346 ..	£964,750
Excise ....Ditto..............	6,580	413,281	.... 6,491	768,795
Stamps ....Ditto..............	521	78,746	.... 519	134,065
Taxes......Ditto..............	291	58,331	.... 347	74,190
Post-Office..Great Britain	957	54,030	.... 1,377	85,970
Ditto ......Ireland............	153	9,278	.... 333	21,961

An important consideration is the comparative remuneration of placemen in 1797 and at present. In the year 1797 there were 16,267 persons employed in the public departments ; and they received £1,374,561 a year. In 1827 there were 22,912 persons, and they received £2,788,907 : the average income of each individual was £84 in 1797, and about £121 in 1827, being at the rate of *thirty-three per cent.* increase of salary.

---

* Parliamentary Paper, No. 552, Session 1828.

† The Custom returns for this year are incorrect, owing to the returns for the Port of London having been destroyed by fire in 1814. The persons employed in the Port of London, in 1815, were 2,043. The return of the amount of salaries, at the two periods, is accurate. To obviate another objection, it must be observed, that in 1806-7, all fees to the annual amount of £40,000 were abolished, and equivalent salaries substituted. This, however, accounts only for a very small part of the enormous increase in the charge of this department.

Now, can any just cause be assigned, why the whole mass of salaries should not be reduced to the rate of 1797, thereby effecting a
saving of upwards of one-third in an expenditure of £2,788,907 per
annum. All the reasons which have ever been alleged for an augmentation in the pay of public servants have ceased to exist. The price of
wheat in consequence of the corn laws is rather higher in 1832 than in
1797 ; but manufactured articles and articles of domestic use are mostly
one-third or two-thirds cheaper than in 1797. How much better
circumstanced are placemen now than in 1810; in that year there
were 22,931 persons receiving £2,822,727, averaging about the same
income as in 1827 : but, at the former period, wheat was 105s. a quarter ; while, at present, it is 61s. a quarter. Why should those who
live on the taxes enjoy such advantages over those who pay them ?
Rents, profits, wages, every description of income, the produce of
industry and capital, has fallen at least one-third since 1810, and why
should not those who are paid by the public be compelled to retrench in
an equal ratio ?   Do not let a suffering community be insulted by the
declaration, that there is no *room for retrenchment*—that it has
already been carried to the utmost limit. Here is the proof to the contrary ; here it is shown that, without the least injustice to individuals,
in the single item of SALARIES, one million per annum might be
saved, which is nearly equal to the produce of the window-duties,
and more than double the produce of all the taxes on newspapers, advertisements, and knowledge !

After all, it is not the clerks—the mere underlings of office—that we
wish to see exclusively curtailed ; it is the vultures of the system whom
we wish to see scotched—the chairmen of boards—the commissioners
of stamps, of the excise, the customs, and assessed taxes—the joint
secretaries of the Treasury—the tellers of the Exchequer—the great
officers of the king's household—the judges, masters, registrars, secretary of bankrupt, prothonotaries, filacers, and custos brevium in the
courts of law—the comptrollers, paymasters, treasurers, solicitors of
taxes, and solicitors of stamps : it is these, the great birds of prey,
whom we first wish to be brought down, and then the inferior race may
be pounced upon.

The increase in salaries is not confined to civil offices ; it extends
equally to military, naval, and ordnance pay and allowances. In all
these branches of service, there has been a great augmentation in consequence of the rise in the price of provisions, which is a reason that can
be no longer urged against reduction. In 1792, the pay of a private
soldier in the regular infantry was only £9 : 2 : 6 for 365 days ; it is
now £18 : 5. The pay of the regular cavalry has been increased in
the same proportion. The pay of a commander in the navy, in 1792,
was 20s. per diem ; in 1829, 60s. per diem. The allowance to the
widow of a colonel, in 1792, was £50 per annum ; in 1827, £90 per
annum.* A similar scale of augmentation has been applied to almost

---

* Parliamentary Paper, No. 594, Session 1830.

every other class ; but the time has arrived when they ought all to be reduced to the rate before the war. The productive orders of society have long since been compelled to retrograde, and those who live on the produce of their industry must follow them. While the tide was at flood all officers and placemen were wafted too high on the beach ; now the tide has fallen, they must either voluntarily glide or supinely wait to be forced into the common channel.

One of the greatest abuses in the public service is *pluralities*. When a single individual can adequately discharge the duties of half a dozen different offices, the duties of these offices must be either very small or unimportant, and consequently some of them might either be abolished or united, and the salaries saved or reduced. It is unnecessary to cite examples of either civil, judicial, or military pluralities ; they will be found in abundance in our *List of Places*. The Whig ministers have consolidated some offices : they have also abolished some offices, and reduced the salaries of others : the changes they have introduced or contemplated we shall notice in a separate section ; but it does not appear they have determined to act on the general principle of reducing all salaries and emoluments to the standard existing prior to the war. There is, however, no good reason why this course should not be followed. Look at the enormous fall in the prices of Sheffield cutlery and Birmingham hardwares recently published ! All articles of domestic use and consumption, except *bread*, have fallen in a corresponding proportion, and many of them have fallen greatly below the prices they were at in 1797. In 1797 the average price of sugar, per cwt., was 60s. ; in 1832 it is only 23s. per cwt. ; in 1797 coffee was 124s., in 1832 it is 33s. 6d. ; sheeting calicoes in 1797 were 1s. 6d. per yard, in 1832 *sixpence ;* broad cloth 22s. 6d. per yard in 1797, in 1832 *nine shillings ;* iron per ton in 1797 £23, in 1832 £5 : 10. While the prices of these articles have fallen from 60 to 75 per cent. *below* what they were in 1797, the price of corn has *risen*. In 1797, the average price was 44s. per quarter at Mark-lane ; in January 1832 it was 61s. 6d. These are the different results of *free* and *restricted* trade—free, as respects manufactures—restricted as respects the produce of the soil.

The price of tea has been kept up from the same cause—monopoly in the East India Company. The high price of corn is no reason whatever for not returning to the standard before the war, because the high price is voluntary—the result of the selfish and pernicious policy of the Aristocracy—of those who chiefly profit not only by the exorbitant price of corn, which they have artificially created, but by exorbitant salaries.

MILITARY AND NAVAL HALF-PAY AND CIVIL SUPERANNUATIONS.

The sums expended under the head of *Dead Weight*, consisting of retired full-pay, half-pay, civil superannuations, and allowances to the army and navy, are equal to the revenue of many powerful states. The number of military officers, on full-pay, is 6,173 : the number of military officers on half-pay, is 6,009. In the navy, there are 5,528 officers : of this number, 200 are admirals, of whom only *ten are in actual service;* 803 are captains, of whom only seventy-nine are employed ; 836 are commanders, of whom only seventy are employed ; and 3,689 are lieutenants, of whom only 669 are employed. The total sum annually paid in retired full-pay, half-pay, superannuations, pensions, and allowances to officers in the army and ordnance ; to militia-adjutants, local-militia-adjutants, and serjeant-majors ; to foreigners on half-pay, and to foreigners receiving pensions, &c. is £3,314,632:17:7.* The total sum annually payable under similar heads in the navy, is £1,583,797 : 16 : 10. The Dead Weight altogether, including the superannuations, grants, and pensions, in the Metropolitan Police, Excise, Customs, Treasury, Stamp, Tax Offices, Revenue, and Military Boards, £5,363,640 : 7 : 11½.†

Such, in addition to the public debt of eight hundred millions, the conflagrations and special commissions, is the fatal bequest of aristocratic government; of that government which vainly sought to avert domestic reform by foreign war and intervention!

There is, however, something so peculiar in the Dead Weight, that it deserves more particular investigation. It might have been thought, during a period of peace and reduced establishments, and more especially by the deaths of annuitants, that the burthen imposed on the community under this head would have been lightened. But it is not so; the Dead Weight is too good a thing for the Aristocracy to be suffered to expire, and it seems likely to be, at least, co-existent with the system which created it. In 1822, this precious entail of the Borough-mongers' war expenditure amounted to £5,289,087,‡ which is only less, by £74,553 per annum, than it was in March, 1830. All the time government was loud and unceasing in professions of economy, of a desire to reduce every possible charge,—to make every possible saving ; yet, in face of all this, one great and most objectionable branch of expense, under circumstances most favourable for reduction, was actually suffered to increase !

All the extravagance of which we complain has resulted from a negligent—not to say deliberate—and indefensible system of profusion. We do not complain of the expense of maintaining those who are actually worn-out or disabled in the public service, no more than we complain of supporting, by a poor-rate, the aged and infirm in civil life ; but we may justly complain of supporting those who are in health and strength,--who never served their country, and have no claim on its gratitude. The half-pay of the Army and Navy, on the present plan, is decidedly objectionable. It is not a *remuneration for past service ;* since every holder of a commission, though he has held it only for a day or an hour, is as much entitled to claim half-pay, when not actually

---

* Parliamentary Paper, No. 185, Session 1830.   † Ibid, page 5.
‡ Parliamentary Paper, No. 424, Session 1826.

employed, as another who has served for twenty years. Such being the rule of the service, ought not government to have adopted every precaution against the multiplication of claimants; ought it not to have guarded against *new* admissions into the naval and military departments, while there remained officers in abundance on half-pay able to fill up every vacancy? Their conduct has been the reverse of so obvious a principle. Thousands of new commissions have been given away in the Army and Navy, while, at the same time, we had upwards of 16,000 officers in both branches of service totally unemployed. Hence the *perpetuity of the Dead Weight.* The Aristocracy look upon the Army, the Navy, the Church, and Public Offices, as so many branches of their patrimony, and that a reduction in them would lessen the amount of patronage, diminish the funds for the maintenance of younger children, illegitimate offspring, collateral relatives, favourites, and dependents.

Besides the granting of first commissions, other causes have operated to keep up the amount of the Dead Weight. Previous to the year 1820, no half-pay was payable to officers holding any other office, civil or military, under the crown; but this regulation did not extend to officers on *full-pay,* the receipt of which was compatible with the holding of civil employment. Another regulation, previous to 1818, was that widows should not be allowed pensions, unless their husbands had been on full pay; and all widows having pensions ceased to receive them if they married. Further, in the Navy, a widow lost her pension if her income from any other source equalled twice its amount. All these regulations have been abrogated;* and the consequence has been an annual increase of charge to the amount of £147,624; and a loss to the public from 1818 of upwards of £1,300,000.

What we have said will, we apprehend, be sufficient to enable our readers to comprehend the nature of the Dead Weight, and the causes of its longevity. We shall proceed with other subjects, first referring to the *Appendix* for a more detailed statement of the Half-Pay and Superannuation Expenditure.

SINECURES, REVERSIONS, AND PENSIONS.

Sinecures are offices without employment! The bare description is sufficient to decide the fate of appointments like these; but how infatuated the government must be, which obstinately retains them amidst a discontented and famishing population. Let us shortly inquire into the origin and present state of these corruptions.

Sinecures have mostly originated from changes in the usages of society, from alterations in the management of the revenue, the administration of justice, and partly from the unions of the three kingdoms. They ought all to have ceased with the duties attached to them; but

---

* Third Report of the Committee on Public Income and Expenditure, Parliamentary Papers, vol. v. Session 1828.

have been kept up for sake of patronage. Of the first description of sinecures, the office of master of the hawks, in the royal household, held, with a salary of £1,392, by the Duke of St. Albans, is an example. The chief-justices in Eyre, with salaries amounting to £4,566, have been kept up for centuries, after such a mode of administering the laws had terminated. In Scotland and Ireland is a host of offices of which the holders, without employment or responsibility, have only to receive their salaries and emoluments. Of this class are the offices of Vice-admiral of Scotland, held by *general* Lord Cathcart; the Keeper of the Privy Seal of Scotland, held by the late first Lord of the Admiralty, Lord Melville; the offices of Keeper of the Signet and Register of Sasines, held by the brother of Lord Melville; the office of Chancellor of Scotland, held by lieutenant-general the Earl of Rosslyn; and the office of Justice-general of Scotland, held by the late Lord Chamberlain, the Duke of Montrose. All these are absolute sinecures, with salaries varying from £1500 to £5000 per annum. The offices of Chief Justices-in-Eyre, now held by Lord Clarendon and the Right Hon. T. Grenville, are to cease with *existing interests;* but when that will be no one can tell, since many of these lucrative appointments have been made *hereditary* in particular families, or patent offices granted for a long term of years.

Next to absolute sinecures are offices of which the salaries are vastly disproportioned to the employment, and of which the duties are discharged wholly by *deputy*. This forms a very numerous class. As specimens may be mentioned, the Auditorship of the Exchequer, held by Lord Grenville, with a salary of £4000; the Registrarship of the Admiralty, held by Lord Arden, with an income, during the war, of £10,500; the four Tellerships of the Exchequer, each with salaries of £2700; and the four Clerkships of the Pells, with salaries of £1500, held by the Bathursts, Dundasses, and Percevals. In the departments of the Army, the Navy, and Revenue, are numerous sinecures, which ought to have been long since extinguished.

But the COURTS OF JUSTICE present the most rank and unweeded garden of lucrative offices without employment, or of which the employment is executed by deputy. Among the foremost of these is Lord Ellenborough, who is clerk in the Court of King's Bench, with an income of £9,625; he is also *custos brevium* of the same court. This pompous man threw out an insolent threat, last session, on some comment being made on the heavy contributions levied by legal sinecurists on suitors for justice. Lord Kenyon is joint *custos brevium* with Lord Ellenborough, with an income of £2,696; and his lordship's brother, the Hon. Thomas Kenyon, is filazer and clerk of outlawries, with emoluments averaging £7,000 a year. Next, is the Duke of Grafton, sealer in the King's Bench, £2,888, though we dare say his grace never sealed a writ in his life, nor ever once entered the dark and dirty hole in Inner Temple Lane, where that function is performed by his representative. Charles Short, clerk of the rules and orders of the King's Bench, receives *from fees*, £5,172 per annum. What can be the grave and responsible duties of Mr. Short to entitle him to this enormous tribute, we cannot precisely state. Again ; there is John Waters, clerk to the chief justice, *from fees*, £2,169. Lord Tenterden receives £10,000 a year as chief judge of this court; but his lordship's office is no sinecure, whatever may be the offices held by his son and nephew, who receive, respectively, £2,985, and £1,000 per annum.

Let us next step into the *Court of Common Pleas* ; we pass over the judges, whose salaries are well known, and perhaps not greatly to be complained of. Not so with others. The three prothonotaries have returned their emoluments at £7,800, " or *thereabouts*," arising from " ancient fees, payable solely by suitors."* Mr. Mansfield, filacer of the court, receives £1,450 for filing writs and affidavits, taking bail, and other small matters. Keene Fitzgerald, Esq. clerk of the warrants, £1,252; W. Woodroffe, Esq. associate of the chief justice, £1,198 ; the *custos brevium*, Sir E. Mostyn and partners, from fees on actions, £1,122; and last, and not least, William R. H. Brown, Esq. warden of the Fleet Prison, " £2,000, or *something upwards*,"—the words of the return. The *Court of Chancery* has been called the " Mint of justice ;" but it is, in fact, a mint for coining into enormous fees the effects of minors, legatees, bankrupts, widows, orphans, and lunatics. The office of the chief fee-gatherer of the court is about to be *regulated ;* that is, in lieu of gleaning £15,000 a-year from writs, petitions, supersedeas, &c. the Lord Chancellor is to be paid a fixed salary to an equal amount. The emoluments of the Rev. Thomas Thurlow amounted, in the year 1830, to £8,502, as patentee of bankrupts ; and the emoluments of the same Reverend Person, in the same year, as clerk of the hanaper, amounted to £2,500. The sinecures, or offices nearly sinecures, in this court, are so numerous, that we must be content with indicating them in clusters, referring to the *List of Places* for particulars. The ten masters, whose chief duties consist in three or four hours' attendance per day, in adjusting accounts and swearing affidavits, receive each, on the average, £4,500 per annum ; and their chief clerks, each, £1,400 a-year. The *Six Clerks*, as they are termed, are nothing more than sinecurists, and their incomes average £1,200 each. The Registrar levies £4,861 in fees, for *copying* proceedings in equity, and the master of the Report Office as much, though his duties are of the same humble description, performed by hireling quill-drivers, who receive less than a curate's stipend. Our task would never be finished, were we to pursue our inquiries minutely through the entire labyrinth of law in the United Kingdom. Edinburgh presents similar enormities in judicial administration, in the fees and emoluments of keeper of signet, and register of sasines, the clerks of sessions, sheriffs' clerks, &c. Dublin has also her flight of vultures perched on the temple of Astræa, under the denomination of masters in chancery, prothonotaries, clerk of the hanaper, and clerks of papers, and what not. In the provinces justice is impeded by clerks of the peace, appointed by lords lieutenant of counties, and who have princely

---

* Parliamentary Paper, No. 55, Session 1830.

emoluments. Then what purlieus of sinecurism there are in the counties palatine and duchy courts of Lancaster, Durham, and Cornwall, in the nominal capacities of chancellors, registrars, receivers, attorney and solicitor-generals, auditors, king's counsel, ushers, and other mimicry of the regal and imperial government!

Knowing, as we do, what a gradation of pillage the course of justice is in this country; knowing how the unfortunate suitor is fleeced at every step of his proceeding, by the harpies of the law; knowing all this, we do often wonder at the proneness of our countrymen to litigation, and cannot behold, without both surprise and indignation, the readiness with which they furnish *pabulum* to the monstrous legal extortions we have shortly indicated. We hear much said about the "hells" of St. James's-street, and of the "hells" of Bond-street, where brainless creatures are stripped of their fortunes ; but are these more ruinous and plundering than others, under a very different name, in the vicinity of Chancery-lane, Temple-bar, and Palace-yard?

We pass on to another description of sinecures, under the titles of governors, lieutenant-governors, town-adjutants, town-majors, constables, gunners, wardens, lord-wardens, and God knows what beside, of the cities, towns, forts, castles, garrisons, &c. of Great Britain and Ireland. Berwick-on-Tweed, Chester, Hull, Blackness-Castle, Dover-Castle, Edinburgh-Castle, Walmer-Castle, and Tilbury-Fort, are examples of these appointments, and which cost the country upwards of £35,000 per annum.* Numerous commissioners of revenue, comptrollers, inspectors of taxes, and distributors of stamps, are little more than sinecurists, the duties, where any exist, being discharged by deputies. But the chief *nidus* of sinecures is in the Colonies. The duties of nearly all offices in the West Indies, civil or judicial, are discharged by *deputy*, while the principal resides in England. They form an immense branch of patronage to the crown. It is impossible to estimate correctly their total value, the incomes being paid in fees, received by the deputy, who stipulates to pay a fixed annual sum to the principal. The total value of colonial sinecures, exclusive of those at the Cape of Good Hope, the Isle of France, and Malta, has been estimated at £76,546.

The subjoined statement, taken from the Supplementary Report of the Committee of Public Expenditure in 1809, shews the *net* value of the principal sinecures in the gift of the Crown, and otherwise. It is now twenty-two years since this report was made ; and during that long iuterval, we doubt whether the *profits* of a single sinecure have been saved to the public: some which we have noticed are to cease on the termination of existing interests. The offices of patentee of bankrupts, and clerk of the hanaper, and of justice-general in Scotland, and a few more, have been abolished ; but then the holders are to have *compensations ;* so that, we repeat, we doubt whether, by the extinction of sinecures, the community has been saved a farthing ; and this monstrous

* Parliamentary Paper, No. 426, Session 1826.

abuse is just as flagrant as ever, to the everlasting reproach of the members of both houses of parliament, who have not raised their voices, not only once but many times, against the further toleration of this shameless robbery, under any shape or pretext. Here is the return to which we have referred:—

	£
Sinecures in the English Law Courts, mostly in the gift of the Judges	62,462
Sinecures in England, not in Law Courts	115,589
Ditto in Scotland	25,523
Ditto in Ireland	76,435
To which add Colonial Sinecures	76,546
	£356,555

Having spoken of Sinecures, we come next to their natural offspring—REVERSIONS. It was very natural that the holders of situations, to which large emoluments and no duties were attached, should not only wish to preserve them during their lives, but also, if possible, transmit them to their relatives and friends after death : hence originated grants in reversion. Another reason, however, may be assigned; ministers not having situations in sufficient abundance to satisfy all their adherents, endeavoured to satisfy them by anticipation. Those for whom they could not immediately provide, they satisfied by obtaining grants from the king, making them the *heirs* of places at the death of the present possessors. Sometimes these reversions were granted to two or three persons at once; first to one, and if *he* or *she* should die, to *another ;* and if he or she should die, to another; in this way have been granted most of the places on the Irish establishment for sixty or seventy years to come, and many of the most valuable legal sinecures in England.

The absurdity of this practice is sufficiently obvious. Nothing could be more ridiculous than to appoint persons to offices who were, perhaps, yet in the nursery, and of whose future capabilities it was impossible to have any knowledge. To be sure, many of these reversionary situations had no duties attached to them, and, of course, it could not be of much importance by whom they were discharged.

From the large emoluments of Sinecures, and the granting them in reversion, have originated some ludicrous incongruities. Many noble lords and their sons, right honourable and honourable gentlemen, fill the offices of clerks, tide-waiters, harbour-masters, searchers, gaugers, packers, craners, wharfingers, prothonotaries, and other degrading situations. Some of these offices are filled by women and some by children. The *Countess* of Mansfield receives £1000 a year from the Barbadoes planters; and the *duchess dowager* of Manchester £2928 a-year, as late collector of the customs outwards! Not long since a right honourable lady, a baroness, was *sweeper* of the Mall in the Park ; another lady was *chief usher* in the Court of Exchequer; and the Honourable Louisa Browning and Lady B. Martny

were *custos brevium :* some of these offices, we see, from the
Law List, have been recently merged in and executed by the husbands and children of these *high-born* dames. Then of noble Lords;
the Beresfords hold the appropriate offices of *wine-tasters, storekeepers,
packers, and craners*, in Ireland; the Duke of Grafton, and Lords
Ellenborough and Kenyon, with deputies to help, are clerks, sealers,
and keepers of writs. Lord Henley is master in chancery; the
late lord Walsingham was in the petty office of comptroller of
first fruits in the Court of Exchequer; and Lord Wm. Bentinck, now
located in India as governor-general of Bengal, is clerk of the pipe, part
of whose office it is to attend or assist the man who holds up Lord Chancellor Brougham's train!

We could enumerate a great many more, but they will be noticed in
our *List ;* we shall pass on to PENSIONS.

As nearly as can be collected from the various official returns submitted to Parliament, it would appear there are upwards of fifteen hundred pensioners, who receive about £805,022 per annum. This is exclusive of colonial pensions, and of all grants, allowances, half-pay, and
superannuations for civil, military, and naval services. We subjoin a statement of the objects and sources from which this vast sum
is paid.

	£
Pensions payable out of the consolidated fund of England and Ireland	455,444
Pensions payable out of the hereditary revenues of the Post Office and Excise	22,439
Pensions to American loyalists	5,056
Pensions to Toulonese and Corsican emigrants	14,380
Pensions to St. Domingo sufferers and Dutch naval officers	1,820
Pensions to ambassadors and other foreign ministers charged on the civil list	57,377*
Court pensions on the English civil list, about	95,000
Pensions on the Irish civil list, about	75,000
Pensions on the Scotch civil list	35,000
Pensions to Spanish refugees, who had co-operated with the British armies in the Peninsular war	18,040†
Pensions payable out of the 4½ per cent. Leeward Island duties	27,466
Total of Pensions	£805,022

The funds out of which pensions are paid are so numerous that we
are not sure, though we have all the official returns about us, some of

* This and the preceding items are taken from the Fourth Report of Sir H.
Parnell's Finance Committee, page 67, Session 1828.
† Parliamentary Paper, No. 127, Session 1830. This item, perhaps, ought
to be omitted, being only, we presume, a temporary allowance to individuals,
many of whom had just claims on the hospitality of the country.

them have not escaped our researches. However, we had rather be under the mark than be accused of exaggeration. Exclusive of sinecures, and the millions expended on objects nearly as unjustifiable, a Pension Roll, in times like these, to the amount of £805,022, is enough to make a man start from his seat, especially if he reflect, for one moment, on the dreadful state of the labouring population of the empire. In our humble opinion the salaries of public servants ought to be their only reward, and the granting of pensions is altogether unjustifiable, unless for casualties in the service of the country ; but when they are squandered on persons of whom the public knows nothing, nor for what, they are an unbearable grievance. Who, for instance, knows any thing of the services of the Giffords, the Cockburns, the Bathursts, Arbuthnots, Hays, Fitzhums, and scores more who are living on the earnings of the industrious. Foreigners, too, are on the Pensions List ; men have been brought from all parts of the earth, from America, from Germany, from France, and myriads from Scotland, to eat our bread, and devour the wages of labour and the profits of trade and agriculture.

It would be quite impossible, within reasonable limits, to enter into an analysis of the Pension List ; but there is one class of pensioners who have got upon our backs in such a peculiar way, and they have such peculiar claims on national gratitude, that we must needs crave the reader's patience while we shortly describe their origin and pretensions.

In the year 1817, there was a pretty general call for retrenchment, and a Select Committee of Finance, consisting mostly of placemen and pensioners, recommended as a sort of tub to the whale, the abolition of a few of the more obnoxious sinecures. Three acts were accordingly introduced to abolish certain useless offices ; as supervisor of his Majesty's printing-press, compiler of the Dublin gazette, master of the revels, chief justices in Eyre, clerk of the pipe, receiver of the bishop's rents, and some others were to be abolished : all which are subject to *existing interests*. But mark the sequel: having recommended the abolition of these sinecures, the committee next recommend the creation of others ; having cut down the places without any duties to perform, they create so many new pensions of retirement and superannuations, as actually to entail a greater burthen on the country after this mock retrenchment than before !

With this view, the 57th Geo. III. c. 65, was introduced. The act begins by reciting that, " the abolition and regulation of various offices, which deprive the crown of *part of the means* by which his Majesty has been heretofore enabled to recompense the service of persons who have held *high and efficient civil offices ;*" and it modestly enacts, that, from henceforth and evermore, all the high and low " *efficient public officers*" of the country, from the first lord of the treasury down to the secretaries of the treasury, under-secretaries of state, clerk of the ordnance, first and second secretaries of the Admiralty, all included, shall be supported by pensions paid out of the pockets of the people.

This was reforming with a vengeance! A committee, appointed expressly to abolish useless places, finishes by recommending the *purchase* of them, and the establishing of a perpetual fund to reward the holders thereof; most of the members of the committee themselves being the parties to be benefited by this admirable mode of retrenchment.

This truly extraordinary Pension Act assumes, as a principle, that the different sinecures are the absolute property of our hereditary legislators and their dependents; and thence concludes, because these offices are abolished, they have a claim to be provided for in some other way. " Here is a considerable mass of property," they say, " taken from our grasp, and it must be made up to us by equivalent pensions." This is exactly the principle, and what must the constitution of the government be which sanctions, by its authority, so monstrous an assumption?

What right had these " high and efficient public men" to compensation at all? The sinecures were *abuses*, and they ought to have been swept away without equivalent. If other classes are injured by reform or improvement, what compensation do they receive for their loss? The workman suffers by the substitution of machinery, the merchant and manufacturer by the vicissitudes of commerce, and the farmer by alterations of the currency; but they receive no equivalent; no fund is provided to make up the loss of their capital and industry. How many individuals have been ruined by the introduction of the *steam-engine;* yet no one thinks of making up the loss of the sufferers. No one thinks of establishing a perpetual fund to compensate the loss of the stocking-weavers, printers, cloth-dressers, or coach-proprietors : no one would think of compensating the loss of the publicans and brewers, from the throwing open of the *beer trade.* Yet the rights of all these classes are as sacred as those of the pensioners and sinecurists. They have all *vested interests* in their pursuits ; they have all served apprenticeships or laid out their capital : and if the sacrifice of their property be a public good, they are as much entitled to compensation as the " high and efficient public men."

Absurd as the principle is, it pervades the whole system : all abuses are *private property*, and you cannot reform them without raising an outcry that the interests of some class or other are violated. If you meddle with tithe, you are violating the property of the church. If you attempt reform in courts of justice, you are attacking the emoluments and patronage of the judicial classes. If you attack the rotten boroughs, you are accused of invading the property of the aristocracy. And, lastly, if you touch sinecures, they are the property of our " *high and efficient public*" men.

Under such a system there can be *no reform ;* there can be only transformation of abuse ; you can only transmute a sinecure into a pension, or an enormous salary into a superannuation; but, as to extirpating the evil altogether, it is chimerical. That can only be done by a reformed Parliament, which shall have no vested interests in the abuses it undertakes to remove.

Having explained the origin and principle of the Pension Act, let us next glance at some of the worthies who, up to this time, under the designation of " high and efficient public men," have fastened their greedy talons on the earnings of the industrious. First on the list is Lord Sidmouth, £3000 a year for life: his lordship, besides, has Richmond-park Lodge, and for many years has been receiving, as deputy-ranger, from £1000 to £2000 per annum, out of the rents and profits of the crown lands. The sinecure of clerk of the pells was many years held by his son; and there are several other Addingtons in the church, and on foreign missions. Altogether £5000 a year may be put down as the reward of the famous circular, the memorable *letter of thanks*, to the Manchester magistrates, for the massacre of the 16th of August, and other high and efficient public services of Henry Viscount Sidmouth.

The next is the honourable Robert Ward £1000, late auditor of the civil list, we believe, and who has run through various ranks and degrees as clerk of the Ordnance, M.P. for Haslemere, &c. This gentleman is only to receive half his pension, if he hold office of less annual value than twice its amount.

The right honourable Henry Goulbourn £2000, the Duke's luminous and most efficient chancellor of the Exchequer. Then follows a Mr. Hamilton £1000, of whom we know nothing, unless he be a late consul or clerk of the Treasury. Afterwards we have Thomas Peregrine Courtenay, M.P. for Totness, colonial agent for the Cape of Good Hope, and late secretary of the India Board. This is the "family man," with a wife and fourteen children, for whom Canning once made so melting an appeal to the guardians of the public purse;—they must be provided for. Mr. Courtenay is the cousin of a peer—let him be put down for £1000, and his sons have the first vacancies in the Mint, the Treasury, or Exchequer!

Now, right honourable John Wilson Croker, come forth; don't be ashamed; who can begrudge any thing to the paymaster of the widows' charity, and a twenty-one years' secretary of the Admiralty, with £3000 per annum. Put John down for £1500 a year for life—but stop; do not let him receive his pension, any more than his brother pamphleteer, Peregrine Courtenay, if he hold offices yielding £3000 a year.

Joseph Planta, Esq. we congratulate you; enrolled among the high and efficient public men; a secretary of the Treasury, with £3500 a year, and a pension for life of £1000 a year. Mr. Planta, you are a happy man; your calling and election are sure, and you are now placed beyond the risk of accident, by " flood or field." Next to Castor and Pollux, whom you have so good a right to follow, you have been one of the most humble and industrious labourers in the borough vineyard.

We pass over Canning and Huskisson ; at the time of their death, each was down for £3000 ; they were amongst the most greedy and audacious of corruptionists ; but they are gone to their audit elsewhere ;— not, however, without leaving long trails of calamities behind, of which more hereafter.

Next is a Hobhouse £1000 ; but we pass over him also to come to the last and greatest of our " high and efficient public men," the right honourable Lord Bexley.   How ought a statesman like this to be rewarded : the great Sieur Vansittart, the steadfast coadjutor of the " Thundẽrer," the astounding financier, the man of infinite resource, who, in the period of our greatest tribulations, did, by the mere force of native genius, make a pound note and a shilling equal to a guinea, when the former was depreciated thirty per cent.   Put Nicholas down for £3000 a year for life, and make him a LORD !

Here ends the muster-roll of " high and efficient public men. "   There are other names ; but these are enough to illustrate the application of the Pension Act of 1817, and the supplementary act to it in 1825, and which acts ought to have been long since repealed by the Whig ministry.

There is another description of pensioners whom we must shortly touch — the noble and learned lords :—Here is Lord Eldon still preying upon us, at the rate of £4000 a year.   Surely £15,000 a year, and upwards, for more than a quarter of a century, and a disposition naturally parsimonious, afforded the means of making a comfortable provision for old age.   Lord Manners, another ex-chancellor, draws £3,892 a-year ; Wynford £3,756.   Then there is lord Tenterden impending, and Bayley and others menace us in the distance.   Lyndhurst for a time hung out a flag of distress, but, after receiving £505 : 14 : 11¼ (*Finance Accounts*, p. 122) as temporary relief, he retreated into the court of Exchequer.   Brougham, or his friends for him, have put in a claim for £6,000 as a retiring pension,—but avast there, good lord !   Surely such doings must have an end !   At this rate the whole Bar may file through the judgeships, and come upon us, after a quarter's service, for pensions for life, each of which, at the present rate of labourers' wages, would maintain eight hundred persons.

COMPENSATIONS AND RETIRED ALLOWANCES.

A most indefensible principle has long been acted upon by the Government,—namely, if a person has only once been so fortunate as to have had the fingering of the public money, he shall for ever after be supported out of the public purse.   It is exactly the principle of the poor-laws ; let a man obtain a settlement, and he thenceforward claims subsistence from the parish, and let a placeman once get into a government office, and he immediately, and for ever, sets up the pauper's claim of being fed and clothed at the charge of the community.

Exactly upon this principle was framed the infamous Act of 1817 ; most of the pensions, we have seen, were granted conditionally ; provided the parties were not *in office*, then they should receive their

£1000, £1500, or £3000 per annum, as a trifling allowance, to keep the poor creatures from starving while unemployed ! What a pity such old and faithful servants should perish of hunger, especially as they could not possibly have had an opportunity, from the lowness of their wages, to lay up a store for a rainy day ! Still we like even-handed justice to all mankind. Many object to that mode of administering the poor laws, which allows a labourer in health and strength his parish-pay, merely because he happens to be *out of work*. But why not extend the same rule to state paupers ? Why should such able-bodied men as Croker, Planta, and Courtenay entail upon the industrious classes such heavy rates, merely because they are just now in want of a job ?

The practice of granting compensations and retiring allowances is just as indefensible as granting pensions. We have now before us two official returns of the session of 1830, the bare titles of which are enough to make one sick : one is—" Returns of all Persons who receive Compensation Allowances for the loss of their Offices until *otherwise provided for;*" the other a " Return of the Number of Clerks and Officers who have been SUPERANNUATED, and who have been *again introduced into the service.*"

What practices are these ? on what principle can they be justified ? A merchant or banker retires from business, reduces his establishment, or is forced into the *Gazette*, by alterations in the currency, or commercial vicissitudes, and what compensation does he give to his clerks and servants thrown out of employment ? None : nor do they expect any, having previously received salaries equivalent to the value of their services. Let us revert to our former illustration ; suppose that, by the discovery of a new machine, a certain manufacture can be carried on at a cheaper rate, and, of course, the public be benefited by its substitution for manual labour, owing to the less price at which they could obtain the manufactured articles. Again ; suppose that, by some new mode of managing the business of government, a number of offices may be abolished, and, of course, their salaries saved to the community. Here, then, are two cases exactly similar ; in one, a number of working people are thrown out of employment ; and, in the other, a number of the officers of government. The public is benefited alike in both cases : in one, by saving of salaries ; and, in the other, by the less price at which it purchases commodities. But how differently these two classes of sufferers have been treated. One receives a pension or compensation, perhaps to the amount of his salary ; and the other is suffered to perish for want of employment, and his privations aggravated by contributing to the maintenance of persons whose claims at all events are not greater than his own.

The same gross injustice is perpetrated in lord Brougham's Bankruptcy Court Act. Under this act, the monstrous sinecures of patentee of bankrupts and clerk of the hanaper, held by the Rev. Thomas Thurlow, and yielding £11,000 a-year, are abolished ; but then the reverend sinecurist is to be compensated during his natural life by an equivalent annuity, payable out of bankrupt estates. This is not the worst part of the arrangement. Lord Eldon had granted these valuable sinecures in reversion to his son, William Henry John Scott, or William Henry Scott, (for with admirable precision he is called by both names in the 52d clause of the statute,) on the death of Thomas Thurlow ; and thus during two lives the public will have to pay £11,000 per annum, without even the pretext of service, and when these lives drop, probably some device will be hit upon for inserting a third, in the same manner as the Dead Weight and other government annuities are perpetuated. Even the commissioners of bankrupts, many of whom had only just finished eating their commons, and whose very names were offensive as synonymous with all that is sponging, imbecile, and parasitical—even these are to receive pensions for life. And last, and not least, the *purse-bearer* to the Lord Chancellor is to be compensated by an equivalent life annuity. Only think of this, the lord chancellor having a purse or sack-bearer to carry his fees—just as if we lived in the time of the Henries or Edwards, and such a contrivance as bank notes had never been heard of. Really we are startled at the Gothic barbarisms of the system at every turn, whether we look into the law-courts, the Exchequer, the royal household, or the Church Establishment, and we almost despair of ever seeing it brought into usefulness and symmetry.

Much as we desire to see legal reforms, we had rather they were altogether postponed than accompanied with such interminable incumbrances. A bill is now in the house for abolishing fines and recoveries, but a long train of vested interests and expectances are to be satisfied and compensated before it can be carried. Our opinion is, we had better stop at once than proceed at this rate; we are evidently in a slough, and the further we go, the deeper we are in the mire. It is obviously better policy to leave abuses in a state of sufferance than to sanction their existence by act of parliament.

It was chiefly by a profuse grant of pensions and compensations to the members of the Irish parliament—which immaculate body Mr. O'Connell is so anxious to see revived—that Mr. Pitt, through the agency of lord Castlereagh and marquis Cornwallis, was enabled to accomplish the Union. From page 488, it appears that more than £75,000 is annually paid to persons for the loss of office, in consequence of that legislative movement. Sir Jonah Barrington relates that, " Among other curious claims for Union compensations, appears one from the Lord-lieutenant's *rat-catcher* at the castle, for decrease of employment ; another from the *necessary-woman* of the privy council of England for the increased trouble in her department ; with numerous others of the same quality." Besides compensations, there was super-added a liberal grant of peerages, and £1,500,000 was raised to compensate refractory members for loss of boroughs ; Lords Ely, Shannon, Clanmorris, Belvidere, and Sir Hercules Langrishe, received £143,000, the first noblemen being paid £90,000 for their six members !

It is, however, to the fatal wars of the Aristocracy we are principally indebted for the immense number of compensations, as well as every other national calamity. The vast extent of our establishments, during the period of hostilities, and their reduction since the peace, has made one very considerable portion of the community sinecure dependents on the other for support; and the extent to which the public is now burthened, in providing for *non-effective* services, is almost incredible.

It appears from the inquiries of Sir H. Parnell's committee, that the non-effective of the army, navy, and ordnance costs the country £4,904,499 a-year; while the effective of the same costs £15,616,354: so that nearly one-third, or thirty-three per cent., is paid for no manner of service whatever. Again, in the civil departments of the government, the sum of £4,371,000 is paid for salaries, and other effective services; and £440,000 for compensations, and other non-effective services, the latter being actually one-tenth part of the former.*

Such a monstrous system could never have grown up, except under a most negligent and lavish administration, directly interested in the corruptions it tolerated. It would be easy to cite examples of the most shameless abuses, in granting compensations and retired allowances. The attempts to fasten the sons of Earl Bathurst and Lord Melville on the public, under these denominations, must be still remembered. In the official returns, to which we have alluded, we find Mr. Penn, a clerk of the customs, was superannuated upon £750 a-year for his important services; but though superannuated for the customs, he was made agent for Ceylon, at a salary of £1050. In 1822, Alfred Johnson, agent-victualler at the Cape of Good Hope, retired on a pension of £400, and reappeared in 1826 as secretary to the commissioners of the navy at Plymouth. Thomas Alexander, store-keeper at Martinique, was superannuated in 1815, at £175 a-year, and just ten years after *debouched* again as store-keeper at Mauritius, at £400 salary.†

Of those who are receiving compensations until *otherwise provided for*, the following may be taken as specimens. Henry Hallam, Esq. late commissioner of stamps, £500 a-year; Charles Jolly, examiner of taxes, £230; J. D. Smith, landing waiter, £375; Alexander Cleghorn, inspector of imports, £416; John Hughes, an unattached barrack-master, £182; W. R. Marshall, clerk of survey, Woolwich, £450; Pierce Edgecumbe, clerk, Chatham-yard, £416. Separately these *pro tempore* allowances are not of much consequence; but when the number of them comes to be considerable, it raises the total amount to a serious sum. After all, it is not clerks and other small fry whom we first wish to see cut down; it is the great consumers of taxes—the high Aristocracy, who, with extensive domains, enjoy valuable sinecures, and receive enormous salaries, and especially such pensioners as Eldon, Bexley, Grenville, Wynford, Sidmouth, and others of that calibre, whom we desire to see curtailed.

---

* Third Report on the Public Income and Expenditure; Parliamentary Papers, vol. v. Sess. 1828.
† Parliamentary Paper, No. 450, Sess. 1830.

Commissioners of Inquiry.—These form a numerous and burthen-some class, most of them receiving salaries of from £1000 to £1500. They are a sort of servants of servants; being set on foot by those who ought to be the servants of the people, to do the work which they themselves have been deputed to perform. The ostensible objects of most of the commissions now in operation are, to inquire into the laws and judicial administration, to inquire into the state of public charities, the national records, the duties, salaries, and emoluments in courts of justice in Ireland, the management in certain branches of the revenue in Great Britain, and the state of the Scotch Univer-sities. The labours of some commissions, it cannot be denied, have been productive of the most beneficial results; others have been in-stituted merely as pretexts for jobs, to extort more plunder from the people. The unpaid services of parliamentary committees have con-tributed, more than any other form of inquiry, to the exposition and amendment of public abuses.

SALARIES AND PENSIONS EXCEEDING ONE THOUSAND POUNDS.

Great as are the salaries, pensions, and emoluments of individuals, it must be constantly borne in mind that these constitute the smallest part of the advantages, or perhaps we may term it corruptive influence, to which official men are exposed. The most important, the most seduc-tive, and most tempting adjuncts to public offices of the higher grade are the vast patronage, the power and personal consideration they confer on the possessors. In this consists the great difference between government employments and the pursuits of trade and commerce. There are, we doubt not, individual merchants and manufacturers who do—or at least have—realized an annual profit equal to the salaries of a first lord of the Treasury, Secretary of State, the Chief Justice, or even the Lord Chancellor. But observe the difference in their respective situations; observe the dazzling and glittering elevation of the state functionaries; observe the good things they have at their disposal—the benefices, bishoprics, commissionerships of customs and excise; the clerkships, registrarships, and secretaryships, worth from £1000 to £10,000 a-year—and think of the opportunities afforded by these splen-did gifts for enriching their families and friends—and think, too, of the delightful incense of adulation and obsequiousness the dispensers of such favours must inhale, and of the host of fawning sycophants, ex-pectants, and dependents, they must every where raise up around them. Here are the real *sweets of office*, the delicious flavour of which can never be tasted by a mercantile man, however successful in his vocation.

What is it which makes individuals seek anxiously to be placed in the magistracy, or sacrifice a fortune for a seat in the House of Com-mons? It is not the direct salary or emoluments, for there are none; it is the power and the chance of obtaining power, and the personal con-

sideration it gives.   A directorship in the Bank of England, or in the
East-India Company is comparatively unprofitable, except from opening
a wide field for valuable appointments and individual influence.   But if
objects like these can rouse up to an intense degree human cupidity,
how much more must it be excited by a chance of obtaining the great
prizes of state, which yield not only great direct emolument, but boundless patronage, and an authority and pageantry almost regal!

In considering, therefore, the salaries of civil and judicial officers, it
is always necessary to bear in mind that they form only a single element
in the multifarious advantages of their situations.   The patronage of
most public officers would be ample remuneration; and were it limited
to that alone, we have no apprehension there would be a dearth of
candidates for official employments, no more than there are for the
magistracy, shrievalties, custos rotulorum, lord lieutenancies, and other
unpaid services.

We have been drawn into these observations from reflecting on a
singular public document before us, and of the contents of which we
shall give the reader some account.   We have hitherto spoken of placemen and pensioners generally; we shall now direct attention to the
highest class, whose emoluments *exceed* £1000 *per annum*, and of which
a return has been made to parliament.*   Why Sir James Graham restricted his motion to tax and fee-eaters of the transcendental order, it is
not easy to conjecture; perhaps it is the intention of the Whig ministry
to make £1000 the maximum of official remuneration,—a proposition
which the community would hail with great thankfulness as one of the
most effective blows ever aimed at sinecurism, deputyships, and aristocrat idlers.   Our opinion indeed is that, with a few exceptions, the
emoluments of no public officer ought to exceed £1000; few persons
with higher incomes will *work*, and they only tend to generate a taste
for luxury, equipage, club-houses, gambling, and the frivolities and dissipation of fashionable life.

To come, however, to an analysis of the return to which we have
alluded.   It comprises 956 individuals whose incomes amount to
£2,161,927, averaging £2261 each; there are *forty-two* persons whose
incomes are not less than £5000 each, and whose united incomes
amount to £339,809; and there are ELEVEN individuals whose incomes
are not less than £10,000 each, and who altogether receive £139,817
per annum.   Of the whole 956 names the following is a classification,
showing the total income of the several classes, and the average income
of each individual.

---

* Parliamentary Paper, No. 23, Session 1830-1.

CLASSIFICATION *of* 956 *Placemen and Pensioners whose Salaries, Profits, Pay, Fees, and Emoluments exceeded, January* 5, 1830, £1000 *per Annum.*

No. of Officers.	Description.	Total Emoluments.	Average Income.
350	Civil Officers	£698,805	.... £1997
50	Court of Chancery	137,216	 2744
112	King's Bench and other Judicial Officers..	338,651	 3023
100	Ambassadors and Consuls................	256,780	 2567
134	Military Officers........................	240,847	 1794
36	Ordnance and Artillery..................	50,155	 1390
19	Naval Officers..........................	39,835	 2076
147	Colonial Officers.......................	378,996	 2578
8	Officers of the House of Commons........	20, 642	 2567

The lawyers evidently profit most by the system; their average emoluments exceed those of any other class; the civilians of all classes are better remunerated than the military; and the officers of the army rather better than those of the navy. The worst paid are *employés* in the Ordnance; this branch of the service requiring men of science and application, is not sought after by the great families, and hence we observe the *working* of our aristocratical government in this department as in every other; the most meritorious and arduous duty not being performed by the Oligarchy and their dependents, it is rewarded by the fewest number and least valuable prizes.

It is not, however, by *averaging* the incomes of public functionaries that we see the iniquities of the System in its most conspicuous light. In the state, as in the church, the most flagrant abuse consists in *pluralities*, in the power which individuals of title, influence, and connexion have to heap upon themselves, families, and friends, a multiplicity of offices. Next to this abuse is that of patronage. We know that the direct income of a lord of the Treasury, or a secretary of state, is very considerable, and that of a lord chief justice or lord chancellor is enormous; but what is that to the value of their patronage. All their immense patronage is so much direct revenue, and we know that it is applied as such in making provisions for sons, sons-in-law, and collaterals. We might cite the Bathursts, Manners, Abbotts, Scotts, and others; but we think the subject has been already sufficiently illustrated, and further proof will be found in our *Place and Pension List.*

Of all classes who prey on the community the lawyers require to be most narrowly watched. By the classification above it is evident they have contrived to have more sumptuous pickings than any other description of *employés*, official, military, or naval. They are talkers by profession, and the gift of tongues enables them to set forth their claims and withstand reduction of emolument with superior effect and clamour. The claim for legal fees has been a principal obstacle to judicial reform, and it has only been by the most extravagant concessions this

obstacle has been surmounted.   The lavish settlement for the sinecures
in equity under the Bankruptcy Court Act we have before noticed.   It
has been the same in the common law courts.   Under the 1 Will. IV.
c. 58, commissioners were appointed to ascertain the value of legal fees
received in the superior courts, and fix a rate of compensation for them
according to their average amount in the ten preceding years.   But it
was found on inquiry that several fees and emoluments had been received
in the courts, the *legality* of which it was difficult to determine.   Here
then was a case of *doubt*, and the question was, who were to have the
benefit of it, the public or the profession.   The " Guardians of the
Public Purse" certainly ought to have guarded the weal of the former ;
but they did not.   Under the same legal intelligence, we presume, as
that which advised the continuance of the payment of the Russo-Dutch
loan, another act was passed the 1 & 2 Will. IV. c. 35, by which it was
provided that all fees, whether legal or extortionate, which had arisen
or been received within the preceding fifty years, should be allowed by
the commissioners.   Further, if any more doubts arose as to the legality
or reasonableness of such fees, to whom does the reader imagine the
commissioners were to refer ?—To the lords of the treasury, to
Mr. Gordon, or to some other impartial tribunal perhaps—No ! by all
that is inept and ridiculous, they were to refer to the judges of the court
in which the questionable fees had been received, and by whom the fee-
gatherers are appointed !

REDUCTIONS OF THE WHIG MINISTRY.

It is much more agreeable to our nature to praise than to blame, and
we regret the subject of this section is not more copious.   From some
paragraphs in the newspapers we were led to infer the Whigs had
effected great things in the public departments ; but on examining more
authentic sources of information we find that all they have effected is,
to adopt the expressive phraseology of the Paymaster of the Forces, a
mere flea-bite.   It is only by a general reduction, as contended at the
commencement of this chapter, of one-third or other fractional part in
all public salaries, pensions, fees, and emoluments, that any material
improvement can be accomplished.   Next to this, a plan of direct
taxation ought to be substituted for the expensive, trumpery, and
inquisitorial fiscal system matured under Mr. Pitt and his successors.
We have before alluded to this subject, and shall leave it to proceed to
our more immediate object.

First, it appears that the salary of the Lord Chancellor is to be
regulated, but it is not said it is to be reduced.   We affirm, however,
it ought to be reduced, and greatly too.   It is monstrous that a man
who, perhaps, the day before was squabbling at the circuit mess, or
pleading some paltry cause for a five-guinea fee, should be at once
thrust into an office worth £15,000 a year.   It is an income enough for
a KING, and is a great deal too much for a king's clerk.   The salaries
of the other equity judges, as also of the judges of the common law

courts, ought all to be reduced; they are enormously too high, and wholly unsuited to the times.

The salary of the First Lord of the Treasury is to be continued at £5000 per annum, but if the office is held in conjunction with the chancellorship of the Exchequer, the salary of the latter is to be reduced one-half, making the net income of the two £7500. Here not a farthing is given up, but a contingent saving may be effected by the Whig successors in office, for whose benefit no doubt this admirable arrangmeent is intended.

The salary of the Chancellor of the Exchequer is £5,398 : it is to be reduced to £5000 net—Here, JOHN BULL, £398 is saved—take it and be thankful!

The junior lords of the Treasury are paid £1220 each : they are to be reduced to £1200—Here, JOHN, is a whole *twenty pounds* saved. This is economy at any rate. Upon my word this is cutting away right and left in grand style! But here follows something more substantial. The joint secretaries of the Treasury are to receive £2500 in lieu of £3500; the three principal secretaries of State £5000 in lieu of £6000; and the under-secretaries of State £1500 in lieu of £2000. My Lord President of the Council is to receive £2000, by which £840:17:4 is saved—a sum not to be sneezed at in these times, and for which many a man would be truly thankful. My Lord Privy Seal, who is my Lord Grey's son-in-law, is to receive the net income of his predecessor in office : but lord Durham is a noble-minded man, and has declined receiving any salary. The first Lord of the Admiralty to be reduced from £5000 to £4500; the first secretary from £3000 to £2000, with an addition of £500 after five years' service. Nothing is said about the junior lords of the Admiralty. The income of the President of the Board of Control to be reduced from £5000 to £3500; that of the paid commissioners from £1500 to £1200; and that of the secretary from £1500 to £1200. The Judge Advocate General is to be reduced to a net salary of £2000, which is enough during peace, when standing armies are unlawful. The reductions at the Ordnance Board are too meagre to merit special notice. The salary of the Postmaster General is to be continued, in consideration of his *real* duties, and of the laborious duties of Sir F. Freeling, who is amply remunerated at the rate of £5000 a year. The rangership of the parks, a sinecure, to be abolished. The Master of the Mint to receive £2000 in lieu of £3000. The Keeper of the Great Seal of Scotland to receive nothing *except fees*. The chief secretary of Ireland to receive £5500—a responsible office—but too highly paid and out of proportion with the incomes of the Premier and Home Secretary. The auditorship of the Civil List has been annexed to the Treasury, by which a saving of £1500 a year has been effected. The offices of receivers general of the taxes, except in the London district, have been abolished, and their duties annexed to the offices of inspectors of taxes. Other offices abolished or reduced, are considerable; among them the Vice-Treasurer, king's Stationer, and Post-Master-General in Ireland;

the Lieutenant-General of the Ordnance and Clerk of Deliveries ; Treasurer of the Military College and the Treasurer of the Military Asylum ; sixty inferior offices in the Post-Office department ; four Commissioners of the Navy and Victualling departments, two Commissoners of the Dockyards, seventy-one clerks, and the Paymaster of Marines ; two Commissioners each of the boards of Excise and Customs : in all 210 officers have been reduced. Considerable savings have been made in diplomatic and consular charges and naval superannuations. The Board of Woods and Forests and Board of Works have been consolidated. Several offices too have been consolidated, which will be noticed in the List.

Upon the whole, after going more minutely into the subject than we had done at the commencement of this section, we are bound honestly to declare that the Whigs merit the gratitude and confidence of the country for the reductions effected ; they have not been idle, and some allowance must be made for the momentous question they have had to battle in the Legislature, from the moment of first entering into office. They have, however, delayed too long the repeal of the vile Pension Act of 1817.

Having treated on the several subjects of this chapter, it only remains to recapitulate : the public documents, from which the several accounts have been taken, having been already cited, need not be repeated in the subjoined summary. It will also be observed, that the expenditure of the Crown and Royal Family is omitted, that having been fully detailed in a former part of this work.

A Statement of the Annual Expenditure of the United Kingdom, in Salaries, Pensions, Sinecures, Half-pay, Superannuations, Compensations, and Allowances.

Salaries of 22,912 persons employed in the public offices £2,788,907
Retired full-pay, half-pay, superannuations, pensions, and allowances
  in the army... 2,939,652
Ditto   ditto   in the Navy 1,583,797
Ditto   ditto   in the Ordnance 374,987
Superannuated allowances in the civil departments of government.. 478,967
Pensions.. 777,556
Pensions in the nature of compensations for the loss of offices
  in England... 12,020
Ditto in Ireland, chiefly in consequence of the Union 89,245
Annual value of sinecure offices.. 356,555
Commissioners of Inquiry 56,299

£9,457,985

Can any one believe that, in these few items, a saving of at least three millions might not be effected ? And with a saving even to this amount, how many oppressive taxes might be repealed ! If we further extend our view to other departments of the government, and to the courts of law, the civil list, the colonies, the monopolies of the Bank and East-India Company, the established church, and the corn-laws, what an ample field presents itself to our consideration for the relief of this suffering and oppressed community.

But will government ever avail itself of these vast resources as the means of national amelioration ? Not under the existing system. Effective retrenchment, without a previous parliamentary reform, is a chimera. To retrench is to *weaken;* the true policy of the Oligarchy is to spend, not to save. There are, no doubt, scores, nay, hundreds of offices and establishments useless, indeed, to the people, but invaluable to their rulers. The greater the sinecure, the greater its importance to the Aristocracy ; and the very reason urged by the people for its extinction, is the strongest argument for its retention by their oppressors. Could government only reward its servants according to their deserts, what inducement would there be to enter into its service ? Who would incur the odium of such employment ! How could it obtain adherents ? How could it so long have had zealous supporters in every part of the empire, and carried on a detestable system, subversive of the rights, and incompatible with the happiness of the community ?

Ever since the death of Fox and Pitt there has been scarcely an individual with the least pretension to the endowments of a statesman in the administration. Look over the roll of the Percevals, Vansittarts, Castlereaghs, Jenkinsons, Cannings, Sidmouths, Huskissons, and Scotts, and say, if there is one that did not deserve a halter, or whose proper place was not behind a counter, in lieu of directing the resolves of a legislative assembly. Yet by these, and such as these, were the destinies of this great empire swayed for upwards of twenty years. Can we wonder at the frightful results of their empyrical statesmanship ? Can we wonder that they bequeathed to their successors, convulsion, decay, and death, in every fibre of the kingdom ? But incapable, vile, and unprincipled as these men were, ignorant and reckless, as experience has proved them to be, of the ultimate issues of their measures ; still these scions of the Pitt school were too sagacious ever to think that retrenchment and rotten boroughs were compatible elements of the constitution. They knew better ; they had been too long familiar with the secret pulses and springs of the state machinery to commit so egregious a mistake. Their dependence was on *force* and *corruption;* on the bayonets of the military, and the annual expenditure of eighty millions of money. These formed the right and left hands, the master principles of their policy. The support they could not bribe they sought to intimidate. Such was their black and iron system ; it lasted *their time,* or the time of most of the pillaging and hypocritical crew ; and for any thing beyond they did not care a rush !

Let us hope that we are on the eve of better times, that we shall not be deluded by temporary expedients and professions, put forth merely to gain time for plundering, nor quack remedies to be followed by mortal maladies; in short, let us hope the Whig ministry will proceed on scientific principles, and that we shall have a parliamentary reform first, and next such an effective retrenchment and disposition of public burthens as will afford real national relief.

" Corruption wins not more than honesty;" and the true end of government is not difficult to attain.   It is simply to augment social happiness—affording equal security to the property and persons of every individual,—protecting the weak against the strong,—the poor against the rich; in short, by guarding against the extremes of indigence and crime, luxury and vice, and spreading an equilibrium of comfort and enjoyment through all ranks, by good laws, wisely conceived, promptly and impartially administered.

It is a cheap and admirable contrivance, when established on the rights, and supported by the confidence of the public.   There is then no need of standing armies in time of peace.   There is no need of expending sixteen millions a year in support of naval and military establishments. There is no need of a Sinking Fund as a resource for future war. Government is strong in the affections of the people.   It is prepared for every exigence, and must always be invincible against domestic foes and foreign aggressors.   But, if government has not this support; if it is looked upon only as an instrument of rapacity and extortion; if it is looked upon as a legalized system of pillage, fraud, and delusion; if it is looked upon only as an artful cabal of tyrants united for plunder and oppression; then must such a government, instead of being a cheap and simple institution, be a complex and expensive establishment— strong, not in the people, but in its means of corruption, delusion, and intimidation.

The English government had been long approximating to the latter predicament.   It had ceased to possess the respect and confidence of the people, and governed by over-awing the weak, deluding the ignorant, and corrupting the baser part of the community.   The latter —its power of corruption—its means of rewarding its adherents by the *spoil of the people*, is the great lever by which it has operated.   This power, its connexion and influence, as exhibited in the church-establishment, the judicial administration, the public offices and departments, chartered monopolies, and corporate bodies, we have fully exposed; and it only now remains to record the *names* and emoluments of those who chiefly profit by its abuses and perversions.

ALPHABETIC LIST

OF

PLACES, PENSIONS, SINECURES,

GRANTS, AND COMPENSATIONS.

EXPLANATIONS.

THE subjoined *List* has been principally prepared from the Parliamentary Papers Nos, 480, 479, 95, 273, 587, and 58, of the Sessions, 1830 ; from Nos. 23, 42, and 56 of Session, 1830-1 ; and from Nos. 345, 249, 167, 55, 108, and 337 of the Session of 1831. We have been also indebted to the Annual Finance Accounts, and to other official returns for pensions payable by the East-India Company, and out of the fee-funds of the public departments.

The same system of mystification and perplexity is observable in the payment of salaries and pensions as in other departments of the public accounts. The incomes of placemen, for example, arise partly from salaries paid by government and partly from fees paid by individuals. Pensions are paid out of at least half a score of different funds and by nearly as many different authorities. Some are parliamentary pensions charged on the revenue of taxes ; others are court pensions, charged on the Civil List ; others are ministerial pensions, charged on the 4½ per Cent. Leeward Island Duties ; and other pensions are granted under the authority of the 57 Geo. III. and 6 Geo. IV. ; and then again an immense number of pensions have been granted under authority of 50 Geo. III. c. 117, which empowers the lords of the Treasury to award pensions payable out of the fees received in the public offices. These are exclusive of pensions payable by the East-India Company, and out of the colonial revenues of Ceylon, Mauritus, and other dependencies. Some individuals have been fortunate enough to obtain pensions on several funds ; others again have had two or three or four pensions granted in succession, charged on the same fund. This complication of funds and payments has been the growth of centuries ; it has been partially remedied during earl Grey's ministry, but the disorder is of too long standing and too widely spread to admit of easy and effectual cure.

To the people the distinctions of the Civil List, Consolidated Fund, 4½ per Cent. Fund, Fee Fund, Regium Donum, &c. are comparatively unimportant ; it is sufficient for them to know that all salaries, pensions, fees, compensations, and allowances, by whomsoever granted, or out of whatever fund paid, ultimately proceed from the produce of industry, and that the misapplication of them for any other than effective *public services,* or for services that have been already sufficiently remunerated by patronage or emolument, is nothing better than peculation and robbery, whether committed by the king, his ministers, or the houses of parliament.

We thought at first of giving separate lists of the members of the Privy Council, the House of Peers, and the House of Commons, holding places, pensions, commissions, or emoluments, but on this plan the reader might have been often at a loss under what head to look for individuals ; whereas, having adopted an alphabetic arrangement, every facility is afforded for direct reference to any name or title. All the sums put down, whether salaries, pensions, compensations, or other denomination, are *annual* payments, and with respect to salaries they are the amount agreeably to the scale of reduction of the present Ministers. Where a *date* is inserted, it refers to the year when the place was obtained or the pension first granted. From the salaries and pensions returned have been deducted all exchequer fees and duties, and they are the net amount actually received. It is unnecessary to observe that all the salaries are not exorbitant, nor all the pensions undeserved, but this is a point we leave to the reader's discrimination.

The *List* is corrected to Feb. 1832 without the alteration of a single item in the official returns, further than by the omission of the *shillings* and *pence*, with which, though the honourable and right honourables have condescended to receive them, we did not think necessary to occupy our pages. In our illustrative notes of the pensioners we have been much aided by the searching expositions of Colonel Jones.

Abbot, Thomas, clerk at nisi prius to the chief justice······	£1000
Abbott, John, Henry, marshal and associate to the chief justice	2665
The last is the son of lord Tenterden, and the preceding a nephew. It is said the principal difficulty in the retirement of the chief justice of the king's bench, is the condition his lordship insists upon, that the Hon. John Henry shall retain his offices, and affords another instance of the obstacles presented by exorbitant fees and emoluments to needful improvements. No new appointment ought to be made, nor the old one much longer continued without the abolition of the remanet fees. It is no fault of the suitor which makes his case a remanet, and the delay of his trial accumulates legal expenses enough upon him, without being heavily taxed every term by the marshal and asssociate for court fees.	
Aberdeen, R. collector of customs, Bridge Town, Barbadoes··	2000
Abergavenny, earl of, compensation for inspectorship of prosecutions in customs ················ ···········	1545
A sinecure abolished twenty years since, and surely the public has paid money enough for an office so long declared useless by statute. The earl has sixteen rectories and two vicarages in his gift ; two sons and a nephew in the church.	
Abercrombie, lord, hereditary pension by act of parliament··	2000
Abercrombie, J. brother of the preceding ; lord chief baron of the court of exchequer, Scotland ················	4000
Adair, Robert Sir, minister to Belgium ··················	3600
Adair, Robert, Diana, and Elizabeth, pension Irish civil list··	445
Adam, W. G. accomptant-general, court of chancery······	3184
Adam, William, lord chief commissioner of jury court, Scotland	4000
Adam, major-gen. Sir F. col. 73d foot, unattached pay······	434
Staff pay as lieut.-gen. in the Ionian Islands········	1383
Pension for wounds·····························	300
Adams, W. D. commissioners of woods and forests ········	1200
Late comptroller of the lottery ··················	375
Addington, Henry Unwin, minister at Madrid ············	3802
Aiton, W. T. director-general of his majesty's gardens······	1400
Alexander, sir W. late chief baron of the court of exchequer··	3500

Albemarle, earl of, master of the horse ··················	£3350

Can the magnitude of the civil list be matter of surprise when such enormous salaries as this are paid out of it? £1000 would be enough for any master of the horse. It might have been expected such a great county meeting patriot as my lord Albemarle and the father-in-law of the veteran Whig, Mr. Coke, would have made his *first* appearance in public in some other capacity than a court lord.

Alderson, sir E. H. puisne judge common pleas·············	5500
Alison, John, distributor of stamps for Dundee, *Sept.* 1828··	445
Late stamp-master of linen, Scotland···············	151
Allen, Frances, viscountess, pension, civil list, *July* 1799 .··	266
Additional, on civil list, *Oct.* 1800··············· ·······	88
Allen, viscount, pension on civil list, *Sept.* 1821 ··········	266

Could not this noble lord pay his subscriptions at White's, Brookes's, and Crockford's—his journeys to and from Paris, and his cabriolet, without the paltry pension attached to his name?

Allen, L, B. one of the six clerks in chancery ·············	1217
Althorp, lord, chancellor of the exchequer················	5000

One cannot help agreeing in the high opinion commonly entertáined of lord Althorp, but he has fallen in troublesome times, and got the most irksome post in the administration. The halcyon days for chancellors of the exchequer were during the sway of Pitt, Perceval, and Vansittart; those days of increasing establishments—granting pensions—multiplying boards and offices—and dispensing the other sweets of official life. It was then all plain sailing ; the chief difficulty was to spend enough, not to raise the means—a sweeping loan of twenty or thirty millions, backed by a never-failing majority of three or four hundred members, covered every deficit. But these are times of pinching economy and abridgment, and all schemes of finance, except such as are comprised in the simple recipe of a reduction of expenditure, are repudiated. The truth is the Whigs have succeeded to a bankrupt concern, and when ministers announced in the Gazette in January that the expenditure exceeded the income, the *docket was struck.* We hope, however, when lord Althorp next gets hold of a good thing, he will neither be baffled out of it by jobbers in city articles, nor jobbers in 'Change-Alley. For our parts we could never see any valid objection to the proposed tax on the transfer of funded property in a country where the transfer of property ef every other description, down to a trumpery receipt or promissory note, is subjected to duty. If by any contrivance mere stock-jobbing could be made a source of revenue, it would be an improvement in morals and police as well as finance. It is quite preposterous to be constantly taking out executions against the " hells" at the West End, or to legislate against thimble-ring and little-goes, while the giant Pandemonium adjoining the Auction Mart is tolerated in all its exuberance and ramifications of iniquity.

Alves, H. S. senior clerk, India board ··················	900
Master of the mint, Scotland ···················· ······	390
Amedroz, K. F. clerk of first class, Admiralty, *Jan.* 1799 ··	780
Translator of foreign papers, 1800··············· ····	100
Amherst, earl, lord of the bedchamber ··················	800
Hereditary pension, by act of parliament ···········	3000

This is one of the most objectionable of the *hereditary* pensions. It was transmitted by the uncle of the peer, sir Jeffrey Amherst, a favourite of George III. and placed by him at the head of the army ; when, as commander-in-chief, he introduced and protected such bare-faced jobbing and traffic in commissions as both disgraced and ruined our military power. The loyalty of that day was not to entertain even a suspicion of the misconduct of the individual who had the ear of royalty, however flagrant, and thus the court favourite died in the full enjoyment of the rewards of his baseness, and left the army of England to his successor as a body in name than in reality.

The services of lord Amherst in Canada were of no great importance, yet they were rewarded with the extravagant pension of £3000 a year—£1000 more than was ever voted by a squandering house of commons to the heroes of the peninsular war. The present Earl cannot object to have one-half, or at least one-third of his unearned hereditary allowance cut-off. It may be urged, indeed, that this pension was granted by act of parliament, and therefore irrevocable ; but what more mutable and evanescent than acts of parliament? are they not constantly being repealed, altered, and amended ? what progress could be made in the improvement of the judicial administration were not hundreds of unintelligible and inapplicable statutes abrogated. Grants and conveyances of property are constantly being set aside in courts of equity for want of a *good title* or *adequate* consideration ; and why should the whole mass of pensions, allowances, and compensations be held more sacred ? It is sheer nonsense to think about the existing generation and posterity being tied up for ever by the folly, ignorance, prodigality, and short-sightedness of their progenitors.

Amyot, T. registrar of colonial slaves	£800
Compensation for loss of office of registrar in Canada	400
Anglesey, marquis of, lord lieutenant of Ireland	20000
Colonel of the 7th dragoons	1800

The salary of the viceroy was reduced £7,000 in 1830 ; it still looks great, but according to the evidence of Mr. Stanley, the lord-lieutenant is constantly out of pocket by the appointment. The marquis is a brave and well-intentioned man, and we should be glad to hear he had got rid of the *tic douloureux.*

Angell, J. chief clerk, ordnance office	1162
Anson, sir George, M.P. for Lichfield ; lieut.-gen. and col. of 4th dragoon guards	1500

His nephew, lord Lichfield, is master of the stag-hounds. Another nephew a lieutenant-colonel—and other relations in the army and church—one, a nephew, is prebendary of Southwell.

Anstruther, P. collector of revenue, Ceylon	1538
Antrobus, G. C. M.P. for Plympton ; sec. of legation, Naples	1500
Arden, C. G. Perceval, lord, registrar of the court of Admiralty	38574

This sum was the gross amount of his lordship's income during the war ;—deductions were given in to the amount of £26,012, making his net income £12,562. In the late return of incomes exceeding £1000, the court of Admiralty was omitted, so we have no authentic means of estimating his lordship's emoluments since the peace. His disinterested loyalty was marvellously exemplified in an animated speech he once made in the upper house, in defence of reversionary grants ; asserting that an attempt to abolish them was an " *indecent attack upon the king's* LAWFUL *prerogative*." His lordship has two sons in the church and another in the navy. Two nephews hold sinecures in the exchequer. Other relatives are in the army and colonies—one, R. Bourke, is governor of New South Wales.

Arthur, Colonel, lieutenant-governor, Van Dieman's Land ··	£1500
Arnaud, E. collector of customs, Liverpool·················	2500
Arbuthnot, major-gen. sir T. staff, western district, Ireland ··	891
Unattached pay as major-general ·················	310
Pension for a wound ·························	300
Arbuthnot, Henry, commissioner of audit ·················	1200
Arbuthnot, Catharine, pension on civil list, 1804 ···········	138
Arbuthnot, Harriet, pension on civil list, 1823 ·············	938

Wife of a veteran placeman, whose pension on the death of George IV. was the subject of amusing discussion and inquiry.

Archdall, Mervyn, M.P. for Fermanagh ; a general and lieutgovernor of the Isle of Wight····················	1397
Argyle, duke of, keeper of the great seal, Scotland ········	fees

A sinecure ; the salary, which constituted nearly the whole emolument of this appointment, has been withdrawn by ministers.

Arnold, J. R. lieut.-col. royal engineers, 1814 ············	330
Extra pay, commanding engineers, northern district··	165
Allowance for a servant ·························	27
Pension for wounds, 1816 ······················	300
Ashworth, Robert, pension on civil list, 1787 ·············	1072
Ashworth, Henrietta, pension on civil list ·················	266
Ashworth, Frederick, pension on civil list·················	266
Ashworth, Charles, pension on civil list···················	177
Ashton, A. secretary and chargé d'affaires at Rio de Janeiro··	1368
Athlone, earl of, hereditary pension, by act of parliament····	2000

This family, the *De Ginkells*, came over with William III. in 1688, and was one of his instruments of oppression in Ireland. It was rewarded by a grant of 26,000 acres of land, the forfeited possessions of the earl of Limerick. This grant was reversed by parliament, and the family retired to Holland, whence they returned on the expulsion of the Stadtholder. The Earl took his seat in the Irish house of lords in 1795, and reclaimed his pension. In 1823 the ninth Earl of the name died, and he was succeeded in the title and pension by his son George, a child now in the eleventh year of his age.

Auckland, lord, master of the mint and pres. board of trade··	2000
Pension on civil list, *July* 1814····················	300
Pension out of 4½ per cent. fund, *July* 1820········	400
Audley, lord, pension on civil list, 1821 ·················	462

Ross Donnelly, father-in-law of the pensioner, a vice-admiral.

Avonmore, viscount, late registrar, court of chancery, Ireland	4199
Aylmer, lieut.-gen. lord, colonel 56th foot, and governor of Canada ········(········)·····················	10,000
Pension on the civil list, *Feb*. 1783 ··············	356
By act of parliament, Ireland·····················	553
Backhouse, John and J. Lewis, pensions out of 4½ per cents.··	500

Backhouse, John, under secretary of state··················	£500
Receiver-general of excise ······ ················	1500
Badger, A. auditor for land revenue, Wales ··············	750
Bagot, W. receiver of taxes for the Westminster district ····	1200
Bagot, sir C. ambassador to the Hague ···················	4000

Brother of the bishop of Oxford and of lord Bagot, whose niece Emily is maid of honour to the Queen. Other Bagots are in the army, and the next, the *fiscal*, is a member of the family also. *W. C. Bagot*, receiver-general of taxes, about whose retention of office we are doubtful, after the abolition of these appointments in the country.

Bagot, G. second fiscal, Demerara····················	1228
Bankhead, Penelope Mary, pension on civil list, 1825 ······	350

Widow of the physician of the late lord Castlereagh.

Barber, — chief registrar, bankrupt court (*exclusive of fees*)	800
Barnard, Edw. pension on civil list, 1823 ················	500
Barraud, William, receiver of duties, customs ·············	1160
Bathurst, earl, teller of his majesty's exchequer ···········	2700
Clerk of the crown in chancery ····················	1105
Bathurst, Charlotte, pension on civil list, 1823·············	600
Pension on civil list, 1825 ·························	200
Pension on civil list, 1829 ·······················	100
Bathurst, Mary, pension on civil list, 1826 ··············	250
Bathurst, hon. Charles, pension on civil list, 1826··········	350
Late commissioner of bankrupts···················	200
Receiver of duchy court of Lancaster··············	500
Bathurst, hon. W. deputy teller, exchequer ···· ··········	1000
Clerk in privy council office·····················	2000
Bathurst, hon. S. treasurer to government, Malta··········	1560

Few persons have evinced a more exemplary appetite for the public money than lord Bathurst. His lordship's family has mostly been in the receipt of £10,000 or £12,000 a year, from fees, pensions, and taxes. He still retains two valuable sinecures, his son William Lennox one, and an office nearly a sinecure, and his son Seymour Thomas another. On the eve of the breaking up of the Wellington ministry, his lordship made strenuous efforts to obtain *firmer hold;* first he tried to superannuate his second son, who had been a couple of years in the victualling office, as a retired commissioner; failing in that, he next, with the most indecent precipitancy and almost by absolute force, thrust him into the office of the late Mr. Buller, as clerk of the privy council. If one did not know that the assurance of men is mostly in the inverse proportion of their deserts they would be surprised at the pecuniary audacity of this nobleman. Lord Bathurst is notoriously a person with the least possible claims to public honour and emoluments: he is altogether without talent; a most feeble, awkward, and puzzled speaker; and in every sense of the word a most trifling personage.

Bannatyne, sir W. M'Leod, late lord of session, Scotland····	1500
Baring, F. M.P. for Portsmouth, nephew-in-law of earl Grey;	
lord of the treasury ······ ················ ·······	1200
Bates, Edw. husband of the 4½ per cent. duties, *Jan.* 1831 ··	400
Secretary to the board of taxes, *Feb.* 1823 ········	1500

Ballantyne, W. police justice, Thames-office ··············	£800
Barrow, John, second secretary to the Admiralty ···········	1500
Barlow, P. mathematical master, Woolwich-academy·········	380
Barton, J. deputy comptroller, mint office ················	600
Barnard, Edward, retired allowance as clerk, colonial office ··	200
Agent for New South Wales, Van Dieman's Land ··	600
Barker, John, consul-general in Egypt ···················	6151
Batley, W. collector of customs, Ipswich ·················	350
Barnes, J. H. petition-clerk, customs····················	350
Barnard, major-gen. sir A. col. rifle brigade, 1st. batt. ·······	1182
Equerry and clerk-marshal to the king ·············	749
Baker, A. St. John, consul-general at Washington···········	1600
Baker, lady Elizabeth Mary, pension civil list, 1814·········	461
Sister to the duke of Leinster, and widow of an under secretary of state.	
Baker, rear-adm. Tho. South America (part of the year) ····	1545
Baker, sir Robert, pension on civil list, 1822···············	500
Late Bow-street magistrate, dismissed and pensioned after queen Caroline's funeral. If he neglected his duty, he ought not to have got a pension.	
Bankes, G. M.P. Corfe Castle; cursitor baron, exchequer····	455
Baillie, G. clerk in colonial secretary's office···············	739
Agent for Sierra Leone and the royal African corps ··	639
Barnouin, J. H. chief clerk to clerk of ordnance ···········	1062
Barry, colonel, secretary to government of Mauritius ·······	3150
Barrington, hon. G. son-in-law of earl Grey, cursitor of county palatine of Durham, and captain in the navy; lord of the admiralty ·······························	1000
Bandinel, James, clerk in office of secretary for foreign affairs	1200
Bayley, sir John, one of the barons of the court of exchequer	5516
Bayley, sir D. consul-general at St. Petersburgh ···········	1000
Bayly, lieut.-gen. H. col. 8th foot, pay and emoluments ····	1320
Pension for wounds································	350
Beauclerk, John, late commissioner of bankrupts, 1797······	200
Recorder of Northampton, 1828····················	750
Beaufort, capt. F. hydrographer to admiralty, *May* 1829····	691
Bedingfield, John, pension on civil list, 1822 ·············	250
Bedwell, F. B. registrar in court of chancery··············	3877
Bell, lieut.-col. J. secretary to governor of Cape of Good Hope, Colonel of 27th foot, and governor of Tilbury Fort··	2000
Bedford, G. C. clerk to auditor of exchequer ··············	1200
Bernard, John F. clerk in the secretary's office, customs ····	50
Clerk of the postage ··························	500
Belfast, earl of, M.P. for Antrimshire; vice-chamberlain in the king's household ····· ····················	600
Belhaven, lord, lord high commissioner of Scotland ········	2000
Belmore, earl of, governor of Jamaica ···················	7000

Bentham, sir S. pension as late civil architect and surveyor ··	£1000
Pension for late employment in Russia, 1797 ········	500
Beresford, William, groom of the privy chamber ·········· ····	no return.
Beresford, general, W. C. viscount, col. 16th foot, pay and	
emoluments ······ ······· ······ ······ ·········	1182
Governor of Jersey········· ······· ············	1100
Pension by act of parliament ················ ········	2000
Beresford, H. B compensation as late joint-storekeeper,	
customs ····· ············ ······· ··········	2157
Beresford, J. C. compensation as late joint-storekeeper, customs	2157

These offices, held by patent, are abolished—and what a compensation! it is a genuine Irish job, and worthy of the plundering family who participate in it. *J. C. Beresford* is the man of the riding-house flogging celebrity. *Sir J. B. Beresford*, brother of the viscount, is a vice-admiral, and major-general lord G. R. Beresford is colonel of 3d dragoons.

Bentinck, gen. lord W. governor-general of Bengal ········	25000
Clerk of the pipe in the exchequer, England ········	1131
Colonel of 11th hussars, pay and emoluments ······	2511

Look at this nobleman's offices, emoluments, and localities, and then think of the incongruities tolerated under the system.

Bentinck, Jemina Helen, pension on civil list, *Nov.* 1809····	300
Bessy, J. F. second under clerk, teller's office ············	600
Bexley, lord, pension as late chancellor of the exchequer ····	3000

Here is a reward for the most consummate ignorance and laxity of principle. Lord Bexley left the Exchequer from sheer incapacity, and then skulked under the Canning ministry as chancellor of the duchy of Lancaster, and after enriching himself in that sinecure, finally graduated on his pension under the profligate 57 Geo. III.

Bidwell, Thomas, clerk in office of secretary for foreign affairs	1250
Deputy clerk of the signet ····· ····· ········ ,·····	95
Bidwell, John, clerk in the office of secretary for foreign affiairs	1400
Binning, D. M. commissioner of customs ·············· ······	1400
Bipland, Thomas, collector of customs, Greenock ········	800
Birch, J. W. assistant reading clerk, house of lords········	1200
Bird, C. clerk, receiver of duties and registrar, Berbice ····	1730
Bingley, Robert, king's assay-master, mint-office········ ·····	900
Birnie, sir. R. chief magistrate, Bow-street-office, salary and	
extra allowance for attendance at home-office ··· · ··	1200
Bicknell, H. E. clerk to registrar in chancery ············	1622
Bingham, C. col- royal artillery, and fire-master royal laboratory	731
Pension for wounds ············· ,············	300
Bingham, major-gen. sir G. R. staff, southern district, Ireland	891
Unattached pay as lieut.-colonel···· ············· ·····	310
Blake, A. R. chief remembrancer of the exchequer, Ireland··	2817
Blackwood, vice-admiral sir H. commander-in-chief at the Nore	2555
Groom of the king's bedchamber ···············	400
Pension on civil list, 1809··············· ······	300

Commanded a frigate at Trafalgar; but other captains in that action have neither obtained a place at court nor a pension.

Blackwood, lady Harriet, pension out of 4½ per cent. fund ··	£206
Blakeney, major-gen. sir E. staff, south-western district, Ireland	691
Unattached pay as lieut.-colonel ·················	310
Blackburn, F. attorney-general of Ireland ·············	3000
Black, Jean and Mary, pension each, civil list *Aug.* 1823··	50
Blair, Mrs. Isabella Cornelia, pension on civil list, *Oct.* 1811	276
Isabella and Cornelia, pension on civil list, 1810, each	138
William, pension on civil list, 1812 ··············	184
Blaquiere, John, lord de, pension on civil list, 1794 ······	1107
Additional pension on civil list, 1802 ············	830
Pension by act of parliament, Ireland ············	500
Well known in the Irish parliament, and who with a handsome person and good address succeeded well at the vice-regal court.	
Blackwell, major-gen. governor of Tobago ·················	3027
Bloomfield, lord, envoy and min. plenipo. in Sweden ······	4900
Colonel of artillery ····························	1003
Blunt, Joseph, solicitor to the mint ···················	800
Borough, sir R. during pleasure, pension on civil list, 1794··	184
Booth, W. deputy commissary-general, half-pay ··········	267
Clerk of the survey, ordnance-department··········	560
Bowen, Jas. late commissioner of navy ···················	956
Boothby, sir W. receiver-general of customs·············	1500
Agent for New Brunswick ······················	150
Paymaster of band of gentlemen pensioners ········	230
A relation by marriage of the " stern path of duty man."	
Bolton, lieut.-general sir R. col. 7th dragoon guards ······	1334
Equerry to the king ·························	750
Bosanquet, sir J. B. a judge of the common pleas··········	5500
Bosanquet, G. secretary and chargé d'affaires at Madrid ····	2260
Bolland, sir W. one of the barons of the court of exchequer··	5516
Bowles, William, comptroller of coast-guard, *July* 1822 ··	1000
Captain in the navy, half-pay ·················	228
Bowles, Charles and Elizabeth his wife, on Irish civil list, 1827	192
Mr. C. Bowles married the sister of Mrs. Goulburn, wife of the late chancellor of the exchequer; was afterwards dubbed private secretary to his brother-in-law; and on the unaccountable promotion of this last in England, finally settled for life on poor Ireland at the pittance mentioned.	
Bowden, J. chief clerk to the receiver-general at post-office ··	600
Inspector of stamps for excise, *Aug.* 1826 ········	150
Bouverie, major-gen. sir H. F. commanding northern district	874
Unattached pay as major in the coldstream guards····	700
Bouverie, H. I. commissioner of customs ················	1400
Bouverie, hon. Arabella, pension on civil list, 1821········	300
It is certainly not the politics of the present lord Radnor, which obtained for the Bouveries their civil and more numerous ecclesiastical appointments.	
Boulton, K. J. attorney-general, Upper Canada ··········	1534
Bousfield, deputy registrar, Bankrupt-court··············	600

Bourchier, Chas. assistant solicitor to the treasury	£1900
Bowden, J. W. commissioner of stamps	1012
Boyd, Chas, surveyor-general, customs	800
Boyd, hon. R. deputy inspector of hospitals and commissioner of revenue and commerce	3000
Boyle, David, lord justice clerk, Scotland	4000
Boyle, hon. C. commissioner of navy, 1823	1000
Bradshaw, J. H. clerk and registrar, post-office	625
Brande, W. T. superintendent of the irons, mint-office	700
Brandon, William, baron, pension on civil list, *Nov.* 1820	276
Briggs, J. T. deputy secretary to victualling-board	800
Brickdale, comptroller of customs, Bristol	666
Brisbane, lieut. gen. sir Tho. colonel 34th foot	1095
Brackenbury, J. M. consul at Cadiz	1216
Brent, T. secretary, board of green cloth	1185
Secretary to the lord steward	124
Groom and clerk of the robes	156
Bradford, lieut.-general sir T. col. 30th foot	1311
Pension for wounds	350
Brougham and Vaux, lord, lord high chancellor of England	14500

The sum we have put down is the average annual emoluments of the chancellor-ship during the three preceding years, and a Parliamentary Committee, of which Mr. Baring was chairman, has proposed to fix the future salary of the lord chancellor at £14,000 a-year, in lieu of all fees and perquisites. We have before expressed an opinion that this is too much. To be sure the Lord Chancellor is a sort of legal chattel moveable with the administration to which he is appendant, whereas the judges seated on the bench of common law have mostly a tenancy for life. But with the precedent of lord Lyndhurst there appears no absolute reason future ex-chancellors should, after the manner of the late lord Erskine, while away time in the gossip of coteries and drawing rooms. It is alleged the lord chancellor has an hereditary peerage to support, which he is compelled to accept, whether he will or not. To this we answer—grant peerages for life! How much better it would have been for the Giffords, Kenyons, Loughboroughs, Ellenboroughs, Thurlows, Fitzgibbons and Avonmores, had their dignities terminated with the individuals who acquired them: we should have heard less of poor peers, and of the necessity of hereditary pensions and hereditary sinecures to support them. Every new chancellor has an allowance for *outfit* to the amount of £2000, and the salary itself is only one of the advantages of the appointment: its great attractions consist in the official precedency it confers, and the vast extent of legal and ecclesiastical patronage it places at the disposal of the possessor. Lord Brougham will not be alone in his penury, if such be his lot; there are other law lords whose pecuniary acquisitions must be much less commensurate to the support of a coronet.

In England the public mind is so diseased by the pursuit of wealth, we are accustomed to hear so much of the necessity of great incomes to maintain the dignity of the Crown, the dignity of the Peerage, and the dignity of the Prelacy; we really seem to think—so much has the judgment been perverted by the worship of Mammon—that there is no honour, no dignity, no happiness, except in the grasping of large heaps of money. It is, however, not so—a man with £500 a-year—if he so will it—may just as well support his dignity as one with half a million. Our notious differ greatly from other ages and nations. The Roman worthies could retire to their farms without disparagement, after the exercise of sovereign power. How much our wealth-seeking aristocracy sinks in comparison with the American democracy—the glorious names of Jefferson, Adams, and Maddison, who needed neither hereditary honours nor pensions to dignify retirement, and transmit their fame to posterity. But we shall leave the subject : all we have said has no reference to the Lord Chancellor ; no one can have read the testimony he gave before the Committee to which we have alluded, without being convinced that he has higher objects in view than pecuniary gain—that he is only actuated by a regard to what is suitable to the office, not to the individual who fills it.

Many persons were surprised that a person possessing such transcendent abilities and unwearied industry as lord Brougham should merge them in the stagnant pool of the house of peers. But ought not the harassing and stormy course of his lordship's previous career to be borne in mind, and may he not, in his latter days, have chosen the woolsack from the same motives which prince *Talleyrand* chose a belle and bonhomie spouse,—namely, as convenient for *repose?* As cabinet minister, head of the law department, keeper of the king's conscience, and what not, his lordship's sphere and power of usefulness are vastly extended and augmented. All the manifold abuses, which he has so long forcibly and eloquently set forth in the administration of justice, in charitable foundations, in corporate and collegiate endowments, and in West Indian slavery, he may now hunt down with a power and means of accomplishment increased a hundred fold. To the pursuit of these objects lord Brougham is solemnly pledged ; and we confess we have seen nothing in his lordship's official career to lessen public confidence in the steadfastness of his engagements. The establishment of the Court of Bankruptcy was a vigorous and disinterested effort at judicial improvement. His lordship's speech, however, on the first introduction of the Reform Bill, was, to say the least of it, a *queer one ;* it had many *readings*, for which we could only account from some misgivings of the Speaker respecting the *future*. As to what his lordship has thrown out on the tenure of ecclesiastical property, we do not attach much importance to it : when the noble Baron alleged that the church was a *sleeping partner* with the state, we considered it a joke, intended for the *blind* side of the House. The spirit of the People is roused ; events are crowding onward at a giant pace, which will practically determine the rights of the Clergy with much less preliminary discussion than has been consumed about the immunities of hares and partridges, the African slave-trade, and Catholic emancipation.

Brougham, W. brother of the preceding ; a master in Chancery, *circa* ·····································	£4250
Brown, W. R. cocket-writer in the customs ············	1088
Brown, N. commissioner, victualling-office ········ ·······	800
Brown, Thomas, master-attendant, Woolwich··············	650
Brown, R. H. warden of Fleet Prison, see p. 486 ··········	2000
Browne, Charles, under-secretary, excise ················	800
Browne, P. secretary and chargé d'affaires at Copenhagen ··	1151

Browne, R. solicitor to the stamp-board, Ireland ··········	£2000
Browne, R. late teller of exchequer, *Aug.* 1824 ··········	400
Late commissioner of musters, 1798 ··············	151
Browne, sir H. pension on civil list, 1829 ·················	200
Brown, R. examiner of army accounts ·····················	1200
Half-pay as deputy-commissary general, 1807 ······	273
Agent for paying retired or officiating chaplains ······	250
Allowance as private secretary to a secretary of war ··	150
Brooking, A. H. collector of customs, Newfoundland ······	1400
Brownrigg, gen. sir R. colonel 9th foot, pay and emolumeuts	1323
Governor of Landguard fort ·····················	339
Pension from Ceylon ····························	1000
Brooksbank, Stamp, clerk in the treasury and auditor ······	1650
Brooksbank, T. C. chief clerk in treasury·················	1200
Agent and paymaster of Chelsea out-pensioners ······	750
Agent for the Bahamas ·························	150
As late commissioner of lottery ··················	150
Brooksbank, Ann, pension on civil list, 1783··············	155
Brooksbank, Elizabeth, Isabella, and Hermoine, civil list, 1827	300
Brooke, R. clerk in customs, Liverpool ·················	500
Bromley, lady Louisa, (late Dawson,) pension out of 4½ per cent. duties, *Nov.* 1820······························	250
Bruce, sir S. pension on civil list, 1817·················	177
Bryce, major-gen. sir A. colonel commandant royal engineers, and deputy inspector-general of fortifications······	1875
Pension for good services ·····················	182

Brydges, sir John W. H. uncle-in-law of marquis of Water-
    ford, and M.P. for Coleraine; a major in the army,
    capt. of Sandgate-castle, and colonel in the Portu-
    guese service ·································
	no return.

The city of London has had a brush with the Beresfords, as well as Mr. O'Connell, and, last election, attempted to rescue from their monopolizing grasp the borough of Coleraine. The borough is indebted for its charter to the corporation of London; they are the proprietors of the soil, and endowed it with upwards of 400 acres of land, for the general benefit of the inhabitants. By some means the Beresfords have contrived to render the common council a *select* body, consisting of the members of their own family and dependents, through whose agency, for upwards of a century, they have returned the parliamentary representative. For the last fifteen years sir John Brydges has been their nominee; and, at the general election, the gallant knight, for the first time, went to pay his respects to his constituents, when, in answer to the inquiries of the townspeople, he told them " that, though he had never before been amongst them, and was an Englishman, he had an *Irish heart.*" Some of the inhabitants claimed the right to which they are entitled by the charter, to the exercise of the elective franchise, and objected to the Major being returned by about twenty non-resident burgesses. These claims and objections were over-ruled by the worshipful mayor; and, after the usual farce of a nomination by a clergyman, and a seconding by another corporate official, the captain of Sandgate-

castle, and colonel in the service of Don Miguel, was declared duly
elected to the imperial parliament. The corporation of London
have protested against these proceedings of the Beresford puppets,
and expressed their intention, by a deputation of their body, to re-
establish, in a court of law, the general rights of the burgess agreeably to their charter. It is probable, however, their laudable endeavours will be rendered unnecessary by the general legislative
measure, which will at once cut off such rotten concerns as Coleraine, Truro, Berealston, and scores more.

Buchanan, lady Janet, pension on civil list, *Oct.* 1827······	£150
Buchanan, Susanna, pension on civil list, *Nov.* 1827 ······	200
Burton, W. W. puisne-judge, Cape of Good Hope··········	1500
Bull, John, clerk of journals and papers, house of commons··	1656
Buller, James, retired allowance as late commis. of customs ··	1100

    This gentleman, we are told, a mild, amiable person, possessed
the borough or boroughs of East and West Looe : therefore, disposing of his seats to the government, was made a commissioner of
the customs ; was unfortunately attacked with deafness ; marries ;
is tired of London ; retires to the country ; makes room for some
other *protegé* of government ; and saddles the country with a pension of **£1100.**

Bulley, A. clerk of issues, auditor's office, *Oct.* 1822 ······	750
Receiver of pensions and officers' duties············ ······	108
Allowance on moneys paid into the Exchequer ······	144
Burgh, Elizabeth, pension on civil list ·················	276
Burgh, Catharine, pension on civil list ·················	230
Burke, J. clerk of crown quit-rents, Dublin ·············	461
Burke, executors of Mrs., pension on the 4½ per cent. fund··	2500

We have touched on this notorious abuse at p. **203,** and shall here
pass it over.

Bushe, C. K. chief justice of the king's bench, Ireland······	5076
Bursey, J. inspector in the audit-office ················	600
Burrows, Peter, commis. for relief of insolvent debtors, Ireland	2092
Burraud, Rev. G. compensation allowance for loss of the office	
of searcher in the customs ···················	1100

    Some boroughmongering job this, no doubt ; otherwise, no cler-
gyman could have held the office of *searcher* in the customs.

Burrard, Hannah, pension on civil list, 1815·············	400
Butler, G. chief clerk, ordnance department ······ ········	900
Butcher, J. store-keeper in the ordnance, Dublin ··········	750
Burghersh, major-gen. Lord, minister plenipo. at Florence ··	3900

    His lordship was receiving a large salary as envoy at Florence,
while spending the last winter in London, busily engaged in
bringing out his new opera.

Burgoyne, J. lieut.-col. royal engineers, 1814 ·············	330
Extra pay, commanding royal engineers, Portsmouth··	165
Allowance for servant·························	27
Pension for good services, 1817 ·················	182
Burnell, Dr. W. commissioner, victualling-office ··········	1000
Burton, Charles, third justice of the king's bench, Ireland····	3692
Burton, T. allowance as late secretary to board of excise ····	1500

Burton, gen. N. C. col. 60th foot (1st batt.)	£1331
Butterwich, M. registrar of deeds, Yorkshire	650
Byham, R. secretary to the board of ordnance	1400
Byng, F. clerk in foreign secretary's office	903
Byng, lieut.-gen. right hon. sir J. M.P. for Poole, col. 29th foot	793
Byng, hon. E. commissioner, colonial audit-office	1000
Byron, lord, captain, R.N. ; lord of the bedchamber	500
Calvert, J. M.P. for Huntington ; late sec. to the lord chamberlain	750
Camden, marquess, one of the four tellers of the exchequer	2700

The great sinecures being about to be attacked, in 1817, the marquis, who had held the tellership thirty-six years, and received, on account of it, probably upwards of a million of money, resigned the fees and emoluments of his office, amounting to £27,000, retaining only the regulated salary of £2500. Previously to this his lordship contributed sums to the public service. In 1819, the house of commons tendered a tardy vote of thanks for this munificent offering. An expectation was entertained, which is not yet realized, that the patriotic example would have been followed by the Grenvilles, the Ardens, the Bathursts, and other great sinecurists. Had the registrar of the admiralty court surrendered the emoluments of his office for the last half century, he would have done more, we imagine, to quench the fires in the county, of which he is lord-lieutenant, than by getting up magisterial resolutions to put down the incendiaries.

Cameron, lady, pension on civil list, *Dec.* 1819	500
Cameron, maj.-gen. sir J. commanding western district	691
Unattached pay as major	310
Lieutenant-governor of Plymouth	493
Pension for injuries received in the service	300
Cane, Richard, sub-agent, Ireland, for Chelsea hospital	1650
Agent to yeomanry corps, ditto	461
Capper, J. H. clerk for criminal business in the home depart.	670
Superintendent of convict establishment	400
Carter, M. consul at Coquimbo	1254
Cartwright, John, consul-general at Constantinople	1600
Carr, hon. Jane, (late Perceval) pension by act of parliament	2000

Our readers may have read or heard of a mild, specious, cold-hearted, self-complacent minister—exactly of the Addington impress—named Spencer Perceval : this pension was granted to his widow, who, within the *annum luctus*, forgot her little lawyer, and married major Carr, of the guards. Some of the minister's children have been well provided for in the public offices ; and in political demeanour, present no contrast to their progenitor.

Carr, Morton, solicitor to excise, Scotland	1500
Campbell, major-gen. sir J. staff at Grenada, staff pay	828
Governor of Grenada, pay and emoluments	3775
Unattached pay as major-general	310
Campbell, lieut.-gen. sir H. commissioner of taxes	1000
Military pay in 1829	1294

Campbell, sir A. late lord of session, Scotland ··············	£1950
Campbell, Patrick, sec. and chargé d'affaires in Colombia ····	3125
Campbell, D. retired allowance as registrar of forfeitures, Ireland	276
Ditto as commissioner of military accounts, Ireland ··	367
Pension on Irish civil list ········· ············	266
Accountant to board of general officers ··· ········	130
A servant of all work, this, at the Castle, and the work there has been mostly *black-jobs.*	
Campbell, gen. A. col. 3d foot, pay and emoluments········	1351
Campbell, D. inspecting commander of customs, Aberdeen ··	344
Captain in the navy····························	191
Campbell, major-gen. sir C. commanding south-west district··	691
Unattached pay as major in the coldstream guards ····	500
Governor of Portsmouth······················	168
Campbell, John, comptroller of customs, Greenock ········	600
Campbell, gen. D. col. 91st foot, pay and emoluments ······	1241
Campbell, Alexander, commissioner of excise··············	1400
Campbell, Eliza, pension on civil list ·····················	389
Campbell, Mary, pension on civil list. *Sept.* 1810 ··········	200
Campbell, Mrs. A. pension out of 4½ per cent. duties, 1820··	219
Campbell, sir Ilay, late president court of session ········ ····	3225
Campbell, Thomas, pension on Scotch civil list, *Oct.* 1806 ··	184
Really the Campbells are a host! We find them in all offices and departments, and in all parts of the world. Those enumerated are only part of the clan. The last we always took to be the author of the celebrated *Pleasures of Hope.* Mr. Campbell's pension, we believe, was given to him by his friends, the WHIGS, but we never could learn by what " high and efficient *public* services" he became entitled to it. If it were bestowed when Mr. C. was a *poor*, but elegant scholar, and man of genius, well and good ; we do not grudge the boon, had it been five times the amount.	
Canning, H. consul-general at Hamburgh ················	1836
Canning, sir Stratford, ambassador at Constantinople········	4460
Canning, trustees for the family of the late Mr., pension, by act of parliament ·· ······ ·······················	3000
The life of the late Mr. Canning was undistinguished by public virtue, and at his death he merited no public reward. He was an open corruptionist and trimmer for place; his political principles were superficial and aristocratic; and by his abilities—specious sophistry, and tinsel eloquence—he kept up a party which inflicted on the country incalculable evils. The friends who deserted him *knew him;* they hated and feared him. If not too late, we would suggest that the monument in honour of this adventurer had better be erected somewhere else than Palace-yard; that is no *place* for George Canning, and the times are coming when it will certainly not be allowed to stand there.	
Carter, Thomas, provost-marshal, Barbadoes ··············	1500
Cathcart, earl of, late ambassador at Petersburgh ···· ······	1784
Colonel of 2d life guards·······················	1816
Vice-admiral of Scotland ······················	1015
Governor of Hull ······························	

Camperdown,visc. hereditary pension for lord Duncan's victory	£3000
Cathcart, Elizabeth, baroness, pension on civil list, 1798	389
Caithness, Jean, countess of, pension on civil list, 1800 ...	200
Additional pension on civil list, *July* 1802	100
Additional pension on civil list, *Sept* 1825	100
Cavan, gen. the earl of, col. 45th foot, pay	613
Governor of Calshot-castle	43
Pension on civil list, *June* 1796..................	260
Chapman, J. commissioner of audit	1200
Chapman, col. S. R. secretary and registrar, Gibraltar	1200
Chapman, J. allowance as late clerk in colonial-office	1100
Late clerk of council, Trinidad	1427
Chad, G. W. foreign minister in Prussia	5500
Charsley, W. assistant-clerk in tally-office	500
Compensation for loss of office in *tally cutting*	150
Junior clerk in tally-office	133
For labour *in locking up the king's treasure*, 1826 ..	40
Christie, col. sir Arch. unattached pay as colonel of 1st royal	501
Commandant of Chatham depot	726
Pension for wounds	600
Chamberlain, sir H. consul at Rio (to 5th June, 1830)	1041
Champagne, gen. Josiah, col. 17th foot..................	1315
Chambers, R. J. police justice, Union Hall	800
Late commissioner of bankrupts, 1803	200
Chambers, Geo. inspector and receiver of taxes, 1825	771
The number of inspectors of taxes for England and Wales is seventeen, and their salaries £400 each, exclusive of allowances for travelling and other expenses. By 1 and 2 William IV. c. 18, the receivers of taxes are abolished, with the exception of one for the London district, and their duties transferred to the inspectors, who receive an additional salary of £100, and a further allowance of £100 for a clerk. We have stated their salaries and emoluments from the Parliamentary Return (No. 167, Sess. 1831), including the additional remuneration for the receipt of the taxes.	
Chatham, earl of, governor of Gibraltar..................	4000
Receives also military allowances, and is col. of 4th foot.	
In trust for seven children of lady Lucy R. Taylor, out of 4½ per cent. Leeward Island duties, for each	139
Chowne, lieut.-gen. C. colonel 76th foot	1321
Christian, J. assistant inspector-gen. of customs, Dublin	400
Commander in the navy	182
Church, John, late clerk in navy pay office, *March* 1822	292
Clerk in stationery-office, *Jan.* 1808	600
Christmas, C. G. deputy auditor for land revenue	2193
Clarendon, earl of, chief justice in Eyre, North of Trent	2250
Prothonotary county palatine of Durham	450
A nephew, G. W. F. Villiers, commissioner of customs; and a cousin, T. H. Villiers, secretary to the India Board.	
Clare, dowager lady, and lady Fitzgibbon, pension on c. l. 1830	780

Mother and daughter; the former, widow of an Irish lord chancellor, who was long in office, realized money, purchased estates, and ought to have been in good circumstances. It was he who was said to have alarmed George III's conscience as to the coronation oath; and, if so, was really the cause of retarding the Catholic claims thirty years, and for which we are now suffering. The present lord is governor of Bombay, with a salary of 15,000 a-year, and his brother, Fitzgibbon, is usher of the Court of Chancery, Ireland.

Clarke, J. inspector and receiver of taxes, 1805 · · · · · · · · · · · ·	£718
Clarke, gen. sir Alured, col. 7th foot, pay and emoluments · ·	1153
Clarke, rev. Dr. receiver of clergy returns, 1804 · · · · · · · · · · ·	500
Late auditor of the royal naval asylum · · · · · · · · · · · ·	300
Clark, E. H. clerk of the warrants, customs · · · · · · · · · · · · · ·	2682
Clerk, John, late lord of session, Scotland · · · · · · · · · · · · · · ·	1500
Clifden, viscount, clerk of the privy council, Ireland · · · · · · · ·	1450
Clancarty, earl of, late ambassador to the Netherlands · · · · ·	2000

A brother, *Poer Trench,* archbishop of Tuam: another brother, Charles Trench, archdeacon of Ardagh; William Gregory, brother-in-law, late under secretary of Ireland, is a pensioner on the civil list.

Clanricarde, marquis, captain of yeomen of guard · · · · · · · · · ·	1341
Clancey, James, taxing officer in common law business, Ireland	1107
Clarina, Penelope, baroness, pension on civil list, 1813 · · · ·	333
Clinton, lieut.-gen. sir W. H. col. 55th foot · · · · · · · · · · · · · · ·	1109
Clinton and Say, lord, col. and aid-de-camp to the king; lord of the bedchamber ·	500

C. R. Trefusis, a brother, commissioner in the excise; another brother capt. R. N; E. Moore, a son-in-law, is in the church. Lady Clinton is lady of the bedchamber.

Clifton, M. W. secretary to the victualling-board · · · · · · · · · ·	1000
Clogstone, S. M. collector of customs, Trinidad · · · · · · · · · · · ·	1500
Cochrane, Maria, lady, pension on civil list, *Oct.* 1800 · · · · · ·	300
Cochrane, Sir T. James, governor of Newfoundland · · · · · · · ·	3000
Cockburn, Henry, solicitor-general, Scotland · · · · · · · · · · · · · ·	2000
Cockburn, A. late minister to Wurtemberg · · · · · · · · · · · · · ·	1700
Cockburn, sir Geo. M.P. admiral and major-gen. of marines · ·	1630
Cockburn, Fanny, Mary, and Harriet, civil list, 1791, each · ·	100
Cockburn, Marianne, pension on civil list, 1800 · · · · · · · · · ·	115
Cockburn, Augusta Harriet, pension on civil list, 1827 · · · ·	200
Cockburn, dame Mary, pension on civil list, 1825 · · · · · · · ·	680
Cockburn, dame Augusta, pension on civil list · · · · · · · · · · · ·	358

Of this singular cluster, probably dame Augusta is the mother of sir James, sir George, the dean of York, and the Columbian or Mexican ambassador. She was of a noble family, and fell in love with her husband, who was either a merchant, or held an office in the India-house. To reconcile her marriage with this person to her family he was made a baronet.

Cockane, Barbara, pension on civil list, *June* 1798 · · · · · · · ·	230
Codd, major-general superintendent, Honduras · · · · · · · · · · ·	1200
Coke, Elizabeth Ann, pension on civil list, 1818 · · · · · · · · · ·	100

This certainly cannot be the lady of the member for Norfolk, and lessee of Dungeness lighthouse!

Colchester, lord, capt. R. N. hereditary pension, by act of parl.	£3000

The father of this lord was speaker of the house of commons for many years with a sufficiently large salary, and held till death the valuable sinecure of keeper of the privy seal, Ireland. He was a shuffling, time-serving lawyer, and the vote of censure on his conduct, moved by lord W. Russell, stands recorded on the journals of the house. Were not such a person adequately rewarded in his lifetime, and ought the country to be burthened with a pension to his heir?

Coleridge, John Taylor, late commissioner of bankrupts······	200

By the Bankruptcy Court Act the Lords of the Treasury are authorised to grant annuities for life, to the amount of £200, to the late commissioners of bankrupt, provided they hold no other public employment.

Colman, George, examiner of plays ····················	400
Lieutenant of the yeomen of the guard ·············	350

Besides the military duties of this court functionary, his business is to examine theatrical pieces before they are licensed for representation, by the Lord Chamberlain; and in the discharge of this office he has latterly acquired considerable notoriety, by his captious and puritanical expurgation of what he considered objectionable passages. The performance of The Bride of Ludgate, we are told in the *Tatler*, was delayed by the extraordinary official sensitiveness of Mr. Deputy Colman, who refused to license the piece until *Charles the Second* (one of the dramatis personæ), who was made by the author to disguise himself as a *parson*, should masquerade it under another less objectionable character! A king appearing as a priest seemed to the deputy as savouring of irreverence towards the cloth! The truth seems to be, that the merry Mr. Colman, of auld lang syne, has turned *Methodist*. It is time, however, the office was abolished; it is too much that talent and genius should be subject to the hypocondriacal whims of repentant prodigals.

Colborne, major-gen. sir J. lieut.-governor, Upper Canada ··	3000
Cowper, earl, hereditary pension out of excise revenue······	1600

Here we have a most singular instance of the application of the revenue. The present noble lord holds it as an inheritance, acquired by the marriage of his grandfather with the heiress of the son of general Overkerken, created lord Grantham. This general was greatly distinguished in the wars of the duke of Marlborough; but whether the pension was granted by king William for the services of the father, or for a loan of money from the son, is not known, no document being extant to establish it; but this pension has been made part of the family settlements of the noble earl, who succeeded to it at his brother's death, as he did to his estates: he may dispose of it at his pleasure. The present possessor, in his political life, has been distinguished by high liberalism, and the most perfect independence. Though frequently invited to Windsor, he was never influenced by it, or ever swerved from his public duty. In the examination of votes, his will be found to have been correctly given. As an *inheritance*, his lordship cannot be blamed for drawing this sum regularly from the public purse; but it becomes the duty of ministers to make arrangements with the noble earl for the extinction of this pension. He is entitled to some compensation; but yet his vested right in it is not such that he can look for so many years' purchase as if it were a landed property. No improvement has been made—no outlay incurred; and what was apparently so lavishingly given, and has been so long enjoyed, may be resumed, with some regard to the present times and the general interests of the country. —Colonel Jones, *Dec.* 15, 1830.

Cowley, lord, brother of the duke of Wellington, late ambassador at Vienna ·························	£2500
Cole, B. and W. Herbert Mullens, brokers, national debt office	750
Combermere, gen. viscount, colonel 1st life guards ··········	1800
Governor of Sheerness ··· ······················	200
Pension, by act of parliament ····················	2000
Congreve, dame Isabella, pension on civil list, 1829 ········	311

Widow of the gentleman of *share-notoriety*, who was himself a pensioner, and at one time much about the person of George IV.

Conway, lord H. S. and lord R. S. Conway, late prothonotaries of the court of king's bench, Ireland ············	7137
Conyngham, marquis, late lord steward of the household, and constable of Windsor castle; lieut.-gen. unattached	636
Conyngham, sir F. N. lieut.-governor of Lower Canada ····	3100
Conyngham, lord A. D. secretary of legation, Berlin ········	1050
Conyngham, G. Lennox, seventh senior clerk in foreign office ··	695

The Conynghams were in high favour at the court of George IV. Dr. Sumner, one of the "*Lady's Bishops,*" was *tutor* in the Conyngham family, and flatterer of the late king, by whose special favour he was raised to the *throne* of Winchester.

Cooksey, J. H. inspector and receiver of taxes ············	814
Corbett, C. H. assistant secretary, excise ················	600
Cooper, George, assistant surveyor, customs ··············	1093
Cooper, sir W. H. and sir F. G. auditor for land revenue in England, salary and emoluments, in year 1829 ····	4071

This is a patent office, held for the lives and life of the survivor; the former is a clergyman, and sir F. G. Cooper was lately an officer in the guards.

Cooper, J. S. comptroller-general of stamps, Ireland ········	900
Cooke, lieut.-general sir G. col. 77th foot ················	1249
Pension for wounds ·························	350
Cooke, Frances, pension on civil list, 1821 ··············	200
Cooke, Eliza, pension on civil list, 1793··················	135

The widow of the celebrated navigator of the name still survives, and probably receives this pension; if so, it is one of the few state annuities of which the public will not complain.

Cornwall, Jos. collector of excise, Edinburgh··············	600
Cornwall, J. warehouse-keeper, excise, Dublin ·· ·········	600
Cole, lieut.-gen. sir G. L. governor of Cape of Good Hope ··	7000
Cope, Walter, consul at Guayaquil··· ,···················	1033
Cotton, William, chief clerk in the treasury ··············	1400
Colles, Joseph, clerk to registrar in chancery···············	1447
Collingwood, hon. S. pension on consolidated fund··········	500
Colville, E. D. registrar in chancery ················ ····	2759
Colby, lieut.-col. F. lieut.-col. royal engineers ············	384
Extra pay for survey of Great Britain ············	495
Superintendent of the trigonometrical survey, Ireland	500
Conant, J. E. police justice, Great Marlborough-street ······	800
Corry, James, late sec. to linen board, Ireland ······ ·····	616
Late clerk of the journals, Irish house of lords ······	609

Colville, lieut.-gen. sir C. governor of Mauritius	£8000
Courtenay, William, patentee of subpœna office in chancery	no return
Clerk in parliament	4000
Courtenay, T. P. agent for Cape of Good Hope	600
Pension under 57 Geo. III. 1825	1000
Courtenay, T. P. in trust for Elizabeth, Catharine, and Frances Courtenay, pensions on civil list, 1806	1000
Courtenay, Ann, pension on civil list, 1827	300

Daughters, we believe, of the above *Thomas Peregrine Courtenay*, cousin of lord Devon, and one of the faction whose future prospects are very much marred by the Reform Bill, and of course very bitter in his hostility.

Connor, Edw. clerk in secretary's office, Dublin	923
Compensation for losses at the union	161
Pension, *May* 1819	184
Allowance on abolition of office of sec. to board of general officers, 1823	92
Connor, R. master in chancery, Ireland	3323
Pension as late clerk, Irish house of commons	55
Conroy, sir John, late commis. colonial audit-office, 1824	800
Captain on half pay, royal artillery, 1822	
Cox, S. C. master in chancery, for year ending *June 5*, 1830	3994
Couper, lieut.-col. G. sec. to master-general of the ordnance	1000
Court, C. T. accountant-general, post-office	700
Cointe, J. F. Le, clerk to registrar in chancery	1230
Craigie, Robert, lord of session, Scotland	2000
Creevey, Thos. M.P. for Downton, treasurer to the ordnance	1000
Crafer, Thomas, clerk assistant to secretaries, treasury	1100
Paymaster of American loyalists	300
Crampton, P. C. solicitor-general of Ireland	3000
Cranstoun, G. lord of session, Scotland	2000
Cranstoun, lady, pension on civil list, *July*, 1826	100
Cranstoun, lady, pension on civil list, *Aug.* 1826	100
Cranstoun, Edward lord, pension on civil list, *Nov.* 1821	200
Crocker, J. accountant to medical board	350
Crofton, hon. Caroline, pension on Irish civil list, 1817	141

Given by Lord Talbot : the lady's father, a man of large fortune, and her mother created a peeress in her own right; sister to Mr. St. George, and aunt of present lord Crofton.

Croomes, John lord, clerk of estimates, war-office	393
Croke, A. LL.D. pension on the consolidated fund	1000
Croker, Rosamond, pension on civil list, 1827	300
Croker, John Wilson, pension under 57 Geo. III. 1826	1500

In a recent pamphlet, imputed to this veteran placeman, written in answer to two pamphlets, imputed to lord Brougham, but no more like Brougham's than Hyperion to Satyr, and much more like the flippant production of some lawyerling, with his pockets stuffed with fees, looking greedily forward to the Rolls, a solicitor-generalship, or some other prize of party-subserviency ;—well, in this pamphlet, Croker—for it must be his—actually resorts to the old bugbear of *property being in danger !* But this, we can assure him, will never do; people do not now believe in stories of ghosts and hobgoblins; we doubt even whether the alarm of a revolution would frighten them. Spoliation, massacre, and infidelity, are no longer associated with resistance to bad government. What, indeed, have political reforms to do with *private* property? they are directed only against public men and public abuses; they are the purifying storms which agitate for a moment the upper regions, while all beneath is secure and tranquil. During the worst period of the French revolution property was respected, and it was only the estates of such of the noblesse as had emigrated and taken up arms against their country, which were confiscated. They had committed high treason against the state, and the same punishment of forfeiture is annexed to high treason in this country. But it is not, we apprehend, the security of *private* property about which the ex-secretary is apprehensive; the property he means, no doubt, is pensions and sinecures; or, perhaps, the lease of crown-land he obtained for the erection of a mansion on the site of Carlton-house, to which he purposes hereafter to retire from the retreat in Kensington-palace, to enjoy in dignified leisure his official gatherings. The bitterness with which this votary of a faction has pursued the Reform Bill, recommended it strongly to all thinking persons: doubtless, a portion of the venom in the Old Pensioner was generated by the terrible scourging his *Boswell* received from the Edinburgh Review.

Croft, Wm. chief clerk ordnance department	£900
Croft, F. Master in chancery for year ending *Jan.* 1830	3799
Crokat, C. examiner of spoiled stamps	500
Crosse, R. inspector and receiver of taxes, 1820	827
Cumberland, lady Albinia, a pension on civil list, 1794	311
Cumming, Ann, pension on civil list, 1822	200
Cust, hon W. commissioner of customs	1200

Most of these commissioners of customs, excise, stamps, and taxes, are *honourables.* The amount of their salaries is still extravagant, and ought to be further reduced.

Cuppage, lieut.-gen. W. col. commandant royal artillery, and inspector of royal carriage department, Woolwich	1430
Cunningham, C. late commissioner of the navy	981
Cuthbert, G. W. assistant-secretary, national debt-office	600
Curtis, Joseph, distributor of sea-policy stamps	500
Dalans, Rev. W. W. assistant chaplain-general	210
Chaplain to the forces serving in London, *March*, 1810	292
D'Albiac, major-gen. sir J. C. unattached pay as lieut.-col.	419
Staff pay as major.-gen.	690

The officer, we apprehend, who distinguished himself by his stern theories of military duty at the Bristol Courts Martial; but as sir Charles drew his chief legal weapons from the armoury of sir Nicholas Tindal, we shall reserve a remark or two till we come to that judge.

Dampier, John L. late commisssioner of bankrupts, 1819	200
Recorder of Portsmouth, 1829	
Dashwood, Charles, consul at Guatemala	1500
Davis, Hart, commissioner of excise	1400
Day, C. late justice of the King's Bench, Ireland	2400
Darby, E. inspector and receiver of taxes, 1827	969

Day, W. Keeper of criminal registers, home department, and conductor of the police horse-patrol establishment ··	£480
Keeper of the accounts, *April*, 1805 ··············	450
Darling, lieut.-gen., governor-in-chief of New South Wales ··	4200
Daly, S. G. late justice of King's Bench, Ireland ···········	2344
Dawkins, E. J. resident in Greece ····················	2900
Dawkins, H. commissioner of woods and forests ·········	1200
Dawkins. R. retired allowance as commissioner of excise ····	1050
Dawson, Lady A. M. pension out of 4½ per cent. duties······	250
Davis, T. H. surveyor-general, customs ··············	800
Dancer, J. N. one of the examiners in chancery; salary and emoluments for year ending *Jan.* 5, 1830 ··········	1600
Darlot, H. deputy comptroller, post-office ···············	814
D'Aguilar, George, brevet lieut.-col., assistant adjutant.-gen.	346
Major, half-pay, 91st foot, *Sept.* 1821 ···········	168
Allowance for mustering life and foot guards ·········	100
Dehany, W. K. solicitor to the excise, in lieu of bills········	2500
De Haekel, J. P. and Ann Ernesline, pension civil list, 1813	200
Delavaud, Geo. retired allowance as late secretary of customs	1500
Dealtry, P. king's clerk, crown-office, salary ··············	30
Secondary clerk in court, clerk of the affidavits, and chief usher, court of king's bench; fees ··········	1672
Dew, E. examiner of dry goods, customs ···············	2141
Dean, R. B. chairman of the board of customs ············	2000
Clerk to master in chancery, alienation office ········	50
Dean, Mary and Laura, pension on civil list, 1830 ········	300
Delamotte, W. master of landscape drawing, military college ··	300
Denman, sir Thomas, M. P. for Nottingham, attorney-general	6200
Desbrow, lieut.-col., capt. and lieut.-col. of grenadier guards	494
Assistant to the general commanding in chief ········	600
D'Este, sir A. equerry to the king ····················	500
Pension on civil list, 1830 ····················	467
Colonel in the army ·····························	1200
D'Este, miss, pension on civil list, 1830····················	467
Children of the duke of Sussex, by his marriage with lady Augusta Murray, (D'Ameland, see page 204,) but which was set aside by the severity of our feudal laws. The royal marriage-act is one of great cruelty ; but if our princes form attachments, they should take care to make provision for their offspring from the handsome allowances they receive, and should not seek to quarter them on the public : we expected better from the high-mindedness of his highness of Sussex.	
Dejoncourt, S. clerk of Connaught-road ··················	724
Devonshire, duke of, lord chamberlain of the household······	3058
Disney, lieut -gen. sir M. col. 15th foot ·················	1272
Dickson, Jane, Caroline, and Louisa, each, civil list, 1806 ··	100
Dickinson, A. assistant clerk of the journals, house of commons	1304
Dickie, Jos. paymaster, Belfast ······················	551
Disbrowe, E. C. envoy extra, and min. plen. at Stutgard ····	3300

Dickson, sir A. lieut.-col. and dep. adj.-gen. artillery ········	£1350
Pension for good services·······················	365
Disbrowe, lieut.-col. assistant military secretary, *Feb.* 1806 ··	600
Lieut.-col. grenadier guards, *July*, 1828 ···········	477
Dixon, col. W. col. commandant royal artillery ···········	1003
Doherty, John, chief justice common pleas, Ireland ········	4615
D'Olier, Isaac, secretary first fruits office, Ireland ··········	313
Dowding, C. inspector-general of customs, Liverpool ········	700
Dowdeswell, T. E., M.P. for Tewkesbury; a master in chancery for year ending *Jan.* 1830 ··················	3896
Dorington, J. E. parliamentary agent to the English and Irish departments of the treasury··············· ·········	1100
Donkin, lieut.-gen. sir R. S. col. 80th foot··················	1412
Don, gen. sir G. col. 3d foot, pay and emoluments ···········	1318
Lieutenant governor of Gibraltar····················	4211
Donoughmore, gen. earl of, col. 18th foot ·················	1258
Searcher of Strangford and Donaghadee·············	929
Governor of Stirling Castle ·······················	857
Pension for military services ·····················	2000
A meritorious officer, but with his other emoluments, and possessed of a large inheritance, he would bear reduction. The presumptive heir to the honours and pension, the late captain Hutchinson, of the guards, distinguished himself in assisting the escape of the French general, Lavalette. But all hereditary rewards are objectionable, except such as history accords.	
Donne, J. G. clerk privy seal office, *July*, 1823············	300
Surveyor of hawkers' licenses, *July*, 1827 ···········	100
Doyle, Sir F. H. deputy chairman, excise board ···········	1700
Deputy lieutenant of the Tower ···················	786
Doyle, gen. sir John, bart. colonel 87th foot ··············	1228
Governor of Charlemont ·························	665
Douglas, col. Sir J. lieut.-col. of Portuguese army, half-pay ··	200
Deputy quarter-master-general in Ireland ··········	746
Inspector of army clothing ······················	346
Pension for loss of leg·························	350
Douglas, sir Howard, lieutenant-governor of New Brunswick	2900
Dombrain, Jos. inspector-general of coast guard, Dublin ····	800
Dorchester, lady, pension on consolidated fund ············	1000
Pension on civil list, 1764 ·····················	115
Drake, Mr. clerk to master Dowdeswell, (whom see)········	1426
Drake, gen. dep. commissary in the West Indies ···········	1317
Drinkwater, lieut.-col. comptroller of army accounts ········	1500
Late commissary-general···················· ·····	525
Drummond, rev. C. E. pension on civil list, 1822 ···········	100
Drummond, Edw. late private secretary to the duke of Wellington, who, on the resignation of the premiership, placed him on the court pension list ··············	250
Drummond, Percy, colonel royal artillery, 1827 ··········	474

Lieut.-governor royal military academy, Woolwich, 1829	£400
Forage and servant allowance ··················· ······	127
Duncan, H. brother of lord Camperdown; storekeeper of the Ordnance ·· ·······························	1200
Duncannon, viscount, son of lord Besborough, and brother of general Ponsonby, commissioner of woods and forests	2000
Dunglass, lord, chamberlain of Ettrick forest·············	300
Durham, lord, lord privy seal ·······················	—
The salary of the privy seal has been fixed at £2000 : but we believe lord Durham has given up the whole of his emoluments to the public. It is an office to which no direct or necessary duties appear to be attached ; but we presume it forms one more of those costly appendages of monarchy, which, like the mysteries of faith, and lord Brougham's wig and train, must not be too closely investigated.	
Durell, Martha, pension on civil list, 1810 ·············	500
Dutton, W. C. minute-clerk, customs ····· ·············	600
D'Urban, sir B. lieut.-governor, Demerara ·············	5877
D'Urban, W. J. government secretary, Demerara ··········	1596
Duntze, sir J. bart. late receiver general of taxes, Devon ····	400
Dundas, lady Elizabeth, pension on civil list, 1801 ········	300
Dundas, William, M.P. for Edinburgh, and brother of viscount Melville ; lord clerk register, keeper of the signet, and register of sasines, Scotland, *circa* ··········	3500
Dundas, dame Charlotte, pension on civil list, 1812 ········	780
Dundas, rear-adm. hon. G. H. L. lord of the admiralty······	1000
Duff, lieut.-gen. hon. Alex. M.P. for Elgin, col. 92d foot ··	1307
Duhigg, Mary, pension on civil list, 1815···············	66
Durnford, col. E. colonel commanding royal engineers, Canada	1195
Dunlop, lieut.-gen., colonel 75th foot···················	1135
Durell, Patty, pension on civil list, 1825 ················	100
Dwyer, F. late six clerk, chancery, Ireland ·············	1088
Dwight, Susannah, widow, pension on civil list, 1820 ······	50
Dyer, H. M. police justice, Great Marlborough-street ······	800
Dyer, H. M. pension out of consolidated fund ··········	1000
Dyer, John, chief clerk in the admiralty ···············	1150
Dyer, John, receiver of receipts of customs ·············	1824
Dyke, P. A. collector of customs, Ceylon ···············	1343
Dyson, Jeremiah, George, and Henry, or survivor, civil list ··	893
Dyneley, Charles, deputy-register, prerogative court of Canterbury ; from fees ······················	1193
Dyneley, John, secretary of presentations to lord chancellor ··	750
Dyott, lieut.-gen. Wm. col. 63d foot, pay and emoluments····	1245
Earl, E. retired allowance as commissioner of customs ······	1500
Earle, P. H. assistant clerk in the treasury, *July*, 1802 ····	689
Retired commissioner of lottery, *March*, 1827 ······	133
Earnshaw, W. assistant solicitor of customs ·············	1500
Eden, Emily and Frances, pension on civil list, 1818, each ··	203
Sisters of lord Auckland, himself a pensioner and a minister.	

Ebbs, John, clerk, privy council office, Dublin ·············	£659
Compensation for wine-warrants, *Jan.* 1828 ········	35
Usher and keeper of council chamber, *March*, 1828 ··	266
Clerk in military department of chief secretary ······	184
Compensation for losses at the union ··············	65
Edwardes, James, head distributor of stamps, Scotland ······	900
Edwards, John, retired allowance as solicitor of excise ······	1292
Edwards, dep. commissary general in Jamaica ·············	1040
Edgecombe, J. collector of customs, Newcastle ·············	700
Edgecombe, F. late commissioner, victualling office ·········	400
Elderton, M. clerk to Master Wingfield,(whom see) ········	1476
Eldon, lord, pension out of consolidated fund ··············	4000

The patriarch of the Pitt and plunder system has survived to witness the final issues of his politics. All the calamities under which the country is suffering are the consequences of the war, of the burthens it entailed, and of the cessation of those dram-shop expedients, which were " strength in the beginning, but weakness in the end." The politicians of this school must have had some misgivings of the soundness of their dogmas; they could not but know that there must be a limit to the magnitude of the debt, and that a load of taxes, which absorbed wages and profits, must end in general poverty and privation. But they were reckless adventurers, who looked only to the present hour, and were regardless of what the future might bring forth. Patriotism, with them, was out of the question: their objects were power and emolument. " If we," said Lord Eldon, on the trial of Mr. Perry, " by our industry, have acquired a degree of opulence and distinction which we could not reasonably have looked for, let us be thankful to *that government* to whose favour we are, in a great measure, indebted for success. And do not let us, by any rash attempt upon our constitution, put it out of the power of *our children* to rise to similar situations." (*Erskine's Speeches*, vol. ii. p. 445.) Here is a distinct avowal of the pure *selfism* which attached his Lordship to the constitution; it had *worked well for* HIM, and it might work well for his *children.* But how it had worked for the country, formed no part of the consideration.

A late repentance is better than none, and we would suggest to this votary of the " immortal memory" the propriety of surrendering his pension in aid of a deficient revenue, caused by the improvident measures of himself and colleagues. The time was when ex-chancellors received no pensions; they have little need of them now, possessing abundant means in outfits, patronage, and direct emoluments for making provision for the future. As respects his lordship individually, his necessities must be much less than others; his official gatherings during the long term he held the great seal must be enormous. Upon the average of three years, 1808, 1809, and 1810, the net receipt of the chancellor was £19,233 : 2 ; and in one year, 1811, the chancellor's emoluments were £22,737 : 13. (*Parl. Rep.*322,*Sess.*1831.) His lordship's son, W. H.J. Scott, is entrenched chin-deep in sinecures and reversions, and if he survive Mr. Thurlow, will have an income of £14,000 a year *for doing nothing.* With so much in possession and in the future, why, my lord, cling to this disgraceful and redundant allowance? Why not offer it up as some poor atonement for past errors—for the inheritance of debt,

difficulty, and civil strife which for the next ten or twenty years
your fatal measures have entailed on the country?

Elgin, earl of, late ambassador to the Ottoman Porte········	£2000
Also, as lieutenant-general············ ··········	595
Elibank, Alexander Murray, pension on civil list, 1826······	150
Elibank, lady, pension on civil list, 1830 ···············	138
Elphinstone, lord, pension on civil list, *Feb.* 1814··········	150
Ditto, additional, *Aug.* 1826···················	150
Ellenborough, lord, chief clerk of court of king's bench ····	9625

A brother, H. C. Law, capt. in the army, and *custos brevium* in
the King's Bench jointly with lord Kenyon ; C. E. Law, a brother,
common serjeant of the city of London ; John Law, a brother in the
army ; W. J. Law, a cousin, commissioner of Insolvent Debtors'
Court ; G. H. Law, uncle, bishop of Bath and Wells ; J. T. Law, a
cousin, prebend of Lichfield ; Henry Law, a cousin, archdeacon of
Wells ; Robert V. Law, a cousin, prebendary of Chester ; E. Law,
a cousin, in the church : Harkness, Barlow, Crofts, and Dynely,
are relations, and hold offices and preferments. Lord Ellenborough
has some reason for disliking the spreading spirit of resistance to
the tithe tax, and has suggested that the person be *attached* for non-
payment of tithe, but the amphibious baron and clerk has not said
where prisons and gaolers are to be found for the confinement of a
whole community.

Elley, major-gen. J. col. 17th light dragoons, pay ········	580
Governor of Galway ··························	348
Pension for wounds ···,·················,··········	300
Ellicombe, C. G. lieut.-col royal engineers, *May,* 1825 ····	720
Allowance for house-rent, forage, and servants ······	182
Brigade major, *Jan.* 1821 ····················	182
Ellice, Edward, brother-in-law of earl Grey, and M.P. for	
Coventry ; joint-secretary to the treasury ········	2500
Ellis, H. clerk of the pells in the exchequer (a *sinecure*) ····	1400

Full brother, born before wedlock, of the earl of Bucking-
hamshire, and lately a civil servant of the East-India Company.

Ellis, Thomas, master in chancery, Ireland ··············	3323
Elliott, H. secretary to military boards ·················	600
Elliott, H. late minister to the two Sicilies ··············	2000
Elliott, hon. capt. Geo. secretary to the admiralty·········	2000
Emmett, brevet-major A. captain, royal engineers, 1825 ····	238
Extra commanding engineers, at Manchester········	119
Allowance for a servant ·····················	27
Pension for a wound, 1817·····················	100
Emerson, J. commander of post-office packet, Liverpool ····	400
Master in the navy, 1810 ·····················	109
Englebach, L. G. inspector in audit-office, 1806 ··········	600
Inspector of foreign department, 1822 ············	100
Erskine, lord, envoy and plenipotentiary at Munich ········	3500
Erskine, lady Louisa, pension on civil list, 1801 ··········	233

Daughter of the old lord Uxbridge, and married a colonel Erskine

who died pending proceedings instituted for a divorce. She has
since married sir George Murray, the late colonial secretary, who
appears from our *List* to have large military emoluments, and who
can hardly sanction his wife drawing a pension as the widow of the
late sir James Erskine.

Erskine, Euphemia, Helen, and Marianne, each, civil list····	£50
Erskine, Mrs. widow of H. Erskine, civil list, 1818········	300
Erskine, Mary Henrietta, pension on civil list, 1797········	400
Erskine, sir T., brother of lord Erskine and of the Misses Erskine, chief judge, bankrupt court··············	3000
Errol, earl of, pension on civil list, 1819 ··············	276
Master of horse to the queen, 1830 ··············	
Errol, countess dowager of, pension on civil list, 1809 ······	92
Errol, Harriet, countess of, civil list, 1820 ··············	300
Esten, C. chief justice of Bermuda ···· ··············	1020
Evans, J. commissioner, bankrupt court ················	1500
Everett, W. receiver of taxes, London and Middlesex ······	1900
Ewart, John, Elizabeth, and Mary, each, civil list, 1794····	121
Ewbank, Jas. general accountant, excise ················	600
Exmouth, admiral lord, pension by act of parliament ······	2000
Admiral in the navy ························	760

    Several sons in the navy and church. See Pellew in the *List of
Pluralists.*

Falconar, John, consul at Leghorn·····················	1144
Fane, J. T. M.P. for Lyme Regis; clerk in privy-seal office	320
Half-pay lieut.-col. in 22d dragoons, 1824··········	200

    Nephew of the anti-reform peer, lord Westmoreland, who has
spent a long life in jobs and offices. His son, major-gen. lord
Burghersh, is envoy in Tuscany ; H. S. Fane, a son, major 34th foot ;
sir H. Fane, cousin, lieut.-gen. and col. 1st dragoon guards ;
Mildmay Fane, a relation, lieut.-col. 54th foot ; F. W. Fane, capt.
R. N.; and R. G. C. Fane, commissioner of bankrupt court, vice-
chamberlain of Chester, and king's sergeant duchy court of Lancaster : these are a few branches, exclusive of numerous others,
struck off in the female line.

Farran, Jos. clerk of the pleas, exchequer, Ireland········	1384
Falkland, viscount, pension on civil list, *June*, 1816 ······	200
Fagel, Louis, baron de, pension on civil list, *Nov.* 1814····	130
Fall, Richard, assistant-surveyor, customs ·············	1420
Farr, W. D. first marshal, Demerara ·················	5100
Fabian, Robt. pension on civil list, 1828 ················	111
Falk, Lucius Bentinck, pension on civil list, 1816 ········	184
Farmer, sir Geo. R. pension on civil list, 1822············	185
Farrer, Ann and Mary, pensions on civil list, 1771 ········	311
Farrer, J. W. master in chancery ·····················	3622
Fauquier, Edward, senior clerk in the treasury···········	849
Superintendent of St. James's and Hyde Parks······	207
Ferguson, Joseph, superintendent of mail-coaches, Ireland ··	369
Manager, money-order office, ditto·········· ······	150

Fergusson, lieut.-gen, sir R. M.P. for Kirkcudbright, col. 79th foot, pay	£612
Fergusson, Isabella, Mary, and Margaret, civil list, 1799	184
Fergusson, Elizabeth, pension on civil list, 1805	97
Finch, H. clerk 1st class, war-office	595
Finch, hon. and rev. E. chaplain and principal of schools, Ceylon	1070
Finch, gon. hon. E col. 22d foot	1231
Finlaison, O. J. actuary, national-debt-office	1330
Findlay, lieut.-col. governor of Sierra Leone	2000
Fisher, major-gen. G. B. unattached gen. Woolwich-garrison	1247
Fisher, Lucy, pension on civil list, 1813	136
Figg, Fanny, pension on civil list, 1829	47
Fitzwilliam, G. deputy-vendue-master, Trinidad	1500
Fitzclarence, misses, pension out of 4½ per cent. fund, 1820	2500

The children of the king by the late Mrs. Jordan. The husbands of the ladies are, the earl of Errol, the hon. J. E. Kennedy, (second son of earl Cassilis), Mr. P. Sidney, (only son of sir James Sidney,) the hon. col. Fox, (son of lord Holland), and lord Falkland. The male scions of this connexion are, G. Fitzclarence, earl of Munster, a colonel in the army, lieutenant of the Tower, and aid-de-camp to the king; lord Adolphus Fitzclarence, capt. R. N. and yeoman of the robes; lord F. Fitzclarence, colonel in the army, lieut. col. 7th foot, and aid-de-camp to the king; and lord Augustus Fitzclarence, rector of Maple-Durham.

Fitzhum, madam, pension on civil list, 1825	40

The pension granted during his viceroyship, by marquis Wellesley, who can, perhaps, explain it, as well as that to lady Montgomery, and other followers to the Emerald isle.

Fitzgibbon, Thomas, pension on civil list, 1826	70
Fitzroy, lady Mary, pension on civil list, 1821	200
Fitzgerald, lord, late minister to Lisbon	1700
Fitzgerald, lord Robert, pension on civil list, 1801	800
Fitzgibbon, R. H. brother of earl of Clare, and M.P. for Limerickshire; usher and registrar of affidavits in court of chancery, Ireland	3560
Fleming, vice-adm. hon. C. E. commander-in-chief, West Indies	2555
Fleming, Jean, Elizabeth, and Catharine, each, civil list	49
Flint, sir C. W. resident secretary, Dublin, 1803	1551
Comptroller of Killybegs	87
Pension on Irish civil list, 1815	266
Foley, lord, captain of gentlemen pensioners	1000
Fonblanque, J. G. commissioner of bankrupt court	1500
Forbes, Dr. superintendent of vaccine establishment, London	1270
Forbes, F. chief-justice of New South Wales	2000
Forbes, J. H. lord of session, Scotland	2000
Forster, T. clerk of debentures, auditors' office	900
Foster, J. L. baron of court of exchequer, Ireland	3692
Foster, A. J. brother-in-law of the earl of Buckinghamshire; envoy and minister plenipotentiary at Turin	4249

Forbes, lord, high commissioner to the church of Scotland ··	£2000
Fox, H. J. minister plenipotentiary, Buenos Ayres ········	3300
Fox, Mrs. Bridget, lord Holland in trust for, civil list, 1806··	938

Widow of the late right hon. Charles James Fox, the idol of the
Whig party. Mr. Fox was an amiable good-natured man, but a
factious, mistaken, and aristocratic politician. Party had never a
more devoted leader; no chieftain of banditti was more faithful to
his troop than Mr. Fox to his followers. He fought for them, apos-
tatized for them : he would resort to any stratagem, disgrace himself with any alliance, adopt any contrivance, domineer over his
sovereign, revile his minister, or court the people : and all this not
for himself, for no man was more disinterested—nor for his country,
for of that he thought little—but solely for the chosen few ranged
under his banner. There never was a more whole-length partizan ;
his whole soul was devoted to the interests of his followers; beyond
that circle he had neither eyes, ears, nor understanding. If Mr.
Pitt's ruling passion was ambition, Burke's base lucre, the god of
Mr. Fox's idolatry was party ; in that " he lived, breathed, and
had his being." That he should be loved by his friends, and enthu-
siastically admired by his followers, may be easily conceived ; but
that he should be held up, after the full discovery of his inconsistent
and mistaken conduct, as an object of *national* gratitude, cannot be
so readily explained.

Mr. Fox was originally bred a Tory. His conversion is ascribed
to Burke, the organ of the Whig, or Rockingham party. Under his
auspices he imbibed those mischievous principles, which ever after
formed his political creed. The system Burke taught was briefly
this :—*First,* that the House of Brunswick being indebted for the
throne to the union of a few great families at the Revolution, it was
right that these families should possess the entire control of the
government. *Secondly,* for the more effectual maintenance of this
claim, it was necessary they should act in a body, so as to be able
to resist the power and influence of the Crown. These two principles embrace the whole system of the Whig school. It is evidently
void of public principle ; the people are excluded from consideration ; it is a mere scheme for the monopoly of power and emolument. The Whigs, indeed, of that day professed that *Retrenchment* and *Reform* formed also a part of their doctrines; but
experience demonstrated to the country, that these were mere pretexts to catch popular support, to enable them to make head against
their opponents, and that real practical Whiggism consisted in acting
en masse, and the *divine indefeasible* right of a few superannuated
nobles to govern the country.

Now, on such principles and partizanship, Mr. Fox's life was
thrown away. Though he beheld the overwhelming influence of
the crown, from enormous taxation, the augmentation of the peerage, and the letting in the whole tribe of contractors, money-jobbers, and paper-dealers, yet he never would cordially join in building up the democratic branch of the constitution, which they had
subverted. His whole mind was contracted to party, to the augmentation of his little knot of followers, the re-union of the *New* and
the *Old Whigs ;* and then, when the whole, by dinners and meetings and caballing, was brought into more perfect discipline and
organization—doing what ? Why, forsooth, not accomplishing any
great and substantial plan for reformation ; but solely renewing the
old war against the king ; thwarting his measures, bearding him in
his closet, quarrelling about the appointment of grooms and bed-

chamber lords, the disposal of ribbons and garters, and rods and wands—and then, having obtained entire control of the palace, from the kitchen to the drawing-room, and placed the sovereign in that state of blessedness in which he can do no wrong, because he can do nothing, completed the grand climacteric of Whiggism!

That this is no exaggerated picture of the principles of Mr. Fox, it is only necessary to advert to his conduct in the extortion of the peerage for sir Fletcher Norton—his petulant abandonment of office, on the King's appointing the duke of Portland successor to the marquis of Rockingham—his coalition with lord North—his conduct on the regency question—and his virulent and unprincipled opposition to the early administration of Mr. Pitt. "I have heard," says Mr. Nichols, "Mr. Fox use this expression :—' Our party is formed on the principle of confederacy ; ought we not then to confederate with him (lord North) who can give us the greatest strength?'"* These memorable words contain a full exposure of the utter littleness and profligacy of Mr. Fox's political system. They need no comment. He never deviated from his " principle of confederacy." Even in 1803, after his long, able, and, so far as the revolutionary war was concerned, praiseworthy opposition to Mr. Pitt, he was most anxious to unite with that minister in order to form a grand party combination. This union did not take place, solely from Mr. Pitt's reluctance to enter, after the Whig fashion, into a systematic opposition to the court. He would, however, have gone into power with Pitt on the overthrow of the Addingtonians, had not the King been " impracticable."

After the full exposure of Mr. Fox's party views, it is needless to show that he was no friend to Parliamentary Reform. " When finally separated," says Mr. Allen, " from his *old aristocratic connexions*, and convinced, from fatal experience, that the House of Commons had sunk into the passive instrument of ministerial power, his opinion became gradually *more inclined* to Parliamentary Reform, from utter despair of seeing the revival of those *party connexions* to which he had been accustomed to look for the preservation of *public liberty*."† Here is the admission of his partial biographer, that Mr. Fox only considered Parliamentary Reform a *dernier resort*, not a great substantive measure, which alone could stem the overwhelming tide of regal, aristocratic, and moneyed influence. As to the revival of *public liberty* by *party connexions*, that language is well understood by those who have read the history of their country from the Revolution, especially of the ill-concocted Administration of 1806.

We shall make no further observations on Mr. Fox. How far he is entitled to the appellation of " the *Friend of the People*," the preceding observations may perhaps enable the reader to determine. Without detracting from his amiable qualities, or the great powers with which Nature had gifted him, we must be permitted to say, that he was a very objectionable statesman ; and that, with the exception of the Libel Law, and the Abolition of the Slave Trade, he neither conceived nor executed a single great measure for the honour and benefit of his country. If he understood, as sir James Mackintosh says he did, the constitutions, both in " an exactly legal and comprehensively philosophical sense" better than any man, and his life was a practical commentary on that knowledge ; then we must say the constitution is a very different thing from what

---

* Recollections of the Reign of George III. p. 172.
† Sup. to Ency. Britt. art. Fox, written by Mr. Allen.

we conceived it to be. And we must also add, that if true patriotism consists in spending a long life in abortive attempts to bolster up the interests of a contemptible Oligarchy, that, too, is a thing we do not understand.

Fox, Mrs. Anne, pension on civil list, 1816 ••••••••••••	£276
A natural daughter, we fear, of Charles James Fox, and who, if need be, ought to have been provided for by the Fox club.	
Fortescue, Jane, and after death to misses Young, civil list••	266
Fortescue, H. postmaster, Cork ••••••••••••••••••••••	520
Fowlis, lady, pension on civil list, 1799 •••••••••••••••	184
Frampson, sir G. F. late commissioner of bankrupts••••••••	200
Franklin, sir W. principal inspector, army medical board••••	1200
Fraser, Charlotte, Charles, and Jane, pension civil list, 1799	389
Fraser, col. sir A. director of the royal laboratory••••••••••	967
Pension for good services •••••••••••••••••••	182
Frere, B. late minister to the Ottoman Porte ••••••••••••	1200
Frere, right hon. J. H. late minister of Spain ••••••••••••	1700
Freeling, sir F. sec. to the post-office, salary and emoluments	4165
Sir F. Freeling has furnished apartments, coals, candles, &c. in addition to these emoluments. He is a meritorious public servant; but it must be conceded, he and his family are sufficiently paid for their services.	
Freeling, G. H. assistant-secretary, post-office••••••••••••	800
Freeling, J. C. secretary to the excise ••••••••••••••••••	1500
Freemantle, sir W. H. treasurer of his majesty's household••	904
Late solicitor for Irish affairs •••••••••••••••••••	924
Freemantle, Georgiana, Albinia, and Frances, pensions on civil list, each, 1813 •••••••••••••••••••••••••••••	43
Freeman, lieut.-gen. Q. J. lieut-gen. in the army ••••••••	593
Late barrack-master and commiss. board of works, Ireland	972
Frewin, Rebecca, pension on civil list, 1824•••••••••••••	100
Fyers, lieut.-gen. W. col. royal engineers, Ireland ••••••••	2184
Fuller, major-gen. sir J. colonel 96th foot ••••••••••••••	1119
President of the consolidated board of general officers••	197
Fullarton, J. moiety of the earl of Bath's hereditary pension out of the excise••••••••••••••••••••••••••••••	1200
Fullarton, John, lord of session, Scotland••••••••••••••••	2000
Fry, J. C. registrar in chancery•••••••••••••••••••••••••	4224
Gambier, E. J. deputy and 1st clerk, tellers' office ••••••••	1000
Gambier, sir J. late consul-general in the Netherlands ••••••	1200
Garrall, capt. H. governor of Haslar-hospital, Plymouth••••	800
Garrow, sir W. late baron of the exchequer ••••••••••••	3500
Gascoyne, gen. I. colonel 54th foot, pay •••••••••••••••	613
Gardiner, col. deputy-adjutant-general, Ireland, 1823 ••••••	693
Contingent allowance •••••••••••••••••••• ••••••••	150
Lieut.-colonel half-pay, 1825•••••••••••••••••••••••	200
Gardiner, sir R. lieut.-col. royal artillery, 1828 •••••••••	293
Pension for good services, 1813 ••••••••••••••••	91

Garvock, capt. J. deputy-assistant adjutant-general, 1809 ··	£260
Allowance in lieu of half-pay as captain of infantry ··	127
Secretary to commiss. of royal military coll. 1814····	200
Gaselee, sir G. a judge of the common pleas··············	5500
Gawler, H. secretary to master of the rolls ··············	1487
One of the six clerks in chancery ················	1200
Gibbs, major John, landing surveyor, Hull ·············,	700
Gibbs, G. T. W. collector of customs, Yarmouth··········	700
Gibbons, Edw. assistant-clerk in the treasury ············	672
Gifford, R. F. lord, pension on civil list, 1827 ············	800
Additional on Irish civil list, 1827················	204
Additional on Scotch civil list, 1827 ··············	198
The pensions are for the benefit of the present lord, and the other children of the late lord Gifford, attorney-general during the trial of Queen Caroline.	
Gillies, Adam, lord of session and justiciary, Scotland······	2600
Commissioner jury court, ditto ················ ······	600
Gillies, Dr. John, pension on civil list, 1813··············	200
Gillon, Catharine and Elizabeth, pensions each, civil list, 1805	97
Giminghan, 2d under-clerk, tellers' office ··············	600
Glenlyon, lord, lord of the bedchamber·················	500
Major-gen. and governor of Isle of Man ··········	
Brother and heir presumptive to the duke of Athol.	
Glennie, Ven. J. M. S. archdeacon, Ceylon ··············	2000
Gloster, H. protector of slaves, Trinidad ················	1300
Gloucester, duch. of, pension out of 4½ per cent. fund, 1820.	1000
For the parliamentary allowances of the royal family see p. 237. The duke of Gloucester was formerly a Whig. When the present government came in he expected to have been put at the head of the army. Finding that lord Grey considered that a general officer, who had seen actual service, was a fitter person for the situation than H. R. H. he went into bitter opposition.	
Goddard, Isabella, pension on civil list, 1812 ············	662
Goddard, Louisa, pension on civil list, 1825 ··············	40
Goderich, viscount, secretary of colonial department ······	5000
Gostling, N. deputy-register of the prerogative court of Canterbury; from fees ······················ ········	1317
Gordon, gen. Geo. duke of, col. of 1st regt. of foot········	2325
Governor of Edinburgh castle ················	1046
Gordon, sir R. late ambassador at Constantinople ··········	2000
Gordon, sir George, pension on civil list, 1821 ············	150
Gordon, J. collector of customs, Bristol············ ······	1000
Gordon, capt. sir Jas. A. governor of Plymouth hospital ····	800
Gordon, lieut. gen. sir J. W. M.P. for Launceston; col. 23d foot	1034
Quarter-master-general ······················	1883
Gordon, A. chief-clerk, secretary colonial-office············	1500
Agent for Demerara ························	400
Agent for Lower Canada ····················	200
Gordon, R. governor and vice-admiral of Berbice ··········	4000

Gort, viscount, constable of Limerick castle	£336
Gore, F. 1st clerk in tellers' office	1000
Goodenough, G. T. late commissioner of taxes, 1801	150
Late sec. for reduction of the national debt, 1818	500
Gosset, Elizabeth and Gertrude, pensions on civil list, 1828 ..	198
Gosset, Ralph-Allen, pension on civil list, 1829	95
Gomez, A. assessor to the governor, Trinidad	1500
Godby, A. secretary post-office, Edinburgh	600
Goulbourn, H. pension as late Irish secretary, 1825	2000

The Tories ought to put on sack-cloth and ashes in lieu of
assailing the Grey ministry, on account of its financial difficulties,
knowing that these difficulties are the result of their own lavish
expenditure. It would be more becoming in them to throw up
their pensions and sinecures as a set-off against the waste of public
money in palace 'building, the Rideau canal and Belgic fortresses.
As to Mr. Goulburn he is certainly no conjurer in finance. He is
all hodge-podge, subterfuge, and deception. Witness his blundering
exhibitions in respect of the sugar duties, his oversight in respect
of life annuities, and the tricks he played in respect of the French
claims and custom duty on West India produce ! Such a specimen
of imbecility and mystification as his speech on the introduction of
the civil list in 1830 was never before presented to parliament. To
expatiate on the *frugality* of the late King in not having exceeded
his income ! Why, had he been HELIOGABALUS himself, and supped
on diamonds, he could not have dissipated his immense revenue.
Then to talk about the inexpediency of separating the various items
of the civil list expenditure, lest the Radicals should discover the
personal expenses of the monarch, and thence institute invidious
comparisons between royal and republican institutions—what ina-
nity ! All these matters are now thoroughly understood by every
body. Only read our chapter on the civil list and the *economy* of
George IV. and the cost of a KING will be as clear as day-light.
But ought it to be inferred from thence we are unfavourable to monarchical government? No ! we know too well what *is*, to think
for a moment of what *de novo* might be ; we know, too, that though
the key-stone is not the arch, there could be no arch without it—at
least not a *Gothic* arch !

Goodman, J. A. vendue master, Demerara	2986

What enormous emoluments to governors, registrars, secretaries,
and other officers in the colonies. Well may the British dependencies be unable to yield revenue to the mother country; or, even,
to defray the expense of their own establishments.

Grady, H. G. allowance as late counsel to excise, Dublin	1333

An Irish job. The office abolished, there should have been no
allowance.

Graham, sir J. M.P. for Cumberland, 1st lord of the admiralty	4500

Sir James by improvements in the civil administration of the
navy, and reductions in the estimates nearly to the amount of a
million, has almost silenced Mr. Hume, and set a splendid example
to the heads of departments. That the baronet possesses abilities of
the first order was evident, from his forcible and eloquent exposition
of the emoluments of privy-councellors, the salaries of public officers,
and the costs of foreign missions, which greatly contributed to fix
public attention on a lavish government expenditure. We trust so
able a man has discovered his' errors on the currency question, and
he no longer entertains the vulgar notion of that class who wrongly

ascribe national distress to the withdrawal of the *rag-money*, and the substitution of a metallic circulation. In other respects the sentiments of the first lord of the Admiralty are liberal and enlightened, as is apparent from the following extract from a pamphlet published by him some years ago :—

" The paramount duty of every government is attention to the interests of the community, of which the labourers must form the great majority ; the right of property itself is instituted for the good not of the few who possess wealth and honour, but of the many who have them not; if the majority be deeply injured, the public peace is in danger; if the majority want food, private property becomes a nuisance."—*Corn and Currency*, p. 75.—Sir James may have trimmed his ideas since these sentiments were published, but we trust the substance remains engraven where it ought to be, in all those entrusted with power over the happiness of the community.

Graham, sir R. late baron of the exchequer ··············	£3500
Graham, M. Kay, Isabella, and Caroline, c. l. *June* 1816··	276

These ladies' father was a man of large fortune, but who dissipated it, and are near relatives of lord Lynedoch. But every one relieves himself to burthen the public. This proves the great necessity that there should be no pension list. In no other country are the poor and decayed relations of the privileged classes so provided for as in England.

Grafton, duke of, hereditary pension out of the excise revenue	7200
Ditto, ditto post-office ditto ·····················	4700
Sealer of king's bench and common pleas ··········	2888

One of the four illegitimate descendants of Charles II. raised to ducal peerages. It might be right in this profligate king to quarter the produce of his debauchery on the people's industry, but it is with surprise and indignation we find it continued to the present day. How happened it the revolution Whigs of 1688 did not rid the country of this infamy? The present duke returns two or three members to the lower house: he is said to be an " excellent gentleman ;" whether the motto—*Et decus et pretium recti* —" the ornament and recompense of virtue," refers to the pensions or descent of his grace it is not easy to determine.

Graves, C. G. cashier of widows' pensions ··············	700
Granville, W. vice-treas. and commissioner of stamps, Ceylon	2000
Granard, earl of, clerk of crown and hanaper, Ireland ····	886
Granville, viscount, ambassador to France ··············	10000
Grange, James, senior clerk in the treasury··············	1000
Pension on 4½ per cent. fund ·········· ··········	250
Grant, major-gen. governor of Trinidad·····················	5535
Grant, J. T. clerk of the cheque, Portsmouth ··············	460
Grant, D. M. collector of customs, Kingston, Jamaica ····	2500
Grant, sir W. late master of the rolls ····················	3750
Grant, maj.-gen. sir C. col. 15th light dragoons ···· ······	1237
Grant, C. M.P. for Invernessshire; president of India board	3500
Grant, R. M.P. for Norwich; judge advocate-general ······	2000
Commissioner of the India board ··· ············	1200
Grant, Sophia and Charlotte, pension each on civil list, 1784	49
Grant, Catharine, Ann, and Harriet, pension each on c. l. 1790	97
Grant, Ann, pension on civil list, 1827 ················	100
Gratton, Lucia, Caroline, and Frances, pension each on c. l. 1803	32

Gravatt, col. W. inspector, royal military academy, 1814 ··	£264
Lieut -colonel invalid engineers, 1811 ············	326
Gregg, — deputy registrar, bankrupt court ·············	600
Gregory, O. professor of mathematics, Woolwich academy ··	558
Gregory, Wm. and lady Ann Gregory, and survivor, civil list	461
Gregory, William, late under secretary for Ireland ········	1000
Green, gen. sir C. col. 37th foot ······················	1123
Greene, Wm. comptroller of customs, Liverpool ··········	600
Gregg, Robert F. clerk in vice-treasurer's office, Dublin ····	390
Allowance as clerk in late Irish treasury, 1817 ······	55
Grenville, lord, auditor of the exchequer *(a sinecure)* ······	4000
Grenville, Thos. chief justice in Eyre ·················	2316
Brother of the preceding sinecurist and uncle of the duke of Buckingham, the nobleman so noted for his love of stationery, of which he carried off a great deal for private use from the office he held in 1806.	
Greville, A. F. commissioner of alienation office, 1828 ······	150
Late private sec. to lord Wellington, pension on c. l.	250
Bath king at arms, 1829 ·····················	90
Greville, Charles, comptroller of cash in the excise········	600
Secretary of the island of Tobago ················	350
Allowance as naval officer, Trinidad ··············	572
Greville, C. C. F. clerk of the council ·················	2000
Secretary and clerk of the enrolments, Jamaica······	3000
As late naval officer, Demerara ·················	500
The duke of Wellington, at the period of his resignation, in lieu of providing out of his own pocket for *A. F. Greville,* as his private secretary—if he needed provision—threw him on the court pension list to be provided for by the people.	
The next of the name, *Charles Greville,* married a daughter of the duke of Portland, who provided for her amply, as above, in the excise, Tobago and Trinidad. The duke also took good care of her *son, C. C. F. Greville.* The pleasures of the turf may be fairly indulged in, the britska in summer, and the post-chariot in winter, when not at the pulbic expense.	
Grey, hon. H. G., gen. brother of earl Grey ; col. 13th light	
dragoons pay ···· ····················	1057
Grey, earl, first lord of the treasury ·················	5000
Commissioner for the affairs of India ··········	

The noble premier is mostly represented as too *exclusive* in his notions to conciliate popular esteem. We should be loth to hang a man for a word or a phrase, any more than a single action of life, unless it were a deliberate and very flagrant atrocity. Besides, although lord Grey did say he would " stick to his order," it ought to be remembered, as a set-off, that in a session or two preceding, he actually took a brother peer to task, for having in his harangue too freely applied the disparaging epithet of *lower orders* to the working classes. The aristocracy of his lordship is, we apprehend, more in words than in any thing else. His early history and the Reform Bill, with which his future fame and character will be identified, sufficiently show that he is now and always has been a sincere friend of popular rights,

Griesbach, Caroline, Elizabeth, and Frances, pension each, on civil list, 1826	£ 50
Griffith, E. police justice, Mary-le-bone	800
Griffith, Walter, Anne, Mary, Henry, George, Charlotte, William, Charles, Arthur, and Harriet, pension, each, on civil list, 1821	18
Grove, H. L. collector of customs, Exeter	590
Groom, R. assistant secretary, tax-office	700
Grosvenor, gen. T. col. 65th foot	1241
Grosvenor, lord Robert, third son of earl Grosvenor, and M.P. for Chester; comptroller of the king's household	920
Gurney, sir J. baron of the court of exchequer, 1832	5510
Guydicker, Frances, pension on civil list, 1793	240
Gwilt, Robert, clerk, Chelsea-hospital	500
Agent for Newfoundland	100
Gwynne, Thomas, comptroller of legacy duties	100
Gwynne, Georgiana, pension on civil list, 1800	115
Gwyn, Mary, pension on civil list, 1821	400
Hatton, Edw. F. late paymaster of widows' pensions, 1799	600
Retired pension as commis. of stamps, 1819	600
Inspector-general of tea and coffee, 1819	292
Uncle of that undefinable peer lord Winchilsea. At the Kent meeting his lordship praised the Reform Bill, and afterwards voted against it; he eulogized lord Grey for bringing it forward; afterwards he abused him for the same cause. In a similar manner he abused and fought the duke of Wellington, and now praises him.	
Haldane, Maria, pension on civil list, 1819	200
Hamilton, lieut.-col., inspecting field-officer, Ireland	466
Pension for loss of a leg, Dec. 1811	200
Hamilton, Mrs. pension out of 4½ per cent. fund, July, 1820	250
Hamilton, Arabella, Elizabeth, Mary, Isabella, and survivors of them, civil list, March, 1796	461
Hamilton, John, in trust for children of	461
Hamilton, R. prothonotary king's bench, Ireland	1384
Hamilton, W. R. pension on consolidated fund	1000
Hamilton, R. principal clerk of session, Scotland	1000
Professor of public law	280
Hamilton, H. C. J. secretary of embassy at Paris	1100
Hamilton, admiral, sir Charles, pension on civil list, 1790	155
Hamilton, sir J. col. 69th foot	1200
Governor of Dungannon fort	
Handfield, Catharine, Anne, Eliza, Jane, Mary, Julia, and Sarah, pensions, each, on Irish civil list, 1816	88
Hart, C. inspector and receiver of taxes, 1806	810
Hart. gen. G. V. unattached pay as general officer	593
Governor of Londonderry and Culmore	499
Harrison, T. commissioner of excise	1200

Harrison, W. parliamentary counsel to the Treasury	£1000
Law clerk, war-office	400
Harrison, G. allowance as late assistant secretary, Treasury··	2000
Harrison, J. allowance for loss of office, customs, Dublin ····	1207
Harrison, Ann, pension on civil list, 1828················	400
Haines, H. gentleman of the chamber to the lord chancellor; net emolument from fees in the year ending *Jan.* 5, 1830	1755
Hallam, Henry, late distributor of stamps ················	500

Can this be the historian of the *Middle Ages* and anti-reformer?
It is one of those objectionable allowances on which we have before
commented; granted conditionally, " until *otherwise provided for*."

Hallifax, Gertrude, Charlotte, Marianne, Caroline, Catharine, and Elizabeth, each, out of the civil list, 1793 ····	60

Daughters, we believe, of a bishop, and connected with the Cockburns through the Littletons.

Hammond, lieut.-gen. sir T. unattached pay as lieut.-gen. ····	593
Hammond, George, Edmund, Margaret, and William, each out of civil list, 1806·························· ··········	150
Harvey, F. clerk of Ulster-road and vice-president, Inland-office	637
Harvey, dame Louisa, pension on civil list, 1826 ············	300
Hardinge, lieut.-col. sir H. pension for wounds ············	300

The recent wanton attack of sir Henry on lord Ebrington was
more worthy of the rejected candidate for the county of Clare than
of a really brave soldier.

Hartwell, sir F. H. late deputy comptroller of the navy ······	1164
Hanmer, W. clerk of Nisi Prius, north and Norfolk circuits··	580
Clerk of the inner treasury, court of king's bench····	602
Hardy, rear-admiral sir Thomas, commissioner of the admiralty	1000
Haultain, Terrick, accomptant, army pay-office············	1200
Hassard, col. Jn. commanding royal engineers, Ionian Islands	1195
Hasler, Sarah, pension on civil list, 1780 ················	132
Hastings, Selina, Georgina, Louisa, Edward, and Richard, pension, each, on civil list, 1829················	50
Hammond, G. late minister to United States ¿············	1200
Hay, Dorothea, Lewis, Elizabeth, Mary, Jane, and Isabella, pensions, each, on civil list, 1806 ··············	79
Hay, lady Fanny, pension on civil list, 1822 ··············	100
Mary, additional on civil list, 1823 ··············	200
Ditto, additional, civil list, 1824········ ··········	100

Of the Tweeddale family these, and as Sir John Cam Hobhouse
has married one, he can best explain the origin of the pensions.

Hay, D. consul-general Tangiers ·····················	2000
Hay, R. W. under secretary of state for the colonies········	2000
Hayman, Ann, pension on civil list, 1823 ················	266
Hayne, Henry, commissary judge at Rio Janeiro ··········	1326
Hayter, Elizabeth and Sophia, pension on civil list, 1818 ····	101

Hailes, Daniel, late envoy, &c. to different courts · · · · · · · · · ·	£1127
Halls, Thomas, police justice, Bow-street · · · · · · · · · · · · · ·	800
Hankey, sir F. chief secretary, Malta· · · · · · · · · · · · · · · · · ·	1500
Hawker, Dorothea, Julia, and Mary, pension on civil list, 1827	300
Henn, W. master in chancery, Ireland · · · · · · · · · · · · · · · ·	3323
Heatly, Mary, pension on civil list, 1790 · · · · · · · · · · · · · · ·	177
Headfort, marchioness of, pension on civil list, 1821· · · · · · · ·	88
Heathcote, Antoinette, pension on civil list, 1802· · · · · · · · · ·	233
Heneage, G. H. W. hereditary proclamator in common pleas· ·	100
Hebden, John, superintendent of dead letter office, Ireland · ·	230
Taxing clerk in the inland office, Ireland · · · · · · · · · ·	173
Henley, lord, brother-in-law of sir R. Peel, master in chancery	4644

Some aristocratical stuff lately appeared in the *Morning Chronicle*, —not from the editor, we are sure, he is incapable of such nonsense —representing the degradation of the peerage by lord Henley, after succeeding to the family title, continuing to hold his appointment of master in chancery, part of whose duty it is to act as messenger from the lords to the commons. We presume this scribe considers it only compatible with the dignity of lords to live by plunder, as in the days of Burke's chivalry, not by the pursuit of some useful vocation. But we wonder what can degrade the aristocracy lower: look at their scrambling, intriguing, and apostatizing for office ; look at them condescending to fill the places of *port-searcher, sealers, clerks,* and *wharfingers,* for the sake of the emoluments ; look at the still greater infamy of quartering themselves, their mothers, children, and relatives on the industry of a starving people ; look at these degradations, and say if proud nobility can fall lower.

Hereford, viscount, pension on civil list, 1806 · · · · · · · · · · · ·	600
Heard, H. G. late six clerk chancery, Ireland · · · · · · · · · · · ·	1348
Herbert, Geo. clerk and auditor in the treasury· · · · · · · · · · · ·	819
Henderson, James, consul-general at Bogota· · · · · · · · · · · · ·	2000
Hertford, marquis of, lord warden of duchy of Cornwall · · · ·	no return

One of the greatest of borough proprietors ; returning two members for Orford, two for Aldeburgh, one for Lisburn, one for Bodmin, and two for Camelford. For illustration of the practical working of these nomination boroughs to the benefit of the relations of the marquis, see *Seymour.*

Hertslet, L. librarian, foreign secretary's office · · · · · · · · · · · ·	700
Superintendent of king's messengers · · · · · · · · · · · · · ·	450
Compensation for loss of fees in Ceylon· · · · · · · · · · · ·	300
Hesketh, Robert, consul at Maranham · · · · · · · · · · · · · · · ·	1105
Herries, J. C. late commissary-in-chief, 1816· · · · · · · · · · · · · ·	1350
Herries, Isabella, pension on civil list, 1814 · · · · · · · · · · · · ·	230
Herries, lieut.-colonel sir W. comptroller of army accounts · ·	1500
Pension for loss of leg· ·	300
Herbert, C. first fiscal, Demerara ·	3078
Hervey, lord W. secretary of legation in Spain · · · · · · · · · · ·	550

Son of lord Bristol, and grandson of the famous absentee bishop of Derry.

Hepburne, Catharine, pension on civil list, 1829 · · · · · · · · · ·	184
Hewitt, W. clerk of the papers, king's bench prison, from fees	1000

Hewett, gen. rt. hon. sir G. col. 61st foot, pay and emoluments	£1221
Hewett, hon. J. commissioner of excise	1200
Hewgill, Elizabeth, pension on civil list, 1801	233
Hervey, L. late minister at Madrid	1200
Heytesbury, lord, ambassador at St. Petersburgh	11000
Heyland, Rowley, clerk of the rules, Ireland	1107
Hill, lord M. C. secretary to embassy in Turkey	800
Hill, gen. rt. hon. R. lord, colonel 53d foot	1350
General commanding in chief	3458
Pension granted by parliament in 1814	2000
Hill, Capt. J. commissioner, victualling establishment, Deptford	800
Hill, W. N. brother of lord Berwick, envoy at Naples	4400
Hill, sir Geo. F. pension as clerk, Irish house of commons	2091
Governor of St. Vincent, West Indies	4000
Hill, lady, pension on civil list, 1830	467

This lady the duke brought in as well as his private secretary, and the *whipper-in*, Mr. Holmes, at the death of his administration. Lady Hill, one of the Beresfords, is the wife of the preceding, who has always held large sinecures in Ireland, but who, from his imprudence, has always been greatly embarrassed. Sir George sold his Irish pension, and was named governor of the Leeward Islands. With the claims of his wife the ex-premier is best acquainted ; but there are strong reasons, it is said, why the public should not be burthened with this pension.

Hicks, John, clerk in home department	1129
Higham, S. secretary, national debt office	1300
Hislop, lieut.-gen. sir T. col. 48th foot, pay and emoluments	1081
Hinchcliffe, H. pension on consolidated fund	1000
Hobhouse, Sir John Cam, secretary at war	2580
Hobhouse, rt. hon. H. keeper of state papers	811
Pension as late under secretary of state	1000
Holland, lord, chancellor of the duchy of Lancaster	3563

Well! who would have thought of lord Holland ever being a chancellor. Sinecures are good for something if it be only for the convenience of the *gout*. But the Aristocracy come upon us in so many different shapes, it is rather too bad, these nests of abuse, the counties palatine should be kept up as a kind of hospital for the aged and infirm of the " order." The Jenkinsons, Bathursts, and Bexleys, have enriched themselves in these retreats, and we regret no better appointment could be found for the nephew of Charles James Fox.—By the bye it was rather ill-natured of so good-natured a man as lord Holland to write the note he did in answer to the inquiries of the parliamentary committee relative to the emoluments of his sinecure. It was a subterfuge worthy only of a Tory, to declare that the duties of his office, " without the express commands of the king," precluded him from making the requisite return. His lordship will wonder how we have learnt the amount of his income ; the fact is we took it from the return of one of his predecessors, less scrupulous about royal commands.

Holroyd, Edw. commissioner of bankrupt court	1500

Holdsworth, Elizabeth, pension on civil list, 1789	£233
Hosier, W. clerk to auditor of land revenue	861
Hope, Elizabeth, pension on civil list, 1806	100
Hornage, clerk to master lord Henley in chancery	1650
Horton, sir R. W. governor and vice-admiral of Ceylon......	10,000
Hood, lord, pension on 4½ per cent. fund	1875
Can any one tell the public services of lord Hood?	
Hood, T. S. consul at Monte Video......................	1250
Howard, L. computer of wine and plantation duties, customs..	1463
Houston, lieut.-gen. sir W. colonel 20th foot, pay..........	1200
Groom of the bedchamber	500
Howard, lieut.-gen. lord, col. 70th foot..................	1343
Howick, viscount, son of earl Grey, and M.P. for Higham Ferrars ; under secretary of state for the colonies..	1500
Hope, John, king's solicitor for Scotland	500
Hough, T. S. clerk to master Trower in chancery	1209
Houghton, Penelope, pension on civil list, 1787	88
Hosier, J. and T. Bernard, pension 4½ per cent. fund, 1796 ..	600
Hornby, Phipps, distributor of stamps, Lancashire..........	562
Half-pay as captain in the navy....................	182
Horne, sir William, solicitor-general	4000
Hobart, hon. H. and rt. hon. J. Sullivan, pension out of 4½ per cent. fund, *July* 1820	600
Holloway, C. W. lieut.-col. royal engineers, Cape of Good Hope	869
Pension for a wound, 1817	200
Hoblyn, Thomas, chief clerk in the treasury	1400
Hope, lieut.-gen. sir J. colonel 72d foot	1158
Hope, lieut.-gen. sir A. col. 47th foot, pay and emoluments ..	900
Lieut.-gov. of Chelsea Hospital	464
Pension for wound	400
Hope, Charles, lord president court of session, Scotland......	4300
The three preceding relations of lord Hopetoun.	
Holmes, T. collector of customs, Grenada	1500
Holmes, Thomas, Knox, pension on civil list, 1830	500
Had the celebrated Mr. W. Holmes been the *whipper-out* in lieu of the whipper-in of many of the honourable members, we should have deemed him a more meritorious public servant, and better entitled to a pension during the life of his son at the close of his official labours.	
Home, sir E. sergeant-surgeon to the king................	277
Surgeon to Chelsea Hospital	546
Retired pay	187
Home, Alexander, earl of, pension on civil list, 1792........	276
Hombourg, princess of Hesse, pension, 4½ per cent. duties, 1820	1000
Honyman, sir W. of Armadale, late lord of session	1950
Honyman, dame Mary, pension on Scotch civil list, 1814....	138

Honyman, Mary, Catharine, Margaret, and Jemima, pension on civil list, 1815, each ⋯⋯⋯⋯⋯⋯⋯⋯⋯⋯	£37
Daughters of the preceding dame Mary ; the lady's husband was a lord of sessions, a baronet, and possessed a considerable estate. The son was a major while a child. How they came chargeable on the pension list is most extraordinary.	
Hudson, T. prothonotary of the common pleas ⋯⋯⋯⋯⋯	2600
Hume, J. D. joint assistant secretary, board of trade ⋯⋯⋯⋯	150
Hume, A. teller of exchequer, Ireland ⋯⋯⋯⋯⋯⋯⋯⋯⋯	1000
Hume, David, one of the barons exchequer, Scotland ⋯⋯⋯	2000
Hume, John, clerk in the victualling-office ⋯⋯⋯⋯⋯⋯	720
Hume, Elizabeth, pension on civil list, 1826 ⋯⋯⋯⋯⋯⋯	200
Humphrey, Louisa, pension on civil list, 1827 ⋯⋯⋯⋯⋯	150
Hunt, Mary, pension on civil list, 1816 ⋯⋯⋯⋯⋯⋯⋯⋯	150
Hunter, sir R., pension on Irish civil list, 1826 ⋯⋯⋯⋯⋯	177
Additional pension on civil list, 1827 ⋯⋯⋯⋯⋯⋯⋯	111
Physician, we believe, to marquis Wellesley during his viceroyship—and so rewarded for medical skill and attendance !	
Huskisson, T. paymaster of the navy ⋯⋯⋯⋯⋯⋯⋯⋯⋯	1200
Huskisson, G. collector of customs, St. Vincent ⋯⋯⋯⋯⋯	1500
Huskisson, J. W. collector of customs and judge, Ceylon ⋯⋯	1184
Huntingdon, earl of, pension on civil list, 1829 ⋯⋯⋯⋯⋯	400
This nobleman is reckoned among the *poor peers;* his brothers and sisters are on the pension list for £222. 10s. The earldom was in abeyance in 1819, and the title claimed on the speculation of receiving a pension to support it.	
Hutchinson, A. A. H. brother of lord Donoughmore, commissioner of customs ⋯⋯⋯⋯⋯⋯⋯⋯⋯⋯⋯⋯⋯⋯	1200
Inglis, doctor, bishop of Nova Scotia ⋯⋯⋯⋯⋯⋯⋯⋯⋯	2000
Iggulden, I. dep. reg. prerog. court of Canterbury ; from fees	1200
Innes, James, secretary and registrar, Berbice ⋯⋯⋯ ⋯⋯⋯	2000
Irvine, A. one of the lords of session, Scotland ⋯⋯⋯⋯⋯	2000
Irving, W. inspector-general of imports and exports ⋯⋯⋯⋯	900
Irving, Lucy, pension on 4½ per cent. duties ⋯⋯⋯⋯⋯⋯	120
Jackson, major-gen. sir R. D. colonel 81st foot, pay ⋯⋯⋯	613
Deputy quarter-master general ⋯⋯⋯⋯ ⋯⋯⋯⋯⋯⋯	691
Jackson, George, commissary judge at Sierra Leone ⋯⋯⋯	2145
Jackson, J. clerk in foreign office ⋯⋯⋯⋯⋯⋯⋯⋯⋯⋯	720
Jackson, Laura Harriet, pension on civil list, 1816 ⋯⋯⋯⋯	100
Jacob, W. comptroller of corn returns ⋯⋯⋯⋯⋯⋯⋯⋯⋯	765
Jadis, Henry, paymaster, exchequer-bills ⋯⋯⋯⋯⋯⋯⋯	600
Clerk in India board office ⋯⋯⋯ ⋯⋯⋯⋯⋯⋯⋯	500
Jardine, sir H. king's remembrancer court of excheq. Scotland	1700
Jarnac, madame de, pension on civil list, 1794 ⋯⋯⋯⋯⋯	177
Jeans, rev. Thomas, pension on civil list, 1780 ⋯⋯⋯⋯⋯	178
Jebb, R. second justice king's bench, Ireland ⋯⋯⋯⋯⋯	3730
Jefferey, T. N. collector of customs, Nova Scotia ⋯⋯ ⋯⋯	2000
Jeffrey, Lucia, pension on civil list, 1816 ⋯⋯⋯⋯⋯⋯⋯	200

Jeffrey, sir Francis, lord advocate of Scotland ············ £2500
We never heard any thing but to the honour of the late prime feather of the Edinburgh Review, and shall give the lord Advocate a fair
name even in *The Black Book*. He possesses, as is well known,
first-rate power as a writer in English, and a speaker in Scotch; and,
after a somewhat arduous course, sir Francis may sit down rejoicing,
either as lord or commoner, in as bright a career as any man, who
begins life with dubious prospects, and all to achieve, need covet
withal.

Jenkinson, R. H. registrar of excise ···················   400
   Receiver of stamps ····························   800
   Lieutenant of Dover-castle·····················   168
Jenner, R. collector of excise, Glasgow ···············   500
Jennings, Ann, pension on civil list, 1801 ············   252
Jeremie, J. chief justice, St. Lucia ··················   2000
   Registrar of slaves ····· ·····················   500
Jesse, Edward, deputy-surveyor of royal parks, &c.········   400
   Gentleman of the ewry (king's household)·········   285
Joddrell, Augusta, pension on civil list, 1794 ············   177
Jones, J. Edw. assist. deputy-adj-gen. royal artillery, 1818··   273
   Lieutenant-colonel royal artillery, 1828 ··········   273
   Forage allowance ···························   73
Jones, W. marshal of the king's bench prison; from fees, *about*   2804
Jones, W. clerk to master Cross, in chancery ············   1443
Jones, B. S. assistant secretary, India board ············   1200
Jones, W. cashier of half-pay ·····················   900
Jones, J. T. lieut.-col. royal engineers, Woolwich, and for *in-
   specting fortresses in the Netherlands* ········   1170
   Pension for wounds ·························   300
Johnson, Robert, late justice common pleas, Ireland ······   1107
Johnson, William, third justice common pleas, Ireland ····   3692
Johnson, J. Irish secretary's office, London ·············   829
Johnson, W. F. chief clerk, ordnance department ········   800
Johnston, L. F. C. judge of criminal inquiry, Trinidad ····   2217
Johnston, sir Alexander, retired judge of Ceylon··········   1600
   Married a cousin of the duke of Argyle
Johnston, sir W. pension on civil list, 1794··············   738
An old bachelor of large property at Gilford, county Downe;
well known at Bath and other watering places, being altogether an
absentee.
Johnston, E. J. pension on civil list, 1827 ··············   400
Keane, major-gen. sir J. col. 94th foot···················   425
   Unattached pay, and staff pay in Jamaica··········   1901
   Pension for wounds ·························   350
Kelly, Patrick, vice-consul at Lima; salary·· ···········   1177
Kekwith, George, puisne judge, Cape of Good Hope ······   1500
Kempt, sir James, master general of the ordnance ········   3000
   Colonel of 40th regiment of foot ···············   1020
Kemmis, Henry, assistant barrister, Kildare ···········   369

Commissioner of inquiry, Ireland	£990
Kenyon, lord, custos brevium, court of king's bench; from fees	2696
Kenyon, hon. Tho. brother of preceding ; filazer, exigenter, and clerk of outlawries in the court of king's bench ; fees	1254
Compensation, per act 6 Geo. IV..................	5463
Kennedy, T. F., M. P. for Ayr ; clerk of the ordnance	1200
Kennedy, Elizabeth, Susanna, Sarah, and Ellen, their lives and survivor, each, civil list	92
Kensit, H. clerk to master Stratford, in chancery	1075
Keppel, gen. right hon. sir W. col. 2d foot, pay and emoluments	876
Kerr, lady Mary, pension on civil list, 1825	200
Kilmorey, gen. F. earl of, colonel 86th foot..............	1220
Kilwarden, viscount, pension out of consolidated fund	600
Kingston, J. commissioner, colonial audit-office	800
Kinsale, lord, pension on civil list, 1823................	369
Kingsland, viscount, pension on civil list, 1826	200
Kinnoul, earl of, pension out of 4½ per cent. duties	1000
Lyon king at arms, Scotland	600
King, sir A. B. his majesty's stationer, Ireland	335
Compensation as printer to Irish house of commons ..	850
King, Harriet M. widow, pension on civil list, 1792	431

A set of creatures have lately disgraced the public press, by advertising for wives, with small properties, which the knaves promise shall be at the ladies' disposal *during their lives*. Speculators of this class will find our *Pension List* of great convenience ; they will be able to select suitable matches from the widows and sempstresses of all ages, rank, and income ; and though some, perhaps, a little the worse for the wear and tear of official duty, in attendance on the court and grandees of the land, quite good enough for them.

Kirkland, J. receiver of crown rents in London and Middlesex	500
Agent for Nova Scotia and Cape Breton	200
Agent for recruiting service	834
Kirkcudbright, baron, pension on civil list, 1828	200
Kirwan, Wilhelmina, pension on civil list, 1807	266
Knight, G. W. H. inspector-general of customs, Leith, 1817	600
Captain in the navy	191
Knight, Cornelia, pension on civil list, 1814	300
Knighton, Dr. sir William, receiver of duchy court of Lancaster and of duchy court of Cornwall..............	no returns

Keeper of the privy purse to George IV. This retired and wealthy favourite might usefully employ his leisure in his Hampshire retreat, in affording the burthened community information of the nature of the services of those troops of females who crowd the *Court Pension List ;* to many of whom the Magdalen, or tread-wheel, would have been more appropriate, than annuities for life out of the taxes. There is an ambassador, long kept out of the way at a northern court ; and a certain major-general, loaded with military emoluments and offices, though no soldier, further than wearing an uniform, who would be well qualified to assist in the undertaking. The *names*, especially the *Georginas, Georgianas,* the Arbuthnots,

the Bathursts, the Lennoxes, the Herries, and sundry selections
from the Continent, are significant enough; but there are others,
to whom there is no clue, and the denomination under which they
are set forth cannot be depended upon. Sir John Newport mentioned an instance, in the house of commons, illustrative of the
way they managed these things at the Castle. A pension of £1000
for many years stood in the Irish civil list, in the name of *George
Charles*; no such person was known to exist any where; and on
inquiry, it turned out that this was a pension to the count de Verry,
who received it under the name of Charles, and was for some services
rendered at Paris.

For the last 70 years the pensions charged on the civil list of the
three kingdoms, exclusive of the immense sums paid for similar
objects out of the Leeward Island duties, and other sources, have
amounted to nearly £200,000 per annum. And for what, or on
whom has this immense sum been squandered? On ———; but
the truth will out one day; the Circean and Paphian rites at the
Cottage will be shown up, and form an appropriate supplement to
the *Parc aux Cerfs*, and other recorded debaucheries of the Bourbon
and German courts.

Leaving these abominations, we cannot help expressing a wish
that, as soon as the Reform Bill is disposed of, the Whigs will institute an inquiry into the Duchy of Cornwall and the stannary
courts. There is no prince of Wales, nor at present, we believe,
any in prospect; so the time of reform could never be more appropriate. Besides *Dr. Knighton*, with immense emoluments, as
receiver-general, there are other officers—among them, an assay-
master for tin, a brother of lord Dorset, who has never even visited
that, to him, remote principality—the sinecure of his infancy, man-
hood, and maturity.

Knollys, gen. W. unattached pay as late major 3d foot guards	£800
Governor of Limerick	306
Pension on civil list, 1814	399
Knox, John, pension on civil list, 1800	177
Knox, John, pension on civil list, 1802	535
Knox, Mary Anne, pension on civil list, 1801	177
Knox, H. V. joint prothonotary, common pleas, Ireland	3575
Kuper, Rev. W. pension on civil list, 1816	400
This person must be a German—probably an Hanoverian. What claim can he have on the taxes of England?	
Kyd, T. clerk and inspector of taxes, Edinburgh	545
Lance, J. H. commissary judge at Surinam	1500
Lack, John, clerk of the rates, customs	1100
Lack, T. assistant secretary board of trade	1500
Laffan, sir Joseph de Courcey, pension on civil list, 1828	192
Went to Ireland as physician to the marquis of Anglesey, having been first made a baronet; and who granted the pension about the time, it is said, he refused to sign the pension of the marchioness of Westmeath.	
Lamb, George, brother of lord Melbourne, and M.P. for Dun-garvon; under sec. of state in the home department	1500
Lamb, sir F. brother of Lord Melbourne, ambassador at Vienna	9900
Lang, Charles, master-shipwright, Deptford	400

Lang, Oliver, master-shipwright, Woolwich ••••••••••••	£650
Lake, viscount, pension on consolidated fund •••••••••••	2000
Lieutenant-general •••••••••••••••••••••••••	456

Pension obtained by his father for services in India and Ireland ; the last, at least, did not merit it. The present viscount is better known as a late lord of the bedchamber than in his military capacity.

Langrishe, Hannah, pension on Irish civil list •••••••••••	460
Langrishe, Anne, pension on Irish civil list, 1796 ••••••••••	177

There was a sir Hercules Langrishe, bart. who received large compensations at the Union, and well known as a good companion. These ladies may probably be his relatives, and the lord lieutenant's generosity moved by the boon companionship of the baronet.

Lansdowne, marquis of, lord president of the council ••••••••	2000

The marquis, who is an estimable and enlightened man, was long silent on the vital question of parliamentary reform ; in the session of 1831, however, he declared himself favourable to an extension of the elective franchise ; not merely for the sake of change, but amendment, by more adequately representing the property and intelligence of the community. The lord president will certainly not gain by recent alterations. His lordship has lost nearly one-third of his salary by Whig retrenchment, and the Reform Bill carries off a moiety of the borough of Calne.

Larpent, F. S. chairman of the board of audit •••••••••••	1500
Lambert, lieut.-gen. sir J. col. 10th foot •••••••••••••	1224
Lane, Thomas, secretary and registrar, Barbadoes ••••••••••	1469
Lavington, Frances, baroness, pension on civil list, 1812 ••••	400
Lascelles, R. late receiver-general for Monmouth •••••••••	200
Chamberlain of Brecon •••••••••••••••••••••••	245
Laing, A. S. police justice, Hatton-garden•••••• •••••••••	800
Latham, J. inspector and receiver of taxes, 1803 •••••• ••••	706
Lawes, Edw. chief registrar bankrupt court (exclusive of fees)	800
Lawrence, T. chief clerk, post-office ••••••••••••••••••	586
Layard, C. E. civil and military paymaster-general ••••••••	2000
Leach, sir John, master of the rolls •••••••••••••••••••	7000
Leake, S. R. M. assistant clerk in the Treasury •••••••••••	672
Leake, S. M. retired allowance as compt. of army accounts ••	2000
Leake, R. M. master of report-office in Chancery •••••••••	4589

Sir E. Sugden might well lift up his eyes in astonishment, when he discovered the enormous emoluments of this gentleman. The report office is a mere copying office ; and why the duty should be remunerated at this extravagant rate is wholly unaccountable. The chief clerkship is a sinecure, the work being done at a low rate by subalterns. In 1798 the receipts of the office amounted to £1069, having increased upwards of fourfold. These enormous sums are all derived from copies of documents in suits ; for which Mr. Spence suggests as a remedy the mutual interchange between the solicitors of the opposite parties the various copies required. The increase in the emoluments of all officers in chancery has been enormous. For an account of other chancery officers see *Pugh, Utterson, Raynsford,* and *Wingfield.* We refer to these gentlemen, not from any personal motive, or from a wish to imply any peculiarity in their mode of discharging judicial duties, but simply because the spirit moved us, in reading their names, to hang a note to them.

Le Blanc, Thomas, master of court of king's bench	£2000
One of the registrars for Middlesex	852
Leigh, George, pension on civil list, 1819	700

This gentleman was in the 10th hussars, and held some office under George IV., and has apartments at St. James's Palace. He married the sister of the poet Lord Byron.

Leigh R. inspector-general, tax-office	600
Leigh, F. allowance as late collector of excise	1384
Lees, sir E. S. clerk of a road post-office, Ireland	1424
Lees, T. O. clerk of a road post-office, Ireland	816
Searcher, packer, and gauger, Wexford	504
Lees, W. clerk, ordnance department	825
Leeds, duke of, constable of Middleham-castle	46
Lee, W. clerk of ships' entries, customs	1215
Leggatt, Horatio, solicitor of taxes, in lieu of bills	1500
Lennard, J. B. receiver of fees, privy council-office	830
Lennox, lady Louisa, pension on civil list, 1764	445
Lennox, lady Georgiana, pension on civil list, 1819	150
Leeves, E. clerk in privy-council for trade	137
Pension on civil list, having been private secretary to the late Mr. Huskisson, 1828	200
Legge, hon. H. commissioner of customs	1200
Legge, hon. H. deputy comptroller of the navy	1200

Brothers of lord Dartmouth, whose uncle was bishop of Oxford.

Lemon, Robert, deputy-keeper of state papers, 1818	467
Secretary to commissioners to state papers, 1825	200
Leitrim, earl of, *port-searcher*, Dublin	1359

Colonel of the Donegal militia; his son, William, is in the army; and his cousin, J. M. Clements, is M. P. for Leitrimshire.

Lewis, J. M. naval commissioner, Sheerness	1100
Ley, W. second clerk assistant, house of commons	2500
Ley, J. H. clerk, house of commons	2300
Leybourn, Thomas, professor of mathematics, Military College	390
Lifford, viscount, commissioner of Excise	1200
Lichfield, earl of, master of the staghounds	2606

Here is another shameful salary payable out of the civil list. Good God, if the king had two millions in lieu of half a million, he might waste them on the Aristocracy at this rate. It has been declared by high authority, the days are past when government depends on patronage for support. Why then was not this feudal sinecure abolished, or its emoluments greatly reduced, on the resignation of lord Maryborough? It is not sufficient to allege such useless dignities are unavoidable in a monarchy; individuals have long since been compelled to give up luxuries, and even comforts, and even royalty must give up *trappings*, of which William IV. we believe is no way tenacious.

Lightfoot, J. accountant and comptroller of stamps	800

Liston, sir R. late ambassador to the Ottoman Porte········	£2300
Littledale, sir J. judge of the court of king's bench ········	5500
Littledale, J. collector of customs, Whitehaven ··········	500
Lipscombe, right rev. W. bishop of Jamaica ··············	4000
Lock, Georgiana and Lucy F. out of 4½ per cent. duties, each	200
Lloyd, John, commiss. for relief of insolvent debtors, Ireland	2062
Lloyd, Mary-Anne and Emma, pension on civil list, 1815 ··	266
Lloyd, Mary-Harriet, pension on civil list, 1829··········	200
Longmore, A. clerk, remembrancer's office, Edinburgh ····	450
Marshal of exchequer and clerk for land-tax········	130
Longey, E. J. clerk in tally-writer's office ················	700
Compensation for loss as *tally-cutter*, 1826········	187
Lowe, major-gen. sir H. 2d in command, Ceylon···········	4000
Colonel of 93d foot ······················ ········	——
Low, Peter, commissioner of inquiry, Ireland ·············	1200
Loughborough, lord, clerk of chancery, Scotland···········	1135
Lieutenant-colonel of 9th Lancers ················	419
Lowdham, L. A. secretary of lunatics to lord chancellor ····	1301
Lowry, John, 2d professor of mathematics, military college··	267
Lulham, Edw. clerk in the tax-office·····················	629
Lumley, lieut.-gen. hon. sir W. col. 6th dragoons, pay ····	911
Pension for wounds ························ ······	400
Groom of bed-chamber ························	360
Lushington, sir H. consul general at Naples ··············	1350
Lushington, E. H. late commiss. colonial audit-office, 1824 ··	600
King's coroner in the court of king's bench ········	1160
Lushington, S. G. commissioner of customs··············	1200
Lushington, S. R. pension, 1825 ·····················	1500
Brother-in-law of lord Harris. What are Mr. Lushington's claims to a pension we are at a loss to discover. Always filling lucrative offices, and now governor of Madras, for which post he deserted his twenty pound Canterbury constituents.	
Lushington, dame Fanny, pension on civil list, 1813 ······	350
Ludlow, gen. Geo. J. Earl, col. 38th foot, pay ··········	613
Governor of Berwick ························	169
Pension for loss of an arm ·····················	400
Lutwidge, C. collector of customs, Hull ···············	1000
Luttrell, H. F. commissioner of audit ··················	1200
Luttrell, J. F. clerk of the pipe, in Ireland···············	450
Lukin, R. 1st clerk, war-office ·······················	1400
Lyndoch, gen. T. lord, col. 14th foot, pay ··············	613
Governor of Dumbarton Castle ··················	164
Pension by act of parliament ················ ······	2000
Lyndhurst, lord, chief baron, court of Exchequer ········	7000
Lyon, major-gen. sir J. col. 24th foot ·················	1514
Staff pay as lieut.-gen. Leeward Islands············	1383
Governor of Barbadoes ························	3767
Pension by Queen Charlotte ················ ······	100
Maberly, lieut.-col. W. L. surveyor-general, ordnance······	1200

Machen, E. deputy surveyor of Dean Forest, 1816 ········	£350
Joint deputy graveller of Dean Forest, 1815···· ···	100
Magenis, Richard, commis. civil accounts, Dublin, 1813 ····	738
Captain half-pay list 7th fusileers, 1811············	220
Pension for loss of an arm, 1811 ············ ······	100
Magra, Emily and Harriet, pension on civil list, 1805, each··	194
Macleod, George, inspector-general of stamps ············	600
M'Nair, R. collector of customs, Leith ····· ············	800
Maclean, A. receiver-general of Scotland ················ ····	2000
Maclean, lieut.-gen. sir F. col. 84th foot, pay and emoluments	1286
M'Clintock, J. and W. F. union compensation as chief ser-geant at arms, Ireland···················· ······	2545
M'Clelland, Thomas, receiver-general of post-office, Ireland··	553
M'Gregor, sir J. director-general army medical board, and physician to garrison, at Portsmouth ············	2172
M'Gregor, M. consul at Panama ················	1377
M'Causland, W. J. brother-in-law of lord Plunket; solicitor for minors and lunatics ······················	1400
Law agent and commis. of charitable bequests ······	600
Law agent to commis. of education·················	400
Solicitor to board of Erasmus Smith ····· ·········	1200
M'Causland, W. J. son of the preceding ; joint secretary of the lord chancellor ·························	1200
Maconochie, A. lord of session and justiciary, Scotland······	2600
M'Kenzie, J H. lord of session and justiciary, Scotland ····	2600
Commissioner of the jury court, Scotland ··········	600
Macdonald, sir James, M.P. for Hampshire ; commissioner of the India board ······ ················· ····	1200
Clerk of the privy seal·························	

This last is a patent office worth £500 a year, the whole of which
sir James has surrendered to the public without any compensation.
Though our work is called the *Black Book,* we are always prompt
to record any deeds of an opposite complexion.

Macdonald, major-gen. J. colonel 67th foot, pay ··········	613
Deputy adj.-gen. to forces ····· ·················	691
Macleay, W. S. commissioner of arbitration at the Havanna··	1850
Macintosh, sir James, commissioner for the affairs of India	1200
Pension from the E. I. Company as late recorder Bombay	1200

Not many public men can boast of having run so long and devious
a course, with so few backslidings, as sir James Macintosh. During
our *evil* days, when England was under the sway of that pestiferous
triumvirate, Sidmouth, Canning and Castlereagh, sir James delivered
speeches which did honour to his principles, his consistency, and
independence.

Macleod, lieut.-gen. sir John, colonel commandant horse artil-lery, director general of artillery, and master gunner, St. James's Park························· ············	2782
Mann, gen. G. col. engineers, inspector-gen. fortifications····	2964
M'Leay, A. secretary and registrar, New South Wales······	2000
Allowance in lieu of pension, per annum···········	700

M'Mahon, sir W. master of the rolls, Ireland··············	3969
M'Murdo, D. collector of customs, Glasgow ··············	500
Macauley, J.S. captain royal engineers, 1829 ············	202
Professor of fortification, military academy ········	250
Macauley, Z. commissioner for inquiring into charities······	1000
Macauley, T. B., son of the preceding M.P. for Calne; late commissioner of bankrupts·············· ········	200
Mackreth, R. inspector and receiver of taxes ··············	767
Maister, H. W. registrar of deeds for east riding of Yorkshire	650
Maitland, lieut.-gen. sir P. col. 1st West-India regiment ····	
Unattached pay as late captain of grenadier guards ··	500
Staff pay and emoluments as lieut.-governor of Nova-Scotia and governor of Anapolis·················	6093
Maitland, gen. F. colonel Ceylon rifle regiment·············	921
Lieut.-governor of Dominica ·····················	366
Cousin of lord Lauderdale, standard-bearer of Scotland, first a republican, then a Whig, and now a Tory. Lieut.-gen. sir William Houston is brother-in-law of the earl. Other relations are in the army and navy, and one, a cousin of the peer, is director of the bank of Scotland. The celebrated T. Garth, capt. R.N. is also a member of the family.	
Mallet, J. L. secretary in the audit-office ················	1000
Maling, major T. assistant military sec. to commander-in-chief, and captain 2d West India regiment ············	1043
Marsden, Alexander, pension on civil list, during lives of his daughters ······························ ·······	645
Marsden, W. retired allowance as secretary to the admiralty··	——
This gentleman voluntarily resigned his pension of £1500 a year to the public, and we retain his name in this edition as an example to others, and to record so meritorious an act.	
Marsden, rev. G. senior chaplain New South Wales, with house	578
Marsden, Elizabeth and Maria, pensions on civil list, 1806 ··	300
Marshall, W. R. clerk of survey, Woolwich, till *otherwise provided for* ····························· ·······	450
Marshall, Edward, clerk in war-office·····················	800
Clerk of estimates in war-office ·············· ······	150
Marshall, H. A. auditor and accountant-general, Ceylon ····	2000
Manners, lord T. late lord chancellor of Ireland············	3692
Manning, W. T. third clerk to clerk of ships entries········	1811
Manning, John, surveyor-general customs··············· ··	800
Martin, vice-admiral sir T. B. late comptroller of the navy ··	1000
Martin, D. cashier of foreign half-pay, and retired full pay ··	700
Martin, Henry, master in chancery, 1831, about ··········	4500
This gentleman had retired from the profession some years, but lord Brougham appears to have thought Mr. Martin was still equal to the discharge of the duties of a master in chancery.	
Mangin, A. clerk secretary's office, Ireland················	1074
Manningham, C. W. deputy and first clerk, teller's office ····	1000
Mascall, E. J. retired allowance as collector of customs······	1750

Mash, T. B. comptroller of accounts lord chamberlains's dep. ··	£1445
Malcolm, vice-adm, sir P. commander-in-chief, Mediterranean	2555
Maxwell, C. W. governor of St. Christopher··············	3490
Maturin, Harriet, widow, pension on Irish civil list, 1826 ····	46

A miserable pittance to the relict of a man of genius, who amused, if he did not instruct the world by his writings.

Matthews, J. R. consul-general at Lisbon ················	1370
Mansfield, J. filacer, court of common pleas ··············	1450
Mansfield, countess of, pension 4½ per cent. duties, 1814····	1000

Mother of general Geo. Murray, and of the enemy of all reform, lord Mansfield, and of Fulke-Greville, and mother-in-law of the hon. Finch-Hatton, brother of lord Winchilsea.

Manchester, duchess dowager of, compensation allowance for loss of the office of collector of customs outwards, held by the late duke of Manchester ············	2928

Here is a curious case—a dowager duchess, ninety years of age at least—receiving compensation for loss of office as searcher of customs! What services can this lady have rendered? Her husband was known some fifty years ago as a court lord, and if the marriage was improvident, why must the widow be quartered on the public? Has not a labourer's or a mechanic's wife an equal claim? Must we have a pauper nobility to support the dignity of the crown? Why is she not maintained by her son, the late governor of Jamaica ; or her grandson, lord Mandeville, who married a rich heiress?

Marlborough, duke of, hereditary pension out of post-office ··	5000

Father of that mysterious reformer, the marquess of Blandford, and of many others in the navy, army, and church. The pension is a proof of the inutility of hereditary honours in guaranteeing hereditary *nobility*. John, the first duke, might deserve the pension, but can it be said his descendant does?

Master, Isabella F. pension out of 4½ per cent. fund········	200
Mayo, earl of, pension as chairman of the committees of the late house of lords, Ireland····················	1332

This pension was given by an act of parliament; it was an abuse, and ought to be revoked by another.

May, sir G. collector of customs, Belfast ················	1000
Maynard, George, computer of duties on East-India calicoes	1449
Mayer, G. C. librarian in colonial-office ················	721
Mayne, Richard, commissioner of metropolitan police ······	800
Maule, George, solicitor to treasury, salary ··············	2000
Emoluments ·······························	850
Mayow, P. W. assistant solicitor of excise················	2000
Meade, hon. J. consul-general at Madrid ················	1613
Meade, lieut.-gen. Robert, colonel 12th foot ·············	1266
Pension for wounds ·······················	400
Melbourne, viscount, secretary of state, home affairs········	5000
Merry, A. late envoy, &c. to the United States ··········	1700
Mellish, Amelia, Eleanora, Elizabeth, and Wilhelmina, pension on civil list, 1825, each ······················	50
Melluish, H. E. captain royal engineers, 1814···········	220
Extra pay, employed in Canada··················	202

Pension for a wound, 1814	£100
Melville, viscount, lord keeper of privy seal, Scotland	2675
Merivale, J. H. commissioner bankrupt court	1500
Mitford, R. chairman board of taxes	1600
Agent for herring fishery	230
Mitford, B. commissioner of inquiry, Ireland	1200
Mitford, John, late commissioner of bankrupts, clerk of inrolments in chancery, deputy register for Middlesex, commissioner for appeals from board of excise, and auditor of duchy of Lancaster	no return
Mitchell, E. clerk vice-treasurer's office, Ireland	720
Computor of off-reckonings	184
Allowance as late clerk in Irish treasury	507
Miller, J. referee and partidon, Trinidad	1902
Milne, A. secretary to commissioner of woods and forests	1650
Miller, sir W. lord of session, Scotland	2000
Millar, major-gen. W. unattached general officer, 1825	479
Inspector of artillery, 1827	350
Inspector of royal brass foundry	100
Allowance for one servant	27
Mills, F. R. precis writer in home department, 1820	300
Librarian in home department, 1820	675
Mingin, W. first puisne judge, Cape of Good Hope	1500
Minto, earl of, pension on civil list, 1800	938
Milnes, sir R. S. and during lives of dame Milnes and daughters, pension on English civil list, 1809	557
Pension on Irish civil list, 1809	445

Lady Milnes is, we believe, a near relative of the house of Bentinck ; the gentleman was formerly in the Blues. On his marriage was appointed a deputy governor of Canada, or of some colony, as a provision. A pension on retiring is, of course, a natural consequence of previous employment.

Minshull, G. R. *superannuated* allowance as receiver-general of taxes for Buckinghamshire, 1825	300
Police magistrate, 1818	800
Moncrieff, sir J. W. lord of session and justiciary, Scotland	2600
Moneypenny, David, lord of session and justiciary, Scotland	2000
Commissioner of the jury court, Scotland	600
Montagu, H. S. commissioner of stamps	1012
Montagu, G. W. A. deputy chairman, board of stamps	1412
Montrose, duke of, justice general of Scotland (sinecure)	2000
Money, W. T. consul-general at Venice	1043
Morier, D. R. consul-general at Paris	1874
Morier, J. late minister to Mexico	1100
Morier, J. P. late minister to Saxony	1700
Morris, Thomas, surveyor-general of customs	800
Morrison, J. W. deputy master and worker, mint-office	800

Morrison, gen. E. colonel 13th foot, pay · · · · · · · · · · · · · · ·	613
Governor of Chester ·	169
Mortlock, sir J. commissioner of excise · · · · · · · · · · · · · ·	1200
Morisset, J. T. superintendent of police, New South Wales · ·	600
Governor of Norfolk, and half-pay as lieut.-col. in army	—
Molleson, Eleanor, pension on civil list, 1793 · · · · · · · · · · · ·	233
Montford, lord, pension on civil list, *March* 1813· · · · · · · · · ·	611
Montgomery, R. lord treasurer remembrancer, Scotland · · · ·	400
Montgomery, sir Joseph, presenter of signatures, Scotland · ·	610
Montgomery, lady S. pension on civil list, 1826 · · · · · · · · · ·	152
And her daughter, miss Marian, civil list, 1827 · · · ·	97
Molesworth, viscount, pension on civil list, 1820 · · · · · · · · · ·	354
Molesworth, Elizabeth, pension on Irish civil list, 1756 · · · ·	61
This lady must have been in the cradle or earlier state of existence, when the pension was granted. As sometimes a life in Ireland has been carried on to the next generation, an inquiry should now be made who really enjoys this pension.	
Mountmorres, F. H. viscount, pension on civil list, 1826· · · ·	277
Mountjoy, lord, representatives of, pension, Irish civil list· · · ·	360
That the representatives of this nobleman should have had any pension, is unaccountable. He had large estates, which descended to his only son, and he left his three daughters large fortunes.	
Moore, R. deputy inspector of hospitals, Ireland · · · · · · · · · ·	641
Surgeon to house of industry ·	75
Moore, Arthur, second justice common pleas, Ireland · · · · · ·	3692
Moore, James, pension on civil list, 1809 · · · · · · · · · · · · · ·	780
Mooyaart, J. N. collector of customs, Ceylon · · · · · · · · · · · ·	1041
Mostyn, sir E., sir W. Eden, and C. Browning, custos brevium, common pleas ·	1122
Mountain, Eliza, M. W. pension on civil list, 1826 · · · · · · · ·	300
Muddle, R. H. harbour master, Demerara · · · · · · · · · · · · · ·	1019
Munday, George, clerk to master Farrer, in chancery · · · · · ·	1479
Murray, major-gen. hon. G. unattached pay as major general	492
Auditor of exchequer, Scotland · · · · · · · · · · · · · · · · · ·	1200
Murray, sir P. baron of the exchequer, Scotland · · · · · · · ·	2000
Murray, lady Charlotte, pension on civil list, 1803 · · · · · · ·	300
Murray, C. K. police justice, Union Hall · · · · · · · · · · · · · ·	800
Cursitor for Essex and Berks ·	—
Murray, hon. Deborah, pension on civil list, 1821· · · · · · · · · ·	200
Murray, E. registrar of slaves, Trinidad · · · · · · · · · · · · · · ·	2653
Murray, lieut.-gen. right hon. sir G. M. P. for Perthshire; colonel 42d foot, pay and emoluments · · · · · · · · · ·	1168
Governor of Fort George ·	141
Murray, J. W. lord of session, Scotland · · · · · · · · · · · · · · ·	2000
Commissioner of the jury court · · · · · · · · · · · · · · · · · ·	600
Murray, lady Virginia, pension on civil list, 1784· · · · · · · · · ·	184
Musgrave, T. M. retired allowance as clerk in alien-office, 1816	333
Comptroller of twopenny post-office, 1824 · · · · · · · · · ·	500

Muskerry, baroness, pension on civil list, 1825 · · · · · · · · · · · ·	£233
Widow of a brave officer, whose father's profligacy left pennyless.	
Mulgrave, Sophia, countess of, pension on civil list, 1829 · ·	800
There is a famous act of Elizabeth, which renders it imperative on children, when of sufficient ability, to maintain their parents, and we know no reason why his grace of Manchester and my lord Mulgrave should be exempt from its operation.	
Napier, Louisa Mary, pension on civil list, 1805 · · · · · · · · · ·	251
Napier, Catharine, Caroline, and Sophia, each, on civil list · ·	97
Nairne, lord, pension on civil list, 1822 · · · · · · · · · · · · · · · · ·	184
Nairne, Caroline, baroness, pension on civil list, 1829 · · · · · ·	184
Nelson, earl, pension, by act of parliament · · · · · · · · · · · · ·	5000
Brother of admiral Nelson. A striking instance this of the injustice of hereditary honours. The present possessor, a Norfolk parson, and now prebendary of Canterbury, could have had as little claim to the rewards of the Nile as any other chance person picked up in St. Paul's-church-yard.	
Nepean, sir M. H. clerk of supreme court, Jamaica · · · · · · · ·	1850
Nepean, Margaret, pension on civil list, 1792 · · · · · · · · · · · ·	501
Nesbit, S. secretary and registrar, Bahamas · · · · · · · · · · · · · ·	1186
Newenham, Thomas, pension on Irish civil list, 1792 · · · · · ·	177
Newenham, Robert C. Callaghan, pension on civil list, 1792	88
Newenham, Mary, pension on Irish civil list, 1792 · · · · · · · ·	177
Newburgh, Mary, pension on civil list, 1782 · · · · · · · · · · · ·	177
Newcome, George W. late clerk in army account's office, 1826	583
Late commissioner of lottery, 1827 · · · · · · · · · · · · · · · ·	150
Neyle, G. N. auditor of accounts of registrar, Admiralty · · · ·	500
Retired allowance as commissioner of stamps · · · · · · · ·	600
Nicholls, colonel G. royal engineers, Nova Scotia · · · · · · · · · ·	1195
Nicholl, sir J. M.P. for Bedwyn; judge of the arches and prerogative courts of Canterbury, about · · · · · · · · · ·	3350
Nicolay, major-general, governor of Dominica · · · · · · · · · · · ·	2565
The father of the general, we believe, was a German, a violin player, and great favourite of queen Charlotte, with whom he came over to this country.	
Nicolay, Mary Georgiana, pension on civil list, 1818 · · · · · ·	322
Nicolay, Augusta Louisa, pension on civil list, 1813 · · · · · · · ·	130
Noble, H. clerk in office of home secretary · · · · · · · · · · · · · ·	925
Allowance as late naval officer, Newfoundland · · · · · ·	379
Norris, John F. fourth senior clerk in the treasury · · · · · · · ·	679
Northland, vis. joint prothonotary of common pleas, Ireland · ·	3575
Nugent, lord, a lord of the treasury ·	1200
Nugent, gen. sir G., M.P. for Buckingham, col. 6th foot, pay	613
Captain of St. Mawes ·	102
Nugent, C. R. consul-general in Chili · · · · · · · · · · · · · · · · ·	2500
O'Brien, Madelina, widow, pension on civil list, 1818 · · · · · ·	155
O'Connell, Louisa and Alicia, pension on civil list, 1821, each	23
O'Callaghan, major-gen. sir R. col. 97th foot · · · · · · · · · · · ·	494
Commanding forces in North Britain, staff pay · · · · · ·	1183

558 PLACES, PENSIONS, SINECURES, AND GRANTS.

O'Connor, A. distributor of stamps for Antrim	£1076
O'Gorman, C. T. consul general at Mexico	2000
Ogle, rear-admiral sir Charles, commander-in-chief at Halifax and Newfoundland	2190
Ogle, J. W. cocket-writer, customs	1103
O'Grady, S. late chief baron exchequer, Ireland	3500
Oliphant, Anthony, attorney-general, Cape of Good Hope	1500
Oldham, Adam, deputy judge advocate; superannuation	400
O'Reilly, M. J. pension on civil list, 1812	222
Osborn, sir J. commissioner of audit	1200
Oswald, lieut.-gen. sir J. col. 35th foot	1287
Otway, rear-admiral sir R. W. commander-in-chief, South America, (part of the year)	1367
Ottley, sir R. chief justice, Ceylon	4500
Ouseley, sir G. late ambassador to Persia	2000
Owen, adm. sir E. commander, East-Indies	2190
Oxenford, W. clerk to register of debentures, customs	1190
Pack, Arthur, Denis, Elizabeth, and Catharine, each, pension on civil list, 1825	100
Paget, gen. hon. sir E. col. 28th foot	1062
Governor of the royal military college	1500
Pension for loss of a limb	400
Paget, rear-admiral sir Charles	2190
Groom of the bedchamber	400
Paget, hon. B. commissioner of excise	1200
Paget, sir A. late ambassador to the Ottoman Porte	2000
The Pagets are brothers of the marquis of Anglesey.	
Pakenham, T. late master general ordnance, Ireland	1107
Pakenham, Richard, secretary of legation in Mexico	2825
Several other Pakenhams in Navy and Church, Relations of the earl of Longford.	
Palmer, lady Madelina, pension on civil list, 1801	184
Sister to the duke of Gordon, and wife, by second marriage, to the popular member for Reading.	
Palmerston, visc. secretary of state, foreign affairs	5000
Palk, Robert, late commissioner of bankrupts, 1828	200
Counsel to Duchy of Lancaster	unknown
Palgrave, W. collector of customs, Dublin	1200
Papendiech, Augusta Amelia, pension on civil list, 1827	100
Parish, W. consul general at Buenos Ayres	3795
Parish, W. commissioner of excise	1200
Parke, sir James, one of the judges of the king's bench	5500
Park, sir J. A. one of the judges of the common pleas	5500
Parks, Wm. pension on civil list, 1794	321
Parker, lieut.-col. J. B. captain royal artillery, 1825	239
2d captain gent. cadets, 1822	120
Pension for loss of leg, 1816	300

Parsons, Mary, pension on civil list, 1813 · · · · · · · · · · · · · · ·	£177
Parsons, Thomas, postmaster, Waterford · · · · · · · · · · · · · · ·	580
Parkinson, John, consul at Pernambuco · · · · · · · · · · · · · · ·	1751
Passmore, U. consul at Arequipa ·	1265
Pasley, C. lieut.-col. royal engineers, 1814 · · · · · · · · · · · · ·	310
Extra pay, inspector field works, Chatham, 1812 · ·	310
Pension for a wound, 1814 · · · · · · · · · · · · · · · · · · ·	300
Allowance for servants ·	54
Patterson, sir J. puisne judge court of king's bench · · · · · · · ·	5500
Parnell, lady C. pension out of 4½ per cent. duties, 1821 · · · ·	200
Parks, W. pension on civil list, 1794 · · · · · · · · · · · · · · · · · ·	333
Payne, gen. sir W. col. 3d dragoon guards · · · · · · · · · · · · ·	1424
Peacock, M. B. solicitor to the post-office · · · · · · · · · · · · · · ·	1800
Peche, J. clerk ordnance department · · · · · · · · · · · · · · · · ·	500
Pechell, capt. sir Samuel, M. P. for Hallestone ; a lord of the admiralty ·	1000

Peel, sir Robert, M. P. for Tamworth, late secretary of state
for the home department · · · · · · · · · · · · · · · · · · ·

Of late years we have often had occasion to speak of sir Robert,
and have mostly reported favourably of his intentions and abilities.
But we lately washed our hands of him. That he could ever so far degrade our gracious king, by recommending, or suffering himself for a
moment to form part of a ministry that had recommended such a speech
as the one with which his majesty opened parliament, in 1830,
fills us with astonishment. In this business we blame the Baronet
more than the Duke ; the latter is a soldier merely, and some excuse
may be found for his prepossessions in favour of the Polignac system ; but the former has always been a civilian, and never slaugh-
tered any thing beyond hares and partridges :—he ought to have
known better the signs of the times, the change in sentiment among
the middling orders, and that it was absolute insanity to think of
foreign intervention, and of resorting to alien bills, espionage,
habeas corpus suspension acts, bank restriction act, and other
et ceteras of the Pitt machinery, for the purpose of putting down
internal discontent. It is due, however, to sir Robert to observe
that, though we have an opinion he is only a tiny statesman and
better qualified for a peerage than premiership, his opposition to
the Reform Bill was not distinguished by the factious spirit, which
animated the subalterns of his party—the Goulbourns, Crokers, and
Courtenays.

We have left out the Baronet's retiring pension, for the same reason we have left out those of his late colleagues, being uncertain
whether or not they have been claimed under the vile act of Castlereagh. Sir Robert is rich, and may be disposed to save us from the
additional burthen ; and we are more inclined to think such will be
the case, as we find none of his family on the pension list.

Next to judicial reforms, the most praiseworthy act of sir R.
Peel is the introduction of the bill which bears his name ; and we
cannot help expressing our surprise at the errors of Messrs. Atwood, Sadler, sir F. Burdett, sir James Graham, and we believe,
too, the premier is or was slightly smitten with the same blindness
—on so plain a matter as the restoration of the currency. The whole
rationale of the question lies in a nutshell. The power of bankers to
issue paper gave them an uncontrolled influence over prices, wages,

and profits; this power, in the eagerness to gain on their issues, they abused, fostered a pernicious system of credit, gave an artificial impulse to over-trading and speculation, which were followed by the disastrous revulsions witnessed in the years 1811, 1815–16, 1819, and 1825.

Such were the evils of the banking system. What was the remedy? The issue of small notes of less value than five pounds was interdicted; the amount of this denomination of notes in circulation never exceeded six millions; and when they were withdrawn they were replaced with sovereigns, so that there was no diminution or next to none, in the amount of the circulation. What national calamity, then, could flow from this transition, from the transmutation of six millions of rag-money into an equivalent gold currency?

We know there has been a great collapse in the mercantile world since 1826—it has been felt in every part of England, but it is the greatest error ever committed—if error it be—to ascribe it to the withdrawal of the small notes. It has been caused by the *destruction of private credit*—of that baseless and vicious credit, of which the banking system had been the parent, and to which some would again resort as a remedy.

Here are the facts. In 1825 the circulation consisted of specie, bank-notes, and mercantile paper, amounting altogether to about 420 millions. The small notes, amounting to about one-seventh part of the bank paper issued, and to one-seventieth part of the whole circulation, were withdrawn, and sovereigns substituted. And what then? Could this cause a deficiency in the circulating medium? could it cramp the operations of industry and trade, and check individual enterprise? or could it have any sensible effect in lowering the prices of commodities? Certainly not; even if there had been no equivalent issue of specie.

But this was the way it operated. Upon the little pivot of small notes an immense superstructure of kite-flying, bills, and private paper, to the amount of 380 millions, had been erected, all of which tumbled down on the shrinking of bank paper, and consequent ruin of domestic credit. By this means was the death of the paper system hastened, but not produced; the catastrophe was impending before, since the system had been carried to its utmost limit, and would have fallen upon this country, as it fell upon France in the course of the summer of 1830, though Peel's bill had never been introduced.

The cause of mercantile depression has not been a scarcity of small notes, but a scarcity of bills of exchange, and there is a want of bills, because there is a want of credit; there is a want of credit, because there is want of objects on which capital can be profitably employed; there is a want of objects on which capital can be profitably employed, because there are heavy taxes, tithes, corn-laws, commercial monopolies; and there are these evils, because there is an unreformed parliament.

If our readers will only excuse this hasty sketch, we shall leave it just as it is. Were we to proceed, we should only repeat our ideas. One word, however, on a recent observation of lord Grey, whom we should be sorry to see commit a mistake on the subject. His lordship has intimated that it is rather strange small notes should circulate without mischief in Scotland and Ireland, and not in England. Why now, in the first place, Scotland has a somewhat better system of banking; but let it proceed, and mind if it does not ultimately prove as rotten and ruinous as it ever

did in England. But contrast the different circumstances of
the three kingdoms, and compare the wealth, the population,
the manufacturing and mercantile transactions of England with
those of Ireland and Scotland. A system of banking, which may
be safe, manageable, and wholesomely stimulative of commercial,
manufacturing, and rural industry in the latter, may, in the former,
be unnecessary and destructive of national wealth and prosperity.

Pell, sir A. puisne judge, bankrupt court	£2000
Penson, John, late commissioner of bankrupts, 1811	200
Cursitor of court of chancery	unknown
Penn, R. agent for Ceylon	800
Retired allowance as late clerk	750
Penn, R. pension on consolidated fund	1000
Penn, John, hereditary pension on consolidated fund	3000
This pension is a parliamentary compensation granted to the Penn family, to indemnify them for the loss of territorial rights in Pennsylvania, consequent on the separation of the American colonies from the English government.	
Pennefather, R. baron of the exchequer, Ireland	3692
Pennefather, John, William, Mary, Catharine, and Margaret,	
pension each, on Irish civil list, 1771	26
Pelham, hon. Catharine, widow, pension on civil list, 1818	233
Pent, Maria, pension on civil list, 1820	155
Pennell, Rosamond, pension on civil list, 1830	100
Pennell, William, consul at Rio Janeiro	1350
Pennington, Geo. Jos. late commissioner of bankrupts, 1823 ..	200
Steward of courts to Eton col. and dep. recorder	
Lincoln	——
Perceval, D. M. junior clerk teller's office	520
Perceval, Spencer, teller of the exchequer	2700
This is the man that sought a *fast*. Let him give all that he hath to the poor, especially his sinecure, and retire to Spitalfields.	
Percy, hon. A. minister plenipotentiary at Berne	2900
Percy, hon. W. H. commissioner of excise	1200
The last is also captain in the navy. Jocelyn Percy, a captain in the navy. Hugh Percy, bishop of Carlisle. They are brothers of lord Beverley, whose son, lord Lovaine, is an officer in the Guards.	
Perdue, J. inspector and receiver of taxes, 1828	768
Perry, R. superintendent of mail coaches	840
Pemberton, C. R. assistant clerk in treasury, and private secretary to one of the secretaries, 1821	495
Agent for Russian Dutch loan, 1827	300
Phillips, S. M. under secretary of state, home office	1500
Pickford, Jacob, pension on civil list, 1776	222
Pierrepont, hon. H. late envoy, &c. to Stockholm	1200
Pilkington, major-gen. R. unattached major-gen. royal engineers, Gibraltar	1742
Pigot, gen. H. col. 82d foot, pay and emoluments	1073
Planta, Joseph, M.P. for Hastings ; pension, 1827	1500

Planta, Barbara, pension on civil list, 1827 ··············	£200
Plumer, Thomas H. late commissioner of bankrupts, 1819····	
Clerk of the petty bag, chancery, 1820············	unknown
One of the examiners in chancery, 1821···········	2000
Plunket, W. commissioner of excise······ ·············	1200
Plunket, hon. David, son of lord Plunket; prothonotary common pleas, Ireland ····························	1384
Examiner in common pleas·····················	600
Plunket, hon. John, assistant barrister, Meath ············	700
Crown counsel, Munster circuit ··················	500
Counsel to the police ·························	400
Commissioner of inquiry······················,··	1300
Plunket, hon. Pat. son of lord Plunket, purse-bearer to the lord chancellor·····································	500
Secretary of bankrupts ·······················	550
Counsel to chief remembrancer ··················	450
Crown counsel, Leinster circuit ·················	400
Plunket, lord, lord chancellor of Ireland····· ·············	8000

Hon. W. T. Plunket is dean of Down, with other church income. Hon. W. Plunket is in the church. Hon. R. Plunket holds church preferment in England, presented by lord Goderich. Sir R. F. L. Blosse, son-in-law of lord Plunket, is chaplain to the lord lieutenant.—See also M. Causland in the *List*.

The connivance of lord Plunket, at the exaction of magisterial fees by his purse-bearer and secretary, and his contest with the master of the rolls about the patronage of a secretaryship, have not tended to obliterate the impression of a shuffling and greedy politician. The Whigs almost moved heaven and earth to raise his lordship to the Irish chancellorship. And for what purpose? His predecessor, the late Sir Anthony Hart, was wholly unexceptionable—almost the *beau ideal* of what a judge should be— unconnected with politics—and discharging his high duties with the same singleness of mind that admiral Blake commanded the fleet during the time of the Commonwealth — intent only upon faithfully executing his individual trust, regardless of the intrigues and mutations of party and faction. Ought such a person to have been removed, to make way for a successor—who is partizanship, ambition, and avarice personified? If lord Plunket possess abilities, why were they not as available to the service of the country in his former situation, as in his present appointment? Are all our public men so void of patriotism—so degraded in principle—such sordid hirelings, that not one can be found to serve the community, unless he first receive a place, title, pension, or patronage to the full value of his labour? The country is more in need of political honesty than splendid abilities; and the Irish chancellor has certainly brought the ministry no accession of character. For the three years preceding his elevation no one heard of him, either as judicial reformer or statesman; and solely, as far as we could learn, because he deemed his appointment in the common pleas not an adequate *price for his services*. Here was disinterested patriotism! Look again at his conduct in 1821, when included in the *sale* of the Grenvillites, he joined the Liverpool administration, and, after receiving the attorney-generalship as the price of silence or apostacy, openly abandoned Catholic emancipation, under the convenient pretext that it was not the *proper time* to agitate the question.

Lord Plunket's notions on church property are not worth answering, being obviously at variance with the most obvious truths of history and analogy. It is not likely, however, an adventurer of his stamp will flinch on this question without strong necessity, especially after fastening so many members of his family on the ecclesiastical and judicial establishments of Ireland.

Plaskett, T. H. chief clerk home office · · · · · · · · · · · · · · · · · ·	£1329
Pollen, R. one of the six clerks in chancery · · · · · · · · · · · · · · ·	1217
Pond, John, astronomer royal, Greenwich · · · · · · · · · · · · · ·	500
Ponsonby, major-gen. hon. F. C. inspecting field-officer · · · ·	383
Lieutenant-governor of Malta ·	4000
Pension for wounds ·	300
Ponsonby, lord, envoy and min. plenipo. at Rio de Janeiro · ·	4500
Ponsonby, George, lord of the treasury · · · · · · · · · · · · · · · · ·	1200
Richard Ponsonby, a third brother, is bishop of Derry.	
Ponsonby, Sarah, pension on civil list, 1829 · · · · · · · · · · · · · ·	200
Porter, sir R. Ker, consul at Caraccas · · · · · · · · · · · · · · · · · ·	1261
Porrett, R. chief clerk storekeeper's office · · · · · · · · · · · · · · ·	750
Portmore, earl of, pension on civil list, 1825 · · · · · · · · · · · ·	233
Well known in the gay world some years ago as lord Milsingtown. He has also £276 on the Scotch civil list.	
Polchet, Alfonce, professor of fortification, military academy · ·	297
Pope, C. surveyor of warehouses, Bristol · · · · · · · · · · · · · · ·	500
Pope, rev. E. archdeacon of Jamaica · · · · · · · · · · · · · · · · ·	2000
Popham, Elizabeth M. pension out of 4½ per cent. duties · · · ·	500
Power, D. protector of slaves, Berbice · · · · · · · · · · · · · · · · ·	1017
Poulett, hon. G. flag captain of H. M. S. " Prince Regent" · ·	799
Late receiver-general of taxes ·	400
Pringle, lieut.-gen. sir W. H. nephew to the earl of St. Germains, and M.P. for Liskeard; col. 64th foot · · · ·	1245
Prior, J. H. inspector and receiver of taxes, 1803 · · · · · · · · · ·	772
Price, J. collector of revenue, Ceylon · · · · · · · · · · · · · · · · ·	1173
Price, J. pension on civil list, 1821 · · · · · · · · · · · · · · · · · · ·	200
Pressly, C. secretary to the board of stamps · · · · · · · · · · · · · ·	700
Pugh, John, clerk to master Wilson, in chancery · · · · · · · · · ·	1520

There are ten masters in chancery, with average incomes of £4000, and each master has a chief clerk with an income of £1200 or £1500 a year. These incomes, like most other judicial emoluments in equity, arise almost entirely from fees paid by suitors, and it is worthy of remark that while the emoluments have increased two or three fold, the time devoted to the public has in a similar inverse proportion decreased. That some reform is needed here there can be no doubt. With respect to the salaries of Mr. Pugh and his brother clerks they are made up in a most objectionable manner : there is a head called " gratuities," under which the chief portion of them is derived. In one office the fees amount to £500 and the gratuities to £800, and in others they present a similar disproportion. Such gratuities are indefensible, for they are sums given—levied we should say—to expedite business, which ought to be done expeditiously without them.

Radcliffe, John, judge of the prerogative court, Ireland · · · · · ·	3000
Radstock, Cornelia, baroness, pension on civil list, 1814 · · · ·	389

Ram, Abel and Elizabeth, pension on civil list, 1827	£95
Ramshaw, John, clerk in the secretary's office, customs	550
Registrar of officers' sureties	600
Rance, W. inspector and receiver of taxes, 1822	717
Rae, dame Mary, pension on civil list, 1830	660

This is a grant made under the Wellington ministry. The lady is the wife of the late lord advocate for Scotland,—an official legal situation resembling our attorney-general as public prosecutor. The only pretext for such a pension is, that this gentleman has lost his practice, that he gave up the office of sheriff-depute, worth some £600 a year, and that a seat in parliament being held essential to the office, he has been put to considerable expense in procuring it, A pity may be felt for the lady, but is the public deserving of no compassion? Let sir W. Rae have the sheriff-deputeship that falls vacant, and let dame Rae be provided for as other dames are, whose husbands do not sell themselves to ministers.

Raper, C. C. clerk in war-office	800
Paymaster of pensions to widows and children of *foreign* officers	250
Rattray, baron of the exchequer, Scotland...............	2000
Raynsford, T. A. registrar in chancery, for year 1830	4861

Of this enormous income £4201 arose from *fees* payable by suitors for copying and registering proceedings in equity. Lord Eldon, for upwards of a quarter of a century, sat cowering over the abuses of chancery, like a miser over his hoard, and would neither touch them himself nor suffer them to be touched by any other person. In 1826 the attorney-general, afterwards lord Lyndhurst, professed his intention to bring in a bill on the subject, but no such bill ever saw the light. Afterwards, however, he introduced an illusive measure, which did not embrace half the objects he originally professed ; and the unfortunate suitors were left to be fleeced as heretofore, and more unmercifully than any poor gudgeon is who ventures within the precincts of the most nefarious gaming house in the metropolis. With respect to the registrars, they are in keeping with most branches of our political and judicial administration, presenting a vast accumulation of abuse and emoluments since the commencement of the revolutionary war. From a parliamentary report of 1813 it appears that in the year 1797 the senior registrar received the annual sum of £1134, and the whole fees of the office did not exceed £4847. Mr. Raynsford alone, it seems, receives more than the whole amount of these fees ; and the fees of the entire registrar's office have increased to £19,119 per annum, (*Parliamentary Paper*, No. 23, *Sess.* 1830-1.) And how has this increase been produced? It has been produced by enlarging the pleadings' bills to such an extent as to allow the enormous charges to be incurred in their registry, which is the consequence of the unnecessary length to which proceedings in chancery are extended. Besides their regular emoluments each registrar has the liberty of taking a clerk, without previous examination, for which he receives a fee of about £1000, and this person succeeds to the office.

Ray, H. B. prothonotary of court of common pleas	2600
Reade, sir T. consul general, Tunis	1800
Reade, W. assistant to collector, outwards	1000
Ready, John and Charles, pension on Irish civil list, 1817, each	177
Renny, W. solicitor of legacy duties, Scotland	500

Renny, Dr. G. director general of hospitals, physician and surgeon to Kilmainham-hospital··················	£1296
Renny, Mary, Elizabeth, and Isabella, pension on civil list, 1821, each ································	88
Reid, J. clerk and chamberlain of Lindores ··············	457
Reed, S. secretary to medical board ····················	500
Reynolds, J. G. clerk commissary dept. of treasury ········	700
Reynolds, J. S. clerk of securities, treasury ··············	1050
Rice, T. S. son-in-law of the earl of Limerick; joint secretary of the treasury ····························	2500
Richardson, —, deputy registrar, bankrupt court··········	600
Richmond, duke of, postmaster general of the United Kingdom	2500
The office of postmaster-general has been abolished in Ireland; one of the two formerly existing, has been dropped in England, and the impression of the duke of Richmond, on his first appointment, being, that the other was only a *sinecure*, he nobly declined receiving any salary. Experience proved this to be a mistake. Numerous and important duties are annexed to the postmaster-generalship, and really, economists as we are, we do not think £2000, or so, too much for the faithful discharge of them.	
Richmond, Henry, commissioner of customs ··············	1200
For loss of fees ·····························	800
Rich, sir Geo. pension on civil list, 1817 ················	132
Rickman, John, clerk assistant, house of commons ········	2500
Richardson, sir J. late justice of the king's bench··········	3500
Richardson, Fanny, Elizabeth, and Sarah, pension on c. l. 1824	101
Richards, R. accountant general and master, court of exchequer	1820
Richards, H. solicitor of stamps, Scotland ···············	1000
Ricketts, C. M. consul-general at Lima ·················	1600
Ricketts, maj. H. J. royal African corps, pay ············	292
Lieut.-governor of Sierra Leone················	2095
Ricketts, Mrs. S. pension out of 4½ per cent. fund, 1820····	411
Ripley, J. J. principal clerk, customs ··················	650
Rippon, T. agent at the bank for national debt ············	300
Ritemeyer, R. J. colonial receiver, Demerara ············	1571
Roberts, W. commissioner for inquiry into charities, 1818 ··	1000
Roberts, W. H. receiver of fees, exchequer ··············	1350
Rogers, F. L. inspector in the audit-office················	800
Robertson, W. late lord of session, Scotland···· ··········	1500
Robinson, lieut.-gen. sir F. P. colonel 59th foot ··········	1171
Robinson, C. collector of customs, Demerara ············	2000
Robinson, sir C. judge of the high court of admiralty ······	2402
Robinson, J. R. chief justice, Upper Canada·············	1500
Robinson, Catharine, pension on civil list, 1793 ··········	407
Rodney, lord, hereditary pension, by act of parliament······	2923
The admiral might have deserved this pension; but titles should not be granted with a perpetual charge on them. This pension originally was £2000, but increased £1000, to put the present possessor on a level with earl St. Vincent and lord Camperdown, and with them should be reduced.	

Rodney, hon. John, chief secretary, Ceylon	£3200
Rodney, hon. W. secretary comptroller, army account office	700
Rodney, John, Jane, Ann, Sarah, and Catharine, pension on civil list, 1781, each	88
Roden, earl of, late auditor of the exchequer, Ireland	2700
Rodmell, Thomas, comptroller of customs, Hull	600
Roe, W. T. commissioner of customs	1200
Steward of the Savoy	15
Roe, F. A. police justice, Great Marlborough Street	800
Rooke, dame H. pension on civil list, 1808	233
Rook, Jane and Mary, pension on civil list, 1816, each	60
Rollo, Isabella and Mary, pension on civil list, 1807	184
Rolland, Adam, principal clerk of session, Scotland	1000
Clerk to his majesty's processes, Scotland	40
Rolleston, H. clerk in foreign secretary's office	880
Romilly, C. late commissioner of bankrupts, 1830	200
Rose, sir George, M.P. for Christchurch; clerk of parliament	3300
Rose, sir G. puisne judge, bankrupt court	2000
Rose, Theodore, pension on civil list, 1785	233
Rose, Ann Fraser, pension on civil list, 1803	92
Rose, Mary, pension on civil list, 1808	97
Ross, major-gen. J. commanding at Guernsey and Alderney, staff pay as colonel	560
Pay and emoluments as lieut.-governor of Guernsey	627
Unattached pay as lieut.-colonel	310
Pension for injuries received in service	350
Ross, C. B. commissioner of the navy, Plymouth	1000
Ross, sir Patrick, governor of Antigua	4859
Ross, Charlotte, widow, pension on civil list, 1823	194
Rosslyn, gen. earl of, col. of 9th lancers	1415
Director of chancery, Scotland	1852
Rothesay, lord Stuart de, late ambassador to Paris	2500
Roscommon, countess of, pension on civil list, 1817	88
Roscommon, earl of, pension on civil list, 1829	192
Rotton, J. deputy comptroller general, excise	600
Rothes, G. W. earl of, pension on civil list, 1821	270
Rothes, Charlotte, dowager countess of, pension on civil list	431
Roupell, J. B. master in chancery, circa	4000
Routh, commissary-general in the Canadas	1862
Rowan, lieut.-col. Charles, commissioner of metropolitan police	800
Rowley, O. secretary and registrar, Malta	1044
Rudlen, J. second clerk to auditor of land revenue	710
Rumbold, Emily and Caroline, pension on civil list, 1826, each	115

Emily, sister to sir William, who was taken out to India by the marquis of Hastings, and has married a wealthy Prussian jew, of the name of Delmar; yet she still continues on the *List*, but this lady may follow the fashion, and pay it over to her sister Miss Caroline Eliza, who has not been so fortunate.

Russell, W. late commissioner of bankrupts, 1828 ········ £200
    Deputy recorder of Bedford ···················
Russell, lord John, paymaster of the forces ············· 2000

The perseverance of the noble paymaster in the cause of parliamentary reform and the able manner in which he introduced the new ark of the constitution have fairly won him a niche in the temple of Fame. We have only one charge to urge against his lordship. Upon one occasion he ventured to insinuate an apology for the shameless cost of foreign embassies, and hinted that the pension roll was almost too insignificant for legislative notice. If the right hon. lord will only condescend to look at page 489 of our publication, he will find he labours under a trifling mistake in this matter, and that the sums paid in pensions only are more than double the produce of all the taxes on knowledge, and which as a friend to the diffusion of intelligence and member of a society instituted expressly for the purpose, he must needs deem a serious consideration : but the waste of public money is not the whole of the evil ; it is the political and social consequences—the vicious influence it creates—the corrupt expectancies excited—and the encouragement of immorality and political prostitution, to which it has been often made subservient.

Ruthven, Wilhelmina, pension on civil list, 1801·········· 230
Ryder, F. D. clerk foreign office ····················· 750

Son of lord Harrowby, and brother of lord Sandon, M.P. for Liverpool. An uncle, bishop of Lichfield and Coventry; another uncle registrar in consistory court ; other Ryders are in the Navy and Church. It is, like the Grenvilles, a keen family.

St. Albans, duke of, hereditary grand falconer············ 1372
    Hereditary registrar of court of chancery ·········· 640
St. George, C. M. secretary and chargé d'affaires at Turin ·· 1401
St. George, Maria and Jane, pension on civil list, 1828 ···· 144
St. John, Henry, pension on civil list, 1780 ············ 101
St. John, R. W. consul-general, Algiers ················ 2000
St. Helens, lord, late ambassador to Russia ············· 2300
    Gentleman of the king's bedchamber ············· 712
St. Vincent, viscount, pension on consolidated fund········ 3000

The uncle, who was a successful naval commander and meritorious first lord of the admiralty, might deserve the pension, but his successor, the nephew of the admiral, can have no claim on the public.

Sandford, Frances, pension on civil list, 1830············· 97
Sansomi, L. collector of customs, Ceylon ··············· 1025
Sargeant, J. late commiss. for auditing public accounts, 1821 1500
    Late secretary to the treasury, 1804········ ······ 800
Sargent, William, principal clerk in the treasury·········· 600
Sargent, Mrs. C. pension out of 4¼ per cent. duties, 1804 ·· 610
Salkeld, George, consul at New Orleans ················ 1136
Sanford, Henry, senior clerk in the treasury ············ 1000
Saurin, Edw. commissioner of stamps, 1826·············· 1000
    Half-pay as captain in the navy, 1819 ············ 57
Saurin, M. A. solicitor to excise, Ireland··············· 1500
Saumarez, adm. lord de, vice-adm. of Great Britain, and admiral of the red ····················· £1230

General of marines, *(a sinecure)* 1832	£1728
Pension, by act of parliament	1200
Saunders, E. clerk in commissariat	511
Clerk in office for civil list accounts, 1816	200
Sawkins, J. inspector and receiver of taxes, 1821	656
Sayer, B. comptroller of accounts, tax-office	1131
Sellon, J. B. police justice, Hatton Garden	800
Seppings, sir R. late surveyor of the navy	500
Pension	400
Selwyn, Charlotte, Albinia, Louisa, and Henrietta, pension on civil list, 1807, each.........................	81
Semphill, hon. Maria and Sarah, pension each, 1826	49
Semphill, Hugh, lord, pension on civil list, 1826	97
Sewell, hon. Harriet, pension on civil list, 1821	88

One of the Beresford family, daughter of the late archbishop of Tuam, sister to present lord Decies, and to Mrs. Thomas Hope of the gay world.

Sewell, J. pension out of consolidated fund	1000
Sewell, Jonathan, chief justice Quebec, and speaker of the legislative council	2400
Seward, lieut.-gen. T. colonel commandant royal artillery····	1003
Seymour, G. H. minister resident in Tuscany	2300
Seymour, lord George, chairman of the excise board	2000

The chairmen and commissioners of the boards of excise, customs, stamps, and taxes, are mostly filled by members of the aristocratical families. The Liverpool administration was pre-eminent for the lavish grant of pensions and increase of salaries. By an order of the lords of the treasury in 1816, the salaries of the chairman of customs and excise were augmented from £1700 to £2000 a year, and the junior members of the two boards from £1400 a year. The Whigs have applied the pruning knife to the exuberances of their predecessors, by directing that two commissioners of customs and as many of excise should retire forthwith, and that each board should be diminished two more as they drop off. The salaries of the commissioners are reduced from £1,400 to £1,200 a year; and the secretaries of the board at the rate of twenty-five per cent. This seems like retrenchment.

Seymour, lord H. compensation allowance for loss of office as *craner and wharfinger*, port of Dublin	1251
Seymour, capt. sir M. naval commissioner, Portsmouth ····	1100
Seymour, lord R. commiss. and prothonotary, King's B. Ireland	7137
Seymour, Henry, sergeant-at-arms, House of Commons ····	2300
Seymour, Capt. G. H. Sergeant-at-Arms, House of Lords ··	3400
Seymour, H. B. gentleman usher, privy chamber··········	——

The Seymours are uncles and cousins of the marquis of Hertford, one of the greatest borough-proprietors, and affords practical proof of the working of this sort of property under, we hope shortly to be able to call, the *old system*.

Scott, W. L. F. registrar of deeds for West Riding of Yorkshire	1200
Scott, W. H. J. son of lord Eldon, receiver of fines, court of chancery, for the year ending 1830	240
Registrar of affidavits, court of chancery	1816

Clerk of the letters patent, court of chancery ·····	£553
Reversion of rev. T. Thurlow's annuity under 1 and 2 William IV. c. 56 ······················	11,000

Under the 39 Geo. III. c. 110, in the year 1800, the salaries of the judges at Westminster and the lords of session at Edinburgh were greatly augmented, chiefly on account of the *high price of provisions.* Why then, it may be asked, are they not now reduced? But this is not the precise point we are aiming at. Under the same act a retiring pension was for the *first time* granted to the lord chancellor to the amount of £4000 a year, without limitation as to the previous time of holding the great seal ; and this pension— greater than is ever given to an admiral or general for the most long and splendid services—was granted, on the pretext that sinecures in the gift of the chancellor had been abolished, whereby his lordship was less able to make a provision for his family than his predecessors in office. Here, however, we find lord Eldon's son entrenched behind three tier of sinecures, and fortified in his rear by the reversion of Parson Thurlow's sinecures, worth £11,000 per annum, all given to him by his father subsequent to the passing of the statute mentioned. Does not this, independent of his official income of £18,000 or £20,000 a year, prove that lord Eldon had ample means of providing for a family, without granting him in addition, a retiring pension out of the taxes. We would suggest to the wealthy Patriarch of the Tories the prudence of making a voluntary sacrifice to the public, without waiting to have these matters revised and settled by that Reformed Parliament, to which his lordship and friends entertain so natural an aversion. The abandonment of the pension at least, with a fortune of £30,000 or £40,000 a year, realized out of the bankruptcies, lunacies, wardships, and supersedeases of the Pitt system, would not be missed, and certainly not abridge the hospitalities of Encombe or Hamilton-Place.

Scott, sir Walter, principal clerk of session, and sheriff of the shire of Selkirk, Scotland ·····················	1600
For loss of fees under 50 Geo. III. c. 112·········	300
Scott, H. R. collector of customs and provincial judge, Cloyne	1041
Scott, sir David, pension on civil list, 1827 ··············	300

Are the magisterial services of this gentleman at Brighton so valuable as to deserve this pension?

Scott, Ann Lindsay, pension on civil list, 1825············	250
Scott, dame Harriet, pension on civil list, 1802 ··········	84
Schenley, E. W. H. consul at Hayti ····················	1200
Schomberg, heir of the duke of, hereditary pension out of post-office revenue ····························	4000

One of king William's followers, and killed, it is su posed, by a random shot from his own troops at the battle of the Boyne. There is no peerage of the name, and to whom the pension is paid, or for what, we are unable to ascertain.

Scovell, sir Geo. col. lieut.-governor of military college, 1829	383
Lieut.-col. royal waggon train ··················	599
Scovell, C. assistant secretary, customs·················	1200
Shadwell, sir Launcelot, vice-chancellor···················	6000
Shaftesbury, earl of, chairman of committees, house of lords··	3000
Shannon, earl of, late clerk of the pells, Ireland ··········	3133

Shawe, lieut.-col. Merrick, pension on civil list, 1824 ······	£500
Pension on Irish civil list, 1825 ····················	499

We are not aware of any claims col. Shawe had to his pensions, further than court favour and having acted as private secretary to the marquis Wellesley. It seems the regular practice of noble lords to throw their private secretaries on the public : this example was followed by the duke, in the cases of Messrs. Drummond and Greville. Every want is provided for out of the taxes, whether it be for the support of an aged parent, sister, niece, illegitimate child, or cast-off mistress.

Shaw, Robert, representative of, pension on civil list, 1786 ··	714

Sir R. Shaw, of Dublin, enjoys this pension ; and he explains, that he *inherits* it ; that it was " purchased," by his father, of course, upwards of forty-four years ago, and that he, of course, inherits it as executor of another. So that this pension may continue for ever, and be transmitted like a freehold estate. The famous pension of Edmund Burke has been sold many times ; and if sir R. Shaw's doctrine be correct, some of these incumbrances may be perpetual.

Shawe, Mary, Catharine, and Ann, pension on civil list, 1828	95
Sharp, sir C. collector of customs, Sunderland ············	600
Shepherd, sir S. late chief baron exchequer, Scotland ······	3000
Shepherd, H. John, late commissioner of bankrupts, 1827 ··	
Judge advocate of fleet and counsel to admiralty, 1828	43
Recorder of Abingdon, 1818 ····················	
Clerk of custodies of lunatics in chancery, 1829 ····	450
Clerk of presentations in chancery, 1829 ··········	43
Shee, sir Geo. under secretary of state, foreign department ··	1500
Shee, dame Maria, pension on civil list, each ············	334
Sherwood, Susan, Rebecca, Ann, and Elizabeth, pension on civil list, 1803, each ····················	15
Shield, W. late naval commissioner ···················	950
Sheridan, Richard Brinsley, Caroline, Thomas Berkeley, Frances, Charles, and Helen, pension on civil list, 1818, each ····························	57

Poor Sheridan's legacy to his friend George IV. who thus disposed of it. As the duke of Somerset's son has married one of the family, he will, it is hoped, do something for his wife's relatives.

Short, Charles, clerk of the rules and orders of the court of king's bench, *from fees* ····················	5172

We are not exactly acquainted with the official duties of Mr. Short, but the nature of them and the sources of his vast emoluments require investigation. It is curious to remark that the greatest portion of public taxes is levied on articles of general consumption, and paid by the industrious classes ; and the emoluments of the most lucrative judicial offices arise principally from fees paid out of the property of bankrupts, insolvents, and imprisoned debtors.

Short, H. T. clerk, secretary of state's office, colonial ······	855
Agent for Trinidad ···· ····················	344
Shrapnell, maj.-gen. H. colonel commandant royal artillery ··	1003
Pension for inventions·························	1200

Sinclair, sir John, compensation on abolition of office of cashier of excise, Edinburgh ························	£2000
From the incessant publications of this person, his duties of office could not have been very great, and we believe he never served any apprenticeship to entitle him to compensation for loss of employment.	
Sinclair, lord Charles, pension on Scotch civil list, 1788 ····	184
Sinclair, Elizabeth, pension on civil list, 1775 ············	138
Sinclair, lady Isabella, pension on civil list, 1790 ··········	115
Sinclair, Ann, pension on civil list, 1791 ················	37
Sinclair, Catharine, pension on civil list, 1791 ············	97
Sidmouth, viscount, late secretary of state ················	3000
Skinner, J. M. com. of a packet, Holyhead, 1793···········	800
Commander in the navy, 1821 ·················	115
Slow, Ann and Catharine, pensioners on civil list, 1817, each	45
Smith, lieut.-col. sir C. F. royal engineers, West Indies ····	1234
Pension for wound ····························	300
Smith, lieut.-gen. John, colonel commandant royal artillery··	1003
Smith, major-gen. J. F. S. colonel, royal artillery, Ireland ··	1870
Smith, J. clerk Irish department, treasury················	1000
Pension for loss of office in Irish house of commons ··	304
Smith, G. late secretary to the navy board················	600
Smith, W. commissioner of arbitration at Sierra Leone ······	1831
Smith, J. S. late envoy, &c. to Stutgard ···············	1200
Smith, sir W. C. baron of the exchequer, Ireland··········	3692
Smith, sir W. Sydney, pension on consolidated fund········	1000
Pension on 4½ per cent. duties ·················	1250
Admiral of the white ·····················	—
Lieut.-gen. of marines·····················	—
Smith, Culling Charles, commissioner of customs··········	1200
Smith, lady Ann Culling, pension on civil list, 1812········	600
Smith, Dame Carterette, pension on civil list, 1813 ········	155
This last is, probably, mother-in-law of the preceding, who is wife of sir George Culling Smith,—mother-in-law twice over to the marquis of Worcester, who married two of her daughters,—sister to marquis Wellesley,—ditto to lord Maryborough,—ditto to the duke of Wellington,—ditto to lord Cowley,—ditto to the rev. Dr.Wellesley, prebend of Durham, rector of Chelsea, and rector of Bishop's Wearmouth, and who would, doubtless, have been a bishop, had he not, by such promotion, been obliged to relinquish more valuable preferments.	
Smith, P. clerk, secretary of state's office, colonial ········	726
Agent for Mauritius ····················	500
Smith, R. Vernon, lord of the treasury ······ ···········	1200
Smyth, sir J. C. baronet, unattached gen. officer, 1825······	479
Pension for good services, 1817···················	456
Governor of the Bahamas ····················	2650
Smythe, the hon. G. A. F. S. pension on civil list, 1828 ····	104
Smyth, James, collector of customs, Cork··············	1000
Smollett, Susan, pension on civil list, 1806···············	97

Soady, B. clerk in audit office ·	£350
Pension for special services ·	100
Private secretary to chairman of audit board, 1826 · · · ·	50
Somerset, lieut.-gen. lord, R. E. H. col. 1st reg. of dragoons · ·	1520
Somerset, major-gen. lord, F. unattached pay as major-gen. · ·	500
Military secretary to the general commanding in chief	2000
Colonel 53d foot, about ·	1200
Pension for wound ·	300

Brothers of the duke of Beaufort, an old ultra-Tory family, whose ramifications in church and state are almost untraceable.

Somerville, William, physician, Chelsea hospital · · · · · · · · · ·	576
Retired pay as inspector, medical department · · · · · · · ·	187
Sergeant surgeon to the king · · · · · · · · · · · · · · · · · ·	277
Sneyd, Elizabeth, and her daughter, pension on civil list, 1776	445
Sneyd, Hannah, pension on civil list, 1781 · · · · · · · · · · · · ·	266
Sneyd, Ann, pension on civil list, 1807 · · · · · · · · · · · · · · · ·	356

These are Irish, and we wonder who they can be. There is a great wine-merchant, named Sneyd, who was in parliament, and who regularly voted with ministers.

Soane, John, clerk of the works, Chelsea hospital · · · · · · · · · ·	749
South, William, clerk to registrar in chancery · · · · · · · · · · · ·	1576
Southey, Robert, pension on civil list, 1807 · · · · · · · · · · · · · ·	155
Poet laureate, circa ·	100
Sparshott, S. deputy comptroller, coast-guard · · · · · · · · · · · ·	500
Commander in the navy, half pay · · · · · · · · · · · · · · · ·	155
Spencer, W. ordnance storekeeper, Portsmouth · · · · · · · · · · · ·	1002
Spearman, A. Y. assistant clerk of parliamentary accounts · ·	875
First clerk, civil list audit office · · · · · · · · · · · · · · · · · ·	400
Spearman, A. and Margaret Young, pension civil list, 1827 · ·	120
Spicer, W. H. deputy treasurer, Chelsea hospital · · · · · · · · · ·	1016
Spottiswoode, George, commandant Hibernian society, 1820 · ·	310
Pension for wounds, 1815 ·	200
Half-pay as major in the army, 1816 · · · · · · · · · · · · · · ·	173
Spottiswoode, Eyre, and Strahan, king's printers · · · · · · · · · ·	no return

These gentlemen hold the valuable patent of King's printer, conferring the exclusive right to print acts of parliament, proclamations, bibles, books of common prayer, and works the copyright of which is vested in the crown. It is impossible to assign the annual profits accruing from this privilege; they must be very great, as their bills against the treasury, ordinarily, amount to £10,000 or £15,000 per annum. Besides the profits from this source, they have another from the *sale* of acts to the public, above the number required by law to be delivered to the houses of parliament, the magistracy, and public bodies; and which profit has been estimated to amount to £30,000 per annum. It appears doubtful whether the terms of the patent entitle the grantees to the *bookseller's profit* on the sale of the acts of parliament to the public; their privilege being restricted to the office of printer to the king.

The patent of Messrs. Eyre and Strahan expired in 1829, and report says, it has been renewed for another period of thirty years, without inquiry, or other terms being exacted than the old understood condition of one of the firm sitting in parliament and voting on all occasions with the treasury. If this report be correct, the profligacy of the arrangement can only be equalled by other acts which signalized the Wellington ministry, when, at the moment of dissolution, they thrust, *en masse*, on the pension list their private secretaries, parasites, and *attachés*, of a still less reputable description. We believe, however, certain formalities remain to be gone through before the grant is finally renewed; and from some expressions, which have fallen from lord Althorp, it is probable measures will be adopted to quash a monopoly which is at variance with the knowledge of the age, and the general policy of an enlightened government.

That the public sustains a great loss from the exclusive privilege of the king's printer is evident from the transactions with the late John Reeves, esq. well known some forty years ago as the getter-up of a *loyal association* for putting down republicans and levellers. Mr. Pitt was desirous of rewarding the services of this redoubtable champion of monarchical institutions; to have placed him openly on the pension list might have given rise to comments rendering questionable the purity of John's loyalty, which dilemma was avoided by the wary minister making it a condition of the renewal of the patent of the king's printer in 1799, that Mr. Reeves should be admitted a *sleeping* partner, receiving for his share of the profits £1500 per annum. In 1807, Mr. Reeves became dissatisfied with the arrangement, having discovered that his share of the profits was far more considerable, amounting, according to the statement he made in a bill of discovery, filed by him against his co-partner in the patent, to £6500 a year. The result of this proceeding was a more favourable agreement with the loyal associator against levellers, the precise nature of which has not transpired. What we have said is perhaps sufficient to elucidate the privileges of the king's printer, the purposes to which they have been applied, and the propriety of their abolition.

Spranger, late commissioner of bankrupts, 1882	200
Master of court of exchequer, 1820	no returns
Speer, W. chief clerk in treasury and auditor	1700
Stack, Annabella and Mary, pension on civil list, 1828	66
Stace, W. ordnance storekeeper, Woolwich	680
Pension	365
Stanley, Edw. G. S. grandson of the earl of Derby; chief secretary for Ireland, salary and emoluments	5500

Mr. Stanley is reputed not to be a bird of sweet voice, but he has eagle talons, and Mr. O'Connell appears never to have forgotten the terrible grip he received from the chief secretary about the affair of the prosecution. We should admire the Liberator more if we saw him zealous in forwarding measures really tending to the relief of Ireland, in lieu of consuming session after session in bagatelle and impossible motions, which seem intended only as an excuse for doing nothing at all, or nothing practically beneficial to his country. Indeed, we are sometimes inclined to think the Great Agitator views with jealousy, if not with absolute aversion, the abolition of tithes, the introduction of poor laws, or any other efficient measure of improvement, lest it should defeat his darling panacea of a repeal of the Union. This last, however, has always appeared to us more a scheme of personal ambition than of national amelioration. Having towed the Emerald Isle along the English line of battleship for centuries, we will never consent that the rope shall be cut just at the moment when, from a beggarly tender, she is about to be manned into a beautiful sailing-yacht, under the auspices of a Reformed Parliament. We have no wish to see awakened into life the dry bones of College-green,—there let them lie,—the relics of all that is corrupt and factious—the remains of those base men, who, after passing the unprincipled Tithe Agistment act, sold their country for the gold of Castlereagh. Infamy and incapacity are associate with the name of Irish parliament, and were it revived it would only be a focus for civil conflict and treason to the empire. The Irish have not legislative *heads*, and their soil, fruitful in men of talent and men of intrigue, has never produced a man with intellectual aptitude for sober government—for maturing comprehensive and enlightened projects of popular advantage. Better far, then, we say, for the Irish nation, whatever it may be for plotters and tribute-gatherers, that they should have the benefit of the concentrated intelligence of the united parliament of the three kingdoms, assembled under the new charter of the constitution.

Stanley, Jane, pension on civil list, 1799	356
Stanhope, A. comptroller of foreign office in the General Post-office, emoluments paid by individuals	1915
Stanhope, lady H. Lucy, pension on 4½ per cent. duties	900
The eccentric foreign lady mentioned page 204.	
Stanhope, Caroline, pension on civil list, 1805	155
Stables, Ann, widow, pension on civil list, 1821	200
Standish, Olivia and Diana, pension on civil list, 1815, each	66
Stapleton, G. A. commissioner of customs	1200
Agent for Grenada	172
Clerk of the signet	300
Stapylton, hon. G. A. C. late chairman of the victualling board	600
Staniforth, J, distributor of stamps, Lancashire	1599
Stavely, John, 8th senior clerk in foreign office	635
Stephen, James, law adviser, colonial and board of trade	1500
Stephen, J. M. judge surrogate, St. Lucia	1046
Stephenson, B. C. surveyor-general of works	1500
Riding forester, New Forest	452
Stephenson, hon. Jane, pension on civil list, 1803	100
Stevens, C. clerk of introitus, pell-office, exchequer	950
Stevens, W. senior, military draftsman, Military-College	330
Sterky, Rev. Alexander, pension on civil list, 1816	400
Wherefore? Had the gentleman no *parish?*	
Sterling, Edward, pension on civil list, 1780	177
Stepney, Dame, pension on civil list, 1826	200
Stevelley, Jones, late six clerk, chancery, Ireland	1498
Stewart, major-gen. D. governor St. Lucia	2500
Stewart, hon. E. deputy chairman of the customs	1700
Stewart, hon. J. H. K. assistant secretary, treasury	2500
Stewart, R. H. second clerk in war-office	333
Private secretary to deputy secretary at war	100
Stewart, lady Lucy, pension on civil list, 1806	184

Steward, Uriana, pension on civil list, 1823 ··············	£266
Stoddart, sir John, chief justice, Malta ·· ···············	1507
Stoddart, Jane and Caroline, pension on civil list, 1824 ····	65
Stoddart, Susan, Ann, Barbara, Jean, and Mary, each pension on civil list, 1809 ··························	49
Stirling, James, consul at Leghorn ······· ···· ··········	1061
Still, Peter, late commissioner of bankrupts, 1793··········	—
Clerk of court of requests, Manchester, 1808 ······	unknown
Stopford, admiral sir R. commander-in-chief, Portsmouth ··	2920
Stopford, lieut.-gen. hon. sir E. colonel 41st foot, pay ······	613
Stockes, J. W. taxing officer common law business, Ireland ··	1107
Stone, William, master shipwright, Chatham··············	720
Stow, D. clerk of a road, in general post-office—salary······	530
Emoluments paid by individuals ···················	1110
Stowell, lord, master in the faculty office ················	no return

Elder brother of lord Eldon, and in the eighty-seventh year of his age; his son-in-law, viscount Sidmouth—*the letter of thanks man*— is in his seventy-fifth year. Lord Stowell retired from the court of admiralty in 1828, having presided there for the term of twenty years, and during the war his emoluments from the office of judge averaged £10,000 per annum. It is a singular fact that the great acquisitions of his lordship, and his brother Eldon, arose principally from the French revolutionary war. A period of national hostilities or distress, by increasing the number of bankruptcies, increased, under the old system of equity, the emoluments of the Chancellor, nearly half his profits accruing from that source. It was the same with lord Stowell, who was interested to the amount of £8,000 a-year in the continuance of the war, his emoluments in peace being only £2000 a-year. It would, perhaps, be unjust to impute to these individuals that they prostituted the great power they possessed, during the late reigns, to the encouragement of war, for the sake of *official gain*. It is inconceivable, that any men, with their eyes open, would act so base and detestable a part; yet, as lord Brougham has most justly remarked, on this very subject, " that human frailty operates so, that without stating to ourselves the points we are erring upon, our interests work upon us unknown to ourselves." The civil and judicial, and, in short, all the governing authorities of the state, had a deep interest in the prolongation of the French war; and the Bank of England, we have seen, was enriched by hostilities. Even the sovereign had a direct motive of the same sort, in the state of the law respecting droits of the Crown and of Admiralty; and though it is improbable any prince, in modern times, can be swayed by such a consideration, yet it is well known that Charles the Second plunged the nation into a most shameful war with Holland, for the sake of the droits of Admiralty, upon the capture of the Smyrna fleet. Both the government and judicial administration must surely need reform, which admits the working of such interest-begotten motives on national affairs.

Stracey, sir Edward, clerk in house of commons, 1830······	1382
Council to chairman of committees, house of lords····	1582
Strangford, Mary, dowager viscountess, pension on English civil list, 1804 ····························	333
Ditto, pension on Irish civil list, 1809 ··················	266

Strangford, viscount, late ambassador to Russia············	£2300
Strangford, lord, pension on civil list, 1797 ··············	88
Stratton, lady Emily, pension on civil list, 1813 ··········	177
A sister of the duke of Leinster. Her husband had a large fortune, and got through it all in a few years.	
Stratton, J. late minister to Sweden ····················	1500
Strathmore, lady Ann, pension on civil list, 1828 ··········	230
If this lady be the wife of the present earl, is it because he may be always in difficulties, that the public should maintain her? If the widow of the late lord, it is more reprehensible, as she was married just in his dying moments, to rob his heirs of rank and fortune.	
Stuart, sir Simeon H. pension on civil list, 1822 ··········	200
Stuart H. retired allowance as clerk, colonial office, 1816 ····	562
Secretary and registrar, St. Lucia, 1803············	200
Stuart, Jane, pension on civil list, 1784 ················	172
Sullivan, L. deputy secretary at war ················ ······	200
Sullivan, I. and H. Hobart, pension on 4½ per cent. duties, 1820	600
Sullivan, J. A. provost marshal, Jamaica ················	1500
Sullivan, J. A. sec. registrar, and king's receiver, Demerara	7800
A relation of the earl of Buckinghamshire. John Sullivan, uncle of the earl, is a commissioner of the India board, and another Sullivan is member of the council, Madras.	
Sutherland, R. consul at Maracaibo ····················	1250
Sutton, right hon. C. M. speaker of the house of commons ··	6000
Surtees, William Villiers, late commissioner of bankrupts, and cursitor for Middlesex, clerk of the jurats, and filazer common pleas, 1799 ······························	no returns
For loss of cursitorial fees in 1829, Mr. Surtees received £1176. He is a relative of John lord Eldon, see page 331.	
Swinton, Margaret, Mary, Isabel, Ann, and Harriet, pension on civil list, 1800 ························	276
Talbot, Robert, late commissioner of bankrupts, 1793 ······	—
Cursitor for London and Middlesex, *for loss of fees*··	1176
Tapp, John W. storekeeper, Halifax, 1818 ··············	406
1st lieutenant invalid artillery (reduced 1819), 1800··	142
Tanner, T. clerk of ship's entries, customs················	3232
Tarleton, gen. sir B. col. 8th dragoons, pay and emoluments··	1243
Governor of Berwick ··························	647
Pension for wounds ··························	300
Taunton, sir W. E. puisne judge of the court of king's bench	5500
Taylor, lieut.-gen. sir Herbert, colonel 85th foot ··········	938
Adjutant-general··························· ··········	1884
Pension on civil list, 1813 ····················	913
Private sec. and aid-de-camp to the king ········	no returns
Master of St. Catharine's hospital ··············	ditto
Taylor, gen. the hon R. col. 6th dragoon guards ··········	1578
Taylor, sir B. clerk of the signet, 1801 ················	291
Late minister plenipotentiary to Berlin, 1828 ······	2300

Taylor, T. deputy keeper of privy seal, Dublin, 1829 ······	£73
Clerk in chief secretary's office, 1799 ··············	712
Taylor, T. comptroller-general of customs ·················	1000
Temple, the hon. W. secretary of embassy at St. Petersburgh	1100
Tenterden, rt. hon. lord, chief justice of the court of king's bench	10000
Terrill, W. pension out of consolidated fund ··············	1000
Thackeray, S. assistant-solicitor, customs ·················	800
Thomson. T. principal clerk of session, Scotland ··········	1000
Deputy clerk register, ditto ····················	500
Thomson, W. deputy commissary-general, half-pay, 1818 ··	267
Prothonotary of Nova Scotia ·····················	600
Thomson, C. Poulett, M.P. for Dover, treasurer of the navy, and vice-president of board of trade ··············	2000
Thompson, T. solicitor to post-office, Ireland ··············	1457
Thornborrow, J. chief clerk in office of woods ·············	700
Thornton, J. chairman of the board of stamps ·············	2012
Thornton, W. T. clerk of the securities, excise ·············	600
Thornton, W. C. late commissioner of hackney coaches ····	150
Lieutenant-governor of Hull ····················	182
Aide-de-camp to the king ······················	182
Pension and retired military allowance ············	591
Thornton, sir E. late envoy to Portugal ···················	2000
Thurlow, rev. Thomas, late patentee for execution of bankrupt-laws; emolument from fees on commissions, writs of supersedeas, and proceedings in bankruptcy, for the year ending *Jan.* 5, 1830 ················	8502
Clerk of hanaper in chancery; emoluments from *June 5,* 1829, to *Jan. 5,* 1830·· ··············	1192

These judicial sinecures were abolished under the Bankruptcy
Court Act, and an equivalent life annuity, payable out of bankrupt
effects, granted with reversion, on the death of Mr. Thurlow, to
W. H. I. Scott, son of lord Eldon. It has been often urged as a
favourable trait in the English constitution that it allows the humblest individual, possessed of merit, to aspire to the highest rewards
and offices in the state; but this advantage is in some measure counterbalanced by the principle which permits those rewards and
honours to be hereditarily transmitted to descendants. Of the practical working of this part of the system the families of Marlborough,
Nelson, and Thurlow, afford striking examples. The founder of the
honours of the last, it is well known, was the lord chancellor of the
name, and during the short period of sixty years, within which it
emerged from the obscurity of a Suffolk parsonage, it has presented
some very singular incongruities. Lord Chancellor Thurlow, whose
father was the rector of Ashfield, died unmarried, but not before
he had, by the influence of his office, pushed his brother Thomas
into the rich see of Durham. This Thomas left two sons, Edward,
the late peer, who succeeded the chancellor, and Thomas, in holy
orders, who succeeded, on the death of his brother, in 1829, to the
valuable reversions mentioned above. The claims of the two
nephews to the honours and emoluments of their uncle, the first
Lord Thurlow, it would be invidious to investigate. Edward is

chiefly known from having married Miss Bolton, the actress, and from having been an unfortunate aspirant in verse-making; the fruits of his marriage were three sons, the eldest of whom is now in his eighteenth year, destined, in due course, to form one of our hereditary legislators.

Tierney, Geo. secretary of legation, Bavaria ·············· £500

Tierney, Mrs. pension on civil list, 1830 ················· 400

Widow of the late M.P. for Knaresborough, and who, if in need of assistance, ought to have obtained it from the wealthy banker, her relative; or, if not from him, from the duke of Devonshire and other party connexions of her husband. But aristocracy is the grave of virtue. The rich lords, like the rich clergy, immersed in luxury and dissipation, are strangers to sympathy, with indigence and misfortune. They do not even provide for the destitute of their "order," and seldom come forward to support any work of utility or benevolence. There are exceptions among the nobility, but this is the general character of the *corporation;* all useful, meritorious, and charitable undertakings are planned, supported, and executed by the middling and industrious classes. It is the same in Ireland, as we learn from the parliamentary report of the session of 1830; there all institutions for the education of the people, and for their relief in sickness and old age, have been established, and are supported, not by the absentee landlords, bishops, and pluralists, but by the farmer, the poor tenantry, and tradesmen. But can there need further proof of the vicious nature of aristocracy in church and state, than the deplorably ignorant and destitute state of our agricultural population? Of the one hundred and thirty-eight miserable creatures on the Berkshire calendar, only twenty-five could *write,* and only thirty-seven could *read;* yet, in face of this evidence of the neglect of the people by their "natural protectors," justices Park, Vaughan, and others of the special commissioners, would insinuate the clergy and lords of the soil had done *their duty,* and that the risings of the peasantry did not proceed from want of food or want of education, but from the wicked machinations of seditious writers, itinerant lecturers, and foreign incendiaries.

Tindal, sir N. C. chief justice of common pleas ············ 8000

This judge, we believe, is better known for prerogative leanings and supple politics than as a high judicial authority. His copious charge to the Bristol grand jury, (Jan. 2, 1832,) was singularly deficient in precision, and has formed a proper subject of animadversion. The two chief legal dicta of sir Nicholas are that *private* persons may *arm* themselves for the suppression of riots; and, secondly, that the duties imposed on the citizen are equally obligatory on the soldier. Both these positions are of dangerous application, and ought to have been laid down within stricter limits than they were by chief justice Tindal.

A *private* person, we conceive, has no general right to interfere in the execution of the laws. A constable, for the maintenance of the peace, may call in the aid of a by-stander, and the by-stander is bound to assist him; but no private person has authority to arrest an offender, without the warrant of a magistrate, for any offence less than *felony.* All riots are not *felonious.* Unless *twelve* persons or more are unlawfully assembled, and continue together *one hour* after being commanded by a magistrate to disperse, they are not guilty of a capital offence. Should any private person interfere, without lawful authority, to suppress a riotous assemblage of a less aggravated description than this, we apprehend he would himself become a transgressor of the law; and if he *armed* himself with any dangerous weapon, as a gun, and thereby occasioned the death of an individual, he would be guilty of manslaughter at the least, and perhaps murder. Similar obligations and restraints are imposed on the military. A soldier is invested with all the rights of other citizens, and is bound to all the duties of other citizens, *Burdett* v. *Abbott* : granted ; but nothing beyond this. He has no general right to interfere for the preservation of the peace, either as citizen or soldier, unless called upon so to do by lawful authority; and if he employ *fire-arms* to suppress a riot of a less dangerous character, and under other circumstances than those described in the statute 1 Geo. I. c. 5, and thereby occasion death, he would be guilty of the highest offence known to the law.

Until recently, game-keepers thought they had a right to carry fire-arms, for the capture of poachers. This error was distinctly refuted by Mr. Justice Bayley, (*Lancaster Assizes, March* 23*d*, 1827,) who expressly stated that no gamekeeper had a right to carry fire-arms for any such purpose, nor to fire at any poacher whatever. No proprietor of game had any earthly power to give such authority to his keeper, who might certainly take into custody any poacher, but it was at his peril to use fire-arms.

The legal authority of Chief Justice Holt is so high, and the anecdote related of him so apposite to our subject, that we cannot forbear incorporating it, though well known, and has appeared in *The Plain Dealer*, and other vehicles of intelligence.

" There happened," says the narrator, " in the time of this chief justice, a riot in Holborn, occasioned by an abominable practice then prevailing, of decoying young persons, of both sexes, to the plantations. The persons so decoyed they kept prisoners in a house in Holborn, till they could find an opportunity of shipping them off; which being discovered, the enraged populace were going to pull down the house. Notice of this being sent to Whitehall, a party of the guards were commanded to march to the place ; but they first sent an officer to the chief justice, to acquaint him with the design, and to desire him to send some of his people to attend the soldiers, in order to give it the better countenance. The officer having delivered his message, Holt said to him, 'Suppose the populace should not disperse at your appearance, what are you to do then ?' ' Sir,' answered the officer, ' we have orders to fire upon them.' ' Have you, sir?' replied Holt, '*then take notice of what I say ; if there be one man killed, and you are tried before me, I shall take care that you, and every soldier of your party, shall be hanged.*' ' Sir,' added he, ' go back to those who sent you, and acquaint them, that no officer of mine shall attend soldiers ; and let them know, at the same time, that *the laws of this kingdom are not to be executed by the sword ;* these matters belong to the civil power, *and you have nothing to do with them.*' Upon this, the chief justice, ordering his tipstaves, with a few constables, to attend him, went himself in person to the place where the tumult was ; expostulated with the mob ; assured them that justice should be done upon the persons who were the objects of their indignation : and thus they all dispersed quietly."

Tighe, G. W. pension on Irish civil list, 1815 ············	£358
Tighe, Charlotte, pension on Irish civil list, 1828··········	47
Tildesley, Sophia, pension on civil list, 1825 ····· ·········	61
Tomlins, A. clerk, Irish revenue, 1817 ··················	500
Private secretary to vice-treasurer, 1817 ··········	75
Allowance for index to journals house of lords ······	400

Tomlins, sir Thomas, counsel to chief secretary, 1810 ······	£400
Counsel to treasurer for Irish revenue·············	500
Pension on Irish civil list, 1825·················	168
For compiling index to acts relative to Ireland ······	200
Torrens, R. fourth justice in common pleas, Ireland········	3692
Torrens, dame Sarah, pension on civil list, 1820············	624

Widow, probably, of the late general sir H. Torrens, adjutant-general. This officer was most fortunate in his advancement, and held high situations; but lived so extravagantly as to leave his family upon the public.

Toole, J. deputy commissary-general, half-pay, 1817········	267
Pension as civil auditor of Malta ················	91
Townsend, J. S. master in chancery in Ireland············	3138

There are *nice pickings* in judicial offices in Ireland as well as in England and Scotland.

Trafford, Trafford, late receiver general of taxes, Chester ····	

Whether Ministers intend granting retiring pensions to the late receivers-general we are uncertain, and for this reason have omitted them in our *List*. The receiverships were mostly given by the Tories to their thick and thin supporters. Trafford is, if we mistake not, the magistrate, who, in conjunction with Hulton and Parson Hay, who immediately after received the valuable living of Rochdale from the late Archbishop Sutton, directed the memorable outrage of Manchester in the year 1819.

Trail, rev. Anthony, pension on Irish civil list, 1794········	132
Trail, Clarissa, pension on Irish civil list, 1809 ··········	356
Treasure, Elizabeth, widow, pension on civil list, 1820 ······	100
Trefusis, hon. C. R. commissioner of excise ··············	1200
Trevor, C. solicitor of legacy duties ···················	600
Trower, J. master in chancery, for year ending Jan. 5, 1830··	3340
Troy, J. J. collector of customs, Limerick················	500
Turner, R. deputy surveyor of New Forest, 1815··········	350
Allowance for Parkhurst Forest ···················	50
Turner, Sir H. governor of Bermuda·····················	3035
Turner, W. envoy extraordinary in Colombia··············	3400
Turton, sir Thomas, clerk of juries, common pleas··········	96
Turton, W. one of the six clerks in chancery ············	1217
Tywll, col. baron, private secretary to lord lieutenant········	829
Tyrconnel, earl of, pension on English civil list, 1813 ······	600
Pension on Irish civil list, 1813·················	445

His brother, the late lord, was in the army, and shipwrecked in the Baltic returning from St. Petersburgh with despatches. Why this lord has got two pensions ought to·be explained.

Tyndale, W. pension on civil list, 1820 ·················	200
Tyton, A. retired allowance as *late solicitor to the customs*··	1800

Pretty well this for a retired solicitor, whose salary and emoluments had averaged, perhaps, £3000 or £4000 per annum. All the government solicitors and assistant solicitors would bear considerable reduction. The solicitor of the treasury has returned his emoluments at £2800 a year, of customs £2500, of excise £2500, of stamps £1200, and of assessed taxes £1500.

Unwin, John, senior clerk in the Treasury······· ······	£1000
Ure, James, comptroller of customs, Leith················	540
Utterson, E. V. one of six clerks in chancery···············	1217

As the name implies there are six of these officers enjoying incomes of £1200 a year; they are sinecurists and their offices might be abolished without detriment to the public. They have so little duty that the custom of these gentlemen is to divide the year into six portions of two months each, and the attendance of one of them at a time is enough. Can any one be surprised at the expense of proceedings in chancery, when there is a judge with £15,000 a year, sinecures worth £11,000 per annum, registrars with £5000 income, masters £4000, and clerks with average incomes of £1200 and £1400 a year—and all these great emoluments, or nearly so, accruing from fees levied on the unfortunate suitor—widow, orphan, lunatic, or bankrupt? We say nothing of the fleecings he undergoes in the *honorariums*, refreshers, consultations, and half-guinea "motions of course," paid to counsel; nor of the term-fees, six-and-eight-penny touches, copy charges, and court attendancies of solicitors.

Usher, Alicia, Frances, Margaret, and Sarah, pension on civil list, 1827···· ······ ··············· ······ ········	100
Udney, Martha, pension on civil list, 1816 ··············	445
Van Spiegle, A. senior clerk in the treasury ···············	1008
Van de Spiegle, Adolph, pension on civil list, 1810 ········	60
Van de Spiegle, Maria, pension on civil list, 1810 ········	68
Vallancey, Catharine, pension on Irish civil list, 1790 ······	132
Vallancey, Mary, pension on Irish civil list, 1770 ········	66

A poor woman was recently convicted in the Metropolis of defrauding the parish, in having continued to receive the allowance for the maintenance of a natural child after its death. We suspect similar cajollery among the state paupers. It is hardly likely so many pensioners should be alive whose grants are dated sixty or seventy years back; dead-weight and annuity people, we know, are proverbially tenacious of vitality; still, we trust lord Althorp will make inquiry and not suffer to be added to our other grievances in this matter, the vexation of being imposed upon by absolute *counterfeits*.

Vallancey, Isabella, pension on Irish civil list, 1823········	61
Vallancey, Fanny, pension on Irish civil list, 1820 ········	42
Vandeleur, lieut.-gen. sir. J. O. col. 14th light dragoons····	1501
Pension for wounds······························	350
Vandeleur, T. B. fourth justice of the king's bench, Ireland ··	3692
Vanderkiste, F. W. comptroller of customs, Cork··········	600
Vaughan, C. R. envoy and minister plenipo. at Washington··	6000
Vaughan, sir J. baron of the court of exchequer ··········	5516
Venables, J. junior clerk in home department, 1803········	612
Private secretary in home department, 1823 ········	300
Receiver of the eight police offices, 1822 ··········	500
Receiver of tenths, 1827 ······················	300
Verbeke, J. F. deputy commissary general, half-pay, 1815 ··	267
Consul of the Netherlands····················	600

Vernon, sir Charles, pension on civil list, 1823 · · · · · · · · · ·	£266
Vernon, Caroline, pension on civil list, 1763 · · · · · · · · · · · ·	88
A sight of this fair spinster would needs be gratifying to admirers of the antique !	
Vernon, Joseph, receiver of fees in the treasury · · · · · · · · · ·	700
Vesey, Francis, one of the six clerks in chancery, 1811 · · · ·	1200
Vie, H. inspector and receiver of taxes, 1828 · · · · · · · · · · · ·	816
Villiers, G. W. F. commissioner of customs · · · · · · · · · · · · ·	1200
Villiers, T. H. secretary to the India board · · · · · · · · · · · · ·	1500
Vivian, lieut.-gen. sir R. H. col. 12th light dragoons, staff, regimental pay and emoluments · · · · · · · · · · · · · · · · · ·	2225
Commander of the forces, Ireland · · · · · · · · · · · · · · ·	3607
Pension for wounds ·	350
Vizard, J. deputy registrar bankrupt court · · · · · · · · · · · · · · ·	600
Vizard, William, secretary of bankrupts · · · · · · · · · · · · · · · ·	2000
Wade, Mary, pension on Irish civil list, 1829 · · · · · · · · · · · ·	100
Wadman, J. first under clerk tellers' office · · · · · · · · · · · · · ·	800
Walker, J. inspector and receiver of taxes, 1803 · · · · · · · · · ·	721
Walker, sir P. hereditary usher of the black rod, Scotland · ·	250
Walpole, Edward, clerk in the treasury and private secretary to chancellor of the exchequer · · · · · · · · · · · · · · · ·	900
For making out East-India accounts · · · · · · · · · · · · · ·	300
Walpole, F. junior clerk in home department, 1811 · · · · · · · ·	506
Joint distributor of military commissions, 1817 · · · · · ·	76
Allowance for yeomanry correspondence, 1820 · · · · · ·	100
Walton, F. clerk foreign department post-office · · · · · · · · · · · ·	580
Walker, J. K. cocket writer, customs · · · · · · · · · · · · · · · · ·	1051
Walker, Thomas, police justice, Lambeth-Street · · · · · · · · · ·	800
Ward, R. P. late clerk in ordnance · · · · · · · · · · · · · · · · · · ·	1000
Ward, John, inspector of aliens at Dover, 1825 · · · · · · · · · ·	100
Collector of customs, Dover · · · · · · · · · · · · · · · · · · ·	700
Ward, E. M. minister plenipotentiary at Dresden · · · · · · · · · ·	2301
Ward, Robert, inspector and receiver of taxes, 1815 · · · · · ·	859
Warde, lieut.-gen. sir H. colonel 68th foot · · · · · · · · · · · · ·	1170
Wardlow, sir W. pension on Scotch civil list, 1824 · · · · · · · ·	72
Warrington, H. consul-general, Tripoli · · · · · · · · · · · · · · · · ·	1800
Walford, J. G. solicitor to the board of customs · · · · · · · · · ·	2500
Warner, A. chief judge, Trinidad ·	1075
Warren, C. W. clerk first class in the war-office · · · · · · · · · ·	661
Warren, Mary, Sarah, Anne, and Rebecca, pension on Irish civil list, 1787, each ·	43
Wallace, J. collector of customs, Waterford · · · · · · · · · · · · ·	700
Walbeoff, J. superintendent of cinnamon plantations · · · · · · · ·	1688
Watson, sir F. B. master of his majesty's household · · · · · ·	1158
Pension on civil list, 1827 ·	931
Waters, John, clerk to chief justice of court of kings's bench; from fees ·	2169

To fees are often added the corruptive agency of gratuities, so that when an income arises from the former it is hardly possible to fix the amount ; depending, too, a good deal on the cupidity or liberality of the fee-gatherer. We wonder who this Mr. Waters can be, and what can be the nature of his duties to entitle him to tax the king's lieges, suing for justice in the highest court, to the tune of £2169 per annum.

Watlington, G. prothonotary of court common pleas	£2600
Watson, T. clerk to clerk of the rates, customs	3114
Watts, R. clerk of a road, general post office	1331
Late clerk in tax-office	400
Watts, E. consul at Carthagena	2100
Webb, W. deputy commissary-general, half-pay, 1822	267
commissioner for valuation of houses, Dublin	560
Wedderburne, sir D. deputy postmaster-general, Edinburgh	800
Welfit, W. late commissioner of bankrupts, 1801	—
Cursitor of court of chancery, 1814	560
Wellesley, marquis, pension from the East-India company	5000
Lord steward of the household	2436
Late joint chief remembrancer of court of exchequer, Ireland	5387

The Wellesleys derive a greater revenue from the taxes than any other family, and since Mr. Pitt first introduced into official employment lord Mornington, they cannot have received, in grants, salaries, pensions, and sinecures, less than two millions of the public money. But how can we complain of the income of the duke, or of his brother, both eminent for their exploits ; while there are bishops with £20,000 or £30,000 a year, and legal sinecurists with £10,000 or £12,000 per annum? The following piece of information appeared in the *Limerick Chronicle*:—The marquis W. late viceroy of Ireland, has *seventy-two* sons, all provided for by the public." The " Hero of the East," as the conquerer of Tippoo Saib used to be styled, has certainly been viceroy of Ireland, but the intelligence cannot refer to him ; for, though his lordship has been twice married, he has no issue by either union. It is, we know, a very general complaint that scarcely any person without family influence and born in lawful wedlock, can obtain a situation in the public offices, owing to the numerous illegitimate progeny of the " order" claiming to be provided for.

Wellington, Charlotte, pension on civil list, 1800	115
Wellington, duke of, pensions out of consolidated fund	8926
Constable of the Tower	950
Colonel of rifle brigade	238
Colonel of 1st regiment of foot guards	2695
Lord-warden of Cinque ports	295
Interest on grants by parliament	35000

Some oversight, some providential *mischance*, generally brings the guilty to judgment. The oversight of the Wellington ministry was the King's speech, and the comments thereupon by his highness of Waterloo. The Duke has since attempted to qualify the fatal declaration against parliamentary reform, by dividing himself into two parts—one *ministerial*, the other *individual*, and holding out a hope of something better for the future, in case of a *second* trial of his civic talents. But it is of no use : the objection is to the entire mass—the history of the Duke—his connexions—the past deeds and capabilities—the foreign and domestic proceedings of the confederacy to which he belongs.

In his foreign policy the Duke is the steadfast partizan of the Turk, Don Miguel, Ferdinand, and the Holy Alliance ; in his domestic policy he belongs to the Tory faction ; that besotted crew of plunderers, possessed of neither common sense nor common honesty, and whose demon ascendancy of forty years has entailed on the empire all its calamities. Agreeably with the views of this party the Premier had prepared to open the Parliamentary campaign. Retrenchment was to proceed no further ; the principle of free-trade was not to be persisted in ; judicial, ecclesiastical, and above all, parliamentary reform, and every thing new or novel was to be repudiated and discountenanced. Abroad the continental system was to be upheld—the vile treaties of 1815 maintained inviolate—and after a million of bayonets had been silently assembled on the Rhine, the Moselle, and the Adige, the kingdom of the Netherlands forcibly re-established, and the liberties of Frenchmen subverted by another victory of Waterloo. Such was the train of mischief laid by the Field Marshal ! one hundred millions more were to be added to the Debt—the dead weight doubled—and Europe deluged with blood, that half-a-dozen crowned conspirators might be guaranteed in their usurpations over the liberties of the human race.

And what averted these calamities? *It was the spirit of the People acting on the fears of parliament.* Such was the deep and universal feeling of indignation excited by the royal speech and the declarations of the Duke, that we are not sure both monarchy and aristocracy would have been laid in the dust, had not the premier made a timely retreat. Perhaps his abdication was not the most favourable issue : had the Captain been allowed to follow up his mad resolves, it is probable, from the pervading spirit of the continent, Germany, Italy, and Prussia, would have been free by the discomfiture of their tyrants in open battle ; but the day is not far distant, when that emancipation will be effected by reason and example, which the insane arrogance of despotism failed to accomplish.

The Duke being naturally shrewd and selfish, and mostly judicious in his conduct, it is surprising how he could adopt such a mistaken course of proceeding. Would none of the parasites, pensioned dowagers, and demireps, who haunt his steps, open his eyes? Even sir R. Peel might have told him England is not in the state it was in 1793 —that there has been a complete revolution in public sentiment— that an individual is hardly to be found who is not convinced of the blunders, profligacy, and mis-government of the last half century— and that all classes—rich and poor—are either dismayed by the overwhelming embarrassments of the system and quiescent in its defence, or the open and determined partizans of its thorough reform. Under such altered circumstances what a brainless project to think of reviving the Pitt system—resorting to Algerine acts—appealing to persons of property—and coercing the entire population, the most favourably disposed portion of which is resolved to be *neutral*, and all the rest in fierce and determined opposition !

It is hardly worth while inquiring now how far lord Wellington participated in the plans of the miserable Polignac. The wretched outcasts would not have sought refuge here had they not been previously apprised of the *spirit* of those who presided over the public councils. Subsequently the ex-Premier was pleased to designate the glorious *three days* a " bad example,"—an opinion, no doubt, he shares in common with prince Metternich, and the autocrat of Russia. France had not much to gain by her immortal triumph ; she had only to defend, not to conquer free institutions.   Her first revolution had swept away an oppressive tithe system, a privileged noblesse, a feudal game-code, and a plundering and barbarous judicial administration.   Would to God our revolution of 1688 had done as much for us, and then we should not have had still to struggle through the Augean stable of aristocratical, legal, and ecclesiastical abuse!   We shall leave the Duke with a fervent prayer that he will never again be premier of England.   His ideas and sentiments are wholly alien to the happiness and liberties of Englishmen, and we verily believe his return to power would be the signal for a general rising throughout the United Kingdom.

West, Robert B. clerk dead letter office, Ireland, 1800 ····	£184
Taxing clerk inland-office, Ireland, 1800 ··········	184
West, F. N. escrivans to the court, Trinidad ············	1821
West, G. clerk in treasury, and for making special payments	1100
Weston, W. surveyor-general, customs ················ ······	800
Weston, J. C. cocket-writer, customs ···················	1868
Westmeath, countess of, by act of parliament (*Irish*) ······	923
Westmeath, marchioness of, lady of the Queen's bed-chamber	105
Pension on Irish civil list, 1829·····················	386

The Westmeath (Nugent) family have been singularly unfortunate in matrimonial engagements.   The late earl of Westmeath, married for a first wife Marianne, niece of the first earl of Clare, by whom he left the present marquis of Westmeath.   This marriage being dissolved by act of parliament in 1796, the earl married in the following year Elizabeth Emily, daughter of the second marquis of Drogheda.   Both wives we believe survived the earl, who died in 1814, and we are uncertain whether the countess in our *List*, whose pension is charged on the consolidated fund, is the lady Marianne of the first or the lady Elizabeth Emily of the second nuptials. We are also ignorant of the public services performed by which the countess of Westmeath became entitled to her pension.   Nor are we less in the dark in respect of the services of the marchioness of Westmeath.   This lady, it is well-known, obtained her pension through one of these brilliant coup de mains of the Duke, for which he is as famous about court as in the field.   All however the public knows of her ladyship is that she is sister to the marquis of Salisbury, who has large estates ; that she has for many years been on bad terms with her husband ; that they have parted several times and again lived together, and not long since the marquis instituted a suit in Doctors' Commons for the *restitution of conjugal rights!*   The marchioness, it appears, has obtained an appointment near the person of the queen, which we take to be a way-lay of the field marshal, that concerns the Whigs more than any body else : we verily believe no man knows better than the Duke how to post his troops—take up a position—throw up entrenchments—and prepare for defensive or offensive warfare ; and we never knew the Captain to be out-generalled in these matters, except on one occasion, when opposed to the chivalry of viscount Combermere.

Weir, Dr. John, late commissioner, victualling-office········	1000
Wharton, Henrietta, pension on civil list, 1813············	501

Is this the widow of the former chairman of the house of commons? or of the member for Beverley ?   A job in either case.

Whitelow, Elinor, pension on Irish civil list, 1813··········	177

White, W. D. clerk in the office of woods and forests, 1810··	£450
Receiver of crown rents in London and Middlesex, 1827	500
Whitmore, col. G. royal engineers, Malta ················	1195
Whitmore, T. secretary to the board of customs············	1700
Whittingham, Maria, pension on civil list, 1822 ··········	400
Is this the wife of general Whittingham, who is on the staff in India ? If so, too bad.	
Whishaw, J. commissioner of audit ···················	1200
Wilmot, Sarah Ann Eardly, widow, pension on civil list, 1797	311
Wickham, rt. hon. W. late minister to Swiss Cantons ······	1200
Wickham, Eleanor, pension on civil list, 1803 ··············	526
Wilson, sir George, master in chancery for year 1830 ·····.	3273
Wilson, W. principal clerk army-pay-office ··· ··········	600
Wilson, Dr. Isaac, physician to Halsar-hospital ············	600
Wilson, Ann, children of, pension on civil list, 1797········	276
Wilson, G. allowance as late commissioner of customs ······	1050
Wilson, R. late commissioner of Bankrupts, 1802··········	—
Cursitor for London and Middlesex, 1823 ··········	1176
Wilson, major.-gen. W. col. commandant 14th royal artillery	1003
Wilkin, John, receiver of crown rents in Wales, 1819 ·······	439
Late receiver of duties on offices and pensions, 1811 ··	395
Wilkinson, Robert, clerk in war office, 1802···············	620
Compiler of army lists, 1808 ·······················	231
Joint collector of fees on military commissions, 1808··	95
Wilkinson, E. clerk of the affidavits, customs···············	2199
Willis, John, pension on civil list, 1791·················	509
Wilkins, Eliza, pension on civil list, 1800 ················	115
Wilkie, David, limner to the king of Scotland, 1823 ······	300
Wilcox, Elizabeth, pension on civil list, 1821 ········ ····	100
Williamson, D. lord of sessions, Scotland ················	2000
Williamson, John S. col. royal artillery, 1825 ············	474
Superintendent of royal military repository, 1828 ····	200
Allowance for one servant ···················· ····	27
Williams, C. northern clerk in the secretary's office, customs	800
Comptroller of the housekeeper's accounts········ ····	50
Williams, John, M. P. for Winchilsea; queen's attorney-gen.	no return.
Williams, C. F. commissioner bankrupt-court ············	1500
Williams, R. J. clerk to receiver of custom duties, outwards··	1182
Williams, rev. J. P. rector of St. Elizabeth, Jamaica ······	1157
Willimott, R. distributor of stamps, excise··············	1000
Receiver-general post-office·· ················ ······	800
Willimot, W. receiver of wine and plantation duties, customs	1436
Willimott, T. S. vice-consul and pro-consul at Lima ······ ··	1150
Willimot, T. collector of customs ·····················	2400
Willimot, Mary, pension on civil list, 1827 ·············	100
Willoughby, Harriet, pension on civil list, 1806 ··········	276
Willoughby, T. E. registrar-general of shipping············	500

Wilde, sir J. chief justice, Cape of Good Hope ············	2500
Wingfield, W. master in chancery for year ending *Jan.* 5, 1830	4161

The masterships are ten in number, and in the gift of the lord chancellor. The duties of the masters are to receive affidavits, and examine accounts, and other matters referred to them by the equity judges; they are also the messengers of the house of lords, in communicating with the commons. Some of the duties of these officers are of the first importance, but, like every thing else in chancery, have been, hitherto, discharged in the worst possible manner for the convenience of suitors. In the reign of Charles II. the masters sat from seven in the morning till twelve, and again from two till six in the afternoon; being nine hours each day. In 1816 they sat from ten to three, and from six to eight, being seven hours; but at present the average time is less than five hours a day. As the hours of attendance have decreased, in similar inverse proportion the emoluments have increased. In 1798, the average, for fifteen years preceding, gave to the masters a salary of £1615 to the highest, and to the lowest £976. The average of the following nineteen years gave to the highest paid master £1914, and to the smaller ones £1060. The average at present is from £3800 to £4500 per annum. Their chief clerks have undergone corresponding increase in remuneration, and realize about £1400 per annum. The abuses in the master's offices are manifold, but as lord Brougham has signified his intention to introduce a legislative measure for thir removal, we forbear to enumerate them. One grievance, however, is so oppressive on suitors, that we cannot help noticing it. The practice is to issue hourly warrants; in consequence of which the parties are put to the expense of paying counsel and attorneys for attending hourly to no purpose. Thus, suppose the master has four cases to hear, he appoints four separate hours, each hour to be appropriated to a case, which, if unfinished, is postponed to a future day, and this, though it is previously known that any one of the cases would occupy the whole four hours.

Wittwer, T. N. allowance as late accountant to India Board··	1150
Accountant between public and E..I. Company ······	300
Wiseman, Harriet, pension on civil list, 1825 ············ ··	100
Winning, Henrietta, pension on civil list, 1808 ············	233
Winchester, Marquis of, groom of the stole ··············	2130

Here is another of those courtly offices, which ought to be abolished, augmenting unnecessarily the expenditure of the civil list. It is not sufficient to say these costly appendages are essential to support the royal dignity. The dignity of the crown is a senseless sound, unless tending to increase the respect and veneration of the people; impoverished by aristocratic wars and misgovernment, we are disabled, if otherwise inclined, from supporting the gewgaws of royalty: and the less we have of them, the more estimable the kingly office will appear in popular estimation. Milton says, "the very trappings of monarchy cost more than the whole establishment of the most costly republics." The nearer we approximate regality to the simplicity of republican institutions, the more permanent and commanding will be its influence. We would neither deprive royalty, nor any public office, of due respect and support, but we would abridge every useless expenditure, which only promotes the corruption of politicians and courtiers. To what public purport, or private gratification of the king, are the offices of groom of the stole, master of the hawks, master of the buck-hounds, master of the horse, or grooms and lords of the bedchamber? These are menial offices, and unbecoming the dignity of noblemen, if endowed with the genuine feelings of nobility. At best, they have served only to purchase the support of some needy boroughmonger, or provide for some low parasite, or ruined aristocrat.

Wood, major-gen. sir G. major-general, unattached	£590
Pension for services	456
Wood, R. R. clerk, secretary of state's office	935
Naval officer, Grenada	200
Late vendu-master, Malta	904
Woodford, C. senior clerk in the treasury	1000
Woodroffe, Wm. associate to chief justice, common pleas	1198
Woolley, capt. Isaac, late deputy chairman, victualling office	1000
Pension for wounds	250
Worthington, T. surveyor-general, customs	800
Wray, Charles, president and judge, vice-admiralty, Demerara	3500
Wray, John, receiver of new metropolitan police establishment	700
Wraxall, Jane, pension on civil list, 1793	311
Wright, Alexander, Alfred, and Caroline, pension, each, on civil list, 1827	25
Wright, Thomas, collector of customs, Plymouth	500
Wulbier, W. R. minute clerk, audit-office	450
Pension for special services	150
Clerk for paying fees on passing accounts, 1815	150
Wulff, major-gen. G. col. commandant royal artillery	1003
Wyndham, hon. P. C. secretary of council, remembrancer of court of exchequer, and clerk of common pleas, Barbadoes	1476
Registrar in chancery, and clerk of the patents, Jamaica	4050

The duties of the hon. Percy Charles Wyndham, brother of lord Egremont, are discharged by *deputy ;* the emoluments are principally paid by the inhabitants of the islands, who are twitched up for *judicial fees* in the same fleecing manner that suitors for justice are in the courts of the United Kingdom.

Wylde, John, pension on Scotch civil list, 1796	138
Wynford, lord, late chief justice common pleas	3750
Wynne, Robert, pension on Irish civil list, 1805	443
Wynne, W. commissioner of appeals, Ireland	738
Commissioner of inquiry, ditto	1200
Wynn, H. W. W. son-in-law of lord Carrington ; envoy and min. plenipo. at Copenhagen	4900
Wynyard, gen. H. col. 46th foot, pay	613
Wynyard, lady, pension on civil list, 1819	467
Wyon, Thomas, chief engraver, mint-office	500
Yates, Jane, pension on Irish civil list, 1814	61
Ditto, Mary, pension on civil list, 1794	177
Yonge, dame, pension on English civil list, 1812	300
Ditto, pension on Irish civil list, 1804	445

There was a sir George Yonge of old in the war-office, but from the date of the pension she cannot well be his widow.

Young, J. W. protector of slaves, Demerara · · · · · · · · · · · · ·	£2000
Yorke, C. P. brother of lord Hardwicke; teller of the exchequer (*sinecure*) ·	2700
Zachary, M. cocket writer, customs · · · · · · · · · · · · · · · · · · ·	1698

A copious introduction to the Place and Pension List renders unnecessary many observations at the conclusion. We might have multiplied notes, but made a point of passing over the Grenvilles, Sidmouths, and other individuals already sufficiently known, whose *merits* have been canvassed and long since settled in public estimation. Many names illustrate themselves, others by juxta position; and really we cannot help thinking that our alphabetical arrangement has been the means of our performing a task very usual at certain seasons of the year—that of assembling families together—from the royal household, the colonies, courts of law, army, navy, and public offices, exhibiting them face to face, their incomes, emoluments, relationships, and prospects.

Our *List* has one striking advantage over every other previously given to the public. All the individuals enrolled upon it are *living*, or were living within a few months of the period of publication. From it the people will be able to learn who receive exorbitant emoluments, and the amount of them in every branch of the public service —civil, judicial, naval, and military. Since the last edition, issued within the preceding twelvemonths, many names have disappeared through death, some few have voluntarily resigned their annuities ; those have of course been omitted, except in the latter case, two or three have been retained, purposely to remark on such a rare example of disinterestedness.

With respect to the pensions generally, though their claims appear at present recognized by the settlement of the Civil List, we apprehend they will ultimately have to undergo the ordeal of another examination. There are some deserving objects, but they are only a grain of sand on the sea-shore—the mass are too vile for description, and their plunderings must speedily have an end. We are told, indeed, " to pause before we plunge *noble* families into distress." But if noble families can only maintain their nobility by living on the public, perish their nobility. Surely tithes and corn-laws are sufficient for the maintenance of the Order, or, if they be still indigent, let them appear in their proper character, and not assume to rank above other paupers. What claim have the Mulgraves, Manchesters, Mansfields, Arbuthnots, Grevilles, Courtenays, Crokers, Herries, and Bathursts; or the lady Anns, Emilys, Bettys, and Jennies, of any titled beggar, to the money wrung from the labours and necessities of the industrious and now deeply depressed people. If they think carriages and fine clothes, titles and fine houses, essential to their existence, let them pay for them out of their own purses ; if they cannot pay for them, what right have they to them?

or what right have they to make the people pay for them? The whole affair is a gross insult to common sense; and those silken creatures, and their dandy brothers, etherial and exquisite as they may be, must do like others, earn their bread by honest industry, or have no bread to eat. Noble families have long been under a delusion, and seem to think they have a hereditary right to be fed and clothed at the public expense, whatever be their improvidence, folly, or worthlessness; but they must be undeceived:—no more lordly plunderings by the sons and daughters of corruption; if they cannot support themselves by useful services, they must descend from their fictitious rank and learn the duties of their proper station in society. They will gain a great deal by the change, lose nothing in point of real dignity, or perhaps comfort; for there can be no dignity not founded in justice, nor comfort in enjoying the rewards which no desert has required.

HOUSE OF COMMONS,

PAST, PRESENT, AND TO COME.

WE have reserved the subject of this chapter to the last, and have been much at a loss what title to give the observations we are about to submit. At this moment the Reform Bill, for the *third* time, is in its last stage in the House of Commons, and we are just on the eve, as we fervently trust, of the birth of a new constitution. Under such circumstances it would be mere folly to do, as we have often done before, drag our readers through the iniquities of the Borough System. That system is doomed, and we will not believe that any event can intervene to avert its fate. We will not believe there is any peer of parliament, however great his prepossessions against reform may be, however great his apprehensions of its ultimate issues ; we will not believe there is any man who will not deem it a less evil to pass the Bill than risk the fearful consequences which would inevitably result from opposing the two constituted authorities of the state, supported by the almost unanimous power, wealth, and intelligence of the community. We will therefore consider the Reform Bill the law of the land, and will throw behind us, as a portion of past history, the abominations it, entombs, like the prerogatives of the Tudors, the oppressions of Feudality, and the corruptions of Popery.

Having thus cleared our course of a loathsome nuisance, we will state the chief points to which we are desirous of calling attention. 1. In order to dispose of some popular errors, we will briefly indicate the progress of the constitution up to the era of the Reform Bill. 2. We will give an estimate of the adequacy of the Bill to the national wants, and advert to the principal objections urged against it by its two classes of antagonists—namely, those who think it concedes too much, and those who think it does not concede enough. 3. And last, we will endeavour to show the future improvements likely to be effected in the country by the practical operation of this great public measure. Our readers need not be alarmed from the general import of these propositions we are going to lead them into any dissertation ; we shall despatch the whole in a very few pages, our aim being only to indicate a few leading problems,—a sort of landmarks, which, at the existing crisis, it may be useful to keep in mind. As we deem the battle won, and seek not victory, we shall submit our remarks in that spirit of truth, candour, and fairness, in which we doubt not they will be received.

1.—PROGRESS OF THE CONSTITUTION UP TO THE REFORM BILL.

We have long been of an opinion that the English constitution is the result of successive improvements advancing with the increasing intelligence of the people.* It is a tree of slow but magnificent growth, in which decayed parts have at intervals appeared, and been partly abscinded, and new and more perfect branches engrafted. Those who entertain a different opinion, rely, we apprehend, either on descriptions purely imaginary, or refer to a period too remote for authentic intelligence. The surest test of the excellence of public institutions, and the extent of popular rights, is the administration of justice. The executive government may claim and exercise a transitory power, dependent on the character of the sovereign or his ministers, or imposed upon them by the emergencies of the moment; but the administration of justice is that permanent and wide-spread divisions of social machinery which touches all the members of society; and accordingly as their rights are respected or violated under it, we may infer the general existence or absence of civil liberty among the people.

Let us apply this test to the Saxon era. We are not accurately informed of the institutions existing at this remote period, but it is certain they were those of a nation little advanced from a state of barbarism. According to Mr. Turner, the laws ascribed to Alfred, and so highly extolled, comprised the decalogue and the principal provisions in Mosaic legislation contained in the three chapters following the decalogue. However applicable such a code may have been to the Jews and Judea, it could not have been well suited to a community placed under widely different circumstances. The existence of the *were* and the *mund* afford further testimony of the rude state of society among the Anglo-Saxons : the former was the *legal* value of a man's life, which varied according to his rank ; the latter was the security afforded to the safety of the house, and like the *were* varied with the rank of the party. If human life and property were thus made to vary in value, it is not surprising personal estimation varied in the same way : thus the oath of a twelve hynd man was equivalent to the oaths of six churls. With such uncouth and partial judicial notions, the condition of the great body of the people may be easily conceived. It was that of mere personal slavery. The labouring classes were considered the property of their masters, and at their absolute disposal as much as the cattle on their estates. They might put them in bonds, whip them, brand them, yoke them in teams like horses, or openly sell them in the market like any other commodity.† This state of society continued till long after the Conquest. In the reign of Henry II. we read that the number of slaves exported to Ireland was so great that the market was absolutely over-stocked; and from William I. to that of John, scarcely a cottage in Scotland but what pos-

---

* Macintosh's History of England, vol. i. p. 72.
† Turner's History of the Anglo-Saxons, 5th edit. v. iii. p. 91.

sessed an English slave,—the spoil of the border wars.* It was only in the year 1102, it was declared in the great council of the nation, held at Westminster, unlawful for any man to *sell slaves openly in the market*, which before had been the common custom of the country.

The state of society described is obviously that existing at this day in the islands of Dominica and Jamaica, and the great mass of the people were no more in the enjoyment of civil rights than the Negroes of the West Indies. It must then be quite indefensible in any one to revert to the times of the Saxons, or to a period long subsequent, for models of constitutional liberty and government.

Let us advance to the era of *Magna Charta*. The concessions extorted by the barons at Runnymede were concessions extorted for themselves, not the people. But even this indicates a progression in society. Two orders at least in the state were recognized, namely, the king and nobility, and the idea of prescribing their respective immunities by a public law shows a growth of intelligence, and may be deemed, perhaps, the first visible germ of the Constitution.

From the reign of king John, to that of Charles I. the constitution underwent no decided improvement; the powers of the several parts of which it consisted were the subject of dispute, but were not fixed or materially altered by any public act. Great changes however had taken place among the people. Vassalage was entirely extirpated; commerce and manufactures had been introduced and flourished; comforts and luxuries unknown to preceding ages were placed within the reach of all ranks. But what most distinguished this interval was the growth of an entirely new order of vast power and influence who claimed for the first time a share in political government—namely, the MIDDLE CLASSES; consisting of the smaller freeholders and copyholders living in the county, and of merchants, manufacturers, and retailers resident in cities and towns. These, hitherto unknown as an independent cast, had gradually and almost imperceptibly become influential enough to contest the prerogatives of the monarch in the legislature—make war upon him—and, after beating him and his feudal chivalry in open battle, consolidate all authority in themselves. But their day had not yet come. They conquered, but knew not how to preserve their conquest. Political knowledge was not sufficiently diffused to enable them to frame and maintain a system of government, greatly superior to that which previously existed, and as a consequence, the power of the state fell back into the hands of its former possessors. The new influence, however, manifested in this great struggle was never lost; though the political power reverted to the King and Aristocracy, a vast influence was ever after exercised over public affairs by the middling classes; and we consider the Reform Bill of 1832 nothing more than an open and constitutional recognition of that authority in the body of the People, which, for the last century and a half, has never ceased to be indirectly, though often inefficiently, exercised over the national government.

---

* Sir Frederick Eden's History of the Poor, p. 7.

In this sketch we have taken no notice of the rise of the HOUSE OF COMMONS. The fact is, we consider the House of Commons had hardly begun to exist for any useful purpose, till a short time anterior to the Civil Wars of the commonwealth. What was the constitution of this body previously? Why, it was an assemblage of persons, summoned or not, at the pleasure of the crown or of the sheriff, to raise a sum of money for the public treasury, by taxing themselves and constituents. It was not a legislative assembly, in any proper sense of the term, any more—perhaps not so much—than the Court of Star Chamber, or High Commission. It was a meeting of deputies to assess aids and scutages, not *to make laws*. That was a branch of the royal authority to be exercised by the summary process of *edict* and *proclamation*, not by mean burgesses, the delegates of mushroom towns, who it is true might have *money* to spare for princely extravagance—the produce of their industry—but whom it was assumed had not intellects sufficiently refined for the high·task of legislation, though they might be great adepts in the mysteries of felt-hats, hose, and woollen cloths! So little did the M. P.s of those days value the representative function that they considered it a task imposed, not an honour conferred, and actually received *wages* for the discharge of so unpleasant a duty.* All sorts of evasions were practised to avoid sending representatives to parliament ; some boroughs pleaded poverty, others their insignificance, and the honourable members were almost constrained by force to appear at Westminster, Oxford, or other place of royal residence. The whole proceeding was analogous to what takes place in a city taken by storm. The victorious general calls together the principal inhabitants, not to make laws for the government of the town, but to determine how great a sum they can raise to save themselves from pillage. It was the same with the House of Commons, and so continued till the advent of Hampden, Pym, Hollis, Eliot, and other master minds, claimed for the third estate a nobler and more independent vocation.

Such, we apprehend, is an unvarnished representation of the constitutional importance of the House of Commons up to a comparatively recent period ; and for its truth we have only to appeal to the recollections of those who have even cursorily studied the histories of Henry VIII. and Queen Elizabeth, and the notions of prerogative entertained by the princes of the Stuart race. The English government for a long period was a despotism, occasionally checked and controlled by the clergy and nobility ; but though its arbitrary powers were often and bravely disputed, no permanent constitutional barrier was erected against them, till the next great era of our history, the Revolution of 1688.

The expulsion of the Stuarts was a great achievement in favour of constitutional government; but it left the industrious orders in their former state as to the exercise of political power. The limits of the royal prerogatives were defined, and the basis of public freedom declared by the Bill of Rights, but it failed to confer the great desideratum of

---

* Allen's short History of the House of Commons, p. 12.

the period—a system of representation commensurate with the augmented wealth and intelligence of the community. The classes who chiefly profited by the revolution were the Clergy and Aristocracy. The reformed church was in danger from the revival of popery; the aristocracy from both popery and prerogative : the two interests in jeopardy united for their common security and obtained it. From the despotism of the monarch the people fell under the despotism of an Oligarchy, divided into two factions—equally corrupt and inveterably hostile to each other. Though their professions were different, their practice was the same, and neither party, when circumstances gave them an ascendency, pursued measures for the general advantage. Abroad, the country was involved in unceasing, unnecessary, and expensive wars ; while, at home, public happiness was a mere pretext, the emoluments of administration being the end of their policy. Government became *a game*, played at by the rival parties ; the king being the occasional umpire, and the people the prize!

The chief reason which can be assigned, for the people remaining so long quiescent under such a defective national administration, has been the internal prosperity of the country, the result of their own unpatronized energies. During two centuries, the career of improvement has been steady and uniform; each reign closed with an augmentation of wealth and knowledge ; but in this increase government had no share. It is hardly possible to fix on any period, under any minister, when the spirit of improvement was fostered by government, when men of genius were patronized, or when any anxiety was manifested to facilitate the operations of industry, by abstaining from burdening it with imposts. On the contrary, history exhibits only the virtues of the people struggling against the vices of power,—of liberty against oppression,—of industry against the rapacity of taxation,—of truth against established error. Nevertheless, in spite of these obstacles, the country continued to flourished ; but its prosperity is not the creation of a day nor a century; it is not to be dated from the Revolution, nor the reign of George III. nor the Pitt system, nor any other system. No; it is to none of these causes: the great towns of Liverpool, Bristol, Manchester, Birmingham, Leeds, and Glasgow, have not emerged into opulence and magnificence under the favouring auspices of any of these *dynasties ;* their growth may be ascribed to the people themselves, who, while they had to surmount the disadvantages of their own condition, had to contend against the spirit of institutions hostile to improvement.

How little government, at any time, has been identified with public prosperity may be instanced in this. The worst period of our history may be reckoned from the restoration of Charles II. to the expulsion of James II. ; it was a period remarkable for the profligacy of the Court, arbitrary principles, bigotry, and parliamentary corruption; yet Mr. Hume observes, that the commerce and riches of England never encreased so fast as during that time.*

---

* History of England, vol. viii. p. 329.

In the period which followed the Revolution, the policy of government was not more favourable to industry. It was a shameless picture of war and misrule; the King the slave of faction, the People of fiscal extortion, and the mere profession of patriotism rendered ridiculous by the profligacy of public men. Yet even this vile system did not repress the energies of the people; the country flourished, but it flourished not in consequence of the vices of administration, but in spite of them. There was nothing in it paradoxical, it demonstrated no natural connexion between bad government and national prosperity; it merely showed that the seeds of improvement may be so powerful, that they will triumph over the most defective institutions.

The causes of public prosperity during the reign of George III. are too obvious to be pointed out. On the accession of that prince, the country was in the full tide of wealth and glory, and his reign was a mere continuation of the impetus it had previously received. The general progress, no doubt, was greatly accelerated by the invention of machinery: the discoveries of Watt and Arkwright, doubling the productive power of industry, gave to our manufactures an unrivalled superiority, which, in their turn, laid the foundation of agricultural prosperity. In all this, however, government did not participate: indeed, the contrast between the struggling energies of industry and the vices of power was remarkable; while the people were acquiring *within*, their Rulers were wasting *without*. It was a singular contest: genius and industry ministering to the calls of folly and prodigality. The result is now before us; and, after all our inventions, toil, and enterprise, we find ourselves worse situated than a century ago. Instead of exhibiting an unexampled picture of real opulence, social enjoyment, and general comfort, we are a woeful spectacle of embarrassment and privation. The first was the portion provided by the Genius of the people, the last is the evil entailed by the Demon of faction and misrule.

Had government ever directed its attention to the intellectual or physical improvement of the people, how different would have been the result. Five things at least might have been expected from an enlightened administration :—First, a general system for the education of the people, founded, not on any system of religious exclusion or political injustice, but on social utility. Secondly, a provision for the clergy, independently of tithe, which is so oppressive on agriculture, and adapted only to a different state of society. Thirdly, a more simple and economical mode of taxation, embracing an abolition of such internal duties as, without adding proportionately to public revenue, interfere with the operations of commercial and manufacturing industry. Fourthly, a revision of the civil and criminal jurisprudence. Lastly, as a necessary preliminary to the rest, an extension of the basis of representation, so as to embrace the power, intellect, and property of the community.

These ameliorations might have been all quietly effected within the last century. Instead, however, of government being occupied on these truly national objects, it has been a mere arena for aristocratical contention, on which these pseudo-patriots—these " Great Men," as they are sometimes called, the Godolphins, the Somers, the Harleys, the Bolingbrokes, the Chathams, Foxes, Burkes, and Pitts, have displayed their selfishness and ambition, their want of real patriotism, and enlarged views of public justice and happiness.

We have thus run through the historical part of our subject, and brought out those propositions which mark the progress of the Constitution at different epochs; it only remains to show their application to the great question of parliamentary reform in progress through the Legislature.

Our first inference is, that England never had a constitution in which equality of civil rights and equal protection to all interests were recognised; and that it is in vain to look for such a model of government in any anterior period of our history.

Secondly, we infer, that in England, as in most infant communities, political power was originally exercised by a single person, and that it was afterwards divided between the monarch and nobility.

Thirdly, that the power of the government continued to be exercised by the two estates, and almost to be unquestioned by any antagonist claim till the accession of the Stuarts, when the rise into importance of the Middle Classes called for a new partition of political authority; that these classes succeeded in wresting the government from the king and nobility, but failed to retain it, and that they also failed in securing a direct share in the government in the Revolution of 1688: but, though excluded on both these occasions, they have ever since the great struggle in the sixteenth century succeeded in exercising an indirect influence on national affairs by their numbers, wealth, and intelligence—aided by the Press, access to the debates of the Legislature, and a fragment of popular representation in the House of Commons.

Fourthly, we infer that the period has arrived when the productive classes can no longer be excluded from a direct share in the constitution; that the indirect influence they have hitherto exercised must be converted into an integral and operative part of government; and that this is really the object sought to be accomplished by the Reform Bill.

Fifthly, we infer that we have arrived at a crisis when this change is wholly irresistible :—1. Because the interests to be benefited and enfranchised by it so greatly preponderate over the minor interests by which it can be opposed. 2. Because the change is expedient as well as just; and this is shown by contrasting the past history of the people with the past history of the government: for while the latter presents a congerie of abuse, incongruities, and embarrassments, the results of the partial interests it has embodied; the former have been eminently successful in all their pursuits, and have only been retarded in their progress to social happiness by the folly and incapacity of their Rulers. The conclusion is manifest; the people ought to be admitted to a share of that political power for which experience has proved them qualified, and the Aristocracy deprived of the irresponsible authority, which they have perverted to their exclusive benefit, and the detriment of the nation.

II. ADEQUACY OF THE REFORM BILL TO THE WANTS OF THE NATION.

Two considerations appear to have principally influenced Ministers in framing the Reform Bill; first, to introduce a measure commensurate with the wishes of sincere and rational reformers; and, secondly, to introduce a measure which should not involve greater changes in established institutions than were essential to the accomplishment of this end. Had they introduced a measure less extensive than it is, it would have been unsatisfactory—it would, certainly, have been no *resting-place*—and would have left the national grievance precisely in its original state. Had they introduced a measure more extensive, it would have had to encounter increased opposition, which opposition, though it could not possibly have averted an efficient parliamentary reform, might have caused its postponement, and, in the intervening struggle, involved us in those internal calamities which every well-wisher to his country is anxious to avoid.

With great ability Ministers have pursued a medium course; if there has been any leaning contrary to popular expectation we candidly confess it has been to the democratic rather than the aristocratic side, and for this bent the people will know how to be thankful. By the extinction of the nomination boroughs they have, with a bold and dexterous hand, cut out the cancer of the Constitution, and by enfranchising the great towns they have conceded that political controul to the people which every intelligent community ought to possess over the government under which they live, and on whose administration their happiness so greatly depends.

Judicious as we humbly conceive the Reform Bill to be, happily as it has steered through the middle passage, well-adapted as it is to the times —to the expectations it has to satisfy—the interests to reconcile—and the prejudices to conciliate; still it has failed to give universal satisfaction, and is opposed by two opposite and very different classes of antagonists —by one class who conceive the Bill concedes *too much*, and by another who conceive it does not concede *enough*. We shall submit a few observations to each of these denominations, not in the vain hope that we can add to their previous knowledge, but simply with the view of recalling to their recollection considerations which, in our opinion, will shew that the apprehensions of one party and the *non-expectations* of the other are alike unfounded, or greatly exaggerated.

We shall first address ourselves, as in courtesy bound to do, to my lords Harrowby, Wharncliffe, Wellington, Winchilsea, and those who constitute what may be termed the "*Alarmists.*" We may premise to these noble persons, in the first place, that if the Reform Bill be an evil, it is an evil wholly unavoidable; we have reached such a crisis in national affairs, that either the bill, or a measure equally effective with the bill, must necessarily be passed, and that, therefore, it behoves them to submit to it, as one of these dispensations of Providence to which we must be resigned, however painful to be borne. It is true they may flatter themselves a measure less perilous would have done; in this we can assure them they are mistaken; not an atom less than the bill gives would have satisfied us, neither would it have satisfied that numerous and influential class with which we conceive we hold community of interest and sentiment.

But the great spectre which haunts the imaginations of the Alarmists is that the Bill involves consequences of direful import, that it is only the first of a series of constitutional changes, which will follow in rapid succession, and ultimately sweep away the Order, the Throne, the Altar, and even property itself. These are dreadful apprehensions, but more worthy of the dowagers of Grosvenor-Square than of statesmen seated in the highest chamber of legislation. What the people of England require is not alteration in the frame of the constitution, nor in its constituent parts. All they require is to live under cheap and enlightened institutions—institutions which shall preserve them from unnecessary wars—institutions which shall not take more from the produce of industry, neither under the pretext of religion, nor of law, nor of civil government, than is necessary to the efficient administration of public affairs—institutions which shall purge off the foul opprobrium of men claiming honour and worship from their fellow citizens, though holding lucrative offices without employment, and pensions without desert—institutions which shall not be supported by the offerings of want, but the redundancies of the rich—institutions, in short, that shall assimilate with the altered mind and altered circumstances of the community. It is not the form of the government the people wish changed, but its better administration; and what is there in this, we ask, that any just or wise man need to dread or protest against?

The apprehension of indefinite change is unwarranted by all previous experience. The country has been constantly undergoing great changes without altering the *status* of the Aristocracy. The Reformation was a great change, but when made it stopt, and did not subvert the Peerage. The rise of the House of Commons was a great change; so were the abolition of feudal tenures in the reign of Charles the Second—the revolution of 1688—the Septennial Act—the Scotch and Irish unions—the publication of the debates—the Catholic relief act—the separation of the American colonies—the rise of the Bank of England and East-India Company: all these were great changes, but the Order buffetted through these storms, and not only outlived them, but, positively, attained a higher, more palmy, and enviable state of existence than before. The English government has been a perpetual menstruum of changes. The king, as we have seen in the last section, at first engrossed all political authority; he afterwards shared it with the clergy —next with the nobility—next with the House of Commons—next, indirectly, with the middle classes—and, ultimately, perhaps, he may share it with the labouring classes, when circumstances render them sufficiently independent and intelligent for the beneficial exercise of it; and this last we deem the utmost subdivision and diffusion of political power. In all this efflux there is nothing alarming; it has been the work of two thousand years, and is the natural progress of events which it is vain to try to stop. As classes rise in wealth and intelligence they must necessarily be incorporated in the government. There is no help for it ; and it is just to be so. But because men seek what is just and useful, are we to infer they aim at something further? because they seek the abolition of an oppressive and impolitic impost, called *tithe*, is it to be inferred, as sir R. Peel most fatuously insinuated, they seek the abolition of rent? The boundary which mostly limits the demands of mankind is the just and expedient: beyond that, it is against the general feeling of human nature to trespass.

But it is alleged dangerous opinions are abroad—opinions menacing the security of property and all social institutions. There are the followers of Robert Owen, of Thomas Paine, of Joseph Spence, of Parson Irving, and the " Lady of the Rotunda." This is all true, and " 'tis a a pity 'tis true." But when was it otherwise? Men's minds have bubbles in them as " the earth and air have." In the civil wars of the Commonwealth there were the Levellers and Republicans, there were Fifth Monarchy men and Millennium men, who thought the period had arrived when Jesus was to descend and reign a thousand years. The fact is, we are at the *crisis of transition*, we are about to undergo a great change ; and such periods are now, and always have been, the very Carnival of conceits, theories, and fancies. But does any sane person believe that the vast rational mass of English society, set in its solid frame-work of a thousand years' duration, can be endangered by such puny assailants? We shall not utter another word on the subject. Let us have the renovated constitution, based on the general interest, and all the system-mongers, who with their new-born idea vainly think to subvert a social edifice which, with its habits and usages, is the result of ages of experience, will disappear with the excitement that gave them birth, and be no more heard of, except for fire-side laughter ; certainly not to be mentioned in the street, much less alluded to in the legislature.

Having tried to allay the fears of the Alarmists, we shall next turn to the honest portion of the RADICALS, who fancy they will reap no benefit from the Reform Bill, by its not including Universal Suffrage, or a scheme of suffrage co-extensive with taxation, which last, we believe, is the opinion of the M.P. for Preston, and which in this land of imposts would give the franchise to every person who eats and drinks, whether male or female, child or adult.

Before alluding, however, to the Bill, let us advert to the general principles that ought to govern the elective qualification about which extremely vague notions are entertained. It is a question of time and place, and circumstance, not of theory. A right of suffrage adapted to France or the United States may be unsuited to England. In no country is the franchise exercised without some condition being annexed. In America the slave-population, which forms so large a portion of the inhabitants, is entirely excluded ; and, if we recollect Mr. Cobbett rightly, in none of the States of the Union is the suffrage exercised unaccompanied with *residence* or other qualification in the elector. Were it otherwise, it would not be a conclusive argument for the adoption of a similar scheme of representation in the United Kingdom. In the cheap and universal circulation of newspapers—in the independent circumstances of the industrious—and in the absence of that mass of vagrancy, poverty, and destitution, which is found among ourselves, the Americans possess advantages for the exercise of political power which unhappily do not exist in England.

Take another illustration of the elective qualification, in which a higher standard of suffrage would be sufficiently protective of the people than would be adequate to the same purpose in England. In France, the number of electors amount to 250,000 ; but the electors who returned the Chamber of Deputies of 1830, which so nobly withstood the encroachments of the Bourbons, did not exceed 85,000. In England, the number of electors who actually voted in the general election of 1830, has been estimated at 87,000, which exceeds the number of electors in France under the old system : but mark the difference in the two systems of representation. What class, interest, or section of society do the English electors represent ? None, not a single social element, either of numbers, intelligence, or property. Omitting county freeholders and metropolitan electors, THREE-FOURTHS of the remaining body of the electors of England are of the labouring classes in the lowest state of indigence, non-resident, and the hireling tools of the candidates. Contrast these with the conditions under which the French constituency exercise their suffrages. First, the ballot excludes corruption and intimidation ; and every elector, according to his judgment, may be supposed to vote for the man best qualified to advance the general interests : he can have no other motive ; his only grounds for preferring one person to another must be *public*, not *personal* to himself, like those of the English elector. Secondly, the French electors comprise nearly the entire proprietary and intelligence of the community ; they consist of householders, retailers, shopkeepers, and of the classes more opulent than these : hence they embody, either directly, or through dependence on the working classes, the chief interests of the community. These are not the only points of contrast between the two countries : in France there is no richly endowed Church nor Aristocracy to make head against ; there are no interests like the Bank, or the East-India company, or West-India planters, or brewers, or old chartered corporations to counterpoise. The constitution of society is essentially *democratic ;* there is no monied aristocracy, nor landed interest : having no primogeniture or entail laws, property is more equally divided. Hence it is, that a much smaller body of electors in France would adequately represent and sustain the interests of the community, than would be adequate to similar purposes in England : for it must be borne in mind, that the excellence of any system of representation does not consist in the number of voters, but in the unbiassed and intelligent exercise of their suffrages, and in their being sufficiently numerous to touch on and constitute a fair and aliquot proportion of every social interest. After duly considering these points, the reader will not be at a loss to account for the different results presented in the history of the French chamber of deputies and the English house of commons, though both deriving their origin from an elective basis of similar extent, but differently constituted, differently exercised, and with widely different interests to contend against.

The examples we have mentioned of America and France must, we apprehend, demonstrate that the elective qualification cannot be determined by any general law, but must be governed by the circumstances of communities—the division of property—the diffusion of intelligence —and the independent condition of the people.

So far as abstract right is concerned, no good reason can be alleged why every one should not share in the making of laws to which he is amenable. The person is not less precious than property; and laws which affect the security of the former are certainly not less important to every individual than those which affect the security of the latter. It is not, therefore, residence, householdership, nor the payment of taxes, but *legal responsibility* which prescribes the strictly equitable limit to the right of suffrage.

But the admission of such a principle is clearly incompatible with any practicable form of government : it would entitle all, with scarcely any exception, to participate in legislation, it would embrace females as well as males ; all minors would be included, of whatever age, provided they were judicially responsible : in short, none would be disqualified, except the insane and infants of so tender age, that they are unable to distinguish right from wrong. The introduction of such an unlimited scheme of suffrage, no one can seriously contemplate. Still, if we are asked, why we would adopt any other principle of exclusion ; why disfranchise women in preference to men, or minors to majors ; why we would allow a person to vote at the precise age of twenty-one, and not at twenty or eighteen ; we confess, in answer to these inquiries, we can only give one reply, namely, that *expediency*, not strict justice, dictates their exclusion. Universal suffrage is as much governed by expediency as any other scheme ; for in this plan some classes are excluded, so that the difference is in degree not in principle.

We are thus compelled to resort to the only principle by which political questions must be invariably decided. They must be determined, not on any abstract view of justice, but general advantage. It is not by reverting to rights, or, more correctly, *powers* appertaining to man in a natural state, that we can ascertain his civil immunities ; we can only look to the general good ; or, as Mr. BENTHAM significantly terms it, " the greatest happiness of the greatest number, for the longest period of time."

Upon this principle we exclude minors from voting, because their interests may be presumed to be indentified with those of their parents ; we exclude females from voting, because their interests are merged in those of their husbands, fathers, or brothers. How much farther the principle of exclusion should be carried, is a practical question only

—one of utility, not theory. Whether the right of suffrage should be universal, or limited to householders, or to rent-payers of £10 or £20 a year, or to those assessed to the poor-rate, or direct taxes, is a consideration which must be decided by ascertaining which would be most conducive to public happiness. The end of just government is the equitable and adequate protection of *all interests* ; and provided this is attained, the object for which the suffrage is exercised becomes amply secured. The task of legislation is a part of the labour of society; and it is only a clumsily contrived social machinery—approaching to the organization of the savage state—if it demand the participation and exertion of every individual.

This we think is sufficient to show that no condition of suffrage is of universal application, and adapted to all times and places. For further proof we may inquire what would be the tendency of a scheme of universal suffrage, aided by the *ballot*, in Spain and Portugal. It would, evidently, revive the inquisition; increase and perpetuate the domination of the priesthood ; confirm the despotisms of Don Miguel and Don Ferdinand ; and strengthen all interests opposed to liberal ideas, to the developement of internal resources, and the promotion of the prosperity of the Peninsula. Universal suffrage and the ballot would operate in a similar manner in Ireland. There the people are so lamentably ignorant as to be entirely at the mercy of a fanatical priesthood, who pillage them without mercy, under the pretext of saying masses for the *repose of the dead!* The condition of Ireland in the nineteenth century—to the eternal reproach of our Oligarchical government—is a living type of the state of England anterior to the Reformation. And what, we ask, would universal suffrage have done for us at that era? Would it have broken the power of the monks, or of the feudal barons ? Certainly not; it would have perpetuated vassalage ; and had such a regime continued, the body of the people would have been in no better condition at this day than that of the barbarians of Russia, who, like droves of cattle, have trodden under foot the liberties of the heroic Poles.

Having said thus much on the general tendency of Universal Suffrage, we may be permitted to say a few words on its practicability. In the existing state of opinion it would be wholly unattainable by *peaceable means* ; nothing but absolute force, nothing short of a convulsive movement, subversive of every thing, would accomplish it; and then it would not subsist a twelvemonth without leading to Anarchy and Despotism. The middling classes, with hardly an exception, are indisposed to such a sweeping measure ; but without the co-operation of the middling classes no political reform can be obtained. In France the encroachments of the Bourbons were resisted, and they were, finally, expelled from the soil they had polluted, by the co-operation of the industrious orders. It is only by a similar united effort that the Church and Aristocracy of this country can be successfully resisted. What was it that rendered the efforts of the Reformers abortive in 1817 and 1818 ? Upwards of a *million and a half* of petitioners prayed for parliamentary reform , yet this numerical array was powerless of effect, and disappeared like water on a sandy bed. The cause of this memorable failure may be readily found in the fact that the people were not seconded by any portion of the proprietary; the consequences of the revolutionary wars had not penetrated deep enough into the substance of society: the case is now altered, and it is because it is altered that the Boroughmongers are disposed to concession. But though the middling classes are as fully bent on parliamentary reform as any other section of society, it is such a reform as would restore, not destroy.

Before concluding, we would beg to inquire whether by universal suffrage it is meant the floating population of towns should be eligible to vote? Vagrants, Irish emigrants, and persons of that description, for instance. We apprehend the idea has not been sufficiently analyzed; if it had, we feel convinced a scheme so indefinite could have few advocates, except among such mock reformers as Harlequin Sheridan, who professed to be the advocate of universal suffrage, because he deemed it utterly unattainable, and an excellent device for creating divisions, by which every plan of public improvement might be ridiculed and frustrated. Our reasons for preferring a more limited scheme of suffrage are practical; they are that such limitation renders reform attainable, while a more indefinite scheme defeats it; and the fact of keeping house of a certain rental, though it confers no natural right, indicates a class of persons settled in life, of mature age and fixed abode, and that such qualification is adequate to the protection of *all interests*, conciliates the timid, and preserves the suffrage itself from degradation. Lastly, let it be borne in mind that persons are not excluded from the suffrage on the ground of right, on the pretext that they have no stake, no interest in the country; but simply because the exercise of it would be unprofitable to themselves and the community, and as useless as two persons holding a pen in place of one.

Leaving the subject of universal suffrage, let us come to the positive benefits likely to result to the people from the Reform Bill. It is unnecessary we do not anticipate from it the extirpation of all social evils; it will not avert the calamities, unhappily so frequent—of commercial vicissitudes and unemployed industry and capital; these, and other difficulties in our internal state, the best of governments can only mitigate when aided by the co-operative intelligence of the community. But though it will not bring down the golden age, it will accomplish the main object Reformers have been anxious to attain.

In the first place, by the extinction of the nomination boroughs, a mass of legislative power is at once transferred from the Aristocracy to the people. This is a positive gain, without any countervailing loss. Not a particle of democracy previously existing in the Constitution is extinguished by the Bill. As before observed, three-fourths of the voters under the old system (leaving out the Counties and Metropolis) were of the working classes; they will continue voters under the new, and less exposed to bribery and intimidation. Thus there is an addition without subtraction from popular power.

An entirely new influence will be thrown into parliament—an influence emanating from the people and identified with the people in interest, sentiment, and opinion. This influence will not be measured by the additional number of members returned for the metropolis and enfranchised towns, but by the masses of population they will represent and of which they will be the organs and representatives. The ten-pound qualification is not an uniform qualification; it is one thing in London and another in the country; but both in London and the country it includes the working classes, or those chiefly dependent on the working classes. On whom are the Middle Orders, the class of shopkeepers, the butchers, bakers, hatters, grocers, inn-keepers, and alehouse-keepers chiefly dependent? Why, on the working people, to be sure. Their profits accrue more from wages than rents or tithe, or any other source of income. Whatever tends to lessen wages will lessen their gains; whatever tends to impair the condition of the labourer and operative, will impair their own. They will, in consequence, exercise the elective franchise, under an influence favourable to the poor, not to the rich.

The ten-pound qualification has been adopted not as a test of property, but of fitness for the elective function. The object sought was not to create a class of voters representing the wealth of the community, but its virtues, intelligence, and public spirit. How was this to be done? It was impossible to do in this case as is done in schools and colleges— go through the country and submit every individual to personal examination. Some *external* sign—some general rule must be adopted; the ten-pound qualification is one; it is not the best perhaps; it is not infallible; it neither demonstrates invariably moral or intellectual fitness; but it shews, at least, the elector is not a minor, nor a beggar, nor a vagrant.

That it is not a *property-qualification* may be instanced in this. In England there are thousands of persons ineligible to the proposed franchise, though in possession of millions of income—incomes derived from the funds, from colonial property, from the copyrights of books, from government annuities, from professions, trades, and other sources; many of these are persons in opulent circumstances; they are a class of people whom it might have been thought the Government would have been desirous to attach to its interest by granting them the suffrage: yet a great portion of them, not being occupiers of houses, from dislike to the trouble of housekeeping or other motive, will be totally without political power in the State; they will have no share in making militia laws, nor laws of any other description, though bound to obey them; they will be as void of political rights as the man who has not a sixpence, nor a rag to cover him, nor a shed wherein to lay his head. If the new qualification be unjust, it is, at least, impartially so; it does not strike one class and leave another unscotched; it does not exclude all the poor, and incorporate all the rich: it embraces a part of every grade of society and omits a part; and in this, in our opinion, consists the great excellence of the scheme; for, by means thereof, not a single interest is left without legislative protection.

Very erroneous notions are abroad as to the greater popular power the people would derive from the adoption of the household or universal suffrage scheme in preference to the ten-pound qualification. Facts are stubborn things, and we shall avail ourselves of a few from the mass of returns to parliament, and of which a digest will be found at the end of this article. Owing to the great wealth, intelligence, and population, concentrated in the metropolis, the character of the Reform Bill greatly depends on its application to this division of the kingdom. The capital comprises one-tenth of the population of England; it contains 116,279 qualifying tenements, while through the whole kingdom there are only 378,786. But as few houses in London are tenanted at a less rent than £10 a-year, the household plan may be considered in operation in this great influential district of the empire. In some towns, household suffrage and universal suffrage nearly coincide. Thus, in Bishop's Castle there are of household votes 344, of universal suffrage votes 345. This is a small borough; but take some of the large ones, Southwark for instance, with a population of 77,799; here the household voters are 13,187, the universal suffrage voters 15,559. In Hull are 5,350 household, and 6,591 universal suffrage electors; in Ipswich the proportions are 3,412 to 4,090; King's Lynn 2,323 to 2,674; Knaresborough 976 to 1,045; Lancaster 1,803 to 2,028; Leicester 6,627 to 8,102; Ludlow 1,006 to 1,050; Lichfield 1,151 to 1,126; Norwich 11,031 to 12,219. It is unnecessary to proceed; other and as striking examples of coincidence will be found on reference to our Tables. The conclusion to be drawn is important. Universal suffrage is not a bugbear to excite alarm; nor is it of such general concernment as to be worth contending for by the people.

We have been repeatedly told that the constituency to be created by the Bill is too limited—that it gives the suffrage to one man and leaves ten without it. Look to the Tables, and let facts speak. In Birmingham the proportion between the male adult population in possession of the franchise and those without it will be 1 to 3, in Greenwich 1 to 2, in Lambeth 1 to 1½, and in Mary-le-bone 1 to 1. In no case, with one or two exceptions, does the proportion exceed 1 to 4.

On the whole, we conclude the £10 qualification is a happy medium. Had it been higher the elective basis would have been too narrow. As it is, it touches on the different schemes of suffrage which have been proposed: it embraces every class and excludes none. We should object to a plan of representation which embodied only one interest, whatever interest it might be; for instance, we should object to the constitution of a House of Commons which represented only the working classes or the middle classes, just as much as we object to the constitution of that which exists, because it represents only the interests of the Aristocracy.

III.—PRACTICAL RESULTS OF A REFORMED HOUSE OF COMMONS.

Constitutional changes, like the circulating medium, are valueless in themselves. They are not the good sought, but the instrument of its production. A reformed parliament is the machinery which is to extirpate the abuses of our institutions. When it has been obtained the discussion of forms of government, theories of civil rights, and plans of elective qualification will cease to be of interest; the people will naturally turn to subjects of more direct benefit—to the practical measures by which the condition of society can be improved. Let us, then, endeavour to ascertain the sort of materials which will be brought to the new legislative manufactory—the measures which will probably engage the attention of a reformed House of Commons. As this part of our task will be little more than a brief recapitulation of the preceding topics of our work, it will appropriately form the concluding section of our publication.

The first and most important result of the adoption of the Reform Bill will consist in the substitution for the government of an oligarchy with selfish and limited interests—a national government responsible to 500,000 electors, every one of whom has an interest in domestic peace, order, and prosperity.

For the interests of the *few* the Reform Bill would substitute the interests of the *many*; it would lay the axe to the root of all monopolies, and the community no longer be compelled to enrich the Bank Proprietary by exclusive privileges; nor profit the Shipping Interest by the consumption of the dear and inferior timber of Canada; nor the East-India Company, by paying double the price for tea the consumer pays on the Continent; nor would industry be impeded by corn laws which are only favourable to high rents—of no benefit to the farmer—and only tend to limit the exchange of our manufactures for the produce of America and continental Europe.

Reform would equalize taxation, and the redundant incomes of the great, not the wages and profits of the industrious, be made the chief fund of fiscal exaction.

It would remedy the glaring abuses of our judicial administration, and render justice prompt, protective, and attainable to every individual.

It would reduce the public expenditure to the lowest possible scale; abolish sinecures, unmerited pensions, and exorbitant salaries; cut off Colonies that are burdensome to the nation, and which, like useless Boards, Diplomatic Missions, and Consular Establishments, have been kept up solely to provide lucrative appointments for the Boroughmongers and their families.

It would destroy the oppressions of the tithe system, abolish the monstrous inequalities in ecclesiastical income, and improve the condition of the Working Clergy, who reside among their parishioners, and benefit them by their example and ministry.

It would reform the abuses of Corporate Bodies and render them, not only the faithful trustees of the poor, but the centres of local government, police, and judicial administration.

It would provide for the general education of the people—their profitable employment—and open new channels for redundant capital and industry.

It would put an end to the perjuries, drunkenness, riots, and immoralities of parliamentary elections.

It would be a guarantee against future liberticide wars; if wars were waged they would be the wars of the nation, not of an Oligarchy; they would be wars for, not against, the people.

Lastly, it would consolidate the empire, uniting in the bonds of equal rights and reciprocal advantages England, Ireland, and Scotland, and render them what, from superior wealth and intelligence, they ought to be, " the envy and admiration of the world!" England would recover her rank among nations, and be again the model of constitutional governments. Her government would be founded on Public Opinion, not on that sinister opinion fostered by a lavish expenditure of public money—by the abuse of collegiate and ecclesiastical endowments—by the restraint of discussion—but an opinion, the result of impartial investigation and expanded views of social happiness.

Such, we apprehend, are a few of the advantages that would result from the adoption of the Reform Bill, and which would form the subjects of deliberation of a reformed parliament, and which, in due course, it would endeavour to accomplish. That the people can be frustrated in the pursuit of so many national blessings, we cannot for a moment believe; we cannot believe that from supineness or want of union among themselves they will continue the serfs of the Boroughmongers, who, for their own emolument, have cherished every abuse in our institutions, and entailed on the country all its embarrassing calamities.

Our enemies are few in number, but mighty in influence. They are an united, active, and desperate band, exasperated almost to madness at being kept for the last fifteen months from their accustomed prey. If they succeed, they well know all the sacrifices they make will be amply repaid by the plunder of the people. But their rapacious hopes will be baffled. Corruption will never triumph over true patriotism—a mock representation over one that is real—private interests over the public weal—a mere faction over the king, his ministers, the public press, and the nation!

Cheap government—cheap bread—cheap justice—and industry unfettered and productive will reward our efforts in the triumph of the Reform Bill!

———

N.B. Whatever changes the Reform Bill may finally undergo in either House of Parliament, the subjoined "Statistical Tables" will be useful for reference; comprising as they do the elements of representation on any proposed plan, whether founded on population, on rental, the amount of taxation, or the household or universal suffrage scheme.

Totness, in No. IV., which formed one of the semi-disfranchised boroughs, has been removed in the committee of the Lower House; but as it originally stood in the Bill, it has been here retained.

STATISTICS OF REPRESENTATION.

No. I.

The Year of Election, and greatest Number of Freeholders who have exercised the right of voting in ENGLAND and WALES for County Members since 1811.

Counties.	Year of Election.	Freeholders on the Poll Books.
Bedford	1826	2546
Berks.	1812	1992*
Bucks.	1831	2593
Cambridge	1830	3717
Chester.	No polling for last century in this county.	
Cornwall	1831	2762
Cumberland	1811	1396
Derby.	No contest since 1811.	
Devon	1818	7793
Dorset	1831	2961
Durham	1820	2712†
Essex	1830	5317
Gloucester.	No contest since 1811.	
Hereford	1818	3505
Hertford.	No contest since 1811.	
Huntingdon	1826	1884
Lancaster.	No contest in the county since 1811.	
Leicester	1830	5420
Lincoln	1818	5598
Monmouth.	No contest since 1811.	
Norfolk	1817	7217
Northumberland	1826	2985
Nottingham.	No contest for a century past.	
Oxford	1831	2934
Rutland.	No contest since 1811.	
Salop	1831	2534
Somerset	1818	4644
Stafford	1831	12
Suffolk	1830	1691‡
Surrey	1826	3743
Sussex	1820	4440
Warwick	1820	3122
Westmoreland	1826	3455
Anglesey.	No contest since 1784.	
Brecon	1818	1611
Cardigan.	No contest for a century.	
Denbigh.	No poll-books filed.	
Flint.	No contest.	
Glamorganshire	1820	1598
Montgomery	1831	1005
Pembroke	1812	2723
Radnor.	No contest since 1811.	

---

* The number of freeholders in this county is estimated at 4000.—*Parl. Pap.* 149, Sess. 1831.

† The election continued only six days, and supposed half the number of freeholders polled.

‡ The election continued only one day. The number polled in 1790, when the election lasted two days, was 4849.

No. II.

The Number of Freeholders in the different Counties in IRELAND, Registered up to the 1st May, 1831; distinguishing the £50, £20, and £10 Freeholders.

Counties.	Number of £50.	Number of £20.	Number of £10.	Total Number.
Antrim....	752	395	1296	2443
Armagh ..	295	231	1087	1613
Carlow ..	321	97	193	611
Cavan	462	344	781	1587
Clare	579	293	930	1802
Cork	2280	452	447	3179
Donegal ..	811	92	66	969
Down	887	338	1902	3127
Dublin ..	1223	496	109	1828
Fermanagh	273	251	920	1444
Galway ..	897	299	1812	3008
Kerry	632	355	178	1165
Kildare ..	682	122	190	994
Kilkenny..	767	798	383	1948
King's	788	202	318	1308
Leitrim ..	336	181	554	1071
Limerick..	1418	1126	1369	3913
Londonderry	488	215	836	1539
Longford ..	204	85	463	752
Louth	295	113	380	788
Mayo	583	346	335	1264
Meath	784	160	302	1246
Monaghan	464	254	946	1664
Queen's ..	941	183	303	1427
Roscommon	468	357	470	1295
Sligo	399	315	299	1013
Tipperary	2015	411	475	2901
Tyrone ..	265	316	701	1282
Waterford	458	476	488	1422
Westmeath	395	163	366	924
Wexford ..	661	328	697	1686
Wicklow..	314	122	513	949

No. III.

Population, Electors, &c. of the FIFTY-SIX Boroughs totally disfranchised, forming Schedule A of the Reform Bill.

Boroughs.	Population, 1831.	Houses, 1821.	Resident Electors.	Houses over £10.	Houses, over £20.	Assessed Taxes, 1830.	Electors Uni.Suf.
Aldborough	2475	258	147	39	10	574	495
Aldeburgh	1538	268	57	31	7	297	307
Amersham	2816	494	79	126	7	880	563
Appleby ..	1359	145	——	65	6	487	271
Bedwin, Gt..	2191	125	120	2	—	627	438
Berealston..	——	——	——	1	—	3	375
Bishop's Cast.	1729	344	183	83	4	311	315
Blechingley .	1203	85	6	5	1	390	240

Boroughs.	Population, 1831.	Houses, 1821.	Resident Electors.	Houses over £10.	Houses over £20.	Assessed Taxes, 1830.	Electors Uni.Suf.
Boroughbridge	950 ..	158 ..	70 ..	18 ..	4 ..	358 ..	190
Bossiney ..	1006 ..	52 ..	15 ..	1 ..	— ..	46 ..	201
Brackley ..	2107 ..	354 ..	33 ..	25 ..	1 ..	302 ..	421
Bramber ..	97 ..	35 ..	— ..	— ..	— ..	16 ..	12
Callington ..	1388 ..	232 ..	153 ..	32 ..	— ..	221 ..	277
Camelford ..	1359 ..	110 ..	26 ..	14 ..	1 ..	127 ..	271
Castle Rising	888 ..	111 ..	— ..	2 ..	2 ..	127 ..	177
Corfe Castle	960 ..	156 ..	— ..	11 ..	2 ..	104 ..	192
Downton ..	3961 ..	582 ..	86 ..	94 ..	— ..	361 ..	792
Dunwich ..	232 ..	38 ..	25 ..	2 ..	1 ..	75 ..	46
Fowey	1767 ..	310 ..	275 ..	46 ..	5 ..	273 ..	353
Gatton	145 ..	23 ..	6 ..	6 ..	4 ..	206 ..	29
Grinstead, E.	3364 ..	444 ..	8 ..	42 ..	8 ..	855 ..	672
Haslemere..	849 ..	124 ..	— ..	16 ..	4 ..	369 ..	169
Hedon	1080 ..	182 ..	331 ..	44 ..	8 ..	270 ..	216
Heytesbury .	1413 ..	26 ..	— ..	21 ..	7 ..	306 ..	282
Higham Ferrars	965 ..	154 ..	— ..	6 ..	— ..	168 ..	123
Hindon	921 ..	163 ..	— ..	11 ..	1 ..	100 ..	184
Ilchester....	975 ..	165 ..	181 ..	12 ..	3 ..	145 ..	195
Looe, West .	593 ..	107 ..	34 ..	8 ..	1 ..	53 ..	118
Looe, East .	865 ..	142 ..	40 ..	20 ..	1 ..	92 ..	173
Lostwithiel .	1074 ..	206 ..	23 ..	37 ..	15 ..	344 ..	214
Ludgershall.	535 ..	116 ..	— ..	4 ..	1 ..	122 ..	107
Milborne Port	2072 ..	302 ..	169 ..	11 ..	1 ..	210 ..	414
Minehead..	1494 ..	265 ..	261 ..	36 ..	3 ..	316 ..	298
Newport, C.	1084 ..	180 ..	81 ..	8 ..	— ..	116 ..	216
Newtown, I. W.	68 ..	14 ..	26 ..	— ..	— ..	— ..	13
Newton, L. .	2137 ..	275 ..	52 ..	19 ..	2 ..	151 ..	427
Okehampton	2055 ..	313 ..	93 ..	42 ..	7 ..	383 ..	411
Orford	1302 ..	217 ..	— ..	20 ..	1 ..	144 ..	260
Plympton ..	804 ..	128 ..	24 ..	39 ..	12 ..	314 ..	160
Queenborough	786 ..	175 ..	300 ..	11 ..	6 ..	82 ..	157
Romney, New	378 ..	165 ..	16 ..	24 ..	1 ..	352 ..	75
St. Germains	2586 ..	99 ..	30 ..	15 ..	1 ..	341 ..	597
St. Mawes..	459 ..	101 ..	— ..	9 ..	— ..	31 ..	91
St. Michael .	97 ..	24 ..	— ..	1 ..	— ..	34 ..	19
Saltash	3092 ..	234 ..	— ..	134 ..	2 ..	126 ..	618
Sarum, Old..	12 ..	2 ..	— ..	7 ..	2 ..	12 ..	2
Seaford	1098 ..	217 ..	124 ..	36 ..	5 ..	315 ..	219
Steyning ..	1436 ..	127 ..	— ..	18 ..	5 ..	369 ..	287
Stockbridge.	851 ..	134 ..	138 ..	31 ..	5 ..	252 ..	170
Tregony	1127 ..	188 ..	233 ..	11 ..	3 ..	110 ..	225
Wendover ..	2008 ..	148 ..	117 ..	14 ..	— ..	272 ..	401
Weobly	819 ..	118 ..	— ..	5 ..	1 ..	231 ..	163
Whitchurch.	1673 ..	268 ..	— ..	21 ..	2 ..	343 ..	334
Winchelsea .	772 ..	187 ..	8 ..	13 ..	6 ..	217 ..	154
Wootton Bas.	1896 ..	379 ..	300 ..	36 ..	5 ..	321 ..	379
Yarmouth, I.W.	586 ..	97 ..	9 ..	14 ..	4 ..	172 ..	177

No. IV.

Population, Electors, &c. of the THIRTY Boroughs of which the Representatives have been reduced to One, forming Schedule B of the Reform Bill.

Arundel	2803 ..	472 ..	463 ..	200 ..	33 ..	877 ..	560
Ashburton..	4165 ..	341 ..	— ..	54 ..	11 ..	413 ..	833

Boroughs.	Population, 1831.	Houses, 1821.	Resident Electors.	Houses over £10.	Houses over £20.	Assessed Taxes, 1830.	Electors Uni. Suf.
Calne	4795	461	18	208	45	1581	959
Christchurch	1599	936	20	300	18	557	319
Clitheroe	5213	550	7	60	19	406	1042
Dartmouth	4597	607	100	234	48	656	919
Droitwich	2487	474	4	69	19	519	497
Eye	2313	340	129	29	5	411	462
Grimsby	4225	734	394	94	3	461	845
Helston	3293	466	52	234	20	883	658
Horsham	5105	288	78	23	165	1209	1021
Hythe	2287	437	36	77	20	640	457
Launceston	2231	253	14	176	17	537	446
Liskeard	2853	414	24	235	16	542	570
Lyme Regis	2621	401	25	270	26	852	524
Malmesbury	2785	275	13	158	6	338	557
Midhurst	1478	234	20	65	23	802	295
Morpeth	5156	478	240	162	31	946	1031
Northalltn.	5118	567	—	107	30	1128	1023
Petersfield	1423	262	56	54	12	513	284
Reigate	3397	217	8	78	11	662	679
Rye	3715	574	50	95	28	815	743
Shaftesbury	3061	546	359	158	7	528	612
St. Ives	4776	772	496	26	—	337	—
Thirsk	2835	591	6	110	15	606	567
Totness	3442	356	40	247	86	1088	688
Wareham	2325	417	20	53	6	560	465
Westbury	7324	—	—	318	—	995	1464
Wilton	1997	299	20	150	14	492	399
Woodstock	1320	258	145	90	23	487	264

No. V.

Boroughs not included either in Schedule A or B, and to continue to return two Members to Parliament.

	Population, 1831.	Houses, 1821.	Resident Electors.	Houses over £10.	Houses over £20.	Assessed Taxes, 1830.	Electors Uni. Suf.
Abingdon	5622	1114	253	148	39	1355	1124
Andover	4748	810	24	207	94	1704	949
Aylesbury	4450	886	1500	120	21	1220	890
Banbury	5906	701	16	169	62	1305	1181
Barnstaple	6840	805	731	344	88	1455	1368
Bath	38063	5494	29	1243	1062	15885	7812
Bedford	6959	1104	914	209	43	2047	1391
Berwick	8920	1061	527	415	185	2130	1784
Beverley	7432	1513	870	328	130	3000	1486
Bewdley	4003	918	24	121	22	925	800
Bodmin	3375	467	37	178	60	984	675
Boston	11240	2231	503	446	219	2953	2248
Bridgenorth	5298	1021	986	220	73	1363	1059
Bridgewater	7807	1110	460	452	216	2711	1561
Bridport	4242	604	260	338	343	762	848
Bristol	59034	8451	5188	5022	2719	33641	11806
Buckingham	3610	287	13	75	8	842	722
BurySt.Edm.	11436	1960	37	585	262	4994	2287
Cambridge	20917	2682	130	1106	514	7751	4183

Boroughs.	Population, 1831.	Houses, 1821.	Resident Electors.	Houses over £10.	Houses over £20.	Assessed Taxes, 1830.	Electors Uni.Suf.
Canterbury .	12190	2621	1988	667	218	4585	2438
Carlisle	19069	1014	850	587	275	3798	3813
Chester	21331	4076	1504	1040	504	37732	4266
Chippingham	4333	541	126	180	52	1057	866
Chichester..	8270	1328	828	456	194	3785	1654
Cirencester..	4520	900	573	329	127	2731	904
Cockermouth	4536	766	——	101	11	609	907
Colchester..	16167	2768	1406	612	285	5713	3233
Coventry ..	27298	4470	2763	953	241	6658	5459
Cricklade ..	11661	2266	1188	——	——	——	2332
Derby	23627	3516	700	801	336	5488	4725
Devizes	4562	488	40	336	99	1746	912
Dorchester..	3033	405	210	333	112	2103	606
Dover......	14381	2047	1866	273	43	3340	2872
Durham....	9262	1175	987	448	155	3783	1852
Evesham ..	3976	746	155	178	78	1297	795
Exeter	28242	3432	1300	1856	886	22497	5648
Gloucester..	11373	1794	1703	760	360	4765	2276
Grantham ..	7427	766	864	228	114	2196	1485
Guildford ..	3813	565	178	213	93	1630	762
Harwich ..	4297	699	20	170	28	906	859
Hastings ..	10097	1068	17	596	319	5144	2019
Hereford ..	10351	1929	884	617	248	4155	2070
Hertford ..	4028	656	659	273	132	2394	805
Honiton....	3509	697	506	303	69	1125	701
Huntingdon.	3267	538	78	200	77	1773	365
Hull......	32958	5350	2299	2136	781	16182	6591
Ipswich ..	20454	3412	1003	592	180	5025	4090
King'sLynn	13370	2323	284	334	71	2596	2674
Knaresboro	5226	976	28	203	56	1148	1045
Lancaster .	10144	1803	2490	554	265	4100	2028
Leicester..	40512	6627	4781	855	405	5278	8102
Leominster	4300	854	716	195	41	1051	8600
Lewes	6353	808	626	230	79	2475	1270
Lincoln	13102	2145	1233	434	230	3048	2620
Lichfield ..	6281	1151	763	321	149	2476	1256
Liverpool..	165175	27792	4401	14127	5936	59086	33033
London ..	121344	17534	8639	13600	1888	198101	24268
Ludlow ..	5253	1006	16	292	116	1995	1050
Lymington..	3361	417	20	295	66	1077	672
Maidstone	15387	2276	752	685	283	4784	3677
Maldon	3831	606	251	274	53	1114	766
Malton....	4173	774	625	146	60	952	834
Marlborough	3426	488	10	227	37	1276	685
Marlow	2863	494	444	192	11	1741	572
Monmouth	13815	——	——	1279	535	7383	2763
Newark ..	9557	1691	1362	351	198	2856	1911
Nwcstl.UL	8192	1510	800	267	139	1764	1638
Nwcstl.UT	42760	4317	3000	2916	1223	14961	8552
Nwprt.I.W.	4398	731	22	270	118	1841	879
Nrthmpton.	15351	2086	2300	691	266	4127	3070
Norwich ..	61096	11031	4202	2316	810	15550	12219
Nottingham	50216	7676	4051	1436	523	9359	10043
Oxford....	18460	2520	1779	1460	443	2735	3692
Penryn ..	4490	498	429	112	23	521	899
Peterboro'	6511	983	548	245	139	2379	1362
Plymouth ..	31080	2384	177	2059	651	8753	6216
Pontefract..	9349	960	806	484	64	1811	1669

Boroughs.	Population, 1831.	Houses, 1821.	Resident Electors.	Houses over£10.	Houses over£20.	Assessed Taxes 1830.	Electors Uni.Suf.
Poole	6459	1180	95	298	71	1702	1291
Portsmouth.	50389	8506	59	—	—	—	10077
Preston	33112	4229	7122	976	510	7394	6622
Reading	15595	2585	1010	1050	657	8661	3119
Retford	—	6724	1283	152	31	924	—
Ripon	5080	178	—	195	70	3076	1016
Richmond	3900	748	41	175	77	1899	780
Rochester	9891	1646	841	400	608	2356	1978
St. Albans.	4772	744	623	286	93	1964	954
Sandwich	3084	578	468	125	28	785	616
Salisbury	9338	1684	57	567	286	5365	1867
Scarborough	8752	1883	44	387	173	2503	1750
Shoreham	—	210	1041	26	5	196	—
Shrewsbury	16055	3155	974	989	471	8695	3211
Southamptn.	19324	2249	839	1284	656	11378	3864
Southwark	77799	13187	5000	4658	2629	26271	15559
Stafford	8956	1013	864	190	80	1331	1391
Stamford	5837	919	667	340	168	3224	1167
Sudbury	4677	843	730	108	21	1131	935
Tamworth	7118	747	470	137	44	914	1423
Tavistock	5602	560	27	269	72	1282	1120
Taunton	—	800	739	336	225	2699	—
Tewkesbury	5780	1132	318	262	108	1575	1156
Thetford	3462	602	23	77	21	887	692
Tiverton	9566	1357	25	213	86	1651	1913
Truro	8644	464	25	190	90	1278	1728
Wallingford.	2545	386	286	218	43	1073	509
Warwick	9109	1590	186	354	152	3227	1821
Wells	4048	505	308	173	85	1355	809
Wenlock	17435	3667	485	36	6	2723	3487
Westminster	202050	19275	17060	17681	15163	303421	40410
Wymth & M.	7655	1213	745	490	300	3747	1531
Wigan	20774	3288	97	474	204	2686	4514
Winchester	5280	769	140	307	136	2805	1056
Windsor	8661	811	363	374	181	3538	1732
Worcester	18590	2926	2173	909	511	6900	3718
Wycombe	6299	519	124	446	46	1737	1219
Ymth. Nrflk.	22028	4403	929	420	129	3192	4405
York	26260	3326	3715	1589	807	11514	5254

WELSH BOROUGHS.

Boroughs.	Population, 1831.	Houses, 1821	Resident Electors.	Houses over 10l.	Houses over 20l.	Assessed Taxes, 1830.	Electors Uni. Suf.
Beaumaris	13697	462	—	152	43	1404	2739
Brecon	4139	977	—	186	75	1259	838
Caernarvon	18106	1148	—	434	72	2498	3621
Cardiff	32777	671	702	654	250	4053	6555
Cardigan	8120	448	1096	219	35	1478	1624
Carmarthen	15552	1128	633	372	74	2192	3110
Denbigh	11697	1400	546	442	121	2668	2339
Flint	28338	—	1217	236	30	1427	5667
Haverfordw.	10882	806	500	369	95	2703	2106
Montgomery	16283	227	85	322	15	2090	3256
Pembroke	10098	862	1401	229	91	2422	2041
Radnor	7245	422	922	81	—	830	1449

No. VI.

New Boroughs forming Schedule C, which are to return Two Members.

Names.	Population, 1831.	Houses at 10*l.* and upwards.	Houses at 20*l.* and upwards.	Assessed Taxes, 1839.	Electors Uni. Suff.
Birmingham	142251 ..	6532 ..	1545 ..	28350 ..	28450
Blackburn	27091 ..	1578 ..	176 ..	2325 ..	5418
Bolton	41195 ..	1712 ..	322 ..	4215 ..	8239
Bradford	23233 ..	1083 ..	128 ..	2444 ..	4646
Brighton	40684 ..	2673 ..	2131 ..	31800 ..	8126
Devonport	44454 ..	—— ..	—— ..	9678 ..	8890
Finsbury	244077 ..	23626 ..	17448 ..	206848 ..	48815
Greenwich, &c.	62009 ..	4177 ..	1573 ..	21341 ..	12401
Halifax	15382 ..	1044 ..	183 ..	3186 ..	3076
Lambeth	203229 ..	16872 ..	9224 ..	108814 ..	40645
Leeds	123393 ..	6683 ..	1278 ..	18800 ..	24678
Macclesfield	23129 ..	1206 ..	140 ..	2416 ..	4625
Manchester	187022 ..	12639 ..	2126 ..	40628 ..	37404
Marylebone	240294 ..	22637 ..	19618 ..	290376 ..	48058
Oldham	50513 ..	1128 ..	138 ..	2436 ..	10102
Sheffield	90657 ..	4573 ..	473 ..	12605 ..	18131
Stockport	25469 ..	854 ..	187 ..	2652 ..	5093
Stoke-upon-Trent	52946 ..	—— ..	—— ..	4950 ..	10589
Stroud	13721 ..	—— ..	—— ..	2274 ..	2744
Sunderland	43078 ..	2270 ..	306 ..	4682 ..	8615
Tower Hamlets	359821 ..	26297 ..	13467 ..	118546 ..	71964
Wolverhampton	67514 ..	2125 ..	1451 ..	6229 ..	13502

No. VII.

New Boroughs forming Schedule D, which are to return One Member.

Names.	Population, 1831.	Houses at 10*l.* and upwards.	Houses at 20*l.* and upwards.	Assessed Taxes, 1830.	Electors Uni. Suff.
Ashton-under-Line	33597 ..	—— ..	—— ..	1434 ..	6719
Bury	15086 ..	639 ..	128 ..	2161 ..	3017
Cheltenham	22942 ..	1939 ..	1225 ..	21184 ..	4588
Dudley	23043 ..	595 ..	131 ..	2536 ..	4608
Frome	12240 ..	1354 ..	91 ..	1960 ..	2448
Gateshead	15177 ..	795 ..	140 ..	2036 ..	3035
Huddersfield	31041 ..	1709 ..	248 ..	3941 ..	6208
Kendal	11265 ..	—— ..	—— ..	3027 ..	2253
Kidderminster	14981 ..	473 ..	117 ..	1920 ..	2998
Rochdale	35764 ..	1044 ..	N. D. ..	3143 ..	7521
Salford	50810 ..	1244 ..	463 ..	8970 ..	10162
South Shields	18756 ..	987 ..	N. D. ..	1627 ..	3751
Swansea	19093 ..	739 ..	303 ..	3644 ..	3818
Tynemouth	16926 ..	974 ..	N. D. ..	2467 ..	3385
Walsall	15066 ..	750 ..	N. D. ..	1735 ..	3013
Wakefield	12232 ..	675 ..	271 ..	5530 ..	2446
Warrington	16018 ..	799 ..	252 ..	2914 ..	3203
Whitby	10399 ..	—— ..	—— ..	2035 ..	2079
Whitehaven	17808 ..	468 ..	130 ..	2842 ..	3561

No. VIII.

A LIST of the PLACES contained in Schedule (C.) and (D.); 1. specifying the Parishes, Townships, or Hamlets, of which the whole or any part is recommended in the Reports of the Commissioners as the appropriate limits of each place contained in Schedules (C.) and (D.) 2. The Population, Number of Houses, Number of Qualifying Tenements, and Amount of Assessed Taxes, within such limits, or as nearly as can be ascertained.

SCHEDULE (C.)

Birmingham.—Parish of Birmingham, parish of Edgbaston, township of Bordesley, township of Deritend, township of Duddeston with Neachels :—containing town of Birmingham and its immediate neighbourhood.

Population .... 142,000 | Qualifying tenements....   7,000
Houses................ 30,000 | Assessed taxes £28,000

Blackburn.—The township of Blackburn ;—containing the town of Blackburn and its immediate neighbourhood.

Population.............. 27,000 | Qualifying tenements   600
Houses .... 4,800 | Assessed taxes £2,300

Bolton.—The township of Great Bolton, the chapelry of Little Bolton, the township of Haulgh ;—containing the town of Bolton.

Population.............. 42,000 | Qualifying tenements   1,600
Houses .... 7,600 | Assessed taxes £4,300

Bradford.—The township of Bradford, the township of Bowling, the township of Little Horton ;—containing the township of Bradford and its neighbourhood.

Population.............. 34,000 | Qualifying tenements....   1,100
Houses .... 4,100 | Assessed taxes £2,444

Brighton.—Parish of Brighton, parish of Hove ;—containing the town of Brighton with its immediate neighbourhood, which includes the village of Hove.

Population.............. 42,000 | Qualifying tenements....   3,000
Houses .... 9,000 | Assessed taxes £31,800

Devonport.—The parish of Stoke Damerill, the township of Stonehouse ;—containing the town of Devonport, with its neighbourhood, which includes the suburbs of Stoke and Morrice town.

Population.............. 44,000 | Qualifyiᴜg tenements....   3,000
Houses .... 4,600 | Assessed taxes £9,700

Finsbury.—Part of the parish of St. Mary, Islington, part of parish St. Andrew, Holborn, part of the parish of St. James and St. John, Clerkenwell, part of the parish of St. Sepulchre, part of Furnival's-inn, part of Staple's-inn, Lincoln's-inn, Gray's-inn, the parish of St. Luke, the parish of St. George-the-Martyr, the parish of St. Giles-in-the-Fields, the parish of St. George, Bloomsbury, the liberties of Saffron-hill, Hatton-garden, and Ely-rents, the liberty of Ely-place, the liberty of the Rolls, the liberty of Glasshouse-yard, the precinct called the Charter-house,—containing the northern portion of the metropolis.

Population .... 225,000 | Qualifying tenements ..   23,600
Houses .... 30,000 | Assessed taxes £201,000

Greenwich.—The parish of St .Paul, Deptford, the parish of St. Nicholas, Deptford, part of the parish of Woolwich, part of the parish of Greenwich, part of the parish of Charlton, part of the parish of Plumstead ;—containing the towns of Woolwich, Greenwich, Deptford, and the intermediate space, including the village of Charlton.

Population.............. 64,000 | Qualifying tenements....   6,000
Houses .... 12,000 | Assessed taxes..........£21,500

Halifax.—The township of Halifax, part of the township of South Ouram, part of the township of North Ouram;—containing the town of Halifax.

Population.............. 31,000 | Qualifying tenements....   1,300
Houses .... 9,000 | Assessed taxes £3,200

Lambeth.—Part of the parish of Lambeth, part of the parish of St. Giles, Camberwell, the precinct of the Palace, the parish of St. Mary, Newington;—containing the southern portion of the metropolis.

Population .... 154,000 | Qualifying tenements ..   16,400
Houses .... 29,000 | Assessed taxes £91,000

Leeds.—The borough of Leeds;—containing the town of Leeds, with its surrounding neighbourhood.

Population .... 123,000 | Qualifying tenements....   6,700
Houses................ 27,000 | Assessed taxes £18,800

Macclesfield.—The borough of Macclesfield, part of the township of Sutton, part of the township of Hurdsfield;—containing the town of Macclesfield and its immediate neighbourhood.

Population.............. 30,000 | Qualifying tenements   1,100
Houses .... 6,000 | Assessed taxes........... £2,500

Manchester.—Township of Manchester, township of Chorlton-row, township of Ardwick, township of Beswick, township of Hulme, township of Cheetham, township of Bradford, township of Newton, township of Harpur Hey;—containing the town of Manchester and its immediate neighbourhood, with the exception of the town and township of Salford.

Population .... 187,000 | Qualifying tenements ..   12,700
Houses................ 32,000 | Assessed taxes £40,600

Marylebone.—The parish of St. Marylebone, the parish of Paddington, part of the parish of St. Pancras;—containing the north-western portion of the metropolis.

Population .... 234,000 | Qualifying tenements ..   21,600
Houses................ 28,000 | Assessed taxes £274,000

Oldham.—The township of Oldham;—containing the town of Oldham and its neighbourhood.

Population.............. 32,000 | Qualifying tenements....   1,100
Houses .... 6,000 | Assessed taxes.......... £2,000

Sheffield.—The township of Sheffield, the township of Attercliffe-cum-Darnell, the township of Brightside Bierlow, the township of Netherhallam, part of the township of Eccleshall Bierlow;—containing the town of Sheffield and its surrounding neighbourhood, which includes the village of Attercliffe.

Population.............. 90,000 | Qualifying tenements....   4,300
Houses .... 20,000 | Assessed taxes..........£12,000

Stockport.—The borough of Stockport, part of the township of Heaton Norris, part of the township of Brinnington, the hamlet of Brinksway, the hamlet of Edgeley;—containing the town of Stockport.

Population.............. 41,000 | Qualifying tenements....   1,500
Houses .... 7,600 | Assessed taxes.......... £4,000

Stoke-upon-Trent.—The township of Tunstall, the township of Burslem, the vill of Rushton Grange, the hamlet of Sneyd, the township of Hanley, the township of Shelton, the township of Fenton Vivian, the township of Lane-end, part of the township of Penkhull, part of the township of Fenton Culvert, part of the township of Longton;—containing the district of the Potteries, including the towns of Lane-end, Stoke, Shelton, Hanley, Burslem, and Tunstall.

Population .... 53,000 | Qualifying tenements   1,500
Houses................ 9,000 | Assessed taxes £4,900

Stroud.—Parish of Stroud, parish of Bisley, parish of Painswick, parish of Pitchcomb, parish of Randwick, parish of Stonehouse, parish of Eastington, parish of Leonard Stanley, with the exception of that part called Lorridge's Farm, parish of King's Stanley, parish of Rodborough, parish of Minchinhampton, parish of Woodchester, parish of Avening, parish of Horsley :—containing the Clothing District, situate on the Stroud Water, or River Frome, and its tributary streams.

Population .... 41,000 | Qualifying tenements 1,600
Houses .... 9,300 | Assessed taxes £7,000

Sunderland.—The parish of Sunderland, the township of Bishop Wearmouth, the township of Bishop Wearmouth Panns, the township of Monkwearmouth, the township of Monkwearmouth Shore, the township of Southwick ;— containing the town of Sunderland and its neighbourhood.

Population.............. 43,000 | Qualifying tenements 2,500
Houses .... 5,000 | Assessed taxes £4,500

Tower Hamlets.—Parish of St.'Leonard, Shoreditch, parish of St. Matthew, Bethnal-green, parish of Christ Church, Spitalfields, parish of All Saints, Poplar and Blackwall, parish of St. Anne, Limehouse, parish of St. George-in-the-East, parish of St John, Wapping, parish of St. Mary, Whitechapel, the liberty of East Smithfield, the hamlet of Mile-end Old-town, the hamlet of Mile-end New-town, the hamlet of Ratcliff, the precinct of St. Catharine, the liberty of Nortonfalgate, the several divisions of the liberty of the Tower ;— containing the north-eastern suburbs of the metropolis.

Population .... 293,000 | Qualifying tenements...... 23,000
Houses .... 65,000 | Assessed taxes £93,000

Wolverhampton.—The township of Wolverhampton, the township of Bilston, the township of Wednesfield, the township of Willenhall, the parish of Sedgeley ; containing the towns of Wolverhampton and Bilston, and their surrounding neighbourhood, including the villages of Sedgeley, Wednesfield, and Willenhall.

Population.............. 67,000 | Qualifying tenements........ 2,400
Houses .... 14,000 | Assessed taxes £6,200

SCHEDULE (D.)

Ashton-Under-Line.—Part of the parish of Ashton ;—containing the town of Ashton-under-Line, as limited by its Police Act.

Population .... 15,000 | Qualifying tenements........ 600
Houses .... 2,900 | Assessed taxes £1,400

Bury.—Township of Bury, part of the township of Elton ;—containing the town of Bury and its immediate neighbourhood.

Population.............. 19,000 | Qualifying tenements........ 750
Houses ....3,500 | Assessed taxes..............£2,200

Chatham.—Part of the parish of Chatham, part of the parish of Gillingham ; —containing the towns of Chatham and Brompton.

Population.............. 19,000 | Qualifying tenements........ 1,200
Houses .... 3,500 | Assessed taxes..............£3,500

Cheltenham.—The parish of Cheltenham ; containing the town of Cheltenham and its neighbourhood.

Population.............. 23,000 | Qualifying tenements........ 2,100
Houses .... 4,350 | Assessed taxes £21,000

Dudley.—The parish of Dudley ;—containing the towns of Dudley and its immediate neighbourhood, which includes the village of Netherton.

Population.............. 23,000 | Qualifying tenements........ 800
Houses .... 4,700 | Assessed Taxes £2,500

Frome.—Part of the parish of Frome ;—containing the town of Frome.

Population.............. 12,000 | Qualifying tenements........ 400
Houses .... — | Assessed taxes £1,960

Gateshead.—The parish of Gateshead, part of the chapelry of Heworth ;— containing the town of Gateshead and its neighbourhood south of the river Tyne.

Population .... 15,000 | Qualifying tenements...... 750
Houses................ 4,000 | Assessed taxes £2,000

Huddersfield.—The township of Huddersfield ;—containing the town of Huddersfield.

Population	19,000	Qualifying tenements	1,100
Houses	4,000	Assessed taxes	£3,900

Kidderminster.—The borough of Kidderminster, part of the foreign of Kidderminster ;—containing the town of Kidderminster.

Population	16,000	Qualifying tenements	500
Houses	3,100	Assessed taxes	£1,000

Kendal.—The township of Kirby Kendal, the township of Kirkland, the township of Nethergraveship ;—containing the town of Kendal and its neighbourhood.

Population	11,600	Qualifying tenements	680
Houses	2,200	Assessed taxes	£3,000

Rochdale.—Part of the township of Castleton, part of the township of Wandleworth, part of the township of Spotland, part of the township of Wuerdale with Wardle ;—containing the town of Rochdale.

Population	20,000	Qualifying tenements	1,000
Houses	3,000	Assessed taxes	£3,100

Salford.—The township of Broughton, the township of Salford, the township of Pendleton, part of the township of Pendlebury ;—containing the town of Salford and its neighbourhood north-west of the river Irwell.

Population	50,000	Qualifying tenements	1,300
Houses	9,500	Assessed taxes	£9,000

South Shields.—The township of South Shields, the township of Westoe ;—containing the town of South Shields and its neighbourhood, which includes the village of Westoe.

Population	18,600	Qualifying tenements	1,150
Houses	2,200	Assessed taxes	£1,600

Tynemouth.—The township of North Shields, township of Chirton, township of Tynemouth, township of Preston, township of Cullercoats ;—containing the towns of North Shields and Tynemouth, and their neighbourhood.

Population	25,000	Qualifying tenements	1,150
Houses	3,500	Assessed taxes	£2,800

Wakefield.—The township of Wakefield, part of the township of Alverthorpe, part of the township of Stanley ;—containing the town of Wakefield, and its immediate neighbourhood.

Population	12,500	Qualifying tenements	800
Houses	2,800	Assessed taxes	£1,730

Walsall.—The borough of Walsall ;—containing the town of Walsall with its neighbourhood.

Population	15,000	Qualifying tenements	800
Houses	3,000	Assessed taxes	£1,730

Warrington.—Township of Warrington, township of Latchford, part of township of Thelwall ;—containing the town of Warrington and its immediate neighbourhood.

Population	18,000	Qualifying tenements	1,000
Houses	3,400	Assessed taxes	£2,914

Whitehaven.—Township of Whitehaven, part of the township of Preston Quarter ;—containing the township of Whitehaven.

Population	15,700	Qualifying tenements	900
Houses	3,000	Assessed taxes	£2,000

Whitby.—Township of Whitby, the township of Ruswarp, the township of Hawsker-cum-Stainsacre ;—including the town of Whitby and its neighbourhood, which includes the villages of Hawsker, Ruswarp, and Stainsacre.

Population	10,300	Qualifying tenements	500
Houses	—	Assessed taxes	£2,000

No. IX.

Population, Electors, &c. of the Cities and Burghs of SCOTLAND.*

City or Burgh.	Population.	Houses.	Number of Electors.	Houses rated at £10 and upwards.
Aberdeen	26484	2187	19	1166
Inverbervie	1092	217	15	7
Aberbrothock	5817	734	19	136
Montrose	10338	1150	19	239
Brechin	5906	858	13	64
Ayr	7455	962	17	297
Irvine	7007	1037	17	105
Rothsay	4107	503	17	124
Campbeltown	6445	413	16	65
Inverary	1137	103	16	27
Crail	1854	344	21	11
Kilrenny	1494	247	15	—
Anstruther, East	1090	191	19	13
Anstruther, West	429	65	15	3
Pittenweem	1200	219	24	8
Dumfries	11052	1436	25	417
Sanquhar	1357	268	17	32
Annan	4486	808	21	123
Lochmaben	2651	591	15	8
Kirkcudbright	2595	348	17	62
Dysart	6529	959	24	20
Kirkaldy	4452	451	28	167
Kinghorn	2443	365	21	11
Burntisland	2136	260	21	32
Edinburgh	138253	9925	33	9382
Elgin	5308	1122	16	127
Cullen	1152	341	19	13
Banff	3855	708	17	118
Inverary	735	164	9	17
Kintore	312	79	13	5
Forfar	5897	827	19	72
Perth	19068	5304	26	561
Dundee	30575	2773	21	910
Cupar	5892	897	26	131
St. Andrews	4899	828	29	160
Fortrose	not stated	not stated	15	14
Inverness	12264	2240	21	221
Nairn	3228	699	17	38
Forres	3540	775	17	72

* The cities and burghs sharing together in the return of a member are placed between brackets. The number of persons in whom the elective franchise is vested is here stated.

City or Burgh.	Population.	Houses.	Number of Electors.	Houses rated at £10 and upwards.
Glasgow	147043	33805	32	6357
Renfrew	2646	366	19	8
Rutherglen	4091	549	18	49
Dumbarton	3481	365	15	77
Haddington	5255	834	25	71
Dunbar	5272	750	20	45
North Berwick	1694	237	12	8
Lauder	1845	359	17	9
Jedburgh	5251	826	25	76
Inverkeithing	2512	384	39	18
Dunfermline	13681	2106	22	147
Queensferry	690	80	21	21
Culross	1434	269	19	3
Stirling	7113	727	21	261
Kirkwall	2212	311	23	33
Wick	6713	1078	12	113
Dingall	2031	360	15	35
Dornoch	630	137	15	4
Tain	2861	583	15	27
Selkirk	2728	451	33	40
Peebles	2701	451	17	60
Linlithgow	4692	568	27	53
Lanark	7085	797	23	65
Wigton	2042	347	18	18
Stranrear	2463	417	18	28
New Galloway	not stated	not stated	18	2
Whithorn	2361	421	18	116

No. X.

Number of Parliaments held in each Reign, from 27th Edward I. A.D. 1299, to the End of the Reign of George IV.; also the respective length of each Reign.

	No. of Parliaments.	Length of Reign.		No. of Parliaments.	Length of Reign.
Edward I. from 1299,	8	8 years.	Mary	5	5 years.
Edward II.	15	20	Elizabeth	10	45
Edward III.	37	50	James I.	4	22
Richard II.	26	22	Charles I.	4	24
Henry IV.	10	14	Charles II.	8	36
Henry V.	11	9	James II.	3	4
Henry VI.	22	39	William III.	6	13
Edward IV.	5	22	Anne	6	12
Richard III.	1	2	George I.	2	13
Henry VII.	8	24	George II.	6	33
Henry VIII.	3	38	George III.	11	59
Edward VI.	2	6	George IV.	2	10

From this table it appears that in the 461 years preceding the reign of George III. there were 202 parliaments, whose average duration was 2½ years; and that in 210 years preceding the reign of Henry VIII. there were 143 parliaments, averaging rather less than 1½ year each. In the 69 years of the reigns of George III. and IV. there were only thirteen parliaments, averaging *five years and one-third* each. Hence we learn how greatly the duration of the same parliament has been extended in these latter days, resulting, no doubt, from the better understanding subsisting between the ministers of the Crown and the representatives of the people, which rendered frequent dissolutions unnecessary.

No. XI.

A List of those Places which formerly sent Members to Parliament and now do not.

Alresford.	Dunstable.	Kidderminster.	Pickering.
Aulton.	Dunster.	Kingston-on-	Raveners.
Axbridge.	Dudley.	Thames.	Ross.
Bamborough.	Doncaster.	Ledford.	South-Molton.
Basingstoke.	Dedington.	Langport.	Sherborne.
Berkhampstead.	Egremont.	Lidbury.	Spalding.
Blandford.	Exmouth.	Leeds.	Stoke.
Bishops-Stortford.	Ely.	Mere.	Tickhill.
Bradnesham.	Fareham.	Montacute.	Tonbridge.
Bradford.	Farnham.	Manchester.	Teignmouth.
Bromyard.	Fremington.	Melton-Mowbray.	Torrington.
Burford.	Glastonbury.	Medbury.	Wainfleet.
Chelmsford.	Grampound.	Newbury.	Wisbeach.
Conebrig.	Greenwich.	Odyham.	Whitney.
Crediton.	Halifax.	Overton.	Whitby.
Chard.	Highworth.	Poligreen.	Ware.
Chipping-Norton.	Jarvell.	Pershore.	Watchet.

In all *sixty-nine* boroughs, which sent members to parliament in different reigns, and which are now deprived of that right. Besides these, Mr. Oldfield has given a list of *ninety-seven* other boroughs which have charters, and most probably sent members at some former period since the reign of Edward I. but which are now disfranchised. From the reign of Edward I. to that of Charles II. boroughs have been created and annihilated, at the caprice of each successive monarch. The following will show at one view, the gradual alterations in the representation of the people.

No. XII.

SHIRES AND UNIVERSITIES.

		No. of Members.
Edward I.	and preceding monarchs, 37 counties	74
Henry VIII. ...	{ shires of Chester and Monmouth .... 4 } { 12 Welsh counties, 1 member each ....12 }	16
James I.	the two universities	4
Charles II.....	Durham county	5
Anne	30 Scotch counties, with one member each	30
George III. ..	Irish county members	64
	Irish university	1
George IV.....	Yorkshire county	2

193

CITIES AND BOROUGHS.

Edward I.	{ and preceding monarchs, created 78 boroughs, with 2 members each, and London with 4 }	160
Edward II....	created 6 boroughs, with 2 members each	12
Edward III. ..	{ created 9 boroughs, with 2 members each 18 restored 2 boroughs, with 2 members each 4 }	22
Henry VI.	{ created 5 boroughs, with 2 members each 10 restored 2 boroughs, with 2 members each 4 }	14
Edward IV. ..	{ created 3 boroughs, with 2 members each 6 restored 1 borough, with 2 members 2 }	8
Henry VIII. ..	{ created 4 boroughs, with 2 members each 8 created 12 Welsh boroughs 1 member each 12 created 1 borough, with 1 member 1 }	21
Edward VI. ..	{ created 14 boroughs, with 2 members each 28 restored 10 boroughs, with 2 members each 20 }	48
Mary	{ created 7 boroughs, with 2 members each 14 created 3 boroughs, with 1 member each 3 restored 2 boroughs, with 2 members each 4 }	21
Elizabeth	{ created 24 boroughs, with 2 members each 48 restored 8 boroughs, with 2 members each 16 }	64
James I.	{ created 3 boroughs, with 2 members each 6 created 1 borough, with 1 member each 1 restored 8 boroughs, with 2 members each 16 }	23
Charles I.	restored 9 boroughs, with 2 members each	18
Charles II.....	created 2 boroughs, with 2 members each	4
Anne	added 15 Scots boroughs 1 member each	15
George III. ..	added 35 Irish cities and boroughs	35
		465

RETROSPECTIVE GLANCE AT PAST HOUSES OF COMMONS.

> Hence chartered boroughs are such public plagues,
> And burghers, men immaculate perhaps
> In all their private functions, once combined,
> Become a loathsome body, only fit
> For dissolution, hurtful to the main.—*Cowper.*

In the puerile debates on the East Retford bill, sir R. Peel took up a sophism dropped by the late Mr. Canning; namely, that however just and expedient a reform in the representation might be, still he should oppose it, since it would compromise the safety of the monarchy. What an argument to address to the United Kingdom! Is the safety of the Crown and the Aristocracy to be put in competition with the wishes and welfare of twenty-four millions of people; or, if we include the population of the colonies and dependencies of the empire, with one hundred and fifty millions? The kingly office is only a trust for the public benefit, and the Peerage is instituted for a similar purpose: and shall the prerogatives of these be made a pretext for withholding justice and happiness from such an assemblage of human beings? But we deny either the Crown or Peerage would be compromised by parliamentary reform, between which and a governmeut of three orders we cannot discern an inherent incompatibility. Every community must have a head : we prefer a king to any other designation, and between the monarch and the commons an intermediate body may be interposed, without deranging the harmony of the system or erecting a barrier to popular rights. This intermediate body is the Peerage, or Aristocracy, and ought to be a real aristocracy, consisting of the *élite* of society, not deriving their functions from the accident of birth, but chosen, like the judges, *for life*. Such an innovation as this might compromise the corruptions of monarchy and aristocracy, they might involve a reduction in the civil list, and in the pensions and unearned salaries of the nobility; and it may be these Sir Robert contemplated ; but the loss of them would not be greatly deplored by the people of England, so long as the substance of the regal office and the legitimate functions of an upper chamber were preserved inviolate. It would relieve them at least of the pain of beholding the descendants of statesmen, heroes, and lawyers, dependent on sources of income which true nobility ought to spurn. They inherit name, and fame, and rank, but no bread. A poor lord is a poor thing, and the natural prey of a corrupt or ambitious Minister. What will not a pauper peer, dependent on a paltry sinecure or pension, with a fashionable wife and a crowd of infant nobility about her—very hungry, and what is worse, very capricious and luxurious— do for *quarter day*?

It may be truly said England has yet to establish a constitution. France and America are the only countries which can answer the challenge—If you have a constitution produce it? An Englishman, if asked, where is the constitution of which you boast? must answer, it exists by a sort of inference from what a half hundred hirelings have written, and in which they all contradict each other, and are the whole of them contradicted by daily practice in every transaction of state. In every part the renovated French constitution, under king Philip, is an improvement on the principles of the English government. We shall select a few points of comparison.

The French charter is announced as the right of the people, not the grant of the Crown. It abolishes the censorship of the press. The dramatic censorship exists in England in great rigour, and the powers of the attorney-general are an indirect censorship—a suspended despotism—which, aided by the stamp-duties, and the law of securities, fetter the freedom of discussion. The sittings of the two chambers are declared public : the debates of our parliament are by law declared secret, and are published only by connivance at the illegality. The French deputies are elected only for five years, ours for seven. A confiscation of goods is abolished ;—in England, children may be attainted in blood for the delinquencies of their parents, and punished by confiscation of their father's property. Peers in France cannot vote till they are twenty-five years of age : in England they vote at twenty-one, and by proxy, without hearing the discussion. Half the members must be resident: in England, one-half the members have no knowledge of the boroughs they represent.   The French government, without professing to be of any religion, grants not only equal toleration, but equal provision for the maintenance of every Christian sect: the English government adopts one creed, and subjects to neglect every other.   In short, the French constitution is, in all respects, what the English pretends to be, except in the impossible theory of three equal and co-existing branches of the legislature.   In France, the commons are triumphant, the peers subordinate, and the king only the premier, or first public minister: in England, a surreptitious branch of the constitution has been predominant—the boroughmongers.

To all complaints against our defective representation, Mr. Canning had but one reply—*It works well.*   Any government is better than no government; and, consequently, they must all work well.   It was time, however, for that great Pacific Ocean, the English public, to look about them, and see whether other governments did not work better. While John Bull has been dozing under the political drug, it works well, his more vigilant neighbours in France have laughed him to scorn, and bravely achieved a government that works better.   Having compared the principles of the two governments, let us next compare, not theories, charters, and paper-constitutions, but simply the working well; acknowledging, however, *imprimis*, that in *working a people*, no government ever worked half so well as that of England.

Who does not remember the incessant goadings in the house of commons to acknowledge the free republics of South America, and the sophistry, concealments, and shuffling to put off the recognition?   The French government, before it was a month old, declared its recognition.

We have been chuckling and rejoicing over Mr. Fox's libel bill for the last forty years.   The French have at once determined that all offences of the press shall be subject to the adjudication of a jury.

What nauseating debates have occurred session after session, to induce the government to rescue the black population of our Colonies from a brutal tyranny.   The French have already given all the rights and privileges of citizenship to their negroes, and are adopting measures for the effective protection of the African race.

What eloquent and endless declamation there has been on the increasing influence of the Crown, from the increased expenditure, and the augmentation of the Peerage.   Within a few days of its first sitting, the French Chamber struck off the roll ninety-three peers of the creation of Charles X. and last year made a bolder step by the abolition of the hereditary right of legislation.

Every session has produced its exposure of jobs, which generate like the polypus, and are quite as indestructible.   The Dundas and Bathurst and the South-American missions were the jobs of the Tories, and the Plunket doings those of the Whigs.   The French are subjecting their pension-list, their dead weight, and the ecclesiastical and civil salaries to rigid investigation and close curtailment.

Every session produced its scores of motions for economy, finance committees, judicial inquiries, and what not.   They all ended in nothing but bills of charges for commissioners, secretaries, office-keepers, and so forth. The most ridiculous, and almost the last farce of the Tories, was the mock trial of the East Retford electors, and the passing laws to indemnify witnesses for their evidence in proof of corruption! Lastly, observe what the French have done in regard to capital punishments. We have been nibbling for half a century at our savage treason laws : in the session of 1830 an abortive attempt was made to abolish capital punishment for forgery; the French have voted for the abolition of the punishment of death for *all political offences.*

Instead of a working government, the Borough System has been the laziest institution in the world for any purpose save evil doing—a mere congerie of formalities, parade, and ostentation. The Parliament, for a century, has been little better than a common debating club, where a mob of gentlemen met, during the winter season, to spend their evenings in cracking jokes and spouting nonsense. It has been mere play at shuttlecock between the rival disputants, who, in alternately changing from one side of the house to the other, have amused themselves in reciprocally throwing back their opponents' arguments, phrases, and opinions : all the time the nation has been looking on the logomachy quite seriously, as if it were real business, instead of a sham fight— harmless pastime for those who had no better employment : but the game is up!

ANALYSIS OF THE HOUSE OF COMMONS ELECTED IN 1830.

Relations of peers	256
Placemen and pensioners	217
Officers in the army	89
Officers in the navy	24
Lawyers	54
East India interests	62
West India interests	35
Bankers	33
Agricultural interests	356
Miscellaneous	51

Many of the members belonged to several classes or interests, and have been enumerated in each, which swells the nominal number of individuals. It is apparent that the vast majority were connected with the Peerage, the Army, Navy, Courts of Law, Public Offices, and Colonies; and, in lieu of representing the People, only represented those interests over which it is the constitutional object of a real House of Commons to exercise a watchful and efficient control.

APPENDIX.

INNS OF COURT AND CHANCERY.

IN our chapter on Corporations we might have properly included a short notice of the present state of the Inns of Court. They form incorporated foundations, originally intended for the study of the law and advancement of legal science; and grew out of the violent contests between the clergy and laity respecting the introduction of the civil law into this country, the former being anxious to make it the law of the land, and the latter, with equal pertinacity, insisting on being governed by the municipal or common law. As the clergy had the control of the universities, the professors of the common law were excluded from them, and constrained to establish an university for themselves. This they did by purchasing, at various times, certain houses and lands between the city of Westminster, the place of holding the king's courts, and the city of London, for advantage of ready access to the one, and plenty of provisions in the other.—*Chit. Bl. C.* 18. Here they naturally fell into collegiate order—exercises were performed, lectures read, and other immunities of the regular universities assumed. After being established some time, the crown took them under protection ; and more effectually to encourage them, Henry III. issued an order, directed to the mayor and sheriffs of London, prohibiting law to be taught any where else in the metropolis, except by these bodies. He also formed the members of each inn or lodging house into a corporation, and established rules for their regulation. The societies, feeling their importance, began to exercise the privilege of bestowing rank upon their students of a certain standing, and conferred the degrees of barrister and serjeant, corresponding to those of bachelor and doctor in the universities.

From Dugdale and Stow it appears James I. made a grant by letters patent of the premises of the middle and inner temple to the benchers of both societies, to have and to hold the same mansions, gardens, and appurtenances, &c. to themselves, their heirs and assigns for ever, for lodging, reception, and *education of the professors and students* of the laws of the realm, yielding and paying to the same king, &c. the sum of £10 a year for each of the temples. That a similar grant for *the same purpose* was made of Gray's Inn, by Henry VIII. for a rent of £6 : 13 : 4; that the fee simple of Lincoln's Inn was conveyed to the benchers of that society, for the same object, in the reign of Elizabeth; that the fee simple of Clements Inn and Lyons Inn is vested in the society of the Inner Temple ; that of the New Inn, in the Society of the Middle Temple; that of Barnard's Inn and Staple's Inn, in the society of Gray's Inn ; that Thavie's Inn and Furnival's Inn belonged to the Society of Lincoln's Inn. The latter was sold by that society a few years ago. Such is a brief outline of the origin and objects of the inns of court and of chancery. To enter more minutely into the history of these societies would be foreign to our purpose ; our object in stating the foregoing facts is to shew that these institutions were founded for the purpose of *promoting legal knowledge ;* that the different estates above enumerated were conferred on the societies for the advancement of that object; that the mode prescribed for carrying it into effect was by giving public instructions in the different inns, and that such instructions were actually given at the period when those estates were granted to the benchers. It is unnecessary to state that the benchers have ever since been in the reception of the profits of these estates, and that no legal instructions have for a long time been given in the inns of court, or any measures adopted to direct the application of those who may feel disposed to study. At the Inner Temple the exercises are compounded for by the payment of money. In the Middle Temple the form is observed, but with no real utility. These inns, with Gray's Inn and Lincoln's Inn, are the only societies the members whereof are called to the bar. Admission to the inns of chancery, which are Barnard's Inn, Staple's Inn, Furnival's Inn, Lyon's Inn, Thavies' Inn, Clement's Inn, Clifford's Inn, and New Inn, would now be of no avail in obtaining a call to the bar.

Two reasons may be assigned for the decline of the inns of court as seminaries of legal instruction. First, the more eminent of the profession find it more advantageous to aspire to the receipt of the profitable fees in the courts of law, the possession of rich legal sinecures, and the higher offices of state, than to devote themselves to the teaching the principles of judicial knowledge. The second reason we consider to be that assigned by a writer in the *Legal Examiner*—namely, the irresponsible character of the benchers, who, not being accountable for the revenues at their disposal, feel no disposition to part with them, nor listen to improvements which might disturb the exercise of their authority. They also possess irresponsible power in conferring the degree of barrister, and may even refuse to admit any person a student in the inns of court, and cannot be compelled to assign reasons for such refusal *(King's Bench, M.T.* 1825*):* thus possessing authority arbitrarily to exclude any individual from the most seductive department of the profession.

From the known character of many of the Benchers, it is a subject of surprise the defective administration of the inns of court has so long escaped notice; it can only have arisen from that *esprit de corp* which usually renders individuals averse from any proceeding which savours of a betrayal of their own cast; and, if they be of a reforming spirit, induces them to apply to objects foreign or extraneous to their fraternity. In the list of benchers of Lincoln's Inn we find the distinguished name of Henry Brougham, synonymous with universal hostility to abuses. There is also sir Thomas Denman, the ex-officio prosecutor of malversation and violated trusts by incorporated bodies. There is also the celebrated Jeremy Bentham, who has devoted a long life to the task of legal improvement, not only in this but most other countries. Those eminent individuals, we doubt not, are wholly guiltless of participation in the mal-administration of their brethren; perhaps there are few subjects with which they are so little acquainted. The government of the inns of court, we suspect, like that of the city companies and most corporations, has fallen into the hands of a few intriguers, or of those who have no higher or more lucrative objects of ambition. But this is no justification of the specific abuses of the law establishments. The benchers are self-elected bodies, accountable to no superior, consisting of about one hundred and twenty individuals, in the receipt, it has been calculated, of £60,000 a year, granted to them in trust to promote legal knowledge, yet not one shilling of these revenues do they expend in forwarding that object. This is quite as bad as the Gresham lectures in the city; it is a state of things that ought not to pass uninvestigated: every student, we apprehend, who is entered of the inns of court, is a shareholder in the funds of the society to which he belongs, and may rightfully demand that they shall be administered in the advancement of these ends for which they were originally granted.

Some years ago sir James Scarlett had a project on foot for raising the scholastic and other qualifications of aspirants to the bar. Should this design still be entertained, an improvement in the institutions of the inns of court, and the administration of the revenues, might be rendered auxiliary to the proposed undertaking. If it be true, that out of one thousand and fifty-four barristers there are only *twenty* capable of filling the situation of puisne judge, it is high time some change was introduced, both for the advantage of the community and legal students. With such a limited number of individuals qualified for judicial appointments, the choice of Ministers is restricted, and the salaries of the judges maintained at a monopoly standard.

TRINITY COLLEGE, DUBLIN.*

THE revenues of " The College of the Holy and undivided Trinity of Queen Elizabeth, near Dublin" are kept so masonically secret, that, up

---

* We have received the account of this institution from a correspondent in Dublin, well known in that city and also to the English Public. With respect to its accuracy, we can only say, that we will promptly correct any error that may be pointed out from an authentic source; but at the same time we warn the College that partial contradictions, unaccompanied by plain statements of income and expenditure, can do no service to that establishment.

to this hour, all is mystery without. Conjectures and statements have been, at different times, made by men supposed to be capable of judging, and who had graduated within the blessed precincts, but they are all vague and uncertain. A general opinion is, that the land revenues are about £60,000 a year, and that the profit on the board and lodging of the fellow commoners and pensioners, fees, fines, and other sources of income, pay so much of the expenses as to leave £30,000 or, as some think, £40,000 surplus. One account has been published, stating that it had in one county alone (Armagh) 60,000 acres, but that a good part was let so low as 6s. per acre. Those old leases are, however, occasionally dropping, and of course increasing the college revenue. It has also very good estates in Donegal and Kerry, estimated some fifteen or twenty years ago at upwards of £15,000 rent. Besides, it possesses many excellent Dublin holdings in ground rents and houses, that are all valuable. It was James I. who gave the Ulster estates, and also a pension of £358 : 15. In your list of composition tithes (page 148) Trin. Col. Dub. is sprinkled here and there, but that is nothing to the actual presentation which it holds as a matter of right, and dispenses at pleasure. A writer, evidently favourable to the college, says that it has nineteen benefices of from £500 to £1000 a year, and that their value is constantly increasing. That was thirty years ago—what must they be worth now ?

There are seven senior and eighteen junior fellows. The latter, who are the teachers, have, *it is said*, £400 (some say £500) a year, with lodging and commons (board); but they make from £800 to £1000, and even above £1800 more by tuition ; for all the students, whether intern or extern, must pay for that separately, and they can choose their own teacher, though great efforts were made to deprive them of that right. Some restrictions would, however, be judicious, as I shall hereafter shew. The charges for tuition will be noticed in another place.

The senior fellows have, *it is said*, £1000 (some say £1200) a year, a church living in some particular cases, and a lucrative post or two, as vice-provost; bursar, librarian, and catechist (here are three); senior proctor ; senior dean and auditor, &c. &c.; though these were formerly distinct places. The junior fellows also hold places like the senior, though less valuable, as registrar, censor, junior dean, junior proctor, sub-librarian, professorships, assistant ditto, morning lecturers, preachers, &c. &c.

We now come to the door, for we can get no farther, of the grand arcanum. Those seven senior fellows with the provost form the actual government of the college, and it is believed that none else are let into the mysteries of revenue, and that until a junior gets to be a senior, which he one day devoutly expects, he is not entrusted with the grand secret, which has been kept with a fidelity almost unexampled. The question then is, what is done with the alleged surplus ? Here we non-masons are all left to guesses, and I can only tell you what people think. No one supposes that any of the junior fellows get much of it— indeed, the popular opinion is, they get none ; because if they did they would not work so hard as they do at tuition. The common opinion is, that a good part is shared amongst the senior government; and surely, if this be false, it would be very easy for the college to disprove what brings it into, perhaps, unmerited disrepute. While the public are left to mere conjecture, they will inevitably believe in the worst reports.

Let it not be thought by Englishmen, that Trinity College, Dublin, is merely a local Irish subject, with which they have no concern. If " what every one says must be true," it is *the wealthiest university in the world*, although it has scarcely 2000 students, while Oxford and Cambridge together have nearly 10,000, and it is the duty of English members to bring the subject under parliamentary investigation. Concealment in one great instance sanctions it in another, and it is this that leads to such abuses and misapplications of the public money. We know how the *honest* portion of the London press advocated secrecy in the Bank of England, when, a few years ago, a wish was expressed for a yearly exposé similar to the Bank of Paris. Old Trinity, like the church, always appears to be much hurt by the frequent guesses at her wealth; but, until we have an authentic statement, it is natural for the public to presume that its income is enormous, and that a vast portion of it is not applied as intended. Why not set all those conjectures, that it would call malicious, or ill founded—why not set them at rest for ever by a candid statement? The public have a right to such statement, for the college is endowed with the property of the nation, no matter by what name, royal grants or otherwise, it might have been given; and parliament has also lavished large sums in the buildings at different times. While authentic information is unattainable by the public, can they be blamed for believing in the worst reports? Can they be blamed for believing that there is something which will not bear the light? The college threatens actions—that is the way it answers charges. About four years ago the Freeman's Journal ventured on some animadversions, but it was silenced by a threat of law proceedings. Now this never did any thing for a public establishment but to excite and confirm suspicion, hatred, and disgust, nor will it ever make people believe in the purity of the college. What though the directors are all in holy orders, they are but men, and therefore peccable. The charter of Charles I. granted in lieu of Elizabeth's, requires that the bursar give in, on the 20th November in each year, an accurate account of all receipts and disbursements, and copy same into a book. Now that book is kept—else the charter is void. " Show, show, show " (Macbeth). That would be the proper way to answer alleged libels.

Old Trinity is, like the church, so very tenacious of change in technicals, that it is still " near " Dublin, though it has been above a century *in* it, and is now more in the centre of our city than Ludgate-hill is in London. This very absurdity would form cogent grounds for a new and improved charter for Trinity College *in* Dublin, there being now no such thing as Trinity College *near* Dublin. There is something more than humour in this remark, and I wish it to be taken very seriously.

Yet, still, like the church, Old Trinity permits changes beneficial to revenue. In 1793 Catholics were admitted as students in this orthodox

establishment, which assuredly was a great innovation on its unsullied
Protestant charter.   No matter for that—it materially served the fiscal
department, for the students, who had been fluctuating between 5 and
700, rose in a few years to 1000, and are now nearly 2000.   But
again—there were then fifteen junior fellows or teachers for 500, and
now there are but three additional for three times the number.   What
prodigious spirit and liberality !   Their labours are indeed so great, that
even an archbishop of Dublin, in defending the University from the
charge of " silent sister," did not hesitate to declare them excessive.
His grace clearly showed that they left the teachers no leisure for au-
thorship, but it did not occur to him at the time, that he was making
a heavy charge against the college itself, which the worthy prelate
otherwise treats with all the tenderness due to a high-church-loving
establishment.   The charter sets no limit to the number of junior fellows, and Charles began with nine, " in the name of more," when there
were not, perhaps, 100 students.

The following are some extracts of yearly salaries and charges from
the charter : —

Provost, £100 ; senior fellow, £9. 13. 4.; junior fellow, £3 ; catechist, £13. 6. 8.; sub-dean, £4 ; junior ditto, £2 ; lecturer, £4 ;
bursar, £10 ; librarian, £3.   With lodging and commons.

Scholars.—Natives, £3, not natives 10s.   With lodging and commons.

The junior fellows or teachers not to charge more for tuition than £4
for a fellow commoner, £2 for a pensioner, and 20s. for a sizer.

College to be charged no more than 4s. 4½d. a week for the commons
of a fellow, and 1s. 9½d. for a scholar.   This was fixed by George II.,
who also raised the salary of the librarian to £60, to which office he
attached great importance and responsibility ; but he left all other
salaries and charges as in the charter   No official mention of sub-
librarian appears any where.

Having given these very necessary extracts, we must now speak
particularly of scholars and sizers.   Scholars are deserving students,
not lower than junior sophister, who stand an examination in logic, and
though the post cannot be held beyond the five years, and the advantages are very trifling, it is eagerly sought.   What must we then think
of Old Trinity's liberality, when the number is still but 70, as fixed
by Charles ?   Yes, this college, which has made such numerous bye-
laws and changes for renewal and other purposes, here sticks religiously
to the charter !   Do we wish them to break it ?   No, but we wish no
partial observances.   Let it be either " the whole charter, and nothing
but the charter," or let the deviations be generally liberal.   The provost
and senior fellows know full well, that leave would be readily granted to
increase the scholars, and why not here apply to government ?   But we
have more to say about the scholars, and shall leave them for the present,
in order to notice the sizers.

The free students or sizers were directed, by the statutes of Charles,
to be used as servants, to wait at table, feed on the fragments, and do
menial offices in the college.   Of the baseness, the meanness, and the
cruelty of this, we cannot form a just estimation without recollecting

that they were Protestants—were they Papists, the thing might find a justification in the persecuting spirit of the times, but we have seen that none were admitted till 1793. Can we possibly imagine any mode of giving charity more revolting or detestable? Is it not something like inhumanly flinging our alms in the face of the humble mendicant? A show is made of fostering indigent talent, while it is wounded and repressed by the bitterest mortification that can be well conceived. This was Charles's refined notion of rearing up spirited Protestants, who were afterwards to declaim against the slavish and degrading institutions of popery. Yet, on a vacancy occurring, it is common to have 150 candidates, who must already know more Greek and Latin than is necessary for a *filius nobilis* to obtain a degree at Oxford. The best answerer in a most severe examination is admitted; and he, though a mere boy, has often sufficient *lore* to qualify, as times go, for a classical professor. It is but justice, however, to say that, about the beginning of the present century, the college relaxed a great deal of its *authorised* severity towards those interesting objects, from whose ranks have sprung some of the finest geniuses that could adorn any country. Yet the number is still but thirty, as originally fixed by Charles! O the charter—how beautifully inviolable it appears in some cases! So, then, the scholars must never exceed seventy, nor the sizers thirty, no matter how the college revenues augment!

Come we now to some most important considerations. No one will maintain that the salaries of Charles, though doubtless liberal enough at the time, would answer for the present day. Accordingly, we find, on the authority of T. Swift, of whom we shall have occasion to speak hereafter, that thirty-seven years ago the provost had £3000, the bursar £2000, and the junior fellows £90. Look now to preceding page, and it will be seen that the first and last exhibit an increase of exactly thirty fold, and the bursar two hundred fold, over the charter salaries. And if it be true that the junior fellows have now £400, that is an increase of one hundred and thirty-three fold. Now, how were these augmentations made? Through bye-laws, no doubt; but why not keep *cæteris paribus* in view. Why keep the scholars to the now miserable allowances of Charles? Answer that. Tell us why, at only taking thirty fold as a standard, they are not allowed £90 a-year; for they are now, perhaps, all natives? Tell us whether 1s. 9d. a week is not still, in some cases, the calculation for their commons; and tell us, is there no more than 4s. 4½d. for that of a fellow?

Look again to former page for tuition. The charge for a pensioner now is, entrance (of which there is no mention in the charter) £14 : 5 : 0, and £6 : 8 : 0 for first *half* year, and it goes on rising according to class. I have not ascertained, precisely, the charges for a fellow commoner, but I find that they are *considerably* higher. So much for the sacred charter and tuition. I do not know what is now allowed for the sizers, but, as there are not two a piece for the teachers, it is of no consequence.

All the fellows, " big and little," are, with the exception of three, obliged to be *priested*, in order to fill up the college benefices as they become vacant. We are now approaching some of the university mysteries. No institution has succeeded so well in getting favourable reports in books as this. Look into any of the most independent English works that mention Trinity College, Dublin, and you would suppose it faultless as any thing human could be expected; but the truth is, that they have all been deceived for want of authentic information. The only attempt worth notice, at a fearless exposé, of which I have heard, was by a gentleman named Theophilus Swift, in a pamphlet published 1794, which is now out of print and very scarce. He brings numerous grave charges against the entire college system, and particularly as regarding not only education, but competency for tuition. Those I shall pass, but he makes one accusation of great importance,—that mulcts and fines were vexatiously multiplied on the pupils, so as to amount to no less than £8000 a-year, " which was all swept into the fobs of the fellows." For this, and, particularly observe, for this only, he was served with notice of an action for " libel." Swift called for a fair account of receipts and disbursements, and this is the way that he is answered ! He also states that a living worth £1000 a-year was refused by eight junior fellows, and was only accepted by the ninth in rotation, because he wished a quiet life. See what an answer this is to the *authentic* accounts we read, of a senior fellowship being worth "perhaps" £1000 a-year, and a junior " perhaps" £700 or £800 a-year, when £1000 was actually spurned at by a junior near forty years ago. To us, in Dublin, such accounts are quite mawkish—they appear, at best, like the miracle of the five loaves and fishes, when we see senior fellows keeping splendid town mansions, beautiful country seats, carriages, livery servants, and living altogether at a rate immeasurably above our notions of a thousand a-year. The fact is that we know nothing of fellowship incomes, for the whole machinery is managed with admirable dexterity. Thus the present (now the late) provost, Kyle, has accepted the bishopric of Cork, estimated at £6000 a-year, and, of course, that would seem to say that the provostship was not worth so much. We have seen what Swift says of the salary, and there is, besides, a princely mansion, with all the other nameless &c.'s, and the place is at this day so valuable, that some carry their estimates as high as £8,000 or £10,000 a-year. Why, then, accept one of only a-third the amount ? In explaining this, it is necessary to observe that the patronage of the Cork see is said to be worth from £10,000 to £30,000 a-year,—no contemptible source for a family provision ; but suppose it had no patronage, the new bishop does not calculate on remaining there always. There is, you know, such a thing as translation—you, Mr. Editor, as a learned man, understand that. So, if a senior fellow is vacated to accept a living of £1000 a-year, it is no proof that his fellowship was not worth above treble. But these apparent phenomena help to silence the vulgar inquirer, who understandeth not translation, collation, or the beauties of Christian-like expectancy.

We can now plainly see that Trinity College, Dublin, is, in essence and substance, a church establishment, and some light on its political character may be interesting. The suppression of the celebrated Historical Society, that produced so many great men, is well known, and I shall only observe that, about sixteen or eighteen years ago, Locke on Government was expelled to make room for Butler's Analogy of revealed Religion. You know the two works, Mr. Editor, and you can judge of the spirit that actuates the only university in a country with eight millions of inhabitants.

No Catholic can remain in college after he have finished his course, as he cannot be a scholar, nor be admitted to a higher degree than Bachelor of Arts.

None but the provost, fellows, and scholars, have a vote for the parliamentary representative.

From all these considerations, the following are among some improvements that naturally suggest themselves : —

1. That the real yearly revenue of the college, in lands and otherwise, and from fines, entrance, or other fees, board and lodging of fellow commoners and pensioners, tuitions, &c. and the total expenditure, say for ten years last past, be published. This is necessary, to inspire confidence and respect ; for no one can conceive why there should be any secrecy in the pecuniary concerns of a NATIONAL establishment, assuredly for the advancement of learning.

2. That, if any surplus appear over and above a reasonable fund for contingencies of building or repairing, it should, in the first instance, be applied to giving the scholars the increased allowances to which they are as fairly entitled as the provost and fellows.

3. That, after adjusting the rights of the scholars, any further surplus should be applied to extending the sizers to one hundred — a number which would still be by no means proportioned to other augmentations. The scholars, too, should be increased, but not until after the sizers were one hundred. And a charge, now exacted from the sizers for lodging, not mentioned in the charter, should be abolished.

4. That the number of junior fellows should be regulated by that of the students, which would be very easy ; for if they decreased, a vacant junior fellowship need not be filled up. None of them to have less than a certain number of pupils, say fifty, and while that remained uncompleted, no new student should be allowed to choose his teacher. Such a regulation would be found most equitable and serviceable.

5. That the junior, or, at least, the senior sophisters have the right of voting for a parliamentary representative for the college.

6. That Catholics should be eligible to scholarships. For fellowships, the church being the fountain of college promotion, I do not think they could or would expect a participation, as the constitution of the establishment should be entirely changed to allow their admission : but to scholarships there cannot be any reasonable objection.

I now tell the college that petulant or dogmatical contradictions, or actions at law, will avail nothing, while the whole revenue and disbursement are unknown to the public. A new charter and statutes for Trinity College in Dublin, should certainly be recommended to parliament. We shall, no doubt, hear a great deal of *fudge* about the sacredness of charters, but that is mere fustian, with the precedent of Charles before us, who did nothing less than *abrogate* the original of Elizabeth—with the example of George II., who altered as much as he thought proper of Charles's; and, finally, with the admission of Catholics by the act of an Irish parliament, and which was rather aided than opposed by the college, as could be easily demonstrated. An improved charter would ultimately serve the college itself, by making it a popular and respected establishment, instead of being, as it now is, an object of suspicion, monopoly, and unfavourable report, and one of which the public are ready to believe the very worst rumours.

PARLIAMENTARY REPRESENTATION.

RETURN of the population, according to the census of 1821 and 1831, of all towns or cities in *England*, exceeding a population of ten thousand, to which it is not intended by the Reform Bill to give representatives.

City or Town.	Population in 1821.	Population in 1831.
LANCASHIRE:		
Toxteth Park	12,829	24,067
Spotland	13,453	15,325
MIDDLESEX:		
Chelsea	26,860	32,371
Kensington	14,428	20,902
STAFFORDSHIRE:		
Kingswinford	11,022	15,156
Tipton	11,546	14,951
YORKSHIRE:		
Saddleworth	13,902	15,986

An Account of the Amount actually Expended under each Head of Service in the years 1829 and 1830; and an Estimate for the Year 1831.

Heads of Service.	The Amount Actually expended in 1829	1830	The Estimated Expenditure in the Year 1831.	Savings on Grants as stated in the Finance Accounts for the Years ended Jan. 5, 1829 and 1831. pages 162 and 154. as granted, and parts of the Ways and Means for 1829 and 1831.	The probable Amount of Grants Unexpended on the 5th Jan. 1832.	Total Amount which might have been Expended in 1829, 1830, & 1831.
	£ s. d.	£ s. d.	£ s. d.	£ s. d.	£ s. d.	£ s. d.
For Army	7,709,372 6 9	6,991,163 7 4¼	7,404,416 0 0	126,475 5 0½	1,745,087 0 1¾	23,979,513 19 3½
,, Navy	5,902,339 1 10	5,399,605 17 5	5,675,787 0 0	..	1,619,692 18 3	18,407,354 17 4
,, Ordnance	1,569,150 0 0	1,613,908 0 0	1,362,444 0 0	..	640,817 0 0	5,186,919 0 0
,, Miscellaneous	2,410,105 7 1	1,891,608 13 4	..	97,014 9 2	..	8,455,986 17 2¼
,, Services formerly paid out of the Civil List	..	160,415 3 11¼	2,307,316 0 0	..	1,589,596 3 7½	
,, Interest on Exchequer Bills	..	720,873 0 2	..	..	29,126 19 10	2,142,252 5 10
	17,590,968 15 6	16,687,574 2 3	16,659,963 0 0	..	..	
,, Interest on Exchequer Bills not voted	792,252 5 10	..	600,000 0 0	..	..	
Services not voted	75,555 5 3	58,500 0 0	..	..	..	191,055 6 3
	18,458,774 6 7	16,746,074 2 3	17,259,963 0 0	223,489 14 2½	5,624,180 1 10½	58,305,481 4 10¾

SUMS EXPENDED UNDER THE HEAD OF CIVIL CONTINGENCIES
IN 1831.

The amount expended for furniture, ironmongery, &c. for Whitehall Chapel, apartments of the officers of the guards, and for
the Tower, in the three quarters ended June 30, 1831 · · · · · · £336
Ditto for robes, collars, badges, &c. for knights of the several
orders, in the same period · 2578
Ditto for repairing the King's crown, maces, badge, &c., gold
and silver sticks, officers attending proclamation of His Majesty's accession, in the same period · · · · · · · · · · · · · · · · · 511
Ditto for plate supplied to Lord Melbourne, upon his appointment
as secretary of state, in the quarter ended 30th June 1831 · · 488
The commission for inquiring into the state of His Majesty's settlements, the Cape of Good Hope, Ceylon and Mauritius · · 14830
The commission for inquiring into fees in the courts of justice;
on account of remuneration and expenses · · · · · · · · · · · · · · 3662
The commission for inquiring into the law of real property; on
account of expenses · 1044
The commission for inquiring into the practice, &c. of the ecclesiastical courts · 1639
The commission for carrying into effect the convention signed at
London on the 29th September 1827, between His Majesty
and the United States of America, stipulating the reference
to the arbitration of a friendly sovereign, of the disputed points
of boundary under the 5th article of the Treaty of Ghent · · · · 3000
The commission for carrying into effect certain stipulations relative to the demarcation of the boundaries of the new state of
Greece, agreed upon between the plenipotentiaries of the
allied powers, parties to the treaty signed at London on the
6th July 1827 · 962
The amount paid on account of R. Lander's late expedition of
discovery to Africa · 853
The amount paid for relief of certain distressed Spanish subjects
residing in this country, wholly without the means of subsistence, who had been employed with the British army, or under
British authorities in Spain, or who had otherwise rendered
service to our military operations in that country · · · · · · · · · 12420
Expense of creating Admiral sir James Saumarez a baron of
the United Kingdom, in reward for public services · · · · · · · · 556
T. Wyon, esq. chief engraver of His Majesty's Mint, for en-
graving great and other seals for the courts of Exchequer,
&c., and for silver medals for native chiefs on the River
Gambia · 1428

The amount issued to C. Babbage, to enable him to proceed in constructing a machine for the calculation of various tables £2000

Ditto to defray the expenses incurred in publishing the natural history of the late expedition to Behring's Straits 236

Ditto to J. Richards, for salary to himself and clerk, and for travelling and other contingent expenses of his mission of survey in North America ································· 1600

Ditto to pay the fees on the nomination of certain officers to be Honorary Knights Commanders and Companions of the Order of the Bath ································· 210

Ditto to pay the fees on the installation of his serene Highness Augustus William Maximilian Frederick Lewis, reigning Duke of Brunswick, Knight Companion of the most noble Order of the Garter ································· 439

Ditto to pay the fees on the nomination of Count Munster, to be a Knight Grand Cross of the most honourable Order of the Bath ································· 330

Ditto ditto for the maintenance and care of two incurable lunatics, for three years to 5th April 1831 ····················· 300

Ditto ditto in removing the records belonging to the court of common pleas, from Westminster Hall to the Old Mews, Charing-cross ································· 849

Ditto to the minister and churchwarden of St. James's, in the island of Nevis, towards erection of a church there ········ 500

Ditto to Dr. J. Bowring, in reimbursement of the expenses incurred by him and in remuneration for his services in reporting upon the public accounts of France ····················· 908

Ditto to T. Telford, to defray expenses already incurred in his survey for supplying the metropolis with pure water, and to enable him to proceed with the same ················· 1000

Ditto to defray the expenses incurred on account of, and for services connected with the Cholera Morbus ················· 1934

Ditto to defray the expenses incurred in England and Scotland, in procuring information relative to the boundaries of different cities and boroughs ································· 6623

Ditto to T. Marshall, to enable him to complete a series of statistical tables of the resources of the British empire ········ 500

Ditto to pay rewards offered by His Majesty's proclamation of the 23d November 1830, for the discovery, &c. of the offenders in the districts at that time in a disturbed state, and to discharge expenses connected therewith ····················· 32000

His excellency the Marquess of Anglesey, the usual equipage money allowed the lord lieutenant on his arrival in Ireland ·· 2769

Right honourable lord Plunket, lord chancellor of Ireland, the like on his appointment························· 923

N. B. We have only extracted a few of the items; the total expenditure under the head of civil contingences in 1831, was £174,657.

An Account of the Sum paid in 1829, for Half Pay and Retired
Superannuated Allowances ; distinguishing the amount under separate
Heads and Departments.

ARMY.

Army pay of general officers	140,362	12	6
Retired full pay, half pay, and military allowances	866,431	12	7
Militia adjutants and serjeant majors	11,202	17	6
Local militia adjutants	17,205	14	0
Out-pensioners of Chelsea and Kilmainham hospitals	1,328,797	7	1
In-pensioners of do. do.	40,215	0	9
Widows' pensions	151,226	5	9
Compassionate list	37,592	5	0
Royal bounties	31,561	0	9
Pensions for wounds	119,167	17	7
Foreign half-pay	79,067	13	8
Foreign pensions, including allowances to widows and children of deceased foreign officers	18,712	10	0
Superannuation allowances	48,462	19	0
Commissariat	46,545	5	9
Royal military asylum	345	13	9
			—2,939,896 15 8

NAVY.

HALF-PAY :

To flag-officers, captains, commanders, lieutenants, pursers, masters, and surgeons	824,504	6	4
To royal marine officers	51,113	2	10

SUPERANNUATIONS, PENSIONS, AND ALLOWANCES :

To officers, &c. in the military line of service	127,174	16	5
To commissioners, secretaries, clerks, &c. formerly employed in the civil departments of the navy	130,518	7	11
Victualling department	33,331	12	6
Bounty to chaplains	1,372	10	0
Allowances to widows and orphans on the compassionate list	12,808	0	0
Widows' charity	148,327	0	0
Greenwich hospital, out-pensioners	250,000	0	0
			—1,579,149 16 0

ORDNANCE.

MILITARY :

Superannuated and half-pay officers	£55,118	0	0
Retired as general officers	13,039	0	0
Allowances for good services	5,099	0	0
Pensions in remuneration for inventions and improvements in artillery service	1,200	0	0
Superannuated and disabled men	189,004	0	0
Pensions to wounded officers	7,393	0	0
Pensions to widows and children	22,910	0	0
Retired officers of the late Irish artillery and engineers, and pensions to widows	8,590	0	0

CIVIL :

Superannuated and half-pay to civil officers, artificers, and labourers ; retired pay and pensions to civil officers, in consequence of reduction and ill-health	36,838	0	0
Pensions to widows	4,666	0	0
Superannuated and half-pay to Irish civil officers and artificers and labourers ; and pensions to widows	4,429	0	0
Barrack department	17,340	0	0

	365,626	0	0
	4,884,672	11	8
To which add the Civil Departments of the government, including pensions, superannuations, and allowances in the treasury, tax-office, customs, excise, stamps, police, &c.	478,967	16	3
Grand Total, military, naval, and civil	£5,367,640	7	11

DEAD WEIGHT.

Year 1822	£5,289,087	19	10
—— 1823	5,311,248	2	4
—— 1824	5,317,445	3	7
—— 1825	5,302,499	18	0
—— 1826	5,376,674	2	1
—— 1827	5,455,990	19	4
—— 1828	5,362,670	16	1

DIVIDENDS PAYABLE ON THE PUBLIC DEBT.

An Account of the Total Number of Persons to whom a Half-Year's Dividend on Three per Cent. Consols became due on 5th January last; specifying the Number respectively of those whose Dividend for the Half-Year did not exceed £5, £10, £50, £100, £200, £300, £500, £1000, £2000, and the Number of those whose Dividend exceeded £2000; —a like Account of Dividends on Three per Cent. Reduced, payable on 10th October last;—a like Account of the Dividends on Three and a Half per Cents, payable on 10th October last;—a like Account of Dividends on Four per Cents, payable on 10th October last;—a like Account of the Dividends on Long Annuities, payable on 10th October last;—a like Account of the Dividends on New Four per Cents, payable on 5th January last;—and, a like Account of the Dividends on Three per Cent. Annuities, Anno 1726, payable on 5th January last.—*Vide page* 361.

	Not exceeding £5.	Not exceeding £10.	Not exceeding £50.	Not exceeding £100.	Not exceeding £200.	Not exceeding £300.	Not exceeding £500.	Not exceeding £1,000.	Not exceeding £2,000.	Exceeding £2,000.	TOTAL.
£3 per cent. Consolidated..	26,596	12,779	30,651	9,326	6,163	2,192	1,421	820	239	82	90,269
£3 per cent. Reduced......	10,078	4,653	11,460	3,491	2,110	775	455	222	85	32	33,361
£3. 10 per cent. Reduced ..	6,933	4,381	10,365	2,978	1,613	428	291	124	39	15	27,167
£3. 10 per cent. 1818......	222	186	489	192	155	53	40	32	7	7	1,383
£4 per cent. Annuities, 1826	1,269	735	1,486	430	266	80	71	29	8	5	4,379
Long Annuities	9,077	4,008	9,210	1,985	1,017	339	209	95	20	2	25,962
New £4 per cent. Annuities	29,307	15,403	33,451	7,874	3,857	1,037	589	233	52	18	91,821
£3 per cent. Annuities, 1726	127	82	195	40	28	8	1	Nil.	Nil.	Nil.	481
Totals......	83,609	42,227	97,307	26,316	15,209	4,912	3,077	1,555	450	161	274,823

Bank of England, 15th Feb. 1830.

WILLIAM SMEE, Deputy Accountant.

COLONIAL STATISTICS.

RETURN from each COLONY or FOREIGN POSSESSION of the BRITISH CROWN; stating the Number of the POPULATION, distinguishing White from Coloured, and Free from Slaves; also, the Value of EXPORTS and IMPORTS into each of those Colonies, for each of the past Three Years.
N.B.—Those with a * affixed have a Legislative Assembly; those without are governed by the Orders of the King in Council.

COLONIES.	POPULATION 1829, OR LATEST CENSUS.		Imports into the United Kingdom. Official Value.	Exports from the United Kingdom, Official Value.	Number and Tonnage of Vessels to and from the United Kingdom and the Colonies.			
					Inwards.		Outwards.	
NORTH AMERICA.		Total.			Ships	Tons.	Ships	Tons.
Lower Canada	...............423,630..............	}	569,451	1,117,421	778	327,909	760	321,694
Upper Canada	...............188,558..............							
*New Brunswick	...............72,932..............	....	213,842	274,922	562	155,249	460	133,469
Nova Scotia............ }								
Cape Breton ....}	....142,548..............	}	61,701	297,966	121	30,146	126	31,738
Prince Edward's Island	...............23,473..............	....						
Newfoundland	...............60,088..............	....	243,628	373,817	148	17,820	306	31,246
		911,229						
Totals..		911,229	1,088,629	2,064,126	1,609	431,124	1,652	418,147

	Whites.	Free Coloured.	Slaves.							
WEST INDIES.										
Antigua	1,980	3,895	29,839	35,714	285,500	146,657	46	9,781	43	9,367
Barbadoes	14,959	5,146	81,902	102,007	489,214	369,828	65	17,190	82	20,887
Dominica	840	3,606	15,392	19,838	141,911	27,478	12	3,011	12	2,921
Grenada	801	3,786	24,145	28,732	359,813	93,015	41	12,349	37	11,031
Jamaica	No census taken.		322,421	322,421	3,741,179	2,761,483	286	85,710	276	82,558
Monserrat	330	814	6,262	7,406	40,958	8,302	5	1,253	4	944
Nevis..................	700	2,000	9,259	11,959	78,278	25,223	8	1,892	8	1,996
St. Kitts	1,612	3,000	19,310	23,922	192,280	97,234	24	6,224	26	6,804
St. Lucia	972	3,718	13,661	18,351	157,593	51,505	22	5,290	19	4,209
St. Vincent	1,301	2,824	23,589	27,714	414,548	99,891	53	14,379	42	12,084
Tobago................	322	1,164	12,556	14,042	158,385	51,368	26	6,594	29	6,913
Tortola	477	1,296	5,399	7,172	33,243	5,666	5	1,317	3	606
Anguilla	365	327	2,388	3,080						
Trinidad....	4,201	15,956	24,006	44,163	694,001	361,077	94	22,224	82	20,474
Bahamas...............	4,240	2,991	9,268	16,499	17,915	51,524	7	1,360	7	1,338
Bermudas	3,905	738	4,608	9,251	4,901	24,817	3	620	9	2,256
Demerara & Essequibo	3,006	6,360	69,467	78,833	1,762,409	502,236	190	55,250	183	53,687
Berbice...............	552	1,151	21,319	23,022	325,051	51,587	29	7,710	23	6,070
Honduras	250	2,266	2,127	4,643	190,795	792,278	42	11,184	33	8,847
Totals..				798,769	9,087,914	5,521,169	958	263,338	918	252,992
Gibraltar..............	17,024	nil.	nil.	17,024	34,535	1,117,615	16	1,795	93	10,426
Malta ....} Gozo ....}	104,489 } 15,480 }			119,969	20,784	505,359	11	2,034	46	7,906
Cape of Good Hope	55,675	37,852	35,509	129,036	238,133	383,427	36	8,069	35	7,705
Sierra Leone and.......	87	15,123		15,210 }						
Gambia	24	2,192		2,216 }	258,570	511,779	103	27,912	116	31,909
Ceylon.	6,414	906,389	20,464	933,267	202,668	46,496	4	1,309	9	3,048
Mauritius	8,844	15,851	76,774	101,469	451,998	280,530	41	12,824	27	6,391
New South Wales	20,930		36,598	92,528	250,620					
Van Dieman's Land....	9,421 {	Aborigines not ascertained	15,668 Convicts. 8,484 Convicts.	17,905	33,191	58,915	} 30	8,970	81	28,719
Swan River	850			850		37,210				
General Totals..	2,229,725 White and Free.		829,665 Slaves, exclusive of Convicts.	3,083,542 Total Population.	11,508,943 Imports.	10,777,244 Exports.	2,808 Ships	757,375 Tons.	2,977 Ships	767,243 Tons.

HOUSE OF LORDS.

" There must be a period and an end of names and dignities and whatsoever
is terrene ; and why not of De Vere? For where is Bohun? Where's Mortimer?
Nay, which is more and most of all, where is Plantagenet?"—*Speech of Lord
Chief Justice Crewe*, 1662.

WE have taken some pains to view the House of Lords under its various
aspects. It presents itself in the way of the Nation's wish ; and it is
natural that the Nation should seek to understand the character of the
obstacle which impedes its progress. We have looked into the history
of the Peerage, and what is the result? Who are they that, generally
speaking, have been made peers—and why? Is a peerage the reward
of virtue, of talent, of disinterestedness, of grand patriotic efforts, of a
long course of noble doings? No one who has looked with any care to
the family annals of the British peers will venture to say that, even in
the selection of a virtuous man for a peer, his virtue has been the cause
of his ennoblement; or if a man of talent, that he has been chosen
because his talent has been patriotically directed. No – the peerage has
been one of the means employed for several ages to carry on the great
JOB of government. If a patriot was troublesome, he was bought off by a
peerage; if a powerful individual was importunate, he was quieted by a
peerage ; if votes were in demand, the possessor or manager was paid by
a peerage; if a minister's place was desired, he vacated it for a peerage.
The lawyer, who proved the ablest instrument of government, was
rewarded by a peerage. In short, the honour of the peerage has mostly
been the Treasury of Corruption.

If the House of Lords, by the natural progression of things, is
hastening to an *euthanasia* because of its want of correspondence and
sympathy with public opinion, what is so well calculated to postpone that
inevitable hour, as the adoption of that for the want of which they must
wither and decay? A large and copious addition of popular peers would
revivify the antique and mouldering mass, and cause it to rise up with
much of the ardour and beauty of a veritable rejuvenescence. Unless
this plan be acceded to, the days of the peerage, as at present constituted, are numbered; and yet it is against this very measure that the
greatest number of prejudices are arrayed.

The peers are jealous of NEW MEN. What are they themselves?
Take even the oldest of them, they are but of a few centuries ; and the
majority are the merest *novi homines*—mushrooms, whom a shower of
wealth, or an accidental fall of borough rottenness, has caused to spring
from the earth within the last few years. The peerage of England is
the most modern in Europe : it is a contemptible upstart, compared with
that either of Germany or of France. Where are the true ancestors of
Englishmen, the men of Saxon blood? where even the descendants of
the butchers and bakers that came over with the Norman Conqueror?
Not all the lies of all the heralds can give us a creation six hundred
years old; and such as go even two hundred years back are very thinly
scattered indeed. Some of the most ancient blood of England is repre-

sented by men of private station, or by baronets, whose ancestors did not happen to receive the king's summons to parliament in former reigns, and whose descendants, if they were to receive it now, would carry into the House of Peers all that depends " upon Norman blood, or whatever else it is they are so proud of." But the day is gone past when a legislator is to be chosen on such grounds.

It would be a curious phenomenon, if the obstacle which the peers have thrown in the way of the people's measure, should lead to an immediate change in their own body. It was a reform in the Commons that was demanded; we may come to see that a virtual reform in the House of Lords is a necessary preliminary. The House of Commons has confessed its corruption: are the Lords immaculate? They debate as if their House stood upon the foundations of the earth, and as if angels guarded its keystone. It would seem they deemed it the very sun of our political constellation: they are mistaken—it is but a lamp, and may want trimming—may be worn out, and renewed—may have grown useless, and be removed : a more cynical illustrator of its nature might even term it a will-o'-the-wisp, which, when the bog of corruption in the other House comes to be dried up by Reform, may die out of itself.

What then are our conclusions? They are these—

I. The history of the origin and progress of the House of Peers indicates that it was calculated for another order of things; and that it is only by its having been used as an instrument in the hands of ministers and their masters, that it has been made tolerable, under the increased wealth and intelligence of the people.

II. The House of Peers has maintained its existence by usurping an influence over the representation of the people, which it has turned to its sole advantage.

III. The history of the peerage is a series of JOBS. It is a coinage ; and represents place, pension, commission, civil employment, government contract—in one word, public money. *The actual peerage is chiefly an efflorescence of taxation.*

IV. Whenever the minister has wanted votes, he has created peers ; whenever he has wished to get quit of votes, he has created peers. A peerage is the grave of the patriot—the throne of the placeman.

V. The antiquity of the families of the existing peerage is a farce ; the Herald's College and the Alienation Office are the managers of this noble melodrama. When a line becomes extinct, by some trick of marriage, or by some interpretation of a patent, a trap-door is struck, and out comes a representative of the Mortimers or the Mowbrays. To such an extent is this carried, that the same family name is changed almost every other year in the peerage ; and some peers do not know their own name. For instance, lord Oriel wished to vote against the Reform Bill ; his real name is Foster—he signed his proxy Ferrard, he *ought* to have written something else. The proxy was useless—there was one vote less against the people.

VI. The most numerous and the most active of the existing peers are the creations of the long reign of George the Third: they may be considered as a body of unconscious conspirators, bound together by the minister, for the secret purpose of swelling the national debt. With the exception of the military and naval chiefs, they are titled contractors for a loan, who have received their per centage in peerage.

VII. When the personal characteristics of the descendants of this motley society of born legislators are looked to—this assemblage of " accidents of an accident,"—we are not led to believe that station and fortune have redeemed them from the stain of their original creation, but that, on the contrary, it would be difficult to select from any class the same number of men less competent to create laws or propagate legislation.

If there be any truth in these conclusions—and we have come to them not by rhetoric, but rather by arithmetic—can any thing be more absurd, more drivelling, than the affected hesitation which has been shown in creating at once a due number of King and People's Peers,—a class which, when the object of their ennoblement is considered, and the character of the parties who instal them in their elevated niche, may be assuredly maintained as the most honourable and distinguished division of the House to which they will belong? We have proved, in every possible way, that the peers as a body may derive honour from such a creation, but can lose none. Is not all the world convinced, that this is a course which may *save* the House, not only from contempt, but destruction; and that though the people may by it gain the immediate passing of " the Bill," the Lords will gain much more—they will snatch their political existence out of the flames of discord and civil war.—Abridged from the *Spectator* newspaper.

BOROUGH LORDS AND THEIR REPRESENTATIVES.

Should there be found in some not distant year—
[*Oh, how I wish to be no* PROPHET *here !*]
Amongst our British Lords should there be found
Some great in pow'r, in principles unsound,
Who look on Freedom with an evil eye,
In whom the springs of loyalty are dry,
Who wish to soar on wild Ambition's wings,
Who hate the Commons, and who love not Kings—
Who would divide the people and the Throne,
To set up separate interests their own ;—
Should there be found such men in after-times,
May HEAVEN, in mercy to our grievous crimes,
Allot some milder vengeance,—nor to them,
And to their rage this wretched land condemn.—CHURCHILL.

The Names printed with R, were in favour of the Bill in 1831 ; those with A against it.

Names of Patrons.	Places.	Members returned.
Anglesey Marquis, R	Milborne Port	Mr. S. G. Byng
Aylesbury, Marquis, A ..	Marlborough	Mr. W. J. Bankes

Names of Patrons.	Places.	Members returned.
Aylesbury, Marquis, A ..	Marlborough	Mr. T. Estcourt
	Great Bedwin..........	Mr. J. J. Buxton
		Sir J. Nichol
Bath, Marquis, A	Weobley	Lord E. Thynne
		Lord H. Thynne
Bandon, Earl	Bandonbridge..........	Lord Bernard
Bathurst, Lord, A......	Cirencester	Lord Apsley
Beaufort, D. A..........	Monmouth	Marquis of Worcester
Bedford, D. R..........	Tavistock	Mr. J. Hawkins
		Lord J. Russell
Balcarras, E. A	Wigan	—
		Mr. J. H. Kearsley
Beverley, E. A..........	Beeralston	Mr. D. Lyon
		Lord Lovaine
Bristol, M. A	Bury St. Edmund's	Earl Jermyn
Brownlow, E. A........	Clitheroe	Hon. P. F. Cust
Buckingham, D. A......	Buckingham	Sir T. Freemantle
		Sir G. Nugent
	St. Mawe's	Sir E. Sugden
		Mr. G. W. Pigott
	Winchester............	Mr. J. B. East
Bute, M. A	Cardiff	Lord J. Stuart
Caledon, L.............	Old Sarum	Mr. J. Alexander
		Mr. J. D. Alexander
Calthorpe, L. A	Bramber	Mr. W. S. Dugdale
	Hindon	Mr. J. Weyland
Carrington, L. A........	Wendover	Mr. S. Smith
		Mr. A. Smith
Carlisle, E. R..........	Morpeth	Hon. W. Howard
Castlemaine, L.........	Athlone	Mr. H. Handcock
Charleville, E. A........	Carlow................	Lord Tullamore
Cholmondeley, M. A	Castle Rising	Lord Cholmondeley
Clarendon, L. R	Wootton Basset	Lord Mahon
Cleveland, M. R........	Camelford	Mr. M. Milbank
		Mr. S. Cradock
	Ilchester	Dr. Lushington
		Hon. E. Petre
	Winchilsea	—
		Mr. J. Williams
Clifford, L. de, R........	Kinsale	Captain J. Russell
Clinton, L. R	Ashburton	
Delewarr, E. A	East Grinstead	Mr. F. R. West
		Viscount Holmesdale
Devonshire, D. R	Derby	Mr. W. Cavendish
	Dungarvon	Hon. George Lamb
	Knaresborough	Lord Waterpark
		Sir J. Mackintosh
	Youghall	Hon. G. Ponsonby
Donegal, M. R..........	Belfast	Sir A. Chichester
Downshire, M. R	Carrickfergus..........	Lord G. A. Hill
Dundas, L. R	Richmond	Mr. I. C. Dundas
		Sir R. L. Dundas
Edgecumbe, E. Mt. A....	Plympton..............	Sir C. Domville
	Lostwithiel	Mr. E. Cust
		Lord Valletort
Egremont, E.	New Shoreham	Sir C. Burrell
Ely, M. A..............	Wexford	—
Enniskillen, L. A	Enniskillen............	Hon. A. H. Cole

Names of Patrons.	Places.	Members returned.
Exeter, M. A	Stamford	Lord T. Cecil
Falmouth, E. A	Truro	Lord Encombe
		Mr. N. W. Peach
	St. Michaels	Hon. L. Keynon
		Hon. W. Best
Fitzwilliam, E. R	Malton ,..............	Mr. H. J. Ponsonby
		Mr. H. G. Knight
	Peterborough	Mr. Fazakerley
		Sir R. Heron
	Higham Ferrars	Viscount Howick
Foley, Lord, R........	Droitwich	Mr. J. H. Foley
		Sir T. Winnington
Forester, Lord, A	Wenlock	Mr. G. Forester
		Mr. P. B. Thomson
Grafton, D. R..........	Bury St. Edmunds......	C. A. Fitzroy
	Thetford	Lord J. Fitzroy
Grantley, Lord, A	Guildford..............	Mr. C. F. Norton
Guilford, E. A..........	Banbury	
Hardwicke, E. A	Reigate................	Captain J. Yorke
Harewood, E. A........	Northallerton	Hon. H. Lascelles
		Sir J. Beresford
Harrowby, E. A	Tiverton	Mr. S. Perceval
		Mr. G. D. Ryder
Hertford, Marquis, A....	Bodmin	Mr. H. B. Seymour
	Lisburne	Mr. Henry Meynell
	Orford	Mr. T. H. Kilderbee
		Sir H. F. Cooke
	Aldeburgh	Mr. J. W. Croker
		Marquis of Duoro
Heytesbury, L.	Heytesbury............	Mr. E. H. A'Court
		Sir G. Staunton
Howe, E. A.	Clitheroe..............	Hon. R. Curzon
Huntingfield, L.........	Dunwich..............	E. of Brecknock
Kilmorey, E.	Newry	Hon. J. H. Knox
Lansdowne, M. R	Calne	Colonel Fox
		Mr. T. B. Macauley
Leeds, D. A............	Helstone	Lord J. Townshend
		Mr. S. L. Fox
Lichfield, E.	Lichfield	Sir G. Anson
Lonsdale, E. A	Haslemere	Sir J. Beckett
		Mr. W. Holmes
	Cockermouth	Sir J. Scarlett
		Col. Lowther
	Carlisle	
	Appleby	Viscount Maitland
Manvers, E. R..........	Bassetlaw	Lord Newark
Marlborough, D. A......	Woodstock	Lord Stormont
		Lord S. C. Churchill
Middleton, L.	Newark	
Monson, L. A	Gatton	Hon. J. Ashley
		Viscount Pollington
Mulgrave, E. R	Scarborough	Hon. E. Phipps
Newcastle, D. A........	Aldborough............	Mr. J. F. C. Clinton
		Mr. M. T. Sadler
	Boroughbridge	Sir C. Wetherell
		Mr. M. Attwood

Names of Patrons.	Places.	Members returned.
Newcastle, D. A	Bassetlaw	—
	Newark	—
Norfolk, D. R	New Shoreham	Mr. H. Howard
	Steyning	Mr. G. R. Phillips
		Mr. E. Blount
	Horsham	Earl of Surrey
		Mr. N. W. Colborne
Northumberland, D. A	Launceston	Mr. J. Brogden
		Sir J. Malcolm
	Newport, Corn.	—
		Sir H. Hardinge
Orford, Lord, A	King's Lynn	—
Pembroke, E.	Wilton	Mr. J. Dawkins
		Mr. J. Penruddock
Primate of Ireland, A	Armagh	
Portarlington, E.	Portarlington	Sir W. Rae
Portland, D. R	King's Lynn	Lord G. Bentinck
Powis, E. A	Bishop's Castle	Mr. E. Rogers
		Mr. J. Knight
	Ludlow	Viscount Clive
		Hon. R. H. Clive
	Montgomery	Mr. H. Clive
Radnor, E. R	Downton	Mr. J. Brougham
		Mr. T. Creevey
	Salisbury	Hon. D. Bouverie
Ranfurley, E. R	Dungannon	Hon. T. Knox
Richmond, D. A	Chichester	Lord A. Lennox
Roden, Lord, A	Dundalk	Hon. J. H. Cradock
Rutland, D. A	Bramber	Mr. J. Irving
	Cambridge	Marquis of Graham
		Col. F. W. Trench
Salisbury, M. A	Hertford	
Sandwich, E.	Huntingdon	Col. J. Peel
		Mr. F. Pollock
Seaford, L. R	Seaford	
Shaftesbury, E. A	Dorchester	Lord Ashley
Sidney, V. A	Whitchurch	Hon. H. Townshend
Somers, E.	Reigate	Capt. J. Yorke
St. Germains, E. A	Liskeard	Sir H. Pringle
		Lord Eliott
	St. Germain's	Mr. C. Ross
		Mr. W. M. Praed
Thanet, E. R	Appleby	Mr. H. Tufton
Verulam, E. A	St. Alban's	
Warwick, E. A	Warwick	—
Waterford, M.	Berwick	Captain Beresford
Westminster, M. R	Chester	General R. Grosvenor
	Shaftesbury	Mr. L. Maberly
		Mr. E. Penrhyn
	Hindon	Mr. J. Weyland
	Stockbridge	Mr. W. S. Stanley
		Mr. G. Wilbraham
Westmoreland, E. A	Lyme Regis	Mr. H. S. Fane
		Mr. J. T. Fane
Wharncliffe, L. A	Bossiney	Hon. J. S. Wortley
Yarborough, L. R	Newtown	Mr. C. A. W. Pelham

CHURCH PATRONAGE OF THE NOBILITY,

Exhibiting the Number of Rectories and Vicarages in the gift of each, with the Valuation annexed of all Livings not exceeding £150 per annum as returned to Parliament in 1818.

EXPLANATIONS.

The following Table of the Ecclesiastical Patronage of the Nobility is abstracted from the *Patroni Ecclesiarum,* published in 1831. *k.b.* is the value of the living in the King's Book, taken in the reign of Henry VIII. and of which an account will be found at pp. 43 and 131. *p.r.* is the real value of livings *not exceeding* £150 as presented to parliament: for a return has been made of the present value of *poor* livings but none of the *rich* ones; *r.* rectory, *v.* vicarage, *c.* chapelry, *p.c.* perpetual curacy, *d.* donative; *w.* signifies the living is held *cum* or with another.

Living	County	type	KB/PR	£	s	d
ABERGAVENNY, Earl of						
Byr'ing	*Kent*	*v.*	KB	6	9	4
Bryngwm w .. }	*Mnm.*	*r*	PR	150	0	0
Clytha c .... }			KB	5	0	6
Goytrey	—	*r.*	PR	150	0	0
Llanfihangells- } ternllewryne }	—	*r.*	—	150	0	0
Llanfoist	—	*r.*	KB	7	4	4
Llangattock	—	*r.*	—	11	7	3
Llanhilleth......	—	*r.*	PR	50	0	0
Llanvapley......	—	*r.*	KB	10	15	2
Llanvetherine ..	—	*r.*	—	14	17	8
Llanwenarth w. } Aberystwith c }	—	*r.*	—	26	6	6
Brunstead	*Norf.*	*r.*	—	6	5	7
Holveston w. } Burgh Apton }	—	*r.*	—	13	6	8
Sutton St. Mich..	—	*r.*	—	6	16	8
Otley	*Suffolk*	*r.*	—	16	6	5
Chiltington, West	*Sussex*	*r.*	—	12	16	10
Easthothley	—	*r.*	—	7	6	3
Rotherfield	—	*r.*	—	27	12	6
Inkberrow	*Worc.*	*v.*	—	16	2	1
ABINGDON, Earl of						
Cumnor	*Berks.*	*v.*	PR	120	0	0
So. Hinksey w. } Wootten c. }	—	*p.c.*	—	70	0	0
Wightham	—	*r.*	KB	7	5	2
Bothenhampton	*Dorset.*	*p.c.*	PR	45	0	0
Aldbury	*Oxon.*	*r.*	KB	9	2	8
Weston on the } Green ...... }	—	*v.*	PR	125	0	0
ABOYNE, Earl of						
Chesterton......	*Hunts*	*r.*	—	17	3	4

Living	County	type	KB/PR	£	s	d
Haddon ...... } w. Holme c. }	—	*r.*	—	11	5	0
Orton Long- } ville w..... } Botolph Br. }	*Hants*	*r.*	—	20	13	4
Ranton	*Staff.*	*pc.*	PR	84	0	0
AILESBURY, Marquess of						
Maulden........	*Beds*	*r.*	KB	15	9	7
Bedwin, Great ..	*Wilts.*	*v.*	PR	146	0	0
—— Little....	—	*v.*	KB	9	6	8
Collingb. Ducis..	—	*p.c.*	—	not in char.		
Easton	—	*p.c.*	—	not in char.		
East Witton	*Yksh.*	*v.*	PR	111	0	0
Wath	—	*r.*	KB	17	17	1
West Tanfield ..	—	*r.*	—	13	0	5
Marlbro' Gram. Sch.	*Wilts.*			*Mastership.*		
ALBEMARLE, Earl of						
Southwd. Hay- } ling w. N. } Hayling c.. }	*Hants.*	*v.*	KB	8	10	0
Quiddenham .. } w. Snetterton }	*Norf.*	*r.*	—	{ 8 { 12	4 17	6 1
Shottisham All Sts.	—	*v.*	—	6	18	4
——St. Mary	—	*v.*	—	6	0	0
Thetford, St Mary	—	*p.c.*	PR	70	0	0
——St. Cuth- } bert w Trinity }	—	*p.c.*	—	86	0	0
——St. Peter } w St Nicholas }	—	*r.*	—	50	0	0
Winfarthing	—	*r.*	KB	2	0	0
AMHERST, Countess						
Middleton on } Leven ...... }	*Yksh.*	*p.c.*	—	43	13	6
East Rownton ..	—	*p.c.*	—	37	7	6

Place	County			£	s	d
Flitwick........	—	v.	—	7	17	0
Goldington......	—	v.	PR	140	0	0
Houghton Regis	—	v.	KB	11	3	4
Ravensden......	—	v.	PR	120	0	0
Steppingley	—	r.	KB	6	16	3
Stevington......	—	v.	PR	111	18	0
Wilden	—	r.	KB	18	7	1
Willington	—	v.	—	7	17	0
Woburn	—	p.c.	—	not in char.		
Cheney East- manstead .. }	Bucks.	r.	—	12	16	0
Chesham	—	v.	—	13	1	5
——— Boys ..	—	p.c.	—	5	6	8
Thorney	Camb.	r.	—	not in char.		
Awliscombe	Devon.	v.	—	12	10	10
Brent Tor	—	p.c.	PR	14	19	10
Denbury........	—	r.	KB	12	7	6
Milton Abbot ..	Devon.	v.	KB	19	13	6
North Petherwin	—	v.	PR	124	0	0
Tavistock	—	v.	—	111	0	0
Whimple	—	r.	KB	30	0	0
Swyre..........	Dorset.	r.	PR	80	0	0
Stibbington	Hunts.	r.	KB	7	13	6
Westminster, St. Paul, Covent Garden }	Midd.	r.	—	not in char.		
Thornhaugh w. Wansford c. }	Npn.	r.	—	17	1	3
Streatham	Surry.	r.	—	18	13	9
BERKELEY, Earl of						
Berkeley........	Glouc.	v.	—	32	15	7
Cranford	Midd.	r.	—	16	0	0
West Thorney ..	Suss.	r.	—	10	8	4
BERWICK, Lord						
Thornton Mayow	Chesh.	r.	—	24	7	8
Berrington w. Little Ness.. }	Salop.p.c.		PR	70	0	0
Shrewsbury .. St. Giles & . Holy Cross.. }	—	v.	KB	8	0	0
Sutton St. John..	—	r.	—	3	0	0
Shenstone	Staff.	v.	—	6	5	8
Fornham St. .. Gen. w Risby }	Suff.	r.	PR	94	4	11
BOLINGBROKE, Lord Viscount						
Manston........	Dorset.	r.	KB	12	5	0
BOLTON, Lord						
Chickerell	Dorset.	r.	—	18	16	0
Frome Vau- .. church with Batcombe .. }	—	r.	—	7 9	11 9	0 9
Hooke	—	r.	PR	80	15	0
Herryard	Hants.	v.	—	105	7	0
Kingsclere w. Itchinswell c. & Sidmont c. }	—	v.	KB	17	19	7
Winslade	—	r.	PR	97	0	0
Wensley with Bolton and Radmire p.c. }	Yksh.	r.	—	149	9	9

Place	County			£	s	d
West Witton	Yksh.	p.c.	—	75	0	0
BOSTON, Lord						
Llanddona......	Angl.	p.c.	PR	74	10	0
Llanidan .... with Llan-. ddaniel c .. Llanfair y .. Cwmmwd c. and Llaned- wan c .... }	—	v.	KB	10	0	0
Penrhos-lligwy..	—	p.c.	PR	48	0	0
Hedsor, alt.	Bucks.	r.	—	59	8	5
Dolwyddelan....	Carn.	p.c.	—	48	0	0
Whiston with.. Deynton c... }	Npn.	r.	KB	14	11	0
BRADFORD, Earl of						
Hughley	Salop.	r.	PR	145	0	0
Knockin	—	r.	—	130	0	0
Walsall	Staff.	v.	KB	10	19	7
Weston under Lizard .... }	—	r.	—	6	7	8
Wigan	Lanc.	r.	—	80	13	4
Teddington	Midd.	d.	—	not in char.		
Castle Bromwich, in Aston Birming. Parish .... }	Warw.p.c.		—	———		
Clifton on Dunsmore w. Brownsoverc. }	—	v.	PR	113	0	0
BRAYBROOK, Lord						
Arborfield	Berks	r.	KB	7	19	10
Wargrave	—	v.	—	13	13	6
Saffron Walden..	Essex	v.	—	33	6	8
Shadingfield	Suff.	r.	—	12	0	0
BRIDGEWATER, Countess of						
Tottenham	Beds.	v.	PR	98	0	0
Cheddington	Bucks.	r.	KB	15	9	7
Edlesboro'......	—	r.	—	13	17	0
Ivinghoe	—	v.	PR	70	0	0
Nettleden	—	p.c.	—	30	0	0
Pightlesthorne ..	—	p.c.	KB	20	0	0
Wingrave	—	v.	—	9	9	7
Aldbury........	Herts.	r.	—	20	8	6
Little Gaddesden	—	r.	—	11	12	8
Ellesmere w. Cockshut and Dudlaston p.c. }	Salop.	v.	PR	17 90	18 0	1 0
Middle	—	r.	KB	12	7	3
Tilstock	—	p.c.	PR	110	0	0
Whitchurch w. Marbury, c. }	—	r.	KB	44	11	8
Settington	Yksh.	r.	—	42	12	6
Dunnington	—	r.	—	19	0	0
BRIDPORT, Lord						
Cricket, St. Thomas .... }	Som.	r.	PR	145	0	0
BRISTOL, Marquess of						
Chesterford, Gt.	Essex.	v.	—	10	0	0
——— Little....	—	r.	—	11	0	0

Wendon, Great. }	—	r. PR	75	0	0
—— Little v. }					
Asgarby with }					
Kirby Lay- }	Linc.	r. KB	16	6	10
thorpe .... }					
Metheringham ..	—	v. PR	120	0	0
Normanton	—	r. —	100	0	0
Quarrington	—	r. KB	7	2	3
Sleaford, New ..	—	v. PR	130	0	0
——, Old, sin.	—	v. KB	4	10	0
Bredfield, St. }					
George, w }	Suffolk	r. —	11	17	3
Rushbrook.. }			8	1	5
Bromeswell ..:.	—	r. —	4	15	7
Chedburg w. }					
Ickworth .. }	—	r. —	11	14	2
Horningsheath..	—	r. —	10	17	8
Playford	—	p.c. PR	36	0	0
Rushmere	—	v. —	80	0	0
Shotley	—	r. KB	20	0	0
Sproughton	—	r. —	20	18	9
Tuddenham	—	r. —	10	17	6
Anwick, alt. w. }					
Brauncewellr. }	Linc.	v. —	15	2	11
and Dunsby r. }					
BROWNLOW, Earl					
Cockayne-hatley.	Beds.	r. —	8	0	0
Belton	Linc.	r. PR	150	0	0
Carlton Scropp..	—	r. KB	13	1	5
Faldingworth ..	—	r. —	15	8	1
Hereby	—	r. —	6	4	7
Hough on the Hill	—	v. PR	83	4	8
Raisin Tupholm .	—	v. —	108	0	0
Saltfleetby, East .	—	r. KB	7	0	1
Snelland..	—	r. PR	145	12	9
Little Billing....	Npn.	r. KB	10	2	11
Overston	—	r. —	12	16	3
Sywell	—	r. —	11	1	5
Marnham	Notts.	v. —	8	19	2
Horndon, E. alt.	Essex.	r. —	10	0	0
Warley, Lit- }					
tle, alt. .... }	—	r. —	11	3	9
BUCCLEUGH, Duke of					
Beaulieu	Hants.	d. PR	61	0	0
St. Andrew, Holb.	Midd.	r. KB	18	0	0
St. George.... }					
Queen's Sq.. }	—	r. — not in char.			
St. Matthew & }					
St. Peter }					
Cheap. alt. }	—	r. PR	250	0	0
Friday St.. }					
Barton Seagrave.	Npn.	r. KB	10	17	1
Broughton......	—	r —	21	9	7
Geddington w. }					
Newton d.. }	—	v. PR	140	0	6
Little Oakley ..	—	r. —	108	0	0
Scaldwell	—	r. KB	14	0	10
Warkton	—	r. —	18	16	3
Weekly	—	v. PR	135	0	0

BUCKINGHAM, Duke of					
Foscot	Bucks.	r. KB	9	9	4
Stowe..........	—	v. PR	91	18	0
Water Stratford .	—	r. KB	7	0	5
Wootton Un- }					
derwood.... }	—	p.c. PR	82	0	0
Gosfield	Essex	v. KB	8	0	0
Bighton	Hants.	r. —	19	8	1
East Wellow....	—	v. —	5	0	0
Finmere	Oxon.	r. PR	126	6	6
Compton Mart. }					
w.Nempnet c. }	Som.	r. KB	10	6	3
Doddington	—	r. PR	122	0	0
Keynsham	—	v. KB	11	19	7
Saltford	—	r. —	10	5	0
Burton Dasset ..	Warw.	r. —	14	0	0
BUCKINGHAMSHIRE, Earl of					
GreatHampden }					
with Great }	Bucks.	r. KB	9	9	7
Kimb. v .... }			6	10	5
Werrington	Corn.	d. — not in char.			
Welborne	Linc.	r. —	11	12	9
BUTE, Marquess of					
Luton	Beds	v. KB	35	12	1
Kelligaer with }					
Birthdir c.. }	Glam.	r. —	20	7	11
Llandough w. }					
Leckwith & }	—	r. —	8	8	4
Cogan c .... }					
Llanmaes	..	r. —	10	2	3
Merthyr Tydvil..	—	r. —	20	5	7
Neath with }					
Llantwit c. & }	—	r. —	16	2	3
Resolven c.. }			13	0	0
Roath..........	—	v. —	7	0	0
Llanbaddock ..	Mnm.	p.c. PR	52	15	0
Wroxton .... }					
w. Balscot c. }	Oxon	v. —	50	0	0
CADOGAN, Earl of					
Santon Downh...	Suff.	p.c. KB not in char.			
Chelsea	Midd.	r. —	13	6	8
CALTHORPE, Lord					
Elvetham	Hants.	r. KB	9	0	0
Acle	Norf.	r. —	20	0	0
Ampton	Suff.	r. PR	121	12	6
Blakeney w. }					
Cockthorper }					
Glandford c. }	Norf.	r. KB	35	0	0
and Little }					
Langham v. }					
Pakenham	Suff.	v. —	10	8	9
Edgbaston	War.	p.c. PR	110	13	0
CAMDEN, Marquess					
Llanspydded w }					
Pennybont c. }	Brecon	v. PR	80	0	0
Merthyr Cynog..	—	v. —	32	0	0
CARDIGAN, Earl of					
Cranoe	Leic.	r. —	143	0	0
Glooston........	—	r. —	$10\frac{3}{4}$	14	0

			£	s	d
Stanton Wyvel ..	—	r. KB	9	18	11
Corby	Npn.	r. —	13	16	3
Dean	—	r. —	24	3	6
East Ardsley....	Yksh.	p c. —	27	0	0
West Ardsley ..	—	p.c. —	31	5	0
Sheckling w. } Burstwick. c {	—	v. —	7	0	0
Sproatley	—	r. —	7	0	10
Batley, alt	—	v. PR	150	0	0
CARLISLE, Earl of					
Denton	Cumb.	p.c. —	68	0	0
Lanercost w.. } Farlam .... {	—	p.c. —	156	0	0
Stapleton	—	r. —	88	10	0
Morpeth w. .. } Ulgham c... {	North.	r. KB	32	16	8
Hovingham	Yksh	p.c. PR	57	0	0
Slingsby........	—	r. KB	12	1	10
Brampton	Cumb.	v. —	8	0	0
CARNARVON, Earl of					
Burghclere w. } Newtown c. {	Hants.	r. —	30	0	0
Highclere	—	r. —	7	13	9
Brushford	Som.	r. —	15	1	5
Seagry	Wilts	v. PR	120	0	0
CARRINGTON, Lord					
Bledlow	Bucks.	v. KB	16	9	7
Humberston	Linc.	v. PR	72	0	0
CARTERET, Lord					
Bedford, St. Paul	Beds.	v. —	10	0	0
Willhampstead ..	—	v. —	9	9	7
Kilkhampton....	Corn.	r. —	26	13	11
Brown Cando- ver w.Wood- mancote c ..	Hants.	r. —	23	4	2
CAVENDISH, Lord G. A H.					
Broughton Field .	Lanc.	p.c. PC	90	0	0
Cartmell with } CartmellFell {	—	p.c. —	134	16	9
Flockborough ..	—	p.c. —	93	4	0
Lindale	—	p.c. —	111	0	0
Staveling	—	p.c. —	90	0	0
Jevington	Suss.	r. KB	20	0	0
Rye............	—	v. —	42	13	4
Uddimore	—	v. PR	35	0	0
Westham	—	v. KB	21	10	10
Wilmington	—	v. PR	96	0	0
Hawnby........	Yksh.	—	147	0	0
Hilton	—	p.c. —	47	0	0
CAWDOR, Earl					
Llandeveyson ..	Carm.	p.c. PR	52	0	0
Llanfihangel } Kilvargen .. {	—	r. —	55	0	0
Ystradffyn	—	p.c. —	46	16	4
Botheston	Pemb.	r. —	140	0	0
Loweston	—	r. —	106	0	0
Penboyr with } Ydrindod c. {	—	r. KB	9	9	4
Stackpool Ba- } sher {	—	r. —	11	6	8

			£	s	d
— Elidu, s:n..	—	r. —	15	12	11
......	—	v. PR	90	0	0
St. Petrock	—	r. —	116	0	0
Wiston	—	p c. —	130	0	0
CHANCELLOR, Lord					
Six PREBENDAL STALLS in Bristol Cathedral					
Five DITTO in Gloucester Cathedral					
Five DITTO in Norwich Cathedral					
Five DITTO in Rochester Cathedral					
RECTORIES 428, VICARAGES 357					
CHANDOS, Marquess of					
Bristol, St. Ma- } ry Magdalen {	Som.	r. PR	110	0	0
CHATHAM, Earl of					
Curry Rival	Som.	r. —	13	16	4
CHESTERFIELD, Earl of					
Aston Abbots....	—	v. —	150	0	0
Grove	—	r. —	40	12	3
Ilmer	—	v. —	97	0	0
Wing	—	v. KB	18	16	3
Cubley with Marston Montgom. c.	Derb.	r. —	13	16	3
Horsley	—	v. PR	94	0	0
Somershall......	—	r. KB	4	18	10
Bingham	Notts.	r. —	44	7	11
Burton Joyce } w. Bulcote c. {	—	v. PR	121	0	0
Gedling	—	r. KB	21	2	0
Shelford	—	p.c. PR	40	0	0
CHICHESTER, Earl of					
Falmer w. .... }	Suss.	v. —	6	10	10
Stanmer r... {		PR	130	0	0
Hastings, St. } Mary:nCastle {	—	p.c. KB	not in char.		
Hellingley	—	v. —	6	16	8
Laughton	—	v. —	9	11	3
CHOLMONDELEY, Marquess					
Barrow	Chesh.	r. KB	19	6	5
Houghton in the } Hole {	Norf.	v. PR	52	0	0
Gt. Massingham	—	r. KB	33	6	8
Stalham	—	v. —	5	0	0
Syderstrand	—	r. PR	133	12	4
CLARENDON, Earl of					
Wootton Bassett	Wilts.	v. —	12	0	0
Llanganna, alt. ..	Glam.	r. PR	150	0	0
CLEVELAND, Marquess of					
Tregony........	Corn.	v. —	10	4	2
Darlington	Durh.	p.c. PR	133	3	10
Staindrop with }	—	p.c. —	98	0	0
Cockfield r. {		KB	9	18	0
Brigstock with } Stannyon {	Npn.	v. —	11	17	3
Botterell Aston } w. Bold p. c. {	Salop.	r. —	7	1	0
Billingsley......	—	r. PR	129	0	4
Eaton Constanti.	Salop.	c. KB	not in char.		
Hope Bagot	—	r. PR	100	0	0

Wem with Ed-⎫ — r. KB 26 4 4
staston c. and ⎬   PR 54 0 0
Newtown p.c. ⎭
Wroxeter with ⎫ — v. KB 11 8 0
Eyton on Se- ⎬
vern c.   ⎭
Wrington with ⎫ Som. r. — 39 9 4
Burrington c. ⎭   3 7 11
Donnington Gram. Sch. Salop. Mastership
CLIFFORD, LORD
Wappenbury .... Warw. v. PR 70 4 0
Westan u. We- ⎫ — v. — 70 0 0
therley .... ⎭
CLINTON, Lord
Huish .... Devon. r. — 150 0 0
West Putford.... — r. KB 9 11 0
Southill .... Corn. r. — 38 0 0
Callington ...... — c. — not in char
Merton .... Devon. r. — 20 15 7
St. Petrock Stowe — r. — 17 0 2
COMBERMERE, Viscount
Burledam ...... Chesh. p.c. PR 100 0 0
COURTENAY, Viscount, Trustees of
Honiton .... Devon. r. — 40 4 2
Milton Damerel ⎫ — r. — 26 13 6
with Cook-   ⎬
bury c.   ⎭
MoretonHampstead — r. — 49 19 7
Woolboro' with ⎫
Newton Ab-   ⎬ — d. — not in char.
bot c.   ⎭
COVENTRY, Earl of
Oxenton ...... Glouc. p c. PR 80 0 0
Woolston ...... — r. KB 13 6 0
Edgeware ...... Midd. d. — not in char.
Croome D' A- ⎫
bitot with   ⎬ Worc. r. — 15 3 0
Pirton ...... ⎭
Grafton Flyford.. Worc. r. KB 20 0 10
Powick .... — v. — 10 2 7
Severnstoke .... — r. — 21 17 4
Wolvey, alt. .... Wa?w. v. PR 144 0 0
CRAVEN, Earl
Enborne .... Berks. r. KB 10 0 0
Hampstead ⎫ — r. — 12 14 4
Marshall.... ⎭
Elkstone........ Glouc. r. — 12 9 2
Yelvertoft ...... Npn. r. — 25 0 10
West Felton .... Salop. r. — 20 12 6
Onibury........ — r. — 8 17 8
Staunton Lacy .. — v. — 16 0 0
Wistantow ...... — r. — 18 0 0
Binley .... Warw. p.c. PR 53 0 0
Rugby.......... — r. KB 17 19 2
Wykin .... — p.c. PR 96 0 0
Allington ...... Wilts. r. KB 14 13 4
Burnsall, 1st ⎫
portion with ⎬ Yksh. r. PR 63 0 0
Rilstone c. .. ⎭

CREWE, Lord, Trustees of
Barthomley .... Chesh. r. — 25 7 1
Nantwich ...... — r. PR 100 0 0
Warmingham .. — r. KB 12 4 7
Bamborough ⎫ North. p.c. PR 165 18 0
with Lucker ⎭
Blanchland .... — p.c. — 115 0 0
Great Madely .. Staff. v. PR 94 0 0
DACRE, Lord
Carlton with..⎫ Camb. r. KB 9 0 0
Willingham c...⎭
Kimpton........ Herts. v. — 12 0 0
Royston........ — v. PR 117 1 4
DARNLEY, Earl of
Cobham .... Kent. v. PR 63 0 0
Sandgate, in ⎫
Folkstone   ⎬ — c. KB not in char.
parish ...... ⎭
DARTMOUTH, Earl of
Olney .... Bucks. v. PR 100 0 0
Lewisham ...... Kent. v. KB 23 19 2
Westbromwich .. Staff. p c. PR 20 0 0
———— .. — c. KB not in char.
DE DUNSTANVILLE, Lord
Camborne ...... Corn. r. — 39 16 10
St. Illogan ...... — r. — 22 7 6
Redruth .... — r. — 20 0 0
St. Eweny ...... — r. — 20 0 0
West Buckland.. Devon. r. — 13 3 4
DEERHURST, Lord and Lady
Hatfield with ⎫ Yksh. p.c. PR 80 4 3
St. Laur. c. ⎭   KB 42 14 0
DE GREY, Countess
Blunham ...... Beds. r. — 46 2 11
Clophill .... — r. — 12 0 0
Harrold ········.. — v. PR 144 8 0
Pulloxhill ...... — v. — 113 7 0
Colchester, St. ⎫
Michael My-   ⎬ Essex. r. KB 7 10 0
land........   ⎭
Great Horkesley — r. — 15 0 0
Fordham........ Essex. r. KB 14 4 2
Aston Flamville .. Leic. r. PR 124 1 4
Leir .... — r. KB 9 14 9
DELAMERE, Lord
Whitegate ...... Chesh v. PR 90 0 0
DE LA WARRE, Earl
Ashurst .... Kent. r. KB 5 4 7
East Grinstead .. Suss. v. — 20 0 0
DE LA WARRE, Earl, &c.
Stratford on Avon Warw. v. — 20 0 0
DERBY, Earl of
Chester, Trinity Chest. r. KB 8 15 5
Forrest .... — p.c. PR 60 0 0
Bury .... Lanc. r. KB 29 11 5
Huyton .... — v. PR 70 0 0
Ormskirk ...... — v. KB 10 0 0
Winwick ...... — r. — 102 9 9
Badsworth ...... Yksh. r. — 32 5 10

De Tabley, Lord						
Knutsford	Chesh.	v.	KB	26	16	2
Peover Nether ..	—	p c.	PR	146	2	0
Witton	—	p.c.	—	85	0	0
De Vesci, Viscount, &c.						
Silchester	Hants.	r.	—	9	6	0
Devonshirf, Duke of						
Ault	Derby.	v.	—	6	0	0
Bealey.........	—	p c.	—	10	18	0
Blackwell	—	v.	PR	40	0	0
Bradborne with ⎫ Ballidon p.c. ⎪ and Brassing- ⎬ ton p.c. .... ⎭	—	v.	—	160	0	0
Buxton	—	p.c.	—	54	0	0
Doveridge	—	v.	—	12	2	1
Edensover	—	v.	PR	40	0	0
Eyam..	—	r.	KB	13	15	5
Hartington w. ⎫ Earlstern- ⎬ dale c....... ⎭	—	v.	PR	151	11	7
Hathersage w. ⎫ Middleton ⎪ Stoney p. c. ⎬ & Peake Fo- ⎪ rest p. c..... ⎭	—	v.	—	123	0	0
Heath.........	—	v.	—	132	0	0
Upper Langwith	—	r.	—	134	18	0
Marston on Dove	—	v.	KB	7	15	2
Pentridge	—	v.	PR	80	0	0
Scarcliffe	—	v.	—	32	11	0
Staveley........	—	r.	KB	12	7	6
South Wingfield	—	v.	—	6	13	4
Youlgreave	—	v.	PR	103	0	0
Sawtry, All Sts.	Hunts.	r.	KB	8	15	7
Brindle	Lanc.	r.	—	12	8	4
Barrowby	Linc.	r.	—	31	1	5
Arnold	Notts.	v.	—	7	17	8
Beeston, St. John	—	v.	—	4	15	0
Clareborough ..	Notts.	v.	—	9	15	4
Everton	—	v.	—	7	2	2
Hucknall Torkard	—	v.	PR	100	0	0
Normanton on ⎫ Trent ...... ⎭	—	v.	—	118	11	8
Sutton Ashfield..	—	p.c.	—	87	6	8
Martinthorpe, sin.	Rutl.	r.	—	66	0	0
Kingsley	Staff.	r.	KB	16	15	0
Tutbury	—	v.	PR	130	0	0
Burnby	Yksh.	r.	—	98	19	6
Londesborough ..	—	v.	KB	16	0	0
Barden	—	p c.	—	not in char.		
Bolton.........	—	p c.	—	32	10	0
Kirkby Mal- ⎫ hamdale.... ⎭	—	v.	PR	43	10	0
Keighley	—	r.	KB	21	0	7
Digby, Earl						
Castletown......	Dors.	p.c.	—	7	0	0
Bishops Caundle	—	r.	—	11	10	0
Heydon	—	v.	PR	116	17	0

Oborne	—	v.	KB	6	5	10
North Wootton ..	—	p.c.	PR	60	0	0
Goathill	Som..	r.	—	90	0	0
Coleshill........	Warw.	v.	KB	10	13	6
Sheldon	—	r.	—	8	10	10
Water-orton	—	p.c.	PR	75	0	0
Dillon, Lord Viscount						
Marston Fleet ..	Bucks.	r.	KB	8	2	8
Cuddington	Oxon.	r.	—	7	9	4
Dorchester, Lord						
Nately Scures ..	Hants.	r.	—	100	0	0
Dorset, Duke of						
Welford	Glouc.	r.	KB	29	15	10
Weston on Avon	—	v.	PR	80	0	0
Islip	Npn.	v.	KB	15	6	8
Lowick	—	r.	—	16	18	11
Slipton	—	v.	PR	100	0	0
Drayton, St. ⎫ Leonard ....⎭	Oxon.	r.	—	75	0	0
—— Hanwell ..	—	r.	KB	17	13	0
Chiddingley	Suss.	v.	PR	150	0	0
Rottingdean	—	v.	KB	9	10	0
Watlington......	—	r.	PR	140	0	0
Downe, Lord Viscount						
Ashwell	Rutld.	r.	KB	20	16	3
Danby..........	Yksh.	p c.	PR	90	0	0
Thormanby......	—	r.	KB	8	2	11
Downshire, Dowager Marchioness of						
Eversholt	Beds.	r.	—	16	11	8
Ombersley	Worc.	v.	—	15	7	3
Downshire, Marquess of						
Hampstead ⎫ Norris with ⎬ Langley c. .. ⎭	Berks.	v.	—	9	18	11
Somerton	Suff.	r.	—	6	16	8
Seaseay	Yksh.	r.	—	17	0	2
Ducie, Lord						
Frocester........	Glouc.	r.	PR	140	0	0
Woodchester	—	r.	KB	10	0	0
Dudley, Earl of						
Stonar..........	Kent	r.	—	3	6	8
Broome	Staff.	r.	—	5	3	4
Himley	—	r.	—	3	13	4
Kingswinford ..	—	r.	—	17	3	4
Sedgley	—	v.	—	5	12	8
Dudley, St. Tho.	Worc.	v.	—	7	18	6
Dundas, Lord						
Marske	Yksh.	r.	PR	72	0	0
Dungannon, Viscount						
Llansantffraed ⎫ Glynkeriog ⎭	Denb.	p.c.	KB	7	16	6
Dunraven and Mountearle, Earl of						
Coity w. Nol- ⎫ lon c. ...... ⎭	Glam.	r.	KB	21	12	3
Little St. Bride's	—	r.	PR	120	0	0
Llanmihangel ..	—	r.	—	72	11	3
Michaelstow, ⎫ nr.Cowbrid. ⎭	—	r.	KB	4	12	8
Llanganna, alt...	—	r.	PR	150	0	0

DYNEVOR, Lord

Place	County			£	s	d
Great Barrington	Glouc.	v.	KB	7	6	4
—— Rissington	—	r.	—	22	0	5
Teynton	Oxon.	v.	PR	56	6	8

DYSART, Earl of

Place	County			£	s	d
Acton	Ches.	v.	KB	19	9	7
Harrington	Npn.	r.	—	15	9	7
Framsden	Suff.	v.	—	10	0	2
Pettaugh	—	r.	—	9	12	1

EOMONT, Earl of

Place	County			£	s	d
Enmore	Som.	r.	PR	85	0	0

EGREMONT, Earl of

Place	County			£	s	d
Egremont	Cumb.	r.	KB	7	12	1
Beercrocombe w.Copelandc.	Som.	r.	PR	150	0	0
SouthBradon,sin.	--	r.	—	36	0	0
St. Decumans....	—	v.	—	140	0	0
Barlavington....	Suss.	r.	—	54	19	0
Bodecton w. Coates	—	r.	—	7	3	11
North Chapel ..	—	r.	—	not in char		
Combes with Shipley, p. c.	—	r.	KB / PR	10 / 99	0 / 0	2 / 0
Duncton........	—	r.	KB	not in char		
Egdean	—	r.	PR	68	17	0
Iping with Chichurst, c.	—	r.	KB	7	0	0
Kirdford	—	v.	—	11	0	0
Ludgershall	—	r.	—	8	0	0
Petworth	—	r.	—	41	10	5
Pulborough	—	r.	—	19	0	7
North Stoke	—	v.	PR	24	0	0
Sutton..........	—	r.	KB	15	0	10
Tillington	—	r.	—	13	10	0
Upwaltham	—	r.	PR	125	0	0
Catton	Yksh.	r.	KB	21	12	8
Leckonfield	—	v.	PR	66	7	4
Scarborough	—	r.	KB	7	0	0
Wressle	—	v.	PR	90	7	1
Kirkby Overblow	—	r.	KB	20	1	0
Spofforth	—	r.	—	73	6	8
Tadcaster	—	r.	—	8	4	9

ESSEX, Earl of

Place	County			£	s	d
Little Raine	Essex	r.	—	14	13	4
Watford........	Herts	v.	—	21	12	1
Thrussington....	Leic.	v.	—	6	0	0

EXETER, Marquess of

Place	County			£	s	d
Calby, alt.......	Linc.	r.	KB	9	1	10
Stamford, St. Andr. & St. Mich. w. St. Stephen, 2 turns in 4	—	r.	PR	128	17	1
— St. Geo. w. St. Paul	—	r.	—	125	7	10
— St. J. Bap. w. St. Clem. 1 turn in 3 ..	—	r.	—	144	3	0
— All Saints w. St. Peter 2 turns in 3	Linc.	r.	KB	12	7	8
— St. Mary	—	r.	PR	80	0	0
— Barron......	Npn.	r.	—	91	0	0
Easton, All Sts.	—	r.	KB	19	8	9
Wakerley	—	r.	PR	100	0	0
Whittering......	—	r.	—	104	0	0
Barrowden	Rutl.	r.	KB	14	13	1
Great Casterton	—	r.	—	11	2	11
Pickworth	—	r.	—	4	0	0
Ryhal w. Eson-dine, c.	Rutl.	r.	KB	13	17	0
Stoke Dry	—	r.	—	11	2	1
Tinwell	—	r.	—	12	10	5

EXMOUTH, Viscount

Place	County			£	s	d
Christowe......	—	v.	PR	138	0	7

FALKLAND, Lord Viscount

Place	County			£	s	d
Skinnand, sin. ..	Linc.	r.	PR	100	0	0

FALMOUTH, Earl of

Place	County			£	s	d
Lamorran	Corn.	r.	—	145	0	0
St. Mabyn	—	r.	KB	36	0	0
St. Michael Penkevil ..	—	r.	PR	106	0	0
St. Stithian w. Peran Arwo-thal c.	—	v.	KB	14	0	10

FEVERSHAM, Lord

Place	County			£	s	d
Sutton Full	Yksh.	r.	—	130	0	0
Helmsley on Black Moor	—	v.	KB	11	3	6
Kirkby Cold....	—	d.	PR	53	5	0
Misperton	—	r.	KB	25	1	10

FITZWILLIAM, Earl

Place	County			£	s	d
Dore	Derby	p.c.	PR	70	0	0
Glossop with Charles-worth c. and Ludworth v.	—	v.	— / KB	109 / 4	6 / 4	9 / 4
Covington	Hunts	r.	PR	135	0	0
Fletton	—	r.	KB	9	3	9
Great Gidding ..	—	v.	PR	114	0	0
Keystone	—	r.	KB	29	5	0
Billinghay w. Walcot c. ..	Linc.	v.	—	13	14	0
Etton	Npn.	v.	—	9	9	9
Harpole........	—	r.	—	18	13	4
Harrowdn Magna	—	v.	—	13	3	8
—— Parva ..	—	p.c.	—	18	0	0
Higham Fer-rers w. Cal-decott and Chelveston c.	—	v.	—	33	4	4
Irthingboro', All Saints w. St. Peter v.	—	r.	—	5	6	8
Lutton with Washingley	Npn. Hunts.	r.	KB	21	11	0 / — not in char

Marholme ...... Npn.	r. KB	9	2	3
Hutton Bushel .. Som.	v. —	14	17	6
Yeddingham .... Yksh.	r. —	5	4	2
Bulmer .... —	r. —	11	0	0
Swinton .... —	p.c. —	24	0	0
Malton, Old } —New, viz. St. Mich.& St. Leon. c.	— p.c. FR	117	0	0
Ecclesfield...... —	v. —	150	0	0
Greasborough .. —	p.c. —	110	0	0
Hooton Roberts —	r. KB	7	11	8
Smeaton Kirk .. —	r. —	10	1	0
Tankersley .... —	r. —	26	0	2
Thornscoe ...... —	r. —	11	7	8
Tinsley .... —	p.c. PR	111	0	0
Wentworth .... —	p.c. —	120	0	0
FITZWILLIAM, Earl, and others				
Thorpe Basset .. —	r. —	144	0	0
FOLEY, Lord				
Great Witley .. Worc.	r. KB	7	6	3
Holt w. Little } Witley c....	— r. —	15	17	8
Kidderminster } with Lower Mitton c.....	— v. —	30	15	7
Oddingley...... —	r. —	4	19	4
Oldswinford w. } Lye c.......	— r. —	26	6	8
Pedmore ...... —	r. —	9	10	0
Shelsley Beau- } champ......	— r. —	9	4	4
Shelsley Walsh.. —	r. PR	67	3	0
FORESTER, Lord				
Broseley ...... Salop	r. —	7	18	6
Lit.Wenlock w. } Salop	r. —	11	13	4
Barrow ...... —	p.r. —	80	0	0
Willey .... —	—	117	14	9
FORTESCUE, Earl				
Challacombe.... Devon.	r. —	11	9	3
Filleigh with } E. Buckland	— r. —	21	6	10
Wyer Gifford .. —	r. —	13	5	0
Billingborough Linc.	v. —	6	1	8
Sempringham } w. Pointon c. & Birthorpe c...........	— v. PR	28	0	0
GAGE, Lord Viscount				
Staunton ...... Glouc.	r. —	94	10	9
Dixton .... Monm.	v. PR	130	0	0
Maresfield ...... Suss.	r. KB	12	0	0
GODERICH, Viscount				
Bennington .... Linc.	r. —	33	8	11
Conisholme	r. PR	128	0	0
Wyham .... —	r. KB	80	0	0
GOSFORD, Earl of				
Wysall .... Notts.	v. —	4	11	0

Beccles, St.Mary Suff.	v. KB	7	6	3
—— St. Mich. —	r. —	21	12	3
Ellough........ —	r. —	12	0	0
Kettleborough ..		16	0	0
Pakefield .... } 1st Mediety 2d Ditto....	— r. —	14	0	0
Redisham...... —	p.c. PR	40	0	0
GOWER, Earl				
Kinnersley .... Salop.	r. KB	6	1	8
GOWER, W. L.				
Limpsfield...... Surry	r. —	20	0	5
Tatsfield ...... —	r. —	5	0	5
Titsey.......... —	r. —	7	17	3
GRAFTON, Duke of				
Barnham, St. } Gregory .... Suff.	r. —	7	11	10
— St. Martin } w. Euston & Little Fa- kenham	— r. —	21	13	4
Great Fakenham —	r. —	11	10	5
Sapiston........ —	p.c. PR	34	0	5
GRANTHAM, Lord				
Bracewell ...... Yksh.	v. PR	60	0	0
GRANTLEY, Lord				
Wonersh-........ Surry	v. —	119	0	0
GRENVILLE, Lord				
Boconnoc w. } Broad Oak Corn.	r. KB	18	11	0
Ladock .... —	r. —	18	0	0
New Milford .. Pemb.	p.c. —	not in char		
GROSVENOR, Earl (marq. of Westminster)				
Alford .... Chesh.	r. —	16	17	8
Chester, St. Mary —	r. —	52	0	0
Eccleston ...... —	r. —	15	13	11
Farndon........ —	p.c. PR	104	0	0
Pulford .... —	r. KB	6	15	10
Prestwich...... Lanc.	r. —	46	6	9
Ratcliffe,St Thos. —	p.c. —	not in char		
GUILFORD, Earl of				
Ashley w. Sil- } verley v..... Camb.	r. KB	15	17	3
Kirtling .... —	v. —	10	0	0
Harlow .... Essex	v. —	15	7	11
Lindsell........ —	v. PR	99	8	0
East Langdon .. Kent	r. —	136	0	0
ChippingWarden Npn.	r. KB	26	10	0
Elsfield .... Oxon	v. PR	134	0	6
Shotteswell .... Warw.	v. KB	5	13	4
GUILFORD, Earl of, and others				
Eythorne........ Kent	r. —	15	12	6
HARBOROUGH, Earl of				
Saxby.......... Leic.	r. —	120	0	0
Stapleford ...... —	v. —	100	0	0
Stainby with } Gunby .... Linc.	r. KB	10	10	10
Teigh .... Rutl.	r. --	14	2	11

Whisendine	Rutl.	v. PR	144	0	0
HARCOURT, Earl					
North Hinksey ..	Berks.	p.c. —	90	0	0
Nuneham-Courtney .. }	Oxf.	r. KB	15	6	0
HARDWICKE, Earl of					
Foulmire	Camb.	r. —	20	14	2
Wimpole	—	r. —	18	0	0
Shenfield	Essex.	r. —	14	18	4
Haresfield	Glouc.	v. PR	113	13	4
Aspeden	Herts.	r. KB	15	5	2
Ayott, St. Peter..	—	r. —	7	8	6
Ridge	—	v. PR	110	0	0
St. Alban's, St. Peter Colney }		— p. c. KB not in char.			
Westmill	Herts	r. KB	20	0	0
Crudewell	Wilts.	r. —	17	5	2
Buntingford Gram. Sch. Herts, Mastership					
HARLWOOD, Earl of					
Goldsborough ..	Yksh.	r. —	10	1	0
Harewood, alt. ..	—	v. —	14	1	10
HARROWBY, Earl of					
Aston-sub-edge..	Glouc.	r. —	10	2	2
Mark	Som.	p. c. PR	75	0	0
Sandon	Staff.	r. KB	7	10	0
HARRINGTON, Earl of					
Gawsworth	Chesh.	r. KB	7	4	4
HASTINGS, Marquess of					
Smisby	Derby.	p.c.—	35	0	0
Piddletown	Dorset.	v. —	31	2	11
Ashby de la Zouch	Leic.	v. —	14	10	4
Belton	—	v. PR	68	0	0
Castle Don-nington .... }	—	v. —	8	2	3
Markfield	—	r. —	6	1	3
Osgathorpe	—	v. —	7	0	0
Stanton Stoney ..	—	r. —	14	13	1
West Leake	Notts.	r. —	25	4	7
HENNIKER, Lord					
Catcott	Som.	p.c. —	50	0	0
Ashfield with Thorpe c... }	Suff.	p.c. —	32	0	0
Debenham	—	v. KB	15	2	6
Kenton	—	v. PR	130	0	0
Great Thornham.	—	r. KB	7	11	3
Little Thornham.	—	r. —	4	14	4
Worlingworth w. Southolt c. }	—	r. —	19	12	3
HERTFORD, Marquess of					
Laughton	Leic.	r. KB	10	10	5
Laughton	Linc.	v. PR	140	0	0
Alcester	Warw.	v. KB	14	8	10
Arrow	—	r. —	10	10	7
Binton	—	r. PR	140	0	0
Birdsall	—	p.c. —	49	0	0
HOLLAND, Lord					
Ampthill	Beds.	r. —	10	6	8
Milbrook	—	r. —	9	16	3
Brinkworth	Wilts.	r. —	23	9	2
Foxley	—	r. —	3	17	8

HOTHAM, Lord					
South Dalton....	Yksh.	r. KB	12	0	0
Hutton Crans-wick ...... }	—	v. PR	53	1	0
Scarborough	—	v. —	60	0	0
HOWARD OF EFFINGHAM, Lord					
Rotheram	Yksh.	v. KB	16	8	6
Whiston	—	r. —	10	0	0
HOWE, Earl					
Little Minster ..	Bucks.	v. —	93	0	0
Penn	—	v. KB	9	13	4
Altham	Lanc.	p.c. PR	73	10	10
Clithero	—	p c. —	110	0	0
Downham	—	p.c. —	128	0	0
Newchurch in Pendle .... }	—	p.c. —	105	0	0
Ratcliffe on Soar.	Notts.	v. KB	10	11	3
Acton	Suff.	v. —	9	6	3
Whitacre Over..	Warw.p.c.PR		140	0	0
Gotham, alt.	Notts.	r. KB	19	8	6
HUNTINGFIELD, Lord					
Aldham	Suff.	r. KB	10	13	4
Aldringham w. Thorpe c. }	—	p.c. PR	40	18	0
Huntingfield w. Cookley .... }	—	r. KB	13 / 6	6 / 13	8 / 4
Laxfield with Cratfield.... }	—	v. —	15	1	3
Great Linstead ..	—	p.c. PR	82	0	0
Little Linstead ..	—	p.c. —	65	10	0
Ubbeston	—	v. KB	6	13	4
HUNTINGTOWER, Lord					
Buckminster	Leic.	v. PR	150	0	0
Silk Willoughby .	Linc.	r. KB	14	8	1
ILCHESTER, Earl of					
Rewe	Devon.	r. —	22	4	2
Abbotsbury	Dorset.v. PR		125	4	0
Bridport........	—	r. —	135	0	0
Maiden Newton .	—	r. KB	30	5	0
Melbury Bubb ..	—	v. —	11	10	5
——— Osmond .	—	r. ..	8	3	4
——— Sampford	—	r. —	5	6	5
Stinsford........	—	v. —	12	17	1
Winterborne Monkton .. }	—	r. PR	130	0	0
Middle Chinnock	Som..	r. KB	7	9	7
Chiselborough with West Chinnock c. }	—	r. —	14	6	7
Kilmington	—	r. —	21	9	4
Milton Clevedon	—	v. —	6	13	4
Penselwood	—	r. PR	147	16	0
Shepton Montagu	—	p.c. —	46	0	0
Somerton	—	r. KB	16	0	7
WestGrimstead w.Plaitford c. }	Wilts.	r. —	7	10	2
Little Somerford	—	r. —	8	7	1
ILCHESTER, Earl of, &c.					
Lustleigh	Devon.	r. —	16	7	6
Silverton	—	r. —	51	8	4

JERSEY, Earl of				
Britton Ferry ..	Glam. p.c. PR	105	0	0
Glyncorriog	— p.c. —	62	17	4
KENYON, Lord				
Peel	Lanc. pc. PR	93	0	0
Pulverbatch	Salop. r. KB	10	13	4
KING, Lord				
Culborne	Som. r. PR	51	0	0
East Clandon ..	Surry. r. KB	10	6	10
Ockham	— r. —	11	2	1
LANSDOWNE, Marquis of				
High Wycombe..	Bucks. v. PR	122	0	0
Calstone........	Wilts. r. KB	4	13	4
LE DESPENCER, Lord				
Mereworth......	Kent r. —	14	2	6
Tudeley w. Ca- } pel le Perne c. }	— v. —	4	16	0
LEICESTER'S (Earl of) HOSPITAL, Govs. of				
Hampton in } Arden with } Knowle c. .. }	Warw. v. —	15	6	8
LICHFIELD, Earl of				
Marsham	Norf. r. KB	10	17	9
Paston	— v. PB	107	0	0
Swanton Abbot..	— r. KB	6	10	9
Ellenhall	Staff. p.c. PR	91	18	2
Norbury........	— r. KB	10	2	6
LILFORD, Lord				
Leigh	Lanc. v. PR	94	0	0
Warrington	— r. KB	40	0	0
Aldwinkle, St. } Peter ...... }	Npn. r. —	11	6	3
Pilton	— r. PR	136	11	3
Thorpe Achurch } w. Lilford v. }	— r. KB	22	8	11
Titchmarsh	— r. —	45	0	0
Warrington Gram. Sch. Lanc. Mastership				
LINDSAY, Earl of				
Uffington	— r. —	21	5	2
LISBURNE, Lord				
Ystrad-meiric ..	Card. r. KB not in char.			
Ysotty Ystwith..	— p c. PR	83	18	0
LIVERPOOL, Earl of				
Hawkesbury w. } Tresham c... }	Glouc. v. PR	140	0	0
Pitchford	Salop. r. KB	6	5	5
LONDONDERRY, Marquess of				
Durham, St. Giles	Durh. p.c. PR	50	0	0
—— St. Nichol	— p.c. —	90	0	0
Great Asby	Westm. v. KB	23	13	4
LONSDALE, Earl of				
Aikton	Cumb. r. KB	14	13	1
Beaumont w. } Kirk Andrs. } on Eden.... }	— r. PR / RB	80 / 9	0 / 9	0 / 8
Bolton Gate	— r. —	19	18	4
Bootle..........	— r. —	19	17	3
Bowness	— r. —	21	3	11
Brigham........	— v. —	20	16	0
Cockermouth....	— p.c. PR	97	0	0
Corney	Cumb. r. KB	9	17	1
Dittington	— r. —	7	1	0
Embleton	— p.c. PR	36	0	0
Hayle..........	— p.c. —	79	0	0
Hensingham	— p.c. —	136	0	0
Kirkbampton ..	— r. —	86	0	0
Lorton	— p.c. —	60	0	0
Lowswater	— p.c. —	46	16	6
Moresby........	— r. —	107	4	8
Mossar	— p c. —	54	0	0
Patterdale......	— p.c. —	70	0	0
St. Bees	— p.c. —	66	0	0
Whitehaven, } St. Nicholas }	— p.c. —	140	0	0
—— St. James ..	— p.c. —	108	16	0
—— Trinity	— p.c. —	92	0	0
Whiteham	— r. KB	8	15	0
Melling	Lanc. p.c. PR	63	0	0
High Barton	West. v. PR	150	0	0
Lowther	— r. KB	25	7	3
Ravenstondale ..	— p.c. PR	120	0	0
Shap	— v. —	91	10	0
Arkingarthdale..	Yksh. p.c. —	92	0	0
Startforth	— v. —	128	19	8
Wilton	— p.c. —	114	10	0
LYTTELTON, Lord				
Halesowen w. } Offchurch c. }	Salop. Worc. v. KB	15	8	11
Penkridge and } Copnall w. }	—	24	0	0
Dunston c. }	Staff. p.c. PR	70	8	0
and Wood- } baston c..... }	KB	10	0	0
Shareshill	— p.c. PR	105	0	0
Churchill, near } Kiddermins. }	Worc. r. KB	5	6	8
Hagley with } Frankley c.& } St. Kenelm c. }	— r. — Salop.	10	6	5
MALMESBURY, Earl of				
Dibden	Hants. r. KB	5	12	11
MANCHESTER, Duke of				
Quedgeley	Glouc. d. —	40	0	0
Breamore with } Hale ...... }	Hants. d. —	92	0	0
Kimbolton	Hunts. v. —	137	14	9
Holywell with } Needing- } worth c. }	— r. KB	30	6	3
Swinestead	— r. —	12	13	6
MAN-CORNWALLIS, Earl of				
Llandewi Brery .	Card. p.c. —	110	10	6
Linton	Kent. v. KB	7	13	4
Little Saxham ..	Suff. r. —	8	11	5
Palgrave	— r. —	19	11	3
Thrandeston	— r. —	13	6	3
Packwood	Warw. p.c. PU	66	0	0
MANVERS, Earl				
Langton, by } Wragby .... }	Linc. v. —	4	13	4

Cotgrave, 1st and 2d Mediety ...... }	Notts.	r.	PR	20	2	1
Cuckney........	—	v.	—	150	0	0
Eakring	—	r.	KB	9	16	0
Fledborough	—	r.	—	9	7	6
Holm Pierrepoint with Adbolton .. }	—	r.	—	15	7	6
				2	13	9
Laxton	—	v.	PR	129	0	0
Lowdham	—	v.	KB	4	18	4
Nottingham, St. Mary & St. Paul c... }	—	v.	—	20	5	8
Radcliffe on Trent ...... }	—	v.	—	4	12	6
Snenton	—	p.c	PR	87	0	0
Weston in the Clay ...... }	—	r.	KB	19	2	11
MARLBOROUGH, Duke of						
Hurley	Berks.	v.	PR	138	17	9
Long Crendon ..	Bucks.	p c.	--	98	0	0
Low Winchendon	—	p.c.	—	80	0	0
Waddesdon, three portions }	—	r.	KB	45	0	0
Ardley	Oxon.	r.	—	5	12	8
Bladon with Woodstock c. }	—	r.	—	16	0	5
				5	5	0
Noke	—	r.	PR	130	0	0
Sandford	—	d.	—	50	0	0
Stonesfield	—	r.	KB	4	19	9
Hardwick Priors w. Marston Priors c. and Low Shuckburg c. }	Warw.	v.	—	23	16	0
Liddington, sin...	Wilts.	r.	—	14	0	0
West Overton with Alton Priors c. & Fifield c. .. }	—	v.	—	23	0	5
MAYNARD, Lord Viscount						
Great Easton....	Essex.	r.	KB	18	13	4
Little Easton....	—	r.	—	10	0	0
Thaxstead	—	v.	—	24	0	0
Tiltey..........	—	d.	PR	30	0	0
Thornton with Bagworth c. and Stanton under Bardon c....... }	Leic.	v.	KB	6	10	2
Passenham	Npn.	r.	—	20	0	0
MELBOURNE, Lord Viscount						
Boothby Grafton	Linc.	r.	KB	11	12	3
Willesford	—	r.	—	10	0	0
Duston	Npn.	v.	PR	93	5	5
Greasley with Kimberley c. }	Notts.	v.	—	51	0	0
Hertford Gram. Sch.			Mastership.			
MIDDLETON, Lord						
Carlton in Moorland w. Stapleford c. }	Linc.	v.	PR	5	3	4
Grimoldby	—	r.	—	116	13	3
Saundby........	Notts.	r.	—	78	9	1
Trowell, 1st & 2d Med..... }	—	r.	KB	9	8	9
North Wheatley	—	v.	PR	105	0	0
Wollaton with Cossall c... }	—	r.	—	88	11	4
Middleton	Warw.	p.c.	not in char.			
Wharram in the Street ...... }	Yksh.	v.	PR	70	0	0
Smeaton	—	r.	KB	13	13	4
Henbury with Aust c. and Northwick c. 1 turn in 4 .. }	Glouc.	v.	—	30	0	0
MOLESWORTH, Lord						
Edlington	Yksh.	r	—	130	0	0
MONSON, Lord						
Broxholme......	Linc.	r.	—	9	10	0
Bucknall	—	r.	—	9	11	10
Burton	—	r.	—	11	15	2
Camringham	—	v.	PR	137	10	0
Croft	—	v.	KB	23	7	3
Dalby..........	—	p.c.	PR	73	0	0
Donnington on Baine ...... }	—	r.	—	110	0	0
North Carlton ..	—	p.c.	—	35	0	0
Owersby with Kirby Osgarby ...... }	—	v.	—	103	10	0
			KB	8	18	4
South Carlton ..	—	p.c.	PR	37	0	0
MONTACUTE, Lord						
Eastbourne, n. Midhurst .. }	Suss.	v.	PR	35	0	0
MONTAGU, Lord						
Copmanford w. Upton c. .... }	Hunts.	r.	KB	18	13	1
Winwick	—	v.	PR	44	10	0
Luddington	Leic.	r.	KB	8	8	9
Barnwell, AllSts.	Npn.	r.	PR	120	0	0
—— St. Andrew	—	r.	—	150	0	0
Hemington	—	v.	—	99	8	0
Church Lawford with Newnham Regis p. c. }	Warw.	r.	KB	11	15	5
				5	0	0
MONTFORD, Lord						
Westwicken	Cam.	p.c.	PR	50	0	0
MORLEY, Earl of						
Morley with Smalley c... }	Derby	r.	—	13	6	8
Charlton	Devon.	r.	—	31	8	4
Morleigh	—	r.	PR	102	16	5
North Moulton w. Twitchin c. }	—	v.	—	81	8	5

Zele Mona-chorum .. } *Devon. r.*   KB   17   8   9
MOUNT EDGECOMBE, Earl of
Landrake ...... *Corn. r.*   KB   18   12   4
Lostwithiel .... — *v.*   PR   92   10   0
Megavissey .... ← *v.*   KB   6   4   2
Rame .... — *r.*   —   12   7   6
St. Michael on } the Mount.. } — *p.c.* — not in char.
Truro, St. Mary — *r.*   PR   140   0   0
MOUNTNORRIS, Earl of
Arley Over ....*Staff. p.c.* KB not in char.
MUNCASTER, Lord
Irton ....*Cumb. p.c.* PR   110   0   0
Muncaster...... — *p c.* —   40   14   0
Wabberthwaite.. — *r.*   —   107   0   0
Warter .... *Yksh. v.* —   27   0   0
NEWCASTLE, Duke of
Bamber .... *Linc. p.c.* —   30   0   0
Bothamsall ....*Notts. p.c.* —   50   0   0
Cromwell ...... — *r.*   KB   13   2   3
Elksley .... — *v.*   PR   110   0   0
Kirton .... — *r.*   KB   7   14   9
Mapplebeck .... — *p.c.* PR   37   0   0
East Markham } with West } —. *v.* KB   11   18   11
Drayton *c...*
Damerham w. } Martin *c.* .. } *Wilts. v.* —   25   10   10
NORFOLK, Duke of
Bixley with } Framlingham } *Norf. r.* KB   8   6   8
Earl
Bressingham.... — *r.*   —   15   0   0
Great Poringland — *r.*   —   6   13   2
Shelfanger...... — *r.*   —   17   0   0
Thwaite, St. Mary — *r.*   PR   138   17   2
Worksop ...... *Notts. v.* KB   12   4   2
Bungay .... *Suff. p.c.* PR   44   0   0
Ilketshall, St. } Margaret .. } — *r.* KB   5   13   9
Capel ....*Surry. d.* PR   50   0   0
Dorking .... — *v.*   KB   14   13   11
Arundel .... *Suss. v.* —   5   0   10
South Stoke .... — *r.*   —   11   15   10
Storrington .... — *r.*   —   18   0   0
Thakeham ...... — *r.*   —   14   9   9
Worminghurst.. — *p.c.* PR   40   0   0
Handsworth .... *Yksh. r.* KB   12   4   7
Treeton .... — *r.*   —   12   0   0
NORTHAMPTON, Marquis of
Moulsoe........*Bucks. v.* KB   16   16   8
Castle Ashby.... *Npn. r.* —   17   9   7
Yardley Hastings — *r.*   —   13   16   0
Compton Wy-neate with } *Warw.v.* —   20   0   0
Tysoe
Whatcott ...... — *r.*   —   12   17   3
NORTHUMBERLAND, Duke of
Haslebury Bryan *Dorset. r.* KB   19   13   9

St.Mary at Hill } and St. And. } *Lond. r.* PR   333   6   8
Hubbard,*alt.*
Alnham .... *North. r.* —   70   0   0
Alnwick .... — *p.c.* —   106   0   0
Birtley .... — *p.c.* —   120   0   0
Chatton .... — *v.*   KB   12   16   0
Doddington .... — *p.c.* — not in char.
Elsdon .... — *r.*   —   20   0   0
Long Houghton.. — *v.* PR   140   0   0
Ilderton .... — *r.*   —   80   0   0
Tynemouth } with North } — *v.* KB   24   19   4
Shields *c. alt.*
Kirkby Wiske .. *Yksh. r.* —   27   16   5
Kirkheaton .... — *r.*   —   25   13   9
NORTHWICK, Lord
Harrow .... *Midd. v.* —   33   4   2
ONSLOW, Earl
West Clandon .. *Surry r.* —   124   13   0
Merrow .... — *r.*   —   111   1   0
Send w. Ripley *c.* — *v.* KB   8   18   1
Wisley w. Pir-ford *v.*....... } *Surry r.* KB   40   19   0
Woking .... — *v.*   —   11   5   0
ORFORD, Earl of
Huntshaw ......*Devon. r.* PR   100   0   0
Aldby ......,..*Norf. r.* —   115   8   7
Bircham New-ton and Tofts } — *r.* KB   7   13   4
Burnham Thorpe — *r.*   —   19   10   0
Itteringham w. } Mannington . } — *r.* —   12   10   5
North Barsham.. — *r.*   —   6   0   0
Sloley .... — *r.*   —   5   6   8
Tivetshall, St. } Mary and St. } — *r.* —   20   0   0
Margaret ..
Waborne ...... — *p.c.* —not in char.
Wickmere w. } Woolierton. } — *r.* —   17   0   0
OXFORD, Earl of
Aylton ....*Heref. r.* PR   75   0   0
Brampton .... } Bryan, *alt...* } — *r.* KB   5   11   0
Cusop .... — *r.*   —   5   19   7
Kenderchurch .. — *p.c.* PR   32   0   0
Leintwardine.... — *v.*   KB   7   15   8
St. Margaret .... — *p.c.* —   6   0   0
Walterstone .... — *p.c.* PR   62   0   0
Old Castle......*Mon. p.c.* —   76   0   0
Presteigne, w. } Discoyd *c.* & } *Radn. v.* KB   20   0   0
Kinsham *c. alt.* ....
PEMBROKE, Earl of
Langeinwen w. } Langaffo *c...* } *Angl. r.* —   16   4   -4
Chalbury ......*Dorset. r.* —   7   10   2
Abdon ....*Salop. r.* PR   95   10   0

Bishopstone n. } Wilts. r. KB 19 14 2
Swind. sin. }
Ditto .... — v. — 12 1 3
Chilmark ...... — r. — 19 13 4
Fovant .... — r. — 17 0 0
Fuggleston, }
  St. Peter w. } — r. — 24 0 0
  Bemerton c. }
Little Lanngford Wilts. r. PR 110 0 0
North Newington — r.&p. KB 2 15 7
South Newton .. — v. PR 115 0 0
Stanton St. }
  Bernard .... } — v. KB 7 0 0
Wilton with }
  Bulbridge v. }
  Ditchampton } — r. — 23 18 4 / 10 0 0
  v. and Nether }
  Hampton c. }
Wylye.......... — r. — 21 14 2
PLYMOUTH, Earl of
Pennarth St. }
  Austin with } Glam. r. PR 119 6 0
  Llavernock }
St. Fagan with }
  Llaniltern c. } — r. KB 14 9 7
Radir.......... — v. PR 57 0 0
Kempsing w. } Kent. v. KB 19 13 4
  Seal c. .... }
Stratford on } Warw. v. — 23 0 0
  Avon, alt. .. }
Tanworth ...... — v. — 6 13 4
Tardebig ......Worc. v. — 8 0 0
POMFRET, Earl of
Bourne ....Linc. v. KB 8 0 0
Cold Higham ..Npn. r. PR 124 0 0
Easton Neston .. — v. KB 8 0 0
PORTLAND, Duke of
Bolsover ......Derby. v. PR 117 0 0
Botley ....Hants.r. KB 5 10 2
Bothall with } North. r. — 28 17 1
  Sheepwash.. }
Kirkby in Ash- } Notts. r. — 18 1 8
  field ...... }
Mansfield
  Woodhouse } — p.c. PR 142 0 0
  w. Skegby.. }
Muskham, 2d } — p.c. KB 8 19 7
  Mediety .... }
Sibthorpe ...... — d. PR 28 0 0
Sutton on }
  Lound with } — v. KB 10 0 0 / PR 57 0 0
  Scrooby .... }
Gotham, 1 tu. } — r. KB 19 8 6
  in 3 ...... }
PORTMORE, Earl of
Thorne ....Yksh. p.c. PR 72 0 0
PORTSMOUTH, Earl of
Farley Wallop } — r. — 20 8 9
  w. Cliddesden }
Over Wallop.... — v. — 27 5 2

Weild ....Yksh.p.c. PR not in char.
POULETT, Earl
Chafcombe......Som. r. — 120 2 0
Chillington .... — p.c. — 46 0 0
Lympsham .... — r. KB 38 5 2
Seavington, St. }
  Mary and St. } — p.c. PR 163 0 0
  Michael r. w. } KB 30 0 0
  Dinnington c. }
Hinton, St. Geo. — r. — 13 13 4
POWIS, Earl
Bishops Castle..Heref. v. — 9 12 11
Llanwddun ....Mont. p.c. PR 57 10 0
Bromfield w. } Salop. v. KB 6 0 0
  Hawford c. }
Clunbury ...... — p.c. — not in char.
Clunn with }
  Bettws p.c. } Salop. v. — 13 10 5 / PR 34 10 0
  & Edgton c. }
Llanfair Wa- }
  terdine and } — p.c. — 100 0 0
  Shipton c. .. }
Monsford ...... — v. KB 4 18 6
Mindtown ...... — r. PR 60 0 0
Shrawardine .. — r. KB 9 12 6
RADNOR, Earl of
Coleshill ...... Berks v. — 17 11 8
Hambledon ...Surry r. — 6 7 11
Great Civerhall Wilts r. — 16 0 0
Little Ditto .... — r. — 11 17 3
Odstock........ — r. — 11 17 11
Pewsey ...... — r. — 26 16 8
t anton, St. }
  Quintin .... } — v. — 10 5 7
RANCLIFFE, Lord
Bunney with }
  Bradmore c. } Notts. v. — 6 14 0
Costock........ — r. — 7 18 4
Keyworth ...... — r. — 7 5 0
Thorpe in Glebis — r. — 12 9 4
RAVENSWORTH, Lord, &c.
Lamesley ......Dur. p.c. — 90 0 0
Tanfield........ — p.c. — 85 0 0
REDESDALE,Lord
Lower Leming- } Glouc. p.c. KB 10 0 0
  ton .... }
Goring ....Suss. v. PR 130 0 0
RICHMOND, Duke of
Boxgrove ...... Suss. v. — 9 5 5
Tangmere ...... — r. PR 145 0 0
Singleton w. }
  Eastdam v. }
  and Friston v. } — r. KB 18 17 8
  1 turn in 3 .. }
RIVERS, Lord
Belchalwell w. }
  Fifehead } Dorset r — 12 16 5
  Neville .... }
Cerne Abbas .... — v. PR 95 5 0
Chesselborn .... — r. KB 18 10 5

Burton Brad-stock w.	*Dorset*	r.	KB	25	0	0
Sheppington George p.c.						
Ibberton........	—	r.	—	19	13	9
Iwerne Courtney	—	r.	—	25	8	1
Melcomb Horsey	—	r.	—	16	0	0
Okeford Fitz-paine	—	r.	—	21	12	8
Pimperne	—	r.	—	19	12	6
Shapwick w. Ashcott p.c.	—	v.	—	7	9	4
Sturminster Newton	—	v.	—	16	16	8
Sudely	*Glouc.*	r.	PR	46	0	0
Winchcombew. Gretton c. ..	—	v.	—	61	11	10
ROCHFORD, Earl of						
Easton	*Suff.*	r.	—	10	18	6
RODNEY, Lord						
High Roding....	*Essex*	r.	—	20	0	0
ROKEBY, Lord						
Coveney with Maney c....	*Camb.*	r.	—	5	0	0
Arthingworth ..	*Npn.*	r.	—	12	2	8
ROLLE, Lord						
Abbots Bick-ington......	*Devon* p.c.		PR	83	0	0
Bickton........	—	r.	KB	12	13	4
Chittlehampton..	—	v.	—	34	18	11
Harpford with Fen Ottery c.	—	v.	PR	139	10	6
Lancross	—	r.	--	40	0	0
Langtree	—	r.	KB	29	1	3
North Tamerton	—	d.	—	not in char		
Otterton........	—	v.	—	22	0	0
ROLLE, Lord, &c.						
Little Torrington	—	r.	—	14	18	11
West Chelboro'..	—	r.	PR	133	0	0
ROMNEY, Earl of						
Allington	*Kent*	r.	—	114	0	0
Paddlesworth,des.	—	r.	KB	not in char		
ROSEBERY, Earl of						
Postwick	*Norf.*	r.	—	10	0	0
ROSSLYN, Earl of						
Knaresborough..	*Yksh.*	v.	KB	9	9	4
RUTLAND, Duke of						
Borough Green..	*Camb.*	r.	—	18	10	0
Newmarket w. WoodDittonv.	—	r.	—	46	5	5
Whitwell	*Derby*	r.	—	20	3	4
Sturmer	*Essex.*	r.	—	8	10	0
Aylestone with Lit. Glen c. and Lubbesthorp c.	*Leic.*	r.	—	31	8	11
Barkston	—	v.	—	7	5	5
Bottesford	—	r.	—	51	5	0
Branston	--	v.	—	15	10	5
Croxton Kerrial	*Leic.*	r.	KB	7	14	17
Croxton South ..	—	r.	PR	125	0	0
Knaptoft with Shearsby c.	—	r.	KB	32	12	0
Knipton	—	r.	—	16	12	3
Redmile	—	r.	—	12	9	2
Scalford	—	v.	—	8	1	10
Sproxton and Saltby	—	v.	PR	100	0	0
Thorpe Arnold with Brentingby	.—	v.	KB	6	17	8
WalthamleWolds	—	r.	—	11	0	0
Harby	—	r.	—	20	0	0
Plungar........	—	v.	PR	120	0	0
Gunby	*Linc.*	r.	—	140	0	0
Osbourny	—	v.	KB	7	0	5
Ropesley	—	r.	—	11	14	2
South Witham ..	—	r.	PR	95	0	0
Woolsthorpe	—	r.	KB	12	2	8
Granby with Sutton c.....	*Notts.*	v.	PR	120	0	0
Gringley	—	v.	—	140	0	0
Bisbrooke	*Rutl.*	r.	KB	6	0	4
Lidgate	*Suff.*	r.	—	15	10	5
Trowbridge w. Staverton c.	*Wilts*	r.	—	20	12	8
SALISBURY, Marquess of						
Cranborne	*Dorset*	v.	—	120	0	0
Long Burton w. Holnest c.	.—	v.	—	100	0	0
Pebworth	*Glouc.*	v.	—	55	0	0
Lit. Berkhampst.	*Herts.*	r.	KB	7	8	6
Bygrave	—	r.	—	17	9	7
Clothall........	—	r.	—	16	0	7
Essendon with Bayford c. ..	—	r.	—	18	0	0
Bishops Hatfield	—	r.	—	36	2	1
Great Offley	—	v.	—	9	0	0
—— Edstone ..	*Yksh.*	v.	PR	140	0	0
SANDWICH, Earl of						
Little Ravely...	*Hunts* p.c.		PR	30	0	0
SAY AND SELE, Lord						
Mursley........	*Bucks*	r.	KB	10	0	0
SCARBOROUGH, Earl of						
Blyton	*Linc.*	v.	KB	12	0	0
Glentworth w. Spittle c...	—	v.	PR	56	0	0
Saxby St. Helens	—	r.	KB	7	4	2
Scothern	—	v.	PR	100	0	0
Skegness ··....	—	r.	—	90	0	0
Stainton St. John	—	v.	KB	4	18	4
Willoughton, alt.	—	v.	PR	143	12	3
Maltby	*Yksh.*	v.	—	30	0	0
Stainton	—	v.	—	80	0	0
SCARSDALE, Lord						
Kedlaston	*Derby*	r.	PR	90	0	0
Quarndon	—	p.c.	—	40	0	0
Worthington	*Leic.*	p.c.	—	110	0	0

SCOTT, Lord, alt.

Parish	County			£	s	d
Dunchurch	Warw.	v.	KB	14	1	10

SEFTON, Earl of

Parish	County			£	s	d
Altcar	Lanc.	p.c.	PR	37	10	0

SELSEY, Lord

Parish	County			£	s	d
Elstead	Suss.	r.	PR	31	10	0
Stedham with } Heyshot .. }	—	r.	KB	17	18	6
Treyford with } Didling.... }	—	r.	PR	127	0	0

SEYMOUR, Lord Robert

Parish	County			£	s	d
Taliaris........	Carm.	p.c.	PR	52	0	0

SEYMOUR, Lord H. &c.

Parish	County			£	s	d
Bonchurch	Hants.	r.	—	140	0	0

SHATESBURY, Earl of

Parish	County			£	s	d
Cann, St. Rumbold	—	r.	—	9	2	1
Edmondisham ..	—	r.	PR	100	0	0
Hinton Martel ..	—	r.	KB	16	18	6
Horton	—	v.	PR	50	0	0
Loders with } Baunton c.alt. }	—	v.	—	105	0	0
Shaftesbury, } St. James .. }	—	r.	KB	1	11	0
——St. Peter & } Holy Trinity }	—	r.	PR	140	0	0
—— St. Rumb.	—	r.	KB	9	2	1
Wimborne, All } Saints & St. } Giles ...... }	—	r.	—	9	4	4
—— Minster	—	r.	—	12	13	4
Beeby	Leic.	r.	PR	107	3	0
Purton	Wilts.	v.	KB	22	17	6

SHERBORNE, Lord

Parish	County			£	s	d
Sherborne......	Glouc.	v.	KB	15	6	8
Windrush	—	v.	—	5	0	0

SHREWSBURY, earl of

Parish	County			£	s	d
Burghfield	Berks.		KB	14	19	8
Cotfield, alt.....	Norf.		RV	7	10	0

SOMERS, Earl

Parish	County			£	s	d
Eastnor........	Heref.	r.	—	7	19	5
Pixley	—	v.	PR	65	12	0
Droitwich, St. } St. Peter .. }	Worc.	v.	KB	6	0	0
Leigh with } Bransford c. }	—	r.	—	13	9	4
Little Malvern..	—	p.c.	PR	15	0	0
North Piddle ..	—	r.	—	116	12	11
Stoulton	—	p c.	—	60	0	0

SOMERSET, Duke of

Parish	County			£	s	d
Berry Pomeroy	Devon.	v.	KB	18	19	7
Witham Friary	Som.	p.c.	PR	40	0	0

SOMERVILLE, Lord

Parish	County			£	s	d
Aston Somerville	Glouc.	r.	KB	9	3	4

SONDES, Lord

Parish	County			£	s	d
Wendy with } Shengay c. }	Camb.	r.	PR	42	0	0
Badlesmere w. } Leveland .. }	Kent.	r.	KB	9	2	0
Selling	—	v.	—	6	13	4

Parish	County			£	s	d
Garthorpe......	Leic.	v.	KB	7	5	3
Kettering	Npn.	r.	—	34	13	4
Rockingham....	—	r.	PR	107	0	0
Stoke Albany ..	—	r.	KB	13	6	8
Weston on } Welland w. } Sutton Bas- } set .... }	—	v.	—	11	17	1
Wilbarston	—	v.	—	7	17	1

SOUTHWELL, Lord Viscount, &c.

Parish	County			£	s	d
Garway........	Heref.	p.c.	PR	45	0	0

SOUTHWELL, Lady

Parish	County			£	s	d
Asterby........	Linc.	r.	—	135	10	6

SPENCER, Earl

Parish	County			£	s	d
Dunton........	Beds.	v.	PR	104	16	0
....	Bucks.	r.	KB	9	9	7
Stanton Bury ..	—	v.	PR	30	0	0
Sandridge	Herts.	v.	KB	8	0	0
Bozeat with } Strixton r. }	Npn.	v.	—	15	0	0
Brampton Church	—	r.	—	21	6	8
Great Brington..	—	r.	—	40	0	0
N. Creake, alt.	Norf.	r.	KB	33	6	8
Hinton with } Steane.... }	—	r.	—	10	0	0
				5	9	7
Battersea	Surry.	v.	—	13	15	2
Wormleighton ..	Warw.	v.	PR	75	0	0

SPENCER, Lord Charles

Parish	County			£	s	d
Wheatfield	Oxon.	r.	KB	9	10	10

SPENCER, Lord Robert

Parish	County			£	s	d
Woolbeding	Suss.	r.	—	7	0	1

STAFFORD, Marquess of

Parish	County			£	s	d
Brackley, St. } Peter w. St. } James c. & } St. John c. }	Npn.	v.	—	19	1	6
Donnington	Salop.	r.	—	13	6	8
——, } St. George }	—	c.	PR	93	10	0
Lillershall	—	v.	KB	6	17	11
Barlaston	Staff	p.c.	PR	147	10	8
Blurton........	—	p.c.	KB	\multicolumn{3}{l}{not in char.}
Sheriffhales w. } Burleton c.& } Woodcote c. }	—	v.	—	11	1	8
Trentham with } Blurton c... }	—	p.c.	PR	13	9	2

STAFFORD, Earl of

Parish	County			£	s	d
Carrington	Chesh.	p.c.	—	100	0	0
Risley with } Breason c... }	Derby.	p.c.	—	125	6	8
Ashton under } Lyne .... }	Lanc.	r.	KB	26	13	4
Staley Bridge ..	—	p c.	PR	98	0	0
Breedon with } StauntonHar- } rold c. }	Leic.	v.	—	98	0	0
Rathby cum } Groby .... }	—	v.	—	86	0	0

Wolverhamp- ton, St. John }	*Staff.p.c.* PR	130	0	0
STOWELL, Lord				
Hampnet with }	*Glouc.* r. KB	10	0	0
Stowell .... }		5	17	1
STRADBROKE, Earl of				
Bedfield........	*Suff.* r. —	14	0	0
Brusyard	— *p.c.* PR	54	13	4
Darsham	— *v.* —	70	0	0
Eyke	— *r.* KB	15	0	0
Reydon with }	— *v.* —	13	6	8
Southwold *p.c.* }	PR	83	2	0
Wangford	— *p.c.* KB	not in char.		
Yoxford........	— *v.* —	5	14	2
STRATHMORE, Earl of				
Romaldkirk	*Yksh.* r. KB	58	14	2
SIDNEY, Viscount				
Bexley	*Kent.* v. —	13	4	7
Paul's Cray	— *r.* —	22	0	0
ST. ALBANS, Duke of				
Little Grimsby ..	*Linc.* v. KB	78	13	4
Pickworth......	— *r.* PR	137	2	7
Redbourn	— *v.* —	126	0	0
ST. GERMAINS, Earl of				
Jacobstow......	*Corn.* r. —	19	0	0
Eisey	*Wilts.* v. —	11	14	4
Latton	— *v.* PR	46	8	6
ST. HELEN'S, Lord, &c.				
Westminster,				
St. Clement }	*Midd.* r. —	52	7	1
Danes...... }				
ST. JOHN, Lord				
Bletsoe	*Beds.* r. KB	17	0	0
Melchburn	— *v.* PR	75	10	0
Risley..........	— *v.* —	124	5	0
Tilbrook........	— *r.* KB	13	10	0
Woodford, 1st Mediety }	*Npn.* r. —	11	8	1
—— 2d Mediety	— *r.* —	11	11	5
SUFFIELD, Lord				
Aldborough	*Norf.* r. —	8	0	0
Antingham, St. Mary .. }	— *r.* —	6	3	1
Blickling with }	— *r.* KB	10	13	4
Erpingham, }		9	18	0
alt. .... }				
Bradfield	— *r.* PR	119	0	0
Colby	— *r.* KB	8	15	10
Frettenham w. }	— *r.* —	10	0	0
Stanninghall }		1	13	6
Gunton with Hanworth v. }	— *r.* —	5	1	8
Hunworth with }	— *r.* —	10	3	4
Stody ...... }				
Knapton alt.....	— *r.* —	13	7	1
Overstrand	— *r.* —	2	1	5
Suffield	— *r.* —	14	0	0
Thorpe Market..	— *v.* PR	68	16	4
SUFFIELD, Lady				
Middleton	*Lanc.* r. —	36	3	11

SUFFIELD, Dowager Lady				
Norwich St.				
Michael at }	*Norf.p.c.* PR	87	0	0
Thorn ...... }				
TALBOT, Earl				
Church Eaton ..	*Staff.* r. —	14	19	9
Gratwich	— *r.* PR	140	0	8
Ingestrie	— *r.* KB	10	6	8
TANKERVILLE, Earl of				
Shrewsbury, St. Julian .. }	*Salop. p.c.* —	130	0	0
THANET, Earl of				
Hothfield	*Kent.* r. —	17	5	0
Framfield	*Suss.* v. —	13	6	8
Brougham	*West.* r. —	16	10	7
Dufton	— *r.* PR	120	0	0
Kirby Thore	— *r.* KB	37	17	11
Mallerstang	— *p.c.* PR	97	0	0
Long Marton....	— *r.* KB	21	15	7
Milborn........	— *p.c.* PR	94	0	0
Sowerby Temple	— *p.c.* —	86	0	0
Stainmore	— *p.c.* —	92	3	0
Silsdon on the }	*Yksh. pc..* —	86	0	0
Moor ...... }				
Hatfield... ...	*Suss.* r. KB	10	0	0
THURLOW, Lord				
Great Ashfield ..	*Suff. p.c.* KB	16	0	0
TOWNSHEND, Marquess				
Walton on				
Trent with }	*Derby* r. KB	17	2	8
Rolleston c. }				
Norwich, St. MaryCoslany }	*Norf.* r. PR	96	0	0
East Rudham w.W.Rudham }	— *r.* —	13	13	4
Sherford........	— *r.* KB	9	0	0
Stiffkey, St. John w. St. Mary and Morston .... }	— *v.* —	43	0	0
Toftres	— *v.* PR	86	14	0
TOWNSHEND, Lord John				
Colkirk with Stibbard ....}	*Norf.* r. KB	21	13	4
VALLETORT, Viscount				
Beerferris	*Devon.* r. —	24	1	0
Dittisham	— *r.* —	34	15	0
Plympton, St. Maude Gr.Sch. *Devon. Mast*				
VERNON, Lord				
Sudbury........	*Derby.* r. —	14	12	0
Aberavon with Bagland c. .. }	*Glam.* v. PR	160	0	0
Llandilo Talybont	— *v.* KB	4	14	7
Llangwinor	— *p.c.* PR	42	0	0
Llangonoyd	— *v.* —	145	0	0
Penrice	— *p.c.* —	36	0	0
Nuthall	*Notts.* r. KB	3	14	9
VERULAM, Earl of				
Colne Wake	*Essex.* r. KB	12	0	5
Messing	— *v.* —	8	0	0

Parish	County			£	s	d
Pebmarsh	*Essex.*	r.	KB	10	0	0
Redburn	*Herts.*	v.	—	16	5	0
St. Alban's, St. Michael }		v.	—	10	1	8
WALDEGRAVE, Earl of						
Borley	*Eseex.*	r.	—	9	0	0
Lapgenhoe	—	r.	—	14	3	4
Peldon	—	r.	—	16	15	10
Radstock	*Som.*	r.	—	6	11	0
WALSINGHAM, Lord						
Copdock with Washbrook v. }	*Suff.*	r.	KB	17	19	4
Merton	*Norf.*	r.	—	6	0	5
Sturston, *sin*	—	p.c.	PR	35	0	0
WARWICK, Earl of						
Milverton	*Warw.p.c.*		PR	58	0	0
WATERFORD, Marquess of						
Ford	*North*	r.	KB	24	0	0
WELLINGTON, Duke of						
Strathfieldsaye	*Hants.*	r.	KB	24	13	0
—— Turgis	—	r.	—	6	10	2
WESTMINSTER, Marq. of, (see *Grosvenor*)						
WESTMORELAND, Earl of						
Cotterstock w. Glapthorne }	*Npn.*	v.	PR	100	0	0
Kingscliff	—	r.	KB	13	16	3
Warmington	—	v.	PR	141	10	0
WHARNCLIFFE, Lord						
Barnstaple	*Devon.*	v.	—	15	8	9
Ordsall	*Notts.*	r.	—	19	10	7
Hardrow	*Yksh.p.c.*		PR	65	0	0
WHITWORTH, Lord, &c.						
Drayton	*Oxon.*	r.	PR	75	0	0
WILLOUGHBY DE BROKE, Lord						
Kimcot	*Leic.*	r.	—	20	16	3
Tothill	*Linc.*	r.	PR	135	12	0
Pointington	*Som.*	r.	KB	13	8	4
Bramshall	*Staff.*	r.	—	4	3	9
East Lavant	*Suss.*	r.	—	20	18	1
Chesterton	*Warw.p.c.*		PR	128	0	0
Kingston with Combrook c. }	—	v.	—	45	6	2
Leighthorn	—	r.	KB	14	7	3
WILLOUGHBY D'ERESBY, Lord						
Bellau w. Aby v. & Greenfield v. }	*Linc.*	r.	KB	19	7	3
Careby	—	r.	PR	117	12	0
Edenham	—	p.c.	KB	not in char.		
Partney with Spilsby p.c. }	—	r.	PR	164	10	0
Skendleby	—	v.	KB	4	5	0
Somerby cum Humby }	—	r.	—	11	12	5
West Theddlethorpe with Mablethorpe St. Peter }	—	r.	—	18	10	2
Little Stepping	*Linc.*	r.	PR	53	0	0
Swinestead	—	v.	PR	100	0	0
Tallington	—	v.	KB	8	9	9
Toynton	—	r.	—	12	0	2
——All Saints	—	v.	PR	94	0	0
——Low	—	r.	KB	11	1	8
WILTON, Earl of						
Radcliffe	*Lanc.*	r.	KB	21	0	5
Farthingoe	*Npn.*	r.	—	16	0	0
Batley, *alt.*	*Yksh.*	v.	PR	150	0	0
WINCHELSEA, Earl of						
Middleton Keynes }	*Bucks.*	r.	—	20	0	0
Ravenstone	—	v.	PR	100	0	0
Foulness	*Essex.*	r.	PR	98	12	0
Eastling	*Kent.*	r.	KB	16	0	0
Eastwell	—	r.	PR	110	0	0
Wye	—	p.c.	—	120	0	0
Burley	*Rutl.*	v.	KB	10	13	1
Greetham	—	v.	PR	127	0	0
WINCHESTER, Marquess of						
Yateley	*Hants.*	pc.	—	28	0	0
WODEHOUSE, Lord						
Carlton Forehoe	*Norf.*	r.	KB	5	17	1
Crownthorpe	—	r.	PR	125	10	0
Hingham	—	r.	—	29	5	0
Kimberley w. Barnham Broom r. }	—	v.	KB	12	8	1
				6	12	3
East Lexham w Litcham }	—	r.	—	17	8	6
West Lexham	—	r.	—	5	11	8
Runhall	—	r.	PR	48	0	0
YARBOROUGH, Lord						
Eyworth	*Beds.*	v.	PR	65	0	0
Bonby	*Linc.*	v.	KB	6	4	4
Brocklesby	—	r.	PR	59	7	2
Cabourn	—	v.	—	36	6	0
Cadney	—	v.	KB	7	18	4
East Halton	—	v.	PR	112	10	0
Horkstow	—	v.	KB	4	18	4
Irby on Humber	—	v.	—	18	0	0
Keelby	—	v.	PR	60	0	0
Killingholme	*Linc.*	v.	PR	132	4	4
Kirmington	—	v.	—	130	0	0
Ruckland with Farforth and Maiden Well c. }	—	r.	—	115	15	0
Swallow	—	r.	KB	7	10	10
Counde with Cressage c. }	*Salop.*	r.	—	33	0	0
St. Lawrence	*I. of W.*	r.	PR	112	14	0
ZOUCH, Baroness						
East and West Angmering }	*Suss.*	r.&v.	KB	21	9	8
Parham	—	r.	PR	90	0	0

AMOUNT of Highway Rates, Church Rates, Poor Relief, County Charges, Constables Charges, Militia, Litigation, and all other incidental local charges, for the Year 1827, in each County in England and Wales; also the annual value of Real Property Assessed in 1815 to the Property Tax, and the Population according to the last census.

Year ending 25th March, 1827,	Highway Rates.	Church Rates.	Expended in Relief of the Poor, County Rate, &c.	Total Expenditure.	Annual Value of Real Property, April 1815.	Population, 1831.
	£	£	£	£	£	
Bedford	8,045	6,826	91,359	106,230	343,682	95,383
Berks	11,979	7,015	114,970	133,964	652,082	145,289
Bucks	15,207	7,118	152,515	174,810	644,129	146,529
Cambridge	16,511	5,698	104,863	127,072	655,220	143.955
Chester........	26,449	9,135	147,124	182,708	1,083,083	334,410
Cornwall	24,086	8,072	115,453	147,611	916,060	302,440
Cumberland ..	13,734	3,758	58,785	76,277	705,445	169,681
Derby	16,049	8,793	99,518	124,360	887,659	237,170
Devon	39,588	19,567	244,887	304,042	1,897,515	494,168
Dorset	10,767	6,913	94,923	112,603	698,395	159,252
Durham	17,363	9,518	94,181	121,062	791,359	253,827
Essex	29,444	19,808	306,794	356,046	1,556,836	317,233
Gloucester	31,755	11,560	200,596	243,911	1,463,259	386,904
Hereford	13,367	5,999	69,433	88,799	604,614	110,976
Hertford	14,034	9,305	108,054	131,393	571,107	143,341
Huntingdon	5,335	2,387	48,276	55,998	320,187	53,149
Kent	46,693	32,715	392,253	471,661	1,644,179	479,155
Lancaster	96,615	27,111	539,388	663,114	3,087,774	1,336.854
Leicester	24,315	8,775	138,904	171,994	902,217	197,003
Lincoln	76,731	18,186	214,368	309,285	2,061,830	317,244
Middlesex......	34,246	94,359	711,874	840,479	5,595,536	1,358,541
Monmouth	6,766	4,387	31,851	43,004	295,097	98,130
Norfolk........	25,240	14.236	344,950	384,426	1,540,952	390,054
Northampton ..	21,441	8,577	167,352	197,370	942,161	179,276
Northumberland	16,067	5,337	79,117	100,521	1,240,594	222,912
Nottingham	27,703	6,208	99,685	133,596	737,229	225,320
Oxford	12,984	5,829	135,886	154,699	713,147	151,726
Rutland........	4,128	947	13,873	18,948	133,487	19,385
Salop,.........	17,032	9,865	96,461	123,358	1,037,988	222,503
Somerset	34,680	18,314	186,809	239,803	1,900,651	403,908
Southampton ..	16,096	10,077	210,526	236,699	1,130,951	314,313
Stafford	19,108	13,542	158,808	191,458	1,150,281	410,485
Suffolk	24,849	13,557	252,283	290,689	1,127,404	296,304
Surrey	34,086	36,597	291,830	356,513	1,579,172	486,326
Sussex	27,087	9,442	273,664	310,193	915,384	272,328
Warwick	20,003	11,198	178,425	209,626	1,236,726	336,988
Westmorland ..	3,099	1,158	31,514	35,771	298,198	55,041
Wilts	21,231	8,851	190,043	220,125	1,155,458	239,181
Worcester	17,506	10,030	92,078	120,244	799,605	211,356
York, E. R.	24,503	8,227	119,911	152,641	1,190,325	168,646
—— N. R.....	26,564	6,320	96,730	129,614	1,145,252	226,235
—— W. R.....	102,776	21,632	388,730	513,138	2,392,405	976,415
Wales	46,550	23,417	313,771	383,783	2,153,801	805,236
TOTAL of England and Wales ..	1,121,834	564,388	7,803,465	9,489,687	51,898,423	13,894,574

RETURN of Lay and Clerical Magistrates in each County in England and Wales who have qualified, appointed by the Lord Chancellor.

Names of the Counties.	Names of the present Lord Lieutenants.	Number.		
		Clergy	Lay.	Total.
Bedford	Lord Grantham............	19	27	46
Berks	Earl of Abingdon	28	95	123
Bucks	Duke of Buckingham	54	90	144
Cambridge	Earl of Hardwicke	23	28	51
Chester	Earl of Stamford	16	58	74
Cornwall	Earl of Mount Edgecumbe ..	36	54	90
Cumberland	Earl of Lonsdale	15	39	54
Derby	Duke of Devonshire........	..	79	79
Devon	Earl of Fortescue	42	144	186
Dorset	Earl Digby................	25	43	68
Durham	Marquis of Cleveland	23	59	82
Essex	Viscount Maynard	51	119	170
Gloucester	Duke of Beaufort, K.G.....	49	127	176
Hants	Duke of Wellington........	19	131	150
Hereford	Earl Somers	58	97	155
Hertford	Earl of Verulam	44	102	146
Huntingdon	Duke of Manchester........	7	18	25
Kent	Marquis Camden, K.G.	2	145	147
Lancaster	Earl of Derby	24	151	175
Leicester	Duke of Rutland	17	27	44
Lincoln	Earl Brownlow............	52	59	111
Middlesex	Duke of Portland..........	16	153	169
Monmouth	Duke of Beaufort..........	13	44	57
Norfolk	Hon. John Wodehouse	78	119	197
Northampton	Earl of Westmoreland	35	49	84
Northumberland	Duke of Northumberland ..	6	40	46
Nottingham	Duke of Newcastle	10	44	54
Oxford	Earl of Macclesfield........	18	53	71
Rutland	Marquis of Exeter	3	6	9
Salop............	Earl of Powis	38	106	144
Somerset	Marquis of Bath	53	97	150
Stafford............	Earl Talbot	16	70	86
Suffolk	Duke of Grafton	58	98	156
Surrey	Lord Arden	39	215	254
Sussex	Earl of Egremont	..	189	189
Warwick	Earl of Warwick	24	42	66
Westmoreland	Earl of Lonsdale	15	18	30
Wilts	Marquis of Lansdowne	18	71	89
Worcester..........	Earl of Coventry	44	92	136
York—East, West, & North Ridings ...	Earl Carlisle, Earl Harewood, and Duke of Leeds	103	311	414
Anglesea	Marquis of Anglesea	7	14	21
Brecon	Duke of Beaufort..........	24	37	61
Cardigan	W. E. Powell, Esq	11	53	64
Carmarthen	Lord Dynevor	9	75	84
Carnarvon	Lord Willoughby de Eresby .	14	17	31
Denbigh	Sir W. W. Wynn, Bart	24	41	65
Flint	Earl Grosvenor............	15	26	41
Glamorgan	Marquis of Bute	18	36	54
Merioneth..........	Sir W. W. Wynn, Bart.	9	14	23
Montgomery........	Lord Clive................	13	31	44
Pembroke	Sir John Owen, Bart.......	10	35	45
Radnor	Lord Rodney	4	29	33
	Total	1324	4017	5371

COMMISSIONERS OF SEWERS.

" Out of evil sometimes comes good, but do not evil that good may come."—

FIELDING'S PROVERBS.

WHILE a malignant distemper is either actually amongst us or impending, it seems a suitable moment for referring to a subject directly bearing on the general health of the community. Except in periodical calls for *rates* the public know and hear little of the Commissioners of Sewers. They are, however, a branch of the ancient institutions of the country, and the people have a right to be informed of the derivation of their powers, their duties, and the abuses in their administration.

From the lectures of Challis at Gray's Inn, in 1662, public sewers appear to have been first vested in commissioners in the reign of Henry III.; and after several acts to extend their powers, became consolidated in the 23d of Henry VIII. c. 25; when authority was granted to certain individuals, in various districts of the kingdom, to construct sewers for drainage, and levy rates for the purpose. The authority of the Commissioners is almost absolute, and still continues with little abridgement. They can summon, examine, and even imprison; and it is even doubtful whether the superior courts of law can interfere. As regards the qualifications and appointment of the Commissioners, the statute of Henry VIII. directs that substantial persons, having a freehold qualification of £20 per annum, shall be nominated by the lord Chancellor, lord Treasurer, and two chief justices, for " making and repairing ditches, banks, gutters, gates, sewers, calcies, bridges, streams, trenches, mill-ponds, and locks." Each commission is to continue ten years; and six are to form a quorum. Commissioners acting without being duly qualified, to forfeit £40 each sitting; they may proceed either by inquisition or survey; each commissioner to be allowed 40s. a day while engaged in the duty of the commission, and the rates to be assessed in proportion to land, rents, profits, and fisheries.

Besides this and other general acts, local acts have been obtained by several commissions, the provisions of which extend only to the particular jurisdiction for which they have been passed. In the district of the metropolis, north of the Thames, are four principal commissions. Monthly committees, clerks of the works, surveyors, inspectors, messengers, &c. are attached to each commission. Every one who receives a benefit or avoids a damage is liable to be assessed to the sewers' rate. The average expenditure under the Westminster commission is £24,000 per annum;* the Holborn and Finsbury, £10,000; the Tower Hamlets,

----

* Parl. Paper, vol. v. No. 542, Sess. 1832.

under £2,000; the city of London, £8,000: making a yearly expenditure of £44,000 for the maintenance of the sewers of one district of the kingdom.

Having shortly noticed the origin and powers of Commissions of Sewers, we shall instance their defective administration. We shall call attention to the state of that portion of the environs of this great metropolis on the south side of the river. It may be thought by some, perhaps, so obscure and remote a corner of the realm is totally unworthy of legislative notice, but it ought to be borne in mind that it is the principal seat of productive industry in the capital, and that it comprises a dense population of half a million of persons, every one of whom is equally entitled with other of his majesty's lieges to the enjoyment of health and the blessings of life. If the inhabitants of this portion of the suburbs be peculiarly subject to the cholera or other malignant disease, it cannot be matter of astonishment. They are compelled to drink the most deleterious beverage, and the sewers, ditches, and channels for carrying off the foul and redundant water are in a state of disgraceful neglect. In all that thickly-peopled area, of at least sixteen square miles, embracing the entire parishes of Rotherhithe, Bermondsey, Horseley Down, Walworth, Newington-Butts, and a considerable portion of Lambeth, extending from Deptford and the Kent Road to the New Camberwell Road, and the roads in the vicinity of the Surrey Zoological Gardens, the channels and ditches for carrying off the water remain in their natural state, overflowing with filth and impurity. If, for want of descent, it might not be easy to drain them, they might at least be widened, cleansed, and covered over. If, by economy in the expenditure of the existing assessment, it could not be made adequate to the undertaking, at such a moment of apprehension of infectious disease, and for such a salutary end, the inhabitants would hardly complain of an additional rate for the purpose; in fact they would save it in the reduction of poor-rate, caused by the employment created for men who now burden the parish for want of work. As it is, the nuisance of which we complain is personally dangerous to the passenger, offensive to the eye, and most injurious to the constitution.

It is gratifying to think the Surrey parishes are about obtaining representatives in parliament, were it only for the sake of local improvements. At first we thought of calling the attention of Mr. Warburton to the power and duties of commissioners of sewers, but this gentleman has his hands full with the Anatomy Bill, and moreover is in some measure a *particeps criminis*, having been recently presented for a nuisance on his own lands, by the Surrey grand jury. However, we trust some honourable Member will take up the subject. A parliamentary committee sat on the state of the public sewers in 1823, but it had an indifferent chairman in the late Mr. Peter Moore—made no report, and nothing came of its inquiries.

PROGRESS OF POPULATION.

	1801.	Increase per cent.	1811.	Increase per cent.	1821.	Increase per cent.	1831.
England....	8,331,434	14¾	9,551,888	17⅛	11,261,437	16	13,089,338
Wales......	541,546	13	611,788	17	717,438	12	805,236
Scotland ..	1,599,068	14	1,805,688	16	2,093,456	13	2,365,807
Army, Navy, &c.	470,598	—	640,500	—	319,300	—	277,017
	10,942,646	15¼	12,609,864	14	14,391,631	15	16,537,398

The increase in population has been rapid and nearly at an uniform rate per cent. for the last thirty years, notwithstanding the increase or diminution of the Army, Navy, &c. The population of Ireland amounted in 1831 to 7,734,365, making the aggregate population of the three kingdoms 24,271,763. With such an augmented number of people, cribbed in by corn laws, anti-emigration prejudices, and monopolies, can it be matter of surprise that capital is redundant—bread *dear* and labour *cheap*? Is it possible, while society is progressively increasing in numbers, wealth, and intelligence, public institutions can be stationary? Is it possible that an Aristocracy, daily becoming more disproportionatè in every element of power to the mass of the community, can maintain a monopoly of political authority? Either they must speedily repair the few decayed pillars by which the State is supported within, or be crushed from the superincumbent pressure without!

POSTSCRIPT.

Two or three changes occasioned by deaths and removals, have occurred while the work has been printing, but they are of too great publicity to need particularizing. We may also remark that the observations at pages 376 and 502 were printed prior to the publication of the Navy Estimates. The energy with which sir J. Graham has proceeded to new-model the department over which he presides will leave, we apprehend, little to desire in that branch of the public service.

After the explanations of the Duke of Wellington (House of Lords, March 16th) we suppose we must acquit his Grace of the design imputed to him, p. 584, and conclude that he had no intention of joining the continental despots in a crusade against the liberties of France and Belgium.—May not this be an *after-thought* of the ex-Premier, like his famous explanation on the subject of Parliamentary Reform?

Page 498, line 14, for *custos* read *custodes;* page 592, line 15, for *divisions* read *division;* page 597, line 27, for *sixteenth* read *seventeenth* century.

In the printed Reform Bill, as amended in committee by the House of Commons, *Wallingford* forms one of the semi-disfranchised boroughs, and ought to have been inserted in No. IV. instead of No. V. of our Tables, page 614.

In No. VII. page 615, Chatham should be inserted and Swansea omitted.

On bringing up the Report, *Merthyr Tydvil* was included in the number of enfranchised boroughs.

INDEX.

—

THE END.